Contents

↘ **1 Introduction**
4 Highlights map

↘ **13 Essentials**
14 Planning your trip
17 Getting there
20 Getting around
25 Sleeping
27 Eating
30 Entertainment
31 Festivals and events
35 Shopping
36 Activities and tours
41 Responsible tourism
43 Essentials A-Z

↘ **53 Kuala Lumpur**
56 Ins and outs
61 Background
62 Modern Kuala Lumpur
63 Sights
73 Around Kuala Lumpur
81 Listings

↘ **105 Northern Peninsula**
108 Highlands and
hill stations
124 Ipoh and around
141 Penang
167 Alor Star and around
174 Pulau Langkawi

↘ **189 Southern Peninsula**
192 Melaka and around
216 Johor Bahru
221 Pulau Tioman and around
240 Endau Rompin
National Park

↘ **243 East Coast Peninsula**
246 Ins and outs
246 Background
247 Kuantan and around
257 Pahang's national parks
265 Kampong Cherating
and around
273 Kuala Terengganu
and around
281 Redang archipelago
284 The Perhentian Islands
290 Kota Bharu and around

↘ **301 Sarawak**
304 Kuching and around
331 Bandar Sri Aman
and around
336 Sibu, Kapit and Belaga
350 North coast
369 Northern Sarawak
379 Background

Footprint story

It was 1921

Ireland had just been partitioned, the British miners were striking for more pay and the federation of British industry had an idea. Exports were booming in South America – how about a handbook for businessmen trading in that far away continent? The Anglo-South American Handbook was born that year, written by W Koebel, the most prolific writer on Latin America of his day.

1924

Two editions later the book was 'privatized' and in 1924, in the hands of Royal Mail, the steamship company for South America, it became The South American Handbook, subtitled 'South America in a nutshell'. This annual publication became the 'bible' for generations of travellers to South America and remains so to this day. In the early days travel was by sea and the Handbook gave all the details needed for the long voyage from Europe. What to wear for dinner; how to arrange a cricket match with the Cable & Wireless staff on the Cape Verde Islands and a full account of the journey from Liverpool up the Amazon to Manaus: 5898 miles without changing cabin!

1939

As the continent opened up, the South American Handbook reported the new Pan Am flying boat services, and the fortnightly airship service from Rio to Europe on the Graf Zeppelin. For reasons still unclear but with extraordinary determination, the annual editions continued through the Second World War.

1970s

Many more people discovered South America and the backpacking trail started to develop. All the while the Handbook was gathering fans, including literary vagabonds such as Paul Theroux and Graham Greene (who once sent some updates addressed to "The publishers of the best travel guide in the world, Bath, England").

1990s

During the 1990s the company set about developing a new travel guide series using this legendary title as the flagship. By 1997 there were over a dozen guides in the series and the Footprint imprint was launched.

2000s

The series grew quickly and there were soon Footprint travel guides covering more than 150 countries. In 2004, Footprint launched its first thematic guide: *Surfing Europe*, packed with colour photographs, maps and charts. This was followed by further thematic guides such as *Diving the World, Snowboarding the World, Body and Soul escapes, Travel with Kids* and *European City Breaks*.

2010

Today we continue the traditions of the last 89 years that have served legions of travellers so well. We believe that these help to make Footprint guides different. Our policy is to use authors who are genuine experts who write for independent travellers; people possessing a spirit of adventure, looking to get off the beaten track.

↘ 395 Sabah
398 Kota Kinabalu
418 Off the coast and south
   of Kota Kinabalu
435 North of Kota Kinabalu
439 Gunung Kinabalu
   National Park
450 East coast
483 Background

↘ 493 Background
494 History
503 Modern Malaysia
506 Economy
509 Culture
522 Religion
529 Land and environment
541 Books

↘ 547 Singapore
552 Planning your trip
553 Getting there
558 Getting around
561 Sleeping
562 Eating
565 Festivals and events
567 Shopping
570 Essentials A-Z
576 Sights
616 Listings
641 History
647 Modern Singapore

↘ 653 Footnotes
654 Malaysian words and phrases
657 Glossary
660 Malaysian and Singaporean
   food glossary
663 Index
672 Credits

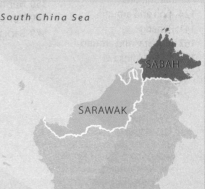

South China Sea

NORTHERN
PENINSULA
EAST COAST
PENINSULA
KUALA
LUMPUR
SOUTHERN
PENINSULA
SINGAPORE
SABAH
SARAWAK

Malaysia

Contents

14 Planning your trip
  14 Where to go
  16 Itineraries
  17 When to go

17 Getting there
  17 Air
  19 Rail
  19 Road
  20 Sea

20 Getting around
  20 Air
  21 Rail
  22 Road
  24 Sea
  25 Maps

25 Sleeping

27 Eating

30 Entertainment

31 Festivals and events

35 Shopping

36 Activities and tours
  36 Birdwatching
  36 Cookery courses
  36 Diving
  40 Motorbike tours
  40 Spas
  40 Spectator sports
  41 Trekking and climbing
  41 Whitewater rafting

41 Responsible tourism

43 Essentials A-Z

Footprint features

  15 Packing for Malaysia
  21 Sample air fares
  23 Important road signs
  26 Sleeping price codes
  29 Eating price codes
  42 Travelling light

Malaysia Essentials

Planning your trip

Where to go

Getting around Peninsular Malaysia and Singapore is not difficult and even making the trip from Kota Bharu at the northern extremity of the east coast, down to Melaka, towards the southern end of the west coast, need only take a day's travelling by road. Air links between the major towns are, obviously, faster still. However, many visitors with only, say, a fortnight in the area wonder whether it is possible to combine a trip to Peninsular Malaysia, Singapore and the East Malaysian states of Sabah and Sarawak. This requires a little more thought. There are regular domestic air connections between Kuala Lumpur (KL), Johor Bahru, and Singapore to the major cities of East Malaysia, and from there with smaller towns in the Bornean interior. For those intending, for example, to fly to Kota Kinabalu, Sabah, stay a few days at Tanjung Aru Beach, and then return to the Peninsula, taking in East and West Malaysia should pose no difficulties. However, if you're intending to do more than this, such as climbing Gunung Kinabalu, travelling upriver on the Baram, Rejang or Skrang rivers, or hiking through one of the national parks, then a little more leeway in terms of time is required. A minimum period to just scratch the surface would be one week; more preferable would two to three weeks. Of course, some people spend many weeks in just one area and still profess to have seen only a fraction of what is on offer. The ideas below cover only a selection of places of interest and the list is not exhaustive. It is designed to assist in planning a trip to the region. Any 'highlight' list is inevitably subjective.

Hill stations
Fraser's Hill and the **Cameron Highlands** offer a taste of colonial Malaysia, and there are good walks around the Cameron Highlands. The Genting Highlands is more ersatz and kitsch, a favourite haunt of Kuala Lumpur's nouveau riche and stressed Singaporeans in search of a weekend refuge from the heat of their island. Maxwell Hill is the quietest of the hill stations.

Wildlife and jungle
The national parks of the Peninsula do not compare with those of East Malaysia. Nonetheless, **Taman Negara** and the **Endau Rompin National Park** are both well worth visiting. **Rantau Abang** on the east coast is a stretch of shoreline where turtles come to lay their eggs. In East Malaysia, Sarawak and Sabah offer a wealth of parks and conservation areas. Some, like the **Semonggoh Orang-Utan Sanctuary** and the **Bako National Park** outside Kuching, and the **Sepilok Orang-Utan Rehabilitation Centre** and the **Turtle Islands National Park** outside Sandakan, are accessible as short trips from Kuching and Sandakan respectively. Other parks, like the Niah and Gunung Mulu national parks, require several days to explore properly.

Natural features
The caves at the **Niah** and **Gunung Mulu** national parks and **Gunung Kinabalu**, Malaysia's highest mountain, are stupendous natural features worth visiting in themselves. There are many islands you can visit off both the west and east coasts of the Peninsula, although the east coast islands come closer to popular notions of palm-fringed island idylls. **Penang** has a wide selection of hotels and tourist facilities and a fantastic historical centre. **Pulau**

Packing for Malaysia

Remember that almost everything is available in the main towns and cities – often at a lower price than in Western countries – and that laundry services are cheap and rapid, so there is no need to bring loads of supplies. More remote areas are inevitably less well supplied.

Dress in Malaysia (and, but to a lesser extent, Singapore) is relatively casual, even at formal functions. Suits are not necessary except in a few of the most expensive restaurants. However, although formal attire may be the exception, dressing tidily is the norm. Women should note that in many areas of Malaysia, they should avoid offending Muslim sensibilities and keep shoulders covered and wear below-knee skirts or trousers. This is true on the east coast of the Peninsula, especially in Kelantan, but doesn't apply in most beach resorts.

The following lists provide an idea of what to take with you on a trip to Malaysia: money belt, first-aid kit, insect repellent (with high DEET concentration recommended for jungle treks), international driving licence, passports (valid for at least six months), photocopies of essential documents, spare passport photographs, sun protection, sunglasses, Swiss Army knife, torch, umbrella and a phrase book. Those intending to stay in budget accommodation might also include: cotton sheet sleeping bag, padlock (for room and luggage), soap, student card, towel and travel wash. For women travellers: a supply of tampons (although these are available in most towns) and a wedding ring for single female travellers may help ward off the attentions of amorous admirers.

There is a good smattering of camping grounds in Malaysia, both in Peninsular Malaysia and in Sabah and Sarawak. If you're intending to camp, then all the usual equipment is necessary: a tent, stove, cooking utensils, sleeping bag, etc. Iodine drops – for purifying water, sterilizing jungle cuts and scratches and loosening leeches – are difficult to come by in Malaysia but easily obtained in UK camping and outdoor shops. They are distributed by **Lifesystems** in the UK, www.lifesystems.co.uk.

Langkawi has developed rapidly and is more the haunt of upmarket resorts than budget-friendly guesthouses. Also off the west coast and just a few hours by road from Kuala Lumpur is Pulau Pangkor. Pulau Tioman, off the Peninsula's east coast, is less developed than Langkawi and Penang and there are also numerous other islands which are still less touched by the hands of humans. On the Peninsula itself, **Kampong Cherating** is the best known beach resort, and was once a well-established stop on the backpacking trail, but is now gaining popularity with local tourists from KL. There are also other groups of hotels and chalets dotted up and down the east coast. Sabah and Sarawak do not have beach resorts to compare with those – at least in scale – of the Peninsula. However, there are some fine beaches and excellent snorkelling and diving, especially in the **Tunku Abdul Rahman National Park** and the **Sipadan Island Marine Reserve**. Small resorts include those at Damai, north of Kuching; Tanjung Aru, outside Kota Kinabalu; and Labuan.

Historical sites

Melaka is one of Malaysia's two historic gems. There are buildings dating from the Portuguese and Dutch periods, as well as some fine Chinese shophouses. **Georgetown**, the capital of Penang, is Malaysia's second city of architectural and historical note, with probably the finest assembly of Sino-colonial architecture in the region. Both cities were awarded UNESCO World Heritage Site status in 2008, gazetted jointly as the Historic Cities of the Straits of Malacca. Whilst the government is undoubtedly pleased with the status, activists complain of rampant development and further erosion of culture, many worrying that the fascinating hearts of the two cities will turn into some kind of historical theme park.

Culture

Traditional Malay culture is best preserved on the east coast of the Peninsula and especially in the Malay heartland of **Kelantan** (Kota Bharu), with its rural kampongs, or villages, and thriving craft industry. The **Sarawak Cultural Village** near Kuching offers an anaesthetized vision of tribal life and culture; the upriver 'tribes' and longhouses give a taste of the real thing. The Rejang and Skrang rivers, dotted with towns and small tribal settlements, are all worth exploring by boat. For information on visiting longhouses in Sarawak, see page 334.

Shopping

KL is the best place to buy the full range of handicrafts from batik to blowpipes, although prices are higher than at their source. The east coast is the centre of the Peninsula's Malay handicraft industry, particularly Kelantan (Kota Bharu). Sabah and Sarawak (especially Kuching) are the places to find tribal handicrafts. Many are on sale in the main towns, although smaller communities potentially offer the best buys.

Museums

KL's museums are less impressive than those in Singapore but are still worth visiting. The **Islamic Arts Museum** in KL is, perhaps, the city's best. The best museum in East Malaysia is the **Sarawak Museum** in Kuching with its superb ethnographic collection.

Itineraries

Itineraries for Peninsular Malaysia and Singapore are easy to customise to meet your own needs and interests. Distances are not enormous, transport is good and the seasons rarely put particular places off-limits. (The exception to this is the east coast, where the monsoon between November and February brings rough seas and heavy rains. Some islands are difficult or impossible to reach at this time, and some national parks are also closed.) Most travellers arrive either in Singapore or KL, although a good number also enter Malaysia overland across its northern border with Thailand. From all these points of arrival it is possible to reach any of Malaysia's beach resorts, bar some of the islands off the east coast which require a morning boat departure from the mainland. The main question is how to combine, say, a visit to Melaka, to the south, with a few days on the beach in Penang, to the north, or east to Tioman island.

It requires a little more effort to co-ordinate and plan a visit to one of the Peninsular's national parks where two, three or four days may be necessary to explore the area to any degree. And, as noted above, for those who want to combine a visit to the Peninsula with a trip to East Malaysia, and particularly if this includes river trips, trekking and longhouse stays, even more time should be put to one side. As a rule-of-thumb, one week is the minimum length of time to get a taster of Peninsular Malaysia and Singapore, and two weeks if this is to be combined with East Malaysia.

When to go

Climate

When planning a trip to Malaysia, always take into account the rainy seasons; the best time to visit the Peninsula's east coast is between March and September. Trips along the east coast and interior jungles are not advisable between November and February, during the northeast monsoon. The east coast suffers flooding at this time of year, and it is inadvisable and also impossible to take fishing boats to offshore islands such as Pulau Tioman as the sea can be very rough. Taman Negara National Park is closed from November to the end of January. Other parts of Peninsular Malaysia can be visited year round as the rainy season is not torrential, although it is fairly wet during the northeast monsoon period. Rainfall is worst from May to September on the west coast of the Peninsula, but it is never very heavy.

In East Malaysia, March and June are the best times to visit the interior, the worst rains are usually from November to February and some roads are impassable in these months. Conversely, in the dry season, some rivers become unnavigable. In recent years the onset of the wet and dry seasons in both Sabah and Sarawak has become less predictable; environmentalists ascribe this to deforestation and/or global warming, although there is no scientifically proven link. ▸▸ *For more information on climate, see page 530.*

Festivals and events → *See also page 31.*

School holidays run from mid- to late February, mid-May to early June, mid- to late August and late November to early January. During these periods it is advisable to book hotels. Room rates also increase significantly during these holidays. During Ramadan (see Festivals, page 33) travel can be more difficult and many restaurants close during daylight hours, especially in the east coast states of Kelantan and Terengganu. After dusk many Muslims break their fast at stalls which do a roaring trade, although Ramadan is usually a period when Muslims eat at home.

Getting there

Air

The majority of visitors arrive at one of two international airports: Kuala Lumpur (KLIA), see page 56, or Singapore (page 553). Those headed to Borneo can also fly to Brunei. Some international flights go direct to Penang, Langkawi, Kota Kinabalu (KK) and Kuching. Smaller airlines also run services between Singapore and island resorts such as Langkawi and Pulau Tioman.

Airport departure tax is RM15 for domestic flights and RM51 for international, but these are usually included in the ticket price.

Flights from Europe

Malaysia Airlines (MAS, www.malaysiaairlines.com) offers direct services from London Heathrow to KL (12½ hours). MAS also operates non-stop services from Amsterdam, Frankfurt, Paris, Rome and Stockholm. **KLM** (www.klm.com) flies from Amsterdam non-stop. From other cities a change of plane is usually necessary en route, often in the Middle East. Budget airline **AirAsia** (www.airasia.com) has direct flights between London Stansted and KL at very reasonable rates. Book online at www.airasia.com.

Flights from the USA and Canada

MAS flies from LA and New York. Many North American and Asian carriers require a stopover in Japan, Hong Kong or Taipei.

Flights from Australasia

MAS offers direct flights from Sydney, Melbourne, Adelaide, Brisbane, and Perth (flight times seven to nine hours). **AirAsia** has direct flights between KL and Perth, Melbourne and the Gold Coast.

Flights from Northeast Asia

KL is very well connected to cities in Northeast Asia with regular flights on to Hong Kong with **MAS** and **Cathay Pacific** (www.cathaypacific.com), Shanghai with **China Eastern** (www.flychinaeasten.com) and MAS, Tokyo with **Japan Airlines** (www.jal.com) and MAS, Beijing with **Air China** (www.airchina.com.cn). **AirAsia** has a good selection of flights to this region with flights to Chengdu, Guilin, Hangzhou, Tianjin, Shenzhen and Guangzhou.

Flights from Southeast Asia

There are flights to KL from all regional capitals. **AirAsia** has flights connecting KL with Jakarta, Bali, Singapore, Hanoi, Phnom Penh, Siem Reap, Manila and Bangkok, and Bangkok with Penang and Johor Baru. Many airlines fly from Hong Kong and Tokyo. Budget carriers fly between KL and Singapore. Airlines include **Tiger Airways** (www.tigerairways.com), **Jet Star Asia** (www.jetstar.com) and AirAsia.

Flights from South Asia

From Delhi (India), **MAS**, **AirAsia** and **Air India** (www.airindia.co.in) fly to KL. AirAsia fly from Kolkata, Mumbai, Hyderabad, Chennai, Bangalore, Kochi and Trivandrum to KL and direct from Chennai to Penang. **Sri Lankan Airlines** (www.srilankan.aero) and **AirAsia** fly from Colombo to KL, while **Bangladesh Biman Airlines** (www.biman-airlines.com) and AirAsia fly from Dhaka (Bangladesh). **Pakistan International Airlines** (www.piac.com.pk) and **MAS** fly from Karachi. **Royal Nepal** (www.royalnepal- airlines.com) operates flights from Kathmandu.

Note that budget airlines such as AirAsia arrive and depart from KLIA LCCT (Low Cost Carrier Terminal), some 20 km from the main KLIA terminal building.

Discount flight agents

UK and Ireland

STA Travel, 86 Old Brompton Rd, London, SW7 3LH, T0871-230 0040, www.statravel.co.uk. (Other branches across the UK and in major cities worldwide). Specialists in low-cost student/youth flights and tours, student IDs and insurance.
Trailfinders, 194 Kensington High St, London, W8 7RG, T0845-058 5858, www.trailfinders.com. (Other branches across the UK and in major cities worldwide).

North America

Air Brokers International, 323 Geary St, Suite 411, San Francisco, CA94102, T01-800-883 3273, www.airbrokers.com. Consolidator and specialist on RTW and Circle Pacific tickets.
Discount Airfares Worldwide On-Line, www.etn.nl/discount.htm. A hub of consolidator and discount agent links.
STA Travel, 5900 Wilshire Blvd, Suite 2110, Los Angeles, CA 90036, T1-800-781 4040, www.sta-travel.com. Branches across US.
Travel CUTS, 187 College St, Toronto, Ontario, M5T 1P7, T1-866-246 9762,

www.travelcuts.com. Specialist in student fares, IDs and other travel services. Branches in other Canadian cities.
Travelocity, www.travelocity.com. An online consolidator.

Australia and New Zealand
Flight Centre, 82 Elizabeth St, Sydney, T1-300-733867, www.flightcentre.com.au;

205 Queen St, Auckland, T09-309 6171. Plus other branches.
STA Travel, www.statravel.com.au. Offices across New Zealand and Australia. Good deals on flights, insurance and hotels.
Travel.com.au, 80 Clarence St, Sydney, T02-929 01500, www.travel.com.au.

Rail

Keretapi Tanah Melayu (KTM), www.ktmb.com.my, runs express trains daily between Singapore and the major cities on the west coast of Malaysia. There is a daily express train between Bangkok (Thailand) and Butterworth. This connects with the KL service, and from KL onwards to Singapore. Another railway line, known as the jungle railway, runs from Gemas (halfway between KL and Johor Bahru) to Kota Bharu, on the northeast coast.

The most luxurious way to travel by train to Malaysia is aboard the **Eastern & Oriental (E&O) Express**, www.orient-express.com. This air-conditioned train consisting of 66 carriages a quarter of a mile long, including a salon car, dining car, bar and observation deck. Carrying just 132 passengers, it runs from Singapore to Bangkok and back. Now that the line across Isaan in Thailand has been completed, it is possible to extend a trip as far north as Vientiane, Laos. Elegant carriages, fine wines and food designed for European rather than Asian tastes make this not just a mode of transport, but an experience. The journey takes two days with stops in KL, Butterworth, Hua Hin and the River Kwai. But such luxury is excruciatingly expensive.

Road

It is possible to travel to and from Malaysia by bus or share-taxi from Thailand and Singapore. Direct buses and taxis are much easier than the local alternatives which stop at the borders. Singapore is five hours by taxi from KL (via Johor Bahru) and about seven hours by bus (see page 102). Taxi fares are approximately double bus fares.

From Thailand

There are direct buses and taxis to destinations from Thailand to most major towns in northern Malaysia (see relevant sections) and six border crossing points. For those using the North-South Highway – which is most people – the crossing point is at Bukit Kayu Hitam, which links up with the Thai city of Hat Yai. On the western side of the Peninsula there are also crossings at Wang Kelian and Padang Besar. The Wang Kelian crossing (to Satun in Thailand) is convenient if you are driving; it is quiet and usually pretty rapid. The Padang Besar crossing is easy on foot and makes sense if you're travelling to or from Pulau Langkawi. In Perak the crossing is at Pengkalan Hulu, and in Kelantan, on the eastern side of the Peninsula there are two more crossing points, the more important at Pengkalan Kubar, and the second from Kota Bahru to Rantau Panjang/Sungai Golok although this is not considered to be safe (see page 290). The more popular of these is the Rantau Panjang crossing; few people cross at Pengkalan Kubar. The FCO warns against travel to the four southern Thai provinces of Songkhla, Pattani, Yala and Narathiwat due to the continuing violence and civil unrest. Check www.fco.gov.uk for the latest updates. Check the situation if you intend to cross the border. Local buses and taxis terminate at the border crossing points, but there are regular connections to towns and cities from each side.

From Kalimantan and Brunei

It is also possible to cross overland to the East Malaysian state of Sarawak from Kalimantan (Indonesian Borneo) and Brunei. The main crossing point is in the west at Entikong, between Kuching in Sarawak and Pontianak in Kalimantan and regular buses (11 hours) run between these two towns.

Sea

Most passenger ships and cruise liners run between Port Klang, west of KL, Georgetown (Penang), Singapore, Kuantan, Kuching and Kota Kinabalu. There are hopes that **Feri Malaysia**, a former service that connected East and West Malaysian ports, will be revived in the near future. However, with domestic air fares so low, it seems that any ferry service will be doomed to struggle from the outset.

There are also regular ferry services from Melaka to Dumai in Sumatra and from Georgetown (Penang) to Medan, also in Sumatra (see relevant sections). Passenger boats connect Langkawi Island with Satun in South Thailand (see page 187). Small boats run between Johor state and Singapore's Changi Point. In East Malaysia, there are connections between Tawau and Tarakan and Nunukan in East Kalimantan, Indonesia. There is also a regular ferry service between Sandakan in Sabah and Zamboanga in the southern Philippines.

Getting around

Transport around the East Malaysian states of Sabah and Sarawak is not as easy as it is on the Peninsula since there are fewer roads and some are not in a good state of repair. There are excellent coastal and upriver express boat services in Sarawak and national airline Malaysian Airlines (MAS), its subsidiary MASwings, and AirAsia have an extensive network in both states; flying is by far the easiest way to travel around Sabah and Sarawak, with frequent and inexpensive flights between the main towns. Speed ferries skirt the northern parts of the island of Borneo, passing immigration points either en route or at the departure and arrival points. The cheapest (and slowest) means of travelling here is by bus. Remember that Sarawak has its own immigration rules (independent to those of Malaysia), with visitors receiving a one-month entry stamp, which needs to be renewed in Kuching for longer stays.

Air

MAS operates an extensive network of flights to domestic destinations. On the Peninsula, MAS serves Alor Star, Ipoh, Johor Bahru, Kota Bahru, Kuala Lumpur, Kuala Terengganu, Kuantan, Langkawi and Penang. MAS subsidiary on the Peninsula, **Firefly** (www.fireflyz.com.my) based at Subang International Airport outside KL has an excellent network of flights including Alor Star, Kerteh, JB, Kota Bharu, Kuala Ternengganu, Kuantan, Langkawi, Melaka, Penang and international destinations in Indonesia, Thailand and Singapore. In the east Malaysian states of Sabah and Sarawak, another MAS subsidiary **MASwings** (www.maswings.com.my) has a superb network with very

Sample air fares

Destination Malaysia Air	One-way (RM)		Destination	One-way (RM)
			KL-Sandakan	228 AirAsia
JB-Kota Kinabalu	109	AirAsia	KL-Sibu	185 AirAsia
JB- Penang	84	AirAsia	Kuching-Bintulu	45 MasWings
JB- Kuching	69	AirAsia	Kuching-Miri	132 AirAsia
Kota Kinabalu- KL	179	AirAsia	Kuching-Penang	198 AirAsia
Kota Kinabalu – Tawau	76	AirAsia	Kuching-Sibu	67 AirAsia
Kota Kinabalu-Kuching	153	AirAsia	Kuching – Singapore	99 AirAsia
Kota Kinabalu-Penang	181	AirAsia		
KK-Sandakan	45	MasWings	**Singapore Air**	**One-way (SGD)**
Subang -Alor Setar	95	Firefly		
Subang-Kuantan	65	Firefly	Singapore – KL	58 Jet Star Asia
Subang – Singapore	45	Firefly	Singapore – KK	49 AirAsia
KL-Langkawi	85	AirAsia	Singapore – Kuching	49 AirAsia
KL-Kota Bahru	82	AirAsia	Singapore – Penang	44 Tiger Airways
KL-Kota Kinabalu	176	AirAsia		
KL-Kuala Terengganu	89	AirAsia	All flight prices are for online fares	
KL-Kuching	133	AirAsia	booked two weeks in advance and	
KL-Penang	84	AirAsia	include all taxes and fees.	

reasonable prices. MASwings offers services to many rural parts of Sabah and Sarawak on its ATRs, Fokker 50s and Twin Otters. Flights get booked up quickly so it's best to book online as soon as possible. MASwings serves Ba'kelalan, Bario, Bintulu, Kota Kinabalu, Kuching, Lahad Datu, Pulau Labuan, Lawas, Limbang, Long Akah, Long Banga, Long Seridan, Long Lellang, Marudi, Miri, Mukah, Mulu, Sandakan, Sibu, Tanjung Manis and Tawau. Local MAS offices are listed under each town; the head office is at Bangunan MAS (opposite Equatorial Hotel), Jalan Sultan Ismail, 50250, Kuala Lumpur, T1300-883000 (within Malaysia, 24 hours), T606-(0)3-7843 3000 (outside Malaysia, 24 hours). The budget airline **AirAsia** (www.airasia.com) flies to Alor Star, Bintulu, JB, KL, Johor Bahru, KK, Kuala Terengganu, Kuching, Labuan, Langkawi, Miri, Penang, Sandakan, Sibu and Tawau. Domestic flights from KL leave from the LCCT (Low Cost Carrier Terminal) near KLIA, see page 56. Flights get very booked up on public holidays.

Rail

The Peninsular Malaysian Railway System or Keretapi Tanah Melayu (KTM) was privatized in 1992 and became the **Keretapi Tanah Melayu Berhad**. The KTM is an economical and comfortable way to travel around the Peninsula. Privatization pumped much needed investment into the system. However, buses are usually much faster than trains, many of which arrive at awkward times in the middle of the night.

There are two main lines. One runs up the west coast from Singapore, through KL, Ipoh and Butterworth, connecting with Thai railways at Padang Besar (where half of the extra-long platform is managed by Malaysian officials and the other half by Thais) and from there continues to Hat Yai in Southern Thailand and north to Bangkok. The other line branches off from the west coast line at Gemas (halfway between KL and Singapore) and heads northeast to Kota Bahru. From Kota Bahru it is possible to take buses/taxis to Rantau Panjang/Sungai Golok for connections with Thai railways. (See page 290 for warning on travel to this area). The express service (Ekspres Rakyat or Ekspres Sinaran) only stops at major towns; the regular service stops at every station but is slightly cheaper. All first- and second-class coaches have sleeping berths on overnight trains and all classes have air conditioning. Reservations can be made for both classes. First- and second-class carriages are equipped with videos. **Note** Air conditioning on Malaysian trains is very cold.

In East Malaysia, in the state of Sabah, there is only one railway line, running from Kota Kinabalu to Tenom, via Beaufort (see page 426). It passes through the spectacular Padas River Gorge. However, this railway line is currently being upgraded and is due to reopen in late 2010.

Rail passes for five, 10 and 35 days are available to all foreign visitors, except those from Singapore, for every class, and there are no restrictions other than seat availability. Passes are available from railway stations in Singapore, KL, Johor Bahru, Butterworth, Padang Besar, Rantau Panjang, Wakaf Bahru (Kota Bahru). A 15-day pass costs US$70, US$35 (child); a 10-day pass, US$55, US$28 (child), and a five-day pass, US$35, US$18 (child). There are additional charges for international express services. Tickets bought in Singapore cost around twice the price of those purchased in Malaysia. It therefore makes sense to purchase a ticket to JB and then make onward purchases from there.

Road

Bus

Peninsular Malaysia has an excellent bus system with a network of public express buses and several privately run services. Air-conditioned express buses (and VIP buses on the more popular routes) connect the major towns; seats can be reserved and prices are reasonable. Prices quoted are for air-conditioned buses. Prices vary according to whether the bus is express or regular, and between companies.

Recommended companies are **Plusliner** (T03-2274 0499, www.plusliner.com), with super VIP buses and **Transnasional** (T1300-888582, www.transnasional.com.my). Although these may cost a few ringgit more, it's usually money well spent. In larger towns there may be a number of bus stops; some private companies may also operate directly from their own offices. Bus stations are often located several kilometres outside of town, but taxis are usually waiting to drive passengers onwards to their destination. **Note** Buses are less frequent on the east coast.

Buses in East Malaysia are more unreliable because of the poorer road conditions. Recently the governments of Sabah and Sarawak have started to invest extensively in road infrastructure; in some places road surfacing has outpaced public transport, which has yet to establish itself in many areas. Air or water transport may be the only choice or provide at least the more comfortable options.

Car and motorcycle

You can find car hire companies listed in individual towns under transport. Visitors can hire a car provided they are in possession of an international driving licence, are aged 23-65 and have had a licence for at least a year. Car hire costs up to RM250 daily depending on the car model and the company. Cheaper weekly and monthly rates and special deals are available. Please note that driving in Malaysia carries its risks – local

Important road signs

awas caution
beri laluan give way
berhenti stop
dilarang berhenti no stopping
dilarang meletak kereta no parking
dilarang memotong no overtaking
ikut kiri keep left

jalan bahaya dangerous road ahead
jalan licin slippery road
jalan sehala one way
kawasan kemalangan accident area
kurangkan laju slow down
utara/selatan north/south
timur/barat east/west

drivers don't always obey traffic lights or road signs and hardly ever give way. Drink driving can be a problem, particularly in Sarawak. Some expats strongly urge visitors not to risk hiring a car because of the dangers of sharing the road with Malaysian drivers.

Driving is on the left; give way to drivers on the right. Within towns the speed limit is 50 km per hour; the wearing of seat belts is compulsory for front-seat passengers and the driver. Most road signs are international but *awas* means caution; see also box above. Road maps are on sale at most petrol stations; Petronas (the national oil company) produces an excellent atlas, *Touring Malaysia by Road*. Most roads are kept in good repair. However, during the monsoon season, heavy rains may make some east coast travel difficult and the west coast roads can be congested.

In Sarawak the road network is extremely limited: air or water transport are the only option in many areas. In Sabah, 4WD vehicles are de rigeur; they are readily available, but expensive. On some islands, such as Penang, Langkawi and Pangkor, motorbikes are available for hire, starting around RM35 per day. If bringing your own car into the country, no carnet or deposit is required. The vehicle is allowed to stay in the country as long as the owner has permission to stay.

Cycling

Bicycles are available for hire from some guesthouses and specialist hire shops, especially on islands such as Pangkor, Penang, Langkawi and Tioman, but also in some towns and hill resorts. Compared with hiring motorbikes, bike hire can seem expensive – around RM20 per day and substantially more (hour-for-hour) from those places that hire by the hour. Price also vary a good deal depending on the machine; locally or Chinese-made sit-up-and-beg bikes are cheaper than new mountain bikes.

Malaysia plays host to the annual Le Tour de Langkawi attracting cyclists from all over the world. For more information, see www.ltdl.com.my.

We have had a number of letters from people who have cycled through various parts of Southeast Asia. The advice below is collated from their comments, and is meant to provide a general guideline for those intending to travel by bicycle. There may be areas, however, where the advice does not hold true, and some of the letters we have received even disagree on certain points.

Touring, hybrid or mountain bikes are fine for most roads and tracks in Malaysia – take an ordinary machine, nothing fancy. Mountain bikes have made a big impact in the country, so accessories and spares are widely available. Less common are components made of unusual materials – titanium and composites. As cycling is becoming more common, clubs are springing up across the country. Unlike Indonesia and Thailand, a foreigner on a bike is not such an object of interest. Cars and buses rarely give way to a bicycle and so be very wary, especially on main roads; avoid major roads and major towns. Non-air-conditioned, cheaper buses are more accommodating of bicycles; air-conditioned tour buses may refuse to carry a bike. Many international airlines take bicycles for no extra cost, provided they are not boxed. Take the peddles off and deflate the tyres.

Cyclists may consider taking: pollution mask if travelling to large cities; a basic toolkit including a puncture repair kit; spare inner tubes; spare tyre; pump; a good map of the area; bungee cords; and a water filter.

Hitchhiking

It is easy for foreigners to hitch; look reasonably presentable and it shouldn't be long before someone will stop. Hitching is not advisable for lone women.

Taxi

There are two types of taxi in Malaysia – local and 'out-station' – or long distance. The latter – usually Mercedes or Peugeot – connect all major towns and cities. They operate on a shared-cost basis – as soon as the full complement of four passengers turns up the taxis set off. Alternatively, it is possible to charter the whole taxi for the price of four single fares. Taxi stands are usually next door to major bus stations. If shared, taxi fares usually cost about twice as much as bus fares, but they are much faster. For groups travelling together taking a taxi makes good sense. Note that it is easier to find passengers going your way in the morning than later in the day.

Local taxi fares in Malaysia are fairly cheap, but it is rare to find a taxi with a meter; you will need your bargaining skills.

Trishaws

In KL it has long been too dangerous for trishaws, apart from around Chinatown and suburban areas. In towns such as Melaka, Georgetown and Kota Bharu, as well as in many other smaller towns, trishaws are still available, but they have largely become an expensive way to travel for well-heeled tourists. Trishaw fares in Melaka are fixed. Signs around popular trishaw congregation areas display the hourly fee.

Sea

On the Peninsula, there are regular scheduled ferry services between the main islands – Pulau Pangkor, Penang and Pulau Langkawi – and the mainland. There are services from Mersing to Pulau Tioman. There are passenger and car ferries between Butterworth and Georgetown, Penang, every 20 minutes. For other offshore islands, mostly off the east coast, fishing boats, and sometimes regular boats, leave from the nearest fishing port.

Local water transport comes into its own in Sarawak, where lack of roads makes coastal and river transport the only viable means of communication. On larger rivers in Sarawak, such as the Rejang and the Baram, there are specially adapted express boats. If there is no regular boat, it is nearly always possible to charter a local longboat, although this can be expensive. In the dry season the upper reaches of many rivers are unnavigable except by smaller boats. In times of heavy rain, logs and branch debris can make rivers unsafe. There is still some river transport on the Peninsula's east coast.

Maps

Maps are widely available in Malaysia and Singapore. Both the Singapore and Malaysian tourist boards produce good maps of their respective capital cities and in the case of Malaysia a series of state maps, although these are much poorer in quality. The Sabah and Sarawak tourist boards also publish reasonable maps.

In the UK, the best selection is available from **Stanfords** ① *12-14 Long Acre, London WC2E 9LP, T020-7836 1321, www.stanfords.co.uk*. Also recommended is **McCarta** ① *15 Highbury Place, London N15 1QP, T020-7354 1616*.

City maps **Nelles Singapore; Bartholomew Singapore**.

Country maps **Bartholomew Singapore and Malaysia** (1:150,000); **Nelles Malaysia** (1:1,500,000); **Nelles West Malaysia** (1:650,000); **Nelles Singapore** (1:22,500); **Nelles Indonesia** (1:4,000,000).

Sleeping → See also box, page 26.

Malaysia offers a good selection of international-standard hotels as well as simpler hotels and mid-range business hotels. It also has some of Southeast Asia's best guesthouses and hostels for those travelling on a budget. Room rates are subject to 5-10% tax. Many of the major international chains have hotels here, such as **Hilton, Holiday Inn** and **Hyatt**. Room rates in the big hotels have been fairly stable for the last few years. The number of four- and five-star hotel rooms has also multiplied. This, combined with the global economic crisis, has forced hotels to keep prices highly competitive. By world standards even the most expensive hotels are good value.

It is also worth noting that in tourist resorts, many hotels have two, sometimes three, room tariffs: one for weekdays, one for weekends and sometimes a third for holiday periods. Room rates can vary substantially between these periods. In the more popular holiday destinations such as the Cameron Highlands, accommodation can become scarce during the school holidays – April, August and December -- and prices sky rocket. During these months it is worth booking ahead.

On the east coast of Peninsular Malaysia and in East Malaysia, it is often possible to stay with families in Malay kampongs (villages) as part of the homestay programme (contact the local tourist office or travel agent for more information). The most popular place to do this is at Kampong Cherating, north of Kuantan, although it has been getting progressively quieter in recent years, as backpackers hunt out newer pastures; it is also possible to stay in a kampong house in Merang and Kuching.

Towns and cities on the tourist trail also often have guesthouses with dorms for the seriously shallow of pocket. These vary in quality, but most major tourist centres have a good selection to choose from and there are some superb dorms in Malaysia.

The accommodation scene in East Malaysia has improved immeasurably in recent years with places such as Kuching, Miri, Kota Kinabalu and Sandakan boasting excellent value accommodation. Other towns do not offer as good value for money as hotels on the Peninsula, but there are some bargains. For accommodation in national parks it is necessary to book in advance. In Sarawak and Sabah it is possible to stay in longhouses, where rates are at the discretion of the visitor (see page 340).

Reflecting Malaysia's enthusiastic embrace of all things high-tech, most hotels, and even many guesthouses, have internet access and Wi-Fi is becoming standard in tourist centres.

Sleeping price codes

L	Over US$200		AL	US$91-200
A	US$41-90		B	US$21-40
C	US$12-20		D	US$7-11
E	US$3-6		F	Under S$3

Price codes refer to the cost of two people sharing a double room in the high season.

Top-end hotels (L-A)

Hotels at the top of this bracket are few and far between in Malaysia. KL's splendid **Carcosa Seri Negara** is one such hotel. The **Datai** on Langkawi is another and the **Pangkor Laut Resort** on the private island of Pangkor Laut is also in the top league. Hotels in the lower ranges of this category are regarded as among the best value in the region and are beautifully appointed, offering impeccable service and an array of facilities and business services.

Mid-range hotels (B-D)

Hotels in this bracket have a good range of services and facilities, sometimes including a swimming pool, gym and maybe a spa. They can be very competitively priced, given the standards of service. Hotels at the lower end in this category provide a basic range of services and facilities, including a coffee shop and/or simple restaurant and all rooms should have air conditioning. Many will also provide Wi-Fi access and cable TV.

Budget hotels (E-F)

While there are some excellent economy hotels in this bracket, few provide much in the way of services. There will be air-conditioned or fan-cooled rooms and a choice of attached/shared bathrooms. Backpacker-oriented hostels and guesthouses fall into this bracket, and usually offer good travel advice, a laundry service, Wi-Fi, breakfast facilities and maybe a common fridge and kitchen. They are often suitable for families on a budget. Places in the mid-range of this bracket are mainly Chinese run and located in town centres. They are therefore often noisy and many are pretty scruffy with few services or facilities. Rooms may have air conditioning and attached bathrooms; cheaper rooms have fans and communal bathrooms. Some fine, old, tumbledown colonial relics in this range offer good value for money. Youth hostels fall into this price range.

At the lower end of this bracket are lodging houses, guesthouses and hostels, offering very simple rooms with shared bathroom and fan. Some backpacker places will have simple rooms and dorms. The price for a shared dorm or a bed in a simple A-frame by the beach are almost always per person.

Eating → See also box, page 29.

Cuisine

Malaysians, like their neighbours in Singapore, love their food, and the dishes of the three main communities – Malay, Chinese and Indian – comprise a hugely varied national menu. Even within each ethnic cuisine, there is a vast choice; every state has its own special Malay dishes and the different Chinese provincial specialities are well represented In addition there is North Indian food, South Indian food and Indian Muslim food. Nyonya cuisine is found in the old Straits Settlements of Penang and Melaka. Malaysia also has great seafood, which the Chinese do best, and in recent years a profusion of restaurants, representing other Asian and European cuisines, have set up, mainly in the big cities. In the East Malaysian states of Sabah and Sarawak, there are various tribal specialities.

With a large ethnic Indian population, vegetarian food is usually available, especially on the Peninsula. In East Malaysia it can be harder to find vegetarian alternatives. There are also numerous Chinese and Malay vegetarian dishes, although it is not unusual to find slivers of meat even when a vegetable dish is specifically requested. In tourist areas and more cosmopolitan towns, vegetarian restaurants are becoming popular. Many of the more religiously inclined ethnic Chinese are strong adherents to vegetarianism and in towns with a major Chinese population, it is usually easy to find a decent Chinese pure vegetarian eatery complete with authentic pieces of mock meat made from soya.

Malay The best Malay food is usually found at stalls in hawker centres. The staple diet is rice and curry, which is rich and creamy due to the use of coconut milk. Herbs and spices include chillis, ginger, tamarind, turmeric, coriander, lemongrass, anise, cloves, cumin, caraway and cinnamon.

Chinese Each province of China has its own distinct cuisine. A balanced meal should contain the five basic taste sensations: sweet, bitter, salty, spicy and acidic to balance the yin and yang.

Cantonese and Hainanese cooking are the most prevalent Chinese cuisines in Malaysia. Some of the more common Malaysian-Chinese dishes are Hainanese chicken rice (rice cooked in chicken stock and served with steamed or roast chicken), *char kway teow* (Teochew-style fried noodles, with eggs, cockles and chilli paste), or *luak* (Hokkien oyster omelette), dim sum (steamed dumplings and patties), and *yong tow foo* (beancurd and vegetables stuffed with fish). Good Chinese food is available in restaurants, coffee shops and from hawker stalls.

In **Cantonese** cuisine, light and delicately flavoured dishes are often steamed with ginger and are not very spicy. Shark's fin and birds' nest soups, and dim sum (mostly steamed delicacies served from a trolley at your table, but only until early afternoon) are Cantonese classics. Other typical dishes include fish steamed with soy sauce, ginger, chicken stock and wine; wan ton soup; blanched green vegetables in oyster sauce; and suckling pig.

Hainanese cooking is simple cuisine from the southern island of Hainan. Chicken rice with sesame oil, soy sauce and a chilli and garlic sauce is their tastiest contribution.

Hakka cuisine uses plenty of sweet potato and dried shrimp and specializes in stewed pigs' trotters, *yong tau foo* (deep-fried beancurd), chillis and other vegetables stuffed with fish paste.

Being one of Singapore's biggest dialect groups means **Hokkien** cuisine is prominent, particularly in hawker centres, although there are very few Hokkien restaurants. Hokkien Chinese invented the spring roll. Their cooking uses lots of noodles and in one or two places you can still see them being made by hand. Hokkien cuisine is also characterized by clear soups and steamed seafood, eaten with soya sauce. Fried Hokkien *mee* (yellow wheat noodles stir fried with seafood and pork), *hay cho* (deep-fried balls of prawn) and *bak kut teh* (pork rib herbal soup) and *bee hoon* (rice vermicelli cooked with prawns, squid and beansprouts with lime and chillies) are specialities.

Hunanese cuisine is hearty and spicy and well known for its glutinous rice, honeyed ham and pigeon soup.

In **Peking** (Beijing) cooking, dumplings, noodles and steamed buns predominate, since wheat is the staple diet, but in Singapore, rice may accompany the meal. Peking duck, *shi choy* (deep fried bamboo shoots) and hot and sour soup are among the best Peking dishes. Peking duck (with the skin basted with syrup and cooked until crisp) is usually eaten rolled into a pancake and accompanied by hoisin sauce and spring onions. Fish dishes are usually deep-fried and served with sweet and sour sauce. Chefs at the imperial court in Peking had a repertoire of over 8000 recipes.

Seafood dominates **Shanghainese** cuisine and many dishes are cooked in soya sauce with sugar added, giving the food a sweeet taste. Braised fish-heads, braised abalone (a prized large shellfish) in sesame sauce and crab and sweetcorn soup are typical dishes. Wine is often used in the preparation of meat dishes, hence drunken prawn and drunken crab.

Steamboat, the Chinese answer to fondue, is a popular dish in Malaysia and can be found in numerous restaurants and at some hawker centres. Thinly sliced pieces of raw meat, fish, prawns, cuttlefish, fishballs and vegetables are gradually tossed into a bubbling cauldron in the centre of the table. They are then dunked into hot chilli and soy sauces and the resulting soup provides a flavoursome broth to wash it all down. Often a lot of MSG is added to the stock resulting in a parched thirst after dining. Try and find a place that doesn't use MSG in its stocks.

Very spicy (garlic and chilli are dominant) **Sichuan** food is one of China's most celebrated cuisines. It includes heaps of hot red peppers, traditionally considered to be protection against cold and disease. Among the best Sichuan dishes are smoked duck in tea leaves and camphor sawdust; minced pork with beancurd; steamed chicken in lotus leaves; and fried eels in garlic sauce.

Teochew is famous for its muay porridges. This is a light, clear broth consumed with side dishes of crayfish, salted eggs and vegetables.

Indian This cuisine can be divided into three schools: northern and southern (neither eat beef) and Muslim (no pork). Northern dishes tend to be more subtly spiced, use more meat and are served with breads. Southern dishes use fiery spices, emphasize vegetables and are served with rice. The best-known North Indian food is tandoori, which is served with delicious fresh naan breads, baked in onsite ovens. Other pancakes include roti, dosai and chapati. Malaysia's famous mamak-men are Indian Muslims who are highly skilled in everything from teh tarik (see Drink below) to rotis.

Nyonya Through intermarriage with local Malays a unique culture evolved and, with it, a cuisine that has grown out of a blend of the two. Nyonya food is spicier than Chinese food and it uses pork. Nyonya dishes in Penang have adopted flavours from neighbouring Thailand, whereas Melaka's Nyonya food has Indonesian overtones. In traditional Straits

Eating price codes

¶¶¶ over US$12	¶¶ US$4-12	¶ under US$4

Prices refer to the average cost of a two-course meal for one person, not including drinks or service charge.

Chinese households, great emphasis was placed on presentation and the fine-chopping of ingredients. See also Glossary, page 660.

Sabahan The Kadazans form the largest ethnic group in Sabah. Their food tends to use mango and can be on the sour side.

Eating out

Malaysia, like Singapore, has just about got it all on the restaurant front: from the swankiest restaurants where international cuisine is served at prices that are usually rather less than one would expect, through to stalls and hawker centres where a meal can cost less than a Coca-Cola back home. There's also a huge range to choose from because, as noted above, Malaysia is a plural society and home to significant Malay, Chinese and Indian populations that have, at times, intersected in gastronomically interesting ways. Furthermore, and again as in Singapore, good food is not confined to restaurants; some of the best local dishes can be sampled at hawker centres, which are cheap and often stay open late into the night.

The cheapest places to eat are in hawker centres and roadside stalls (often concentrated in or close to night markets) where it is possible to eat well for less than RM5. Stalls may serve Malay, Indian or Chinese dishes and, even, some food that approximates to 'Western' – think deep-fried chicken thighs, chips and cold baked beans. Next in the sequence of sophistication and price come the ubiquitous *kedai kopi* (coffee shops), which can be found in every town and almost every street, and where a meal will cost upwards of RM5. Usually run by Chinese or Indian families, rather than Malay, they open at around 0900 and close in the early evening, many are 24 hours. However some open much earlier, at dawn, to serve dim sum to people making their way to work. Chinese-run *kedai kopi* tend to be the last to close – sometimes as late as midnight – and they are also the only coffee shops where it is possible to track down a cold beer. Malay-run *kedai kopi* are good for lunch with their *nasi campur* spreads, while Indian-run coffee shops offer what you would expect them to offer. Above the *kedai kopi* come a phalanx of restaurants from the basic to the extremely pricey. A special category are the restaurants geared to travellers' culinary needs, which tend to be concentrated in beach resorts. Here it is possible to live off banana pancakes, fudge cake, smoothies, jaffles and all the other dishes that backpackers on the move seem to need to keep body and soul together. Hotel restaurants regularly lay on buffet spreads, which are good value at about RM30, often much cheaper than the price of a room would suggest.

Drink

Soft drinks, mineral water and freshly squeezed fruit drinks are available. Anchor and Tiger beers are widely sold, except in the more Islamic states of the east coast, especially Kelantan, and are cheapest at the hawker stalls (RM5-7 per bottle). A beer will cost

RM8-15 per bottle in coffee shops. Potent Malaysian-brewed Guinness Foreign Extra is popular, mainly because the Chinese believe it has medicinal qualities as it has been successfully sold on the 'Guinness Stout is good for you' line (and recent studies suggest there is some truth in that). Malaysian tea is grown in the Cameron Highlands and is very good. One of the most interesting cultural refinements of the Indian Muslim community is the Mamak-man, who is famed for *teh tarik* (pulled tea), which is thrown across a distance of about a metre, from one cup to another, with no spillages. The idea is to cool it down for customers, but it has become an art form; mamak-men appear to cultivate the nonchalant look when pouring. Malaysian satirist Kit Leee says a tea stall mamak "could 'pull' tea in free fall without spilling a drop – while balancing a beedi on his lower lip and making a statement on economic determinism". Most of the coffee comes from Indonesia, although some is locally produced. Malaysians like strong coffee and unless you specify *kurang manis* (less sugar), *tak mahu manis* (no sugar) or *kopi kosong* (black, no sugar), it will come with lashings of condensed milk. To ask for tea or coffee without sugar or milk as for *teh/kopi o kosong*.

Entertainment

Bars and clubs

If you want to stagger down the street five sheets to the wind on a nightly basis, it should be remembered that Malaysia is most certainly not Glastonbury or Ayia Napa. There has never been a really happening club and dance circuit in Malaysia, although KL has a range of decent clubs and bars and the nightlife is becoming increasingly sophisticated in the city. Karaoke is more the average Malaysians cup of *arak* than hip hop. The main towns where there is a nightlife of sorts are KL, Penang, Kuching and Kota Kinabalu. Despite the lack of booze on the east coast, the Perhentians and Pulau Tioman can get lively after dark if you know the right spots.

Cinema

Most of the big cities have multiplex cinema – these are usually tucked away in shopping malls. As a general rule, big cities or towns such as KL, JB, Ipoh, Melaka, Penang, Kuantan, Kuching, Miri and Kota Kinabalu have a choice of cinemas. Outside those, cinemas are few and far between.

Mainstream Hollywood movies are shown along with an Asian selection including local offerings, Bollywood blockbusters and Japanese, Chinese and Korean cinema. While Bollywood movies and local films are unlikely to have English subtitles, East Asian movies often have them.

Movies are rated U (general viewing), 18SG (for over 18s with non-excessive horrifying or violent content), 18SX (for over 18s with non-excessive sex scenes), 18PA (for over 18s with political/religious counter-culture elements) or 18PL (for over 18s with a combination of two or more undesirable elements).

KL's Berjaya Times Square shopping mall has an IMAX cinema, see page 96.

Comedy

Stand-up comedians and comedies are most likely to be performed at the Actor's Studio Theatre in KL. Many shows, however, will be in Malay. If you are lucky you may catch a bilingual show which will be half in Malay and half in English. It's unlikely you'll be able to catch any comedy in English outside of KL. During the Mahathir era comedy was an occasional 'safe' outlet for local artists to poke fun at their prime minister.

Dance and theatre

Malaysia is not a mecca for the performing arts. For contemporary dance and theatre your best bet is KL; see page 97 for a list of venues. See www.kakiseni.com for more information on Malaysia's arts scene. You are unlikely to see any English-language theatre outside of KL.

For traditional dance performances contact the Malaysia Tourism Centre or visit their website, see page 60. Some of the fancier hotels and restaurants also stage shows while guests eat. Tourism Malaysia also hosts an annual theatre festival, but many of the offerings are in Malay.

Festivals and events

The timing of Islamic festivals is an art rather than a science and is calculated on the basis of local sightings of various phases of the moon. Thus dates are approximations and can vary by a day or two. Muslim festivals move forward by around nine to 10 days each year. To check on dates, see www.tourism.gov.my.

Chinese, Indian (Hindu) and some Christian holidays are also movable. To convert the Gregorian calendar to the lunar calendar see www.mandarintools.com/calendar.html. To make things even more exciting, each state has its own public holidays when shops and banks close. This makes calculating public holidays in advance a bit of a quagmire of lunar events, assorted kings' birthdays and tribal festivals. Note that most government offices (including some tourist offices) are closed on the first and third Saturday of each month.

Schools in Malaysia have five breaks through the year, although the actual dates vary from state to state. They generally fall in the months of January (one week), March (two weeks), May (three weeks), August (one week) and October (four weeks).

Only sultans' and governors' birthday celebrations are marked with processions and festivities. State holidays can disrupt travel itineraries, particularly in east coast states where they may run for several days.

January/February

New Year's Day (1 Jan: public holiday except Johor, Kedah, Kelantan, Perlis and Terengganu). Thaipusam (movable: public holiday Johor, Negeri Sembilan, Perak, Penang and Selangor only). Celebrated by many Hindus throughout Malaysia in honour of their deity Lord Subramanian (also known as Lord Muruga); he represents virtue, bravery, youth and power. Held during full moon in the month of Thai, it is a day of penance and thanksgiving. Devotees pay homage to Lord Subramanian by piercing their bodies, cheeks and tongues with sharp skewers and hooks weighted with oranges, and carrying kevadis (steel structures bearing the image of Lord

Muruga). There are strict rules the devotee must follow in order to purify himself before carrying the kevadi; he becomes a vegetarian and abstains from worldly pleasures. Women cannot carry kevadis as they are not allowed to bare their bodies in order to be pierced. Although a kevadi carrier can have as many as 100 spears piercing his flesh, he only loses a small amount of blood in his trance. Each participant tries to outdo the others in the severity of his torture. At certain temples firewalking is also part of this ceremony. Many Hindus disapprove of the spectacle and believe that their bodies are a gift from Siva; they should serve as a temple for the soul and should not be abused. This festival is peculiar to Hindus in Malaysia, Singapore and Thailand and is a corruption of a Tamil ceremony from South India. The biggest gatherings are at Batu Caves just outside KL, when thousands of pilgrims congregate in a carnival-like atmosphere (see page 74); there are also festivals held in Melaka, Penang and Singapore (see page 565).

Chinese New Year (late Jan/early Feb, movable: public holiday, two days in most states, one day in Kelantan and Terengganu). A 15-day lunar festival. Chinatown streets are crowded for weeks with shoppers buying traditional oranges which signify luck. Lion, unicorn or dragon dances welcome in the New Year and, unlike in Singapore, thousands of firecrackers are ignited to ward off evil spirits. Chap Goh Mei is the 15th day of the Chinese New Year and brings celebrations to a close; it is marked with a final dinner, another firecracker fest, prayers and offerings. The Chinese believe that in order to find good husbands, women should throw oranges into the river or sea on this day. In Sarawak the festival is known as Guan Hsiao Cheih (Lantern Festival).

Hari Raya Haji (movable: public holiday in Kedah, Kelantan, Perlis and Terengganu). Hari Raya Qurban is also a public holiday celebrated by Muslims to mark the 10th day of Zulhijjah, the 12th month of the Islamic calendar when pilgrims celebrate their return from the Haj to Mecca. In the morning, prayers are offered and later, families hold an open house. Those who can afford it sacrifice goats or cows to be distributed to the poor. Many Malays have the title Haji in their name, meaning they have made the pilgrimage to Mecca; men who have been on the Haj wear a white skullhat. The Haj is one of the five keystones of Islam.

Sultan of Kedah's birthday (20 Jan, state holiday). Kedah.

Federal Territory Day (1 Feb, state holiday). KL and Labuan.

March/April

Easter (movable). Celebrated in Melaka with candlelit processions and special services. Good Friday is a public holiday in Sabah and Sarawak.

Maal Hijrah (Awal Muharram) (movable: public holiday). The first day of the Muslim calendar, marking the Prophet Muhammad's journey from Mecca to Medina on the lunar equivalent of 16 July AD 622. Religious discussions commemorate the day.

Installation of Sultan of Terengganu Day **(4 Mar**, state holiday). Terengganu.

Sultan of Selangor's birthday (11 Dec, state holiday). Selangor.

Sultan of Kelantan's birthday (30-31 Mar, state holiday). Kelantan.

Sultan of Johor's birthday (8 Apr). Johor.

Declaration of Melaka as Historic City (15 Apr). Melaka.

Sultan of Perak's birthday (19 Apr). Perak.

May

Labour Day (1 May, public holiday).

Kurah Aran (1 May) celebrated by the Bidayuh tribe in Sarawak (see page 385) after the paddy harvest is over.

Wesak Day (movable: public holiday except Labuan). The most important day in the Buddhist calendar, celebrates the Buddha's birth, death and enlightenment. Temples throughout the country are packed with devotees offering incense, joss sticks and prayers. In Melaka there is a procession at night with decorated floats and dancers.

Birthday of the Prophet Muhammad (Maulidur Rasul) (movable: public holiday). Commemorates Prophet Muhammad's birthday in AD 571. Processions and Koran recitals in most big towns.

Pahang Hol Day (7 May, state holiday). Pahang.

Rajah of Perlis' birthday (17 May, state holiday). Perlis.

Harvest Festival (30-31 May, state holiday). Sabah and Labuan.

June

Birthday of Yang di-Pertuan Agong ('His Majesty the King') (1st Sat of the month: public holiday). Mainly celebrated in KL with processions.

Dragon Boat Festival (movable). Honours the suicide of an ancient Chinese poet hero, Qu Yuan. He tried to press for political reform by drowning himself in the Mi Luo River as a protest against corruption. In an attempt to save him fishermen played drums and threw rice dumplings to try and distract vultures. His death is commemorated with dragon boat races and the enthusiastic consumption of rice dumplings; the biggest celebrations are in Penang.

Dayak Day (**1-2 Jun**, state holiday). Sarawak.

July

Governor of Penang's birthday (2nd Sat of the month, state holiday). Penang.

Yang Di-Pertuan Besar of Negeri Sembilan's birthday (**19 Jul**, state holiday). Negeri Sembilan.

Sultan of Terengganu's birthday (**20 Jul**, state holiday). Terengganu.

August/September

Awal Ramadan (movable: Aug 2010, public holiday Johor and Melaka). The first day of Ramadan, a month of fasting for all Muslims – and by implication, all Malays. During this month Muslims abstain from all food and drink (as well as smoking) from sunrise to sundown; if they are very strict, Muslims do not even swallow their own saliva during daylight hours. It is strictly adhered to in the conservative Islamic states of Kelantan and Terengganu. Every evening for 30 days before breaking of fast, stalls are set up selling traditional Malay cakes and delicacies. The only people exempt from fasting are the elderly and women who are pregnant or menstruating.

Hari Kebangsaan or **National Day** (**31 Aug**, public holiday). Commemorates Malaysian independence (*merdeka*) in 1957. It's a big celebration in KL with processions of floats representing all the states. The best places to see it are on the Padang (Merdeka Square) or on TV. In Sarawak, Hari Kebangsaan is celebrated in a different divisional capital each year.

Hari Raya Puasa or **Aidil Fitri** (movable: Sep 2010, public holiday). Marks the end of the Muslim fasting month of Ramadan and is a day of prayer and celebration. In order for Hari Raya to be declared, the new moon of Syawal has to be sighted; if it is not, fasting continues for another day. It is the most important time of the year for Muslim families to get together; Malays living in towns and cities balek kampong (return home to their village), where it is open house for relatives and friends, and special Malay delicacies are served. Hari Raya is also enthusiastically celebrated by Indian Muslims.

Mooncake or **Lantern Festival** (movable). This Chinese festival marks the overthrow of the Mongol Dynasty in China; celebrated, as the name suggests, with the exchange and eating of mooncakes. According to Chinese legend secret messages of revolt were carried inside these cakes and led to the uprising. In the evening, children light festive lanterns while women pray to the Goddess of the Moon.

Festival of the Hungry Ghosts (movable). On the 7th moon in the Chinese lunar calendar, souls in purgatory are believed to return to earth to feast. Food is offered to these wandering spirits. Altars are set up in the streets and candles with faces are burned.

Governor of Sarawak's birthday (**14 Sep**, state holiday). Sarawak.

Governor of Sabah's birthday (**16 Sep**, state holiday). Sabah.

October

Festival of the Nine Emperor Gods or **Kiew Ong Yeah** (movable). Marks the return of the spirits of the nine emperor gods to earth. The mediums whom they are to possess purify themselves by observing a vegetarian diet. The gods possess the mediums, who go into trance and are then carried on sedan chairs whose seats are comprised of razor-sharp blades or spikes. Devotees visit temples dedicated to the nine gods. A strip of yellow cotton is often bought from the temple and worn on the right wrist as a sign of devotion. Ceremonies may end with a firewalking ritual.

Governor of Melaka's birthday (2nd Sat of the month, state holiday). Melaka.
Sultan of Pahang's birthday (**24 Oct**, state holiday). Pahang.

October/November

Deepvali (movable: public holiday except Sarawak and Labuan). The Hindu festival of lights commemorates the victory of light over darkness and good over evil, the triumphant return of Rama after his defeat of the evil Ravanna in the Hindu epic, the Ramayana. Every Hindu home is brightly lit and decorated for the occasion.
Hari Hol Almarhum Sultan Ismail (movable, Johor). Israk and Mikraj (movable, Kedah and Negeri Sembilan).
Nuzul Quran (movable). Kelantan, Pahang, Perak, Perlis, Selangor and Terengganu.

December

Christmas Day (**25 Dec**, public holiday). Christmas in Malaysia is a commercial spectacle these days with fairy lights and decorations and tropical Santa Clauses – although it does not compare with celebrations in Singapore. It's mostly celebrated on the west coast and ignored on the more Muslim east coast. Midnight mass is the main Christmas service held in churches throughout Malaysia.

Festivals in East Malaysia

Besides those celebrated throughout the country, Sabah and Sarawak have their own festivals. Exact dates can be procured from the tourist offices in the capitals.
Kadazan Harvest Festival or Tadau Keamatan (movable: public holiday, Sabah and Labuan only). This festival marks the end

of the rice harvest in Sabah; the magavau ritual is performed to nurse the spirit back to health in readiness for the next planting season. Traditionally, the ritual world would have been performed in the paddy fields by a *bobohizan* (high priestess). Celebrated with feasting, *tapai* (rice wine) drinking, dancing and general merrymaking. There are also agricultural shows, buffalo races, cultural performances and traditional games. The traditional sumazal dance is one of the highlights of the festivities.

Gawai (movable: public holiday Sarawak only). The major festival of the year for the Iban of Sarawak; longhouses party continuously for a week. The Gawai celebrates the end of the rice harvest and welcomes the new planting season. The main ritual is called *magavau* and nurses the spirit of the grain back to health in advance of the planting season. Like the Kadazan harvest festival in Sabah, visitors are welcome to join in, but in Sarawak, the harvest festival is much more traditional. On the first day of celebrations everyone dresses up in traditional costumes, singing, dancing and drinking *tuak* (rice wine) until they drop.

Gawai Burung (Sarawak). The biggest of all the gawais and honours the war god of the Ibans. Gawai Kenyalang is one stage of Gawai Burung and is celebrated only after a tribesman has been instructed to do so after a dream.

Gawai Antu (Sarawak Jun). Also known as **Gawai Nyunkup** or **Rugan**, this is an Iban tribute to departed spirits. In simple terms, it is a party to mark the end of mourning for anyone whose relative had died in the previous 6 months.

Gawai Batu (Sarawak Jun). A whetstone feast held by Iban farmers.

Gawai Mpijong Jaran Rantau (Sarawak). Celebrated by the Bidayuh before grass cutting in new paddy fields.

Gawai Bineh (Sarawak). An Iban festival celebrated after harvest. It welcomes back all the spirits of the paddy from the fields.

Gawai Sawa (movable). Celebrated by the Bidayuh in Sarawak to offer thanksgiving for the last year and to make the next year a plentiful one.

Festivals in Sarawak

Most of Malaysia's mainstream festivals are celebrated in Sarawak, including Chinese New Year, Christmas and Hari Raya. But there are also some festivals that are peculiarly Sarawakian.
Mid-Mar-early Apr (movable), **Kaul**. Celebrated by the Melanau community. Although the Melanau are now largely Muslim and Christian, this animist festival continues to be celebrated, most enthusiastically in the coastal town of Mukah. Fishermen appease the spirits of the sea before the onset of the fishing season by launching miniature wooden boats. Young men compete in a game known as *tibou* where they see how many can swing from a single rope.
31 May-1 Jun Gawai Dayak. Sarawak's major home-grown festival, marking the end of the rice harvest. Vast quantities of food are prepared and *tuak* brewed. Urban residents return to their rural roots for a major binge.

Shopping

Most big towns have modern shopping complexes as well as shops and markets. Department stores are fixed price, but nearly everywhere else it is possible – and necessary – to bargain. In most places, at least 30% can be knocked off the asking price; your first offer should be roughly half the first quote.

What to buy
The islands of Langkawi, Tioman and Labuan have duty-free shopping; the range of goods is poor, however. But the selection of booze is generally excellent, with wine and beer going for a fraction of the price on the mainland.

Kuala Lumpur and most of the state capitals have Chinatown, which usually have a few curio shops and nearly always a *pasar malam*, or night market. Indian quarters, which are invariably labelled 'Little India', are only found in bigger towns; they are the best places to buy sarongs, longis, dotis and saris (mostly imported from India) as well as other textiles. Malay handicrafts are usually only found in markets or government craft centres.

Handicrafts
The Malaysian arts and crafts industry used to enjoy much more royal patronage, but when craftspeople went in search of more lucrative jobs, the industry began to decline. The growth of tourism has reinvigorated it, particularly in traditional handicraft-producing areas, such as the east coast states of Terengganu and Kelantan. The Malay Arts and Crafts Society has also been instrumental in preventing the decline of the industry. Malaysian Handicraft and Souvenir Centres (Karyaneka centres) were set up to market Malaysian arts and crafts in KL and some state capitals. Typical Malaysian handicrafts that can be found on the Peninsula include woodcarvings, batik, songket (cloth woven with gold and silver thread), pewterware, silverware, kites, tops and wayang kulit (shadow puppets). For more information on Malaysian crafts, see page 520.

Other than the Peninsula's east coast states, Sarawak is the other place where the traditional handicraft industry is flourishing (see page 392). The state capital, Kuching, is full of handicraft and antique shops selling tribal pieces collected from upriver; those going upriver themselves can often find items being sold in towns and even longhouses en route. Typical Sarawakian handicrafts include woodcarvings, *pua kumbu* (rust-coloured tie-dye blankets), beadwork and basketry (see page 326). Many handicraft shops on Peninsular Malaysia also sell Sarawakian handicrafts – particularly those in KL – although there is a considerable mark-up.

Activities and tours

Birdwatching

Malaysia is home to hundreds of birds including many migratory species and there are great facilities for birdwatchers. Notable sites in Peninsular Malaysia include Fraser's Hill, page 109; Maxwell Hill, page 130; and Taman Negara National Park, page 257. In Sabah: Gunung Kinabalu Park, page 439; Kinabatangan Riverine Forest area, page 459; Lahad Datu, page 460; Layang Layang Island, page 406; Tempasuk River, page 435. In Sarawak: Bako National Park, page 318; Gunung Mulu National Park, page 369; Lambir Hills National Park, page 359; Similajau National Park, page 352. For organized birdwatching holidays, see www.birdtours.co.uk.

Cookery courses

For those wishing to learn more about Malaysian cuisine, several state tourist boards offer short courses. Enquire at Tourism Malaysia information centres. A wide variety of Malaysian cookery books is available at leading bookshops.

Diving

Malaysia's underwater world is as diverse as anywhere can be: from pristine vistas of immaculate corals with enormous whale sharks or schools of hammerheads to shallow waters rich with tiny and rare marine creatures. Like her land environment, Malaysia's seas are incredibly diverse and it's this diversity that attracts divers from all over the planet. Peninsular Malaysia has the East Sea (South China Sea) to the east and the Straits of Melaka to the west. Borneo's two states, over 500 km away, are surrounded by the East, Sulu and Celebes seas. Each has its own weather patterns and consequent dive styles. Choosing where to dive will be governed by the time of year and where you happen to be, but no matter where that is, there will be a delightful island resort and a friendly dive centre to help you submerge. Tourism Malaysia, www.tourism.gov.my, has plenty of diving information on its website.

Malaysian Borneo

The outstanding region of Malaysian Borneo is *the* destination for serious divers who travel here for no other reason but to submerge. Sabah has many well-established and well-run island resorts completely dedicated to diving. Sea and wind conditions vary, so diving can be hard, but there are many places suitable for novices.

Located one hour by plane north of Kota Kinabalu, **Layang Layang**, page 406, is a tiny, man-made island sitting on a stunning lagoon. Around the edge of the lagoon is a large atoll whose steep-sided walls drop off to unimaginable depths. Strong currents drag nutrients across the reefs, which, in turn, ensure prolific hard coral growth and create a haven for masses of pelagic life. However, most people come for the curious hammerhead phenomena every Easter, when large schools swarm around Layang for a few weeks. At other times turtles, reef sharks and schooling fish are common. As the diving here can be challenging – and there is little else to do – it is perhaps not a place for novices. The resort is also a bird sanctuary where rare boobies nest.

Around one hour by boat from Sandakan into the Sulu Sea, idyllic **Lankayan**, page 454, is ringed by an iridescent white beach and covered in a labyrinth of unruly jungle. The reefs surrounding the island are gently shelving, flat plateaus. There is high biodiversity, but visibility can be low at times, due to the proximity of the mainland and the high concentration of plankton. Diving here is about looking for the animals that thrive in these nutrient-rich conditions. There are plenty, including rare rhinopias and occasional whalesharks. Several shipwrecks ensure good variety, including one straight off the jetty.

Sipadan, page 465, is the most famous of Borneo's dive destinations, a tiny spit of land that sits off the eastern tip of Borneo on the Litigan Reefs. It is an all-out magnet for divers. The walls off the island drop to well over 600 m and this unique geography has created a spectacular marine environment. If you are looking for big stuff, this is the place. Turtles are everywhere, so prolific and curious that they will follow you around on a dive. Sharks are easy to spot: white tips snooze on sandy shelves and hammerheads are frequently sighted. On the aptly named Barracuda Point, huge schools of this fish just hang about. There are plenty of small and colourful creatures to see as well. Dive conditions are variable, currents can be strong and dives are done as drifts. A few years ago all resorts were either closed or moved to Mabul Island (see below) or nearby Semporna. This closure was largely due to environmental concerns and now diver numbers in the Sipadan area are limited by a strict permit system. Licences to dive around Sipadan are usually booked weeks in advance; no surprise given its fame. A good website is www.scuba-junkie.com, with descriptions and maps detailing Sipadan and Mabul dives.

Sipadan's nearest neighbour is **Mabul**, page 465, known as a special place for spotting small creatures. The island is large compared to both Sipadan and nearby Kapalai, with a village and several resorts. Offshore is an ugly oil rig, but beneath it is one of the best muck dives in the region. Shore dives are equally spectacular, with seahorses, frogfish and ghost pipefish. Conditions are mostly easy, although occasional currents can restrict dive choices.

Although charted on maps, **Kapalai**, page 466, is only a sand bar remaining from what was once a small island, a short motor from Sipadan. The flat topography extends underwater, yet visibility is reasonable as the reef mounds are washed daily by gentle tides. Corals tend to be low lying to the contours of the landscape and are a great haven for masses of sea creatures. Leaffish, hawkfish and frogfish appear on virtually every dive. Diving is year round and suitable for everyone.

Miri, page 356, the coastal region off northern Sarawak, has a growing dive reputation but is sadly affected by weather and the coastal marine environment. Miri sits on the mouth of a river which extends seawards as a flat plateau, never dropping far beyond 15 m. The areas can be awash with sediment, caused by both man-made and natural erosion. But arrive on a clear day, when there has been little rain, and the diving can be excellent. Further offshore are some dive sites that reach 30 m and several oil rigs that make great artificial reefs, attracting pelagics like barracuda and turtles. The reefs here are 'undiscovered' but whether you enjoy the diving will depend much on the visibility.

Mataking, page 466. As Sipadan becomes ever busier, the resorts around her grow and develop. Mataking is the newest and has built an excellent reputation. The reefs here are shallow and gentle and in the past, there has been some damage. However, the resort is working hard to regenerate the reef with the introduction of a well-regarded reef ball project. These artificial reefs give baby corals a foundation to latch onto and help attract fish species by giving them protection. Meanwhile there is a proliferation of small, colourful creatures plus rays, turtles and so on. In 2006 the resort sank a 40-ft wooden cargo ship as part of its conservation programme. The wreck will create a new artificial reef and also contains one of only five underwater post offices on earth. The island itself is quite large and ringed by a stretch of white sandy beach. There's even an outdoor spa set under the mangrove trees. Just watch out for the coconut crabs who come to visit at night. Diving is year round and the island is perfect for everyone, even non-diving friends.

Pulau Labuan, page 420, is a Malay Federal Territory 8 km off the west coast of Sabah and a short hop from the Sultanate of Brunei. The marine park off Labuan's south coast consists of three small islands with pretty beaches, ringed by some shallow reefs that are suitable for snorkelling. However, the real draw is the cluster of accessible wrecks. A couple – the American and Australian wrecks – date from the Second World War, while the Blue Water and Cement wrecks are more recent. This last is suitable for beginners, but the others require more advanced diving experience. Fish and coral growth on the structures are both reasonable, which is a good thing as the local reefs suffer from sediments and low visibility. The best dive season is May to September.

Peninsular Malaysia

The dive reputation of this area lags far behind highly respected Borneo. It's not that there isn't good diving, it just isn't quite as spectacular. West coast reefs have suffered due to the commercial nature of the region, however, the good news for divers is that the easily reached and relaxing east coast has a huge variety of resorts and islands. The best time to visit is in the drier season, from April until October, but even then visibility can drop way down to 3 m – or be as high as 30 m. All these places are suitable no matter what your experience is, although serious divers may find them not quite enough of a challenge. If no accommodation is listed below it's because the dive centres work with several options. Just tell them your budget and they'll find you somewhere appealing to stay.

Perhentian Islands, page 284. Inside the Terengganu Marine Park are the two Perhentian Islands. These tiny, pretty, Robinson Crusoe-like islands are ringed by dive sites. These tend to be rocky outcrops with cracks and crevices to investigate. There's plenty of coral growth and all the typical fish species – angels butterflies, jacks and so on. In July and August bigger pelagics, even whale sharks, may make an appearance.

Redang Archipelago, page 281. This is just below the Perhentian Islands and also part of the marine park. Redang consists of a main island surrounded by a cluster of smaller ones. This was Malaysia's first marine park and has the best visibility as there are deeper drop-offs. Dive sites circle outcrops which have sandy terrain on the eastern side and rocky terrain on the west. This makes for quite a variety of sites with plenty of hard corals and fans. Occasional mantas and whale sharks have been spotted.

Pulau Lang Tengah, page 282. Regarded as one of the nation's best-kept secrets, this small island has virgin beaches and an unspoilt tropical jungle interior. It is also undeveloped, with only a few tiny resorts that give it a sense of exclusivity. Diving is, like its neighbours, gentle and easy going.

Tenggol Island, page 267. Located further south, this island is regarded as having some of the best diving on the Peninsula. It's a bit further offshore and has better visibility. The west of the island is a steep-sided wall that descends down to 30 m where interesting boulders can be found. There's plenty of colour, with soft corals and fans, while on the east of the island you may find some intriguing critters lurking in the sand.

Tioman Island, page 222. The movie *South Pacific* was filmed on Tioman and it is as lovely as you might recall (if you're old enough). At less than one hour's flight from KL and Singapore, it is an ideal add-on, but possibly as much for its jungle walks, birdlife and flora as its diving. The island is a designated marine park, but the water is very shallow so best suited to beginners. In fact, this can be a good place to take a course. There is more challenging diving a little way offshore, with all the usual suspects to spot, and a couple of small wrecks lurking in the shallows.

Langkawi and **Pulau Payar**, pages 174 and 179. The west coast of Malaysia's Peninsula is not regarded as a dive-specific destination by those in the know. A history of heavy shipping, trade and industry has taken its toll on the marine realm, but if you're heading this way for another reason, there is diving available. The Payar Marine Park has some reasonable coral reefs and plenty of life in them, but the area tends to suffer from low visibility.

Liveaboards

There are a fair number of liveaboards cruising the waters of Malaysia. Many offer combination packages to nearby diving spots in Indonesia. Try **White Manta** ⓘ *18 Sin Ming Walk, 02-03, Singapore, T9677 8894, www.whitemanta.com,* which cruises the Peninsula's east coast in summer visiting Tioman, Redang, Perhentian and Tenggol. Winter trips take in dive sites around Thailand. **Celebes Explorer** ⓘ *book via Adventure Journey World Travel, Ground Floor, Lot 4, Block A, Taman Fortuna Shoplots, Jln Penampang, PO Box 12248, 88825 Kota Kinabalu, Sabah, T088-248331, www.borneo.org/liveaboard,* offers the only regular sailings around the top of Borneo. Itineraries cover Sipadan and nearby islands, depending on the length of cruise.

Diving practicalities

It is hard to be general about diving seasons and conditions across Malaysia. Although it is warm and humid all year round, the mainland and Borneo are governed by very different wind patterns and currents. For example, monsoons from the northeast will affect the mainland's east coast, but make little difference to Borneo's east coast. Consequently, best dive seasons are listed after each resort or region.

No matter what time of year you visit, or what area, the water temperature is invariably warm. Temperatures hover between 25°C and 29°C but may occasionally drop as low as 23°C. A 3 mm wetsuit is as much as you are likely to need unless you plan to do more than three dives a day.

Almost every dive centre will rent good-quality equipment but bringing your own will considerably reduce costs. Prior to departure, check your baggage allowance with the airlines and see if you can come to some kind of arrangement for extra weight.

There are masses of world-class dive destinations on almost as many islands – and the good news is that there are just as many operators. In general, dive businesses are extremely professional and run by friendly and helpful staff. Some, on smaller or newer resorts, may have limited diving facilities. Many work closely with one of the international governing bodies (PADI, NAUI, CMAS or BSAC). It's always worth asking around if you're unsure of what you are being offered.

As always, there are a few simple rules to avoid getting bent: don't dive too deep; don't ascend too quickly; use – and obey – your computer; always do a safety stop (three minutes at 3 m minimum); and drink plenty of water to avoid dehydration. Should you become victim to a suspected decompression attack, contact one of the recompression facilities listed below immediately or the **Malaysian Diving Emergency Hotline** ① *T05-930 4114 (24 hrs), for advice.*

Recompression facilities can be found in the following places. Sipadan Island: **Borneo Divers** ① *T088-222226, www.borneodivers.info*, runs a single chamber on Mabul Island. Labuan: chamber owned and operated by the Malaysian Navy, **Labuan Recompression Chamber** ① *Labuan Pejabat Selam, Markas Wilayah Laut Dua, 87007, Labuan, Labuan T087-412122.* East Coast: **Kuantan Naval Base** ① *Kuantan Mawilla Sail Diving Team, Tg Gelang, 25990, Kuantan, Pahang T09-433444.* West Coast: **Armed Forces Hospital** ① *RMN Base, 32100 Lumut, Perak, Malaysia, T05-683 7090 ext 4071, divemed@hatl.gov.my.* Singapore: **Naval Medicine and Hyperbaric Centre** ① *36 Admiralty Rd, West Singapore T6750 5632 (appointments), T6758 1733 (24-hr emergencies).*

Note that air-evacuation services if available are extremely expensive and hyperbaric chambers can charge as much as US$800 per hour. Good diving insurance is imperative. It is inexpensive and well worth it in case of a problem. Many general travel insurance policies will not cover diving. Contact **DAN (Divers Alert Network)** ① *www.diversalertnetwork.org*, **DAN Europe** ① *www.daneurope.org*, or **DAN South East Asia Pacific** ① *www.danseap.org*, for more information. If you have no insurance you can join online.

Motorbike tours

Those interested in seeing Malaysia on two wheels might want to check out the following reputable tour operators: **Ride Malaysia** ① *www.ridemalaysia.com.my*, and **Borneo Biking Adventures** ① *www.borneobikingadventures.com*, founded by five-times British Motorcross champion, Bryan Wade.

Spas

Many luxury hotels have cashed in on the popularity of pamper-yourself holidays by adding spas to their resorts. You'll find spas, aromatherapy and massage centres in most of the upmarket hotels all over the country – on the Peninsula and in East Malaysia.

Spectator sports

The best place to see traditional sports such as **silat** (the Malaysian art of self defence), **kite flying** and **top-spinning** is at the Cultural Centre in Kota Bahru on the east coast where performances and competitions are held at fixed times every week.

All over the country, a good way to make friends is by watching village **football** matches – you may be asked to take part. Head to the village green.

There are **horse-racing** tracks in Penang, T04-229 3233, www.penangturfclub.com and near KL at Selangor, T03-9058 3888, www.selangorturfclub.com.

For **motor racing**, there is the state-of-the-art Malaysian F1 Grand Prix stadium with its 15-turn track in Sepang, 60 km south of KL. See www.malaysiangp.com.my for details of events and how to get there.

Trekking and climbing

There are numerous opportunities for climbing, especially in Sarawak and Sabah. Most national parks in this region offer hiking trails, but the best are in the parks listed below. Climbing Mount Kinabalu in Sabah, to be at the summit for sunrise, is one of the most popular hikes. New and exciting multi-day hikes are opening up in more remote regions of Sabah and Sarawak, such as the spectacular route between waterfalls in the Maliau Basin Conservation Area, Sabah. There are good jungle treks in Taman Negara and in the Endau Rompin National Park and hiking in the Cameron Highlands on the Peninsula.

Whitewater rafting

Wild or whitewater rafting is not a well-established activity in Malaysia although there are some good spots to take to the swirl, such as Fraser's Hill, Northern Peninsula, page 109; Kiulu river (Grade II), Sabah, page 415 (under Riverbug/Traverse Tours); and Padas river (Grade III), Sabah, page 416.

Responsible tourism

Conduct

As elsewhere in Southeast Asia, in Malaysia 'losing face' brings shame. Even when bargaining, using a loud voice or wild gesticulations will be taken to signify anger and, hence, 'loss of face'. Similarly, the person you shout at will also feel loss of face, especially if it happens in public. In Muslim company it is impolite to touch others with the left hand or with other objects – even loose change. Men shake hands but men don't usually shake a woman's hand. Using the index finger to point at people, even at objects, is regarded as insulting. The thumb or whole hand should be used to indicate something, or to wave down a taxi. Before entering a private home, remember to remove your shoes; it is also usual to take a small gift for the host, usually not opened until after the visitor has left.

Dress

Malaysians dress for the heat. Clothes are light, cool and casual most of the time, but also fairly smart. Some establishments, mainly exclusive restaurants and clubs, require a shirt and dress shoes or local batik shirt. Those wearning shorts and flip flops will be left outside to stew in the heat.

Those visiting the Cameron Highlands or other upland areas are advised to take a light sweater. For jungle treks, a waterproof is advisable, as are canvas jungle boots, which dry faster than leather. Although many Malaysian business people have adopted the Western jacket and tie for formal occasions, the batik shirt, or *baju*, is the traditional formal wear for men, while women wear the graceful *sarung kebaya*.

Malaysians dress smartly, especially in cities. Dress codes are important to observe from the point of view of Islamic sensitivities, particularly on the Peninsula's east coast. In some places such as Marang, bikinis are banned and wearing them will cause great offence. Topless bathing is completely taboo in Malaysia; this should be remembered even if you see other tourists stripping off. It is better to dress modestly out of respect for local tradition.

Malaysia's cross-cultural differences are most apparent on the streets: many Chinese girls think nothing of wearing brief mini-skirts and shorts, while their Malay counterparts

Travelling light

The point of a holiday is, of course, to have a good time, but if it's relatively guilt-free as well, that's even better. Perfect ecotourism would ensure a good living for local inhabitants, while not detracting from their traditional lifestyles, encroaching on their customs or spoiling their environment. Perfect ecotourism probably doesn't exist, but everyone can play their part. Here are a few points worth bearing in mind:

- Think about where your money goes and be fair and realistic about how cheaply you travel. Try to put money into local people's hands; drink local beer or fruit juice rather than imported brands and stay in locally owned accommodation wherever possible.
- Haggle with humour and appropriately. Remember that you want a fair price, not the lowest one.
- Think about what happens to your rubbish. Take biodegradable products and a water filter to avoid using lots of plastic bottles. Be sensitive to limited resources such as water, fuel and electricity.
- Help preserve local wildlife and habitats by respecting rules and regulations, such as sticking to footpaths, not standing on coral and not buying products made from endangered plants or animals.
- Don't treat people as part of the landscape; they may not want their picture taken. Ask first and respect their wishes.
- Learn the local language and be mindful of local customs and norms. It can enhance your travel experience and you'll earn respect and be more readily welcomed by local people.
- And finally, use your guidebook as a starting point, not the only source of information. Talk to local people, then discover your own adventure.

are clad from head to toe. The *tudung* (or *telukung*) veil signifies adherence to the puritanical lifestyle of the fervently Islamic dakwah movement; during the 1980s, this almost became a fashion among women at universities as well as among blue-collar workers in factories. Some women dressed in the full black purdah until it was forbidden by the government. Much of this was the result of peer pressure and reflected a revival of strict Islamic values in Malaysia during and after the 1970s.

Eating
When picking up and passing food, do not use the left hand in Muslim company. It is worth remembering that Malays do not make pork satay and that Hindus do not make beef curries. Chinese cooking on the other hand seems to incorporate almost anything, although Buddhists often avoid beef.

Religion
Remove shoes before entering mosques and Hindu and Buddhist temples; in mosques, women should cover their heads, shoulders and legs and men should wear long trousers.

Essentials A-Z

Accident & emergency

Ambulance, **police** or **fire**, T999.
The worldwide emergency number T112
used on GSM phones is redirected to the
emergency services in Malaysia.

Children

Travelling with children is a touch more
difficult than in child-friendly Singapore, but
is nonetheless an awful lot easier – and safer –
than in many other so-called developing
countries. Food hygiene is good, bottled water
is sold almost everywhere, public transport is
cheap (including taxis) and ubiquitous and
most museums and other attractions provide
good discounts for children. Powdered milk
and baby food and other baby/child items,
including disposable nappies, are widely sold
and high chairs are available in most
restaurants (and even coffee shops).

Many people are daunted by the prospect
of taking a child to a 'developing' country,
but Malaysia's level of development is high
and if you are thinking of a place in the
Asian tropics to travel with your child then
Malaysia – and particularly the Peninsula – is
one of the easiest and safest bets. Naturally,
it is not something to be taken on lightly;
travelling is slower and more expensive and
there are additional health risks for the child
or baby. But it can be a most rewarding
experience. Children are excellent passports
into a local culture. You will also receive the
best service, and help from officials and
members of the public when in difficulty.

Children in Malaysia are given 24-hr
attention by parents, grandparents and
siblings. They are rarely left to cry and are
carried for most of the first 8 months of their
lives since crawling is considered animal-like.
A non-Asian child is still something of a novelty
and parents may find their child frequently

taken off their hands, even mobbed in more
remote areas. This can either be a great relief
(at mealtimes, for instance) or most alarming.
Some children love the attention, others react
against it; it is best simply to gauge your own
child's reactions.

Disposable **nappies** can be bought in most
towns in Malaysia but can be expensive. If you
are staying any length of time in one place, it
may be worth taking reusable nappies. Cotton
nappies also dry quickly in the heat.

The advice given in the health section on
food and drink should be applied even more
stringently where young children are
concerned. Be aware that expensive hotels
may have squalid cooking conditions; the
cheapest street stall can be more hygienic.
Where possible, try to watch the food being
prepared. Stir-fried vegetables and rice or
noodles are the best bet; meat and fish may be
pre-cooked and then could be left out before
being reheated. Various fruits can be bought
very cheaply right across Southeast Asia:
papaya, banana and avocado are all excellent
sources of nutrition, and can be self-peeled
ensuring cleanliness. Powdered milk is also
available throughout Malaysia, although most
brands have added sugar. But if taking a baby,
breastfeeding is strongly recommended.
Powdered food can be bought in most towns;
the quality may not be the same as equivalent
foods bought in the West, but it is perfectly
adequate for short periods. Bottled water and
fizzy drinks are also sold widely. If your child is
at the 'grab everything and put it in mouth'
stage, a damp cloth and Dettol (or equivalent)
are useful. Frequent wiping of hands and
tabletops can help minimize infection.

At the hottest time of year, a/c may be
essential for a baby or young child's comfort
when sleeping. This rules out many of the
cheaper hotels, but a/c accommodation is
available in all but the most remote spots.
Guesthouses probably won't have cots, so
it is worth bringing a travel cot, but more

expensive hotels should be able to provide them (it's worth emailing or phoning to check). When the child is bathing, be aware that the water could carry parasites, so avoid letting him or her drink it.

Public transport may be a problem; trains are fine but long bus journeys are restrictive and uncomfortable. Hiring a car is undoubtedly the most convenient way to see a country with a small child. Seatbelts in the back seats are fitted in more recent models and it is possible to buy child seats in capital cities or rent them from larger car hire firms.

Checklist Pack your own standard baby/child equipment and include baby wipes; child paracetamol; disinfectant; first-aid kit; immersion element for boiling water; oral rehydration salts (such as Dioralyte); sarong or backpack for carrying child; Sudocreme (or similar); high-factor sun-block; sunhat; thermometer; powdered or instant food.

Customs and duty free

Allowances are 200 cigarettes, 50 cigars or 250 g of tobacco and 1 litre of liquor or wine. Cameras, watches, pens, lighters, cosmetics, perfumes and portable radio/cassette players are also duty free in Malaysia. Visitors bringing in dutiable goods such as video equipment may have to pay a refundable deposit for temporary importation. It is advisable to carry receipts to avoid this problem.

Export permits are required for arms, ammunition, explosives, animals and plants, gold, platinum, precious stones and jewellery (except reasonable personal effects), poisons, drugs and motor vehicles. Unlike Singapore, export permits are also required for antiques (from the Director General of Museums, Muzium Negara, Kuala Lumpur; see page 68).

Disabled travellers

Before travelling, contact a specialist travel agent or organization dealing with travellers with special needs. In the UK, contact **RADAR** (Royal Association for Disability and Rehabilitation) ① *12 City Forum, 250 City Rd, London, EC1V 8AF, T020-7250 3222, www.radar.org.uk.* In North America, contact **SATH** (Society for Accessible Travel Hospitality) ① *Suite 610, 347 5th Av, New York, NY 10016, T1-212-447 7284, www.sath.org.*

Disabled travellers are not well catered for in Malaysia and this stands in contrast with the situation in Singapore, see page 571. Pavements are treacherous for those in wheelchairs, crossing roads is a hazard, and public transport is not well adapted for those with disabilities. This is surprising for a country which in so many other ways presents itself as cutting edge. But it is not impossible for disabled people to travel in Malaysia. For those who can afford to stay in the more expensive hotels, the assistance of hotel staff makes life a great deal easier, and there are also lifts and other amenities. And even those staying in budget accommodation will find that local people are helpful, sometimes heart warmingly so.

Electricity

220-240 volts, 50 cycle AC. Some hotels supply adaptors.

Embassies and consulates

Australia, Malaysian High Commission, 7 Perth Av, Yarralumla, Canberra, ACT 2600, T61-02-6273 1543.
Brunei, Malaysian High Commission, 61 Simpang 336, Jln Kebangsaan BA 1211 kg. Sungai Akar, PO Box 2826, Bandar Seri Begawan BS8675, T673-238 1095.

Canada, Malaysian High Commission, 60 Boteler St, Ottawa, Ontario K1N 8Y7, T1-613-241 5182.

France, Malaysian Embassy, 2 bis rue Benouville, Paris, T33-1-4553 1185.

Germany, Malaysian Embassy, Klingelhoefer St 6, D-10785 Berlin, T49-30-885 7490.

Italy, Malaysian Embassy, Via Nomentana 297, 00162 Rome, T39-06-841 5764.

Japan, Malaysian Embassy, 20-16, Nanpeidai-Machi, Shibuya-ku, Tokyo 150, T081-3-3476 3840.

New Zealand, Malaysian High Commission, 10 Washington Av, Brooklyn, Wellington, T64-4-385 2439.

Spain, Malaysian Embassy, Paseo de la Castellano 91-10, Centro 23, 28046 Madrid, T34-91-5550684.

Sweden, Malaysian Embassy, Karlavagen 37, PO Box 26053, 10041 Stockholm, T46-8-440 8400, F46-8-791 8760.

Switzerland, Malaysian Embassy, Jungfrau-strasse 1, CH-3005 Berne, T41-31-350 4700.

UK, Malaysian High Commission, 45 Belgrave Sq, London SW1X 8QT, T44-(0)20-7235 8033.

USA, Malaysian Embassy, 3516 International Court, NW, Washington DC 20008, T1-202-572 9700.

For countries not listed here check www.kln.gov.my.

Gay and lesbian travellers

Like Singapore (see page 571), Malaysia – officially at least – is not particularly accepting of what might be regarded as alternative lifestyles and homosexuality remains a crime. (Bear in mind that even Malaysia's former deputy prime minister, Anwar Ibrahim, was charged with sodomy in 1999 and at the time of writing is facing another charge of sodomy after being controversially accused by one of his aides.) However, there is a buzzing gay scene in KL and, to a lesser extent, in Penang,

Kota Kinabalu and Kuching. There are 2 good websites for gay and lesbian travellers to the region: www.fridae.com, which has city listings, features on local gay and lesbian issues, an events page and a personals section with a search by region; and www.utopia-asia.com, which provides a listing of gay clubs, bars, discos, gyms and meeting spots. But the site's homepage states: "Gay life in Malaysia is blossoming. However, Muslims, both Malay and visitors, are subject to antiquated religious laws which punish gay or lesbian sexual activity with flogging and male transvestism with imprisonment. Police may arrest and harass any gay person (Muslim or non-Muslim) in a public place (ie cruise spots), so discretion is advised."

Health

See your GP or travel clinic at least 6 weeks before departure for general advice on travel risks and vaccinations. Try phoning a specialist travel clinic if your own doctor is unfamiliar with health conditions in Malaysia. Make sure you have sufficient medical travel insurance, get a dental check, know your blood group and, if you suffer a long-term condition such as diabetes or epilepsy, obtain a Medic Alert bracelet/necklace (www.medicalert.co.uk). If you wear glasses, take a copy of your prescription.

Contact your embassy or consulate for a list of doctors and dentists who speak your language, or at least some English. Doctors and health facilities in major cities are also listed in the Directory sections of this book. Good-quality healthcare is available in the larger centres of Malaysia but it can be expensive, especially hospitalization. Make sure you have adequate insurance.

Vaccinations
You should confirm your primary courses and boosters are up to date (diphtheria, tetanus, poliomyelitis, hepatitis A, typhoid). Hepatitis A is recommended as the disease can be caught

easily from food and water. The final decision, however, should be based on a consultation with your GP or travel clinic. A yellow fever certificate is required by visitors over 1 year old, who are coming from, or have recently passed through, an infected area.

Health risks

The most common cause of travellers' **diarrhoea** is from eating contaminated food. In Malaysia, drinking water is rarely the culprit, although it's best to be cautious (see below). Swimming in sea or river water that has been contaminated by sewage can also be a cause; ask locally if it is safe. Diarrhoea may also be caused by viruses, bacteria (such as E coli), protozoal (such as giardia), salmonella and cholera. It may be accompanied by vomiting or by severe abdominal pain. Any kind of diarrhoea responds well to the replacement of water and salts. Sachets of rehydration salts can be bought in most chemists and can be dissolved in boiled water. If the symptoms persist, consult a doctor. Tap water in the major cities is in theory safe to drink but it may be advisable to err on the side of caution and drink only bottled or boiled water. Avoid having ice in drinks unless you trust that it is from a reliable source.

Fresh water can also be a source of diseases such as **leptospirosis** (present in Malaysia) so it is worth investigating before bathing in lakes and streams.

Travelling in high altitudes can bring on **altitude sickness**. On reaching heights above 3000 m, the heart may start pounding and the traveller may experience shortness of breath. Smokers and those with underlying heart or lung disease are often hardest hit. Take it easy for the first few days, rest and drink plenty of water, you will feel better soon. It is essential to get acclimatized before undertaking long treks or arduous activities.

Mosquitoes are more of a nuisance than a serious hazard but some, of course, are carriers of serious diseases such as **malaria**, which is present in Malaysia though the risk is low on Peninsula Malaysia and coastal areas of Sabah and Sarawak. Anti-malarial antibiotic doxycyclone is available without a prescription from pharmacists on the Peninsula, but specialist advice should be taken on the best anti-malarials to use. **Dengue fever** is a viral disease spread by mosquitoes that tend to bite during the day. There are no effective vaccines or antiviral drugs though. Fatal cases are reported annually in Malaysia and Singapore.

Rabies is a problem in Malaysia so be aware of the dangers of the bite from any animal. If bitten always seek urgent medical attention – whether or not you have been previously vaccinated – after first cleaning the wound and treating with an iodine-based disinfectant or alcohol.

Useful websites

www.btha.org British Travel Health Association. **www.cdc.gov** US government site that gives excellent advice on travel health and details of disease outbreaks.
www.fco.gov.uk The British Foreign and Commonwealth Office travel site has useful information on each country, people, climate and a list of UK embassies/consulates.
www.fitfortravel.scot.nhs.uk A-Z of vaccine/health advice for each country.
www.numberonehealth.co.uk Travel screening services, vaccine and travel health advice, email/SMS text vaccine reminders and screens returned travellers for tropical diseases.

Insurance

Always take out comprehensive insurance before you travel, including full medical cover and extra cover for any activities (hiking, rafting, riding, etc) that you may undertake. Check exactly what's being offered, the maximum cover for each element and also the excess you will have to pay in the case of a claim. Keep details of your policy and the insurance company's telephone number with you at all times and get a police report for any lost or stolen items.

Internet

Malaysia is one of the most forward thinking countries in Asia when it comes to information technology and the internet. In line with this, internet cafés have sprung up all over the place and every town, however small, down-at-heel and apparently forgotten by the wider world, will have a place offering internet services. Rates are cheap too: RM2 per hour at the bottom end, with most places charging around RM3 per hour. Generally, internet cafés geared to tourists are more expensive than those serving the local market, where teenage boys spend hours playing online games. For travellers with laptops, guesthouses, hotels, cafés and coffee shops routinely offer free Wi-Fi.

Language

Bahasa Melayu (the Malay language, normally shortened to Bahasa) is the national language. It is very similar to Bahasa Indonesia, which evolved from Malay. All communities, Malay, Chinese and Indian, as well as tribal groups in Sabah and Sarawak, speak Malay, as most are schooled in the Malay medium. Nearly everyone in Malaysia speaks some English, except in more remote rural areas. Chinese is also spoken, mainly Hokkien but also Cantonese, Hakka and Mandarin. The Indian languages of Tamil and Punjabi are spoken too.

For those wanting to get a better grasp of the language, it is possible to take courses in KL (ask at the Tourism Malaysia office, see page 60) and other big cities. The best way to take a crash course in Malay is to buy a teach-yourself book; there are several on the market, but one of the best ones is *Everyday Malay* by Thomas G Oey (Periplus Language Books, 1995), which is widely available. A Malay/English dictionary or phrase book is a useful companion too; these are also readily available in bookshops.

The basic grammar is very simple, with no tenses, genders or articles, and sentence structure is straightforward. Pronunciation is not difficult either as there is a close relation between the letter as it is written and the sound. Stress is usually placed on the second syllable of a word. The **a** is pronounced as *ah* in an open syllable, or as in *but* for a closed syllable; **e** is pronounced as in *open* or *bed*; **i** is pronounced as in *feel*; **o** is pronounced as in *all*; **u** is pronounced as in *foot*. The letter **c** is pronounced *ch* as in *change* or *chat*. The **r** is rolled.

For further information, see Useful words and phrases, page 654.

Media

Newspapers
The main English-language dailies are the *New Straits Times*, www.nst.com.my; *Business Times*, www.btimes.com.my; *The Star* (best for local news), www.thestar.com.my; and the *Malay Mail* (afternoon, basically a gossip rag), www.mmail.com.my. The main Sunday papers are *The New Sunday Times*, *The Sunday Mail* and *The Sunday Star*. The main English-language newspapers in **Sarawak** and **Sabah** are the *Daily Express*, www.dailyexpress.com.my, and the *Eastern Times*, www.easterntimes. com.my. *Aliran Monthly*, www.aliran.com, is a high-brow but fascinating publication offering current affairs analysis from a non-government perspective. The *Sarawak Tribune* was forced out of business in 2006 in a controversy over the Jyllands-Posten Mohammed cartoons, about which the paper claimed the cartoons had made no impact in Sarawak, and reprinted the cartoon pulling enormous amounts of criticism from the pro-Islamic Malaysian government. The English-language dailies are government owned and this is reflected in their content which tends to be relentlessly pro-government. *The Rocket* is the Democratic Action Party's opposition newspaper, and also presents an alternative perspective. International editions of leading foreign newspapers and news magazines can be obtained at main news stands and

book stalls, although some of these are not cleared through customs until mid-afternoon. One of the most popular online news portals is *Malaysia Kini*, www.malaysiakini.com, offering fairly independent coverage of news and politics.

For what's on listings, the best sources are *Time Out KL*, www.timeoutkl.com, and the What's On section of the *Malay Mail*.

Radio

There are 6 government radio stations broadcasting in various languages including English. Radio 1 broadcasts in Bahasa Melayu; Radio 2 is a music station; Radio 3 is Malay; Radio 4 is in English; Radio 5, Chinese; Radio 6, Tamil. In KL you can tune into the Federal Capital's radio station and elsewhere in the country there are local stations. The BBC World Service can be picked up on FM in southern Johor, from the Singapore transmitter. Elsewhere it can be received on shortwave. The main frequencies are (in kHz): 11750, 9740, 6195 and 3915.

RTM1 and RTM2 are operated by Radio Television Malaysia, the government-run broadcasting station. Apart from locally produced programmes, some American and British series are shown. Programmes for all channels are listed in daily newspapers. Satellite TV is popular in Malaysia and many hotels routinely carry the ASTRO service which offers HBO. STAR movies, ESPN, CNN, BBC, Discovery and MTV as well as a host of Chinese channels.

Money

Currency

The unit of currency in Malaysia is the Malaysian dollar or ringgit (RM), which is divided into 100 cents or sen. Bank notes come in denominations of RM1, 5, 10, 50, and 100. Coins are issued in 5, 10, 20 and 50 sen. The exchange rate in March 2010 was RM3.34 = US$1.

Exchange

Most of the bigger hotels, restaurants and shops in **Sarawak** and **Sabah** accept international credit cards with Mastercard and Visa being the most widly accepted. Cash advances can be issued against credit cards in most banks. Many ATMs wll accept foreign credit and debit cards. Banks with such ATM services include Maybank, HSBC and OCBC. Traveller's cheques can be exchanged at banks and money changers although rates and charges vary.

Cost of travelling

It is best not to calculate your budget simply by multiplying the number of days you intend to stay by the figures given below: a couple of days' diving or the need to hire a guide on a trek, for example, would throw such careful calculations right out.

Malaysia is relatively cheap for overseas visitors. However, with the global credit crisis raging, currencies are going up and down. Nevertheless, Malaysia remains excellent value for overseas visitors. It is possible to travel on a shoestring, and getting by on US$15-20 (RM60-80) per day – including accommodation, meals and transport – is certainly possible, if you stay in the bottom-end guesthouses, eat at stalls or in hawker centres and travel on public transport. Cheaper guesthouses charge around US$8-15 (RM30-50) a night for two. Dorm beds are less common these days, but are available in big towns for around RM10-25. It is usually possible to find a simple a/c room for US$10-20 (RM40-80). A room in a top-quality, international-class hotel will cost US$80-130 (RM300-500) and in a tourist-class hotel (with a/c, room service, restaurant and probably a swimming pool), US$26-40 (RM100-150). Eating out is also comparatively cheap: a good curry can cost less than US$1.50 (RM5). Finally, overland travel is a bargain; the bus network is extremely good and fares are very good value.

Post

Malaysia's post is cheap and quite reliable, although incoming and outgoing parcels should be registered. Sending postcards and aerograms overseas costs RM1.50, while letters cost RM1.50 (up to 10 g) or RM1.50 (up to 20 g). Post office opening hours are Mon-Sat 0830-1700 (closed 1st Sat of every month). Fax services are available in most state capitals. Poste restante, available at general post offices in major cities, is reliable; make sure your surname is capitalized and underlined. Most post offices provide a packing service for a reasonable fee (around RM5). You can also buy **AirAsia** tickets at post offices.

Prohibitions

Malaysia is well known around the world for its stringent laws against **drugs**. The Dadah Act – *dadah* is the Malay word for drugs – stipulates a mandatory death sentence upon conviction for anyone in possession of 15 g or more of heroin or morphine, 200 g of cannabis or hashish or 40 g of cocaine. Those caught with more than 10 g of heroin or 100 g of cannabis are deemed to be traffickers and face lengthy jail sentences and flogging with a rotan cane.

While **alcohol** is not illegal in any part of Malaysia, be aware of Muslim sensibilities, particularly in the east coast states of Kelantan and Terengganu.

Safety

Normal precautions should be taken with passports and valuables; many hotels have safes. Pickpocketing and bag snatching are problems in KL, JB and Penang. Women travelling alone need have few worries – although take the usual precautions, such as not walking alone in deserted places at night.

Student travellers

Anyone in full-time education is entitled to an International Student Identity Card (ISIC). These are issued by student travel offices and travel agencies across the world and offer special rates on all forms of transport and other concessions and services. The ISIC head office is **ISIC Association** ① *Box 9048, 1000 Copenhagen, Denmark, T45-3393 9303*. Students can benefit from discounts on some entrance charges and special deals on transport. But there is no institutionalized system of discounts for students.

Taxes

Sales tax is generally 10%.

Telephone

IDD access code 00. **International country code** +60. **Operator** T101. **Directory enquiries** T102/103. **International assistance** T108.

There are public telephone booths in most towns; telephones take RM0.10 and RM0.20 coins. Card phones are now widespread and they make good sense if phoning abroad. **iTalk** offers good IDD (international direct dialling) rates. Cards come in denominations from RM10 to RM100 and are available from airports, petrol stations, most outlets of **7-Eleven** and also from magazine stalls on the street.

You can use your mobile phone in Malaysia if you have a GSM model, but the service will be expensive. A better idea is to get a pre-paid SIM card when you arrive; these are available from most mobile phone shops with Maxis, Celcom and DiGi offering the widest service and extraordinarily cheap international calls. You can use TM **iTalk** cards to make international calls through your mobile.

Time

Official time is 8 hrs ahead of GMT.

Tipping

Tipping is unusual, as a service charge of 10% is automatically added to restaurant and hotel bills, plus a 5% government tax (indicated by the + and ++ signs). Nor is tipping expected in smaller restaurants where a service charge is not automatically added to the bill. For personal services, such as porters, a modest tip may be appropriate.

Tour operators

In the UK

Audley Travel, New Mill, New Mill Lane, Whitney, Oxfordshire OX29 9SX, T01993-838000, www.audleytravel.com. Tailor-made eco-tour itineraries.

Eastern Oriental Express, Sea Containers House, 20 Upper Ground, London SE1 9PF, T020-7921 4000, www.orient-express.com. Offices worldwide. Luxury train trips in Thailand, Laos, Malaysia and Singapore.

Exodus, Grange Mills, Weir Rd, London SW12 0NE, T020-8675 5550, www.exodus .co.uk. Wide range of trips to Southeast Asia. The Borneo Explorer tour includes river journeys and caves at the Niah National Park.

Explore Worldwide, Nelson House, 55 Victoria Rd, Farnborough, Hampshire GU14 7PH, T0870-333 4001, www.explore.co.uk. Arranges small group tours, including cultural excursions, adventure holidays and natural history tours.

Kuoni Travel, Kuoni House, Dorking, Surrey, T01306-747002, www.kuoni.co.uk. Consistently high-quality tour operator that organizes trips all over Southeast Asia.

Magic of the Orient, 14 Frederick Place, Clifton, Bristol BS8 1AS, T0117-311 6050, www.magicoftheorient.com. Knowledgeable staff specializing in tailor-made holidays.

Realworld-travel, Lower Farm, Happisburgh,

Norwich NR12 0QQ, T0709-23322, www.4real.co.uk. Everything from self-drive tours to beaches and rainforest treks.

Regaldive, 58 Lancaster Way, Ely, Cambs CB6 3NW, T0870-220 1777, www.regal-diving. co.uk. Diving tours around Sipadan and Mabul islands on Sabah's southeast coast.

Silk Steps, Compass House, Rowdens Rd, Wells, Somerset BA5 1TU, T01749-685162, www.silksteps.co.uk. Tours of Borneo.

Trans Indus, Northumberland House, 11 The Pavement, Popes Lane, London W5 4NG, T020-8566 2729, www.transindus.com. Tailor-made and group tours and holidays.

Travel Mood, 214 Edgware Rd, London W2 1DH; 1 Brunswick Ct, Bridge St, Leeds LS2 7QU; 16 Reform St, Dundee DD1 1RG, T0207-087 8400, www.travelmood.com. 21 years of experience in tailor-made travel to the Far East and specialists in adventure and activity travel.

Trekforce Expeditions, Way to Wooler Farm, Wooler, Northumberland NE71 6AQ, T0845-241 3085, www.trekforce.org.uk. A UK-based charity offering programmes consisting of sustainable projects, language, teaching and cultural experiences.

In North America

Asian Pacific Adventures, T1-800-825 1680, www.asianpacificadventures.com. Small group, tailor-made and family adventure tours to Borneo.

In Australia

Intrepid Travel, 11 Spring St, Fitzroy, Victoria, T61-1300-360887, www.intrepid travel.com.au. Australian company with agents all over the world. Dozens of different tours of Malaysia, including some that take in neighbouring countries such as Thailand.

Tourist information

The main **Tourism Malaysia** is in KL, see page 60. It has a tourist information bureau in most large towns, is very efficient, and can supply further details on tourist sights, advise on itineraries, help place bookings for travel and cultural events and provide updated information on hotels, restaurants and air, road, rail, sea and river transport timetables and prices. If there is no Tourism Malaysia office in a town, head for a travel agent, who are usually helpful.

The **Malaysia Tourism Centre** is another tourist information bureau, see page 60. Regional tourism offices in state capitals are all reasonably efficient.

Malaysia tourist offices

Australia, Level 2, 171 Clarence St, Sydney, NSW 2000, T61-02-9299 4441, mtpb.sydney@tourism.gov.my; 56 William St, Perth, WA 6000, T08-9481 0400, mtpb.perth@tourism.gov.my.
Canada, 1590-1111 W Georgia St, Vancouver, BC, V6E 4M3, T1-604-689 8899, mtpb.vancouver@tourism.gov.my.
France, 29 rue des Pyramides, 75001 Paris, T33-1-4297 4171, mtpb.paris@tourism.gov.my.
Germany, Rossmarkt 11, Frankfurt Am Main, D-60311, T49-69-283782, mtpb.frankfurt@tourism.gov.my.
Indonesia, Jln HR Rasuna Said, Kav.x/6, No 1-3, Kuningan, Jakarta Selatan 12950, T62-021-522 0765 (ext 3030), www.tourism.gov.my.
Italy, Via Priviata della Passarella, No 4, 20122 Milan, T39-02-796702.
Japan, 5F Chiyoda Bldg, 1-6-4 Yurakucho Chiyoda-ku, Tokyo 100, T81-3-3501 8691, mtpb.tokyo@tourism.gov.my.
Singapore, 01-01B/C/D, 80 Robinson Rd, Singapore 068898, T65-6532 6321, mtpb.singapore@tourism.gov.my.
South Africa, 1st floor, 5 Commerce Sq, 39 Rivonia Rd, Sandhurst, T27-011-268 0292, mtpb.johannesburg@tourism.gov.my.
Sweden, Klarabergsgatan 35, 2tr Box 131, 10122 Stockholm, T46-8-249900, mtpb.stockholm@tourism.gov.my.
UK, 57 Trafalgar Sq, London WC2N 5DU, T44-(0)20-7930 7932, mtpb.london@tourism.gov.my.

USA, 120 East 56th St, Suite 810, New York 10022, T1-212-745 1114, mtpb.ny@tourism.gov.my.

Useful websites

headlines.yahoo.com/full_coverage/ world/malaysia/ An excellent news site for Malaysian current affairs.
www.aseansec.org Homepage of the Asean Secretariat, the Southeast Asian regional organization of which Singapore is a founder member. Lots of government statistics, acronyms, etc.
www.journeymalaysia.com A great web resource that covers the majority of Malaysia's tourist sites in an entertaining and factual way. You can also book tours.
www.sabahtourism.com A well-designed but hard-to-navigate site about Sabah by the state's tourism board.
www.sabahtravelguide.com A great travel site with links to the official tourist board. There are interactive maps, tour agents, up-to-date descriptions of destinations, good travel advice and travel features.
www.sarawaktourism.com Heaps of information on the state.
www.tourismmalaysia.gov.my Tourism Malaysia's website.
www.virtualtourist.com A good website with content by other travellers. Put in your destination and find information on hotels, restaurants, things to see and even tourist traps and places to avoid.

Visas and immigration

No visa is required for a stay of up to 3 months in Malaysia (provided you're not going to work) for citizens of the UK, the US, Australia, New Zealand, Canada, Ireland and most other European countries. If you intend to stay in the country for longer, 2-month extensions are usually easy to get at immigration offices in KL, Penang or JB. Note that Israeli passport holders are not allowed to enter Malaysia.

Visitor passes issued for entry into Peninsular Malaysia are not automatically valid for entry into the states of **Sabah** and **Sarawak**. (The reason for this anomaly is that Sabah and Sarawak maintain control over immigration and even Malaysian visitors from the Peninsula are required to obtain a travel permit to come here.) On entry into these states from Peninsular Malaysia, visitors will have to go through immigration and receive a new stamp in their passport, usually valid for a month. If you want to stay for longer, then you must ask the official. Apply to the immigration offices in Kota Kinabalu and Kuching for a 1-month extension; 2 extensions are usually granted with little fuss. There are certain areas of East Malaysia where entry permits are necessary; for example, Bario and the Kelabit Highlands in Sarawak. These can be obtained from the residents' offices (see appropriate sections).

Weights and measures

Metric, although road distances are marked in both kilometres and miles.

Women travellers

Women, if not accompanied by men, usually attract unwarranted attention, especially in more Islamic areas, like the east coast.

Most male attention is bravado and there have been few serious incidents involving foreign female tourists (or male, for that matter). However women should be sensitive to the fact that Malaysia is a predominantly Muslim country. In the east coast states of Kelantan and Terengganu particularly, women should dress appropriately, avoiding short skirts and singlets. In beach resorts, clothing conventions are more relaxed but topless bathing is unacceptable. If swimming outside beach resort areas bear in mind that Malay women usually bathe fully clothed, so stripping off and running like a gazelle into the sea with nothing more than a bikini may raise one or two eyebrows.

When travelling it is best to keep to public transport and to travel during the day. Hitching is not advisable for women travelling on their own.

Working in Malaysia

For jobs, tips and links on working there, see www.escapeartist.com/as/pac.htm. The Centre for British Teachers offers teaching opportunities for qualified teachers to work in Malaysia and offers fairly reasonable compensation. Check www.cfbt.com for more information. Occasional ESL teaching gigs are offered in KL, though salaries are generally poor. Check www.tefl.com for more information. The Malaysian government has an incentive programme for foreigners to move or retire to the country called 'Malaysia: My Second Home'. This scheme offers a renewable 5-year multiple-entry visa called a Social Visit Pass. The catch is that you need at least RM350,000 banked (depending on age and pension income) in Malaysia and a minimum RM10,000 monthly income. If you are retired, you only need one of these. Apply at Malaysian embassies or **Tourism Malaysia** offices. Check www.mm2h.com for more information. The **Ministry of Human Resources** (MOHR) provides details of labour law and practice in Malaysia, details of which can be found on www.mohr.gov.my.

Contents

56 Ins and outs
61 Background
62 Modern Kuala Lumpur

63 Sights
63 The colonial core
66 Chinatown
68 Little India
68 Lake Gardens and around
69 Kuala Lumpur City Centre
and Jalan Ampang
72 The Golden Triangle
73 Outer Kuala Lumpur

73 Around Kuala Lumpur
74 North
75 East
75 West and southwest
77 South

81 Listings

Footprint features

54 Don't miss...
57 24 hours in Kuala Lumpur
80 Minangkabau:
the buffalo-horn people

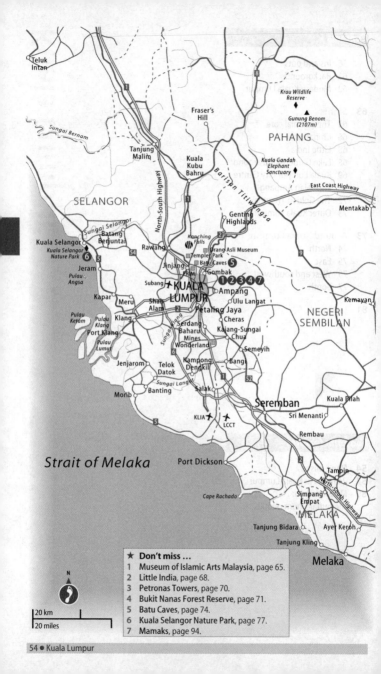

★ **Don't miss ...**
1 Museum of Islamic Arts Malaysia, page 65.
2 Little India, page 68.
3 Petronas Towers, page 70.
4 Bukit Nanas Forest Reserve, page 71.
5 Batu Caves, page 74.
6 Kuala Selangor Nature Park, page 77.
7 Mamaks, page 94.

Introduction

In the space of a century, Kuala Lumpur grew from a trading post and tin-mining shantytown into a colonial capital. Today, it is a modern, cosmopolitan business hub and centre of government.

The economic boom that started in the late 1980s has caused a building bonanza. In downtown Kuala Lumpur, old and new are juxtaposed. The jungled backdrop of the copper-topped clocktower of the Supreme Court of 100 years ago has been replaced by scores of stylish, high-rise office blocks, dominated by the soaring, angular-roofed Maybank headquarters. The Victorian, Moorish and Moghul-style buildings, the Art Deco Central Market and the Chinese shophouses stand in marked contrast to these impressive skyscrapers. The Petronas Twin Towers offer the most impressive addition to the modern skyline; part of the Kuala Lumpur City Centre (KLCC) development, these are the tallest twin towers in the world.

Around the city are the intriguing Batu Caves and some good entertainment in the form of the Sunway Lagoon and Mines Wonderland. Seremban, a former tin-mining centre and window on the world of the Minangkabau culture, is south of the capital.

Getting there → *Population:1,500,000.*

As befitting Malaysia's capital, Kuala Lumpur (KL) is well linked both to other areas of Malaysia and to the wider world.

The international airport at Sepang, **KLIA** ① *www.klia.com.my*, provides a slick point of entry to the country. It lies over 70 km to the south, with a KLIA Exspres rail link to the KL Sentral train station in the city centre. Domestic air connections (including to Sabah and Sarawak) also pass through KLIA.

Opened in 2006, the **Low Cost Carrier Terminal (LCCT)** ① *20 km south of KLIA, www.lcct.com.my*, is used by most budget airlines. Shuttle buses connect KLIA and the LCCT (20 minutes) for RM1.50. Always check your ticket to confirm which terminal you're flying from. The LCCT terminal is dominated by the hugely successful **Air Asia** ① *T03-8775 4000, www.airasia.com*, which is the region's main low-cost carrier, with flights as far afield as China, Australia and the UK. Internet bookings provide the best deals. Tickets booked a few weeks in advance are the cheapest and most travellers moving onto Malaysian Borneo find this is the most convenient option.

Sultan Abdul Aziz Shah Airport (Subang) ① *T03-746 1833*, 25 km west of the city centre, is used by **Berjaya Air**, www.berjaya-air.com, to fly to Pulau Tioman, Pulau Pangkor and Koh Samui in Thailand, and by MAS subsidiary **Firefly**, www.fireflyz.com.my, to fly to JB, Kerteh, Kota Bahru, Kuala Terrenganu, Penang, Koh Samui in Thailand, Medan and Pekanbaru in Indonesia, and Singapore. To get there take Metro Bus 9 from Puduraya or RapidKL Bus U81 from Pasar Seni LRT or KL Sentral (45 minutes). A taxi should take around 30 minutes and cost RM40-50. **Car hire** firms have desks at the airport terminal. Arrange hotel pick-up service in advance or at the office outside the terminal.

International departure tax is RM51 and domestic departure tax is RM15 – though these taxes are usually included in the price of the ticket.

Getting to and from the airport The **KLIA Ekspres train** ① *T03-2267 8000, www.klia ekspres.com, 30 mins, RM35 (child RM15) one way*, runs between 0500 and 0100 between the airport and **KL Sentral** train station in the city centre, every 20 minutes. If using the KLIA Ekspres you can check your luggage in at KL Sentral for outgoing flights.

Alternatively you can take the **KLIA transit** ① *35 mins, RM35*. It stops at three intermediate stations and leaves between 0550 and 0100.

The **Airport Coach Service** ① *T03-8787 3894, RM10*, provides an efficient service from KLIA to KL Sentral from 0630 to 0000. The journey takes 1½ hours. For those travelling to or from the LCCT Terminal, with budget airlines such as AirAsia, Tiger Air etc, there are a couple of excellent bus companies: **Star Shuttle** ① *T03-4043 8811, www.starwira.com/index.htm*, have frequent departures from Puduraya Bus Terminal to the LCCT from 0430 until 0145 (RM12, 1½ hours). **SkyBus** ① *T016-217 6950, www.skybus.com.my*, runs from KL Sentral to the LCCT from 0330 to 2200. You can purchase AirAsia tickets on the bus for those in a spontaneous mood.

Bargain hard for a **taxi** to the city. For a taxi from the city to KL Airport, expect to pay around RM80-100 when you buy a coupon; the journey takes one hour. Hotels can arrange a good fare in the RM75 range. Make sure the taxi fare includes the motorway toll for either direction.

24 hours in Kuala Lumpur

Begin the day by heading to the **Petronas Twin Towers**. Queue for a free ticket to the **skybridge** (closed Mondays) to survey the city from above. Head back to earth, pick up a copy of the *New Straits Times* and enjoying a leisurely *kopi* before making a foray for the classic Malay breakfast: *nasi lemak* – rice cooked in coconut milk served with prawn sambal, *ikan bilis* (like anchovies), hard boiled egg and peanuts.

Make your way to Chinatown and discover the two facets of Malaysia's cultural heritage: the **Sri Mahamariamman Temple** and the **Chan See Shu Yuen Temple**. For the sake of cultural balance, make your way to the **Masjid Negara** (National Mosque), stopping en route at the art deco **Central Market** to browse handicrafts and souvenirs.

Enjoy a dim sum buffet lunch followed by a walk in the 90-ha **Lake Gardens** before looking around the **Islamic Arts Museum** near its southern tip.

Then shake off the past and witness Malaysia's tryst with modernity. Start the evening with a cold beer at the **Coliseum Café** before heading to Chinatown around 1930 when the copy-watch sellers and all kinds of other hawkers emerge.

For dinner, sample another slice of this culinary melting pot in the unique Nyonya cuisine of the Straits Chinese.

While KL doesn't have the liveliest nightlife, there is still a reasonably hot stock of bars and clubs on Jln Pinang and Jln P Ramlee, and less touristy options in **Bangsar Baru** west of the city centre and near the university of Malaya. If your stomach grumbles after midnight, 24-hour *mamak* canteens are plentiful in Bangsar.

Lie on your bed and reflect on what's in your stomach or in your head: Indian, French, Taoist, Hindu, Chinese, Malay, Muslim and Western. Quite a cultural score for one day.

KL Sentral is a transport hub; from this train station you can hop off the KLIA Exspres and onto a KTM train going to Singapore, Penang, Kota Bharu and Bangkok, or catch a taxi to your hotel or change to the underground/overground trains that zip around the city. Lines that have an interchange with KL Sentral are: the Monorail (actually across the road, not in the same building), the KTM Komuter, and the Kelana Jaya LRT line (only the Ampang and Sri Petaling LRT lines do not go through KL Sentral. These last three are in the KL Sentral building). **Puduraya bus station** also has international connections south to Singapore and north to Bangkok, as well as to many towns on the Peninsula. For a good map of the lines, see www.rapidkl.com.my/int_map.htm. ▸▸ *See also Transport, page 101 and Airport Information, Essentials, page 553.*

Getting around

Kuala Lumpur is not the easiest city to navigate, with its sights spread thinly over a wide area. Pedestrians have not been very high on the list of priorities for Malaysian urban planners, with many roads, especially outside the city centre, built without pavements, making walking both hazardous and difficult. In addition, with the exception of the area around Central Market, Chinatown and Dayabumi, distances between sights are too great to cover comfortably on foot, both because of the lack of pavements and because of heavy pollution and the hot and humid climate. Like other Southeast Asian cities, with the notable exception of Singapore, the internal combustion engine rules. The bus system is labyrinthine and congested streets mean that travelling by taxi can make for a tedious

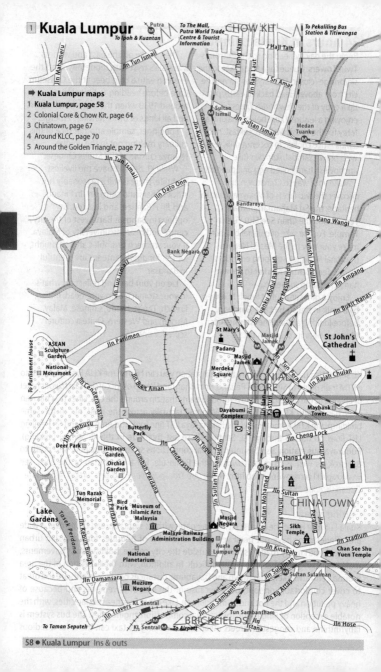

1 Kuala Lumpur

To The Mall, Putra World Trade Centre & Tourist Information

To Ipoh & Kuantan

To Pekeliling Bus Station & Titiwangsa

CHOW KIT

➡ **Kuala Lumpur maps**

1 Kuala Lumpur, page 58
2 Colonial Core & Chow Kit, page 64
3 Chinatown, page 67
4 Around KLCC, page 70
5 Around the Golden Triangle, page 72

Jln Mahameru
Jln Tun Ismail
Jln Thong Nam
J'Haji Taib
Jln Raja Laut
J'Sri Amar
Sultan Ismail
Jln Sultan Ismail
Medan Tuanku
Jln Kuching
Gombak River
Jln Tun Ismail
Jln Dato Onn
Bandaraya
Jln Dang Wangi
Jln Munshi Abdullah
Bank Negara
Jln Raja Laut
Jln Tengku Abdul Rahman
Jln Masjid India
Jln Ampang
Jln Tun Ismail
Jln Bukit Nanas
St Mary's
Masjid Jamek
St John's Cathedral
Padang
Masjid Jamek
Jln Tun Perak
Merdeka Square
COLONIAL CORE
Jln Rajah Chulan
ASEAN Sculpture Garden
Jln Parlimen
National Monument
Jln Bukit Aman
Jln Cenderawasih
To Parliament House
Dayabumi Complex
Jln Benteng Kasturi
Maybank Tower
2
Jln Tembusu
Butterfly Park
Jln Cenderasari
Jln Tugu
Kiang River
Jln Cheng Lock
Deer Park
Hibiscus Garden
Jln Tembah Perdana
Orchid Garden
Jln Hang Lekir
Pasar Seni
Jln Sultan Mohamed
Jln Sultan
CHINATOWN
Tun Razak Memorial
Bird Park
Museum of Islamic Arts Malaysia
Jln Perdana
Jln HS Lee
Sikh Temple
Jln Peteling
Lake Gardens
Tasek Perdana
Malaya-Railway Administration Building
Masjid Negara
Jln Stadium
Jln Sultan Hishamuddin
Kuala Lumpur
Jln Kinabalu
Chan See Shu Yuen Temple
3
Jln Kebun Bunga
National Planetarium
Jln Sulaiman
Sultan Sulaiman
Jln Damansara
Muzium Negara
Jln Kg Atrap
To Taman Seputeh
Jln Travers
KL Sentral
Jln Tun Sambanthan
Tun Sambantham
Jln Istana
Jln Hose
KL Sentral
To Airport
BRICKFIELDS

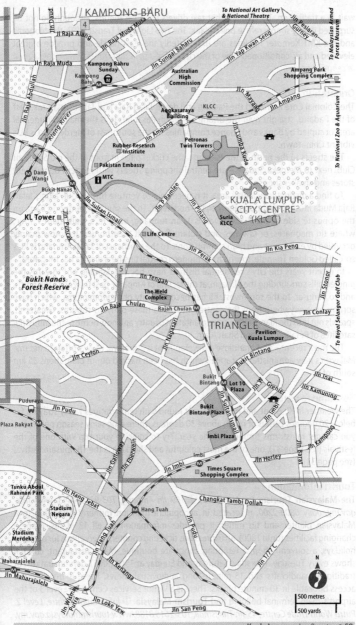

wait in a traffic jam. Try to insist that taxi drivers use their meters, although do not be surprised if they simply refuse point blank. The two Light Rail Transit (LRT), the Monorail and the KMT Komuter rail lines are undoubtedly the least hassle and provide a great elevated and air-conditioned view of the city. ▶▶ *See also KL Rail Transit System colour map in centre of book.*

Orientation

The Colonial Core is around the Padang and down Jalan Raja and Jalan Tun Perak. East of the Padang, straight over the bridge on Lebuh Pasar Besar, is the main commercial area, occupied by banks and finance companies. To the southeast of Merdeka Sq is KL's vibrant Chinatown.

The streets to the north of the Padang – the cricket pitch in front of the old Selangor Club, next to Merdeka Square – are central shopping streets with modern department stores and smaller shops.

To find a distinctively Malay area, it is necessary to venture further out, along Jalan Raja Muda Musa to Kampong Baru, to the northeast. To the south of Kampong Baru, on the opposite side of the Klang River, is Jalan Ampang, once KL's 'millionaires' row', where tin magnates, or *towkays*, and sultans first built their homes. It is now mainly occupied by embassies and high commissions. To the southeast of Jalan Ampang is KL's so-called Golden Triangle, to which the modern central business district has migrated.

In recent years the city's residential districts have been expanding out towards the jungle hills surrounding the KL basin, at the far end of Ampang, past the zoo to the north, and to Bangsar, to the southwest. KL has become a city of condominiums, which have sprung up everywhere from the centre of town to these outlying suburbs. Greater KL sprawls out into the Klang Valley, once plantation country and now home to the industrial satellites of Petaling Jaya and Shah Alam.

The most recent – and grandiose – development is Putrajaya, www.putrajaya.net.my, Malaysia's new administrative capital, which has been hacked out of plantations 35 km south of KL.

Best time to visit

The weather in KL is hot and humid all year round with temperatures rarely straying far below 20 degrees celsius or much above 30 degrees. There is no rainy season per se, but you can get rainstorms throughout the year. Try to coincide your trip with one of the festivals (see page 31), one of the most colourful and shocking is the Thaipusam festival (see page 31).

Tourist information

The **Malaysian Tourism Centre** (**MTC**) ⓘ *109 Jln Ampang, T03-9235 4848, www.mtc. gov.my, daily 0800-2200,* is located in an opulent mansion formerly belonging to a Malaysian planter and tin miner. It provides information on all 13 states, money-changing facilities (until 1800), an express bus ticketing counter, reservations for package holidays, a souvenir shop, a tempting chocolate boutique, Malay restaurant, cultural shows every Tuesday, Thursday, Saturday and Sunday at 1500 (RM5), demonstrations of traditional handicrafts and 15-minute-long audiovisual shows. There is free internet access bookable in 30-minute blocks. There is a Visitor Services Centre on Level 3 of the airport's main terminal building and **Tourism Malaysia** ⓘ *Information Centre, Level 2, Putra World Trade Centre, 45 Jln Tun Ismail, T03-2615 8188, www.tourismmalaysia.gov.my,*

Mon-Fri 0900-1800. Other useful contacts are **KL Tourist Police** ① *T03-2149 6593*, and the **Wildlife and National Parks Department** ① *KM10, Jln Cheras, T03-9075 2872.*

Many companies offer city tours, usually of around three hours, which include visits to Chinatown, the National Museum, the Railway Station, Thean Hou Temple, Masjid Negara (the National Mosque), the Padang area and Masjid Jamek – most of which cost about RM30. City night tours take in Chinatown, the Sri Mahmariamman Temple and a cultural show (RM60). Other tours visit sights close to the city such as Batu Caves, a batik factory and the Selangor Pewter Complex (RM30), as well as day trips to Melaka, Port Dickson, Fraser's Hill, Genting Highlands and Pulau Ketam (RM40-80). Helicopter tours are also available. ▶ *See also tour operators, page 101.*

Background

Kuala Lumpur means 'muddy confluence' in Malay – as apt a description today as it was in the pioneer days of the 1870s. This evocative name refers to the Klang and Gombak rivers that converge in the middle of the city – there is also some evidence that the *kopi-susu*-coloured (literally 'milky-coffee-coloured') Gombak was once known as the Sungai Lumpur. Kuala Lumpur, commonly known simply as KL, has grown up around the Y-shaped junction of these rivers in the area called Ulu Klang – the upper reaches of the Klang River.

In 1857, members of the Selangor royal family (including Rajah Abdullah, the Bugis chief of the old state capital of Klang) mounted an expedition to speculate for tin along the upper reaches of the Klang River. Backed by money from Melakan businessmen, 87 Chinese prospectors travelled up the river by raft to the confluence of the Klang and the Gombak. After trekking through dense jungle they stumbled across rich tin deposits near what is now Ampang. On this first expedition 69 miners died of malaria within a month.

This did not stop Rajah Abdullah from organizing a second expeditionary labour force, which succeeded in mining commercial quantities of tin, taking it downriver to Klang. Until then, Malaya's tin-mining industry had been concentrated in the Kinta Valley near Ipoh, to the north. At about this time, the invention of canning as a means of preserving food led to strong world demand for tin. Spotting a good business opportunity, two Chinese merchants opened a small trading-post at the confluence in 1859. One of them, Hiu Siew, was later appointed Kapitan Cina – the first headman of the new settlement. But secret-society rivalries between groups such as the Hai San (who controlled KL) and the Ghee Hin (who controlled a nearby settlement) retarded the township's early development. Malaria also remained a big problem and fires regularly engulfed and destroyed parts of the town.

By the mid-1860s, KL, which was still predominantly Chinese, began to prosper under the guiding hand of its sheriff, **Yap Ah Loy**. He was a Hakka gang leader from China, who arrived in Melaka in 1854, fought in Negeri Sembilan's riots at Sungei Ujong in 1860 (see page 79), then went to KL in 1862 where he became a tin magnate (*towkay*) and ran gambling dens and brothels. But he emerged as a respected community leader and in 1868, at the age of 31, he was appointed Kapitan Cina of KL by the Sultan of Selangor. He remained the headman until his death in 1885.

Frank Swettenham, the British Resident of Selangor, then took the reins, having moved the administrative centre of the Residency from Klang in 1880. The same year, KL replaced Klang as the capital of the state of Selangor; shortly after Yap's death, it became the capital of the Federated Malay States. Swettenham pulled down the ramshackle shanties and rebuilt the town with wider streets and brick houses. In the National Museum there is a remarkable photograph of the Padang area in 1884, showing a shabby line of *atap* (palm thatch) huts where the Sultan Abdul Samad Building is today. By 1887 the new national capital had 518 brick houses and a population of 4050. By 1910, when the magnificent Moorish-style railway station was completed, the city's population had risen more than 10-fold and nearly four-fifths of the population was Chinese. The town continued to grow in the following decades, becoming increasingly multiracial in character, as the British educated the Malay nobility, then employed them as administrators. The Indian population also grew rapidly; many were brought from South India to work on the roads and railways and the plantations in the Klang Valley.

During the Second World War, the city was bombed by the Allies, but little real damage was incurred. The Japanese surrendered in KL on 13 September 1945. Three years later, with the start of the Communist Emergency, there was a massive influx of squatters into the city. The city area quickly became overcrowded, so in 1952 Petaling Jaya, KL's satellite town (see page 75), was founded to relieve the pressure. It subsequently went on to attract many of Malaysia's early manufacturing industries. Following the end of the Emergency, Malaya became the independent Federation of Malaya on 31 August 1957. Independence was declared by the first prime minister of the independent federation, Tunku Abdul Rahman ('Papa Malaysia'), in the newly built Merdeka Stadium (see page 67). Not until the almagamation of Malaya, Sarawak and Sabah, in 1963 was the name Malaysia given to the new nation.

Modern Kuala Lumpur

In 1974, the 243-sq-km area immediately surrounding the city was formerly declared the Federal Territory of Kuala Lumpur, with a separate administration from its mother state of Selangor. Today, although one of the smallest capitals in Southeast Asia, it is a rapidly growing business centre, with its industrial satellites gaining the lion's share of the country's manufacturing investment. The skyline is dominated by the Petronas Twin Towers, in the Kuala Lumpur City Centre (KLCC) complex, which, on completion in 1996, became the tallest building in the world at 452 m and 88 storeys. It has now been knocked back into second place by the Taiwan 101 tower in Taipei. The bridge connecting the two towers claims the title of the highest bridge in the world. When the building was being built in 1995 and 1996 the contractors were completing a floor every four days – and were being paid around RM2.2 million (US$579,000) per day.

There have been efforts to create a 'new Malaysian architecture', to lend the city a more integrated look and a national identity. Such buildings include the modern-Islamic Masjid Negara (the National Mosque), the National Museum and the Putra World Trade Centre (the latter two have Minangkabau-style roofs) and the 34-storey Dayabumi complex, by the river, with its modern-Islamic latticed arches. At the same time, KL has also been trying to cultivate a 'garden city' image like neighbouring Singapore; from the top of its skyscrapers, KL looks green and spacious, although green areas are fast being taken over by building developments.

Once a relatively quiet capital city, KL is becoming increasingly noisy and congested, as well as suffering from serious air pollution – or 'the haze', which is caused by the fires that burn uncontrollably in Sumatra and Kalimantan from July to September. Pollution is sometimes so bad it makes landings at KL's airport difficult. Locals note how convenient it is for the authorities to blame fires in another country for pollution problems at home. Environmentalists' initiatives to reduce pollution have got nowhere. Instead, while KL hospitals fill up with children suffering from bronchial problems, the health ministry feebly recommends that Malaysians wear surgical masks and give up exercising outside.

Sights

KL is a bit of a sprawl of a city. The big shopping malls, trendy restaurants and bars are clustered around The Golden Triangle and the KLCC. Here too are the Petronas Towers, once the tallest in the world, and the KL Tower, another mighty spike on the landscape. The ethnic neighbourhoods lie southwest of here – there's Chinatown, a web of bustling streets filled with temples, funeral stores, restaurants and shophouses, and Little India, packed with stores selling Bollywood DVDs, saris and spices. Also here is the colonial core where the remnants of the British empire ring Merdeka Square. You can escape from the hustle a few streets southwest of here in the Lake Gardens, which house the fine Islamic Arts museum and a bird and orchid park.

The colonial core

Mederka Square and around

Behind the mosque, from the corner of Jalan Tuanku Abdul Rahman and Jalan Raja Laut, are the colonial-built public buildings, distinguished by their grand, Moorish architecture. All were the creation of AC Norman, a colleague of Hubbock's, and were built between 1894 and 1897. The photogenic former State Secretariat, now called the **Sultan Abdul Samad Building**, with its distinctive clock tower and bulbous copper domes, houses the Supreme Court. To the south of here is another Moorish building, the **Textile Museum** ① *26 Jalan Sultan Hishamuddin, T03-2691 7136, daily 0930-1800, RM1.* It has excellent content, with an emphasis on weaving, as well as beadwork, batik and some embroidery. There is a video presentation and a shop.

The Sultan Abdul Samad Building faces on to the **Padang** on the opposite side of the road, next to **Merdeka Square**. The old Selangor Club cricket pitch is the venue for Independence Day celebrations. The centrepiece of Merdeka Square is the tallest flagpole in the world (100 m high) and the huge Malaysian flag that flies from the top can be seen across half the city, particularly at night when it is floodlit. The Padang was trimmed to make way for the square, which is also the venue for impromptu rock concerts, and is a popular meeting place. A shopping complex, the Plaza Putra, has been built underneath the square.

The very British mock-Tudor **Royal Selangor Club** fronts the Padang and was the centre of colonial society after its construction in 1890. Much of the building was damaged by a fire in the late 1960s and the north wing was built in 1970. The Selangor club is still a gathering place for KL's VIPs. It has one of the finest colonial saloons, filled with trophies and pictures of cricket teams. The famous Long Bar (known as 'The Dog'), which contains a fascinating collection of old photographs of KL, is still an exclusively male preserve. On the north side of the Padang is **St Mary's Church**, one of the oldest Anglican churches in Malaysia, built in 1894.

The **Bank Negara Money Museum** ① *on the ground floor of the Bank Negara Building, Jln Dato Onn, T03-2698 8044, www.moneymuseum.bnm.gov.my, Mon-Fri 0900-1630, free,* is a must for numismatic collectors. Founded in 1989, it houses a collection of Malaysian money.

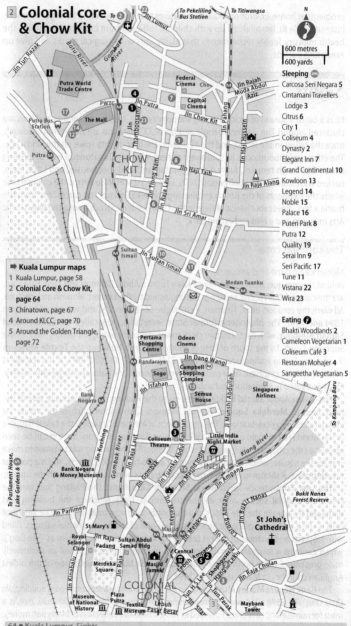

To ❷
To Pekeliling
Bus Station
To Titiwangsa

Jln Lumur

N

600 metres
600 yards

➡ **Kuala Lumpur maps**

1 Kuala Lumpur, page 58
2 Colonial Core & Chow Kit, page 64
3 Chinatown, page 67
4 Around KLCC, page 70
5 Around the Golden Triangle, page 72

Sleeping 🛏

Carcosa Seri Negara 5
Cintamani Travellers
  Lodge 3
Citrus 6
City 1
Coliseum 4
Dynasty 2
Elegant Inn 7
Grand Continental 10
Kowloon 13
Legend 14
Noble 15
Palace 16
Puteri Park 8
Putra 12
Quality 19
Serai Inn 9
Seri Pacific 17
Tune 11
Vistana 22
Wira 23

Eating 🍴

Bhakti Woodlands 2
Cameleon Vegetarian 1
Coliseum Café 3
Restoran Mohajer 4
Sangeetha Vegetarian 5

Putra World
Trade Centre

Batu River
Gombak River

Federal
Cinema

Capitol
Cinema

Jln Rajah
Muda Abdul
Aziz

PWTC

Jln Putra

The Mall

Jln Thamboosamy

Putra Bus
Station

Putra

CHOW
KIT

Jln Chow Kit

Jln Pahang

Jln Haj Hussein

Jln Tiong Nam

Jln Haji Taib

Jln Raja Laut

Jln Sri Amar

Jln Raja Alang

Sultan
Ismail

Jln Sultan Ismail

Medan Tuanku

Jln Kampong Baru

Pertama
Shopping
Centre

Odeon
Cinema

Jln Dang Wangi

Bandaraya

Campbell
Shopping
Complex

Sogo

Jln Isfahan

Semua
House

Singapore
Airlines

Bank
Negara

Coliseum
Theatre

Jln Hutching

Jln Raja Laut

Gombak River

Jln Tuanku Abdul Rahman

Little India
Night Market

LITTLE
INDIA

Jln Masjid India

Klang River

Jln Ampang

To Parliament House,
Lake Gardens & ❺

Bank Negara
(& Money Museum)

Jln Parlimen

St Mary's

Royal
Selangor
Club

Jln Raja
Padang

Merdeka
Square

Museum
of National
History

Jln Raja

Sultan Abdul
Samad Bldg

Masjid
Jamek

Plaza
Putra

Textile
Museum

Lebuh
Pasar Besar

COLONIAL
CORE

Jln Melaka

Masjid Jamek

Central

Leboh Ampang

Jln Gereja

Jln Bukit Nanas

Bukit Nanas
Forest Reserve

St John's
Cathedral

Jln H S Lee

Shophouses

Jln Hang

Jln Tun Perak

Jln Raja Chulan

Maybank
Tower

On the south side of Merdeka Square is the **Museum of National History** ① *T03-2694 4590, www.nationalhistorymuseum.gov.my, daily 0900-1800, free,* which has only limited displays including rocks, skulls and coins.

The Dayabumi Complex and National Market

North of the mosque, back towards the Padang, is the 35-storey, marble **Dayabumi Complex** (see Chinatown map, page 67). Located on Jalan Raya, it is one of KL's most striking modern landmarks. It was designed by local architect Datuk Nik Mohamed, and introduces contemporary Islamic achitecture to the skyscraper era. The government office-cum-shopping centre used to house Petronas, the secretive national oil company, which has since moved to the even more grandiose Petronas Twin Towers. Try getting permission to stand on the 30th floor helipad where a superb, but fading (and increasingly obsolete), pictorial map of all the city's sights has been painted on the rooftop. Next door to the Dayabumi Complex is the General Post Office.

On the opposite bank to the Dayabumi Complex is the **Central Market**, ① *www.centralmarket.com.my*, a former wet market built in 1928 in art deco-style, tempered with 'local Baroque' trimmings. In the early 1980s it was revamped to become a focus for KL's artistic community and a handicraft centre – KL's version of London's Covent Garden or San Francisco's Fisherman's Wharf. It is a warren of boutiques, handicraft and souvenir stalls – some with their wares laid out on the wet market's original marble slabs. On the second level of the market are several restaurants and a good foodcourt serving regional cuisines.

The railway station and around

In 1910, Hubbock designed the fairytale Moorish-style **Railway Station**, Jalan Sultan Hishamuddin (now a hotel and replaced by the new Sentral station a few streets further south) and, in 1917, the **Malaya Railway Administration Building** opposite (see Chinatown map, page 67). Beneath the Islamic exterior of the former, the building resembles the glass and iron railway stations constructed in England during the Victorian era – except this one was built by convict labour. The station's construction was apparently delayed because the original roof design did not meet British railway specifications; it had to be able to support snow a metre deep. The refurbished interior now includes restaurants and souvenir stalls.

To the northwest of the old railway station is the National Mosque, **Masjid Negara** ① *open to tourists daily 0900-1230, 1400-1530 and 1700-1830, women must use a separate entrance*, the modern spiritual centre of KL's Malay population and the symbol of Islam for the whole country. Abstract, geometric shapes have been used in the roofing and grillwork, while the Grand Hall is decorated with verses from the Koran. Completed in 1965, it occupies a 5-ha site at the end of Jalan Hishamuddin. The prayer hall has a star-shaped dome with 18 points, representing Malaysia's 13 states and the five pillars of Islam. The 48 smaller domes emulate the great mosque in Mecca. The single minaret is 73 m tall and the grand hall can accommodate 8000 worshippers. An annexe contains the mausoleum of Tun Abdul Razak, independent Malaysia's second prime minister.

Close to the National Mosque is the **Museum of Islamic Arts Malaysia** ① *Jln Lembah Perdana, T03-2274 2020, www.iamm.org.my, daily 1000-1800, RM10, children RM5,* which provides a fascinating collection of textiles and metalware and is a wonderful oasis of calm in the midst of the city. It is possible to get on to the roof, at a level with the mosque's mosaic dome.

Chow Kit

The US$150 million **Putra World Trade Centre** (Kompleks Seni Budaya, Jalan Conlay), to the north of the city centre on Jalan Tun Ismail, took nearly 15 years to materialize, but when it opened in 1985, Malaysia proudly announced that it was finally on the international convention and trade-fair circuit. The luxurious complex of buildings includes the Pan-Pacific Hotel, a sleek 41-storey office block and an exhibition centre, adorned with a traditional Minangkabau roof. The headquarters of former Prime Minister Dr Mahathir Mohamad's ruling United Malays National Organization (UMNO) occupies the top floor and there is a tourist information centre on the second floor.

Chinatown

Southeast of the Central Market lies Chinatown, roughly bounded by Jalan Tun HS Lee (Jalan Bandar), Jalan Petaling and Jalan Sultan. It was the core of Yap Ah Loy's KL (see page 61) and is a mixture of crumbling shophouses, market stalls, coffee shops and restaurants. This quarter wakes up during late afternoon, after about 1630, and in the evening its streets become the centre of frenetic trading and haggling. Jalan Petaling and parts of Jalan Sultan are transformed into an open-air night market, pasar *malam*, and foodstalls selling Chinese, Indian and Malay delicacies, fruit stalls, copy watch stalls, pirate DVDs, leather bag stalls and all manner of impromptu boutiques line the streets. Jalan Hang Lekir, which straddles the gap between Jalan Sultan and Jalan Petaling, is full of popular Chinese restaurants with their tables set up on the pavement. Off the north side of Jalan Hang Lekir, there is a lively covered fruit and vegetable market in two intersecting arcades.

Sri Mahamariamman Temple

ⓘ *South of Jln Hang Lekir, tucked away on Jln Tun HS Lee (Jln Bandar).*

The extravagantly decorated **Sri Mahamariamman Temple**, incorporating gold, precious stones and Spanish and Italian tiles, was founded in 1873 by Tamils from southern India who had come to Malaya as contract labourers to work in the rubber plantations or on the roads and railways. Its construction was funded by the wealthy Chettiar money-lending caste, and it was rebuilt on its present site in 1985. It has a silver chariot dedicated to Lord Murugan (Subramaniam), which is taken in procession to the Batu Caves (see page 74) during the Thaipusam festival, when Hindu devotees converge on the temple. Large numbers flock to the temple to participate in the ritual; this is usually preceded by about half-an-hour's chanting, which itself is accompanied by music.

Chinese temples

There are two prominent Chinese temples in the Chinatown area. The elaborate **Chan See Shu Yuen Temple**, at the southernmost end of Jalan Petaling, was built in 1906 and has a typical open courtyard and symmetrical pavilions. Paintings, woodcarvings and ceramic sculptures decorate the façade. It serves both as a place of worship and as a community centre. The older **Sze Ya Temple**, close to the Central Market on Lebuh Pudu, off Jalan Cheng Lock, was built in the 1880s on land donated by Yap Ah Loy. He also funded the temple's construction and a photograph of him sits on one of the altars. Ancestor worship is more usually confined to the numerous ornate clan houses (*kongsis*); a typical one is the **Chan Kongsi** on Jalan Maharajalela, near the Chan See Shu Yuen Temple.

Merdeka Stadium

ⓘ *RM1.*

Southeast of Chinatown, off Jalan Stadium, is the 50,000-capacity Merdeka Stadium, the site of Malaysia's Declaration of Independence on 31 August 1957 (*merdeka* means 'freedom' in Malay). National and international sports events are held at the stadium (the famous boxing match between Mohammad Ali and Joe Bugner was staged here in 1975), as well as the annual international Koran reading competition, held during Ramadan.

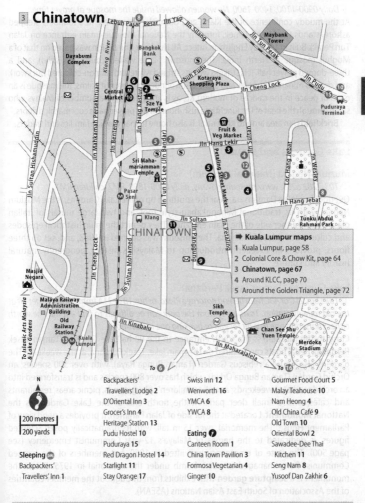

③ Chinatown

➡ **Kuala Lumpur maps**
1 Kuala Lumpur, page 58
2 Colonial Core & Chow Kit, page 64
3 Chinatown, page 67
4 Around KLCC, page 70
5 Around the Golden Triangle, page 72

200 metres
200 yards

Sleeping 🛏
Backpackers'
Travellers' Inn **1**

Backpackers'
Travellers' Lodge **2**
D'Oriental Inn **3**
Grocer's Inn **4**
Heritage Station **13**
Pudu Hostel **10**
Puduraya **15**
Red Dragon Hostel **14**
Starlight **11**
Stay Orange **17**

Swiss Inn **12**
Wenworth **16**
YMCA **6**
YWCA **8**

Eating 🍴
Canteen Room **1**
China Town Pavilion **3**
Formosa Vegetarian **4**
Ginger **10**

Gourmet Food Court **5**
Malay Teahouse **10**
Nam Heong **4**
Old China Café **9**
Old Town **10**
Oriental Bowl **2**
Sawadee-Dee Thai
Kitchen **11**
Seng Nam **8**
Yusoof Dan Zakhir **6**

Little India

Little India's streets – Jalan Masjid India and nearby lanes – echo to the sounds of Bollywood CDs and hawker cries. There are stalls and stores selling garish gold, saris, fabrics, great *kurta* (pyjama smocks), traditional medicines, flowers and spices. It is also a good place to eat cheap Indian snacks and sip on sweet lassis. Although the streets are fairly scruffy, the smells and colours make up for its lack of gloss.

Masjid Jamek
ⓘ *Daily 0900-1100, 1400-1600. No women allowed inside the mosque at prayer time.*
At the muddy confluence of the Klang and Gombak rivers where KL's founders stepped ashore, stands the Masjid Jamek, formerly the National Mosque (main entrance on Jalan Tun Perak). Built in 1909 by English architect, AB Hubbock, the design was based on that of a Moghul mosque in North India. The mosque has a walled courtyard, (*sahn*), and a three-domed prayer hall. It is striking with its striped white and salmon-coloured brickwork and domed minarets, cupolas and arches. Surrounded by coconut palms, the mosque is an oasis of peace in the middle of modern KL, as is apparent by the number of Malays who sleep through the heat of the lunchtime rush-hour on the prayer hall's cool marbled floors.

Brickfields, an area around KL Sentral, is also home to many Indian families and traders.

Lake Gardens and around

Muzium Negara (National Museum)
ⓘ *T03-2282 6255, www.museum.gov.my, daily 0900-1800, RM2, children RM1.*
Overlooking Jalan Damansara, near the southern tip of the Lake Gardens, is the Muzium Negara, with its traditional Minangkabau-style roof, and two large murals of Italian glass mosaic either side of the main entrance. They depict the main historical episodes and cultural activities of Malaysia. The museum was opened in 1963, and, set on three floors, provides an excellent introduction to Malaysia's history, geography, natural history and culture.

Lake Gardens (Taman Tasek Perdana)
ⓘ *Take bus 21C or 48C from behind Kotaraya Plaza, or bus 18 or 21A from Chow Kit, get off at the old railway station. Taxis away from the park can be difficult to find – it may be worth either chartering one to wait for you or booking one in advance.*
Close to the museum is the south entrance to the 90-ha Lake Gardens (Taman Tasek Perdana). Pedal boats can be hired on the main lake, Tasek Perdana, at the weekend. The gardens also house a Hibiscus Garden (Taman Bunga Raya), with over 500 species; an Orchid Garden (Taman Bunga Orkid), which has over 800 species and is transformed into an orchid market at weekends; as well as children's playgrounds, picnic areas, restaurants and cafés, and a small deer park. At the north end of the Lake Gardens is the **National Monument**. Located at the far side of Jalan Parlimen, it provides a good view of Parliament House. The memorial, over 15 m tall, with its dramatically posed sculpted figures, is dedicated to the heroes of Malaya's 12-year Communist Emergency (see page 500). The state of emergency was lifted in 1960, but members of the banned Communist Party managed to put a bomb under the memorial in 1975. Below the monument is a **sculpture garden** with exhibits from throughout the member countries of the Association of South East Asian Nations (ASEAN).

The showpiece of the Lake Gardens is the **Bird Park (Taman Burung)** ⓘ *T03-2272 1010, www.birdpark.com.my, daily 0900-1900, RM28, children RM20*. Opened in 1991 in an effort to outdo neighbouring Singapore's famous Jurong Bird Park, this aviary at 20.9 acres is twice the size of Jurong and is billed as the world's largest covered bird park. It encloses more than 3000 birds from 200 species, ranging from ducks to hornbills. Spread out over landscaped gardens, most of the birds are free and very accustomed to being around people. The hornbill area is particularly exciting. It houses seven varieties of hornbill, most of which are indigenous to Malaysia. There are bird shows and feeding sessions of eagles, ostriches and hornbills which kids love. There is a reference centre, refreshment kiosk and binoculars for hire.

The **Butterfly Park (Taman Rama-rama)** ⓘ *T03-2693 4799, daily 0900-1800, RM17, children RM8*, is a five-minute drive from the main entrance of the Lake Gardens, coming in from Jalan Parlimen. It is a miniature jungle, which is home to almost 8,000 butterflies, from 150 species. There are also small mammals, amphibians and reptiles, and rare tropical insects in the park. There is an insect museum and souvenir shop on the site.

On the southeast edge of the park is **Tun Abdul Razak Memorial** ⓘ *T03-2693 7740, Tue-Sun 1000-1730 (except Fri 1200-1500), closed Mon, free,* the former residence of Malaysia's revered second prime minister, the late Tun Abdul Razak, whose great, great, great, great, great grandfather, Sultan Abdullah of Kedah, ceded Penang to the British (see page 143). In recognition of his services – he is popularly known as the father of Malaysia's development – his old home has been turned into a memorial with the aim of preserving his documents, speeches, books and awards, as well as housing his collection of walking sticks and pipes. At the southeastern end of the Lake Gardens is the **National Planetarium** ⓘ *T03-2273 5484, daily 0930-1700, RM1, children under 12 free, Sky movie: RM6, children RM4*, which has a theatre with a 20-m-diameter domed screen where the Space Science Show and Sky movies are projected. Other facilities include an exhibition hall, an observatory, a viewing gallery and a 14-in telescope.

The modern 18-storey **Parliament House** and its Toblerone-shaped House of Representatives is on the west fringe of the gardens. When parliament is in session, visitors may observe parliamentary proceedings (permission must be formally obtained, and visitors must be smartly dressed). In years gone by, many of the administrative arms of government were housed in the State Secretariat (now renamed the Sultan Abdul Samad Building) on the Padang.

Kuala Lumpur City Centre and Jalan Ampang

Kuala Lumpur City Centre
ⓘ *www.klcc.com.my.*
The old Selangor Turf Club racecourse, which lies to the southeast of this intersection, has been the focus of extraordinary redevelopment in the guise of the Kuala Lumpur City Centre (KLCC), a 'city within a city'. High-rise development came late to KL but has rapidly gained a foothold; the city's offices, hotels and shopping complexes are mostly concentrated in the Golden Triangle, on the east side of the city. The complex is one of the largest real-estate developments in the world, covering a 40-ha site and including the Petronas Towers, see below. The Ampang Tower, a mere 50-storey office block; the Suria KLCC, a crescent-shaped retail and entertainment centre on the junction of Jalan Ampang and Jalan P Ramlee; the Esso Tower; a 20-ha park with a children's playground; and the Mandarin Oriental, a five-star hotel with over 600 rooms, are all part of the KLCC project.

Jalan Bukit Bintang and Jalan Sultan Ismail was where the first modern hotels and malls went up: the Regent, Hilton (now the Mutiara), Equatorial, Holiday Inn, Shangri-La and Concorde. In front of the Suria KLCC complex and to the southeast lies the pleasant KLCC Park, a welcome patch of green beneath the twin towers with its elegant lakes and fountains.

Petronas Towers

ⓘ *The Skybridge, which links the two towers on the 41st floor, is open to the public Tue-Sun 0900-1900. Visitors must queue for a ticket which gives free access to the bridge and some stunning views. Only a limited number of people are allowed up every day, so it is advisable to get there before 1000.*

The towers were designed by American architect Cesar Pelli and the surrounding park by Brazilian landscape artist Roberto Marx Burle. On Level 4, Suria KLCC Petrosains, **The Discovery Centre** ⓘ *T03-2331 8181, wwwpetrosains.com.my, Tue-Sun 0930-1830, Fri 1330-1730, RM12, children RM4*, which is really a petroleum promotion exercise, has rides and hands-on computer games all glorifying this industry, but is also a great place for kids.

Aquaria KLCC ⓘ *Concourse Level, KLCC, T03-2333 1888, www.klaquaria.com, daily 1100-1900, RM38, children RM22*. Kids will love this giant fish bowl, reputed to be the largest aquarium on earth at over 5000 sq ft. The aquarium contains over 150 species, including scary tiger sharks, lethal sea snakes and more delightful bright coral fish and seahorses. It

⁴ Around KLCC

Sleeping	Eating
Concorde 1	Bharath's 3
Corus 5	Bombay Palace 4
Crown Princess 2	Ciao 7
Equatorial 9	D'Tandoor 1
Mandarin Oriental 3	Seri Angkasa 1
Nikko 7	Studio 123 5
Renaissance 6	Tamarind Springs 6
Shangri-La 8	Top Hat 2

500 metres
500 yards

➡ **Kuala Lumpur maps**
1 Kuala Lumpur, page 58
2 Colonial Core & Chow Kit, page 64
3 Chinatown, page 67
4 Around KLCC, page 70
5 Around the Golden Triangle, page 72

takes visitors on a journey from the highlands and flooded jungles of Malaysia and the Amazon basin to coral reefs and the open ocean. There's a 90-m walk through tunnel and feeding of tiger sharks takes place on Monday, Wednesday and Saturday.

Jalan Ampang

Jalan Ampang became the home of KL's early tin-mining millionaires and an important leafy adjunct to the colonial capital. The styles of its stately mansions range from art deco and mock-Palladian to Islamic. Today many of these buildings have become embassies and consulates (although the government is trying to persuade foreign missions to decamp to Putrajaya). One of the lovelier art deco-style buildings now houses the **Rubber Research Institute**. Further into town, another renovated house is now the **Malaysian Tourism Centre** (MTC); see also page 60. It was the headquarters of the Japanese Imperial Army during the Second World War, but was originally built in 1935 by Eu Tong Seng, a wealthy Chinese rubber planter and tin mogul. More recently, the area around Jalan Ampang and Jalan Tun Razak has been transformed into a commercial centre; several towers have sprung up in the area in recent years, including the extraordinary hour-glass-shaped Pilgrims' Building, which co-ordinates the annual Haj and looks after the pilgrims' funds. There are several further developments including a Sheraton and Hyatt, both five-star tower-block hotels. The area has become a booming shopping area in the shape of Ampang Park and City Square shopping centres.

Menara KL

① *T03-2020 5444 (reservations), T03-2020 5055, www.menarakl.com.my, daily 1000-2200, RM20, children RM10. No public transport; take a taxi or walk from one of the surrounding roads.*

Near the intersection of Jalan Ampang and Jalan Sultan Ismail, atop Bukit Nanas, stands the **Menara KL** (KL Tower). This 421-m-high tower is the second tallest telecommunications tower in Asia and the fourth tallest in the world (the viewing tower stands at 276 m). The views from the top are vastly superior to the views from the Skybridge at the Petronas Towers. Characteristically, the tower is the brain-child of former Prime Minister Dr Mahathir Mohammed. There are 22 levels and 2058 stairs, so the lift is recommended. At ground level there are several shops, fast-food restaurants and a mini amphitheatre. Above the viewing platform is the Seri Angkasa revolving restaurant. It has excellent Malay cuisine and revolves once every 60 minutes, so diners get to see the whole city between hors d'oeuvre and ice cream.

Bukit Nanas Forest Reserve

① *There are a couple of entrances into this reserve and various tracks running through it – you can get onto one of these tracks from the road going up to KL Tower. There are also ways in from Jln Ampang and Jln Bukit Nanas (off Jln Raja Chulan) (look for signposts). Free.*

Combine a visit to the tower with a walk in the surrounding **Bukit Nanas Forest Reserve**, a beautiful 11 ha of woodland in the centre of the city with marked trails.

KL is perhaps the only city with a patch of rainforest at its heart. Butterflies, monkeys, squirrels and birds live in the forest. There are warnings about dangerous snakes.

The Golden Triangle

The **Rumah Penghulu Abu Seman** ① *T03-2144 9273, www.badanwarisan.org.my, Mon-Sat 1000-1700 (tours at 1100 and 1500 including a video presentation, RM5)*, on Jalan Stonor, otherwise known as the Heritage Centre of the Badan Warisan Malaysia, is in a mock-Tudor building off Jalan Conlay, on the northern edge of the Golden Triangle. In the garden is a reconstructed headman's house made of timber – it displays detailed carvings and is furnished in the style of a 1930s house. Just to the east of the Heritage Centre is the **Komplex Budaya Kraf**, a local handicraft centre offering visitors the chance to dabble in batik or watch artists at work.

⑤ Around the Golden Triangle

Sleeping ⓖ	Bintang Warisan 2 C1	Shuttle Inn 16 B2	Johnny's Thai
Agora 1 B2	Cardogan 3 C1	Swiss Garden 18 C1	Steamboat 3 C2
Berjaya Times	Comfort Inn 6 B1	Tai Ichi 19 C1	Marco Polo 14 A1
Square 5 C2	Federal 7 C1		Mark's Asam Laksa 6 A1
	Fortuna 8 B2	Eating ❼	Michaelangelo's 8 A2
	Imperial 9 B1	Athena 5 A2	Restoran Sari Ratu 9 B2
	Istana 10 A1	Bangkok Jam 3 C2	Sakura Café &
	JW Marriott 13 B2	Delaney's at Parkroyal	Cuisine 15 C3
	Pondok Lodge 21 B1	Hotel 1 C2	Tarbush 13 B2
	Putra Bintang 20 B1	Eden Village 2 A2	The Ship 7 B2
	Replica Inn 11 B1	Esquire Kitchen 10 C2	

➡ Kuala Lumpur maps
1 Kuala Lumpur, page 58
2 Colonial Core & Chow Kit, page 64
3 Chinatown, page 67
4 Around KLCC, page 70
5 **Around the Golden Triangle, page 72**

200 metres
200 yards

One of the newest shopping plazas in the Golden Triangle is Times Square on Jalan Imbi, which features a roller coaster, an Imax cinema, and a hotel complex, as well as the usual retail and dining suspects.

The **Karyaneka Handicraft Centre** (Kompleks Seni Budaya) ① *T03-2162 7533, daily 0900-1730, RM3, children RM1; minibus or Intrakota no 40 from Jln Tuanku Abdul Rahman*, is on Jalan Conlay to the east of the city centre and is popular with tour groups. There is a small museum illustrating the batik, weaving and pottery processes. Craft demonstrations are held from 1000 to 1800, and there are crafts on sale from each of the 13 states of Malaysia.

South of the Karyaneka Handicraft Centre, on Jalan Bukit Bintang, is the **Jade Museum** ① *daily 1000-1900, RM10; 10-min walk from Bukit Bintang Monorail station*. This small museum houses a private collection of 80 jade artefacts from China. Replicas and jade souvenirs are for sale.

Outer Kuala Lumpur

Titiwangsa

The **National Art Gallery** ① *T03-4025 4990, www.artgallery.gov.my, daily 1000-1800, free; to get there take the Monorail to Titiwangsa station, from where it's a 15-min walk eastwards along Jln Tun Razak, the gallery is on the left-hand side*, has moved from its location near the old railway station to north of the city at Jalan Temerloh next to the National Theatre and National Library. The gallery showcases some 2000 works by Malay artists.

Taman Seputeh

Thean Hou Temple (Temple of the Goddess of Heaven) ① *take minibus 27 from Klang bus terminal to Jln Syed Putra*, is situated at Jalan Klang Lama (off Jalan Tun Sambathan, to the southwest of the city). Perched on a hill, it has a panoramic view over KL. A contemporary Buddhist pagoda and Buddha images are enshrined in the octagonal hall. It stands between a sacred Bodhi tree and a Buddhist shrine, built by Sinhalese Buddhists in 1894.

Around Kuala Lumpur

The most popular day trip from KL is to Batu Caves, around half an hour's drive north (or an hour by public bus). This series of caverns, with their entrances, wreathed in mist, reached by a sweat-inducing flight of steps and with colourful Hindu paraphernalia everywhere, make a fun day out. Further north, Templer Park is a great place for picnics and escaping the city. KL's satellite towns have become destinations in themselves with hotels, restaurants, bars and shopping centres such as Petaling Jaya, Shah Alam and Putrajaya. Petaling Jaya or PJ, in the southwest, also has the Sunway Lagoon, a fun water park, Shah Alam has an impressive mosque, while bustling Port Klang is the country's main port. To the south around the airport are the Mines Wonderland theme park and the Sepang International circuit for world-class motor-racing. Seremban, the state capital of Negeri Sembilan and Port Dickson can also be visited from KL. ►► *For listings, see pages 81-104.*

Batu Caves

ⓘ *The caves stay open until about 2100; RM1. Take bus 11 or 11D from near Central Market or taxi. The caves are a short walk off the main road.*

This system of caverns set high in a massive limestone outcrop, 13 km north of KL, was 'discovered' by American naturalist William Hornaby in the 1880s. In 1891 Hindu priests set up a shrine in the main cave dedicated to Lord Subramaniam and it has now become the biggest Indian pilgrimage centre in Malaysia during the annual Thaipusam festival (see page 31), when over 800,000 Hindus congregate here.

The main cave is reached by a steep flight of 272 steps. Coloured lights provide illumination for the fantasy features and formations of the karst limestone cavern. There are a number of other, less spectacular caves in the outcrop, including the Museum Cave (at ground level) displaying elaborate sculptures of Hindu mythology. During the Second World War, the Japanese Imperial Army used some of the caves as factories for the manufacture of ammunition and as arms dumps; the concrete foundations for the machinery can be seen at the foot of the cliffs.

Templer Park

The park, covering 500 ha and about 10 km further on up the main road from the turn-off to the Batu Caves, serves as KL's nearest jungle playground, apart from the tiny Bukit Nanas Forest Reserve in the middle of the city. It opened as a park in 1954 and is named after the last British High Commissioner of Malaya, Sir Gerald Templer, 'the Tiger of Malaya', who oversaw the tactical defeat of the Communist insurgents during the Emergency (see page 500). The park is dominated by several impressive 350-m-high limestone hills and outcrops, the biggest being **Bukit Takun** and **Bukit Anak Takun** (similar to the Batu Caves outcrop).

There are extensive networks of underground passages and cave systems within the hills, thought to have formed 400 million years ago. Unfortunately, two huge floodlit golf courses have impinged on the boundaries of the park making access to some of these massifs more difficult. The park has a wide variety of jungle flora and fauna and is a popular venue for boy scout and youth camps. Nearby are the **Kanching Falls** ⓘ *buses from Puduraya bus terminal*, which drop 300 m in several stages and are a good place for swimming. They are sometimes incorrectly referred to as Templer Park Falls.

Orang Asli Museum

ⓘ *Sat-Thu 0900-1700, free. Take a bus from Lebuh Ampang terminus or it is a 15-min walk from Titiwangsa Monorail station.*

Situated 25 km north of KL on the old Gombak Road, this museum preserves the traditions of Malaysia's indigenous Orang Asli aboriginals, who number about 60,000 on the Peninsula. There are displays giving the background to the 18 different tribes and their geographical dispersal. There are also models of Orang Asli village houses and a souvenir shop attached to the museum selling Orang Asli crafts.

Jungle canopy walk

ⓘ *It's important to book with FRIM, T03-6279 7575, www.frim.gov.my, Tue-Sun 1000-1300.*

It's possible to do this walk through the treetops at the Forestry Research Institute of Malaysia (FRIM) at Kepong, some 30 minutes north of KL, on the Jabayan Perhutanan.

East

The **Malaysian Armed Forces Museum** ① *Jln Padang Tembak, T03-2071 9966, Sat-Thu 0900-1800, 20 mins in taxi*, exhibits pictures, paintings and weapons, including those captured from the so-called Communists Terrorists during the Emergency (see page 500). The **Royal Selangor Complex** ① *4 Jln Usahawan 6, T03-4145 6122, www.visitorcentre.royal selangor.com, daily 0900-1700, free, take the Putra LRT to Wangsa Maju station, and then take a taxi (fare around RM4)*, on Jalan Pahang, in Setapak Jaya, to the north of the city, is the biggest pewter factory in the world, employing over 500 craftsmen. Royal Selangor was founded in 1885, using Straits tin (over 95%) which is alloyed with antimony and copper. Visitors can watch demonstrations of hand-casting, pewter working, jewellery making and the handpainting of porcelain. You can also make your own pewter by enrolling in a day class at the 'school of hard knocks'. Call the centre in advance. One of the most photographed sights at the complex is the massive pewter tankard outside the building; it's in *The Guinness Book of Records* as the largest in the world. As well as the Setapak Jaya Complex, there are showrooms throughout the city (see page 98).

The **National Zoo and Aquarium** ① *T03-4108 2219, Mon-Fri 0900-1700 Sat-Sun 0900-2300, RM10, children RM5; take the Putra LRT to Wangsa Maju station followed by a taxi*, is 13 km from the centre of KL, down Jalan Ampang to Ulu Klang. The zoo encompasses a forest and a lake and houses 1000 different species of Malaysian flora and fauna in addition to collections from elsewhere in the world. It also has an aquarium with over 80 species of marine life. There are performances by orang-utans, elephants and sea lions and a chance to see nocturnal animals at their prime at the weekends in the Zoo By Night.

West and southwest

Asian Art Museum
① *Mon to Fri 0900-1600, Sat 0900-1200, free, to get there, take the LRT to the university and then take a taxi.*
The Asian Art Museum is housed within the university campus, about 4 km southwest of the Lake Gardens. The museum exhibits Asian art objects, sculpture, ceramics, textiles and handicrafts.

Petaling Jaya
Located 15 km southwest of KL, this is a thriving industrial satellite and middle-class dormitory town for the capital and is known as PJ. Initially built to provide low-cost housing for squatter resettlement, it is now a satellite city in its own right, with shopping and administration centres. The whole town, with its streets running in semi-circles, was planned on a drawing board but, despite its unimaginative street names (or rather, numbers), it is not as sterile as it might sound. In recent years it has become quite lively, with its own nightlife scene and several gourmet restaurants (particularly around Damansara Utama, where clubs stay open until 0300 or 0400), which cater for PJ's expatriate and wealthy Malaysian population.

Also nearby is the water theme park **Sunway Lagoon** ① *T03-5631 1452, www.sunway.com.my/lagoon/, Mon, Wed-Fri 1100-1800 and Sat-Sun 1000-1800, RM90 for all the park, children RM70 (cheaper packages depending on the number of parks visited, check website); take the Kelana Jaya LRT to Kelana Jaya and catch the shuttle service from there. Alternatively, buses to most parts of Petaling Jaya can be boarded at Bangkok Bank stop* *and Klang bus terminal,* with a variety of watery rides on offer and some dry-land activities too. Surfing and body-boarding sessions are held at weekends in the wave pool. A new addition at Sunway is the **Extreme Park** ⓘ *T01-8232 1426, www.extreme park.com.my,* a good place for adrenaline junkies. This fun place offers paintball, water sports, including diving lessons on a 50-acre lake, go-karting and golf. Pay separately for each activity – check website for times and rates.

Shah Alam
ⓘ *1 hr from Klang bus terminal or take a taxi (RM75).*
The state capital of Selangor, situated between KL and Port Klang, has the reputation of being Malaysia's best-planned city, and is an ultra-modern showpiece town. The skyline is dominated by the State Mosque, **Masjid Sultan Salahuddin Abdul Aziz Shah,** which has a huge, blue aluminium dome, said to be the largest aluminium dome in the world. Completed in 1988, it is reputed to be the largest mosque in Southeast Asia and can accommodate up to 16,000 worshippers. **Wet World** ⓘ *Mon-Tue, Thu-Fri 1300-1900, Sat-Sun 1000-2000, RM7, children RM5,* a water theme park, provides some entertainment for children, including the Monsoon Buster – a watercoaster, which at one point reaches a height of 220 m.

Klang and its offshore islands
ⓘ *The KTM Komuter line runs to Port Klang, where it's a short walk into town.*
This royal town, 30 km southwest of KL, is also known as Kelang, a name thought to derive from an old Sumatran word for tin. It has a magnificent mosque and attractive royal palace, the **Istana Alam Shah**, set in well-cared-for grounds. The palace is closed to the public, but can be seen from the road. Klang had been the capital of Selangor for centuries before the tin-mining town of Kuala Lumpur assumed the mantle in 1880. Klang was the name for the whole state of Selangor when it formed one of the Negeri Sembilan (the nine states of the Malay Federation).

Today **Port Klang** (previously known as Port Swettenham, after former British Resident Frank Swettenham) is KL's seaport and is a busy container terminal. Klang is also an important service centre for nearby rubber and palm oil plantations, which, in the early decades of the 20th century, spread the length of the Klang Valley to KL.

The **Gedung Rajah Abdullah** warehouse, built in 1857, is one of the oldest buildings in the town. Rajah Abdullah was the Bugis Chief who first dispatched the expedition to the upper reaches of the Klang River, which resulted in the founding of KL. There is a **fort** in Klang, built by Rajah Mahdi (a rival of Raja Abdullah), which guarded the entrance to the Klang valley from its strategic position overlooking the river.

The town is well known for its seafood; most of the restaurants are close to the bus terminal. Ferries leave from Klang for offshore islands such as Pulau Ketam (see below), Pulau Morib and Pulau Angsa.

Pulau Ketam (Crab Island) ⓘ *about 10 km west of Port Klang, www.pulauketam.com, from KL, take the Komuter train to Port Klang and then a ferry, 30 mins, 10 a day, RM7,* is like a downmarket Venice, Malaysian-style, with the whole village on stilts over the water. It is a good spot for seafood.

Kuala Selangor
Kuala Selangor is a coastal town on the banks of the Sungai Selangor river, 64 km northwest of KL. In the 19th century, it was a focal point of the Sultanate of Selangor. The

Dutch built two fortresses here in 1784, overlooking the Sungai Selangor estuary, to blockade the Sungai Selangor in retaliation for Sultan Ibrahim of Selangor's attacks on Melaka. In 1871, British gunboats bombarded the forts – then occupied by Malays – for several hours, marking the first British intervention in the Selangor Civil War, over the possession of the tin-rich Klang Valley. The larger of the two, **Fort Altingberg** ① *on Bukit Melawati, daily during daylight hours,* serves as a royal mausoleum and museum.

Kuala Selangor Nature Park
① *The actual riverside site is around 8 km from Kuala Selangor, near a village called Kampong Kuantan. There are regular direct buses from KL's Puduraya bus terminal to Kuala Selangor. Taxis can be chartered from Kuala Selangor to Kampong Kuantan, a boat trip can then be taken from Kampong Kuantan, RM10 each for 4 people. The Malayan Nature Society, which operates the park, will arrange private transport to Kampong Kuantan and back, for approximately the same price, when pre-arranged with their KL office, T03-3289 1439.*
Fort Altingberg overlooks the Kuala Selangor Nature Park, 250 ha of coastal mangrove swamp and wetland. It has several observation hides, and more than 156 bird species, bee eaters, kingfishers and sea eagles have been recorded here. There are also leaf monkeys. It is also one of the best places to see Malaysia's famous synchronized fireflies – the only fireflies in Southeast Asia that manage to co-ordinate their flashing; they are best observed on a moonless night, from about one hour after sunset. Accommodation is available here (see page 87). All-in tours can be arranged at numerous hostels and agencies in KL starting at around RM160.

South

Mines Wonderland
① *Batu 10 1/2, Jln Sungai Besi, T03-8942 5010, Tue-Fri 1800-2300, Sat-Sun 1700-2300, RM35, children RM23. Take KTM Komuter from KL railway station to Serdang station (walkable from here).*
This adventure playground, next to the site of Sepang International Airport in Sungai Besi, about 20 minutes south of KL, has been constructed on a 60-ha plot, which used to be the largest tin-mining lake in the world. Attractions include a Snow House, where you can see sculptures carved out of ice by artists from China. Alternatively, take a ride on a water taxi or see the Musical Fountain or any of the other sound and light attractions. The whole 'Mines Resort City' consists of a sizeable conference centre set within a five-star hotel, a 'Beach Resort' (although there is no beach here), a shopping mall, a business park and an international-standard golf course.

From Kuala Lumpur to Seremban and Port Dickson
The drive south from KL through Seremban to Melaka runs on the first stretch of the much-vaunted North-South Highway, and is an easy, pleasant drive through rubber and oil palm plantations. Like the route north from KL, the towns are predominantly Chinese, while the rural kampongs are almost exclusively Malay. Negeri Sembilan, a confederacy of nine small states, is renowned for its Minangkabau-style architecture. This is characterized by buffalo-horn shaped roof peaks, reflecting the influence of the state's first inhabitants who came from Sumatra.

On the coast, southwest of Seremban, off the main highway, is the seaside resort town of Port Dickson (PD), which serves as a popular weekend retreat from KL, but is not generally frequented by tourists from abroad. The drive southeast from PD to Melaka is much more interesting along the coastal backroads that run through open countryside and Malay kampongs.

Seremban → *Colour map 2, B2.*

ⓘ *Tourist information, State Economic Planning Unit, 5th floor Wisma Negeri, T06-762 2311.*
Seremban is the capital of the state of Negeri Sembilan, which translates from Bahasa as 'nine states', and was historically a loose federation of districts, lorded over by four territorial chiefs. Seremban (formerly known as Sungei Ujong) started life as another rough and ready tin-mining centre with a large population of Chinese. A lively town, its major sight is the Teman Seni Budaya (Cultural Complex), which offers an interesting insight into the Minangkabau culture. The town, 62 km south of KL, is easily accessible and can be visited in a day from either KL or Melaka.

Tin-mining flourished in the early years of the 19th century, and is one of the reasons Melaka continued as a thriving trading port. The control of the river, Sungai Linggi, which was the route Sungei Ujong's tin took to the sea, became a great source of contention between the 1820s and 1860s. The Dato Klana, or territorial chief of the Sungei Ujong

Seremban

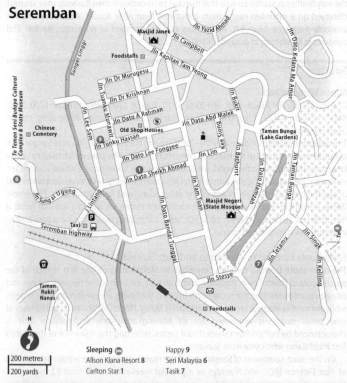

200 metres	Sleeping 🛏	Happy **9**
200 yards	Allson Klana Resort **8**	Seri Malaysia **6**
	Carlton Star **1**	Tasik **7**

district, frequenty clashed with other members of the council of chiefs over the highly profitable river taxes and port dues. All wanted a share of the river tolls and erected illegal forts along the river to levy tolls from the Chinese merchants from Melaka and the Chinese miners. In 1857 the British sent an expedition up the river to destroy these fortified toll booths, but this did not work and in no time they were back in business. In 1860 the confrontation came to a tumultous head when the tin miners in Sungei Ujong rebelled against the chiefs; hundreds were killed in the subsequent riots. One of the Chinese ring-leaders was a ruthless young Hakka ruffian named **Yap Ah Loy**, who went on to become headman of a new tin boomtown called Kuala Lumpur in 1862.

Along the fringe of the outstanding **Lake Gardens** (Taman Bunga) is the **State Mosque** (Masjid Negri), with its nine pillars representing the nine old mine-states of Negeri Sembilan. The Cultural Complex (**Teman Seni Budaya**) is on 4-ha site at the junction of Jalan Sungai Ujong and the KL-Seremban road, 2 km from the centre of town. The main building is the Terak Perpatih, originally constructed as the pavilion for an international Koran-reading competition in 1984 and now a museum. On the ground floor are handicraft displays and upstairs there is an exhibition of historical artefacts. Also within the complex is a beautifully carved traditional Minangkabau wooden house, Rumah Contoh Minangkabau, built in 1898 (originally at Kampong Air Garam). In 1924 it was shipped to England and exhibited as an example of Malay architecture. On its return it was reassembled near the Lake Gardens in Seremban before being moved to Taman Seni Budaya.

The **State Museum** ① Tue-Wed 1000-1800, Thu 0815-1300, 1000-1215, Fri 1445-1800, Sat-Sun 1000-1800, is also part of the complex and is itself a good example of Minangkabau architecture; it is a reconstructed 19th-century palace (Istana Ampang Tinggi), a high stilt building with an atap roof. The museum houses a small collection of ceremonial weapons and tableaux depicting a royal wedding and some photographs and other memorabilia from the time of the Malayan Emergency.

Sri Menanti
① A taxi from Seremban costs about RM20, or else take a Kuala Pilah bus.
Sri Menanti, the old Minangkabau capital of Negeri Sembilan, is 30 km east of Seremban, about 10 km before Kuala Pilah. This area is the Minangkabau heartland. Sri is the Minangkabau word for 'ripe paddy', and Menanti means 'awaiting' – although it is colloquially translated as 'beautiful resting place'. It was also common for early kings to add the Sanskrit honorific 'Sri' to their titles and palaces. The former royal capital is on the upper reaches of Sungai Muar, which meanders through the valley that was known as Londar Naga, or the tail of the dragon. The **Istana Lama Sri Menanti** ① Sat-Wed 1000-1800, Thu 0815-1300, is a beautifully carved wooden palace built in Minangkabau style in 1908. It has 99 pillars depicting the 99 warriors of the various luak-luak (clans). It was, until 1931, the official residence of the Yang di-Pertuan Besar, the state ruler. On the fourth floor is a display of royal treasures. It is not officially a museum but is open to visitors. This royal town also has a large mosque. Most people come here on a day trip from Seremban, but there is a reasonable resort hotel next to the Istana Lama, see page 88.

Port Dickson
Port Dickson, typically shortened to PD, is 32 km from Seremban and is one of the most popular seaside resorts in Malaysia, as testified by all the modern condominium developments. The pace of development has given the little fishing port a pollution

Minangkabau: the buffalo-horn people

Negeri Sembilan's early inhabitants were immigrants from Minangkabu in Sumatra. They started to settle in the hinterland of Melaka and around Sungai Ujong (modern Seremban) during the 16th and 17th centuries and were skilled irrigated paddy farmers. Minangkabau roughly translates as 'buffalo horns' and the traditional houses of rural Negeri Sembilan and Melaka have magnificent roofs that sweep up from the centre into two peaks. The Minangkabau architectural style has been the inspiration behind many modern Malaysian buildings, notably the Muzium Negara (National Museum) and the Putra World Trade Centre in Kuala Lumpur.

The Minangkabau introduced Islam, a sophisticated legal system and their matrilineal society to the interior of the Malay Peninsula. In 1773 they appealed to the Minangkabau court at Pagar Ruyong in Sumatra to appoint a ruler over them and a Sumatran prince – Raja Melewar – was installed as the first king (Yang di-Pertuan Besar) of the confederacy of mini-states, with his capital at Sri Menanti.

But Negeri Sembilan's four *undang* (territorial chiefs) saw to it that he wielded no real power. In all there were four kings from Sumatra, all of them ineffectual, and the link with Sumatra finally ended in 1824 with the establishment of an indigenous hereditary royal family. The current Sultan of Seremban, educated at Oxford, continues to reside in his palace outside the town.

---

problem in recent years and many people regard the sea as so toxic that it is best not to swim at all. This is a narrow point of the Melaka Strait and large ships use the deep-water channel, which cuts close to the Malaysian coast. Rarely a month goes by when the Malaysian authorities aren't giving chase to tankers, which have an increasingly alarming tendency to dump thousands of tonnes of sludge, oil and effluent into the strait. Although for KL's residents it may be a convenient destination for a day trip or weekend, it is, frankly, hard to imagine why those with more time on their hands would wish to come here.

The port town, originally called Tanjung Kamuning, was renamed after Sir Frederick Dickson, British Colonial Secretary and acting Governor in 1890. Port Dickson itself is quiet and undistinguished but to the south is a long, sandy beach, stretching 18 km down to the **Cape Rachado** lighthouse, although there are cleaner places to swim in Malaysia. Built by the British on the site of a 16th-century Portuguese lighthouse, Cape Rachado has panoramic views along the coast. At **Kota Lukut**, 7 km from Port Dickson, is Raja Jamaat fort, built in 1847 to control the tin trade in the area.

⊙ Kuala Lumpur listings

Hotel and guesthouse prices
L over US$200 AL US$91-200 A US$41-90
B US$21-40   C US$12-20   D US$7-11
E US$3-6   F under US$3
Restaurant prices
††† over US$12 †† US$4-12 † under US$4
See pages 26-29 for further information.

⊖ Sleeping

With the success of AirAsia and other regional budget airlines giving increasing numbers of people in Southeast Asia the opportunity for travel, room occupancy rates at the lower end of the scale have picked up significantly.

By international standards KL's hotels are excellent value for money, but because of the city's traffic problems, the location of a hotel has become an increasingly important consideration. Most top hotels are between Jln Sultan Ismail and Jln P Ramlee, in KL's Golden Triangle. South of Jln Raja Chulan, in the Bukit Bintang area, south of the Golden Triangle, there is another concentration of big hotels. There are also lots of mid-range hotels in the Golden Triangle, particularly along Jln Bukit Bintang, convenient for upmarket restaurants, bars and shopping. The Chinatown area is home to rock-bottom budget places which are looking the worst for wear and, in many cases, offer nothing more than a bare, windowless cell.

It is possible to live with a Malaysian family, sharing their home and eating meals together as part of a **homestay**. At least one member of the family will be able to speak English. Tourism Malaysia has a list of homestays and can advise on how to arrange one. Homestays vary in cost from RM40 a night for all meals and a simple bed in a village house to RM100 or more with expensive tour agencies who provide transport and day trips to sites and activities such as white water-rafting, farms and scenic spots etc. Some even offer golf. The Tourism Malaysia office has an excellent booklet on homestays, including sections on agrovisits, and cultural homestay options.

You'll probably have a more satisfactory stay if you organize it once you get there and meet locals and ask for their advice than going through a tour agency.

For accommodation at the airport, see KLIA Airport, page 86.

The colonial core *p63, map p64*
AL Seri Pan Pacific, Jln Putra, T03-4042 5555, www.seripacific.com. Popular choice for business travellers, with an excellent range of business facilities, rooms with broadband access and a range of eateries including Japanese and dim sum. Spa, nightclub and help with arranging golf trips outside the city. Next to the PWTC LRT station.
A AnCasa, Jln Cheng Lock, situated next to the Puduraya bus station, T03-2026 6060, www.ancasa-hotel.com. International hotel with well-furnished, clean a/c rooms that have a TV, internet access, minibar and in-room safe. There's a restaurant and bar and breakfast is included. Walking tours of KL and homestay packages are available. There are good discounts; check online. Recommended.
A Citrus, Jln Tiong Nam (off Jln Raja Laut), T03-9195 9999, www.citrushotelkl.com. Popular new hotel with excellent discounts, modern rooms with Wi-Fi, cable TV and electronic safe. Colour schemes follow the hotels refreshing minimalist style. De luxe rooms have great views of the Petronas Towers. Recommended.
A Dynasty, 218 Jln Ipoh, T03-4043 7777, www.dynasty.com.my. Bright, comfortable hotel with distinctly late 80s design undertones. There are 788 a/c rooms, a pool, Chinese and Mediterranean restaurants and a business centre. It's a short distance from the Putra World Trade Centre.
A Grand Continental, Jln Belia/Jln Raja Laut, T03-2693 9333, www.ghihotels.com.my. A/c, restaurant, but nowadays looking a tad dated. 300-odd unremarkable rooms,

impersonal atmosphere, but reasonable facilities. The main draw here is the rooftop pool area which has incredible skyline views at night. Wi-Fi access in lobby.

A Legend, 100 Jln Putra, T3-40429888, www.legendhotelkl.com. Next to the PWTC LRT station, this is a gargantuan hotel, with 600 rooms and apartments and a regal atmosphere. It was opened by Joan Collins and pursues a filmstar image. The a/c rooms are spacious, comfy and have cable TV and good views. There are Chinese, Japanese and health food restaurants (7 in total), a pool and a health centre. Staff are friendly and helpful. Breakfast is included.

A Puteri Park, Jln Raja Laut, T03-4047 9999, www.puteriparkhotel.com.my. Business hotel with functional but comfortable a/c rooms in a slightly inconvenient location. Wi-Fi available. Excellent discounts; check their website.

A Quality, Jln Raja Laut, T03-2693 9233, www.quality.com.my. This is a big a/c hotel with over 250 rooms, but things seem to be a bit squashed. Rooms are well appointed and feature cable TV and a bathtub. There's also a Sichuan restaurant, Malay coffee house, a small pool, squash, health club and a small gym.

A-B Vistana, 9 Jln Lumut, off Jln Ipoh, T03-4042 8000, www.ytlhotels.com. An easy walk from the Putra World Trade Centre, a short taxi ride from Chinatown and within comfortable walking distance of Titiwangsa LRT and Monorail station, this classic business hotel is of an excellent standard but is unpretentious. There is a/c, a restaurant, coffee house, business centre and pool.

A-B Wira, 123 Jln Thamboosamy, T03-4042 3333, www.wirahotel.com.my. This place is off the main street, so is slightly quieter than other typical business hotels in the area. There are clean and simple rooms with a/c, large TV (de luxe rooms have 29-in flatscreen TV), telephone and fridge. Staff are friendly and there's a coffee shop.

B City, 366 Jln Raja Laut, T03-4041 4466. It doesn't look much from the exterior, but the 101 rooms are clean with hot-water showers and a/c. There's no restaurant, but

it's competitively priced and has professional management. Most guests are Malaysians. Recommended.

B Elegant Inn, 164 Jln Raja Laut, T03-4045 2288, F4045 6973. Located on a busy main street, this hotel has aged, musty mid-range, a/c rooms with attached bathrooms, TV (domestic channels only) and telephones.

B-E Tune, 316 Jln Tuanku Abdul Rahman, T03-7962 5888, www.tunehotels.com. Owned by AirAsia's Tony Fernandez, this hotel follows the no-frills budget airline model with clean, bright and functional rooms emblazoned with advertising. Wi-Fi, towels and a/c are available at additional costs on a daily basis. For best rates, book well in advance (5 months for the cheapest rates). There's a newsagents, Subway and shuttle bus service to the airport (RM75). It's very popular at weekends.

C Putra, 50-52 Jln Putra, T03-4041 2232, reservation@hotelputra.com. A little out of town, this place has clean, simple, slightly old a/c rooms, with attached bathrooms, TV and telephone. There's an internet café adjoining. Breakfast is included.

Chinatown *p66, map p67*

A Swiss Inn, 62 Jln Sultan, T03-2072 3333, www.swissgarden.com. Fair value lodgings in the heart of Chinatown. Rooms in the new wing are a little on the small side, but feature flatscreen TVs, good mattresses and new, spotless bathrooms. Rooms in the older wing have no windows. There's free internet access but no Wi-Fi. Breakfast is included.

A-B Wenworth, Jln Yew, southeast of the city, T03-9283 3888. In a good location for the North-South Highway – approaching KL from the south, it is one of the first hotels in the city. There's a/c, a Chinese restaurant, café, rooftop pool, health spa and simple but comfortable rooms.

B D'Oriental Inn, 82 Jln Petaling, T03-2026 8181, www.dorientalinn.com. Newly renovated hotel offering clean, well-furnished a/c rooms with attached bathrooms and free Wi-Fi access. Friendly staff. Recommended.

B Heritage Station, Banguanan Stesen Keretapi, Jln Sultan Hishamuddin, T03-2272 1688, www.heritagehotel malaysia.com. Part of the magnificent Moorish-style railway station. After its redevelopment it managed to retain some of its colonial splendour, but disappointingly the standard rooms have been furnished in a contemporary style. It's more of a faded elegance these days, with cranky lifts, saggy floors and lukewarm food. But it's unbeatable for atmosphere and location. The family rooms are big enough for groups of up to 8.

B Puduraya, 4th floor, Puduraya Bus Station, Jln Pudu, T03-2072 1000, F2070 5567. Excellent location above the bustling coach station. This hotel is tired, and looks dated, but rooms are clean and some have incredible views over the city.

B-C Stay Orange, 16 Jln Petaling, T03-2070 2208, www.stayorange.com. Somewhat akin to living inside an Easyjet 737, the bright orange walls and branding can be a tad off-putting, but rooms here are spotless and all feature free Wi-Fi, a/c and good bedding. Book online in advance for excellent rates.

C Red Dragon Hostel, 80 Jln Sultan, T03-2070 6000, hostelrd@yahoo.com. Converted from the old Rex cinema, this sprawling complex of nondescript a/c and fan doubles, and dorms, all have shared bathrooms. Many rooms have no windows and some smell of bug spray. Free Wi-Fi access in lobby area.

C Serai Inn, Jln Hang Lekiu, T03-2070 4728, www.seraiinn.com. Rooms here are tiny with paper-thin walls, but are kept spotless and all have free Wi-Fi access. Bathrooms are shared, but kept very clean. Pleasant rooftop terrace for smokers, and communal area with TV, internet access and free tea and coffee all day. Recommended.

C Starlight, 90-92 Jln Hang Kasturi, T03-2078 9811. Seriously dated and with plenty of character, this hotel features an ancient lift, psychedelic floor tiles and tatty furniture from bygone days. A/c and fan rooms are spacious and many come with (basic) en suite facilities. Well situated for

Central Market, Chinatown, bus stations, eateries, shops and sights. Being opposite the Klang bus station, it can be noisy.

C YWCA, 12 Jln Hang Jebat (to the east of Chinatown and south of Jln Pudu), T03-2078 3225, www.ywcamalaysia.org. Good selection of a/c and fan rooms with hot and cold water, quiet and clean with a friendly atmosphere. Offers short- and long-term accommodation for women, and also caters for married couples (no single men allowed). There's a restaurant and access to a TV and fridge. It looks a bit grim, with wire mesh on the windows, and is a bit of a trek into Chinatown (15 mins' walk).

C-E Backpackers' Travellers' Inn, 2nd floor, 60 Jln Sultan, T03-2078 2473, www.backpackerskl.com. Well-run hotel with attached travel agency and relaxed rooftop bar/café with good views and cheap beer. Rooms are simple and the owner is proactive in the fight against bugs, with each room having bug deterrents and seamless mattress covers. Rooms are small, dark and unattractive, but generally clean, ranging from a/c dorm rooms (RM11 per night), to single windowless fan rooms, to a/c rooms with facilities. Also available is a book exchange, video, TV and laundry. Wi-Fi access (RM5 per day).

C-E Backpackers' Travellers' Lodge, 158 Jln Tun HS Lee, T03-2031 0889, www.backpackerskl.com/lodge.htm. Fairly uninspiring digs with clean, basic a/c and fan rooms, often without a window. Under same management as **Backpackers' Travellers' Inn**.

C-E Grocer's Inn, 78 Jln Sultan, T03-2078 7906, www.grocersinn.com.my. This is one of the better cheap places to stay, with cheery yellow walls, hallways with antique Chinese furniture and bright simple a/c and fan rooms all with shared bathroom. Dorm available for RM13. Recommended.

D-E Pudu Hostel, 3rd floor, Wisma Lai Choon, 10 Jln Pudu (opposite Puduraya bus station), T03-2978 9600, www.puduhostel.com. Handily located for the coach station, this hostel has a big lounge area with a pool table, cable TV (DVDs for rent at RM3), and washing and ironing facilities. Wi-Fi access in lobby area.

All rooms have a shared bathroom, are cramped, often windlowless and shabby but clean overall. Dorms are available (RM12).

Little India p68

B Kowloon, 142-146 Jln Tuanku Abdul Rahman, T03-2693 4246, www.kowloonhotelkl.com. Old-style, a/c business rooms with faded blue furniture, TVs and attached bathrooms. There is an 'executive' health club and coffee shop. Rooms facing the main street can be noisy.

B Noble, 165 Jln Tuanku Abdul Rahman, T03-2711 7111, www.hotelnoble.com. Although without much character, this hotel is reasonable value and is modern, clean and tastefully finished. Rooms have a/c, TV and showers. Some have free Wi-Fi access and wonderful city views at night. Breakfast and a newspaper are included. Recommended.

B Palace, 40-46 Jln Masjid India, T03-2698 6122, www.palacehotel.com.my. Slightly decrepit but clean and comfortable a/c rooms with cable TV and attached bathroom with small bathtub. Staff are friendly and the atmosphere is good.

C Coliseum, 100 Jln Tuanku Abdul Rahman, T03-2692 6270. For those on a budget who want a taste of the 1920s, this place is certainly worth a try. It has large, simply furnished rooms (fan or a/c) that have seen better days, a famous bar and restaurant and friendly staff. There are no attached bathrooms. Rooms facing main street are very noisy. If arriving out of hours, knock on one of the side doors.

Lake Gardens and around p68

L Carcosa Seri Negara, Taman Tasek Perdana, T03-2282 1888, www.ghmhotels.com. This former residence of the British High Commissioner, built in 1896, is now a luxury hotel, where Queen Elizabeth II stayed when she visited Malaysia for the Commonwealth Conference in 1989 and where other important dignitaries, presidents and prime ministers are pampered on state visits. Situated in a relatively secluded wooded hillside and overlooking the Lake Gardens, it has a/c, a

restaurant and a pool. It's truly fit for royalty. Recommended.

KLCC and Jalan Ampang p69, map p70

L-AL MiCasa Hotel Apartments, 368b Jln Tun Razak, T03-2618 8333, www.micasahotel.com/malaysia/default.htm. Recently reopened, this a/c place is truly first rate, especially for longer stays. It has 240 suites, which include fully equipped kitchens as well as sitting rooms. Facilities include an Italian restaurant, tapas bar, pool, shopping arcade, hair salon, dentist and doctor, children's pool, jacuzzi, tennis, squash, gym, sauna, children's playhouse and a business centre. Recommended.

AL Corus, Jln Ampang, T03-2161 8888, www.corushotelkl.com. An upmarket hotel with some rooms enjoying a great view of the Petronas Towers. Rooms are functional but comfortable and there's broadband internet, a pool and Chinese and Japanese restaurants.

AL Crown Princess, City Square Centre, Jln Tun Razak, T03-2162 5522, www.crownprincess.com.my. This a/c hotel features opulent decor and over 550 spacious rooms with panoramic views. On the 10th floor is a pool and a restaurant, good for a 'High Tea' buffet. The award-winning **Taj** Indian restaurant is on the 11th floor, along with the lobby lounge and baby grand piano, and cafés. There's a ladies-only floor, a couple of cyber floors and the Crown Club floor, with access to an executive lounge. There is also a business centre and an adjacent shopping centre with 168 shops. Recommended.

AL Mandarin Oriental, KLCC (next door to Petronas Towers), T03-3380 8888, www.mandarinoriental.com. Luxury chain hotel, with all that you would expect for its prestigious location, including some stunning views and bookmarks with thought-provoking quotes left on pillows. There are several bars and restaurants including the excellent **Pacifica**, as well as a health spa, pool, tennis court and sauna and massage rooms.

AL Renaissance, corner of Jln Ismail and Jln Ampang, T03-2162 2233, www.marriott.com. A hotel with more than 900 rooms and an over-the-top lobby of massive black marble pillars. Furnishings in rooms are verging on the pretentious, but the lovely pool makes up for this. Except in rooms, which are wired, there is Wi-Fi throughout. There are also 5 lounges and restaurants and 2 tennis courts.

AL Shangri-La, 11 Jln Sultan Ismail, T03-2032 2388, www.shangri-la.com. With its grand, marble lobby and 720 rooms, the 'Shang' has remained KL's ritziest hotel, despite the arrival of swish upstart competition. It's constantly playing host to political leaders and assorted royalty for dinner. Stylish, plush a/c rooms with all mod cons, including broadband internet access, Chinese, Japanese and French restaurants, a small and rather old-fashioned pool, health club, sauna, jacuzzi and tennis. Recommended.

AL-A Equatorial, Jln Sultan Ismail, T03-2161 7777, www.equatorial.com. This is one of KL's earlier international hotels, and has had several revamps over the years. Choose a room at the back to reduce disturbance by traffic noise. Good dining choices with a Cantonese and a Japanese restaurant, both of which are held in high regard. There's also a pool.

A Nikko, 165 Jln Ampang, T03-2611 1111, www.hotelnikko.com.my. Near City Square and Ampang shopping centres, this a/c hotel has an oriental atmosphere with a very minimalist Japanese feel to it. With excellent service, it offers some super dining options in its Japanese and Chinese restaurants. There's also a pool and a spa. Recommended.

A-B Concorde, 2 Jln Sultan Ismail, T03-2144 2200, www.concordehotelsresorts.com. This is the old Merlin (KL's first big modern hotel) masquerading behind a facelift and rather sterile interior decor. It has a/c, a decent-sized pool, gym and 2 non-smoking floors. There are also 4 good restaurants, a coffee shop and, next door, the **Hard Rock Café**.

The Golden Triangle *p72, map p72*
L Istana, 73 Jln Raja Chulan, T03-2141 9988, www.hotelistana.com.my. Striking, almost grotesquely extravagant, hotel in the heart of KL's business district. It has comfortable, modern rooms with Wi-Fi and cable TV. The excellent freeform pool has lovely views.

L JW Marriott, 183 Jln Bukit Bintang, T03-2715 9000, www.marriott.com. Next to Star Hill shopping mall, this place is magnificent in its extravagance. It has a pool, fitness centre and conference facilities.

L-AL Federal, 35 Jln Bukit Bintang, T03-2148 9166, www.federalhotel.com.my. Once glam, but now looking a tad out of date, this hotel has spacious a/c rooms with internet access and cable TV. There is an Indian 'fun pub', an Irish pub, a revolving restaurant on 18th floor, an ice-cream bar, cafés, bowling, shopping arcade, business centre and a pool. When it opened in the early 1960s it was the pride of KL: its **Mandarin Palace** restaurant was once rated as the most elegant eatery in the Far East, and is still good, but it does not compare with the world-class glitz in contemporary KL.

AL Swiss Garden, 117 Jln Pudu, T03-2141 3333, www.swissgarden.com. Handy for Puduraya bus terminal, this a/c hotel has 310 good-sized rooms over 15 storeys, but facilities are disappointing and it's expensive for what you get. There's a Chinese restaurant, a tiny pool, a fitness centre with limited equipment, a business centre and a spa.

AL-A Berjaya Times Square, 1 Jln Imbi, T03-2117 8000, www.berjayahotel.com. Shares the same building as Times Square. Its mind-boggling 900 suites have lounges, kitchenettes and separate bathtubs and showers, as well as fabulous views of the city. Great facilities include a big pool, a gym, jacuzzi and restaurants, but the atmosphere is a bit sterile. It's popular with tour groups.

A-B Fortuna, 87 Jln Berangan, T03-2141 9111, www.fortunakl.com. With a/c, coffee house with live band, health centre. Just off Bukit Bintang, tucked away and slightly quieter than most. Good value for money with clean, comfortable rooms with cable TV and attached bathrooms. Recommended.

B Agora, 106-110 Jln Bukit Bintang, T03-2142 8133, www.agorahotel.com.my.

Small 50-room hotel, small and past its prime but functional. Located on a busy intersection in the shopping area of the Golden Triangle, rooms on the front tend to be noisy. There's a/c and a restaurant but no internet access.
B Bintang Warisan, 68 Jln Bukit Bintang, T03-2148 8111, www.bintangwarisan.com. Well-managed hotel offering clean, spacious a/c room with TVs and attached bathrooms. Most rooms have windows, some have excellent views of Petronas Towers and some have their own garden. There are 2 small cafés. Breakfast is included. Recommended.
B Cardogan, 64 Jln Bukit Bintang, T03-2144 4883, www.cardogan.com. Simple a/c rooms, clean but a little old, with small, attached, white-tiled bathrooms. There 's a coffee house, health centre and a business centre.
B Imperial, 76-80 Jln Cangkat Bukit Bintang (Jln Hicks), T03-2142 9048, www.hotelimperial.com.my. Good-value Chinese hotel in an otherwise pricey part of town, well located for shopping centres and nearby eateries. Recently revamped, it has a a/c rooms with attached bathrooms and cable TV.
B Replica Inn, Cangat Bukit Bintang, T03-2142 1771, www.replicainn.com. Newish place in a super location for shops and foodstalls. The excellent value rooms have good bedding, TVs, attached bathrooms and windows. There's a good Malay café downstairs. Another branch is on Jln Petaling in Chinatown.
B-C Comfort Inn, 65 Cangkat Bukit Bintang, T03-2141 3636, www.hotelcomfort.biz. Tiny rooms with tiny TVs, old a/c units and small attached bathrooms make a stay here akin to a sojourn in Hong Kong's Chungking Mansions. But rooms are clean, there's Wi-Fi access in the lobby and staff can help organize tours. They also run **Comfort Lodge**, 52 Tengkat Ting Shin (just around the corner).
B-C Tai Ichi, 78 Jln Bukit Bintang, T03-2142 7533, F2148 6294. Another basic Chinese hotel in this strip. A bit shabby, but very clean, popular and serviceable with good management. Rooms are all a/c and have TVs. Most have some natural light. There is a **Subway** sandwich store by the reception.

C-D Pondok Lodge, 20 Jln Cangkat Bukit Bintang, T03-2142 8449, www.pondoklodge.com. Rooms are simple and comfortable with a/c. What sets this place apart is the rooftop garden, and the funky upper floor lounge area, which has a kitchen, big comfy sofas and a breakfast dining area. Breakfast is included.
C-D Putra Bintang, 72 Jln Bukit Bintang, T03-2141 9228, F2142 9678. Efficient, clean and popular hotel which offers short-stay rates and gets crowded on weekends with locals seeking a little love break. Rooms are basic, with a/c, attached shower and shiny tiles. There's a 24-hr internet room downstairs.
C-D Shuttle Inn, 112 Jln Bukit Bintang, T03-2145 0828. Cleanish, slightly decrepit rooms with attached shower room, TV and a/c. Acceptable for a night.

Around Kuala Lumpur p73
B-C YMCA, 95 Jln Padang Belia, T03-2274 1439, www.ymcakl.com. The good facilities – barber, gym, language courses, shop, a/c rooms and standard rooms with attached bathroom – are neutralized by the inconvenient location in the Brickfields district on the southwest outskirts, off Jln Tun Sambathan. It is, however, within sniffing distance of Raju's tandoori ovens (see Eating, page 93), and it's a short walk to KL Sentral train hub.

KLIA airport p56
AL Pan Pacific, T03-8787 3333, www.panpacific.com. Linked to the airport via a skybridge, there are well over 400 rooms, plenty of sports facilities and dining options.
A Airside Transit Hotel, T03-8787 4848, airsidetransit@klia.com.my. Located within the airport at satellite A with 80 comfortable rooms, a gym, bar and café.

LCCT p56
B-E Tune, T03-7962 5888, www.tunehotels.com. A no-frills, comfy and heavily branded lodgings, handy for morning departures from the LCCT. Book well in advance for sizeable discounts.

Petaling Jaya p75

AL Allson Sunway Lagoon Resort, Jln Lagun Timur, Bandar Sunway, T03-7492 8000, www.sunway.com.my/hotel. Dazzling resort with the world's largest surf 'n' wave pool, a health and spa club, 3 tennis courts, squash, 170-m man-made beach, kids' camp, shuttle service to KL, restaurants with Japanese, Chinese and American/Italian cuisine, a coffee house and a poolside bar. Recommended.

AL Holiday Inn Glenmarie Resort, Jln Sultan, T03-7803 1000, www.holidayinn.com. Resort hotel with over 300 rooms set in more than 1000 ha of grounds, with sports facilities including 2 golf courses, an Olympic-sized pool, a spa, squash and tennis courts.

AL Hyatt Regency Saujana Hotel & Country Club, 2 km off Sultan Abdul Aziz Shah Airport Highway, T03-7846 1234, www.hyatt.com. 5 mins from the airport and 2 mins from the golf course (it has 2 18-hole championship courses). Low-rise hotel set in landscaped gardens, a convenient stopover for early morning flights, with shuttle service to and from airport.

AL Petaling Jaya Hilton, 2 Jln Barat, T03-7955 9122, www.hilton.co.uk. Large white block, a 45-min drive from the airport. There's a pool, spa, tennis courts and golf course.

A Shah's Village, 3 & 5 Lorong Sultan, T03-7956 9322, www.shahsresorts.com. Boutique-style hotel set around a garden and pool, with 91 comfy a/c rooms and a restaurant.

Klang and its offshore islands p76

C SeaLion Guest House, T03-3110 3142, Pula Ketam. The only guesthouse on the island.

Kuala Selangor Nature Park p77

A-E Chalets, T03-3289 2294. The Malaysian Nature Society, www.mns.org.my, runs simple accommodation in Kuala Selangor Nature Park, a short walk from the last bus stop. Accommodation ranges from simple A-frame huts, to a couple of chalets and a hostel. These must be booked a few days in advance for weekend visitors. Some have bathrooms, others have to share. Dorm available (RM110).

Mines Wonderland p77

AL Mines Wellness Hotel, Jln Dulang, T03-8943 6688, www.mineswellness hotel.com.my. Low-rise hotel in well-landscaped gardens, a pleasant alternative to the bustle of KL. It's furnished to a high standard and has even created a sandy beach.

AL Palace of the Golden Horses, Jln Kuda Emas, T03-8943 2343, www.palaceofthegoldenhorses.com.my. Set on the shores of the old tin-mining lake, this hotel has 400-plus rooms, luxury fittings, a range of cuisines, state-of-the-art conference centre, an exquisite spa, a fitness centre, a free-form lagoon pool and a children's camp.

B Mint, 8th km, KL-Seremban Highway, T03-8943 8888. Convenient for the Mines Exhibition Centre, Wonderland and airport, this is an ugly block of over 400 rooms, with a sizeable pool, health and business centre.

Seremban p78, map p78

Seremban has only a few hotels, one of which is among the best of Malaysia's resort hotels, the Allson Klana. There are 3 mid-range hotels; the rest are basic, Chinese-run establishments of an almost uniformly poor quality.

AL Allson Kiana Resort, PT4388 Jln Penghulu Cantik, Taman Tasik Seremban, T06-762 7888, www.allsonklana.com.my. This offers a good alternative to staying in KL, the airport being only 20 mins away. Set in 24 acres of landscaped gardens, this is a luxurious and well-established resort, overlooking one of the largest lagoon-shaped pools in Malaysia. It has over 200 very comfortable and spacious rooms with a/c, in-house video, showers and baths and minibars. There's also tennis, a health club, sauna, business centre, deli and a boutique. There are outstanding food outlets including **Yuri Japanese Restaurant** and **Blossom Court Chinese Restaurant**, as well as a coffee house.

B Carlton Star, 47 Jln Dato Sheikh Ahmad, T06-763 6663, F762 0040. Good central position, clean though slightly small a/c rooms with TVs and attached bathrooms. There's also a coffee house, fitness centre and a karaoke lounge. One of the better budget places.

B Seri Malaysia, Jln Sungai Ugung, T06-764 4181, www.serimalaysia.com.my. A bit out of the way, but handy for the bus terminus and good value for money. The building is topped with a Minangkabau-style roof.

B Tasik, Jln Tetamu, T06-763 0994. This place has seen better days but has a good central position overlooking the Lake Gardens. A/c, TV, shower, restaurant and a pool .

D Happy, 35 Jln Tunku Hassan, T06-763 0172. Probably the best of the budget places to stay, although that isn't saying much. The rooms are dark but fairly clean.

Sri Menanti p79

B Sri Menanti Resort, T06-497 0242. Good, well-equipped rooms with a/c. There's also a pool and a restaurant.

Port Dickson p79

Because PD is a favourite family getaway for KL's weekenders, beach hotels are often quite full – and rates are comparatively high. During the week, discounts are often on offer. There is not much selection for the budget-minded traveller, who may be wise to give Port Dickson a miss.

AL Guoman, Km 16, Jln Pantai, T02-662 7878, www.guomanhotels.com. A top-class resort set in 90 acres on the beachfront. There are over 250 rooms and suites, a golf course, a pool, 7 restaurants and cafés.

AL Ilham Resort Tanjung Biru, T02-662 6800, www.ilhamresort.com/. Resort comprising 59 apartments inspired by the architecture of the Melaka Sultanate. All rooms have a/c and phones. Facilities include a pool, tennis court, squash court and spa on site. A babysitting service is available.

A Bayu Beach Resort, Batu 4½, Jln Pantai, T02-647 3703, www.bayu.com.my. Luxury 300-room beach resort, with good water sports facilities and a pool. All rooms have a/c, kitchenette, TV and minibar. There's a Chinese restaurant, coffee house and karaoke lounge.

A Corus Paradise Resort, 3.5 km, Jln Pantai, T02-647 7600, www.corusparadisepd.com. This luxury hotel, the best on the strip, has over 200 rooms, all with ocean views, bath, TV, in-house video, minibar and tea/coffee-making facilities. Other amenities include a pool, children's playground, tennis, squash, water sports, business centre and coffee house.

A Tanjung Tuan Beach Resort, Batu 5, Jln Pantai, T06-647 3013. A/c, restaurant, pool, good sports facilities and weekday discounts.

B Seri Malaysia, Batu 4, Jln Pantai, T02-647 6070, www.serimalaysia.com.my. One of newer additions to this budget chain, good value and beach views. Recommended.

B-C Golden Resort, Batu 10, Jln Pantai, T02-662 5176. Rooms have a/c, mini-fridge and TV. Facilities include a restaurant and pool.

C Beach Point Motel, Batu 9, Jln Pantai, T02-662 5889. Located down a track off the main road, with a/c and showers. Basic but spotlessly clean.

D Kong Meng, Batu 8, Teluk Kemang, T02-662 5683. On the beachfront, reasonable for the price. Restaurant.

E Port Dickson Youth Hostel, Km 6 Jln Pantai, T02-647 2188. YHA card holders only (although some non-members seem to land a room), separate dorms for men and women, dining/cooking area, large compound and camping.

Eating

Many of KL's big hotels in the Jln Sultan Ismail/Bukit Bintang areas serve excellent-value buffet lunches and offer a selection of local and international dishes. One of the best ways to sample various cuisines is to graze among the foodstalls. In the past few years, Cangkat Bukit Bintang and Tingkat Tong Shin, a couple of streets west from Jln Bukit Bintang, have emerged as trendy eating areas.

The colonial core p63, map p64

The Museum, Legend Hotel, The Mall, Putra Pl, 100 Jln Putra, T03-4042 9888. Open 1200-1500 and 1830-2230. This place aims to look like a museum, with Chinese antiques and columns everywhere. It has Teochew and Cantonese cuisine and adventurous food promotions. Winner of the Malaysian Tourism and Promotion best Chinese award.

Hai Tien Lo, Seri Pan Pacific Hotel, Jln Putra, T03-4049 4510. Open 1200-1500 and 1900-2300. Excellent dim sum, steamed fish with suet and plates of spicy Sichuan grub. Recommended.

Cameleon Vegetarian Restaurant, 1 Jln Thamboosamy (off Jln Putra, near The Mall and Pan Pacific). Thai and Chinese, good *kway teow*. Vegetarians with carnivorous instincts rate the soya bean roast duck and other ersatz meat and fish dishes whose presentation (and sometimes taste) is convincing.

Food courts

There is a clean food court in the basement of **The Mall** on Jln Putra with stalls dishing up good-value plates of local, Thai and Japanese fare. There are also a couple of cheap restaurants in the basement including **Kyros Kebab** and **The Chicken Rice Shop**.

Foodstalls

Chow Kit is the best area for foodstalls. On Jln Raja Muda Abdul Aziz there is a food court with great Indian and Afghan food. Jln Haji Hussien has a picturesque collection of superb foodstalls. Walk up Jln Haji Hussien and turn right. The food court on the top floor of The Mall, built like rows of old Chinese shophouses, is run down but has an attractive ambience. The Indian, Malay and Chinese food are all good, but most places to eat here close by 2000. It's cheap too; tandoori chicken, naan, dal and drink, all cost just RM8. Jln Raja Alang and Jln Raja Bot stalls, off Jln Tuanku Abdul Rahman, have mostly Malay cuisine.

Next to Keramat supermarket there is a South Indian stall with good mutton soup. In the alleyway between Keramat supermarket and the Pakistani mosque are many good foodstalls during the day. On the riverfront behind Jln Mesjid India are good Indian and Malay night stalls.

Munshi Abdullah Food Complex, off Lorong Tuanku Abdul Rahman (near Coliseum), has good satay.

Scores of rough-and-ready Chinese pavement restaurants line Jln Alor, parallel to Jln Bukit Bintang.

Chinatown *p66, map p67*
Chinese

China Town Pavilion, Jln Hang Lekir. One of the open-air restaurants that gets out the tables in the evening. Lively place for a beer and good for people-watching, although fending off hawkers and monks asking for donations can get tiresome after a while. The food is overpriced and not too dissimiliar to what can be found at Chinese takeaways in the UK, hence it is patronized mainly by tourists.

Ginger, 1st floor Central Market. Slightly dim, but elegant and popular eatery dishing up spicy tongue-twisting Nyonya favourites.

Oriental Bowl, 587 Leboh Pudu, T03-2202 5577. A/c restaurant above Chinese spice shop, convenient location for Central Market, rather formal atmosphere and a fascinating array of Chinese herbal soups (very good for stomach problems), as well as some tasty antelope and fish maw dishes.

Old China Café, 11 Jln Balai Polis, T03- 2072 5915, www.oldchina.com.my. Good, interesting Nyonya and Malay favourites, like *asam* prawns (prawns cooked with candlenuts and tamarind), *mee siam* and plenty of seafood dishes. The walls are covered in old photos of Malaysia and the tables are topped with marble. Lots of olde-worlde ambience. Fine choice for a romantic evening out.

Canteen Room, 8 Jln Hang Kasturi, T03-2070 7091. Open 0800-2200. New place with comfy seating and some excellent-value set meals, like the RM16.50 set lunch and filling breakfasts. The *nasi lemak* is recommended.

Formosa Vegetarian, 48 Jln Sultan. Mammoth menu of fake meat and fish, beancurds and other creative veggie dishes. Recommended.

Gourmet Food Court, Jln Petalin. A local favourite with a great vegetarian counter with a dozen choices of tasty vegetables and beancurd to pile on rice. Also, stalls serving up the usual Chinese food court fare.

Hameeds, Jln Hang Kasturi. Open 1000-2200. This simple and popular place offers up a selection of Asian favourites, from sumptuous biriyanis to freshly made naan and tandoori chicken. The *tom yam* soup and fish-head curry are the most sought-after dishes. Ahmedia next door offers more of the same.

Malay Teahouse, G/F Central Market Annexe, T017-300 7811. Open 0900-2100. Charming place playing Chinese and Malay music of the 1950s and serving a simple menu of Malay favourites including *mee rebus*, *nasi lemak* and tea from the highlands.

Nam Heong, 54 Jln Sultan. Open 1000-1500. Clean and non-fussy place specializing in delightful plates of delicious Hainanese chicken rice, but also some wonderful Chinese delights, including pork with yam (truly outstanding), *asam* fish and fresh tofu.

Old Town, ground floor, Central Market, www.oldtown.com.my. With a menu of simple *kopitiam* fare, this place is jammed at breakfast with locals hunting out the thick *kaya* toast with butter, dark thick coffee and well-priced meals such as *rending* and *mee siam*.

Sawadee – Dee Thai Kitchen, ground floor, Plaza Warisan, Jln Tun HS Lee, T03-2070 4788. Open 0900-2100. Superb value, authentic Thai dishes served up in a bright, fresh setting. The seafood fried rice is excellent. Recommended.

Seng Nam, Lebuh Pasar Besar. Hainanese. The steamboats in the restaurant area of Chinatown are worth sampling at one of the outdoor tables.

Yusoof Dan Zakhir, opposite the Central Market. Simple food hall with blaring music, and bright yellow and green decor. Cheap and good grazing. Recommended.

Food courts

The clean food court on the 1st floor of the Central Market has an excellent selection of regional Malay cuisines, Chinese and Thai food served in generous portions on large plates. Recommended.

Foodstalls

Puduraya Bus Station, Jln Pudu. A good variety of stalls open at all hours.

Little India *p68*

Coliseum Café, 100 Jln Tuanku Abdul Rahman (Batu Rd), next door to the old Coliseum Theatre. Long-famed for its sizzling lamb and beef steaks, Hainanese (Chinese) food and Western-style (mild) curries. There's a good range of cocktails, all served by frantic waiters in buttoned-up white suits. During the Communist Emergency, planters were said to come here for gin and curry, handing their guns in to be kept behind the bar; it's easy to believe it. Great little bar to sit around. Recommended.

Bhakti Woodlands, 55 Leboh Ampang, T03-2034 2399. Good selection of vegetarian Indian food with set lunches, tasty *masala dosai* and lashings of sugary tea.

Sangeetha Veg Restaurant, 65 Jln Lebuh Ampang, T03-2032 3333. Open 1100-2230. With branches all over India, this tidy restaurant is a great place to sample some true Indian veg fare (including Jain) in a/c comfort. The thalis (served 1100-1500) are truly gargantuan, and the *papad* are deliciously peppery. Recommended.

Foodstalls

Jln Masjid India, has many good Indian and Malay foodstalls.

Lorong Raja Muda Food Centre, off Jln Raja Muda, on the edge of Kampong Baru. This place has mainly Malay food.

Sunday Market, Kampong Baru (main market actually takes place on Sat night). This market has many Malay hawker stalls.

Lake Gardens and around *p68*

Carcosa Seri Negara, Persiaran Mahameru, Taman Tasek Perdana, Lake Gardens, T03-2282 1888 (reservations). Daily 1530-1800. Built in 1896 to house the British Administrator for the Federated Malay States, Carcosa offers English-style high tea in a sumptuous, colonial setting. Expensive Italian lunches and dinners are also served in the Mahsuri dining hall on fine china plates with solid silver cutlery. Continental cuisine. Recommended.

ⵉⵉ Seri Melayu, 1 Jln Conlay, T03-2145 1833. Open 1100-1500 and 1900-2300 (reservations recommended for groups of 4 or more – although it seats 500). The brainchild of former Malaysian PM Dr Mahatir Mohamad, this is one of the best Malay restaurants in town, in a traditional Minangkabau-style building. It has a beautifully designed interior in the style of Negeri Sembilan palace. Don't be put off by cultural shows or the big groups – the food is superb and amazing in its variety, including regional specialities. It's very popular with locals too. Individual dishes are expensive, so the buffet is the best bet (with a choice of over 50 dishes). Those arriving in shorts will be given a sarong to wear. Recommended.

KLCC and Jalan Ampang *p69, map p70*
ⵉⵉ Bharath's, Suria KLCC, T03-2163 2631. Classy South Indian restaurant with great views. Some of the seating is provided by wooden swings. Very kitsch.

ⵉⵉ Ciao, 428 Jln Tun Razak, T03-9285 4827. Tue-Sun 1200-1430 and 1900-2230. Authentic, tasty Italian food served in a beautifully renovated bungalow. Recommended.

ⵉⵉ D'Tandoor, KL Tower, T03-2021 2020. Fancy Indian restaurant (part of an international chain) in the KL tower.

ⵉⵉ Golden Phoenix, Hotel Equatorial, Jln Sultan Ismail, T03-2161 7777. Open 1200-1430. Gourmet Chinese establishment, which has been recently revamped with sleek undertones. Serves up delicious dishes such as double-boiled bamboo pith with seafood soup and Shanghainese favourite sautéed prawns with salted egg.

ⵉⵉ Kampachi, Hotel Equatorial, Jln Sultan Ismail, T03-2161 7777. Japanese restaurant with Ginza-trained chefs and private tatami rooms. Winner of a Malaysian Tourism award.

ⵉⵉ Lafitte, Shangri-La Hotel, 11 Jln Sultan Ismail, T03-2074 3900. Open 1200-1500 and 1900-2300. Excellent French restaurant, but

very expensive, with award-winning wine list. Formal dress in the evenings. Recommended.

ⵉⵉ Shang Palace, Shangri-La Hotel, Jln Sultan Ismail, T03-2032 2388. Open 1200-1430 and 1830-2230. Sleek, posh eatery famed for its Cantonese cusine, this restaurant often has a superb value dim sum lunch of over 40 varieties; check with the hotel for current offers.

ⵉⵉ Tamarind Springs, 1 Jln Kerja Air Lama, T03-4256 9100. Indochinese cuisine served in leafy elegance to a well-heeled crowd.

ⵉⵉ Toh Lee, Hotel Nikko, 165 Jln Ampang, T03-2782 6128. Open 1200-1430 and 1830-2230. Offers one of the city's most celebrated dim sum lunches. Broad selection of southern Chinese cuisine after dark.

ⵉⵉ Zipangu, Shangri-La Hotel, 11 Jln Sultan Ismail, T03-2032 2388. Regular winner of best restaurant, with a small Japanese garden. Limited menu but highly regarded with cigar lounge and walk-in wine and sake cellar. Recommended.

ⵉⵉ Bangles, 270 Jln Ampang, T03-4532 4100. This is reckoned to be among the best North Indian tandoori restaurants in KL. It's often necessary to book in the evenings. Recommended.

ⵉⵉ Bombay Palace, 215 Jln Tun Razak, next to US Embassy, T03-2145 4241. Open 1200-1500 and 1830-2300. Good-quality North Indian food in tasteful surroundings with staff in traditional Indian uniform. The menu includes a vegetarian section.

ⵉⵉ E'Toile Bistro, Basement, Equatorial Hotel, Jln Sultan Ismail. Coffee and pastries with free internet access to all customers. Recommended.

ⵉⵉ Seri Angkasa, at the top of the KL Tower (see page 71), T03-2020 5055. A sister Malay restaurant to **Seri Melayu**. The tower revolves, achieving a full rotation in 60 mins. Good food. Booking is advisable for the evenings. There is also a good-value buffet lunch available.

ⵉⵉ Spices, Concorde Hotel, 2 Jln Sultan Ismail, T03-2244 2200. Mon-Sat 1130-1500 and 1830-2300. Ironically, considering its name, the food is not overly spicy. Eclectic Asian cuisine as well as traditional Malay. There's a

4-piece band for background music, a/c indoors or poolside outdoor seating. On the varied drinks list is *setengah*, a stiff whisky drink popular in colonial times.

¶ **Studio 123**, 159 Jln Ampang. Easily missed – it's opposite the **Corus Hotel** – this is an unassuming place with friendly staff and excellent, good-value seafood. Recommended.

¶ **Top Hat**, 7 Jln Kia Peng, T03-2241 3611. Open 1200-1500, 1900-2400. Good Nyonya set menu. Some Western dishes are available, such as chicken pie. This restaurant, set in a 1930s colonial bungalow, is just south of KLCC. Recommended.

Foodstalls

Ampang Park Shopping Complex, along Jln Tun Razak. A popular but small centre, with a good variety of stalls.

The Golden Triangle *p72, map p72*

¶¶¶ **Sakura Café & Cuisine**, 165-169 Jln Imbi. Excellent variety of Malay, Chinese and Indian dishes, including fish-head curry. Located in an area with many other good cheap restaurants. Recommended.

¶¶¶ **Scalini's**, 19 Jln Sultan Ismail, down from the **Istana Hotel**. A perennial favourite among expats and locals, this place serves delightful Italian food, including excellent pasta. It's in trendy surroundings and has friendly staff and a superb wine list. Pricey, but recommended.

¶¶¶ **Shook!**, The Feast Floor, Starhill Gallery, Jln Bukit Bintang, T03-2719 8535. Emphasizing seasonal trends, the fusion menu here includes Japanese, Chinese, Italian and a Western grill. It's popular with celebrities and has a huge walk-in wine cellar with over 3000 bottles.

¶¶ **Athena**, Pavilion Mall, T03-2141 5131. The bright blue and white decor screams Greece and there are a few Greek dishes on the menu. Other Western-inspired options include Worcester striploin and nutmeg fish fillet.

¶¶ **Bangkok Jam**, BB Plaza, Jln Bukit Bintang, T03-2142 3449. Popular Thai eatery, recommended by locals.

¶¶ **Chikuyo-Tei**, 2nd floor, **Istana Hotel**, Jln Raja Chulan, T03-2141 4328. Open 1200-1500 and

1830-2230. One of the first Japanese restaurants in KL, serves up quality teppanyaki, seafood and steak.

¶¶ **Delaney's**, Park Royal Hotel, Jln Sultan Ismail. Open 1200 until late. This offers the manufactured Irish experience available at most cities around the world. With Asian snacks, hearty pies and a pint of Guinness you can't go wrong.

¶¶ **Eden Village**, 260 Jln Raja Chulan, T03-2141 4027. Wide-ranging menu, but probably best known for seafood, resembles a glitzy Minangkabau palace with garden behind, cultural Malay, Chinese and Indian dances every night. There's a less touristy outlet in PJ 25-31 Jln 5322/23, Damansara Jaya).

¶¶ **Federal Hotel Revolving Restaurant**, 35 Jln Bukit Bintang. This was once one of KL's tallest buildings, now rather dwarfed but still a good spot for ice-cream sundaes with a view.

¶¶ **Marco Polo**, Wisma Lim Foo Yong, 86 Jln Raja Chulan, T03-2142 5595. Open 1200-1400, 1830-2230. This restaurant with 1970s-style decor has an extensive menu. The barbecue roast suckling pig is recommended. It gets very busy at lunchtimes.

¶¶ **Michaelangelo's**, Pavilion Mall, T03-2141 1123. Open 0900-0100. Whilst the atmosphere is a tad sterile, the portions in this Italian joint are good, with a menu that's sweeps effortlessly from superb seafood, good pizza and knots of spaghetti.

¶¶ **Sari Ratu**, 42 Jln Sultan Ismail, T03-2142 1811. Open 1000-2200. Huge, informal place with a large *nasi padang* spread, featuring fish heads, *rendang* and *dendeng paru* (spicy beef lungs).

¶¶ **The Ship**, 40 Jln Sultan Ismail. Open from lunch until 0230. This place is in the Malaysia *Book of Records* as being the longest running 'Western Thematic Restaurant'. It has a very dark interior with a confused 'Lord Nelson in the Orient' fusion feel. There is an extensive menu of steaks, chicken, salads. The stone grills are particularly popular.

¶¶ **Tarbush**, 138 Jln Bukit Bintang, T03-4253 4177. Lebanese cuisine served in a simple setting. Locals recommend it for the good service and the authentic Middle Eastern taste with no Malay influence. There are a number of excellent Middle Eastern eateries in this area; also recommended are **Zaytoun**, **Sahara Tent Restaurant** and **Restoran Lebanese** (all around the corner from Tarbush on Jln Sultan Ismail).

⍦ **Esquire Kitchen**, Level 1, Sungai Wang Plaza, Jln Sultan Ismail. Good-value dumplings and pork dishes and popular Shanghai dishes.

⍦ **Johnny's Thai Steamboat**, basement, Bukit Bintang Plaza. Good-value, spicy Thai dishes.

⍦ **Mark's Asam Laksa**, 12 lower ground floor, The Weld, Jln Raja Chulan. Delightful bowls of spicy, fish-infused laksa.

⍦ **Sri Penang**, lower ground floor, Menara Aik Hua, Cangkat Raja Chulan (Jln Hicks). Variety of Nyonya and North Malaysian dishes.

⍦ **Teppanyaki**, 2nd floor, Sungai Wang Plaza, Jln Bukit Bintang and Lot 10, Jln Sultan Ismail. Excellent Japanese fast food, set meal RM10.

Teahouses

Chinese teahouse. Try out the traditional Chinese teahouse opposite **Sungai Wang Hotel** on Jln Bukit Bintang.

Foodcourts

The basement of the **Pavillion Mall** has one of the city's best (and most expensive) food courts, with a wonderful variety of food including Vietnamese, Thai, Japanese, Indonesian and Malay. A meal costs around RM10. There are also a number of other good-value restaurants in the basement, including **Bombay Spice**, **Peppersteak Lunch** and **Pasta Mania**.

Foodstalls

Lot 10 Shopping Complex, Jln Sultan Ismail. There is an excellent choice of food here, if you can tolerate the high-volume music.

Around Kuala Lumpur *p73*

ⅢⅢⅢ **Jake's**, 21 Jln Setiapuspa, Medan Damansara, off Jln Damansara, towards PJ, T03-2094 5677. Open 1200-1500 and 1830-2300. Jake's steaks are highly rated in KL,

served by cowboys and cowgirls. There's another branch in **Starhill Gallery**, Jln Bukit Bintang. Recommended.

ⅢⅢ **Bangsar Seafood Village**, Jln Telawi Empat, Bangsar Baru. Open 1200-1430 and 1800-2300. Large restaurant complex with reasonably priced seafood, fresh from tanks lining the inside of the restaurant. Specialities include crab in butter sauce and Thai-style tiger prawns (and a good satay stall).

ⅢⅢ **Hai Peng Seafood Restaurant**, Taman Evergreen, Batu Empat, Jln Klang Lama (Old Klang Rd). Open until 0100. The smallest and least assuming restaurant in a row of Chinese shophouses (red neon sign), but one of the very best seafood restaurants in Malaysia, where the Chinese community's seafood connoisseurs come to eat (the other seafood restaurants in the cluster include **Chian Kee**, **Pacific Sea Foods** and **Yee Kee**, most of which are good, but not as good as Hai Peng). Its specialities include butter crab (in clove and coconut), belacan crab, sweet-and-sour chilli crab and bamboo clams. The *siu yit kum* (small gold-leaf tea) is a delicious, fragrant Chinese tea, which is perfect with seafood. Recommended.

⍦ **Annalakshmi**, ground floor, Mid-Valley Megamall, T03-2284 3799. Excellent Indian, vegetarian restaurant run by the Temple of Fine Arts, dedicated to the preservation of Indian cultural heritage in Malaysia. The buffet is particularly recommended.

⍦ **Halfway to Kajang**, near Sungai Besi (take the Seremban highway, exit to the left at Taman Sri Petaling – before the toll gates, turn right at the T-junction, go over the railway line and past the Shell and Esso stations, turn left towards Sungai Besi tin mine, then branch right to Balakong, the restaurant is signposted). Little more than a tin shed (with a fruit stall outside), it's famed among KL's epicureans for its deep-fried, paper-wrapped chicken, wild boar curry and vinegar pork. Recommended.

⍦ **Sri Vani's Corner (Raju's)**, Jln Tun Sambathan 4 (next to the YMCA tennis courts). Overgrown hawker stall rated among its dedicated clientele as the best place for

tandooris and oven-baked naan in KL.
Recommended.

¶ Valentine Roti, 6 Jln Semark (close to the National Library). This place was reviewed in the *Far Eastern Economic Review*, billed as the best roti restaurant in town. Ilango Arokias-amy's rotis are a treat and so light and flaky. As he says "I think God wanted me to do this".

Foodstalls

Brickfields, Jln Tun Sambathan. A string of small outdoor restaurants.

Mamaks For a good, cheap eat, *mamaks*, canteens run by Muslim Indians, are found everywhere. Many open 24 hrs. The most famous *mamak* is **Mamak SS2 Mumi**, in the SS2 area of Petaling Jaya. It's so well known that taxi drivers know where it is just by its name.

Petaling Jaya *p75*

¶¶¶ Ampang Yong Tau Foo, 53 Jln SS2/30. Closed Mon. *Yong tau foo* (stuffed beancurd dishes) in a coffee shop. Recommended.
¶ Wan Kembang (Cik Siti), 24 Jln 14/22, in front of the mosque. Specializes in Kelantanese food.

Seremban *p78, map p78*

¶¶¶ Blossom Court, Allson Klan Resort. A classy Chinese restaurant with expensive-looking decor. Popular for extensive range of *dim sum*, good Peking duck and Cantonese dishes.
¶¶¶ Yuri, Allson Klan Resort. Excellent-quality, traditional Japanese. It has good, private Tatami rooms, a sushi bar and a Teppanyaki counter. Good-value set meals.

Foodstalls

Jln Tuanku Antah, near the post office; Jln Dr Murugesu, opposite Masjid Janek mosque.

Port Dickson *p79*

¶ Haw Wah Seafood, Teluk Kamang. Simple but clean coffee shop at the end of a row of modern shophouses on the main road. Good seafood.
¶ Kemang Seafood, Batu 7. Malay seafood, crab sold by weight (1 kg RM25).

◑ Bars and clubs

Kuala Lumpur now has a vibrant bar scene and several streets have emerged over the past 5 years or so as hip places to be seen. Bars, restaurants, coffee shops and even *mamaks* have sprouted along the same street, serving food and drink well into the early hours of the morning. The Golden Triangle is a good place to find bars and clubs, the main bar and club street being Jln P Ramlee, but a few bars have begun setting up in Cangkat Bukit Bintang, and this area is set to grow more. Bangsar and Desi Sri Hartamas are 2 areas just outside the centre of KL that have developed into popular night spots. Bars, restaurants, coffee shops and *mamaks* stand side by side in a network of streets in both of these areas. Most stay open until the early hours of the morning.

The Metro section in *The Star* (Malaysia's most widely read English-language daily) is devoted to what's on and where. Also check out freebie magazines such as *KL Lifestyle*, and *KL Vision* (usually free in hotels, if not they are available in newsagents for about RM5).

Since the mid-1980s, with the rise of the KL yuppy, the city has shaken off its early-to-bed image and now has a slightly more lively club scene. Several old colonial buildings have been converted into night spots. Most nightclubs and discos in KL stay open until 0300 during the week and until 0400 on Fri nights and weekends. Clubs are concentrated in Jalan P Ramlee and Bangsar.

Gay clubs cannot freely advertise themselves as 'gay' here because of the illegal status of homosexuality. However, there are a couple of well-established gay clubs like **Liquid** and **Velvet** and several gay-friendly venues that host gay functions, including the new **Zouk** superclub. While some women will hang out in gay bars, there is no lesbian bar per se. Occasional women's events are held at various venues; check www.fridae.com or www.forplu.com. The Fridae website also has an up-to-date gay and gay-friendly bar and club listing section.

Chinatown *p66, map p67*

Liquid, Mezzanine, Central Market Annexe, T03-2078 5909, www.liquidbar.com.my. A predominantly gay club and bar; they advertise themselves as the place for those with "an alternative lifestyle". There is a laid-back bar on the 1st floor with balcony seating. Upstairs is a thumping club, regularly hosting international Djs.

Reggae Bar, 158 Jln Tun H S Lee. Large, friendly bar, popular with backpackers as it's the only bar in Chinatown and within staggering distance of their dorms. Cheap spirits for women on most nights.

KLCC and Jalan Ampang *p69, map p70*

Bar Blonde, 50, Jln Doraisamy, Asian Heritage Row, T03-2691 1088, www.barblonde.com.my. Shamelessly contemporary design, cool house grooves and a roof terrace used for occasional moon parties make this a very trendy venue.

Bar Ibiza, 924 Jln P Ramlee, T03-2713 2333, www.modestos.com.my. Open 1600-0300. Trying to capture the laid-back old Ibiza vibes, this bar has beams of light shone on walls to look like lava. Podium dancing, drinks promotions. Ladies' night Wed and Sun.

Beach Club, 97 Jln P Ramlee, T03-2166 9919. Casual Hawaiin resort-style club decorated with palm leaves and drift wood. The music is mostly 'oldies'. Centrepiece is a tank with baby sharks (which must be uncomfortable for them since sharks 'see' through vibrations). Gets packed and is popular with tourists.

Bed, Heritage Row, 33, Jln Yap Ah Shak, T03-2693 1122, www.bed.com.my. Trying hard to attract the beautiful people, beds are scattered around this venue for the cool to lounge to a backdrop of slick contemporary tunes.

Club Quattro G/F Avenue K, Jln Ampang, www.clubquattro.com. Tries to encompass the atmosphere of the 4 seasons into its club with the icy Winter Bar at only 8 °C and a comedy bar in the Spring Bar. This place is loaded with gimmicks but makes for a fun night out.

Hard Rock Café, basement and ground floor, Wisma Concorde, 2 Jln Sultan Ismail, T03-2144 4062. The **Hard Rock**, with its Harley Davidson chopper poised on the rooftop, opened in 1991 and quickly became one of the most popular and lively bars in town. Good atmosphere and a small disco floor.

Nouvo, 5 Jln Sultan Ismail, T03-2170 6666. A chic club for a youngish crowd. R&B and hard house nights, currently one of the coolest venues in town.

The Red Chamber, 33 Jln Telawi 3, Bangsar. Funky bar splashed in red from floor to ceiling.

Red Square, Cap Square E-Centre, 8 Jln Ampang, T03-2692 2310, www.redsquarekl.com. After taking Jakarta by storm, this Russian-themed vodka bar is a new arrival on the scene, with groovy lighting and serious drinking. Very stylish bar and restaurant with romantic lighting and incense. Popular with locals. Recommended for its ambience.

Zouk, 113 Jln Ampang, T03-2171 1997, www.zoukclub.com.my. Perhaps KL's trendiest nightclub, following in the footsteps of Singapore's **Zouk**. A glowing futuristic domed exterior encapsulates the groovy interior. Hosts occasional gay parties. Attracts international DJs such as Tiesto and has a great chillout bar, **Velvet Underground**. Now expanded, Zouk features three new clubs with distinct vibes; **Barsonic**, **Phuture** and **Aristo** – check website for more details. Recommended.

The Golden Triangle *p72, map p72*

Delaney's Pub, corner of Jln Imbi and Jln Pudu. Quite expensive, standard Irish pub.

Frangipani, 25 Cangkat Bukit Bintang, T03-2144 3001. An elegant French restaurant and bar with a premoninantly gay clientele.

Fun Theatre (also known as **Funtheque**), 102-104 Jln Bukit Bintang. Cavernous bar on the 2nd floor with live cover bands.

QbA, Westin Hotel, 199 Jln Bukit Bintang, T03-2731 8333. Latin grill, wine and cigar lounge. The Latin American bar has a resident Colombian band. Popular with expats.

Viper Room, D5 KL Plaza, 179 Jln Bukit Bintang, T03-2148 8471. Attracts an interesting bag of characters for pre-clubbing drinks.

Around Kuala Lumpur *p73*

Wine@Nine, Plaza TTDI, 3 Jln Wan Kadir, Taman Tun Dr Ismail, T012-286 1688. Off Jln Damansara and next to KL Golf and Country Club is this relaxing venue with a good wine list, snacks and a couple of spanking new snooker tables.

● Entertainment

Art galleries

KL is gradually becoming a centre for local and some international artists, but the art market is not exactly flourishing, and much of the work around is mediocre. The following are some of the main galleries.

AP Art Gallery, ground floor, Central Market, off Jln Hang Kasturi, near Chinatown.

Art Salon, 4 Jln Telawi Dua, Bangsar Baru, T03-2282 2601. Open Tue-Sun. Contemporary Malaysian art. All work is by local contemporary artists. Prices range from a few hundred ringgit to thousands.

Artfolio Gallery, 1st floor City Sq, Jln Tun Razak, T03-2162 3339.

Galeri Petronas, Suria KLCC, T03-2331 7770, www.galeripetronas.com.my. Tue-Sun 1000-2000. There are multimedia terminals to learn about Malaysian art, plus regular exhibitions of contemporary local and regional work, including cartoon art.

National Art Gallery Jln Temerloh (off Jln Tun Razak), T03-4025 4990, www.artgallery.gov.my. Daily 1000-1800. Displays paintings and sculptures by leading Malaysian artists.

Sandra Knuyt, Shangri-La Hotel, T03-2032 4073. Daily 0900-2230. Work from around the world including works in porcelain and glass, and an expensive shop.

Cinemas

Cinemas are open daily from 1100. The first showing is usually a 1300 matinee with the last show at 2115 (Sat 2400).

The Sun newspaper's weekly listings magazine *Time Out* publishes details of what's on at the cinemas, and screenings are also listed in *The New Straits Times* and the *Star*. Tickets cost around RM11. Cineplex, small cinema complexes, are increasingly popular and many are incorporated into the shopping plazas.

Alliance Française, 15 Lorong Gurney, off Jln Semarak, T03-2694 7880. Hosts art house movies and art exhibitions.

Berjaya Times Square IMAX Theatre, T03-2117 3046, www.timessquarekl.com.

Capitol, Jln Raja Laut, T03-442 9051.

Coliseum, Jln Tuanku Abdul Rahman, T03-292 5995.

Federal, Jln Raja Laut, T03-442 5014.

Odeon, Jln Tuanku Abdul Rahman, T03-292 0084.

Odeon Cineplex, Central Sq, T03-230 8548.

President, Sungai Wang Plaza, Jln Sultan Ismail, T03-248 0084.

Tanjong Golden Village, at the KLCC, T03-7492 2929. 12 screens.

Classical music

Petronas Philharmonic Hall (KLCC), T03-2051 7007, www.dfpmpo.com. The KL Symphony Orchestra and the Malaysian Philharmonic Orchestra perform here.

Cultural shows

Eden Village, 260 Jln Raja Chulan, T03-2141 4027. Malay, Indian and Chinese cultural performances on Thu, Fri, Sat between 2030 to 2130 (RM55, includes a meal).

Malaysia Tourism Centre (MTC), 109 Jln Ampang, T03-2164 3929. Shows on Tue, Thu, Sat and Sun at 1500 to 1545 (RM 5).

Seri Melayu Restaurant, 1 Jln Conlay. Traditional Malay folk dances and singing daily between 2030 and 2115 (RM66.70, includes dinner) in KL's best Malay epicurean experience (see page 91).

Temple of Fine Arts, 116 Jln Berhala, Brickfields, T03-2274 3709. This organization, set up in Malaysia to preserve and promote Indian culture, stages cultural shows every month with dinner, music and dancing. The temple organizes an annual Festival of Arts (call for details), which involves a week-long stage production featuring traditional and modern Indian dance (this is free, since "the Temple believes art has no price"). It also runs classes in classical and folk dancing, and in playing traditional musical instruments.

Theatre

The Actors Studio, Bangsar, level 3, New Wing, Bangsar Shopping Centre, Jln Maarof, Bangsar, T03-2094 0400, www.theactorsstudio.com.my. Most local theatre is performed here.

Genting International Showroom, Genting Highlands Resort, Genting Highlands, 51 km from KL, T03-2162 2666, www.mice.genting.com.my/venue_gis.htm. 2 theatres with seating for over 1000 each; where the majority of international acts play. Major performances, including occasional international acts, play here.

National Theatre (Istana Budaya) Jln Tun Razak, T03-4025 2525, www.kakiseni.com.

Plaza Putra. Underneath Merdeka Sq. Occasional performances are performed here.

O Shopping

In the past, Malaysians and KL's expats used to go on shopping trips to neighbouring Singapore. These days, however, the city has most things, with new shopping complexes springing up every year. They are not concentrated in any particular area and ordinary shopping streets and markets are also dotted all around the city.

Antiques

Oriental Spirit, 1st floor, Central Market (northern end). A stunning emporium of mostly mainland Southeast Asian treasures. It's quite pricey, but the interior is an Aladdin's cave of goodies and is well worth a look for the imaginative way in which it's been laid out.

Artefacts

For a general range of Southeast Asian artefacts, the best areas are Jln Ulu Klang,

Jln Pudu and Bangsar Town Centre. **Tibetan Treasures**, 16 Cangkat Bukit Bintang, is great for antique Tibetan furniture and paintings.

Batik

Aran Novabatika Malaysia, 174 ground floor, Ampang Park Shopping Centre, Jln Ampang.

Batik Corner, Lot L1.13, the Weld Shopping Centre, 76 Jln Raja Chulan. Excellent selection of sarong lengths and ready-mades in batiks from all over Malaysia and Indonesia.

Batik Permai, Lobby Arcade, Hilton hotel, Jln Sultan Ismail.

Central Market, Jln Hang Kasturi. Hand-painted silk batik scarves downstairs, many shops sell batik in sarong lengths.

Evolution, G24, Citypoint, Dayabumi Complex, Jln Sultan Hishamuddin. Fashionable range of ready-mades and other batik gift ideas by designer Peter Hoe.

Globe Silk Store, 185 Jln Tuanku Abdul Rahman. The city's oldest department store, founded in 1930, mainly selling fabrics.

Heritage, 38 1st floor. A big selection of original Kelantanese batiks (RM15-90 per m), most ordinary batiks cost about RM7 per m.

Khalid Batik, 48 ground floor, Ampang Park Shopping Centre, Jln Ampang.

Books

There is a second-hand bookshop on the first floor of Central Market. Guesthouses are good for second-hand books and book exchanges.

Berita Book Centre and **MPH Bookstores**, Bukit Bintang Plaza, 1st floor and ground floor respectively, Jln Bukit Bintang.

Kinokuniya, Isetan Dept Store, 2nd floor, 50 Jln Sultan Ismail and level 4 of Suria KLCC. Excellent selection of books.

Popular Book Co, Jln Petaling, Jln Hang Lekir, Sungai Way Plaza.

Times Books, KLCC, Yow Chuan Plaza, 6-7 Jln Tun Razak and Weld Shopping Complex. A good selection of English-language books.

Cameras

KL is a good place to buy cameras, as they are very competitively priced here.

Bukit Bintang Plaza and Sungai Wang Plaza, Jln Sultan Ismail, Golden Triangle, have good choices.

Clothing

A good place to look for custom-made shoes is along Jln Tuanku Abdul Rahman.
Berjama Times Square, Jln Imbi. Designer clothing and accessories.
Sogo, Jln Tuanku Abdul Rahman. One of Southeast Asia's largest department stores. This Japanese store has international brands spread over 8 floors.
Starhill Shopping Centre, Jln Bukit Bintang, Golden Triangle; located at Lot 10 on the corner of Jln Sultan Ismail and Jln Bukit Bintang, Golden Triangle. 6 floors of upmarket designer brands next to the Marriott Hotel.
Sungai Wang Shopping Plaza, Jln Sultan Ismail, Golden Triangle. For custom-made clothing and discount fashion brands.
Weld Shopping Centre, Jln Raja Chulan, near the KL Tower, and **City Square**, Jln Tun Razak, northeast of Golden Triangle. Good for discount fashion brands.

Fabric

A good place to look for fabrics is along Jln Tuanku Abdul Rahman.

Furniture

Rattan furniture is available from Bangsar Town Centre and Ampang Point.
Oriental Style, 1st floor, Central Market (southern end), and at 64 Jln Hang Kasturi. Reproduction Asian furniture. Pricey.
Oriental Spirit, 1st floor, Central Market (northern end). Antique furniture. Expensive but beautiful objects.

Gems

City Sq, Jln Tun Razak. Sell gold, pearls and precious gems.
Petaling St; Lot 10, Jln Bukit Bintang.
Semua House, Lorong Tuanku Abdul Rahman (at northern end of Jln Masjid India). Gems and stones.

Handicrafts

Many of the handicrafts are imported from Indonesia. The areas to look for Chinese arts and handicrafts are along Jln Tuanku Abdul Rahman and in Bangsar town centre. Jln Masjid India, running parallel with Jln Tuanku Abdul Rahman, is an Aladdin's cave of all things Indian, from saris to sandalwood oil, and bangles to brassware incense burners.
Andida Handicraft Centre, 10 Jln Melayu.
Borneo Crafts, 1st floor, Central Market. Mostly wooden pieces and a good selection of puppets and boxes.
Central Market, Jln Hang Kasturi. The old wetmarket is now full of handicraft stalls; not always the cheapest but a wide selection.
Golden Triangle, 1st floor, Central Market. Sell a cornucopia of wooden figures.
Karyaneka Handicraft Village, Kompleks Budaya Kraf, Jln Conlay. Government run, exhibiting and selling Malaysian handicrafts. Batik demonstrating on the ground floor.
Lavanya Arts, 116A Jln Berhala Brickfields. Run by the Temple of Fine Arts, of **Annalakshmi** vegetarian restaurant fame, which aims to preserve Malaysia's Indian heritage. The shop sells Indian crafts: jewellery, bronzes, wood carvings, furniture, paintings and textiles.
Peter Hoe, 139 Jln Tun HS Lee or 2 Jln Hang Lekir. For a range of small items, such as candlesticks, mirrors, table decorations. All his products are sourced in the region. He also sells jewellery and some locally printed clothing.

Pewter

Royal Selangor Pewter Showrooms, 231 Jln Tuanku Abdul Rahman.

Markets and shopping streets

For apparel, shoes, bags and textiles try Jln Sultan and Jln Tun HS Lee, close to Klang bus station. In Petaling St (Chinatown) you can barter for Chinese lanterns, paintings and incense holders.
Central Market, next to Jln Hang Kasturi. A purpose-built area with 2 floors of boutiques and stalls selling just about every conceivable

craft – pewter, jewellery, jade, wood and ceramics for a start. Stalls of note include one that sells all kinds of moulds and cutters for baking, a wonderful spice stall, another one for nuts and a third for dried fruits.

Jln Melayu. This is another interesting area for browsing – Indian shops filled with silk saris and brass pots and Malay shops specializing in Islamic paraphernalia such as *songkok* (velvet Malay hats) and prayer rugs as well as herbal medicines and oils.

Jln Tuanku Abdul Rahman, Batu Rd. This was KL's best shopping street for decades and is transformed into a pedestrian mall and night market every Sat between 1700 and 2200.

Kampong Baru Sunday Market (Pasar Minggu), off Jln Raja Muda Musa (a large Malay enclave at the north end of KL). An open-air market which comes alive on Sat nights. Malays know it as the Sunday market as their Sun starts at dusk on Sat (so don't go on the wrong night), when a variety of stalls selling batik sarongs, bamboo birdcages and traditional handicrafts compete with dozens of food stalls. However, the Pasar Minggu has largely been superseded by Central Market as the place to buy handicrafts.

Leboh Ampang, off Jln Gereja. The first area to be settled by Indian immigrants and today remains KL's 'Little India', selling everything from samosas to silk saris.

Pasar Malam, Jln Petaling, Chinatown. This is a night market full of 'copy watches', pirate DVDs and cheap clothes.

Pudu Market, bordered by Jln Yew, Jln Pasar and Jln Pudu. A traditional wet market selling food and produce, mainly patronized by Chinese.

Shopping complexes

The majority of KL's shopping complexes are to be found in this area, listings are east to west.

Ampang Park, Jln Tun Razak, opposite City Sq, Ampang. One of the oldest shopping complexes in town, noted for its jewellery boutiques.

Bukit Bintang Plaza, corner of Jln Bukit Bintang and Jln Sultan Ismail. One of KL's oldest shopping centres, houses the popular department store Metrojaya and a labyrinth of other shops, which lead into Sungai Wang.

Imbi Plaza, corner of Jln Sultan Ismail and Jln Imbi. Good for computer hardware and software.

Jln Sultan Ismail/Bukit Bintang, Berjaya Time's Square, Jln Imbi. A hotel, a roller coaster, and scheduled to have an IMAX cinema.

Kota Raya Shopping Complex, Jln Cheng Lock, close to the Puduraya bus station. Cut-price goods.

Kuala Lumpur Plaza, Jalan Bukit Bintang. Tower Records is here, also good for watches, bags, jewellery and shoes.

Lot 10, Jln Sultan Ismail. Distinctive green and blue striped façade, Isetan Department Store, British India, Moschino, Knickerbox, plus an excellent food court.

Low Yat Plaza Shopping Centre. The most recent addition to the Bukit Bintang scene, it houses BB Chinatown and Computer City.

The Mall, Jln Putra. Right across from Putra World Trade Centre. This a trendy, large shopping mall. It's good for fashion, housing Yaohan Department Store, Starlight Express indoor theme park, lots of fast-food outlets, including Delifrance, Pizza Hut etc.

Mid-Valley Megamall, Federal Highway, Lingkaran Syed Putra (a suburb of KL). This is indeed 'mega'. It has a wide range of shops and a choice of restaurants. There is also a multiplex cinema here.

Pavillion Mall, Jln Bukit Bintang. The city's newest mall, gleaming and chic with a host of designer clothing outlets, excellent dining options and a cinema.

Pertama Shopping Complex, Jln Abdul Tunku Abdul Rahman. In the Chow Kit area near the Bandaraya LRT station, one of the older complexes and a great place for the bargain hunter. It has a wide range of mid-budget products from souvenirs to fashion and a basement bazaar, as well as photographic and electronic goods. KL's original department store.

Sogo Pernas Department Store, Jln Tuanku Abdul Rahman, Ampang. A huge store on 10 floors.

Star Hill Plaza, next to JW Marriott Hotel. Prestigious marble-clad shopping centre housing Tang's Department Store (of Singapore fame) and many designer boutiques.

Subang Parade, Subang Jaya. Houses Parkson Grand Department Store and Toys 'R' Us, an amusement park and fast-food outlets.

Sungai Wang Plaza, Jln Sultan Ismail. One of the largest complexes in KL, houses over 500 shops and Parkson Grand Department Store, and a basement food court.

Suria KLCC, in the KLCC complex. Without doubt the grooviest shopping centre in town, housing, among other things, designer fashions and jewellery shops and some good bookshops.

The Weld, on the corner of Jln Raja Chulan and Jln P Ramlee. A large Times Bookstore, art gallery and a selection of fashion/leather shops, food outlets, etc.

Yow Chuan Plaza, Jln Tun Razak, Ampang. Antiques, curios, souvenirs and designer goods, and is linked to City Sq next door which has a Metrojaya department store and Toys 'R' Us.

▲ Activities and tours

Bowling

Bangsar Bowl, Bangsar Shopping Centre, T03-2094 3498. 24 lanes.

Cosmic Bowl, Mid-Valley Megamall, T03-2287 8280.

Megalane Bowl, Endah Parade Shopping Centre, T03-9543 1181. 34 lanes.

Golf

There are over 40 courses in and around the city with green fees ranging from RM60-400. Check www.mgaonline.com.my for more information of golfing around the city.

Royal Selangor Golf Club, Jln Kelab Golf, off Jln Tun Razak, T03-9206 3333. Exclusive championship course (including 2 18-hole

courses and a 9-hole course). One of the oldest in the country, non-members can only play on weekdays.

Saujana Golf & Country Resort, Subang (near Subang International Airport), T03-7846 1466. Two 18-hole championship courses.

Sentul Golf Club, 84 Jln Strachan, Sentul, T03-4041 5068. Built in 1928, recently refurbished and a swimming pool added.

Sultan Abdul Aziz Shah Golf Club, Subang (near Subang International Airport), T03-5510 5872. 27 holes.

Templer Park Country Club, T03-6091 9617, 21 km north of KL. Fully flood-lit course for 24-hr golf, frequented by Japanese golf package tourists. It is developed and part-owned by Japanese company. The more environmentally minded have complained that the course has ruined the north end of Templer Park.

Spas

Komleks Selangor, Jln Sultan Ismail.

Martha Tilaar Spa, Crown Princess hotel, City Square Centre, T03-2775 3868. Women-only spa.

Samsara Spa, Swiss Garden hotel, 117 Jln Pudu, T03-2141 3333. Separate male and female spa with outdoor pool and a range of treatments, including Balinese and Thai.

Thalgo Marine Spa, Mandarin Oriental hotel, KLCC, T03-2380 8888. Posh spa with jacuzzi, steam bath, consultations and marine spa treatments.

Spectator sports

Merdeka Stadium and the stadium on Jln Stadium, off Jln Maharajalela. Inter-state Malaysia Cup football matches are played here. The (rather more successful) Selangor team play at the Shah Alam Stadium.

Cricket, rugby and hockey are played on the Padang, in KL centre, most weekends.

Swimming

Bangsar Sports Complex, Jln Terasek Tiga, Bangsar Baru, T03-2284 6065. Mon-Sat 0800-1300.

KLCC park. Has a pleasant swimming pool which can be used free of charge.

Tour operators
There are plenty of travel agents in the Angkasaraya Building on the corner of Jln Ampang and Jln Ramlee.

Asia Tenggara Aviation Services, T03-7783 0097, F7783 0095. Helicopter tours of the city are available. 20-min tours in 3-seater Piper 28 planes. There must be 3 passengers and it's RM240 each. Note that aerial photography is not allowed.

Asian Spooks Experience, T03-2092 5626 ext 137. One of the weirdest tours on offer. It is a night city tour, popular with Westerners, but not with Asian visitors. For their money, would-be thrill seekers get a steamboat dinner, a creepy tour of an Indian temple and a Chinese cemetery, a drive past Pudu prison, and a getting-to-know the Asian vampire session. At RM168 per person (minimum of 2 people), it's a little pricey.

Reliance Travel, 3rd floor, Sungei Wang Plaza (T1300-882828, www.tourworld.com.my/). For student/cheap outbound tickets.

STA, 5th floor, Magnum Plaza, Jln Pudu, T03-2148 9800, www.statravel.com.my.

Utan Bara Adventure Team (UBAT), Suite 284014003, The Heritage, Jln Pahang, T03-4022 5124, www.ubat.com.my. A jungle tour with a difference. The people who run this outfit are ex-security personnel and the names of their tours speak for themselves: 'Practical jungle survival course', 'cross-country jungle raid' and a daily tour to an elephant orphanage where you get to scrub clean and feed baby elephants.

⊘ Transport

Air
Long distance
KLIA at Sepang (T03-8776 2000, www.klia.com.my) lies 72 km south of the city. **MAS** and **AirAsia** flights to other Malaysian destinations include connections with **Alor Star**, **Ipoh**, **Johor Bahru**, **Kota**

Bharu, **Kota Kinabalu**, **Kuala Terengganu**, **Kuantan**, **Kuching**, **Labuan**, **Lahad Datu**, **Langkawi**, **Miri**, **Penang**, **Sibu** and **Tawau**.

Airline offices
Aeroflot, Suite 17.03, level 17, Menara HLA NO:3, Jln Kia Peng, T03-2141 6000.

Air India, Bangunan Ankasa Raya, 123 Jln Ampang, T03-2142 0166.

AirAsia, KLIA, T03-2171 9222.

Bangladesh Biman, Bang Angkasaraya, T03-2148 3765.

British Airways, 8th floor, West Wing, Rohas Perkasa 8, Jln Perak, T03-2167 6188 .

Cathay Pacific, Level 22, Menara IMC, 8 Jln Sultan Ismail, T03-2078 3355.

China Airlines, 22 Jln Imbi, T03-2148 9417

Emirates, Shangri-La Hotel, Annexe Lot 25, 1st floor, UBN Tower, 10 Jln P Ramlee, T03-2058 5888.

Garuda, Suite 3.01, Level 3, Menara Lion, Jln Ampang, T03-2162 2811. Opposite Ampang Park Shopping Mall.

Japan Airlines, Menara Citibank, T03-2161 1722

Gulf Air, Mezzanine Floor, Wisma Abadi 79, Jln Bukit Bintang, T03-2141 2676.

KLM, Unit 106, 1st floor, Grand Plaza Parkroyal, Jln Sultan Ismail, T03-2711 9811.

Korean Air, 17th floor, MUI Plaza, Jln P Ramlee, T03-2142 8616.

Lufthansa, 18th floor, Kenanga International, Jln Sultan Ismail, T03-2052 3428.

MAS MAS Bldg, Jln Sultan Ismail, T13-0088 3000.

Northwest Airlines, UBN Tower, Jln P Ramlee, T03-2143 3542.

Philippine Airlines, 2.29 Angkasa Raya Building, Jln Ampang, T03-2141 0767.

Qantas, T18-0088 1260.

Qatar Airways, Suite 18+6+603-04, 18th floor, Central Plaza, Jln Sultan Ismail, T03-2141 8281.

Royal Brunei, 2nd floor, UBN Tower, 10 Jln P Ramlee, T03-2070 6628 (T03-2070 7166 reservations).

Scandinavian Airlines, Bangunan Angkasa Raya, 123 Jln Ampang, T03-2142 6044.

Singapore Airlines, 10th floor, Menara Multi-Purpose, Capital Square, No 8, Jln Munshi Abdullah, T03-2698 7033

Sri Lankan Airlines, MUI Plaza, T03-2072 3633.

Thai International, Suite 30.01, 30th floor, Wisma Goldhill 67, T03-2031 1913.

Turkish Airlines, Wisma Goldhill, T03-2031 2900.

United Airlines, Bangunan MAS, Jln Sultan Ismail, T03-2161 1433.

Virgin Atlantic, 77 Jln Bukit Bintang (2nd floor), T03-2143 0322/3.

Bus

Local

Rapid KL (T03-7625 6999, www.rapidkl.com.my) has a good system of a/c buses plying the streets. See website for routes. All-day bus tickets start at RM1.

KL Hop-on Hop-off City Tour, T03-2691 1382, www.myhoponhopoff.com, daily 0830-2030, RM38, is a hi-tech variant on the London tour bus theme. Tickets are for 24 hrs and can be bought at hotels, travel agents and on the bus itself, which stops at 22 clearly marked points around town. A recorded commentary is available in 8 languages as the bus trundles around a circuit that includes KLCC, the Golden Triangle, Petaling St (Chinatown), KL Central Station, the National Mosque and the Palace of Culture.

Long distance

KL's main bus terminal is Puduraya, T03-2070 0145, on Jln Pudu. Buses leave here for destinations across the Peninsula as well as to **Singapore** and **Thailand**. Most large bus companies have their offices inside the terminal, above the departure hall. Many hotels and guesthouses will arrange tickets, which saves a journey to Puduraya. There are bus offices opposite the terminal along Jln Pudu and, due to overcrowding within, quite a few buses drop off and pick up along this road. Avoid buying tickets from touts. Inside there is an information desk, post office, tourist police booth, left luggage office

(Mon-Sun 0800-2200) and foodstalls. Puduraya serves most travellers needs – the exception being those wishing to visit Taman Negara National Park.

Pekeliling Station, T03-4044 9022, is in the north of the city, off Jln Tun Razak. Buses to towns in **Pahang State**, including **Jerantut** (for **Taman Negara**) and **Kuala Lipis**, leave from here, not from Puduraya. Other destinations include **Kuantan** and the **Genting Highlands**.

Putra Station, T03-4043 8984, facing the Putra World Trade Centre, serves the east coast and has connections with places in **Kelantan, Terengganu** and **Pahang**, including **Kuantan, Kuala Terengganu** and **Kota Bharu**.

Klang Station in Chinatown, on Jln Hang Kasturi, serves Port Klang and Shah Alam suburb.

Seremban

Newish, brightly coloured station on Jln Sungai Ujong. Connections with **JB, Melaka, KL, Kota Bharu** and **Port Dixon**.

Port Dickson

The station is on Jln Pantai, just outside the main centre, but buses will normally stop on request anywhere along the beach. Regular connections with **KL** and **Melaka**.

Car hire

Apex Rent-A-Car, T03-2142 1926; Avis, T03-9222 2558; Hertz, T03-2148 6433; Mayflower, T03-6253 1888; Sintat, T03-2145 7988.

Taxi

Local

KL is one of the cheaper cities in Southeast Asia for taxis and there are stands all over town, but you can hail a taxi pretty much anywhere you like. Most are a/c and metered, but it is a challenge sometimes to get the driver to use the meter: RM2 for the first 1 km and RM0.10 for every 150 m thereafter. Extra charges apply between 2400 and 0600 (50%

surcharge), for each extra passenger in excess of 2, as well as RM1 for luggage in the boot. Waiting charges are RM2 for the first 2 mins, RM0.10 for every subsequent 45 secs. During rush hours, shift change (around 1500) or if it's raining, it can be difficult to get a taxi to the centre; negotiate a price (locals claim that waving a RM10 bill helps) or jump in and feign ignorance.

For 24-hr taxi service try the following: **Comfort**, T03-8024 2727; **Teletaxi**, T03-92211011; **KL Taxi**, T03-9221 4241. **Supercab**, T03-7875 5333; A surcharge of RM1 is made for a phone booking.

Long distance
These leave from Jln Pudu, outside the Puduraya bus station. Share taxis run to most large towns on the Peninsula; fares are about double those of the equivalent bus journeys. There are no scheduled departures; just turn up.

Seremban
For **Port Dickson**, **KL** and **Melaka**, T06-7610764.

Port Dickson
T02-761 0764, shared taxis to **Melaka**, **KL** and **Seremban**.

Trains
Local
Within the city there are 5 rail systems: 3 LRT lines – the Ampang line (yellow) and Sri Petaling line (lime green and the Kelana Jaya Line (dark green) – 2 **KTM Komuter** lines (blue and red), and the new **monorail** (light blue). There is also the **KLIA Ekspres and Transit line** running from KL Sentral to the airport. Trains leave every 5-15 mins, and tickets cost from RM1.20. Going from one line to the other often means exiting the station and crossing a road. All lines except Sri Petaling and Ampang lines go through KL Sentral. The trains are a great way to see the city as they mostly run on elevated rails, some 10 m above street level. ▸▸ *See also the colour map in the centre of the book.*

Long distance
The **Sentral Railway Station**, Jln Stesen, T03-2730 2000, www.klsentral.com.my. There is a left-luggage office and information desk. The desk is helpful and can advise on schedules. KL is on the main line from **Singapore** to the south and **Butterworth** (Penang) to the north; some of these trains go on through to Bangkok. To get on the east coastline you have to go to **Gemas**, the junction south of KL or to **Kuala Lipis** or **Mentakab**, 150 km to the west of KL. Regular connections with **Alor Star**, **Butterworth**, **Taiping**, **Ipoh**, **Tapah Rd** (for **Cameron Highlands**), **Tampin**, **Gemas**, **Johor Bahru** and **Singapore**. Tourists, on production of their passport, can buy a KTM rail pass, which offers unlimited rail travel, although it is not valid on the Thai system. There are plenty of fast-food restaurants inside the station. For more information, see www.ktmb.com.my.

Seremban
The blue KTM Komuter line ends in Seremban. The journey takes less than an hour.

❶ Directory

Banks
Money changers are in all the big shopping centres and along the main shopping streets and they generally give better rates than banks. Most branches of the leading Malaysian and foreign banks have foreign exchange desks, although some (for example Bank Bumiputra) impose limits or charge card cash advances. There are bank ATMs everywhere that will provide ringgit for cards with Cirrus, Visa, MasterCard, Maestro or Plus. **American Express**, 18th floor, The Weld (near KL Tower), Jln Raja Chulan, T03-2050 0000.

Seremban
Bumiputra, Wisma Dewan Permagaa Melayu; Maybank, 10-11 Jln Dato Abdul Rahman; OCBC, 63-65 Jln Dato Bandar Tunggal; Public Bank, 46 Jln Dato Lee Fong Yee;

Standard & Chartered, 128 Jln Dato Bandar Tunggal; UMBC, 39 Jln Tuanku Munawir.

Port Dickson

Bumiputra, 745 Jln Bharu; Public, 866 Jln Pantai; Standard Chartered, 61 Jln Bharu.

Embassies and consulates

Australia, 6 Jln Yap Kwan Seng, T03-2146 5555, www.australia.org.my.

Canada, 17th floor, Menara Tan & Tan, 207 Jln Tun Razak, T03-2718 3333, www.international.gc.ca/missions/malaysia-malaisie/.

France, 192-196 Jln Ampang, T03-2162 0671, www.ambafrance-my.org.

Germany, 26th floor, Menara Tan & Tan, 207 Jln Tun Razak, T03-2170 9666, www.german-embassy.org.my/.

Indonesia, 233 Jln Tun Razak, T03-242 1354, www.kbrikl.org.my/.

Netherlands, Suite 7.01, 7th floor, The Ampblock, 218 Jln Ampang, T03-2168 6200, www.netherlands.org.my/.

New Zealand, 21st floor, Menara IMC, Jln Sultan Ismail, T03-2078 2533, www.nzembassy.com/home.cfm?c=23.

UK, 185 Jln Ampang, T03-2148 2122, www.britain.org.my/.

USA, 376 Jln Tun Razak, T03-2168 5000, www.malaysia.usembassy.gov/.

Internet

There are internet cafés everywhere, many of them open 24 hrs. There are dozens along Jln Bukit Bintang and a handful around Chinatown. The Chinatown internet venues are often packed with gaming schoolboys

which can make it very noisy. Many backpacker places will offer internet. Expect to pay upward of RM3 per hr. Many hotels and guesthouses offer free Wi-Fi access for those travelling with laptops.

Language schools

Courses are available at many places (see the Yellow Pages), but they are not cheap.

Time Spoken Language Centre, 2nd floor, 226-227 Campbell Complex, T03-2692 1595. Recommended but not especially, based on 'travelling bahasa'. Flexible schedules. Also offers classes in Mandarin and Cantonese.

Medical services

Casualty wards are open 24 hrs.

Assunta Hospital, Petaling Jaya, T03- 7782 3433. Damai Service Hospital, 115-119 Jln Ipoh, T03-4043 4900. Pudu Specialist Centre, Jln Baba, T03-2142 9146. Tung Shin Hospital, 102 Jln Pudu, T03-2072 1655.

Port Dickson

Hospital, on the waterfront by the bus station, Jln Pantai.

Post office

General Post Office Dayabumi Complex, Jln Sultan Hishamuddin (Poste Restante).

Telephone

Overseas telephone service: Kedai Telekom at the airport. Kaunter Telegraf STM, Wisma Jothi, Jln Gereja; Syarikat Telekom Malaysia, Bukit Mahkamah. Assisted International Calls: T108. Directory Enquiries: T103. Trunk Calls Assistance: T101.

Contents

108 Highlands and hill stations
108 Ins and outs
108 Genting Highlands
109 Fraser's Hill
110 Cameron Highlands
116 Listings

124 Ipoh and around
124 Ins and outs
126 Around Ipoh
127 Kuala Kangsar
128 Taiping
130 Pulau Pangkor
132 Listings

141 Penang
141 Ins out outs
143 Background
144 Georgetown
150 The island
154 Listings

167 Alor Star and around
167 Ins and outs
168 Sights
171 Listings

174 Pulau Langkawi
174 The main island
179 Neighbouring islands
179 Listings

Footprint features

106 Don't miss...
112 Jungle walks:
    Cameron Highlands

Northern Peninsula

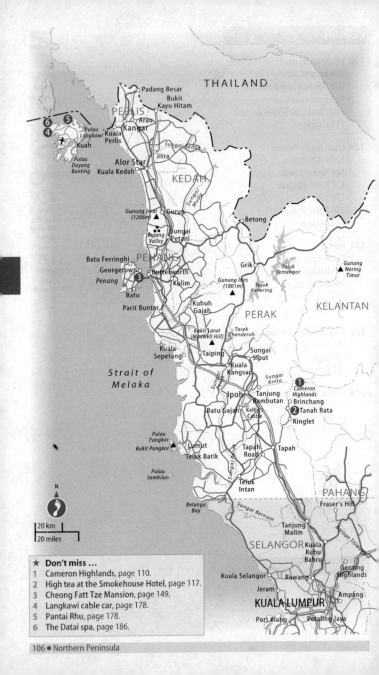

★ **Don't miss ...**
1 Cameron Highlands, page 110.
2 High tea at the Smokehouse Hotel, page 117.
3 Cheong Fatt Tze Mansion, page 149.
4 Langkawi cable car, page 178.
5 Pantai Rhu, page 178.
6 The Datai spa, page 186.

Introduction

North of KL are the temperate hill resorts and tea plantations of the Cameron Highlands and Fraser's Hill and the entertainment gambling hub of the Genting Highlands.

The former tin-rush town of Ipoh offers Straits Chinese architecture and some superb food. It's off the beaten track for many tourists and so makes a welcome break from the usual travel network.

Offshore, there's the 25 km-long island of Penang with its fine capital Georgetown, which is packed with Chinese shophouses, temples and clan houses. On the north shore is an array of beachside hotels. Less developed than Penang are the islands of Pulau Pangkor to the south and Pulau Langkawi to the north, the latter being closer to Thailand than to mainland Malaysia. Langkawi has world-class resorts, fine beaches and jungle adventures.

Highlands and hill stations

On the road north, Peninsular Malaysia's mountainous, jungled backbone lies to the east. It is called the Barisan Titiwangsa or Main Range. It remains largely unsettled, apart from the Genting Highlands and the old British hill stations of Fraser's Hill, the Cameron Highlands and Maxwell Hill, as well as some scattered Orang Asli aboriginal villages. During the Malayan Emergency in the late 1940s and early 1950s, the Communist guerrillas operated from jungle camps in the mountains and later used the network of aboriginal trails to infiltrate the Peninsula from their bases in southern Thailand. ➤➤ *For listings, see pages 116-123.*

Ins and outs

Getting there
The highland resorts are all easily reachable by bus from Kuala Lumpur – ranging from less than an hour for the casino mecca of the Genting Highlands, to four to five hours for the Cameron Highlands. Genting and Fraser's Hill are also close enough to KL to make a shared taxi a reasonable proposition. There are several buses a day to Fraser's Hill or alternatively you can take a train to Kubu Bharu and then a taxi or bus.

Getting around
Genting's sights are more or less within walking distance of each other. The best way to tour the Cameron Highlands' flower and tea gardens is by taking a tour or sharing a taxi. Fraser's Hill is best negotiated on foot or by taxi.

Best time to visit
Due to their altitude, the highland resorts are a good escape from the heat of the plains all year round. However, it might be worth avoiding it during school and public holidays to escape the crowds. It gets chilly at night, so bring warm clothes.

Tourist information
For more information on the Genting Highlands see www.genting.com.my or contact **Fraser's Hill Development Corporation Office** ① *between the golf club and the Merlin Hotel, 9th floor, Terentum Complex, T09-517 1623, www.pkbf.org.my*, which also has maps.

There is no official tourist information centre in Tanah Rata in the Cameron Highlands and information is best picked up from the backpacker guesthouses and the tour agencies dotted around the main street. One of the better ones is **Golden Highlands Adventure Holidays** ① *T05-490 1880, www.gohighadventure.com, 1000-1930*, which has an office in the bus station and offers inexpensive half-day and full-day tours of the area including forest treks and visits to tea plantations and strawberry, rose and bee farms. Friendly Gil Rozells mans the office and offers plenty of good advice on where to stay and what to do. **Tourism Pahang** publish small and moderately useful guides to both Fraser's Hill and the Cameron Highlands, available free. Also see www.cameronhighlands.com.

Genting Highlands → *For listings, see pages 116-123. Colour map 2, A2.*

The Genting Highlands, just 51 km northeast of KL, is the city's closest hill resort and a popular source of entertainment, Las Vegas-cum-Disneyland style. The Highlands were first developed as a resort in the 1960s by a prominent Malaysian businessman, Tan Sri Lim Goh Tong. At the time, investing in construction at an altitude of 2000 m above sea level was considered a harebrained idea. Building the tortuous and impossibly steep road through the dense, jungle-covered hills took seven years alone. However, the idea took off, and the government conceded to allow Malaysia's only casino to operate here. The casino attracts an estimated 30,000 clients a day and provides the main source of revenue in the Highlands. The resort's main attraction is the **Casino de Genting**, which is one of the largest casinos in the world, with endless rows of slot machines, games tables and even a computerized racetrack where it is possible to bet on the Royal Ascot. The decor is glitzy; red plush and glittering chandeliers abound. Occasional grand sweeps are made: people still talk of an Indonesian who put a RM4 keno token into a machine and came away with RM1.5 million. Other attractions in the resort include an outdoor and indoor theme park, which is rated among the best in Malaysia and is constantly being expanded; see page 120. There is a leisure zone to cater for the wet-weather days, particularly frequent in the Highlands at the end of the year. It takes at least a day to get around this bonanza of entertainment and at least as long to work out how to get around. Weekends and public holidays are very busy; Chinese New Year and Hari Raya are two of the peak holiday times.

Fraser's Hill → *For listings, see pages 116-123. Colour map 2, A2. Altitude: 1524 m.*

Fraser's Hill is named after Englishman Louis James Fraser, who ran a gambling den, traded in tin and opium and operated a mule train in these hills at the end of the 19th century. He went on to manage a transport service between Kuala Kubu and Raub. Before Mr Fraser lent his name to them the seven hills were known as Ulu Tras. The development of the hill station began in the early 1920s. In 1925, British High Commissioner Sir George Maxwell wrote that Fraser's Hill "would always be the most exquisite and most dainty hill station in Malaya" and, although he foresaw that development would come to this hitherto remote slice of Pahang, he cannot have anticipated the changes that would transform the station over the coming years.

It was along the road from Kuala Bubu Bharu that the British High Commissioner, Sir Henry Gurney, was ambushed and killed by Communist insurgents during the Malayan Emergency in 1951 (see page 500). A few years earlier British soldiers were involved in the massacre of suspected Communist sympathizers near Kuala Kubu. They shot dead a number of rubber tappers from a local village. There are a number of Orang Asli villages along rivers and tracks leading from the twisting road up the hill.

Fraser's Hill is close enough to KL to be a favoured weekend resort. Because it was easily accessible by train from Kuala Kubu Road, it was a popular weekend retreat long before the Cameron Highlands. Most of colonial Malaya's big companies, such as Sime Darby, Guthries' and Harrisons and Crosfield, built holiday bungalows among the hills. More and more luxury bungalows are now being built here to cater for wealthy Malaysians, but it is still more tranquil and attractive than Genting. Although it is not as varied as the Cameron Highlands by way of attractions, there is one trail (a three-hour walk), which starts just to the south of the tennis courts and ends at the Corona Nursery Youth Hostel, offering good opportunities for birdwatchers (260 species of migratory and local birds have been identified here) and wildflower enthusiasts. There is also a golf course, tennis courts and gardens. Swimming at **Jeriau waterfalls**, 4 km from Fraser's Hill town centre, is limited as the concrete pool has all but silted up so that the water is only knee deep, but standing under the powerful waterfall is very refreshing.

The biggest and best known of Malaysia's hill stations lies on the northwest corner of Pahang, bounded by Perak to the west, and Kelantan to the north. On the jungle-clad 1500m-high plateau the weather is reassuringly British – unpredictable, often wet and decidedly cool – but when the sun blazes out of an azure-blue sky, the Camerons are hard to beat.

Most of the tourist attractions are on and around the plateau, but there are a handful of sights on the road from Tapah. These are listed in order from the bottom of the mountain up. There are three main townships in the Highlands: **Ringlet**, **Tanah Rata** (literally 'flat land') and **Brinchang**. The latter two are in the plateau area, either side of the golf course.

There are a number of worthwhile forest walks/treks in the Camerons. Good walking boots and a water bottle should be taken (see box, page 112). It is advisable for women travelling alone only to trek with a guide or with other travellers.

Unfortunately, the Cameron Highlands is no longer a peaceful bolthole in the sky. Frenetic development is turning the area, in critics' eyes, into a building site where forest is fast making way for golf courses and luxury tourist developments. A new highway now links Ipoh to the Cameron Highlands and runs to Gua Musang for connections to the east coast, promising to bring a wave of development to the area.

Ins and outs

Getting there There are buses from KL's Puduraya terminal and Georgetown (Penang) direct to the Cameron Highlands and various tour buses make the journey too. There is a direct taxi service from Georgetown. Alternatively, catch a bus to Tapah, the main railway station for the Camerons. There are numerous connections from KL to Tapah, as well from Ipoh, Butterworth, Kuantan, Melaka and Singapore. From Tapah there are local buses every two hours to the Highlands. Alternatively, take a train to Tapah Road, Tapah's train station (outside town to the west), a bus or taxi into Tapah town, and a bus from there to the Camerons. There are twice daily rail connections with Tapah Road from KL, Ipoh and Butterworth.

Getting around Buses from Tapah all pass through Tanah Rata and Brinchang and it is usually possible to climb aboard to travel between these centres (RM2). There are also taxis available for hire by the hour or for specific journeys.

Best time to visit Daytime temperatures in the Cameron Highlands average around 23°C, and in the evening, when it drops to 10°C and the hills are enveloped in swirling cloud (known as 'the white witch'), pine log fires are lit in the hilltop holiday bungalows. The weather has become more unpredictable in the last 50 years – torrential downpours and landslides are no longer confined to the monsoon months of November and December. But the mountain air is still bracing enough to entice thousands of holidaymakers to the Camerons from the steamy plains. Today, coachloads of Singaporeans wind their way up the mountain roads and, together with well-heeled KL businessfolk, fork out extortionate sums for weekends in timeshare apartments and endless rounds of golf.

History

Fifty years elapsed between the discovery of the highland plateau and the arrival of the first settlers. William Cameron, a government surveyor, first claimed to have stumbled across "a fine plateau, shut in by lofty mountains" while on a mapping expedition in 1885. The irony was that Cameron's name was bestowed on a place he never set eyes on. What

Cameron Highlands

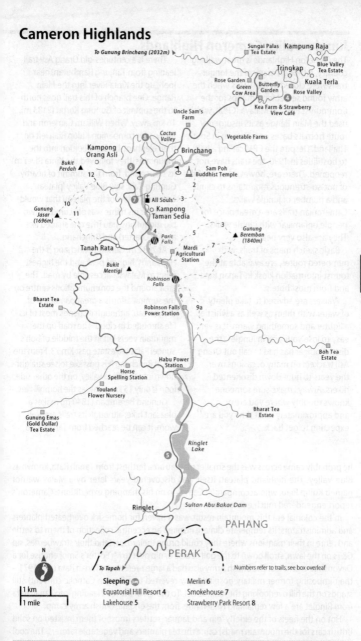

To Gunung Brinchang (2032m)

Sungai Palas Tea Estate   Kampung Raja

Tringkap

Blue Valley Tea Estate

Rose Garden

Green Cow Area

Butterfly Garden

Kuala Terla

Rose Valley

Kea Farm & Strawberry View Café

Uncle Sam's Farm

Vegetable Farms

Cactus Valley

Kampong Orang Asli

Brinchang

Bukit Perdah

Sam Poh Buddhist Temple

All Souls'

Kampong Taman Sedia

Gunung Jasar (1696m)

Gunung Bereman (1840m)

Parit Falls

Mardi Agricultural Station

Tanah Rata

Bukit Mentigi

Robinson Falls

Bharat Tea Estate

Robinson Falls Power Station

Boh Tea Estate

Habu Power Station

Horse Spelling Station

Youland Flower Nursery

Gunung Emas (Gold Dollar) Tea Estate

Bharat Tea Estate

Ringlet Lake

Ringlet

Sultan Abu Bakar Dam

PAHANG

PERAK

N

1 km

1 mile

To Tapah

Numbers refer to trails, see box overleaf

Sleeping
Equatorial Hill Resort 4
Lakehouse 5
Merlin 6
Smokehouse 7
Strawberry Park Resort 8

Jungle walks: Cameron Highlands

The Cameron Highlands is great walking country, although many of the longer trails were closed in the 1970s when the army found secret food dumps for the Communist Party of Malaya (CPM), which used the Main Range as its insurgency route from its bases near Betong in South Thailand. Despite the CPM calling a halt to hostilities in 1990, the trails have not reopened. There are, however, a handful of not-so-strenuous mountains to climb and a number of jungle walks. Cameronian trails are a great place for people unfamiliar with jungle walks. They are also very beautiful.

Basic sketch maps of trails, with numbered routes, are available at the tourist information kiosk in Tanah Rata and from most hotels.

Walkers are advised to take plenty of water with them as well as a whistle, a lighter and something warm. It is very easy to lose your way in jungle – the district officer has had to call out Orang Asli trackers on many occasions over the years to hunt down disoriented hikers. Always make sure someone knows roughly where you are going and approximately what time you are expecting to get back.

There is a centuries-old Orang Asli trail leading from Tanjung Rambutan, near Ipoh, up the Kinta River into the Main Range. One branch of this trail goes north to the summit of Gunung Korbu (2183 m), 16 km away. When William Cameron and his warrior companion Kulop Riau left on their elephant-back expedition into the mountains, they followed the Kinta River to its source and, from the summit of nearby Gunung Calli, saw Blue Valley 'plateau'. Cameron's view of the plateau that would later bear his name was obscured by two big mountains, Irau (the one shaped like a roller coaster) and Brinchang.

At 2032 m, Gunung Brinchang is the Highlands' highest peak and the highest point in Malaysia accessible by road. The area around the communications centre on the summit affords a great panorama of the plateau, although it spends most of its life shrouded in cloud. The road up the mountain veers left in the middle of Boh's Sungei Palas tea estate past Km 73. From the top of Brinchang it is possible to see straight down into the Kinta valley, on the other side. Ipoh is only 15 km away, as the hornbill flies.

Gunung Beremban (1840 m) makes a pleasant hike, although its trails are well worn. It can be reached from Tanah Rata

he probably came across was the smaller plateau area farthest from Tanah Rata, known as Blue Valley. The highland plateau itself was discovered years later by a Malay warrior named Kulop Riau, who accompanied Cameron on his mapping expeditions. Cameron's report engendered much excitement.

In the colonial era this mountain resort was a haven for homesick overheated planters and administrators. Its temperate climate inspired an eccentric collection of them to settle and retire in their mansions where they could prune their roses, tend their strawberries, sip G&Ts on the lawn, stroll down to the golf course or nip over to Mr Foster's Smokehouse for a Devonshire cream tea. The British Army also had a large presence in Tanah Rata until 1971 – their imposing former military hospital (now reverted to a Roman Catholic convent) still stands on the hill overlooking the main street. To the left of the road leading into Tanah Rata from Ringlet are a few remaining Nissen huts from the original British army camp.

Hot on the heels of the elderly 'gin and Jaguar' settlers (most of them insisted on solid British cars for the mountain roads) came the tea planters and vegetable farmers. The cool (trail No 7 goes up through the experimental tea in the MARDI station past the padang off Jalan Persiaran Dayang Endah); the more arduous route from Brinchang (trail No 2 leads up from behind the Sam Poh Buddhist temple); or the easiest route from the golf course (follow trail No 3 past the Arcadia bungalow where the road stops). Allow about four hours to get up and down. There is a good view down Tanah Rata's main street from the top. It is also possible to climb Gunung Beremban from Robinson Falls (trail No 8 leads off trail No 9). The trail heading for the latter is from the very bottom of the road leading past MARDI from Tanah Rata.

Gunung Jasar (1696 m), between the golf course and Tanah Rata, is a pleasant – but gentler – walk of about three hours (trail No 10). The trail goes from halfway along the old back road to Tanah Rata near the meteorological station (the road – Jalan Titiwangsa – leaves Tanah Rata from behind a hotel south of town and emerges at the golf course, on the corner next to the Golf Course Hotel). The Jasar trail also forks off to Bukit Perdah (trail No 12, which branches off the Jasar trail) and takes two to three hours to the top and back. The path down from the summit comes out on a road leading back into the top end of Tanah Rata.

The trails to Robinson Falls (trail No 9, an hour's walk) and Parit Falls (trail No 4, 30 minutes' walk) are more frequently trampled. The trail branches off to No 9a, which leads down to the BOH tea estate road near Ringlet Lake. The walk to the BOH tea estate is a long one, but it is possible to hitch along the road or catch a bus with great views when you get there. There are tours every hour. The estate is closed on Monday, and closes at 1700 on other days; the last bus leaves the factory at 1730. The short trail to Parit Falls starts behind the Garden Hotel and mosque on the far side of Tanah Rata's padang and ends up below the Slim army camp. Parit Falls is a small waterfall in between the two, with what was once a beautiful jungle pool before it became cluttered with day trippers and their rubbish.

There are hundreds of other trails through the Camerons, traversing ridges and leading up almost every hill and mountain. Most are Orang Asli paths, some date from the Japanese occupation in the Second World War (these are marked by barbed wire) and some aren't really trails at all – beware!

mountain climate was perfect for both. The forested hillsides were shaved to make way for more tea bushes and cabbages and the deforestation appears to have affected the climate. The local meteorological station reports that the average temperature has risen 2°C in the past 50 years.

Southern Cameron Highlands

Tapah is a centre for making the large bamboo baskets that are used to collect the tea grown in the Highlands. The town itself is very small, a single street of dilapidated shophouses with a couple of basic hotels and a few eating places. The bus station is on Jalan Raja, just off the main road. There are connections every two hours with Tanah Rata, as well as occasional departures for KL and Penang. Most long-distance bus departures from Tapah (including for KL, Melaka, Penang, Kuantan, and Ipoh as well as connections with Hat Yai in southern Thailand) are from the Caspian Restaurant on the main highway. The Tapah Road Railway Station is about 10 km from the town. **Kuala Woh**, a jungle park with a swimming pool, fishing and natural hot pools, is only 13 km from Tapah, on the road to the Camerons and has a basic camping area. **Lata Iskandar Waterfall**, 22.5 km from Tapah, is a beautiful jungle waterfall, right by the roadside, which has been ruined by commercial ventures capitalizing on the picnic spot. However, it is a good place to pick up the local terracotta pottery, crafted in Kampung Kerayung. The **19th Mile**, further up the hill, is a better spot for stopping off. To the right of the shop, a path leads along the side of the river, up into the jungle, past Asli villages, waterfalls and jungle pools. It's a good spot for birdwatching and butterflies.

Ringlet, the first township on the road to the Cameron Highlands, just inside Pahang state, was relocated to its present site in the 1960s when the original village was flooded to make way for the Sultan Abu Bakar hydroelectric scheme. Ringlet is the Semai aboriginal word for a jungle tree. The town itself is unattractive, with shabby 1960s apartment blocks. There is also a cluster of hawker stalls in the town centre and a well-used temple.

After Ringlet, the road follows a wide river to a large, murky brown lake, connected to a hydroelectric dam. The lake is overlooked by the famous **Lakehouse**, a Tudor-style country house, formerly the home of Colonel Stanley Foster and now an 18-room hotel, and food and souvenir stalls. At the Habu power station, a road leads to two of the tea-growing estates of the BOH plantations. The BOH Estate is 6 km from the junction; 12 km away is the **Fairlie Estate** ⓘ *free guided tours of the factory given almost every hour, Tue-Sun*. The letters BOH stand for 'Best Of the Highlands'.

Youland Flower Nursery is on the road to Gold Dollar tea estate, left off the main road to Tanah Rata from Ringlet (milestone 32). Before reaching Tanah Rata, on the right is a waterfall and picnic spot, on the left is the Cameron Bharat tea shop; which has a fine view over the Bharat tea estate.

Tanah Rata

A further 5 km up the mountain is Tanah Rata, the biggest of the three Cameronian towns. Having said this, it is still not very large, comprising a row of shophouses straddled along the main road where there are two or three restaurants, imitating British cafés with fish and

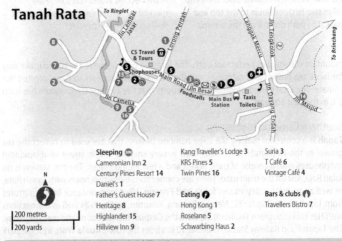

Sleeping 🛏	Kang Traveller's Lodge **3**	Suria **3**
Cameronian Inn **2**	KRS Pines **5**	T Café **6**
Century Pines Resort **14**	Twin Pines **16**	Vintage Café **4**
Daniel's **1**		
Father's Guest House **7**	**Eating** 🍴	**Bars & clubs** 🍸
Heritage **8**	Hong Kong **1**	Travellers Bistro **7**
Highlander **15**	Roselane **5**	
Hillview Inn **9**	Schwarbing Haus **2**	

chips on most menus. It is a friendly little town, with a resort atmosphere rather like an English seaside town. There are also several souvenir shops, including the Yung Seng Souvenir Shop, which is more upmarket than the others and has an interesting selection of well-priced Asli crafts, ranging from blowpipes to woodcarvings. It is also worth looking in local shops for teas from surrounding estates: **Gan Seow Hooi** ⓘ *seowhooigan@ hotmail.com*, is the only shop that will let customers sample the high-grade leaf tea grown in the area. It is worth a visit for the traditional tea ceremony as well as the tea itself. The shop also stocks traditional Chinese clay teapots and other Chinese handicrafts.

Brinchang and around

In recent years Brinchang, 7 km beyond Tanah Rata, on the far side of the golf course, has grown fast: since the mid-1980s several new hotels have sprung up, mainly catering for mass-market Malaysian Chinese and Singaporean package tourists. It is not a very beautiful little town, although the central square, with its craft centre, offers a small ray of interest. **Sam Poh Buddhist Temple**, a popular sight with Chinese visitors who arrive by the coachload, is located just outside Brinchang, along Jalan Pecah Batu, overlooking the golf course. It is backed by the Gunung Beremban hills and comprises both a temple and monastery, which were built here in 1971. Emphasis is on size and grandeur, with monumental double gates with dragons at either side leading into the complex. The inner chamber with its six red-tiled pillars holds a vast golden effigy of a Buddha.

Up the hill from Brinchang the Cameron Highlands becomes one big market garden and the terrain becomes increasingly steep and hilly. **Cactus Valley** is five minutes' walk from the town. The centre grows an amazing variety of the desert plants, some as old as 60 years, as well as a host of flowers including roses, bird of paradise, and an orchard of apples, peaches and passion fruit trees. Just after the army camp on the left is **Uncle Sam's Farm**. The farm specializes in the cultivation of the kaffir lily, as well as strawberries, oranges, apples and a selection of cacti. Beyond Uncle Sam's, 4 km up the road from Brinchang, there is a large market selling local produce to eager customers from the plains below.

The Cameronian climate is especially suited to the cultivation of vegetables more usually associated with temperate climates. Cabbages, cauliflowers, carrots and tomatoes, as well as fruit such as strawberries and passion fruit, are taken by truck from the Camerons to the supermarkets of KL and Singapore. **Kea Farm**, with its neatly terraced hillsides, is down the first right turn after the market area. At the Kea turning, on the main road, the farm has a small shop and café/ restaurant called the Strawberry View. Here, perched on the hillside, is the Equatorial Hill Resort.

Brinchang

To Tringkap & Kampong Raja

Jade Shopping Centre

KS Mini Market & Dept Store **7**

2

Balai Kraftangan (Craft Centre)

Main Road (Jln Besar)

2
@
5

Toilets
Titiwangsa Tours & Travel

1

8

Hawker's Centre

3

Jade Holidays

4

To Tanah Rata   To Sam Poh Buddhist Temple

Sleeping	Eating
Country Lodge **2**	Brinchang Hotel **1**
Iris **4**	Fong Lum **2**
Kowloon **5**	Parkland Hotel **3**
Rainbow **7**	
Rosa Passadena **8**	

N

Not to scale

The **Butterfly Garden** ⓘ *daily 0800-1700, RM5, children RM2,* is past the Kea Farm turning; be warned that there are some steep stairs here. There is a large shop attached to the garden, where everything from framed dead butterflies to Cameronian souvenirs (beetles embedded in key rings) is on sale. Outside there are fruit and vegetable stalls – all very popular with Chinese visitors. There is also a Butterfly farm located in Kea Farm.

The **Rose Garden** is 2 km further up the mountain. To get there, take the first left turn after the butterfly farm, on Jalan Gunung Brinchang, at what is known as the Green Cow area; a village there was burned to the ground by the Communists during the insurgency. A few kilometres beyond the Rose Garden, continue up Jalan Gunung Besar, which is a very picturesque narrow road. On the right is a turning for one of the BOH tea plantations – the **Sungai Palas** ⓘ *www.boh.com.my, Tue-Sun 0900-1630, free guided tours of the tea-processing factory every 30 mins; the visitors' centre has a video about tea cultivation and a shop, as well as a charming terrace where you can enjoy a pot of tea and the dramatic view across the steeply terraced tea plantations.*

Back at the Green Cow area, the main road, the C7, continues into the mountains, finally ending at the **Blue Valley Tea Estate**, 13 km from the junction with Jalan Gunung Brinchang. Midway along the C7, at the village of Trinkap, a right turn leads to a large rose-growing establishment, **Rose Valley** ⓘ *daily 0800-1800, RM3, children RM1.50.* It boasts 450 varieties of rose including the thornless rose, the black rose and the green rose, said to be the ugliest of the rose family. It also has a cactus plantation where some of the plants are 40 years old and lays claim to having the largest flower vase in Malaysia.

⦿ Highlands and hill stations listings

For Sleeping and Eating price codes and other relevant information, see Essentials pages 25-30.

⦿ Sleeping

Genting Highlands *p108*

The accommodation in the Genting Highlands comes under the umbrella of the **Genting Highlands Resorts**. Weekends and holidays have the disadvantage of visitors having to queue at check-in and check-out times. It is best to visit on a weekday if possible; special deals are often available online.

AL Genting, T03-2718 1118, F6101 1888. Centrally located, rooms here are de luxe. The hotel features a heated pool and jacuzzi, restaurant, coffee house, casino (see page 120) and easy access to all the resort facilities.

AL Genting Highlands Resort, T03-2718 1118, www.genting.com.my. Next door to the Genting Hotel. This is a massive place (with around 900 rooms) and very smart. It calls its decor London-style. This hotel has all the trimmings, and was the venue for the 2008 MTV Asia Music Awards

A Awana Golf & Country Resort, T03-6436 9000, www.awana.com.myag/index.htm. The 30-storey octagonal tower dominates this resort, which is 10 km below the main resort peak, and overlooks an 18-hole golf course. All rooms have a/c, bath, TV and balconies offering panoramic views. Facilities include a heated pool, tennis, gym, sauna, children's library, restaurant, cocktail lounge and golf course. Good selection of dining choices including hearty Korean, and a restaurant specializing in Imu, the Hawaiian technique of underground cooking.

A First World, T03-2718 1118, F6101 1888. Splashed in rainbow colours this place is hard to miss. Another Malaysian World Record holder, as the biggest hotel in the world. This psychedelic beast of a hotel has 7000 rooms, the lobby is opulent, but rooms are well priced. Good value and gets good reviews.

Fraser's Hill *p109*

Many of the hotels offer tennis, squash, riding and snooker.

AL Smokehouse, T09-362 2226, www.thesmokehouse.com.my.
Small 16-room hotel in the 'olde English' style of the **Smokehouse Hotel** in the Cameron Highlands; with breakfast, a/c, TV, minibar, bath, in-house movie, restaurant and pool. Rooms are spacious, clean, with bathroom and some balconies overlooking the golf course, offering excellent views. Price includes traditional English breakfast, so it's good value.

A Silverpark Resort, Jln Lady Maxwell, T09-362 2888, www.fraserssilverpark.com. Apartments only, no cooking facilities, associated with Fraser's Hill Golf Club, pool, restaurant and excellent outdoor activities including archery, horse riding and go-karting.

A-B Shahzan Inn, Jln Lady Guillemard, T09-362 2300. Sterile rooms in a rather ugly white block, although some have very nice views.

C Fraser Hill Travel Lodge (YHA), MC G/5 Taman Setia (Sg Hijua), Fraser Hill, T09-362 2443. Run by Mike Chan, who is very helpful and informative. The best budget option in town. Bedroom apartment with shared kitchen and bathroom with hot water. It's 15 mins' walk from town or 5 mins on a shuttle bus.

C Gap Resthouse, T09-362 2227, 8 km before Fraser's Hill. Large rooms, excellent value and a very characterful place to stay. Restaurant serves good Chinese food but poor Western and Malay-Indian food.

C Seri Berkat Rest House, T09-804 1026, book through district office at Kuala Kubu Bharu. Another colonial building with high ceilings and big rooms.

Cameron Highlands *p110, map p111*

There are some excellent mid-range and budget choices here, with hotels and guesthouses usually offering tour and ticketing services. Touts meet new arrivals at the bus station and can take them to a hotel. Popular places get booked well in advance.

During public holidays, accommodation is fully booked and prices rise by 30-50%.

It is also busy at peak school holiday periods: Apr, Aug and Dec. It's cheaper to share a bungalow; most have gardens, log fires and are away from the centre.

A Lakehouse, T05-495 6152, www.lakehouse-cameron.com. A few kilometres outside of Ringlet, this Tudor-style country house, the final brainchild of Colonel Stanley Foster, has fantastic lake views. It has 18 rooms of antique furnishings, 4-poster beds and en suite rooms. The restaurant serves English food and the bar has an English country pub atmosphere. A great place to stay and reasonable value.

Tanah Rata *p114, map p114*

LL Smokehouse, 30 mins' walk from Tanah Rata, T05-491 1215, www.thesmokehouse.com.my. This place is modelled on its namesake, the **Smokehouse** in Mildenhall (UK) and preserves its home counties ethos and 'ye olde English' style of old-time resident Colonel Stanley Foster. Its rooms are first class, there is an original red British telephone box in the garden and the restaurant serves expensive English food.

L Heritage, T05-491 3888, www.heritage.com.my. Located just west of Tanah Rata next to the Convent School. This place has a rather bland international look, out of keeping with its surroundings, although the intention is to make it look colonial/chalet-esque. It has 170 spacious rooms, bath, TV, in-house video, Chinese restaurant, coffee house, sauna, health centre, squash, a bar and a chemist.

B Century Pines Resort, Jln Masjid, T05-491 5115, www.thongsin.com. Although there's no colonial charm, the 59 newish luxury cottages, reminiscent of an English middle-class housing estate, offer excellent value at the quiet edge of town and within calling distance of the mosque's minarets. There are another 149 in an apartment complex. All rooms have 5-star hotel facilities with DVD players and internet access.

B Merlin, 72 Jln Pekeliling Tun Abd Razak, T05-491 1211. Excellent position overlooking the golf course, north of Tanah Rata, but a bit stuck out by itself, and not very atmospheric.

B Strawberry Park Resort, T05-491 1166, www.strawberryparkresorts.com. Magnificent setting some 6 km above Tanah Rata, dominating a hilltop with its 8 blocks of rooms and apartments, built in Tudor/Swiss-chalet style. Although the interior is starting to look dated, rooms are designed to hold maximum capacity; even the smallest studio rooms and 1-room apartments can sleep 4 people. All rooms with bath (inadequate water heaters), TV, in-house video. Indoor pool (the only one in the Cameron Highlands), tennis, squash, sauna, indoor games rooms, mini-putting green, kids' play area, 7-km jogging track, **Monroe's Pub** (with the only disco in the Cameron Highlands and karaoke rooms), coffee house, **Tudor Grill** steakhouse and a Chinese restaurant. Good rates in low season.

B-E Father's Guest House, Jln Gereja, T05-491 2484, www.fathers.cameron highlands.com. Near the convent, up a long flight of steps (look for the Bob Marley sign). This former seminary is the best budget bet in town and is consistently full. It's tranquil and friendly and has a great communal area with beautiful views. It occupies the entire hill and has plenty of lawn, gardening plots and a small lounge for evening beers and cable TV. Dorms and cheaper rooms are in old Nissan huts, a unique place to stay. There is also a good selection of clean, comfortable rooms with terrace and some with Wi-Fi. Daily tours to the tea plantations and butterfly garden. The **Secret Garden Café** is a great place for breakfast. Free pick-up from the bus station and transfers to the Perhentian Islands, Taman Negara and other popular sites. Book in advance. Highly recommended.

C Hillview Inn, 17 Jln Mentigi, T05-491 2915, www.hillview-inn.com. Charming house with spacious rooms with balcony. Facilities include TV, internet service (Wi-Fi in some rooms, RM10 for unlimited use), laundry, book exchange, beautiful garden and restaurant. Very quiet and spotlessly clean. Recommended.

C-D Cameronian Inn, 16 Jln Mentigi, T05-491 1327, www.thecameronianinn.com. Sparkling floors make this one of the cleanest budget digs in the Highlands, with simple, but comfortable rooms, most of which have windows. An inexpensive café serves toasted sandwiches and there's a TV room, internet access (Wi-Fi in some rooms) and a decent expanse of lawn with chairs for soaking up the mountain rays. Recommended.

C-D Kang Travellers Lodge, 38 Jln Besar, T05-491 5828, www.kangtravels.google pages.com. Well-managed and clean place offering simple rooms with Wi-Fi. Travel agency and café downstairs.

D Highlander, 80B Persiaran Camelia 4, T05-491 4934, www.highlanders.cameron highlands.com. The 12 spacious rooms are carpeted and have TV but are tatty and have limited ambience.

D KRS Pines, 7 Jln Mentigi, T05-491 4069, krspines@yahoo.com. Close to the **Twin Pines** and with the same owners, this place has good-sized rooms (pricier with en suite) and friendly and enthusiastic management.

D-E Daniel's, 9 Lorong Perdah, T05-491 5823, www.daniels.cameronhighlands.com. Just past the market and a few kampong houses, this is the town's budget option with average rooms. Friendly staff and plenty to keep backpackers happy. Laundry, internet, movies, jungle bar and nightly log fires.

D-E Twin Pines, 2 Jln Mentigi, T05-491 2169, www.twinpines.cameronhighlands.com. Decent guesthouse a short walk from the bus station. Small, clean rooms and dorm, more expensive rooms have own hot showers. Leafy garden, internet, TV room and friendly staff. Good value. Bus tickets and tours bookable here, good source of information (especially for transport around Malaysia).

Brinchang and around *p115, map p115*

As elsewhere in the region, during public holidays places are fully booked and prices rise by 30-50%. It's also busy at peak school holiday periods of Apr, Aug and Dec. The cheapest place is a shared bungalow; most have gardens, log fires and are away from the towns.

AL Equatorial Hill Resort, near Kea Farm, north of Brinchang, T05-496 1777, www.equatorial.com/cam/. This monstrosity of more than 500 rooms, mock-Tudor in style, has a heated pool, tennis, squash, bowling alley and a Cineplex. Not very intimate.

A-B Country Lodge, Lot 47, section 3, T05-491 3071, F491 1396. Located on a hillside above Brinchang, this is in typical black and white Tudor-style. The decor is rather on the severe side, with parquet floors and rattan furniture. Spacious standard and de luxe rooms as well as suites, restaurant and karaoke lounge. Prices for hotel room or apartment; great value – dinner is sometimes included. Recommended as the most tasteful place to stay in Brinchang, away from noisy karaoke.

A-B Rosa Passadena, 1 Bandar Baru Brinchang, T05-491 2288, F491 2688. Large mock-Tudor concrete block dominating the town centre. 120 rooms with bath, TV, in-house video, restaurant and karaoke lounge. Rooms offer superb views of the surrounding Highlands. Restaurant serves everything from steaks to Chinese steamboats.

B Iris, 56 Jln Kuari, T05-491 1818, irish@tm.net.my. Although this place looks pretty hideous – a doll's house on a grand scale – it's good value. Sparsely furnished rooms have hot water and TV. Average restaurant.

B Rainbow, Lot 25, T05-491 4628, F491 4668. Same owner as the Rosa Passadena. Fairly bland corner hotel with 36 good-value, comfortable rooms (but don't expect Conran, it's more like a dentist's waiting room) with TV and minibar. Good views on one side. Recommended, but there is no restaurant.

C Kowloon, 34-35 Jln Besar, T05-491 1366, F491 1803. Above a popular Chinese restaurant, nice rooms with shower, good value for money (under the same management as the Parkland Hotel).

② Eating

Genting Highlands p108
Eating places are all within the resort, which caters for most tastes and budgets.

††† **Awana Golf and Country Resort**, see page 116. This place has many places to eat including: Japanese Restaurant, which is recommended for sushi and Genting Theatre Restaurant, where you can dine at tables while watching a show. There's also Kampong, which has traditional Malay fare, a good-value buffet and a set lunch, and Sidewalk Café, a 24-hr café.

††† **Highlands**, see page 116. There are a couple of places: The Bistro, with continental food and pizza and Good Friends Restaurant, with Chinese food.

† **Happy Valley**, Theme Park Hotel. Houses a large and very popular Chinese restaurant.

Fraser's Hill p109
†† **Smokehouse**, see page 117. Similar to the Smokehouse Hotel in the Cameron Highlands, serving English-style dishes such as beef Wellington and Devonshire cream teas.

†† **Spices**, Jln Genting, T09-362 2510. Serves Guinness and has a small but interesting menu (Indian, Chinese and Western). The place has a 1950s feel to it.

† **Satay's Corner**, up the hill from the main town, next to the mosque. Chinese. Serves a good breakfast.

Cameron Highlands p110, map p111
There are a lot of Chinese and Indian eateries along Jln Besar, although the quality is generally lower than in less touristy places.

††† **Lakehouse**, see page 117. Traditional English food, typical Sun lunch fare and cream teas.

Tanah Rata p114, map p114
Indian restaurants on Jln Besar (†) include D'Chennai, Number One Restaurant and KS Curry, all serving similar dishes, including dosai, vegetarian options and good set meals. D' Chennai has an excellent tandoori set menu for RM7.

††† **Smokehouse**, see page 117. Similar to Lakehouse. Favourites include beef Wellington, roast beef, Yorkshire pudding, steak and kidney pie and Devonshire cream teas.

Roselane, 44 Jln Besar. Open 1000-2200. Pseudo-Western food in abundance, with a smattering of Chinese dishes. Also a bistro, serving meals in a slightly upmarket setting and a coffee shop with a selection of cakes.

Schwarbing Haus, 59B Jln Persiaran Camellia 3, T05-491 5667. Interesting little restaurant up a flight of stairs, offering a comprehensive menu of German specialities including soup, potato dishes and sausages to keep the mountain chills at bay.

Suria, 66A Jln Perisan Camellia 3. Open 24 hrs. Excellent South Indian food served on a banana leaf, good range of vegetarian options, breakfast buffet and friendly staff.

Vintage Café, 13 Jln Besar. Decent breakfast, afternoon teas and pancakes.

Hong Kong, Jln Besar. Steamboat and herbal soups are popular at this typical Chinese place with a long menu of meat and veg dishes and some good noodle options.

T Café, 1F, 4 Jln Besar, T019-5722 8833. Entry up a flight of steps at the side of the building. Homely travellers' café serving Western versions of Chinese and Malay dishes as well as sandwiches, burgers, pasta and a wicked selection of cakes, scones and pies. Very friendly and good atmosphere. Recommended.

Foodstalls
Next to the bus station, opposite the main row of shops on Jln Besar, serve good selection of Malay, Indian and Chinese food.

Brinchang and around *p115, map p115*

Parkland, Parkland Hotel. Grill restaurant with steaks, breakfast menu.

Brinchang, below hotel of same name on Jln Besar. Popular for its steamboat, good selection of vegetable dishes. Recommended.

Fong Lum, 24 Jln Besar. In the same vein as **Kowloon**, with a very meaty menu. It is lit with fairy lights after dark.

Kowloon, Jln Besar. A busy restaurant, with red tablecloths and clean, tiled floors. The menu is priced according to size of portion. Lemon chicken and steamboat are popular.

Foodstalls
Hawker stalls in the central square open after 1600; they're especially good for satay and roti.

⚓ Bars and clubs

Tanah Rata *p114, map p114*
Strawberry Park Resort, see page 118. The only nightlife takes place here, where there is the only disco in town, karaoke, and a bar.
Travellers Bistro, Jln Persian Camellia. This bar with outdoor seating, 80s rock music and mugs of cold beer is a fun place to meet some locals.
The **Lakehouse** and **Smokehouse** hotel bars are also popular venues for their country pub atmosphere and air of exclusivity.

Brinchang and around *p115, map p115*
Big Rock Disco Café. The resort's main disco.
Rosa Passadena Hotel. Apart from a rash of karaoke bars, the nightlife takes place here.

⚙ Entertainment

Genting Highlands *p108*
Casino de Genting, Genting Hotel, see page 116. Formal dress required, a tie for men or hire a batik shirt at the door. Blackjack, baccarat, roulette, Tai-Sai are among the table games, along with slot machines, computerized racing. The International Room, for cardholders only, caters for more serious players.
First World Theme Park, see page 116. This has more esoteric entertainment including a snow slide (uses 'real' manufactured snow from Japanese technology), an amazing skydiving simulator, a branch of the kooky Ripley's Believe It Or Not, a ghost train and water park.
Indoor Theme Park, www.rwgenting.com, Mon-Fri 1000-1800, Sat 0800-2200, Sun 0800-2000; these hours are extended during peak season. RM26 (RM30 peak season), child RM24 (RM28 peak season).

The usual video games as well as train rides, safari expedition, along with plenty of rides for children.

Outdoor Theme Park, www.rwgenting.com, Mon 0900-1900, Tue-Fri 1000-1900, Sat 0800-2200, Sun 0800-2200; these hours are extended during peak season. Day pass RM38, children and senior citizens RM27, family (2 adults, 2 children) RM125. This park is packed with rides including a water flume, go-kart track, Rolling Thunder Mine Train roller coaster, double loop Corkscrew roller coaster, gravity drop space shot and the Matahari Ferris wheel. A monorail makes a circuit of the park and offers good views on a clear day. A cable car runs across the park which is also good for views.

▲ Activities and tours

Genting Highlands *p108*
Awana Golf & Country Resort, Km 13, T03-6436 9000, www.awana.com.my. Open daily 0730-1730. An 18-hole, international-class course featuring bunkers, ponds and streams, putting green and 3-tiered driving range. Not open to public at weekends.
Awana Horse Ranch, T03-211 2026. Daily 0800-1800. Pony rides for children, jumps and horse trekking.

Fraser's Hill *p109*
Allan's Water, far end of Fraser's Hill. Paddle boats for hire.
Fraser Golf & Country Club, T09-362 2888. 18-hole course.
Jeram Besu, Countryview Recreation Park, near Benta. Whitewater rafting.
The Paddock, by the golf course. Small bajau ponies are saddled for vast westerners.

Tanah Rata *p114, map p114*
Cameron Highlands Golf Club, T05-491 1126. Located north of Tanah Rata and connected by a pleasant footpath, this club was founded in 1885 by the British surveyor

William Cameron. The 18-hole course is magnificently appointed, occupying pride of place in the centre of the plateau, surrounded by jungled hills. It is a favourite haunt of Malaysian royalty. Note that players are expected to wear appropriate clothing, which rules out vest tops and revealing shorts. Shoe and club hire available. Tennis courts are across the road from the golf clubhouse, rackets and balls on hire at clubhouse shop.

Tour operators
Cameron Secrets at Father's Guest House, T05-4912 888, www.cameronsecrets.com. A well-run outfit offering tours of Orang Asli villages, night walks and sunrise jaunts.
CS Travel & Tours, 47 Jln Besar, T05-491 1200, www.cstravel.com.my. For local tours, tickets and accommodation reservations.
Golden Highlands Adventure Holidays, Main Bus Station T05-490 1880, www.gohigh adventure.com. For local tours, good information, ticketing and hotel bookings. It also runs a bus tour from Tanah Rata to Ipoh for sights around Ipoh as well as hot springs and a waterfall in the Highlands.

Brinchang and around *p115, map p115*
Cameron Highlands Golf Club, see Tanah Rata, above.

Tour operators
See also Tanah Rata, above.
Jade Holidays, 37a and b Jln Bandar, T05-491 2318, F491 2071. For local tours, air and bus tickets, accommodation bookings and jungle trekking.
Titiwangsa Tours & Travel, 36 Jln Besar, T05-491 1452, www.titiwangsatours.com. Similar services to Jade Holidays.

◉ Transport

Genting Highlands *p108*
Bus
The Awana resort operates an a/c express bus service between **KL**'s Puduraya bus station

and the Genting Highlands (Genting Skyway Lower Station); from here you must take the cable car or a bus. The express bus service runs every 30 mins from 0700 to 1900, RM6.80. The journey takes 1 hr, inclusive of the cable car, which runs from near the Awana Hotel to the resort at the peak. The ticketing office at Puduraya is at counter 43. For advance reservations T03-6251 8398. A free shuttle service operates every 2 hrs between the Awana and the Resort Hotel. An hourly, 24-hr free shuttle service connects the Resort Hotel, Genting Hotel and Ria Apartments. There is an express bus service between **KL** Sentral station and the Skyway Lower Station, operating between 0800-1900, RM6.80. The ticketing office is on level 2 of KL Sentral. There is also a shuttle service to the highlands from **KLIA**.

Cable car

The Skyway cable car operates between the resort at the peak and a station near Awana. It runs every 20 mins, single RM5, return RM10; hotel guests receive a 50% discount if you buy tickets with evidence of your purchase of accommodation at the resort. Mon-Thu 0730-2300 and Fri-Sun 0730-2400. Travelling time is 12 mins. See also www.rwgenting.com under Getting there.

Fraser's Hill *p109*

There are 2 routes to Fraser's Hill. Either take the KL–Karak highway and turn off at Bentong towards Raub and then left again at Tranum for The Gap. (The Gap is an 8-km one-way road that climbs up Fraser's Hill. It's uphill on odd hours, and downhill only on even hours.) If you have more time and would like something a little more scenic, take the road to Ipoh and then turn off at Kuala Kubu Bahru for The Gap.

Bicycle hire

From Fraser's Hill Development Corporation Office.

Bus

Regular connections from **KL**'s Pudaraya bus station to **Kuala Kubu Bahru**, at the foothill of Fraser's Hill. Change here to Fraser's Hill. The bus only runs at 0800 and 1200 from Kubu Bahru to Fraser's Hill, with return buses departing from Fraser's Hill at 1000 and 1400.

Car

A one-way traffic system operates from 0600-1940, 8 km from Fraser's Hill: uphill traffic gets right of way on the odd hours, downhill traffic on the even hours (with 40 mins of traffic permitted during those hours).

Train and taxi

Kubu Bahru is a stop on the KTM train from KL. From here, shared taxis go direct to Fraser's Hill. KL (RM20 from Kubu Bahru, or RM70 for the whole cab).

Tanah Rata *p114, map p114*

Those who suffer from travel sickness are advised to take some anti-nausea medication before setting out on the mountain road.

Bus

Kurnia Bistari has 5 express buses which ply between **KL**'s Pudaraya terminal and the Cameron Highlands, first one at 0900, last one at 1530 (4½ hrs). Leaving from Tanah Rata, the first one departs at 0800 and the last one at 1630 (VIP RM30, economy RM25). Most other buses for the Cameron Highlands leave from **Tapah**, 67 km from Tanah Rata. There are 4 buses a day, to Tapah the first one at 0800 and the last bus at 1730. There is a bus hourly between Tanah Rata and **Kampong Raja** (in the north of the Camerons) via **Brinchang** from 0630 until 1830. Tickets for the return journey can be booked at travel agents or at the bus station in Tanah Rata. From **Tapah** there are express buses to KL every 2 to 2½ hrs, first one at 1020, last one at 1815. There are 4 express buses to **Ipoh** and then onto **Georgetown**, Penang, at 0800, 0900 and 1430 and 1830 (RM30-35). Buses coming down from the Camerons tend to be more expensive. For the east, it is necessary to buy a through ticket that involves a change of bus in Ipoh. Destinations served in the east include **Kota Bharu**. There is a daily bus to **Singapore** departing at 0900 and one to JB at 0830. Note the bus station is open 0730 to 1800.

Nearly all the buses from Tapah (last bus 1730) go through **Ringlet**, Tanah Rata and on to **Brinchang** and it is easy enough to climb aboard one of the buses that do this route through the day, every 2 hrs.

Car hire

Because visitors pose a serious insurance problem on the mountain roads, the car rental business is not well developed in the Camerons. The only one available is semi-official: contact **Ravi** at Rainbow Garden Centre (between the Smokehouse and Tanah Rata), T05-491782. If driving, remember to sound your horn at bends and beware of lorries that hurtle along.

Taxi

Taxis are available for local travel – they can be chartered for individual journeys or by the hour. It is also possible just to take a seat in a taxi, going from Tanah Rata to **Brinchang**, for example. Taxis and the local bus station (T05-491 1485) are on either side of the Shell station in Tanah Rata. To order a taxi, T05-491 1234.

Train

The nearest station to the Camerons is Tapah Rd in **Tapah**, 67 km from Tanah Rata. There are 2 connections daily with **Ipoh**. Many travellers use the railhead at Ipoh (rather than Tapah) from where there are excellent bus connections to the Cameron Highlands.

Brinchang and around p115, map p115
See also Tanah Rata, page 122.

Bus

For travel between **Tanah Rata**, Brinchang and **Tapah** it is easy enough to climb aboard

one of the buses that travels this route through the day or take a taxi (RM15).

Taxis

Taxis are available for local travel and can be chartered for about RM 40 per hr.

❶ Directory

Genting Highlands p108
Bank Maybank, Genting Hotel.
Post Genting Hotel.

Fraser's Hill p109
Banks It is possible to change money at Maybank, in the Shahzan Inn, and at the Malaysia Bank, along from the Shahzan Inn entrance in the same complex of shops.

Tanah Rata p114, map p114
Banks All the banks are on Jln Besar and Jln Camelia. HSBC, Maybank. It is also possible to change money at **CS Travel & Tours**.
Emergencies District office, T05-491 1455. Alert this office if someone you know is long overdue after a jungle walk.
Internet Almost all the backpacker places and the hotels have internet and many have Wi-Fi. You could try **Highlands Computer Centre**, 39 Jln Besar, a few doors down from Roselane Coffee Shop, 0900-2200 or **Pusat Komputer**, 1/F, 55B Persiaran Camellia 3, 1000-2200. Both charge around RM4 per hr.
Medical services Hospital: opposite gardens at north end of town, on Jln Besar, T05-491 1966. **Police** T05-491 1222, opposite gardens at north end of town.

Brinchang and around p115, map p115
Banks Public Bank, next to Garden Lodge.
Internet There's an internet café next door to the Fong Lum, on the 2nd floor. **Post office** Opposite the Petronas petrol station at the north end of the town. **Medical services** See Tanah Rata, above. **Police** In central square, next to children's playground.

Ipoh and around → Colour map 1, C3.

The northern state of Perak is known for its tin ore (mainly in the Kinta Valley) and Ipoh, its capital, is Malaysia's third city. The city is situated in the Kinta Valley, between the Main Range and the Keledang Mountains, to the west. There are some fine examples of colonial architecture in the Old Town and outer areas housing among other notable sights the Perak Darul Ridzuan Museum, which provides an interesting insight into Ipoh's history. Within easy reach of the city is the Sam Poh Tong, the largest cave temple in the area, and Perak Tong, one of the largest Chinese temples in Malaysia.

Close to Ipoh is the royal town of Kuala Kangsar; the ancient town of Taiping with its strong Chinatown, Lumut; a holiday destination on the coast and the pleasant island of Pulau Pangkor with good beaches and coral. ▶ *For listings, see pages 132-140.*

Ins and outs

Getting there
Sultan Azlan Shah Airport ① *15 km south of town, T05-312 2459*, is a RM20 taxi ride from the centre. The train station is on the edge of town and there are trains from Butterworth and KL as well as from Singapore and north from Hat Yai in Thailand. The long-distance bus terminal, Medan Gopeng, is 4 km north of town, a RM9 taxi trip or take a bus to the centre. There are share taxis for journeys from KL, Butterworth, Taiping, Alor Star and Tapah.

Getting around
Local car hire firms and taxis are also available (note taxi drivers do not use meters). However, Ipoh is not a large place and it is perfectly possible to walk around the town. The grid layout of the town's streets makes navigation a doddle.

Tourist information
None of Ipoh's three tourist offices offer much in the way of help and assistance, bar a map. **Ipoh City Council Tourist Office** ① *Jln Abdul Adil, Mon-Thu 0800-1245 and 1400-1615, Fri 0800-1212 and 1400-1615, Sat 0800-1245.* **Perak Tourist Information Centre** ① *Lot 7, Jln Medan Istana 3, T05-255 2772, mtpbperak@tourism.gov.my, Mon-Thu 0800-1245 and 1400-1615, Fri 0800-1215 and 1445-1615, Sat 0800-1245.* **Tourist Information** ① *Casuarina Hotel, 18 Jln Gopeng, T05-253 2008.* Also see www.perak.gov.my and www.ipoh.com.my.

Background
Ipoh is named after the abundance of the huge, elusive ipoh (*upas*) trees that once grew there. The city also has an abundance of imposing limestone outcrops. These jungle-topped hills, with their precipitous white cliffs, are riddled with passages and caves, many of which have been made into cave temples.

In its early days, Ipoh's citizens became wealthy on the back of the tin-mining industry. In 1884 the Kinta Valley tin rush brought an influx of Chinese immigrants to Ipoh; many made their fortunes and built opulent townhouses. Chinese immigrants have bequeathed what is now one of Malaysia's best-preserved Chinatowns (the 'Old Town'). In the 1880s Ipoh vied with Kuala Lumpur to be the capital of the Federated States of Malaya, and long after KL took the title, Ipoh remained the commercial 'hub of Malaya'. The city has long had an active 'flesh trade'; there are frequent round-ups of Thai and Burmese prostitutes who are smuggled across Malaysia's north border.

Few tourists spend long in Ipoh; most are en route to Penang, KL or Pulau Pangkor. Those who do stay rarely regret it: there are excellent Chinese restaurants (a speciality is the rice noodle dish, *sar hor fun*, which literally means 'melts in your mouth'), Buddhist temples and examples of Straits Chinese architecture. It is also a good place to pick up Chinese imported goods, such as baskets and chinaware. The shophouses on and around Jalan Yau Tet Shin make for good browsing. Ipoh also has a handful of very well-established bakers. On Jalan Raja Eleram the two bakeries here have been in the business for well over 50 years. They specialize in French bread, buns and cakes.

Sights

The Kinta River, spanned by the Hugh Low Bridge, separates the old and new parts of town. The **Old Town** is centred on the river between Jalan Sultan Idris Shah and Jalan Sultan Iskander Shah, and is known for its old Chinese and British colonial architecture, particularly on Jalan Sultan Yusuf, Jalan Leech and Jalan Treacher.

Prominent landmarks include the **Birch Memorial**, a clocktower erected in memory of the first British resident of Perak, JWW Birch. His murder in 1875 was one of colonial Malaya's first anti-British incidents and the three perpetrators, after being hanged,

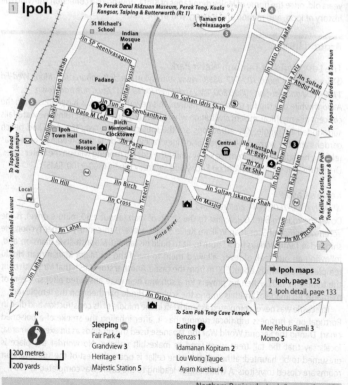

1 Ipoh

To Perak Darul Ridzuan Museum, Perak Tong, Kuala Kangsar, Taiping & Butterworth (Rt 1)

To Tapah Road & Kuala Lumpur
To Long-distance Bus Terminal & Lumut
To Japanese Gardens & Tambun
To Sam Poh Tong Cave Temple
To Kellie's Castle, Sam Poh Tong, Kuala Lumpur &

St Michael's School
Indian Mosque
Taman DR Seenivasagam
Padang
Ipoh Town Hall
Birch Memorial Clocktower
State Mosque
Central

Jln SP Seenivasagam
Jln Sultan Yusuf
Jln Dato Onn Jafar
Jln Raja Musa Aziz
Jln Sultan Abdul Jalil
Jln Tun Sambantham
Jln Dato M Lela
Jln Sultan Idris Shah
Jln Pasar
Jln Laksamana
Jln Mustapha Al-Bakri
Jln Yau Tet Shin
Jln Dato Tahwil Azhar
Jln Raja Ekram
Jln Leech
Jln Treacher
Jln Hill
Jln Birch
Jln Cross
Jln Sultan Iskander Shah
Jln Masjid
Jln Lahat
Jln Yang Kalsom
Jln Ali Pitchay
Kinta River
Jln Lahat
Jln Datoh
Jln Panglima Bukit Gantang Wahab

N
200 metres
200 yards

Sleeping	Eating	
Fair Park 4	Benzas 1	Mee Rebus Ramli 3
Grandview 3	Idamanan Kopitam 2	Momo 5
Heritage 1	Lou Wong Tauge	
Majestic Station 5	Ayam Kuetiau 4	

promptly became local heroes, which they remain to this day. The four panels decorating the base of the tower depict the development of civilization; the upper part of the tower holds a bust of JWW Birch who was, local history relates, not well-liked in the area. The Moorish-style **railway station** (off Jalan Kelab), built in 1917, bears close resemblance to its Kuala Lumpur counterpart, and is known as the 'Taj Mahal' of Ipoh. The **Station Hotel** is a colonial classic. **Ipoh Town Hall**, with its Palladian façade, stands opposite. A solitary ipoh tree stands in the centre of **Taman DR Seenivasagam** (a park north of the centre). The park also contains an artificial lake and a children's playground. Nearby, there are also the tiny **Japanese Gardens** ① *Jln Tambun, T05-241 3733, daily 0600-2400*, complete with a typical Japanese carp pond.

The **Geological Museum** ① *Lorong Hariman, T05-545 7644, Mon-Thu 0800-1230, 1400-1630, Fri 0900-1200, 1445-1630*, out of the town centre, was set up in 1957. It is known for its exhibition of tin ore and collection of fossils and precious stones, as well as over 600 samples of minerals. On Jalan SP Seenivasagam there is an old **colonial mission school** with an impressive white stone façade and an Indian mosque next door.

Heading out of town past **St Michael's School**, on Jalan Panglima Bukit Gantang Wahab, after about 500 m on the right, is an elegant white colonial building housing the **Perak Darul Ridzuan Museum** ① *Sat-Thu 0900-1700, free*. The building, which is over 100 years old, once the home of Malay dignitaries of Kinta, now holds a collection showing the history of Ipoh, and mining and forestry within the state.

Around Ipoh

The Lost World Of Tambun Water Park
① *Sunway City Ipoh, T05-542 8888, www.sunwaylostworldoftambun.com, Mon, Wed-Fri 1100-1800 and Sat-Sun 1000-1800, RM25, children RM19. RM12 taxi ride from town.*
A worthwhile day trip for those with children, this new theme park is based loosely on the concept of a mythical ancient civilization where rides are built amongst ruins and waterfalls surrounded by jungle. Key attractions are the musical body wash, the river and beach gardens and the wave pool. There's also Tiger Valley, with daily tiger feedings, as well as relaxing hot springs for parents to enjoy whilst the kids are running wild on the water slides. Or visit the hot springs at night on Friday and Saturday (open 1800-2100, RM5).

Kellie's Castle
① *Daily 0900-1800, RM4, children RM3.*
Down the road to Batu Gajah, just to the south of Ipoh (about a 30-minute drive), is the eccentric edifice of Scotsman William Kellie Smith, a late 19th-century rubber tycoon. He shipped in Tamil workers from South India to build his fanciful Moorish-style mansion, and, following an outbreak of fever, allowed them to build the Sri Maha Mariamman Hindu temple in the grounds, about 500 m from the castle. Another story has it that Mr Smith built the temple in 1902, when his prayers for a son and heir were answered after six years of marriage. An image of Smith is among the sculpted Hindu pantheon on the temple roof.

The castle was never completed as Smith left in the middle of its construction and died in Portugal on a business trip (local rumour has it, after inhaling the smoke of a poisoned cigar). During the Second World War the Japanese used the grounds as an execution area; locals say that the tall trees were used as makeshift gallows. No wonder the place is presumed to be haunted: although the wine cellar is open, the rest of the subterranean rooms are closed to visitors. A white bridge leading to the castle was completed in 1994.

Sam Poh Tong

ⓘ *T05-312 0813, 0900-1800. Take Kampar bus No 66. En route for KL, it is on the left-hand side of the road, but watch out, as you need to take a sudden turn to enter the car park; the entrance is opposite a Mobil petrol station and the temple is named Ling Sen Tong.*

At Gunung Rapat, 5 km south of Ipoh, is the largest of the cave temples in the area. There are Buddha statues among the stalactites and stalagmites. The temple was founded 100 years ago by a monk who lived and meditated in the cave for 20 years and it has been inhabited by monks ever since. The only break was during the Japanese occupation, when the cave was turned into a Japanese ammunition and fuel dump. There is a pond at the entrance where locals release turtles to gain merit while young boys sell turtle food to earn money.

Perak Tong

ⓘ *0900-1600. Take Kuala Kangsar bus or city bus No 3.*

One of the largest Chinese temples in Malaysia is 6.5 km north of Ipoh on Jalan Kuala Kangsar. Built in 1926 by a Buddhist priest from China, the temple houses over 40 Buddha statues and mystical traditional Chinese-style murals depicting legends. It is visited by thousands of pilgrims every year and is the most ornately decorated of the many cave temples at the base of the 122 m limestone hill. A path beyond the altar leads into the cave's interior and up a brick stairway to an opening 100 m above ground with a view of the surrounding countryside. Another climb leads to a painting of Kuan Yin, Goddess of Mercy, who looks out from the face of the limestone cliff. A 15-m-high reinforced concrete statue of the Buddha stands in the compound.

Gua Tambun (Tambun Cave)

ⓘ *Caves open 0900-1600, RM5. A 15-min drive from Ipoh; taxi with a 3-hr wait, RM80.*

Traces of a civilization dating back 10,000 years were discovered at these caves, 3 km from Ipoh near Tambun, in the 1930s. The ochre drawings on the cave walls and the limestone cliffs depict the life of prehistoric man; especially interesting is the 'Degong' fish, a drawing of a large fish that feeds on meat, rather like a piranha. **Tambun Hot Springs** nestle at the foot of this limestone hill. Two swimming pools have been built – one filled with lukewarm water and one with hot. There are also saunas.

Kuala Kangsar → *For listings, see page 132-140. Colour map 1, B2.*

Though at first glance this royal town halfway between Ipoh and Taiping on the Kangsar River seems unassuming, it is a pleasant place to stop off, with plenty of atmosphere.

On the east bank of the Kangsar River lies the **Sultan of Perak's home** ⓘ *find the main roundabout in the town, which has a distinctive clocktower at its centre, and head southeast towards the gates marking the start of the road to the palace estate. The road twists alongside the Perak River where there is also a back walkway for those on foot.* The first monument you come to is the **Ubudiah Mosque**, built on the slopes of Bukit Chandan. Completed in 1917, it is one of the most beautiful mosques in the country with its golden domes and elegant minarets. Next to it are the graves of the Perak royal family.

Present members of the Perak royal family are resident in the beautiful **Istana Iskandariah** (and south bank of the Perak), which was built in 1930 and sits on the summit of Bukit Chandan, overlooking the Perak River and Ubudiah Mosque. It is a massive marble structure with a series of towers, topped by golden onion domes set among trees and rolling lawns. It is not open to the public, but the former yellow palace, Istana Kenangan (next door to the current Istana), is now the **Museum di Raja** (Perak Royal Museum) ⓘ *T05-776 5500, open 1000-1700, closed Fri lunchtime for prayers, free,* and exhibits royal regalia. It is a fine example of Malay architecture and was built by Sultan Idris of Perak between 1913 and 1917, without recourse to any architectural plans or even a single nail.

In the vicinity of the palaces are several grand **traditional wooden Malay homes**, which used to house court officials. There is also another **former palace** (not open to public) near the Ubudiah Mosque. This imposing white building was erected in 1903 for the 28th Sultan of Perak. For many years it housed the Mazwin School for Ladies, but has now been renovated into the **Sultan Azlan Shah museum** ⓘ *open until 1700.* Besides these buildings, in the grounds of the district office near the Agricultural Department, is one of the first three rubber trees planted in Malaysia. HN Ridley, also known as 'Crazy Ridley', was responsible for developing Kuala Kangsar as a rubber planting district. He obtained rubber seeds from London's Kew Gardens and brought them, first to Singapore, and then to Kuala Kangsar where the seeds were sown in 1877, when Sir Hugh Low was British President in Perak. The sole tree to remain is now marked with a memorial plaque to Ridley. Across the road from Kuala Kangsar's famed rubber tree is a charming pavilion, built in 1930 as a viewing gallery from which the sultan could watch polo on the padang. The padang is also overlooked by the attractive red-roofed building of the **Malay College**. Considered the Eton of Malaysia, the school was built in 1905 for the children of the Perak royal family. During the Japanese occupation in the Second World War, the college was turned into administration offices for the Japanese Imperial Army who interrogated and subsequently beheaded anyone found to be a traitor. A school once again in the 1950s, it attracted a celebrated crowd – Anthony Burgess taught here (see page 541 for a listing of his novels with a Malaysian theme).

Taiping → For listings, see page 132-140. Colour map 1, B2.

With a backdrop of the Bintang Mountains, Taiping is the old capital of Perak and one of the oldest towns in Malaysia. Around 1840, Chinese immigrants started mining tin in the area and it is the only big Malaysian town with a Chinese name. The town is busy and friendly, with a close-knit, community-oriented atmosphere similar to that in the other Chinatowns of Terengganu and Melaka.

In the 1860s and 1870s the Larut district of Taiping, then known as Kelian Pauh, was the scene of the Perak War, caused by bloody feuding between two rival Chinese secret societies, the Hai San and Ghee Hin, over rights to rich tin deposits. The fighting between these Hakka and Hokkien groups resulted in British armed intervention and, when it subsided, the town was renamed *thai-peng* (everlasting peace). The Japanese built a prison in Taiping during the Second World War (next to the Lake Garden), which was converted into a rehabilitation centre for captured terrorists during the Communist Emergency. Some of the executions carried out under Malaysia's draconian drugs legislation now take place in Taiping jail.

One of the main reasons for coming here is to visit Maxwell Hill (see below). There is more colonial-era architecture here than in many of Malaysia's towns; there are some fine examples on Jalan Kota, including the former District Office, and on Jalan Main and Jalan Station. Jalan Iskandar has some fine examples of Chinese shophouse architecture.

Sights

As early as 1890 the **Lake Garden** (Taman Tasik) was set up on the site of an abandoned tin mine by Colonel ESF Walker. It is very lush due to the high rainfall and is the pride of the town. Covering 66 ha, the park lies at the foot of Bukit Larut (Maxwell Hill).

At one end of the park is **Taiping Zoo** ① *www.zootaiping.gov.my, daily 0830-1800, including public holidays, RM5, children RM3, extra charge for use of the tram, camera or video camera*, which is one of the oldest in Malaysia and boasts over 800 animals, including Malaysian elephants, tigers and hornbills, as well as an assortment of animals from Africa. Animals are normally fed between 1000 and 1200. In the early morning locals use the park for their tai chi exercises. Rowing boats are available for hire on lake. There is also a **night safari** ① *Sun-Fri 2000-2300, Sat 2000-2400, RM10, children RM6.*

Built in 1883, the lovely colonial **Perak Museum** ① *Jln Taming Sari (Main Rd), T05-807 2057, opposite the prison, Sun-Thu 0900-1700, Fri 0900-1215 and 1445-1700, free*, is the oldest museum in Malaysia, dating from 1883. It contains a collection of ancient weapons, aboriginal implements, stuffed animals and archaeological finds. The bull elephant skull on show was extracted from an animal that was killed after derailing a train at Telok Anson in 1894. Near the museum is **All Saints' Church**. Built of wood in 1889, it is the oldest Anglican church in Malaysia. The graveyard contains graves of early settlers and those who died in the Japanese prisoner-of-war camp nearby. Also next to the museum is the **Ling Nam Temple**, worth a visit for the Chinese antiques inside, said to be the oldest Chinese temple in Perak State. The **railway station** on Jalan Stesen, now a school, is the oldest in Malaysia.

Around Taiping
Kuala Sepetang lies 16 km west of Taiping and has a Mangrove Forest Museum, the first of its kind in Malaysia, which aims to highlight the country's forestry operations. The site is in 40,700 ha of mangrove swamp, more than half the swamp area in Peninsular Malaysia.

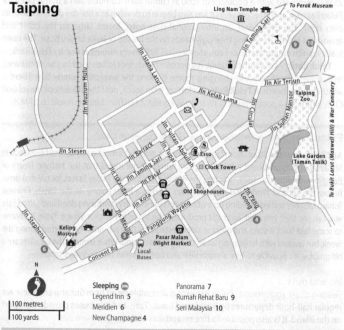

Taiping

Sleeping 🛏
Legend Inn 5
Meridien 6
New Champagne 4

Panorama 7
Rumah Rehat Baru 9
Seri Malaysia 10

100 metres
100 yards

The foot of **Bukit Larut**, formerly known as **Maxwell Hill** ① *for information phone the superintendent, T05-806 6789, daily 0800-1700; Tulip Greehouse opening hours daily 0800-1600*, is just 12 km or so east of the Lake Garden. Most people climb the hill, whether on foot or by Land Rover (RM7 to the summit), as a day excursion from Taiping. At an elevation of 1034 m it was once a tea plantation. Bukit Larut is a small resort with limited facilities compared to the Peninsula's other hill stations. The road up was built by prisoners of war during the Japanese occupation in the Second World War. It is in such bad repair that it is virtually inaccessible in anything other than a 4WD; in any case, private transport is not permitted.

On the way up you pass a **Commonwealth War Cemetery**. Many of the gravestones here are marked December 1941, which was the date a single company from the Argyle Regiment tried to hold back the Imperial Japanese 42nd Infantry on the road north of Kuala Kangsar. Another stop is the **Tea Gardens** (or what is left of them) at the Batu 3.5 mark. The administration office is at the Batu 6 marker and about 1 km on from here is the end of the road – at the Gunung Hijau Rest House. From here travel is on foot. On clear days, from the summit, it is possible to see for miles along the coast. The walk to the top takes about 30 minutes and is a good trail for birdwatchers. There are jungle walks near the top of the hill, but leeches can be a problem. To walk all the way down takes around two to three hours.

Lumut
① *Lumut Tourist Information Centre, Jln Sultan Idris Shah, opposite the jetty, T05-683 4057, Mon-Fri 0900-1700, Sat 0900-1345.*

Lumut is primarily a base for the Royal Malaysian Navy, which has a population of around 25,000 compared with a populace of 1000 in Lumut itself. Lumut is also a transit point for Pulau Pangkor and in recent years it has also begun to develop as a holiday destination in its own right. The Orient Star, an international-class hotel, looms large on the coast and apartment blocks are rearing their ugly heads on the hill top of Bukit Engku Busu. The town is at its zenith during the Pesta Laut, a sea festival, held every August at nearby Teluk Batik.

Teluk Batik, 7 km south of Lumut, is a popular beach spot (often used by the naval base), with chalets, foodstalls and changing rooms backing the sweeping, sandy bay. There is another sandy beach at **Teluk Rubiah** a further 6 km south, near the Teluk Rubia Royal Golf Club, which has a pool, tennis courts and golf course. A taxi from Lumut should cost RM20.

Pulau Pangkor → *For listings, see page 132-140. Colour map 1, B2.*

Just 7 km across the Straits from Lumut is Pangkor, one of the most easily accessible islands in Malaysia. It was on board a British ship anchored off the island that the historic Treaty of Pangkor was signed in 1874, granting the British entry into the Malay States for the first time. Before the Second World War the island was used as a leper colony. In the 1950s, Chinese fishing families settled, building up a vibrant cottage industry producing dried and salted fish; you can see their wrinkled, aromatic produce in the shops in Pangkor village. Now, it's home to some laid-back resorts and great seafood restaurants that are virtually deserted during the week, but packed with holidaying locals during the weekend. While some of the beaches are a bit grubby, it's possible to hire a motorbike and laze on some fine secluded sands.

Ins and outs
Getting there and around Pulau Pangkor is accessible by air from Subang and there are regular half-hour departures by boat from Lumut. Taxis and minibuses provide transport on the island. It is also possible to hire motorbikes and bicycles.

Sights Pangkor is one of the largest fish suppliers in Peninsular Malaysia. Old Pangkor has the fishing villages of Sungai Pinang Kecil (the first stop-off for the ferry from Lumut), Sungai Pinang Besar and Pangkor (main village). Modern Pangkor to the north has a modern luxury resort. To the southwest is the tiny island of Pangkor Laut. The main island is pretty but, as it is one of the few places on the west coast with good beaches, it is very busy at weekends and during school holidays (although on weekdays it can feel deserted). While

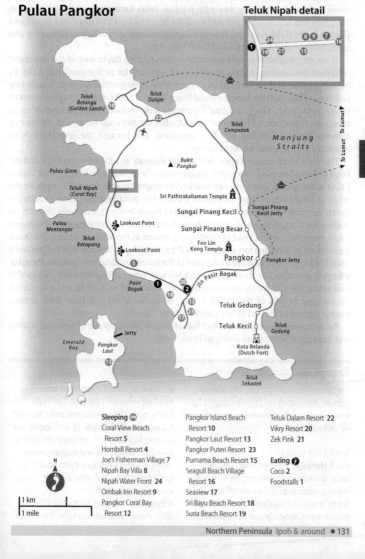

Pulau Pangkor

Teluk Nipah detail

Teluk Belanga (Golden Sands)
Teluk Dalam
Teluk Cempedak
Manjung Straits
To Lumut
To Lumut
Pulau Giam
Bukit Pangkor
Pulau Mentangor
Teluk Nipah (Coral Bay)
Lookout Point
Sri Pathirakaliaman Temple
Sungai Pinang Kecil
Sungai Pinang Kecil Jetty
Teluk Ketapang
Lookout Point
Sungai Pinang Besar
Foo Lin Kong Temple
Pangkor
Pangkor Jetty
Pasir Bogak
Jln Pasir Bogak
Teluk Gedung
Teluk Kecil
Teluk Gedung
Emerald Bay
Pangkor Laut
Jetty
Kota Belanda (Dutch Fort)
Teluk Sekadek

1 km
1 mile
N

Sleeping
Coral View Beach Resort 5
Hornbill Resort 4
Joe's Fisherman Village 7
Nipah Bay Villa 8
Nipah Water Front 24
Ombak Inn Resort 9
Pangkor Coral Bay Resort 12

Pangkor Island Beach Resort 10
Pangkor Laut Resort 13
Pangkor Puteri Resort 23
Purnama Beach Resort 15
Seagull Beach Village Resort 16
Seaview 17
Sri Bayu Beach Resort 18
Suria Beach Resort 19

Teluk Dalam Resort 22
Vikry Resort 20
Zek Pink 21

Eating
Coco 2
Foodstalls 1

it does not have the same heady atmosphere of the east coast islands, it has a much more laid-back, local feel, comparable to that of Langkawi, but on a smaller scale.

Some of the best beaches and coral can be found on nearby islands, such as **Emerald Bay** on Pangkor Laut, a private island only open to guests of the resort (see page 135). Emerald Bay is the spot where F Spencer Chapman escaped from Malaya after three years fighting the Japanese behind enemy lines, all recounted in his book *The Jungle is Neutral*. There are some hidden beaches on the main island. North of **Pasir Bogak**, the most developed beach, turtles lay their eggs right on **Teluk Ketapang** beach, mainly during May, June and July. North of this are two of the best beaches **Coral Bay** (Teluk Nipah) and **Golden Sands** (Teluk Belanga). The most popular beach is at Pasir Bogak. Visitors can also take boats to Pulau Mentangor and Pulau Sembilan.

There are good walks around the island: it takes nearly a day to walk all the way round (although the winding, narrow roads are not very safe for pedestrians); half a day by bicycle; and two to three hours by motorcycle. Note, however, that the route is quite hilly and the parkland past the Pangkor Island Beach Resort is a difficult ride for all but the most determined cyclist. The west coast is comparatively secluded with stretches of quiet beach and the occasional fishing settlement, while the east coast hums with commercial activity, like boat building and fish processing, and because the population is so ethnically diverse, there is a lot of variety.

There is a South Indian temple, **Sri Pathirakaliaman**, at Sungai Pinang Kecil, and the **Foo Lin Kong Temple** at the foot of Sungai Pinang Besar, with a miniature Great Wall of China in the garden and some sad monkeys in desperately old and rusty cages. To the south at Teluk Gedung there are ruins of a Dutch fort, **Kota Belanda**. It was built by the Dutch East India Company in 1680 to protect Dutch interests, especially the rich tin traders, from attack by Malay pirates. It was heavily fortified and apparently its cannon could protect the whole Strait of Dinding also known as the Manjung Straits. The Dutch were forced to leave the fort after an assault by the Malays, although they reoccupied it from 1745 to 1748. Little more than a shell of the former building now remains. **Pangkor village** is also attractive. Its main street is lined with stores selling dried fish packaged in pink plastic bags. There are also souvenir shops, mostly selling T-shirts, and a handicraft centre. One or two of the coffee houses along the street still have their original marble-topped tables and Straits wooden chairs.

Pulau Sembilan lies 27 km south of Pulau Pangkor. This is a group of nine small islands and outcrops offering good diving and marine life.

◉ Ipoh and around listings

For Sleeping and Eating price codes and other relevant information, see Essentials pages 25-30.

● Sleeping

Ipoh *p124, maps p125 and p133*
AL-A Heritage, Jln Raja DiHilir, T05-242 8888, www.heritage.com.my. An 11-storey business hotel with 265 rooms off the North-South Highway just before you come to Ipoh town. Rooms are well equipped with

a/c, minibar, cable TV and some with excellent views over the Ipoh Turf Club. Sauna, gym, a few restaurants and a 'fun' pub.
A Casuarina Park Royal, 18 Jln Gopeng, out of town, T05-255 5555, gmcaspr@tm.net.my. Over 200 comfortable and well-decorated rooms. There is a restaurant and pool. Ipoh's finest hotel, but set in a rather inconvenient location.
A Syuen, 88 Jln Sultan Abdul Jalil, T05-253 8889, www.syuenhotel.com.my. This hotel is

set in a striking building with a delightful outdoor rooftop pool, commanding superb views over the old part of the city. The rooms are decorated with a gentle Asian twist and have cable TV, minibar, and views of the bougainvillea park. Plenty of dining choices and a bar, disco, pool, business centre, sauna and tennis. Recommended.

B Excelsior, 43 Jln Sultan Abdul Jalil, T05-253 6666, www.hotelexcelsior.com.my. This is the city's first international-class hotel, built in 1994, the unattractive tower block has over 150 rooms, restaurants and a bar (ladies' night Wed and Sun). Rooms are clean and comfortable but nothing wildly exciting. Hotel organizes golf trips to local courses. Friendly staff.

B-C Grandview, 36 Jln Horley, T05-243 1488, F05-243 1811. A/c rooms with TV in a fairly unexciting building. Rooms are looking a little tatty, but offer fair value.

B-C Majestic Station, Bangunan Stesen Keretapi, Jln Panglima Bukit Gantang Wahab, T05-255 5605, www.majesticstationhotel.com. Set on the 3rd floor of the railway station, this hotel offers an excellent opportunity to stay in a gorgeous colonial building on the cheap. Rooms are large but a bit gloomy. There is a wonderful terrace with a café overlooking the Ipoh Town Hall. Stay here before developers get their hands on it. Recommended.

B-C Merloon, 92-98 Jln Mustapha al-Bakri, T05-253 6755. Big old airy building with large, clean rooms and attached bath.

B-C Robin, 106-110 Jln Mustapha al-Bakri, T05-241 3755, F254 1818. Same owner as the Merloon next door, but about RM10 pricier. This hotel is rambling, empty corridors and spacious, clean a/c rooms, TV and fridge. What this hotel lacks in ambience, it makes up for in location and price. Recommended.

C Fair Park, 85 Jln Kamaruddin Isa, T05-548 8666, www.fairparkhotel.com.my. One of the newer budget hotels, near DBI Sports Centre and with a selection of clean carpeted a/c rooms with (temperamental) Wi-Fi, cable TV and attached bathroom. One of the best value places to stay in Ipoh, but 25 mins' walk from the city centre. Recommended.

C New Caspian, 6 Jln Jubilee, T05-242 3327, F243 3329. This garish blue and purple building has a selection of clean and comfortable rooms offering reasonable value for money with TV, fridge and a/c. A good location with lots of late-night cafés and Chinese restaurants.

C-D Ritz Kowloon, 92-96 Jln Yang Kalsom, T05-254 7778, F253 3800. Chinese run with a/c, TV, in-house video, safe, tastefully furnished rooms. Very helpful staff.

Homestays

Tourism Malaysia has a list of homestay options around Perak. Contact the Ipoh tourism office or phone any of these

② Ipoh detail

➡ **Ipoh maps**
1 Ipoh, page 125
2 Ipoh detail, page 133

200 metres
200 yards

Sleeping 🛏
Casuarina Park Royal 1
Excelsior 4
New Caspian 3
Merloon 6
Ritz Kowloon 8
Robin 2
Syuen 10

Eating 🍴
Hainam 2
Kopitian Junction 3
Restoran Impressive Foodstalls 1
Restoran MP 5
Sushi King 6

homestays for more information on what they offer: **Homestay Bukit Gantang** (T05-855 4967), **Homestay Bagan Datoh** (T05-646 6829), **Homestay Gopeng** (T05-242 7277), **Homestay Klah** (T05-438 6869) and **Homestay Selama** (T013-506 2597).

Kuala Kangsar p127

Although Kuala Kangsar is not a popular stopover spot, due to the limited number of rooms, it is best to book in advance. There are very few places to stay in Kuala Kangsar; none is particularly desirable apart from the **Rest House**, and all are small – the largest hotel has 14 rooms.

B Rest House (Rumah Rehat Kuala Kangsar), Bukit Candan, T05-776 5872. In a pleasant position just inside the gates to the palace road is this old colonial mansion. There are huge rooms with a/c, bathroom and hot water; some rooms face the river (fabulous views). There are friendly, helpful staff.

C-D Ban Cheong, 79 Jln Kangsar, T04-976 1184. Clean rooms with washbasin and shared bathrooms. One of the cheapest places in town. No great shakes, but adequate for a night.

Taiping p128, map p129

B Legend Inn, 2 Jln Long Jaafar, T05-806 0000, www.legendinn.com. Hotel block with 88 rooms, bath, TV, video channel, coffee house. The plushest place in town with well-equipped rooms.

B Panorama, 61-79 Jln Kota, T05-834111, www.panoramataiping.com. A/c, TV, in-house video, bath, mini fridge, coffee-making facilities, joined to a 3-storey supermarket, the **Fajar**, restaurant. The hotel has a central location and 79 ordinary rooms.

B Seri Malaysia, 4 Jln Sultan Mansor, T05-806 9502, www.serimalaysia.com.my. One of the new chain of budget hotels, located outside town, near the Lake Garden, spotlessly clean to the point of being sterile.

B-C Meridien, 2 Jln Simpang, T05-808 1133. With a/c, TV, shower, coffee house and restaurant.

C New Champagne, 17 Jln Lim Swee aqun, T05-806 5060, www.newchampagnehotel.com. Opposite Cathay Cinema and round the block from **Furama Hotel**. Friendly, helpful staff; this place is pleasant and clean.

C-D Rumah Rehat Baru (New Resthouse), 1 Jln Sultan Mansor, Taman Tasek, T05-807 2044. Rooms with fan or a/c. Restaurant, a little out of town and the new block is hardly attractive but rooms are large, with attached bathrooms. It overlooks the Lake Garden and is good value. Recommended.

Around Taiping p129

For bungalows it is essential to book in advance (between 0900-1200), T05-807 7241 or write to: Officer in charge, Bukit Larut Hill Resort, Taiping.

B Cendana and **Tempinis**, both between the 6th and 7th milestones, Bukit Larut.

D Bukit Larut. Large bathrooms, excellent value.

E-F Rumah Hijau, Bukit Larut. Also has a campsite.

Lumut p130

AL Swiss-Garden Golf Resort and Spa, 101-107 Jln Titi Panjang, T05-618 3333, www.swissgarden.com. New, clinical feel, but has good facilities.

AL-A Orient Star Resort, Lot 203 and 366, Jln Iskandar Shah, T05-683 3800, www.orientstar.com.my. A hotel with 150 a/c rooms, TV, in-house video, mini fridge, freeform pool with swim-up bar, paddling pool, gym, jet ski hire, bicycle hire, coffee house, bar, palatial in size and decor, pleasantly furnished rooms with balconies and sea views but no beach. A classy place that sometimes offers excellent discounts.

A-B Blue Bay Resort, T05-683 6939, F683 6239. Rooms with TV, tea/coffee-making facilities and complimentary newspaper. Late check-out (1500), pool, a/c and breakfast included. Jungle and fishing treks organized, also island cruises. 2 restaurants. Great value, although it looks a little spartan.

B Lumut Country Resort, 331 Jln Titi Panjang, T05-683 5109, F683 5396. A hotel with 44 a/c rooms, pool, paddling pool, tennis courts, does not quite measure up to the **Orient Star**, but has some attractive features such as hand-printed batik bed covers and wooden floors. Disco, function room. Very good value; one of the best deals in town.

B Putra, Jln Iskandar Shah, T05-683 8000, dayaent@po.jaring.my. A/c, baths in all bedrooms, TV, telephone, tea/coffee-making facilities, some rooms with lovely view over bay towards Pangkor. Restaurant. Breakfast included. Good value.

B-C Galaxy Inn, Jln Sultan Idris Shah, T05-683 8731, F683 8732. Clean and simple rooms with attached bathrooms, a/c, apartments available for monthly rental. Seating area with TV in foyer. On seafront.

C Harbour View, Lot 13 and 14, Jln Titi Panjang, T05-683 7888, F683 7088. Small, quiet hotel on main road along seafront, a/c, TV, mini fridge, tea/coffee-making facilities, bathroom. Recommended. Good value.

C Indah, 208 Jln Iskandar Shah, T05-683 5064, F683 4220. One of the budget hotels on the main road along the coast, a/c, TV, hot shower, adjoining coffee house, simple and very clean, with pleasant views over the esplanade. Family run with seating area and café.

C-D Lumut Villa Inn, Batu 1, Jln Sitiawan, T05-683 5982, F683 6563. Inconveniently located outside the town if you do not have your own transport, but good value for money, rooms without a/c (**D**).

D ERA, opposite bus station, T013-505 4991, sykna@hotmail.com. 6-bed dorms and big clean doubles, shiny tiled floors, shared bathrooms, some with balcony, washing facilities and kitchen. Friendly family atmosphere; owner Mr Syed has a wealth of information for travellers. Recommended budget option if you have to stay overnight in Lumut.

Pulau Pangkor *p130, map p131*
Room rates are discounted during the week, especially at the more expensive hotels. Most of the mid- and upper-range accommodation is at Pasir Bogak and can be reached from Pangkor village by taxi. Many of the budget places are at Teluk Nipah on the west coast,

which requires a longer taxi ride in one of the vehicles belonging to Pangkor's taxi mafia. Note that many places increase their room rates by around 50% during public holidays.

L Pangkor Laut Resort, T800-9899 9999, www.pangkorlautresort.com. One of Malaysia's most idyllic resorts. The chalets, a blend of Malay and Balinese architecture, are magnificently set, either over the sea (linked by wooden walkways) or on the jungled hillside. Each is beautifully furnished, with carved wood and rattan work. Luxurious bathrooms with recessed tubs and orchids floating on the water's surface greet you upon arrival. A/c, minibar, CD player (TV in lounge only), immaculate kimonos, fresh fruit. Other facilities include well-stocked library (books and CDs), 3 pools, squash, water sports, health club, gym, sauna, spa, jacuzzi. A steep hike, or a short shuttle ride, takes you to Emerald Bay, one of the most perfect sandy bays in Malaysia. The wildlife on Pangkor Laut is also remarkably abundant and diverse – from hornbills to macaques – and the jungle treks are recommended. Paradise it may be, but some kayakers who said they had paddled secretly to the island report seeing dregs of litter along the island's waterline, similar to the detritus that spoils the beaches on the main island. Even so, this place is highly recommended if you have no limit to your budget.

L-AL Sri Bayu Beach Resort, Pasir Bogak, T05-685 1929, sribayu_hotels@hotmail.com. Chalets, suites and rooms. With oriental-style decor, a/c, TV, bath, pool, tennis, karaoke, restaurant and children's club. Rather overpriced, but a good place to stay on Pasir Bogak.

AL Pangkor Island Beach Resort, Teluk Belanga, T05-685 1091, www.pangkorisland beach.com. Secretive resort tucked away in the north corner, serviced by its own ferry with a private 1.2 km beach. A/c, restaurants, 2 pools, limited golf course, tennis, water sports, limited business facilities. Pricier rooms have sea views, cheaper ones look onto the garden. Excellent location on wide sandy bay, 240 rooms of varying standard and price.

AL Teluk Dalam Resort, T05-685 0000, www.pangkorresorts.com. Unique retreat set in 40 acres of gardens with 160 wooden chalets built to resemble upmarket kampong village homes, but decorated with bland Western furniture. Very peaceful and elegant with hornbills in the garden, pool, tennis courts, nursery and video games room.

A Pangkor Coral Bay Resort, Pasir Bogak, T05-685 5111, www.pangkorcoralbay.com.my. 6-storey tired white building, the only hotel of this size on this part of the island. Great value for money considering the facilities: TV, a/c, pool, small gym, disco/karaoke, sauna. 2 restaurants and water sports. The interior needs sprucing up. It's a 5-min walk to the beach.

A-B Coral View Beach Resort, Pasir Bogak, T05-685 2190. Cute chalets on hillside surrounded by trees, a tranquil spot with hornbills and macaques. Upper level chalets have great sea views. Simple accommodation away from the backpacker crowd. Simple restaurant and sea tours arranged. Good views, friendly staff, motorbike hire. Quiet strip of beach. The 10-min walk to Pasir Bogak makes it a little isolated and hard to find a taxi.

A-B Hornbill Resort, Teluk Nipah, T05-685 2005, F685 2006. All rooms with sea views and balcony, a/c, TV, hot shower, good breakfast menu, seafood restaurant, popular bar with local and imported brews and recommended at sunset.

A-B Pangkor Puteri Resort, Pasir Bogak, T05-685 3409, www.pangkorputeri.net. Housed in 2 incongruous orange box-like buildings, inside there are big, clean suites with fully equipped kitchen, living room, bedrooms, balcony and a sea view for rooms in front. Great value for 3 people sharing on a weekday (RM120).

A-B Seaview, Pasir Bogak, T05-685 1605, F685 1970. A/c, restaurant, water sports, fishing, boat trips, pool, tennis and badminton, breakfast included in room rate. (Package for 3 or more people including all meals RM85-120.)

B Nipah Bay Villa, Teluk Nipah, T05-685 2198, www.pangkornipahbay.com. A/c, shower, attractive wooden cottages, well

equipped. Video library and internet, laundry service, motorbike hire, traditional massage, also restaurant, breakfast included. Discounts for stays of over 1 night.

B-C Nipah Water Front, Teluk Nipah, T05-685 5485. Beachfront place, one of the more upmarket backpacker choices. Big comfy beds, clean and roomy. Same family ownership as Vikry Resort at Pasir Bogak (see below).

B-C Ombak Inn Resort, Teluk Nipah, T05-685 5223, www.ombakinnchalet.com. Small and simple resort. A few a/c and fan wooden chalets with cable TV and attached bathroom. Good-value backpacker option.

B-C Purnama Beach Resort, Teluk Nipah, T05-685 3530, www.purnama.com.my. Chalets with fan or a/c, breakfast included, some rooms with TV, restaurant, internet access and games, karaoke, mini swimming pool, motorbike hire and laundry service.

B-C Seagull Beach Village Resort, Teluk Nipah, T05-685 2878, www.seagullbeach villageresort.com. Longhouse, mini-cabins and chalets all with bathroom and television. A/c or fan. Good location and quiet. Clean, friendly, Western breakfast (not included), games and badminton. Recommended.

B-C Suria Beach Resort, Lot 4441, Teluk Nipah, T05-685 3922, www.suriaresort.tripod.com. A/c, shower, rooms are clean enough but spartan and lacking in character. Over-capacity of rooms means bargaining is possible. Restaurant serves Malay and Western food.

C Mizam Resort, Teluk Nipah, T/F05-685 3359. A/c chalets with attached bathrooms. Restaurant serving Malay, Chinese and Western dishes. Clean and in a quiet location at the end of a row of resorts. Friendly staff, good value. Recommended.

C Zek Pink, Teluk Nipah, T05-685 3529, zek_pink@tm.net.my. Curiously named but well-equipped resort popular with Malaysian tourists. Rooms with a/c or fan, attached bathroom, TV, restaurant. Island trips.

C-D Vikry Resort, Pasir Bogak, T05-685 4258. 10 a/c chalets in spacious grounds. Rusty A-frames reserved for school trips. There are plans to build beachfront rooms. The Indian restaurant is one of the best places to eat on the island. Friendly staff. Recommended.

D Joe's Fisherman Village, Teluk Nipah, T05-685 2389. One of the most popular budget places to stay with simple A-frame chalets with 2 mattresses on the floor and a fan, bicycles for hire, meals available.

⊘ Eating

Ipoh *p124, maps p125 and p133*
Ipoh is well known for its Chinese food, especially Ipoh chicken rice and *kway teow* – liquid and fried versions. The pomelo and the seedless guava are both grown in the state of Perak, and the state is also known for its delicious groundnuts. Ipoh white coffee is a well known local tipple, roasted with palm-oil margarine and it has the colour of cappuccino.

† **Momo**, 13 Jln Tun Sanbatham. Closed Sun. Tasty Malay dishes and great iced drinks (try iced cappuccino mix) served in a stylish café, also tables on the street facing the Padang.

† **Sushi King** and **Restoran MP**, G/F Ipoh Pde. Both have sushi on a conveyer belt and are spotless but lacking in atmosphere. MP offers hearty steamboats.

† **Benzas**, Jln Tun Sambantham. Lovely setting, outdoor seating facing the Padang, great north Indian fare. Recommended.

† **Hainam**, Jln Mustapha Al-Bakri. Good place to go for a plate of authentic Hainan chicken rice.

† **Idamanan Kopitiam**, 27-29 Jln Tun Sambantham. Cosy coffee shop with superb Penang laksa. Also, desserts and sandwiches

† **Kopitian Junction**, G/F Ipoh Parade Mall. Popular eatery serving Malay snacks and cooling desserts and drinks such as delicious mango ice, cucumber and lemon juice. There's even a local take on sausage and mash.

† **Lou Wong Tauge Ayam Kuetiau**, 49 Jln Yau Tet Shin. Big corner restaurant with tables spilling onto the street, good for late-night Chinese fare.

† **Mee Rebus Ramli**, Jln Raja Ezram. Excellent selection of Malay dishes specializing in noodles like *mee jawa* and *mee rebus* but also serves a fair choice of rice dishes.

Foodstalls
Jln Clarke, Jln Dewan, Ipoh Garden and Jln Sultan Idris Shah have mainly Chinese stalls. The **Railway Station**, Jln Kelab is recommended. **Wooley Food Centre**, Canning Gardens. On Jln Ali Pitchay is **Restoran Impressive Foodstalls**, which is cheap and clean. Recommended. **Pusat Makanan Man Utd**, near Jln Mustapha Al Bakri, is cleanish, gets packed with football fans at the weekend and has excellent beer promotions.

Kuala Kangsar *p127*
Many restaurants only open at lunchtime, it can be a problem eating after dusk. The smartest restaurant is the overpriced **Hotel Seri Kangsar**. In front is an Indian restaurant open early morning until late evening serving good *roti canai* and chapati. The market has foodstalls serving Malay food and there's a bakery beside the **Double Lion Hotel**. There's a supermarket on Jln Kangsar.

Taiping *p128, map p129*
† **Dragon Phoenix**, Jln Kota. Chinese food.
† **Malaysia Restoran**, 36 Jln Eastern. Chinese.
† **Nagaria Steak House**, 61 Jln Pasar. Dark interior, popular for beer drinking.
† **Panorama**, 61-79 Jln Kota. Mediocre Western food and steakhouse.

† **Restoran Bumi**, Jln Kota (next door to Kum Loong). Malay restaurant. Also serves some Western dishes.

Foodstalls
Large **night market** on Jln Panggung Wayang. Hawker Centre in Metro Arcade (Shopping Centre), 54 Medan Simpang (5 km from town centre, on road to Kuala Kangsar). **Malay hawker stalls** on Jln Tupai. Burger, rice and fried chicken stalls near foot of Bukit Larut (Maxwell Hill).

Around Taiping p129
¶ **Rumah Hijau** or **Bukit Larut** guesthouses.

Lumut p130
¶¶ **Capri**, 4174 Jln Sultan Idris Shah, T05-683 3112. Soups, salads, ice cream and a long list of pastas and oven-baked pizzas.
¶¶ **Ocean Seafood**, 115 Jln Tit Panjang. A/c, specializes in Chinese and seafood.
¶¶ **Sin Pinamhui**, 93-95 Jln Titi Panjang. Traditional Chinese food.
¶ **Kedai Makan Sin Pinamhui** (Green House), 95 Jln Titi Panjang. Fri-Wed 1030-1445 and 1715-2045. Another good Malay place to try.
¶ **Makanan Laut Ocean**, Jln Titi Panjang. Fresh fish dishes available.
¶ **Nasi Kandar**, 46 Jln Sultan Idris Shah. Friendly and clean, with excellent rice and roti. Serves good vegetarian rice. Recommended.
¶ **Restoran Samudera Raya**, 39 Jln Sultan Idris Shah. Indian and Malay food.

Pulau Pangkor p130, map p131
Most hotels and chalets have their own restaurants – most people end up eating where they are staying. Seafood is always on the menu.
¶¶¶ **Pangkor Laut Resort**, see page 135. Eating here is a delight: top-quality seafood at the **Fisherman's Cove**, steamboat at **Uncle Lim's**, or Western fare at the **Sumudra** where chimes blow in the breeze.
¶¶ **Coco**, Pasir Bogak. Outdoor seafood restaurant and local dishes. Recommended.
¶¶-¶ **Fook Heng**, Pangkor village. Simple coffee shop but excellent quality Chinese food, seafood prices are high.
¶ **Juo**, same street as Hornbill Resort. Superb food and fresh fish in this Indonesian place.
¶ **Vikry Resort**. Excellent home-cooked dishes served on banana leaves. One of Pangkor's best-kept secrets. Recommended.
¶ **Wah Mooi**, Sungai Pinang Kecil. Steamed carp recommended by locals.
¶ **Ye Lin Seafood Garden**, 200 Jln Pasir Bogak. Popular outdoor restaurant, prides itself on its low prices.

Foodstalls
On Pasir Bogak and Teluk Nipah.

🍸 Bars and clubs

Ipoh p124, maps p125 and p133
Apart from the bars and discos in 4-star hotels, there are a couple of bars near the train station.
Babyface, Jln Dato Mahaaraja Lela. Look for the blacked out windows and massive Guinness ads. Chinese drinking den with beer girls and mix of Chinese and Western pop.
Miner's Arms, Jln Dato Mahaaraja Lela. A British-themed pub.

⛰ Activities and tours

Ipoh p124, maps p125 and p133
DBI Sports Complex, Perak Sports Centre, Lebuh Raya Thivy, T05-546 0651. Open 0900-2100. Largest swimming complex in Southeast Asia. Also tennis, indoor badminton, table tennis, volleyball, basketball, velodrome rugby pitch, stadium. Admission charge.
Perak Turf Club, Jln Raja Dihilir, Perak, T05-254 0505. Races held every Sat and Sun. Free entry for last race of the day. For details of the race calendar, see www.turfonline.com.
Royal Perak Golf Club, Jln Sultan Azlan Shah, 3 km from centre, T05-547 3266, www.royal perak.com.my. 18-hole course over 420 ha, members only at weekends and holidays. Bowling alley, billiards room and bar.

Tour operators
HWA Yik Tour & Travel, 23 Jln Che Tak, T05-250 4060, F253 0118. Tours, hotel reservation, domestic and international air ticketing, minibus rental.
K&C Travel, 250 Jln Sultan Iskandar, T05-250 6999, F250 2154. Airline ticketing, hotel reservation, travel insurance, foreign exchange.

Kuala Kangsar p127
No 3 MDKK, Jln Tebing, T05-776 9717. 3-day canoe safaris on the Perak.

Taiping *p128, map p129*
Bukit Jana Golf & Country Club, Jln Bukit Jana, T05-883 7500. Clubhouse has pool, tennis, squash, kids' playground and card room.

Tour operators
Trans Asia Pacific, 112 Jln Barrack, T05-828451. Ticketing, hotel reservations, car hire.

Pulau Pangkor *p130, map p131*
Pangkor Yacht Club, Teluk Gedung, T05-685 3478. Water sports facilities, including jet skis, sailing and snorkelling, and fishing trips.

⊖ Transport

Ipoh *p124, maps p125 and p133*
Air
Ipoh has daily connections with **Singapore** on Firefly Airlines and MAS.
Airline offices MAS, Lot 108 Bangunan Seri Kinta, Jln Sultan Idris Shah, T05-241 4155.

Bus
Ipoh is on the main north-south road and is well connected. Buses to **Taiping** (RM7), **Lumut** (RM6.50), **Cameron Highlands** (2 hrs, RM8) and **Kuala Kangsar** (RM5) leave from the local bus terminal, 200 m from the railway station. Regular connections from the long- distance terminal at Medan Gopeng with **Butterworth** (RM11), **KL** (3 hrs, RM14), **Penang** (2½ hrs, RM15) **Alor Star** (RM16.80), **Kuantan, Sungai Petani, Johor Bahru, Kangar, Kuala Perlis, Lumut** and **Kuala Kangsar**. Star Shuttle (www.starwira.com) run services to **KLIA** and the **LCCT** (4 hrs, every few hours 24 hrs a day, RM42).

Car hire
Avis, Sultan Azian Shah Airport, T05-206586. Hertz, Royal Casuarina Hotel, 18 Jln Gopeng, T05-250 5533, and Sultan Azlan Shah Airport, T05-312 7109.

Taxi
BK Taxi, T05-253 4188. Kinta Radio Taxi, T05-545 8384. Sample taxi fares: KL RM200, Penang RM170, Cameron Highlands RM120, Taiping RM80, Tapah RM50. Shared taxis leave from beside the bus station for **KL, Butterworth, Taiping, Alor Star** and **Tapah**. Connections with **Hat Yai** in southern Thailand.

Train
Ipoh is on the main north-south line. 2 daily connections north with **Butterworth** (5½ hrs, departures 1733, 2328); daily departure to **Hat Yai** (2328); and 3 daily going south to **KL**, (4 hrs, 0119, 1049, 1800). T05-254 7987.

Kuala Kangsar *p127*
Bus
The terminal is in the centre on Jln Raja Bendahara. Regular services to **Ipoh, KL, Lumut, Butterworth, Taiping** and **Kota Bharu**.

Taxi
The only local transport available. Taxis leave close to the bus station for places including **Butterworth, KL, Ipoh** and **Taiping**.

Train
The station is out of town to the northeast, on Jln Sultan Idris. Trains on the KL–Butterworth route also stop here.

Taiping *p128, map p129*
Bus
The main long-distance bus station is 7 km out of town; take a town bus or a taxi. Regular connections with **Butterworth, Ipoh, Sungai Petani** and **KL**. A morning bus goes to **Kuantan** on the east coast. For other connections, change at Ipoh. Local buses for **Ipoh, Grik, Lumut** and **Kuala Kangsar** leave from the local bus station, which is more conveniently located in the centre at the intersection of Jln Masjid and Jln Iskandar.

Train
The station is on the west side of town. On the north-south railway line, there are twice daily connections with **Ipoh**, **KL** and **Butterworth**.

Around Taiping p129
The steep walk from Taiping Lake Gardens takes about 2½-3½ hrs. The road is restricted and private cars are not permitted. A Land Rover service runs from the foot of the hill just above the Lake Garden in Taiping, every hour 0700-1800, T05-827243.

Lumut p130
Bus
The station is in the centre, a few mins' walk from the jetty. Regular connections with **Ipoh**, **KL** and **Butterworth** and less regular ones with **Melaka**. Bus every 30 mins from Ipoh (1 hr 45 mins). Buses also run to **Singapore**.

Ferry
Pan Silver Ferry has regular crossings, every 30 mins from 0700 to 2100 from Lumut Jetty to **Pangkor village** on **Pangkor Island**. It takes under 30 mins, one way RM10. Crossings every 30 mins from 0645 to 2030 to Pangkor Island Beach Resort.

Taxi
Services to **Ipoh**, **KL** and **Butterworth**.

Pulau Pangkor p130, map p131
Air
The airport on the north of the island is used by Berjaya Air's 48-seater Dash-7s to carry passengers between Pangkor and **Subang**. The 50-min flight leaves Subang for Pangkor 1040, returns at 1140 on Mon, Wed, Fri, Sat and Sun, one way RM225, return RM450. T05-685 4516, www.berjaya-air.com.

Boat
Ferries leave from **Lumut** jetty (watch out for the hotel touts). Every 30 mins to Pangkor Jetty (one way RM10, 30 mins, 1st boat 0645, last boat 2030), also regular connections with Pangkor Island Beach Resort, jetty close to Golden Sands

(one way RM12). There are inter-island ferries or hire a fishing boat from the main villages. Large hotels organize trips to the islands.

Bus/taxi
There is a fleet of pink taxis, or more accurately minibuses (Kereta Isewa), from Pangkor village to **Pasir Bogak**, **Teluk Nipah** and Pangkor Island Beach Resort. There are no meters, and the prices are fixed. Share a taxi to cut costs. RM10 to Pasir Bogak, RM14 to **Coral View Resort**, RM20 to Telok Nipah, RM28 to **Pangkor Island Beach Resort** and RM20 to Teluk Dalam. Cabs wait at the jetty and at the above sites.

Motorbike/bicycle hire
You can hire motorbikes from Pangkor village for RM20-30 per day. Most resorts and chalets have both motorbikes and bicycles for hire.

⑦ Directory

Ipoh p124, maps p125 and p133
Banks Banks on Jln Sultan Idris Shah, Jln Yang Kalsom and Jln Sultan Yussuf. Tour operators (see page 138) have foreign-exchange facilities.
Internet Infoweb Station, Jln Dato Onn Jaafar, near Jln Sultan Idris Shah. **Post** Next to the railway station on Jln Panglima Bukit Gantang Wahab or on Jln Dato Onn Jaafar.

Kuala Kangsar p127
Post Jln Taiping, near the clocktower.

Taiping p128, map p129
Banks On Jln Kota and Jln Sultan Abdullah. Poly Travels, 53 Jln Mesjid and **Fulham Tours**, 25 Jln Kelab Cina, have foreign exchange facilities. **Internet** Discover de Internet, 3 Jln Panggong Wayang, T05-806 9487, RM2.50 per hr. Helm Computer Technology Centre, Jln Kota, T05-808 2454. **Post** Jln Barrack.

Pulau Pangkor p130, map p131
Banks Large hotels will change money and there's a **Maybank** in Pangkor village.

Penang

→ Colour map 1, B1. Population: 1.2 million.

Penang – or, more properly, Pulau Pinang – is the northern gateway to Malaysia and is the country's oldest British settlement. It has been sold to generations of tourists as 'the Pearl of the Orient', but in shape Penang looks more like a frog than a pearl. Although the island is best known as a beach resort, it is also a cultural gem with Chinese, Malay and Indian influences. Georgetown has the largest collection of pre-war houses in all Southeast Asia.

Penang State includes a strip of land on the mainland opposite, Province Wellesley – named after Colonel Arthur Wellesley, later to become the Duke of Wellington, who went on to defeat Napoleon at Waterloo. Covering an area of 738 sq km, Province Wellesley is also known by its Malay name, Seberang Perai. Georgetown's founder, Captain Francis Light, originally christened Penang 'Prince of Wales Island'. In Malay, pinang is the word for the areca nut palm, an essential ingredient of betel nut. The palm was incorporated into the state crest in the days of the Straits Settlements during the 19th century. Today Pulau Pinang is translated as 'betel-nut island'. Light named Georgetown after George, the Prince of Wales, who later became King George IV, as it was acquired on his birthday; most Malaysians know the town by its nickname, Tanjung, as it is situated on a sandy headland called Tanjung Penaga. ▸▸ For listings, see pages 154-167.

Ins and outs

Getting there

From **Bayan Lepas International Airport** ① *T04-643 4411, 20 km south of Georgetown and 36 km from Batu Ferringhi,* take a taxi (which operate on a coupon system, 30 minutes to Georgetown, RM30) or a Rapid Penang bus (U401 or U401E, RM2, every 30 minutes from 0635 to 2300, stops at KOMTAR and Pengkalan Weld). Long-distance buses arrive at Sungai Nibong, 7 km from town (a negotiable RM25 trip). Those wishing to take the train need to alight at Butterworth, see page 154, and make their way across the bridge from there (or take the ferry). Taxis also tend to terminate there, with local taxis making the run across the bridge to the island; long-distance taxis will, however, cross the bridge for an extra charge. ▸▸ See also Transport, page 164.

Getting around

There are bus services including a free shuttle bus that does a circuit stopping at most tourist destinations in Georgetown (daily 0600-2400, every 15 minutes; the 19 stops are marked with red circular signs enclosing a number) and in the tourist areas there are plenty of taxis. It is also possible to hire self-drive cars and motorbikes from local and international firms. In Georgetown there are city buses and taxis as well as a number of trishaws. There are also bicycles for rent.

Orientation

Georgetown, the capital of Penang state, is on the northeast point of the island, nearest the mainland; Bayan Lepas Airport is on the southeast tip. The 13 km Penang Bridge, linking the island to Butterworth, is halfway down the east coast, just south of Georgetown. Batu Ferringhi, now a strip of luxury hotels, is Penang's most famous beach and is on the north coast. There is still a handful of small, secluded coves with good beaches on the northwest tip of the island. The west of the island is a mixture of jungle-covered hills, rubber plantations and a few fishing kampongs. There are more beaches and fishing villages on the south coast. A short, steep mountain range forms a central spine, including Penang Hill, overlooking Georgetown, at 850 m above sea level.

Tourist information

Penang Tourist Centre ① *Penang Port Commission Building, Jln Tun Syed Sheikh Barakbah (off Victoria Clocktower roundabout, opposite Fort Cornwallis), T04-262 0202, www.tourismpenang.com.my, Mon-Fri 0900-1800, Sat 0800-1300, closed 1st and 3rd Sat.*

① Penang

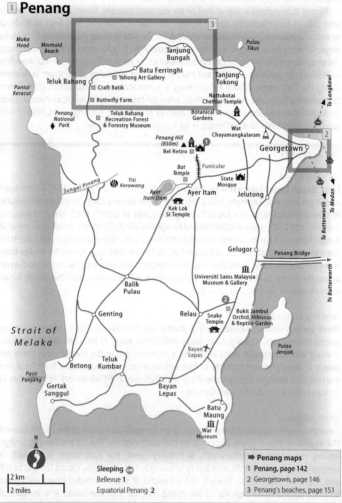

Sleeping 🛏
Bellevue **1**
Equatorial Penang **2**

➡ **Penang maps**
1 Penang, page 142
2 Georgetown, page 146
3 Penang's beaches, page 151

This tourist office is known to be unreliably informed on occasions. Often your best bet for finding out information is to ask the locals; restaurant and café owners are particularly helpful. You could also try **Tourism Malaysia Northern Regional Office** ① *10 Jln Tun Syed Sheh Barakbah, round the corner from the Penang Tourist Association, T04-262 0066*. One of the best places is the **Tourist Information Centre** ① *3rd floor, KOMTAR Tower, Jln Penang, T04-261 4461, the office is hidden around a bend opposite the McDonald's; and at Bayan Lepas Airport, T04-643 0501, Mon-Sat 1000-1800*. It has a list of tour companies in Georgetown.

The three main **tours** offered by companies are: the city tour; the Penang Hill and temple tour; and the round-the-island tour. All cost RM35-55 with two departures a day, usually one at around 0900 and one at 1400. Longer tours usually include lunch in the price. The cheapest tours are bookable at guesthouses around Lebuh Chulia and Lebuh Muntri. Star Lodge (see page 155) is recommended for its efficiency. See also Tour operators, page 163.

Background

Before the arrival of Francis Light, who captained a ship for a British trading company, in 1786, Penang was ruled by the Sultan of Kedah. The sultanate had suffered repeated invasions by the Thais from the north and Bugis pirates from the sea. Sultan Muhammad Jawa Mu'Azzam Shah II was also beset by a secession crisis and when this turned into a civil war he requested help from Francis Light, then based at Acheen in Sumatra, whom he met in 1771. Light was in search of a trading base on the north shore of the Strait of Melaka, which could be used by his firm, Jordain, Sulivan and De Souza, and the British East India Company. In 1771, Light sent a letter to one of his bosses, De Souza, in which he first described Penang's advantages, but before De Souza made up his mind, Light struck a private deal with the Sultan of Kedah. The Sultan installed Light in the fort at Kuala Kedah and gave him the title of Deva Rajah, ceding to him control of the Kedah coast as far south as Penang. In turn, Light promised to protect the Sultan from his many enemies.

A frisson between Sultan Muhammad and the East India Company brought developments to a standstill in 1772. Light left Kedah and sailed to Ujung Salang, which English sailors called 'Junk Ceylon' and is now known as Phuket, where he built up a trading network. Eleven years later he finally repaired relations with Kedah and the newly installed Sultan Abdullah agreed to lease Penang to the British – again, in return for military protection. On 11 August 1786, Light formally took possession of Penang. The island was covered in dense jungle and was uninhabited, apart from a handful of Malay fishermen and a few Bugis pirates.

A township grew up around the camp by the harbour. A wooden stockade was built to defend the island on the site of the original camp and the cantonment was called Fort Cornwallis, after Marquis Cornwallis, the then Governor-General of India. Light declared Prince of Wales Island a free port to attract trade away from the Dutch, and this helped woo many immigrant traders to Penang. Penang's status as a free port was only withdrawn in 1969. Settlers were allowed to claim any land they could clear. The island soon became a cultural and religious melting pot. By 1789, Georgetown had a population of 5000 and by the end of century the number had more than doubled.

The Sultan of Kedah was upset that the East India Company had not signed a written contract setting out the terms of Penang's lease. When the company began to haggle with him over the price and the military protection he had been promised, Sultan Abdullah believed the British were backing out of their agreement. In alliance with the Illanun pirates, the Sultan blockaded Penang in 1790 and tried to force the Company's hand. Light went on the offensive and quickly defeated the Sultan's forces. The vanquished Sultan Abdullah agreed to an annual fee of 6000 Spanish dollars for Penang. Francis Light remained the island's superintendent until his death, from malaria, in 1794. The disease, which struck down many early settlers, earned Penang the epithet of 'the White Man's Grave'.

Despite Georgetown's cosmopolitan atmosphere, there remained a strong British influence: the British judicial system was introduced in 1801 with the appointment of the first magistrate and judge, an uncle of novelist Charles Dickens. The previous year, Colonel Arthur Wellesley had signed a new Treaty of Peace, Friendship and Alliance with Kedah's new Sultan Diyauddin, which superseded Light's 1791 agreement and allowed for Penang's annexation of Province Wellesley, on the coast of the Peninsula, in return for an annual payment of 10,000 Spanish dollars.

In 1805 Penang's colonial status was raised to that of a Residency. A young administrative secretary, Stamford Raffles, arrived to work for the governor. Georgetown became the capital of the newly established Straits Settlements, which included Melaka and Singapore (see page 495). But the glory was shortlived. Following Raffles's founding of Singapore in 1819, Georgetown was quickly eclipsed by the upstart at the southern tip of the Peninsula and by the 1830s had been reduced to a colonial backwater. From an architectural perspective, this proved a saving grace; unlike Singapore, Penang retains many of its original colonial buildings and rich cultural heritage.

Colonial Penang prospered, through tin booms and rubber booms, until the outbreak of the Second World War. When the Japanese raced down the Peninsula on stolen bicycles, Penang was cut off, without being formally taken. The British residents were evacuated to Singapore within days, leaving the undefended island in the hands of a State Committee, which, after three days, put down the riots that followed the British withdrawal. The Japanese administration lasted from December 1941 to July 1945; remarkably, Georgetown's buildings survived virtually unscathed, despite Allied bombing attacks.

Today, Chinese make up 42% of Penang's population, while around the same number are Malay and 10% Indian. Like in many other places in Malaysia, the ethnic Chinese population is shrinking in comparison to that of the Malays. Penang, along with the other two Straits settlements of Melaka and Singapore, was a centre of Peranakan culture. Peranakans, also known as Babas or Straits Chinese, evolved their own unique blend of Malay and Chinese cultures (see page 194). The Babas of Penang, however, have almost disappeared as a distinctive group.

Georgetown

The original four streets of Georgetown – Beach (now known as Lebuh Pantai), Lebuh Light, Jalan Masjid Kapitan Kling (previously Lebuh Pitt) and Lebuh Chulia – still form the main thoroughfares of modern Georgetown. Lebuh Chulia was formerly the Cantonese heartland of the Ghee Hin triad, one of the secret societies involved in the 1867 Penang Riots. The older part to the west of Weld Quay, overshadowed by Kapitan Kling Mosque, is mainly Indian.

Georgetown is, however, mainly Chinese; the main Chinatown area is contained by Jalan Kapitan Kling Mosque, Lebuh Chulia, Jalan Penang and Jalan Magazine. The shophouses were built by Chinese craftsmen: the rituals, burial customs, clan associations, temples and restaurants make up a self-contained Chinese community. Despite the traffic and a skyline pierced by the Kompleks Tun Abdul Razak (KOMTAR) skyscraper, the streets still have charm. There are an estimated 12,000 pre-war houses still standing in Georgetown, making it an architectural gem in Southeast Asian terms.

Penang has managed to preserve at least some of its heritage while that in other Malaysian towns has been torn down partly because of a rent control act – on the statute books for years – which have frozen rents and therefore made redevelopment unprofitable. While the houses may be mouldering, at least they aren't (usually) being demolished. This, however, may all change, as this rent control was lifted a few years ago. In 2008, Georgetown was made a UNESCO World Heritage Site. However, not all of the island is worthy of such a status. Pollution and litter have spoiled parts of Penang in recent years. Some beaches are dirty and very few people swim in the sea. The coral that used to line the shore at Batu Feringghi has all gone, mainly due to the silt washed around the headland during the construction of the Penang Bridge. But the sea is not as dirty as in some of the region's other big resorts, as testified by the presence of otters on the beach at Batu Feringghi in the early morning.

Street names in Georgetown are confusing as many have been rechristened with Malay names; streets are known by both their Malay and English names.

Clocktower, Fort Cornwallis and ABN-AMRO Arts Centre

At the junction of Lebuh Light and Lebuh Pantai is the Penang Clocktower, which was presented to Georgetown by a Chinese millionaire, Chen Eok, in 1897 during Queen Victoria's Diamond Jubilee celebrations. The tower is 60ft (20 m) tall: one foot for every year she had been on the throne. Opposite the clocktower is **Fort Cornwallis** ① *T04-261 0262, Mon-Sat 0830-1830, RM3*. There are many colonial buildings on Lebuh Farquhar, such as the high court, mariners' club and the town hall on the north tip of the island. Named after Marquis Cornwallis, a governor-general of India, it stands on the site of Francis Light's wooden stockade. It was built by convict labour between 1808 and 1810 and only its outer walls remain. The main cannon, *Serai Rambai*, which was cast in the early 17th century, is popularly regarded as a fertility symbol; offerings of flowers and joss sticks are often left at its base. It was presented to the Sultan of Johor by the Dutch in 1606 and ended up in Penang. The modern amphitheatre hosts concerts and shows. There is an example of a wooden Malay kampong house near the entrance.

The **ABN-AMRO Arts Centre** ① *9 Lebuh Pantai, T04-262 9675, Mon-Sat 0900-1700, free*, is a stately colonial-era building, donated by the bank, and now home to a small stage where occasional gamelan recitals are held and an upstairs art gallery which has some great photo exhibitions. Recommended.

Cathedral of Assumption and around

The twin-spired Roman Catholic Cathedral of Assumption houses the only pipe-organ in Penang. The Convent of the Holy Infant Jesus – slightly further east, is the site of Francis Light's original house. Light was Adelaide's architect and planner. His grave can be found on Jalan Sultan Ahmad Shah.

Close to the cathedral is the **Penang Museum and Art Gallery** ① *on the junction of Lebuh Light and Lebuh Farquhar, T04-261 3144, Sat-Thu 0900-1700, RM1, children RM0.50*. The building was the first English-language public school in the east, established in 1816. A statue of Francis Light, cast for the 150th anniversary of the founding of Penang, stands in front of the building. As no photograph of Georgetown's founding father was available, his features were cast from a portrait of his son, Colonel William Light, founder of Adelaide in Australia. The statue was removed by the Japanese during the Second World War and later returned, minus the sword. The museum also has a 19th-century bust of Germany's Kaiser Wilhelm II, which turned up in Wellesley primary school. How it came to be there in the first place is a mystery.

② Georgetown

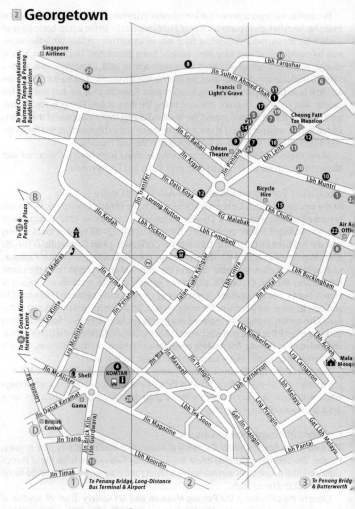

200 metres
200 yards

Sleeping

75 Travellers
  Lodge **1** *B3*
Banana Guesthouse **8** *B3*
Bayview **6** *A3*
Berjaya
  Georgetown **21** *B1*
Broadway Budget **3** *B4*
Cathay Heritage **11** *B3*

Cheong Fatt Tze
  Mansion **12** *A3*
Cititel **5** *A3*
Continental **7** *A3*
Eastern & Oriental **10** *A3*
Grand Continental **15** *D1*
Love Lane Inn **18** *B4*
Malaysia **19** *A3*
Old Penang **14** *B4*

Oriental **24** *B2*
Paramount **25** *A1*
SD Guesthouse **17** *B4*
Stardust Guesthouse **20** *B3*
Star Lodge **22** *B3*
Sunway **9** *C1*
Traders **28** *D1*
White House **33** *A2*

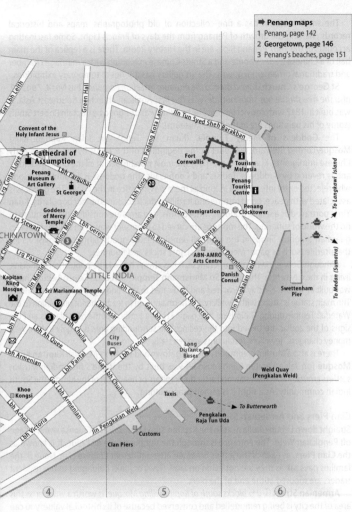

➡ **Penang maps**
1 Penang, page 142
2 Georgetown, page 146
3 Penang's beaches, page 151

Eating

Beach Blanket
  Babylon **1** A3
Café Tower Lounge **4** C1
Di Tai Tong **2** C2
Ecco Café **15** B3
Goh Thew Chik **22** B3
Jin Xim Teahouse **10** B3
Kaliaman's **6** C5

Kapitan **3** C4
Kassim Mustafa **5** C4
Lum Fong **10** B3
Maple **7** B3
May Garden **14** A2
My Thai **9** B2
Obake Ya **12** A3
Ocean-Green **16** A1
Passage Thru' India **12** A3

Red Garden Night
  Market **18** B3
Ros Mutiara **19** C4
Sea Palace **17** A3
Sire Museum **20** B5
Thirty Two **8** A2

Bars & clubs

Garage **11** A3

Soho **21** A3

The small museum has a fine collection of old photographs, maps and historical records charting the growth of Penang from the days of Francis Light. Some fascinating accounts of the 1867 Penang Riots are in the History Room. There is a replica of the main hall of a Chinese trader's home and a Straits Chinese exhibition with a marriage chamber and traditional ornamental gowns. The art gallery has a series of temporary exhibitions.

St George's Church ① *next door to the museum on Lebuh Farquhar; bus Nos 4, 7 and 10, also the free shuttle bus stops outside*, was the first Anglican church in Southeast Asia. It was built in 1817 with convict labour. The building was designed by Captain Robert Smith (some of his paintings are in the State Museum).

The **Goddess of Mercy Temple**, (Kuan Yin Teng), on Jalan Kapitan Kling Mosque/Lorong Steward, was built at the beginning of the 1800s by the island's early Chinese immigrants. Kuan Yin is probably the most worshipped of all the Chinese deities, and is revered by Buddhists, Taoists and Confucians. The goddess is a Bodhisattva, one who rejected entry into nirvana as long as there was injustice in the world. The goddess is associated with peace, good fortune and fertility, which accounts for her popularity. Kuan Yin is portrayed as a serene goddess with 18 arms; two arms are considered inadequate to rid the world of suffering. The rooftops are carved to represent waves, on which stand two guardian dragons. Shops in the area sell temple-related goods: lanterns, provisions for the afterlife (such as paper Mercedes cars), joss sticks and figurines.

Although Georgetown is mainly Chinese, it has always had a large population of Indians, living in the city centre. The Hindu **Sri Mariamann Temple**, on Lebuh Queen/Lebuh Chulia, was built in 1883. It is richly decorated and dedicated to the Hindu god Lord Subramaniam. The main statue is strung with jewellery. It is normally used to lead a chariot procession to the Waterfall Temple during Thaipusam (see page 31). The symbols of the nine planets and the signs of the zodiac are carved into the ceiling. The surrounding area is largely Indian, with money changers, jewellers, restaurants and tea stalls.

There is also a Muslim community in Georgetown and the Indo-Moorish **Kapitan Kling Mosque** (on Jalan Kapitan Kling Mosque) was built by the island's first Indian Muslim settlers around 1800. It was named after the 'kapitan' or headman of the Kling – the South Indian community. As a sight it is rather disappointing.

Clan Piers and Armenian Street

Straight down Lebuh Chulia next to the Kapitan King Mosque is the Chinese water village off Pengkalan Weld. The entrance is through the temple on the quayside. It is known as the **Clan Piers**, as each of the jetties is named after a different Chinese clan. None of the families pays tax as they are not living on land. Rows of junks belonging to the resident traders are moored at the end of the piers.

Armenian Street ① *1½ blocks south of Kapitan Kling Mosque*, is worth a wander as this area of the city is being remodelled and conserved because of its historical value; you can see the house of the rich Arab merchant who constructed the mosque opposite the park and a bit further down the road can be found the traditional Chinese house where Dr Sun Yat Sen is said to have planned the Canton Uprising. The uprising started in Canton (modern Guangzhou in China) against the Qing dynasty, and eventually led to the downfall of the child emperor, hence the birth of modern China.

Khoo Kongsi and Malay Mosque

① *T04-261 2119, Mon-Fri 0900-1700, Sat 0900-1300, RM5. The free shuttle bus stops nearby.*
Located on Jalan Acheh, off Lebuh Pitt, Khoo Kongsi is approached through an archway to

Cannon Square and is one of the most interesting sights in Georgetown. A *kongsi* is a Chinese clan house, which doubles as a temple and a meeting place. Clan institutions originated in China as associations for people with the same surname. Today they are benevolent organizations that look after the welfare of clan members and safeguard ancestral shrines. Most of the *kongsis* in Penang were established in the 19th century when clashes between rival clans were commonplace.

The Khoo Kongsi is the most lavishly decorated of the *kongsis* in Penang, with its ornate Dragon Mountain Hall. It was built in 1898 by the descendants of Hokkien-born Khoo Chian Eng. A fire broke out in it the day it was completed, destroying its roof. It was rebuilt by craftsmen from China and was renovated in the 1950s; the present tiled roof is said to weigh 25 tonnes. The *kongsi* contains many fine pieces of Chinese art and sculpture, including two huge carved stone guardians, which ensure the wealth, longevity and happiness of all who came under the protection of the *kongsi*. The interior hall houses an image of Tua Sai Yeah, the Khoo clan's patron saint, who was a general during the Ch'in Dynasty in the second century BC.

There are other kongsis in Georgetown, although none is as impressive as the Khoo Kongsi. The Chung Keng Kwee Kongsi is on Lebuh Gereja and the Tua Peh Kong Kongsi on Lebuh Armenian. The Khaw Kongsi and the modern Lee Kongsi are both on Jalan Burmah; Yap Kongsi on Lebuh Armenian and the combined *kongsi* of the Chuah, Sin and Quah clans at the junction of Jalan Burmah and Codrington Avenue. Every *kongsi* has ancestral tablets as well as a hall of fame to honour its 'sons' or clansmen who have achieved fame in various spheres of life. Today women are honoured in these halls of fame too.

Near the Khoo Kongsi, on Jalan Acheh, is the **Malay Mosque**. Its most noteworthy feature is the Egyptian-style minaret – most in Malaysia are Moorish. In the past it was better known as the meeting place for the notorious White Flag Malays, who sided with the Hokkien Chinese in street battles against the Cantonese (Red Flags) in the Penang Riots of 1867. The hole halfway up the minaret is said to have been made by a cannonball fired from Khoo Kongsi during the clan riots. The mosque is one of the oldest buildings in Georgetown, built in 1808.

South Georgetown

ⓘ *1030-2230, RM5. All buses stop at Komtar.*

Apart from the RM850 million Penang Bridge and several new hotels, one of the few visible architectural contemporary monuments is **Kompleks Tun Abdul Razak (KOMTAR)** on Jalan Penang. This cylindrical skyscraper, which houses the state government offices and a shopping centre, dominates Georgetown. There should be spectacular views of the island and across the straits to the mainland from the 58th floor, but unfortunately the windows are filthy and even if they were clean the smog usually prevents a clear view. The viewing gallery encircles the souvenir centre and has coin-operated telescopes.

West of the cathedral

Cheong Fatt Tze Mansion ⓘ *14 Lebuh Leith, T04-262 0006, www.cheongfatttze mansion.com, fully guided restoration tours every 1100 or 1500 daily, RM12,* was winner of the UNESCO Conservation Award 2000 and is now a state monument. Built by Thio Thiaw Siat, a Kwangtung (Guangdong) businessman who imported craftsmen from China, this Chinese equivalent of a stately home is one of only three surviving Chinese mansions in this style; the others are in Manila and Medan (Sumatra). There is also a chance to stay in one of the decadent 16 bedrooms. Parts of the film *Indochine* were shot here.

Jalan Sultan Ahmed Shah (previously Northam Road Mansions) became known as Millionaires' Row as it was home to many wealthy rubber planters in the wake of the boom of 1911-1920. Many of the palatial mansions were built by Straits Chinese in a sort of colonial baroque style, complete with turrets and castellations. Many of them now have gone to seed as they are too expensive to maintain; a few have been lavishly done up by today's generation of rich Chinese businessmen. The largest houses are the Yeap family mansion, known as the White House, and the Sultan of Kedah's palace.

West of the town centre

On Lorang Burmah, just off Jalan Burmah, is **Wat Chayamangkalaram** ① *Rapid Penang bus Nos 101, 103, 104 and 105 stop here*, also known as Wat Buppharam, the largest Thai temple in Penang. It houses a 32-m-long reclining Buddha, Pra Chaiya Mongkol. There is a nine-storey pagoda behind the temple. The Thais and the Burmese practise Theravada Buddhism as opposed to the Mahayana school of the Chinese. Queen Victoria gave this site to Penang's Thai community in 1845. Opposite Wat Chayamangkalaram is Penang's only **Burmese temple**. It has ornate carvings and two huge white stone elephants at its gates. The original 1805 pagoda (to the right of the entrance) has been enshrined in a more modern structure.

The **Penang Buddhist Association** ① *168 Jln Anson, T04-228 0910, www.thepba168.org, bus No 202*, holds meditation sessions, retreats and lectures. The Buddha statues are carved from Carrara marble from Italy, the glass chandeliers were made in what was Czechoslovakia and there are paintings depicting the many stages of the Buddha's path to enlightenment. Next door at Number 184 is a 1960s art deco-style building, which is a clan hall for the Lee family.

The island → *For listings, see pages 154-167.*

From Georgetown, the round-island trip is a 70-km circuit. It is recommended as a day trip as there is little or no accommodation available outside Georgetown apart from the north coast beaches.

Batu Ferringhi and Teluk Bahang → *Colour map 1, B1.*

The main beach, Batu Ferringhi, whose hot, white sands were once the nirvana of Western hippies, has been transformed into an upmarket tropical version of the Costa Brava. There are scores of hotels along the beach strip and graffiti is splashed across the famous Foreigner's Rock. Ferringhi – which is related to the Thai word *farang* (foreigner) – actually means Portuguese in Malay. Portuguese Admiral Albuquerque, who captured Meleka in 1511, stopped off at Batu Ferringhi for fresh water on his way down the Straits. St Francis Xavier is said to have visited Batu Ferringhi in 1545. In the late 16th century, Captain James Lancaster, who later founded the East India Company in 1600, also came ashore at the beach.

For many package tourists, Batu Ferringhi *is* Penang. The area is currently very much in vogue with visitors from the Middle East, hence the number of Arabic (not Jawi) signs in the resort. The beach is just over 3 km long but it has been extended to the fishing village of Teluk Bahang at the west end. Most holidaymakers and honeymooners prefer to stick to their hotel swimming pools rather than risk bathing in the sea, which for much of the year looks like coffee. Pollution, silt and an influx of jellyfish have affected water quality, but of late, the hotels have taken much more care of the beach itself. With its palms and casuarina trees, it retains at least some of its picture-postcard beauty. The hotels offer many different activities: windsurfing, waterskiing, diving, sailing and fishing, as well as jungle walks and sightseeing tours of the island.

Apart from the string of plush modern hotels, the Batu Ferringhi area also has many excellent restaurants, hawker stalls and handicraft shops.

The small fishing kampong of Teluk Bahang is situated at the westerly end of this northern stretch of beach. It is where the Malabar fishermen used to live and has now been dramatically changed by the Penang Mutiara Beach Resort. Beyond Teluk Bahang, around **Muka Head**, the coast is broken into a series of small secluded coves separated by rocky headlands; there are several tiny secluded beaches. Some of these are only accessible by boat, which can be hired either from the beach hotels, or from fishermen in Teluk Bahang, which is much cheaper. Trails also lead over the headland from the fishing kampong. One trail goes along the coast past the University Malaya Marine Research Station to Mermaid Beach and Muka Head lighthouse (1½ hours); another leads straight over the headland to Pantai Keracut (two hours).

The **Teluk Bahang Recreation Forest** has several well-marked trails and a **Forestry Museum** ① *Mon-Thu 0900-1700, Fri 0900-1200 and 1425-1700*. About 1 km up the road from the Teluk Bahang junction, the **Butterfly Farm** ① *Butterfly House, 830 Jln Teluk Bahang, T04-885 1253, www.butterfly-insect.com, Mon-Fri 0900-1730, Sat-Sun 0900-1800, RM20, children RM10, additional charges for video camera, take bus No 101 to get here*, claims to be the largest tropical butterfly farm in the world. It has 4000 butterflies, representing over 120 species of Malaysian butterflies. The best time to visit is in the late morning or early afternoon when they are most active. The farm is also an important research centre and breeding station. Around 20% of the butterflies are released into the wild to help secure the future of the different species. A small but excellent reptile and insect museum is next door.

③ Penang's beaches

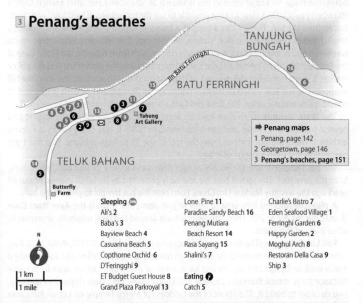

➡ **Penang maps**
1 Penang, page 142
2 Georgetown, page 146
3 Penang's beaches, page 151

Sleeping 🛏
Ali's 2
Baba's 3
Bayview Beach 4
Casuarina Beach 5
Copthorne Orchid 6
D'Feringghi 9
ET Budget Guest House 8
Grand Plaza Parkroyal 13

Lone Pine 11
Paradise Sandy Beach 16
Penang Mutiara
   Beach Resort 14
Rasa Sayang 15
Shalini's 7

Eating 🍴
Catch 5

Charlie's Bistro 7
Eden Seafood Village 1
Ferringhi Garden 6
Happy Garden 2
Moghul Arch 8
Restorán Della Casa 9
Ship 3

Northern Penang

The **Nattukotai Chettiar Temple** ① *take bus No 102 and get off at the stop before the Botanical Gardens,* on Waterfall Road was built by members of the Indian Chettiar money-lending fraternity and is the biggest Hindu temple on the island. It is a centre of pilgrimage during the Thaipusam festival (see page 31).

The **Botanical Gardens** ① *T04-227 0428, daily 0500-2000; the more interesting plants are kept under lock and key and are open to visitors Mon-Fri 0700-1900, bus No 102,* also on Waterfall Road, are situated in a valley surrounded by hills 8 km from Georgetown. The gardens are well landscaped and contain many indigenous and exotic plant species. They were established in 1844. A path leads from the gardens' Moon Gate up Penang Hill, see below; the 8-km hike takes about 1½ hours. The resident macaques are a bit frisky, it's wise to watch them from a distance.

Central Penang

A short distance from Kek Lok Si is the **funicular railway** ① *every 30 mins between 0630 and 2115 (until 2315 Fri, Sat),* which started operating in 1922. It climbs 850 m up **Penang Hill** ① *take bus No 204 to Ayer Itam Station, then shuttle bus No 8 to the railway. Most buses from Stand 3 go to Penang Hill, but if unsure the bus drivers are helpful – provided you have the right change for the fare.* A vintage steam engine is on display at the Penang Museum. The railway was originally completed in 1899, but on its inauguration by the governor it didn't work and had to be dismantled. Penang Hill is about 5°C cooler than Georgetown and was a favoured expat refuge before the advent of air conditioning. Indeed, it was the first colonial hill station developed on Peninsular Malaysia. **Bel Retiro**, designed as a getaway for the governor, was the first bungalow to be built on the hill. There is a small hotel. The ridge on top of Penang Hill is known as Strawberry Hill, after Francis Light's strawberry patch. On a clear day it is possible to see the mountains of Langkawi and North Kedah from the top. There's also a temple, a mosque, a post office, a few restaurants, a small hawker centre and police station on the top. The hill gets very crowded on weekends and public holidays. A well-marked 8-km path leads down to the Moon Gate at the Botanical Gardens (about an hour's walk) from between the post office and the police station; a steep but delightful descent, with plenty of places to sit along the way. The hill supports the last relic patch of tropical rainforest on Penang and as such is deemed of considerable natural value. The flora and fauna here have been protected since 1960.

The **State Mosque** ① *Jln Ayer Itam/Jln Masjid Negeri, bus No 101,* is the largest and newest mosque in Penang and can accommodate 5000. It was designed by a Filipino architect. There are good views from the top of the 57-m-high minaret. You must get permission first from mosque officials.

The **Bat Temple** ① *take bus No 204,* at Ayer Itam is a sanctuary for fruit bats, which hang from the cave roof. The sacred bats are zealously protected by Buddhist monks. About 60 years ago the wealthy Madam Lim Chooi Yuen built the bat temple to protect the bats.

A pleasant wooded hilly area to relax in just above the town is the **Ayer Itam Dam** ① *take bus No 201 or 203.* There are several trails around the lake, originally shortcuts to other parts of the island.

Kek Lok Si Temple (The Monastery of Supreme Bliss) ① *T04-828 3317, 0900-1800, free, voluntary contribution to climb the 30-m-high tower, bus No 201, 203 or 204, followed by a 5-min walk or Transit Link shuttle bus No 8, south of Ayer Itam,* can be seen from some distance away. It took Burmese, Chinese and Thai artisans, who were shipped in specially, two decades to build it. The abbot of the Goddess of Mercy Temple on Lebuh Pitt came from China in 1885 and the landscape around Ayer Itam reminded him of his homeland. He collected money from rich Chinese merchants to fund the construction of the huge temple, modelled on Fok San Monastery in Fuchow, China. On the way up the 'ascending plane' is a pond for turtles, which are a symbol of eternity. The temple sprawls across 12 ha and is divided into three main sections: the Hall of Bodhisattvas, the Hall of Devas and the sacred Hall of the Buddha. The seven-tier pagoda, or Ban Po, the Pagoda of a Thousand Buddhas, is built in three different styles: the lower follows a Chinese design honouring the Goddess of Mercy, Kuan Yin; the middle is Thai-Buddhist and commemorates Bee Lay Hood (the Laughing Buddha); and the upper Burmese levels are dedicated to the Gautama or historic Buddha with thousands of gilded statues. The topmost tier contains a relic of the Buddha, a statue of pure gold and other treasures, but it is closed to visitors. It's all pretty tacky stuff and more than half the complex has been turned into a shopping centre. All in all, it's an impressive building compromised by tack.

South Penang

Universiti Sains Malaysia Museum and Gallery ① *Mon-Thu 0900-1630, Fri 0900-1215, 1445-1630*, is at Minden near the Penang Bridge interchange. It has a large ethnographic and performing arts sections with a special exhibition on wayang kulit (shadow puppets; see page 517). There is also an art gallery with works by Malaysian artists and visiting temporary exhibitions.

Snake Temple ① *T04-643 7273, 0600-1900, free, bus No 401*, also known as Temple of the Azure Cloud, was built in 1850 at Bayan Lepas 12 km from Georgetown. Snakes were kept in the temple as they were believed to be the disciples of the deity Chor Soo Kong, to whom the temple is dedicated. The temple was built as the result of a donation from a Scotsman, David Brown, after he was cured by a local priest of an 'incurable disease', using local medicines. Nowadays the reptilian disciples (almost exclusively Wagler's pit vipers) are a bit thin on the ground. The number of snakes in the temple varies from day to day – there are usually more around during festivals. The incense smoke keeps them in a drugged stupor, and most of them have had their fangs extracted. Photographs with (defanged) snakes can be posed for in a new annexe next door to the temple (RM5). The temple is surrounded by factories and a highway and most locals say the place is a con, given the paucity of reptiles.

Batu Maung ① *take bus No 401*, is a Chinese fishing village near Bayan Lepas and is known for its 'floating' seafood restaurant, built out over the water. Around the south coast, there are a few beaches and a couple of unremarkable fishing kampongs. The southern beaches are more secluded than the beaches along the north coast; the drawbacks are the litter and the absence of accommodation.

Also here, is Penang's latest tourist venue, the **War Museum** ① *Mukim 12, Daerah Barat Daya, T04-421 3606, daily 0900-1900, RM15, children RM7.50; shuttle bus from Tourism Malaysia Office 0930 and 1430, or take bus 401*, built around a 1930s military fortress. The fort sprawls across 20 acres on Bukit Batu Maung, a supposedly haunted hill. It is gradually being restored, but currently visitors can clamber over a torture chamber, medical infirmary, canon firing bay and scoot along tunnels.

The **Bukit Jambul Orchid and Hibiscus and Reptile Garden** ① *T04-644 8863, daily 0930-1830; snake show Sat, Sun and public holidays at 1130 and 1530, RM10, children RM5*, is found along Persiaran Bukit Jambul, close to the Hotel Equatorial and five minutes' drive from the airport. As its name suggests, it specializes in orchids and hibiscus. There is also a reptile house here.

Veering north towards the centre of the island, however, beyond Barat, is **Balik Pulau**, a good *makan* stop with restaurants and cafés. Around the town, known as the durian capital of Penang, there are a number of picturesque Malay kampongs.

West Penang

Further up the west side of the island is the **Penang National Park** (formerly the Pantai Acheh Forest Reserve) ① *T04-881 3530, daily 0800-1800, visitors are required to register at this office before entering the national park, entrance to the park is through Telok Bahang at the end of Batu Ferringhi Rd, take bus No 101 to Telok Bahang; either walk from here or take a boat from the fishing jetty; longer fare stages cost anything up to RM2; as the island buses are infrequent, check departure times at each place to avoid being stranded*, which also has well-marked trails into the jungle and to the bays further round; for example, to Pantai Keracut (one hour). After the Pantai Acheh junction, and on up a twisting, forested section of road, there is a waterfall with a pleasant pool, suitable for swimming, just off the road (20th milestone), called **Titi Kerawang**. This is the world's smallest national park and contains over 410 species of flora and 143 of fauna including dolphins, otters, hawksbill turtles, snakes, macaques and leaf monkeys. There are camping facilities; enquire at the Wildlife Office in Teluk Bahang (see above).

Butterworth → *Colour map 1, B2. Phone code: 04*

This industrial harbour town and base for the Royal Australian Air Force was billeted here under the terms of the Five Powers Pact. It is the main port for ferries to Penang and most tourists head straight for the island; Butterworth is not a recommended stopping point.

⦿ Penang listings

For Sleeping and Eating price codes and other relevant information, see Essentials pages 25-30.

⦿ Sleeping

Georgetown *p144, map p146*

Most upmarket hotels are concentrated in the Jln Penang area. Most cheaper hotels are around Lebuh Chulia and Lebuh Leith. Many of the backpacker places offer Thai and Indonesian visa services as well as laundry and ferry ticketing for Medan and Langkawi.
L Eastern & Oriental (E&O), 10 Lebuh Farquhar, T04-222 2000, www.e-o-hotel.com. With a/c, restaurant and pool, this hotel was built in 1885 by the Armenian Sarkies brothers, who operated Singapore's **Raffles Hotel** (see page 581) and the **Strand Hotel** in Rangoon (Yangon). Noël Coward and Somerset Maugham figured on former guest lists. This stunning hotel has been restored to its former glory. Staff are friendly and efficient

and the atmosphere is luxurious. There are fair options for varied cuisine, both international fine dining and local, from coffee houses to ballrooms. There's also a shop, business centre, pool and gym. Excellent promotional rates available; check the website.
L-AL Bayview, 25a Lebuh Farquhar, T04-263 3161, www.bayviewhotels.com/georgetown/. Large top-of-the-range hotel, although with a less formal atmosphere than others in this category. Facilities include 24-hr room service, laundry, dry cleaning, tour desk, pool, health centre (at additional cost), gym, internet access and a revolving restaurant. The cheaper rooms have a city view, and the higher the price range you climb, the better the views of the sea become. Rooms are comfy, well decorated – if slightly unimaginatively – and have Wi-Fi, cable TV and piped music.
L-AL Traders, Jln Magazine, T04-262 2622, www.shangri-la.com. Comfortable hotel mainly patronised by business types. Facilities

include a restaurant, 24-hr coffee garden, pool and small fitness centre. Central location.

AL Berjaya Georgetown Hotel, T04-227 7111, www.berjayahotels-resorts.com. Fairly new luxury hotel with over 320 rooms, part of the one-stop Midland Park Complex. All the usual amenities including pool, health centre, 2 restaurants and business centre. Top floors have superb views over the city. Good promotional rates available; check the website.

AL-A Cheong Fatt Tze Mansion, 14 Leith St, T04-262 0006, www.cheongfatttzemansion.com. This indigo 19th-century mansion, beautifully restored, has a selection of 16 elegant themed rooms all furnished with period pieces and modern facilities. Rate includes breakfast and valet service. A unique, albeit pricey, experience. Recommended for those who want to live Penang's history and culture first-hand.

AL-A Cititel, 404 Jln Penang, T04-370 1188, www.cititelpenang.com. Large hotel in central location. Comfortable rooms with long bathtub, Wi-Fi and some excellent sea views. 24-hr café, Chinese and Japanese restaurants and a sports bar. Breakfast included. Recommended.

A Grand Continental, 68 Brick Kiln Rd (Jln Gurdwara), T04-263 6688, www.ghihotels.com. With a/c, restaurant, pool, health club, coffee lounge, massage centre and karaoke lounge. Good value.

A-B Continental, 5 Jln Penang, T04-263 6388, www.hotelcontinental.com.my. Large hotel with over 200 carpeted a/c rooms. 18 storeys with great views from higher rooms. The top draw here is the rooftop pool, a great place to dream away the hours.

A-B Sunway, 33 New Lane, T04-229 9988, www.sh.com.my. Pleasant decor, good facilities in rooms including Wi-Fi, a/c, TV, pulsating shower, in-house video, iron, fridge, complimentary tea/coffee. There is also a pool, jacuzzi, restaurant and a tea-house. Breakfast included. Not much character, but great value for money.

B Malaysia, 7 Jln Penang, T04-263 3311, www.hotelmalaysia.com.my. Dated high-rise hotel in the centre with faded decor, a/c rooms, coffee house, disco and health centre.

B Oriental, 105 Jln Penang, T04-263 4211, www.oriental.com.my. This hotel towers over Lebuh Chulia and offers a variety of entertainment options, including a massage parlour, Japanese and Indian restaurants and a bar with all-day happy hour. The rooms are looking tired, but all have a/c, TV and attached bathroom and are often heavily discounted. Good views from the upper floors.

B-C Cathay Heritage, 15 Lebuh Leith, T04-262 6271, cathayhbh@gmail.com. Huge fan and a/c rooms in a detached colonial mansion filled with 1920s furniture including a gorgeous art deco staircase. Fittings are somewhat ancient, giving the place a rustic, well-used feel, but this hotel is packed with rogueish charm. Recommended.

C Paramount, 48F Jln Sultan Ahmad Shah, T04-227 3649. A/c and restaurant. Big rooms in run-down colonial house, right on the sea, but not central.

C-D Star Lodge, 39 Lebuh Muntri, T04-2626378, 75lodge@gmail.com. Owned by the same people as the **75 Travellers Lodge**, this is a slightly more upmarket option with spotless new rooms with window and attached bath and Wi-Fi. Staff are very friendly and knowledgeable about Georgetown and its environs. Recommended.

C-E Banana Guesthouse, 355 Lebuh Chulia, T04-262 6171, www.banananewguest house. com. Located above a cavernous café/bar, this place has a broad selection of a/c and fan rooms with a communal area littered with seats taken out of a minibus. It could do with a good clean, but offers fair value for money.

C-E Old Penang, 53 Lorong Cinta, T04-263 8805, www.oldpenang.com. Clean budget lodgings in a former restaurant with space aplenty, high ceilings and smallish but comfortable rooms with Wi-Fi and a/c or fan. Some rooms are without window. Dorm available (RM10). Recommended.

D White House, 72 Jln Penang, T04-263 2385, F264 1409. Fan and a/c rooms. Lovely staff, communal eating area, clean attached or common bathroom with hot water. Excellent value for money. Recommended.

D-E 75 Travellers Lodge, 75 Lebuh Muntri, T04-2626378, 75lodge@gmail.com. Hugely popular old-school traveller hostel with plenty of communal vibes, cheap dorms and lots of dusty corners. Offers plenty of tourist info and internet access, but don't expect anything fancy.

D-E Broadway Budget Hotel, 35F Jln Masjid Kapitan Kling, T04-262 8550, www.broadway budgethotel.com. This place is not wildly atmospheric but has 18 comfy, spotless a/c and fan rooms on 3 levels in the heart of town. Free Wi-Fi access. Recommended.

D-E SD Guesthouse, 35 Lebuh Muntri, T04-264 3743, www.sdguesthouse.com.my. Clean, simple guesthouse with good management and a/c and fan rooms. Free internet access.

D-E Stardust Guesthouse, 370-D Lebuh Chulia, T04-263 5723, www.stardustguest house.com. Simple, clean lodgings located above a busy and at times noisy café. Mixture of fan and a/c rooms with shared bath and free Wi-Fi access. Popular.

D-F Love Lane Inn, 54 Love Lane, T016-419 8409, ocean008@hotmail.com. Perennial backpackers' favourite with a wide variety of simple, clean rooms in a rambling 3-storey building. Some rooms are windowless. Dorm available (RM12). Shared, cold-water bathroom.

Batu Ferringhi and Teluk Bahang
p150, map p151

The big international hotels all have excellent facilities, including tennis, water sports, sailing and sightseeing tours. They also offer free shuttle services at least once a day to Georgetown. With fewer European customers, many have turned to the incentive travel business and the Asian market, targeting Singaporeans in particular. While middle to upmarket tourists are spoilt for choice, budget travellers' options on the north coast are rather more limited. All the budget guesthouses are in a little strip close to the sea edge just next to turn-off by the **Grand Plaza Parkroyal**.

L Penang Mutiara Beach Resort, Jln Teluk Bahang, Teluk Bahang, T04-886 8888, www.mutiarahotels.com. With a/c, restaurant,

pool, luxurious spa and over 400 rooms. This is the last outpost of 5-star luxury along the beach. The **Mutiara** (Malay for 'pearl') has landscaped gardens, a great pool with a bar and every conceivable facility, including a children's wonderland. A drink at the Mutiara bar costs the same as a huge meal in some nearby restaurants. Recommended.

L-AL Bayview Beach, T04-881 2123, www.bayviewbeach.com. With a/c, 2 restaurants, pool and over 400 rooms, in a pleasant location, away from others on the strip. Plush interior, sophisticated, but not strikingly different from other 5-star hotels here. Staff are friendly.

L-AL Casuarina Beach, T04-881 1711, www.penang-hotels.com/casuarina. Elegant rooms, a/c, restaurant and pool. This place is named after the trees that line Batu Ferringhi beach. There are particularly nice grounds and a good beach; a variety of water sports can be arranged. Tennis courts and table tennis available. Doctor on call and laundry service.

L-AL Copthorne Orchid Penang, Tanjung Bungah, T04-892 3333, www.copthorne. com.my. A/c, 2 restaurants, pool. A very formal atmosphere. A little dated.

L-AL Golden Sands Resort, T04-886 1911, www.shangri-la.com. A/c, restaurant, pool (arguably the best), popular and central on the beach. The restaurant and bar are situated on the beachfront. A well-equipped large resort.

L-AL Grand Plaza Parkroyal, T04-881 1133, www.parkroyalhotels.com. Huge hotel popular with tour groups and conventions. A little dated from the outside, but the interior is stylish, airy and contemporary. Comfortable rooms with all the usual mod cons. The Francis Light suite has its own garden and huge lounge. Numerous cafés and restaurants, spa and massage centre, pool and tennis courts.

L-AL Lone Pine, T04-881 1511, www.lone pinehotel.com. Recent renovations have almost hidden the fact that this is one of the oldest hotels in the area. Accommodation is in private villas with walled gardens, many with shady veranda. There's a pool near the beach and a good restaurant. Peaceful atmosphere away from the package tour masses. Excellent promotional rates available.

L-AL Paradise Sandy Beach, 527 Jln Tanjung Bungah, T04-899 9999, www.paradise sandybeach.com. Over 300 suites of varying size with kitchenette, balconies, sea views, TV, complimentary coffee/tea, a/c and bath. The decor is tasteful and facilities are good, with a free-form pool, paddling pool, water sports, tennis, squash and gym, 24-hr coffee house and lounge overlooking the sea. Stunning views. Recommended.

L-AL Rasa Sayang, T04-888 8888, www.shangri-la.com. A/c, restaurants, pool, another of the **Shangri La** group. Over 500 rooms, probably the most popular along the beach strip, modern interpretation of Minangkabau-style, horse-shoe design around central pool and garden area. More sophisticated style than others on the strip, still welcoming. Recommended.

A-B D' Feringghi, 66 Jln Batu Feringghi, T04-881 9000, www.dferingghi.com. New hotel with superb midweek promotional rates and a good restaurant. Located on the wrong side of the road for the beach, but some of the rooms at the back have good hill views. Rooms are on the small side, with TV, attached bathroom and a/c. Temperamental Wi-Fi.

B-D Ali's, 53b Batu Ferringhi, T04-881 1316, alisguesthouse_pg@yahoo.com. Efficiently run budget guesthouse with clean rooms, a/c and fan, with long shady common veranda and Wi-Fi access. One of the best budget options along this strip. Recommended.

B-D Baba's, 52 Batu Ferringhi, T04-881 1686, www.geocities.com/babaguesthouse2002. Chinese-owned place with a selection of fan and a/c rooms that are clean and functional. The fan rooms upstairs, though comfy, are merely partitioned boxes and have shared bathrooms. Spacious communal veranda and Wi-Fi. The owner here is well informed and a good source of information.

B-D ET Budget Guest House, 47 Batu Ferringhi, T04-881 1553, www.geocities.com/ etguesthouse. An offshoot of **Baba's** with a friendly family vibe and a good selection of

spotless rooms. Fan rooms have shared bathroom, a/c rooms a private bathroom. Good tour and bus information, laundry service. Another good-value option with travel information and tickets available.

C-D Shalini's, 56 Batu Ferringhi, T04-881 1859, ahlooi@pc.jaring.my. Lovely little house with shady balcony overlooking the sea. Clean and homely, mostly cold water, shared bathrooms.

Central Penang p152

A Equatorial Penang, 1 Jln Bukit Jambal, T04-643 8111, www.equatorial.com/pen/ index.html. With a/c and restaurant, this place is between the airport and town, on a hill with a view over the Penang Bridge. It's mostly used by visiting business people as it's conveniently located for Penang's duty-free industrial zone, which lies between it and the airport. There's a monstrous block of 600-plus rooms with good sports facilities and adjacent 18-hole golf course.

B Bellevue, Penang Hill, T04-829 9600, F4-8292052, penbell@tm.net.my. A/c and restaurant serving steamboat. This is a colonial-style house and a cool retreat up on the hill. Good views over Georgetown. Pleasant accommodation, small and quite isolated from the real action – other than the sights and attractions on Penang Hill.

Butterworth p154

Nearly all hotels are a good 20 mins' walk from the bus terminal, so a taxi ride is advisable.

B Berlin, 4802 Jln Bagan Luar, T04-332 1701, F332 3388. A/c, TV. Next to **Sayang Coffee House**, which serves meals. The best option, if you are unfortunate enough to require accommodation in Butterworth.

C Apollo, near the **Capital**, T04-331 1355. Very clean, a/c and fan rooms, private bathroom.

❶ Eating

Georgetown p144, map p146
Penang's specialities include *assam laksa* (a hot-and-sour fish soup), *nasi kandar* (curry),

mee yoke (prawns in chilli-noodle soup) and *inche kabin* (chicken marinated in spices and then fried). Penang and Melaka are the culinary centres of Nyonya cuisine (see page 28). Penang's Little India is bounded by Lebuh Bishop, Lebuh Pasar and Lebuh King, close to the quay. There is a string of good Indian restaurants along Lebuh Penang in this area. Try the foodstalls for great Malay food, see page 159.

There are a multitude of uninspiring but busy backpacker cafés on Lebuh Chulia including **Banana Café** and **Betel Hut** (both ¶), all serving simple Asian and Western cuisine and ice cold beer.

¶¶¶ **Ocean-Green**, 48F Jln Sultan Ahmad Shah (in quiet alleyway in front of **Paramount Hotel**). Specialities include lobster and crab thermidor, drunken prawns and fresh frogs' legs ('paddy chicken'). Lovely location overlooking fishing boats. Recommended.

¶¶¶ **Shang Palace**, Traders Hotel, Jln Magazine, T04-262 2622. Hong Kong, dim sum brunch, Cantonese dishes.

¶¶¶-¶¶ **Thirty Two**, 32 Jln Sultan Ahmad Shah, T04-262 2232. Set in a beautifully maintained Italian-style mansion built in the 1920s, this restaurant includes a bar and lounge area with live jazz bands, a terrace by the water and a no-smoking room with a/c. Varied menu, Asian fusion cuisine. Beautiful building, friendly staff and sophisticated ambience.

¶¶ **Beach Blanket Babylon**, Lot 81, The Garage, 2 Penang Rd, T04-2610 289. Trendy bar-restaurant with a good selection of international dishes, reasonable set menus and jugs of frosty beer.

¶¶ **Brasserie**, Traders Hotel. Californian cuisine.

¶¶ **Café Tower Lounge**, 59th floor, KOMTAR. Buffet lunch, good view over the city and afterwards free entrance to viewing gallery.

¶¶ **City Bayview**, 14th floor, 25a Lorong Farquhar. Asian cuisine served while the room gently rotates a circuit in about an hour, giving spectacular views of the city and coast.

¶¶ **Ecco Café**, 400 Lebuh Chulia. Open at 1800. Atmospheric bar/Italian café crammed with bizarre objects and Indian tapestries.

Very relaxed and friendly hangout. The owner makes his own pizza dough and pasta, to create some of Penang's best Italian food for a reasonable price. Freshly ground coffee, pastas, sandwiches and pizzas including the unconventional banana pizza. Highly recommended.

¶¶ **Hide No Ya**, 8 Abu Siti Lane. T04-228 2359, small, friendly restaurant, especially good for its *tempura chauonmushi*, *karagi* and sashimi/sushi. Recommended.

¶¶ **Kashmir**, base of **Oriental Hotel**, 105 Jln Penang (not Lebuh Penang). North Indian food in an a/c restaurant. Popular.

¶¶ **Maple**, 106 Jln Penang (near Oriental Hotel). Same management as **May Garden** and the food is in the same league.

¶¶ **May Garden**, 70 Penang Rd (next to **Towne House**). Reckoned to be among the best seafood restaurants in Georgetown, with an aquarium full of fish and shellfish to choose from. The crab is excellent and May Garden's speciality is frogs' legs, fried with chilli and ginger or just crispy. Recommended.

¶¶ **Obake Ya**, 11c Leith St. Immaculate traditional decor, *teppenyaki* and set lunches. Recommended.

¶¶ **Passage Thru' India**, 11A Leith St, T04-262 4644. One of the city's most highly regarded Indian restaurants serving an award-winning blend of frontier and southern Indian cuisine.

¶¶ **Sea Palace**, 50 Jln Penang (next to **Peking Hotel**). Huge menu, popular, a/c, Chinese tableware, good value. Recommended.

¶¶ **Sire Museum**, 4 King St, T04-264 5088. Closed Sun. Attractive restaurant covered in Asian artwork and with a menu offering tasty dishes such as baked Portobello mushrooms, crab cakes and a selection of pasta dishes and sandwiches. Excellent choice of beers. Recommended.

¶ **Banana Leaf**, Lebuh Penang, about 2 blocks south of Lebuh Gereja. Serves excellent southern Indian food; an especially good place for a thali and the lassis are good.

¶ **Di Tai Tong**, 45 Lebuh Cintra. Lunch and dinner. Locals rave about its delicious Cantonese delights. Limited English menu.

♯ **Goh Thew Chik**, 338 Lebuh Chulia. Famed for its Hainanese chicken rice, this simple restaurant is a popular lunchtime favourite.

♯ **Jin Xiu Tea House**, 58 Lebuh Muntri, T04-263 8595. Café with long list of Chinese teas and simple noodle dishes in a beautifully restored shophouse with a gallery featuring work of respected local artists.

♯ **Kaliaman's**, 43 Lebuh Penang. One of Penang's best Indian restaurants with an atmosphere that transports the diner to the streets of Chennai. Excellent South Indian set lunches and a good selection of north Indian à la carte dishes all day. The menu includes favourites such as rogan josh, dopiaza and spicy Chettinad curries. Recommended.

♯ **Kapitan**, 93 Lebuh Chulia (nr Sri Mariamman Temple), T04-264 1191. Patrons flock to this restaurant for a taste of their Indian Muslim cusine, fabulous tandoori set menus and clay pot biryanis. Recommended.

♯ **Kassim Mustafa**, 12 Lebuh Chulia. Basic coffee shop that prides itself in cooking a handful of dishes very well, most trade is done between 0500 and 1200, specialities are *nasi dalcha* (rice cooked with ghee and cinnamon), *ayam negro* and mutton *kurma*. Good *roti bom* and *teh tarik*. Staff are friendly, and this is also an excellent place for breakfast. Recommended.

♯ **Kassim Nasi Kandar**, 2-1 Jln Brick Kiln. Hot Indian Muslim food, open 24 hrs, recommended by locals.

♯ **Lum Fong**, 108 Muntri St. Lively coffee shop with an arcaded front, old wooden tables and chairs, good noodles.

♯ **My Thai**, 84 Jln Penang. Tourist-friendly spot with Thai salads, soups, curries and noodles. Popular.

♯ **Ros Mutiara**, 128 Lebuh Chulia, T04-261 9239. Tandoori dishes and veg and non-veg set meals.

♯ **Sin Kheng Hooi Hong**, 350 Lebuh Pantai. Hainanese cuisine, *lor bak* (crispy deep-fried seafood rolls, with sweet-and-sour plum sauce). Recommended.

♯ **W&O Café**, Lebuh Muntri (next to 75 Traveller's Lodge). Popular breakfast hangout

with fry-ups, BBC World on TV and internet and Wi-Fi access.

Coffee shops

Most Chinese coffee shops are along Jln Burmah and Jln Penang, with some in the financial district along Lebuh Bishop, Lebuh Cina and Lebuh Union. **Khuan Kew** and **Sin Kuan Hwa**, both in Love Lane, are particularly popular. The latter is well known for its Hainan chicken rice.

Kek Seng, 382 Jln Penang. Founded in 1906 and still serving *kway teow* soup and colourful *ais-kacangs*. It's the oldest in Georgetown.

Maxim Cakehouse and Bakery, Penang Rd. A popular stop.

Foodstalls

Penang's hawker stalls are famous in Malaysia, serving some of the island's best food. There are also popular stalls along Jln Burmah, Love Lane and at Ayer Itam. Good *roti-canai* opposite **Golden Plaza Hostel**, Lebuh Ah Quee.

Datuk Keramat Hawker Centre (also called **Padang Brown**), junction of Anson and Perak roads. One of the venues for Georgetown's roving night market – it is possible to check if it's on by calling the tourist information centre, T04-261 6663. Recommended.

Kota Selera Hawker Centre, next to Fort Cornwallis, off Lebuh Light. Recommended.

Lebuh Keng Kwee. Famed locally for its *cendol* stalls (cocktails of shaved ice, palm sugar and jelly topped with *gula melaka* and coconut milk).

Lebuh Kimberley (called noodle-maker street by the Chinese). Good variety of hawker food at night.

Lorong Selamat hawker stalls, highly recommended by locals.

Padang Kota Lama/Jln Tun Syed Sheh Barakbah, Esplanade. Busy in the evenings. Recommended.

Pesiaran Gurney Seawall (Gurney Drive), hawker stalls opposite the coffee shops. Good range of Malay, Chinese and Indian food, very popular in the evenings. Recommended.

Red Garden Night Market, Lebuh Leith. An excellent hawker centre that comes alive after dark and offers ice-cold beers, Japanese, Thai and local dishes such as chicken rice, *yong tau foo* and fresh seafood. Busy at weekends. Recommended.

Batu Ferringhi and Teluk Bahang
p150, map p151

Virtually every cuisine is represented along this stretch. Many of the big Batu Ferringhi hotels have excellent restaurants. They have to be good as there is plenty of good-quality competition from road-side restaurants.

Feringgi Grill, Rasa Sayang Resort, Batu Ferringhi. This popular restaurant aims to imitate an English club. Specialities include prime US rib of beef served with Yorkshire pudding, expensive but memorable.

Honjin, Bayview Beach, Batu Ferringhi. Peaceful, Japanese-style setting with a garden at the centre of the restaurant, good-quality food, set meals are best value.

House of Four Seasons, Penang Mutiara Beach Resort, Jln Teluk Bahang. Closed Tue. Good old-fashioned opulence, black marble, silk and carpets and an interesting menu with Cantonese and Szechuan dishes.

Japanese Restaurant, Rasa Sayang Resort, Batu Ferringhi. Typically spartan Japanese decor, main items on menu are sushi and sashimi, and *teppanyaki*.

Marco Polo, Bayview Beach, Batu Ferringhi. Wide selection of Cantonese dishes, bright lighting and typical Chinese decor with tables set around a courtyard.

The Ship, Batu Ferringhi (next to Eden Seafood Village). Set inside a recreated wooden schooner, this slightly tacky restaurant serves up large portions of Western grub and purports to have the finest steak in Penang.

The Catch, Jln Teluk Bahang, next to Mutiara Hotel. Malay, Chinese, Thai and international seafood dishes, huge fish tanks for fresh fish, prawns, crabs, lobster and more. 1-hr cultural show daily. In a pleasant setting, this is one of the best seafood restaurants on the island. Recommended.

Charlie's Bistro, Batu Ferringhi (opposite Lone Pines Hotel). Tables and chairs are set in a recreated beach atmosphere here, so tourists can dine with their toes in the sand, but facing a busy road rather than the sea. Dishes include Western-style Asian food, soups and salads.

Eden Seafood Village, 69a Batu Ferringhi. If it swims, **Eden** cooks it – things are priced according to weight so it's not cheap. Nightly cultural shows, **Eden** has now expanded to include 2 other big, clean red restaurants, adjacent and opposite the original, the **Ferringhi Village** at 157b and **Penang Village**.

End of the World, end of Teluk Bahang beach. Huge quantities of fresh seafood, its chilli crabs are superb and its lobster is the best value for money on the island (about RM25 each). This is in a pleasant setting on the beach, with not too many tourists. Recommended.

Ferringhi Garden, 34 Batu Ferringhi. Spotlessly clean and sleekly stylish, this top-notch restaurant serves Malay cuisine and delectable seafood including lobster and tiger prawns.

Fok Lok Sow, Mar Vista Resort, Batu Ferringhi. Good-value buffet and 7-course set dinner.

Moghul Arch, Batu Ferringhi, near Yahong Art Gallery. Good-value north Indian cuisine with a few Western favourites and Arabic dishes to ensure they have covered all bases.

Restoran Della Casa, Jln Batu Ferriringhi (20 m to the east of Yahong Art Gallery). Curious little place with a mixed Middle Eastern and Italian menu. Good value.

Happy Garden, Batu Ferringhi, left after police station and **Eden** restaurant. Pretty garden, Chinese and Western dishes.

Papa Din's Bamboo, 124-B Batu Ferringhi (turn left after police station and **Eden** Restaurant, 200 m up the Kampong Rd by **Happy Garden** Restaurant). Home-cooked Malay fish curries made by loveable *bumoh* who prides himself on being able to say thank you in 30 languages. Papa Din Salat is also a renowned masseur.

🎵 Bars and clubs

Georgetown *p144, map p146*

Most of the big hotels have in-house clubs and discos. Expect to pay cover charges if you are not a guest.

Chillout Club, The Gurney Hotel, 18 Persiaran Gurney, Georgetown, T04-370 7000. Good dance club with R&B and house music. Very popular with 20-somethings; Wed night is ladies' night.

The Garage, 2 Penang Rd (opposite E&O Hotel), T04-263 6868. Open 1100-0300. There are several bars and clubs inside this restored art deco garage including **Slippery Senoritas**, a tapas and salsa bar with live South American music and performing bar staff. Recommended.

Soho, 50 Penang Rd, T04-263 1111. Situated beneath the Peking Hotel, the purple façade of this archetypal English pub is hard to miss. Proper pints, DJs and long happy hours all add to the charm. Recommended.

There is an abundance of small bars with outside seating on Lebuh Chulia that are popular with tourists and locals alike. Notables include **Hong Kong**, **Reggae Club** and **Monaliza**.

Batu Ferringhi and Teluk Bahang
p150, map p151

Borsalino, Grandplaza Parkroyal. Open 2100-0200. Sunken dance floor, fun disco.

Cool Bananas & Sunset Bar. Good selection of beers, some draught, low prices, darts and snooker nights. There's a 2-for-1 happy hour on Fri evenings until 0100.

Ozone, Mar Vista Resort, Batu Ferringhi. Open 2100-0200. Disco, karaoke and live music area.

Sapphire, Ferringhi Beach Hotel. Open until 0100. 30% discount on pouring brands and draught beer, ladies' night Tue.

Sunset Bistro, Batu Ferringhi. Relaxed beachside shack with excellent daily happy hour specials; low prices and gorgeous sea views.

🎬 Entertainment

Georgetown *p144, map p146*

Cinemas

All cinemas are now to be found in cineplexes, within the shopping centres.

Prangin Mall, best of the bunch in the shopping complex opposite KOMTAR. The old **Odean Theatre** still shows Indian and southeast Asian offerings.

Batu Ferringhi and Teluk Bahang
p150, map p151

Most of the larger hotels have cultural shows in the evening.

Eden Seafood Village, Batu Ferringhi.

🎉 Festivals and events

Georgetown *p144, map p146*

Feb/Mar Chap Goh Meh, celebrated on the 15th night of the 1st month of the Chinese lunar calendar. Girls throw oranges into the sea for their suitors to catch.

May/Jun Penang International Dragon Boat Race, Tuen Ng festival near Penang Bridge. (Movable.) Teams from around the region and beyond compete.

Floral Festival at the Botanic Gardens held at the end of May/Jun. City parades by Malays (at Fort Cornwallis), Chinese (at Khoo Kongsi) and Indians (at Market St). See tourist office for details.

Sep Penang Lantern Festival held at the end of Sep. A parade with lanterns.

Oct/Nov Deepavali Open House. (Movable.) Festivities in Little India.

🛍 Shopping

Georgetown *p144, map p146*

This requires a lot of wandering around the narrow streets and alleyways off Jln Penang. The main areas are Jln Penang, Jln Burmah and Lebuh Campbell.

Antiques

An export licence is still required for non-imported goods. Shops are concentrated on and around Jln Penang with the best ones at the top end opposite **Eastern and Oriental Hotel**. There are also antique shops along Rope Walk (Jln Pintal Tali). Most stock antiques from Burma, Thailand, Indonesia and Malaysia, as well as a few local bargains. Another street with a number of crafty-cum-antique shops is Rope Walk or Jln Pintal Tali.

Oriental Arts Co, 3f Penang Rd. Well-established with a fine collection of antiques.

Penang Antique House, 27 Jln Patani, showcase of Peranakan (Straits Chinese) artefacts – porcelain, rosewood with mother-of-pearl inlay, Chinese embroideries and antique jewellery.

Arts and crafts

Jln Penang is a good place to find handicrafts: **China Handicraft Co**, 3d Jln Penang; **Federation Arts & Crafts**, 3c Jln Penang; **Peking Arts & Crafts** at 3b Jln Penang.

ABN-AMRO Arts Centre, 9 Lebuh Pantai. Formerly the ABN-AMRO bank building, beautiful colonial house with great photo exhibitions.

The Art Gallery, 36B Burmah Rd, T04-229 8219.

Yahong Art Gallery, Batu Ferrenghi, T04-881 1093. Open 0930-2100. Has a variety of batik exhibits as well as some jewellery and other works of art.

Books

There are several bookshops in Lebuh Chulia near Swiss Hotel, selling second-hand books.

HS Sam Bookstore, 144 Lebuh Chulia. Prides itself on being well organized and runs a sideline in travel services: Thai visas, bus ticketing, car/bike rental and has a luggage storage. It has the best selection of travel books and fiction of all the second-hand bookshops. You can exchange books here too.

MPH Bookstore, Island Plaza, Jln Tanjong Tokong.

Parvez Book Store, 419 Lebuh Chulia. As well as dealing in books they arrange Thai visas and trips, and car/motorbike hire.

Times Bookshop, Penang Plaza, 1st floor, 126 Burmah Rd.

Camping equipment

Tye Yee Seng Canvas, 162 Chulia St. Good stock of tents, rucksacks, sleeping bags and beach umbrellas.

Food and drink

There are a number of outlets in Georgetown, mostly Chinese-run, selling locally produced specialities.

Eu Yan Sang, 156 Chulia St. Chinese teas and ginseng in a variety of forms are the speciality of this shop, which offers a herb-boiling service in a cauldron that bubbles inside the doorway.

Gama, behind the KOMTAR Tower, is excellent for stocking up on basics.

Him Heang, 162 Jln Burmah. Similar products to **Wee Ling** including *pong pneah* (pastry filled with molasses or caramel).

Wee Ling, 132 Chulia St. Dragon Ball biscuits, pastry balls filled with a mung bean paste.

Markets

The night market changes venue every night and is more often than not out of town. There are illegal street vendors selling CDs etc, and you might also beat the odds of receiving a faulty disk. There may be plans in the future to set up a permanent night market in Chinatown but these are as yet unfulfilled. Jln Chulia and the surrounding streets have a busy and friendly atmosphere with good late-night cafés. It is popular with westerners and most bars offer international football games on the television or a film.

Shopping complexes

Gurney Plaza, Jln Gurney, www.plazagurney. com.my. This may not be the biggest shopping mall in Georgetown, but it's certainly the flashest. Designer shops, the north's biggest multiplex cinema and alfresco dining options.

Island Plaza, Jln Tanjung Tokong, on road to Batu Ferringhi. Upmarket shops, East India Company, Guess, Fila, Coca Restaurant, the Forum, a food court and a new cinema.
KOMTAR. Hundreds of boutiques, 2 department stores, fast food restaurants, amusement arcade.
Queensbay Mall,100 Persiaran Bayan Baru. The largest mall in Penang, located near the airport, has a good selection of eateries, branded clothing and electronics and a cinema. Take bus 307 to get here.
Prangin Mall, complex opposite KOMTAR. There are restaurants, fast-food outlets and a few upmarket shops and an ice rink and cinema.

Souvenirs
Many of the curios are imported from China and are very well priced.
Lebuh Chulia, Bishop and Rope Walk (Jln Pintal Tali).
Tan Embroidery Co, 20 Lebuh Pantai. Has a good selection.

Batik Ferringhi and Teluk Bahang
p150, map p151
Craft Batik, opposite the Grandplaza ParkRoyal. Batik cloth sold by metre and as ready-made garments, demonstrations can be seen to rear of showroom.
Deepee's Silk Shop, 591 Batu Ferringhi. Offers a reasonable tailoring service.
Sim Seng Lee Batik and Handicrafts, 391 Batu Ferringhi.
Yahong Art Gallery, 58d Batu Ferringhi Road, T04-8811251, F881 1093. Displays batik paintings by the Teng (born in China in 1914) family. The elder Teng is regarded as the father of Malaysian batik painting. Entrance is free and the batik works are certainly worth it. Also offers packaging and transport of bought goods to any international destination.

▲ Activities and tours

Georgetown *p144, map p146*
Golf
Kristal Golf Resort, 364 Jln Valdor, Seberang Perai Selatan, T04-582 2280. Green fees weekdays RM105, weekends RM150.
Penang Golf Resort, Lot 2462, Mk6, Jln Bertram, T04-578 2002, www.penanggolf resort.com.my. Green fees weekdays RM94 weekend RM150.
Penang Turf Club, Jln Batu Gantong, T04-226 6701, www.penangturfclub.com. 18-hole.

Horse racing
Penang Turf Club, Jln Batu Gantung, T04-229 3233.

Snorkelling and diving
While Pulau Payar (Payar Island) is usually accessed from Langkawi, it is possible to organise diving and snorkelling day trips out there from Penang.
East Marine Holidays, 5 Lengkok Nun, Penang (for the office), T04-226 3022, www.eastmarine.com.my. Costs around RM240 for snorkelling and RM340 for diving at Pulau Payar, including the return ferry and buffet lunch.

Tour operators
Most of the budget travel agents are along Lebuh Chulia. There are quite a few agencies around the Swettenham Pier.
MS Star Travel Agencies, 475 Lebuh Chulia, T04-262 2906.
MSL Travel, Ming Court Inn Lobby, Jln Macalister, T04-227 2655 or 340 Lebuh Chulia, T04-261 6154. Student and youth travel bureau.
Renae Agency, 2 Penang Port Commission Complex, T04-262 2369.

Batu Ferringhi and Teluk Bahang
p150, map p151
Boat trips
Trips can be arranged through fishermen at Teluk Bahang. Negotiate prices in advance.

Traditional massage

Simple on-the-beach foot reflexology place opposite Baba's. Nice setting for a foot massage. Health clubs – such as the Do-Club in the Mar Vista Resort, Batu Ferringhi – in all major hotels offer massage.

⊖ Transport

Georgetown *p144, map p146*
Air

Penang is well connected internationally with frequent daily flights to **Medan** (Lion Air, AirAsia, MAS), **Jakarta**, **Bangkok** (AirAsia), **Hong Kong** (Cathay Pacific) and **Singapore** (AirAsia, Jet Star Asia). Other international connections on MAS via KL.

Regular connections on MAS and AirAsia with **KL**. Daily departures to **JB**, **Kuching**, **Kota Kinabalu**, **Kota Bahru**, **Kuala Terengganu** and **Kuantan** with AirAsia and Firefly. Firefly also has 2 daily flights to **Langkawi** (0955 and 1445, 30 mins).

Airline offices AirAsia, 332 Lebuh Chulia T04-261 5642, with computers for online booking in a/c comfort; **Cathay Pacific**, AIA Building, Lebuh Farquhar, T04-226 0411; **Emirates**, T04-263 1100; **MAS**, Kompleks Tun Abdul Razak (KOMTAR), Jln Penang, T04-262 0011 (the ticket office is on the ground floor, at the southern side of KOMTAR, and can only be entered from outside the complex) or at the airport, T04-643 0811; **Singapore Airlines**, Wisma Penang Gardens, 42 Jln Sultan Ahmad Shah, T04-226 3201; **Thai International**, Wisma Central, 202 Jln Macalister, T04-226 6000.

Boat

Passenger and car ferries operate from adjacent terminals, Pengkalan Raja Tun Uda, T04-331 5780.

Ferries leave from Georgetown for Belawan, on **Sumatra**, Indonesia and for **Langkawi** and from there to **Thailand**.

There's a ferry service between Georgetown and **Butterworth**. Ferries leave every 20 mins 0600-0100, one-way RM1.20. Car RM7.70, motorbike RM2. **Selasa Express Ferry Company** has its office by the Penang Clocktower, next to the Penang Tourist Office, T04-262 5630. **Sejahtera** and **Fast Ferry Ventures** operate boats between Georgetown and **Langkawi** daily, 2 departures from each company a day, one at 0815 and another at 0830 (via Pulau Payar) (3 hrs), one way RM60 (children RM45), return RM115 (children RM85). Tickets can be bought from travel agents all over town. Boats leave from Swettenham Pier. You can take a motorcycle or bicycle aboard. Some guesthouses sell tickets including a minibus trip to the pier for RM66.

International boat connections
Several ferry companies including **Fast Ferry Ventures** operate a service between Penang and Belawan (Medan's port), **Sumatra**, from Swettenham Pier. There are currently 3 departures a week, on Tue, Thu and Sat (0830, one way RM150, children RM100, return RM220, children RM140, 4½ hrs). Sat departure is often full, so book a ticket beforehand if possible. Tickets can be bought from most guesthouses and travel agents. Many nationalities including citizens of all EU countries, USA, Australia, Canada and Japan are eligible for a VOA (Visa On Arrival) at Medan's Belawan port; check with nearest Indonesian embassy for details.

Note Belawan is located 15 km outside the city and a further RM4 is charged for onward bus connections into Medan proper (enquire at travel agent in Penang for more details). There is plenty of local transport at Belawan. A taxi into Medan should costs around 50,000Rp.

Bus

Local Leave from Lebuh Victoria near the Butterworth ferry terminal and serve **Georgetown** and the surrounding districts. All buses leave for various points around the island from Pengkalan Weld (Weld Quay) – next to the ferry terminal, and all buses stop at KOMTAR. **Rapid Penang** covers most places and offers a/c comfort. Check routes at www.rapidpg.com.my.

To the **airport**, take **Rapid Penang** bus U401 or U401E (RM2, every 30 mins from 0635 until 2300 and pick up at KOMTAR and Pengkalan Weld).

Long distance At Sungai Nibong, 7 km from town. Direct bus connections link the island via the 13-km-long Penang Bridge with **KL** and a host of Peninsula towns as well as international services to **Thailand** and **Singapore**.

Booking offices along Lebuh Chulia and inside KOMTAR. Some coaches depart from KOMTAR and head to Butterworth to pick up more passengers whereas others depart from Sungai Nibong and travel direct to major towns on the Peninsula. Make sure you know whether the coach departs from KOMTAR or Sungai Nibong.

Masa Mara Travel, 54/4 Jln Burmah, is an agent for direct express buses from Penang to **Kota Bharu** and **KL** (5 hrs).

Minibus companies now organize an early morning pick-up from your hotel, to **Hat Yai** (4 hrs, RM30), from where there are connections north to Thailand. Pick-ups are 0500, 0830, 1200, and 1600. Destinations include Hat Yai. Other destinations include a change of bus at Hat Yai: **Bangkok** (18 hrs, RM118), **Surat Thani** (8 hrs, RM60) and **Phuket** (10 hrs, RM75). Buy tickets at Swiss Travel, 395 Lebuh Chulia, T04-262 0133. Also, many guesthouses organize minibuses to destinations in Thailand.

There is an overnight bus to **Singapore**.

Car hire

The journey from Penang to KL is reasonably painless, at 4½ hrs. There is a RM7 toll to drive across the Penang Bridge to the mainland. No payment required for the inbound journey. **Budget**, 28 Jln Penang, T04-643 6025 and Bayan Lepas Airport. **Hawk Rent-a-car**, T04- 881 3886. **Hertz**, 38 Lebuh Farquhar, T04-263 5914 and Bayan Lepas Airport. **New Bob Rent-a-car**, 7/F Gottlieb Rd, T04-229 1111, and Bayan Lapas Airport, T04-642 1111. **Orix**, City Bayview Hotel, 25A Lebuh Farquhar, T1800-881555.

Motorcycle hire

In Georgetown there are several motorbike rental shops, many of them along Lebuh Chulia. It costs from around RM35 per day to hire a motorcycle depending on size.

Taxi

Long-distance taxis to all destinations on the Peninsula operate from the depot beside the Butterworth ferry on Pengkalan Weld. There are taxi stands on Jln Dr Lim Chwee Leong, Pengkalan Weld and Jln Magazine. Fares are not calculated by meter, so agree a price before you set off; short distances within the city cost RM8-16. A trip to the airport costs RM30 (fares are always negotiable). **Radio taxis**, T04-890 9918 (at ferry terminal). **City Radio Taxi Service**, T04-229 9467. Direct taxis from Penang to Thailand: overnight to **Hat Yai; Surat Thani** for Koh Samui, **Krabi** (for Phuket).

Train

The station is Butterworth ferry terminal, T04-331 2796. Make advance bookings for onward rail journeys at the station or ferry terminal, Pengkalan Weld, Georgetown, T04-261 0290. From Butterworth: 2 daily connections with **Alor Star**, **Taiping**, **Ipoh**, **KL** (6 hrs) and **JB**.

Trishaw

Bicycle rickshaws that carry 2 people are one of the most practical and enjoyable ways to explore Georgetown. Cost RM3 per half mile or RM35 per hr; if taking an hour's trip around town, agree on the route first, bargain and set the price in advance.

Batu Ferringhi and Teluk Bahang
p150, map p151
Bus

Rapid Penang bus 101 goes to Batu Ferringhi/ Teluk Bahang from Pengkalan Weld (Weld Quay), Lebuh Chulia or KOMTAR in **Georgetown**, every 30 mins, 30-40 mins, RM2.

Car hire

Avis, Rasa Sayang Hotel; Hertz, Casuarina Beach Hotel; Kasina Baru, 651 Mukim 2, Teluk Bahang (opposite Mutiara Beach Resort), T4-8811988; Mayflower, Casuarina Beach Hotel; Ruhanmas, 157B Batu Ferringhi, T4-8811576; Sintat Rent-a-Car, Lone Pine Hotel.

Motorbike hire

Quite a few places along Batu Ferringhi offer motorbike hire, all of them clearly signposted on the road and most of the guesthouses also hire bikes. Expect to pay around RM150 per day for a car, RM50 for a motorbike. Saber Holidays, Batu Ferringhi Beach, T04-881 1882.

Taxi

Stands on Batu Ferringhi (opposite Golden Sands Hotel). The big hotels along the strip are well served by taxis. Be warned though that some taxis operate on commission for certain resorts and guesthouses. Try and work out roughly where you want to stay before you get there and ring up your destination in advance to check rates. Of course, not all taxi drivers are quite so manipulative; many are friendly, honest and a good source of information. Taxi from airport to Batu Ferringhi, 40 mins, RM60.

Butterworth p154

Butterworth is the main transport hub for Penang, and buses and trains operate into Thailand, and down to KL and Singapore.

Bus

The bus station is next to the ferry terminal. There are regular connections with KL, Taiping, Kuala Kangsar, Melaka, Johor Bahru, Kota Bharu, Kuala Terengganu, Kuantan and Ipoh (2 hrs). Buses leave at least every hour from Butterworth for Kuala Kedah (Langkawi ferry). There are also buses to Keroh, on the border with Thailand, from where it is possible to get Thai taxis to Betong.

Ferry

Ferries for pedestrians and cars and leave for Georgetown every 15-20 mins. Ferries leave every 20 mins 0600-0100, one-way RM1.20. Car RM7.70, motorbike RM2.

Taxi

These leave from next to the ferry terminal. If you take a taxi to Penang you must pay the taxi fare plus the toll for the bridge.

Train

The railway station is beside the Penang ferry terminal. There are 2 daily connections with Alor Star, Taiping, Ipoh, KL and JB and trains to Bangkok, (1 daily, departing at 14.20,19 hrs), Hat Yai (2 daily, 05.19 and 14.20, 5 hrs) and Singapore (0700, 14 hrs). Butterworth is one of the main stopovers on the Eastern and Orient Express, which travels in style from Singapore to Bangkok. Passengers disembark here to make the 3-hr trip by ferry and rickshaw to Georgetown.

❶ Directory

Georgetown p144, map p146
Banks Most banks in Georgetown are in or around the GPO area and Lebuh Pantai. Most money changers are in the banking area and Jln Masjid Kapitan Keling and Lebuh Pantai, close to the Immigration Office. Bank Bumiputra, 37 Lebuh Pantai; Citibank, 42 Jln Sultan Ahmad Shah; HSBC, Lebuh Pantai; Maybank, 9 Lebuh Union (branches everywhere!); Standard Chartered, 2 Lebuh Pantai. Consulates Denmark, Bernam Agencies, Hong Kong Bank Chambers, Lebuh Downing, T04-262 4886; France, 82 Bishop St, Wisma Rajab, T04-262 9707; Germany, Bayan Lepas Free Trade Zone, T04-647 1288; Indonesia, 467 Jln Burmah, T04-227 5141 (60-day visas available from here – take bus 101 and get off at the Adventist Hospital, next door to the consulate.) ; Japan, 2 Jln Biggs, T04-226 3030; Netherlands, Algemen Bank Nederland, 9 Lebuh Pantai, T04-261 6471;

Thailand, 1 Jln Tunku Abdul Rahman, T04-226 8029 (visas arranged in 2 days – it's a fair distance from town, RM16 in a taxi); UK, Birch House, 73 Jln Datuk Keramat, T04-262 5333. **Immigration** Immigration Office, on the corner of Lebuh Light and Lebuh Pantai, T04-261 5122. **Internet** There are a number of internet cafés along Lebuh Chulia, all offering similar rates of RM3 per hr, and many of the guesthouses and cafés offer Wi-Fi. **Libraries** Alliance Française, 46 Jln Phuah Hin Leong T04-227 6008, **The British Council**, 3 Weld Quay, T04-262 0330. **Penang Public Library**, Dewan Sri Pinang, Lebuh

Light, T04-229 3555. **Medical services** General Hospital (government), Jln Residensi, T04-229 3333; Lam Wah Ee Hospital (private), 141 Jln Batu Lancang, T04-657 1888.
Post Lebuh Pitt, efficient poste restante, also has a parcel-wrapping service, T04-261 8973.
Telephone Telecoms office (international calls, fax), Jln Burmah.

Butterworth p154
Banks Maybank, UMBC and HSBC on Jln Bagan Luar. **Internet** Genesys, 4922 Jln Bagan Luar, T04-324 3710. RM6 per hr.

Alor Star and around

→ Colour map 1, A2.

Alor Star is the capital of Kedah State on the road north to the Thai border. It is the home town of former Prime Minister Dr Mahathir Mohamad and is the commercial centre for northwest Malaysia. Its name, which has been corrupted from Alor Setar, means 'grove of setar trees' (which produce a sour fruit). Kedah is now Malaysia's most important rice-growing state; together with neighbouring Perlis, it produces 44% of the country's rice, and is known as jelapang padi (rice-barn country).

Nearby is the Bujang Valley Historical Park, where the remains of an ancient Hindu kingdom lie, Gunung Jerai, the highest mountain in the northwest and Kuala Perlis a small fishing port, the jumping-off point for Pulau Langkawi, see page 174. ▸▸ *For listings, see pages 171-173.*

Ins and outs

Getting there

Alor Star's airport is 13 km north of town. There are direct domestic connections with KL. Firefly, MAS and AirAsia fly from here to KL and Subang. From the railway station near the town centre trains connect with KL and Singapore (and points between) and north to the border with Thailand and Hat Yai. Alor Star is also on the main North-South Highway and there are bus connections with all the major destinations on the Peninsula as well as Singapore and Hat Yai. The bus terminal is several kilometres outside town. For Kuala Kedah and the ferry to Langkawi, catch bus No 106 from the local bus station. Share taxis leave from the stand near the centre of town.

Getting around

Taxis are available for out-of-town trips from the stand on Jln Langgar in Alor Star and the town bus station is not far away on Jalan Stesyen, also close to the train station. It's easy enough to walk around the town centre.

Tourist information

Kedah State Tourist Office ① *20 Jln Raja, T04-7301322, Sun-Thu 0800-1215 and 1445-1700*, has a limited choice of brochures, but not much on Alor Star or Kedah.

History

Kedah is the site of some of the oldest settlements on the Peninsula and the state's royal family can trace its line back several centuries. The ancient Indian names for the state are Kadaram and Kathah and archaeologists believe the site of the fifth-century kingdom of Langkasuka was just to the southeast of Kedah Peak (Gunung Jerai), in the Bujang River valley, halfway between Butterworth and Alor Star.

Sights

Alor Star has some interesting buildings, most of which are clustered round the central Padang Besar (Jalan Pekan Melayu/Jalan Raja); apart from them, the town is unremarkable. The most interesting building is the **State Mosque**, the Moorish-style Masjid Zahir, completed in 1912 and designed by state architect James Gorman. Almost directly opposite is the Thai-inspired **Balai Besar**, (audience hall), built in 1898, which is still used by the Sultan of Kedah on ceremonial occasions; it houses the royal throne. Close to the mosque is the **Balai Seni Negeri** (State Art Gallery) ① *daily 0900-1700, except Fri closed 1230-1430, free*, which contains a collection of historical paintings and antiques, including Malay handicrafts and colonial collections. The building was formerly the High Court and was built in the early 20th century. Further down Jalan Raja is the 400-year-old **Balai Nobat**, an octagonal building topped by an onion-shaped dome. This building houses Kedah's *nobat* (royal percussion orchestra); it is said to date back to the 15th century. It is not open to the public.

Royal Museum Kedah (Muzium Di Raja) ① *daily 0900-1700, except Fri closed 1230 1430, free*, is next to the Balai Besar and gives an insight into the heritage and traditions of the Sultans of Kedah.

The **State Museum** (Muzium Negeri) ① *daily 0900-1700, except Fri closed 1230 1430, free*, situated around 2 km north of the centre, is styled on the Balai Besar and was built in 1936. The museum houses exhibits on local farming and fishing practices, a collection of early Sung Dynasty porcelain and some finds from the archaeological excavations in the Bujang Valley (see below).

The **Pekan Rabu** (Wednesday market), which is now held all week long, is a good place to buy local handicrafts and try some of the traditional food of Kedah. It does not cater for tourists, and is therefore a good place to find local foods and see everyday Malay life.

Two other places of interest are the **Royal Boat House**, near the Sungai Anak Bukit, west of the clocktower. It houses boats belonging to former rulers of Kedah.

The house where former Prime Minister Dr Mahathir Mohamad was born on 20 December 1925, has been opened as a **museum** ① *18 Lorong Kilang Ais, off Jln Pegawai, daily 0900-1700, except Fri closed 1230-1430, free*, giving an insight into his early days of 'simple' living. Photographs and various items of Mahathir memorabilia including his 'favourite' bicycle are on display.

Menara Alor Star ① *99 Lebuhraya Darul Aman, T04-720 2234, www.menaraaalor star.com.my, daily 0900-2100, RM6, children RM3*, is a TV tower-cum-observation point. Standing at 165 m, it's the 19th tallest such tower in the world. Opened in 1997 by Matahir Mohamed, it's a good place for visitors to get their bearings. The views over the town's older buildings are good and it is usually possible to see Gunung Keriang and the Kedah river meandering its way to the Straits of Malacca. Base jumpers occasionally use the tower, taking around 18 seconds to reach the ground from a height of 105 m.

Bujang Valley

ⓘ *To get there, change buses at Bedong; it is easier to take a taxi from Alor Star.*

Situated near the small town of **Sungai Petani**, to the southeast of Kedah Peak (Gunung Jerai), is this site of some of Malaysia's most exciting archaeological discoveries; finds there have prompted the establishment of the **Bujang Valley Historical Park**, under the management of the National Museum. The name Bujang is derived from a Sanskrit word, *bhujanga*, meaning serpent. It is thought to be the site of the capital of the fifth-century Hindu kingdom of Langkas, the hearthstone of Malay fairytale romance. While the architectural remains are a far cry from those of Cambodia's Angkor Wat, they are of enormous historical significance.

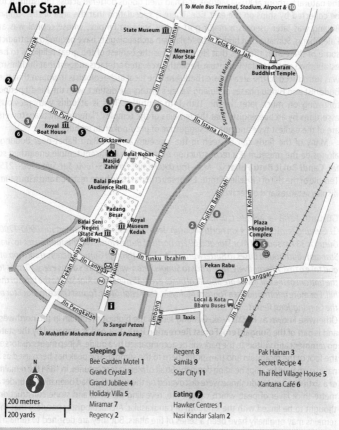

Alor Star

To Main Bus Terminal, Stadium, Airport & ⑩

State Museum 🏛

Menara Alor Star

Nikradharam Buddhist Temple

Jln Perak

Jln Lebuhraya Darulaman

Jln Telok Wan Jah

Sungei Alor Malai Malai

②

⑪

Jln Putra

① ③

① ④ ⑨

Jln Istana Lama

③

Royal Boat House

⑤

⑥

Clocktower

Balai Nobat

Masjid Zahir

Jln Raja

Balai Besar (Audience Hall)

Padang Besar

Jln Sultan Badlishah

Jln Kolam

Balai Seni Negeri (State Art Gallery) 🏛

Royal Museum Kedah 🏛

②

⑧

Plaza Shopping Complex

④ ⑤

@

Jln Pekan Melayu

Jln Langgar

Jln S A Halim

Jln Tunku Ibrahim

Pekan Rabu M

Jln Langgar

Jln Steyen

Jln Pengkalan

🏲

To Sungai Petani

To Mahathir Mohamad Museum & Penang

Limbong Kapal

Local & Kota Bharu Buses

Taxis

N

200 metres
200 yards

Sleeping 🛏
Bee Garden Motel **1**
Grand Crystal **3**
Grand Jubilee **4**
Holiday Villa **5**
Miramar **7**
Regency **2**

Regent **8**
Samila **9**
Star City **11**

Eating 🍴
Hawker Centres **1**
Nasi Kandar Salam **2**

Pak Hainan **3**
Secret Recipe **4**
Thai Red Village House **5**
Xantana Café **6**

The city is thought to represent one of the very earliest Hindu settlements in Southeast Asia, several centuries before Angkor, and at least 200 years before the founding of the first Hindu city in Java. The capital of Langkasuka is thought to have been abandoned in the 6th century, probably following a pirate raid. There have been some remarkable finds at the site, including brick and marble temple and palace complexes – of both Hindu and Buddhist origin – coins, statues, Sanskrit inscriptions, weapons and jewellery. In 1925 archaeologists stumbled across "a magnificent little granite temple near a beautiful waterfall" on a hillside above the ancient city. One of them, Dr Quarith Wales, the director of the Greater-India Research Committee wrote of the temple: "It had never been robbed, except of images, although the bronze trident of Shiva was found. In each of the stone post-holes were silver caskets containing rubies and sapphires." More than 50 temples have now been unearthed in the Bujang area, most of them buried in soft mud along the river bank.

For several centuries, Indian traders used the city as an entrepôt in their dealings with China. Rather than sail through the pirate-infested Melaka Strait, the traders stopped at the natural harbour at Kuala Merbok and had their goods portered across the isthmus to be collected by ships on the east side. There is speculation that the area of the Sungai Bujang was later used as a major port of the Srivijaya Empire, whose capital was at Palembang, Sumatra. But findings by Malaysian archaeologists have begun to contradict some of the earlier theories that Hinduism was the earliest of the great religions to be established on the Malay Peninsula. Recently excavated artefacts suggest that Buddhism was introduced to the area before Hinduism. The local archaeologists maintain that the Buddhist and Hindu phases of Bujang Valley's history are distinct, with the Hindu period following on much later, in the 10th-14th centuries. This is at odds with previous assertions by archaeologists that the remains of the temples' "laterite sanctuary towers are of the earliest type and not yet suggestive of pre-Angkorian architecture".

Many of the finds can be seen in the museum at Bukit Batu Pahat near Bedong; alongside the museum is a reconstruction of the most significant temple unearthed so far, **Candi Bukit Batu Pahat** ① *Mon-Thu 0900-1600, Fri 1445-1600, Sat-Sun 0900-1215*, Temple of the Hill of Chiselled Stone. Eight sanctuaries have been restored and a museum displays statues and other finds.

Gunung Jerai → *Altitude: 1206 m*

① *Gunung Jerai is about 4 km north of Garun. Jeeps from Gurun to the resort run 0900-1700. Gurun is 33 km south of Alor Star and 60 km north of Butterworth. Northbound buses to Alor Star and southbound buses to Butterworth will all pass through Gurun where you can hop off and take a taxi. Alternatively, take a bus to Sungei Petani where there's a bus every 30 mins to the bottom of the hill. There are also local buses every 45 mins from Alor Star to the base of the hill. For more information see Tourism Malaysia, the Kedah State Tourist Office in Alor Star or the Gunung Jerai Resort.*

Otherwise known as Kedah Peak, Gunung Jerai is the highest mountain in the northwest and is part of the **Sungai Teroi Forest Recreation Park**. This park is managed by the state government and visitors to the park will be accompanied by a guide. A jeep meets visitors at the foot of the mountain and transports them to the summit. The peak has been used as a navigational aid for ships heading down the Strait of Melaka for centuries. In 1884 the remains of a sixth-century Hindu shrine were discovered on the summit. It had been hidden under a metre-thick layer of peat, which caught fire, revealing the brick and stone construction, thought to be linked with the kingdom of Langkasuka. Archaeologists speculate that the remains may originally have been a series of fire altars. But they are destined to remain a mystery as a radio station has now been built on top. About 3 km north of Gurun, between Sungai Petani and Alor Star, a narrow road goes off to the left and leads to the top of the mountain (11 km). There is even a small hotel just below the summit and the Museum of Forestry on top. There are good views out over Kedah's paddy fields and the coast.

Kuala Kedah

Historically, this town has been an important port for trade with India and there are the ruins of an old fort, built between 1771 and 1780. The fort was built for defence of the state capital from pirate attacks. It fell into the hands of the Siamese army, under the leadership of Raja Ligor in 1821 and was occupied by Siam until 1842, after which it was abandoned. Kuala Kedah, 12 km W of Alor Star, is renowned for its seafood stalls. It is also a departure point for Langkawi (see page 174).

Kuala Perlis

This small fishing port, 14 km from Kangar, (the capital of the state of Perlis, the smallest in Malaysia) at the delta of the Sungai Perlis is mainly a jumping-off point for Pulau Langkawi and Phuket (in Thailand). It is noted for its local fast food, *laksa*, and there are foodstalls by the jetty. There is a night market every Tuesday.

● Alor Star and around listings

For Sleeping and Eating price codes and other relevant information, see Essentials pages 25-30.

● Sleeping

Alor Star *p167, map p169*

AL Holiday Villa, 162/163 Jln Tunku Ibrahim , Plaza shopping centre, T04-734 9999, www.holidayvillaalorstar.com. Large, luxury hotel in the centre of town. There's not a great deal of character about this Lego-block building, but it does have a great swathe of facilities including IDD telephone, in-house video, 24-hr restaurant, pool, jacuzzi, bowling alley, gym and massage.

AL The Regency, 134 Jln Sultan Badlishah, T04-733 5917, www.theregencyhotel.com.my. Formerly the Grand Continental, this place has been reborn with elegant contemporary design, comfortable rooms and a great location in the heart of the city.

A Grand Crystal, 40 Jln Kampong Perak, T04-731 3333, www.ghihotels.com.my. Popular with domestic business types, this place has a/c rooms with attached bathroom, a great Chinese restaurant and a pool. Good promotional rates offered.

A Star City, 88 Jln Pintu Sepuluh, T04-735 5888, www.starcity.com.my. New hotel that has comfortable modern rooms with Wi-Fi access, cable TV and choice of daily newspaper. Facilities are limited, but include a babysitting service and restaurant.

B Regent, 1536 Jln Sultan Badlishah, T04-731 1900, F731 1291. All 25 rooms have a/c and are good value for money. TV with cable channels and movies, bathrooms and bright, friendly atmosphere. Wi-Fi available in lobby. Recommended.

B Samila, 27 Jln Lebuhraya Darulaman, T04-731 8888. Friendly hotel, established in 1974 and still going strong. The heavy colouring of the decor gives the hotel a dated look, but rooms are functional and comfortable with a/c, cable TV and attached bathroom. Check that the windows in the room open, as some seem to be broken. Coffee shop downstairs with Wi-Fi access.

B Seri Malaysia, Mukim Alor Malai, Daerah Kota Setar, Jln Stadium, T04-730 8738, www.serimalaysia.com.my. A 100-room hotel, one of the 'amazingly affordable' chains, with a/c, TV, shower, tea/coffee-making facilities, in-house video and café. Clean, functional and good value, located between the stadium and public pool at north end of town.

B-C Bee Garden Motel, 2512 Kompleks Tunku Yaccob, Lebuhraya Darul Aman, T04-733 5355, beemotel@streamyx.com. Bounding ahead of all competition in the mid-range category is this new upstart with excellent promotional rates. Spacious, clean modern rooms with attached bath, cable TV and Wi-Fi access. Recommended.
C Grand Jubilee, 429 Jln Kancut, T04-733 0055, F733 0197. Clean and well managed, although staff are mirthless. It's worth paying a little more for an a/c room here, with hot-water bath. All rooms have cable TV and Wi-Fi. Very reasonable prices.
C Miramar, 246 Jln Putra, T04-733 8144, F731 1668. The modern exterior and lobby are somewhat at odds with the dated room design. Rooms on the ground floor are windowless, so ask for a room on the upper floors. All rooms are clean and have Wi-Fi, TV, a/c and attached bathroom. Fair value.

Bujang Valley *p169*
B Sungai Petani Inn, Jln Kolam Air, Sungai Petani, T04-421 3411. The plushest in town with a/c and pool.
B-D Duta, 7 Jln Petri. Best of the budget hotels.

Gunung Jerai *p170*
B Gunung Jerai Resort, T04-441 4311. 1920s resthouse, rooms and chalets, garden.
B Peranginan Gunung Jerai, Sungai Teroi Forest Recreation Park, T04-422 3345. A/c, restaurant, attached bathrooms with showers, slightly worn but reasonable.

Kuala Perlis *p171*
B Seaview, T04-985 2171. Across from the taxi rank with plain rooms and a coffee house if you miss the boat to Langkawi.

🍴 Eating

Alor Star *p167, map p169*
🍴🍴 **Secret Recipe**, Plaza Shopping Complex. This chain restaurant can occasionally be a saviour for those that can't face another local meal, and who can't deal with the guilt of a visit to the usual junk-food outlets. Fair pasta dishes, chicken Kiev, and cordon bleu and some Asian dishes.
🍴 **Nasi Kandar Salam**, Jln Perak (opposite Miramar Hotel). Simple standard Indian place with curries and rotis. Locals recommend the tandoori, which is tender and delicious.
🍴 **Pak Hainan**, Kompleks Tunku Yaacob (next to **Bee Garden Motel**, another branch in basement of Plaza shopping complex). Contemporary take on a traditional *kopitiam* with simple, good-value Chinese dishes including Hainan chicken rice. Clean, Wi-Fi access and fair range of coffees.
🍴 **Rose**, Jln Sultan Badishah. Local café serving good roti and *nasi*. Recommended.
🍴 **Sri Pumpong**, Jln Pumpong. Highly recommended by locals who flock here nightly for the barbecued fish.
🍴 **Thai Red Village House**, Jln Putra. Popular spot for Thai-style seafood and other Thai dishes.
🍴 **Xantana Café**, 57 Jln Kampung Perak. Good local fare, with claypots, half-boiled eggs and toast and loads of ice-cream sundaes.

Foodstalls
'Garden' Hawker Centre, Jln Stadium, for a good range of cuisines, next to stadium, Jln Langgar (in front of cinema); **Old Market** (*Pekan Rabu*), Jln Tunku Ibrahim. There is a street of hawker centres on the road turning east past the Grand Jubilee. They get packed in the evenings with predominantly Chinese customers waiting for a dinner of fresh seafood, satay and laksa. Popular centres include **May Hiang** and **Jai Huat Seafood**.

🛍 Shopping

Alor Star *p167, map p169*
An extensive shopping plaza can be found in the multi-storey building at the end of Jln Tunku Ibrahim (it also houses the **Holiday Villa Hotel**). Handicrafts can be found in the Old Market, Pekan Rabu, on Jln Tunku Ibrahim.

⊖ Transport

Alor Star *p167, map p169*
Air
The airport is 13 km north of town. Daily connections on MAS and AirAsia with **KL** and with **Firefly** to **Subang** and **Singapore**.
Airline offices AirAsia office at the airport; MAS office at the airport, T04-711 106.

Bus
The main bus terminal is 2 km north of the town centre, at Shahab Perdana, and all long-distance buses leave from here. Hop on a bus from Pekan Rabu (RM2) or take a taxi (RM10). Destinations include **KL** (6 hrs, RM39, every 2 hrs), **Melaka** (8 hrs, RM51), **Ipoh** (3 hrs, RM21.80), **JB** (10 hrs, RM69), **Kota Bharu** (6 hrs, RM35), **Kuantan**, **Butterworth** (every 45 mins) and **Kuala Terengganu**. Local southbound buses, including buses to **Kuala Kedah** (45 mins for **Langkawi**, RM1.50), leave from Pekan Rabu in the centre of town, as well as the express bus station.
International connections The northern section of the North-South Highway runs to the Malaysian border crossing at Bukit Kayu Hitam, from where it is easy to cross to **Sadao**. Most of the buses leave from Penang/Butterworth for **Bangkok** and other destinations on the Kra Isthmus. To get to the border it is necessary to take a local bus from Shahab Perdana to Changlun and from there a taxi following the North-South Highway from Changlun to **Bukit Kayu Hitam**. It is then a shortish walk past the paraphernalia of the border to the bus and taxi stop where there are connections with the Thai town of **Sadao** (a few kilometres on) and **Hat Yai**. A less popular alternative is to travel to **Padang Besar** (accessible from Kangar in Perlis), where the railway line crosses the border. From here it is an easy walk to the bus or train station for connections to **Hat Yai**. The other option is to take a taxi from Sungai Petani to **Keroh** and cross the border into Thailand's red-light outpost at **Betong**. There are also bus connections with **Singapore** from the main long-distance terminal at Shahab Perdana.

Taxi
These leave from the stand just south of Jln Langgar, near the town centre, for **Penang**, **Kuala Kedah** (for **Langkawi**) and **Kangar** (**Perlis**).

Train
The station is off Jln Langgar. There is one train a day at 1807 to **KL** and **Butterworth**. There are 2 express trains to **Hat Yai** daily at 0748 and 1633. The 1633 train continues on to Hualamphong Station in **Bangkok**.

Kuala Kedah *p171*
Bus
Buses leave at least every hour from **Alor Star** to Kuala Kedah (RM1.50, 45 mins). For long-distance bus connections, change at Alor Star.

Boat
Regular connections with **Langkawi**. The ferry leaves at least every hour between 0700 and 1900, 1hr 45 mins, RM23, children RM17.

Kuala Perlis *p171*
Bus and taxi
Both leave from the ferry terminal. Regular connections by bus and taxi with **Butterworth**, less regular links with **Alor Star**, **KL** (around every 2 hrs, 0900-2200), **Kota Bharu** (0800 and 1945) and **Padang Besar** (for connections with Thailand see below) and local buses to **Kangar**. High-speed ferry departs from Kuala Perlis jetty approximately every hour 0700-1900 to **Pulau Langkawi**, 1hr 15 mins, RM18 (children RM13). Last ferry back to Kuala Perlis leaves around 1900.

⊙ Directory

Alor Star *p167, map p169*
Banks Bank Bumiputra, Jln Tunku Ibrahim; Chartered Bank, Overseas Union Bank and UMBC are all on Jln Raja. **Internet** There are cafés in the Plaza shopping centre at the end of Jln Tunku Ibrahim. **Post office** GPO, Jln Langgar, opposite the police station.

Pulau Langkawi

→ *Colour map 1, A1.*

The Langkawi group is an archipelago of 99 islands around 30 km off the west coast of Peninsular Malaysia, and Pulau Langkawi itself, by far the largest of the group, is a mountainous, palm-fringed island with scattered fishing kampongs, paddy fields and sandy coves. Some of the islands are nothing more than deserted limestone outcrops rearing out of the turquoise sea, cloaked in jungle, and ringed by coral.

The name Langkawi is the last surviving namesake of the ancient kingdom of Langkasuka, known as negari alang-kah suka, or 'the land of all one's wishes'. Langkasuka, whose capital is thought to have stood at the base of Kedah Peak, south of Alor Star, is mentioned in Chinese accounts as far back as AD 500. According to a Chinese Liang Dynasty record, the kingdom of 'Langgasu' was founded in the first century and its Hindu king, Bhagadatta, paid tribute to the Chinese Emperor. The names of its kings – known as daprenta-hyangs – resurface in Malay legends and fairytales.

The main settlement of locals is in the dusty town of Kuah, while upmarket resorts are at Pantai Cenang, Pantai Tengah, Burau Bay, Datai Bay and Pantai Rhu. Pantai Cenang and Tengah also have a smattering of cheaper guesthouses. ▸▸ *For listings, see pages 179-188.*

The main island

Getting there

Langkawi's **airport** ① *T04-955 1311*, is 20 km from Kuah (the main town and location of the jetty). It has regular connections with KL, and Penang. There are also flights direct from Bangkok and Singapore. Ferries from Kuala Perlis and Kuala Kedah leave roughly every hour to Langkawi and there are two daily departures from Penang by sea and three daily departures to Satun in Thailand. ▸▸ *See also Transport, page 187.*

Getting around

Taxis offer reasonably priced travel around the island (prices are fixed according to the distance). Cars, motorcycles and bicycles are available for hire. Boats are also available for hire to explore the neighbouring islands.

Best time to visit

Langkawi's wet season usually runs between April to October. The water clarity is poor between July and September, the months of the monsoon, and the sea can be rough.

Tourist information

Langkawi Tourist Information Centre ① *Jln Pesiaran Putra, Kuah, T04-966 7789, F966 7889, daily 0900-1300 and 1400-1700.* The monthly magazine, *Senses of Langkawi*, which you can pick up from hotels and touristy restaurants, has some articles on Langkawi life and some ideas of things to do and where to eat on the island. The privately run www.langkawi-online.com and www.best-of-langkawi.com websites have some good information.

Background

In January 1987 the Malaysian government conferred duty-free status on Langkawi to promote tourism on the island. The promotion campaign and improved transport links to the mainland means the islands can no longer be touted as 'Malaysia's best-kept secret'. New hotels, shopping centres and restaurants have sprouted with typical Southeast Asian speed and, for some former visitors at least, the Langkawi of old is just a memory. But development has been concentrated in a handful of places, so much of the island remains relatively unspoilt. Budget accommodation is still available and the construction of upmarket hotels and resorts means that a broader spectrum of tourists is being attracted.

Kuah
The main town is strung out along the seafront and is the landing point for ferries from Satun (Thailand), Kuala Perlis, Kuala Kedah and Penang. The jetty is 2 km from Kuah itself. The town is growing fast and developers have reclaimed land along the shoreline to cope with the expansion. There is a rather stark park area overlooked by a giant effigy of an eagle on Dataran Lang (Eagle Square), symbol of the island's flight to prosperity. The park area itself, Chogm Park, was built to commemorate the Commonwealth Heads of Government Meeting (CHOGM) in 1989. The old part of Kuah has several restaurants, a few grotty hotels, banks, plenty of coffee shops and a string of duty-free shops, which do a roaring trade in cheap liquor, cigarettes and electronics. There is also an attractive mosque.

The town's name Kuah (gravy) is said to derive from a legend about a fight that broke out between two families who fell out over the breaking of a betrothal. Kitchen pots and

Pulau Langkawi

Chinchin Straits

Datai Bay

Ibrahim Hussein Museum

Crocodile Adventureland Langkawi

Gunung Mat Chinchang

Cable Car

Telaga Tujuh

Burau Bay

Teluk Nibong

Kuala Muda

Beras Terbakar

Padang Matsirat

Makam Purba

Makam Mahsuri

Pantai Kok

Kampong Kuala Teriang

Pulau Rebak Besar

Muzium Laman Padi

Kedawang

Bukit Malut

Underwater World

Pulau Rebak Kecil

Pantai Cenang

Pulau Tepor

Pantai Tengah

Pulau Kentut Kecil

Pulau Kentut Besar

Pulau Beras Besar

Gua Langsir

Lake of Pregnant Maiden

Pulau Singa Besar

Pulau Dayang Bunting

Melaka Straits

Pulau Gasing

Gua Cerita

Pantai Rhu

Pulau Jemurok

Pulau Dangli

Teluk Ewa

Pasir Hitam

Pulau Pasir

Pulau Tanjung Tembus

Pulau Langgun

Padang Lalang

Telaga Air Hangat

Langkawi Bird Paradise

Galeria Perdana

Durian Perangin

Gunung Raya (911m)

Belanga Pecah

Pantai Syed Omar

Kuah

Jetty

Pulau Timun

Pulau Chorong

Pulau Bunbun Besar

Pulau Bunbun

Pulau Tuba

Pulau Paku

To Kuala Perlis

To Kuala Kedah, Penang & Pulau Payar

N

3 km

3 miles

pans were thrown around and a cooking pot smashed on to Belanga Pecah (broken pot); its contents splashed all over Kuah. A saucepan of boiling water landed at Telaga Air Hangat (the motley hot springs on the north of the island).

Makam Mahsuri
ⓘ *0800-1700, RM2.*

The road west to the golf course goes to Makam Mahsuri, the tomb of the legendary Princess Mahsuri, in the village of Mawat 12 km from Kuah. The beautiful Mahsuri was condemned to death for alleged adultery in 1355. She protested her innocence and several attempts to execute her failed. According to the legend, the sentence was finally carried out using her own *tombak* (lance) and her severed head bled white blood, thus confirming her innocence. Before Mahsuri died she cursed the island, saying it would remain barren for seven generations. Shortly afterwards, the Thais attacked, killing, plundering, looting and razing all the settlements to the ground. At the time of the Thai attacks, villagers buried their entire rice harvest on Padang Matsirat in Kampong Raja, but the Thais found it and set fire to it too, giving rise to the name Beras Terbakar (field of burnt rice) nearby. The legend is far more interesting than the field, which is just a field.

Pantai Cenang
Southwest of Mahsuri's tomb, past some beautiful paddy fields and coconut groves, are the two main beaches, Pantai Cenang and Pantai Tengah. Pantai Cenang is a strip about 2 km long, with accommodation that runs the gamut from budget through mid-range chalet operations to a couple of more upmarket resorts. It is also possible to hire boats to the islands off Pantai Cenang from the beach.

Note The sea at Pantai Cenang and Pantai Tengah will come as a disappointment to those who have experienced the Thai islands to the north and the beaches on Malaysia's east coast. Unfortunately, plastic and rubbish from tour boats and larger vessels has dirtied the sea, which can be a little murky anyway. It is best to swim at high tide rather than low tide. Zackry (see page 182) has a weekly tide chart posted at reception.

Pantai Cenang also has water sport facilities and the **Langkawi Underwater World** ⓘ *T04-955 6100, www.undeterworldlangkawi.com.my, daily 1000-1800, RM38, children RM28,* one of the largest aquariums in Asia, stocked with more than 100 tanks and over 5000 types of marine life. The highlight of the aquarium is the 15 m-long walkthrough tunnel tank. One part features rockhopper and blackfooted penguins and harbour seals.

Just north of Pantai Cenang the **Muzium Laman Padi** (rice museum garden) ⓘ *T04-955 4312, www.langkawigeopark.com.my, 1000-1800, free,* has a gallery explaining all the stages of rice farming, a multi-tiered rooftop rice garden, ducks and buffalo. There is an 8.6 acre paddy field, where visitors can have a wander and a herb garden where guides offer informative tours describing medicinal uses of the herbs. Of course, you can also taste cooked rice at their restaurants, Café d'Padi and Laman Ria. There's also a spa on site.

Pantai Tengah
Most of the beach development is along the 3 km stretch of coast from Pantai Cenang to Pantai Tengah, which is at the far southern end, around a small promontory. Pantai Tengah is less developed and quieter and has a more relaxed feel than Pantai Cenang. Also, visitors here do not have to put up with the bothersome sounds of jet skis with such frequency. Beaches can get crowded at weekends and during school and public holidays.

Pantai Kok and Burau Bay

The road west leads past the airport to Pantai Kok, once a magnificent unspoilt bay with a dramatic backdrop of the forested Gunung Mat Chinchang. The area is now spotted with upmarket resorts and a fancy marina. Ever proud of their Hollywood connections, irrespective of whether it offended their neighbour Thailand or not, Malaysia has recreated part of the set of *Anna and the King* at **Pantai Kok** ① *daily 1000-1900, RM3.50, children RM2*. Much of the movie was filmed here and on the mainland, as Thailand, who found the story offensive to the memory of its royal family, refused to have anything to do with it. However, as just some wooden huts filled with props and costumes, it's of little interest except to hardened fans of the movie.

Pantai Cenang & Pantai Tengah

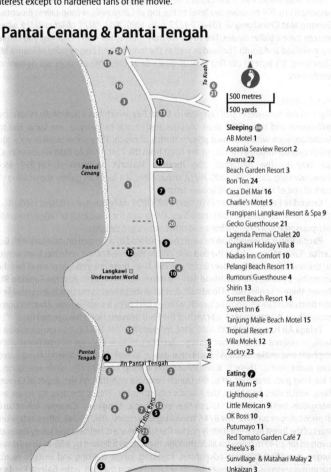

500 metres
500 yards

Sleeping
AB Motel **1**
Aseania Seaview Resort **2**
Awana **22**
Beach Garden Resort **3**
Bon Ton **24**
Casa Del Mar **16**
Charlie's Motel **5**
Frangipani Langkawi Resort & Spa **9**
Gecko Guesthouse **21**
Lagenda Permai Chalet **20**
Langkawi Holiday Villa **8**
Nadias Inn Comfort **10**
Pelangi Beach Resort **11**
Rumours Guesthouse **4**
Shirin **13**
Sunset Beach Resort **14**
Sweet Inn **6**
Tanjung Malie Beach Motel **15**
Tropical Resort **7**
Villa Molek **12**
Zackry **23**

Eating
Fat Mum **5**
Lighthouse **4**
Little Mexican **9**
OK Boss **10**
Putumayo **11**
Red Tomato Garden Café **7**
Sheela's **8**
Sunvillage & Matahari Malay **2**
Unkaizan **3**
Yellow Café **12**

There are several isolated beaches along the bay, accessible by boat from either Pantai Kok itself, Pantai Cenang (12 km away) or Kampong Kuala Teriang, a small fishing village en route. On the west headland, the **Telaga Tujuh** waterfalls used to be the island's so-called 'most wonderful natural attraction'. It can no longer claim to be that, as the area has been bought by Berjaya Leisure Berhad, 'mother' of the Berjaya Hotels Group. A pipeline running next to the pools, and the waterfall, goes all the way to the Berjaya Langkawi Beach Resort on nearby Burau Bay, reducing the falls to a trickle in dry season and a modest cascade in wet. The falls run down the steep hillside, between huge rocks and through seven (*tujuh*) pools (*telaga*); so much for development.

Also near Burau Bay is Langkawi's newest attraction, a cable-car station that jerks passengers to 709 m above sea level to the top of Langkawi's second tallest mountain, **Gunung Mat Chinchang** ① *T04-959 4225, daily 1000-2000, RM25, children RM10*, where you can have a buffet dinner. The views are truly spectacular – on a clear day you can see the mainland and South Thailand as well as the forested and craggy sides of Mount Mat Chinchang. It's best to call first to arrange a ride as the cable car does not operate on windy days.

North coast

Right on the northwest tip of Langkawi is **Datai Bay**, which has a beautifully landscaped golf course and two of the most sophisticated resorts in Malaysia: the Datai and the Andaman, each with their own private stretch of beach. They are accessible via a road which cuts up through the hills to the coast from the Pantai Kok to Pasir Hitam road. On the way to the Andaman, the **Ibrahim Hussein Museum** ① *T04-959 4669, www.ihmcf.org, daily 0900-1800, RM12, children free*, is a funky art gallery showcasing the work of one of Malaysia's well known artists.

Crocodile Farm ① *T04-959 2559, daily 0900-1800, daily shows at 1100 and 1500, RM15, children RM5*, houses over 1000 crocodiles. Along with the usual array of caged crocodilia, this gruesome place has pythons and other shows and delights.

Pantai Rhu is a beautiful white sand cove, enclosed by a jungled promontory with **Gua Cerita**, (Cave of Legends), at the end of it. Within the cave, Koranic verse has been written on the walls. Beneath the sheer limestone cliff faces there are a couple of small beaches accessible by boat. The Thai island Koh Turatao is just 4 km north. Past the **Tanjung Rhu Resort**, there is a collection of foodstalls and small shops next to the beach. It is possible to hire boats and canoes from the beach, which is backed by a small lagoon. Another sign of encroaching development – a branch of the **Four Seasons Hotel** has opened here.

Telaga Air Hangat ① *0900-1800, RM4, children RM2, T04-959 1357*, 14 km northwest of Kuah, is centred on some hot springs. Activities include displays of traditional crafts, elephant and snake 'displays', traditional dance, as well as an 18 m-long, hand-carved river stone mural. There is a restaurant and a shop here. At the ninth milestone, a 3 km-long path branches off to the Durian Perangin waterfall, on the slopes of Gunung Raya, which rises to 911 m, the island's tallest mount. This is the area for forest and mangrove trekking. For a tarzan-like experience, **Langkawi Canopy Adventures** ① *phone Jurgen on T012-484 8744, www.langkawi.travel/, RM210-240*, offers airtrekking tours of the forest here – definitely not for the faint-hearted. Helmets and safety ropes are involved for a 140 m flying fox slide through the canopy followed by a 30-m abseil down. Jurgen also offers triathlon adventures, kayaking, jungle trekking and visits to nearby mangrove swamps. Not far away, on the seaward side of the road, is the **Galeria Perdana** ① *T04-959 1498, Tue-Sat 1000-1700, RM10, children RM5. Extra charges for camera and* *video camera*, which houses around 2500 gifts given to long-serving former Prime Minister Dr Mahathir Mohamad. Just past this is Taman Burung, **Langkawi Bird Paradise** ⓘ *T04-966 5855, daily 0900-1800, RM12, children RM6*, housing 150 feathered species. It has a covered walkway, peacocks, a flamingo pond, and the Macaw Courtyard. Kids will love the well-trained cockatoos and mynah birds.

Neighbouring islands

Pulau Dayang Bunting
ⓘ *Boat trips are organized to Pulau Dayang Bunting by many of the larger hotels and travel agents, or boats can be chartered privately from Pantai Cenang. Most trips also include a chance to snorkel off Pantai Singa Besar.*

This island, whose name means 'Island of the Pregnant Maiden', is the second largest island in the archipelago, and lies just south of Langkawi. Separated from the sea by only a few metres of limestone is a freshwater lake renowned for its powers to enhance the fertility of women; unfortunately it is also said to be inhabited by a big white crocodile, although most people swim there unmolested. The myth surrounding this lake involves a beautiful girl named Telani, who became pregnant by the king's son. This indiscretion so angered the god Sang Kelembai that he brought a drought upon the land and turned the newborn baby into a white crocodile. Telani was turned into a rock and the king's son was transformed into an island. To the north of the lake is the intriguingly named **Gua Langsir** (Cave of the Banshee). The cave is high on a limestone cliff and is home to a large population of bats. Other nearby islands include Pulau Bunbun, Pulau Beras Besar and Pulau Singa Besar; there is some coral between the last two.

Pulau Payar
ⓘ *Several hotels and companies run day trips to Pulau Payar. These islands are also within reach of Kuala Kedah, on the mainland and Pulau Penang.*

This tiny island, 2 km long and 250 m wide, about 45 minutes southeast of Langkawi, is part of a marine park. The other islands are **Segantan**, **Kala** and **Lembu**. A reef platform has been built with an underwater observation chamber and diving facilities, see Activities and tours, page 187. There is also a bar and restaurant and a souvenir shop. There are basic facilities on the island for day visitors, but those intending to camp on the island require permission; see page 183.

⦿ Pulau Langkawi listings

For Sleeping and Eating price codes and other relevant information, see Essentials pages 25-30.

● Sleeping
Langkawi is no longer a haven for backpackers, although there some budget places in Pantai Cenang and Pantai Tengah. There are far more mid- and upper-range places to stay, although prices are a little higher than elsewhere in Malaysia. The island is particularly popular during Nov-Feb and

during school holidays. Outside these periods, room rates are often reduced.

Most hotels in Kuah itself are rather seedy and poor value for money. Tourists are advised to head straight for the beach resorts.

Kuah *p175*
L Westin Langkawi Resort & Spa, Jln Pantai Dato' Syed Omar, T04-960 8888, www.sheraton.com. With a/c, restaurant and pool. Formerly the Langkawi Island Resort. Has

its own private beach with water sports facilities, and all the comforts you would expect of a **Sheraton**.

A Beringin Beach Resort, round the corner from the **Sheraton Perdana**, T04-966 6966, F04-966 7970. A/c, restaurant, own private beach. Recommended.

A-B City Bayview, Jln Pandak Mayah, T04- 966 1818, www.bayviewhotels.com. In a block dominating Kuah town, are 280 rooms with 4-star facilities, including a pool and health centre. There are also 2 restaurants (Chinese and coffee house); breakfast included. Central location.

A-C Asia, 3A-4A Jln Persiaran Putra, T04-966 6216, F04-966 6216. With a/c. Reasonable place with attached bathrooms as well as some dorm beds. 15 mins' walk from the jetty. Clean and quiet in a good location. Recommended.

Pantai Cenang *p176, map p177*
The most popular of the 3 main beaches, with plenty of hotels and chalets to choose from; some are cramped a little too closely together. Despite the development, it is a picturesque beach.

L-AL Bon Ton, T04-955 1688, www.bonton resort.com.my. Langkawi's "something different". Australian owner Narelle has rebuilt 5 100-year-old Malay houses, largely using the original woodwork and stocked them with Indonesian furniture and modern facilities including hot showers, fridge and kettle (TV on request). The homes are comfortable, although they do let in a lot of the wildlife as the windows are glass free. Animal lovers will be especially happy as Narelle also runs an animal shelter and lazy cat residents drape themselves around the resort. Pool, jacuzzi, fantastic fusion restaurant and Chinese bar. The resort has its own mini-guide to Langkawi and staff are very helpful. Although it doesn't face the beach, the reedy lake makes a romantic setting at sunset. Unbeatable for its atmosphere. Voted one of the world's top 101 by *Tatler* in 2009. Highly recommended.

L-AL Casa del Mar, T04-955 2388, www.casa delmar-langkawi.com. One of the best resorts on this stretch of the beach with its strong earthy Mexican hacienda overtones, this place has 27 elegant rooms with nice touches such as DVD player, cold milk in the fridge and separate bath and shower. All rooms have a sea view. The hotel sits astride the beach making it a great place for a sunset cocktail. The resort has a RM1700 royal suite – owned by the Sultan, and only rented out with his permission – complete with a dress-up room and private jacuzzi.

AL Pelangi Beach Resort, T04-952 8888, www.pelangibeachresort.com. This large 5-star resort is styled as a posh Malay village houses and is run by the Meritus group. The Malay theme continues in the rooms which are raised on stilts and command good views. Decor in the rooms varies greatly, but all are very modern, some with pastels and some decorated with more hearty and local woody colours. Rooms are all a/c, cable TV and large veranda. Guests and their baggage are whisked around in electric cars, holiday camp atmosphere, with daily activities. Buffet breakfast included in the price.

A Beach Garden Resort, T04-955 1363, www.beachgardenresort.com. German-owned resort with Malay overtones evident in the rattan furnished rooms with their thatched roofs. Each of the 12 rooms is very comfortable, has marble floor tiling and a/c, There's a small pool and beachside restaurant (with Swiss chef), designed to resemble a Bavarian breakfast room (although the Balinese masks on the walls throw this idea into some chaos). Apart from the **Casa del Mar** and **Pelangi** this is the best hotel along this stretch and certainly the best value for those who are looking for a little character and intimacy. Highly recommended.

A-B AB Motel, T04-955 5278, abmotel@ hotmail.com. Clean a/c rooms with attached bathroom (hot water in more expensive rooms), some right on the beach. Cheaper rooms are on the other side of the road and are charmless. Organizes island hopping and sightseeing tours. Restaurant, internet and car and motorbike hire available.

A-B Nadias Inn Comfort, T04-955 1401, www.nadiasinn.com.my. Clean place with 96 large and characterless rooms mainly patronised by Malay visitors. Rooms are painted in garish pinks and lime greens and are overpriced, given their simplicity. Pool, restaurant and karaoke lounge. No alcohol on site. Local buffet breakfast included.

B Lagenda Permai Chalet, Lot 2014, Jln Pantai Cenang, T04-955 3007, lagenda permai.tripod.com/lagenda1.html. Family-run operation with rows of prim little Malay chalets set back from the beach but in pleasant plots, some with a/c, TV and fridge. Floors are a little bouncy and have light blue carpets. Very clean. Friendly, helpful owners.

B Langkawi Beach Resort, T04-955 7778, www.langkawiholidayresort.com. 3-star hotel lacking the boutique touch and with a frighteningly quiet and cavernous lobby, spookily lit up at night. Rooms are fairly plush and well-equipped rooms with TV, minifridge and are set in a compound facing the pool, set back from the beach.

B Sweet Inn, Lot 792, off Jln Pantai Cenang away from the beach, 100 m down a side road and next to Gecko Guesthouse, T012-493 9718, www.sweetinn.net. This is a great new hotel, offering the best value for money in the mid-range bracket. Rooms are set in an orange concrete block and are simple and clean. All feature TV, minifridge, attached bathroom and Wi-Fi. The downside is its distance from the beach. Recommended.

C Shirin, T04-955 5991. Run by Hiroko and her Malay husband, this cheery place attracts a lot of Japanese tourists and takes the overspill from the Gecko. The brightly coloured a/c chalets in the garden are a good deal. Some fan chalets available too.

C-D Gecko Guesthouse, tucked away up a lane on the other side of the main road to the beach, T019-428 3801. Well-decorated rooms, albeit simple with wooden floors and attached cold-water showers. Good bar, super relaxed atmosphere, movies and all the

regular traveller accessories. This place is prime backpacker territory and is often swarming with people. Can get a bit noisy in the evenings as people take advantage of the cheap booze. The monkeys chained up behind the reception are a bit of a turn-off.

D Rumours Guesthouse, 50 m up a signed path on the other side of the road opposite Underwater World, T017-487 4199. Small but growing new guesthouse offering a few rooms with attached bathroom and a/c. The real steal here are the 2 fan rooms on the 2nd floor of the family house. Tasteful and cheap and with wonderful views of grazing buffalo, padi fields and the hills beyond – a truly Southeast Asian vision.

Pantai Tengah *p176, map p177*
Those seeking a bit of peace and quiet will prefer staying here to Pantai Cenang.

AL Villa Molek, 734 Jln Tasik Anak, T04-9552995, www.villamolek.com. Delightful new place, slightly hindered by lack of sea views, but with gorgeous views of surrounding hills. 12 well-designed villas with balcony, TV and tasteful furnishings. Small pool, and a café serving good breakfasts. Breakfast included. Under 18s are not allowed to stay here.

A Awana Porto Malai, T04-955 5111, www.awana.com.my. Right next to the Star Cruise terminal on the headland. Fantastic views of the bay and islands. 208 spacious 4-star rooms, many with good views although a bit heavy on the pine furniture. Very popular with Chinese tourists. Good online discounts.

A Frangipani Langkawi Resort & Spa, Jln Teluk Baru, T04-952 0000, www.frangipani langkawi.com. A self-styled 'green resort' implementing over 100 environmentally friendly practices with 100 Malay-style bungalows with sea views and stylish, contemporary design. All rooms are a/c, and have bath and shower, cable TV, fridge and private terrace or balcony. Tennis and a pool.

A Langkawi Holiday Villa, T04-955 1701, www.holidayvillalangkawi.com. Huge resort with over 250 rooms, 2 pools, tennis, squash restaurants and all the amenities you would expect of a first-class resort. Not overly charming, and for this price, visitors can find a lot more interesting places to stay.

A Sunset Beach Resort, T/F04-955 1751, www.sunvillage.com.my. Beautiful setting – romantic and sumptuous chalets filled with Balinese furniture and frangipani flowers scattered about the gardens. Large, clean bathrooms. Honeymoon suites available. Stunning. Highly recommended.

B Aseania Seaview Resort, Jln Pantai Tengah, T04-955 2020, F955 2115. This large pink and white building resembles a strawberry gateau, but with a pool complete with waterfalls it is a good option for those looking to relax. Rooms with TV, a/c, shower and fridge. 2 restaurants and a business centre. Water sports organized and bikes can be hired. Breakfast included.

B Tropical Resort, Jln Teluk Baru, T04-955 4975. Owned by the charming Laila from Germany and her local husband, this popular place is quiet, relaxed and lowkey. Rooms are spacious and clean and just a short walk away from a quiet stretch of beach. Recommended.

B-C Charlie's Motel, T04-955 1200, F955 1316. A/c and fan, restaurant, chalets, at the end of Pantai Tengah. Good location but expensive for tacky huts – walls peeling, grubby carpet. Not the best budget option, but bang on a fair stretch of sand. Mostly used by domestic visitors at the weekend.

B-C Tanjung Malie Beach Motel, T04-955 1891. Clean a/c rooms, some with TV, in blocks, some right on the beach. This isn't the most exciting place to stay, but is only a leap from the sea. The cheapest huts have seen their best and are worth avoiding. Prices here are a little high for what you get.

C-D Zackry, right at the south end of Pantai Tengah, T04-955 7595, zackryghouse@gmail.com. Another spot swarming with backpackers. It only accepts online bookings for a minimum of 2 nights. Rooms are a jumbled assortment of a/c and fan, some with attached bathroom. Runs on a unique trust system, with payment for beers and internet done by guests at the end of their stay. Great communal bar area, and a communal kitchen. It's across the road from the beach. There are 3 dogs wandering around so anyone with a phobia will not feel comfortable here. Free bicycle rental. Recommended.

Pantai Kok and Burau Bay *p177*
Having once been the most popular place for those on a lower budget to stay, this area now has a number of exclusive resorts and a few top-class hotels as well as **Telaga Harbour Park Marina** with a clocktower, shops and restaurants.

Most resorts that did spring up at Kuala Muda have now closed, probably due to the rather disappointing beach, which does not offer any of the more spectacular views than can be found in other areas of the island. The area is close to the airport.

AL Berjaya Langkawi Beach Resort, Burau Bay, T04-959 1888, www.berjayaresorts.com.my. Malaysian-style chalets spread over 170 ha of tropical rainforest, some on stilts over water, some on jungled hillside, all serviced by minibuses. Each chalet has a/c, TV, cable TV, in-house movies, minibar, balcony, massage shower and is comfortably furnished with oriental carpets and traditional furniture. Superb facilities include pool, jacuzzi, Japanese restaurant, tennis, water sports, daily organized activities, white sand beach, beach restaurant, Chinese restaurant and good-value buffet served in Dayang café, inside vast main lobby overlooking sea. Surprisingly, this 400-room resort manages to feel friendly and not impersonal. Recommended.

AL Sheraton Beach Resort, Teluk Nibong, T04-955 1901, www.sheraton.com. Pool overlooking the islands, restaurants, children's centre, health club and spa, water sports, rooms arranged in individual Malay- style chalets serviced by resort bus. Total of 6 lounges and bars to choose from. Beautiful hotel, but its beach is a disappointment.

A Mutiara Burau Bay, Jln Teluk Burau, T04-959 1061, www.mutiarahotels.com. A/c, restaurant, at the far end of Pantai Kok, with

Gunung Mat Chinchang behind it, away from other chalets. A fun hotel good for families with a pool, children's play area and forest or beach horse riding. Its **Seashell Beach Café** has won an entertainment award. Recommended.
B Langkasuka Resort, Kauala Muda, T04-955 6888, www.langkasukabeachresort langkawi.com. Large hotel with 214 rooms aimed primarily at Japanese and Korean tourists. Rooms with a/c, shower, TV. Pool and several restaurants, but little else to offer. The bay has a great view of Thailand's Koh Turatao and other islands and arguably the best stretch of beach on Langkawi.

North coast p178
L Andaman, Datai Bay, T04-959 1088, www.theandaman.com. Luxury resort with its own stretch of beach, spa and beautiful pool set among mature trees. Very friendly and helpful staff. Resident naturalist takes guests on nature walks and jungle treks. Great Malay restaurant in Kampong-style house.
L Datai, Datai Bay, T04-959 2500, www.ghm hotels.com. 2 pools, health club, 40 individual 'villas' each with private sunbathing terrace, spacious marble bathroom, a/c, bar, minimalist decor offset by Jim Thompson silks from Bangkok, connected by walkways set in 400 ha of primary jungle where hornbills and flying squirrels roam. There are a further 60 large rooms, designed with panache, with sitting areas and cool wooden floors, own balcony with jungle (and some sea) views, private beach, fine white sand, a wealth of water sports, restaurants (see page 185). 18-hole golf course adjacent, attractive, very luxurious resort. Recommended.
L Tanjung Rhu Resort, Mukim Air Hangat, T04-959 1033, www.tanjungrhu.com.my. Exquisitely laid-out resort of only 100 rooms with understated decor. It's all beautifully presented, with dining on the beach and luxurious facilities; a honeymooners' paradise.

Neighbouring islands p179
L-AL Rebak Marina Resort, T04-966 5566, www.rebakmarina.com. On Pulau Rebak

Besar, the island just opposite Pantai Cenang. 150 chalets, and 200-berth marina.
B-E Sunrise Beach Homestay, Pulau Tuba (the island opposite Kuah), T04-966 9264. Wooden chalets along Pasir Panjang beach, a stretch of secluded sands on Tuba Island. Tents for 2 also available with kitchen facilities. Call to arrange transport from Kuah jetty. Quite isolated.
E Camping, Pulau Payar. Permission is required from of the Fisheries Management and Protection Office, Wisma Tani, Jln Mahameru, KL, T04-298 2011, or Wisma Persekutuan, Jln Kampong Baru, Alor Star, T04-725 573.

❶ Eating

Langkawi's speciality is *mee gulong* – fried noodles cooked with shredded prawns, slices of beef, chicken, carrots, cauliflower rolled into a pancake and served with a thick potato gravy. Langkawi is also known for its Thai cuisine. Being close to the border, Thai influences even creep into the Malay dishes with the use of hot and spicy ingredients.

Virtually all of the beach hotels have their own restaurants, some of which are excellent; seafood is an obvious choice on Langkawi.

Kuah p175
While Kuah is not much to look at, it does have some great Chinese seafood restaurants along the main street, all quite reasonable value for money.
♯♯ Sari Village, Kompleks Pasar Lama, T04-966 751. Built out on stilts over the sea – which is now being reclaimed – with a vast selection of seafood. Beautifully designed restaurant with good views over bay and surrounding islands. Owned by globetrotting architect and landscape architect Ridzuan Aziz. Menu influenced by Pakistani cuisine. Specialities include vegetable curry and fish tandoori. Recommended.
♯ Naga Emas, 31 Pusat Bandar, Jln Pandak Mayah. Thai seafood and steamboat.

Prawn Village, Jln Persiaran Putra (near Asia Hotel). Good seafood. Large open restaurant where diners can play God and choose their own fish for the chop-and-wok.

Sangkar Ikan, Jln Pantai Penarak. Seafood restaurant and fish farm where you can hire rods and catch fish for your own dinner.

Pantai Cenang p176, map p177

Though there is an excellent selection of international food on offer in Pantai Cenang, it's also worth trying out some of the smaller foodstalls, which offer excellent seafood and cheap *nasi lemak* breakfasts.

Nam, inside the **Bon Ton Resort** just north of Pantai Cenang. Beautiful restaurant overlooking a lake, serving fusion food, tapas and meze and a fabulous Nonya platter. Try the seared garoupa and prawns, with a spring onion rice cake, spinach and ginger lime *ponzu* sauce. Fantastic. Highly recommended.

Putumayo, Lot 1584, Jln Pantai Cenang, T04-955 2233. Open for lunch and dinner. Sophisticated fusion menu, heavy on seafood, in a stylish and elegant setting sadly located on the side of the road away from the beach. The lobster and scallop dishes are divine, as is the fare on the lengthy wine list. Highly recommended.

The Dining Room at the Casa del Mar, and the **Beach Garden** next door, offer a good international selection, beautifully prepared. The latter is right on the beach and is highly recommended. The Casa del Mar has the La Luna package for RM500 per head and limited to 2 bookings a night – degustation menu, fine wines, and 100 garden candles on the beach. Worth a splash if you want to impress a special person.

Little Mexican, Lot 22, Jln Pantai Cenang, T04-955 5100. Open 1200-2400. Friendly service complements the fairly authentic Mexican cuisine, juicy cheeseburgers and chocolate cake. Good spot for a relaxed lunch.

Red Tomato Garden Café, T012-513 6046. Closed Fri. Run by a German lady, Tania, and her local husband, this is one of the most popular places to eat with its freshly baked

bread, double-handed sandwiches, extensive breakfast menu and authentic pasta, pizza and salads. Travellers who have been on the road too long will love this place. Recommended.

Yellow Café, on the beach at Pantai Cenang. Great spot for a sunset drink, or a light lunch. This French-owned place has salads, baguettes and a great beachside lounging area.

OK Boss, opens for dinner only, next to the entrance of **Rumours Guesthouse**. Excellent little shack, highly popular with locals for its generous portions, friendly service and, most importantly, superb Melakan *asam pedas* cooking. Recommended.

Pantai Tengah p176, map p177

L'Osteria, Rumah Molek Complex, Jln Tasik Anak. Tue-Sat. This Italian place gets rave reviews for its lobster pasta, superb selection of booze, cosy ambience and friendly service. Recommended.

Unkaizan, T04-955 4118. There are great views from the balcony at this upmarket award-winning Japanese joint. The chef formerly worked at **The Andaman**. Pricey but recommended.

Fat Mum, T04-955 8818. With such a name, it is difficult to go wrong at this local Chinese seafood garden with outdoor seating.

Lighthouse, T04-955 2586. Open 1130-2230. Minimalist place, inspired by its name, with tables right on the beach. Varied lunch and dinner menus. Outrageous desserts, lamb shanks, gnocchi and fresh crunchy salads.

Sheela's, Tue-Sun. Garden restaurant serving European and Malay cuisine although the menu is quite limited.

Sunday Bistro. The owner of the 2 places below also runs this uber cool hangout, designed as beautifully as his other offerings. It has delightful statues of monks with their alms bowls, as well as water features and intimate seating. But the menu, with its steaks, pasta dishes and chicken cordon bleu, is sadly unimaginative.

Sunvillage and **Matahari Malay**, T04-955 6200, F955 1751. 2 spectacular restaurants set in exquisite landscaped surroundings.

The extensive menus at each offer traditionally prepared dishes. Recommended.

Pantai Kok p177
††† **Oriental Pearl**, Berjaya Langkawi Beach Resort, Buran Bay. Upmarket but simple a/c Chinese restaurant, with ocean views. The steamboat is recommended.

North Coast p178
††† **The Dining Room**, Datai, Datai Bay. Quintessentially tasteful in the style of the resort, overlooking a turquoise pool and jungle. The French chef combines Malay and Western cuisine to create an interesting menu.
††† **Pavillion**, Datai, Datai Bay. Stunning setting on a high terrace in jungle treetops, top-class Thai chefs, papaya salad, excellent seafood.
†† **Barn Thai**, Kampong Belanga Pecah, Mukim Kisap, T04-966 6699. Around 9 km from Kuah on the road to Padang Lalang, this is a unique restaurant set in mangrove swamp, reached along a 450 m wooden walkway, housed in a fine wooden building that blends with its natural surroundings. Mixed reviews about the Thai food, but the setting is memorable and they often have live jazz.

❶ Bars and clubs

Nightlife in Langkawi mainly centres on the bars, discos, karaoke and live music of the larger hotels.

Pantai Cenang p176, map p177
Pantai Cenang now has a few standalone bars, but they tend to close by 0100.
Go Slow Café, opposite Nadia's. The big yellow place right on the beach, a good stop for a sunset beer. An unpretentious bar that also serves Malay food and fish and chips. They occasionally hold laser parties.
Irish Bar, T04-955 8151, Jln Pantai Cenang. A great place to go if you're hunkering after TV sports or Irish food with your beer. Run by Debbie, this is a friendly spot for an evening drink.

Pantai Tengah p176, map p177
SunKarma, Jln Teluk Baru. Daily 1800-2400. This upmarket chillout bar has a long list of cocktails, fascinating toilet design and indoor and outdoor seating. Just down the road and owned by the same guy is **Sunba**, with a more homely, pub-like atmosphere playing music long past its sell-by date.

Pantai Kok and Burau Bay p177
Mutiara Burau Bay has the award-winning **Seashell's** which is a fun pub and restaurant with dancing on the beach.

○ Shopping

Kuah p175
Duty-free shops line the main street in Kuah, and alcohol is especially good value. There is a duty-free shopping complex at the jetty. The only shop selling alcohol here, **Sime Duty Free**, is on the 1st floor. Although Langkawi enjoys duty-free status, there is not much reason to come here for the shopping. There is also: **Cenang Duty Free Zone** next to Underwater World; the **Langkawi Fair Shopping Centre**, Persiaran Putra, Kuah (near the jetty); **Langkawi Mall**; the **Saga Shopping Centre**; and **Zone Shopping Paradise**.

Fishing tackle
There is a fishing shop opposite the **Langasuka Hotel** in Kuah.

Handicrafts
Many small shops in Kuah sell textiles.
Batik Jawa Store, 58 Pekan Pokok Asam. The best-stocked handicraft shop is in front of the **Sari Restaurant**.
Flint Stones Handicraft, Jln Pandak Maya. A good range of Asian handicrafts. Both these places above offer 30% discount during the low season.
Sunshine Handicraft, Jln Pandak Mayah (left turning before the Duty Free). Open daily. A range of *songket* products, particularly *songket* sarongs. Recommended.

Pantai Kok and Burau Bay p177
Oriental Village, a shopping development overlooking Burau Bay. Daily 1000-2200. Lots of themed restaurants and duty-free shopping. All in all, there is a lot of shopping – although for visitors from outside Malaysia and Singapore it seems a long way to come to hole up in some surreal tropical shopping paradise.

▲ Activities and tours

North Coast p178
Go-karting
Morac International Karting Circuit, Pantai Cenang, near the airport, T04-955 5827. Daily 1000-1900, RM70 for 10 mins (RM5 for racing suit hire).

Golf
Datai Bay Golf Club, Teluk Datai, T04-959 2700, www.dataigolf.com. Green fees RM400, 18-hole course, magnificent fairways, sea views. Tee-off times daily 0700, 1530. Langkawi International Masters is held here each April.
Gunung Raya, Jln Air Hangat, Kisap, T04-966 8148, www.golfgr.com.my. Daily 0700-1700. RM150 for 9 holes, RM200 for a full round. Designed by Max Wexler on a 750-ha former rubber plantation, an 18-hole course. Tee-off times daily 0700, 1530. Driving range.
Langkawi Golf Club, Jln Bukit Malut, T04-966 6187.

Spas
Langkawi has become a centre for pampered holidaymakers with a great range of spas from the severely upmarket at The Datai, to backpacker-friendly outlets at Pantai Cenang. It's also a good option when it rains, as there's not much else to do in inclement weather.
Alun Alun, T04-955 5570, www.langkawi-spa.com. Branches in Kuah, Pantai Cenang and Pantai Tengah. Full range of treatments including manicures, golfer's massage and body and facial treatments. Held in high regard. Those staying at the **Tropical Resort** in Pantai Tengah get a healthy 20% discount.

Nawa Sari Spa, In the Laman Padi, T04-955 2888. In the tranquil setting of the Laman Sari, this spa uses traditional Malay techniques and has good packages. Reservations are advised.
The Spa, Datai, T04-959 2500. Nothing but the best: a luxurious spa in the rainforest.
Teratai Spa, Pelangi Beach Resort, T04-952 8888. Part of the Aspara chain, with Swedish, Indonesian Thai, hot stone and Yin and Yang massages for around RM300 an hour.

Water sports
The big resorts and hotels all offer water sports facilities.
Cabana Water sports, T01-2470 5325. Offers the most extensive range of water sports activities on the island, including scuba diving and snorkelling, jet and water skiing, parasailing, banana boat rides and island hopping. Friendly staff. Café attached.

Tour operators
Organized tours around Langkawi and neighbouring islands can be booked through almost all the hotels and resorts. There are also scores of agents at the ferry pier. Popular tours include jungle trekking (including canopy trekking), paddling through mangrove swamps, island hopping, eagle spotting and feeding (operators throw chicken guts to swooping white tailed eagles and brahminy kites – a dubious practice you may not want to support) and a round-island trip to take in the waterfalls, mountains and other sites.

Trips to Pulau Rebak Besar (opposite Pantai Cenang) and Palau Dayang Bunting leave from the beach next to **Pelangi Resort** (signposted from the road).
Coral Island, 47 Jln Kelibang, Langkawi Mall, T04-966 1368, F966 1386. Largely diving and marine based tours on the beautiful Pulau Payar.
East Marine, T04-966 3966, www.eastmarine.com.my. Leaves Kuah for Pulau Payar (for snorkelling and scuba diving) daily at 0930 (returning at 1500). The journey each way takes 1 hr and the snorkeller package costs RM240 adult,

RM140 child. Dive package RM340. Non-certified divers can try an introductory dive as part of the snorkelling programme.

Langkawi Canopy Adventures, T012-4848744, www.langkawi.travel/. For air trekking at 30 m, RM210-RM240.

Mahsuri Travel & Tours, 1-S4 Jetty Point Complex, Kuah, T019-479 1009. Tours and services ranging from car and bike rental to multiple island tours, mangrove cruises, jet-skiing and parasailing. Good rates.

Mutiara Burau Bay, call Hamzah on T019-437 9783. Organizes guided horse riding trips through kampongs, forest and a gallop along the beach.

Neighbouring islands *p179*
A reef platform has been built at Pulau Payar with an underwater observation chamber and diving facilities (tank and weights RM50, full diving gear RM70, introductory dive RM100). There's also a bar, restaurant and souvenir shop. Contact **East Marine**, see above.

⊖ Transport

Air
The international airport is the other side of Pantai Cenang, about 20 km from Kuah and 8 km from Pentai Cenang, at Padang Matsirat. A taxi to Kuah from the airport is RM16 and around RM18 to Pantai Kok. Prices are fixed – coupons are on sale in the airport building. Daily connections with **KL** on MAS. AirAsia flies between Langkawi and **KL** and **Singapore**. Firefly has daily connections to **Penang** and **Subang**. MAS and Silk Air and Tiger Airways (www.tigerairways.com) operate frequent connections with **Singapore**. There are also direct flights from **Hong Kong** (Hong Kong Express) and **Bangkok** (Thai Airways).

Airline offices MAS, ground floor, Langkawi Fair Shopping Mall, Persiaran Putra, Kuah, T04-746 3000; Silk Air, c/o MAS, T04-292 3122; AirAsia, T04-202 7777.

Bicycle hire
On the main beaches, RM10-15 per day.

Boat
It is well worth hiring a boat if you can get a large group of people together, otherwise it tends to be expensive – approximately RM150 per day. Many of the beach hotels run boat trips to the islands as well as one or two places in Kuah (see Tour operators above).

Ferries to Langkawi leave from both **Kuala Perlis** and **Kuala Kedah**. Timetables are subject to seasonal change (fewer boats during the monsoon months, Apr-Sep), journey time from Kuala Perlis is 1 hr 15 mins departing every hour from 0700 to 1900, adults RM18, children RM13 and from Kuala Kedah, 1 hr 45 mins, adults RM23, children RM17. **Fortune Express**, Seraya Bayu; and **Labuan Express**. To check the latest schedule, phone the ticketing counter in Langkawi, T04-966 1125. There are 2 departures daily for **Penang** at 1430 (via Pulau Payar) and 1715, adult RM60, children RM45. **Langkawi Ferry Services** and Labuan Express both run connections with **Satun** in **Thailand**, adult RM30, children RM23. There are at least 3 ferries a day departing at 0930, 1300 and 1700. It is possible to buy through tickets in Langkawi to **Phuket** (RM70), **Krabi** (RM55) and **Surat Thani** (RM65) via Satun.

Connections with **KL** are easiest from Kuala Kedah, while if you're heading east to **Kota Bharu** take a ferry to Kuala Perlis. **Qudrat Bistari Agency**, which sells bus tickets, at counter 9 at the Kuah jetty, is friendly and helpful.

Note, leaving Langkawi, there are bus ticket agents at the ferry if you want to book a connection from Kuala Perlis or Kuala Kedah.

Bus
There are infrequent local buses that seem to run on a timetable only known to themselves. It is recommended that visitors hire their own vehicle or use a taxi.

It is a 6-hr journey from KL to Kuala Kedah; from there catch the boat to Langkawi.

Car hire
SBM Travel and Tours, Jln Pantai Cenang (over the road from Kampung Siam restaurant), Pantai Cenang, T04-955 9935. Rates start at RM70 per day.
Tomo Express, 14 Jln Pandak Maya 4, Pekan Kuah, T04-966 9252. Expect to pay about RM80 per day.

Motorcycle hire
Motorbikes are reasonably cheap to hire (RM20-35 per day) and are by far the best way to scoot around the island. There are rental shops in Kuah and on all the beaches. Although Langkawi's roads are wide and not very busy, be warned to drive with extra special care since monkeys and buffalo frequently dart or lumber onto the tarmac.

Taxi
Fares around the island are fixed. From the jetty to **Kuah** is RM6, to **Pantai Cenang** RM24, to **Datai Bay**, RM32.

ⓘ Directory

Kuah *p175*
Banks Maybank and United Malayan Banking Corporation are just off the main street in Kuah in the modern shophouse block. Banks are open all day Mon-Thu and Sun, but only in the morning on Fri and Sat.
Immigration Customs office, T04-966 6227, Immigration office, T04-969 4005.
Internet There are a number of cafés in Kuah, including **Langkawi Online**, ground floor, Langkawi Plaza, daily 0930-2400. **Post office** General Post Office, at the jetty end of the main street in Kuah.

Pantai Cenang and Pantai Tengah *p176, map p177*
Banks There are also a couple of money changers at Pantai Cenang and Pantai Tengah. There is one opposite the **Aseania**, daily 1100-2130, and another opposite **Underwater World**, daily 1000-2000. Maybank ATM is in the Underwater World complex. **Internet** Max Gen2, next to the Sunset Beach Resort, RM3 per hr. **AB Motel** has internet, daily 1000-2300, RM3 per hr. Those with laptops can buy Langkawi Winet coupons for RM10 (24 hrs) and connect to the island-wide Wi-Fi network. Coupons are available at the convenience stores lining the road.

Contents

192 Melaka and around
  192 Ins and outs
  194 Background
  200 Sights
  206 Around Melaka
  207 Listings

216 Johor Bahru
  216 Ins and outs
  217 Background
  217 Sights
  218 Listings

221 Pulau Tioman and around
  221 Ins and outs
  222 Mersing
  222 Pulau Tioman
  228 Other islands
  229 Listings

240 Endau Rompin National Park
  240 Ins and outs
  241 Listings

Footprint features

190 Don't miss …
194 The Nyonas and the Babas
196 The Flor de la Mar: sunken
     treasure beyond measure
203 Chinese cobblers
205 Peranakan table manners

Southern Peninsula

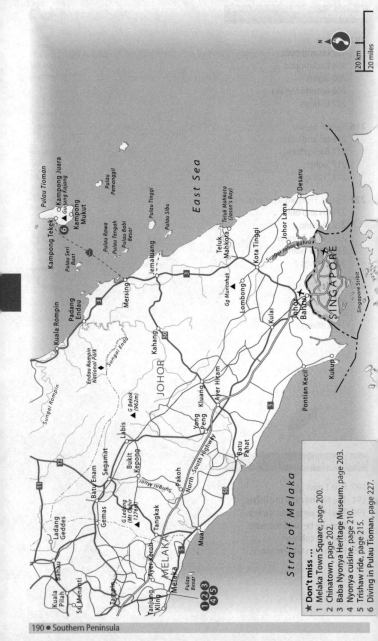

East Sea

Strait of Melaka

Pulau Tioman

Kampong Tekek • 6 Kampong Juara
▲ *Gunung Kajang*
Kampong Mukut

Pulau Pemanggil

Pulau Rawa
Pulau Tengah
*Pulau Babi
Besar*

*Pulau Seri
Buat*

Mersing

Pulau Tinggi

Pulau Sibu

Jemaluang

Padang
Endau

Kuala Rompin

Teluk
Mahkota
(Jason's Bay)

Teluk
Mahkota

Desaru

Kota Tinggi

Johor Lama

Sungai Endau

3

Endau-Rompin
National Park

Gg Muntahak ▲

Lombong

Kahang

50

Sungai Johor Bahru

Kulai

SINGAPORE

Singapore Strait

Johor
Bahru

Kukup

Pontian Kecil

Sungai Rompin

JOHOR

G Bekok
(962m)

Ayer Hitam

Kluang

Yong
Peng

Batu
Pahat

Labis

Bukit
Kepong

Sungai Muar

North-South Highway

Segamat

Pakoh

Batu
Enam

12

Gemas

G Ledang (Mt Ophir)
(1276m)

Tangkak

Muar

5

11

Ladang
Geddes

Kuala
Pilah

Srj Menanti

Bahau

Ayer Keroh

MELAKA

Melaka

*Pulau
Besar*

Tanjung
Kling

1 2 3
4 5

6

★ Don't miss ...
1 Melaka Town Square, page 200.
2 Chinatown, page 202.
3 Baba Nyonya Heritage Museum, page 203.
4 Nyonya cuisine, page 210.
5 Trishaw ride, page 215.
6 Diving in Pulau Tioman, page 227.

N

20 km
20 miles

Introduction

Melaka, a UNESCO World Heritage Site, is one of the Malaysian tourism industry's trump cards, thanks to its Portuguese, Dutch and British colonial history, rich Peranakan (Straits Chinese) cultural heritage, excellent Nyonya restaurants and picturesque hinterland of rural Malay kampongs. The route south from Melaka is a pleasant but unremarkable drive through plantation country to Johor Bahru (JB), on the southernmost tip of the Peninsula.

It's a short hop across the causeway from JB to Singapore, and Malaysia's east coast islands and resorts are within easy reach. One of the most famous of these is Pulau Tioman, a large volcanic outcrop off the east coast, with perfect strips of sandy beaches, good diving and snorkelling, forest trails, mountain hikes and, for the most part, a laid-back atmosphere.

Inland lies Peninsular Malaysia's second-largest national park – Endau Rompin, which covers 800 sq km of lowland forest. Although facilities are limited and the access is trickier than in Taman Negara, the park offers more possibilities of catching a glimpse of rare rhinos, tigers and boars because of the paucity of tourists.

Melaka and around → *Colour map 2, B3.*

Thanks to its strategic location on the strait that bears its name, Melaka was a rich, cosmopolitan port city long before it fell victim to successive colonial invasions. Its wealth and influence are now a thing of the past, and the old city's colourful history is itself a major money-spinner for Malaysia's modern tourism industry. The Jerak Warison Heritage Trail is a great introduction to historical Melaka, with its striking Dutch colonial core and bustling, although somewhat manufactured, Chinatown (which houses the oldest Chinese temple in Malaysia).

After you've exhausted the rich historical sites of Melaka, 11 km up the road towards the North-South Highway is Ayer Keroh, a kind of contrived holiday camp with golf, a zoo, night safari, butterfly park and go-kart racing. Tanjung Kling, 9 km northwest, is well known for its seafood, although the waters around here are, as the tourist bureau puts it, "kind of milky". For serious trekkers, there's the myth-enshrouded Mount Ledang, which is a tough scramble at 1276 m.
▶▶ *For listings, see pages 207-215.*

Ins and outs

Getting there
Batu Berendam International Airport is 9 km from town and at the time of research was being upgraded. There are plans to connect the city with destinations in Malaysia, Indonesia and China. At the moment there is only a four-times weekly connection with Pekanbar in Indonesia, with Riau Airlines. It is a relatively painless overland journey either south from KL (150 km) or north from Singapore (250 km). There are numerous express buses plying the KL – Melaka and Singapore – Melaka routes and there are also connections with numerous other towns on the Peninsula. There is a direct shuttle bus from KLIA and the LCCT seven times daily. The town has a modern bus station, Melaka Sentral, opposite a big branch of Tesco supermarket. This is inconveniently located a few kilometres out of town on Jalan Tun Razak. Taxis are notorious for ripping off tourists as drivers refuse to use their meters anywhere in town. The fare from the bus station to the centre of town should cost around RM12 to RM15. Guesthouse touts occasionally greet new arrivals and, if you are planning on staying in budget accommodation, they are worth paying attention to as places are hard to find without a little help. The railway line does not run through Melaka – the nearest stop is at Tampin some 40 km north of town. There are daily express international ferry connections with Dumai in Sumatra. ▶▶ *See also Transport, page 214.*

Getting around
While Melaka is a largish town it is still possible to enjoy many of the sights on foot; bicycles are also available for hire from some of the guesthouses and shops in town. There is a town bus service; the No 17 bus runs from the bus station to historical Melaka and on to the Portuguese area, while the No 19 runs from the bus station out to Ayer Keroh (where the butterfly farm, reptile park and 'Mini Malaysia' are situated). The Melaka Panorama shuttle service does circuits of the city's main tourist sites and tourists can hop on and off as they please. Tickets can be purchased onboard the bus. Taxis are plentiful. While colourful trishaws are available for rent, these are not part of Melaka's public transport system; they survive by providing a service to tourists.

It is possible to walk around Melaka's historical sights. There is now an interesting walk, called the **Jerak Warisan Heritage Trail**, which starts at the Tourist Office on Jalan Kota, near the quayside, and covers all the major cultural sights of interest. The route crosses the bridge, to the Baba Nyonya Heritage Museum, takes in some temples on Jonker Street and then heads back to Stadthuys, St Paul's Church, St Paul's Hill and the Porta de Santiago Independence Monument. For a handout on the trail, ask at the Tourist Office.

There are boat tours down the river through the original port area and past some of the old Dutch houses, see Activities and tours, page 214. The river is a little pungent, but the 16th-century sanitation adds to the realism.

Tourist information

Tourism Malaysia ① *Jln Banda Kaba (next to the Bangunan Tabung Haji office), T06-288 1549, Mon-Thu 0800-1300, 1400-1700, Fri 0800-1200, 1445-1700, closed Sat-Sun*, has good, free maps. There is also a tourist information desk at **Ayer Keroh** ① *T06-293 3913*, and at **Melaka Sentral bus station** ① *T06-288 1340, www.melaka.org.my*. A new, as yet unopened, office is located inside the Menara Taming Sari ticketing building and should be open by the time you read this.

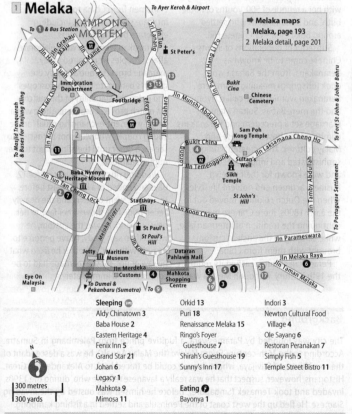

1 Melaka

➡ **Melaka maps**
1 Melaka, page 193
2 Melaka detail, page 201

Sleeping	Orkid 13	Indori 3
Aldy Chinatown 3	Puri 18	Newton Cultural Food
Baba House 2	Renaissance Melaka 15	Village 4
Eastern Heritage 4	Ringo's Foyer	Ole Sayang 6
Fenix Inn 5	Guesthouse 7	Restoran Peranakan 7
Grand Star 21	Shirah's Guesthouse 19	Simply Fish 5
Johan 6	Sunny's Inn 17	Temple Street Bistro 11
Legacy 1		
Mahkota 9	Eating ⑦	
Mimosa 11	Bayonya 1	

The Nyonyas and the Babas

By the early 1400s Melaka was one of the most important ports of call for Chinese trade missions. They arrived between November and March on the northeast monsoon winds and left again in late June on the southwest monsoon; giving them plenty of time to settle down and start families.

Melaka's early sultans made several visits to China, paying obeisance to the Ming emperors to ensure Chinese imperial protection for the sultanate. When Sultan Mansur Shah married the Ming Chinese princess Hang Li Poh in 1460, she brought with her a retinue of 500 'youths of noble birth' and handmaidens who settled around Bukit Cina – or Chinese Hill.

Subsequent generations of Straits Chinese came to be known as Peranakans, from the Bahasa word *anak* (offspring) meaning 'born here'. Peranakan women were called Nyonyas and the men, Babas. Sultan Mansur's marriage set a precedent and Peranakans combined the best of Chinese and Malay cultures. They created a unique, sophisticated and influential society and were known for their shrewd business acumen and opulent lifestyles. When the Dutch colonists moved out in the early 1800s, more Chinese moved in, continuing the tradition of intermarriage, while clinging to the ancient customs brought with them from China.

Peranakan culture reached its zenith in the 19th century. Although Melaka was

the Peranakan hearthstone, there were also large Straits Chinese communities in Penang and Singapore. The Nyonyas adopted Malay dress and were known for their fastidiousness when it came to clothes. The women were renowned for their intricate jewellery and glass beadwork – which are now prized antiques. The Nyonyas imported colourful porcelain from China for ceremonial occasions, which became known as Nyonya-ware and was typically emblazoned with phoenix and peony flower motifs. They also imported craftsmen from China to make their intricate silver jewellery, including elaborate belts and hairpins.

Peranakan weddings were elaborate affairs; couples were paired off by marriage brokers, contracted by the groom's parents to consult horoscopes and judge the suitability of the match. If a match proved auspicious, there was a lengthy present-exchanging ritual for the young couple, who were not permitted to see each other until they finally got to the nuptial chamber.

Wedding rituals often went on for 12 days and ended in a lavish feast before the couple went upstairs and the heavily veiled bride first showed her face to her new husband. As was the custom, he would then say: "Lady, I have perforce to be rude with you", whether he liked what he saw or not, for the marriage had to be consummated immediately.

Background

The city was founded by Parameswara, a fugitive prince from Palembang in Sumatra. According to the 16th-century *Sejara Melayu* (the Malay Annals), he was a descendant of the royal house of Srivijaya, whose lineage could be traced back to Alexander the Great. Historians, however, suspect that he was really a Javanese refugee who, during the 1390s, invaded and took Temasek (Singapore), before he himself was ousted by the invading Siamese. He fled up the west coast of the Peninsula and settled in a fishing kampong.

Peranakan architecture is exemplified in the Chinese Palladian townhouses – the best examples of which are in Melaka – with their open courtyards and lavish interiors, dominated by heavy dark furniture, inlaid with marble and mother-of-pearl.

Aside from their magnificent homes, one of the Peranakans' most enduring endowments is their cuisine, the result of the melding of their cultures. The food is spicy but uses lots of coconut milk and is painstakingly prepared – Nyonya-Baba restaurants are difficult business propositions. For details of particular dishes, see page 662.

The cliquey Peranakan upper-class assimilated easily into British colonial society, following the formation of the Straits Settlements in 1826. The billiard-playing, brandy-swilling Babas, in their Mandarin dresses, conical hats, pigtails and thick-soled shoes, successfully penetrated the commercial sector and entered public office. Many became professionals, such as lawyers, doctors and teachers, although they were barred from entering government above the clerical level.

"Strange to say," wrote Vaughan, "that although the Babas adhere so loyally to the customs of their progenitors, they despise the real Chinamen and are exclusive fellows indeed; [there is] nothing they rejoice in more than being British subjects ..." In Penang they were dubbed 'the Queen's Chinese'. Over the years they evolved their own Malay patois, and, in the 19th century, English was also thrown into their linguistic cocktail. They even devised a secret form of slang by speaking Baba Malay backwards.

Although they chose not to mix with immigrant Chinese, they retained a strong interest in events in China. The Straits Settlements provided a refuge for exiled reformers from the motherland – most notably Dr Sun Yat-sen, who lived in both Singapore and Penang in the early 1900s and became the first president of the Republic of China in 1911.

The Baba community's most famous son was Tan Cheng Lock, who was born into a distinguished Melakan Baba family in 1883. He lent his name to the Peranakans' architectural treasure, Jalan Tun Tan Chen Lock (formerly Heeren Street) in Melaka's Chinatown. Tan served in local government in colonial Melaka from 1912-1935 and vociferously fought British discrimination against the Straits and Malayan Chinese. He charged that the British had done nothing to "foster and strengthen their spirit of patriotism and natural love for the country of their birth and adoption". Tan was the spokesman for Malaya's Chinese community and fought for equality among the races; he founded the Overseas Chinese Association and became a prominent reformist politician in the years leading up to Malaysian independence.

The Malay Annals relate how Parameswara was out hunting one day and, while resting in the shade of a tree, watched a tiny mouse deer turn and kick one of his hunting dogs and drive it into the sea. He liked its style and named his nearby settlement after the *malaka* tree he was sitting under. Sadly it seems more likely that the name Melaka is derived from the Arabic word *malakat*, or market, and from its earliest days the settlement, with its sheltered harbour, was an entrepôt. Melaka was sheltered from the monsoons by the island of Sumatra and perfectly located for merchants to take advantage of the trade winds. Because the Strait's deepwater

The Flor de la Mar: sunken treasure beyond measure

From the early years of the very first millennium, Chinese junks were plying the Nanyang, or South Seas, and by the 1400s a sophisticated trade network had built up, linking Asia to India, the Middle East and Europe. For three centuries, Melaka was at the fulcrum of the China trade route and even before the Europeans arrived, hundreds of merchants came each year from Arabia, Persia, India, China, Champa, Cambodia, Siam, Java, Sumatra and the eastern Isles. By the early 1500s, more than 100 large ships were anchoring at Melaka every year. It was known as the emporium of the east.

But this trade was not without its casualties and the sunken wrecks littering the coastal waters of the South China Sea and the Strait of Melaka have given rise to a new, highly profitable industry: treasure hunting. Divers, in league with marine archaeologists and maritime historians, have flocked to the region in recent years. The most publicized find was the 1987 salvage of a cargo of Chinese porcelain from a vessel that sank off the Riau Islands in 1752; the booty was auctioned by Christie's in Amsterdam two years later for US$16 million. But treasure hunting carries with it political sensitivities over the ownership of wrecks. Salvage operators have been jailed in Indonesia and salvaged antiquities have been confiscated in Thailand.

The ultimate sunken treasure trove lies in what remains of the wreck of the *Flor de la Mar*, at the bottom of the Strait of Melaka. The Portuguese vessel, commanded by Admiral Alfonso d'Albuquerque, is thought to be the richest ship ever lost. Having left Lisbon in 1503, Albuquerque plundered his way from Mozambique, the Red Sea and India to the coastal regions of Burma and Thailand. By July 1511, when he anchored off Melaka, he had amassed untold riches. After capturing the city, he plundered it.

In his book *The Search for Sunken Treasure*, the treasure hunter Robert F Marx wrote: "The spoils the Portuguese took from Malacca stagger the imagination." They included more than 60 tonnes of gold booty in the form of solid gold statues of elephants, tigers, birds and monkeys, all studded with gemstones. There was gilded furniture, gold ingots, gold coins, gold-plated royal litters, chests full of diamonds, rubies and sapphires and several tonnes of Chinese and Arabic coins. And this was just the loot from Sultan Ahmad's palace".

In London, Sotheby's auction house valued the treasure at US$9 billion; by far the world's richest wreck. Albuquerque stole so much gold that Melaka was left without any coinage. Tin coins were minted instead, for the first time.

Two days after setting off for Portugal, his fleet of four ships ran into a storm at the

channel lay close to the Malayan coast, Melaka also had command over shipping passing through it.

In 1405 a Chinese Muslim Admiral, the eunuch Cheng Ho, arrived in Melaka bearing gifts from the Ming Emperor (including a yellow parasol, which has been the emblem of Malay royalty ever since) and the promise of protection from the Siamese. Cheng Ho (Zheng Ho) made seven voyages to the Indian Ocean over the next 30 years and used Melaka as his supply base. The Chinese gained a vassal state and Melaka gained a sense of security: Parameswara was wary of Siamese encroachment. Court rituals, ceremony and etiquette were formalized and an exclusive royal court language evolved. In 1411, three northeastern tip of Sumatra. Two ships went down, then the *Flor de la Marit* self hit a reef. Albuquerque survived the shipwreck and managed to salvage a gold sword, a jewel-encrusted crown, a ruby bracelet and a ring, which today are on display in a Lisbon museum. The rest was lost in 37 m of water. The admiral returned to Portugal on his one remaining ship. With his pilot, who also survived, he drew up a chart indicating where the ship went down – 8 km off Tanjung Jambu Air in Aceh.

It lay there, forgotten, for nearly 500 years. In 1988 an Italian specialist in underwater wrecks and an Australian marine historian claimed to have located the *Flor de la Mar*, hidden under several metres of mud, using satellite imaging. The Indonesian government, in whose territorial waters the wreck lay, then awarded a salvage contract to PT Jayatama Istikacipta, a company linked to the family of President Suharto, which subcontracted the diving operation to an Australian, arrested in Indonesia the previous year for illegal treasure hunting. He hired former divers from the British Navy's Special Boat Squadron to join the search. In 1989 they found a couple of wrecked Chinese junks but no *Flor de la Mar* and, in frustration, the operation was called off.

The same year, the Indonesians granted a search permit to a Singapore salvage firm. After a year's fruitless exploration, they hired Robert Marx, who, with the aid of a facsimile of Albuquerque's chart, located the reef that the ship had struck. Numerous artefacts were recovered, but, he wrote "a thorough sonar and magnetometer survey revealed that the main section of the wreck lies in an area the size of five football fields at a depth of 37 m under 15 m of concrete-like mud."

The discovery sparked a political row. Malaysia and Portugal contested Indonesia's claim to the booty and the matter was passed to the International Court in The Hague for adjudication. Meanwhile, an endless stream of conspiracy stories – none of them confirmed – surrounds the fate of the *Flor de la Mar*.

In 1991, it was reported that "powerful interests linked to President Suharto" had harassed other treasure hunters researching the location of the wreck and had privately tried to force them to help mount a covert salvage operation. In late 1991, following further reports that Indonesian Navy divers had tried again, Jakarta and Kuala Lumpur reportedly entered a joint-venture agreement. Under it, Malaysia agreed to bear the entire cost of the operation and split the booty 50/50. There are constant rumours about secret salvage operations circulating among Singapore's commercial diving community, but the matter is so sensitive and the stakes potentially so high that lips are firmly sealed.

years before his death, Parameswara sailed with Cheng Ho to China with a large retinue and was received by the third Ming Emperor, Chu Ti. Melaka's next two rulers continued this tradition, making at least two visits each to China.

But China began to withdraw its patronage in the 1430s and to make sure Melaka retained at least one powerful friend, the third ruler, Sri Maharaja, married the daughter of the sultan of the flourishing maritime state of Samudra-Pasai in Sumatra. Historian Mary Turnbull says "he embraced Islam and hitched Melaka's fortunes to the rising star of the Muslim trading fraternity". He adopted the name Mohamed Shah, but retained the court's longstanding Hindu rituals and ceremonies. He died without a child from his marriage to the Pasai princess and a succession crisis followed. The rightful royal heir, the young Rajah Ibrahim, was murdered in a palace coup after a year on the throne and Kasim, one of Mohamed's sons by a non-royal marriage, declared himself Sultan Muzaffar Shah. Melaka's first proper sultan made Islam the state religion and beat off two Siamese invasions during his reign. Islam was also spreading through the merchant community. In the latter half of the 15th century the faith was taken from Melaka to other states on the Peninsula as well as to Brunei and Javanese port cities that were breaking away from the Hindu kingdom of Majapahit.

In the late 15th century, Malay power reached its pinnacle. Muzaffar's successor, Sultan Mansur Shah, extended Melaka's sway over Pahang, Johor and Perak, the Riau archipelago and Sumatra. Contemporary European maps label the entire Peninsula 'Malacca'. According to the Malay Annals, the sultan married a Chinese princess in 1460. This marriage and the arrival of the princess and her followers marked the formal beginning of the unique and prosperous Straits Chinese Peranakan culture (see box, page 194).

Another cultural blend that had its roots in medieval Melaka was the Chitty Indian community, the result of Indian merchants intermarrying with local women, including the Malay nobility. Because foreign traders had to wait several months before the winds changed to allow them to return home, many put down roots and Melaka, 'the city where the winds met', had hundreds of permanent foreign residents. There were no taboos concerning cross-cultural marriage: the polygamous Muslim Sultan Mansur Shah even visited the crumbling Majapahit court in East Java where he cemented relations by his second royal marriage, to the Hindu ruler's daughter.

By the beginning of the 16th century Melaka was the most important port in the region. Foreign merchants traded in Indian and Persian textiles, spices from the Moluccas (Maluku), silk and porcelain from China as well as gold, pepper, camphor, sandalwood and tin. The Malay language subsequently became the lingua franca throughout the region.

Tales of luxury and prosperity attracted the Portuguese who came in search of trading opportunities, with the aim of breaking the Arab merchants' stranglehold on trade between Europe and Asia. Spices from the Moluccas came through the Strait and whoever controlled the waterway determined the price of cloves in Europe. The Portuguese – known to Melakans as 'the white Bengalis' – combined their quest for riches with a fervent anti-Muslim crusade, spurred by their hatred of their former Moorish overlords on the Iberian Peninsula. They arrived in 1509, received a royal welcome and then fled for their lives when Gujerati (Indian) traders turned the sultan against them. Alfonso d'Albuquerque, the viceroy of Portuguese India, returned two years later with 18 ships and 1400 men. After an initial attempt at reconciliation he too was beaten off. D'Albuquerque then stormed and conquered the city in July 1511, the year after he seized Goa on India's west coast. The Melakan court fled to Johor where Sultan Ahmad re-established his kingdom.

The foreign merchants quickly adapted to the new rulers and under the Portuguese the city continued to thrive. Tomé Pires, a Portuguese apothecary who arrived with d'Albuquerque's fleet and stayed two years, wrote in his account, *Suma Oriental*: "Whoever is lord of Melaka has his hand on the throat of Venice," adding that "the trade and commerce between different nations for a thousand leagues on every hand must come to Melaka". The port became known as the 'Babylon of the Orient'. Despite the two-year sojourn of Spanish Jesuit priest St Francis Xavier, Christianity had little impact on the Muslim Malays or the hedonistic merchant community. A large Eurasian population grew up, adding to Melaka's cosmopolitan character; there are still many people called Pereira, D'Cruze, de Silva, da Costa, Martinez and Fernandez in the Melaka phonebook.

Back in Lisbon in the early 17th century, the Portuguese monarchy was on the decline, the government in serious debt and successive expeditions failed to acquire anything more than a tenuous hold over the Spice Islands to the east. The Portuguese never managed to subdue the Sumatran pirates, the real rulers of the Strait of Melaka. As Dutch influence increased in Indonesia, Batavia (Jakarta) developed as the principal port of the region and Melaka declined. The Dutch entered an alliance with the Sultanate of Johor and foreign traders began to move there. This paved the way for a Dutch blockade of Melaka and in 1641, after a six-month siege of the city, Dutch forces, together with troops from Johor, forced the surrender of the last Portuguese governor.

Over the next 150 years the Dutch carried out an extensive building programme; some of these still stand in Dutch Square. Melaka was the collecting point for Dutch produce from Sumatra and the Malay Peninsula, where the new administration attempted to enforce a monopoly on the tin trade. They built forts on Pulau Pangkor and at Kuala Selangor, north of Klang, to block Acehnese efforts to muscle in on the trade, but the Dutch, like the Portuguese before them, were more interested in trade than territory. Apart from their buildings, the Dutch impact on Melaka was minimal. Their tenure of the town was periodically threatened by the rise of the Bugis, Minangkabaus and Makassarese, who migrated to the Malay Peninsula, having been displaced by the activities of the Dutch East India Company in Sulawesi and Sumatra. In 1784 Melaka was only saved from a joint Bugis and Minangkabau invasion by the arrival of the Dutch fleet from Europe.

By the late 18th century, the Dutch hold on the China trade route was bothering the English East India Company. In 1795 France conquered The Netherlands and the British made an agreement with the exiled Dutch government, allowing them to become the caretaker of Dutch colonies. Four years later the Dutch East India Company went bankrupt, but just to make sure that they would not be tempted to make a comeback in Melaka, the British started to demolish the fortress in 1807. The timely arrival of Stamford Raffles, the founder of modern Singapore, prevented the destruction from going further, and in 1824, under the Treaty of London, Melaka was surrendered to the British in exchange for the Sumatran port of Bencoolen (Bengkulu).

In 1826 Melaka became a part of the British Straits Settlements, along with Penang and Singapore. But by then, its harbour had silted up and it was a town of little commercial importance. In 1826 it had a population of 31,000 and was the biggest of the settlements; by 1860, although its population had doubled, it was the smallest and least significant of the three. In 1866, a correspondent for the *Illustrated London News* described Melaka (which the British spelled *Malacca*) as "a land where it is 'always afternoon' – hot, still, dreamy. Existence stagnates. Trade pursues its operations invisibly. It has no politics, little crime, rarely gets even two lines in an English newspaper and does nothing towards making contemporary history". In 1867 the Straits Settlements were transferred to direct colonial rule and Melaka faded into obscurity.

Strangely, it was the town's infertile agricultural hinterland that helped reinvigorate the local economy at the turn of the 20th century. The first rubber estate in Malaya was started by Melakan planter Tan Chay Yan, who accepted some seedlings from 'Mad' Henry Ridley, director of Singapore's Botanic Gardens, and planted out 1200 ha in 1896. The idea caught on among other Chinese and European planters and Melaka soon became one of the country's leading rubber producers. In 2008, after years of campaigning, Melaka was awarded UNESCO World Heritage City status along with its sister city of Georgetown, Penang.

Jalan Munshi Abdullah, which runs through the middle of the more recent commercial district, is like any Malaysian main street. While the old city is quite compact, the town itself is neither as small or as medieval looking as visitors are led to suppose. The historical sights from the Portuguese and Dutch periods are interesting because they are in Malaysia – not because they are stunning architectural wonders. That said, the old red Dutch buildings on the east bank of the river and the magnificent Peranakan architecture and stuccoed shophouses on the west side, lend Melaka an atmosphere unlike any other Malaysian town. It also lays claim to many of the country's oldest Buddhist and Hindu temples, mosques and churches.

Town Square
The Dutch colonial architecture in the town square is the most striking feature of the riverfront. The buildings are painted a bright terracotta red and are characterized by their massive walls, louvred windows and chunky doors with wrought-iron hinges. The most prominent of these is the imposing **Stadthuys**. Completed in 1660, it is said to be the oldest-surviving Dutch building in the East and served as the official residence of the Dutch governors. The renovated building now houses a good **history museum** ① *T06-284 1934, Sat-Thu 0900-1730, Fri 0900-1215 and 1445-1730, RM5, free tours on Sat-Sun at 1030 and 1230,* detailing in maps, prints and photographs the history and development of Melaka. Also here is a cultural museum and a literature museum, which are of less obvious interest to the average visitor. Just southwest from Stadthuys on the river is a half-size replica of the galley that the viceroy of Portuguese India arrived in. The **Tang Beng Swee Clocktower** looks Dutch but was built by a wealthy Straits Chinese family in 1886. **Christ Church** ① *Thu-Tue,* was built between 1741 and 1753 to replace an earlier Portuguese church, which was by then a ruin (church records date back to 1641). Its red bricks were shipped out from Zeeland in Holland. It is Malaysia's oldest Protestant church and the floor is still studded with Dutch tombstones. The original pews are intact – as are its ceiling beams, each hewn from a single tree trunk more than 15 m long. On the altar there is a collection of sacramental silverware bearing the Dutch coat-of-arms and there is a beautiful altar carving of the Last Supper.

On Jalan Kota, which runs in a curve round St Paul's Hill from the square is the **Muziam Islam Melaka** (Islamic Museum) ① *Tue-Sun 0900-1730,* which has a rather average display of Islamic cultural pieces.

St Paul's Hill
From behind the gate, a path leads up to the ruins of **St Paul's Church**, built on the site of the last Melakan sultan's *istana*. The small chapel was originally built by the Portuguese in 1521 and called *Nossa Senhora da Annunciada*, Our Lady of the Annunciation. The body of St Francis Xavier (the 16th-century Jesuit missionary who translated the catechism into Malay and visited the church regularly), was temporarily interred in the church vault following his death off the coast of China in 1552. His remains were later sent to Portuguese Goa on the west coast of India. An armless marble statue, erected in 1953, now commemorates Malaysia's best-known missionary. The Portuguese added gun turrets and a tower to the church and it became a fortress between 1567 and 1596. During the Dutch siege of Melaka in 1641, it was badly damaged but the invaders repaired it and renamed it St Paul's. It became a Protestant church and remained so until Christ Church

was completed in 1753. St Paul's ended its life as a cemetery; it was used as a special burial ground for Dutch nobles, whose tombs line the walls. There are good views of the city and over the sea from the top of Saint Paul's Hill. The ruins now host buskers and souvenir sellers. There is a Dutch cemetery in the grounds, with fascinating gravestones showing the grim devastation wrought by the epidemics that sporadically wiped out entire generations of early colonists.

Head down the hill the other side and you reach the **Porta de Santiago**, the remains of the great Portuguese fort A Famosa, said to have been built in four months flat under Admiral Alfonso d'Albuquerque's supervision in 1511. What remains is largely a Dutch reconstruction, the result of repair work carried out following the siege in 1641; it prominently displays the Dutch East India Company's coat-of-arms. The fort originally sprawled across the whole hill and housed the entire Portuguese administration, including their hospitals and five churches. It was flattened by the British between 1806 and 1808 when they occupied Melaka during the Napoleonic Wars. They wanted to

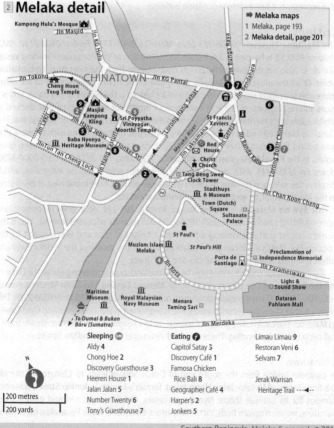

2 Melaka detail

➡ **Melaka maps**
1 Melaka, page 193
2 Melaka detail, page 201

Sleeping 🛏
Aldy 4
Chong Hoe 2
Discovery Guesthouse 3
Heeren House 1
Jalan Jalan 5
Number Twenty 6
Tony's Guesthouse 7

Eating 🍴
Capitol Satay 3
Discovery Café 1
Famosa Chicken
Rice Bali 8
Geographer Café 4
Harper's 2
Jonkers 5

Limau Limau 9
Restoran Veni 6
Selvam 7

Jerak Warisan
Heritage Trail ---◄---

ensure that the fort was not reclaimed by the Dutch. Stamford Raffles arrived for a holiday in Melaka just in time to forestall the destruction of its last remaining edifice.

A wooden replica of Sultan Mansur Shah's 15th-century *istana* is below St Paul's. The **Sultanate Palace** ① *T06-262 7464, daily 0900-1730, RM2, children RM0.50*, has been painstakingly reconstructed from a description in the 16th-century *Serjarah Melayu* (Malay Annals) and was built in 1985 using traditional construction techniques and materials. Mansur – who came to the throne in 1459 – inherited what was reputed to be the finest royal palace in the world, with a roof of copper and zinc in seven tiers, supported by wooden carved pillars. According to the Annals, his magnificent *istana* was destroyed by fire after being struck by lightning the year after his accession.

The **Proclamation of Independence Memorial** ① *T06-284 1231, Tue-Sun 0900-1730, free*, was built in 1912 and formerly housed the Malacca Club. The old Dutch colonial building was the social centre of British colonial Melaka. Perhaps appropriately, it now houses an extensive timeline exhibition covering Malaysia's journey to independence. There are lots of photographs – interesting to those who like that sort of thing – and it also represents a fine example of nation building.

East bank

The **Maritime Museum** ① *T06-283 0926, Mon-Thu 0900-1730, Fri-Sun 0900-2130, RM2, children RM0.50*, is housed in a full-scale reconstruction of the Portuguese trading vessel *Flor de la Mar*, on the riverbank, 200 m downstream from the river boat embarkation point. Of all the museums in Melaka, this is one of the better ones – many of the other museums are rather repetitive, but as Melaka's history is the history of sea trade, this is a more interesting option. It has a collection of models of foreign ships that docked at Melaka during its maritime supremacy from the 14th century to the Portuguese era. The *Flor de la Mar* itself ended its days on the sea bed just offshore, laden with treasure that was bound for Portugal (see box, page 196). Entry to the Maritime Museum also gives access to the **Royal Malaysian Navy Museum** ① *Jln Kota, T06-283 0926, daily 0900-1730, closed Fri 1215-1445, RM2, across the road, hold onto your tickets for inspection*, which displays the salvaged remains of 19th-century vessels that have foundered or been sunk in the Melaka Strait, as well as more contemporary items.

The **Eye on Malaysia** ① *Muara Sungai Melaka, T06-284 1888, www.eyeonmalaysia. com.my, RM20, children RM10, daily 1000-2300*, has recently relocated from KL. This is the world's largest portable viewing wheel with a height of 60m and was inspired by the London Eye. The Eye is located on reclaimed land, at the mouth of the Melaka River and offers some excellent views of the city and the Straits.

If you are wondering what that ugly blot on the landscape is towering above the Dataran Pahlawan, you can sate your curiosity at the **Menara Taming Sari** ① *Jln Merdeka, Bandar Hilir, T06-288 1100, www.menaratamingsari.com, RM20, children RM10, daily 1000-2200*. This is yet another Malaysian record breaker, and is registered as the 'First Revolving Gyro Tower' in Malaysia. The cabin takes groups of tourists up to a height of 80 m and then slowly turns a full circle before descending. There are good views over the city and the Straits.

Chinatown

A concrete bridge from the south end of Dutch Square leads to Chinatown, the old trading section of Melaka. **Jalan Hang Jebat**, formerly known as **Jonker Street**, was once famous for its antique shops: Nyonya porcelain, Melakan-style 'red and gold' carved furniture, wooden opium beds, Victorian mirrors, antique fans and Peranakan blackwood

Chinese cobblers

One of Melaka's most significant cultural assets was removed from 92 Jonker Street as part of the project to lure tourists.

Elderly Mr Yeo, the proprietor, was given three days to move out. For two generations the Yeo family, at **Wah Aik Shoemaker Shop**, have been the only cobblers catering for the country's dwindling population of ageing Chinese women with bound feet. The practice, which was considered *de rigueur* for women of noble stock during the Ch'ing Dynasty (1644-1912), was rekindled among the families of nouveau riche Chinese tin *towkays* during the days of the British Straits Settlements.

The process involved binding the feet firmly with bandages before they were fully formed; it was supposed to add to a woman's sensuality, but in reality it just caused a lot of pain. In China, the practice was outlawed in 1912. There are only a tiny number of women in Malaysia with bound feet, most of them in Melaka and all of them in their 80s or 90s. Mr Yeo Sing Guat made these *san choon chin lian* (3-in golden lotus feet) shoes – with brocade on authentic Shanghai Hang Chong silk – for them and as tourist souvenirs; he also makes the Peranakan *kasut manik* 'pearl shoes', sewn with miniature pearl beads.

Wah Aik Shoemaker Shop is the last of its kind in Malaysia and is now run by Raymond and Tony, grandsons of the original owner Yeo Eng Tong, who originally came from Hainan in China. The shop can be found at 56 Jln Tolong (Temple St).

furniture inlaid with mother-of-pearl. There are some good examples of Peranakan architecture along the street – notably the renowned Jonkers Melaka Restoran. But none of these Peranakan houses compare with the picturesque **Jalan Tun Tan Cheng Lock**. Named after a leading Melakan Baba, instrumental in pre-independence politics (see box, page 194), it is lined with the Straits Chinese community's ancestral homes and is Melaka's Millionaire's Row. Many of the houses have intricately carved doors that were often specially built by immigrant craftsmen from China. Today tour buses exacerbate the local traffic problem, which clogs the narrow one-way street, but many of its Peranakan mansions are still lived in by the same families that built them in the 19th century.

One of the most opulent of these houses has been converted into the **Baba Nyonya Heritage Museum** ① *48-50 Jln Tun Tan Cheng Lock, T06-283 1273, daily 1000-1230 and 1400-1630, RM8*. It is in a well-preserved traditional Peranakan town house, built in 1896 by millionaire rubber planter Chan Cheng Siew. Today it is owned by William Chan and his family, who conduct tours of their ancestral home. The interior is that of a typical 19th-century residence and all the rooms are still as they would have been 100 years ago. The house contains family heirlooms and antiques, including Nyonyaware porcelain and blackwood furniture with marble or mother-of-pearl inlay, and silverware. There is also a collection of traditional wedding costumes, photographs and kitchen utensils. The kitchen sink has the name of William Chan's great grandfather carved on it. The information-packed tours are run regularly throughout the day.

Although at first glance tourists may be impressed by the streets around Chinatown, the sad truth is that the desire to attract mass tourism to this 'heritage' town has probably destroyed more heritage than it has protected. Over 20 buildings have been demolished and many traditional trades evicted in the interests of bigger business. False 'heritage' façades and trinket shops have taken the place of the authentic article. 'Jonker Walk' – the renaming of Jonker Street (Jalan Hang Jebat) – has led to the pedestrianization of the street over the weekends. There are two ways of looking at Jonker Walk. Most visitors come away thinking that the night market here is fun and zingy, they like the shophouse architecture, the hawkers sell tasty snacks, and the pedestrianization of the street makes it all more human. The alternative view is that the street has been transformed from a place with real people running traditional businesses to a contrived and ersatz place geared to the needs of tourists. No local residents were consulted about the project, the original traders and guilds have been displaced and an accumulation of rubbish and associated rats and cockroaches has created health problems.

The **Cheng Hoon Teng Temple** ① *Jln Tokong*, was built in 1645, although there were later additions in 1704 and 1804 and is the oldest Chinese temple in Malaysia. The name literally means 'Temple of the Evergreen Clouds' and was founded by Melaka's Kapitan Cina, Lee Wi King from Amoy, a political refugee who fled from China. All the materials used in the original building were imported from China, as were the craftsmen who built it in typical South Chinese style. The elaborate tiled roofs are decorated with mythological figures, flowers and birds, and inside there are wood carvings and lacquer work. The main altar houses an image of Kuan Yin, the Goddess of Mercy (cast in solid bronze and bought from India in the 19th century), who is associated with peace, good fortune and fertility. On her left sits Ma Cho Po, the guardian of fishermen and on her right, Kuan Ti, the god of war, literature and justice. The halls to the rear of the main temple are dedicated to Confucius and contain ancestral tablets.

Nearby, on Jalan Tukang Emas, is the **Sri Poyyatha Vinayagar Moorthi Temple**, built in 1781 and the oldest Hindu temple in use in Malaysia. It is dedicated to the elephant-headed god Vinayagar (more usually known as Ganesh). Near to this Hindu temple on Jalan Tukang Emas is the **Masjid Kampong Kling**, a mosque built in 1748 in Sumatran style, with a square base surmounted by a three-tiered roof and pagoda-like minaret. Another 18th-century mosque in the same style is the **Masjid Tranquerah**, Jalan Tengkerah, 2 km out of town on the road to Port Dickson. Next door is an unusual freestanding octagonal minaret with Chinese-style embellishments, in marked contrast to Malaysia's traditional Moorish-style mosques. In the graveyard is the tomb of Sultan Hussein Shah of Johor who, in 1819, signed the cession of Singapore to Stamford Raffles.

West bank

On the west bank is **Kampong Morten**, a village of traditional Melakan houses. It was named after a man who built Melaka's wet market and donated the land to the Malays. The main attraction here is Kassim Mahmood's handcrafted house. This a great area for a wander and well worth the walk.

North Melaka

St Peter's Church ① *Jln Taun Sri Lanang, daily until 1900*, was built in 1710 by descendants of the early Portuguese settlers when the Dutch became more tolerant of different faiths. Iberian design is incorporated in the interior, where Corinthian pillars support a curved ceiling above the aisle, similar to churches in Goa and Macau. It is the centre of the Roman Catholic faith in Malaysia. Easter candlelit processions to St Peter's seem strangely out of context in Malaysia.

In 1460 when Sultan Mansur Shah married Li Poh, a Ming princess, she took up residence on Melaka's highest hill, **Bukit Cina**, which became the Chinese quarter. The Malay Annals do not record what became of the princess's palace but the hill, off Jalan

Peranakan table manners

Local food is served with local superstition. The heritage of the Babas and the Nyonyas includes a detailed etiquette of what to do and what to avoid at mealtimes. Food is considered a symbol of *jerki*, meaning luck or fortune. For this reason, food should not be squashed, dropped or trodden upon and anything spilt must be picked up. If food is not treated with due respect this is known as *sway* and brings bad fortune. Meals should be eaten at a circular table; sitting at a corner is to be avoided. Once seated, diners should not sit with their chin in their hand, nor should they move from seat to seat as this will lead to a restless life. Other acts of *sway* include breaking wind or crying at the dinner table, discussing depressing topics while eating, breaking or using chipped crockery, and piling plates one on top of another. If cutlery is clashed together, sibling squabbles will follow.

For women, there are yet further complications. If a woman drinks too much soup it will rain on her wedding day; if she leaves food on her plate she will marry an ugly husband; and if she sings at the table her husband will be old.

These traditions reach out to a wider belief system that sees inanimate objects as potential habitats for spirits. Thankfully they are not followed to the letter by Perankan restaurants in Melaka, although the proprietors are often happy to offer further insights into this culture.

Munshi Abdullah/Jalan Laksamana Cheng Ho, remained in the possession of the Chinese community and because of its good feng shui – its harmony with the supernatural forces and the elements – it was made into a graveyard. The cemetery now sprawls across the adjoining hills of Bukit Gedona and Bukit Tempurong. Some of the graves date back to the Ming Dynasty, but most of these are now overgrown or in the process of disintegrating.

At the foot of the hill is an old Chinese temple called **Sam Poh Kong**, built in 1795 and dedicated to the famous Chinese seafarer, Admiral Cheng Ho (see page 196). It was originally built to cater for those whose relatives were buried on Bukit Cina. This temple has a peaceful and relaxed atmosphere and is interesting to explore. Next to the temple is the **Sultan's Well** (*Perigi Rajah*), also called the **Hang Li Poh Well**, said to have been sunk in the 15th century. It is believed that drinking from this well ensures a visitor's return to Melaka – but anyone foolhardy enough to try this today is liable to contract dysentery and instead stay rather longer than they anticipated. However, while the water may be off-limits to all but the most foolhardy, there is a small market situated beside the well where the visitor can sample the local fruits.

The ruined **Fort St John**, another relic of the Dutch occupation, is southeast of Bukit Cina. Its hilltop location affords some excellent views although its aspect has been spoiled by the water treatment plant and high-rise apartment block on either side of it.

Portuguese Settlement

ⓘ *Take the blue line of the Panorama Melaka shuttle bus from outside Mahkota Parade, or Stadthuys.*

About 3 km from the town centre is the Portuguese Settlement (Medan Portugis) at Ujong Pasir, where the descendants of the Portuguese occupiers settled. A Portuguese community (of sorts) has managed to survive here for nearly five centuries; unlike the subsequent Dutch and British colonial regimes, the Portuguese garrison was encouraged to intermarry and generally treat the Malays as social equals. Today these Malaysians of Portuguese descent number around 2600. In the country as a whole, there are thought to be some 10,000. The process of integration was so successful that when the Dutch, after capturing the city in 1641, offered Portuguese settlers a choice between amnesty and deportation to their nearest colony, many chose to stay. In the 1920s, as their distinctive culture was threatened with extinction, the leaders of the community pleaded with the British to allot them a piece of land on which they could settle. A small area of swampland was duly allocated and the neat and well-planned settlement visible today was built, its street named after Portuguese heroes largely unrecognized in Malaysia. The main square, built only in 1985, is a concrete replica of a square in Lisbon – and is visibly ersatz.

Today there are just a few tourist-oriented restaurants and shops in the modern Portuguese Square, and cultural shows are staged on Saturday nights (see Eating page 212). Other than tourism, the residents of the Portuguese settlement earn their livelihoods by fishing and through a small number of cottage industries including shrimp paste production. The central role that the sea plays in the community's coherence and identity is threatened by a land reclamation project that will cut off its access to the sea. This will destroy the settlement's fishing industry, its fish-based cottage industries and undermine its attraction to tourists. Resident Gerard Fernandis said, "Our history, our culture, songs, dances and food are all linked to the sea", adding that without the sea the "settlement will become an island in a sea of concrete."

Around Melaka → For listings, see pages 207-215.

Tanjung Kling
About 9 km northwest of Melaka, it is a pleasant drive past beachside kampongs – despite the muddy sea and dirty beach from passing tankers that have a habit of swilling out their tanks. This does not seem to affect the taste of the seafood – or perhaps it improves it – and there are several restaurants and hawker stalls along the roadside at **Pantai Kundor**, where there are a number of hotels. Kampong Kling is thought to have got its name from Tamils who originally settled there, having come from Kalingapatam, north of Madras. For the less geographically confident, local tour companies offer organized tours on foot or by car, including visits to the plantation and to Ayer Keroh. Ask at the tourist office in Melaka for details.

Ayer Keroh
① Take bus No 19 from Melaka.
Situated just off the highway to KL, 11 km northeast of Melaka, Ayer Keroh has a lake, a 359-ha forest, a golf course and a country club. It is also the site of **Melaka Zoo** ① T06-232 4053, www.zoomelaka.gov.my, daily 0900-1800, RM7, children RM4. The zoo also has a **night-viewing safari** ① Fri and Sat 2000-2300, RM10, children RM5, where guests are driven around lit-up exhibits by tram. Also on offer are **Elephant and pony rides** ① Sat-Sun 1000-1200, 1400-1600, RM2/RM1. Ayer Keroh also has the **Butterfly and Reptile Sanctuary** ① T06-232 0033, daily 0830-1730, RM5, children RM3, a **go-kart track** ① daily 0900-1800, and a **Mini Malaysia Complex** ① T06-232 1331, daily 0900-1700, RM12, children RM6, where the various states of Malaysia are represented by 13 traditional houses containing works of art and culture (similar to the Karyaneka Handicraft Centre in KL) as well as an Orang Asli village. All the houses look remarkably alike, except the Borneo one. It also stages cultural shows. Children can take part in various activities, such

as learning to play traditional Malay games or honing their skills on an Iban blowpipe. Mini-ASEAN is next door and is more varied (and included in the ticket price). The **Ayer Keroh Golf and Country Club** ⓘ *Km 14.5, Jln Ayer Keroh, T06-233 2000, www.akcc. com.my,* off the main road past the Ayer Keroh Lake, is the longest golf course in Malaysia; take note that handicap cards must be produced.

Pulau Besar

Contrary to its name (*besar* is Malay for big), Pulau Besar is a small, quiet island, about 8 km southeast of Melaka, which is popular at weekends. According to local legend, a princess became pregnant by a Melakan commoner and was banished to the island to die. There is a shrine on the island dedicated to an early Muslim missionary, who is said to have come to Melaka in the 1400s. The island has good beaches (although the sea is not clean and most of the coral is dead) and there are jungle walks.

Gunung Ledang → Altitude: 1276 m.

This is one of the Peninsula's best-known mountains, also called Mount Ophir, located on the east side of the North-South Highway, equidistant from Melaka and Muar and just inside Johor state. It is isolated from the mountains of the Main Range and is sacred to the Orang Asli of Melaka. A Straits Chinese and Malay rumour has it that the mountain is the domain of a beautiful fairy endowed with the local version of the Midas Touch: she has a habit of turning Gunung Ledang's plant life into gold. The mountain is said to be guarded by a sacred tiger, which is possessed by the fairy.

Gunung Ledang is a strenuous climb involving some very steep scrambles, particularly towards the top. In 1884 an expedition reached the summit while trying to demarcate the boundary between Johor and Melaka. Most climbers of Gunung Ledang choose to camp overnight on the summit, although, at a push, it can be done in a day, from dawn to dusk. The mountain is surrounded by and covered in virgin jungle and rises through mossy forest (where there are several varieties of pitcher plant) to the rocky summit. Climbers are strongly advised to stick closely to the trails. The trail is complex in places and the climb should be carefully planned. There are two main trails up the mountain; the best route starts 15 km from Tangkak, just beyond Sagil. Waterfalls (Air Terjun) are signposted off the road that leads to Air Penas, a popular local picnic spot. The trail begins just beyond the rubber factory. Climbers can enquire about guides at the Gunung Ledang Resort, see page 210.

⊙ Melaka and around listings

For Sleeping and Eating price codes and other relevant information, see Essentials pages 25-30.

● Sleeping

Melaka *p192, maps p193 and p201*
There's plenty of choice in Melaka with some charming places to stay right in the heart of town. There are several good hotels around Tanjung Kling; several good budget hotels at Taman Melaka Raya and an increasing number of places around Chinatown. Note

that many of the mid-range places increase prices by around 10% at weekends and 20-30% during public holidays such as Chinese New Year.

L Mahkota, Jln Merdeka, T06-281 2828, www.malaccahotels.com. On the waterfront next to the Mahkota Parade Shopping and Entertainment Complex, this was one of Melaka's first resort hotels, with 617 rooms. 2 pools, a health centre, a tennis court, 2 squash courts, mini golf, and a children's playground, all spread out over several towers. Also suites and apartments with the usual facilities.

L Renaissance Melaka, Jln Bendahara, T06-284 8888, www.marriott.com. 24 storeys high, this the tallest building in the town and can clearly be seen from Melaka Sentral. There are 294 rooms, all of which are spacious and elegantly appointed with Malaccan wood furniture, a/c, mini-fridge, TV, in-house video and grand views either over the town or to the sea. There's also a coffee shop, restaurants, a fitness centre, and a pool on the 9th floor. Excellent promotional rates – check online. Recommended.

AL Aldy Chinatown, 148 Jln Bunga Raya, T06-281 3636, www.aldyhotel.com.my. Not as well located as the other **Aldy** hotel, but this place has newer rooms, with spotless bathrooms and free Wi-Fi in the lobby.

AL-A Legacy, 146 Jln Hang Tuah, T06- 281 6868, www.malaccacityhotels.com. Sophisticated hotel with 235 rooms, business facilities, gym, pool and more. Well designed and popular with business visitors.

A-B Aldy, 27 Jln Kota, T06-283 3232, www.aldyhotel.com.my. This place has spacious rooms tastefully stocked with rattan furniture. Great location at the foot of Bukit St Paul. Only downside is it straddles a bar and restaurant, so could be a bit noisy at night, but this is easily overcome by the existence of a rooftop jacuzzi ideal for sunset drinks and a bit of romance.

A-B Heeren House, 1 Jln Tun Tan Cheng Lock, T06-281 4241, www.heerenhouse.com. This friendly family-orientated guesthouse has 6 a/c rooms furnished simply with colonial and Peranakan antiques. Most rooms have a full river view, but the gem is the family room with a canopied four-poster bed, a day bed for lounging and a spacious bathroom. A full English breakfast is included in the price. Wi-Fi is available in the rooms closest to the reception. Recommended.

A-B Mimosa, 108 Jln Bunga Raya, T06-282 1113, www.mimosahotel.com. Decent, fully carpeted rooms with a/c, TV and shower. Café, Wi-Fi. Popular with Japanese tours.

A-B Orkid 138 Jln Bendahara, T06-282 5555, www.hotelorkidmelaka.com. Smart hotel at an affordable price. A/c, shower, TV. Facilities include a spa, restaurant and bar. Primarily a business visitor's stopover but good value for tourists except for the nightly karaoke warblings from across the street.

A-B Puri, 118 Jln Tun Tan Cheng Lock, T06-282 5588, www.hotelpuri.com. Beautiful hotel set in a restored Peranakan house with 73 rooms and 9 suites. There's a bird room with nesting starlings in the ceiling's covings, a tiny museum depicting the restoration work, a serene Chinese garden café and a lobby with a piano and spiral staircase. The rooms don't have as much character unfortunately, although they are clean and tastefully furnished. Several come with balconies. Wi-Fi available; breakfast is included. Full spa service. Good Nyonya fare in the restaurant. Recommended.

B Fenix Inn, Jln Merdeka, T06-281 5511, www.fenixinn.com. New hotel close to good eating and shopping options on the edge of the Taman Melaka Raya area. Rooms are spacious, with a/c and attached bathroom. Most have windows (ones without windows smell musty). Free Wi-Fi access. Fair value.

B Number Twenty, 20 Jln Hang Jebat, T06-281 9761, www.twentymelaka.com. Charming guesthouse housed in a Dutch edifice built in 1673. With high ceilings, exposed beams and creaking floorboards, there are plenty of ancient vibes, although the owners have managed to blend these features well with simple contemporary furnishings. Rooms have a/c and Wi-Fi access. Shared bathroom only. Breakfast included in the price. The downside of this location is the Malay karaoke that blares from next door until late.

B-C Baba House 125-127 Jln Tun Tan Cheng Lock, T06-281 1216, www.thebabahouse. com.my. In the centre of Chinatown, 60 comfortable, though slightly sterile, rooms with a/c and TV in an attractive traditional Peranakan house. Prices increase for the few rooms with windows. Wi-Fi available in the lobby. Small café attached.

B-C Johan, 210 Jln Melaka Raya 1, T06-286 5703, travellodgemik@yahoo.com. Another hotel catering for budget business travellers. Rooms are clean and have TV, a/c and attached bathroom. Wi-Fi access in the lobby. Not wildly atmospheric, but fair value for money.

D Grand Star, 256b & 257b, Taman Melaka Raya Jalan 3, T06-281 8199, F283 6891. An extensive guesthouse, a little grubby but with friendly staff and good facilities.

D Sunny's Inn, 270 Jln Taman Melaka Raya, T06-226 5446/T019-360 6232, www.geocities.com/sunny_inn2002. Looking a bit worse for wear nowadays, with its checked red lino floor and broken doors. Rooms are clean, and adequate for a short stay.

D-E Chong Hoe, 26 Jln Tukang Emas, T06-282 6102. Simple tidy rooms with a/c smack in the middle of Chinatown, opposite the Masjid Kampong Kling mosque. Reasonable value.

D-E Discovery Guesthouse, 3 Jln Bunga Raya, T06-292 5606, discoverycafe_1999@ yahoo.com. A warren of rooms located above this popular watering hole. Rooms are simple, and can get a little noisy if the bar has a live act on. Shared bathroom with squat toilet.

D-E Eastern Heritage, 8 Jln Bukit China, T06-283 3026, www.eastern-heritage.com. Great old Chinese building with carved wood and gold inlay, spacious and basic rooms on the 2nd floor with interesting murals, a dorm on the 3rd floor and a small dipping pool on 1st floor. Batik lessons are available. They provide a useful town map covering the centre's highlights.

D-E Jalan Jalan, 8 Jln Tukang Besi, T012-612 6665. New backpacker place with small but clean fan rooms in an excellent location. There is a garden out the back and free Wi-Fi access. Good value.

D-E Ringo's Foyer Guesthouse, 46A Jln Portugis, T06-281 6393, www.ringosfoyer.com.my. Highly sociable place owned by a local musician and his pals. The rooms are basic but clean and have a/c or

fan with shared bathroom. The guesthouse is festooned with items salvaged from the dump, and they have made excellent use of old sewing machines, windows and doorways throughout. There's a pleasant rooftop terrace for beers and sunbathing. Howard, one of the owners, takes guests out each night to sample Melaka's cuisine. Single sex dorms (RM13). Wi-Fi available. Recommended.

D-E Shirah's Guesthouse, 207 Taman Melaka Raya, T06-286 1041, shirahgh@ tim.net.my. This place has an interesting choice of rooms, from the dark and gloomy to the spacious and comfy with a/c and attached bathroom. Ask to see a selection. Dorm available.

D-E Tony's Guesthouse, 24 Lorong Banda Kaba, T012-688 0119, cobia43@hotmail.com. Whilst this place is a tad tatty, it has cheap fan rooms, a helpful owner and free Wi-Fi. Rooms are eye-bulgingly colourful and covered in Tony's eccentric art. Shared bathrooms and a café. Recommended.

Homestay

C-D Seri Tanjung, T06-384 5853 (enquire in Tourist Office for booking, or call the number). Located in the village of Seri Tanjung (once winner of nationwide Most Beautiful Village contest), some 24 km outside Melaka, the homestay here focuses on agricultural activities.

Tanjung Kling p206

A Klebang Beach Resort, 92-1, km 9, Batang Tiga, Tanjung Kling, T06-315 5888, www.malacca.ws/klebangmc. This small hotel has 46 clean and comfortable rooms, although the decor is unimaginative. There's a small free-form pool, a paddling pool, a children's playground and 2 restaurants.

A Riviera Bay Resort, 10 km, Jln Tanjung Kling, T06-315 1111, www.malaccahotels.net. Neoclassical architecture on a palatial scale. This U-shaped building on 14 floors has 450 spacious suites, tastefully decorated in shades of green and all sea-facing, with a/c, TV, in-house movies and minibar. Other amenities include 3 restaurants, the Buccaneer pub, hair salon, children's playground, water sports, tennis, pool with swim-up bar, paddling pool. Just 15 mins' drive from Melaka's town centre.

A Shah's Beach Resort, 9 km, Tanjung Kling, T06-315 3120, www.shahsresorts.com. A/c, restaurant, pool, 1950s front with 2 lines of a/c chalets behind, set in tropical grounds. Tennis court and pool can be used by non-guests for a fee. Internet access. Breakfast included.

Ayer Keroh p206

B Seri Warisan Resort, Lebuh Ayers Keroh, next to Mini Malaysia, T06-232 5211. Motel-like atmosphere, a/c, restaurant, pool and sauna.

C-E Ayer Keroh Recreational Forest, off the main road opposite Mini Malaysia, call Malacca Forest Department, T06-529 1244, www.forestry.gov.my/melaka/eng/index_en. htm. Hostel rooms (RM4), cabins (RM20) or chalets (RM50) with kitchenette.

Gunung Ledang p207

A-C Gunung Ledang Resort, 91-a, Jln Sutera, Taman Sentosa; sales office T06-977 2888, www.ledang.com. This place has 60 chalets and 30 jungle huts set in the jungle. Facilities include a pool, gym, health centre, restaurant and convention centre. The resort is about 2 hrs' drive on the North-South Express through Tangkak Town to Sagil; from there drive up the mountain.

● Eating

Melaka p192, maps p193 and p201
Pengkalan Pernu (Pernu Jetty), 10 km south on the way to Muar, has several fish restaurants and stalls where you can pick your own fish and have it grilled. North of Melaka, towards Tanjung Kling, there are a few Chinese seafood restaurants along the beach. A couple of the Indonesian *nasi*

Padang restaurants (see **Indori** below) in the Taman Melaka Raya area specialize in fresh *ikan bakar* (grilled fish)

Most restaurants in the Medan Portugis are expensive tourist traps but some of the spicy seafood dishes are worth trying.

�t♡ Flavours, 145 Jln Bendahara, T012-603 1113. Mon-Sat 1100-1500 and 1830-2230. New place in an airy restored shophouse with a koi-filled pond in the middle. Good Nyonya dishes as well as a smattering of Thai, Chinese and Japanese.

♡ Good New World Restoran, Taman Melaka Raya, T06-284 2528. Large and modern, specializes in Cantonese dishes. Locally recommended.

♡ Harper's, 2 Lorong Hang Jebat, T06-286 6592. Open 1200-1500, 1900-2200. Charming riverside eatery with high ceilings and some outdoor seating. Serves Western and Nyonya fare, but the real focus is on tapas. The menu features fair value combo meals where tapas can be paired with a main course. Wine and decent beer selection. Good place to catch sight of monitor lizards in the river.

♡ Indori, 236 Jln Melaka Raya 1, T06-282 4777. Open 0800-2300. New restaurant serving up tasty portions of authentic Indonesian *nasi Padang*. Choose from the selection in the window, or from the menu. The speciality here is freshly grilled fish. Recommended. There's another good *nasi Padang* restaurant 2 doors down from here which is slightly cheaper and more rustic, but equally authentic.

♡ Jonkers, 17 Jln Hang Jebat. Closes around 1600. Old Nyonya house, with restaurant in the old ancestral hall. Good atmosphere and an excellent place to try different types of laksa. There are also simple noodle dishes and more robust meals such as delicious *rendang* (fiery Indonesian beef stew). Recommended.

♡ Kapitan House, 71 Jln Merdeka, T06-282 6525. With food prepared by eccentric chef Kenny Chan, this excellent restaurant serves up mouthwatering dishes such as Nyonya *otak otak* (minced fish grilled inside a banana leaf), *asam* fish (spicy, sour) and Nyonya chicken roll.

Ole Sayang, Taman Melaka Raya, T06-283 1966. Serves all the Nyonya favourites, including chicken *pongteh* (in sweet and sour spicy sauce). Recommended.

Restoran de Lisbon, Portuguese Square. Run by Senhor Alcantra, this places comes recommended, with its dishes that blend Malaysian and Portuguese cuisines – including devil chicken curry and sea bass roasted in a banana leaf, all washed down with ice-cold Portuguese lager or wines. Cultural shows Sat evenings.

Restoran Peranakan, 107 Jln Tun Tan Cheng Lock, T06-284 5001. Only opens for dinner on weekends, on weekdays last orders are at 1530. Popular with tour groups, this is a decent place to come to try Nyonya dishes such as *asam pedas*, *sambal sotong* and *ayam pong teh*. Authentic atmosphere – eating here will recreate the feelings of dining in an upper-class Straits Chinese house about 100 years ago.

San Pedro, Portuguese Settlement (just off the square). Family run and probably the best at the Portuguese settlement, specialities include spicy baked fish wrapped in banana leaf.

Temple Street Bistro, 82 Jln Tokong, T06-286 9328. Newish place offering Western standards and good beer promos.

Bayonya, 164 Taman Malaka Raya, T06-2292 2192. Open Wed-Mon 1000-2200. Excellent Peranakan cuisine. The establishment is owned by a real enthusiast who will provide a culture lesson with your meal, and the food is certainly autherntic. Recommended.

Capitol Satay, 41 Lorong Bukit Cina, T06-283 5508. It's better to arrive early at this highly popular place serving *sate celup*, meat, seafood (including huge prawns), and veggies impaled on a bamboo stick and cooked in a broth or scalding peanut sauce. Look for the glutton's leaderboard on the wall. Highly recommended.

Discovery Café, 3 Jln Bunga Raya. A little haven for backpackers. A small, friendly café and bar with simple food for homesick foreigners. It has a terrace, pool table, darts board and TV.

Famosa Chicken Rice Ball, 28 Jln Hang Kasturi, T06-286 0121. There are several branches of Famosa in town, as tourists can't seem to get enough of the chicken rice ball – a golf ball-sized ball of rice cooked in chicken stock and served with delicious steamed chicken.

Geographér Café, 83 Jonker St, www.geographer.com.my. A friendly establishment with a good choice of local and Western food. Internet access. This place gets absolutely jammed at weekends and is open late for drinks. There's a pleasant dining area upstairs.

Heeren House, 1 Jln Tun Tan Cheng Lock. Good-value set lunch and cakes. Appeals to Western tastes, but has some Peranakan and Portuguese dishes. A/c and attractive Peranakan furniture. No meals served in the evening.

Hoe Kee Chicken Rice, Jln Hang Jebat. Hainanese chicken rice in Chinatown coffee shop, incredibly popular with workers at lunchtime. Recommended.

Limau Limau Café, 9 Jln Hang Lekiu, T012-698 4917. Open 1000-2100. Comfortable café with a selection of interesting goods to browse. The menu here is distinctly aimed towards Western visitors with chunky roasted vegetable sandwiches, hummus, a distinctive house salad featuring celery, apple and lychee and heavenly fruit juices and lassis. Internet access. Recommended.

Lu Yeh Yen, 154 Jln Bunga Raya. Chinese staples. It's best to come here at night when tables are set up in the temple courtyard. Bustling and popular. Service, albeit friendly, is slow and erratic.

Nyonya Makko, 124 Taman Melaka Raya, T06-284 0737. Located in the bustling Taman Melaka Raya area, this place gets rave reviews from locals. Good selection of dishes. Cheap and friendly. Recommended.

Restoran Veni, 34 Jln Temenggong, T06-284 9570. Open 0700-2200. Highly acclaimed eatery with superb veg and

non-veg sets with daily veg specials. Good fish cutlets, extraordinarily zesty lime pickle and mountains of rice. Recommended.
† **Selvam**, intersection of Bendahara and Temenggong. A great place to come for a breakfast of *masal dosai* and strong tea. This popular place also has a range of set meals and Indian standards.
† **Simply Fish**, 206 Jln Melaka Raya, T06-286 7697. Open 1100-2300. Spotlessly clean café serving an interesting range of mainly European-style fish dishes and the first place in town to go to satisfy fish and chip cravings.

Bakeries and ice cream
Outlets for both are in Mahkota Parade shopping mall and in the Dataran Pahlawan Mall. There's an outrageously popular doughnut shop in the latter serving toppings of every imaginable description including kiwi fruit. **Renaissance Melaka Hotel** has a good bakery shop in its lobby.

Foodstalls
Reassuringly touristy and spotlessly clean, the new **Newton Cultural Food Village**, opposite the Menara Taming Sari has dangling red lanterns and a selection of well-priced stalls serving up Portuguese curries, popiah, Penang fried *kway teow*, fish soups and even sushi. Open 1100-2200. Recommended. **Jln Bendahara**, has several noodle stalls and a *Mamak* man (Indian Muslim) who serves *sup kambing* (mutton soup) and the bits – for marrow suckers (opposite the **Capitol**), Chinese food. **Jln Bukit Baru**, just off the main road past the state mosque, mostly Chinese food. **Jln Bunga Raya**, stalls (next to Rex Cinema), seafood recommended. **Jln Semabok** (after Bukit Cina on road to JB), Malay-run fish-head curry stall, which is a local favourite. **Klebang Beach**, off Jln Klebang Besar, Tanjung Kling – stalls, with several *ikan panggang* (grilled fish) specialists.

Tanjung Kling *p206*
† **Roti John**, Pantai Kundor, on the seafront. Melaka's Roti John specialist.

† **Yashika Traveller Hostel**, Batu 8, Pantai Kundor. Beach restaurant, international.

Bars and clubs

Melaka *p192, maps p193 and p201*
At weekends, **Geographér's Café** and **Ringo's Classic Bar** (both Jln Lekir) get busy and have a superb, bustling ambience, with Ringo's playing an extraordinary selection of music. On the Jln Hang Lekir and Jln Tun Tan Cheng Lock junction is the **EZ and Light Bar**, popular with locals for after-work beers and a game of pool. Backpackers congregate at the **Discovery Café**, although there is awful live music.

Entertainment

Melaka *p192, maps p193 and p201*
Cinemas
Cinemas showing the latest blockbusters can be found in **Dataran Pahlawan Mall** and **Mahkota Parade**.

Clubs
Cosmopolitan Club, 14 Hang Lekir. The site of a club, formerly the Malayan Chinese Literary Association, exclusively for the Babas of Heeren St. Today, it is full of locals playing mah-jong and snooker. Non-members may join in games for a small fee. It's run by a friendly, English-speaking family with insiders' knowledge of their home town.

Cultural shows
At the Portuguese Settlement in Portuguese Sq, every Sat at 2030. With songs and dances. **Light and Sound Show**, on the Padang, opposite St Paul's Hill, T06-282 6526. English version daily 2000-2100, RM10, children RM2. A chronological history of Melaka, an hour-long show with a distinctly Malay nationalist perspective – there's only 5 mins' mention of European rule and no mention of the contribution by the Chinese and

Indian ethnic communities. It's not expertly presented.

Taman Mini Malaysia, Ayer Keroh. Sat, Sun and public holidays 1120 and 1430.

⊕ Festivals and events

Melaka *p192, maps p193 and p201*
March/April Easter Procession (movable), on Good Friday and Easter Sunday, starts from St Peter's Church.
May Saint Sohan Singh's Prayer Anniversary (movable), thousands of Sikhs from all over Malaysia and Singapore congregate at the Melaka Sikh temple, Jln Temenggong, to join in with the memorial prayers.
June 29 Pesta San Pedro (Feast of St Peter) (movable), celebrated at the Portuguese Settlement by fishermen. The brightly decorated fishing boats are blessed and prayers offered for a good season. **Mandi Safar** (movable), bathing festival at Tanjung Kling. **Kite Festival** (movable), on the seafront.

○ Shopping

Melaka *p192, maps p193 and p201*
Melaka is best known for its antique shops, which mainly sell European and Chinese items.

Antiques
Jln Hang Jebat (formerly Jonker St). The best place for antiques, from shadow puppets to Melakan furniture inlaid with mother-of-pearl.

Art
Jonker Art Collection, 76 Jln Hang Jebat, T06-283 6578. A small shop selling prints by local artists, in particular the work of Titi Kwok, son of the well-known Macau-based artist Kwok Se and owner of the **Cheng Hoon Art Gallery** situated a couple of streets away on Jln Tokong. He is often in the shop selling

his own beautiful Chinese-style ink paintings and has plenty of time for his customers. Recommended.
Orang-Utan House, see under Clothes below. Paintings by local artist Charles Cham.

Books
Boon Hoong Sports and Bookstore, 13 Jln Bunga Raya; **Jln Taman Melaka Raya**, english-language books; **Times Bookshop**, Jaya Jusco Stores, Mukim Bukit Baru.

Clothes
Orang-Utan House, 59 Lorong Hang Jebat www.charlescham.com/. Artist Charles Cham sells funky original T-shirts for RM30 from his shop. His place is hard to miss – a huge orange orang-utan is painted on the outside of the building. He has several branches in Melaka.

Furniture
Malacca Woodwork, 312c Klebang Besar, T06-315 4468. Specialist in authentic reproduction antique furniture including camphor wood chests.

Shopping centres
Main shopping centres on Jln Hang Tuah and Jln Munshi Abdullah.
Dataran Pahlawan Melaka Megamall, opposite Mahkota Parade. This is the newest mall in town and has a Carrefour supermarket, cinema and good Western and Asian dining options including pizza, roast chicken and sushi. There is also a food court here, although it is not busy and the food is mediocre.
Mahkota Parade Shopping and Entertainment Complex, including Parkson Grand Department Store and Supermarket, 1 Jln Merdeka, just south of the river mouth. A good choice of shops – the centre won an award for the best shopping centre in the country. A very Western feel with many international chain stores.

▲▲ Activities and tours

Melaka *p192, maps p193 and p201*
Boat tours
Boat tours of Melaka's docks, godowns, old Dutch trading houses, wharves and seafront markets run from the quay opposite the Post Office. Look for the yellow awning. Predictably this area is known as Melaka's Little Venice, but it doesn't live up to the description. However, the guides are generally informative, pointing out settlements and wildlife. There are views of the giant lizards on the banks. Boats leave when full (min 8 people) and usually there is a departure every hour or so between 1400 and 1700 (although departures do vary according to the tides). Tickets for the river boat can be purchased from the tourist office (45 mins, RM15, children RM8). For bookings, T06-642 9864.

Golf
A'Famosa Golf Resort, Jln Kemus, Pulan Sebang, T06-552 0777, www.afamosagolf.com.my. Near the Alor Gajah interchange of the North-South Expressway is this 9-hole course, featuring a novel crocodile pool. It also has a clubhouse, shop and accommodation.

Tour operators
Annah (Melaka) Tours & Travel, 27 Jln Laksamana, T06-283 5626; AR Tours, 302a Jln Tun Ali, T06-283 1977; Satik Tour & Travel, 143 Jln Bendahara, T06-283 5712.

Ayer Keroh *p206*
Golf
Ayer Keroh Golf Club, see page 207.

☉ Transport

Melaka *p192, maps p193 and p201*
Air
Airport is at Batu Berendam, 9 km out of town. Riau Airlines (www.riau-airlines.com)

runs a 4-weekly flight (Mon, Wed, Fri, Sat) to Pekanbaru in **Indonesia**. Tickets cost around RM300 for the short flight. Tourists from EU countries, Japan, USA and Australia are currently eligible for a VOA (Visa On Arrival) at Pekanbaru Airport. Check with your nearest Indonesian Embassy regarding any changes before purchasing a ticket. **AirAsia** has announced Melaka will shortly receive flights from Pekanbaru, Padang, Palembang and Medan in Sumatra. There are also plans to link the city with Penang. Check www.airasia.com for updates.

Bicycle hire
Many of the cheaper hotels/hostels rent out bikes, as do a few shops in town, RM5-8 per day.

Boat
Indomal Express ferries to **Dumai** (Sumatra), leave daily at 1000 from the public jetty on Melaka River, 2 hrs. Indomal Express office, G29, Jln PM10, Plaza Mahkota, T06-283 2506, www.m-sia.com/indomal/index.html. Tickets can also be bought from travel agents. Try **Atlas Travel Service**, Jln Hang Jebat, T06-282 0315. Service leaves Melaka at 0900 and at 1500, one-way RM110; return RM170. Ferries also leave for **Pekanbaru** (Sumatra) from the public jetty on Tue, Thu and Sat, 6½ hrs, one-way RM150; return RM260) at 0950. Tourists need to get an Indonesian visa in advance for Pekanbaru (port), but Dumai has VOA (Visa On Arrival) facilities. However, the visa situation in Indonesia is volatile, so check with the nearest embassy.

Buses
It's about RM1 around town on local buses. Long-distance buses leave from the terminal on Jln Tun Razak. The Panorama Melaka hop-on-hop-off buses do a circuit of the town calling at major tourist sights. There is a stop by the Stadthuys. A ticket, valid for a whole day, costs RM2. There are are 2 routes, clearly marked at each stop. The blue route covers a larger area and passes Kampung Portugiss,

Baba Nyonya Heritage Museum, Bukit China and Melaka Sentral. The smaller red route covers the main tourist spots. Regular connections from Melaka Sentral with **KL** (RM10), **Seremban** (RM6), **Port Dickson** (RM3), **Ipoh** (RM28), **Butterworth** and **Penang** (RM38), **Lumut** (Pulau Pangkor), **Kuantan**, **Kuala Terengganu**, **Kota Bharu**, **Johor Bahru** and **Singapore** (4 hrs, RM22 via JB).

There is a 7 times daily shuttle service from Melaka calling in at **KLIA** main terminal and the **LCCT**. It departs from 125, Jln SP1, Taman Semabok Perdana (2 hrs, RM36). Book tickets at travel agents in town. Check www.bjaya.com/airport.html for timetables.

Car hire
Avis, 124 Jln Bendahara, T06-284 6710; **Hawk**, T06-283 7878; **Sintat**, Renaissance Melaka Hotel, Jln Bendahara, T06-284 8888; **Thrifty**, G-5 Pasar Pelancong, Jln Tun Sri Lanang, T06-284 9471.

Taxi
Taxi drivers in Melaka refuse to use their meters. Bargain hard. When directing a taxi be careful not to confuse street names with general district areas; use the former whenever possible. There are stands outside major hotels and shopping centres, or T06-282 3630. Between 0100 and 0600 there is a 50% surcharge. A taxi to **KLIA** should cost RM150, and to **JB** RM250.

There is a taxi station at the long-distance bus station on Jln Tun Razak. Vehicles leave for **KL**, **Seremban**, **Penang**, **Mersing** and **Johor Bahru**. Passengers for Singapore must change taxis at Larkin terminal in JB.

Train
Nearest station is at Tampin, 40 km north; Tampin railway station, T06-441 1034. See www.ktmb.com.my for timetables.

Trishaws
Mostly for the tourist trade, they congregate at several points in town (there are usually a number near the tourist information centre on the town square). Fares are clearly printed at major trishaw gathering points such as near Christ Church. 1 hr costs RM40. For a single ride hard bargaining is required.

Tanjung Kling *p206*
Patt Hup bus Nos 51, 18, 42 and 47 can be caught from Jln Tengkera (at the north end of Jln Tun Tan Cheng Lock, in Melaka); there are also taxis.

❻ Directory

Melaka *p192, maps p193 and p201*
Banks Bumiputra, Jln Kota; HSBC, Jln Kota. Several banks on Jln Hang Tuah near the bus station and Jln Munshi Abdullah.
Emergencies Central Police Station, Jln Kota, T06-282 2222. **Tourist Police**, Jln Kota, T06-288 3732. **Immigration** Immigration office, Bangunan Persekutuan, Jln Hang Tuah, T06-232 2662 (for visa extensions).
Internet These are many in number, easy to come across and very inexpensive. Internet café, beside the Youth Museum, RM3 per hr; **Geographér Café** and **Discovery Café** also have internet. Nowadays, many guesthouses have free Wi-Fi access for those travelling with laptops. **Medical services** Straits Hospital, 37 Jln Parameswara, T06-282 2344. **Post office** General Post Office, T06-283 3844, just off Jln Kota next to Christ Church.

Johor Bahru → *Colour map 2, C5. Phone code: 07.*

Modern Johor Bahru – more commonly called JB – is not a pretty town. It lies on the southernmost tip of the Peninsula and is the gateway to Malaysia from Singapore. JB is short on tourist attractions but has for many years served either as a tacky red-light reprieve for Singaporeans and/or as a large retail outlet. There is little reason to stay here; most travellers pass through on their way from or to Singapore. ▶ *For listings, see pages 218-221.*

Ins and outs

Getting there

Senai airport ① *www.senaiairport.com*, is 20 km from town and there are connections with KL and several other destinations in East and Peninsular Malaysia. There are international air links with several destinations in Indonesia and with Bangkok. A shuttle bus service runs from the airport to town. There is a regular bus service between Singapore and KL and links with most other towns on the Peninsula. Outstation taxis provide a service to KL, Melaka and Kuantan. The KL–Singapore railway line runs through JB and there are trains to both destinations including commuter trains to Singapore. There is a FerryLink service between Changi Point in Singapore and Tanjung Belungkor. ▶ *See also Transport, page 219.*

Getting around

Hiring cars in JB is considerably cheaper than in Singapore. Cheap taxis (meters not an option) provide the main form of transport for most visitors.

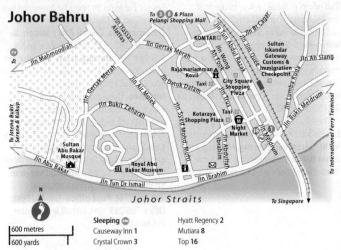

Johor Bahru

600 metres
600 yards

Sleeping
Causeway Inn **1**
Crystal Crown **3**

Hyatt Regency **2**
Mutiara **8**
Top **16**

Tourist information

Located at 2 Jalan Air Molek are the **Johor Tourist Information Centre (JOTIC)** ① *T07-223 4935, www.johortourism.com.my, Mon-Fri 0800-1630, Sat 0800-1230*, and the **Tourism Malaysia Information Centre** ① *T07-222 3591, www.tourismmalaysia.com.my*, but neither is very helpful.

Background

At weekends JB is jammed with Singaporeans, here, it would seem, largely for sex and/or shopping – and, perhaps, the chance to escape for a few hours from the stultifying atmosphere of their own clean and green country.

There are two links with Singapore: the old causeway across the Selat Tebrau (Strait of Johor), built in 1924, is overburdened with road traffic and also carries the railway and water pipelines (Singapore relies on Johor for most of its water supply). A bridge to the west of the causeway, known as the Second Link, is 30 km out of town to the west at Gelang Patah.

The Sultanate of Johor was founded to the east of modern JB in the 16th century by the stepson of Sultan Ahmad who had been forced to flee from Melaka by the Portuguese. Next was to follow almost 200 years of upheaval at the hands of the Achenese, the rival Sumatran kingdom on Jambi, infighting and also squabbling with the Dutch.

Abu Bakar, the grandson of Singapore's Temenggon Abdur Rahman, moved his headquarters to the small settlement of Tanjong Putri in Johor, which he renamed Johor Bahru in 1866. In the early 20th century, Johor attracted many European rubber planters. Johor was the last state to join the colonial Malay Federation, in 1914.

Sights

The renovated **Istana Besar** is the Sultan's former residence on Jalan Tun Dr Ismail (built by Sultan Abu Bakar in 1866). It is now a royal museum, the **Royal Abu Bakar Museum** ① *T07-223 0555, Sat-Thu 0900-1700, US$7 (payable in ringgit at a very poor exchange rate), under 12s US$3*. Today the Sultan lives in the Istana Bukit Serene, which is on the west outskirts of town (it is not open to the public) and locals say the Sultan enjoys great feng shui with his new residence. The Istana Besar is a slice of Victorian England set in beautiful gardens, overlooking the strait. In the north wing is the throne room and museum containing a superb collection of royal treasures, including gruesome hunting trophies such as hollow elephant feet and an array of tusks and skulls, as well as Chinese and Japanese ceramics.

Not far away, on Jalan Abu Bakar, is the **Sultan Abu Bakar Mosque**, which faces the Strait of Johor. It was finished in 1900 and clearly reflects the Victorian climate of the period. The mosque can accommodate 2500 worshippers.

The 32-m-high tower of the 1930s **Istana Bukit Serene** on Jalan Skudai – the home of the Sultan of Johore and not open to the public – is only outdone by the 64-m tower of the State Secretariat, on Bukit Timbalan, which dominates the town.

Kukup

On the Strait of Melaka 40 km southwest of Johor this small Chinese fishing kampong is renowned throughout the country and in Singapore for its seafood, especially prawns and chilli crab. Most of the restaurants, known as *kelong*, are built on stilts over the water. To get there, take bus No 3 to Pontian Kecil and from there take a taxi to Kukup; alternatively take a taxi the whole way.

◉ Johor Bahru listings

For Sleeping and Eating price codes and other relevant information, see Essentials pages 25-30.

◉ Sleeping

Johor Bahru *p216, map p216*
JB's top hotels cater for businesspeople and have all the 5-star facilities. Most budget travellers don't stop in JB so there really isn't much choice at the bottom end, except for seedy short-stay hotels.

AL Hyatt Regency, Jln Sungai Chat, T07-222 1234, www.johorbahru.regency.hyatt.com. Over 2 km west of town centre, all the comforts you would expect of the **Hyatt** chain including pool, tennis and an internet room. 10 mins from downtown JB.

AL Mutiara, Jln Dato Sulaiman, Century Garden, T07-332 3800, www.mutiarahotels.com. A/c, restaurants, pool, gym, 24-hr coffee house. Good views of the city, and complimentary shuttle service between hotel and main shopping plazas. Rooms are large and comfortable.

A Crystal Crown, 117 Jln Tebrau, T07-333 4422, www.crystalcrown.com.my. A/c, restaurants, TV, business centre, tea and coffee-making facilities, minibar, pool, organizes car hire. Breakfast included. Tourist class hotel geared to business visitors.

B-C Causeway Inn, 6 Jln Meldrum, T07-224 8811, F224 8820. A/c, unlike neighbouring premises, this is a clean, quiet, well-run hotel that looks smart and does not overcharge with TV, excellent bathroom (bath). Check the room though because some have no view. Recommended.

C Top, 12 Jln Meldrum, T07-224 4755. Much better value than most of the mid-range

hotels in this area. Large rooms with huge beds. Bathrooms are of a very good standard. Recommended.

◉ Eating

Johor Bahru *p216, map p216*
JB is best known for its seafood, which is considerably cheaper than in Singapore.

♈♈♈ Meisan, Mutiara hotel, see opposite. Superb but expensive Sichuan restaurant, serving spicy specialities.

♈♈ George & Dragon Café, 1 Jln Glsier, far out on the western edge of town. Family-run restaurant serving English and Irish pub grub including pies and steaks. Also serves afternoon tea with scones and cream.

♈♈ Kinsahi, Plaza Pelangi, T07-332 3288. Japanese cuisine served in a relaxing setting inside a shopping mall. Recommended.

♈♈ Marina Seafood, 1d Jln Skudai. Very popular, specialities include drunken prawns, frogs' legs and chilli crabs. Diners may find flashing neon lights and revolving stage unsettling. Good views across the Singapore Straits. Recommended.

♈♈ Newsroom Café, Puteri Pacific hotel, Jln Abdullah Ibrahim, T07-219 9999. Reasonably priced local and continental dishes.

♈♈ Seasons Café, branches in City Square and Plaza Pelangi. Café serving a mixture of Western snacks and breads and some Asian rice dishes.

♈ Sedap Corner, branches in Plaza Kotaraya, Plaza Pelangi and City Square, among other locations. Chain of serving good Chinese and Malay food.

Yamani Café, Plaza Seni. A tiny streetside café serving a mixture of Arabic, Malay and Western food. Good atmosphere opposite stage where evening traditional dance performances are often held.

Coffee shops

There are branches of **Coffee Bean** and **Starbucks** in City Square.

Foodstalls

The night market on Jln Wong Ah Fook is a great place to sample the full array of stall dishes.

Tepian Tebrau, Jln Skudai (facing the sea beside the General Hospital). Good for Malay food, including satay and grilled fish. There is also good stall food at the long distance bus terminal and outside the railway station. There is a sprawling outdoor hawker centre right in the centre of town, adjacent to the Plaza Kotaraya on Jln Trus. **Pantai Lido** is another well-known hawker centre. There is a food court in the **Kompleks Tun Abdul Razak**, Jln Wong Ah Fook, and in **Plaza Kotaraya** on Jln Trus.

O Shopping

Johor Bahru *p216, map p216*
Handicrafts

Craftwork Handicraft Centre, Jln Skudai; Jaro, Jln Sungai Chat; Johorcraft, Kompleks Kotaraya and Kompleks Tun Abdul Razak, Jln Trus; Karyaneka Centre at Kompleks Mawar, 562 Jln Sungeai Chat; Mawar, Jln Sultanah Rogayah, Istana Besar.

Shopping centres

Large shopping complexes include the upmarket **City Square** (once inside you could be in Singapore) on Jln Wong Ah Fook, www.city-square.com. **Holiday Plaza**, Jln Datuk Sulaiman, 3 floors of retails outlets as well as a cinema, nightclub, hawker centre and various fast-food outlets. **Johor Bahru Duty Free Complex**, next to the International

Ferry Terminal and said to be one of the largest such complexes in the world – better known as ZON. **Kompleks Tun Abdul Razak** (KOMTAR), Jln Wong Ah Fook. **Kotaraya**, off Jln Trus, a pink building situated in the centre of the city, opposite the night market – possibly the best place to shop with a hawker centre upstairs. **Plaza Pelangi**, Jln Tebrau, billed as JB's 'most exciting mall', shops include fashion goods, souvenirs, handicrafts and there is also the usual range of food and beverage outlets. **Plaza Seni**, a tiny place selling handicrafts and Arabic hookah pipes. **Sentosa Complex**, Jln Sutera.

▲ Activities and tours

Johor Bahru *p216, map p216*
Golf

Palm Resort Golf and Country Club, Jln Persiaran Golf, off Jln Jumbo (near airport), Senai, T07-599 6222, www.palmresort.com. 3 18-hole championship courses, part of a 5-star resort, which includes tennis, squash, bowls, pool and gym.
Royal Johor Country Club, Jln Larkin, T07-223 3322, www.royaljohorcountryclub.com. 18-hole golf course.

☉ Transport

Johor Bahru *p216, map p216*
Air

MAS and AirAsia fly into Senai, JB's airport, 20 km north of the city. Transport to town: Buses run to/from the City Airport Lounge at Kotaraya 2 bus terminal on Jln Trus. Buses depart roughly every half hour from 0815 to 2055 (40 mins, RM8). Those wishing to travel to Larkin can hop on Maju Bus 207. The taxi ride from the aiport to the city costs RM40, and takes 30 mins. As Senai is viewed as a threat to Changi, transport links from Singapore to Senai are poor and involve a change of vehicle in JB. Regular connections on MAS and AirAsia to **KL**, **Kota Kinabalu**,

Kuching, Sibu and Penang. AirAsia also has direct flights to Jakarta and Surabaya. Firefly has daily flights to Subang and Penang.

Airline offices MAS, 1st floor, Plaza Pelangi, Menara Pelangi, Jln Kuning, Taman Pelangi, T07-334 1003, a little over 2 km from the town centre. AirAsia, JOTIC, 2 Jln Ayer Molek, T07-222 4760.

Boat

JB's ferry terminal to the east of the causeway operates ferry services to **Tanjung Belungkor**. Bumboats leave from various points along Johor's ragged coastline for **Singapore**; most go to **Changi Point** (Changi Village), on the northeast of the island, where there is an immigration and customs post. The boats run from 0700-1600 and depart when full (12 passengers). There is a passenger ferry from Tanjung Belungkor (JB) to Changi Ferry Terminal 3 times a day, T06-5323 6088. JB's ferry terminal east of the causeway has connections with **Batam** in Indonesia.

Bus

Local buses leave from the main bus terminal on Jln Wong Ah Fook.

The Larkin bus terminal is inconveniently located 4 km north of the town centre. Book tickets at agents in town or at the station itself. Regular connections with **Melaka**, **KL** (RM31), **Lumut**, **Ipoh** (RM52), **Butterworth** (RM60), **Mersing** (RM12), **Kuantan**, **Kuala Terengganu** and **Alor Star** (RM69).

International connections From **Singapore** there are 3 bus services. The SBS No 170 runs every 15 mins from Singapore's Ban San Terminal between Queen St and Rochor Canal Rd. Tickets are all priced around RM2 from JB, or S$1.90 (twice as much) from Singapore. The **Johor Singapore Express** is a/c and is faster, slightly more frequent and also leaves from Ban San (S$2.40). Both buses end up at the JB Larkin terminal. The yellow **Causeway Link** bus with a smiley face runs between Kranji MRT station in Singapore and the Larkin terminal. It only takes 20 mins from

the border to the MRT station. All 3 buses require you to get off twice – for the Malaysian border point and its Singaporean counterpart. You have to take all your luggage with you since the bus does not wait for you. You wait for the next bus to come along; each bus has its own stop after exiting immigration. Keep your ticket or you will have to buy a new one. Also have a pen handy to fill in immigration forms as they are not provided.

The new Malaysian border crossing, the Sultan Iskandar Gateway, opened in Dec 2008 and is a huge improvement on the previous border. However, be warned that this border sees busy queues on Sun evenings as waves of Sinagporeans return home. If you plan on staying in JB, you don't need to board the bus again after passing Malaysian immigration. Just walk out of immigration and you are in JB Sentral in the heart of the city. The streets here have lots of budget hotels, or you can catch a taxi. There's little point in going to Larkin bus terminal unless you plan on taking a bus out of JB.

Car hire

It is much cheaper to hire a car in JB than it is in neighbouring Singapore, but check whether the car hire company allows the car to go to Singapore. The causeway between JB and Singapore should be avoided at all costs during public holidays. It gets particularly jammed at rush hours.

Avis, Tropical Inn Hotel, 15 Jln Gereja, T07-224 4824; **Budget**, Suite 216, 2nd floor, Orchid Plaza, T07-224 3951; **Calio**, Tropical Inn, Jln Gereja, T07-223 3325; **Halaju Selatan**, 4M-1 Larkin Complex, Jln Larkin; **Hertz**, Room 646, Puteri Pacific Hotel, Jln Salim, T07-223 7520.

Taxis

Taxis, minus the meter, are plentiful. The main long-distance taxi station is attached to the Larkin bus terminal 4 km north of town. Taxis from here to destinations including **KL**, **Melaka**, **Mersing** and **Kuantan**.

Malaysian taxis leave, when full, for **Singapore** from the taxi rank on the 1st floor of the car park near the KOMTAR building on Jln Wong Ah Fook and go to the JB taxi rank on Rochor Canal Rd in Singapore. Drivers provide immigration forms and take care of formalities, making this a painless way of crossing the causeway. Touts also hang around JB's taxi rank offering the trip to Singapore in a private car. They will take you directly to your address in Singapore, although their geography of the island is not always expert. This is also a fairly cost-effective way to travel and is reliable.

Train
The station is on Jln Campbell, near the causeway, off Jln Tun Abdul Razak. Regular connections with **KL** and all destinations on the west coast, see www.ktmb.com.my for timetables. Malaysian and Singapore immigration desks are actually in the Singapore railway station, so for those wanting to avoid delays on the causeway, this is a quick way to get across the border. A new train station is being built at the Sultan Iskandar integrated border complex.

✪ Directory

Johor Bahru p216, map p216
Banks Bumiputra, HSBC and United Asia are on Bukit Timbalan. Several money changers in the big shopping centres and on/around Jln Ibrahim/Jln Meldrum.
Immigration Immigration office, 1st floor, Block B, Wisma Persektuan, Jln Air Molek, T07-224 4253. **Internet** There are some internet cafés opposite City Square shopping plaza on Jln Wong Ah Fook. There's also internet on the 2nd floor of Larkin Bus Station. **Medical services** Sultanah Aminah General Hospital, Jln Skudai. **Post office** Jln Tun Dr Ismail.

Pulau Tioman and around → Colour map 2, B5.

There are a total of 64 islands off Mersing in the Seribuat archipelago; many are inaccessible and uninhabited. The most accessible of these is Tioman, made famous by the Hollywood movie South Pacific and which has scores of resorts, simple beach huts and dive operators. It is also possibly to island hop to bask on deserted beaches or snorkel in coves – Pulau Rawa, Pulau Tengah and Pulau Besar are nearest the coast. Further afield, the islands mainly cater to serious divers or fishing enthusiasts. ▶▶ *For listings, see pages 229-240.*

Ins and outs

Getting there and around
There is accommodation and boats to Pulau Rawa, Pulau Babi Besar (Big Pig Island), Pulau Tinggi, Pulau Sibu, Pulau Aur (Bamboo Island) and Pulau Pemanggil. The main departure point is Mersing, see below. ▶▶ *See also Transport, page 238.*

Best time to visit
If you plan on visiting any of the beaches or islands on the east coast, and especially if you're hoping to dive, the best time to visit is between February and September to avoid the rainy season. During the winter monsoon, the seas are very rough, many island resorts are closed and boat operators pack up business. Between May and September is the best time for turtle spotting.

This small fishing port is a pleasant little town distinguished only by the Masjid Jamek, a green-tiled mosque, 500 m out of town on the top of a hill. Most people are in a hurry to get to the islands, namely Pulau Tioman, the best known of the East Coast's islands, and spend as little time as possible in the town.

As ferry times can sometimes be erratic, it's possible to get stuck here overnight if you don't arrive early enough. In recent years a number of good little restaurants have sprung up and Mersing is a relaxed place to spend a day or two and has a pleasant kampong area north of the jetty good for an evening stroll. The town is evidently prospering, thanks to the flow of tourists to the islands. There is a plethora of tour and ticketing agencies as well as a shiny shopping plaza. **Mersing Tourist Information Centre** ⓘ *Jln Abu Bakar (about 5 mins from the jetty walking into town), T07-799 5212, Mon-Thu 0800-1300 and 1400-1630, Fri 0800-1200 and 1445-1630, Sat 0800-1245, although it's sometimes closed during these times*, is friendly and is a useful source of information.

Pantai Air Papan is 9 km north of Mersing and is the best mainland beach in the area. (Formerly, the most popular beach was **Sri Pantai**, but it is now stony and unpleasant.) Pantai Air Papan is 5 km off the main road north and the beach is about 2 km long, between two headlands. The beach is quite exposed but is backed by lines of casuarina and coconut palms. There is a liberal scattering of rubbish among the trees. There are a number of places at the end of the road offering budget accommodation and a few beach shelters dotted along the beach. To get there, take the Mersing-Endau bus to Simpang Air Papan (turn-off); there is no bus service connecting with the beach, although it is possible to hitchhike. Chartered taxis are also available; arrangements can be made for pick-ups later in the day.

Pulau Tioman
→ For listings, see pages 229-240.

Tioman, 56 km off Mersing, is the largest island in the volcanic Seribuat Archipelago at 20 km by 12 km. The island is dominated by several jagged peaks, notably the twin peaks of Nenek Semukut and Bau Sirau towards the southern end of the island and in Malay legend its distinctive profile is the back of a dragon whose feet got stuck in the coral. It is densely forested and is fringed by white coral sand beaches, with kampongs around the coast.

Mersing

To Masjid Jamek
To Pulau Tioman & Islands
Plaza R & R
Jetty
Jln Tun Dr Ismail
Jln Dato Mohd Ali
Giant Supermarket
Jln Pasar
To R & Pantai Air Papan
To Pulau Air Papan
Local Buses
Jln Sulaiman
Taxis
Jln Abu Bakar
Jln Ismail
Shell
To Kuantan
Long Distance
Island Connection Travel
Long Distance
To Johor Bahru

N

100 metres
100 yards

Sleeping
Country 1
Embassy 2
Mersing Inn 6
Seri Malaysia 9
Teluk Godek Chalet 3
Timotel 12

Eating
Al-Arip 2
Corner Lot One Seafood 3
Kedai Kek Kile Bakery 1
Mersing Seafood 4
Port Café 5
Restoran P1 6
Sweet Story 7
Yong Seng Seafood 8

Ins and outs

Getting there The airport is in the centre of Tekek. Daily connections with KL and Singapore. The **Berjaya Tioman Beach Resort** (see page 230) sends a bus to meet each plane and various touts approach likely looking passengers. The jetty is just 100 m away where you can catch a sea taxi or ferry to other spots or walk to your hotel. Most people arrive on Tioman by ferry from Mersing. The jetty at Mersing is five minutes' walk out of Mersing next to the blue-roofed R&R Plaza. Tickets can be bought from one of the many ticket offices at the R&R Plaza. The variety can be confusing and slightly concerning but in fact all licensed vendors comply with the regulation price. The ferry timetable is only drawn up a month in advance because it depends on tides.

Getting around There are very few trails around the island and one main road, a 2 km stretch from the airstrip at Tekek to the Berjaya Tioman Beach Resort (to the southwest of the airport) and a new section from Tekek across the island to Kampong Juara on the eastern coast. You can still walk from the west side of the island to the east by a beautiful jungle trail or you can hire a taxi in town, of which 4WDs are probably the best option. To get from one kampong to another, the best way is to go by boat and a sea bus service works its way around the island. To get to Mukut and Nipah you must get off at Genting from where you can hire a boat to the beach. For Paya you need to ask the boat to make the stop.

Best time to visit Many guesthouses and resorts close down between November and February when it is wet and can be windy and rough. Chinese New Year seems to be a popular time for places to open, cashing in on the Singapore market, but as Chinese New Year is a moveable feast the date varies from year to year. Transport from Mersing also becomes more difficult during the off season; ferries will only leave if there is sufficient demand to make it worth their while.

The highest peak is Gunung Kajang (1049 m) or Palm Frond Mountain. It has been used as a navigational aid for centuries and is mentioned in early Arab and Chinese sailing charts. In the mid-1970s, 12th-century Sung Dynasty porcelain was unearthed on the island.

Tourist information The Tioman website, www.tiomanisland.com.my, has lots of local information including details of accommodation and ferries.

Alcohol Many locals are unhappy with the sale of alcohol on the island. However, the upmarket resorts generally cater to alcohol-drinking guests and there is plenty of cheap booze at the duty-free stores. There are a couple of small bars at the larger resort areas such as Salang and Ayer Batang. Many of the simpler chalet operations do not allow alcohol on their premises, while a few others will quietly serve beer or wine at their restaurant.

Background

Despite the growth in hotels and guesthouses, Tioman remains a beautiful island. In the 1950s it was discovered by Hollywood and selected as the location for the musical *South Pacific* where it starred as the mythical island of Bali Hai. All this attention put Tioman on the map; tourism accelerated during the 1970s and 1980s as facilities were expanded. However, over the last decade business has not been quite so brisk and prices, which at some places during the 1980s and 1990s were absurdly high, given the level of amenities on offer, have now levelled out.

The cheaper beach huts are mostly to be found on the northwest side of the panhandle, and despite a growth in the number of places to stay, these little kampongs have retained their charm and are still very laid back, making them an idyllic retreat for anyone who is looking for a deserted beach, snorkelling or diving and some great seafood, although Kampong Salang has developed a slightly brash atmosphere. Thankfully, as yet, there are no nightclubs or fast-food restaurants and the tourist trinket shops are very low key.

Kampong Tekek

Kampong Tekek is the kampong-capital of Tioman and, frankly, is nothing special. However, because boats from Mersing call first at Tekek's large concrete jetty, and the airport is also here, many visitors decide to stay put rather than face another journey. Tekek has the longest beach on the island, but for a large stretch north of the jetty it is rather dirty and with an ugly concrete breakwater. Almost all the coral is dead and broken, the river is polluted and there are rusting oil drums and other paraphernalia littering the town. There are many places to stay at Tekek, mostly south of the jetty or towards the northern end of the bay. However, much of the accommodation is run down and the place doesn't have much of a tropical island resort atmosphere. It feels like a small service centre, which is what it is. Tekek has a couple of duty free shops, small post office, a police post, an excellent clinic, a few money changers, the administrative HQ for the island, a few mini markets and an immigration office. The main area of accommodation is a 10-minute walk south of the jetty. To the north is the Pulau Tioman Marine Park Headquarters, with a jetty and a floating pontoon that offers some good snorkelling. A new road and promenade is being constructed from Tekek to the Marine Park headquarters, further diminishing the area's charm⋙ See also map, page 230.

The island

Kampong Lalang is not really a kampong at all but a beach devoted solely to the Berjaya Tioman Beach Resort and its sister condotel.

The beach is rocky at low tide at **Ayer Batang** (also known as ABC) and the sandy area quite small. The better portion of the beach is south of the jetty. Monitor lizards roam freely and the tall coconut palms are home to scores of bickering fruit bats that are noisiest at dusk. There are a couple of mini markets for supplies and souvenirs, a small beach bar and internet at Bamboo Hill guesthouse. ⋙ See also map, page 231.

Kampong Panuba is a tiny stretch of beach with a single resort just north of Ayer Batang.

Kampong Salang is the northernmost development on the island and is set in a sheltered cove with a beautiful beach. The beach is more rowdy than Ayer Batang, with some concrete development and more of a party scene, and its relaxed atmosphere attracts European backpackers and increasing numbers of domestic visitors. The mangrove swamp to the south of the jetty, though dirty, still holds plenty of monitor lizards that cruise around like primeval monsters. Some are getting on for 2 m in length. There are several minimarts along the main strip for basic supplies and internet at the Salang Indah. A 150-room resort lies unused and now decomposes on the south end of the bay, testament to the fact that Tioman cannot pull the kind of numbers developers had dreamed of, and a big pink concrete monstrosity of a food court stands sadly at the jetty. ⋙ See also map, page 232.

Kampong Paya, south of Tekek, is a quiet place with a small *surau* (prayer hall) and a couple of restaurants. Ferries from Mersing stop here. The beach is attractive enough but at low tide a belt of dead and broken coral makes swimming difficult and there have been reports that sandflies are sometimes a major nuisance. This resort is primarily frequented by package tour visitors from Singapore and elsewhere in Malaysia.

Kampong Genting lies to the south of Kampong Paya and is the second largest village on the island. However, it is not as popular as some of the other kampongs and has the feeling of a locals' resort; tourists are mainly from the mainland and Singapore. The extensive jetty gives an impression that the village had hoped for greater things. The beach here is poor; rocks are exposed at low tide and the coral is largely broken and dead. There is, though, an incredibly modest sight: the graves of Tun Mohamad bin Tun Adbul Majid, the sixth Bendahara of Pahang, and his wife, also of royal blood, the daughter of Sultan Mahmud of Johore-Riau-Lingga-Pahang. In 1803 the Bendahara (who had

Pulau Tioman

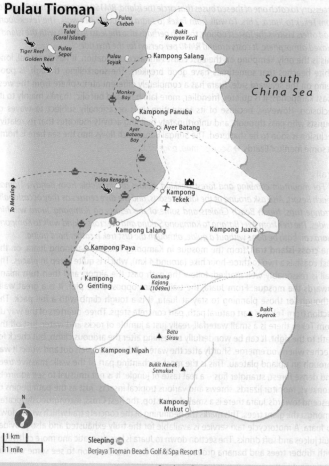

South China Sea

Pulau Chebeh

Bukit Kerayon Kecil ▲

Pulau Tulai (Coral Island)

Tiger Reef
Golden Reef

Pulau Sepoi

Pulau Soyak

○ Kampong Salang

Monkey Bay

Kampong Panuba ○

Ayer Batang ○
Ayer Batang Bay

Pulau Renggis

🏠

○ Kampong Tekek

To Mersing ◄

Kampong Lalang ○

Kampong Juara ○

Kampong Paya ○

Gunung Kajang (1049m) ▲

Kampong Genting ○

Bukit Seperok ▲

Batu Sirau ▲

Kampong Nipah ○

Bukit Nenek Semukut ▲

Kampong Mukut ○

N

|—— 1 km
|—— 1 mile

Sleeping 🛏
Berjaya Tioman Beach Golf & Spa Resort **1**

assumed the position the year before) and his wife were at sea between Tioman and the mainland when their boat foundered in a thunderstorm. With their cabin locked the couple were unable to escape and both drowned. Their bodies, though, were recovered and buried here after having been washed in fresh water from the local river – which is now known as the Sungai Air Rajah. Another version has it that the bodies were never found and the graves are purely symbolic. There is a *surau* (prayer hall) by the jetty.

Kampong Nipah is one of the most secluded and tranquil spots on the island.

Kampong Mukut is in a tiny, isolated rocky bay and doesn't have a great beach and just a handful of resorts but there are plenty of good treks and climbing trails.

Kampong Juara

① *Being on the east side of the island, the ferries from Mersing rarely call here and it is necessary to catch one of the sea buses that circle the island, RM150 per person (min 2 people) from Tekek to Juara, 2 hrs. To walk from Tekek to Juara is a tough 3-hr walk. The Tekek-Juara road offers visitors the fastest option, though perhaps also the least in touch with the island's relaxed atmosphere. It costs around RM40 per person for the taxi ride.*

This is the only kampong on the east coast with accommodation. It has beautiful, long white beaches that sometimes have swell breakers. The snorkelling, though, is poor. Being on the seaward side, Juara has a completely different atmosphere from the west coast kampongs; it is quieter, friendlier, more laid back and bucolic, thanks mainly to its seclusion. However, because of its reputation, it is occasionally subject to waves of tourists who pass through, and unfortunately building activity indicates that its relative seclusion is soon to be shattered. The Sungai Baru which flows into the sea here is home to some monitor lizards. ⏵ *See also map, page 233.*

Trails

① *For mountain climbing and forest trekking, guides are available from Berjaya Tioman Beach Resort. Also ask around at the larger resorts, and the dive centres as they occasionally arrange trips. Nipah Beach Chalets and some of the resorts on Kampong Juara will hire guides. The trek from Ayer Batang to Kampong Salang and the cross-island walk to Kampong Juara can both be done without a guide, although the first trek is rather hard going.*

The **cross-island trail**, from the mosque in Kampong Tekek to Kampong Juara, on the east coast, is a two to three-hour hike (around 4 km), which is quite steep in places. The trail is reasonably well marked: follow the path past the airport and then turn inland towards the mosque. From Juara, the trail begins opposite the pier. It is a great walk, although for those planning to stay at Juara, it is a tough climb with a full pack. The section from Tekek is part natural path, part concrete steps. Three-quarters of the way up from Tekek there is a small waterfall, really just a jumble of rocks and water, just off the path to the right. It can be wonderfully refreshing after the arduous climb, but check for leeches when you emerge. Shortly after the waterfall the route levels out and works its way through an upland plateau. This is the most enchanting part of the walk: massive trees and dense forest, strangler figs – a real taste of jungle. It is not unusual to see squirrels, monkeys, monitor lizards, shrews and various tropical insects. Just as the path begins to descend towards Juara there is a small drinks stop, the Rest Cross, incongruously located amongst the giant trees. This marks the beginning of the concrete trail which winds down to Juara. A motorcycle taxi service is available for the truly exhausted and also provides fruit juices and soft drinks. The section down to Juara is less dramatic and more cultivated with rubber trees and banana groves, but even here it is common to see some wildlife, including monkeys and squirrels. To return to the west coast, there is an expensive daily sea bus service from Juara leaving in the afternoon.

There are also many easier jungle and coastal walks along the west coast: south from Tekek, past the resort to kampongs **Paya** and **Genting** and north to **Salang**. The walk from Ayer Batang to Salang is a difficult one of more than three hours, with a trail that snakes over rocky outcrops, fallen trees and sometimes peters out altogether. About an hour and a half into the walk you will hit **Monkey Bay**, which is a beautiful white sandy beach. If you get fed up with the trek you can always shout down a passing boatman to get you back to civilization. (The sea taxi ride from Monkey Bay back to Penuba, ABC or Salang costs RM15.) There are times when the trail gets very difficult to follow, and the best way is to keep following the power line above it, which runs between ABC and Salang. Bring enough water and don't attempt the walk in flip flops.

Gunung Kajang can be climbed from the east or west sides of the island; an unmarked trail leads from the Tioman Island golf course (advisable to take a guide). It is also possible to trek to **Bukit Nenek Semukut** (Twin Peaks) and **Bukit Seperok**. The trail up Semukut starts from Pasir Burong, the beach at Kampong Pasir.

Diving

① *There are dive shops based in most of the kampongs: at Salang, Tekek, Genting, Paya, Ayer Batang and at the Berjaya Tioman Beach Resort, see page 237.*

Tioman's coral reefs are mainly on the western side of the island, although sadly large areas have been killed off. This is in part due to fishing boats dragging anchor; nimble-fingered snorkellers pilfering coral stalks (thereby killing neighbouring corals); boat activity kicking up sand and retarding the growth or killing the coral; and damage caused by the crown-of-thorns starfish. Wholesale coral 'harvesting' has also been going on, to feed the increasingly lucrative trade in saltwater aquaria. Live coral specimens are loaded into water-filled bags, having been hacked off reefs with pickaxes. This practice has more or less ended around Tioman now, but is still reported to be going on off other east coast islands. Pollution also kills coral. Both sewerage and effluent from building sites can alter water salinity levels, killing coral and resulting in the proliferation of harmful algae.

There are still some magnificent coral beds within easy reach of the island. **Pulau Renggis**, just off the Berjaya Tioman Beach Resort, is the most easily accessible coral from the shore, with a depth of up to 12 m and a good place for new divers to find their flippers. For more adventurous dives, the islands off the northwest coast are a better bet. There is cave diving off **Pulau Chebeh** (up to 25 m) and varied marine life off the cliff-like rocks of the **Golden Reef** (depths up to 20 m) and nearby **Tiger Reef** (for 9-24 m dives). Off the northeastern tip of the island is **Magicienne Rock** (20-24 m dives), where bigger fish have been sighted. Off the southwestern coast is **Bahara Rock** (20 m), considered one of the best spots on the island.

Boat tours

Boats leave from Kampong Tekek, ABC and Salang to Pulau Tulai (or Coral Island, RM70), Turtle Island, to a waterfall at Mukut or an around-island trip (RM100). All boats must be full otherwise prices increase. Boat trips can also be arranged to other nearby islands.

Pulau Rawa

A small island 16 km off Mersing, Pulau Rawa is owned by a nephew of the Sultan of Johor and was one of the first resorts built in the area; it remains highly rated by lots of travellers. The island has a fantastic beach and for those in need of a desert-island break Rawa is perfect, for there is absolutely nothing to do except mellow out. Unfortunately the coral reef is disappointing, but more active visitors can windsurf, canoe and fish. The island gets busy at weekends as it is close enough for day visitors; it is also a popular getaway for Singaporeans.

Pulau Babi Besar, Pulau Tinggi and Pulau Sibuh Tengah

Pulau Babi Besar is larger and closer to the mainland than Rawa. It is a very peaceful island and is particularly well known for its beaches and coral. Pulau Tinggi is probably the most dramatic-looking island in the Seribuat group, with its 650-m volcanic peak, but is less popular than neighbouring Sibuh Tengah. Pulau Sibuh Tengah, formerly a refugee camp for Vietnamese boat people, is an hour away from Mersing. The government has declared it a marine park because of its reef and the fact that giant leatherback turtles (see page 268) lay their eggs there between June and August.

Pulau Sibu and Pulau Pemanggil

Pulau Sibu, otherwise known as the Island of Perilous Passage (also including Pulau Sibu Besar, Pulau Sibu Tengah, Pulau Sibu Kukus and Pulau Sibu Hujung) because it used to be a pirate haunt, has been recommended by many travellers for its beaches and water sports. Sibu is frequented more by Singaporeans and expats than by Western tourists. It is popular for fishing and diving and because it is larger than the other islands there is more of a sense of space and there are also some good walks. The best beaches on Pulau Pemanggil are at kampongs Buan and Pa Kaleh, which is fortunately where the accommodation is sited. Landmarks include the Harimo (Tiger) Caves which are good for snorkelling.

Pulau Aur

Pulau Aur, at 80 km from the mainland, is one of the furthermost islands of the Seribuat Archipelago. It is only really accessible by buying a fairly expensive dive package. Once home to hundreds of fishermen, traders and slaves, and the favourite hunting ground of pirates, the island now only caters to tourists, for the main part divers hungry for wreck dives.

For Sleeping and Eating price codes and other relevant information, see Essentials pages 25-30.

● Sleeping

Mersing *p222, map p222*

B Mersing Inn, 38 Jln Ismail, T07-799 1919, F799 2288. 5 mins' walk from the jetty, this spotless but wholly unexciting hotel has a range of comfortable carpeted a/c rooms with attached bathroom and tiny TV.

B Seri Malaysia, Jln Ismail, T07-799 1876, www.serimalaysia.com.my. Chain hotel with clean a/c rooms, limited ambience and fair prices.

B Timotel, 839 Jln Endau, T07-799 5898, www.timotel.com.my. Looks like a set of offices from the outside and located near the long-distance bus stand, this hotel is a bit of a trek into town. Rooms are comfortable and spacious, making this one of the town's better mid-range options.

B-C Embassy, 2 Jln Ismail, T07-799 3545, F799 5279. Selection of a/c and fan rooms with TV and attached bathroom in the heart of the town. The hotel is efficiently managed and kept spotlessly clean. Small restaurant/bar downstairs. Rooms at the front face a busy road and can be a bit noisy, ask for a room at the back. Recommended.

C Country, 11 Jln Sulaiman, T07-799 1799. Get past the first impression of the grumpy owner and the rooms here are a pleasant surprise; clean and with a/c or fan and attached bathroom.

C-E Teluk Godek Chalet, Pantai Air Papan, T07-799 4469. A/c rooms with cable TV and telephone.

Pulau Tioman *p222, map p225*

Sandflies can be a problem on Tioman and mosquito coils are recommended.

The **Berjaya Tioman Beach Resort** and most of the cheaper places to stay are scattered along the west coast (the island is virtually uninhabited on the southeast and

southwest sides and north of Juara Beach on the east coast, apart from a few fishing kampongs). Most of the accommodation on the island is simple; they are often individually owned by locals who may offer home-cooked meals, and it is often hard to distinguish between them in terms of facilities and quality. Generally *atap* or tin-roofed chalets/huts are in the **C-E** categories and A-frames are in the **E-F** categories. Chalets with attached bathrooms fall into the **C-D** categories and upwards. Rooms are fairly spartan; expect to pay more for mosquito nets and hot water. Inevitably, beachfront chalets cost more. Due to stiff competition, many prices are negotiable depending on the season.

For the island's more luxurious resorts, it's always worth checking their websites a few weeks in advance for specials and package deals; you can find some real bargains, especially in the low season.

Kampong Tekek

A-B Monte Chalets, T07-419 1648. Fair range of comfortable a/c chalets, unfortunately located next to a semi-industrial (for Tioman) area. Good restaurant with sizeable breakfasts and the usual selection of Western and Asian cuisine.

A-C Babura Sea View, T07-419 1139. Right down at the south end of the strip, this place has a mixture of fan and a/c rooms. There is also a fair Chinese restaurant, and **Tioman Reef Divers**, a PADI/NAUI dive shop. The rooms are clean and well maintained although some can be dark; the best are in the block on the beachfront. Recommended.

B Persona Island Resort, T/F07-419 1213. Located a 5-min walk from the beach (turn right at jetty and continue). Blend of unexciting but perfectly comfortable a/c and fan rooms in a concrete block.

B-C Peladang, T07-419 1249, F011-950852. Some a/c, a well-kept little place with clean and comfortable chalets. Its big drawback is that it is on the opposite side of the road

Kampong Tekek

To Juara (4 km)

7 to 7
Mini Mart

Airport Shopping
Plaza & Money
Changers

Souvenir Shop
& Food Court

Jetty

Ferry Terminal
& Immigration

Clinic

School

To Mersing

Storage
Depot

16 hr Stop
Mini Mart

Duty Free
Shop

Eco Divers

Mini
Mart

Tioman
Dive Centre

N

100 metres
100 yards

Sleeping
Babura Sea View 1
Coral Reef Seaview 2
Monte Chalets 4
Peladang 5
Persona Island Resort 6

Sri Tioman Beach Resort 9
Tekek Inn 10

Eating
Liza 1
Malay (no name) 2
Shady Bakery 4

Bars & clubs
Dolphin 5
Kontiki 3

some distance from the beach, so it is neither possible to watch the sun go down over the horizon nor dash headlong from your chalet into the water. The restaurant here serves good seafood and there is also a minimart.
B-D Coral Reef Seaview, T07-419 1137. Tired looking cluster of a/c and fan chalets, some with sea view and others on a grassy compound facing each other.
B-D Sri Tioman Beach Resort, T07-419 1189. Some a/c, restaurant, a popular place and one of the better places to stay in this price range in Tekek. Sea-facing chalets shaded beneath casuarina trees, good restaurant with prawn, squid and fish dishes as well as the usual range of pancakes, etc.
D Tekek Inn, T07-419 1576. This is perhaps the best of the cheaper places to stay. It is on the beach, rooms are OK with attached showers, the management is suitably relaxed and there are snorkels and canoes for hire. No restaurant, just a drinks station. Recommended.

Kampong Lalang
AL Berjaya Tioman Beach Golf & Spa Resort, T07-419 1000, www.berjaya resorts.com. 400 rooms set in 80 ha of land, built on the site of the old Kampong Lalang. It is by far the biggest and most expensive resort on Tioman, with a good range of facilities and a lovely stretch of beach. This is not the place to come if you are hoping for a quiet retreat; during holiday periods, the whole place is heaving with activity. Rooms are adequately equipped, but furnishings are a little dated. Choice of rooms; the cheapest have garden views and are the older 1-storey chalets. The de luxe and superior 2-storey chalets are bigger and are more suitable for families, some overlook the sea (if you crane your neck). All rooms have wooden floors and balconies, a/c, TV and minibar. Rather shabby bathrooms, with hot-water shower only (bath tubs in de luxe rooms only). The suites are very forgettable. Several restaurants (see page 236). Rather cramped area for the freeform pool with children's slides and jacuzzi. Water sports centre with boats for

diving and snorkelling parties to nearby islands (it is possible to snorkel 100 m out from the northern end of the bay and at the very southern end, near the beach), jet skis, windsurfers, 18-hole golf course, gym – with good range of (underused) equipment, donkey and horse riding, tennis courts.

Ayer Batang

This lies just north of Tekek. Accommodation comprising mainly simple chalets is spread out around the bay and is generally good.

B Bamboo Hill Chalets, T09-419 1339, www.geocities.com/bamboosu. Selection of fan and a/c chalets at the far end of the beach, some perched on a hilltop overlooking the bay. The chalets are well designed and comfortable and have hot-water showers and balconies with sea views. Small library and water-refilling service (RM1). Recommended.

B-C Johan's Resort, T09-419 1359. Well-established resort with popular restaurant and simple, clean fan huts near the sea and a/c chalets perched on the hillside overlooking the resort.

B-C Nazri II, www.nazrisplace.com. Tidy place with comfortable a/c chalets with sea views, backed by a raised restaurant serving some delightful fresh seafood and with extensive views over the bay. Cheaper fan chalets are available on the hill behind the restaurant, and are simple, but comfy. Laundry service and tours round the island. Recommended.

B-D Nazri's, T07-419 1329, www.nazrisplace.com. The most southerly of the guesthouses in Ayer Batang. There's a newish concrete block with tiled rooms with a/c, and some huts at the back of the plot, among the mango trees. Spartan but clean rooms, restaurant on seafront, friendly management, good discounts available during low season. Nazri's has the best stretch of beach in Ayer Batang. Recommended.

C-D ABC Bungalows, T07-419 1154. Cramped compound with an assortment of chalets, some in a vastly better state than

others. Fair restaurant and good snorkelling offshore. Popular.

C-E Mokhtar's, T09-419 1148. Simple huts, fan and mosquito nets provided, basic restaurant.

D Mawar, T09-4191 153. Row of simple wooden huts with fan facing the sea. Good restaurant attached. Popular.

D South Pacific, T07-419 1176. The first bunch of chalets to the north of the jetty, with some of the cheapest sea-view fan chalets in ABC (with mosquito net, attached bathroom). Whilst some of the cheaper chalets could do with a bit of a revamp, they are good value. There are currently 2 a/c chalets with 2 more in construction.

D YP Chalets, T07-419 1018. Very simple huts with mosquito nets, fan and attached bathroom with cold shower. The huts are very tightly packed together and face each other, so not really a place for lovebirds seeking some privacy. Bikes for hire. Internet access.

Ayer Batang (ABC)

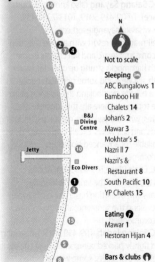

N
Not to scale

Sleeping
ABC Bungalows 1
Bamboo Hill Chalets 14
Johan's 2
Mawar 3
Mokhtar's 5
Nazri II 7
Nazri's & Restaurant 8
South Pacific 10
YP Chalets 15

B&J Diving Centre

Jetty

Eco Divers

Eating
Mawar 1
Restoran Hijan 4

Bars & clubs
Hello 2

Kampong Panuba

C-D Panuba Inn Resort, situated just north of Kampong Ayer Batang, on the next promontory, and has its own jetty, T07-799 2535, panuba@hotmail.com. There's a small forest trail so guests can walk into Ayer Batang. The ferry from Mersing will stop here if you ask the boatmen in advance. Attractively laid out chalets built on stilts on the hillside, wall with seaviews. It has its own rocky beach, with snorkelling in front of the resort, and a busy restaurant. This place can feel a bit ghetto-like as rooms are packed together and unless visitors fancy tramping the trail to ABC, they must eat at the hotel. Popular with package tourists.

Kampong Salang

A-C Khalid's Place (also known as Salang Pusaka Resort), T09-419 5317, www.salangpusakaresort.com. A collection of 48 fan and a/c chalets set back from the beach. Some of the fan chalets do not have a shower, but have running water and a bucket. There is a dive centre and a good restaurant. Family rooms available.

A-C Salang Sayang (also known as **Zaids Place**), T/F09-419 5019, T013-720 6439, www.salangsayangresort.com. Well-managed resort with a wide selection of comfortable a/c and fan chalets (some with hammocks strung up outside), many with sea view and some perched regally on a hillside overlooking the swaying palms. The top rooms here are the concrete a/c suites, with fridge, kettle, narcolepsy-inducing beds and sea views. Excellent package deals available for advanced bookings. Recommended.

B-C Ella's Place, T09-4195004. At the northern end of the strip, this friendly family-run operation has a string of simple huts along the shoreline, all with sea view. Recommended.

B-C Salang Indah, T09-419 5015. Unexciting and tightly packed conglomerate of chalets in all price brackets, some with attached bathrooms right on the sea (2 of the more

expensive rooms are built out over the sea), others with a/c and private stairs down to the sea, plus the original, rather drab, rooms in a U-shaped barrack of a building. There's a minimart, good restaurant serving Malay and seafood dishes and internet café (open 0900-2400). Excellent all-inclusive package deals available.

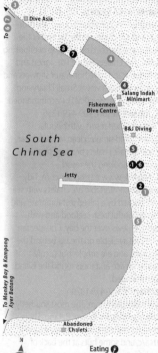

Kampong Salang

South China Sea

Dive Asia

Salang Indah Minimart

Fishermen Dive Centre

B&J Diving

Jetty

To Monkey Bay & Kampong Ayer Batang

To Kampong Ayer Batang

Abandoned Chalets

N

Not to scale

Sleeping ⬤
Ella's Place 6
Khalid's Place 1
Salang Beach Resort 3
Salang Huts 7
Salang Indah 4
Salang Sayang 5

Eating 🍴
Amin's Café 1
Food Court 2
Salang Dreams 6
Warung 3
White House 7

Bars & Clubs 🍸
Four Café & Bar 4
Ng Café 5

B-D Salang Beach Resort, T07-419 5015, F419 2024. Expansive chalet operation offering spacious rooms with verandas set in well-kept grounds, some with a/c. This resort is quiet and the beach is virtually a private one. Good Chinese restaurant.
D Salang Huts, a very isolated choice right at the northern end near a rocky bay. If you don't mind the somewhat abandoned air, there are plenty of hammocks and very cheap simple huts.

Kampong Paya

AL-A Paya Beach Resort, bookings T065-6733 4333. Small resort 30 a/c chalets, all sea-facing. Small pool and spa, and a restaurant serving up some decent seafood. There is a PADI dive school attached to the hotel which charges reasonable rates. Popular with package tourists. Good all-inclusive deals available for those travelling from Singapore.

Kampong Genting

A Island Reef Resort, set back on hillside behind jetty, with chalets side on to beach, so no views except in the restaurant.
A Sun Beach Resort, T09-419 7069, www.sunbeachresort.com.my. Some 50 rambling bungalows built too close together, some on the seafront, others piled up the hill behind. Monstrous restaurant on stilts and bar.
B-C Bayu Chalets, T09-799 6364, tiomanholidays@yahoo.com. At the north end of the beach, quiet and secluded. Upmarket wooden chalets with some attempt to give them a Malaysian village feel. Fan or a/c, some larger rooms can sleep 4. Restaurant and games room.
D Damai, bookable in Mersing at Jln Abu Bakar, T07-419 7055. About 80 rather grotty looking double chalets with balconies, restaurant, minimarket and 24-hr electricity, speedboat to Mersing.

Kampong Nipah

B-D Nipah Beach Chalet, funky place with simple wooden huts decorated with bamboo

and colourful batiks. One chalet sleeps 5 (4 on beds and 1 in rooftop annexe).

Kampong Mukut

A-B Mukut Coral Resort, T09-412 0392. Restaurant, traditional-style *atap*-roofed chalets with balconies, a/c, secluded and beautiful location with a magnificent backdrop.
C Mukut Harmony Resort, T09-799 2275. Simple rows of chalets, fan and bathroom.

Kampong Juara

B Juara Beach, T09-419 3188, www.thejuaraway.com/juarabeach.html. The swankiest place in Juara north of the pier mainly geared at package tourists. This new place has massive rooms set back from the beach, with wooden floors, hot-water showers and comfortable beds.
B-C Juara Mutiara, booking office at 6 Jln Abu Bakar, near Plaza R&R, Mersing, T09-419 3161, www.juaramutiararesort.com. The more expensive rooms sleep 4, all have attached

Kampong Juara

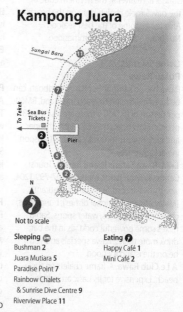

Not to scale

Sleeping 🛏
Bushman **2**
Juara Mutiara **5**
Paradise Point **7**
Rainbow Chalets
 & Sunrise Dive Centre **9**
Riverview Place **11**

Eating 🍴
Happy Café **1**
Mini Café **2**

showers, clean and popular, some chalets right on the beach, can be noisy (for Juara) as there are other chalet operations on both sides. Organizes diving trips and island tours.

C Bushman, T09-419 2109, near the southern end of the beach. Simple huts practically on the sands. Restaurant, bar and a dive shop (see page 238) and the staff are friendly.

D Paradise Point. 1 of only 3 places to stay on the northern side of the beach. Simple rooms, attached showers, the chalets closest to the beach get the breeze, a quiet place with a relaxed atmosphere. Restaurant with extensive menu. Recommended.

D Rainbow Chalets, T07-419 3140. Simple colourful chalets next to Bushman on the beach. Runs the Sunrise Dive Centre, see page 238.

D Riverview Place, T09-419 3168, www.riverview-tioman.com. The cheapest yet most scenic places to stay, between an aquamarine mangrove swamp and the Sungai Baru River at the northern edge of the bay. Simple chalets right on the beach. Also serves some of the best seafood. No karaoke allowed. Recommended.

Other islands p228
Pulau Rawa

Rawa has no kampongs on it. Speedboats can be hired in Mersing to reach the island, RM60 per person or RM250 if there are less than 8 people. Slow boats may be a little cheaper and expensive resorts may include transport in package prices.

L-AL Rawa Safaris Island Resort, Tourist Centre, Jln Abu Bakar, Mersing, T07-799 1204, www.rawasfr.com. Some a/c, restaurant (Malay and international dishes), bungalows, chalets and A-frames, water sports. Sahid mixes some powerful cocktails in the bar; drink more than 2 Rawa specials and you'll be on the island for good.

A Le Club Rawa. A-frame chalets on the beach. Expensive for its basic amenities.

Pulau (Babi) Besar

AL-A D'Coconut Island Resort, T03-4296 5753, www.dcoconut.com. Built on the land of an old coconut plantation, with chalets and a large restaurant that overlooks the sea and beautiful pool. Water sports facilities and recommended as a good diving location with 20 sites within reach. Further 21 luxury rooms added in 2006, with bath tubs, mini-fridges and coffee makers included in the extras.

A Aseania Resort Pulau Besar, www.pulaubesar.net. Some a/c, stylish traditional chalets with jungle hillside backdrop. Restaurant.

A-C Nirwana Beach Resort, T07-799 5929. Choice of chalets, some with a/c, restaurant attached, dorms available.

B Hillside Beach Resort, 5B Jln Abu Bakar, Mersing or book through Suite 125, 1st floor, Johor Tower, 15 Jln Gereja, Johor Bahru, T07-799 4831, F224 4329. Attractively designed kampong-style resort, nestling on jungled slopes above beach, water sports. Restaurant.

B-D Batu Kembar. 18 large chalets on a hillside, for 4 people each in bunks, a/c, hot showers and balconies.

E Bluewater Resort. Chalet or longhouse accommodation in this place in Aur village.

Pulau Tinggi

A Dreamz Tinggi Island (formerly Tinggi Island Resort), T065-8103 1319, www.dreamztinggiisland.com. Fabulous island location under the 650-m volcanic peak of Semundu. Activities include diving, canoeing, jet-skiing, jungle treks to an isolated waterfall and visits to the island's turtle hatchery.

Pulau Sibu
Popular with visitors into sport fishing and diving.

A Sea Gypsy Village Resort, T07-222 8642, www.siburesort.com. Restaurant, chalets and bungalows. Friendly management – the company also work with a Dugong conservation project. Recommended.

A Sibu Island Cabanas, c/o G105 Holiday Plaza, Century Garden JB, T017-755 2690, www.sibuisland.com. Restaurant, chalets and de luxe bungalows.

B-D O & H Kampong Huts, c/o 9 Tourist Information Centre, Jln Abu Bakar, Mersing, T07-799 3124. Good restaurant, chalets, some with attached bathrooms, clean and friendly, trekking and snorkelling. Recommended.

Pulau Pemanggil

There is a small agent at the very front of Mersing's Plaza R&R that deals exclusively with Pemanggil travel and accommodation.
A Lanting Beach Resort, T07-799 3973, www.lantingresort.com.my. Pleasant chalets built on a big rocky platform at the far end of the beach making the resort very secluded. Staff speak good English.

Pulau Aur

F Longhouse. Provides basic accommodation.

🍴 Eating

Mersing *p222, map p222*
¶¶ Mersing Seafood, 56 Jln Ismail, T07-7992550. Open 1100-1430 and 1700-2330. One of Mersing's best spots for seafood lovers with an extensive menu of fresh squid, crab, prawns and fish served in a/c comfort. Highlights include sambai prawns, assam fish-head curry and fresh crab with black pepper sauce. Some vegetarian options. Recommended.
¶¶ Port Café The Jetty, Jln Abu Bakar. Open 1000-0100. Broad menu featuring large portions of pizza, grilled lamb and pasta dishes in a comfortable setting with music and TV. Excellent service.
¶¶ Restoran P1, 20 Jln Dato Mohd Ali, T07-7994603. Open 1120-1500 and 1730-2400. Owned by the affable Urs from Switzerland, this unassuming eatery offers tasty pizza, pasta, salads and ice-cold beer at very reasonable prices. Recommended.

¶ Corner Lot One Seaood, Jln Ismail 1. Open 0700-0200. The bright yellow chairs here can't be missed, neither can the booming cable TV which draws in a fair crowd of locals and tourists alike. Menu features Chinese dishes with a Malay spin, *tom yam* soup and a variety of fried rice dishes.
¶ Sin Nam Kee Seafood, 387 Jln Jemaluang (1 km out of town on Kota Tinggi road). Huge seafood menu and reckoned by locals to be the best restaurant in Mersing. Occasional karaoke nights can be noisy.
¶ Sweet Story, 11 Jln Abu Bakar. Open 0730-1900. Interesting fusion menu of Western staples such as pastas and sandwiches complemented by tasty Malay dishes and a good-value daily special. Good set breakfast menu and outdoor seating.
¶ Yong Seng Seafood, 51 Jln Ismail. Big open coffee shop with vast selection. Speciality is seafood steamboat.

Bakeries
Kedai Kek Kile, Jln Abu Bakar (next to Omar's). A good selection of cakes and pastries cooked on the premises.

Foodstalls
There are a smattering of more traditional stalls alongside the fresh fruit and vegetables in the market on Jln Ismail.

Pulau Tioman *p222, map p225*
Most restaurants are small family-run kitchens attached to groups of beach huts. All provide Western staples such as omelettes and French toast, as well as Malay dishes. On the whole, the food is of a high standard. Understandably it makes most sense to eat seafood: superb barbecued barracuda, squid, stingray and other fish. Not all restaurants sell beer.

Kampong Tekek
¶ Babura Sea View Chinese (separate ownership from the guesthouse). Recommended by expats.

Liza. Malay restaurant serving up huge portions of *nasi campur* (1100-1500), fresh seafood and *tom yam*.

Malay (no name), north of the **Babura** and before the bridge. Serves tasty, simple Malay dishes and some seafood.

Shady Bakery. Cheese slices and baguettes.

Sri Tioman Beach Resort. The food at this restaurant is worth trying, especially the squid and chilli prawns.

Kampong Lalang
Berjaya Tioman Beach Resort, see page 230. A choice of restaurants, none of which are outstanding. The best bet is the buffet meal, which is quite good value and a huge spread is on offer. The other restaurants offer barbecue and steamboat. Service for à la carte meals is painfully slow and pretty inefficient. The golf club offers a snack bar with good pizzas and sandwiches.

Ayer Batang
Restoran Hijau. The elevated restaurant at Nazri's 2 has great sea views, and is popular with families and divers stumbling from the happy hour at Happy Bar. The Western food here is missable, but the Malay and Chinese dishes are generally good.

Mawar. Has tables in the scrubby sand. But the Malay dishes are very good and cheap here, especially the fish.

Nazri's Place. The seafront restaurant is one of the best on this stretch with good seafood and Western backpacker staples like chips and sandwiches. Wine and beer is available. Great view of the ocean. It's possible to carry tables onto the sand. Still cheap, but food costs a couple of ringgit more than the other places – it's worth it.

Kampong Salang
This is a sizeable hamlet, so there are a number of restaurants independent of the guesthouses.

Amin's Café. Good option right by the jetty. Provides breakfast, lunch and dinner; a simple, low-key place.

Salang Dreams, opposite the Salang Indah Minimart. Good Malay food, soups and an evening seafood barbecue.

Warung, just north of the **White House**. Among the best of the *warungs* is this place serving simple dishes, including breakfast.

White House. On the strip north of the Salang Indah, this place has a nightly fresh seafood barbecue (1900-2400).

Foodcourt
The rather gloomy looking foodcourt by the jetty is a good place to grab a cheap lunch with stalls offering local fare, and **Aina's** providing cheap pizza and sandwiches.

Kampong Paya
Mekong, at the south end of the bay. Good Chinese seafood dishes.

Kampong Juara
All the guesthouses serve roughly the same dishes: curries, noodle and rice dishes, pancakes, fish, omelettes, etc.

Happy Café. Open-air restaurant with great views of the turquoise ocean. Malay dishes, seafood the best.

Mini Café. Good Malay seafood; try the chilli fish, sweet and sour or simply grilled.

Riverview Place. Expats recommend this simple place as the best in the village. Serves Malay and seafood.

Bars and clubs

Pulau Tioman *p222, map p225*
Kampong Tekek
Dolphin Bar, next to Tekek Inn, T09-419 1779. Beachside bar. Recommended by expats. Cheap beer.
Kontiki Café, another bar popular with expats, gets a bit rowdy.

Ayer Batang
Hello Bar, just in front of **Nazri's II**. A tiny beachside open-air shack cum bar which attracts a wonderfully diverse clientele of

characters with its happy hour (3 beers for RM10, 1700-1900) and eclectic music. The drinking often goes on until the wee hours.

Kampong Salang

Four Café and Bar. Open 1800-2400. One of the more popular places in Salang to grab a bargain basement cocktail.
Ng Café. A hole in the wall proffering icy takeaway beers for those in the mood for a bit of chalet boozing.

O Shopping

Mersing *p222, map p222*
Arts Souvenir, 1 Gerai MDM, Jln Tun Dr Ismail, next to Malay restaurants on the corner after R&R Plaza. Artist Sulaiman Aziz specializes in colourful T-shirts, shorts and beachware and hand-painted batiks. There are some knick-knack souvenir shops in the R&R Plaza. The **market** on Jln Ismail offers more authentic batiks and is worth wandering around.

Pulau Tioman *p222, map p225*
Kampong Tekek
There are a number of minimarts in the Kampong. There is a very small market area next to the **Peladang Restaurant**.
Pak Ali Nasir's stall is the best place for fruit. There are a handful of souvenir shops in Tekek selling the usual range of nautical knick-knacks.

▲ Activities and tours

Mersing *p222, map p222*
Boats for fishing trips can be chartered by groups of 12 or more from the jetty. Owners may be reluctant to take the long journey out to the far offshore islands.

Diving

Most beaches have dive centres attached to at least 1 guesthouse. PADI, NAUI and SSI (Scuba Schools International) certification available, but PADI is by far the most popular.

Tour operators

Competition is intense at peak season and tourists can be hassled for custom.

Ticketing and travel agents all over town are much of a muchness and visitors are unlikely to be ripped off – although use licensed agents (usually displayed on the door). Agencies tend to promote their own business so expect the truth to be warped, bent and generally polished to a high and unlikely sheen. Many agents are located in the R&R Plaza on Jln Tun Dr Ismail, next to the river and around the jetty. They also promote package deals to specific chalet resorts; sometimes they are good value, but buying a boat ticket puts you under no obligation to stay at a particular place.
Dee Travel & Tours, T07-799 2344, 8 Jln Abu Bakar; **Golden Mal Tours**, 9 Jln Sulaiman, T07-799 1463; **Island Connection Travel & Tours**, 2 Jln Jemaluang, T07-799 2612, fee222@yahoo.com (very helpful folks who generally meet tourists off the bus from Singapore or JB. They offer tours and ticketing. Recommended); **Kebina**, Jln Abu Bakar, T/F07-799 5118 (for boat services and accommodation).

Pulau Tioman *p222, map p225*
Kampong Tekek
Tioman Dive Centre, T09-419 1228, www.tioman-dive-centre.com.
Tioman Reef Divers, Babura Sea View, T09-419 1342, www.tiomanreefdivers.com. Reputedly the best dive shop.

Ayer Batang
Diving B&J Diving Centre, T09-419 5554, www.divetioman.com. Just to the north of the jetty on the beach. Small pool for diving practice and can provide PADI certification. RM1660 for PADI open-water course. Other courses include underwater photography and advanced open water.
Eco Divers, T013-368 7833, www.eco-divers.net. Highly regarded dive shop.

Snorkelling equipment can be hired in plenty of places for RM15 for a day and

RM10 for half a day. The area around ABC Bungalows is a good place to start.

Kampong Salang

Salang has been marketed as a snorkellers' haven but, sadly, that is history – the coral is disappointing. It does, however, get better further out and where the coral cliff drops off to deeper water there is a more interesting variety of marine life including the odd reef shark. Snorkels and fins can be hired just about everywhere, about RM7-12 per day.
Diving B&J Diving Centre, T09-419 5014, www.divetioman.com. Hires out equipment and can organize PADI certification and diving trips to nearby islands. **Dive Asia,** by the Salang Beach Resort, also offers PADI certification. Popular and well managed. **Fishermen Dive Centre,** Salang Indah, Kampong Salang, T09-419 5014, www.fishermenscuba.com, courses and lessons in underwater photography.

Kampong Paya

Diving Dive shop at the **Tioman Paya Resort** with PADI certification courses.

Kampong Genting

Diving Sharkeys, the Tropical Coral Inn, T09-419 7041. Runs SSI-certificated courses.

Kampong Juara

Diving Snorkelling and fishing gear can be hired from most guesthouses.
Bushman, T07-419 3157, www.bushman-diving.com, at the **Bushman** resort, see page 234.
Sunrise Dive Centre, T09-419 3102, www.sunrisedivecentre.com. Next door at **Rainbow Chalets,** see page 234.
Golf Tioman Island Golf Club, T07-419 1000, F419 1718. Beautiful 18-hole course. Most club members are weekend trippers from KL and Singapore. Equipment including clubs, golf shoes, and buggy available for hire.

Ayer Batang

Jungle trekking An experienced local guide takes tourists on 3-hr treks trough the delightful jungle above Air Batang. He puts a herbal spin on things with a lot of information deveoted to flora and local use of herbs in medicine and food. Treks are graded hardcore (4 hrs, RM45) and beginner (3 hrs, RM35). Kids under 12 go free. Minimum 2 people. Contact Rinda's Place, T019-915 4440.
Massage Malay-style massage is also offered at **Rinda's Place** (see above), with costs varying from RM30 for a 30-min foot massage to RM70 for an hour-long healing massage.

Tour operators The majority of resorts can organize trips around the island and boat tickets back to the mainland. Note, though, bus tickets cannot be bought on the island. Guides are available from **Berjaya Tioman Beach Resort** and in Kampong Tekek.

Transport

Mersing p222, map p222
Boat

The jetty is a 15-min walk from the long-distance bus stand. Most of the ticket offices are by the jetty but boat tickets to the islands are also sold from booths near the bus stop. The boat trip to the islands from Mersing can be extremely rough during the monsoon season; boats will sometimes leave Mersing in the late afternoon, at high tide, but rough seas can delay the voyage considerably. During peak monsoon all ferry services are cancelled and the ferry companies move to the west coast to find work there. It is advisable only to travel during daylight hours.

At present, only **Bluewater Express** boats are making the trip over to Tioman. The timetable is highly erratic and dependent on the tides. There are 2-3 boats leaving daily, between 0730 and 1630. Tickets cost RM35 (2 hrs) and stop at **Kampong Genting**, Berjaya Tioman Beach Resort, **Kampong Tekek**, **Kampong Ayer Batang**, and **Kampong**

Salang, and you must tell the boat workers where you want to get off in advance.
Note There is an RM5 marine park conservation fee payable before boarding any boat heading to Tioman and other islands. The payment booth is on the left just as you enter the departure point at the jetty.

Bus

The local bus station is on Jln Sulaiman opposite the Country Hotel.

Long-distance buses leave from 2 locations: those not originating in Mersing leave from the blue bus stand in front of the Timotel (buy a ticket at the bus station first) and those that start from Mersing leave from the new bus station just behind the Timotel (follow the signs from the roundabout). Tickets can be bought from Plaza R&R or from tour agents in town. Regular connections with **KL** (RM30), **Johor Bahru** (R11.30), **Kuantan** (RM16.30), **Cherating** (RM22), **Terengganu** (RM26), **Ipoh** (change in KL, RM42), **Singapore** (RM12) and **Kota Bharu** (RM34).
Tip Buses heading north from Mersing to Kuantan and Kuala Terengganu depart between 1200 and 1400. They are often booked out. It is a good idea to reserve your ticket a few days in advance, before heading to Tioman.

Taxi

Taxis meet travellers off the ferries from Tioman. They linger around the jetty all day and go to **KL**, **JB** (RM160) (for Singapore, change at JB), **Melaka**, **Kuala Terengganu** and **Kuantan** (RM200).

Pulau Tioman p222, map p225
Air

Berjaya Air (www.berjaya-air.com) flies from **Singapore** and **Subang** daily to the airstrip on the island. Baggage allowance is 10 kg. A bus from the **Berjaya Tioman Resort** meets each arrival and transports guests to the hotel. Alternatively, walk to the pier and catch one of the sea taxis to the other

beaches. **Airline offices** Berjaya Air operates from Berjaya Resort, T07-419 1309, www.berjaya-air.com. The single fare from Tioman to Subang is around RM230 and to Singapore around RM300.

Boat

Fast boats from Mersing to **Tioman** depart 2-3 times a day depending on the tides (2 hrs, RM35). During the monsoon season (Nov-Feb) departures can be erratic; boats may not run if there are insufficient passengers and the sea can get quite rough. All boats land on the west coast of Tioman and call at each of the main kampongs so you need to tell the boatman where you want to disembark.

Beaches and kampongs are connected by a sea taxi service. Prices are usually based on a minimum of 2 people chartering the vessel. Single travellers have to pay the price for 2. Bargain hard. It is necessary to charter a boat to get to the waterfalls (on the south coast) and Kampong Juara. Sea taxi fares (per person, children half price) from Kampong Tekek to: **Kampong Ayer Batang**, RM20; **Panuba**, RM20; **Salang**, RM30; **Paya**, RM30; **Genting** RM40; **Nipah** RM60; **Juara**, RM150. The east coast is accessible by taxi, around RM40 per person, by boat or by the jungle trail.

Other islands p228
Boat

Boats to some of the smaller islands leave daily from Mersing, usually around 1100 and return in the afternoon, otherwise arrange boat transfer through your resort. Boats to Tioman sometimes stop off at **Rawa** on the way. Boats to **Rawa**, cost RM35; DCoconut has a boat connection for US$15 return to **Pulau (Babi) Besar**. No regular boats to Pulau Aur or Pulau Pemanggil. Getting to **Pulau Aur** takes 4 hrs or more. Also boats to **Sibu** from **Tanjung Sedili Besar** at Teluk Mahkota (23 km off the Kota Tinggi–Mersing road), south of Mersing.

The boat trip to **Pemanggil** is long – 4-5 hrs, as it is 64 nautical miles offshore.

⊙ Directory

Mersing *p222, map p222*
Banks Maybank, Jln Ismail; UMBC, Jln Ismail, no exchange on Sat. Money changer on Jln Abu Bakar and Giamso Safari, 23 Jln Abu Bakar also changes TCs. **Internet** Eddy's Internet, 16 Jln Abu Bakar, open 1000-2300, RM1.5 per hr, wireless service available.
Medical services Dentists: Klinik Pergigian, 28 Jln Mohd, Ali, T07-799 3135. **Doctors:** Klinik Grace, 48 Jln Abu Bakar, T07-799 2399.
Post office Jln Abu Bakar.

Pulau Tioman *p222, map p225*
Kampong Tekek
Banks There are 2 money changers at Tioman Airport in the blue-roofed shopping plaza. **Internet** Internet café on the 2nd floor of the souvenir shop and food court building opposite the jetty at Tekek. **Medical services** There is a small clinic in Tekek

which is good for minor illnesses. The nearest decompression chamber is at Kuantan, see page 40. **Post office** Mini-post office in Kampong Tekek. **Telephone** Public phones in all villages, IDD calling from **Berjaya** and some guesthouses. There are card phones in Tekek next to the Mini Pos (cards available at Post Office).

Kampong Lalang
Banks TCs can be changed at the Berjaya Resort (large surcharge). Recently, some smaller resorts have begun to accept them.

Ayer Batang
Internet Bamboo Hill Chalets and Mohktar's (RM10 per hr).

Kampong Salang
Banks Some shops will also change money.
Internet Salang Indah at Kampong Salang.

Endau Rompin National Park

→ *Colour map 2, B5. Phone code: 09.*

The endangered Sumatran rhino, tigers, wild boars, tapir, elephant deer and mousedeer roam in this park, one of the biggest remaining tracts of virgin rainforest on the Peninsula. Birdlife includes hornbills and the argus pheasant. Amongst the flora there are fan palms (Endau ensis), walking stick palm (Phychorapis singaporensis), climbing bamboo (Rhopa loblaste), pitcher plants and orchids. The 80,000 ha park straddles the border of Johor and Pahang states and in the late 1980s Endau Rompin was upgraded to the status of a national park to protect the area from the logging companies that ravaged the park in the 1970s. ►► *For listings, see pages 241-242.*

Ins and outs

Getting there

There are two ways of getting to the park; either via Rompin, Pahang (paved road to Selanding and then a rough track for 25 km to the park boundary at Kinchin). The other route is from Johor in the south, on Route 50 from Kahang; it's 48 km on a logging route to Kampong Peta (the visitors' centre and entry point to the park). From the visitors' centre it's another 15 km to base camp at Kuala Jasin (three hours on foot or 45 minutes by boat, RM10 per person upon request). For arrivals to the park by boat, travel to Endau, 33 km up the coast from Mersing, and from there, take a six-hour motorboat ride upstream to Kampong Peta (RM200, one way).

Getting around

Both the Johor and Pahang state authorities recommend that visitors come on an organized tour. Given the convoluted travel instructions and excessive fees, this is a sensible option.

Park essentials and tourist information

The park is managed by the **Johor National Parks Corporation** ⓘ *Jkr 475, Bukit Timbalan 82503, Johor Bahru, T07-223 7471, www.johorparks.com*, a private body set up by local government that has made access to the park easier and has allowed some new accommodation. Because of privatization, prices for entry and accommodation are relatively high. Unlike Taman Negara National Park, trips to Endau require careful planning and are best organized by tour agents who can usually do it cheaper than arranging it independently. Some guides offer one-day treks, but this should not be attempted alone. Entry permits are required and these must be secured in advance from the forestry department in Kuala Rompin, T09-414 5204. A tour operator will take care of this for you. If you do decide to travel independently the costs are RM50 per day for a guide (compulsory; one guide can be shared between 10 people), RM20 for an entry permit at each zone (there is a zone A and a zone B), RM10 for a camera and RM20 for a fishing permit.

If arriving via Endau by boat, at the junction of the Endau and Jasin rivers (nine hours from Endau) is a good campsite and base for trekking and fishing expeditions. Boats go further upstream, but it is advisable to take a guide from Endau or the Orang Asli kampongs (RM20-30 per day). At present it is necessary to take all provisions and camping equipment with you.

Most package trips involve a 70-km jeep trip from Mersing to Kampong Peta followed by a 1½-hour longboat ride to the first campsite. Visitors to the park can trek around the Asli trails and visit spectacular waterfalls, the biggest of which is the Buaya Sangkut waterfall on Sungai Jasin.

Entrance fees must be paid at the Park Headquarters in Kampong Peta where the officer on duty will provide a briefing of rules and regulations that apply in the park. See www.pahangtourism.com.my/tropical for more information on the park.

Best time to visit

The park is closed during the monsoon season, from November to March, and during the rainy season you will need a 4WD to negotiate the tracks thick with mud. Fishing trips are best organized between February and August.

◉ Endau Rompin National Park listings

For Sleeping and Eating price codes and other relevant information, see Essentials pages 25-30.

◉ Sleeping

Endau Rompin National Park *p240*
There is no accommodation available in the park; camping only (including tent hire, RM12.50 per person) at **Kuala Jasin, Batu**

Hampar, Upih Guling and Kuala Marong, which have a combined capacity of 250-300 visitors. Base camp is at Kampong Peta, which also has simple A-frames. At headquarters there is running water and flush toilets and a small grocery shop. There are several other campsites, including Kuala Jasin, with running water, a few A-frames and fire pits. Even more basic are those at Kuala Marong and Batu Hampar (no toilets, water from the river). Contact the Johor Park Corporation, page 241, for more on camping in the park.

▲ Activities and tours

Endau Rompin p240
Hotels and guesthouses in Kuala Rompin also usually organize trips into the park.

Tour operators
Organized expeditions, from RM90-200 per person per day, include return vehicle and boat transfer, camping equipment, cooking utensils and permits.
Giamso Travel, 23 Jln Abu Bakar, Mersing, T07-799 2253. The company can supply camping equipment.
Ping Anchorage, 77A Jln Sultan Sulaiman, Kuala Terengganu, T09-626 2020, www.pinganchorage.com.my. One of Malaysia's most successful tour companies.
Shah Alam Tours, 138 mezzanine floor, Jln Tun Sambanthan, KL, T03-230 7161, F274 5739.

Wilderness Experience, 6B Jln SS 21/39, Damansara Utama, Petaling Jaya, T03-717 8221.

⊖ Transport

Endau Rompin p240
Boat
Speedboats go to the first Orang Asli village (**Kampong Punan**). This can cost RM200-400 for a 2-day trip. It is possible to charter longboats (carrying up to 6) from Kampong Punan to go further upstream.

Bus
There are connections with **JB**, **Terengganu** and **Kuantan**. Buses from JB and Kuantan stop on demand at **Endau** or there are regular local buses from Mersing to Endau. There is a 56-km jungle road from Kahang town to Kampong Peta where there is a visitors' centre and the entry point to the park.

Taxi
From Mersing.

Contents

246 Ins and outs
246 Background

247 Kuantan and around
247 Ins and outs
248 Sights
251 Listings

257 Pahang's national parks
257 Taman Negara
    National Park
262 Kenong Rimba
    National Park
262 Listings

**265 Kampong Cherating
    and around**
266 Ins and outs
266 Sights
269 Listings

**273 Kuala Terengganu
    and around**
273 Ins and outs
274 Sights
276 Listings

281 Redang archipelago
282 Listings

284 The Perhentian Islands
285 Listings

290 Kota Bharu and around
290 Ins and outs
292 Background
293 Sights
296 Listings

Footprint features

244 Don't miss …
268 The giant leatherback turtle

East Coast Peninsula

★ Don't miss ...
1 Taman Negara National Park, page 257.
2 Kampong Cherating, page 265.
3 Pulau Tenggol diving, page 267.
4 Giant leatherback turtles in Rantau Abang, page 268.
5 Kuala Terengganu hawker stalls, page 278.
6 The Perhentian Islands, page 284.
7 Kota Bharu traditional crafts, page 290.

THAILAND

Tumpat • Pantai Cinta Berahi
7 Kota Bharu
Pasir Mas
Pantai Dalam Rhu

Pasir Puteh

Kuala Kerai

Dabong

KELANTAN

Kuala Besut

Pulau Perhentian Kecil • 6 Pulau Perhentian Besar
Pulau Redang
Pulau Lang Tengah
Pulau Bidong Laut

Penarek
Merang
Batu Rakit

G Lawit (1519m)

G Chirgoi (863m)

Taluk Kenyir

Gua Musang

Kuala Berang

TERENGGANU

5 Kuala Terengganu
Cendering

Marang ○ Pulau Kapas

East
Sea

Rantau Abang
4 Kuala Abang
Kuala Dungun

3 Pulau Tenggol

G Perlis (1279m)
G Gagau (1377m)
G Mandi Angin (1473m)
G Tahan (2187m)
1 Taman Negara National Park

Kuala Tahan ○ Park HQ

Kenong Rimba National Park

G Dulang (1063m)

Gunung Tapis Park

Kuala Lipis

Krau Wildlife Sanctuary

G Benom (2108m)

Kuala Gandah Elephant Sanctuary

Kuala Tembeling

Jerantut

PAHANG

G Tapis (1512m)

Charah Caves

Sungai Lembing

Kerteh
Kemasik

Kemaman

2 Kampong Cherating
Kampong Sungai Ular
Sungai Kerang
Beserah
Teluk Chempedak
Kuantan

East Coast Highway

Maran

Mentakab Temerloh

Tasek Chini

Pekan

Kampong Pahang

Triang

Kemayan

Tasek Bera

KUALA LUMPUR

NEGERI SEMBILAN

Nenasi

Kampong Gading

N

30 km
30 miles

Introduction

It might just be on the other side of the Peninsula, but Malaysia's east coast could as well be on a different planet than the populous, hectic and industrialized west coast. Its coastline, made up of the states of Johor, Pahang, Terengganu and Kelantan, is lined with coconut palms, dotted with sleepy fishing kampongs and interspersed with rubber and oil palm plantations, paddy fields, beaches and mangroves.

The string of islands stretching all along the coast offers a mix of lazy getaways. Choose from Pulau Kapas for its acclaimed snorkelling and diving sites, or Pulau Tenggol and Pulau Lang Tengah, or enjoy parties and barbecues on the beach at Pulau Perhentian.

For an insight into Malay traditions and artistry, Kota Bharu, located in the north, stages almost daily events, ranging from kite flying to drumming sessions, while Kuala Terengganu is a souvenir hunting ground with fine silverware and a choice of handicraft markets.

Ins and outs

Getting there and around

The east coast can be reached from various points on the west coast. Routes from Butterworth (Penang) and Kuala Kangsar in the north lead across to Kota Bharu on the northeast coast. There's a highway from KL to Kuantan (halfway down the east coast) and the railway cuts north from Gemas (south of KL) to Kota Bharu. There is a new highway from Ipoh to Gua Musang in Kelantan via the Cameron Highlands.

Best time to visit

If you plan on visiting any of the beaches or islands on the east coast, and especially if you're hoping to dive, the best time to visit is between February and September to avoid the rainy season. During the winter monsoon, the seas are very rough; many island resorts are closed and boat operators pack up business. Between May and September is the best time for turtle spotting.

Background

Until the 19th century, the narrow coastal plain between the jungled mountains and the sea was largely bypassed by trade and commerce and its 60-odd coral-fringed (and largely uninhabited) offshore islands were known only to local fishermen. The mountainous interior effectively cut the east coast off from the west coast, physically, commercially and culturally. The east coast did not have the tin deposits which attracted Chinese speculators and miners to the towns on the other side of the Main Range in the 19th century and in more recent decades it was left behind as Malaysia joined the development race. The rural parts have been buffered from Western influence; traditional kampong lifestyles have been tempered only by the arrival of the electric lightbulb, the outboard motor and Japanese motorbikes. The east coast's fishermen and paddy farmers are Malaysia's most conservative Muslims.

In the 1990 general election, the people of Kelantan voted a hardline Islamic opposition party into power, the Parti Islam Se Malaysia (PAS). Several elections on, the PAS still holds Kelantan, although in the interim they have won and lost the state of Terengganu. The rural Malays of the east coast have not enjoyed much in the way of trickledown from Malaysia's newfound economic prosperity. Although they are *bumiputras* (sons of the soil) – see page 509 – few have reaped the benefits of more than 20 years of pro-Malay policies.

The September 11 atrocities in the US and the war in Afghanistan would seem, however, to have stopped the PAS's expansion in its tracks, for the time being at least (see page 503). Party leaders rather shortsightedly called for a jihad in support of the Taliban, they organized a rather bad-tempered demonstration outside the US embassy in KL and also refused to rule out violence. Former Prime Minister Mahathir played all this to his advantage. In reality, however, while some members of the PAS are somewhat extreme, in the main the party has managed Kelantan and, more latterly, Terengganu, pretty sensibly. However, the people of Terengganu who voted and then ousted the party in the ballot of 2004 realised that with PAS they will also be denied the economic support that states loyal to the Barsian Nasional (BN) ruling party enjoyed. They opted out and voted in the BN.

In 2005 PAS fought another tough race with the Barsian Nasional in their Kelantan stronghold, winning a narrow victory and maintaining what seemed like an increasingly fragile grip on power. However, in the 2008 general elections the PAS trounced all competition, gaining a two thirds majority in the state assembly.

During the Second World War, the Japanese Imperial Army landed at Kota Bharu and sped the length of the Peninsula within six weeks on stolen bicycles (see page 497). The east coast did not figure prominently during the war, except in the realm of literary fiction, starring in Neville Shute's *A Town Like Alice*.

Before and after the war, rubber and oil palm plantations sprang up which changed the shape of the agricultural economy. But the most dramatic change followed the discovery of large quantities of high-grade crude oil and natural gas off the northeast coast in the 1970s. By the mid-1980s, huge storage depots, gas-processing plants and refineries had been built in Terengganu, and the battered old coast road was upgraded to cater for Esso and Petronas tankers. The town of Kerteh, halfway between Kuantan and Kuala Terengganu, is a refinery town, built along one of the best beaches on the Peninsula. The construction boom and the rig work helped boost the local economy and provide employment, but the east coast states (bar Johor, which straddles the entire south tip of the Peninsula) haven't attracted industrial investment like their west coast neighbours have. Oil money has, however, helped transform the fortunes of Terengganu.

On the whole, the east coast has been less sullied by industrial pollution; the East Sea (South China Sea) is a lot cleaner than the Strait of Melaka. Despite the oil, the east coast is still the rural backwater of the Peninsula (95% of state revenues from oil go straight into federal coffers in KL).

Kuantan and around

→ *Colour map 2, A5.*
The modern capital of Pahang has a population of around 280,000 and is a bustling, largely Chinese, town at the mouth of the Kuantan River. Kuantan is the main transport and business hub for the east coast; most visitors spend at least a night here as a base to explore the mystical lake of Tasek Chini, the Semelai aboriginal kampongs of lake Tasek Bera, the Charah Caves and the adventure sports of the Gunung Tapis Park. ▶▶ *For listings, see pages 251-256.*

Ins and outs

Getting there
Kuantan's airport is 20 km away; taxis to town cost around RM30. There are bus connections with all the towns up and down the east coast as well as with key destinations on the west, including KL. Outstation taxis travel to Kuala Terengganu, KL and Mersing. ▶▶ *See also Transport, page 255.*

Getting around
Kuantan is not a large town, despite its importance as a centre for transport connections to regions across the country. City buses provide a regular service to the beach and hotels at Teluk Chempedak and there are also a number of car hire firms.

Tourist information
Pahang Tourist Information Centre ① *Jln Mahkota, 25000 Kuantan, Pahang Darul Makmur, T09-516 1007, www.pahangtourism.com.my, Tue-Sat 0800-1730*, has very pleasant and helpful staff, up-to-date information and covers a large proportion of Malaysia, specifically Pahang state.

Sights

While many tourists pass through Kuantan, not many seem to stay longer than it takes to wipe their feet and take a couple of breaths before moving on, and wandering around the centre you are unlikely to meet many westerners. It is noticeable, for example, that local people, while not unfriendly, do not speak very good English. When people do remain in the Kuantan area for any length of time, they seem to stay in the fishing villages to the north and south of town. The city is no pedestrian utopia and crossing the road takes some patience. Traffic can get pretty bad along Jalan Mahkota and Jalan Besar.

Kuantan's striking **Sultan Ahmad Shah** mosque (Masjid Negeri), in the centre of town, is worth wandering around. Visitors are asked to don oversized hooded cloaks. These enormous cloaks, the time limits given to non-Muslim visitors by the stern, yet surprisingly amused, guards and the restrictions placed on females do not detract from the cool and calming beauty of the building. Freshly decorated in blue, green and white, with a cool marbled interior, the mosque can be seen across the town. It has blue and yellow stained glass windows and the morning sun projects their coloured patterns on the interior walls. Kuantan has several streets of old shophouses which date from the 1920s. Most of the oldest buildings are opposite the padang on **Jalan Mahkota**. The 300-km stretch of coast between Kuantan and Kota Bharu is comprised of long beaches, interspersed with fishing kampongs and the occasional natural gas processing plant and oil refinery.

Kuantan

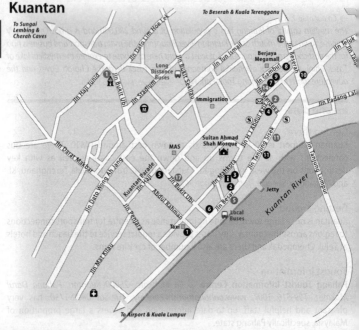

Teluk Chempedak

① *There are regular connections with the Rah Matalan bus company from the local bus station. A taxi should cost RM12.*

This beach resort is just 4 km east of Kuantan and marks the beginning of the beaches. The Pahang state government has reserved the 30 km stretch of coast from Teluk Chempedak beach north to the Terengganu state border exclusively for tourism-related projects, so there is likely to be much more development. Teluk Chempedak was once the site of a quiet kampong, and is now a beach strip with a range of hotels, and a string of bars and restaurants. There is a government-run handicraft shop (Kedai Kraf) beside the beach, specializing in batik. A short walk north of Teluk Chempedak are Methodist Bay and Teluk Pelindong.

Pekan

The old royal capital of Pahang, Pekan has a languid feel to it. Apart from a reasonably picturesque row of older wooden shophouses on the busy street along the river, it is not a particularly photogenic town. Aside from its mosques, Pekan's most distinguishing feature is its bridge, which straddles the Pahang River, the longest river on the Peninsula.

Pekan means town in Malay and it used to be known as Pekan Pahang (town of Pahang). Even before the Melakan sultanate was established in the late 14th century, it was known by the Sanskrit name for town: Pura. It is divided into Old Pekan (Pekan Lama) and New Pekan (Pekan Bharu); the former was the exclusive abode of the Malay nobility for centuries.

There are two mosques in the centre of Pekan: the **Abdullah Mosque**, Jalan Sultan Ahmad (beyond the museum), and the more modern **Abu Bakar Mosque** next door. On the north outskirts of the town is the **Istana Abu Bakar**, the royal palace, just off Jalan Istana Abu Bakar. Its opulent trimmings are visible from the road, but it is closed to the public. The small but interesting **Sultan Abu Bakar Museum** ① *Jln Sultan Ahmad, Tue-Thu 0930-1700, Fri 1445-1700, Sat-Sun 0930-1215, RM1*, is housed in a splendid colonial building and has a jet fighter mounted Airfix-style in the front garden. The museum includes a collection of brass and copperware, royal regalia, porcelain from a wrecked Chinese junk and an exhibition of local arts and crafts. In the back garden there is a depressing mini-zoo which rarely gets visited. It is home to Malayan honey bears, a tapir, a collection of monkeys, a black panther and a fish eagle, all squeezed into tiny cages. A good map of Pekan is provided.

East Sea

Tanjung Api Mosque 🕌

To Teluk Chempedak & Cherating

N

500 metres
500 yards

Sleeping 🛏
Classic 5
Greenleaf 1
Kosma 2
Mega View 11
MS Garden 12
Orchid 14
Shahzan Inn 17
Suraya 7

Eating 🍴
Alif Restoran 1
Chili 11
D'Ummi 4
Khalsa Chapati House 6
Kheng Hop 3
Ming Teck 5
Rasa Bagus 7
Sara Thai Kitchen 8
Taj Restoran 9
Tjantek Art Bistro 2
Zul Satay 10

Tasek Chini→ *Colour map 2, A4.*

ⓘ *Getting there is not easy on public transport. A taxi costs RM100 and take 1½ hrs.*

Tasek Chini is an amalgam of 13 freshwater lakes, whose fingers reach deep into the surrounding forested hills, 100 km southwest of Kuantan. The lake and the adjoining mountain are sacred to the Malays; legend has it that Lake Chini is the home of a huge white crocodile. The Jakun proto-Malay aboriginals, who live around Tasek Chini, believe a *naga* (serpent), personifying the spirit of the lake, inhabits and guards its depths. Some commentators believe that as tourism begins to pick up there, Tasek Chini will acquire similar status to that of Scotland's Loch Ness, although Lake Chini's monster has not been spotted now for more than a decade. Locals call their monster Chinnie.

More intriguing still are tales that the lake covers a 12th-14th century Khmer walled city. The rather unlikely story maintains that a series of aqueducts were used as the city's defence and that when under attack, the city would have been submerged. In late 1992, the *Far Eastern Economic Review* did report that recent archaeological expeditions had uncovered submerged stones a few metres underwater at various points around the lake. But the Orang Asli fishermen don't need archaeologists to support their convictions that the lost city exists. Between June and September the lake is carpeted with red and white lotus flowers.

Lake Tasek Bera

ⓘ *Do not attempt this trip without taking adequate supplies and provisions, including basic cooking utensils. There's no scheduled public transport to the lake. It is possible to take a bus or share taxi to Triang, due south of Temerloh, and then charter a taxi to the lake. Or take a taxi from Temerloh, an expensive option which may make sense in a group. Alternatively, take a bus from Kemayan to Bahau, 45 mins; a bus from Bahau to Ladang Geddes, 30 mins; and hitch or taxi to Kota Iskandar on the south side of the lake (where there are bungalows with cooking facilities, bookable through the Department of Aboriginal Affairs in Temerloh). Kota Iskandar is one of the best places on the Peninsula to visit Orang Asli villages. Boats can be hired to explore the lake but this requires enthusiastic negotiation.*

Temerloh is one of the best access points for Tasek Bera, or the lake of changing colours, the biggest natural lake in Malaysia. There are several Jakun, so-called proto-Malays, and Semelai aboriginal kampongs (including the largest Kota Iskandar) around the lake, once a major centre for the export of jelutong resin, used as a sealant on boats and as jungle chewing gum. Similar to Tasek Chini (see above), Tasek Bera is a maze of shallow channels connecting smaller lakes, in all about 5 km wide and 27 km long. During the dry season it is little more than a swamp, but in the wet it becomes an interconnected array of shallow lakes. The Semelai traditionally exploited the expansion and contraction of the lake(s), fishing during the wet season and collecting non-timber forest products during the dry. When the waters reached their peak, and wild pigs became stranded on the many islands that dot the lake, the Semelai would hunt. One of the lake's resident species is the rare fish-eating 'false' gharial crocodile *(Tomistoma schlegeli)*.

Charah Caves

ⓘ *These lie 25 km northwest of town; take a right fork at the 24-km mark. Catch a Sungai Lembing-bound bus from the local bus station and get off at Panching (RM4 with Seng Heng company), from here it is 3 km to the caves, although it may be possible to catch a lift on the back of a motorbike. A taxi to the caves costs RM50.*

In 1954, the Sultan of Pahang gave a Thai Buddhist monk permission to build a temple in a limestone cave at Pancing, known as the 'yawning skull' cave. A steep climb up 200 stone steps leads into the cave, which contains shrines and religious icons cut into the rock. The collection is dominated by a 9-m-long reclining Buddha, set among the limestone formations. There is always a monk in residence in the cave.

Beyond the caves is **Sungai Lembing** ① T09-541 2378, www.jmm.gov.my, Tue-Sun 0900-1800, RM1, an old tin mine and the site of some of the oldest tin workings on the Peninsula. It claims to be the deepest tin mine in the world. There is also a museum here.

Gunung Tapis Park

① Permits can be obtained from the Sungai Lembing Tapis Resort (T09-541 1339) or made through Pahang Tourism in Kuantan. It is only accessible by jeep via Sungai Lembing; from here accessible via a 12 km track.

This state park, 49 km from Kuantan, offers rafting, fishing (the local fish, ikankelah, is said to be delicious) and trekking. The park is centred on Gunung Tapis, which rises to 1500 m and can be climbed in three days. However, facilities are still poorly developed although there are camp sites.

Beserah and Sungai Karang → Colour map 2, A5

① To get there, take a bus, hourly, from the main bus terminal in Kuantan.

Once a picturesque fishing kampong, 10 km north of Kuantan, Beserah now sprawls and is not much more than a suburb of Kuantan. Beserah is a friendly place, but aesthetically it bears little comparison with villages further north. Like Teluk Chempedak to the south it does provide a slightly quieter place to stay. There is, however, a local handicraft industry still; there is a batik factory to the north of the village. The village's speciality is *ikan bilis* (anchovies), which are boiled, dried and chillied on the beach and end up on Malaysian breakfast tables, gracing *nasi lemak* (rice cooked in coconut milk). Beserah's fishermen use water buffalo to cart their catch directly from their boats to the kampong, across the middle of the shallow lagoon. The kampong has become rather touristy in recent years, but there is a good beach, just to the north, at Batu Hitam.

Kampong Sungai Ular (Snake River Village)

① Catch a bus running up the east coast road and asked to be dropped off at Kampong Sungai Ular.

Sungai Ular, 31 km north of Kuantan, is a typical laid-back and very photogenic Malay fishing village. There is a small island, Pulau Ular, just offshore. The beach is usually deserted, is backed by coconut palms and has fine white sand. The Kampong is signposted to the right, just off the main road.

⊚ Kuantan and around listings

For Sleeping and Eating price codes and other relevant information, see Essentials pages 25-30.

◎ Sleeping

Kuantan p247, map p248
The upmarket hotels are mostly at Teluk Chempedak (4 km north of Kuantan, see page 249). There are plenty of cheap Chinese

hotels in Kuantan itself, mostly on and around Jln Teluk Sisek and Jln Besar. Several smart hotels have sprung up in the **B-C** range, offering excellent value for money.
L-A MS Garden, Jln Lorong Garnbut, T09-517 7899, www.msgarden.com.my.
An enormous 4-star hotel, very elegant inside, at the business end of town. Pool, gym, health centre, restaurant and coffee garden. Breakfast included. Promotional offers available.

A Mega View, 567 Jln Besar, T09-517 1888, www.megaviewhotel.com. Aimed primarily at business visitors, this hotel offers superb promotional rates, comfortable rooms (some with river views), and a pleasant open-air café along the river, great for a sunset beer.

A Shahzan Inn, 240 Jln Bukit Ubi, T09-513 6688, www.shahzaninn.com.my. Brightly coloured edifice towering over the Padang and around the corner from the spectacular Sultan Ahmad Shah mosque. This place is popular with domestic businessmen. The comfortable but dated rooms have cable TV, a/c and those on the top floor command excellent views of the city and surrounding hills. Small pool and Wi-Fi in the lobby area. Discounts available.

B Classic, 7 Bangunan LKNP, Jln Besar, T09-516 4599, classick@streamyx.com. With excellent promotional rates, this is one of the town's best places to stay, with 40 spacious, comfortable a/c rooms with TV, Wi-Fi access and bathroom with tub. Ask for a room at the back for a lovely river view. Buffet breakfast is included in the price. Highly recommended.

B Greenleaf, 60-62 Jln Bukit Ubi, T09-515 9966, sales@greenleafhotel.com.my. Spanking new hotel with excellent discount rates and comfortable modern rooms with cable TV and a/c. Coffee house and daily newspaper each morning. Recommended.

B-C Kosma, 59 Jln Haji Abdul Aziz, T09-516 2214. Owned by a Malay co-operative, this friendly place has clean rooms with a/c and TV.

C Orchid 11 Jln Merdeka, T09-517 7570. Friendly family-run hotel with huge, slightly run-down a/c rooms that are kept spotlessly clean. Some rooms have attached bathroom and TV. Recommended.

C Suraya, 55-57 Jln Haji Abdul Aziz, T09-516 4266. Spacious a/c rooms with attached bathrooms. Caters mainly for business people and the domestic tourist market.

Teluk Chempedak *p249*
Teluk Chempedak provides a more relaxed alternative to the noisier hotels in Kuantan.

AL Hyatt Regency Kuantan, Telok Chempedak, T09-518 1234,

www.kuantan.regency.hyatt.com. With a/c, several restaurants and bars, 2 pools, and a fitness centre. This low-rise hotel is in landscaped gardens in a beautiful setting on the beach. There are good sport (including water sport) facilities, and a well-stocked craft shop. It is well managed with good views. Friendly and efficient staff. Recommended.

B Kuantan, opposite Hyatt, T09-568 0026. With a/c and a restaurant. This place is very clean. Cheaper rooms are fan only but all have attached bathroom, noisy TV lounge, pleasant terrace for sundowners, although it faces the new **Hyatt** extension. The manager here is helpful and friendly. Relaxed atmosphere. Recommended.

Pekan *p249*
There is a poor selection of hotels; the best budget option is the government resthouse.

B Inderapura Country Resort, Kompleks Taman Bandar, Peramu, Pekan, T09-426 6616, F426 6895. Rather bare, functional office-style building with good facilities. En suite rooms have TV and a/c. Restaurant. Inconveniently located 25 mins from Kuantan at Taman Bandar on the Kuantan/Pekan Rd, close to a Petronas garage and Isuzu dealer.

C Rumah Rehat (resthouse), beside the football field (*padang*), off Jln Sultan Abu Bakar. A big, low-slung colonial building in need of a lick of paint with a cool, spacious interior and big, clean rooms, restaurant. It is advisable to try to book accommodation in advance if visiting during the Sultan's birthday celebrations.

Tasek Chini *p250*
A-D Lake Chini Resort, T09-477 8000, tasikchiniresort@hotmail.com. 10 chalets, some with attached bathrooms, a 10-bed dorm and camping, small restaurant attached to the resort serving simple dishes. Fishing is said to be excellent and the resort can arrange visits to local Orang Asli communities.

D Rajan Jones Guest House, 30 mins' walk from **Lake Chini Resort**. The cheapest place to stay, room rate includes all meals but the accommodation is very basic, no running water or electricity, tours and treks arranged.

Beserah and Sungai Karang *p251*

Most of the resort hotels are around Sungai Karang, 3-6 km north of Beserah village itself.

AL Swiss-Garden Resort & Spa, Balok beach, Mukim Sungai Karang, T09-544 7333, www.swissgarden.com. An international-class hotel on the beach with over 300 rooms, gardens, good pool, business facilities, health club and sauna.

A De Ruh Beach Resort, 152 Sungai Karang (6 km north of Beserah), T09-544 7544, www.derhu.com.my. With a/c, restaurants, a pool, a paddling pool, a playground and a good range of facilities including tennis, squash, badminton, gym, jacuzzi and water sports. Next to fine white-sand beach, popular stopover for cruises, all rooms are spacious with a/c, TV, in-house video, minibar, tea and coffee-making facilities, non-smoking rooms available, tour agency.

A-B Duta Village Beach Resort, Lot 1260 Sungai Karang, 8 km north of town, T09-544 7900, www.dutaresorts.com. Pleasant place with pool and tennis, popular with tour groups.

B Blue Horizon Beach Resort, Kampong Balok (5 km north of Beserah), T09-544 8113, F515 7137. North of Beserah on a good beach, pool, clean and spruce with big wooden chalet rooms, built around central area, garden a bit of a wilderness, discounts often available.

B Gloria Maris Resort (1 km north of Beserah), T09-544 7788, F544 7619. A/c, restaurant, water sports, very small pool, sandwiched between road and Pasir Hitam (not such a good stretch of beach), small chalets and friendly management.

B Tiara Beserah Beach Resort, 812 Jln Beserah, T09-544 8101, F514 1979. 32 rooms in new *atap*-roofed chalets, a/c, TV, pool, café.

E La Chaumiere, T09-544 7662. This is the most popular of the budget places to stay, it is well run and pleasant. To get here ask to be let off at Kampong Pantai Beserah and walk towards Kampong Pelidong and the sea for about 1 km.

Eating

Kuantan *p247, map p248*

If you've just come from the tourist havens of Tioman or the Perhentians and are weary of pseudo-Western cuisine, or have been tramping the rainforests of Pahang munching crackers and dried fruit, Kuantan, with its profusion of eateries, is a good place to rediscover the delights of Malaysian cooking.

Tjantek Art Bistro, 46 Jln Besar (opposite Classic Hotel). Open 1800-2300. A funky art-cum-coffee shop also serving pasta, steaks, seafood, tea and juices. There's an art gallery on the 1st floor.

Cantina, 16 Lorong Tun Ismail 1 (off Jln Bukit Ubi). Smart a/c restaurant with waiters in batik *bajus*, Indonesian-style seafood and curries. Recommended by locals.

Chilli, 4A Jln Besar. Simple Chinese eatery offering a good seafood menu, some Malay fare and a 3-person steamboat extravaganza (RM45).

D'Ummi, 60 Jln Teluk Sisek (below Embassy Hotel). Good breakfasts (especially *nasi lemak*). Bright, sunny and friendly.

Khalsa Chapati House, 98 Jln Besar. Tasty Indian dishes including some veg options. The *dosai* here are crisp, and the banana leaf curries go down a treat.

Kheng Hop, 17 Jln Mahkota (on corner), opposite the playing field. Big lively old coffee shop with marble-top tables and good *nasi lemak* and *nasi daggang* in the mornings. Unchanged for 50 years.

Rasa Bagus, Unit A 41 Jln Merdeka (next to Hotel Orchid). Open 0700-1700. Cheery Malay eatery with delicious dishes such as *mee jawa*, *mee udang*, tasty *nasi campur* selection and some seafood curries.

Sara Thai Kitchen, B42 Jln Gambut, T012-946 5591. Open 1300-2300. Excellent Thai restaurant serving delicious, fresh seafood dishes, Thai salads, soups and curries for superb prices in a convivial atmosphere. Very popular. Highly recommended.

Sri Patani, 79 Bangunan Udarulaman, Jln Tun Ismail. Excellent Malay/South Thai food.

Taj Restoran, Jln Gambut (opposite Berjaya Megamall). Very popular restaurant serving delicious fish biryani, fresh naan, juicy tandoori chicken and *tom yam* soups. Just over the road from here is **Alif Restoran** (†), equally popular with locals for its Indian food and open 24 hrs.

Zul Satay, junction of Jln Teluk Sisek and Jln Beserah (known as Kuantan Garden, between Kuantan and Teluk Chempedak). Upmarket satay joint. All the usual, plus rabbit and offal. Recommended.

Foodstalls

The Malay cafés and foodstalls along the riverbank, behind the long-distance bus station, are busy and popular. Recommended, especially for seafood. There are more hawker stalls on junction of Jln Mahkota and Jln Masjid (Taman Salera), next to the local bus station. At **Kuantan Garden**, junction of Jln Teluk Sisek and Jln Beserah (between Kuantan and Teluk Chempedak), there is a large number of Chinese stalls.

Teluk Chempedak p249

Chempedak Seafood, A-1122, Jln Teluk Sisek. Big Chinese restaurant at the crossroads on the way to Teluk Chempedak. Specialities include chilli crab and freshwater fish.

Pattaya, on the beachfront. Good views of the beach, serves crab priced by weight, good food and good value.

Selera Warisan, next door to the Pattaya. Good seafood and pleasant situation overlooking the beach.

Taj Mahal Curry House, 13 Teluk Chempedak. North Indian cuisine plus fish-head curry.

Foodstalls

Group of *gerai makan* in brick kiosks, next to the beach alongside the handicraft centre, serving Malay, Thai, Chinese and Western food.

Pekan p249

There are a couple of reasonable coffee shops in the new town. The foodstalls on Jln Sultan Ahmad, near the bus/taxi stands, are the best Pekan has to offer.

Beserah and Sungai Karang p251

Beserah Seafood, Malay/Chinese, the speciality is buttered prawns.

Gloria Maris Golden Cowrie, near the chalets. Malay/Indian/Thai and traditional Sun lunch, seafood salad by weight.

Pak Su Seafood, popular Chinese restaurant on terrace next to the beach. Recommended.

◑ Bars

Kuantan p247, map p248

Boom Boom Bar, 236 Jln Teluk Sisik. Pool, bands and restaurant. Also on site is **Mini Boom Boom**, an outdoor café.
There are also a couple of bars, some with wailing karaoke, along Jln Merdeka.

Teluk Chempedak p249

The best bars and nightlife are along the beachfront at Teluk Chempedak. New karaoke bars and pubs have sprouted up in town, most with a distinctly Western theme. **Lips** and **Urban Beach**, situated on the main road into Chempedak, opposite the Hyatt car park, both offer beer and karaoke, possibly a bad combination, but they are friendly enough, and make up for the general absence of nightlife in Kuantan, where many restaurants close early in the evening. **Ranch Pub** (formerly the Country Ranch), not far from the Hyatt Hotel. Recommended. **The Sampan Bar**, on the Hyatt beachfront. In the *atap*-roofed shell of a junk which beached in 1978 with 162 Vietnamese refugees aboard. The bar capitalizes on this slightly perverse novelty by charging more.

◑ Shopping

Kuantan p247, map p248

There are several expensive craft shops along Jln Besar.

Berjaya Megamall (close to the MS Garden hotel) with a cinema, fast-food restaurants, bowling lanes and boutiques.

Hamid Brothers, 23 Jln Mahkota. Sells books. (Also a money changer, recommended locally for efficiency and good rates).
Kuantan Parade, corner of Jln Penjara and Jln Haji Abdul Rahman. Fully a/c shopping plaza, offers Western chain stores to those experiencing consumer cold turkey.

⊛ Festivals and events

Pekan p249
October **Sultan's Birthday** (24th: state holiday). Celebrated with processions, dancing and an international polo championship which the sultan hosts on his manicured polo ground at the istana.

▲ Activities and tours

Kuantan p247, map p248
Boat trips
Kuantan River Cruise, for information and booking, Jabatan Perhubungan Awam, Majilis Perbandaran Kuantan, Jln Tanah Putih, T09-512 1555, kbbudaya@mpk.gov.my. Leaving from the jetty at the IBU Pejabat MPK, this cruise takes in the mangrove swamps and jungle surrounding the Kuantan River. The boat trips often stop off at the new Mangrove Boardwalk, a 750 m-long walk over the mangroves. Boats leave Sat-Thu at 0900, 1100, 1430 and 1600. Fri at 0900 and 1500. Trips cost RM15 per person, last 1-2 hrs, minimum 5 people. Night sailings on Fri and Sat for 1 hr 2000-2300 (RM5 per person). Boat trips to see the fireflies, RM250 to charter the boat.

The following operators include trips around the Kuantan area and river tours:
East Coast Holidays, 13 Telok Cempedak, T09-566 5228; **Reliance**, 66 Jln Teluk Sisek, T09-510 2566; **SMAS Travels**, 1st floor, Kompleks Teruntum, Jln Mahkota, T09-511 3888; **Syarikat Perusahaan**, 38, 2nd floor, Bangunan DPMP, Jln Wong Ah Jang; **Taz Ben Travel & Tours**, 2nd floor, Kompleks Teruntum, Jln Mahkota, T09-510 2255.

Golf
Astana Golf & Country Club, KM 13, off Jln Sungai Lembing, T09-568 7311, F567 2519. 27-hole championship-standard course and night golfing at this swanky resort.
Royal Pahang Golf Club, KM5, Jln Teluk Sisek, T09-567 5811, F567 1170. 18-hole course.

Teluk Chempedak p249
Tour operators
East Coast Holidays, 13 Teluk Chempedak, T09- 566 5228. Helpful staff; tours to Lake Chini, the Panching caves and waterfall, Kapas Island, Kuala Terengganu and turtle watching. Also flight reconfirmation, hotel reservation and car rental.
Mayflower Acme Tours, Hyatt Kuantan, Teluk Chempedak, T09-512 1469, www.mayflower.com.my. Well-established operator with an excellent transport network.

Pekan p249
Polo
Royal Pahang Polo Club, Pekan, T09-422 4587. Matches are held in season; Prince Charles is said to have played here. The field is surrounded by traditional Malay houses.

Tasek Chini p250
Tour operators
Malaysian Overland Adventures, Lot 1.23, 1st floor, Bangunan Angkasaraya, Jln Ampang, KL, T03-241 3569. Recommended.

⊖ Transport

Kuantan p247, map p248
Air
Regular flights to **KL** (MAS). **Firefly** has regular connections with **Subang** and **Singapore**.
Airline offices MAS, ground floor, Wisma Bolasepak Pahang, Jln Gambut, T09-538 4291, F515 7870 (T1-300 88 3000, national call centre).

Bus
Local The bus station is on junction of Jln Besar and Jln Abdul Rahman. Connections with **Teluk Chempedak** and **Cherating**.

Buses to Cherating (RM4.70) depart every few hours. The destination is marked as Kemaman, a small town 20 km from Cherating. The bus drops tourists at a bus stop on the road side, where it's a 5-min walk to Cherating's main strip. **Long distance** Since the new highway was opened linking KL and Kuantan the journey to the capital only takes 2½ hrs. The long-distance bus station is on Jln Stadium and companies have their offices on the 2nd floor. Regular connections with **KL** (2½ hrs, RM21.90), **Mersing** (2½ hrs, RM16.30), **JB** (RM26.50), Singapore (RM29.20), **Melaka** (RM27), **Penang** (RM53), **Kuala Terengganu** (RM16.60), **Kota Bharu** (RM31.40) and **Jerantut** (RM16.60) for **Taman Negara** with Transnasional, Utama and Plusliner. To get to **Cherating** take a bus from the local bus station on Jln Besar (RM4.70).

Car hire
Budget, 59 Jln Haji Abdul Aziz, T09-512 6370 or De Ruh Beach Resort, see page 253; Hertz, Samudra River View Hotel, Jln Besar, T09-512 2688; National, 49 Jln Teluk Sisek, T09-512 7303.

Taxi
Taxi station on Jln Besar, next to the local bus station. Long-distance taxi routes are well served from Kuantan. Pahang tourist office has a price list. Taxis serve **KL** (RM280), **KLIA** (RM370), **Mersing** (RM200) and **Kuala Terengganu** (RM200).

Teluk Chempedak p249
Bus
Regular connections from **Kuantan**.

Car hire
Avis, Hyatt Hotel, Teluk Chempedak, T09-566 1234, and ground floor, Loo Bros Bldg, 59 Jln Haji Abdul Aziz, T09-512 3666; Mayflower, Hyatt Kuantan, Teluk Chempedak, T09-513 1234; Sinat, Lot 3, Merlin Inn, Teluk Chempedak, T09-514 1388.

Pekan p249
Bus
Bus stop on Jln Sultan Ahmad in the centre of town. Regular connections with **Kuantan**

(RM10) with **Bee Huat** and **Rahmat Alam**. There are direct buses to **Mersing**.

Taxi
Taxis for **Kuantan** (RM50) and elsewhere from the stand between Jln Sultan Ahmad and the waterfront, opposite the indoor market.

Tasek Chini p250
Bus and boat
Take the KL highway (Rt 2) from Kuantan towards **Maran**; 56 km down the road, Tasek Chini is signposted to the left and onwards to Kampong Belimbing. There are no buses, charter a taxi or use a tour agency. At Belimbing hire a boat across the Pahang River and onto the waterways of Tasek Chini. It is also possible to be dropped off at the resort and picked up at an arranged time.

Alternatively, catch a bus from **Kuantan** or **Pekan** for **Kampong Chini** (12 km from the resort). From here there is a sealed road to the resort but, again, no public transport, although people have managed to persuade local motorcyclists to take them pillion.

Beserah p251
Bus
Several local buses from **Kuantan**'s main bus terminal pass through Beserah, departures at least every hour.

◑ Directory

Kuantan p247, map p248
Banks Along Jln Mahkota and Jln Besar, between GPO and bus station. **Immigration** Immigration Office, Wisma Persekutuan, Jln Gambut, T09-514 2155. **Internet** There are a couple of places on Jln Gambut (RM2 per hr). **Medical services** Hospital, Jln Mat Kilau. **Post** Jln Mahkota (east end).

Pekan p249
Banks Bumiputra, 117 Jln Engku Muda Mansur. **Post** In the middle of town.

Pahang's national parks

→ *Colour map 1, C5, Altitude: 2187 m.*

Taman Negara is in a mountainous area (it includes Gunung Tahan, the highest mountain on the Peninsula) and lays claim to some of the oldest rainforest in the world. This area was left untouched by successive ice ages and has been covered in jungle for about 130 million years, which makes it older than the rainforests in the Congo or Amazon basins.

   Kenong Rimba Park is home to the Batik Orang Asli tribe. It doesn't have the variety of wildlife but is less touristy and cheaper. ▸▸ *For listings, see pages 262-265.*

Taman Negara National Park → *For listings, see pages 262-265.*

Once known as King George V Park, Taman Negara was gazetted as a national park in 1938 when the Sultans of Pahang, Terengganu and Kelantan agreed to set aside a 434,300 ha tract of virgin jungle where all three states meet.

   The range of vegetation in the park includes riverine species and lowland forest through cloud and moss forest at higher elevations and on to a strange subalpine environment rich in strange pitcher plants close to the summit of Gunung Tahan. Over 250 species of bird have been recorded in Taman Negara, and mammals resident in the park include wild ox (gaur), sambar, barking deer, tapir, civet cat, wild boar and even the occasional tiger and elephant herd. However, the more exotic mammals rarely put in an appearance, especially in areas closer to Kuala Tahan.

Ins and outs

Getting there Taman Negara straddles the mountainous interior of three states. Because it is one of the most popular destinations on the Peninsula there are lots of ways to get here – by bus, boat and by train. ▸▸ *See Transport, page 264.*

Best time to visit Between March and September, during the dry season. The park may be closed at the height of the monsoon season from the beginning of November to the end of December, when the rivers are in flood.

Tourist information The Department of Wildlife has a bureau at the Kuala Tembeling jetty (see below) and issues permits and licences. You will need to get your permit before entering the park (bring photocopies of your passport). Park permit RM1; fishing licence RM10; camera licence RM5. Those who risk turning up at the Kuala Tembeling jetty without booking may be turned away if boats are full.

   The **park headquarters** ① *daily 0800-2200*, are at Kuala Tahan, on the south boundary of the park, accessible by boat from Kuala Tembeling, a two- to three-hour beautiful journey (or a more mundane bus journey). At Kuala Tahan all visitors are required to check in at the reception desk. Various companies run tours to Taman Negara. It is sometimes simpler and less hassle to do this than going it alone, but it does cut down on your options. Regardless of what KL tour operators may tell you, there is a local bus (RM6) that runs two to three times a day from Jerantut bus station to Kuala Tahan. **Kuala Tahan** is a sleepy country village on the south bank of the Tembeling River. There is usually plenty of accommodation for all budgets, but it may be booked up during public holidays and in the high season. Many visitors, particularly those unfamiliar with travelling in Malaysia, have recommended tours for their logistical advantages, although the park is also easy to visit independently. The disadvantage of going it along is that tour groups tend to book up the hides. See Activities and tours, page 264, for further information.

Equipment It is worth having walking boots for even the shortest of excursions (as rain turns muddy paths into skiddy patches), as well as a thick pair of socks and long (loose) trousers. Leeches are common in the park after rain; spraying clothes and boots with insect repellent and wearing leech socks helps. If you find yourself providing a free meal for a leech, you can dislodge them with salt or a couple of drops of iodine (also useful for purifying water in the water-poor areas of the park). When crossing jungle rivers, hiking sandles or cheap rubber deck shoes help to keep your balance on the slippery rocks and in the fast current. If you're sticking to the lowlands, minimal clothing is needed, as it's hot work. However, those undertaking the Gunung Tahan trail or similar higher peaks shouldn't underestimate the cooler temperatures at higher altitudes. A good fleece, rain

Taman Negara

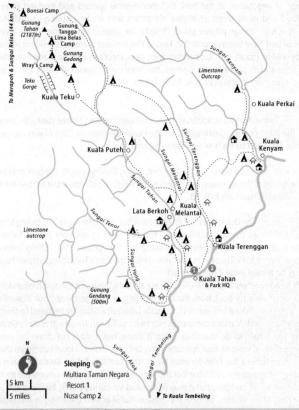

gear and a sleeping bag should be packed as standard. A good torch is essential for those going to hides as is a water bottle for longer walks and treks. A raincover and waterproof bags may be useful. Visitors are not permitted to carry glass into the park. The shop at the park headquarters hires out torches, tents, water bottles, cooking equipment and fishing tackle – even jungle boots. A camera permit is RM5.

Hides Some hides (*bumbun*) are close to the park headquarters, from a five-minute walk to a day's trek or boat ride. Visitors can stay overnight at the hides for a RM5 fee (payable at park HQ in Kuala Tahan), but there are no facilities other than a sleeping space and a pit latrine. Take a powerful torch to spotlight any animals that visit the salt-licks. You are more likely to see wildlife at the hides further from the Park HQ, as the number of people now visiting Taman Negara has begun to frighten the animals away. Rats, monitor lizards and wild pigs are among the animals not so easily frightened: food bags must be tied up securely at night. During popular periods and on weekends it is best to book your spot at a salt-lick.

Background

Gunung Tahan is the highest of three peaks on the east side of the park and marks the Pahang-Kelantan border. Its name means 'the forbidden mountain'; according to local Asli folklore the summit is the domain of a giant monkey, who guards two pots of magic stones. The first expeditions to Gunung Tahan were despatched by the Sultan of Pahang in 1863 but were defeated by the near-vertical-sided Teku Gorge, the most obvious approach to the mountain, from the Tahan River. The 1000-m-high gorge ended in a series of waterfalls which came crashing 600 m down the mountain. Several other ill-fated European-led expeditions followed, before the summit was finally reached by four Malays on another British expedition in 1905.

Until the park was set up, **Kampong Kuala Tahan** – now the site of the park headquarters – was one of the most remote Orang Asli villages in North Pahang, at the confluence of the Tembeling and Tahan rivers. This area of the Peninsula remained unmapped and mostly unexplored well into the 20th century. These days, Kuala Tahan is sometimes overrun with visitors; park accommodation has expanded rapidly under private sector management. But most visitors do not venture more than a day or two's walk from headquarters, and huge swathes of jungle in the north and east sections of the park remain virtually untouched and unvisited. Taman Negara now has scores of trails, requiring varying amounts of physical exertion; the toughest walk is the seven- to nine-day Gunung Tahan summit trek.

Treks

Trails are signposted from Park HQ. Tours are conducted twice daily by guides and these include night walks, cave treks and other walks. Because most visitors tend to stick to the trails immediately around the park headquarters, even a modest day's outing will take you away from the crowds. A full listing and details on various routes can be obtained at park HQ. Independent day walks can be taken to caves, swimming holes, waterfalls, along rivers (again with swimming areas), to salt-licks and hides and through forest. Longer multi-day treks are also possible, but guides must be taken on all these longer forays. The most demanding is climbing Gunung Tahan.

Gunung Tahan → *Altitude: 2187 m.*

There are three possible approaches to climbing the mountain, none should be underestimated, especially during periods of bad weather. A maximum of 48 hikers are allowed on the trail at any one time, so book in advance if planning to trek at peak periods. The first (described below) is a eight- to nine-day tough trek from park HQ at Kuala Tahan, the second route (described below) is for around seven days, following the same route from Kuala Tahan to the Gunung Tahan summit before descending on the northwest side of the mountain and exiting the park at Sungai Relau. From this point (if booked in advance through park HQ), a park pickup can be arranged for a specific date and you can be dropped off at the Western Park HQ near Merapoh. From Merapoh it's possible to continue your journey by train to the north or south. The third and shortest route (four to five days) involves climbing the peak on a return trek from the Merapoh and the park entrance at Sungai Relau.

The first trek is best climbed in spring or early summer, which are usually the drier and clearer months. **Day 1**: Kuala Tahan to Kuala Melantai (four to five hours) – a beautiful trek through lowland rainforest and gently undulating terrain; this is a good introduction of hiking in the forest and getting used to heat and humidity of the lowlands. Good water and some small bathing pools come as a welcome relief on arrival at Melantai camp. **Day 2**: Kuala Melantai to Kuala Puteh (eight hours). No streams en route; succession of tough climbs along the ridge, final one is Gunung Rajah at 571 m (beautiful views of the forest below); 1½-hour descent to campsite by Sungai Tahan. **Day 3**: Kuala Puteh to Kuala Teku (2½-4½ hours). Route follows Sungai Tahan, which must be crossed seven times – care must be taken during periods of high rainfall, either in the valleys themselves or in the surrounding mountains. The campsite is at the Sungai Teku confluence and was the base camp for the first successful Gunung Tahan expedition in 1905. Both Puteh and Teku camps have beautiful riverside locations and plentiful water – make the most of this, as there are limited water resources over the following days. **Day 4**: Kuala Teku to Gunung Tangga Lima Belas (seven hours). Long, uphill slog (4½ hours) to Wray's Camp (named after 1905 expedition member). This is a good campsite; alternatively climb through mossy forest to Gunung Tangga Lima Belas campsite, which has magnificent views, but is very exposed. A third option is a campsite above a steep cliff hike called Gunung Gedong by the locals. This is a long day with limited water and plenty of exposed scrambling using attached ropes and, in some places, some fairly flimsy ladders – with full packs this is around 10 hours hiking from Teku. **Day 5**: Gunung Tangga Lima Belas to summit, returning to the Padang. After a scramble up the side of a rockface on Gunung Gedong, the trail leads to the Padang – a plateau area (three to four hours). Set up tents and leave equipment at campsite; route to summit follows ridge and takes 2½ hours. It's essential to take a raincoat as the summit is often shrouded in mist. A unique and fascinating zone of moss forest and bush replete with pitcher plants surrounds the summit. Begin descent to the Padang by 1600. **Days 6-9**: Padang to Kuala Tahan, following the same route.

For the second route, to continue on the route to Relau (44 km from the summit) and Merapoh, follow the description below.

Day 5 variation: From the summit follow trails to Bukit Botak or Bonsai – both camps are high with great views but limited water. It's cold at night. **Day 6**: The next day is a tough and muddy descent, again using fixed ropes in many areas through rapidly thickening forest. Due to following a ridge there's little water despite passing three 'official' camps – Blumut, Kubang and Permatang. Try to aim for Kem Kor, the first camp to be located close to a river after the summit. This camp has plenty of space and it's incredible to have a proper swim after reaching the summit. **Day 7**: Three to four hours' hike and a couple of river crossings brings you to Sungai Relau and the park entrance point, where there are some good swimming spots, shelter and showers. If you booked previously, a pickup truck will arrive and take you Merapoh HQ on the surfaced road that runs to this point. The very polite Merapoh HQ staff will check your documents at this point and make sure you're taking all your rubbish out of the park. They'll also issue you with certificate confirming your successful ascent of the Tahan mountain! A small additional 'taxi' service will ensure you're dropped off at the Marapoh train station on the Singapore/Kota Bharu train line.

Gunung Gagau and Western Taman Negara

ⓘ *As with Gunung Tahan a guide is necessary for this climb (around RM500 per week, RM50 for each additional day); maximum 12 people with one guide. A sleeping bag and a tent are vital.*

Gunung Tahan might be the highest peak within the park's boundaries, but it's by no means the only one in what is an extremely mountainous area. Far to the east lies Gunung Gagau, a 1377 m peak within the Taman Negara's core zone. This area is currently closed to tourists, being reserved for the area's rich wildlife and members of the indigenous Batik tribe who reside in the area. Scientists or conservationists with specific projects may be allowed into the area with advance notice. Batik guides and national park rangers are often the only people with in-depth knowledge of the area, which is reached by a one-day boat journey up the Tembeling and Sat rivers and around four days' hiking along poorly marked or sometimes nonexistent trails.

Far more accessible and open to visitors are trails to the northeast of Kuala Tahan heading up to Kuala Perkai via several interesting caves and the hide of Bumbun Kumbang – a potential four-day circuit.

Canopy Walk

ⓘ *30-min walk from Park HQ, Sat-Thu 1100-1500 and Fri 0900-1200, RM5.*

This is worth a visit to take in jungle life at close proximity. The walkway is suspended about 40 m above the forest floor and stretches for over 530 m, making it the world's longest canopy walkway.

Fishing

Fishing is better further from Kuala Tahan (be aware that fishing is often prohibited); there are game fishing lodges near the confluence of the Tenor and Tahan rivers, at Kuala Terenggan (up the Tembeling from Kuala Tahan) and at Kuala Kenyam, at the confluence of the Kenyam (often spelt Keniam on tourist maps) and the Tembeling. The best months to fish are February to March and July to August, during the monsoon season. At the height of the monsoon, in November and December travel can be difficult and the park is sometimes closed. The rivers Tahan, Kenyam and the more remote Sepia (all tributaries of the Tembeling) are reckoned to be the best waters. There are more than 200 species of fish in the park's rivers including the *kelasa*, a renowned sport fish. A permit costs RM10, rods are available for hire.

River trips

Boat trips can be arranged from the park headquarters to the Lata Berkoh rapids on Sungai Tahan (near Kuala Tahan), Kuala Terenggan (several sets of rapids to be negotiated) and Kuala Kenyam (from where a trail leads to the top of a limestone outcrop). A trip to the rapids, misleadingly called a waterfall, by park authorities, on a boat that holds four passengers, costs RM80. Although this is a relatively expensive way to see the park, it is probably the most enchanting and when split between a number of people (boats carrying up to 12 people can be booked), it is worthwhile.

Jerantut

This is the nearest town to Kuala Tembeling and the most popular entry point into Taman Negara, some 16 km away and RM25 by taxi. For those travelling to the park on public transport it may be necessary to spend a night here, and there is a range of accommodation on offer, plus backpacker-friendly tour agencies.

Kenong Rimba National Park → *For listings, see pages 262-265. Colour map 1, C4.*

This park is 1½ hours east of Kuala Lipis by boat down the Jelai River to Kampong Kuala Kenong. The park, which encompasses the Kenong River valley and is spread over some 120 sq km, is the home of the Batik Orang Asli tribe, who are shifting cultivators. There is a network of Asli trails around the park and several caves and waterfalls. There are two campsites along the river and chalets.

The park is a good alternative to Taman Negara. Though it may not have the same variety of animal life (and especially large mammals), it is less touristy and trekking here is cheaper. An interesting and useful website is www.endemicguides.com, which outlines some of the park's climbing, trekking and caving options. Treks from two to six days are possible in Kenong Rimba.

Ins and outs

The park is managed by **Kuala Lipis District Forest Office** ① *Government Office Complex, Kuala Lipis, T09-312 3745.* Both a guide and permit are needed before you will be allowed into the park. For tours and treks to Kenong Rimba, see Kuala Lipis Activities and tours, page 264. Entrance to the park is from Batu Sembilan jetty (20 minutes) or an hour's boat ride from the jetty in Kuala Lipis.

Kuala Lipis

Kuala Lipis is a pleasant and relaxed town on the Jelai and Lipis rivers, 100 km north east of Fraser's Hill. Unlike other Malaysian towns it has not been thoughtlessly redeveloped and many colonial buildings still survive. This is probably because Malaysia's development has passed by Kuala Lipis. In the late 19th century it grew to prominence as a gold-mining town and, for a short period, was the area's administrative capital. However, gold fever has passed (although the mines have been reopened since) and the town's administrative role passed to Kuantan in 1955. Today it's a good base from which to trek to Kenong Rimba and is not without charm.

◉ Pahang's national parks listings

For Sleeping and Eating price codes and other relevant information, see Essentials pages 25-30.

◉ Sleeping

Taman Negara National Park *p257, map 258*
Accommodation ranges from the resort, small hotels across the river, fishing lodges, chalets, visitor lodges for hides, hides and campsites.

LL-B Mutiara Taman Negara Resort, Kampong Kuala Tahan, T09-266 2200, www.mutiarahotels.com. Accommodation, which must be booked in advance, runs the gamut from 8-bed dorms with fans, lockers and shared bath, to timber chalets and bungalows, some of them self-catering. Camping is also offered, see page 263.

There are a number of **fishing lodges** (**C-D**) in the park, in which beds and mattresses are provided; there is no bedding or cooking equipment, however. These can be booked at Kuala Tahan HQ. There are chalets (C-D) in various villages around the park, usually booked for tour agencies' guests. Visitor lodges for hides (C-B) at Kuala Terenggan and Kuala Kenyam can also be booked from Kuala Tahan HQ. These are away from the crowds but are surprisingly comfortable with attached bathrooms and restaurant. There is no charge for staying in the hides themselves. It is also possible to spend a night in one of the wildlife observation hides, RM5 per night. These are raised up among the trees at Tabang, Belau, Yong, Cegar Anjing and Kumbang.

Kampong Kuala Tahan

Outside the park, this is on the other side of the river (crossed by a small boat). Places here are much cheaper but slightly less convenient:
B-D Ekotown Chalets, T09-266 9897. Fan and a/c rooms, hot-water showers, generally good reviews, but some plumbing worries.
B-D Teresek Hill View, T09-266 3065. Dorms, chalets and more sophisticated bungalows with attached bathrooms. Simple restaurant.
B-E Nusa Camp, across the river from Park HQ and then 15 mins upriver, T09-266 2369, www.tamannegara-nusaholiday.com.my. Dorms with 2 bunk beds per room, bungalows with attached bathrooms, and also tents for hire, restaurant. The owner is keen to help and will organize trips to the rapids (not particularly exciting), various hikes and trips to an Orang Asli village. To get to Nusa Camp take one of the longboats from Park HQ (there is a shuttle boat every 2 hrs); they also run a direct service from Kuala Tembeling with boats leaving daily at 0900 and 1400 (Fri 1430), RM70 return.
C Agoh Chalets, T09-266 9570, www.agoh. com.my. Basic twins with fan and shower, dorm beds also available in quad chalets.
E Liana Hostel, T09-266 9322. Basic hostel with 4 beds per room.

Camping

E Mutiara Taman Negara Resort, see page 262. Rents out tents (2/3/4-person), as do some of the tourist agencies and shops at Kuala Tahan. There is an additional RM1 fee for use of their campsite. The landscaped campsite can accommodate up to 200, but fortunately never does. Tents, once hired, can be taken with you on treks. Make sure you check the quality of tents before setting off on a major trek – some of the tents being rented are as waterproof as a paper bag – potentially a big problem in the rainforest. See map, page 258, for campsite locations. There are communal toilet facilities and lockers are available.

Jerantut p262

C Wau Hotel and Café, K1, Pusat Perniagaan Sungai Jan, Jln Sungai Jan, T09-260 2255, www.wauhotels.com. A welcome addition to the lodgings scene in Jerantut, this a good-value mid-priced place. Comfy a/c rooms have LCD TV and Wi-Fi. Recommended.
C-D Jerantut Guesthouse, T09-266 6200. Some a/c, restaurant, popular place with range of options including a/c rooms with attached bathrooms, simple fan rooms. Daily trips to the park organized.
C-D Sri Emas, T09-266 4499. Busy little guesthouse with a/c and fan rooms. Rooms are fairly clean, but the shared bathrooms are a bit grotty. Excellent information, free transport from bus/train station. Trips organized to the park, dorms, luggage store, internet available in the lobby, restaurant.

Kuala Lipis p262

C Persona Rimba Resort Kenong, Kuala Lipis, T09-312 5032, F312 1421. Simple wooden huts. Tours organized.
D Jelai, 44 Jln Jelai, T09-312 1562. Near the Jelai River, convenient for boats to Rimba. Small, clean rooms, shared bathrooms with hot water and reasonable value.
D Kuala Lipis (aka Appu's Guesthouse), 63 Jln Besar, T09-312 3142. 4 rooms and 2 dorms, convenient for the train station. Some a/c,

shared bathrooms. Run by Mr Appu who runs highly recommended tours to Kenong Rimba, good source of information.

🍴 Eating

Taman Negara National Park *p257, map 258*

Due to the cost of food at the resort, many tourists prefer to bring their own.
The resort operates one restaurant and bar – the **Seri Mutiara**. On the other side of the river at Kampong Kuala Tahan are many floating restaurants which serve reasonable food at prices considerably lower than those in the park complex.

Jerantut *p262*

There are a number of coffee shops in town as well as the usual stalls in the market area.

🏔 Activities and tours

Taman Negara National Park *p257, map 258*

Tour operators

Mutiara Taman Negara Resort, see page 262. The Mutiara runs the only luxury resort in the park. The package deals include a stay and treks. It also runs several trips and tours around the park and a shuttle service from KL to Kuala Temberling jetty.

Jerantut *p262*

Tour operators

Han Travel, Kuala Tembeling Office, 1A, Bandar Baru, Kuala Tembeling, T/F09-266 2899. Or book through the Chinatown office in KL: Selangor Complex, Lot 6G, ground floor, Jln Sultan, T03-2144 0899, www.taman-negara.com. In direct competition with, and very similar to, NKS travel. Boat and bus transfers from KL, Kota Bharu and the Cameron Highlands (eg Kuala Tembeling to the Cameron Highlands RM55, plus RM25 for Kuala Tembeling Jetty to Kuala Tahan boat

trip) and into the park, hotel/resort bookings in the park plus tour packages. Fairly standard prices, and the bus transfers can be arranged for less if you book outside these agencies – probably worth extra when you take into account the reduction in hassle.

NKS Hotel & Travel, Hotel Sri Emas, T09-260 1777, www.taman-negara.com. Aimed mainly at budget travellers. It arranges bus and boat transfers, hotel or guesthouse stay in Jeruntut, package tours of 3 days and 2 nights for RM450 (a/c accommodation). Tours include boat trips, camping, trekking, stay at Orang Asli village and cave exploring.

Kuala Lipis *p262*

Tour operators

Mr Appu Annandaraja who runs the Kuala Lipis Hotel is highly recommended as a trek organizer. He organizes a 4-day trek including food and boat transport in and out of Kenong Rimba. Another guesthouse which organizes trips to the park for much the same price is the **Gin Loke Hotel**, 64 Jln Besar. Organized treks into Kenong Rimba are also run by **Tuah Travel & Tours**, 12 Jln Lipis, T09-312144.

There are other registered freelance guides who can be hired in Kuala Lipis.

⊖ Transport

Taman Negara National Park *p257, map 258*

Bus and boat

Most visitors get a bus or taxi to **Kuala Tembeling** jetty via Jerantut. There are regular connections from **KL** via Kuantan. Guesthouses and tour operators in KL arrange tickets: **NKS Travel** (T03-2072 0336) shuttle bus leaves from outside the Mandarin Pacific Hotel in KL's Chinatown (0830, 3 hrs, one way RM35). Those staying in the Bukit Bintang area are able to catch the **Ping Anchorage** (T03-4280 8030) daily shuttle from the Mutiara Hotel at 0900 (RM40). Buses connect with a boat to the park. If you want to take a public bus, departures are from Pekeling bus station in **KL** (access via Titiwangsa LRT and Monorail station). You will need to catch the first bus to make the boat connection to the park in time, or you will have to stay in Jerantut overnight.

At Kuala Ternbeling there are boats to the Park HQ at **Kuala Tahan**, 2½ hrs, one way RM25. Boats leave at 1400. **Mutiara Resort** has a boat departing at 1300, RM28.

Nusa Holiday Village also operates a boat service from Kuala Tembeling to their own resort departing daily at 0900 and 1400 (Fri 1430), return RM70.

Bus
It is now possible to go by road all the way to Kuala Tahan from **Jerantut**. A public bus runs around 4 times a day to and from Jerantut bus station (0530, 0830, 1315, 1730), 1½ hrs, one way RM6.

Jerantut *p262*
Bus/taxi
The bus and taxi station is in the town centre. Regular connections from **KL**'s Pekeliling terminal (RM13) – the first bus departs at 0830 – contact Perwira Ekspress for more info T09-266 3919. Taxis direct to Jerantut from KL leave from the Puduraya bus terminal. From the east coast, there 3 daily buses from **Kuantan** (0830, 1300 and 1500); also taxis.

Kuala Lipis *p262*
Bus
Buses to **KL** Pekeliling bus terminal every 1½ hrs 0830-2030 (2 hrs, RM14.50). Daily connections with **Kota Bharu** and **Kuantan** (3 hrs, RM25.80).

Train
There are 2 daily trains to Kuala Lipis from **KL** at 1630 and 2030. From Singapore the mail train leaves at 1800. From **Kota Bharu** (from Wakaf Bharu station, 6 km outside) there are trains at 0335, 1846, and 2028.

❶ Directory

Taman Negara National Park *p257,*
map 258
Useful services Mutiara Taman Negara Resort has an expensive mini-market (selling goods for trekking and camping, 0800-2230); a clinic (Mon-Sun 0800-1615, hospital attendant on call 24 hrs for emergencies); a mini-post office; and a library. There is also a jungle laundry service. In the 'Interpretative Room' there is a thrice-daily film and slideshow on the park's flora and fauna.

Kampong Cherating and around

→ *Colour map 1, C6. Phone code: 09.*
A quiet seaside village, set among coconut palms, a short walk from the beach, Kampong Cherating has become a haven for those who want to sample kampong life or just hang out in a simple chalet-style budget resort. Over the years it has undergone a metamorphosis into something a little more sophisticated and upmarket. In the 1990s the place was a booming resort with a vibrant backpacker scene. However, in more recent times, tourist numbers have dropped considerably and the increasing number of Malaysian visitors has yet to breach the gap.

Kemasik is the best beach close to Cherating but the highlight of the area is Rantau Abang, the nesting site for five different species of turtle. ▶▶ *See listings, pages 269-272.*

Ins and outs

Getting there

It is a 40-minute drive from Kuantan's airport (regular connections by MAS to KL, and with Firefly from Subang, Penang and Singapore). The bus stop is on the main road around 500 m from the kampong itself, down two lanes. There are connections with most destinations on the east coast as well as with Singapore and KL. There are buses to Kemasik. Rantau Abang is also accessible by bus. ▶▶ *See Transport, page 272.*

Tourist information

Cherating Travel Post offers ticketing (buses, taxis and minibuses – for a considerable mark-up); car, motorbike, mountain bike, and boat hire; foreign exchange (including travellers' cheques at a poor rate); book rental; newspapers and tourist information. It organizes tours to Tasek Chini, the night market, turtle hatching in Terengganu National Park and the batik factories, as well as night-time jungle treks. It also offers internet, overseas telephone calls and flight confirmation.

Sights

Cherating never was much of a kampong until the tourists arrived – there was a small charcoal 'factory', using *bakau* mangrove wood, but the local economy is now entirely dependent on falling numbers of Western tourists and, more recently, growing numbers

Kampong Cherating

To Kuantan

Buses for North

CHERATING LAMA

Buses for South

Creek

To Kuala Terengganu, Cendor Beach

Cherating River Sports

Limbang Art   Cherating Travel Post

Evening Food:talls

Kampong Budaya Cherating

CHERATING BHARU

East Sea

200 metres
200 yards

N

Sleeping
Cherating Bay Resort **1**
Cherating Beach Mini
  Motel **3**
Cherating Holiday Villa **5**
Cherating Palm Resort **7**
Club Med **6**
Duyong Beach Resort **10**
Impiana Resort
  Cherating **8**

Legend **12**
Shadow of the Moon at
  Half Past Four **15**
Payung Guesthouse **2**
Ranting Resort **16**
Residence Inn
  Cherating **17**
Tanjung Inn **19**

Eating
Cherating Lagoon
  Seafood **4**
Deadly Nightshade **5**
Payung Café **7**
Surf and Chill Café **8**

Bars & clubs
Don't Tell Mama **1**

of domestic tourists. The beach at Cherating is big, but not brilliant for swimming because the sea is so shallow.

Cherating is named after the sand crabs that are very common along the beach. They may look like heavily armoured tanks, but they are not dangerous. There are a couple of very private and extremely beautiful little beaches tucked into the rocky headland dividing Cherating beach and the **Club Med** next door. These are more easily accessible from the sea (boats can be hired from the kampong) than from the steep trail leading over the promontory. This path goes right over to the **Club Med** Beach, which is private. Bathers and sunbathers should be prepared for periodic low-level fly-pasts by the Royal Malaysian Army, whose helicopters swoop over the beaches.

Cherating has grown explosively in recent years. Big, modern resort complexes have sprung up 3 km south of the original kampong; it is known as Cherating Bharu, (New Cherating). The old roadside village is called Cherating Lama, or Old Cherating. Although the old kampong atmosphere has been irreversibly tempered by the arrival of Anchor Beer and the population explosion, Cherating is still a peaceful haunt with some good places to stay and hang out. Cherating's Malay residents have taken the boom stoically – although their obvious prosperity has helped them tolerate the 'cultural pollution'.

It is possible to hire boats to paddle through the mangroves of the Cherating River, to the south side of the kampong, where there is a good variety of birdlife as well as monkeys, monitor lizards and otters. For a price, there are also demonstrations of silat, the Malay martial art, top-spinning, kite-flying and batik-printing in the village. There are some monkeys in the kampong which are trained to pluck coconuts. A couple of kilometres up the road, on Cendor Beach, green turtles come ashore to lay their eggs; they are much smaller than the leatherbacks that lay their eggs at Rantau Abang, further north.

Cherating is also a good base to visit some of the sights in and around this part of the east coast including Tasek Chini and the Charah Caves (see page 250), for example.

Kemasik
On the road north from Cherating there are several stretches of beach, among the best of which is Kemasik. It is off the main road to the right (85 km north of Kuantan, 28 km north of Cherating), just before the oil and gas belt of Kerteh. Ask buses to stop shortly after the windy stretch through the hills. At Kemasik, the beach is deserted; there is a lagoon, some rocky headlands and safe bathing, but no facilities.

Kuala Abang, Kuala Dungun and Pulau Tenggol
Turtles also come ashore at Kuala Abang, a few kilometres north of Dungun, which is much quieter than Rantau Abang, although there are still a few hotels. There are also several places to stay, although not right on the beach, at the small port of Kuala Dungun, famed for its *kuini*, a local mango. There is a weekly night market (*pasar malam*) in Dungun on Thursdays. From there it is possible to hire a boat to Pulau Tenggol, 29 km out, a small island rumoured to be the best diving site on the east coast. To get there head to Kuala Dungun, then take a speed boat (RM50, 45 minutes) to the island. A boat trip is usually arranged via the **Tenggol Island Resort**, see page 271.

Rantau Abang → *Colour map 1, B6.*
This strung-out beachside settlement owes its existence to turtles. Every year between May and September, five different species of **turtle** (*Penyuin Malay*) come to this long stretch of beach to lay their eggs, including the endangered giant leatherbacks.

The giant leatherback turtle

The giant leatherback turtle is so-called for its leathery carapace (shell). It is the biggest sea turtle and one of the biggest reptiles in the world. The largest grow to 3 m in length and most of the females who lumber up Rantau Abang's beach to lay their eggs are over 1½ m long. On average they weigh more than 350 kg, but are sometimes more than double that. They spend most of their lives in the mid-Pacific Ocean, although they have been sighted as far afield as the Atlantic, and return to this stretch of beach around Rantau Abang each year to lay their eggs.

The beach shelves steeply into deeper water, allowing turtles to reach the beach easily. After selecting a nesting site, the turtle first digs a dummy hole before carefully scooping out the actual nest pit, in which she lays up to 150 soft white eggs between the size of a golf ball and a tennis ball. The digging and egg-laying procedure takes up to two hours, after which she covers the hole and returns to the sea. During the egg-laying period, the turtle's eyes secrete a lubricant to protect them from the sand, making it appear as if it is crying. In the course of the egg-laying season (May to September) this exhausting slog up the beach might be repeated up to nine times.

The gestation period for the eggs is 52-70 days. During this period the eggs are in danger from predators, so the Fisheries Department collects up to 50,000 eggs each season for controlled hatching in fenced-off sections of beach. The eggs are also believed to be an aphrodisiac and can be bought in wet markets for about RM1 each (a small quota is set aside for public consumption). Young hatchlings are regularly released into the sea from the government hatchery. Many are picked off by predators, such as gulls and fish, and few reach adulthood. The turtles have been endangered by drift-net fishing and pollution. They are also prized for their shells which are thought to have the most beautiful markings of any sea turtle.

In 1990 the government started fitting radio transmitters to leather-backs to enable satellites to monitor their movements. French satellite information is providing a stronger database on turtle populations and movements allowing a more effective conservation strategy.

Even so, the leatherback turtle appears to be fighting a losing battle against extinction. There are just five main places in the world where these behemoths lay their eggs. In the 1950s 10,000 turtles were arriving at Rantau Abang; for the past few years there have been none.

Green turtles come ashore to lay their eggs later in the season. For more details on these, see page 455.

Every year, tens of thousands of tourists also make the pilgrimage. During the peak egg-laying season, in August (which coincides with Malaysia's school holidays), the beach gets very crowded. Up until the mid-1980s the egg-laying 'industry' was poorly controlled; tourists and locals played guitars around bonfires on the beach and scrambled onto turtles' backs for photographs as they laid. Conservationists began to press for stricter policing and management. Parts of the beach have now been set aside by the government, and access is prohibited; there are also sections of beach with restricted access, where a small admission charge is levied by guides. The Fisheries Department does not charge. Local guides, who trawl the beach at night for leatherbacks coming ashore, charge tourists RM2 a head for a wake-up call. Turtle watching is free along the stretch around the Turtle Information Centre. The Fisheries Department also runs three hatcheries to protect the eggs from predators and egg hunters: they are a local delicacy. The closest is five minutes' walk from **Awang's**. Officers from the department patrol the beach in three-wheeler beach buggies.

Do not interfere with the turtles while they are laying. There is now a ban on flash photography and unruly behaviour is punishable by a RM1000 fine or six months' imprisonment. Camp fires, loud music, excessive noise and littering are all illegal, although the latter is not well enforced.

Rantau Abang Turtle Information Centre ① *13th Mile Jln Dungun, T09-844 1533, F844 2653, Jun-Aug Sat-Thu 0900-1300, 1400-1900 and 2000-2300, Fri 0900-1200 and 1500-2300; Sep-Apr Sat-Wed 0800-1245 and 1400-1600, Thu 0800-1245,* opposite the big **Plaza R&R**, has an excellent exhibition and film presentation about sea turtles, focusing on the giant leatherback. The Fisheries Department at the centre is very helpful and friendly.

◉ Kampong Cherating and around listings

For Sleeping and Eating price codes and other relevant information, see Essentials pages 25-30.

◉ Sleeping

Kampong Cherating *p265, map p266*
Many new bungalows and chalets have sprung up along the beach in the past decade; there are also larger developments, including the **Impiana** resort which has gone up about 2 km north of Cherating Lama. There is a good range of accommodation available, from simple kampong-style stilt-houses to upmarket chalets. Some accommodation in the kampong proper is family run; chalet accommodation is along the beach. The smarter, plusher hotels 3 km down the road at Cherating Bharu are much closer to the sea – and have a much nicer stretch of beach. Chalets cost from RM30-60. Note that the mid- and upper-range places whose guests are predominantly Malaysians and Singaporeans on weekend breaks, usually offer discounts during the week.
L-A Cherating Holiday Villa, Lot 1303, Mukim Sungai Karang, T09-581 9500, www.holiday villacherating.com. 2 rooms and 13 Malaysian chalets: highly kitsch and pleasant inside. Also offers 12 'Malaysia-style boutique villas' at the Eastern Pavilion, which come with their own pool and jacuzzi. Also 2 pools, 3 tennis courts, gym and water sports centre. Babysitting services offered. Recommended.

AL Impiana Resort Cherating, Km 32, Jln Kuantan, T09-581 9000, www.cherating hotels.impiana.com. Spacious buildings with 250 rooms, elegantly decorated with wood and rattan. All rooms have balconies facing sea, a/c, fan, TV, in-house movies, cable TV, minibar, 4-poster wooden beds with nets. Good facilities including pools, outdoor jacuzzi, tennis, children's playground and playhouse with caretaker, 2 restaurants, pub with happy hour. Recommended.
AL Legend, Lot 1290, Mukim Sungai Karang (Cherating Bharu), T09-581 9818, www.legendcherating.com. 4-star hotel with Mediterranean and international restaurants, huge pool, villas near the beach with smartly appointed rooms, sports centre, tennis courts, water sports facilities and disco. Rooms, which overlook big garden and beach, are pleasant and bright. Recommended.
A Club Med, round the headland from Kampong Cherating, T09-581 9133, www.clubmed.co.uk. Totally self-contained resort designed to resemble a Malay village – private beach, water sports facilities, body-building classes, bungee bounce and a flying trapeze. The 'Circus Village' teaches children and adults to juggle, walk a tightrope or fly a trapeze and will be familiar to those who know Club Meds elsewhere.
A Residence Inn Cherating, T09-581 9252, www.ric.com.my. Located on the same lane as The Shadow of the Moon at Half Past

Four, at the northern end of the village, between the main road and the main strip, this is a charming place to stay with friendly staff and pleasant chalets nestled under palms. There are a couple of pools, restaurant with nightly seafood barbecue and a disco. Comfortable rooms with cable TV, a/c and minibar. Breakfast included. Free Wi-Fi should be available by the time this book hits the shelves. Recommended.

A-B Cherating Bay Resort, T09-581 9988, www.cheratingbay.com. Large family-friendly place with pool and children's play area. Mixture of comfortable a/c apartments and rooms built around a pool. Karaoke and restaurant serving local fare. Wi-Fi in lobby area. Good discounts on weekdays. 5 mins' walk to the beach.

A-B Cherating Bayview Resort, Cherating Lama, T09-5819248, www.cheratingbayview resort.blogspot.com. Chalets on beachfront, some with a/c and TV, simple restaurant, a good mid-range place to stay. Other facilities include a pool, volleyball and free Wi-Fi access.

A-B Cherating Beach Mini Motel, T013-992 9632. A number of chalets right on the beach, metres from the lapping waves. The older fan chalets are a bit run down, but the newer a/c chalets are spacious, and have attached bathroom with hot water. The prices offered are a bit ambitious; bargain for a better deal.

C Cherating Palm Resort, T09-581 9378. This efficiently run place thrives on the coachloads of weekend visitors from elsewhere in Malaysia and Singapore. Chalets are functional and clean and all have a/c, hot water and TV. Very quiet during the week with significant discounts available. 5 mins' walk to the beach.

C Duyong Beach Resort, Batu 28, T019-932 3654 (left at end of lane from main road, at far end). Clean chalets with TV, a/c, bathroom, set in a well-maintained garden. Fair value and busy at weekends.

C Payung Guesthouse, T019-917 1934. New place next to the river, and a 2-min walk from the main junction. This popular guesthouse has simple chalets on stilts with attached bathroom. There's a reiki shed with classes

offered by David, the owner. There are excellent dining options nearby.

C Ranting Resort, T09-581 9068, on the main strip next to the Travelpost. Chalets lined up along the seafront with gorgeous sea views. Pay extra for a/c and the lovely 2-room chalets on stilts overlooking the beach. No TV. Quite smart and deadly quiet during the week.

C Tanjung Inn, turn right at bottom of lane down from main road, after Coconut Inn, T09-581 9081, tanjunginn@jaring.my. The top mid-range spot to stay in Cherating with simple chalets on stilts, some built over a small lake in extensive and well-groomed gardens. This friendly family-run option also has a number of larger bungalows close to the beach. This is a charming place to stay. Recommended.

D-E The Shadow of the Moon at Half Past Four, T09-581 9086 (the northernmost chalet resort on the loop off the main road). This place has fallen from grace a little in recent times, having changed ownership. Nevertheless, the spooky name sums up the bewitching ambience here with simple, rustic cottages set on a quiet forested hillside, with fan and attached bathroom. It offers much more tranquil surroundings than chalet resorts along the beach. Recommended.

Kemasik *p267*

AL Awana Kijal Beach and Golf Resort, Kijal, just south of Kerteh Airport, T03-262 3555, F261 6611. Same management as Genting Highlands, 5-star resort and 18-hole golf course, rather monstrous design, with extensive facilities, surrounded by golf course and the beach.

Kuala Abang, Kuala Dungun and Pulau Tenggol *p267*

AL-A Tanjung Jara Beach, Tanjung Jara, 6 km north of Dungun, T09-844 1801, www.tanjong jararesort.com. A/c, restaurant, pool, the best known 5-star beach resort on the east coast, its Malay-inspired design won it the Aga Khan award for outstanding Islamic architecture. It offers tour excursions, windsurfing, golf and tennis facilities and local tours. Winner of the Best Hotel Spa in Asia Pacific Region in 2008 (*Condé Nast Traveller*).

A Tenggol Island Resort, Pulau Tenggol, T09-849 4822, www.pulautenggol.com. Resort aimed at divers. Wooden chalets with attached bathrooms. As well as a first-class dive centre it offers windsurfing and sailing.
B Merantau Inn, at the south end of the turtle beach, T09-844 1131. Some a/c, restaurant, big, clean chalets above old fish ponds, past its prime, but 3 decent chalets on the beach. Not outstanding but reasonable value.

Rantau Abang *p267*

Accommodation is strung out along the main road; there are many overpriced, unpleasant little hovels. New places are opening and old ones closing all the time. Security is a problem here: it is inadvisable to leave valuables in rooms. The only upmarket place to stay near here is the beautiful **Tanjung Jara Beach Hotel**, which is roughly halfway between Rantau Abang and Kuala Dungun, see above for details. Most hotels have their own restaurants.
B-E Ismail's, T09-844 1054. Next to **Awang's**. Good restaurant (only open in peak season). South of the Visitors' Centre. Average beachside set-up, similar to **Awang's**.
C-D Awang's, T09-844 3500. Restaurant, some a/c, some rooms are very poor, the best are only average. Not good value for money.
C-D Dahimah's, T09-845 2483. 1 km south of Visitors' Centre, restaurant, clean rooms in Malay wooden chalets. Some a/c.

🍴 Eating

Kampong Cherating *p265, map p266*

There is some excellent fresh seafood in Cherating and one of the best places for fresh and cheap food is the collection of evening foodstalls near the **Payung Guesthouse**.
⍦ Cherating Lagoon Seafood Restaurant (next to **Cherating Palm Resort**). Open 1100-0200. Massive menu of Chinese dishes, seafood and some Western food. Cheapest

beers in town (look for the large RM5 bottles of Malaysian beer, Jaz). Busy at the weekend.
⍦ Payung Café, next to the **Payung Guesthouse**. Open 0800-1100 and 1700-2400. Run by a friendly local family, this cheery place next to the river offers Wi-Fi, big-screen TV and ice-cold beers to accompany its menu of great pizza and pasta dishes. Good breakfast of omelette and juice. Recommended.
⍦ Surf and Chill Café, T017-267 9969. Open 1800-2400. Owned by young entrepreneur Nasz, this small bar-cum-eatery offers the finest cheeseburgers on the east coast, as well as beers and a pool table. Recommended.
⍦ Deadly Nightshade (part of **Moon** chalet resort at northwest end of loop off main road), also known as 'the restaurant at the end of the universe'. Enchantingly vague menu, mainly Western with some concessions to local tastes, great atmosphere.
⍦ Restoran Duyong, T09-581 9578 (inside the **Duyong Beach Resort**). Lovely setting on raised wooden terrace at edge of beach, lobster and prawns sold by weight, good selection of Western and local dishes.

Foodstalls

Foodstalls opposite the **Payung Café** offer fresh fish and seafood, cooked with local *sambal* that are great value and good fun. Fish is laid out on display and sold by weight.

Rantau Abang *p267*

Roadside stalls and coffee shops near bus stop.
⍦ Awang's, right on the beach. Awang was formerly the chef at **Tanjung Jara Beach Hotel**.
⍦ Ismail's also has a restaurant and there are some stalls in the **Plaza R&R; Mikinias**, just down from **Awang's**. Big menu but service is slow if it gets busy.

🍸 Bars

Kampong Cherating *p265, map p266*

Don't Tell Mama, 1400-2400. Thatched bar right on the beach selling beers and soft drinks. Friendly staff, big TV and a warm atmosphere.

The Shadow of the Moon at Half Past Four
(part of chalet resort of same name, see
page 270). Fun bar amid *atap* and leafy
foliage. Recommended.

🎭 Entertainment

Kampong Cherating *p265, map p266*
**Kampong Budaya Cherating (Cherating
Cultural Centre)**, western end of the village
street, before the **Cherating Bay View Resort**.
Pavilion-style attraction, in landscaped garden
with a big restaurant, where shows take place.
Batik painting, top-spinning, songkhet
weaving and other east coast activities.
Ayam's work is especially worth a look.

🛍 Shopping

Kampong Cheratang *p265, map p266*
There are several batik shops in Cherating, all
the artists offer classes; prices (including
tuition) are T-shirt RM30-35, sarong RM35.
Limbang Art, left at bottom of lane down
from main road bridge. Mainly shirts, T-shirts
painted by **Munif Ayu Art** (on lane down
from main road bridge).
Matahari Chalets. Local artist Ayu sells his
batik T-shirts and does batik painting classes.

🏃 Activities and tours

Kampong Cherating *p265, map p266*
Travelpost, T09-5819 796. Organizes river
trips (1½ hrs, RM28), Snake Island snorkelling
trips (3 hrs, RM58), excursions to see fireflies
(1 hr, RM25), snorkelling and turtle watching.
Fishing trips are organized from here and by
several beach hotels/chalets. 4 people are
needed to fill a boat (4 hrs, RM250 per boat).

Golf
Kelab Golf Desa Dungun, Dungun, T09-848
1041. 18 holes.

Water sports
Cherating Beach Recreation Centre,
arranges water skiing and windsurfing.
Club Med, see page 269. Water sports.

🚌 Transport

Kampong Cherating *p265, map p266*
Air
Kuantan Airport is 45 mins' drive away.

Bus
Regular buses from Kuantan (Kemaman
bus). Bus stops at the bus stop on the main
road outside the village. Buses to **Rantau
Abang**, **Kuala Terengganu**, **Marang**, **Kota
Bharu** and as far north as the Thai border
at **Rantau Panjang**. For destinations to the
south, it is first necessary to go to Kuantan.
Travelpost can book tickets for destinations
to the north and south.

**Kuala Abang, Kuala Dungun and
Pulau Tenggol** *p267*
Bus
Express buses leave for **Kuantan**, **Mersing**,
KL and **JB/Singapore**.

Rantau Abang *p267*
Bus
Regular connections with **Kuala Terengganu**
and **Kuala Dungun** from opposite **Turtle
Information Centre**. From Kuala Dungun
there are regular connections with Kuantan
and other destinations.

ⓘ Directory

Kampong Cherating *p265, map p266*
Banks See Cherating Travel Post, below.
Nearest bank is at Kemaman, 12 km north.
Internet Cherating Travel Post (RM6 per hr).

Kuala Terengganu and around

→ *Colour map 1, B6.*

The royal capital of Terengganu state was a small fishing port (the state accounts for about a quarter of all Malaysia's fishermen) until oil and gas money started being pumped into development projects in the 1980s. The town has long been a centre for arts and crafts, and is known for its kain songket, batik, brass and silverware. The focal point of the town is the Pasar Besar Kedai Payang market place. The town's colourful history is revealed in the Chinese shophouses and temple, in the Zainal Abdin Mosque and the ceremonial house of istana Maziah, once home to the Terengganu royal family.

Around Kuala Terengganu numerous kampongs specialise in handicrafts. Marang is a colourful Malay fishing village and Pulau Kapas has some laid-back beaches. ➤➤ *See listings, pages 276-281.*

Ins and outs

Getting there and around
Sultan Mahmud airport ① *T09-666 4204*, lies 18 km northwest of town. A taxi costs RM25 from the airport to town. Buses also connect with major destinations across the country. There are plenty of taxis in the area. ➤➤ *See Transport, page 280.*

Kuala Terengganu

Sleeping		Seaview **8**	Naj D'Leaf **9**
Grand Continental **12**		Seri Hoover **9**	Ping Anchorage
Kenangan **3**		Seri Malaysia **10**	Travellers' Café **5**
KT Travellers Inn **4**			Restoran Penyu **7**
Midtown **5**		**Eating**	Restoran Terapung Puteri **2**
Ming Star **1**		Billi's Kopitiam **1**	Taufik **4**
Ping Anchorage **7**		Golden Dragon **3**	Zoq Deli Café **8**
Primula Parkroyal **6**		Madame Bee's Kitchen **6**	

Tourist information

Tourism Malaysia ① *5th floor, Menara Yayasan Islam Terengganu, Jln Sultan Omar, T09-622 1433, F622 1791.* **State Tourist Information Centre (TIC)** ① *Jln Sultan Zainal Abidin, near the Istana Meziah on the jetty, T09-622 1553, www.tourism.terengganu.gov.my, Sun-Thu 0800-1700, Fri-Sat 0900-1500,* is an impressive-looking place bursting with information.

Background

Like neighbouring Pahang, Terengganu state was settled at least as far back as the 14th century, and over the years has paid tribute to Siam and, in the 15th century, to the sultanate of Melaka. When the Portuguese forced the Melaka royal house to flee to Johor, Terengganu became a vassal of the new sultanate. In the 18th century, Terengganu is recorded as having a thriving textile industry; it also traded in pepper and gold with Siam, Cambodia, Brunei and China. A Chinese merchant community grew up in Kuala Terengganu. In 1724, the youngest brother of a former sultan of Johor, Zainal Abidin, established Terengganu as an independent state and declared himself its first sultan. Today's sultan is a direct descendant. The state has always been known for its ultra-conservative Islamic traditions.

Sights

The **Pasar Besar Kedai Payang** (Pasar Payang or central market) ① *0700-1800,* the main market place on Jalan Sultan Zainal Abidin, is the busiest spot in town – particularly in the early morning, when the fishing fleet comes in. On the second floor, the market sells batik, brocade, *songket*, brassware, and basketware, as well as fruit and vegetables on the first floor. **Jalan Bandar**, leading off from the market, is a street of old Chinese shophouses and there is also a busy and colourfully painted Chinese temple. Nearby is the imposing **Zainal Abdin Mosque**, on Jln Masjid. Not far from the mosque (on the other side of Jalan Kota) is the apricot-coloured **Istana Maziah**, the old home of Terengganu's royal family, built in French style. It is now only used on ceremonial occasions and is not open to the public.

Some of Kuala Terengganu's older buildings have fine examples of traditional Malay carvings. Another of these traditional houses was taken apart and reassembled in Kuala Lumpur in the grounds of the National Museum as an example of classical Malay architecture.

The **State Museum** ① *daily 0900-1700, RM5, take a local bus from the local bus station (15-min journey),* one of the largest in the country, is situated in Losong, a town 5 km southwest of the city. The museum is at the end of Jalan Losong Feri, facing Pulau Sekati. It exhibits rare Islamic porcelain, silver jewellery, musical instruments and weaponry, including a fine selection of *parangs* and *krises*. It is an eclectic collection, erratically labelled. **Bukit Puteri**, near the Istana, has fortress remains on it and excellent views of the town.

Around Kuala Terengganu

There is a thriving cottage industry and many of Malaysia's best-known handicrafts are made locally. Surrounding kampongs practise silverwork, batik printing, *songket* weaving and *wau* kite building, but the best way to see these under one roof is in the **Cendering handicraft centres**. Cendering lies 7 km south of Kuala Terengganu. **Kraftangan Malaysia** ① *Sun-Thu 0800-1630; take Marang-bound buses from Jln Syed Hussin, the turning is clearly signposted off the main road,* has a beautifully displayed selection of silver, woodwork, silk, batik, brass and basketware as well as handicrafts from elsewhere in Malaysia. Next door to Kraftangan Malaysia is the huge **Nor Arfa Batik Factory**

① *T09-617 5700*, producing modern and traditional designs and readyrnades. Behind Kraftangan Malaysia is the **Sutera Semai** silk factory.

Pulau Duyung Besar ① *take a minibus from the local station, or take a boat (RM0.50) to the island from the little jetty behind the Seri Malaysia*, is the largest island in the Terengganu Estuary and is famed for its boat-building. It mainly survives by custom-building yachts.

The Floating Mosque ① *located 6 km from town; take any southbound bus*, is situated on the estuary of the Ibai River. Its name is a slight misnomer; it has been built in such a way that it gives the illusion of floating.

Kampong Pulau Rusa ① *take a boat from the jetty on Jln Sultan Zainal Abidin or take a bus from the bus station on Jln Syed Hussin*, is a *songket*-weaving and batik centre, 6 km upriver. It is known for its traditional Petani-Terengganu wooden houses.

Batu Buruk beach, running down the northeast side of KT, is not safe for swimming due to powerful waves and currents. But there are some good beaches near Kuala Terengganu: Merang 30 km (see page 281) and Batu Rakit, 20 km north. There is a guesthouse at the latter. There are regular buses to both beaches from Jalan Syed Hussin.

Numerous **islands** lie offshore from Kuala Terengganu including **Pulau Redang** (see page 281). Boats leave for the islands from Merang and from the Shah Bandar jetty in Kuala Terengganu, from which there are now scheduled departures (you'll need a booking at a resort to take the boat from here). **Pulau Lang Tengah** also has good diving. Boats from Merang jetty are arranged via a resort booking. The best diving, reportedly, on the east coast of Malaysia is off **Tenggol Island**. Boats leave from Kuala Dungun, about a 1½-hour drive from Kuala Terengganu.

Marang → *Colour map 1, B6.*

① *To get into the town from the main road, follow signs to LKIM Komplex from the north end of the bridge.*

This is a colourful Malay fishing kampong at the mouth of the Marang River, although it is not as idyllic as the tourist literature suggests. Marang has been buffeted by the vagaries of the tourist industry over the last couple of decades. In the 1980s and 1990s there was a rush to put up budget accommodation, placing it firmly on the tourist map for the first time. Then, by the mid- to late 1990s the kampong began to acquire a bit of a run-down look as the early developments lost their sheen. Now, a number of new, plusher developments along the shorefront in Marang Town have instilled a slightly more chi-chi atmosphere to the place. Notwithstanding all these twists and turns, it is still a very lovely village, with its shallow lagoon full of fishing boats. The best beach is opposite Pulau Kapas at Kampong Ru Muda. It was the centre of a mini-gold-rush in 1988 when gold was found 6 km up the road at Rusila. On the road north of Marang there are a number of batik workshops, all of which welcome visitors.

Pulau Kapas

Pulau Kapas is 6 km (20 minutes) off the coast, with some good beaches and with a very low-key, laid-back atmosphere. Those wanting a quiet beach holiday should avoid weekends and public holidays, when it is packed. The coral here has been degraded somewhat and there is much better snorkelling at **Pulau Raja**, just off Kapas, which has been declared a marine park. All the guesthouses organize snorkelling and the **Kapas Garden Resort** also has scuba equipment. There is a new resort on the privately owned **Pulau Gemia** (Gem Island), just under 1 km from Kapas. Many hotels can also organize a boat trip to the island.

For Sleeping and Eating price codes and other relevant information, see Essentials pages 25-30.

⊜ Sleeping

Kuala Terengganu *p273, map p273*
There are only a couple of hotels at the top end of the market but there are several cheaper hotels scattered round town, mainly at the jetty end of Jln Sultan Ismail and on Jln Banggol, but the selection is not great.
A Grand Continental, Jln Sultan Zainal Abidin, T09-625 1888, www.grandhotels international.com.my. The swankiest in Kuala Terengganu. A typicalal plush chain hotel with all the usual facilities, including pool and restaurants. Huge rooms, cable TV and in-house movies. The best thing is the great view of the coast – all rooms face the sea.
A Midtown, Jln Tok Lam, T09-623 5288, www.hotelytmidtown.com.my. Old 2-star hotel in greyish block on the street corner. All rooms have a/c, cable TV, Wi-Fi and minifridge. Facilities include laundry, business centre and restaurant. Good promotional rates available.
A Primula Parkroyal, Jln Persinggahan, T09-622 2100, www.primulaparkroyal.com. A/c, restaurant (good Malay buffet), nice pool, high-rise hotel with all mod cons but rooms are shabby and not soundproofed, although they do have a sea view. Breakfast included. Also organizes island excursions.
A Seri Malaysia, Lot 1640, Jln Hiliran, T03-2161 8223, www.serimalaysia.com.my. Well-run chain hotel with spotless a/c rooms with cable TV and decent bedding on the edge of Chinatown. Some rooms overlook the river. Recommended.
B Kenangan, 65 Jln Sultan Ismail, T09-622 2688, www.hotelkenangan.com,my. The a/c rooms here have slightly decrepit decor but are comfortable and have cable TV, attached bathroom and free Wi-Fi. Slightly cheaper than KT Mutiara next door but not quite as good.
B Ming Star, 217 Jln Sultan Zainal Abidin, T09-622 866, www.mingstarhotel.com. New

hotel with small, but well-designed modern a/c rooms with attached bathroom, cable TV and Wi-Fi access. There is a restaurant attached. This is the best option town at this price range, but is hampered by its location, a fair stroll from the centre. Recommended.
B Seaview, 18a Jln Masjid Abidin, T09-622 1911, sv_hotel@yahoo.com. Whilst the paint might be peeling in some rooms, this place is not bad value, given the enormous size of the rooms and general cleanliness. Rooms have Wi-Fi, a/c, cable TV and attached bathroom with hot water. Rooms at the front have good views of the Istana. Recommended.
C KT Travellers Inn, 201, 1st floor, Jln Sultan Zainal Abidin, T09-622 3666, F623 2692. Stuck out on busy road downtown and with uninterested staff, the rooms here are well kept clean and have TV, Wi-Fi and attached bathroom. Cheaper rooms are a bit spartan and have no windows. Some of the better rooms have sea views.
C Seri Hoover, 49 Jln Sultan Ismail, T09-623 3833, F622 5975. Seventy a/c rooms with TV and fridge in an ugly tower block in the heart of town. Rooms are big and clean but could do with being spruced up a bit. Nothing overly inspiring.
C-E Ping Anchorage, 77A Jln Sultan Sulaiman, T09-626 2020, www.pinganchorage.com.my. The most popular backpackers' haunt in town with clued-up management offering excellent local information and tours of the city and beyond. The hotel itself offers functional, unexciting rooms, 3 of which have a/c and attached bathroom. There are fan rooms (shared bathroom) and a dorm (RM8). Wi-Fi is available in rooms nearest the road. The rooftop café here is a great place to mingle and have a beer. Recommended.
E Awi's Yellow House, Pulau Duyung Besar, T09-624 5046, rohanilongvet@hotmail.com. Built out over the river on stilts and popular with budget travellers. Dorm and *atap*-roofed huts, some with balconies over the river, pleasant location with cool breezes, there are

some stalls at the bus stop near the bridge, but most travellers bring their own food and have use of kitchen facilities. **Awi's Yellow House** is not yellow and can be hard to find but is well enough known to sniff out. Take a boat from jetty on Jln Bandar – last boat around 2200 – or by road, via the Sultan Mahmud bridge (taxis or bus from KT).

Around Kuala Terengganu p274

A-C Peladang Setiu Agro Resort, 83 km west of Kuala Terengganu, T09-697 7136, www.pinganchorage.com.my. Set in the midst of tropical forest, it offers a 280-ha plot, complete with lakes, arboretum, mini bird park, pool and – for the enthusiast – an obstacle course. Popular with groups, it also has a campsite, 5 dorm rooms and 31 chalets.

Marang p275

There are hotels and guesthouses in Marang itself and in Kampong Rhu Muda, about 2 km before the bridge over the Marang River.

B Seri Malaysia Marang, Lot 3964, Kampong Paya, T09-618 2889, www.serimalaysia.com. Part of the Seri Malaysia chain, this is good value with views of Pulau Kapas. It has a/c, TV, restaurant and launderette. It organizes island trips. This is the best option along this row of accommodation although not extravagant; breakfast is included. However, the restaurant is overpriced, the variety of food available limited, and the service slapdash.

B-D Angullia Beach House, 12¼ milestone, Kampong Rhu Muda, T09-618 1322, F618 1322. Some a/c, restaurant (with good set meal). This is an extremely friendly, family-run chalet resort on a lovely stretch of beach opposite Pulau Kapas (therefore sheltered). It has leafy, well-kept grounds and very clean chalets. No alcohol is served. Some visitors reckon it is overpriced. Recommended.

C Island View, opposite the lagoon, T09-618 2006. Some a/c, free bicycles, chalets with attached bathrooms and some simpler rooms, popular. Very attractive setting with a central bougainvillea garden to relax in. However, be prepared to share your room

with various visitors from the animal kingdom. It's a little run down.

C-D Travellers Check Point, (aka Marang Guest House and Restaurant). On the hill top above Kamal. Scenic views of the lagoon and sea beyond. Clean and friendly, good restaurant, with TV lounge and seating area with games. Well-built chalets with a/c or fan, excellent value for money. Connected to MGH Travel Centre.

C-E Mare Nostrum Holiday Resort, Kampong Rhu Muda, T09-618 2417. A/c, restaurant, clean and hospitable, boat trips, pleasant little resort next door to **Angullia**, well-kept compound (if a little cramped) and clean chalets. Recommended.

D Nusantara Hostel, Kompleks Pelancongan, T09-618 5733. Opposite the park between the 2 jetties. Basic rooms, including small dorms all with shared cold-water showers. The place has a friendly family environment while the odd furniture gives it some character. Fishing trips, tours and general travel advice offered.

D-E Green Mango Inn, A-71 Bandar Marang, T019-946 9409. Fan, small, bare A-frame chalets, but cheap. Double rooms available. Excellent atmosphere, good views over the bay, a small garden, and sitting area with library and games. Recommended.

D-E Zakaria Guesthouse, Kampong Rhu Muda, T09-618 2328. Basic and further out of the village, dorm or rooms.

Pulau Kapas p275

AL Gem Island Resort, Pulau Gemia, T09-624 5110, www.gemisland.com.my. 52 chalets on this private island. Great place for a bit of rural tranquility with each room offering sea views. Good fresh fish barbecues at night.

A-B Duta Puri, T09-624 6090. Charming wooden and brick chalets set in nice gardens hung with batiks and stocked with dark wood furniture. Beach-facing chalets are more expensive. All rooms have TV and minibar and wooden floors. Recommended.

B Kapas Island Resort, T012-430 2411. This place offers cosy Malay-style chalets set in a tranquil garden. Small pool and restaurant.

B-D Makcik Gemuk Resort, T09-624 5120. Largest outfit on the island with a range of rooms from simple huts with shared facilities through to larger chalets with attached bathrooms. The name **Mac Cik Gemuk** means big, fat Auntie! Very popular with local tourists.
D-E The Lighthouse, T019-215 3558. Owner Din is a real character. The best budget place to stay on the island. All rooms are inside an atmospheric longhouse. Very mellow place, staff make guests feel like part of the family. Lots of beach games, barbecues and the Tropical Hut bar. Highly recommended.

Eating

Kuala Terengganu *p273, map p273*
Nasi dagang is a local speciality. It is aromatic or glutinous rice, served with *gulai ikan tongkol* (tuna fish with tamarind and coconut gravy). *Keropok* (prawn crackers) are another Terengganu speciality. Kuala Terengganu eats and sleeps fairly early, so don't head out too late.
Restoran Penyu, 238 Jln Sultan Zainal Abidin. Open 1200-1500 and 1800-2230, except Fri 1830-2300. Excellent Thai and Chinese seafood.
Billi's Kopitiam, Jln Kampong Dalam. Open 0800-2000. Owned by renowned local gourmand Billi, this little jewel of a place serves up a stunning array of local and fusion options. Billi will gladly recommend dishes. Try the delicious lemongrass-infused chicken *rendang* and the celebrated *nasi lemak goreng*. Highly recommended.
Golden Dragon, 198 Jln Bandar. Fine selection of roasted pork dishes, Chinese economy rice (point and choose buffet) and ice-cold beer in a fun, bewilderingly busy restaurant that eats to a Hokkien musical soundtrack. Next door, **Soon Kee** (¥) serves up more of the same. Recommended.
Madame Bee's Kitchen, 177 Jln Bandar. Small eatery, with marble-topped round tables offering tasty local dishes such as *Terengganu lor mee* and *keropok lekor*, as well as good local Chinese-Malay fusion dishes including *mee jawa* and *nasi ayam*.

Naj D'Leaf, 57 Jln Tok Lam. Open 0800-2000. Clean, friendly place serving good portions of biryani, Malay and Indian curries and dosai.
One-Two-Six, 102 Jln Kampong Tiong 2 (off Jln Sultan Ismail). Big open-air restaurant with hawker stalls, good seafood menu. Speciality is fire chicken wings (comes to table in flames). Recommended.
Pelangi, Jln Pantai Batu Buruk (near the Pantai Primula Hotel). View of the beach, good selection of seafood and renowned for its butter crabs in batter.
Ping Anchorage Travellers' Café, Jln Sultan Sulaiman. Friendly travellers café on an antique-festooned rooftop with views of a leafy kampong to one side and the sea on the other. Dishes are simple Western and Asian and can be washed down with a beer. Good breakfasts. Large TV, used to show football at the weekend. Recommended.
Restoran Terapung Puteri, Jln Sultan Zainal Abidin, T09-623 5396. Floating restaurant opposite the tourist information centre, serving a wide range of Malay and Western food, good fresh fruit drinks available. Well known for its *nasi dagang*.
Taufik, 18 Jln Masjid Abidin (opposite Istana Maziah). North and South Indian dishes, well known for its rotis.
Ziq Deli Café, Jln Paya Keladi Lot 3498, T09-630 9888. Although primarily a cake shop, the owners have changed direction by adding comfy seating, Wi-Fi and a menu of Malay and Nyonya dishes in a cool a/c setting.

Foodstalls

Gerai Makanan (foodstalls) opposite the bus station, Malay; **Jln Batu Buruk**, near the Cultural Centre, some excellent Malay food and seafood stalls, recommended; **Kampong Tiong** (off Jln Bandar), excellent hawker centre with Malay food on one side, Chinese and Indian on the other, open 0800 till late.

Also **Warung Pak Maidin**, nearby on Jln Haji Busu, which is good on seafood; **Kompleks Taman Selera Tanjung** (1st floor), huge area of stalls with good variety of dishes, open-air terrace; **Majlis Perbandaran** stalls, Jln Tok Lam; **Pasar Besar Kedai Payang** (Central Market), 1st floor, Malay snacks, good views over the river. There are also some stalls next to **Stadium Negeri**.

Marang *p275*

Most hotels have good restaurants serving Malay and international dishes. Cheap foodstalls along the waterfront next to the market. Stalls at **Taman Selera**, **Kampong Rhu Muda**, along the roadside are well known for their Malay and Thai-style seafood (closed Fri).

Pulau Kapas *p275*

All the chalet operations have attached restaurants. **Paying Café**, next to the main jetty, is a good spot for a *roti canai* breakfast.

O Shopping

Kuala Terengganu *p273, map p273*
Batik

Some of the best batik in Malaysia can be found in the central market (Pasar Besar Kedai Payang). **Wan Ismail Tembaga & Batik**, near the turtle roundabout, off Jln Sultan Zainal Abidin, is a small, old-fashioned batik factory. There are a number of small craft and batik factories in Kampong Ladang – the area around Jln Sultan Zainal Abidin; **Desa Craft**, 73 Jln Sultan Ismail, in the centre of town, has a good selection of silk and batik readymades and sarongs. Other shops selling batik can be found on Jln Bandar, including the **Batik Gallery** at number 194 and **Yuleza** (Chinese for batik) at number 208. **Noor Arfa**, A3 Jln Sultan Zainal Abidin, T09-623 5173, is an established producer of batik for many years; cloth and ready-made clothes are available and they will take orders. **Teratai Arts and Crafts Shop**, 151 Jln Bandar, T09-625 2157, high-quality craft shop, with batik, woodwork, metalwork and jewellery. Also sells numerous prints and postcards by Malaysian artist Chang Fee Ming. He depicts the colourful nature of local life with stunning watercolours; it's well worth a visit just to see his work.

Handicrafts

The Central Market is touristy, but offers a range of handicrafts, textiles, brassware, etc. **Desa Craft**, on Jln Sultan Ismail, is another good centre.

Marang *p275*
Handicrafts

The market in Marang has a craft section upstairs and there are several handicraft shops along the main street.
Balai Ukiran Terengganu (Terengganu Woodcarving Centre), Kampong Rhu Rendang, near Marang. Master-carver Abdul Malek Ariffin runs the east coast's best-known woodcarving workshop here, making a wide range of intricately carved furniture from cengal wood, carved with traditional floral geometric and Islamic calligraphic patterns. The varnished cengal wood is not to everyone's taste, but everything from mirrors to beds can be ordered for export; because most pieces are made to order there is little on show in Abdul's chaotic workshop, but carvers can be seen at work during the day.

▲ Activities and tours

Kuala Terengganu *p273, map p273*
Golf

Badariah Golf Club, south of town, T09-632 456. Nine holes, requires special permission from the Sultan's private secretary's office.

Tour operators

Ping Anchorage Travel & Tours, 77A Jln Sultan Sulaiman, T09-626 2020, www.pinganchorage.com.my. A very well organized and efficient tour service (islands, jungle trekking, Kenyir Lake), offering tours, accommodation, ticketing, and seemingly everything. Recommended.
Turtleliner (a Reliance franchise), Jln Sultan Masjid Abidin, T09-623 7000, F623 1122. Services include flight booking and confirmation, individual and group tours. Helpful staff.

Marang p275

Half-day river tours and fishing, snorkelling and jungle trips are organized by MGH (Marang Guest House, chalets B-C), from a little office by the small jetty, daily 0900-1700, T09-618 1976, www.marangguesthouse.com.

Pulau Kapas p275
Diving

Aqua Sport, T01-9983 5879, next to Duta Puri, runs scuba trips.

Easy Dive Centre at Kapas Island Resort. Snorkelling gear can be hired at all the resorts. There's some coral in front of the Kapas Garden Resort just off the beach. The resorts run snorkelling and fishing trips around the island, and kayaks can be hired.

Many hotels in Marang offer day trips to the islands. Several companies run boats, the prices are the same (fast boat, 15 mins, RM25 return, 0930-1700). Their offices are crowded around the jetties and they can also arrange accommodation on the island, although this is easy to do yourself once you get there. Zack at the **Suria Link Boat Service** is very helpful and his office is a good place to buy boat tickets (T01-9983 9454). MGH is also recommended. When you pay for your ticket you must tell them what time and day you want to be picked up, or you can get your resort to phone for you, so remember to keep the number of the agency you booked your boat with.

⊖ Transport

Kuala Terengganu p273, map p273
Air

AirAsia has daily flights to **KL**. Firefly connects the city with **Singapore**, **Subang** and **Penang**.
Airline offices MAS and Firefly, 13 Jln Sultan Omar, T09-622 1415.

Bus

Kuala Terengganu's bus station is just off Jln Tok Lam. Local buses leave from the same station with connections to **Merang**, **Marang** and **Kuala Besut**. Connections to **KL** (6 hrs, RM39), **JB** (9 hrs, RM44), **Kota Bharu** (RM14) **Kuantan** (RM17), **Rantau Abang** (RM17), **Mersing** (RM36), **Singapore** (RM46), **Meleka** (RM43), **Butterworth**, (9 hrs, RM41) and **Alor Star** (RM54). Express buses to **KL** leave 0900, 0930, 1000, 2130 and 2200. To **Kuantan** every 90 mins until 2200. To **Mersing**, there are 2 buses, at 1230 and 2200.

For the **Perhentian Islands**, board a bus to Kuala Besut, which goes directly to the jetty. The bus leaves 6 times a day; the most useful departures for travellers leave at 0700, 1000 and 1130 (2½ hrs, RM10.70). After these times, you will have trouble connecting with a boat to the islands.

Car hire

Ping Anchorage, 77A Jln Sultan Sulaiman, T09-626 2020.

Taxi

Taxis operate from next to the bus station on Jln Masjid and from the waterfront. Destinations include **Kota Bharu, Rantau Abang, Marang, Kuantan, KL, JB** and **Penang**. Taxi, T09-621 581.

Marang p275
Bus

Bus stop on the main road up the hill from Marang. Tickets can be bought from the kiosk nearby on Jln Tg Sulong Musa. However, this runs very unpredictable hours so book in advance. Connections with **Kuala Terengganu** every 90 mins and with **Kuala Dungun** for Pulau Tenggol via **Kuala Abang**. If you're stuck without a ticket you will have to head to Kuala Terengganu's express bus station (taxi RM15, local bus, RM1.50, every 90 mins). Taxis wait near the jetty.

❶ Directory

Kuala Terengganu p273, map p273
Banks There are several banks along Jln Sultan Ismail. Bumiputra, UMNO, Jln Masjid

Zainal Abidin; **Hong Kong Bank**, 57 Jln Sultan Ismail; **Maybank**, 69 Jln Paya Bunga; **Public**, 1 Jln Balas Baru; **Standard Chartered**, 31 Jln Sultan Ismail; **UMBC**, 59 Jln Sultan Ismail. There are virtually no money changers in Kuala Terengganu. **Internet** Putra Internet Café, Jln Dato Isaac (a few doors down from Ping Anchorage). **Medical services** Hospital, Jln Peranginan (just off Jln Sultan

Mahmud), T09-623 3333. **Post office** GPO, Jln Sultan Zainal Abidin.

Telephone Telekom, Jln Sultan Ismail.

Marang *p275*

Internet There are a couple of internet cafés on Jln Hakaf Tapai past the school on the other side of the main highway to the jetties.

Redang archipelago

→ *Colour map 1, B6.*

The biggest and best-known of the islands is Pulau Redang, but Pulau Lang Tengah is also catching up. Pulau Bidong was the base for a Vietnamese refugee camp in the 1970s and 1980s and as many as 40,000 were once crammed on this island. The boat people have long gone now, and most of the camp's buildings have rotted away. Tour agencies in Kuala Terengganu offer day trips to the island, where there are few memorials to the refugees and some good snorkelling. The only islands with accommodation are Pulau Redang and Pulau Lang Tengah. ⏩ *See listings, pages 282-283.*

Ins and outs

Getting there There is a daily flight to Pulau Redang from KL. Boats leave from Merang twice daily. ⏩ *See Transport, page 283.*

Tourist information An independently run, excellent website offering news and reviews of places and diving on Pulau Redang and Lang Tengah is www.redang.org. Tourist information from Tourism Malaysia in Kuala Terenggau. Two dives with equipment costs around RM150 on the island, which is fairly reasonable considering the excellent location.

Merang

Merang is a small fishing kampong with a long white sandy beach; it is also the departure point for the many offshore islands.

The nine islands

Redang archipelago is made up of nine islands – the main Redang Island, Lima Island, Paku Besar Island, Paku Kecil Island, Kerengga Besar Island, Kerengga Kecil Island, Ekor Tebu Island, Ling Island and Pinang Island. A number of islands are accessible from Merang, most notably Pulau Redang. Other islands, most of which are uninhabited and all of which are endowed with a good selection of coral, include Pulau Pinang, Pulau Lima and Pulau Ekor Tebu; fishing boats are usually happy to stop off on request.

Pulau Redang is 27 km off Merang in this archipelago. It has some of Malaysia's best reefs, making it one of the most desirable locations for divers. In the months after the monsoon, visibility increases to at least 20 m, but during the monsoon the island is usually inaccessible. Line-fishing is permitted and squid fishing, using bright lights, is popular between June and September; the fishermen use a special hook called a *candat sotong*. The lamps light the surrounding waters, attracting the squid.

Pulau Lang Tengah

Lang Tengah (whose name apparently means 'eagle resting on middle island') is a tiny rocky island protected by a coral reef that sits between Pulau Perhentian and Pulau Redang and is accessible from both by a boat day trip. The five resorts on Lang Tengah are spread over two beaches on the western side of the island, Pasir Air and Pasir Mathasaan. This number could well rise. However, the island is less developed than Pulau Redang and is much more tranquil, although the effect of tourists can be seen on the white beaches – visitors report some sands marred with dead coral and litter. There are more than a dozen dive sites around the island and good snorkelling.

Pulau Redang has a Marine Park Centre, mainly used for research and conservation, on the small island just off its southern coast. The water is shallow, calm and clear around the jetty with quite a few fish, making this a popular spot for snorkelling and with divers practising basic skills. There's a turtle hatchery here, testament to the importance of Redang and surrounding islands as a turtle nesting site. Three species of turtle frequent these waters: green turtles mainly from March to December, with turtle-laying peaking in August. Hawksbill and Olive Ridley turtles can be seen January to September; breeding peaks in May.

◉ Redang archipelago listings

For Sleeping and Eating price codes and other relevant information, see Essentials pages 25-30.

● Sleeping

Merang *p281*

L-AL Aryani Resort, Jln Rhu Tapai-Merang, Pantai Peranginan Merang, T09-653 2111, www.thearyani.com. The original heritage timber suites have private courtyards with outdoor bath, elevated restaurant and pool; all very luxurious.

A-B Sutra Beach Resort, Kampong Rhu Tapai, T09-653 1111, www.sutrabeachresort.com.my. With a/c, restaurants and a pool. This resort overlooks the beach (very pleasant at night). There are 124 chalets, good sports facilities and it is 20 mins from Kuala Terengganu's airport. Malaysian Tourism award winner.

B Stingray Beach Chalet, T09-653 2018. On the beach, fan, bathroom, immaculately run and offers a dive service. Recommended.

C-E Kembara Resort, 474 Pantai Peranginan Merang, 21010 Setiu, T09-6531 770, www.kembararesort.tripod.com. Situated on an endless palm-fringed deserted white beach and in a beautiful garden compound. There's a relaxed atmosphere with just 8 bungalows and

8 rooms all with attached shower and toilet, and fans. Cheap dorm. No restaurant but you can use the large, well-equipped kitchen in the court. A little-known paradise. Recommended.

E Sugi Man's Homestay, 500 m beyond junction, on road to Penarek (signposted from the road). Restaurant, basic kampong farmhouse, quite a walk from the beach, cooking lessons and kite making, includes meals.

The nine islands *p281*

All accommodation is on Pulau Redang. Resorts offer competitive and flexible package deals; check with Tourism Malaysia. If you value privacy and seclusion, avoid weekends and public holidays.

A Berjaya Redang Beach Resort, T09-630 8866, www.berjayahotels-resorts.com. 120 pretty cottage chalets with red roofs. The resort has good reviews but some criticize it (and the rest of the island) for overdeveloping.

A Berjaya Redang Spa Resort, T09-8866 8888. A hotel with 152 rooms with a/c, TV, minibar, pool, restaurants, health spa, gym and an 18-hole golf course. It is a popular destination for business visitors wishing to combine work and golf (limited business facilities). Also dive centre, gym, tennis courts, health spa. Not popular with locals or environmentalists.

A Laguna Redang Island Resort, Pasir Panjang, T09-630 7888, www.lagunaredang.com.my. A luxury resort with pool, private beach, dive shop, restaurants, beach bar, and even mah-jong – a subtle sign that there are plenty of Chinese tourists on Pulau Redang.
A Redang Beach Resort, T09-623 8188, www.redang.com.my Full range of facilities, package deals available. A recently added extension has been scrapped due to lack of state approval, but the original resort is still open for business as before.
A Redang Pelangi Resort, T09-624 2158, www.redangpelangi.com. Pleasant wooden huts on stilts in a traditional Malay style, all with a/c and own bathroom. Dive centre and other activities like beach volleyball. The resort has a popular disco and karaoke so not recommended if it's tranquillity you're after.
A Wisana, T09-622 7840, www.wisanatravel.com. Diving facilities offered. Basic rooms but picturesque, remote location.
A-B Redangkalong Resort/The Divers Den, T03-7960 7163, www.redangkalong.com. 38 en suite comfortable rooms with a/c. Fully equipped PADI dive centre with courses available up to instructor level. **Divers Den** manager AB Lee has 17 years' experience diving in the area and is an enthusiastic underwater photographer. Plenty of other sports facilities, including kayak hire.

Pulau Lang Tengah *p282*
There are now 5 resorts on Lang Tengah spread over 2 beaches on the western side of the island, Pasir Air and Pasir Mathasaan. This number could well rise.
AL-A D'Coconut Lagoon, Pasir Mathasaan, T03-4252 6686, www.dcoconutlagoon.com. Smaller resort with a/c chalets, swimming pool and dive centre.
A Blue Coral Island Resort, Pasir Air, T03-780 5277, www.malaysiaislandresorts.com. 70 a/c rooms, pool, Western and Asian restaurant, reading rooms and dive cente.
A Square Point Resort, Pasir Mathasaan, T09-623 5333, www.bjaya.com. A/c chalets, dive centre and restaurant.

⊖ Transport

Merang *p281*
Bus
2 buses a day from **Kuala Terengganu** to Merang, and then on to **Penarek**. Minibus connections also available from **Kuala Terengganu**, from Jln Masjid.

Taxi
Taxis from Merang to **Penarek**. An a/c taxi from **Kuala Terengganu** to Merang should cost RM30-40.

The nine islands *p281*
Air
There is a small air strip on Pulau Redang operated by **Berjaya Air**, which flies a 48-seater Dash 7 between **Subang** and Redang twice a day in the peak summer season and once a day in the quieter times of the year. The flight takes 1 hr 10 mins. There is a daily flight to and from **Singapore**'s Seletar Airport (1½ hrs). You do not have to stay at **Berjaya** to use this service. Check the website for current flight times and prices.

Boat
These leave for the islands from Merang as well as from the jetty in Kuala Terangganu (but boats leaving from here are only for **Berjaya Redang Holiday** and **Redang Beach** resorts). It has become very expensive to charter boats from Merang (from RM60 per person one way). **Tourism Malaysia** in Kuala Terengganu recommends that tourists take advantage of package deals offered by the island's resorts; further details from the Tourism Malaysia office or see www.redang.org.

Pulau Lang Tengah *p282*
Boat
You can also get to the island by booking with a resort on Lang Tengah – they will direct you to a speedboat pickup at Merang jetty. This will save you around RM45 per person for a single trip to the island.

The Perhentian Islands

→ Colour map 1, A5.

Two more beautiful east coast islands, Pulau Perhentian Besar (big) and Pulau Perhentian Kecil (small), just over 20 km off the coast, are separated by a narrow sound with a strong current. Despite considerable development in recent years, with more hotels, restaurants, bars, diving outfits and much more noise, the Perhentian islands still remain a paradise, with excellent diving and snorkelling, magnificent beaches and some of the best places for swimming on the east coast. ▶▶ *For listings, see pages 285-289.*

Ins and outs

It is important to get to the islands, 20 km offshore, as early as possible on the day of arrival due to high demand for accommodation. Boats leave throughout the day from Kuala Besut which is connected to other towns by regular buses. There are boats between the two islands. ▶▶ *See also Transport, page 289.*

The Perhentian Islands

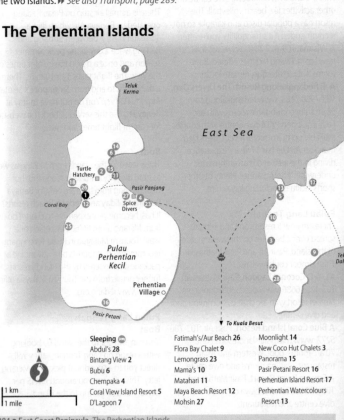

Sleeping
Abdul's **28**
Bintang View **2**
Bubu **6**
Chempaka **4**
Coral View Island Resort **5**
D'Lagoon **7**

Fatimah's/Aur Beach **26**
Flora Bay Chalet **9**
Lemongrass **23**
Mama's **10**
Matahari **11**
Maya Beach Resort **12**
Mohsin **27**

Moonlight **14**
New Coco Hut Chalets **3**
Panorama **15**
Pasir Petani Resort **16**
Perhentian Island Resort **17**
Perhentian Watercolours
Resort **13**

The islands

Of the two islands, Perhantian Besar (big island) is generally more popular with families as it houses slightly more upmarket resorts, although huts on the beach are also available. Perhentian Kecil (small) is simpler and attracts a younger crowd of party-going backpackers. There is a fishing village and a turtle hatchery in the middle of Long Beach (Pasir Panjang) on Perhentian Kecil. Both islands however, are still only developed to a low-key stage and offer beautiful beaches, good snorkelling, and great diving as well as forested trails inland. However, this is changing as more chalet operations are being built every year. Despite the fairly low level of development, there is enough tourist activity to worry environmentalists, in particular damage to the reef from irresponsible divers, litter (although boats come daily to ship it away in bags from the resorts) and the pollution from the generators (almost every resort has their own oil-powered generator).

Kuala Besut

It is possible to spend the night in Kuala Besut. This small fishing village has one main place to stay. Business in this little fishing village has expanded to cater for those tourists passing through and good food can be found at a series of small restaurants along the waterfront. Kuala Besut has lots of travel agents which sell boat and bus tickets and book accommodation on the island. The bus and taxi station is located 100 m to the west of the jetty entrance.

Pulau
Perhentian
Besar

Senja Bay 25
Shari-La Resort 18
Tuna Bay Island
Resort 22

Eating ⑦
Amelia's/Mama's 1

⊙ The Perhentian Islands listings

For Sleeping and Eating price codes and other relevant information, see Essentials pages 25-30.

⊜ Sleeping

The Perhentian Islands *p284, map p284*
All the resorts and chalets now have their own generators; and all have fresh water from wells. Competition for accommodation is fierce due to the ever-increasing popularity of the Perhentians; this must be one of the few places in the world where demand regularly outstrips availability – strict planning laws ensure development is restricted. As the islands are not on the main phone system, many of the numbers provided are mobile numbers, which are liable to change. Bookings are therefore difficult to make, plus most of the guesthouses do not actually accept bookings. Upmarket resorts, though, do and during peak season will only accept people who

have reservations. Upmarket resorts employ booking agents on the mainland. Some of the smaller resorts will accept bookings from tourists about to board a boat in Kuala Besut, and this can save endless walking between beaches and chalets looking for a vacant room. It's advisable to take the earliest boat possible (particularly for Kecil) (see Transport, page 289).

Note There is a RM5 Marine Park conservation payable at the jetty in Kuala Besut before leaving for the islands.

Perhentian Besar

There are a number of bays with accommodation on the larger island. The majority of it is located on the west coast, which is divided into 3 small beaches by outcrops of rock. There are more places to stay in the secluded bay of Telok Dalam.
AL Perhentian Island Resort (bookings c/o 25 Menara Promet, Jln Sultan Ismail, KL), T03-2144 8530, www.perhentianisland resort.net. All of the 106 rooms have a/c. There is a licensed but expensive restaurant, some water sports facilities, diving equipment and courses available. Chalets have hill view or sea view, each with verandas. Pool surrounded by jungle, a good spot for a late-afternoon dip.
A New Coco Hut Chalets, T09-697 7988. This place has renamed itself (added 'New') and shot upmarket with a collection of 93 a/c rooms. Most also have TV and fridge. Cheaper ones have a garden view and cold water.
A Tuna Bay Island Resort, T09-697 9779, www.tunabay.com.my. Pretty wooden chalets all with a/c and attached bathroom with hot water close to a tasty stretch of sand. Breakfast included in price. The lovely open-air restaurant serves up delicious seafood and fair Western cuisine. Dive centre, internet and travel agency. Offers some excellent hotel and dive packages if booked through their website. Recommended.
A-B Coral View Island Resort, (bookings from Kuala Besut), T01-0903 0943. Quite an exclusive resort with 72 chalets rather tightly packed together. All rooms have bathroom

attached, and the cheaper rooms have fan. Sea views more expensive. The fan rooms are quite expensive given what else is on offer in the Perhentians. Diving courses.
A-C Flora Bay Chalet, Telok Dalam, T09-691 1666, www.florabayresort.com. Large resort on the beach with over 80 chalets and 5 different types of spotless, comfortable accommodation, including everything from swanky chalets to A-frames. Wi-Fi access and internet centre and a decent restaurant with nightly seafood barbecue. PADI 5-star dive centre. Recommended.
B-C Mama's, T019-984 0232, www.mamaschalet.com. Fan, shower. Selection of simple chalets mainly used by families or couples. Like every other hostel a daily snorkelling trip is organized. There's also excellent snorkelling offshore and we frequently received reports of shark and turtle sightings a quick swim from the shore. A-frames here a good value. Recommended.
B-C Perhentian Watercolours Resort, T017-938 0952, www.watercolours world.com. Brightly coloured fan rooms (some a/c in the sea-view rooms), near a lovely bit of beach. The restaurant here is renowned for seafood and pizza (although it can take some time coming). Diving, snorkelling and kayaking offered. Internet available.
B-D Abdul's, T09-697 7058. Decent looking chalets on the beach and near the jetty. Rooms are simple and come with fan and shower. The spacious (and expensive) suite room has a/c. Fine restaurant. Good local reputation. This place accepts credit cash if you get stuck here for longer than planned.

Camping This is permitted on the island but not on the beach; anybody found sleeping on the beach will be moved on. Restaurant and dive shop floors go for RM10.

Perhentian Kecil

There are more budget options on Kecil. Accommodation is split, with some huts on the beautiful white sandy beach of Pasir

Panjang (Long Beach), on the east side of the island, and some on Coral Bay, on the west.

Long Beach is the place for parties, while Coral Bay is smaller but with fewer eating choices. The stretch of beach at Coral Bay has mostly dead coral and the growing number of places to eat and sleep gives the place a much more crowded feel than Long Beach. The 2 are separated by a 10-min walk through the forest which is easy by day but not so simple at night after a couple of glasses of jungle juice! There are a couple of places at the southern tip, not far from Perhentian village and an isolated spot at Teluk Kerma.

AL-A Bubu, book through Wisma SBS, 32 Jln Imbi, KL, T03-2142 6688, www.bubu resort.com.my. The most upmarket resort on the island, and situated near a fine stretch of sand at the north end of long beach, this place has a good restaurant, water sports centre and a range of massage therapies on offer. Rooms are a disappointment and vastly overpriced given the competition around; they are pokey, garish and look weathered. Modern bathrooms with hot water. The best views are on the 3rd floor of the concrete block, where rooms overlook the sound to Pulau Besar. The number of self-help books lying on the beach beds suggests this is a bolthole for stressed workers from KL and Singapore.

A Shari-La Resort, Coral Bay, T09-6911 500, www.shari-la.com. New, upmarket place with 74 spacious, colourful a/c rooms with attached bathroom and hot water, and some with excellent sea views. The resort takes up a sizeable portion the promontory at the north end of Coral Bay, and its restaurant is the guilty party for the blaring Bob Marley music which shatters the calm. Internet available. Excellent promotional rates.

B-C Matahari, T09-6911 740. Set back from the beach a little, this large cluster of chalets is often full, and rooms are kept clean. A/c bungalows to A-frames with attached bathroom. Not a great deal of atmosphere, but a stone's throw from the beach.

B-C Maya Beach Resort, Coral Bay, T019-924 1644. Extremely popular operation that constantly has to refuse people due to being full. Trails of disappointed tourists can be seen every afternoon lugging their gear back along the beach in the hunt for somewhere else. The 12 simple fan-cooled chalets are nicely decorated and set in spacious grounds which offer more privacy than most. Excellent little café, internet access and very friendly staff. Internet available. Recommended.

B-C Senja Bay (formerly the Suria Resort), T09-691 1799, www.senjabay.com. Recently refurbished resort, which is equally as popular as the Maya. Chalets and A-frames here are comfortable and have hot water, and some are lined along the beach with glorious sea views. The elevated restaurant serves average Western food but has sublime views, free Wi-Fi for guests and the cheapest internet access on the island for non-guests (RM8 per hr).

B-D Mohsin, T014-548 7863. This place has been through a number of owners in recent years, but seems to have got on top of things now. Accommodation is in rows of blue-roofed huts on a hill, all with excellent views of Long Beach. Rooms are simple, yet modern and have attached bathroom with hot water. Cheerful owner with bizarre pricing system. Make sure to negotiate for your room, and the longer you stay, the larger the discount.

B-D Panorama, T09-691 1598, www.malaysia-panorama.com. One of the better places to stay on Long Beach, with a group of a/c and fan chalets in a leafy garden, on a slight incline. Satellite TV in the café, internet access and the best, most shady place to eat on Long Beach. Excellent value and extremely friendly staff. Recommended.

B-E D'Lagoon, Teluk Kerma, T019-985 7089, www.geocities.com/d_lagoon_my. Remote position at the northern end of the island. Some rooms are in a longhouse; chalets have attached bathrooms. There is a restaurant. A secluded, quiet spot with great snorkelling. Some reports of a lack of cleanliness.

C Pasir Petani Resort, T019-957 1624. At the southern end of the island, simple chalets with fans and attached bathrooms with its own stretch of beach facing the Peninsula.

C-D Bintang View, up the hill on the way to Coral Bay from Long Beach, T013-997 1563. Owned by an Irish lady, Finola, and her local husband Joe, this is a newcomer to the scene. It is refreshingly located far enough away from the beach to be away from any cloying scene, and close enough to be in the sea in 5 mins. The chalets are a mixture of old and new, all with fan, veranda with views and mosquito net. Bathroom facilities are shared, but kept spotless. Restaurant serves some fine pasta dishes and salads. Recommended

C-D Moonlight, T019-985 8222. Simple wooden huts, with fan, shared bathroom which can get dirty. Best point is its location which is on the end of the beach away from the rabble, with lovely views.

D Chempaka, T019-985 7329. Southern end, pleasantly uncramped site with sea views for all the 12 chalets, 12 hours of electricity. Run down but functional.

D Fatimah's/Aur Beach, T09-697 7694. Simple, functional wooden chalets with attached bathroom that take the overspill from the more popular resorts. Notable for its friendly ambience, although rooms are a tad drab. Friendly staff. Best budget option here.

D Lemongrass, T012-956 2392. Next to Rock Garden. Pretty standard place, simple fan chalets with shared showers and toilet of varying cleanliness.

Kuala Besut *p285*

C Nan's Guest House, just around the corner from the jetty, T09-697 4892. A/c rooms with TV or simpler fan rooms all with attached bathrooms. Recommended.

🍴 Eating

The Perhentian Islands *p284, map p284*
There are a couple of restaurants on Perhentian Besar serving simple food, such as banana pancakes, etc. Particularly popular are the restaurants attached to **Coral View Island**

Resort, **New Coco Hut Chalets** and **Tuna Bay**. There are also coffee shops in the kampong on Perhentian Kecil and almost all the chalets here have restaurants at very similar prices. Milkshakes, fruit juices and pancakes are particularly recommended.

On Long Beach, **Panorama's** is particularly good, the food is well presented and you can have dinner and watch movies at the same time.

There are 3 almost identical cafés (🍴) midway down the beach: **Daniel's**, **Family Café**, and **Meeting Point**, serving up generic backpacker-friendly fare.

At Coral Bay, the 2 busiest eateries are **Amelia's** and **Mama's** (both 🍴), with some good local dishes and nightly seafood barbecues. There are lots of good seafood barbecues, although avoid eating shark.

Note Alcohol is not freely available on the island. Some restaurants discreetly offer beer and some spirits, but you need to ask first. A tiny stall outside **Amelia's** on Coral Bay does a roaring trade in cold Tiger (RM10 a can) and local jungle juice (RM25 a bottle).

▲ Activities and tours

The Perhentian Islands *p284, map p284*
Diving and snorkelling
The coral around the Perhentian Islands is some of the best off the east coast. Most guesthouses arrange snorkelling trips and provide masks, snorkels and fins. It's RM30-40 for a half day including the boat trip and gear. It's RM10 to hire gear on the beach.

There are also many PADI dive shops on both islands which run courses and arrange dives for all levels, including night dives. Some of the cheapest diving can be found here, with dives for as little as RM70 including gear. The long-running **Steffen Sea Sports** and **Spice Divers**, both on Perhentian Kecil, have been recommended. Some dive shops offer day trips to Redang Island. It should be about RM1000 to charter a boat for 8-10 people. The diving trip is more expensive; if enough people are going it will cost around RM200 per person for dive equipment and trip to Redang. It is advisable to shop around for the best deal, and seek other tourists' advice to get an idea about the quality of the instructors who tend to vary from season to season. Some dive masters and instructors are European and so dive shops offer tuition in a variety of languages. If you are snorkelling off Long Beach, head for the patch near **Moonlight**.

Kuala Besut p285
MD Traveller's Holiday, T09-690 4028. Sells boat tickets and has a comprehensive travel service.

⊖ Transport

The Perhentian Islands p284, map p284
Boat
Speed boats leave at irregular hours throughout the day; all are booked through travel agents in Kuala Besut. More boats leave in the morning, so the earlier you can get there the better. Fast boats (return RM70) leave **Kuala Besut** generally every hour from 0700-1600 (at peak periods), 30 mins, boats carry 8-14 people. These small boats drive very fast and the ride can get bumpy; try to sit at the back near the driver. The ride is exhilarating to say the least, and you are required to wear a lifejacket. The same boats leave **Pulau Perhentian** for Kuala Besut at 0800, 1200 and occasionally at 1600. Ask a day in advance about the 1600 sailing.

Boats cannot land at the beach. Some resort areas have jetties which the boats can drop you off at, but for others, you'll have to transfer yourself and your luggage to a tiny 13-foot boat (RM2) for a short scoot to the sands. Those staying at the more remote **Pasir Petani Resort** on Perhentian Kecil should pre-arrange a pick-up time. Travellers should be wary of risking the boat trip too close to the beginning or end of the

Dec-Feb monsoon season. If you want to travel between the islands once you are there you will have to hire a water taxi. These motorized dinghies have fixed rates, ask at the guesthouse. A single trip between Long Beach and the opposite beach is RM12.

Bus
There are frequent connections on local buses from the bus station near the jetty to **Kota Bharu** (1½ hrs RM6) and **Kuala Terrengganu** (2½ hrs, RM10.70). To **Kuala Lumpur**: Mahligia Express bus company, T09-690 3699, leaves twice a day, once around 0830 and once at 2030. Buses from KL leave around a similar time. Boats leave from **Kuala Besut** to the Perhentians. Buses from Singapore or JB to Kota Bharu can drop travellers off at Jerteh, where there are frequent local bus connections with Kuala Besut.

Taxi
Kuala Terengganu (RM90); **Merang Jetty** (RM60, for Redang); **Kota Bharu** (RM50). Taxis from **Pasir Puteh** or **Jerteh** to **Kuala Besut** (RM15).

⊕ Directory

The Perhentian Islands p284, map p284
Banks There are no banks or ATM machines on the islands or in Besut and very few of the hotels accept credit cards. If you arrive in Besut short on cash, the nearest bank is 30-min bus journey away, in Jerteh; buses leave every 30 mins. Most guesthouses will change money, but at a poor rate. Note that most dive centres accept credit cards and some will let you have cash on them, but expect to be fleeced.
Internet Upmarket resorts have internet. Connection is slow and expensive: around RM15 per hr. On Long Beach, there's internet at **Panorama** for RM12 per hr. At Coral Bay, Senja Bay has internet access at RM8 per hr, and free Wi-Fi in their restaurant for guests.

Kota Bharu and around

→ *Colour map 1, A5.*

Kota Bharu (KB) is the royal capital of Kelantan, 'the land of lightning', and is situated near the mouth of the Kelantan River. The city is one of Malaysia's Malay strongholds, despite its proximity to the Thai border. This was reinforced during the latest general elections when the opposition PAS once again managed to secure KB and Kelantan (now the only PAS state in the country). While some people react against the state government's enthusiastic support for an Islamic interpretation of public (and private) morals, Kota Bharu is one of Malaysia's more culturally interesting and colourful towns with many eclectic museums, mosques and grandiose royal palaces, including the Istana Batu, Istana Balai and Istana Jahar. The city's wet market is an unmissable experience and an architectural delight, and the Kampong Kraftangan handicraft village forms part of the impressive Kelantan cultural zone.

The crafts for which Kelantan is renowned – such as silverware, weaving and metalworking – were in part the result of the state's close relations with the Siamese kingdom of Ayutthaya in the 17th century. The makyung, a traditional Malay court dance, is still performed in Kelantan and wayang kulit (shadow puppet plays) still provide entertainment on special occasions in the kampongs. Kota Bharu is the centre for Malay arts and crafts, although batik printing, woodcarving, songket-weaving and silver working are more often confined to the villages.

Around KB are Kong Mek, a 100-year-old Chinese temple and KB's most famous beach, Pantai Cahaya Bulan. There are also waterfalls, a Thai village and one of Malaysia's oldest mosques.
▶▶ *For listings, see pages 296-300.*

Ins and outs

Getting there
KB's airport is 8 km from town; it's RM25 per taxi to the centre or take town bus No 9 (RM2). Unusually, the train station is 6 km out of town at Wakaf Bharu; take bus No 19 or 27 to the centre. Many long-distance buses arrive at Jln Hamzah, 2 km from the city centre (RM8 taxi ride). ▶▶ *See also Transport, page 299.*

Getting around
The trishaw used to be the backbone of the town's public transport system, but taxis have elbowed them out of the scene. There is also a city bus service and a number of local and international car-hire firms.

Tourist information
Tourist Information Centre, ① *Jln Sultan Ibrahim, T09-748 5534, www.tic. kelantan.gov.my, Sun-Wed 0800-1300, 1400-1630, Thu 0800-1300 and 1400-1630,* is moderately helpful and has a good map of the town. It will arrange taxis and ferries to the Perhentian Islands (as will almost all hotels and guesthouses), as well as booking accommodation on the islands.

Safety
Since 2004, southern Thailand has been plagued by separatist violence which has in some cases been brutally put down by the Thai police and army. Almost 80 Muslim protesters were suffocated to death in Thai army trucks in October 2004. Militants regularly bomb Buddhist temples and gunmen attack non-Muslims in motorbike drive-by shootings almost daily. It is not recommended for tourists to travel there. At the time of writing more

than 3000 people had been killed by the unrest. In June 2008 four passengers were killed by insurgents on the Sungai Kolok to Yala train. Martial law was imposed throughout Thailand in September 2006 after a coup and the following year Bangkok itself became the scene of several bombings and politically motivated shootings. At the time of writing, the situation remains tense and a state of emergency has been declared in the Thai provinces of Pattani, Yala and Narathiwat (adjoins Kelantan), with martial law imposed. Martial law is also in place in Chana and Thepha districts in Songkhla province. It always

Kota Bharu

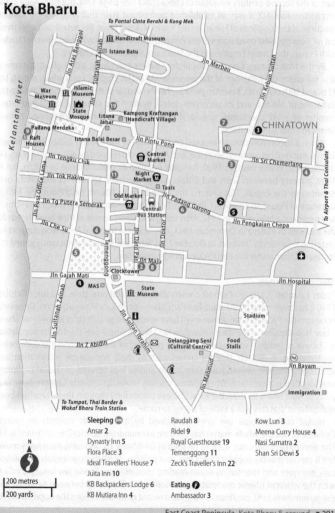

To Pantai Cinta Berahi & Kong Mek

Handicraft Museum

Jln Atas Banggol

Istana Batu

Sultani Zainab

Jln Merbau

Kebun Sultan

War Museum

Islamic Museum

State Mosque

Istana Jahar

Kampong Kraftangan (Handicraft Village)

Kelantan River

CHINATOWN

Padang Merdeka

Raft Houses

Istana Balai Besar

Jln Pintu Pong

Jln Tengku Chik

Central Market

Jln Sri Chemerlang

Jln Tok Hakim

Night Market

Taxis

Jln Post Office Lama

Old Market

Jln Padang Garong

Jln Tg Putera Semerak

Central Bus Station

Jln Doktor

Jln Pengkalan Chepa

Jln Che Su

Jln Dato Pati

Jln Maju

Jln Temenggong

Jln Gajah Mati

MAS

Clocktower

State Museum

Jln Sultanah Zainab

Jln Sultan Ibrahim

Gelanggang Seni (Cultural Centre)

Food Stalls

Stadium

Jln Hospital

Jln Z Abidin

Jln Mahmud

Jln Bayam

Immigration

To Airport & Thai Consulate

To Tumpat, Thai Border & Wakaf Bharu Train Station

N

200 metres
200 yards

Sleeping	Raudah **8**	Kow Lun **3**
Ansar **2**	Ridel **9**	Meena Curry House **4**
Dynasty Inn **5**	Royal Guesthouse **19**	Nasi Sumatra **2**
Flora Place **3**	Temenggong **11**	Shan Sri Dewi **5**
Ideal Travellers' House **7**	Zeck's Traveller's Inn **22**	
Juita Inn **10**		
KB Backpackers Lodge **6**	Eating	
KB Mutiara Inn **4**	Ambassador **3**	

worth checking local news and embassy websites for the latest advice if planning on crossing the border. The UK Foreign and Commonwealth Office (www.fco.gov.uk) gives particularly good assessments of safety in the region.

Background

The fertile alluvial soils of the Kelantan River valley and the coastal plain have supported mixed farming and a thriving peasant economy for centuries. Kelantan may have been part of the second-century kingdom of Langkasuka (see page 170), but from early in the first millennium AD, it was an established agricultural state that adopted the farming practices of the kingdom of Funan on the lower Mekong River. Because it was effectively cut off from the west coast states of the Peninsula, Kelantan always looked north: it traded with Funan, the Khmer Empire and the Siamese kingdom of Ayutthaha.

By the 14th century, Kelantan was under Siamese suzerainty, although at that time it also fell under the influence of the Javanese Majapahit Empire. For a while, during the 15th and 16th centuries, Kelantan joined other Peninsular states in sending tribute to the Sultanate of Melaka, and its successor, Johor. By then the state had splintered into a number of small chiefdoms; one local chief, Long Mohammed, proclaimed himself Kelantan's first sultan in 1800.

When a succession dispute erupted on the death of the heirless Sultan Mohammed, Siam supported his nephew, Senik the 'Red-Mouth' who reigned for 40 peaceful years. On the next succession crisis, in 1900, Bangkok installed its own nominee as sultan. But in 1909, a treaty between Siam and Britain pushed Bangkok to cede its suzerainty over Kelantan to the British. This severed the state from its Islamic neighbour, the former sultanate of Petani, in Southeast Thailand. British interference caused much resentment and provoked a brief revolt in 1912. After using Kota Bharu as one of their beachheads for the invasion of Malaya in December 1941, the Japanese Imperial Army won support for restoring Kelantan to Thailand. In October 1945 however, Kelantan reluctantly joined the Malayan Union, under the British colonial administration.

Modern Kelantan

Today Kelantan is Malaysia's most conservative and traditional state and since October 1990 it has been ruled by the hard-line Parti Islam – or PAS, its Malay acronym. On several occasions the PAS-led state government have voted to introduce strict Islamic – or Sharia – law. Non-Muslims in the state – mainly in Kota Bharu, where one-third of the population is Chinese or Indian – were alarmed by the prospect of the *hudud* criminal code being implemented. It dictates that for crimes such as theft, fornication, intoxication and apostasy, 'criminals' should have their hands and/or legs severed or should be lashed until death if unrepentant. When Islamic officials broke up a rowdy Chinese New Year party in Kota Bharu in 1994, the local Chinese community thought their fears had been realized and that this was a taste of things to come.

Hudud can't become law until it's passed by a two-thirds majority in Federal Parliament, but the whole matter has become a conundrum for Muslim politicians in KL. The government does not want to be seen as un-Islamic by opposing Kelantan's move, but it cannot feasibly support Sharia law, so it polishes its Islamic credentials by building new mosques and sponsoring Koran-reading competitions. Sharia law totally conflicts with the vision of Islamic moderates and modernists. The battle between Kelantan and the government in KL continues. In the most recent general elections the opposition PAS once again managed to hold onto Kelantan despite the most fervent efforts by BN (Barisan Nasional) to secure a victory here and the promise of massive development funds and extensive mosque building. The state is a hotbed of opposition politics.

This highly charged political and religious atmosphere contrasts with the Kelantanese people's laid-back, gentle manner. Tourists visiting the state should be particularly aware of Islamic sensitivities, but the trappings of Islam rarely impinge on the enjoyment of the state's rich cultural heritage.

Sights

The heart of Kota Bharu is the **central market** ① *off Jln Temenggong, daily 0900-2000*, which is one of the most vibrant and colourful wet markets in the country. It is housed in a three-storey octagonal concrete complex painted green with a glass roof and, because it's so bright, is a photographer's paradise. In the modern Buluh Kubu complex across the road on Jalan Tengku Petra Semerak, there are many shops selling Kelantanese batik and other handicrafts. Nearby is the **Istana Balai Besar** ① *not usually open to the public*, the 'palace with the big audience hall', built in Patani-style in 1844 by Sultan Mohammed II. The istana, with its decorative panels and woodcarvings is still used on ceremonial occasions. The palace contains the throne-room and the elaborate royal barge, which the sultan only ever used once for a joy ride on the Kelantan River in 1900. Beside the old istana is the single-storey **Istana Jahar** ① *Sat-Thu, 0830-1645, RM3*, constructed in 1889 by Sultan Mohammed IV; it is now the 'centre for royal customs' and is part of the new cultural complex (see below). It exemplifies the skilled craftsmanship of the Kelantanese woodcarvers in its intricately carved beams and panels. There is a small craft collection including *songket* and silverware.

Kampong Kraftangan (Handicraft Village) is close to the central market. It aims to give visitors a taste of Kelantan's arts and crafts all under one roof. The large enclosure, in which merbuk birds (doves) sing in their bamboo cages, contains four buildings, all wooden and built in traditional Malay style. They are part of the Kelantan cultural zone area which includes several museums, including the Istana Jahar. The complex is quite impressive, but visitors appear few and far between, giving the sprawling place a slightly empty, lackadaisical feel. The **Handicraft Museum** ① *Sat-Thu 1000-1800, RM1*, contains exhibits and dioramas of traditional Kelantanese crafts and customs. There is also a batik workshop and demonstration centre where local artists produce hand-painted batiks. There are several stalls, stocked with handicrafts such as batik, silverware and *songket*, for sale. At ground level there is a pleasant restaurant serving Kelantanese delicacies. Opposite the new complex is the **Istana Batu** ① *Sat-Thu, 0830-1645, RM3*, the sky-blue Stone Palace, which was built in 1939 and was one of the first concrete buildings in the state. The former royal palace was presented to the state by the Sultan for use as a royal museum and contains many personal possessions of the royal family.

A little north of the commercial centre is **Padang Merdeka**, built after the First World War as a memorial. Merdeka Square is also where the British hanged Tok Janggut, 'Father Long-beard', who led the short-lived revolt against British land taxes in 1915. Opposite, on Jalan Sultan Zainab, is the **State Mosque** ① *non-Muslims may visit but must first report to the International Islamic Information Centre a short walk away on Jln Sultana Zainab, T09-747 9376, daily 1000-1800*, which was completed in 1926. Next door is the State Religious Council building, dating from 1914. Next to the mosque on Jalan Merdeka is a magnificent two-storey green-and-white mansion with traditional Islamic latticework carving on eaves, which houses the **Islamic Museum** ① *under renovation at the time of* writing, but should be open by the time you read this. The building itself is more noteworthy than its eclectic contents. The **War Museum** ① *0830-1645, RM2, children RM1*, next to the Islamic Museum, gives visitors an informative account of the Second World War in Southeast Asia. Beginning with Pearl Harbor, it tells the story of the Japanese invasion of Kelantan in December 1941 and the subsequent conquest of Malaya. It includes many pictures and items from the period.

Directly west of the mosque, running north-south along the riverbank is **Jalan Pasar Lama**, off Jalan Post Office Lama. This is an interesting area for a gentle stroll; there are many beautiful but rapidly decaying old Chinese shophouses (there's a large Chinese community in this part of town). Most of the buildings date to the early 1900s. Some have been rendered completely uninhabitable because vast trees have taken root inside them.

At the **Gelanggang Seni** (Cultural Centre), on Jalan Mahmud, opposite the stadium, many traditional arts are regularly performed. The centre tends to get rather touristy but it is the best place to see a variety of cultural performances in one place. Traditional forms of entertainment include: Demonstrations of silat (the Malay art of self-defence); drumming competitions on Saturday and Monday using the *rebana ubi* Kelantan drums, made from hollowed-out logs; top-spinning competitions on Saturday and Monday; wayang kulit (shadow-puppet) performances on Wednesday; kite-flying competitions (Saturday afternoons) with the famous paper-and- bamboo *wau bulan* – or Kelantan moon-kites, the symbol of **MAS**. This has been a Kelantanese sport for centuries; the aim is to fly your kite higher than anyone else's and, once up there, to defend your superiority by being as aggressive as possible towards other competitors' kites. Kite-flying, according to the Malay Annals, was a favourite hobby in the heyday of the Melaka sultanate in the 15th century.

Other cultural performances include traditional dance routines such as the royal *Mak Yong* dance and the *Menora*, both of which relate local legends. Coconut-husk percussion is on Wednesday.

The **State Museum** ① *T09-748 2266, Sat-Thu 0830-1645, RM2*, is situated on Jalan Sultan Ibrahim near the clocktower.

Kong Mek

① *From KB follow the road to PCB; after 500 m, on a sharp right bend, turn left at the vegetable market; go down the dirt track and turn right through Chinese gateway at the bottom.*

Also known as Tin Heng Keong, this Chinese temple is 1 km out of town, on the road to PCB (see below). It is about 100 years old and is very colourful; the best time to visit is 0900-1000 each day when the temple is particularly lively. There is another smaller temple with a grotesque laughing Buddha and a grotto on the riverbank, closer to town.

Pantai Cahaya Bulan and other beaches

① *To get there take minibus No 10, which leaves every 20 mins from Bazaar Buluh Kubu, off Jln Tengku Chik or from Jln Padang Garong, or take a taxi.*

This is KB's most famous beach, formerly **Pantai Cinta Berahi**, but still known as **PCB**, 10 km north of the city. It is really only famous for its name, meaning the 'Beach of Passionate Love'. In 1994 the Islamic state government rechristened it the Beach of the Shining Moon, which conveniently retains the old acronym, PCB. In comparison with some other east coast beaches, it is an unromantic dump. In Malay, the word *berahi* is, according to one scholar, "loaded with sexual dynamite ... a love madness". Local Malays, alluding to this heated innuendo, used to euphemistically call it *pantai semut api* – the beach of the fire ants. Today, young Malay lovers do not even dare to hold hands on the beach, for fear of being caught by the religious police and charged with *khalwat*, the crime of 'close proximity', under Sharia Islamic law. The origin of the name *cinta berahi* is lost. One theory is that it was used as a code word by Malay and British commandos during the Japanese wartime occupation: the site of the Imperial Army's invasion, in 1941, is nearby, on Pantai Dasar Sabak (see below). Despite being rather overrated, there are several resorts along the beach. It gets crowded on weekends and room rates rise accordingly.

Pantai Dalam Rhu, also known as Pantai Bisikan Bayu (Beach of the Whispering Breeze), lies 50 km southeast of KB. This is recommended as an excellent location for windsurfing. **Pantai Irama** (Beach of Melody), 25 km south of KB, is the best of the nearby beaches for swimming. **Pantai Dasar Sabak** is 13 km northeast of KB. Nearby Kampong Sabak is a good place to watch the morning fishing boats come in. To get there, take a bus 8 or 9 from old market terminal.

Other excursions

In the area round Pasir Puteh there are several waterfalls: Jeram Pasu, Jeram Tapeh and Cherang Tuli. **Jeram Pasu** ① *most easily accessible by taxi or bus 3 to Padang Pak Amat and taxi to the waterfalls,* is the most popular, 35 km from Kota Bharu.

Around **Tumpat**, next to the border, are small Thai communities where there are a few Thai-style buildings and wats; they do not, however, compare with the Thai architecture on the other side of the border. **Wat Phothivian** ① *at Kampong Berok 12 km east of KB, take bus No 27 or 19 to Chabang Empat and then a taxi for the last 3-4 km to Kampong Jambu*, on the Malaysian side of Sungai Golok, has a 41-m reclining Buddha statue, built in 1973 by chief abbot Phra Kruprasapia Chakorn, which attracts thousands of Thai pilgrims every year. The last part of the journey also makes for a pleasant enough rural stroll.

Masjid Kampong Laut ① *bus No 44 or express bus No 5 leave every 30 mins,* at Kampong Nilam Puri, 10 km south of KB, was built 300 years ago by Javanese Muslims as an offering of thanks for being saved from pirates. Having been damaged once too often by monsoon floods, it was dismantled and moved inland to Kampong Nilam Puri, which is an Islamic scholastic centre. It was built entirely of cengal, a prized hardwood, and constructed without the use of nails. It vies with Masjid Kampong Kling (in Melaka) for the title of Malaysia's oldest mosque.

From **Kuala Kerai** ① *1½-hr bus trip south from Kota Bharu, bus No 5*, it is possible to take a boat upriver to Dabong, a small kampong nestled among the jungled foothills of the Main Range (the trip takes two hours and departs in the morning, but not on a Friday), where there is a resthouse and restaurant. Dabong, in the centre of Kelantan state, is on the north-south railway, so it is possible to catch the train back to Wakaf Bharu (across the river from KB). Alternatively, take a taxi.

Gua Musang

Gua Musang is the largest town on Route 8, the road through the interior, and lies in Kelantan state close to the border with Pahang. It began life as little more than a logging camp but has now expanded into a thriving administrative centre. The jungle is studded with limestone outcrops in this area of the Peninsula and a particularly impressive one overshadows Gua Musang. The area is challenging for rock climbers, with the Cattle Ranch Wall being a particularly well-known route. There have been reports of large mammals including wild elephants, tigers and tapirs along the roads near here and this is about as wild as Peninsular Malaysia gets outside the national parks and wildlife reserves.

Coast to coast

The East-West Highway makes for a memorable journey. It runs from Kota Bharu to Penang, straight across the forested backbone of the Peninsula, and was one of the biggest civil engineering projects ever undertaken in Malaysia. During its 11-year construction, contractors had to push their way through densely jungled mountains, coping with frequent landslides and hit-and-run-attacks by Communist insurgents.

Grik can be reached from Kuala Kangsar in Perak (see page 127) or from Butterworth via either Kulim (directly east of the town) or Sungai Petani (35 km north of town), which lead first to Keroh, on the Thai border, then on to Grik. The Kuala Kangsar route is a particularly scenic drive along a 111-km road which winds its way up the Perak River valley, enclosed by the Bintang mountains to the west and the Main Range to the east. En route, the road passes Tasek Chenderoh, a beautiful reservoir, surrounded by jungled hills. At **Kota Tampan**, just north of the lake, archaeologists have unearthed the remains of a Stone Age workshop, with roughly chiselled stone tools dating back 35,000 years. The road cuts through the jungle and there are some spectacular viewpoints. There are landslides along this stretch of road during the wet season.

To the east of Grik, the highway runs close to the former bases of the Communist Party of Malaya, which, until 1989, operated out of their jungle headquarters near Betong, just across the Thai border. The area was known as 'Target One' by the Malaysian security forces. The construction of the road opened the previously inaccessible area up to timber companies; there has been much illegal logging – and cross-border drug smuggling – in this 'cowboy country' of North Perak and Kelantan. The 200-km-long highway opened in 1982, and for the first few years was closed to traffic after 1600 because of the security threat posed by Communist insurgents. This threat has now ended. However, road maintenance is something of a hazard, and the journey is slow going with a whole series of road works and places where the road has subsided.

The train trundles along the railway line which cuts a diagonal through the Peninsula, running due north from Gemas (south of KL on the KL–Singapore line) to **Kota Bharu**. Much of the route is through the jungle, and the track skirts the west boundary of **Taman Negara**, the national park (see page 257). The train is slow, but it is an interesting journey. From **Gemas** the line goes through Jerantut, Kuala Lipis, **Gua Musang**, **Kuala Kerai** and on to Kota Bharu. It is possible to catch the train at **Mentakab** (along the Karak Highway, east of KL) or at Kuala Lipis, which can be reached by road via **Fraser's Hill** and **Raub**. It is also possible to drive from Kuala Lipis via Gua Musang to Kota Bharu. There are buses from Kuala Lipis to Gua Musang and Kuala Kerai.

◉ Kota Bharu and around listings

For Sleeping and Eating price codes and other relevant information, see Essentials pages 25-30.

● Sleeping

Kota Bharu *p290, map p291*
None of the hotels, except for the **Murni** and KB Backpackers Lodge, serves alcohol, so minibars are usually a bleak sight. Budget travellers are spoilt for choice in KB; there are

some very pleasant cheaper hostels and guesthouses (most of them in secluded alleyways with gardens) and they are locked in fearsome competition. As a result, new ones start up all the time as old ones fold; the State Tourist Information Centre has a list of budget accommodation and is happy to make recommendations. Homestays can also be arranged with local people. See Activities and tours, page 299, for details.

A-B Dynasty Inn, 2865 D and E Jln Sultan Zainab, T09-747 3000, www.dynastyinn-kota bharu.com. A hotel with 47 rooms with a/c, TV, hot shower, and some rooms with good river views (these cost a premium), rooftop coffee house, Chinese seafood restaurant. Free Wi-Fi in all rooms. Buffet breakfast included.

A-B Raudah, Jln Maju, T09-747 0055. Islamic hotel with prayers lining the walls. The rooms are spacious, modern and comfortable with cable TV and Wi-Fi. Good promotional rates.

A-B Ridel, Block A, Pelangi Mall, Jln Pasar Lama, T09-747 7000, www.ridelhotel.com.my. Large new block by the riverside, giving some rooms superb views. The a/c rooms are spotless, ultra modern and have cable TV, Wi-Fi access, smart bathrooms and a choice of town or river views. Guests can even choose from 4 different colour schemes. Recommended.

A-B Royal Guesthouse, Jln Hilir Kota, T09-743 0008, royalgh@streamyx.com. Excellent value accommodation in the cultural heart of the city, with a selection of comfortable a/c rooms with TV and hot-water bathroom. This is a modern and stylish hotel, and features one of the city's best restaurants on its ground floor. Recommended.

B Ansar, Jln Maju, T09-747 4000, F746 1150. Distinctively ugly 70s concrete block in the heart of town. Nevertheless, the interior is clean and bright with rooms with cable TV and hot-water bathrooms. The hotel is conveniently located near the night market. It is an Islamic hotel, so no shoes allowed; there are prayers in the hallways and signs mentioning Allah in the lifts.

B Flora Place, 202 Jln Kebun Sultan, T09-7477 888, flora999@streamyx.com. New place mainly used by people in transit to their hotel on the Perhentians. Rooms are not huge, but are smart, clean and modern with a/c, fridge, cable TV and firm new mattresses. They have a hotel on the Perhentians and can arrange transfers and good package deals. Diving equipment shop on the ground floor. Wi-Fi in lobby. Recommended.

B Juita Inn, Jln Pintu Pong, T09-744 6888, hotel@tm.net.my. Attractive hotel with 70 rooms, a/c, TV, minibar, restaurant. Rooms are small but clean and well furnished; note that

the superior rooms have no windows and are not particularly good value. Breakfast included.

B-C KB Mutiara Inn, 269 Jln Sri Cemerlang, T09-747 9888, kbmutiarainn@yahoo.com. Newish place with functional and clean a/c rooms, a fair distance from the town centre.

B-C Temenggong, Jln Tok Hakim (on the corner of Jln Temenggong), T09-744 1481. Popular with local business people. This no-frills place has clean a/c rooms with TV and attached bathroom. Some rooms lack natural light.

D Ideal Travellers' House, 5504a Jln Padang Garong, T09-744 2246, www.ugoideal.com. Quiet family-run option, with rooms echoing to the sound of birdsong, pleasantly located away from the busy city streets. The hotel badly needs some investment as mattresses are squashy, bathrooms are clean but with chipped toilet bowl and broken flush and walls are grubby. Can help with onward travel arrangements. Wi-Fi available (RM5 for length of stay).

D-E KB Backpackers Lodge, 1872 Jln Padang Garong, T09-748 8841, backpackers lodge2@yahoo.co.uk. Popular hostel in the city centre with a selection of clean and functional a/c and fan rooms, some with no natural light. There is a rooftop terrace with a small bar serving beer and internet available in the lobby. Dorms available (RM10).

D-E Zeck's Traveller's Inn, 7088 Jln Sri Cemerlang, T09-743 1613, zecktravellers@ yahoo.com. It's a bit of a hike into town from here, but this place is peaceful and comfortable and offers budget travellers the best value for money. Rooms are generally well kept and bright, mostly fan and shared bathroom but there is an a/c room with attached bathroom and hot shower. Dorm (RM10). Wi-Fi available, friendly owner. Recommended.

Pantai Cinta Berahi and other beaches
p294

A Perdana Resort (also known as PCB Resort), Jln Kuala Pa'Amat, Pintai Cinta Berahi, T09-774 4000, F774 4980. A/c, restaurant, pool, water sports, pleasant stretch of beach, dotted with white chalets colour schemed blue, green and pink according to room type,

not very well maintained, popular with business conventions and meetings.
B-C Motel Irama Bachok, Bachok, T09-778 8462. Clean and reasonable value. To get there, take a bus 2A or 2B to Bachok, which leaves every 30 mins.
D HB Village, Pinta Cinta Berahi, T09-773 4993. Clean, friendly – and with very big crocodiles in attached farm.

Gua Musang *p295*
C Kesedar Inn, T09-912 1229. On the edge of town, attractive lawn, clean rooms, friendly.
E Rest House, rather run down but attractive place to stay, shared facilities.

🍴 Eating

Kota Bharu *p290, map p291*
Beer and other alcoholic beverages are only available in certain Chinese coffee shops, notably along Jln Kebun Sultan.

The Kelantan speciality is *ayam percik* – roast chicken, marinated in spices and served with a coconut milk gravy. *Nasi tumpang* is a typical Kelantanese breakfast; banana-leaf funnel of rice layers interspersed with prawn and fish curries and salad.

Good restaurants are thinner on the ground here than in many other east Malaysian cities and as a result fast-food outlets seem to get superb business from fresh-faced foreigners, new arrivals from Thailand. However, a bit of effort will turn up some decent options.
🍴🍴🍴 Bunga Melati, Royal Guesthouse Hotel, Jln Hilir Kota. One of the town's more upmarket eating venues and a great to place to try Kelantan cuisine in an elegant setting. Sushi and good fusion food also available.
🍴🍴 Ambassador, 7003 Jln Kebun Sultan. Big Chinese coffee shop next to Kow Lun, Chinese dishes including pork satay and other iniquitous substances – like beer.
🍴 Kow Lun, 7005 and 7006 Jln Kebun Sultan. Good lively Chinese coffee shop with large variety of dishes from *curry mee*, *loh mee* to roast duck and pork. Also, there is lots of ice-cold beer.

🍴 Meena Curry House, 3377 Jln Gajah Mati. Indian curry house, banana leaf restaurant.
🍴 Nasi Sumatra, 2527 Jln Kebun Sultan. Open lunch and early dinner. Indonesian-style curries including *ikan gulai*, *rendang* and some good *percedel* make this a good lunch spot. There are a couple of branches throughout town. Look for signs saying the food was prepared by Haji Ismail; each one has it above the glass counter. Recommended. Next door is the Jln Sultan Kopitiam (🍴), with a simple menu of soup, fried rice and coffee. Wi-Fi available.
🍴 Qing Liang, Jln Zainal Abidin. Excellent Chinese vegetarian, also Malay and Western dishes. Recommended.

Foodstalls
Night market (in car park opposite local bus station, in front of Central Market), exclusively Malay food, satays and exquisite array of curries; for a delectable sweet dish to round off the evening, try the banana *murtabak*. Colour-coded tables – if you eat from a certain stall and sit at a blue table, you are obliged to buy your drink from a stall in the blue area. Excellent fruit juices, no alcohol. Open every night from 1800, but closes from 1900-2000 for evening prayers. More choice and atmosphere at the weekends. Recommended.

🎭 Entertainment

Kota Bharu *p290, map p291*
Cultural shows
Regular cultural shows at the Gelanggang Seni (cultural centre), Jln Mahmud.

🎉 Festivals and events

Kota Bharu *p290, map p291*
Ask the tourist office or phone Kelantan State Government who organize the kite festival, T09-748 1957, for information on all festival dates.
May/Jun Malaysia International Kite Festival, Pantai Seri Tujuh (Beach of the Seven

Lagoons), Turnport (adjacent to Thai border), 7 km from KB. To get there take bus 43.

Jul Drum festival, a traditional east coast pastime; **10-12 Jul**, Sultan's birthday celebrations.

Aug Bird Singing Contest, when the prized *merbuk* (doves) or *burong ketitir* birds compete on top of 8 m-high poles. Bird-singing contests are also held on Fri mornings around Kota Bharu.

Sep Top-spinning contest. Another traditional east coast sport which is taken very seriously.

O Shopping

Kota Bharu *p290, map p291*
Antiques
Lam's, Jln Post Office Lama. In contrast to the modern town walk there are several old bamboo raft houses along this street.

Batik
Astaka Fesyer, 782K (3rd floor). Recommended.
Bazaar Buluh Kubu, Jln Tengku Petra Semerak, just across the road from the Central Market. Houses scores of batik boutiques; also in the building are tailors' shops which can turn out very cheap shirts, blouses and dresses within 24 hrs.

Handicrafts
The **Central Market** is the cheapest for handicrafts. There are numerous handicraft stalls, silver-workers, kite-makers and wood-carvers scattered along the road north to Pantai Cinta Berahi. At **Kampong Penambang**, on this road, just outside KB, there is a batik and songket centre.

Silverware
On Jln Sultanah Zainab (near the bridge across the Kelantan River), before junction with Jln Hamzah, there are 3 shops selling Kelantan silver including **KB Permai**, a family business which works the silver on the premises. The

Kampong Kraftangan (Handicraft Village) contains many stalls with a huge range of batik sarongs and ready-mades, silverware, songket, basketry and various Kelantanese knick-knacks.

▲ Activities and tours

Kota Bharu *p290, map p291*
Golf
Royal Kelantan Golf Club, 5488 Jln Hospital. 18-hole course.

Tour operators
Batuta Travel & Tour, 1st floor, Bangunan PKDK, Jln Dato' Pati, T09-744 2652; **Boustead Travel**, 2833 Jln Temenggong, T09-744 9952; **Kelmark Travel**, Kelmark House, 5220 Jln Telipot, T09-744 4211; **KTIC** (Kelantan State Tourist Information Centre) organizes a number of tours – river and jungle-safari trips, staying in kampongs and learning local crafts. It also organizes 3-day 'Kampong Experience' tours which are not as contrived as their name suggests. Full board and lodging provided by host families, which can be selected from list including potters, fishermen, batik-makers, kite-makers, silversmiths, dance instructors, top-makers and shadow puppet-makers. All only available by request. Cost from RM350 (all in); minimum 2 people. It also runs short Kelantanese cooking courses; **Pelancongan Bumi Mars**, Tingkat Bawah, Kompleks Yakin, Jln Gajah Mati, T09-743 1189. The Tourist Information Centre also arrange tours as do several of the guesthouses in town.

⊖ Transport

Kota Bharu *p290, map p291*
Air
Regular connections with **KL** (MAS, AirAsia), **Subang** and **Penang** (Firefly).
Airline offices AirAsia office at the airport. MAS, Ground Floor, Komplek Yakin, Jln Gajah Mati (opposite the clock tower), T09-744 7000 and T09-744 0557 at the airport.

Bus

City buses and some long-distance express buses leave from the Central Bus Station, Jln Hilir Pasar. Many long-distance buses also depart from Jln Hamzah, 2 km from the city centre (RM8 taxi ride); make sure you check which terminal your bus leaves from. Buses to **Gua Musang** and **Pasir Puteh** and Kuala Besut (for the Perhentian Islands, 1½ hrs, RM6) also depart from this station. Regular connections with **Grik**, **Kuala Terengganu** (RM14.30), **Kuantan** (RM31.50), **KL** (RM40.20), **JB** and **Singapore** (both RM77), **Penang** (RM36), **Alor Star** (RM38), **Melaka** (RM52.90), **Mersing**, **Temerloh** and many other destinations.

Note Long-distance buses sell out quickly, particularly those for daytime travel. Book as early as possible. There are booking offices by the Central Bus Station.

Car hire

Avis, Hotel Perdana, Jln Sultan Mahmud, T09-748 4457; South China Sea, airport, T09-774 4288, F773 6288; Pacific, T09-744 7610.

Taxi

Taxi station next to the Central Bus Station, Jln Hilir Pasar. Destinations include **Kuala Besut** (RM50), **Kuala Terengganu**, **Kuantan**, **KL**, **JB**, **Butterworth** and **Grik**. Also taxis to **Rantau Panjang** (for **Sungai Golok, Thailand**).
To the Thai border There are frequent buses from the Central Bus Station to Rantau Panjang. Bus No 29 (RM4.50, 1½ hrs) goes to the border from where travellers make the 1-km walk to cross into Thailand's **Sungai Kolok**. Trishaws and motorbike taxis wait to assist people making the crossing. There are hourly minibuses to **Hat Yai** and 2 daily trains to **Bangkok**.

Another route into Thailand is via **Pengkalan Kubor**, a quieter and much more interesting crossing to **Ta Ba** (Tak Bai). Bus Nos 27, 27a and 43 go to **Pengkalan Kubor**. Small boats cross the river regularly and there is also a car ferry. Long-tails cater for the clientele of the cross-border prostitution industry only. There are also regular bus connections with **Singapore**.

Train

Several daily connections with **Singapore** and **KL** via **Gua Musang**, **Kuala Lipis**, and **Jerantut**. The railway is slow but the scenery makes the journey worthwhile. The daily train to KL leaves at and 1846 to arrive between 0725 and 1846. The daily service to Singapore leaves at 2028 and arrives at around 1055.

Gua Musang p295
Bus

Daily buses from **Kuala Lipis** to Gua Musang (0800 and 1300) and **Kuala Kerai** (1430) with onward connections to Kota Bharu. There is a new road linking Gua Musang to **Tanah Rata** in the Cameron Highlands and through to Ipoh on the west coast. There is a connection between Gua Musang and **Tanah Rata**.

Coast to coast p296
Bus

Grik has connections with **Butterworth, KL, Taiping** and **Ipoh**. For **Kota Bharu** change at Tanah Merah. It is possible to cross the border into Thailand from **Keroh**, 50 km north of Grik. There are regular taxis from Keroh to the border post and Thai taxis and *saamlors* (trishaws) on the other side. Thai taxis to **Betong**, 8 km from the border.

❶ Directory

Kota Bharu *p290, map p291*
Banks Money changers in main shopping area. Bumiputra, Jln Maju; D & C, Jln Gajah Mati; Hongkong & Shanghai, Jln Sultan.
Embassies and consulates Royal Thai Consulate, Jln Pengkalan Chepa, T09-744 0867 (Mon-Thu and Sat 0900-1200, 1330-1530). **Immigration** Immigration Office, Kompleks Yakin, Jln Gajah Mati, T09-744 1133. **Medical services** Hospital, Jln Hospital, T09-748 5533. **Post office** General Post Office, Jln Sultan Ibrahim.

Contents

304 Kuching and around
304 Ins and outs
306 Sights
312 Around Kuching
315 Damai Peninsula
318 Bako National Park
320 Listings

**331 Bandar Sri Aman
and around**
332 Skrang longhouses
335 Listings

336 Sibu, Kapit and Belaga
337 Sibu
338 Kapit
341 Belaga
344 Listings

350 North coast
351 Bintulu
352 Similajau National Park
353 Niah National Park
356 Miri and the Baram River
360 Listings

369 Northern Sarawak
369 Gunung Mulu
    National Park
375 Bario and the
    Kelabit Highlands
376 Limbang
377 Listings

379 Background
379 History
384 Politics and
    modern Sarawak
385 Culture

Sarawak

Footprint features

302 Don't miss …
307 A town called Cat
311 A ceramic inheritance
317 The Penan: museum pieces
    for the 21st century?
333 The longhouse: prime
    location apartments
334 Visiting longhouses:
    house rules
343 Build and be dammed:
    an ecological time bomb
353 Niah's guano collectors:
    scraping the bottom
355 How to make a swift buck
383 Tom Harrisson:
    life in the fast lane
386 The Iban in Borneo
387 Skulls in the longhouses
388 The Kelabit in Borneo
389 The Kayan and
    Kenyah in Borneo
390 Tribal tattoos
391 The palang

★ **Don't miss ...**
1 Sarawak Museum, page 306.
2 Bako National Park, page 318.
3 Kuching waterfront foodstalls, page 324.
4 Longhouse stay, page 334.
5 Pelagus Rapids, page 340.
6 Niah National Park caves, page 353.
7 Gunung Mulu hike, page 372.
8 Kelabit Highlands, page 375.

Introduction

Sarawak, the 'land of the hornbill', is the largest state in Malaysia, covering an area of nearly 125,000 sq km in northwest Borneo with a population of just over two million. Sarawak has a swampy coastal plain, a hinterland of undulating foothills and an interior of steep-sided, jungle-covered mountains. The lowlands and plains are dissected by a network of broad rivers which are the main arteries of communication and where the majority of the population is settled.

In the mid-19th century, Charles Darwin described Sarawak as "one great wild, untidy, luxuriant hothouse, made by nature for herself". Sarawak is Malaysia's great natural storehouse, where little more than half a century ago great swathes of forest were largely unexplored and where tribal groups, collectively known as the Dayaks, would venture downriver from the heartlands of the state to exchange forest products of hornbill ivory and precious woods.

Today the Dayaks have been gradually incorporated into the mainstream and the market economy has infiltrated the lives of the great majority of the population. But much remains unchanged. The forests, although much reduced by a rapacious logging industry, are still some of the most species-rich on the globe; more than two-thirds of Sarawak's land area, roughly equivalent to that of England and Scotland combined, is still covered in jungle, although this is diminishing.

Kuching and around

→ *Colour map 3, C1. Population: around 460,000.*

Due to Kuching's relative isolation and the fact that it was not bombed during the Second World War, Sarawak's state capital has retained much of its 19th-century dignity and charm, despite the increasing number of modern high-rise buildings. Chinese shophouses still line many of the narrow streets. Kuching is a great starting point to explore the state and there are many sights within its compact centre, including the renowned Sarawak Museum and the Petra Jaya State Mosque.

Within easy reach is the Semenggoh Orang-Utan Sanctuary and the national parks of Gunung Gading, Kubah and Tanjung Datu. North of Kuching is the Damai Peninsula, featuring the worthwhile Sarawak Cultural Village and Bako National Park on the Muara Tebas Peninsula.
▸▸ *For listings, see pages 320-331.*

Ins and outs

Getting there
The **airport** ① *T082-457373*, is 10 km south of Kuching. At the time of research, the bus service to and from the airport has been suspended due to lack of custom. To take a taxi to town, buy a fixed-price coupon (RM22) from the counter in arrivals. Alternatively, catch the Tune Hotel shuttle bus which departs every hour 0800-2000 (RM10). This service drops passengers off at the Tune Hotel on Jalan Borneo. ▸▸ *See also Transport, page 329.*

Getting around
The central portion of the city, which is the most interesting, can be negotiated on foot. Sampans (*perahu tambang*) provide cross-river transport and operate as river taxis. There are two city bus companies that provide a cheap and fairly efficient service. Taxis are found outside many of the larger hotels and at designated taxi stands. There are several international as well as local self-drive car hire firms in Sarawak.

Best time to visit
Kuching is hot and humid year-round. While heavy showers can happen at any time, they are more likely during the rainy season (November to February), which could make trekking difficult. May and June are also the months for Gawai Dayak (see page 35), a kind of harvest festival and a time for feasting and partying. There's also the popular Rainforest Music Festival held every July at the Sarawak Cultural Village, see www.sarawaktourism.com for exact dates.

Tourist information
Sarawak Tourism Board ① *Visitors' Information Centre, Jln Tun Abang Haji Openg, T082-410944, www.sarawaktourism.com, Mon-Fri 0800-1800, Sat-Sun 0900-1500*, is housed in the beautiful Old Courthouse Complex. It has a good stock of maps and pamphlets. The staff are very knowledgeable and friendly. The smaller branch office of the **Sarawak Tourism Association** ① *Waterfront, Main Bazaar, T082-240620, F427151, Mon-Thu 0800-1245 and 1400-1645, Fri 0800-1130 and 1430-1645, Sat 0800-1245 (closed 1st and 3rd Sat of the month)*, has a good range of information. There is a desk at **Kuching International Airport** ① *T082-450944*, which has information on bus routes, approved travel agents and itineraries. **Tourism Malaysia** ① *Bangunan Rugayah, Jln Song Thian Cheok, T082-246575, F246442*, has information on Sarawak and Sabah and a good stock of

brochures. The state and national tourism organizations are both well informed and helpful; they can advise on itineraries and travel agents and have up-to-date information on national park facilities.

National parks information

For information and accommodation booking for the national parks of Bako, Gunung Gading and Kubah and Matang Wildlife Centre, contact the **National Parks and Wildlife Booking Office** ⓘ *Old Courthouse, Jln Tun Abang Hj Openg, T082-248088, Mon-Fri 0800-1700*; or see www.sarawakforestry.com, click on online services, and then booking of national park; also npbooking@sarawak.net.gov.my.

Background

Shortly after dawn on 15 August 1839, the British explorer James Brooke sailed around a bend in the Sarawak River and, from the deck of his schooner, *The Royalist*, had his first view of Kuching. According to the historian Robert Payne, he saw "...a very small town of brown huts and longhouses made of wood or the hard stems of the nipah palm, sitting in brown squalor on the edge of mudflats." The settlement, 32 km upriver from the sea, had been established less than a decade earlier by Brunei chiefs who had come to oversee the mining of antimony in the Sarawak River valley. The antimony – used as an alloy to harden other metals, particularly pewter – was exported to Singapore where the tin plate industry was developing.

By the time James Brooke had become rajah in 1841, the town had a population of local Malays, Dayaks and Cantonese, Hokkien and Teochew traders. Chinatown dominated the south side of the river while the Malay kampongs were strung out along the riverbanks to the west. A few Indian traders also set up in the bazaar among the Chinese shophouses. Under Charles Brooke, the second of the White Rajahs, Kuching began to flourish; he commissioned most of the town's main public buildings. Brooke's wife, Ranee Margaret, wrote: "The little town looked so neat and fresh and prosperous under the careful jurisdiction of the Rajah and his officers, that it reminded me of a box of painted toys kept scrupulously clean by a child."

Sarawak's capital is divided by the Sarawak River; the south is a commercial and residential area, dominated by Chinese, while the north shore is predominantly Malay in character with the old kampong houses lining the river. The **Astana**, **Fort Margherita** and the **Petra Jaya area**, with its modern government offices, are also on the north side of the river. The two parts of the city are very different in character and even have separate mayors. Kuching's cosmopolitan make-up is immediately evident from its religious architecture: Chinese and Hindu temples, the imposing state mosque and Protestant and Roman Catholic churches.

Of all the cities in Malaysia, Kuching has been the worst affected by the smog – euphemistically known as 'the haze' – that periodically engulfs large areas of Borneo and the Indonesian island of Sumatra, largely blamed on slash-and-burn deforestation in Kalimantan. This was most severe in mid-1997, but occurs to some extent every year. At the peak of the 'emergency' – for that is what it became – in late September 1997, Kuching came to a standstill. It was too dangerous to drive and, seemingly, too dangerous to breathe. People were urged to remain indoors. Schools, government offices and factories closed. The port and airport were also closed. Tourism traffic dropped to virtually zero and for 10 days the city stopped. At one point there was even discussion of evacuating the population of the State of Sarawak. People began to buy up necessities and the prices of some commodities rose 500%.

Sights

Sarawak Museum

ⓘ *Jln Tun Haji Openg, T082-244232, www.museum.sarawak.gov.my, daily 0900-1630, closed on first day of public holidays, free. There is a library and a bookshop attached to the museum as well as a gift shop, the Curio Shoppe, all proceeds of which go to charity. Permits to visit Niah's Painted Cave can be obtained, free of charge, from the curator's office.*

Kuching's biggest attraction is this internationally renowned museum, housed in two sections on both sides of Jalan Tun Haji Openg. The old building to the east of the main road is a copy of a Normandy town hall, designed by Charles Brooke's French valet. The Rajah was encouraged to build the museum by the naturalist Alfred Russel Wallace, who spent over two years in Sarawak, where he wrote his first paper on natural selection. The museum was opened in 1891, extended in 1911, and the 'new' wing built in 1983. Its best known curators have been naturalist Eric Mjoberg, who made the first ascent of Sarawak's highest peak – Gunung Murudi (see page 376) – in 1922, and ethnologist and explorer Tom Harrisson, whose archaeological work at Niah made world headlines in 1957. The museum overlooks pleasant botanical gardens and the Heroes Memorial, built to commemorate the dead of the Second World War, the Communist insurgency and the confrontation with Indonesia. Across the road, and linked by a footbridge, is the Dewan Tun Abdul Razak building, the newer extension of the museum.

The museum has a strong ethnographic section, although some of its displays have been superseded by the **Cultural Village** (see page 316), Sarawak's 'living museum'. New sections of the museum are being opened, including a contemporary art section, for Borneo's rapidly evolving culture, and a natural history section. The old museum's ethnographic section includes a full-scale model of an Iban longhouse, a reproduction of a Penan hut and a selection of Kayan and Kenyah woodcarvings. There is also an impressive collection of Iban war totems (*kenyalang*) and carved Melanau sickness images (*blum*) used in healing ceremonies. The museum's assortment of traditional daggers (*kris*) is the best in Malaysia. The Chinese and Islamic ceramics include 17th-20th century Chinese jars, which are treasured heirlooms in Sarawak (see box, page 311). Temporary exhibitions are held, often sponsored by major corporations, with a small entry fee (RM5).

The natural history collection, covering Sarawak's flora and fauna, is also noteworthy. The new Tun Abdul Razak ethnological and historical collection includes prehistoric artefacts from the Niah Caves, Asia's most important archaeological site (see page 353); there is even a replica of Niah's Painted Cave – without the smell of guano.

Sarawak Islamic Museum

ⓘ *Jln P Ramlee, T082-244232, Sat-Thu 0900-1630, free.*

Not far from the Sarawak Museum, this collection is housed in the restored Maderasah Melayu Building, an elegant, single-storey colonial edifice. As its name suggests, the museum is devoted to Islamic artefacts from all the ASEAN countries, with the collection of manuscripts, costumes, jewellery, weaponry, furniture, coinage, textiles and ceramics spread over seven galleries, each with a different theme, and set around a central courtyard.

Waterfront

Around Main Bazaar are some other important buildings dating from the Brooke era; most of them are closed to the public. The **Supreme Court** on Main Bazaar was built in 1874 as an administrative centre. State council meetings were held here from the 1870s

A town called Cat

There are a few explanations as to how Sarawak's capital acquired the name 'Cat'. (*Kuching* means 'cat' in Malay, although today it is more commonly spelt *kucing* as in modern Bahasa 'c' is pronounced 'ch'.)

Local legend has it that James Brooke, pointing towards the settlement across the river, enquired what it was called. Whoever he asked mistakenly thought he was pointing at a passing cat. If that seems a little far fetched, the Sarawak Museum offers a few more plausible alternatives. Kuching may have been named after the wild cats (*kucing hutan*) which, in the 19th century, were commonly seen along jungled banks of the Sarawak River. Another theory is that it was named after the fruit *buah mata kucing* (cat's eyes), which grows locally. Most likely, however, is the theory that the town may originally have been known as *Cochin* (port), a word commonly used across India and Indochina.

until 1973, when it was converted to law courts. In front of the grand entrance is a memorial to Rajah Charles Brooke (1924) and on each corner there is a bronze relief representing the four main ethnic groups in Sarawak – Iban, Orang Ulu, Malay and Chinese. The clocktower was built in 1883. The **Square Tower**, also on Main Bazaar, was built as an annexe to Fort Margherita in 1879 and was used as a prison. Later in the Brooke era it was used as a ballroom. The square tower marks one end of Kuching's waterfront esplanade which runs alongside the river for almost 900 m to the **Hilton**.

The **waterfront** has been transformed into a landscaped esplanade through restoration and a land-reclamation project. It has become a popular meeting place, with foodstalls, restaurants and entertainment facilities including an open-air theatre used for cultural performances. There is a restored Chinese pavilion, an observation tower, a tea terrace and musical fountains, as well as a number of modern sculptures. During the day, the waterfront offers excellent views of the Astana, Fort Margherita and the Malay kampongs that line the north bank of the river. At night, the area comes alive as younger members of Kuching's growing middle class make their way down here to relax.

A good way to see the Sarawak River is to take a 90-minute **cruise** ① *tickets from Layar Warisan, Level 9, Medan Pelita Lebuh Temple, T082-240366, info@sarawakrivercruise.com.my, or from tourist agencies, hotels or at the waterfront booths halfway along the esplanade, RM60, children RM30, with a minimum of 2 passengers,* during the day. There are three departures daily at 0900, 1200 and 1500, or in the early evening at 1730.

The **General Post Office**, with its majestic Corinthian columns, stands in the centre of town, on Jalan Tun Haji Openg. Dating back to 1931, it was one of the few edifices built by Vyner Brooke, the last Rajah. It has been renovated and there are long-term plans to make it the home of the Sarawak Art Museum.

The **Courthouse complex**, which now houses the Sarawak Tourism Board's Visitors' Centre, was built in 1871 as the seat of Sarawak's government and was used as such until 1973. It remains one of Kuching's grandest structures. The buildings have *belian* (ironwood) roofs and beautiful detailing inside and out, reflecting local art forms. It also continues to house the state's high court and magistrates' court as well as several other local government departments. The colonial-baroque **Clocktower** was added in 1883 and the **Charles Brooke Memorial** in 1924. The complex also includes the **Pavilion Building** which was built in 1907 as a hospital. During the Japanese occupation it was used as an information and propaganda centre and it is now undergoing renovation with a view to making it the home of a new Textile Museum. Opposite the Courthouse is the **Indian Mosque (Mesjid India)** on Lebuh India, originally had an *atap* roof and *kajang* (thatch) walls; in 1876 *belian* (ironwood) walls were erected. The mosque was built by South Indians and is in the middle of an Indian quarter where spices are sold along the Main Bazaar. When the mosque was first built only Muslims from South India were permitted to worship here; even Indian Muslims from other areas of the subcontinent were excluded. In time, as Kuching's Muslim population expanded and grew more diversified, so this rigid system was relaxed. It is hard to get to the mosque as it is surrounded by buildings. However a narrow passage leads from Lebuh India between shop numbers 37 and 39.

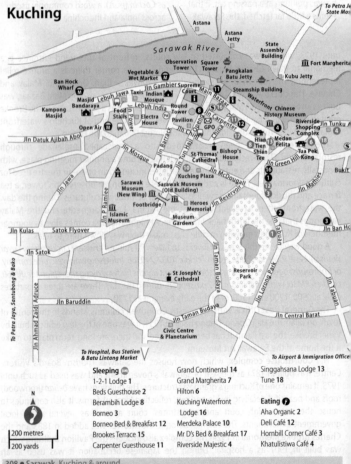

Kuching

Sleeping 🛏
1-2-1 Lodge 1
Beds Guesthouse 2
Berambih Lodge 8
Borneo 3
Borneo Bed & Breakfast 12
Brookes Terrace 15
Carpenter Guesthouse 11

Grand Continental 14
Grand Margherita 7
Hilton 6
Kuching Waterfront
    Lodge 16
Merdeka Palace 10
Mr D's Bed & Breakfast 17
Riverside Majestic 4

Singgahsana Lodge 13
Tune 18

Eating 🍴
Aha Organic 2
Deli Café 12
Hornbill Corner Café 3
Khatulistiwa Café 4

The **Round Tower** on Jalan Tun Abang Haji Openg (formerly Rock Road) was originally planned as a fort in 1886, but was never completed. The whole area is undergoing restoration for future art galleries and cultural exhibits. The **Steamship Building** ① *52 Main Bazaar*, was built in 1930 and was previously the offices and warehouse of the Sarawak Steamship Company. It has been extensively restored and now houses a restaurant, souvenir stalls, a handicrafts gallery and an exhibition area.

The **Bishop's House** ① *off Jln McDougall, near the Anglican Cathedral of St Thomas*, is the oldest surviving residence in Sarawak. It was built in 1849, entirely of wood, for the first Anglican Bishop of Borneo, Dr McDougall. The first mission school was started in the attic – developed into St Thomas's and St Mary's School, which is now across the road on Jalan McDougall.

Chinatown

Kuching's Chinese population, part of the town's community since its foundation, live in the shophouses lining the narrow streets around **Main Bazaar**. This street opposite the waterfront is the oldest in the city, dating from 1864. The Chinese families who live here still pursue traditional occupations such as tinsmithing and woodworking. Kuching's highest concentration of antique and handicraft shops is to be found here. **Jalan Carpenter**, parallel to Main Bazaar, has a similar selection of small traders and coffee shops, as well as foodstalls and two small Chinese temples. Off **Lebuh China** (Upper China Street), there is a row of perfectly preserved 19th-century Chinese houses. The oldest Chinese temple in Kuching, **Tua Pek Kong** (also known as Siew San Teng), in the shadow of the **Hilton** on Jalan Tunku Abdul Rahman, was built in 1876, although it is now much modernized. There is evidence that the site has been in use since 1740 and a Chinese temple was certainly here as early as 1770. The first structure was erected by a group of Chinese immigrants thankful for their safe journey across the hazardous South China Sea. New immigrants still come here to give thanks for their safe arrival. The Wang Kang festival to commemorate the dead is also held here. Just to the east of here, **Jalan Padungan** has some of Kuching's finest Chinese shophouses. Most were built during the rubber boom of the 1920s and have been

Little Lebanon **8**
See Good **6**
The Junk **16**
The Living Room **1**
Tom's **10**
Top Spot Food Court **9**
Waterfront Café **11**

restored. There are also some great coffee shops in this quarter of town. Further east still, the kitsch statue of the **Great Cat of Kuching** – the sort of thing to induce nightmares in the aesthetically inclined – mews at the junction of Jalan Padungan and Jalan Central.

The **Chinese History Museum** ① *T082-244232, daily 0900-1630, free,* stands on the waterfront opposite Tua Pek Kong temple. The museum documents the history of the Chinese in Sarawak, from the early traders of the 10th century to the waves of Chinese immigrants in the 19th century. The exhibits are now a little worse for wear. The building itself is simple, with a flat roof, and shows English colonial influences. It was completed in 1912 and became the court for the Chinese population of Kuching. The Third Rajah was keen that the Chinese, like other ethnic groups, should settle disputes within their community in their own way and he encouraged its establishment. From 1912 until 1921, when the Chinese court was dissolved, all cases pertaining to the Chinese were heard here in front of six judges elected from the local Chinese population. In 1993 it was handed over to the Sarawak Museum and was turned into the museum.

Hian Tien Shian Tee (Hong San) temple, at the junction of Jalan Carpenter and Jalan Wayang, was built in 1897.

The Moorish, gilt-domed **Masjid Bandaraya** (Old State Mosque) is near the market, on the west side of town; it was built in 1968 on the site of an old wooden mosque dating from 1852.

Civic Centre and Planetarium
① *Jln Taman Budaya, Mon-Thu 0915-1730, Sat 0915-1800, viewing platform 0900-1700. Planetarium shows, RM2 (6 shows daily); see www.planetarium-sarawak.org. Take bus No 14A, 14B or14C from Chim Lan Long Bus Station on Jln Masjid.*

On the south side of the river the extraordinary-looking Civic Centre is Kuching's stab at the avant garde. As well as the viewing platform for panoramas of Kuching, the Civic Centre complex houses an art gallery with temporary exhibits (mainly of Sarawakian art), a restaurant and a pub-cum-karaoke bar one floor down, together with a public library. Malaysia's first planetarium is also within the complex. **Sultan Iskandar Planetarium** has a 15-m dome and a 170-seat auditorium.

Astana
① *Take a sampan across the river from the Pangkalan Batu jetty next to Square Tower on the waterfront to the Astana and fort, around RM0.30 with other passengers one way. The boats can also be hired privately for around RM30 per hr.*

Apart from the Sarawak Museum, the White Rajahs bequeathed several other architectural monuments to Kuching. The Astana, a variant of the usual spelling *istana* (palace), was built in 1870, two years after Charles Brooke took over from his uncle. It stands on the north bank of the river almost opposite the market on Jalan Gambier. The Astana was hurriedly completed for the arrival of Charles' new bride (and cousin), Margaret. It was originally three colonial-style bungalows, with wooden shingle roofs, the largest being the central bungalow with the reception room, dining and drawing rooms. The crenellated tower on the east end was added in the 1880s at her request. Charles Brooke is said to have cultivated betel nut in a small plantation behind the Astana, so that he could offer fresh betel nut to visiting Dayak chiefs. Today, it's the official residence of the governor of Sarawak and is only open to the public on Hari Raya Puasa, a day of prayer and celebration to mark the end of Ramadan (see page 33). To the west of the Astana, in the traditionally Malay area, are many old wooden kampong houses.

A ceramic inheritance

Family wealth and status in Sarawak was traditionally measured in ceramics. In the tribal longhouses upriver, treasured heirlooms include ancient glass beads, brass gongs and cannons and Chinese ceramic pots and beads (such as those displayed in the Sarawak Museum). They were often used as currency and dowries. Spencer St John, the British consul in Brunei, mentions using beads as currency on his 1858 expedition to Gunung Mulu. Jars (*pesaka*) had more practical applications; they were (and still are) used for storing rice, brewing *tuak* (rice wine) or for keeping medicines.

Their value was dependent on their rarity: brown jars, emblazoned with dragon motifs, are more recent and quite common while olive-glazed dusun jars, dating from the 15th-17th centuries, are rare. The Kelabit people, who live in the highlands around Bario, in particular treasure the dragon jars. Although some of the more valuable antique jars have found their way to the Sarawak Museum, many magnificent jars remain in the Iban and other tribal longhouses along the

Skrang, Rejang and Baram rivers. Many are covered by decoratively carved wooden lids.

Chinese contact and trade with the north coast of Borneo has gone on for at least a millennium, possibly two. Chinese Han pottery fragments and coins have been discovered near the estuary of the Sarawak River and, from the seventh century, China is known to have been importing birds' nests and jungle produce from Brunei (which then encompassed all of north Borneo), in exchange for ceramic wares. Chinese traders arrived in the Nanyang (South Seas) in force from the 11th century, particularly during the Sung and Yuan dynasties. Some Chinese pottery and porcelain even bore Arabic and Koranic inscriptions – the earliest such dish is thought to have been produced in the mid-14th century. In the 1500s, as China's trade with the Middle East grew, many such Islamic wares were traded and the Chinese emperors presented them as gifts to seal friendships with the Muslim world, including Malay and Indonesian kingdoms.

Fort Margherita
ⓘ *Jln Sapi; to get to the fort, see Astana, above.*

Not far away from the Astana, past the Kubu jetty, is this fort. It was also built by Rajah Charles Brooke in 1879 and named after Ranee Margaret, although there was a fort on the site from 1841 when James Brooke became Rajah. It commanded the river approach to Kuching, but was never used defensively, although its construction was prompted by a near-disastrous river-borne attack on Kuching by the Ibans of the Rejang in 1878. Even so, until the Second World War a sentry was always stationed on the lookout post on top of the fort; his job was to pace up and down all night and shout 'All's well' on the hour every hour until 0800. The news that nothing was awry was heard at the Astana and the government offices.

After 1946, Fort Margherita was first occupied by the Sarawak Rangers and was finally converted into a police museum in 1971. However, in 2008 this museum was closed and the exhibits moved back into police custody. Visitors can't enter the fort, but can have a look at the exterior.

Towering above Fort Margherita is Sarawak's new **State Assembly** building (Dewan Undangan Negeri). In a break from the norm, this huge structure resembles a cross between Brunei's Bolkiah Mosque and an Apollo moon lander. Borneo's take on avant garde, it's a fitting tribute to the rapid modernization of East Malaysia.

The **Malay kampongs** along the riverside next to Fort Margherita are seldom visited by tourists, despite their beautiful examples of traditional and modern Malay architecture.

Petra Jaya

The new **State Mosque** is situated north of the river at Petra Jaya and was completed in 1968. It stands on the site of an older mosque dating from the mid-19th century and boasts an interior of Italian marble.

Kuching's architectural heritage did not end with the White Rajahs; the town's modern buildings are often based on local styles. The new administration centre is in Petra Jaya: the **Bapak** (father) **Malaysia** building is named after the first prime minister of Malaysia and houses government offices; the **Dewan Undangan Negeri** (State Legislative Assembly of Sarawak) next door, is based on the Minangkabau style. Kuching's latest building is the ostentatious **Masjid Jamek**. Also in Petra Jaya, like a space launch overlooking the road to Damai Peninsula, is the **Cat Museum** ① *daily 0900-1700 (closed public holidays), free, camera RM3, take Petra Jaya Transport No 2C or 2D – tell the driver where you want to go, as the museum is a 15-min walk from the nearest bus stop*, which houses everything you ever wanted to know about cats.

Nearby, the **Timber Museum** ① *Wisma Sumber Alam (next to the stadium), Mon-Thu 0800-1300 and 1400-1700, Fri 0830-1140 and 1400-1700, closed public holidays, take a taxi, RM15 as there is no bus*, is meant to look like a log. It was built in the mid-1980s to try to engender a better understanding of Sarawak's timber industry. The museum, which has many excellent exhibits and displays, toes the official line about forest management and presents facts and figures on the timber trade, along with a detailed history of its development in Sarawak. The exhibition provides an insight into all the different forest types. It has information on and examples of important commercial tree species, jungle produce and many traditional wooden implements. The final touch is an air-conditioned forest and wildlife diorama, complete with leaf litter; all the trees come from the Rejang River area. A research library is attached to the museum. While it sidesteps the more delicate moral issues involved in the modern logging business, its detractors might do worse than to brush up on some of the less emotive aspects of Sarawak's most important industry.

Around Kuching → *For listings, see pages 320-331. Colour map 3, C1.*

Semenggoh Orang-Utan Sanctuary

① *Daily 0800-1245, 1400-1615, RM3. The bus service to the sanctuary has been reduced to 2 services a day, departing in front of the Kuching Waterfront Lodge at 0730 and 1330 (one way RM2.60). However, return times are highly erratic and visitors often have to hire a taxi to get back. A good alternative to the public bus is the efficient shuttle service that departs from the waterfront in front of the Old Courthouse at 0800 (returns 1020) and 1400 (returns 1620). RM25 including admission to the sanctuary. A taxi to the sanctuary costs RM45 one way plus RM10 per hour of waiting time. Feeding times 0900-1000 and 1500-1600.*

Semenggoh, 32 km from Kuching, on the road to Serian, became the first forest reserve in Sarawak when the 800 ha of jungle were set aside by Rajah Vyner Brooke in 1920. They were turned into a wildlife rehabilitation centre for monkeys, orang-utans, honey bears and hornbills in 1975. All were either orphaned as a result of logging or were confiscated, having been kept illegally as pets. The aim has been to reintroduce as many of the animals as possible to their natural habitat. In late 1998 many of the functions which previously attracted visitors to Semenggoh were transferred to the Matang Wildlife Centre (see page 315). However, there are a few trails around the park including a plankwalk and a botanical research centre, dedicated to jungle plants with medicinal applications and orang-utans still visit the centre for food handouts. Even when Semenggoh was operating as an orang-utan rehabilitation centre, it did not compare with Sepilok in Sabah, which is an altogether more sophisticated affair.

Gunung Penrissen → Altitude: 1329 m.

This is the highest peak in the mountain range south of Kuching running along the Kalimantan border. The mountain was visited by naturalist Alfred Wallace in 1855. Just over 100 years later the mountain assumed a strategic role in Malaysia's *Konfrontasi* with Indonesia (see page 384) – there is a Malaysian military post on the summit. Gunung Penrissen is accessible from Kampong Padawan; it lies a few kilometres south of Anna Rais, right on the border with Kalimantan. It is a difficult mountain to climb requiring two long days, but affords views over Kalimantan to the south and Kuching and the South China Sea to the north. Prospective climbers are advised to see the detailed trail guide in John Briggs' *Mountains of Malaysia*. The book is usually available in Sarawak Museum bookshop. It's 100 km from Kuching to Anna Rais. There are no buses and visitors need to charter a taxi.

Around Kuching

Sleeping
Damai Puri Resort 2
Permai Rainforest Resort 1
Santubong Kuching Resort 3

Gunung Gading National Park

① *T082-735144, RM10. The park is 5 mins' drive from Lundu; taxis charge around RM10. From Kuching take STC (Green) Bus No EP7 (RM10) to Lundu from the Regional Bus Terminal (3rd mile).*

This park was constituted in 1983 and covers 4104 ha either side of Sungai Lundu, 65 km northwest of Kuching. There are some marked trails, the shortest of which takes about two hours and leads to a series of waterfalls on the Sungai Lundu. Gunung Gading and Gunung Perigi summit treks take seven to eight hours; it is possible to camp at the summit. The park is made up of a complex of mountains with several dominant peaks including Gunung Gading (906 m). The rafflesia, the world's largest flower (see box, page 424), is found here but if you're keen to see one in bloom, phone the Park HQ first, since it has a very short flowering period.

Lundu and Sematan

① *To get there, bus 2 goes from Kuching to Bau from where there are buses to Lundu (2 hrs). STC Bus No EP7 goes directly to Lundu from the Regional Express Terminal (3rd mile) in Kuching.*

These villages have beautiful, lonely beaches and there is a collection of deserted islands off Sematan. One of the islands, **Talang Talang**, is a turtle sanctuary and permission to visit it must be obtained from the **Forest Department** ① *Wisma Sumba Alam, Jln Stadium, Petra Jaya, Kuching, T082-442180, www.sarawakforestry.com.*

Bau

① *Take STC bus No 2 from Jln Masjid; the journey takes 1 hr. Tour companies also organize trips.*

About 60 km from Kuching is **Bau**, which had its five minutes of fame during the 19th century as a small mining town. Today, it is a market town and administrative centre. There are several caves close by; the **Wind Cave** is a popular picnic spot. The **Fairy Cave**, about 10 km from Bau, is larger and more impressive, with a small Chinese shrine in the main chamber and varied vegetation at the entrance. A torch is essential. Another reason to go to Bau is to see the Bindayuh celebrating their Gawai Padi, a festival with animistic roots that thanks the gods for an abundant rice harvest. Singing, dancing, massive consumption of *tuak* (rice wine) and colourful shamans make this a highlight. It's held at the end of May and beginning of June. Ask at the tourist office in Kuching for details.

Kubah National Park

① *T082-845033, but the National Parks and Wildlife Booking Office in Kuching, see page 305, is likely to be more helpful; RM10.*

This is a mainly sandstone, siltstone and shale area, 20 km west of Kuching, covering some 2230 ha with three mountains: **Gunung Serapi**, **Gunung Selang** and **Gunung Sendok**. There are at least seven waterfalls and bathing pools. Flora include mixed dipterocarp and *kerangas* (heath) forest; the park is also rich in palms (93 species) and wild orchids. Wildlife includes bearded pig, mouse deer, hornbills and numerous species of amphibians and reptiles. Unfortunately for visitors here, Kubah's wildlife tends to stay hidden; it's not really a park for 'wildlife encounters'.

There are four marked trails, ranging from 30 minutes to three hours; one, the **Rayu Trail**, passes through rainforest that contains a number of bintangor trees (believed to contain two chemicals which have showed some evidence of being effective against HIV). Visitors may be able to see some trees which have been tapped for this potential rainforest remedy. The park is easy to visit as a day trip, but there is no scheduled bus service. Visitors will need to charter a taxi (one-way RM45) or minivan from Kuching. Travel agents also arrange tours.

The **Matang Wildlife Centre** ① *T082-225012; animal feeding times vary. Animals to see at the feedings include orang-utans, sambar deer, and crocodiles*, is part of the Kubah National Park. It houses endangered wildlife in spacious enclosures which are purposefully placed in the rainforest. The key attraction are the orang-utans, which are rehabilitated for release back into the wild. Other animals include sambar deer, sun bears, civets and bear cats. There is an information centre and education programmes, which enable visitors to learn more about the conservation of Sarawak's wildlife. The centre has also established a series of trails.

Pulau Satang Besar
① *Ask at the Visitor Information Centre, overlooking the Padang, Kuching, T082-410942, for departures from Santubong or Kampong Telaga Air.*
North of Kampong Telaga Air, Pulau Satang Besar has been designated a **Turtle Sanctuary** to protect the green turtles that come ashore here to lay their eggs. It's an excellent spot for snorkelling.

Tanjung Datu National Park
This is the newest and smallest park in Sarawak, first gazetted in 1994, at the westernmost tip, 100 km from Kuching. It is covered with mixed dipterocarp forest, rich flora and fauna, and beautiful beaches with crystal clear seas and coral reefs. To get there, take a bus to Lundu (see Gunung Gading National Park, page 314) and on to Sematan. At the jetty in Sematan, hire a boat (40 minutes, RM100 to hire the whole boat; there is no scheduled service). The seas are too rough for the journey between October and February. The boat will drop you off at the Park HQ's jetty. You can also jump in a boat to Teluk Melano (more regular) from Sematan (about 40 minutes), and then hire a 10-minute boat trip to the park.

Damai Peninsula → *For listings, see pages 320-331. Colour map 3, C1.*

The Peninsula, 35 km north of Kuching, is located at the west mouth of the Santubong River and extends northwards as far as **Mount Santubong**, a majestic peak of 810 m. Its attractions include the **Sarawak Cultural Village**, trekking up Mount Santubong, sandy beaches, a golf course, adventure camp and three resorts which are particularly good value off season when promotional rates are available.

From Kuching, it's a 40-minute bus ride north to **Buntal**. Take bus No 26 from the Petra Jaya terminal. Buses depart every 40 minutes throughout the day. From here, they wind through the foothills to Santubong.

Santubong and Buntal
The village of Santubong itself, located at the mouth of the Santubong River, is small and quiet. Formerly a fishing village, most of the villagers now work in one of the nearby resorts. However, some fishing still goes on, and the daily catch is still sold every morning at the quayside. Nearby are two or three Chinese-run grocery stores and a coffee shop. The rest of the village is made up of small houses strung out along the road, built in the Malay tradition on stilts – many are wooden and painted in bright colours. Another village here is Buntal, which is just off the Kuching-Santubong road and is popular with local Kuchingites, who come to visit at the weekends for the seafood restaurants.

Sarawak Cultural Village

ⓘ T082-846108, www.scv.com.sg. Daily 0900-1730, cultural shows at 1130 and 1600 (45 mins). RM60, children (6-12 years) RM30.00, prices include cultural show.

The Sarawak Cultural Village (Kampong Budaya Sarawak), 35 km north of Kuching, was the brainchild of the **Sarawak Development Corporation** which built Sarawak's 'living museum' at a cost of RM9.5 million to promote and preserve Sarawak's cultural heritage, opening it in 1990. With increasing numbers of young tribal people being tempted from their longhouses into the modern sectors of the economy, many of Sarawak's traditional crafts have begun to die out. The Cultural Village set out to teach the old arts and crafts to new generations. For the State Development Corporation, the concept had the added appeal of creating a money-spinning 'Instant Sarawak' for the benefit of tourists lacking the time or inclination to head into the jungle. While it is rather contrived, the Cultural Village has been a great success and contains some superb examples of traditional architecture. It should be on the sightseeing agenda of every visitor to Kuching, if only to provide an introduction to the cultural traditions of all the main ethnic groups in Sarawak.

Each tribal group is represented by craftsmen and women who produce handicrafts and practise traditional skills in houses built to carefully researched design specifications. Many authentic everyday articles have been collected from longhouses all over Sarawak. In one case the village has served to preserve a culture – pickled – that is already effectively dead: today the Melanau people all live in Malay-style kampongs, but a magnificent traditional wooden Melanau house has been built at the Cultural Village and is now the only such building in Sarawak. Alongside it there is a demonstration of traditional sago processing. A resident Melanau craftsman makes sickness images (*blum*), each representing the spirit of an illness, which were floated downriver in tiny boats as part of the healing ritual.

There are also Bidayuh, Iban and Orang Ulu longhouses, depicting the lifestyles of each group. In each there are textile or basket weavers, woodcarvers or swordmakers. There are exhibits of beadwork, bark clothing, and *tuak* (rice wine) brewing. At the Penan hut there is a demonstration of blowpipe making and visitors are invited to test their hunting skills. There is a Malay house and even a Chinese farmhouse with a pepper garden alongside. The tour of the houses, seven in all (you can collect a stamp from each one for your passport) is capped by an Andrew Lloyd Webber-style cultural show which is expertly choreographed, if rather ersatz. It is held in the air-conditioned onsite theatre.

Special application must be made to attend heritage centre workshops where courses can be requested in various crafts such as woodcarving, mat weaving or batik painting; they also run intensive one-day and three- to four-day courses. There is a restaurant and craft shop, **Sarakraf**, at the village.

A regular shuttle bus service operates from the **Grand Margherita** in Kuching to resort hotels and the Cultural Village (RM12 each way – return RM20; sometimes it's cheaper to buy both the entrance ticket and bus tickets from tour agencies or the Grand Margherita where they often have special offers). These run from 0730 to 2200; the last bus back from Damai is at 2100.

The Cultural Village is also the venue for the fabulous annual **Rainforest Music Festival** ⓘ www.rainforestmusic-borneo.com, which takes place sometime between June and August. There are foodstalls and jamming sessions are held in the different sections, culminating in a great evening show.

The Cultural Village employs 140 people, including dancers, who earn around RM400 a month and take home the profits from handicraft and *tuak* sales.

The Penan: museum pieces for the 21st century?

Economic progress has altered many Sarawakians' lifestyles in recent years; the oil and natural gas sector now offers many employment prospects and upriver tribespeople have been drawn into the logging industry. But it is logging that has directly threatened the 9000-strong Penan tribe's traditional way of life.

Sarawak's nomadic hunter-gatherers emerged as 'the noble savages' of the late 20th century, as their blockades of logging roads drew world attention to their plight. In 1990, Prince Charles's remarks about Malaysia's "collective genocide" against the Penan prompted an angry letter of protest from former Prime Minister Dr Mahathir Mohamad. He is particularly irked by western environmentalists – especially Bruno Manser, who lived with the Penan in the late 1980s. "We don't need any more Europeans who think they have a white man's burden to shoulder", Dr Mahathir said.

Malaysia wants to integrate the Penan into mainstream society, on the grounds that it is morally wrong to condemn them to a life expectancy of 40 years, when the average Malaysian lives to well over 60. "There is nothing romantic about these helpless, half-starved, disease-ridden people", Dr Mahathir said. The government has launched resettlement programmes to transform the Penan from hunters into fishermen and farmers. One of these new longhouses can be visited in Mulu at Batu Bungan (see page 371). It has failed to engender much enthusiasm from the Penan, although 4000 to 5000 Penan have now been resettled. Environmentalists countered that the Penan should be given the choice, but, the government asks, what choice do they have if they have only lived in the jungle?

The Sarawak Cultural Village, opened by Dr Mahathir, offered a compromise of sorts – but the Penan had the last laugh. One tribal elder, Apau Madang, and his grandson were paid to parade in loincloths and make blowpipes at the Penan hut while tourists took their snapshots. The arrangement did not last long as they did not like posing as artefacts in Sarawak's 'living museum'. They soon complained of boredom and within months had wandered back to the jungle where they could at least wear jeans and T-shirts. Today, the Penan hut is staffed by other Orang Ulu. There are thought to be only 400 Penan still following their traditional nomadic way of life.

Gunung Santubong → Altitude: 810 m.

Situated on the Santubong Peninsula, Gunung Santubong's precipitous southwestern side provides a moody backdrop to Damai Beach. The distinctive mountain is most accessible from the east side, where there is a clear ridge trail to the top. There are two trails to the summit; one begins opposite the **Palm Beach Seafood Restaurant and Resort**, about 2.5 km before the **Holiday Inn Damai Beach**. The conical peak – from which there are spectacular views – can be reached in seven to nine hours (the last stretch is a tough scramble). Take your own food and water supplies. Guides are not necessary (but can be provided); check with hotel recreation counters or at the **Santubong Mountain Trek Canteen** ① *T082-846153*. The official Damai guide provides a more detailed description of the trek.

There is a bus to Damai Beach. Alternatively take a minivan from the open-air market on Jalan Masjid, RM5; these only depart when full. A taxi to Damai should cost around RM45 one way.

Kuching Wetlands National Park

Designated in 2002 this relatively small national park encompasses 6610 ha of dense mangrove and heath forest where the Sibu and Salak Rivers meet the South China Sea. The area is rich in wildlife and an important site for a range of water birds, crocodiles and primates, including the proboscis monkey. One of park's truly distinctive inhabitants is the irrawaddy dolphin, a small slow swimming mammal that lives in shallow seas – and often far up major rivers into freshwater areas – throughout Southeast Asia. The dolphin is rare almost everywhere, but the Kuching wetlands is one of the best places to see them in Malaysia.

Several Kuching tour agencies offer dolphin and wildlife spotting boat tours of the park's waterways. These also run in the evening, when it's easier to spot crocodiles and fireflies. Most tours depart from Santubong Boat Club or Damai Beach; from here it's only a 20-30 minute boat ride to the park. A recommended tour operator is **CPH Travel Agency** ① *70 Jln Padungan, Kuching, T082-243708, www.cphtravel.com.my*.

Bako National Park → *For listings, see pages 320-331. Colour map 3, C1.*

Bako is situated on the beautiful Muara Tebas Peninsula, a former river delta which has been thrust above sea level. Its sandstone cliffs, which are patterned and streaked with iron deposits, have been eroded to produce a dramatic coastline with secluded coves and beaches and rocky headlands. Millions of years of erosion by the sea has resulted in the formation of wave-cut platforms, honeycomb weathering, solution pans, arches and sea stacks. Bako's most distinctive feature is the westernmost headland – **Tanjung Sapi** – a 100-m-high sandstone plateau, which is unique in Borneo. Established in 1957, Bako was Sarawak's first national park. It is very small (2742 ha) but it has an exceptional variety of flora and guaranteed wildlife spotting. Its beaches and accessible trails make it a wonderful place to relax for a few days.

Ins and outs

Getting there Bako lies 37 km north of Kuching, an hour's bus journey (RM2.50) from Petra Jaya terminal. Take the orange bus No 6 that leaves every hour between 0700 and 1800 from just below Electra House on Lebuh Market to Kampong Bako. The bus continues just beyond to the Bako NP boat jetty where the driver turns around and heads back to Kuching. There are also minibuses (no fixed schedule) from Lebuh Market, RM4. The last buses returning to **Kuching** depart around 1700 – ask the driver on your way to Bako to confirm the day's last bus. From Kampong Bako, charter a private boat to Sungai Assam (30 mins), which is a short walk from the Park HQ, RM47 per boat each way – ask price before boarding (up to 5 people). Travelling by car, the drive from Kuching takes about 40 minutes. Parking is safe at Kampong Bako and the park offices, from where you rent a boat (see above).

Getting around It also possible to hire boats around the park: speed boats (for up to six) charge a negotiable rate, usually around RM300 per day, good for exploring the park's beaches and the island of Pulau Lakei.

Tourist information On arrival visitors are required to register at the Park HQ; the information centre next door has a small exhibition on geology and flora and fauna within the park. Visitors can ask to see a 40-minute introductory video to the park. The Park HQ has a canteen.

To obtain the necessary permits, contact the the **National Parks and Wildlife Booking Office** ① *Tourist Information Centre, the Old Courthouse, Jln Tun Abang Hj Openg,*

T082-248088, F248087, Mon-Fri 0800-1700; or www.sarawakforestry.com, RM10, children and students RM5, professional photography and filming RM300.

Flora and fauna

There are seven separate types of vegetation in Bako. These include mangroves (*bakau* is the most common stilt-rooted mangrove species), swamp forest and heath forest, known as *kerangas*, an Iban word meaning 'land on which rice cannot grow'. Pitcher plants (*Nepenthes ampullaria*) do however grow in profusion on the sandy soil. There is also mixed dipterocarp rainforest (the most widespread forest type in Sarawak, characterized by its 30- to 40-m-high canopy), beach forest, and *padang* vegetation, comprising scrub and bare rock from which there are magnificent views of the coast. The rare *daun payang* (umbrella palm) is also found in Bako Park; it is a litter-trapping plant as its large fronds catch falling leaves from the trees above and funnel them downwards where they eventually form a thick organic mulch enabling the plant to survive on otherwise infertile soil. There are also wild durian trees in the forest, which can take up to 60 years to bear fruit.

Bako is one of the few areas in Sarawak inhabited by the rare proboscis monkey (*Nasalis larvatus*), known by Malays as Orang Belanda (Dutchmen) or even Pinocchio of the Jungle, because of their long noses (see page 535). Bako is home to approximately 150 proboscis monkeys. They are most often seen in the early morning or at dusk in the Teluk Assam and Teluk Delima areas (at the far west side of the park, closest to the headquarters) or around Teluk Paku (a 45-minute walk from the Park HQ). Another good place to spot them is on the beach when the tide is out and they come down, so you can see them up close.

The park also has resident populations of squirrels, mouse deer, sambar deer, wild pigs, long-tailed macaques, flying lemur, silver leaf monkeys and palm civet cats. Teluk Assam,

Bako National Park trails

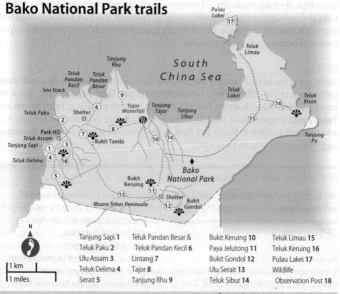

Tanjung Sapi 1	Teluk Pandan Besar &	Bukit Keruing 10	Teluk Limau 15
Teluk Paku 2	Teluk Pandan Kecil 6	Paya Jelutong 11	Teluk Keruing 16
Ulu Assam 3	Lintang 7	Bukit Gondol 12	Pulau Lakei 17
Teluk Delima 4	Tajor 8	Ulu Serait 13	Wildlife
Serait 5	Tanjung Rhu 9	Teluk Sibur 14	Observation Post 18

in the area around the Park HQ, is one of the best places for birdwatching: over 150 species have been recorded in the park, including pied and black hornbills. Large numbers of migratory birds come to Bako between September and November. Other inhabitants of the park are the blue fiddler crab, which has one big claw and is forever challenging others to a fight, and mudskippers, evolutionary throwbacks (resembling half-fish, half-frog), which are common in mangrove areas.

Also in the park there are two species of otter: the oriental small clawed otter and the hairy nosed otter (the best area to see them is at Teluk Assam). The Bornean bearded pig is the largest mammal found Bako and is usually seen snuffling around the Park HQ. There are many lizards too, the largest being the water monitor which is often found near the accommodation. Snakes occasionally seen include the poisonous bright green Wagler's pit viper and sometimes pythons and tree snakes on night walks. Nocturnal animals include flying lemur, pangolin, mouse deer, bats, tarsier, slow loris and palm civet (the beach by the Park HQ is a great place for a night-time stroll).

Treks

There's a good range of well-marked trails throughout the park – over 30 km in total; all paths are colour coded, corresponding to the map available from Park HQ. The shortest trek is the steep climb to the top of **Tanjung Sapi**, overlooking Telok Assam, with good views of Gunung Santubong, on the opposite Peninsula, across Tanjung Sipang, to the west. The 3.5-km trek to Tajor Waterfall is among the most popular, with varied walking (including some steep climbs), spectacular views and a chance of a refreshing swim at the waterfall. A few meters further on you reach a secluded beach.

The longest trek is to Telok Limau; a five- to seven-hour walk through a variety of terrain. You can arrange with Park HQ to lay on a boat to bring you back (around RM200). Some trails are temporarily closed for maintenance – always check with Park HQ. Full day treks and overnight camping expeditions can be arranged. There are plankwalkways with shelters at intervals to provide quiet watching spots, particularly required for viewing the proboscis monkey in the early morning.

Beaches

There are seven beaches around the park, but some are rather inaccessible, with steep paths down to the cliffs. The best swimming beach is at **Telok Pandan Kecil**, about 1½ hours' walk, northeast from the Park HQ. It is also possible to swim at **Telok Assam** and **Telok Paku**. Enquire about jellyfish at the Park HQ before swimming in the sea; it is advisable not to swim in March and April. In the monsoon season, between November and February, the sea can be rough.

⦿ Kuching and around listings

For Sleeping and Eating price codes and other relevant information, see Essentials pages 25-30.

⬤ Sleeping

Kuching *p304, map p308*
It is possible to negotiate over room rates and many of the hotels offer special deals. There is

a good choice of international-standard hotels in Kuching. For an additional listing of hotels and resorts with websites see the Sarawak Tourism Board site, www.sarawaktourism.com.

Recent years have seen unprecedented growth in mid- to budget-priced accommodation and Kuching now has the best selection of guesthouses in Malaysia. With so many options to choose from, finding a bed is rarely a problem. However, guesthouses are booked solid for the annual Rainforest Music Festival and finding somewhere to sleep could be problematic.

For an alternative to the usual hotels and guesthouses, you could try a **Homestay programme**, see page 323.

L-AL Hilton, Jln Tunku Abdul Rahman, T082-248200, www.hilton.com. Minimalistic but very stylish accommodation and the best hotel facilities in town, with many restaurants, gym, tennis courts and pool. Some major discounts make this great value. Good for a treat after a tough jungle trek!

L-AL Riverside Majestic, Jln Tunku Abdul Rahman, T082-247777, www.riversidemajestic.com. Despite a slightly dated feel, this business hotel has spacious rooms and suites. Views blocked by luxury suites on the lower floors. Located in a shopping centre with a cinema.

AL-A Grand Continental, Jln Ban Hock, T082-230399, www.ghihotels.com. Small pool and business centre. Rooms have TV, IDD, minibar and coffee-making facilities.

AL-A Grand Margherita, Jln Tunku Abdul Rahman, T082-423111, contact@gmh.my. Standard business fare with weekend discounts. More expensive rooms have good river views. Rooms are comfortable, with a faux bamboo theme and have bathroom with bathtub, cable TV, safety box and fridge. There is a pool at the back of the hotel and a bar with live music, popular with expats at the weekend.

AL-A Merdeka Palace, Jln Tun Haji Openg, T082-258000, www.merdekapalace.com. Central location overlooking playing field. Pool, health club and business facilities, and broadband in every room. The 214 rooms have minibar and satellite TV. 6 bars and restaurants onsite. Great value. Recommended.

A-B Borneo, 30 Jln Tabuan, T082-244122, F254848. Large and cheerless place, more popular with domestic travellers than with foreign visitors. Rooms are a little musty, and

those with a view (not spectacular by any means) are more expensive. Rooms have a/c, TV and bathroom with bathtub. The hotel is located a good 10-min walk from the centre.

B Brookes Terrace, 231 Jln Abell, T082-427008, www.brookesterrace.org. Run by the friendly font of local knowledge, Seamus, this boutique guesthouse has a relaxed atmosphere, a good mix of local and eccentric international decor. Rooms are comfortable, spacious, and have LCD TV, Wi-Fi and attached bathroom. Highly recommended.

B Tune, Jln Borneo, T082-238221, www.tunehotels.com. Chain based on budget airline model; the earlier you book, the cheaper the room. Rooms are spotless, a little sterile, but comfortable. A/c, towels and Wi-Fi are all chargeable add-ons.

B-C Kuching Waterfront Lodge, Main Bazaar, T082-231111, www.kuchingwaterfront lodge.com. Located along the bustling main bazaar, this hotel is filled with artefacts from around the region with beautifully carved tables and tribal door frames, a stay here will not be short on atmosphere. The dorms are a little dark, as are some of the double rooms on the top floor. Slightly overpriced.

B-D 1-2-1 Lodge, Lot 121, 33 Section KTLD, Jln Tabuan, T082-428 121, www.lodge121. com. Calm and colourful guesthouse with popular TV room, communal dining area and the cheapest laundry in town. Rooms are simple and comfortable, although some lack natural light. All rooms have clean shared bathrooms and toilets and there are numerous washbasins scattered around to prevent lengthy morning queues. Wi-Fi throughout. Owner Henry Lim is a good source of local knowledge. Recommended.

B-D Beds Guesthouse, Lot 91, Section 50, Jln Padungan, T082-424229, www.bedsguest house.com. This small and friendly place has a convivial and comfortable social area, a dining room at the back which is a popular spot for a glass of longhouse *tuak* in the evenings, and free internet and Wi-Fi access throughout. Rooms are comfortable and stylish and kept spotlessly clean. Free breakfast. Highly recommended.

B-D Berambih Lodge, 104 Jln Ewe Hai, T082-231589, www.berambih.com. With its faux longhouse interior and relaxed communal area, this guesthouse is a relaxed option in the heart of town. Rooms are simple and all have a/c, but could do with a good clean. Breakfast included in the price and free Wi-Fi throughout.

B-D Mr D's Bed and Breakfast, 26 Jln Carpenter, T082-248852, www.misterd bnb.com. Functional place with simple, somewhat dark rooms and dorms with shared bathroom. There is free Wi-Fi throughout and free breakfast as well as free tea and coffee.

B-D Singgahsana Lodge, 1 Lebuh Temple, T082-429277, www.singgahsana.com. Well-established guesthouse owned by Donald and Marina Tan whose travel photos from around the world adorn the corridors. Staff here are efficient and the hotel is a well-run and cheerful place with funky decor, a rooftop bar open until the wee hours and free internet and Wi-Fi access. There is a selection of rooms, from large dorms to the stylish and sensual honeymoon suites with attached bathroom. The double rooms on the ground floor have an interesting mezzanine level, although suffer from a lack of natural light.

C-D Borneo Bed & Breakfast, Jln Tabuan (next to Borneo Hotel), T082-231200, borneobedbreakfast@yahoo.com. One of the cheapest options in town, with run-down rooms and plenty of dark nooks and crannies. The family can offer fair value trips to their ancestral longhouse.

Gunung Penrissen *p313*

L-AL Hornbill Golf & Jungle Club, Borneo Highlands Resort, Jln Borneo Heights, Padawan, T082-578980, www.borneo highlands.com.my. As its name suggests, this is a mountain hideaway for golf fanatics. There are luxurious chalets and suites beautifully furnished with golfing touches like paintings of greens. The resort lies at 1000 m and so the weather is cooler and more spring-like. Golf, jungle treks and longhouse tours, a rabbit farm, spas and flower gardens.

Gunung Gading National Park *p314*

A-E National park accommodation. Bookings taken through the National Parks and Wildlife Parks Booking Office, the Old Courthouse, Jln Tun Abang Hj Openg, T082-248088, www.sarawakforestry.com. 2- and 3-bedroom chalets (around RM150 per chalet) and a hostel (RM15 per person). Camping for RM5 per head, although visitors need to bring their own equipment.

Lundu and Sematan *p314*

A Ocean Resort, 176 Siar Beach, Jln Pandan, Sematan, T082-452245 (Kuching office) or T011-225001 (resort). Some rooms in hostel, also 2-bedroom chalets with attached kitchen. The plushest place to stay in Sematan.

C Lundu Gadung, Lot 174 Lundu Town District, T082-735199. A/c, shared bathroom.

Kubah National Park *p314*

A-F National park accommodation. Bookable through the National Parks and Wildlife Booking Office in Kuching, Old Court-house, T082-248088 or www.sarawak forestry.com. There are fan chalets (RM150), an 8-room hostel (RM15.75) and 5 huge bungalows at the Park HQ with full kitchen facilities, 4 beds (2 rooms), a/c, hot water, TV and veranda (RM225 for the whole chalet). Bring your own food.

Damai Peninsula *p315, map p313*

AL-A Damai Puri Resort, Damai Beach, T082-846900, www.damaipuriresort.com. Just below a mansion belonging to the Sultan of Brunei, this upmarket hotel has 207 elegant rooms offering stunning views either of the rainforest and Gunung Santubong on one side or the sea on the other. Facilities include a pool, tennis courts and full spa centre. Discounts available.

A Permai Rainforest Resort, Pantai Damai Santubong, PO Box B91, Satok Post Office, T082-846487, www.permairainforest.com. At the foot of Mount Santubong, this resort markets itself as a low impact eco-resort, and offers lots of green and healthy activities from jungle trekking, night mangrove cruises to sea kayaking. There are comfy a/c treehouses, built on stilts 6 m above ground and with attached hot-water bathroom, or for those with less cash to splash, there are 23 comfortable a/c cabins a little closer to the earth. Camping is also available at RM12 per person. Cafeteria and tents and camping equipment for hire.

A Santubong Kuching Resort, Jln Pantai Damai, Santubong, PO Box 2364, T082-846888, www.santubongresort.com. Surrounded by the Damai golf course, 380 a/c rooms, restaurant, large pool surrounded by greenery, chalets with jacuzzis, tennis, basketball, volleyball, gym, mountain biking, etc. Nestling beneath Mount Santubong, this low-rise resort is particularly popular with golfers who come to hit a few rounds on the Arnold Palmer-designed golf course.

Bako National Park *p318, map p319*
All bookings to be made at the **National Parks and Wildlife Booking Office**, Kuching, T082-248088 (see page 305). **Hostels** have mattresses, kerosene stoves and cutlery; **lodges** offer electricity and fridges. Both have fans. Accommodation is always booked up, so you should reserve as early as possible before you want to go. Bako can be visited on a day trip, although this gives almost no opportunity to explore the parks trails – an overnight or 2 night, 3 days would be preferable. **Lodge**, RM157 per house, RM105 per room. **Hostel**, RM55 per room, RM15.75 per person, checkout time 1200.

Camping
Unless you are intending to trek to the other side of the park, it is not worth camping as monkeys steal anything left lying around and macaques can be aggressive. In addition, the smallest amount of rain turns the campsite into a swimming pool. It is, however, necessary to camp if you go to the beaches on the Northeast Peninsula. Tents can be hired for RM8 (sleeps 4); campsite RM5.

Homestays
It's worth checking with the Sarawak Tourist Board for their latest recommendations and advice on homestay programmes. In Kuching, the tourist offices recommend **Abas Homestay** in the Malay Kampong on the north side of the river. Accommodation is simple and clean and the homestay offers a great way to get a feel for local life. Contact Mr Hj Mahmud Hj Sabli, T019-857 1774, eduquest@streamyx.com.

In Kampung Santubong, there is the Santubong Village Homestay, T082-422495, www.santubonghomestay.com.my. This homestay offers a chance to learn about local cuisine, games and can help organize trips to local attractions. Prices include all meals.

● Eating

Kuching *p304, map p308*
Kuching, with all its old buildings and godowns along the river, seems made for open-air restaurants and cafés – but good ones are notably absent or have quite a high turnover. However, the town is not short of hawker centres. Local dishes worth looking out for include *umai* (a spicy salad of raw marinated fish with limes and shallots) and *laksa* (spicy noodles – a Malaysia-wide dish, but especially good here). Other distinctive Sarawakian ingredients are *midin* and *paku* – jungle fern shoots. See also Food glossaries, pages 660 and 661.

All the major hotels have Chinese restaurants; most open for lunch and dinner, closing in between. There are several cheap Indian Muslim restaurants along Lebuh India.

There is excellent seafood here. On Kampong Buntal are several seafood restaurants on stilts over the sea, 25 km north of Kuching, popular with Kuchingites.
ᵀᵀᵀ Serapi, Holiday Inn, Jln Tunku Abdul Rahman. Specializes in North Indian tandoori, good vegetable dishes, excellent selection of grills and seafood, imported steak, elegant surroundings. Recommended.

Tom's, 82 Jln Padungan, T082-247672. Tue-Sun 1130-2300. Excellent Western dishes including steaks and salads in a slick modern setting. There's a good beer garden out the back, ideal for a pre-dinner tipple.

Aha Organic, No 38, Lot 36, Section 47, Jln Tabuan, T082-420808. Mon-Sat 0830-1830. Smart place with a selection of tasty organic dishes including pastas, salads and excellent soups – the chicken ginseng soup is excellent. There is also a range of juices.

Hornbill Corner Café, 85 Jln Ban Hock. All-you-can-eat steamboat and barbecue, popular.

James Brooke Bistro and Café, on the waterfront, Main Bazaar, T082-412120. Facing the river near the Chinese museum. Open-air restaurant in fine Casablanca style, especially the mirrored bar. Fairly expensive but fine food from Malaysian curries to colonial favourites.

The Junk, 80 Jln Wayang, T082-259450. Closed Tue. Intimate little gem of a restaurant filled with antiques like old cash registers and lit by lanterns. Serves good but not fantastic pasta, steaks and other Western and Asian dishes. Recommended.

Khatulistiwa Café, Waterfront. In a circular pavilion-style building. Great views from this 24-hr café serving Malay and international dishes. There's an R&B music café on the 2nd floor open at 2300. Good breakfast.

Little Lebanon, The Old Courthouse, Jln Barrack, T082-233523. Small place with outdoor seating, *sheesha* pipes with a range of flavoured tobacco and a long menu of Lebanese favourites including kebabs, tabbouleh and hummus.

The Living Room, 23 Jln Tabuan, T082-426608. Stylish and sophisticated restaurant with a tranquil Japanese garden - a good spot to unwind. A wide range of cuisine, excellent fish and they can also order food from **Blah, Blah, Blah** next door, giving you more choice – just don't expect it to be cheap!

Lyn's Tandoori, Lot 62, 10G Lg 4, Jln Nanas. A worthwhile taxi ride from the centre for genuine North Indian tandoori cuisine, excellent naan. Recommended by locals. Closed Sun evenings.

Meisan, Grand Margherita, Jln Tunku Abdul Rahman. Dim sum, set lunch; Sun all-you-can-eat dim sum special, also Sichuan cuisine. Recommended.

Orchid Garden, Grand Margherita, Jln Tunku Abdul Rahman. Good breakfast and evening buffets, international and local cuisine. Recommended.

See Good, Jln Bukit Mata Kuching, behind MAS office. Closed 4th and 18th of every month. Extensive range of seafood. Strong-flavoured sauces, lots of herbs, extensive and exotic menu, unlimited free bananas. Recommended by locals.

Waterfront, Hilton Hotel, Jln Tunku Abdul Rahman. Reasonably priced for the venue. The best pizzas, and a family brunch buffet on Sun which is very popular.

Lok Thian, 1st floor, Bangunan Beesan, Jln Padungan, T082-331310. Good food, pleasant surroundings and excellent service. Booking advisable, especially at weekends.

Minsion Canteen, end of Jln Chan Chin Ann, on right. Speciality is *daud special* (noodles in herbal soup with chunks of chicken).

Waterfront Café, 2nd floor, Lot 10531, Blk 16, Jln Tun Tugah, T082-458311. Pleasant, clean eatery on the waterfront offering a range of Malay and Chinese dishes. Try local dishes such as *laksa Sarawak, umai* and *mee kolok*. Wi-Fi available.

Coffee shops

There are several Malay/Indian coffee shops on Lebuh India including **Madinah Café**, **Jubilee** and **Malaysia Restaurant**. Many Chinese coffee shops serve excellent *laksa* (breakfast) of curried coconut milk with a side plate of *sambal belacan* (chillied prawn paste). **Deli Café**, 88 Main Bazaar, T082-232788. Atmospheric Western-style café, fair sandwiches, snacks and pastries, good coffee. Try the excellent carrot cake. Free internet and plenty of magazines to read.

Foodstalls and food centres

There are great open-air informal places along the waterfront selling everything from kebabs to *ais cream goreng* (fried ice cream) that start opening towards the evening. It makes a great place for an evening meal. Most of the foodstalls are clustered around the Hilton end of the promenade selling Malay dishes and fruit juices (no alcohol). There are beautiful views of the river, accompanied by popular Malay love songs.

Some of the best food centres are located in the suburbs; a taxi is essential.
Batu Lintang open-air market, Jln Rock (to the south of town, past the hospital).
Chinese Food Centre, Jln Carpenter (opposite temple). Chinese foodstalls offering hot and sour soups, fish balls and more.
Hock Hong Garden, Jln Ban Hock, opposite Grand Continental. Finest hawker stall food in Kuching, little English spoken but definitely worth trying to be understood.
King's Centre, Jln Simpang Tiga (bus No 11 to get there). Large range of foodstalls, busy and not many tourists.
Kubah Ria Hawker stalls, Jln Tunku Abdul Rahman (on the road out of town towards Damai Beach, next to Satok Suspension Bridge). Specialities include *sop kambling* (mutton soup).
Petanak Central Market, Jln Petanak, above Kuching's early morning wet market. Light snacks, full seafood selection, good atmosphere, especially early in the morning.
Song Thieng Hai Food Centre, between Jln Padungan and Jln Ban Hock. Every type of noodle available.
The Spring Food Bazaar, Spring Mall, Jln Simpang Tiga. A clean and comfortable setting to eat with a selection of Asian favourites, from Japanese teppanyaki to Sarawak *laksa*.
Top Spot Food Court, Jln Bukit Mata Kuching, top floor of a car park. Range of stalls, popular.

Damai Peninsula *p315, map p313*
❦ **New Dolphin Seafood**, Kampong Buntal, T082-846441. Great position on the coast, about 5 km east of Santubon, good food, above-average prices.

❦ **Santubong Mountain Trek Canteen**, 5 mins' walk from hotels, T082-846153. Rice and noodle dishes, in nearby Buntal village there are excellent seafood restaurants.

Bako National Park *p318, map p319*
The canteen is open 0700-2100. It serves local food at reasonable prices and sells tinned foods and drinks. No need to take food, there is a good seafood restaurant near the jetty.

❶ Bars and clubs

Kuching *p304, map p308*
There are enough clubs, pubs and bars to keep most people reasonably happy. Clubs and discos usually have a cover charge, although there is often a drink or two thrown in with the price. Expect to pay RM10-15 for a beer and RM20-25 for spirits.

Most places have happy hours and 2-for-1 offers. Bars tend to close around 0100-0200, a little later in hotels. Most bars are along **Bukit Mata** off Jln Pandungan and along Jln Borneo next to the **Hilton**.

The main centres of evening entertainment are along **Jln Tunku Abdul Rahman, Jln Mendu, Jln Padungan** and **Jln Petanakin**, an area known locally as Travillion.
Cat City, Jln Chan Chin Ann (turn left at Pizza Hut). Open late. Happy hour 2030-2215, followed by live bands (usually Filipino) playing a mixture of Western rock covers and Malay and Chinese ballads.
Fire, Jln Petanak. New and friendly spot with a long happy hour and a crowd that grooves to Chinese dance music.
Grappa, 58 Jln Padungan. Stylish place popular with the young crowd. Music is famously loud and the beer some of the cheapest in town.
Marina Dangdut, Jln Ban Hock. Fri, Sat and evenings of public holidays. Top 40 hits and plenty of hip-shaking Indonesian and Malay *dangdut* to *joged* to.
Mojo@Denise, on the junction of Jln Padungan and Jln Abell. Wine and cocktail

bar with themed evenings including poetry nights and live music.

Music Café, 100 Jln Petanak, 1800-0200. Good spot to meet locals with live music, DJs and big jugs of beer.

Monsoon, Riverside Complex, Jln Tunku Abdul Rahman. Balcony jutting out over the river. Good mix of locals and tourists.

Rajang Lobby Lounge, Grand Margherita. Small but popular and with plenty of good drinks promotions.

Ruaikitai Tribal Café and Restaurant, 3 Jln Green Hill, T019-8056107, peter@pegari.com.my. Iban local Peter Jaban runs this cool café/bar. Good decor, rockin' music and tasty food make this a good evening venue. There's sometimes a free welcome *tuak* (fiery local stuff) for patrons. Peter also runs tours to longhouses, including the Skrang river, and aims to keep trips as authentic and rugged as possible.

Senso, Hilton Hotel. The best cocktails and good live music, but drinks are pricey.

Tribes, downstairs at Grand Margherita. Open 1600-0100. Ethnic food, tribal decor and a variety of live music.

Damai Peninsula *p315, map p313*
Gecko at Damai Puri Inn, Damai Beach. Lovely tropical-style bar with plenty of comfy seats and a good selection of drinks. Simple Asian and Western snacks served.

⊕ Entertainment

Kuching *p304, map p308*
Cinemas
Riverside Cineplex, Riverside Complex, Jln Tunku Abdul Rahman, in the basement of Riverside Majestic, T082-427061. Check local press for programme details.
Star Cineplex, Level 9, Medan Pelita, top floor of car park on Temple St.

Cultural shows
Cultural Village, Damai Beach. Daily 1130 and 1600. Cultural shows, with stylized and expertly choreographed tribal dance routines.

⊛ Festivals and events

Bau *p314*
May-Jun The Bindanyuh celebrate **gawai padi**, a festival with animistic roots that thanks the gods for an abundant rice harvest. Ask at the tourist office in Kuching for exact details.

O Shopping

Kuching *p304, map p308*
When it comes to choice, Kuching is the best place in Malaysia to buy tribal handicrafts, textiles and other artefacts, but they are not cheap. In some of Sarawak's coastal and upriver towns, you are more likely to find a better bargain, although the selection is not as good. If buying several items, it's a good idea to find a shop that sells the lot, as good discounts can be negotiated. It is essential to shop around: the best-stocked handicraft and antique shops in and near the big hotels are usually the most pricey. It is possible to bargain everywhere. Most shops are closed Sun.

It is illegal to export any antiquity without a licence from the curator of the Sarawak Museum. An antiquity is defined as any object made before 1850. Most things sold as antiquities are not; some very convincing weathering and ageing processes are used.

Antiques, art and handicrafts
Most handicraft and antique shops are along Main Bazaar, Lebuh Temple and Lebuh Wayang, with a few in the Padungan area. There is a Sun market (which starts on Sat afternoon) on Jln Satok, to the southwest of town, with a few handicraft stalls. Sat evening or early Sun morning are the best times to visit. There are rows of pottery stalls along Jln Penrissen, out of town, take a bus (No 3, 3A, 9A or 9B) or taxi to Ng Hua Seng Pottery bus stop. Antique shops sell this pottery too.
Artrageously Ramsay Ong, 94 Main Bazaar, T082-424346, www.artrageouslyasia.com. Art gallery of Sarawak artiste extraordinaire Ramsay Ong who made fame with his tree

bark works. Now showing an eclectic collection of contemporary Malaysian art including some beautiful pieces by celebrated Bidayuh artist Narong Daun. Recommended.

Borneo Art Gallery, Sarawak Plaza, Jln Tunku Abdul Rahman.

Fabriko, Main Bazaar. Set in a beautifully restored Chinese shophouse, interesting souvenirs and gallery.

Galleri M, Hilton lobby, 26 Main Bazaar. Exclusive jewellery, bead necklaces and antiques, best available Iban hornbill carvings. Also paintings from Sarawakian artists.

Karyaneka (handicrafts) Centre, Cawangan Kuching, Lot 324 Bangunan Bina, Jln Satok.

Sarakraf, Upper ground floor, Sarawak Plaza Shopping Complex, sarakraf@tm.net.my. Wide range of souvenirs and handicrafts with outlets in major hotels in Kuching, Damai, Sarawak Cultural Village and Miri airport (chain set up by the Sarawak Economic Development Corporation).

Sarawak Batik Art Shop, 1 Lebuh Temple.

Sarawak House, 67 Main Bazaar. More expensive but better quality crafts, carvings, fabrics and pots.

Thian Seng, 48 Main Bazaar. Good for *pua kumbu*.

Books and maps

Berita Book Centre, Jln Haji Taha, has a good selection of English language books.

HN Mohd Yahia & Sons, Holiday Inn, Jln Tunku Abdul Rahman, and in the basement of the Sarawak Shopping Plaza. Sells a 1:500,000 map of Sarawak.

Times Books, 1st floor, Riverside Shopping Complex, Jln Tunku Abdul Rahman. Biggest and best place for foreign language books.

Markets

Vegetable and wet markets are on the riverside on Jln Gambier; further up is the **Ban Hock Wharf market**, now full of cheap imported clothes. The **Sunday Market** on Jln Satok sells jungle produce, fruit and vegetables (there are a few handicraft stalls) and all sorts of intriguing merchandise;

it starts on Sat night and runs through to Sun morning and is well worth visiting. There is a jungle produce market, **Pasar Tani**, on Fri and Sat at Kampong Pinang Jawa in Petra Jaya.

Shopping malls

Riverside Shopping Complex, next to Riverside Majestic. Has Parkson Department Store and good supermarket in basement.

Sarawak Plaza, next to the Holiday Inn, Jln Tunku Abdul Rahman.

The Spring, Jln Simpang Tiga (on the way to the airport). Kuching's newest shopping mall with a range of high street shops and a good food court.

▲ Activities and tours

Kuching *p304, map p308*
Climbing

Batman Wall, rock climbing at the Fairy Caves outside Bau. 20 routes and rises to 40 m.

Diving

Southern Sarawak has yet to open up as a popular diving centre. Visibility is generally poor most of the year, perhaps due in part to the vast amounts of silt being carried down the major rivers. But the marine life (if you can see it) is rich and relatively undisturbed, so there's a lot of potential for exploration. Apr-Sep are considered the best diving months.

Kuching Scuba Centre, 159 Jln Chan Chin Ann, T082-428842, www.kuchingscuba.com. One possible option.

Fishing

Fui Lip Marketing, 15 ground floor, Wisma Phoenix, Jln Song Thian Cheok. Offshore from Santubong or deep-sea game fishing at Tanjung Datu (near Indonesian border). Contact Mr Johnson.

Golf

Damai Golf & Country Club, see page 328.
Hornbill Golf & Jungle Club, Borneo Highlands Resort, Padawan, T082-790800,

www.borneohighlands.com.my. 18-hole golf
course at 1000 m.
Kelab Golf Course, Petra Jaya, T082-440966.
An 18-hole course.
Sarawak Golf and Country Club, Petra Jaya,
T082-440966.

Mountain biking
Good trails from **Kamppung Singgai**, about
30 mins from Kuching (across the Batu Kawa
bridge). Beginners to intermediate: good trail
near **Kampong Apar**. Advanced trail: **Batang
Ai**. Alternatively, hire a bike from Kuching and
tour the Malay villages adjacent to the Astana
and Fort Margherita. Cross the Sarawak River
by sampan (around RM1 for you and your
bike) and then follow the small road that
runs parallel to the river.
Borneo Adventure, see under Tour
operators. Rents mountain bikes and
can arrange specialized tours.

Spectator sports
Football See Malaysia Cup football matches
in the Stadium Negeri Sarawak, Petra Jaya.
Horse racing The Kuching Turf Club,
Serian Rd, is the biggest in Borneo (see
newspapers for details of meetings).

Swimming
Kuching Municipal Pool, next to Kuching
Turf Club, Serian Rd. Open mornings only.

Tour operators
Most tour companies offer city tours as well
as trips around Sarawak to **Semenggoh, Bako,
Niah, Lambir Hills, Miri, Mulu** and **Bario**.
There are also competitively priced packages
to longhouses (mostly up the Skrang River, see
page 332). It is cheaper and easier to take
organized tours to Mulu, but arrange these
in Miri (see page 365) as they are much more
expensive if arranged from Kuching. Other
areas are easy to get to independently.
Borneo Adventure, No 55 Main Bazaar,
T082-245175, www.borneoadventure.com.
Known for its environmentally friendly
approach to tourism. Offers tours all over

Sarawak. Recommended.
Borneo Exploration, 76 Jln Wayang, T082-
252137, www.borneoexplorer.com.my.
Organizes a variety of longhouse tours,
a city tour and trips to the national parks.
Borneo Fairyland, 18 Main Bazaar, T082-
420194, www.borneofairyland.tripod.com.
Aimed at backpackers with good-value tours
around Sarawk. A 4-day/3-night trip to a
longhouse costs RM750.
Borneo Interland Travel, 63 Main Bazaar,
T082-413595, www.bitravel.com.my. Helpful
staff. The only agency licensed to sell bus and
boat tickets in town.
Borneo Trek and Kayak Adventure, T082-
240571, www.rainforestkayaking.com. Highly
regarded outfit that offers kayaking trips
combined with other cultural activities. Day
trips from RM188 per person. Recommended.
CPH Travel Agency, 70 Jln Padungan,
T082-243708, www.cphtravel.com.my.
Longhouse trips, national park tours, day trips
to the Kuching wetlands. Recommended.
Ibanika Expeditions, Lot 435, ground floor,
Jln Ang Cheng Ho, T082-424022, ibanika@po.
jaring.my. Long-established company offering
longhouse and more general tours, also has
French- and German-speaking guides.
Interworld, 1st floor, 161/162 Jln Temple,
T082-252344, 424515. Can arrange packages
to the Rainforest Music Festival.
Pan Asia Travel, 2nd floor, Unit 217-218,
Sarawak Plaza, Jln Tunku Abdul Rahman,
T082-419754. Half-day trips from Kuching.
Ruaikitai Tribal Café and Restaurant, see
page 326. Peter John Jaban runs rough 'n'
ready but interesting longhouse trips.

Water sports
Permai Rainforest Resort, see page 322.
Aimed at families with many activities on
offer, including kayaking, windsurfing, sailing
and rafting. Also offers trekking.

Damai Peninsula *p315, map p313*
Golf
Damai Golf & Country Club, Jln Santubong,
PO Box 400, T082-846088, www.damaigolf.com.

International-standard, 18-hole golf course designed by Arnold Palmer, laid out over approximately 6.5 km, 10-bay driving range right on the sea. A very long 18 holes, with electric buggies to stop you expiring through perspiring. Caddies, clubs and shoes for hire, spacious clubhouse, restaurant, bar, pro shop, tennis, squash and pool are also available. Due to its popularity, bookings should be made 3 days in advance.

Mountain biking
Damai Cross-Country Track. Close to the Permai Rainforest Resort, this is a purpose-built track where visitors can get very hot, sweaty and dirty as they career around the 3.5-km track; bikes can be hired from hotels.

Water sports
Damai Puri Resort, see page 322. A range of water sports from jet skiing to sailing. Snorkelling trips also arranged.
Permai Rainforest Resort, see page 322. A slightly more limited range of watersports.

⊖ Transport

Kuching *p304, map p308*
Air
For details of transport from the airport to Kuching centre, see Getting there, page 304.

Regular connections with **KL** (8-10 flights daily), **Kota Kinabalu** (**KK**) and **Brunei**. AirAsia flies to KL, KK, JB, **Miri**, **Bintulu**, **Penang**, **Macau**, **Jakarta** and **Singapore**; book online for the best rates. Jet Star Asia and Tiger Airways both offer regular connections with Singapore. Batavia Air flies 3 times a week (Tue, Thu, Sun) to **Pontianak** in West Kalimantan (from RM246) at 1255 and then on to Jakarta.

Malaysian Airlines subsidiary MASwings has a fleet of Twin Otters, Fokker F50s and ATR 72-500s to smaller destinations in Sabah and Sarawak. Tickets can be purchased online. Destinations include Bintulu, **Mukah**, **Tanjung Manis**, **Gunung Mulu National**

Park (via **Miri**) and **Sibu**. There are connections to KK via Sibu and Bintulu.

Airline offices Air Asia, Wisma Ho Ho Lim, ground floor, 291 Jln Abell, T082-283222. **Batavia Air**, T082-626299. MAS, Lot 215, Jln Song Thian Cheok, T082- 246622. **Royal Brunei**, 1st floor, Rugayah Building, Jln Song Thian Cheok, T082-243344. **Sin Hwa Travel Service**, 8 Lebuh Temple, T082-246688.

Boat
Sampans cross the Sarawak River from next to the Square Tower on Main Bazaar to **Fort Margherita** and the **Astana** on the north bank for around RM0.30. Small boats and some express boats connect with outlying kampongs on the river. Sampans can also be hired by the hour (RM40) for a tour up and down the river.

Express boats leave from the Sin Kheng Hong Wharf, 6 km out of town. Take a taxi (RM18). Tickets for **Kuching-Sibu** are only for sale at 2 places in town: **Borneo Interland**, 63 Main Bazaar, T082-413595, and **Lim Magazine bookshop**, 19 Ban Hock Lane, T082-410076. Otherwise turn up at the ferry 30 mins before departure to get a ticket. 1 daily departure for **Sibu** via Sarakei at 0830 (5 hrs, RM45).

Bus
Local 2 bus companies operate here. Blue and white Chin Lian Long buses serve the city and its suburbs; major bus stops are at Jln Masjid and opposite the post office. The green and yellow Sarawak Transport Company (STC) buses leave from the end of Lebuh Jawa, next to Ban Hock Wharf and the market.

Buses depart from the **Regional Express Bus Terminal** on Jln Penrissen at Mile 3.5 (a taxi ride costs around RM10). You either have to buy tickets at the bus station itself a few kilometres outside of the centre, or from **Borneo Interland**, 63 Main Bazaar, T082-413595, closed Sun. Buses to **Sibu** (7 hrs, RM40, first departure 0645, last 2200) **Bintulu** (RM60) and **Miri** (15 hrs, RM80, first 0100 last 2100). Biaramas has an office on Jln Wayang,

T012-883 3410 and sells bus tickets to major cities in Sarawak and to Pontianak.

International connections There are express bus departures to **Pontianak** in Kalimantan, Indonesia, (0730-2300, 10 hrs, RM45, a comfy VIP bus goes daily at 1100, RM75).

Since November 2008, the border crossing at **Entikong** has been given VOA (Visa On Arrival) status, meaning tourists can get a 30-day visa (US$25) on arrival. However, the visa situation in Indonesia is extremely volatile, and it is imperative that travellers contact the consulate in Kuching for the latest updates (see below). Buses leave from the Regional Express Bus Terminal. There are several departures daily from Kuching via Miri and Kuala Belait to **Bandar Seri Begawan** (Brunei, RM130).

Interior towns are sometimes difficult to access by road.

Car

It is possible to enter Sarawak from Kalimantan driving a private vehicle (including rental vehicles) as long as it has international insurance cover.

Car hire Flexi Car Rental, Lot 7050, 2nd floor, Jln Sekama, T082-335282, www.flexicarrental.com. Also at the airport. **Golden System Car Rental & Tours**, 58-1B, 1st floor, Block G, Pearl Commercial Centre, Jln Tun Razak, T082-333609, www.goldencr.com.my. Also has a desk at the airport. A wide range of cars, vans and 4WDs. Free pick-up and delivery in the Kuching area. **Pronto Car Rental**, 1st floor, 98 Jln Padungan, T/F082-236889. **Wah Tung Travel Service**, 7 Jln Ban Hock, T082-248888, www.wahtunggroup.com.my.

Taxi

Local taxis congregate at the taxi stand on Jln Market, or outside the big hotels; they don't use meters, so agree a price before setting off. 24-hr radio taxi service, T082-343343 or T082-342255. Short distances around town should cost RM10.

Damai Peninsula *p315, map p313*
Bus

There are shuttle buses from the **Grand Margherita** in **Kuching** (RM12 each way, RM5 children, 40 mins, first bus at 0730 from Kuching, last return bus at 2200) or take the public bus No 2B, operated by **Petra Jaya Transport** (yellow buses with black and red stripes) to **Santubong** at a fraction of the price (RM3.30) from the market place at the end of Jln Gambier. Tour companies offer packages for various prices including transport, entry to the Sarawak Cultural Village and lunch.

Taxi

From **Kuching** is negotiable and costs between RM40 and RM45 depending on bargaining skills.

Bako National Park *p318, map p319*
For details on transport to and from Kuching, see page 318.

ⓓ Directory

Kuching *p304, map p308*
Banks

Money changers in the main shopping complexes usually give a much better rate for cash than the banks, although for TCs the rates are much the same. ATMs are everywhere. Note that the 1st and 3rd Sat of every month is a bank holiday. **American Express**, 70 Jln Padungan (assistance with Amex TCs), T082-252600; **HSBC**, Bangunan Binamas (near Cat Statue) on Jln Padungan; **Majid & Sons Money Changer**, 45 Jln India; **Mohamed Yahia & Sons** (money changer), GF3, Sarawak Plaza, some of the best rates in Kuching; **Standard Chartered**, Wisma Bukit Mata Kuching (opposite Grand Margherita), Jln Tunku Abdul Rahman. **Embassies and consulates** Australian Honorary Consul, T082-233350; British Honorary Representative, T012-322 0011; French Honorary Consul, Telang Usan Hotel, T082-415588; **Indonesian Consulate**, 111 Jln Tun

Haji Openg, T082-241734; **New Zealand Honorary Consul**, T082-482177. **Immigration** 1st floor, Bangunan Sultan Iskandar (Federal Complex) Jln Simpang Tiga, T082-245661. **Internet** Most guesthouses offer free internet access. Also try **Cyber City**, Taman Sri Sarawak (opposite the Hilton, open 1000-2200, RM4 per hr; **Dot.com**, Wayang St (next to Ting & Ting supermarket and Borneo Hotel), open 0900-2100, RM2 per hr. **Waterfront Cyber Café**, Steamship Building, open 0900-2100, RM4 per hr. International calls can be made from most public cardphones. Major hotels all have cardphones in their lobbies. **Medical services** Abdul Rahman Yakub, T082-440055, private hospital with good reputation; **Doctor's Clinic**, Main Bazaar, opposite Chinese History Museum, said to be excellent and is used to treating travellers' more minor ailments (between RM20 and RM30 for consultation); **Normah Medical Centre**, across the river on Jln Tun Datuk Patinggi, T082-440055; **Sarawak General Hospital**, Jln Tan Sri Ong Kee Hui, off Jln Tun Haji Openg, T082-276666, consultation from RM50; **Timberland Medical Centre**, Rock Rd, T082-234991. Recommended. **Pharmacies: Apex Pharmacy**, 125 1st floor, Sarawak Plaza, open 1000-2100; **UMH**, Ban Hock Rd, Mon-Fri 0900-2030, Sat 0900-1800; **YK Farmasi**, 22 Main Bazaar, 0830-1700. **Police** Tourist Police, Kuching Waterfront, T082-250522. **Post office** General Post Office, Jln Tun Haji Openg, Mon-Sat 0800-1800, Sun 1000-1300. Operates a poste restante service.

Bandar Sri Aman and around

→ *Colour map 3, C2.*

Previously called Simmanggang, Bandar Sri Aman lies on the Batang Lupar, a three- to four-hour journey from Kuching, and is the administrative capital of the Second Division. The river is famous for its tidal bore; several times a year, a wall of water rushes upstream wreaking havoc with boats and divides into several tributaries: the Skrang River is one of these. It is possible to spend the night in longhouse homestays on the river. The Batang Ai National Park is home to hornbills, orang-utans and gibbons. ▸▸ *For listings, see pages 335-336.*

Ins and outs

Bandar Sri Aman is accessible from Kuching and Sibu by bus. To reach Skrang longhouses, buses and then chartered boats must be arranged. There is one hotel in Batang Ai National Park. It arranges transport for its guests. Trips to longhouses and the national park can be organized through **Borneo Adventure Travel Company**, see page 335.

Sights

The major sight in Bandar is the defensive Fort Alice. Most tourists do not stop in Bandar but pass through on day trips from Kuching to visit traditional Iban longhouses sited along the Skrang River. The route to Bandar goes through pepper plantations and many 'new' villages. During Communist guerrilla activity in the 1960s (see page 384), whole settlements were uprooted in this area and placed in guarded camps.

Fort Alice was constructed in 1864. It has small turrets, a central courtyard, a medieval-looking drawbridge and is surrounded by a fence of iron spikes. Rajah Charles Brooke lived in the Batang Lupar district for about 10 years, using this fort – and another downriver at Lingga – as bases for his punitive expeditions against pirates and Ibans in the interior. The fort is the only one of its type in Sarawak and was built commanding this stretch of the Batang Lupar River as protection against Iban raids. The original fort here was built in 1849 and named Fort James; the current fort was constructed using much of the original material. It was renamed Alice in honour of Ranee Margaret Brooke (it was her second name). It is said that every evening, until the practice was ended in 1964, a policeman would call from the fort (in Iban): "Oh ha! Oh ha! The time is now eight o'clock. The steps have been drawn up. The door is closed. People from upriver, people from downriver, are not allowed to come to the fort anymore." (It probably sounded better in Iban.)

Skrang longhouses → *For listings, see pages 335-336. Colour map 3, C3.*

The Skrang River was one of the first areas settled by Iban immigrants in the 16th to 18th centuries. The slash-and-burn agriculturalists originally came from the Kapual River basin in Kalimantan. They later joined forces with Malay chiefs in the coastal areas and terrorized the Borneo coasts; the first Europeans to encounter these pirates called them Sea Dayaks (see page 386). The Ibans took many heads. Blackened skulls – which local headmen say date back to those days – hang in some of the Skrang longhouses. In 1849 more than 800 Iban pirates from the Batang Lupar and Skrang River were massacred by Rajah James Brooke's forces in the notorious Battle of Beting Marau. Four years later the Sultan of Brunei agreed to cede these troublesome districts to Brooke; they became the Second Division of Sarawak.

There are many traditional Iban longhouses along the Skrang River, although those closer to **Pias** and **Lamanak** (the embarkation points on the Skrang) tend to be very touristy – they are visited by tour groups almost every day. **Long Mujang**, the first Iban longhouse, is an hour upriver. Pias and Lamanak are within five hours' drive of Kuching. Jungle trekking is available (approximately two hours). The guide provides an educational tour of the flora and fauna.

Batang Ai and Batang Ai National Park

The Batang Ai River, a tributary of the Batang Lupar, has been dammed to form Sarawak's first hydroelectric plant, which came into service in 1985; it provides 60% of Sarawak's electricity supply, transmitting as far as Limbang. The area was slowly flooded over a period of six months to give animals and wildlife a chance to escape, but it has affected no fewer than 29 longhouses, 10 of which are now completely submerged. The rehousing of the longhouse community has been the topic of fierce controversial debate. The communities were moved into modern longhouses and given work opportunities in local palmeries. However, it now seems that the housing loans that were initially given are not commensurate with local wages and will be very difficult for the longhouse communities to pay off. In addition, modern longhouses were not provided with farmland, so many local people have returned to settle on the banks of the reservoir. Near the dam there is a freshwater fish nursery. These fish are exported to South Korea, Japan and Europe. Those families displaced by the flooding of the dam largely work here and many of the longhouses surrounding the dam depend upon this fishery for their own fish supply.

The Batang Ai dam has created a vast and picturesque man-made lake covering some 90 sq km, stretching up the Engkari and Ai rivers. Beyond the lake, more than an hour's boat ride upriver from the dam, it is possible to see beautiful lowland mixed dipterocarp forest.

The **Batang Ai National Park**, 250 km from Kuching and two hours from the jetty by boat, covers an area of over 24,040 ha and was inaugurated in 1991. It protects the much-endangered orang-utan and is home to a wide variety of other wildlife, including

The longhouse: prime location apartments

Most longhouses are built on stilts, high on the riverbank, on prime real estate. They are 'prestigious properties' with 'lots of character', and with 'commanding views of the river', they are the condominiums of the jungle. They are long-rise rather than high-rise, however, and the average longhouse has 20-25 'doors' (although there can be as many as 60). Each represents one family. The word 'long' in a settlement's name – as in Long Liput or Long Terawan – means 'confluence' (the equivalent of *kuala* in Malay), and does not refer to the length of the longhouse.

Behind each of the doors – which even today, are rarely locked – is a *bilik* (apartment), which includes the family living room and a loft, where paddy and tools are stored. In Kenyah and Kayan longhouses, paddy (which can be stored for years until it is milled) is kept in elaborate barns, built on stilts away from the longhouse, in case of fire. In traditional longhouses, the living rooms are simple with *atap*-roofs and bamboo floors; in modern longhouses, designed on the same principles, living rooms have sofas, lino floors, TV and en suite bathroom.

At the front of the *bilik* is the *dapur*, where the cooking takes place. All *biliks* face out onto the *ruai* (gallery), which is the focus of communal life and is where visitors are usually entertained. The width of the wall which faces onto the *ruai* indicates the status of that family. Attached to the *ruai* there is usually a *tanju* (open veranda) running the full length of the house – where rice and other agricultural products are dried. Long ladders – notched hardwood trunks – lead up to the *tanju*; they can get very slippery and do not always come with handrails.

hornbills and gibbons. As yet there are no visitor facilities, but five walking trails have been created, one of which takes in an ancient burial ground. Trips to one of the 29 longhouses surrounding the dam and to Batang Ai National Park are organized by the **Borneo Adventure Travel Company**, see Activities and tours, page 335.

Visiting longhouses: house rules

There are more than 1500 longhouses in Sarawak. They are usually located along the big rivers and their tributaries, notably the Skrang (see page 332), the Rejang (see page 336) and the Baram (see page 356). The Iban, who are characteristically extrovert and hospitable to visitors, live on the lower reaches of the rivers. The Orang Ulu tribes – mainly Kayan and Kenyah – live further upriver and are generally less outgoing than the Iban. The Bidayuh live mainly around Bau and Serian, near Kuching. Their longhouses are usually more modern than those of the Iban and Orang Ulu, and are visited less often for that reason. The Kelabit people live on the remote plateau country near the Kalimantan border around Bario (see page 376).

The most important ground rule is not to visit a longhouse without an invitation. People who arrive unannounced may get an embarrassingly frosty reception. Tour companies offer the only exception to this rule, as most have tribal connections. Upriver, particularly at Kapit, on the Rejang (see page 338), such 'invitations' are not hard to come by; it is good to ensure your host actually comes from the longhouse you are being invited to. The best time to visit Iban longhouses is during the gawai harvest festival at the beginning of June, when communities throw an open house and everyone is invited to join the festivities.

On arrival, visitors should pay an immediate courtesy call on the headman (the *tuai rumah* in Iban longhouses). It is normal to bring him gifts; those staying overnight should offer the headman around RM20 per person. The money is kept in a central fund and saved for use by the whole community during festivals. Small gifts such as beer, coffee, biscuits, whisky, batik and food (especially rice or chicken) go down well. It is best to arrive at a longhouse during late afternoon after people have returned from the fields. Visitors who have time to stay the night generally have a much more enjoyable experience than those who pay fleeting visits. They can share the evening meal and have time to talk and drink.

If you go beyond the limits of the express boats, it is necessary to charter a longboat. Petrol costs RM2.50-5 a litre, depending on how far upriver you are. Guides charge approx RM60-100 a day and sometimes it is necessary to hire a boatman or frontman as well. Prices increase in the dry season when boats have to be lifted over shallow rapids. Permits are required for most upriver areas; these can be obtained at the residents' or district office in the nearest town.

Visitors should note the following:
→ On entering a longhouse, take off your shoes.
→ Accept food and drink with both hands. If you do not want to eat or drink, the accepted custom is to touch the brim of the glass or the plate and then touch your lips as a symbolic gesture. Sit cross-legged when eating.
→ When washing in the river, women should wear a sarong and men, shorts.
→ Ask permission to take photographs. It's not unusual to be asked for a small fee.
→ Do not enter a longhouse during *pantang* (taboo), a period of misfortune usually following a death. There is normally a white (leaf) flag hanging near the longhouse as a warning to visitors. During this period (normally one week) there is no singing, dancing or music, and no jewellery is worn.
→ Bow your head when walking past people older than you.

⊙ Bandar Sri Aman and around listings

For Sleeping and Eating price codes and other relevant information, see Essentials pages 25-30.

⊖ Sleeping

Bandar Sri Aman and around *p331*
B Bukit Saban Resort, on the rarely visited Paku River, just north of the Skrang and Lemnak rivers, about 4½ hrs from Kuching, T082-477145, F477103 (Kuching sales office), T083-648949 (at the resort). 50 rooms in longhouse style with traditional sago palm thatch, restaurant, a/c, TV, hot water.
B Champion, 1248 Main Bazaar, T082-320140. A small but central establishment.

Skrang longhouses *p332*
All longhouses along the Skrang River are controlled by the Ministry of Tourism so rates are the same – RM40 inclusive of all meals. Resthouses at most of the longhouses can accommodate 20-40 people; mattresses and mosquito nets are provided in a communal sleeping area with few partitions. Basic, with flush toilet, shower, local food, phone and a clinic nearby. If the stay is 3 days/2 nights, on the 2nd night it's possible to camp in the jungle and then get a return boat ride to the longhouse.

Batang Ai and Batang Ai National Park *p332*
Tour companies provide accommodation in longhouses here, in a much more central location within the park than the **Hilton**.
A Hilton International Batang Ai Longhouse Resort, T083-584388, www.hilton.com. On the eastern shore of the lake. Opened in 1995, the resort is made up of 11 longhouses, built of the local *belian* (ironwood) to traditional designs. Despite its lakeside location there are no views, except from the walkways, as longhouses are built, for purposes of defence, to face landwards – in this case, over the buggy track. However, there are compromises to modern comforts: all 100 rooms have a/c, fan, TV, shower room, minibar. Other facilities

include a pool and paddling pool, restaurant, 18-km jogging track, shuttle from **Kuching Hilton International** tour desk. The hotel arranges transport. If the **Hilton** is not your style, there is, unfortunately, not much else.

⊙ Eating

Bandar Sri Aman and around *p331*
¶ Alison Café & Restaurant, 4 Jln Council. Chinese cuisine.
¶ Chuan Hong, 1 Jln Council. Chinese coffee shop, also serves Muslim food.
¶ Melody, 432 Jln Hospital. Chinese and Muslim food.

▲ Activities and tours

Bandar Sri Aman and around *p331*
Many of the restaurant staff in the resort are locals and discreet enquiries may get you a trip to a longhouse and/or Batang Ai National Park for considerably less than the **Borneo Adventure Travel Company** charge.
Borneo Adventure Travel Company, 55 Main Bazaar, Kuching, T082-410569, www.borneoadventure.com, and at the Hilton Batang Ai Longhouse Resort.

⊖ Transport

Bandar Sri Aman and around *p331*
Bus
Regular connections with **Kuching**, RM15 (135 km) and **Sibu** (via Sarikei).

Skrang longhouses *p332*
Bus
Buses No 14 and 19 to **Pias** and bus No 9 to **Lemanak**. Self-drive car rental (return) or minibus (8-10 people, return) from **Kuching** to **Entaban**. From these points it is necessary to charter a boat to reach the nearest

longhouses. Many of the Kuching-based tour agencies offer cut-price deals for 1- to 2-day excursions to Skrang and Lemanak river longhouses (see page 328). Unless you are already part of a small group, these tours work out cheaper because of the boat costs.

Sibu, Kapit and Belaga

The third largest town in Sarawak, Sibu is sited at the confluence of the Rejang and the Igan rivers 60 km upstream from the sea. It is the starting point for trips up the Rejang to the Kapit and Belaga. The Rejang is an important thoroughfare and Malaysia's longest river at 563 km. Tours to upriver longhouses can be organized from Sibu or more cheaply from Kapit and Belaga. **▶▶** *For listings, see pages 344-350.*

Sibu

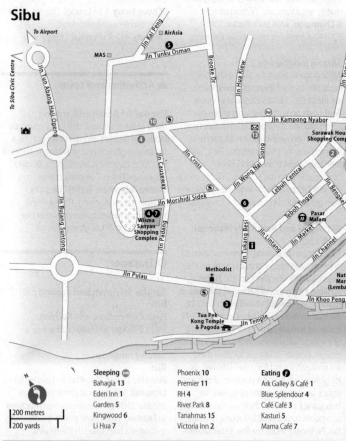

N
200 metres
200 yards

Sleeping		
Bahagia 13	Phoenix 10	**Eating**
Eden Inn 1	Premier 11	Ark Galley & Café 1
Garden 5	RH 4	Blue Splendour 4
Kingwood 6	River Park 8	Café Café 3
Li Hua 7	Tanahmas 15	Kasturi 5
	Victoria Inn 2	Mama Café 7

Ins and outs

Getting there and around The airport is 25 km from Sibu and there are flights to KL, Kuching and KK; **Sibu airport information centre** ⓘ *T084-307755*. To get from the airport by taxi you need to buy a taxi coupon (RM32). Or take Lanang Bus No 3A, which leaves every two hours between 0630 and 1600.

The new long-distance bus station is about 3 km out of town. Take a taxi, RM15, or a Lorong Road bus (no number) or Sungei Merah bus No 12 or 17 to the local bus station near the ferry terminal. There are daily connections with Bintulu and Miri, and Kuching via Sarikei. Boats for Kuching and Sarikei dock at two wharves close to the town centre.

Although this is Sarawak's third largest town, it's still possible to see most of Sibu's sights on foot. ▸ *See also Transport, page 349.*

Rex Food Court **6**
Sri Menanti **2**
Sri Menanti
Chicken Rice **8**

Tourist information The **Visitors' Information Centre** ⓘ *ground floor, 32 Jln Tukang Besi (around the corner from the Methodist Church), T084-340980, www.sara waktourism.com, Mon-Fri 0800-1700 (closed on public holidays)*, is very friendly and helpful. As well as information on Sibu they can advise for trips onwards to Kapit and Belaga. A visit here is highly recommended. For the latest information on riverboats leaving Sibu, phone the **Sarawak Riverboat Information Line** ⓘ *T084-339936*.

Background

Thanks to the discovery of the Kuala Paloh channel in 1961, Sibu is accessible to boats with a sizeable draft. Sibu is a busy Chinese trading town – the majority of the population came originally from China's Fujian Province – and is the main port on the Rejang (also spelt Rajang). In 1899, Rajah Charles Brooke agreed with Wong Nai Siong, a Chinese scholar from Fujian, to allow settlers to Sibu. Brooke had reportedly been impressed with the industriousness of the Chinese: he saw the women toiling in the paddy fields from dawn to dusk and commented: "If the women work like that, what on earth must the men be like?"

The Kuching administration provided these early agricultural pioneers with temporary housing on arrival, a steamer between Sibu and Kuching, rice rations for the first year and tuition in Malay and Iban. The town grew rapidly (its expansion is documented in a photographic exhibition in the Civic Centre) but was razed to the ground in the great fire of 1828. The first shophouses to be constructed after the fire are the three-storey ones still standing on Jalan Channel. At the beginning of the 20th century, Sibu became the springboard for Foochow migration to the rest of Sarawak. Today it is an industrial and trading centre for timber, pepper and rubber, and home to some of Sarawak's wealthiest families, mostly timber *towkays* (merchants).

Sights
The old trading port has now been graced with a pagoda, a couple of big hotels and a smart esplanade. The 1929 **shophouses** along the river are virtually all that remains of the old town. The seven-storey **pagoda**, adjacent to **Tua Pek Kong Temple**, cost RM1.5 million to build; there are good views over the town from the top, you'll need to ask for the key. The pagoda and temple are well worth visiting for the caretaker, Tan Teck Chiang, alone. Chiang speaks great English and gives impromptu animated lectures filled with unique interpretations and humour on the temple, Chinese culture and Taoism. Just turn up and ask for Chiang. In the **Sibu Civic Centre** ⓘ *2.5 km out of town on Jln Tun Abang Haji Openg, Tue-Sun 0800-1700; take Sungei Merah bus No 4 from the bus terminal and ask for the Civic Centre*, there is an exhibition of old photographs of Sibu and a mediocre tribal display. This serves as Sibu's municipal museum. Five aerial photographs of the town, taken since 1947, chart the town's explosive growth.

There are a couple of interesting Chinese temples out of town. The **Taoist Tiger Temple** is unique in that it is the only temple in Malaysia dedicated to the seven tiger deities. The temple has the tigers in various fierce poses dressed in human clothes. The myth goes back to the mountains of rural China, where after years of being attacked and killed by the local human population, seven tiger brothers took their revenge and went on a violent killing spree until they were caught and imprisoned by Kuan Keng, a Chinese general from the Three Kingdoms period. The tigers were released after 400 years of captivity, by which time they had become half human and had vowed to become strict vegetarians. Each of the statues in the temple represents the qualities of a different deity; the tiger nearest the entrance is in charge of the environment, and next to him is Tsai Shen, the fifth tiger deity and God of Wealth. The tigers receive vegetarian offerings from the local Chinese population. To get there, take a taxi to Jalan Trusan, off Jalan Teku (RM12). Recently completed, the Sibu **Yu Lung San Tian Ensi** ⓘ *T019-892 8128*, is the largest Chinese temple in Southeast Asia. It's the temple that turns heads on the road from Bintulu with its enormous size, sweeping gables and multicoloured buildings. To get there, take Lanang bus No 2 (hourly from 0515, RM3) from Jalan Maju. A taxi costs RM30.

Kapit → *For listings, see pages 344-350. Colour map 3, C4. Population: 100,000.*

Kapit, which means 'twin' in local dialect, is the capital of Sarawak's Seventh Division, through which flows the **Rejang River** and its main tributaries, the Batang Baleh, Batang Katibas, Batang Balui and Sungai Belaga. In a treaty with the Sultan of Brunei, Rajah James Brooke acquired the Rejang Basin for Sarawak in 1853. Kapit is the last big town on the Rejang and styles itself as the gateway to 'the heart of Borneo', after Redmond O'Hanlon's *Into the Heart of Borneo*, which describes his adventure up the Batang Baleh in the 1980s. Kapit is full of people who claim to be characters in this book.

The main sights are Fort Sylvia and the Kapit Museum but, like O'Hanlon and his journalist companion James Fenton, most visitors simply use the town as a pit stop before continuing their adventures into the interior to explore the upper Rejang and its tributaries, where there are many Iban and Orang Ulu longhouses. Maps of the Kapit Division and other parts of Sarawak are available from the **Land Survey Department** ① *Jln Beletik on Jln Airport*. Permits for upriver trips are available from the **government administration centre** ① *Resident Office, Kapit Division, 96800 Kapit, T084-796445*, which is outside town near the old airport. Take one of the local buses heading 'downstream' from Kapit town centre for around RM2. Tourists going up the Balleh River or Upper Rejang must sign a form saying they understand they are travelling at their own risk.

Background

There are only a few tens of kilometres of surfaced road in and around Kapit, but the small town has a disproportionate number of cars. It is a trading centre for the tribespeople upriver and has grown enormously in recent years with the expansion of the logging industry upstream. Logs come in two varieties: floaters and sinkers. Floaters are pulled downstream by tugs in huge chevron formations. Sinkers – like *belian* (ironwood) – are transported in the Chinese-owned dry bulk carriers that line up along the wharves at Kapit. When the river is high these timber ships are able to go upstream, past the Pelagus Rapids. The Rejang at Kapit is normally 500 m wide and, in the dry season, the riverbank slopes steeply down to the water. When it floods, however, the water level rises more than 10 m, as is testified by the high-water marks on Fort Sylvia.

Sights

Fort Sylvia near the wharves was built of *belian* by Rajah Charles Brooke in 1880, and is now occupied by the Kapit Museum. It was originally called Kapit Fort but was renamed in

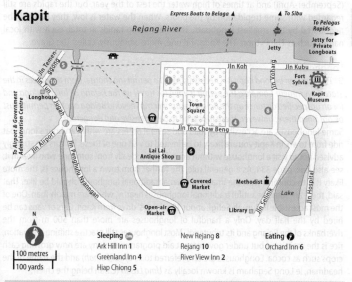

Kapit

Express Boats to Belaga ▲   ▲ To Sibu

To Pelagus Rapids

Rejang River

Jetty for Private Longboats

Jetty

Jln Koh   Jln Kubu

Jln Voharg

Fort Sylvia 🏛

Kapit Museum

Jln Temenggong

Jln Jugah

Longhouse 🏠

To Airport & Government Administration Centre

Jln Airport

Town Square

Jln Teo Chow Beng

Lai Lai Antique Shop 🏠

Jln Penghulu Nyanngan

Covered Market

Methodist ✝

Lake

Jln Selnik

Jln Hospital

Open-air Market

Library 🏛

N

100 metres
100 yards

Sleeping 🛏		Eating 🍴
Ark Hill Inn 1	New Rejang 8	Orchard Inn 6
Greenland Inn 4	Rejang 10	
Hiap Chiong 5	River View Inn 2	

1925 after Rajah Vyner Brooke's wife. Most of the forts built during this time were designed to prevent the Orang Ulu going downriver; Fort Sylvia was built to stop the belligerent Iban headhunters from attacking Kenyah and Kayan settlements upstream.

Kapit Museum ⓘ *Tue-Sun, 1000-1200 and 1400-1700, free (if closed at these times search for the curator to open it)*, was enlarged in the 1990s and moved to Fort Sylvia. It has exhibits (all labelled in English) on Rejang tribes and the local economy. Set up by the Sarawak Museum in Kuching, it includes a section of an Iban longhouse and several Iban artefacts including a wooden hornbill. The Orang Ulu section has a reconstruction of a longhouse and a mural painted by local tribespeople. An Orang Ulu *salong* (burial hut), totem pole and other woodcarvings are also on display. The museum has representative exhibits from the small Malay community and the Chinese. Hokkien traders settled at Kapit and Belaga and traded salt, sugar and ceramics for pepper, rotan and rubber; they were followed by traders from Fujian. The Chinese exhibit is a shop. In addition, there are also displays on the natural history of the upper Rejang and modern industries such as mining, logging and tourism.

Kapit has a particularly colourful daily **market** in the centre of town. Tribeswomen bring in fruit, vegetables and animals to sell; it is quite normal to see everything from turtles, frogs, birds and catfish to monkeys, wild boar and even pangolin and pythons. **Note** If you do see animals such as monkeys, pangolins, wild cats or birds, please remember that most of them are protected species and in serious danger of extinction, due to the wildlife 'pet' trade and the rising demand for 'traditional' medicines like ground bone and body parts such as monkey gall bladders. Please do not buy them or in any way encourage this business.

Pelagus Rapids
Forty-five minutes upriver from Kapit on the Rejang River, this 2.5-km-long series of cataracts and whirlpools is the result of a sudden drop in the riverbed, caused by a geological fault line. Express boats can make it up the Pelagus to Belaga in the wet season (September-April) and at times of high water the rest of the year, but the rapids are still regarded with some trepidation by the pilots. When the water is low, they can only be negotiated by the smallest longboats. There are seven rapids in total, each with local names such as The Python, The Knife and one, more ominously, called The Grave.

Longhouses
ⓘ *To go upriver beyond Kapit it is necessary to get a permit (no charge) from the offices in the State Government Complex; the permit is valid for travel up the Rejang as far as Belaga and for an unspecified distance up the Baleh. For upriver trips beyond Belaga another permit must be obtained there; however, these trips tend to be expensive and dangerous.*

Some longhouses are accessible by road and several others are within an hour's longboat ride from town. In Kapit you are likely to be invited to visit one of these. Visitors are strongly advised not to visit a longhouse without an invitation, ideally from someone who lives in it; see also box, page 334. As a general rule, the further from town a longhouse is, the more likely it is to conform with the image of what a traditional longhouse should be like. That said, there are some beautiful traditional longhouses nearby, which are mainly Iban. One of the most accessible is **Rumah Seligi**, about 30 minutes' drive from Kapit. Cars or vans can be hired by the half day. Only a handful of longhouses are more than 500 m from the riverbanks of the Rejang and its tributaries. Most longhouses still practise shifting cultivation; rice is the main crop but under government aid programmes many are now growing cash crops such as cocoa. Longhouses are also referred to as *Uma* (*Sumah*) and the name of the headman, ie Long Segaham is known locally as *Uma Lasah* (Lasah being the chief).

Longhouses between Kapit and Belaga on the upper Rejang river are accessible by the normal passenger boats, but these express boats travel a limited distance on the Baleh River (2½ hours). To go further upriver it is necessary to take a tour or organize your own guides and boatmen. The sort of trip taken by Redmond O'Hanlon and James Fenton (as described in O'Hanlon's book *Into the Heart of Borneo*) would cost more than RM1800 a head. Large-scale logging operations are currently underway on the Baleh River and although this may increase boat traffic and the opportunities to access this part of Sarawak, brace yourself for a very different experience from that described in *Into the Heart of Borneo*. ➤➤ *See Activities and tours, page 348.*

The vast majority of the population, about 68%, in Sarawak's Seventh Division is Iban. They inhabit the Rejang up to and a little beyond Kapit, as well as the lower reaches of the Balleh and its tributaries. The Iban people are traditionally the most hospitable to visitors but, as a result, their longhouses are the most frequently visited by tourists. Malays and Chinese account for 3.4% and 7% of the population respectively. The Orang Ulu live further upriver; the main tribes are the Kayan and the Kenyah (12%) and a long list of sub-groups such as the Kejaman, Beketan, Sekapan, Lahanan, Seping and Tanjong. In addition there are the nomadic and semi-nomadic Penan, Punan and Ukit. Many tribal people are employed in the logging industry and, with their paid jobs, have brought the trappings of modernity to even the most remote longhouses.

Only enter the **Rumah Tuan Lepong Balleh** longhouse with the local policeman, Selvat Anu, who lives there; ask for him at Kapit police station. During the day Selvat and some members of the longhouse can take visitors on various adventure tours: river trips, visiting longhouses, jungle treks, fishing, pig hunting, camping in the jungle, trips up to logging areas, swimming in rivers and mountain trekking. Selvat is very knowledgeable and has good relations with longhouse communities. Visitors can eat with the family and occasionally have the chance to experience a traditional Iban ceremony.

Belaga → *For listings, see pages 344-350. Colour map 3, C4.*

This is the archetypal sleepy little town, most people while away the time in coffee shops. They are the best places to watch life go by and there are always interesting visitors in town, from itinerant wild honey collectors from Kalimantan to Orang Ulu who have brought their jungle produce downriver to the Belaga bazaar or those who are heading to the metropolis of Kapit for medical treatment. At night, when the neon lights flicker on, coffee shops are invaded by thousands of cicadas, beetles and moths.

A few Chinese traders set up shop in Belaga in the early 1900s and traded with the tribespeople upriver, supplying essentials such as kerosene and cooking oil. The Orang Ulu brought their beadwork and mats as well as jungle produce such as beeswax, ebony, *gutta-percha* (rubbery tree gum) and, most prized of all, bezoar stones. These are gall-stones found in certain monkeys (the wah-wahs, jelu-merahs and jelu-jankits) and porcupines. To the Chinese, they have much the same properties as rhinoceros horn and, even today, they are exported from Sarawak to Singapore, where they fetch S$300 per kilogram.

Belaga serves as a small government administration centre for the remoter parts of the Seventh Division as it is the last settlement of any size up the Rejang.

It's also a major centre for the illegal logging business, with many locals having been paid off handsomely to say nothing negative regarding the huge scale logging operations close to the Kalimantan border. For such a small village Belaga boasts a large number of expensive cars and 4WDs, and the money's not from ecotourism.

Belaga is also a good place to arrange visits to the Kayan and Kenyah longhouses on the Linnau River. There is a very pretty **Malay kampong** (Kampong Bharu) along the esplanade downriver from the Belaga Bazaar. The **Kejaman burial pole** on display outside the Sarawak Museum in Kuching was brought from the Belaga area in 1902.

The **District Office** (for upriver permits) is on the far side of the basketball courts.

Upriver from Belaga

ⓘ *To go upriver beyond Belaga it is technically necessary to obtain a permit from the Residents' Office, T084-321963, and permission from the police station. The situation 'on the ground' is usually a lot more relaxed, with local guides and boat owners able to travel with the minimum of paperwork; ask in Belaga hotels and coffee shops on arrival.*

When the river is high, express boats go upstream as far as the vast **Bakun Dam** (see box opposite). From the dam a paved road connects to Bintulu on the coast, around four hours away, providing the main artery of supply for the Bakun project. Several basic shops and even a couple of 'motels' have been set up in the area to provide for the needs of the workers employed here. Beyond the Bakun dam itself logging roads continue further into the interior and it's sometimes possible to hire a driver and 4WD to explore.

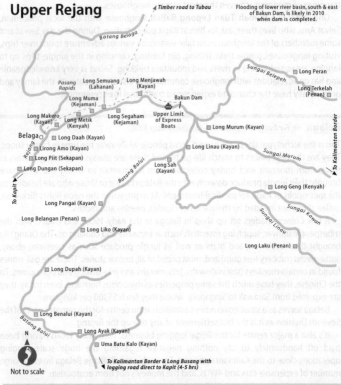

Upper Rejang

Timber road to Tubau

Flooding of lower river basin, south & east of Bakun Dam, is likely in 2010 when dam is completed.

Batang Belaga

Sungai Belepeh

Long Peran

Pasang Rapids

Long Semuang (Lahanan)

Long Muma (Kejaman)

Long Menjawah (Kayan)

Long Terkelah (Penan)

Bakun Dam

Long Makero (Kayan)

Long Metik (Kenyah)

Long Segaham (Kejaman)

Upper Limit of Express Boats

Belaga

Lirong Amo (Kayan)

Long Daah (Kayan)

Long Piit (Sekapan)

Long Dungan (Sekapan)

Long Murum (Kayan)

Long Linau (Kayan)

Rejang

Batang Balui

Long Sah (Xayan)

Sungai Murum

Long Geng (Kenyah)

Long Pangai (Kayan)

Long Belangan (Penan)

Long Liko (Kayan)

Sungai Lindu

Sungai Kawan

Long Laku (Penan)

To Kapit

To Kalimantan Border

Long Dupah (Kayan)

Long Benalui (Kayan)

Batang Balui

Long Ayak (Kayan)

Uma Batu Kalo (Kayan)

N

Not to scale

To Kalimantan Border & Long Busang with logging road direct to Kapit (4-5 hrs)

Build and be dammed: an ecological time bomb

The Bakun Dam Scheme, upriver from Belaga on the upper Rejang and 400 km east of Kuching, has had more twists and turns than the river on which it is being built.

The RM9.12 billion project, one of the largest in Southeast Asia, will flood a tract of virgin rainforest that supports at least 43 species of endangered mammals and birds. In preparation for the flooding, 9000 longhouse-dwelling tribespeople have been displaced from their ancestral homeland.

The dam is going to be twice the height of the Aswan Dam in Egypt and will flood 69,000 ha – an area bigger than Singapore. Environmentalists say it will be an ecological time bomb in the heart of Borneo.

The project has been on and off the books countless times. In 1990 it was scrapped for environmental reasons, but was back on again in 1993. Again, in late 1997, in the midst of Malaysia's economic crisis, when money was scarce, it was shelved only to be restarted in 2001. In 2004, with the government struggling to find buyers for the dam's electricity, it was rumoured that the project would again be scrapped or postponed. Government figures are determined to see the project through, although its original completion date of 2003 was pushed back to late 2007 and then onto 2010. Even during the hiatus preparations for the eventual flooding went on. Thousands of locals were moved from their villages and jungle longhouses and rehoused elsewhere.

The plan is for Bakun to generate 2400 MW of electricity. The power will be consumed within Sabah and Sarawak, and possibly Brunei and Kalimantan, and will involve the construction of 800 km of high-voltage power lines. Plans for an undersea cable more than 600 km long have been revived with a possible completion date of 2015 at a cost of around RM9 billion. The cable is to carry power to Peninsular Malaysia where energy needs are increasing, unlike Borneo where there does not seem to be the growth in demand to warrant the dam's construction. It is also possible that the cable will be used to carry power to other ASEAN members.

Roads need to be carved through dense jungle to bring building materials and engineering equipment to the remote site above the Bakun Rapids. Malaysian lobby groups such as the Environmental Protection Society predict the project will cause severe soil erosion in an area already suffering from the effects of logging. In the early 1990s the river water was clear and fish were abundant; now the river is a muddy brown and water levels fluctuate wildly. Nor is the project a long-term one: even the government admits its productive life is likely to be in the region of 25 years before it silts up. Friends of the Earth Malaysia say: "This project is going to have a tremendous effect on the lives of natives, plants and animals and on the biodiversity of the pristine forests where it is going to be built".

The local tribespeople, mainly Kayan and Kenyah whose ancestors battled for decades against the White Rajahs, have, it seems, finally met their match in Malaysia's relentless thrust towards modernity. Some 9000 of them have been pushed off their ancestral homelands and moved to longhouse settlements in Sungai Asap. Activists claim that many tribespeople were promised jobs on the dam that never materialized. As money concerns have crept in, many of these once proud subsistence farmers have turned to the bottle for comfort.

Many lowlying areas are to be flooded on completion of the dam and boat transport may again be more organized further upriver. Indigenous communities above the Bakun Dam have been resettled in the Sungai Asap area some 40 km away on the Bintulu road. It's possible to stop at Asap when heading back to Bintulu on the coast.

Although these communities have been given compensation, land and housing it seems they had little choice once the dam scheme was finalized. No financial compensation or land was given to upriver longhouses beyond the direct area of flooding in the Bakun Basin – for example, the Kayan Longhouses of Long Benalui, Long Ayak and Uma Batu Kalo. These communities still reside in their original homes. It's possible to stop at the Asap resettlement area when heading back to Bintulu on the coast.

The biggest impact of this project seems to have been felt by the nomadic and semi-nomadic Penan people. Due to their non-agricultural way of life little or no land rights or compensation have been provided, despite having lived in the area for hundreds, perhaps thousands, of years. Logging – and its associated disturbance of the forest – means nomadic people are finding it increasingly difficult to find enough food and make a living in the Upper Rejang basin.

Many of the longhouses around Belaga are quite modern, although several of the Kenyah and Kayan settlements have beautifully carved wooden *salongs* (tombstones) nearby. All the longhouses beyond Belaga are Orang Ulu, upriver tribal groups. Even longhouses which seem to be very remote (such as Long Busang) are now connected by logging roads from Kapit, only four hours' drive away. To get well off the beaten track, into Penan country, it is possible to organize treks from Belaga towards the Kalimantan border, staying in longhouses en route.

About 2 km up the Batang Belaga from Belaga are the **Pasang Rapids** (hire a boat from Belaga), the biggest in Sarawak. No one has deliberately tried to shoot them as they are too dangerous. Boats can get reasonably close, however, and in the dry season it is possible to climb up to a picnic area overlooking the white water.

◉ Sibu, Kapit and Belaga listings

For Sleeping and Eating price codes and other relevant information, see Essentials pages 25-30.

● Sleeping

Sibu *p337, map p336*
Cheaper hotels tend to be around the night market in Chinatown, but there's also a selection within walking distance of the jetty.
AL-A RH, Jln Kampung Nyabor, T084-365888, www.rhhotels.com.my. Huge, sparkling, new hotel overlooking Wisma Sanyan shopping complex and Sibu's spacious new town square. Styling itself as Sibu's No 1 business hotel, this place boasts plenty of luxurious suites (more expensive) with excellent park views and crisp, modern decor. It has a pool and steam bath, and

rooms have Wi-Fi, cable TV and safety deposit boxes. The **Oriental Bistro** serves good coffee and international dishes. Huge discounts often available. Good.
AL-A Tanahmas, Jln Kampong Nyabor, T084-333188, www.tanahmas.com.my. Tall building in the heart of town offering modern, well-furnished rooms with Wi-Fi and good views over the rooftops. There's a pool, karaoke lounge and good restaurant.
A Kingwood, 12 Lorong Lanang 4, T084-335888, kingwood.sibu@yahoo.com.my. Fairly unexciting hotel primarily targeting business visitors. Rooms are comfortable and have cable TV and Wi-Fi. Some have town views and the more expensive ones have good river views. There is a top Chinese restaurant, **Mingziang**, and pool and fitness centre.

A Premier, Jln Kampong Nyabor, T084-323222, www.premierh.com.my. Good restaurant and café with Wi-Fi, clean rooms with a/c, TV, own bath, some with river view. Helpful staff, adjoins **Sarawak House Shopping Centre and Cinema**, discounts often available. Recommended.

B Garden, 1 Jln Huo Ping, T084-317888, gardenhotel_sbw@yahoo.com. This hotel has a flash lobby with a bewildering array of mirrors next to the coffee shop. Rooms are comfortable, but furnishings are a little tatty and old. Renovations are promised in the near future. Staff are friendly and there is Wi-Fi access throughout. Decent buffet breakfast included in the price.

C Li Hua, 18 Lorong 2, Jln Lanang, T084-324000, F326272. Run by one of the local Chinese associations, and often packed with visiting ethnic Chinese, this friendly place has simple, large rooms with TV and attached bathroom. Many rooms offer sweeping views over the Rejang and the dense forest beyond. Highly recommended.

C Phoenix, 1 & 3 Jln Kai Peng (off Jln Kampong Nyabor), T084-313877, F320392. Spotless, slightly old hotel with a selection of clean a/c rooms with attached bathroom and TV. Good value.

C Victoria Inn, 80 Jln Market, T084-320099, F320055. New place with clean rooms, some windowless in the heart of town. Rooms are well furnished and good value.

C-D Eden Inn, 1 Jln Lanang, T084-337277. Next to the 60s-style Sacred Heart Church, this well-run place is owned by a local Catholic association and has a selection of large, spotless a/c rooms with TV and attached bathroom. Excellent value. Recommended.

C-D River Park, 51-53 Jln Maju, T084-316688, F316689. Close to the action on the esplanade, this functional hotel has clean rooms, more expensive with river views.

D Bahagia, 21 Jln Wong Nai Siong, T084-331131, F320536. Small place off a busy street with friendly management and clean rooms with TV, Wi-Fi access and attached bathroom. There's a good restaurant downstairs.

Kapit *p338, map p339*
All are within walking distance of the wharf.

B Greenland Inn, 463 Jln Teo Chow Beng, T084-796388, F797989. This clean place offers 19 well-maintained spacious rooms with a/c, TV and attached bathroom. Often full at weekends. A little expensive given the competition in town.

B-C Ark Hill Inn, Lot 451, Jln Penghulu Gerining (off the Town Square), T084-796168, arkhill@streamyx.com. Fair value place with 20 a/c rooms with attached bath and TV. The single rooms here are small, but doubles offer greater value. Although clean, the walls could do with a lick of paint. Wi-Fi access available.

B-C River View Inn, 10 Jln Tan Sit Leong. Largely uninspiring place with a selection of spacious, clean a/c rooms with Wi-Fi access and TV. Many of the rooms are windowless.

C New Rejang Inn, 28 Jln Temenggong Jugah, T084-796600, F799600. Friendly hotel with 4 flights of steep steps and spotless a/c rooms with TV (1 cable channel), powerful showers and liberally scattered bibles. Room 401 has a good partial view of the murky Rejang. Recommended.

D Hiap Chiong, 33 Jln Temenggong Jugah, T084-796314. This place has a strangely institutional feel but looks like it has survived the test of time. Rooms, though old, are good value with small TV, attached bathroom and TV. Room 307 is huge and offers the finest river views of any hotel in town.

D Rejang, 28 New Bazaar, T084-796709. Archaic place with furniture made before you were born. The TVs and fridges are similarly old, but rooms, though not particularly cheerful, are cheap. The **Hiap Chong** is better value in this price range.

Pelagus Rapids *p340*

A-B Pelagus Resort, set on the banks of the Rejang overlooking the rapids, T084-799051, www.theregencyhotel.com.my. 40 longhouse-style rooms, with restaurant, pool, bar and sun deck, de luxe rooms have a/c, otherwise fans. Trips organized from resort to longhouses, nature treks and river safaris, whitewater rafting on the rapids. Express boats pass through rapids upstream.

Longhouses p340

D Rumah Tuan Lepong Balleh, see page 341. Stay in this longhouse, RM30 inclusive of meals, generator until 2300, basic. It's about 1 hr from Kapit; take a minibus and ask for **Selvat and Friends Traditional Hostel and Longhouse**.

Belaga p341

C-D Belaga Hotel, 14 Belaga Bazaar, T086-461244. Some a/c, restaurant, no hot water, friendly proprietor, good coffee shop, in-house video and cicadas. Best option.

D B&B, 4 Belaga Bazaar (upstairs from **Worldwide Exploration Travel and Tour** office), T086-461512. Run by the Mr Hasbee of Hasbee Enterprises, this mellow place has a dorm and a double room with fan and a/c on offer. This is a good place to source local information and guides.

D Bee Lian, 11 Belaga Bazaar, T086-461439. A/c, 9 rooms, all reasonable.

D Sing Soon Huat, 26-27 New Bazaar. T086-461413, F461346. Smart, friendly, pleasant living area with TV, movies, etc. A good choice.

D-E Sing Soon Hing, 15 New Bazaar. Same owners and contact details as **Sing Soon Huat**. Much cheaper resthouse kind of affair, a little gloomy, but clean, rooms with private shower. Good for those on a tight budget.

❼ Eating

Sibu p337, map p336

With such a large Chinese population, it's no surprise that the many coffee shops and hawker centres are packed with Chinese eateries. One Sibu speciality is *kampua mee*, a fatty dish of noodles and pork lard served with roasted pork or pork balls with soup.

¶¶ Ark Café and Gallery, Jln Maju, T084 313 445. Open 1000-2300. Uber-stylish place on the riverfront with elevated seating and river views. The restaurant is set around a banyan

tree with plenty of water features and has a menu of international and local favourites.

¶¶ Blue Splendour 3rd floor, Wisma Sanyan Shopping Complex. Good Shanghainese, Cantonese and Hokkien cuisine including *nestum* prawns, *kampua mee* and steamed fish dishes. Held in high regard by locals.

¶¶ Café Café, 10 Jln Chew Geok Lin, T084 328 101. Open 1200-1600 and 1800-2300. Friendly and stylish eatery with Nyonya, Thai and Western dishes. Good value.

¶¶ Golden Palace, Tanahmas hotel, Jln Kampong Nyabor. Cantonese and Sichuan.

¶¶ Mama Café, 4th floor, Wisma Senyan Shopping Complex. Relaxed place with large glass windows looking over the eastern side of town. The menu has lots of coffees, mocktails and Korean dishes. Their signature is the Korean steamboat.

¶¶ Peppers Café, Tanahmas Hotel, Jln Kampong Nyabor. A favourite with visiting foreigners, this hotel eatery has a good selection of Western and local food. Popular.

¶¶ Sri Meranti, 1A Jln Hardin. Friendly staff, good seafood, nice sitting-out area with cold beer and tablecloths.

¶ Kasturi, 18 Jln Tunku Osman. One of the town's most celebrated Malay places with great curries and seafood. Also a selection of Melanau dishes and including *tebaloi* and *umai* (raw fish salad – delicious)

¶ Mr and Mrs Yeo's Stall, Lorong Tiong Hua (mornings only). This friendly local spot dishes up a local speciality, *konpia*, a fresh bread roll served with pork broth and slices of pork.

¶ Rafis Café, Jln Kampong Datu. Open 0700-2300. Very popular place with a great *nasi campur* selection. Recommended by locals.

¶ Sri Menanti Chicken Rice, 26 Jln Mission, T084-316 904. Open 0830-2100. Functional a/c restaurant offering chicken rice in every conceivable form with good Chinese vegetable dishes in sauces including *sambal belacan*.

Foodstalls

Jln Market Food Court, Jln Market, near Premier Hotel. Good selection of Chinese and Malay stalls.

Rex Food Court, 28 Jln Cross. New and clean.
Sibu Central Market, 1st floor. Over 30 stalls
serving mainly Chinese dishes, but with a few
interesting local offerings.

Kapit *p338, map p339*

There is nothing very exciting about dining
in Kapit. Most of the locals are content with
eating and relaxing in the town's many coffee
shops. Food to look out for includes fresh river
fish (including the very expensive *emparau*,
Borneo masheer), and Rejang prawns.
🍴 **Orchard Inn**, Jln Teo Chow Beng, T084-
796325. A/c restaurant with a simple menu
of Chinese seafood and meat dishes. Not a
bad choice for a meal and beer. Popular with
the local Chinese.
🍴 **Ah Kau**, Jln Berjaya. Good spot for local
seafood dishes.
🍴 **Chun Cheng**, Jln Pedral. Held in high regard
among the locals, this place offers mainly
Chinese and some halal Malay dishes.
🍴 **MAS Islamic Café**, Jln Pedral. Good choice
for well-made Malay specialities.
🍴 **MI**, Jln Pedral. Good selection of Malay staples
including *ayam bakar*, *laksa Sarawak* and a good
nasi campur spread, all in a/c comfort.

Bakeries and coffee shops

Chuong Hin, opposite the Sibu wharf.
Best-stocked coffee shop in town.
Ung Tong Bakery, opposite the market.
Very friendly family-run bakery offering
sweet treats, simple breakfasts and
Asian-style (soft and sweet) fresh bread.
Big selection of rolls and good coffee, fresh
bread baked daily (1500). Recommended.

Foodstalls

Gelanggang Kenyalang, opposite the
Orchard Inn. Look for the brightly painted
exterior of this covered food court. It's usually
the first place recommended by locals and has
a range of Chinese and Malay stalls. Here you
can find a Kapit speciality, the heart-stoppingly
unhealthy, but fiendishly tasty, deep-fried *roti
canai*, found at the Malay stall on the 1st floor.

Belaga *p341*

Several small, cheap coffee shops along
Belaga Bazaar and Main Bazaar.

O Shopping

Sibu *p337, map p336*
Handicrafts

Stalls along express boat wharves at Jln
Channel, mainly selling basketware.
Chop Kion Huat, Jln Market, just behind the
tourist information office. Sarawak handicrafts:
batik, basketware, T-shirts and carvings.

Markets

Native market (Lembangan market),
Lembangan River between Jln Mission
and Jln Channel. Sells jungle produce.
Pasar Malam (night market), High St, Jln
Market and Lembangan Lane, Chinatown.

Pottery

2 potteries at Km 7 and 12 Ulu Oya Rd.

Supermarket

Sarawak House Shopping Complex,
Jln Kampong Nyabor, has **Premier**
Department Store. There's a good
minimarket opposite **Chop Kion Huat**
handicraft shop on Jln Market with fruit
juice, wine, spirits and Marmite, and is a
good place to stock up on shampoo and
shower gel. There's a book and magazine
shop on the ground floor of Sarawak House
Complex that sells English magazines.

Kapit *p338, map p339*
Handicrafts

Din Chu Café, next to Methodist
Guesthouse. Sells antiques and handicrafts.
Lai Lai Antique Shop, the second floor of the
Gelanggang Kenyalang complex. Small range
of woven rugs/sarongs, prices are high but
similar to the starting prices at longhouses.

Belaga *p341*
Handicrafts

Chop Teck Hua, Belaga Bazaar. An intriguing selection of tribal jewellery, old coins, beads, feathers, woodcarvings, blowpipes, parangs, tattoo boards and other curios buried under cobwebs and gecko droppings at the back of the shop; the owner is noticeably uninformed about the objects he sells.

▲ Activities and tours

Sibu *p337, map p336*
Golf
Sibu Golf Club, Km 17, Ulu Oya Rd.

Tour operators
Most companies run city tours plus tours of longhouses, Mulu National Park and Niah Caves. It is cheaper to organize upriver trips from Kapit or Belaga than from Sibu.
Greatown Travel, No 6 1st floor, Lorong Chew Siik Hiong 1A, T084-211243, www.rajangtourism.blogspot.com. Currently the leading operator offering longhouse tours and rainforest treks. Highly recommended.
Sazhong Trading & Travel, 4 Jln Central, T084-336017, www.geocities.com/sazhong. Director Frankie Ting can arrange budget stays for groups in a longhouse in Kapit and beyond.
Travel Consortium, 14 Jln Central, T084-334455, F330589. Good for air ticketing.

Kapit *p338, map p339*
Tour operators
There has been a number of recent complaints made by tourists who feel they have been overcharged for unsatisfactory tours. Often the guides are young local guys with a fair command of English but limited experience guiding foreigners who are paying handsomely for the experience. The Sarawak Tourist Information Office in Sibu and the Kapit Resident's Office recommend using guides from **Alice Tours and Travel**,

Lorong 6 Jln Airport (a good 25-min walk from town in a residential area past the overgrown airport), T019-859 3126, atta_kpt@yahoo.com. Day trips to visit the longhouse at Bundong start at RM198, and an overnight trip including a stay at the longhouse starts at RM285. Owner Alice Chua recommends booking tours at least a week in advance. Local expert **Joshua Muda**, T084-796600, joshuamuda@hotmail.com, arranges sensitive and authentic longhouse trips. Some hotels will help organize trips, or ask at the police station.

Belaga *p341*
Tour operators
Belaga Hotel will contact guides for upriver trips and the district office can also recommend a handful of experienced guides. In this part of Sarawak, guides are particularly expensive – sometimes up to RM80 a day, mainly because there are not enough tourists to justify full-time work. It is necessary to hire experienced boatmen too, because of the numerous rapids. Guides recommended by Sarawak Tourism include **John Belakirk**, T086-461512, johneddie1@hotmail.com; **Hamdani Louis**, T086-461039, hamdani@ hotmail.com; **Andreas Bato**, T019-3722972, niestabato@yahoo.com, an Orang Ulu guide with perfect English; **Councilor Daniel Levoh**, No.34, Lot 1051, Jln Bato Luhat, New Bazaar, H/P 013-8486351, T086-461176, daniellevoh@ hotmail.com. This guide often seems busy picking up clients for upriver trips, with his family contacts throughout the area, and much of Belaga's tourism business is under his control. While it's true Daniel is good at the arranging and bureaucracy side, he falls pretty short with the guiding itself, spending most his time snoozing away the day.

Prices for longhouse trips upriver vary according to distance and water level, but are similar to those in Kapit. English is not widely spoken upriver so basic Bahasa comes in handy.

O Transport

Sibu *p337, map p336*
Air
The airport is 25 km north of town. Regular connections with **Kuching** on MAS, MASwings and Air Asia (around 7 flights a day), **Bintulu** (on MASwings, 2 flights daily), **Miri** on MASwings (3 flights daily), **KK** (2 direct flights daily with MASwings and Air Asia, 2 daily flights via Bintulu) and **KL** (MAS flies daily and AirAsia, has 3 daily flights).

Airline offices MAS, 61 Jln Tunku Osman, T084-326166. **AirAsia**, Jln Kai Peng.

Boat
All boats leave from the wharf. The time of the next departure is shown by big clock faces on whiteboards; just buy the ticket at the jetty. There is 1 express boat daily between Sibu and **Kuching** (5 hrs, RM45). **Ekspress Bahagia** (T084-319228) leaves at 1130. This boat stops off at **Sarekei** (RM10). There are regular express boats to **Kapit**, every 30 mins from 0545 until 1500, 2-3 hrs RM20 economy/RM25 second class/RM30 first class, and in the wet season, when the river is high enough, they continue to **Belaga**, 5-6 hrs. It is not possible to travel up river to Belaga in a day, as you need a permit from the Resident's Office in Kapit. However, in case the situation changes, there is a daily boat from Sibu to Belaga (RM40) at 0530 when the water is high enough. This service doesn't usually run in the dry season (Jul-Sep). Some Sibu–Kapit boats stop off at **Kanowit** and **Song** on their way upriver.

Bus
Local Buses leave from Jln Khoo Peng Loong.
Long distance Buses leave from the long-distance bus terminal at Jln Pahlawan. To get there take a taxi (a negotiable RM15), or bus No 12 or No 17 from the local bus station. There are 3 main long-distance bus companies: Biaramas Express, Borneo Highway Express and Suria Express which all have routes from Sibu to Bintulu, Miri and Kuching. Regular connections with **Bintulu**, (4 hrs, RM20), and **Miri** (6-7 hrs, RM40), along a surfaced road. First bus leaves around 0630, and last bus at 0100, departures every hour or so. Best to purchase tickets the day before departure – there are ticket offices for the different companies around the jetty or else buy from the bus station. Early morning buses to Bintulu connect with the buses direct to **Batu Niah** (see page 366). There are also daily connections with **Kuching** via **Sarikei** (8 hrs to Kuching, RM40, 2 hrs to Sarikei, RM10). There are around 10 daily departures 0700-2400.

International connections There are evening departures to **Pontianak**, Kalimantan (RM80, 16 hrs).

Kapit *p338, map p339*
Boat
All 3 wharves are close together. A new Kapit/Sibu Express Boat Terminal opened in late 2009. Regular connections with **Sibu**, 0630-1500, RM20-30 depending on class, 2-3 hrs. **Belaga** is not accessible by large express boats during the dry season (Jul-Sep). There is a daily express boat to Belaga at 0930, RM35. In the dry season smaller speed boats sometimes go upriver (RM60-100 per person).

Belaga *p341*
Air
At the time of research flights between Belaga and Bintulu had been suspended. Check www.maswings.com.my for updates.

Airline offices MAS, c/o Lau Chun Kiat, Main Bazaar.

Boat
There is a daily boat from **Kapit** leaving at 0930, RM35, only in the wet season; the journey takes around 5 hrs. In the dry season speedboats leave from Kapit, from RM60 per person. When the river is very low the only option is to drive to Belaga from **Bintulu**.

To **Tubau** and on to **Bintulu**: it is possible to hire a boat from Belaga to Kestima Kem (logging camp) near Rumah Lahanan Laseh

(RM60 per person in a group or RM260 for 2-3 people); from there logging trucks go to Tabau on the Kemena River. Logging trucks leave irregularly and you can get stuck in logging camps. It is a 3-hr drive to Tabau; this trip is not possible in the wet season. There are regular express boats from Tabau to Bintulu (RM12). This is the fastest and cheapest route to Bintulu, but not the most reliable. It is necessary to obtain permission from the Residents' Office and the police station in Belaga to take this route.

Car
At the moment Belaga is comparatively isolated and overland links are poor. During the dry season it is possible to travel by 4WD overland to **Bintulu** (see below), but it is drawn out and expensive. It is likely that road links will keep improving, particularly with the controversial Bakun Dam project still under construction. The Bakun to Bintulu road has been gradually upgraded and is now surfaced along almost its full length. To charter a 4WD for the whole journey to Bintulu costs RM300-400 for 5 people and the journey takes 5 hrs. **Hasbee Enterprises**, 4 Belaga Bazaar, can help with a 4WD or try **Hap Kiat Transport**, T013-807 5598. They have a Toyota Landcruiser that leaves Belaga daily at 0730 and returns from Bintulu at 1330 (RM60). Those wishing to travel overland from Bintulu must report to the Bintulu Resident's Office and the Belaga Resident's Office. For more information phone the Kapit Resident's Office, T084-796445. Keep a close eye on people's driving abilities in this area – many drive while drunk and large logging trucks speeding round the sharp bends can be a significant danger.

<0> Directory

Sibu *p337, map p336*
Banks Standard Chartered, 25 Jln Tukang Besi HSBC, Bangunan Grand Merlin, 131 Jln Nyabor. Apart from the banks, cash can be exchanged at good rates at goldsmiths around town. **Internet** There are a number of good places in the Wisma Sanyan Shopping Complex. **Police** Jln Kampong Nyabor, T084-322222. **Post office** General Post Office, Jln Kampong Nyabor 0800-1800. **Residents' Office** T084-321963.

Kapit *p338, map p339*
Banks There are 2 banks which will accept TCs, one in the New Bazaar and the other on Jln Airport, but it is easier to change money in Sibu. **Libraries** On the other side of the road from 1st floor State Government Complex. Good selection of books on history and natural history of Borneo. There's also internet access. Mon-Sat 1615-2030, Sun 0900-1115, 1400-1630.

Belaga *p341*
Internet Hasbee Enterprises, 4 Belaga Bazaar (RM6 per hr), 0700-1900. Painfully slow connection. **Post office** In the District Office.

North coast

The north coast of Sarawak is fairly remote, with Bintulu, Miri and Marudi being the only significant towns. Close to Bintulu is Similajau National Park where green turtles lay their eggs. Niah National Park boasts famous limestone caves and is home to jungle birds and primates. Miri is the launch pad for river trips into the interior and Marudi is an upriver trading post and the start of a cross-border trek. Bintulu is accessible by air, boat from Tubau in the interior and bus. Miri is accessible by air and bus and Marudi by air and boat. ⏵ *For listings, see pages 360-368.*

On the Kemena River, Bintulu is in the heart of Melinau country and was a fishing and farming centre until the largest natural gas reserve in Malaysia was discovered offshore in the late 1970s, making Bintulu a boom town overnight. **Shell**, **Petronas** and **Mitsubishi** then moved into the town in force. Modern Bintulu has a frontier town atmosphere, with muddy 4WDs ploughing streets lined with an inordinate number of short-time hotels and sleazy *dangdut* and karaoke lounges popular with stimulation-starved oil men on boozy weekend escapades.

Few tourists stay long in Bintulu, despite it being the jumping-off point for the Similajau National Park and the Niah Caves. The longhouses on the Kemena River are accessible, but tend not to be as interesting as those further up the Rejang and Baram rivers. The Penan and Kayan tribes are very hospitable and eager to show off their longhouses and traditions to tourists.

The word Bintulu is believed to be a corruption of Mentu Ulau, which translates as 'the place for gathering heads'.

There is no government tourist information office in Bintulu; for enquiries contact the **Bintulu Development Authority** ① *T086-332011.* The **Sarawak Forestry Department** ① *www.sarawak. forestry.gov.my*, provides information on the national parks around Bintulu. Visitors can also contact the **National Parks Booking Office** ① *T086-331117, ext 50, F331923.*

Background

The remnants of the old fishing village at Kampong Jepak are on the opposite bank of the Kemena River. During the Brooke era the town was a small administrative centre. The **clocktower** commemorates the meeting of five members of the Brooke government and 16 local chieftains, creating Council Negeri, the state legislative body.

The first project to break ground in Bintulu was the RM100-million crude oil terminal at Tanjong Kidurong from which 45,000 barrels of petroleum are exported

Bintulu

To Tanjung Kiderong, Mosque, Taman Tumbina, Miri & Long-distance Bus Terminal

Clock Tower

Lebuh Raya Abang Galau

Local Pasar Bintulu

Kemena River

Wet Market

Jl Tun Razak

Pasar Malam

Jl Law Gek Soon

Jl Market

Taxi

Taxi   Jl Temple

Jl Somerville

Jl Reservoir

To Airport

Jl Keppel

Main Bazaar   Jl Pedada

Jetty

MAS

Jl Sri Dagang

Jl Masjid

Jl Abang Galau

Pasar Malam (Night Market)

100 metres
100 yards

Sleeping
AA Inn **1**
Kintown Inn **3**
Regency **4**
Riverfront Inn **5**

Royal **6**
Sea View **12**
Sunlight Inn **7**

Eating
An Nur Nasi Padang
Sambal Belado **1**
Makan United **5**
Nasi Ayam Singapore **6**
Popular Corner **2**

daily. A deep-water port was built and the liquefied natural gas (LNG) plant started operating in 1982. The abundant supply of natural gas also created investment in related downstream projects. The main industrial area at Tanjong Kidurong is 20 km from Bintulu. The **viewing tower** at Tanjong Kidurong gives a panoramic view of the new-look Bintulu and out to the timber ships on the horizon. They anchor 15 km offshore to avoid port duties and the timber is taken out on barges.

Sights

Bintulu has a modern Moorish-style mosque called the **Masjid Assyakirin**; visitors may be allowed in when it is not prayer time. There is a colourful, centrally located Chinese temple called **Tua Pek Kong**. The **Pasar Bintulu** is an impressive building in the centre of town, built to house a local jungle produce market, foodstalls and some limited handicrafts stalls. A landscaped wildlife park, **Taman Tumbina** ⓘ *www.tumbina.com.my, daily 0800-1800, RM2*, has been developed on the outskirts of town, on the way to Tanjong Batu. It is a local recreational area and contains a small zoo, including a hornbill collection, a botanic garden (the only one in Sarawak) and a newly opened **Butterfly World**.

Longhouses

Trips to the longhouses on the Kemena River (which are rarely visited) can be organized from Bintulu. More than 20 Kemena River longhouses can be reached by road or river within 30 minutes of Bintulu. Iban longhouses are the closest; further upriver are the more traditional Kayan and Kenyah longhouses. Overpriced tours are organized by **Similajau Adventure Tours**; or hire a boat from the wharf.

Similajau National Park → *For listings, see pages 360-368. Colour map 3, B4.*

Lying 20 km northeast of Bintulu, Similajau is a coastal park with sandy beaches, broken by rocky headlands. It is Sarawak's most unusually shaped national park, being more than 32 km long and only 1.5 km wide. Similajau was demarcated in 1978, but has only been open to tourists since the construction of decent facilities in 1991. **Pasir Mas** (Golden Sands) is a beautiful 3.5-km-long stretch of coarse beach, to the north of the Likau River, where green turtles come ashore to lay their eggs between July and September. A few kilometres from the Park HQ at **Kuala Likau** is a small coral reef, known as **Batu Mandi**. The area is renowned for birdwatching. Bintulu is not on the main tourist route and consequently the park is very quiet. Its seclusion makes it a perfect escape.

The beaches are backed by primary rainforest: peat swamp, *kerangas* (heath forest), mixed dipterocarp and mangrove (along Sungai Likau and Sungai Sebubong). There are small rapids on the Sebulong River. Sadly, the rivers, particularly the beautiful **Sungai Likau**, have been polluted by indiscriminate logging activities upstream.

Ins and outs

Permits are available from the **Bintulu Development Authority** ⓘ *T086-332011*. There's also an **information centre** ⓘ *Park HQ, at the mouth of Sungai Likau, across the river from the park*. A boat is needed to cross the 5 m of crocodile-infested river. Because the park facilities are outside the park boundaries, visitors do not need a permit to stay there. This has led to the 'park' becoming popular with Bintulites at the weekend.

Niah's guano collectors: scraping the bottom

Eight bat species live in the Niah Caves. Some are quite common, such as the horseshoe bat and fruit bats, while other, more exotic, varieties include the bearded tomb bat, Cantor's roundleaf horseshoe bat and the lesser bent-winged bat.

The ammonia-stench of bat guano permeates the humid air. People began collecting guano in 1929 and it is used as a fertilizer and to prevent pepper vines from rotting. Guano collectors pay a licence fee for the privilege of sweeping up *tahi sapu* (fresh guano) and digging up *tahi timbang* (mature guano), which they sell to the Bat Guano Cooperative at the end of the plankwalk.

Flora and fauna

On arrival at Kuala Likau there is a prominent sign advising against swimming in the river and to watch your feet around the Park HQ area; Similajau is well known for its saltwater crocodiles (*Crocodylus perosus*). It also has 24 resident species of mammal (including gibbons, Hose's langurs, banded langurs, long-tailed macaques, civets, wild boar, porcupines and squirrels) and 185 species of birds (including many migratory species). There are some good coral reefs to the north and marine life includes dolphins, porpoises and turtles. Pitcher plants grow in the *kerangas* forest and along the beach.

Treks

Several longish but not-too-difficult trails have been cut from the Park HQ by park rangers. One path follows undulating terrain, parallel to the coast. It is possible to cut to the left, through the jungle, to the coast, and walk back to Kuala Likau along the beach. The main trail to **Golden Beach** is a three- to four-hour walk crossing several streams and rivers where estuarine crocodiles are reputed to lurk. Most of these crossings are on 'bridges', which are usually just felled trees with no attempt made to assist walkers; a good sense of balance is required. Another enjoyable walk is the trail to **Selansur Rapids**, around 2½ hours in total. Follow the trail to Golden Beach; after about an hour a marked trail leads off into the forest. The walk ends at the rapids where it is possible to take a dip and cool off.

Niah National Park → For listings, see pages 360-368. Colour map 3, A5.

Niah's famous caves, tucked into a limestone massif called Gunung Subis (394 m), made world headlines in 1958, when they were confirmed as the most important archaeological site in Asia. The park is one of the most popular tourist attractions in Sarawak and more than 15,000 visitors come here every year. The caves were declared a national historic monument in 1958, but it was not until 1974 that the 30 sq km of jungle surrounding the caves were turned into a national park to protect the area from logging.

The park primarily comprises alluvial or peat swamp and mixed dipterocarp forest. Long-tailed macaques, hornbills, squirrels, flying lizards and crocodiles have all been recorded here. There are also bat hawks, which provide an impressive spectacle when they home in on one of the millions of bats which pour out of the caves at dusk.

Ins and outs

Getting there The nearest town to the park is Batu Niah. There are regular bus connections with Miri (just under two hours), Bintulu (two hours) and Sibu. From Batu

Niah it is around 3 km to the Park HQ and the caves. Either walk through the forest (45 minutes), take a longboat, or take a taxi. ▶▶ *See Transport, page 367.*

Getting around From Park HQ there are well-marked trails to the caves. Longboats can be chartered for upriver trips.

Tourist information Park HQ ① *Pangkalan Lubang next to Sungai Niah, park daily 0800-1700, caves daily 0800-1630, RM10, children RM5 (camera RM5, video RM10, professional photography RM200); for more information on the park, contact the Deputy Park Warden, Niah National Park, PO Box 81, Miri Post Office, Batu Niah, T085-737454 or T085-737 450.* Guides are not essential but they provide information and can relate legends about the paintings. Even with a guide, visitors cannot cross the barrier 3 m in front of the cave wall. Guides charge RM40 for groups of up to 20 and can be hired from Park HQ. Longboats can be hired from Park HQ for upriver trips (maximum of eight people per boat). Bring a powerful torch for the caves. Walking boots are advisable during the wet season as the plankwalk can get very slippery.

History
About 40,000 years ago, when the Gulf of Thailand and the Sunda Shelf were still dry ground and a land bridge linked the Philippines and Borneo, Niah was home to *Homo sapiens*. It was the most exciting archaeological discovery since Java man (*Homo erectus*).

Scientist and explorer A Hart Everett led expeditions to Niah Caves in 1873 and 1879, after which he pronounced that they justified no further work. Some 79 years later, Tom Harrisson, ethnologist, explorer, conservationist and curator of the Sarawak Museum, confirmed the most important archaeological find at that time in Southeast Asia at Niah. He unearthed fragments of a 37,000-year-old human skull – the earliest evidence of *Homo sapiens* in the region – at the west mouth of the Niah Great Cave itself. The skull was buried under 2.4 m of guano. His find debunked and prompted a radical reappraisal of

Niah National Park

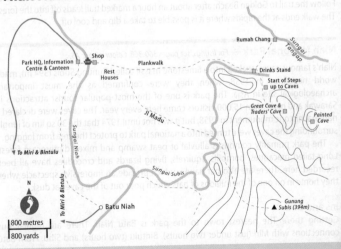

How to make a swift buck

The Malay name for the Painted Cave is Kain Hitam (black cloth), because the profitable rights to the birds' nests were historically exchanged for bolts of black cloth.

The Chinese have had a taste for swiftlets' nests for well over 1000 years, and the business of collecting them from 60 m up in the cavernous chamber of the Great Cave is as lucrative – and as hazardous – a profession now as it was then. The nests are used to prepare birds' nest soup – blended with chicken stock and rock salt – which is a famous Chinese delicacy, prized as an aphrodisiac and for its supposed remedial properties for asthma and rheumatism.

Birds' nests are one of the most expensive foods in the world: they sell for up to US$500 per kg in Hong Kong, where about 100 tonnes of them (worth US$40 million) are consumed annually. The Chinese communities of North America import 30 tonnes of birds' nests a year. Locally, they fetch RM150-600 per kg, depending on the grade.

Hundreds of thousands – possibly millions – of swiftlets (of the *Collocalia* swift family) live in the caves. Unlike other parts of Southeast Asia, where collectors use rotan ladders to reach the nests (see Gomantong Caves, Sabah, page 458), Niah's collectors scale *belian* (ironwood) poles to heights of more than 60 m. They use bamboo sticks with a scraper attached to one end (called *penyulok*) to pick the nests off the cave roof. The nests are harvested three times each season (the seasons run from August to December and January to March). On the first two occasions, the nests are removed before

the eggs are laid and a third are left until the nestlings are fledged. Nest collectors are now all supposed to have licences but, in reality, no one does. Although the birds' nests are supposed to be protected by the national park in the off-season, wardens turn a blind eye to illegal harvesting; the collectors also know many secret entrances to the caves. Officially, people caught harvesting out of season can be fined RM2000 or sent to jail for a year, but no one's ever caught.

Despite being a dangerous operation (there are usually several fatal accidents at Niah each year), collecting has become so popular that harvesters have to reserve their spot with a lamp. Nest collecting is run on a first-come, first-served basis. Nests of the white-nest swiftlets and the black-nest swiftlets are collected – the nests of the mossy-nest and white-bellied swiftlets require too much effort to clean. The nests are built by the male swiftlets using a glutinous substance produced by the salivary glands under the tongue which is regurgitated in long threads; the saliva sets like cement producing a rounded cup which sticks to the cave wall. In the swifts' nest market, price is dictated by colour: the best are the white nests which are without any plant material or feathers. Most of the uncleaned nests are bought up by middle-men, agents of traders in Kuching, but locals at Batu Niah also do some of the cleaning. The nests are first soaked in water for about three hours and, when softened, feathers and dirt are laboriously removed with tweezers. The 'cakes' of nests are dried over-night: if left in the sun they turn yellow.

popular theories about where modern man's ancestors had sprung from. A wide range of palaeolithic and neolithic tools, pottery, ornaments and beads was also found at the site. Anthropologists believe Niah's caves may have been permanently inhabited until around AD 1400. Harrisson's excavation site, office and house have been left intact in the mouth of the Great Cave. A total of 166 burial sites have been excavated, 38 of which are Mesolithic (up to 20,000 years ago) and the remainder neolithic (4000 years ago). Some of the finds are now in the Sarawak Museum in Kuching.

Park Information Centre

ⓘ *Mon-Fri 0800-1230 and 1400-1615, Sat 0800-1245, Sun 0800-1200.*

At the Park HQ is this centre, with displays on birds' nests and flora and fauna. The exhibition includes the 37,000-year-old human skull which drew world attention to Niah in 1958. Also on display are 35,000-year-old oyster shells and palaeolithic pig bones, monkey bones, turtle shells and crabs, found littering the cave floor. There are also burial vessels dating from 1600 BC and carved seashell jewellery from 400 BC.

The caves

To reach the caves, take a longboat across the river from Park HQ at Pangkalan Lubang to the start of the 4-km **belian** (ironwood) plankwalk to the entrance of the **Great Cave**. Take the right fork 1 km from the entrance. The remains of a small kampong, formerly inhabited by birds' nest collectors (see below) and guano collectors, is just before the entrance, in the shelter of overhanging rocks. It is known as **Traders' Cave**. Beware of voracious insects; wear long trousers and plenty of repellent. There are no lights in the Great Cave, so torches are needed.

The **Painted Cave** is beyond the Great Cave. Prehistoric wall paintings – the only ones in Borneo – stretch for about 32 m along the cave wall. Most of the drawings are of dancing human figures and boats, thought to be associated with a death ritual. On the floor of the cave, several 'death-ships' were found with some Chinese stoneware, shell ornaments and ancient glass beads. These death-ships served as coffins and have been carbon-dated to between AD 1 and AD 780. By around AD 700 there is thought to have been a flourishing community based in the caves, trading hornbill ivory and birds' nests with the Chinese in exchange for porcelain and beads. But then it seems the caves were suddenly deserted in about 1400. In Penan folklore there are references to 'the ancestors who lived in the big caves' and tribal elders are said to be able to recall funeral rites using death boats similar to those found at Niah.

Treks

A lowland trail called **Jalan Madu** (Honey Road), traverses the peat swamp forest and ascends Gunung Subis; it is not well marked. Return trips need a full day. The trail leads off the plankwalk to the right, about 1 km from Pangkalan Lubang (Park HQ). The left fork on the plankwalk, before the gate to the caves, goes to an Iban longhouse, Rumah Chang (40 minutes' walk), where cold drinks can be bought.

Miri and the Baram River → *For listings, see pages 360-368. Colour map 3, A5.*

Miri is the starting point for adventurous trips up the Baran River to Marudi, Bario and the Kelabit Highlands. Also accessible from Miri and Marudi is the incomparable Gunung Mulu National Park with the biggest limestone cave system in the world and one of the richest assemblages of plants and animals. The capital of Sarawak's Fourth Division is a prosperous, predominantly Chinese town with one of Malaysia's best selections of restaurants and back streets filled with karaoke lounges and ladies of the night. While there isn't a great deal to do in the town itself, many visitors find Miri a good place to recuperate after the rigours of the road and often spend a couple of days enjoying the bustling streets and bountiful food on offer. The waterfront development on the north side of town has a marina; there is a pleasant walk on the Peninsula here across the Miri River, and some good fishing.

Ins and outs

Getting there The **airport** ⓘ T085-615433, is close to the centre of town. Taxi coupon from the airport into town costs RM22. Bus No 28 (RM2.20) goes almost hourly to the airport 0700-1830. Buses from the airport run almost hourly from 0720-1850 and drop passengers at the local bus terminal near the Tourist Information Centre. The new bus terminal at Pujuk Padang Kerbau, Jln Padang, is around 4 km from the town centre. A taxi to the terminal costs RM15. Or take bus No 33 from outside the tourist centre.

Tourist information The **Tourist Information Centre** ⓘ *Jln Malay (next to bus station and just across from the Park Hotel), T085-434181, www.sarawaktourism.com, Mon-Fri 0800-1800 and Sat, Sun and public holidays 0900-1500,* can offer maps and tourist information, but contrary to popular belief, they do not assist with accommodation booking.

Permits These are now only required for travel to Bario. Apply at the **Residents' Office** ⓘ *Jln Kwantung, T085-433202/03,* with a passport photocopy. For further information visitors can also contact the **National Parks and Wildlife Office** ⓘ *Jln Puchong, T085-436 637, F431975.* Book national park accommodation through the relevant national park office: for **Gunung Mulu** ⓘ *T085-792300 or T085-432561;* for the **Lambir Hills** ⓘ *T085-491030;* for **Loagan Bunut** ⓘ *T085-779410;* for **Niah** ⓘ *T085-737454,* and for **Similajau** ⓘ *T085-391284.*

A **visa extension** this can be obtained at the **immigration office**, see page 368.

Background

In the latter years of the 19th century, a small trading company set up in Sarawak to import kerosene and export polished shells and pepper. In 1910, when 'earth oil' was first struck on the hill overlooking Miri, the small trading company took the plunge and diversified into the new commodity – making, in the process, Sarawak's first oil town. The company's name was **Shell**. Together with the Malaysian national oil company, **Petronas**, Shell has been responsible for discovering, producing and refining Sarawak's offshore oil deposits. Oil is a key contributor to Malaysia's export earnings and Miri has been a beneficiary of the boom. There is a big refinery at Lutong to the north, which is connected by pipeline with Seria in Brunei. Lutong is the next town on the Miri River and the main headquarters for Shell.

The oil boom in this area began on Canada Hill, behind the town (incidentally, this limestone ridge provides excellent views). **Oil Well No 1** was built by Shell and was the first oil well in Malaysia, spudded on 10 August 1910. The well was still yielding oil 62 years later, but its productivity began to slump. It is estimated that a total of 600,000 barrels were extracted from Well No 1 during its operational life. It was shut off in 1972. There are now 624 oil wells in the Miri Field, producing 80 million barrels of oil a year.

Sights

Juxtaposed against Miri's modern boom-town image is **Tamu Muhibba** ⓘ *open 24 hrs,* the native jungle produce market, which is opposite the **Park Hotel** in a purpose-built concrete structure with pointed roofs on the roundabout connecting Jalan Malay and Jalan Padang. The Orang Ulu come downriver to sell their produce and a walk around the market provides an illuminating lesson in jungle nutrition. Colourful characters run

Miri

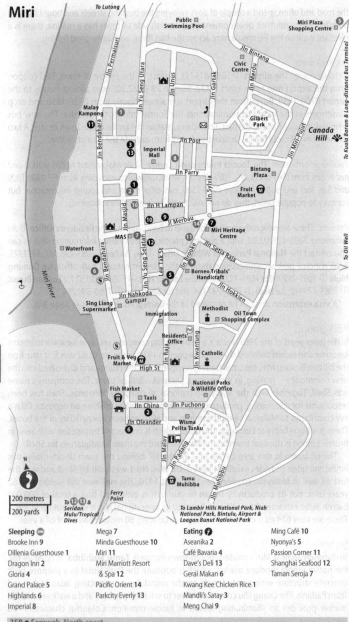

To Lutong

Public Swimming Pool

Miri Plaza Shopping Centre

Jln Bintang

Jln Permaisuri

Civic Centre

Jln Merdu

Gilbert Park

Jln Yu Seng Utara

Jln Gartak

Malay Kampong

Jln Bendahara

Imperial Mall

Jln Post

Jln Unus

Canada Hill

To Kuala Baram & Long-distance Bus Terminal

To Kuala Baram & Long-distance Bus Terminal

Bintang Plaza

Jln Parry

Jln Sylvia

Fruit Market

Jln Maslid

Jln H Lampan

Jl Merbau

Miri Heritage Centre

Jln Setia Raja

Waterfront

Jln Bendahara

MAS

Jln Yu Seng Selatan

Lee Tak Tek

Jln Brooke

Borneo Tribals' Handicraft

Jln Hokkien

To Oil Well

Miri River

Jln Nahkoda Gampar

Sing Liang Supermarket

Immigration

Methodist

Oil Town Shopping Complex

Residents' Office

Jln Raja

Jln Kwantung

Catholic

Fruit & Veg Market

High St

National Parks & Wildlife Office

Fish Market

Taxis

Jln China

Jln Puchong

Wisma Pelita Tunku

Jln Oleander

Jln Malay

Jln Padang

Tamu Muhibba

Jln Muhibbu

200 metres

200 yards

N

Ferry Point

To 12 13 & Seridan Mulu/Tropical Dives

To Lambir Hills National Park, Niah National Park, Loagan Bunut National Park, Bintulu, Airport & Loagan Bunut National Park

Sleeping
Brooke Inn **9**
Dillenia Guesthouse **1**
Dragon Inn **2**
Gloria **4**
Grand Palace **5**
Highlands **6**
Imperial **8**

Mega **7**
Minda Guesthouse **10**
Miri **11**
Miri Marriott Resort & Spa **12**
Pacific Orient **14**
Parkcity Everly **13**

Eating
Aseanika **2**
Café Bavaria **4**
Dave's Deli **13**
Gerai Makan **6**
Kwang Kee Chicken Rice **1**
Mandli's Satay **3**
Meng Chai **9**

Ming Café **10**
Nyonya's **5**
Passion Corner **11**
Shanghai Seafood **12**
Taman Seroja **7**

impromptu stalls from rattan mats, selling yellow cucumbers that look like mangoes, mangoes that look like turnips, huge crimson durians, tiny loofah sponges, sackfuls of fragrant Bario rice (brown and white), every shape, size and hue of banana, *tuak* (rice wine) in old Heineken bottles and a menagerie of jungle fauna – including mouse deer, falcons, pangolins and the apparently delicious long-snouted *tupai* (jungle squirrel). There are handicrafts and a large selection of dried and fresh seafood: fish and *bubok* (tiny prawns) and big buckets boiling with catfish or stacked with turtles.

Taman Bulatan is a scenic, centrally located park with foodstalls and boats for hire on the man-made lake.

Around Miri

Hawaii Beach is a pristine, palm-fringed beach, popular for picnics and barbecues. It's privately owned and visitors are asked to pay RM12 to enter. To get there, it's a 15-minute taxi ride from Miri (RM20) or take bus No 13 (RM2). There are a couple of other beaches closer to Miri including Luak Bay and Taman Selera. Bus No 11 (RM1) runs to both these spots. Don't expect anything akin to Mauritius here; these places are mellow city escapes.

Lambir Hills National Park ① *T085-491030, RM10, children RM5, photography RM5, video camera RM10, professional camera RM200; to get there, take Bintulu or Bakong bus from Park Hotel (40 mins, RM3) or go by taxi (30 mins, RM60)*, mainly consists of a chain of sandstone hills bounded by rugged cliffs, 19 km south of Miri and just visible from the town; the main attractions are the beautiful waterfalls. *Kerangas* (heath forest) covers the higher ridges and hills while the lowland areas are mixed dipterocarp forest. Bornean gibbons, bearded pigs, barking deer and over 100 species of bird have been recorded in the park. There is only one path across a rickety suspension bridge at present, but there are numerous waterfalls, tree towers for birdwatching, and several trails which lead to enticing pools for swimming. The park attracts hordes of day trippers from Miri at weekends. It's possible to stay overnight, see Sleeping, page 363. The Park HQ is close to the Miri–Niah road and contains an audiovisual room.

Loagan Bunut National Park ① *T085-779410, take a local bus from Miri to Lapok Bridge and then hire a car/taxi for the remaining 10 km to the park*, is located in the upper reaches of the Sungai Bunut and contains Sarawak's largest natural lake covering approximately 650 ha. The water level in the lake is totally dependent on the water level of the rivers Bunut, Tinjar and Baram. The level is at its lowest in the months of February, May and June and sometimes, for a period of about two to three weeks, the lake becomes an expanse of dry, cracked mud. The lake's main cultural attraction is the traditional method of fishing (*selambau*), which has been retained by the Berawan fishermen. The surrounding area is covered with peat swamp forest. Common larger birds found here are darters, egrets, herons, bittern, hornbill and kites. Gibbons are also common.

Although visibility might not be comparable to more well known sites, such as Sipadan off the east coast of Sabah, the extensive **coastal reefs of Miri** are an area of rich marine life and unexploited hard and soft coral gardens. With patch reefs, steep drop-offs descending into the depths and diverse wreck sites, there's something to interest divers of any level of experience. Combine that with world-beating biodiversity and divers are in for a little known adventure. So, why isn't this one of the world's most popular diving areas? The answer is that visibility is often low, at many sites 10 m or less, with bad weather sometimes making diving impossible. Miri's sites are fairly easy to access and the Miri-Sibuti area has recently been declared a conservation zone. Some of the more distant regions offshore seem to have become more difficult to access.

Luconia Shoals, more than a day's sail from Miri, is a good example of this with few boats (liveaboards required) prepared to sail out to this area, charging prohibitive fees. A few years ago, some in the diving world claimed that Luconia was one of Malaysia's greatest diving sites, and while that may still be the case, several sources suggest that illegal dynamite fishing has inflicted a heavy price recently. For more detailed and up-to-the-minute information, contact Mr Voo Heng Kong, Miri's own godfather of diving, at **Seridan Mulu/Tropical Dives**, see page 366. The shop is located in a small commercial centre just before the **Park City Everly Hotel**, a RM1 bus or a short taxi ride out of town towards the town's very own Brighton Beach – a good spot for a sunset stroll or a seafood snack.

Marudi → Colour map 3, A5.

Four major tribal groups – Iban, Kelabit, Kayan and Penan – come to Marudi to do business with Chinese, Indian and Malay merchants. Marudi is the furthest upriver trading post on the Baram and services all the longhouses in the Tutoh, Tinjar and Baram river basins. Most tourists only stop long enough in Marudi to down a cold drink before catching the next express boat upriver; as the trip to Mulu National Park can now be done in a day, not many have to spend the night here. Because it is a major trading post, however, there are a lot of hotels, and the standards are reasonably good.

Fort Hose was built in 1901, when Marudi was still called Claudetown, and has good views of the river. It is named after the last of the Rajah's residents, the anthropologist, geographer and natural historian Dr Charles Hose. The fort is now used as administrative offices. Also of note is the intricately carved **Thaw Peh Kong Chinese Temple** (diagonally opposite the express boat jetty), also known as Siew San Teen. The temple was shipped from China and erected in in the early 1900s, although it was probably already 100 years old by the time it began life in its new location.

The **Marudi Kampong Teraja log walk** is normally done from the Brunei end, as the return trek, across the Sarawak/Brunei border, takes a full day, from dawn to dusk. It is, however, possible to reach an Iban longhouse inside Brunei without going the whole distance to Kampong Teraja. The longhouse is on the Sungai Ridan, about 2½ hours down the jungle trail. The trail starts 3 km from Marudi, on the airport road. There's no customs post on the border; the trail is not an official route into Brunei. Trekkers are advised to take their passports in the unlikely event of being stopped by police, who will probably turn a blind eye. Kampong Teraja in Brunei is the furthest accessible point that can be reached by road from Labi.

Three **longhouses** – Long Seleban, Long Moh and Leo Mato – are accessible by 4WD from Marudi.

◉ North coast listings

For Sleeping and Eating price codes and other relevant information, see Essentials pages 25-30.

◉ Sleeping

Bintulu *p351, map p351*
There aren't any places specifically geared towards budget foreign travellers here, and there are plenty of seedy short-time hotels that are worth avoiding.

AL-A The Regency, 116 Taman Sri Dagang, Jln Abang Galau, T086-335111, rihbtu@ tm.net.my. A hotel with upmarket pretensions and a fair number of empty rooms. This place has a decent restaurant, bar with occasional live music, and Wi-Fi access in the lobby. Rooms are comfortable, with all mod cons, including a bathroom with bathtub.
B Riverfront Inn, 256 Taman Sri Dagang, T086-339577, riverf@tm.net.my. One of the

Footprint Mini Atlas
Malaysia & Singapore

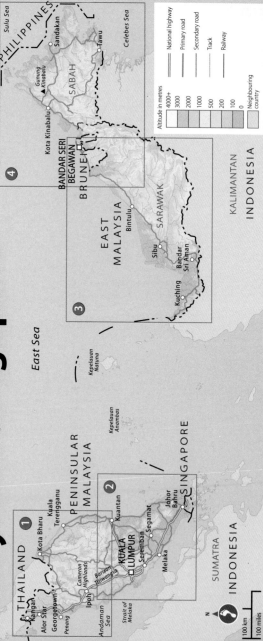

Map 1

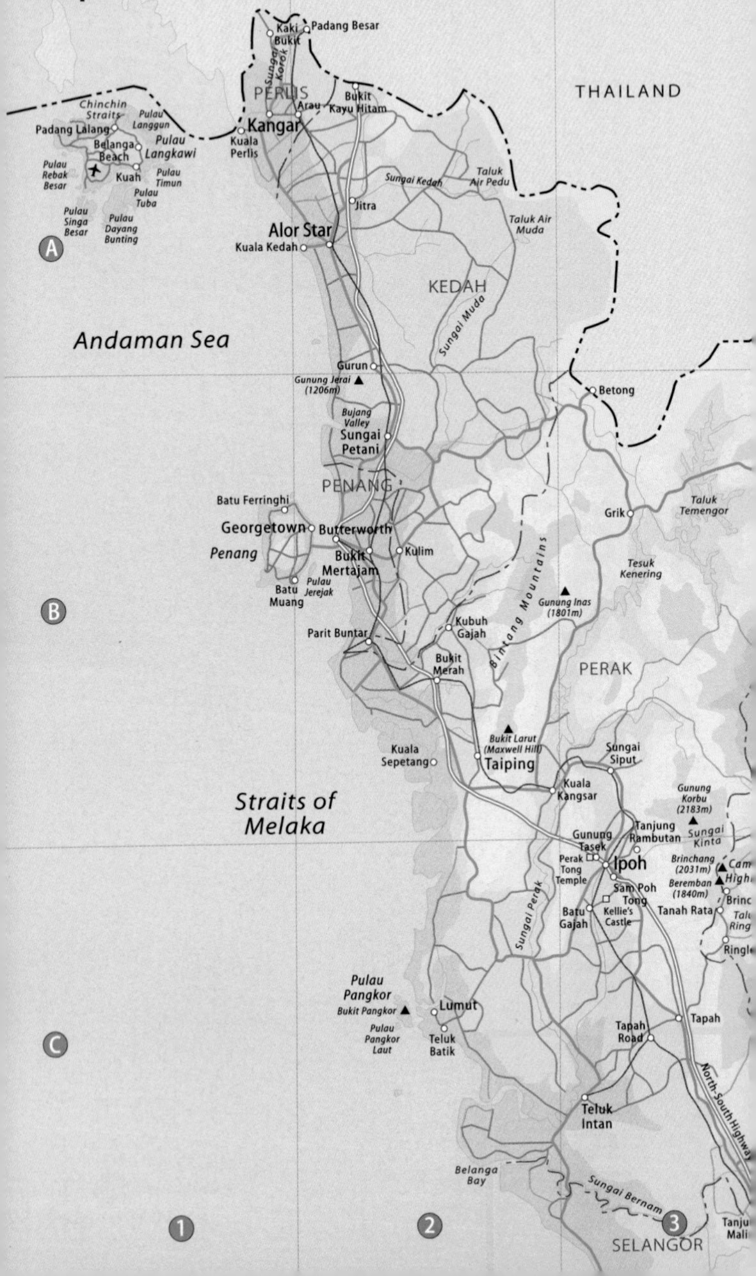

THAILAND

PERLIS

Padang Besar
Kaki
Bukit
Sungai
Kangar
Bukit
Kayu Hitam
Arau
Kuala
Perlis
Chinchin
Straits
Pulau
Langgun
Padang Lalang
Belanga
Beach
Pulau
Langkawi
Pulau
Rebak
Besar
Kuah
Pulau
Timun
Pulau
Tuba
Pulau
Singa
Besar
Pulau
Dayang
Bunting

Jitra

Sungai Kedah
Taluk
Air Pedu

Alor Star
Kuala Kedah
Taluk
Air Muda

KEDAH

Andaman Sea

Gurun
Gunung Jerai
(1206m)
Betong

Bujang
Valley
Sungai
Petani

PENANG

Batu Ferringhi
Georgetown
Butterworth
Grik
Taluk
Temengor

Penang
Bukit
Mertajam
Kulim

Batu
Muang
Pulau
Jerejak

Tesuk
Kenering

Parit Buntar
Kubuh
Gajah
Gunung Inas
(1801m)

Bukit
Merah
PERAK

Kuala
Sepetang
Bukit Larut
(Maxwell Hill)
Taiping
Sungai
Siput

**Straits of
Melaka**

Kuala
Kangsar
Gunung
Korbu
(2183m)
Sungai
Kinta

Gunung
Tasek
Tanjung
Rambutan

Perak
Tong
Temple
Ipoh
Brinchang
(2031m)
Cam
High

San Poh
Tong
Beremban
(1840m)

Batu
Gajah
Kellie's
Castle
Tanah Rata
Brinc

Talu
Ring

Ringle

Pulau
Pangkor
Bukit Pangkor
Lumut
Tapah
Road
Tapah

Pulau
Pangkor
Laut
Teluk
Batik

Teluk
Intan

North-South Highway

Belanga
Bay
Sungai Bernam
Tanju
Mali

SELANGOR

A

B

C

1

2

3

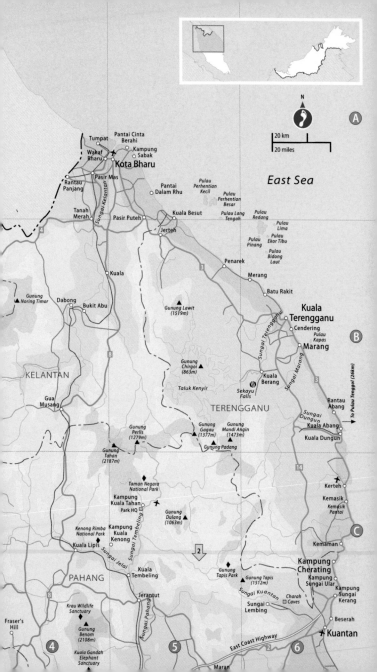

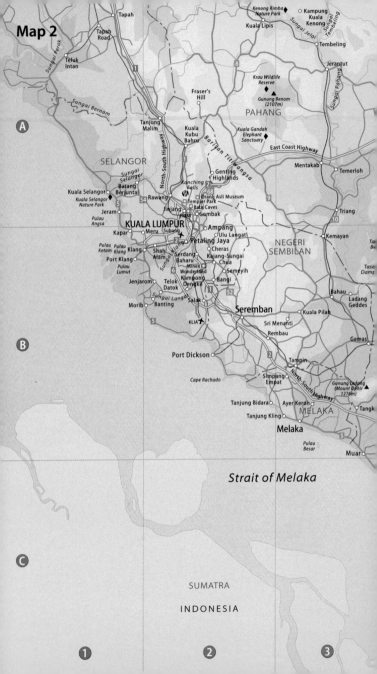

Map 2

Tapah
Tapah Road
Teluk Intan
Sungai Perak
Sungai Bernam

Kenong Rimba Nature Park
Kampung Kuala Kenong
Kuala Lipis
Sungai Jelai
Sungai Tembeling
Tembeling
Jerantut

Fraser's Hill

Krau Wildlife Reserve
Gunung Benom (2107m)
PAHANG
Sungai Pahang

Tanjung Malim
Kuala Kubu Bahru
Kuala Gandah Elephant Sanctuary
East Coast Highway
Mentakab
Temerloh

A

SELANGOR
Sungai Selangor
Batang Berjuntai
Rawang
Genting Highlands
Kanching Falls
Banjaran Titiwangsa

Kuala Selangor
Kuala Selangor Nature Park
North-South Highway
Jinjang
Orang Asli Museum
Templer Park
Batu Caves
Gombak
Triang

Pulau Angsa
Kapar
Meru
Subang
KUALA LUMPUR
Ampang
Ulu Langat
Kemayan

Pulau Ketam
Pulau Klang
Klang
Shah Alam
Petaling Jaya
Cheras
Kajang-Sungai Chua
NEGERI SEMBILAN

Port Klang
Pulau Lumut
Serdang Baharu
Mines Wonderland
Semenyih
Tase Damp

Jenjarom
Telok Datok
Kampong Dengkil
Bangi
Bahau
Ladang Geddes

Morib
Banting
Salak
Sungai Langat
Seremban
Kuala Pilah

B
KLIA
Sri Menanti
Rembau
Gemas

Port Dickson
Sri Menanti
Tampin
Gunung Ledang (Mount Ophir) (1276m)
Tangk

Cape Rachado
Simpang Empat
North-South Highway
MELAKA

Tanjung Bidara
Ayer Keroh
Tanjung Kling
Melaka
Pulau Besar
Muar

Strait of Melaka

C

SUMATRA

INDONESIA

1   **2**   **3**

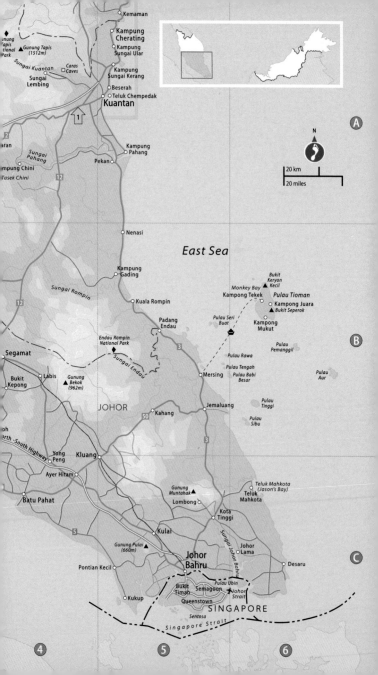

Map 3

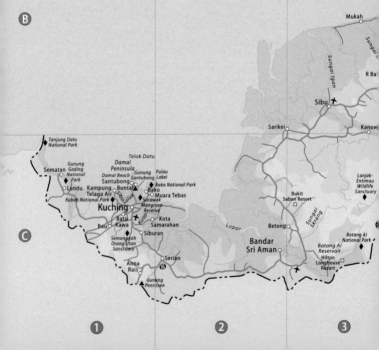

East Sea

A

N

30 km
30 miles

B

Mukah

Sungai

Sungai Igan

R Ba

Sibu

Sarikei

Kanow

Lanjak-
Entimau
Wildlife
Sanctuary

Bukit
Saban Resort

C

Tanjung Datu
National Park

Sematan

Gunung
Gading
National
Park

Lundu

Telaga Air

Kubah National Park

Telok Datu

Damai
Peninsula

Damai Beach

Kampung

Santubong

Buntal

Gunung
Santubong

Pulau
Lakei

Bako National Park

Bako

Muara Tebas

Sarawak
Mangrove
Reserve

Kuching

Batu
Kawa

Bau

Semonggoh
Orang Utan
Sanctuary

Siburan

Kota
Samarahan

Anna
Rais

Serian

Gunung
Penrissen

Lupar

Bandar
Sri Aman

Betong

Sungai
Skrang

Batang Ai
Reservoir

Batang Ai
National Park

Hilton
Longhouse
Resort

1 **2** **3**

Map 4

Inset (top left): Map showing location within Malaysia

To Pulau Layang Layang →

Mantanani Island

East Sea

Tempasuk (Bird Sanctuary)

Kota Belud
Surusup
Tuaran
Mengkabong
Tamparuli
Telipok
Gu
Kin
Natio
(4)
Me
Na
he

Tunku Abdul Rahman Park
Pulau Gaya
Kota Kinabalu
Tanjung Aru
Putatan
Kinarut
Penampang
Kundas
*Rafflesia F
Reserv*
*Gunung Alab
(1964m)*
Papar
Manggis
*Sungai
Papar*
Mawar
Waterfall
Pa
Tambunan
*Gunur
Trusma
(2642m)*

*Pulau Tiga
National Park*

Kuala
Penyuh

LABUAN
*Pulau
Labuan*
Menumbok
Beaufort
Melalap
Keningan
*Agricultural
Research Station
Orchid Centre*

Telok Brunei
Sipitang
Sindumin
Tenom
Tomani

**BANDAR SERI
BEGAWAN**

BRUNEI & MUARA
Muara
Merapok
Lawas
*Gunung
Lumaku
(1966m)*
Sapulut

Tutong
Brunei
Limbang
Labu
Bangar
Kampong
Batong
Duri
TEMBURONG
Partit
Baru
Amo

Lumut
Kuala
Belait
Seria
TUTONG
BRUNEI
BELAIT
Ladan Hills
Sungai Limbang
*Sungai
Trusan*
Long
Semado

Lutong
Miri
Kuala
Baram
baram
Labi
Teraja
Marudi
3

*Lambir Hills
National Park*
*Sungai
Belait*
*Gunung Mulu
(2376m)*
*Gunung Mulu
National Park*

KALIMANTAN

*Niah
National Park*
Niah Caves
Long
Terawan
Long
Seridan
*Gunung Murudi
(2423m)*

INDONESIA

*Loagan Bunut
National Park*
Sungai Tutoh
*Bukit Batu Bali
(2082m)*
Bario

Sungai Tinjar
Sungai Baram
Sungai Patah
Kelabit Highlands

SARAWAK

*Gunung
Skalap*
Long
Peran
*Sungai
Belepeh*
Long
Muma
*Bakun
Dam*
Long Murum
Long Linau
Belaga
Long Sah

1   *2*   *3*

N
30 km
30 miles

Kuala Lumpur Rail Transit System

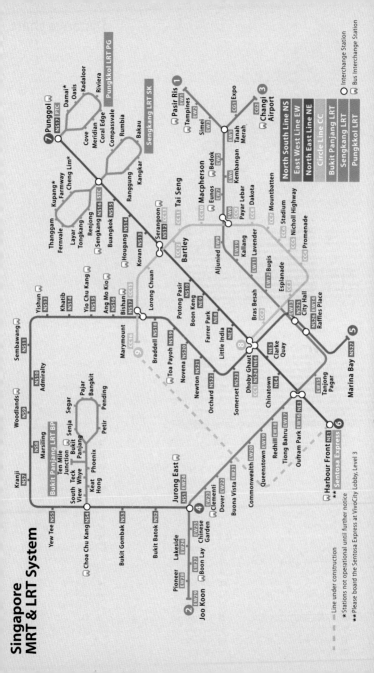

Singapore
MRT & LRT System

Distance chart

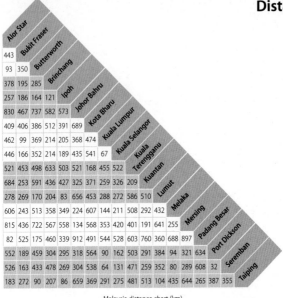

	Alor Star	Bukit Fraser	Butterworth	Brinchang	Ipoh	Johor Bahru	Kota Bharu	Kuala Lumpur	Kuala Selangor	Kuala Terengganu	Kuantan	Lumut	Melaka	Mersing	Padang Besar	Port Dickson	Seremban
Bukit Fraser	443																
Butterworth	93	350															
Brinchang	378	195	285														
Ipoh	257	186	164	121													
Johor Bahru	830	467	737	582	573												
Kota Bharu	409	406	386	512	391	689											
Kuala Lumpur	462	99	369	214	205	368	474										
Kuala Selangor	446	166	352	214	189	435	541	67									
Kuala Terengganu	521	453	498	633	503	521	168	455	522								
Kuantan	684	253	591	436	427	325	371	259	326	209							
Lumut	278	269	170	204	83	656	453	288	272	586	510						
Melaka	606	243	513	358	349	224	607	144	211	508	292	432					
Mersing	815	436	722	567	558	134	568	353	420	401	191	641	255				
Padang Besar	82	525	175	460	339	912	491	544	528	603	760	360	688	897			
Port Dickson	552	189	459	304	295	318	564	90	162	503	291	384	94	321	634		
Seremban	526	163	433	478	269	304	538	64	131	471	259	352	80	289	608	32	
Taiping	183	272	90	207	86	659	369	291	275	481	513	104	435	644	265	387	355

Malaysia distance chart (km)

Map symbols

□	Capital city
○	Other city, town
⌇⌇	International border
⌇⌇	Regional border
⊖	Customs
⬯	Contours (approx)
▲	Mountain, volcano
⇌	Mountain pass
⊥⊥	Escarpment
	Glacier
	Salt flat
	Rocks
	Seasonal marshland
	Beach, sandbank
⦚	Waterfall
~	Reef
══	Motorway
──	Main road
──	Minor road
====	Track
······	Footpath
──	Railway
▪━	Railway with station
✈	Airport
⬤	Bus station
Ⓜ	Metro station

- - - -	Cable car
++++	Funicular
⚓	Ferry
▭▭	Pedestrianized street
⊃ ⊂	Tunnel
→	One way-street
⫯⫯⫯	Steps
⇌	Bridge
▃▃▃	Fortified wall
▫▫	Park, garden, stadium
●	Sleeping
❶	Eating
❶	Bars & clubs
▢	Building
▪	Sight
♰♰	Cathedral, church
🏯	Chinese temple
♟	Hindu temple
♟	Meru
▣	Mosque
△	Stupa
✡	Synagogue
ⓘ	Tourist office
🏛	Museum
✉	Post office
Ⓟ	Police

Ⓢ	Bank
@	Internet
♪	Telephone
ⓜ	Market
✚	Medical services
Ⓟ	Parking
⛽	Petrol
⛳	Golf
⁂	Archaeological site
♦	National park, wildlife reserve
✿	Viewing point
Ⓐ	Campsite
⌂	Refuge, lodge
⌘	Castle, fort
	Diving
☘☘	Deciduous, coniferous, palm trees
⌒	Hide
♣	Vineyard, winery
♨	Distillery
⛵	Shipwreck
✕	Historic battlefield
⇨	Related map

town's more upmarket offerings and popular with foreign oil workers. Rooms are modern and clean, and ones at the front have good views over the river. However, there is a lingering odour of cigarette smoke throughout the hotel which is off-putting. Wi-Fi available in the lobby.

B-C AA Inn, 107 Taman Sri Dagang, T086-313237, F331237. Good-value new hotel with sleek modern bathrooms, comfortable bedrooms with tiny TVs and Wi-Fi access throughout. Recommended.

B-C Kintown Inn, 93 Jln Keppel, T086-333666. Large orange building offering a selection of carpeted a/c rooms with TV and attached bathroom. Wi-Fi. Fair value.

B-C Royal, 12 Jln Pedada, T086-315888, F334028. Fair-value mid-range hotel offering carpeted a/c rooms with attached bathroom and cable TV. Wi-Fi access throughout.

C Sea View, 254 Jln Masjid, T086-339118. Offers a/c, shower and TV in spacious rooms with views over the river.

C Sunlight Inn, 7 Jln Pedada, T086-332577 F334075. Slightly worn a/c rooms with cable TV and attached bathroom. Staff here are friendly, and despite the wear and tear, the hotel is generally clean and rooms are good value. Wi-Fi access available. Recommended.

Similajau National Park *p352*
To book accommodation, contact Similajau National Park, T086-391284.

B-C National park accommodation.
2 chalets, and 2 'forest' hostels with bargain-basement dorm beds (RM15). The hostels have attractive polished hardwood decor. It can get block booked. The more expensive accommodation is in the chalets, which have 8 beds to a room, settees and a sea view. 24-hr electricity. The canteen at Park HQ serves basic food and there are picnic shelters at Park HQ. You can camp for RM5 a night.

Niah National Park *p353, map p354*
It's advisable to book accommodation at least 2-3 days in advance, through the National Parks Booking Office, not the tourist

information office. **Niah National Park**, T085-737454 or T085- 737450; **National Parks Booking Office**, T085- 434184, www.forestry.sarawak.gov.my. Also npbooking@ sarawak.net.gov.my. All places have 24-hr electricity and treated water.

There's a **family chalet**, similar to a hostel but with cooker and a/c, 2 rooms with 4 beds in each, RM150 per room or RM225 per chalet. There is a slightly cheaper chalet with fan for RM100 per room or RM150 per house. **Hostels**, 5 hostels each with 4 rooms of 4 beds each, all rooms have private bathrooms, clean, and Western-style with shower, toilet, electric fans, fridges, large sitting area and kitchen. No cooking facilities, but kettle, crockery and cutlery provided on request. RM40 for 1 room, 4 beds, or RM15 for 1 bed.

C Niah Caves, T085-737726. Some a/c, shared facilities, 6 rooms (singles, doubles and triples available). Basic, but light and clean, next to the river.

C Niah Caves Inn, T085-737333, F737332. With a/c, TV, shower and spacious, fully carpeted rooms. Reasonable value.

There are also 4 small hotels in Batu Niah (4 km from Park HQ).

Camping
There is a campsite with space for 30, RM5 per night. Tents can be hired from Park HQ (RM8) or from the site (RM5).

Miri and the Baram River *p356, map p358*
Most people going to Mulu will have to spend at least a night in Miri. The town has a fair selection of dreary mid-range accommodation and a couple of excellent new budget options, which are good value. Many mid-range hotels are around Jln Yu Seng Selatan. Being an oil town, and close to Brunei, Miri has a booming prostitution industry and the warblings from the karaoke bars go on late into the night.

AL-A Miri Marriott Resort & Spa, Jln Temenggong Datuk Oyong Lawai, T085-421121, www.marriotthotels.com. Luxurious resort-style hotel overlooking the sea a short taxi ride from Miri. 5-star comforts, 220 a/c rooms, all with minibar, TV and internet access. International restaurant, expensive, but excellent coffee house with highly recommended cakes. There's also the largest pool in the Miri area, tennis, a 24-hr gym and a health centre. Balinese-style spa and massage parlour. Good deals are available but watch for pricey extras. **Wildlife Expeditions** arrange tours from their office in the lobby.

A Grand Palace, 2 km Jln Miri-Pujut, **Pelita Commercial Centre**, T085-428888, www.grandpalacehotel.com.my. Imposing peach and pastel building on town outskirts next to **Miri Plaza Shopping Centre**. 125 comfortable rooms with dreary carpet and intense burgundy curtains and decor. Rooms have cable TV, a/c and smart attached bathroom. There is Wi-fi access in the lobby. There's a pool and a couple of good restaurants with occasional theme buffets.

A Imperial, Jln Post, T085-431133, www.imperialhotel.com.my. Set in a towering block to the east of the town centre, this hotel offers comfortable, modern rooms with cable TV and internet access. The suites here are massive and come with full settees. Lovely poolside area with café offering excellent views over the city, particularly at sunset. Part of the **Imperial Shopping Mall**. Serviced rooms or rental apartments. Apartments feature internet, hi-fi, fully equipped kitchen, and, in some cases, a washing machine. The hotel has some excellent dining options.

A Mega, Jln Merbau, T085-432432, www.megahotel.com.my. Another beast of a building, towering over the town with 293 rooms and good promotional rates. Rooms are comfortable and functional though not particularly inspiring, and have the usual range of facilities for this class. There is an oddly shaped pool with a jacuzzi and lounge chairs, bar and karaoke lounge and good Chinese restaurant. Free Wi-Fi throughout. There is a shopping mall below the hotel.

A Parkcity Everly, Jln Temenggong Datuk Oyong Lawai, T085-440288,

www.vhhotels.com. 2 km from town centre, at the mouth of the Miri River, this modern hotel curves around the South China Sea. 168 a/c rooms with cable TV, bathroom, minibar and balcony. You can watch sunsets over sea and colourful but noisy river traffic. There's a palm-lined free-form pool with swim-up bar and a jacuzzi. The beach is too near town to be clean and the sea is not safe for swimming but is good for sunset strolls. Also coffee house, Chinese restaurant, bar, bakery/deli, fitness centre, sauna. Good rates if booked in advance online. Recommended.

B Dragon Inn, Lot 355, Jln Masjid, T085-422266, www.dragoninnmiri.com. A new place with an outrageous psychedelic carpet and flowery wallpaper clash in the corridors, which is quite disturbing after a few hours in the sun. Thankfully, decor in the rooms is toned down, with comfy beds, flatscreen TV, kettle, fridge and free Wi-Fi access. Good value. Recommended.

B Gloria, 27 Jln Brooke, T085-416699, F418866. Selection of bright carpeted a/c rooms with cable TV and attached bathroom with bathtub. Free Wi-Fi in lobby and good Chinese restaurant downstairs. Gets busy at weekends. Rooms here are fair value, but nothing special. Some of the cheaper rooms are windowless.

B Miri, 47 Jln Brooke, T085-421212, F412002. Fair value mid-range option with musty but clean rooms with free Wi-Fi access, TV and attched bathroom. A couple of cafés downstairs serve Western and Chinese fare.

B Pacific Orient, 49 Jln Brooke, T085-413333, pohotel@streamyx.com. Prices have risen considerably here over the years and this place is no longer the great bargain that it once was. Aiming for domestic business travellers, rooms are comfortable, plain and have a/c, TV and attached bathroom. Free Wi-Fi in the lobby and a cheap food court on the ground floor offering local delights.

B-D Dillenia Guesthouse, Lot 846, 1st floor, Jln Sida, T085-434204, dillenia.guesthouse@gmail.com. Superb new guesthouse that gets unanimously good reviews from guests for its

homely atmosphere, simple but spotless rooms, excellent free breakfasts and Wi-Fi access throughout. This place is easily the best of the bunch. Highly recommended.
C Brooke Inn, 14 Jln Brooke, T085-412881, brookeinn@hotmail.com. Unpretentious place with clean, basic rooms with TV and a/c. You get what you pay for here.
C Highlands, Lot 1271, Block 9, Jln Sri Dagang (off Jln Bendahara), Miri Waterfront, T085-422327, highlan@streamyx.net. Well-established backpacker haunt on the top floor of a shophouse with spartan, functional double rooms and dorms with shared bathroom. Joanne, who runs the place enthusiastically, is a good source of travel information.
C Minda Guesthouse, Lot 607, 1st floor, Jln Yu Seng Utara, T085-411422, www.minda guesthouse.com. Another new offering which is well set up for budget travellers, with clean dorms and a couple of doubles. Free Wi-Fi access, breakfast and a good travellers' noticeboard. The roof terrace is a little bare, but is a fine spot for a sunset beer. Recommended.

Around Miri *p359*
Book accommodation through the **National Parks Booking Office**, T085-491030 for Lambir Hills.
A-B Lambir Hills, there's plenty of choice here, from 3-room a/c chalets at RM150 per chalet or RM100 per room and fan chalets for RM75 per chalet or RM50 per room (2 beds in a room). Camping at RM5 per person.
D Loagan Bunut National Park accommodation. To book, call the **National Parks Booking Office**, T085-779410. There is 1 forest hostel with 4 rooms each with 7 double bunk beds with fan and own toilet. RM15 per bed. The park has a canteen. Electricity available from 0600-0200.

Marudi *p360*
B-C Grand, Lot 350 Backlane, T085-755711, F775293. Large but good hotel close to jetty. With restaurant, 30 clean rooms with cable TV and some a/c. Information on upriver trips. Wi-Fi.

B-C Mount Mulu, Lot 80 & Lot 90, Marudi Town District, T085-756671, F756670. A/c; discounts available which make this place excellent value. Internet access.
C Mayland, 347 Mayland Building, T085-755106, F755333. With a/c and 41 rooms. Slightly run down but a good range of accommodation
C Victoria, Lot 961-963 Jln Merdeka, T085-756067. All 21 rooms have cable TV and attached bathroom.

🍽 Eating

Bintulu *p351, map p351*
Umai, raw fish pickled with lime or the fruit of wild palms (*assam*) and mixed with salted vegetables, onions and chillies, is a Melanau speciality. Bintulu is famed for its *belacan* – prawn paste – and in the local dialect, prawns are *urang*, not *udang*.
🍴 **An Nur Nasi Padang Sambal Belado**, Jln Somerville. It's worth getting here early when there is still a good selection of tasty Indonesian-style curries and vegetable dishes.
🍴 **Makan United**, Jln Abang Galau (below Sunlight Inn). Cheap and cheerful place with English menu knocking out plates of fried rice, noodles and soups.
🍴 **Nasi Ayam Singapore**, Jln Somerville. Large place offering up plates of steamed and roast Hainan chicken rice. Good spot for lunch.
🍴 **Popular Corner**, opposite hospital. This place is definitely one of the better places to eat in Bintulu with a range of good fresh seafood dishes, dim sum at lunchtime and refreshing juices. Recommended.

Foodstalls
Chinese stalls behind the Chinese temple on Jln Temple. Stalls at both markets.
Pantai Ria, near Tanjong Batu. Mainly seafood, open evenings only. Recommended.

Niah National Park *p353, map p354*
Emergency rations recommended.
The **Guano Collectors' Cooperative** shop at

the beginning of the plankwalk sells basic food and cold drinks and camera film. There is another basic **shop/restaurant** just outside the park gates. There is a **canteen** at Park HQ, which serves good local food and full Western breakfast, good value, barbecue site provided, the canteen is supposed to be open 0700-2300 but is a little erratic.

Miri and the Baram River *p356, map p358*
Locals take their food pretty seriously in Miri and there are more than enough good places to choose from. A walk after dark along Jln Yu Seng will reveal an array of eateries, from simple Malay stalls to top-notch seafood joints. Below is a selection of the better ones.
†† Café Bavaria, Miri Waterfront, T085-429 4959. Pricey halal German dishes, cheaper Malay food. Run by Monikka from Germany, this place is a quaint slice of Bavaria pasted into Miri. Despite being close to the river, there are no views. But it's open-walled, making it a pleasant place for an iced coffee.
†† Dave's Deli, Jln Yu Seng Utara. Open 0900-2300. The Peninsula has **Kenny Rogers** and Miri has **Dave's** to satisfy the local craving for roast chicken and mash. An interesting menu of American-themed Western food including the mighty 1-ft-long sausage. Ice cream, creamy soups and plenty of cholesterol.
†† Meng Chai, Jln Merbau. Open from 1700. Members of the local Chinese community rave about this place, with a variety of types of fish and shellfish cooked myriad ways. Recommended.
†† Passion Corner, 856 Jln Permaisuri, T085-423213. Small and clean family-run eatery offering MSG-free mini-steamboats, light Chinese and Korean meals and a range of Chinese teas.
†† Shanghai Seafood, Jln Yu Seng Selatan. Open for lunch and dinner. Another popular seafood place where customers happily get stuck into treats such as prawns cooked in Chinese wine and steamed seafish. Recommended.
† Aseanika, Jln Yu Seng Selatan. Serves good Indian and Indonesian food.

† Kwang Kee Chicken Rice, Jln Yu Seng Utara. Plates of delicious fresh chicken rice. Busy at lunctimes.
† Mandli's Satay, Jln Yu Seng Utara. This is the town's top satay joint with delicious beef and chicken satay sold alongside Malay curries and *murtabak*. It's justifiably very popular with locals. Recommended.
† Ming Café, on the corner of Jln Merbau and Jln Yu Seng Utara. Open 0800-2400. Collection of different hawker stalls offering some good Indian fare, Chinese beef noodles and *asam pedas*. This place is popular with tourists and locals and gets a bit boozy in the evenings with its numerous drinks promotions and loud, but inoffensive music. Recommended.
† Nyonya's, 21 Jln Brooke. This place has changed hands recently, although the name plate has stayed the same. Serves cheap and filling Javanese staples doled out to Indonesian workers. The menu includes *ayam penyet, ikan lalapan* and the vegetarian delight of *gado-gado*. Good, cheap lunches.

Foodstalls
Gerai Makan, near Chinese temple at end of Jln Oleander. Malay food.
Taman Seroja, Jln Brooke. Malay food, best in the evenings.
Tamu Muhibba (Native Market), opposite Park Hotel on roundabout connecting Jln Malay and Jln Padang. Best during the day.
Tanjong seafood stalls, Tanjung Lobung (south of Miri). Best in the evenings.

Marudi *p360*
There are several coffee shops in town.
Rose Garden, opposite **Alisan Hotel**. A/c coffee shop serving mainly Chinese dishes.

⊛ Festivals and events

Miri International Jazz Festival is held each year in May at the Park City Everly Hotel with bands from around the world playing their own brands of jazz. Tickets cost around RM60 for a day. See www.mirijazzfestival.com.

O Shopping

Bintulu *p351, map p351*
Handicrafts
Dyang Enterprise, Plaza Hotel, lobby floor, Jln Abang Galau. Rather overpriced because of the Plaza's more upmarket clientele.
Li Hua Plaza, near the Plaza Hotel. The best place for handicrafts.

Miri and the Baram River *p356, map p358*
Books
Parksons Department Store, Bintang Plaza.
Pelita Book Centre, 1st floor, Wisma Pelita Tunku department store.

Handicrafts
Borneo Arts, Jln Yu Seng Selatan (next to Cosy Inn). Daily 0900-2100. T-shirts, pottery, handicrafts, wood carvings, batik, Iban textiles, Chinese porcelain, kris daggers, Dayak warrior swords and shields.
Miri Handicrafts Centre, Jln Brooke (about 15 mins' walk from the local bus station). Stalls with local artists' batik, beads, basketry, musical instruments and some tourist tack, café. Worth checking out.
Olly Dress Making, 2nd floor, Wisma Pelita Tunku, Jln Puchong, T019-8751854. Traditional tailored women's dresses and local handicrafts.
Rong Reng Heritage, Borneo Tribals' Handicraft, 14 Jln Brooke, next to Brooke Inn, T013-833 2406. Straightforward locals George and Eva run this well-stocked craft centre with a diverse range of crafts, from woven mats to beads and T-shirts. George and Eva will tell you the products, origins. Inexpensive.

Shopping complexes
Boulevard (BSC), Jln Pujut Lutong. Miri's biggest shopping complex, food court, supermarket, department store and boutiques.
Imperial Mall, part of the Imperial hotel complex. Money changers, a department store and supermarket in the basement.
Soon Hup Tower, next to Mega Hotel. With Parkwell's supermarket and department store.

Supermarkets
Ngiukee, moving from Pelita to Imperial Mall; **Parkson Grand**, Bintang Plaza; **Pelita**, ground floor, **Sing Liang Supermarket** on Jln Nakhoda Gampar, Chinese store; **Wisma Pelita Tunku**, useful for supplies for upriver expeditions.

▲ Activities and tours

Bintulu *p351, map p351*
Golf
Tanjong Kidurong, north of town, by the sea (regular buses from town). 18-hole course.

Sports complex
Swimming pool (RM2), tennis, football. To get there, fork right from the Miri road at the Chinese temple, 1 km from town centre.

Tour operators
Deluxe Travel, 30 Jln Law Gek Soon, T086-331293, F334995; **Hunda Travel Services**, 8 Jln Somerville, T086-331339, F330445; **Similajau Adventure Tours**, Sublot 5, 4359 Medan Jaya Commercial Centre, T086-331 552, F330 097, offers tours around the city, and to Niah caves, longhouses and Similajau National Park.

Miri and the Baram River *p356, map p358*
Golf
Eastwood Valley Golf and Country Club, Lot 1379, Block 17, KBLD, T085-421010, www.eastwoodvalley.com. Located out near the Miri bypass, this lovely new place has good facilities. A round of 18 holes starts at RM175.

Swimming
Public pool off Jln Bintang, close to the Civic Centre, RM1.

Tour operators
Although most tour companies specialize in trips up the Baram River to Mulu National Park, some are much better than others – in terms of facilities and services offered. Every agency in Miri has a Mulu National Park itinerary covering the caves, pinnacles and

summits. It is also possible to trek to Bario and Mount Murud as well as to Limbang from Mulu. Most agencies employ experienced guides who will be able to advise on longer, more ambitious treks. The Mulu National Park is one destination where it is usually cheaper to go through a tour company than to try to do it independently. Costs vary considerably according to the number of people in a group. For a 3-day Mulu trip, a single tourist can expect to pay at least RM500 with all accommodation, food, travel and guide costs included. An 8-day tour of Ulu Baram longhouses would cost RM2000 for 1 person and RM1400 per person in a group of 10. A 20-day trek will cost 2 people (minimum number) around RM2300 each, and a group of 6-10, RM1500 a head. For remote longhouses, tour companies present by far the best option. Tour fees cover 'gifts' and all payments to longhouse headmen for food, accommodation and entertainment. **Borneo Mainland**, Jln Merpati, T085-433511, www.borneomainland.com; **JJ Tour Travel**, Lot 231, Jln Maju Taman, Jade Centre, T085-418690, F413308, ticketing agents; **KKM Travel & Tours**, 236 Jln Maju, T085-417899, F414629; **Limbang Travel Service**, 1G Park Arcade (near Park Hotel), T085-413228, efficient ticket service. **Seridan Mulu/Tropical Dives**, Lot 273, ground floor, Brighton Centre, Jln Temen-ggong Datuk Oyong Lawai, T085-415582, www.seridanmulu. com. Runs tailor-made land trips in the region. Manager Mr Voo Heng Kong also stands out from others in the area for being Miri's only dive operator, running dives on all local reefs or in more remote locations on request. Superb knowledge of Miri's diving possibilities. Tours for land lubbers also organized. **Tropical Adventure Tours and Travel**, ground floor, **Mega Hotel**, Lot 907, Jln Merbau, T085-419337, www.borneotropical adventure.com. Professional and with lots of experience. Tailor-made trips in Malaysia or Indonesia. Boss Richard Hii has an excellent working knowledge of Kalimantan and its more remote corners – it's worth checking

their website for the latest special deals. There are some excellent offers for those with residence permits in Singapore, Malaysia or Brunei. At the time of writing, they offer the cheapest all-inclusive tours to Mulu, starting at RM399 for 2 days/1 night. Recommended.

☉ Transport

Bintulu *p351, map p351*
Air
Air Asia and MAS have regular connections with **Kuala Lumpur** and **Kuching**. MAS flies to **Miri**, **Sibu** and **Kota Kinabalu**.
Airline offices MAS and MASwings, Jln Masjid, T086-331554.

Boat
Enquire at the wharf for times and prices. Regular connections with **Tubau**, last boat at 1400 (2½-3 hrs, RM22). Connections with **Belaga**, via logging road, see page 349; this route is popular with people in Belaga as it is much cheaper than going from Sibu. However, tourists need a permit to get to Belaga, and there is no accommodation in Tubau for those who get stuck. If you really want to do this, call Mr Hasbee in Belaga (T013-842 9767) and see if any drivers are making the return trip to Belaga from Bintulu (RM60); alternatively, try **Hup Kiat Transport** in Belaga (T013-807 5598), as they have Toyota Landcruisers leaving Bintulu at 1330 daily for Belaga (RM60). If travelling overland from Bintulu, report to the Bintulu Resident's Office and the Belaga Resident's Office. For more information, call the Kapit Resident's Office, T084-796445.

Bus
There are 2 stations in town. The local bus terminal is in the centre. The long-distance Medan Jaya station is 10 mins by taxi from the centre, on the road towards Miri (RM15). Regular connections with **Miri** (RM20), **Sarikei Batu Niah** (RM12) and **Sibu** (RM20) and **Kuching** (RM60). There are at least 10 bus companies, and buses leave frequently

all day. One of the more organized companies ploughing the bumpy roads is Biaramas, T086-314 999, www.busasia.net.

Taxi
For **Miri** and **Sibu**, taxis leave from Jln Masjid. Because of the regular bus services and the poor state of the roads, most taxis are for local use only and chartering them is pricey.

Similaju National Park *p352*
There is no regular bus service to the park. Take a taxi (30 mins, RM50 Bintulu–Similajau trip, RM100 for a return trip). Bintulu taxi station, T086-332009. Boats can be chartered from the wharf at Bintulu, from RM200.

Niah National Park *p353, map p354*
Boat
From Batu Niah (near the market) to Park HQ at Pangkalan Lubang, Niah National Park by boat (RM15 per person or if more than 5 people, RM3 per person) or 45 mins' walk.

Bus
Every 2 hrs for a connection with **Miri** (2 hrs, RM12); 6 buses a day to **Bintulu** (RM12) and **Sibu** via Bintulu to **Batu Niah**.

Taxi
From **Miri** to Park HQ, will only leave when there are 4 passengers. Most visitors jump on a bus from Miri to Bintulu or Sibu and get off at Batu Niah (2 hrs) and then take a taxi for 20 mins (RM20) to get to the park HQ. From **Bintulu** to Batu Niah (RM10). A taxi to Park HQ costs RM20 from the bus station at Batu Niah but the riverboat is far more scenic (see Boat, above).

Miri and the Baram River *p356, map p358*
Air
For details of the airport, see page 357. Take a bus No 28 (RM2.20) to the airport, but ask the driver to drop you off outside, otherwise you will be dropped off on the highway, a 10-min trek from the terminal.

Air Asia and MAS fly to **Kuching**, **Kota Kinabalu** and **Kuala Lumpur**. Air Asia also flies to **JB**. Miri is a hub for MASwings with flights to **Ba'kelalan**, **Bario**, **Bintulu**, **Lawas**, **Limbang**, **Long Akah**, **Long Banga**, **Long Lellang**, **Long Seridan**, **Marudi**, **Mukah**, **Mulu**, **Sibu** and **Labuan**. Sarawak-based airline **Hornbill Skyways** flies to rural parts of Sarawak including Mukah, **Tanjung Manis** (via Mukah), Kuching (via Mukah or Tanjung Manis), and Mulu.

Note that it is crucial to book the excellent-value flights to Bario and Mulu in advance. Travellers hoping to show up and get on a flight will probably be disappointed. There are no flights between Miri and **Brunei**.

Airline offices AirAsia, Jln Asmaram, T085-438022. Hornbill Skyways, T085-611066. MAS and MASwings, 239 Halaman Kabor, off Jln Yu Seng Selatan, T085-414144.

Bus
Regular connections from early morning to early/mid-afternoon with **Batu Niah** (2 hrs, RM12), **Bintulu** (4 hrs, RM20), **Sibu** (7 hrs, RM40) and **Kuching** (13 hrs, RM80).

Regular bus connections with **Kuala Baram** and the express boat upriver to **Marudi**. There are also taxis to Kuala Baram, either private or shared (RM35 or more). Express boats upriver to **Marudi** from Kuala Baram, 3 hrs. Roughly 1 boat every 2 hrs from 0800. Last boat 1500 (RM20). This is the first leg of the journey to Mulu and the interior.

Several departures a day to **Kuala Belait** in **Brunei** and these leave from Miri's central bus station near the Park Hotel and Tourist Information Centre (2 hrs, RM13), via Sungai Tujuh checkpoint, with onward connections to **Bandar Seri Begawan**. These buses are run by the Miri Belait Transport Co. From the checkpoint you need to change buses at Kuala Belait for Seria (B$1) and then onwards to Bandar Seri Begawan (B$6). You can use Singapore dollars in Brunei. Note the last bus from Seria leaves at 1520, which means you need to catch a morning bus from Miri (0700 or 1000) to make the connection, or you will need to stay the night in Kuala Belait or Seria. Travelling by your own means of transport from Miri, it is necessary to take the ferry across the Belait River. This crossing is just served by a small passenger boat, with another bus waiting on the far side – check on the car ferry status before driving across the border. At weekends and public holidays there are long queues for the ferries/boats as well as at immigration. Be warned also that the ferry across the Belait River takes an unscheduled 1-hr break for lunch. The distance itself is nothing – the ferry crossings take no more than 10 mins and Miri to Kuala Belait is just 27 km. Bus passengers sometimes bypass the queues because they board the ferry as foot passengers and then hop on another bus the other side of the river. From Kuala Belait regular connections with Seria, (45 mins, B$1), and from Seria regular buses with Bandar Seri Begawan (1-2 hrs, B$6). It takes at least 5 hrs to reach Bandar Seri Begawan.

Alternatively, there is now a service offered by Mr Foo and his son with a 7-seater Toyota departing Miri daily around 0900 and arriving in BSB around noon. The fare is RM60. Seats can be booked via the Dillenia Guesthouse (see page 362) or by calling Mr Foo, T013-833 2231. Highlands (see page 363) offers a similar service for the same price. It's a slightly less adventurous way of arriving in BSB, but can shave hours off travel time.

There is a daily bus service to **Kota Kinabalu** leaving the long-distance bus terminal at 0800 (RM93). This travels via Limbang and Lawas and takes 9-10 hrs. There is also a bus to **Pontianak** departing daily at 0730 which travels via Kuching. Both services are run by Bintang Jaya Bus Co (T085-432178) from the long-distance terminal.

Car
Car hire Avis, Permaisuri Rd, T085-430222; Lee Brothers, 17 River Rd, T085-410606; **Kong Tek**, Counter 2, Ground Floor, Public Concourse Terminal Building, T085-617 767. Decent range of cars starting at RM128 a day. Also, driver services offered for trips to longhouses and the interior.

Marudi *p360*
Air
The airport is 5 km from town. Connections with **Miri** (3 daily), **Bario** and **Long Lellang** with MASwings.

Boat
These leave opposite the Chinese temple. Connections with **Kuala Baram**, 5 boats a day from 0700-1500 (RM20); **Tutoh**, for longboats to Long Terawan, 1 boat daily at 1200 (RM25); **Long Lama**, for longboats to **Bario**, 1 boat every hour 0730-1400. From Long Terawan the longboat journey takes up to 2 hrs (RM55 each for group of 5 or more). From Miri to Kuala Baram take bus No 1 (RM3, 1st bus 0530) or a shared taxi (RM35).

ⓘ Directory

Bintulu *p351, map p351*
Banks HSBC and Standard Chartered, both on Jln Keppel. **Post office** GPO (Pos Laju) far side of the airport near the Residents' Office, 2 km from centre.

Miri and the Baram River *p356, map p358*
Banks All major banks here.
Immigration Pajabat Imigresen, 2nd floor Tingkat 2&3, Yu Lan Plaza, T085-442118. New office in huge skyscraper at Jln Brooke/Jln Raja. For an extension to your entry stamp or visa. **Internet** There are internet cafés in the Imperial Plaza and Soon Hup Shopping Complex. Most of the popular lodgings offer internet access. **Medical services** Hospital, on the edge of town on Jlln Cahaya, T085-420033. **Police** Police station, Jln Kingsway, T085-433730. **Post office** General Post Office, on Jln Post behind the Imperial Mall. **Telephone** Telecom Office, Jln Gartak, daily 0730-2200.

Marudi *p360*
Banks There are 2 local banks with foreign exchange. **Police** Police station, Airport Rd. **Post office** Post Office, Airport Rd.

Northern Sarawak

The impressive peak of Gunung Mulu is the centrepiece of the eponymous national park. The luscious jungle, home to orchids and hornbills, also boasts the largest limestone cave system on the planet. The cooler climes of the Kelabit Highlands provide good walking opportunities around Bario. Limbang is frontier country and the start of a cross-border trek. ➤➤ *For listings, see pages 377-379.*

Gunung Mulu National Park → *For listings, see pages 377-379. Colour map 3, A6.*

Tucked in behind Brunei, this 529 sq km park lays claim to **Gunung Mulu**, which at 2376 m is the second highest mountain in Sarawak, and the biggest limestone cave system in the world. Mulu is basically a huge hollow mountain range, covered in 180-million-year-old rainforest. Its primary jungle contains an astonishing biological diversity. The park was awarded UNESCO World Heritage status in 2000.

Just outside the national park boundary on the Tutoh River there are rapids which it is possible to shoot; this can be arranged through tour agencies.

Ins and outs

Park essentials RM10, children RM5, camera RM5, video RM10, professional filming RM200.

Equipment A small store at the Park HQ sells basic necessities; there is also a small shop just outside the park boundary, at Long Pala. A sleeping bag is essential for Gunung Mulu trips; other useful items include a good insect repellent, wet weather gear and a powerful torch.

Guides No visitors are permitted to enter the caves without an authorized guide; guides can be arranged from Park HQ or booked in advance from the national parks office in Miri, see page 357. There are some treks around the park that can be done without a guide. Most of the Mulu Park guides are very well informed about flora and fauna, geology and tribal customs. Tour agencies organize guides as part of their fee. Guide fees: from RM20 per cave (or per day) and an extra RM10 per night. Mulu summit trips, RM1000 for a group of up to five (four days, three nights) and Melinau Gorge and Pinnacles, minimum RM400 for five people (three days, two nights). Ornithological guides cost an additional RM10 a day. Porterage: maximum 10 kg and RM30 per day, RM1 for each extra kilogramme. Mulu summit, minimum RM90; Melinau Gorge (Camp 5), minimum RM65. It is usual to tip guides and porters.

Tourist information For up-to-date information on Mulu, see www.mulupark.com. For cavers wishing to explore caves not open to the public (those open to visitors are known as 'show' caves), there are designated 'adventure caves' within an hour of Park HQ. Experienced cave guides can be organized from headquarters. The most accessible adventure cave is the one-hour trek following the river course through **Clearwater Cave**. Cavers should bring their own equipment. Tougher caves such as the Sarawak Chamber can only be visited by advanced cavers who have some experience. The Park Manager needs to approve this trip.

Best time to visit It is best to avoid visiting the park during school and public holidays. In December the park is closed to locals, but remains open to tourists.

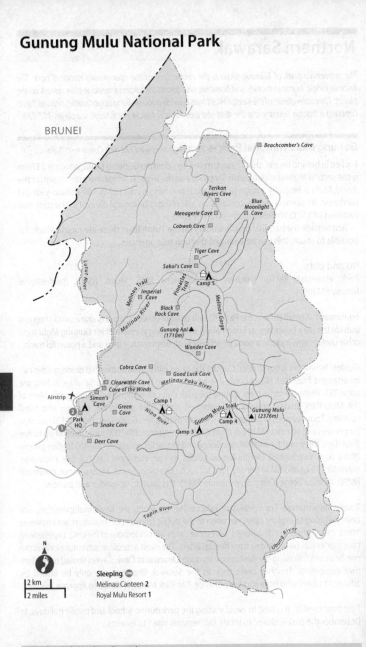

Gunung Mulu National Park

BRUNEI

Beachcomber's Cave

Terikan Rivers Cave

Blue Moonlight Cave

Menagerie Cave

Cobweb Cave

Tiger Cave

Sakai's Cave

Camp 5

Imperial Cave

Black Rock Cave

Gunung Api (1710m)

Wonder Cave

Cobra Cave

Good Luck Cave

Melinau Paku River

Clearwater Cave
Cave of the Winds

Camp 1

Airstrip

Simon's Cave

Green Cave

Nipa River

Gunung Mulu Trail

Camp 4

Gunung Mulu (2376m)

Park HQ

Snake Cave

Camp 3

Deer Cave

Tapin River

Ubun River

Melinau Trail

Melinau River

Pinnacles Trail

Melinau Gorge

Lutut River

N

2 km

2 miles

Sleeping
Melinau Canteen **2**
Royal Mulu Resort **1**

Background

In Robin Hanbury-Tenison's book *The Rain Forest*, he says of Mulu: "All sense of time and direction is lost." Every scientific expedition that has visited Mulu's forests has encountered plant and animal species unknown to science. In 1990, five years after it was officially opened to the public, the park was handling an average of 400 visitors a month. Numbers have increased markedly since then – the area is now attracting more than 12,000 tourists a year – and as the eco-tourism industry has extended its foothold, local tribespeople have been drawn into confrontation with the authorities. In the early 1990s, a series of sabotage incidents was blamed on the Berawan tribe, who claim the caves and the surrounding jungle are a sacred site.

In 1974, three years after Mulu was gazetted as a national park, the first of a succession of joint expeditions led by the British Royal Geographical Society (RGS) and the Sarawak government began to make the discoveries that put Mulu on the map. In 1980 a cave passage over 50 km long was surveyed for the first time. Since then, a further 137 km of passages have been discovered. Altogether 27 major caves have now been found speleologists believe they may represent a tiny fraction of what is actually there. The world's biggest cave, the **Sarawak Chamber**, was not discovered until 1984.

The first attempt on Gunung Mulu was made by Spencer St John, the British consul in Brunei, in 1856 (see also his attempts on Gunung Kinabalu, page 442). His efforts were thwarted by "limestone cliffs, dense jungle and sharp pinnacles of rock". Dr Charles Hose, Resident of Marudi, led a 25-day expedition to Gunung Mulu in 1893, but also found his path blocked by 600-m-high cliffs. Nearly 50 years later, in 1932, a Berawan rhinoceros hunter called Tama Nilong guided Edward Shackleton's Oxford University expedition to the summit. One of the young Oxford undergraduates on that expedition was Tom Harrisson, who later made the Niah archaeological discoveries, see page 354. Tama Nilong, the hunter from Long Terawan, had previously reached the main southwest ridge of Mulu while tracking a rhinoceros.

The cliffs of the Melinau Gorge rise a sheer 600 m, and are the highest limestone rock faces between north Thailand and Papua New Guinea. The limestone massifs of Gunung Api and Gunung Benarat were originally at the same elevation as Gunung Mulu, but their limestone outcrops were more prone to erosion than the Mulu's sandstone. Northwest of the gorge lies a large, undisturbed alluvial plain which is rich in flora and fauna. Penan tribespeople (see page 317) are permitted to maintain their lifestyle of fishing, hunting and gathering in the park. At no small expense, the Malaysian government has encouraged them to settle at a purpose-built longhouse at **Batu Bungan**, just a few minutes upriver from the Park HQ, but its efforts have met with limited success because of the desire of many Penan to maintain their travelling lifestyle. Penan shelters can often be found by riverbanks.

Reeling from international criticism, the Sarawak state government set aside 66,000 ha of rainforest as what it called 'biosphere', a reserve where indigenous people could practise their traditional lifestyle. Part of this lies within the park. In Baram and Limbang districts, the remaining 300 Penan will have a reserve in which they can continue their nomadic way of life. A further 23,000 ha has reportedly been set aside for 'semi-nomadic' Penan.

In 1961 geologist Dr G Wilford first surveyed Deer Cave and parts of the Cave of the Winds. But Mulu's biggest subterranean secrets were not revealed until the 1980s.

Flora and fauna

In the 1960s and 1970s, botanical expeditions were beginning to shed more light on the Mulu area's flora and fauna: 100 new plant species were discovered between 1960 and

1973 alone. Mulu Park encompasses an area of diverse altitudes and soil types – it includes all the forest types found in Borneo except mangrove. About 20,000 animal species have been recorded in Mulu Park, as well as 3500 plant species and 8000 varieties of fungi (more than 100 of these are endemic to the Mulu area). Mulu's ecological statistics are astounding: it is home to 1500 species of flowering plant, 170 species of orchid and 109 varieties of palm. More than 280 butterfly species have been recorded. Within the park boundaries, 262 species of bird (including all eight varieties of hornbill), 67 mammalian species, 50 species of reptile and 75 amphibian species have been recorded.

Mulu's caves contain an unusual array of flora and fauna too. There are three species of swiftlet, 12 species of bat and nine species of fish, including the cave flying fish (*Nemaaramis everetti*) and blind catfish (*Silurus furnessi*). Cave scorpions (*Chaerilus chapmani*) – which are poisonous but not deadly – are not uncommon. Other subterranean species include albino crabs, huntsman spiders, cave crickets, centipedes and snakes (which dine on swiftlets and bats). These creatures have been described as "living fossils... [which are] isolated survivors of ancient groups long since disappeared from Southeast Asia."

Gunung Mulu

The minimum time to allow for the climb is four days, three nights; tents are not required if you stay at Camps 1 and 2. The main summit route starts from the plankwalk at Park HQ heading towards Deer Cave. The Mulu walkway forks left after about 1 km. From the headquarters it is an easy four- to five-hour trek to Camp 1 at 150 m, where there is a shelter, built by the RGS/Sarawak government expedition in 1978. The second day is a long uphill slog (eight to 10 hours) to Camp 4 (1800 m), where there is also a shelter. Past Camp 3, the trail climbs steeply up Bukit Tumau, which affords good views over the park, and above which the last wild rhinoceros in Sarawak was shot in the mid-1940s. There are many pitcher plants (*Nepenthes lowii*) along this stretch of trail. From Camp 4, known as 'The Summit Camp', the path passes the helicopter pad, from where there are magnificent views of Gunung Benarat, the Melinau Gorge and Gunung Api. The final haul to the summit is steep; there are fixed ropes. Around the summit area, the *Nepenthes muluensis* pitcher plant is common – it is endemic to Mulu. From Camp 4 it takes 1½ hours to reach the summit, and a further seven hours back down the mountain to Camp 1.

Equipment Camps 1, 3 and 4 have water (providing the tank has been filled by rain water). Water should be boiled before drinking. It is necessary to bring your own food; in the rainy season it is wise to bring a gas cooking stove. A sleeping bag and waterproofs are also necessary and spare clothes, wrapped in a plastic bag, are a good idea.

Treks from Camp 5

For a three-day trip, a longboat will cost about RM370. It takes two to three hours, depending on the river level, from Park HQ to Kuala Berar; it is then a two- to three-hour trek (8 km) to Camp 5. Visitors to the Camp 5 area are also advised to plan their itinerary carefully as it is necessary to calculate how much food will be required and to carry it up there. There is a fairly well-equipped shelter with kitchen, bathrooms with shower and communal sleeping space which can house a maximum of 50 people. The camp is next to the Melinau River; river water should be boiled before drinking. There is a solar power generator to power radios, pump river water and for low lighting after dark.

Camp 5 is located in the Melinau Gorge, facing Gunung Benarat, about four to six hours upstream from the Park HQ. From the camp it is possible to trek up the gorge as well as to the Pinnacles on Gunung Api. It is advisable to hire a longboat for the duration of your time at and around Camp 5. The boat has to be abandoned at Kuala Berar, at the confluence of the Melinau and Berar rivers. It is only used for the first and last hours of the trip, but in the event of an emergency, there are no trails leading back to the Park HQ and there are stories of fever-stricken people being stuck in the jungle.

Melinau Gorge

Camp 5 nestles at the end of the gorge, across a fast-flowing section of the Melinau River and opposite the unclimbed 1580-m Gunung Benarat's stark, sheer limestone cliffs. The steep limestone ridges, which lead eventually to Gunung Api, comprise the east wall of the gorge. Heading out from Camp 5, the trail fizzles out after a few minutes. It takes an arduous two to three hours of endless river crossings and scrambles to reach a narrow chute of whitewater, under which is a large, deep and clear jungle pool with a convenient sandbank and plenty of large boulders to perch on. Alfred Russel Wallace's *Troides brookiana* – the majestic Rajah Brooke's birdwing – is particularly common at this little oasis, deep in undisturbed jungle. The walk involves criss-crossing through waist-deep, fast-flowing water and over stones that have been smoothed to a high polish over centuries: strong shoes are recommended as is a walking stick. Only occasionally in the walk upstream is it possible to glimpse the towering 600 m cliffs. Mulu can also be climbed from the south ridge of Melinau Gorge; it is three hours to Camp 1, five hours to Camp 3, a steep four- to five-hour climb to Camp 4, and finally two hours to the top.

The Pinnacles

The Pinnacles are a forest of sharp limestone needles three-quarters of the way up Gunung Api. Some of the pinnacles rise above treetops to heights of 45 m. The trail leaves from Camp 5, at the base of the Melinau Gorge. It is a very steep climb all the way and a maximum time of three to four hours is allowed to reach the pinnacles (1200 m); otherwise you must return. There is no source of water en route. It is not possible to reach Gunung Api from the Pinnacles. It is strongly recommended that climbers wear gloves as well as long-sleeved shirts, trousers and strong boots to protect themselves against cuts from the razor-sharp rocks. Explorers on Spenser St John's expedition to Mulu in 1856 were cut to shreds on the Pinnacles: "three of our men had already been sent back with severe wounds, whilst several of those left were much injured," he wrote, concluding that it was "the world's most nightmarish surface to travel over".

Gunung Api (Fire Mountain)

The vegetation is so dry at the summit that it is often set ablaze by lightning in the dry season. The story goes that the fires were so big that locals once thought the mountains were volcanoes. Some of the fires could be seen as far away as the Brunei coast. The summit trek takes a minimum of three days. At 1710 m, it is the tallest limestone outcrop in Borneo and, other than Gunung Benarat (on the other side of the gorge), it is probably the most difficult mountain to climb in Borneo. Many attempts to climb it ended in failure; two Berawans from Long Terawan finally made it to the top in 1978, one of them the grandson of Tama Nilong, the rhinoceros-hunter who had climbed Gunung Mulu in 1932. It is impossible to proceed upwards beyond the Pinnacles.

From Camp 5, cross the Melinau River and head down the **Limbang Trail** towards Lubang Cina. Less than 30 minutes down the trail, fork left along a new trail which leads along a ridge to the south of Gunung Benarat. Climbing higher, after about 40 minutes, the trail passes into an area of leached sandy soils called *kerangas* (heath) forest. This little patch of thinner jungle is a tangle of many varieties of pitcher plants.

It is possible to trek from Camp 5 to **Limbang**, although it is easier to do it the other way (see page 376).

Clearwater Cave

This part of the Clearwater System, on a small tributary of the Melinau River, is 107 km long. The cave passage – 75 km of which has been explored – links Clearwater Cave (Gua Ayer Jernih) with the **Cave of the Winds** (Lubang Angin), to the south. It was discovered in 1988. Clearwater is named after the jungle pool at the foot of the steps leading up to the cave mouth, where the longboats moor. Two species of monophytes – single-leafed plants – grow in the sunlight at the mouth of the cave. They only grow on limestone. A lighting system has been installed down the path to **Young Lady's Cave**, which ends in a 60-m-deep pothole.

On the cave walls are some helictites – coral-like lateral formations – and, even more dramatic, are the photokarsts, tiny needles of rock, all pointing towards the light. These are formed in much the same way as their monstrous cousins, the Pinnacles (see above), by vegetation (in this case algae), eating into and eroding the softer rock, leaving sharp points of harder rock which 'grow' at about 0.5 mm a year. Inside Clearwater you can hire a rowing boat for RM10 and follow the river for 1.5 km upstream, although the current is strong.

Clearwater can be reached by a 30-minute longboat ride from the Park HQ (RM27 per person). Individual travellers must charter a boat for a return trip. Tour agents build the cost of this trip into their package, which works out considerably cheaper. There are daily scheduled guided tours of the cave at 0945 or 1030 (RM10)

Deer Cave
ⓘ *An hour's trek along a plankwalk from Park HQ.*

This is another of Mulu's record breakers: it has the world's biggest cave mouth and the biggest cave passage, which is 2.2 km long and 220 m high at its highest point. Before its inclusion in the park, the cave had been a well-known hunting ground for deer attracted to the pools of salty water running off the guano. The silhouettes of some of the cave's limestone formations have been creatively interpreted; notably the profile of Abraham Lincoln. Adam's and Eve's Showers, at the east end of the cave, are hollow stalactites; water pressure increases when it rains. This darker section at the east end of Deer Cave is the preferred habitat of the naked bat. Albino earwigs live on the bats' oily skin and regularly drop off. The cave's east entrance opens onto 'The Garden of Eden' – a luxuriant patch of jungle, which was once part of the cave system until the roof collapsed. This separated Deer Cave and Green Cave, which lies adjacent to the east mouth; it's open only to caving expeditions.

The west end of the cave is home to several million wrinkle-lipped and horseshoe bats. Hundreds of thousands of these bats pour out of the cave at dusk. Bat hawks can often be seen swooping in for spectacular kills. The helipad, about 500 m south of the cave mouth, provides excellent vantage points. VIPs' helicopters, arriving for the show, are said to have disturbed the bats in recent years. From the analysis of the tonnes of saline bat guano, scientists conclude that they make an 80-km dash to the coast for meals of insects washed down with seawater. Cave cockroaches eat the guano, ensuring that the cavern does not become choked with what locals call 'black snow'.

Lang's Cave

Part of the same hollow mountain as Deer Cave, Lang's Cave is less well known but its formations are more beautiful and it contains impressive curtain stalactites and intricate coral-like helictites. The cave is well lit and protected by bus-stop-style plastic tunnels.

The Sarawak Chamber

Discovered in 1984, this chamber is 600 m long, 450 m wide and 100 m high – big enough, it is said, to accommodate 40 jumbo jets wing-tip to wing-tip and eight nose-to-tail. It is the largest natural chamber in the world. It is now possible for cavers with some experience to visit the cave, with the approval of the Park Manager. It is a three-hour trek to the cave following the summit trail. Access to the cave is through Gua Nasib Bagus, following a river trail bordered by 50-m-high sheer rock faces on both sides for 800 m. After a further scramble, cavers reach the dark mouth of the chamber. It is not permitted to enter any further as it is considered too dangerous. Guide fees are RM500 for a group of up to five.

Bario and the Kelabit Highlands → For listings, see pages 377-379. Colour map 4, C2.

Bario (Bareo) lies in the Kelabit Highlands, a plateau 1000 m above sea level close to the Kalimantan border in Indonesia. The undulating Bario valley is surrounded by mountains and fed by countless small streams that in turn feed into a maze of irrigation canals.

Ins and outs

Bario is only accessible by air or via a seven-day trek from Marudi. For information on Bario and the Kelabits, see www.kelabit.net. The best time to visit the area is between March and October.

Background

The local Kelabits' skill in harnessing water has allowed them to practise wet rice cultivation rather than the more common slash-and-burn hill rice techniques. Fragrant Bario rice is prized in Sarawak and commands a premium in the coastal markets. The more temperate climate of the Kelabit Highlands also allows the cultivation of a wide range of fruit and vegetables.

The plateau's near-impregnable ring of mountains effectively cut the Kelabit off from the outside world; it is the only area in Borneo which was never penetrated by Islam. In 1911 the Resident of Baram mounted an expedition which ventured into the mountains to ask the Kelabit to stop raiding the Brooke Government's subjects. It took the expedition 17 days to cross the Tamu Abu mountain range, to the west of Bario. The Kelabit were then brought under the control of the Sarawak government.

The most impressive mountain in the Bario area is the distinctive twin peak of the sheer-faced 2043 m **Bukit Batu Lawi** to the northwest of Bario. The Kelabit traditionally believed the mountain had an evil spirit and so never went near it. Today such superstitions are a thing of the past since locals are mostly evangelical Christians.

In 1945, the plateau was selected as the only possible parachute drop zone in North Borneo not captured by the Japanese. The Allied Special Forces that parachuted into Bario were led by Tom Harrisson, who later became curator of the Sarawak Museum and made the famous archaeological discoveries at Niah Caves (see page 356). His expedition formed an irregular tribal army against the Japanese, which gained control over large areas of North Borneo in the following months.

Treks around Bario

Because of the rugged terrain surrounding the plateau, the area mainly attracts serious mountaineers. There are many trails to the longhouses around the plateau area, however. Treks to Bario can be organized through travel agents in Miri, see page 365. Guides can also be hired in Bario and surrounding longhouses for RM30-40 per day. It is best to go through the Penghulu, Ngiap Ayu, the Kelabit chief. He goes around visiting many of the longhouses in the area once a month. It is recommended that visitors to Bario come with sleeping bags and camping equipment. There are no formal facilities for tourists and provisions should be brought from Miri or Marudi. There are no banks or money changers in Bario.

Several of the surrounding mountains can be climbed from Bario, but they are, without exception, difficult climbs. Even on walks just around the Bario area, guides are essential as trails are poorly marked. The lower 'female' peak of **Bukit Batu Lawi** can be climbed without equipment, but the sheer-sided 'male' peak requires proper rock climbing equipment; it was first scaled in 1986. **Gunung Murudi** (2423 m) is the highest mountain in Sarawak and it is a very tough climb.

Limbang → For listings, see pages 377-379. Colour map 4, B2.

Limbang is the administrative centre for the Fifth Division and was ceded to the Brooke government by the Sultan of Brunei in 1890. The Trusan Valley, to the east of the wedge of Brunei, had been ceded to Sarawak in 1884. Very few tourists reach Limbang or Lawas but they are good stopping-off points for more adventurous routes to **Sabah** and **Brunei**. Limbang is the finger of Sarawak territory which splits Brunei in two. To contact the **Residents' Office** ① T085-202106.

Sights

Limbang's **Old Fort** was built in 1897, renovated in 1966, and was used as the administrative centre. During the Brooke era, half the ground floor was used as a jail. It is now a centre of religious instruction, Majlis Islam. Limbang is famous for its **Pasar Tamu** every Friday, where jungle and native produce is sold. Limbang also has an attractive small museum, **Muzium Wilayah** ① 400 m south of the centre along Jln Kubu, Tue-Sun 0900-1800. Housed in a wooden beige and white villa, the museum has a collection of ethnic artefacts from the region, including basketry, musical instruments and weapons. To the right of the museum, a small road climbs the hill to a park with a man-made lake.

To trek to the **Gunung Mulu National Park** (see page 369), take a car south to Medamit; from there hire a longboat upriver to Mulu Madang, an Iban longhouse (three hours, depending on water level). Alternatively, go further upriver to Kuala Terikan (six to seven hours when the water's low, four hours when it's high) where there is a simple zinc-roofed camp. From there take a longboat one hour up the Terikan River to Lubang China, which is the start of a two-hour trek along a well-used trail to Camp 5. There is a park rangers' camp about 20 minutes out of Kuala Terikan where it is possible to obtain permits and arrange for a guide to meet you at Camp 5. The longboats are cheaper to hire in the wet season.

Lawas

Lawas District was ceded to Sarawak in 1905. The Limbang River, which cuts through the town, is the main transport route. It is possible to travel from Miri to Bandar Seri Begawan (Brunei) by road, then on to Limbang and Lawas. From Lawas there are direct buses to Kota Kinabalu in Sabah.

For Sleeping and Eating price codes and other relevant information, see Essentials pages 25-30.

⦿ Sleeping

Gunung Mulu National Park *p369, map p370*

Park chalets must be booked in advance at the **National Parks and Wildlife Office Forest Department** in Miri (T085-792300 or T085-792301, enquiries@mulupark.com), www.mulupark.com. Booking fee is RM20 per party (maximum 10 people). Bookings must be confirmed 5 days before visit.

AL-A Royal Mulu Resort, Sungai Melinau, Muku, Miri, a 20-min (RM5) boat ride downstream from Park HQ, T085-790100, www.royal muluresort.com. This resort has 188 well-designed rooms with cable TV and a/c. There is also a pool, a gym, a spa and restaurants. Travellers who are desperate to visit the park and find that all the other accommodation is booked can usually find a (pricey) bed here. It has sparked much resentment among local tribespeople. The Berawan claim the resort's land as theirs by customary right.

A-E Park HQ. The park also offers its own accommodation. Top of the range are the **de luxe longhouses (A)** which have attached bathroom, a/c, and 4 single beds, or a twin share. For 4 people sharing, it works out at RM41 each and breakfast is included. **Rainforest Rooms (B)** sleep up to 4 and have fans and attached bathroom, at just over RM25 per person. There is also a **hostel (C)** with 21 dorm beds, fan and shared bathrooms for RM37 per person. At Camp 5 is a **simple hostel (D)** with kitchen for self-catering, mats for sleeping and shared bathrooms. There are also simple wooden shelters on the summit trail **(E)**. For both of these, bring your own sleeping bag. **D Melinau Canteen**, T085-657884. One of several hostels just outside the park. Privately owned, with dorm beds, about 5 mins' walk downstream from the Park HQ on the other bank of the river.

Camping

E Camping is only allowed at the campsite at Park HQ (RM10). Bring your own sleeping bag.

Bario and the Kelabit Highlands *p375*

C Bariew Lodge, T085-791038, bariew lodge@yahoo.com. Popular backpacker option with simple rooms and a pleasant lounge area. All meals are included, as are airport transfers. Guide service offered for RM65 per half day. Recommended.

C-D De Plateau Lodge, munney_bala@ kelabit.net. 2 km from the airport, this wooden house has plenty of funky native decor and offers simple rooms with meals included. There's a pleasant communal area, and guide services for treks and walks, as well as birdwatching trips around the highlands at RM65 per half day.

D Tarawe. A well-run place to stay with a good source of information. Simple rooms and a veranda overlooking a fish pond. Cable TV and electricity after dark. Recommended.

Limbang *p376*

Limbang has become a sex stop for Bruneians, whose government takes a more hardline attitude to such moral transgressions, and consequently many hotels and guesthouses have a fair share of short-time guests.

B Centre Point Hotel, T085-212922. Newish place, with a/c and restaurant, tops Limbang's limited bill of hotels.

B-C Metro, Lot 781, Jln Bangkita, T085-211133, F211051. A fairly new addition to Limbang's mid-range places, with less than 30 small but clean rooms, all with a/c, TV, fridge, good quality beds. Recommended.

B-C Muhibbah, Lot T790, Bank St, T085-213705, F212153. Located in town centre, this place has seen better days, but rooms are fairly clean with a/c, TV and bathroom.

B-C National Inn, 62a Jln Buangsiol, T085-212922, F212282. Probably the best of the 3 hotels along the river, comfortable a/c rooms with TV, minibar. Higher rates for river view.

Lawas *p376*

A-B Country Park Hotel, Lot 235, Jln Trusan, T085-85522. A/c and restaurant.
C Lawas Federal, 8 Jln Masjid Baru, T085-85115. A/c and restaurant.
D Hup Guan Lodging House, T085-85362. Some a/c, can be noisy, but the rooms are clean and spacious and reasonable value for money.

🍴 Eating

Gunung Mulu National Park *p369, map p370*

There are stoves and cooking utensils available and the small store at Park HQ also sells basic supplies. The Café Mulu at Park HQ (0730-2100) has a range of simple Asian and Western dishes. Alcohol is not available but guests are allowed to bring their own. As an alternative, cross the suspension bridge and walk alongside the road to the first house on the left; down the bank from here is the **Mulu Canteen**, which fronts onto the river. There is also the **Melinau Canteen**, just downriver from the Park HQ. There is a small shop with basic supplies at Long Pala. All tour companies with their own accommodation offer food.

Limbang *p376*

🍴 **Tong Lok**. A/c Chinese restaurant next to National Inn, gruesome pink tablecloths and fluorescent lighting, but good Chinese food.
🍴 **Hai Hong**, 1 block south of **Maggie's**. Simple coffee shop – good for breakfast with fried egg and chips on the menu.
🍴 **Maggie's Café** on the riverside near National Inn. Chinese coffee shop, pleasant location, tables outside next to river in the evening. Braziers set up in evening for good grilled fish on banana leaf. Recommended.

🎉 Festivals and events

Limbang *p376*

May The (movable) Buffalo Racing Festival marks the end of the harvesting season.

▲ Activities and tours

Gunung Mulu National Park *p369, map p370*

Visitors are recommended to go through one of the Miri-based travel agents (see page 365). The average cost of a Mulu package (per person) is RM750 (4 days/3 nights) or RM850 (6 days/5 nights). Independent travellers will find it more expensive arranging the trip on their own.

Limbang *p376*

Sitt Travel, T085-420567. Specializes in treks in this area and is the ticketing agent for Miri tour operators.

🚌 Transport

Gunung Mulu National Park *p369, map p370*

Longboats can be chartered privately from Park HQ (maximum 10 people per boat). The cost is calculated on a rather complicated system which includes a rate for the boat, a charge for the engine based on its horsepower, a separate payment for the driver and frontman, and then fuel. Total costs can be over RM100. How far these boats can get upriver depends on the season. They often have to be hauled over rapids whatever the time of year.

Air

Daily flights from **Miri** to Mulu, 20 mins. The airstrip is just downriver from Park HQ. MASwings currently has 2 flights daily from Miri (book well in advance). The price of a flight is only marginally more expensive than taking the bus and boat from Miri and is much faster. The airline operates thrice-weekly flights to **Kuching** and daily flights to **Kota Kinabalu** via Miri.

Bus/boat/taxi

Bus or taxi from **Miri** to **Marudi** express boat jetty near **Kuala Baram** at mouth of the Baram River (see page 368). Regular express boats from **Kuala Baram** to **Marudi** (3 hrs, RM20) from 0800 until about 1500. One express boat per day (leaves at 1200) from Marudi to **Long Terawan** on the Tutoh River, via **Long Apoh** (RM25). During the dry season express boats cannot reach Long Terawan and terminate at Long Panai on the Tutoh River, where longboats continue to Long Terawan (RM25). Longboats leave Long Terawan for Mulu Park HQ: this used to be regular and relatively cheap; now that most people travel to Mulu by air, longboats need to be privately chartered – an expensive business at RM350 a pop. Mulu Park HQ is 1½ hrs up the Melinau River, a tributary of the Tutoh. As you approach the park from Long Terawan the Tutoh River narrows and becomes shallower; there are 14 rapids before the Melinau River, which forms the park boundary. When the water is low, the trip can be very slow and involve pulling the boat over the shallows; this accounts for high charter rates. The first jetty on the Melinau River is **Long Pala**, where most of the tour companies have accommodation. The Park HQ is another 15 mins upriver. Longboats returning to Long Terawan leave the headquarters at dawn each day, calling at jetties en route.

Bario and the Kelabit Highlands *p375*
Air
The only access to Bario is by air on MASwings. Bario's airstrip is very small and because of its position, flights are often cancelled due to mist. Flights are always booked up. There is at least 1 flight a day

(2 flights on Tue, Thu, Fri, Sun) on MASwings. There is also one connection a day to **Marudi**.

Walking
It is a 7-day trek from **Marudi** to Bario, sleeping in longhouses en route. This trip should be organized through a Miri travel agent (see page 365).

Limbang *p376*
Air
There are 2 daily connections with **Miri** with MASwings. The airport is 5 km from town and taxis ferry passengers in.

Boat
Regular connections with **Lawas**, depart early in the morning (2 hrs, RM20). There is also an early-morning express departure to **Labuan**. Regular boat connections with **Bandar Seri Begawan**, Brunei (30 mins, RM20).

Lawas *p376*
Air
Frequent connections with **Miri** and a twice-weekly flight to **Ba'kelalan** with MASwings.

Boat
Regular connections to **Limbang**, 2 hrs. Daily morning boat departures for **Brunei**.

Bus
Connections with **Merapok** on the Sarawak/Sabah border (RM8). From here there are connections to **Beaufort** in Sabah. Twice-daily connections with **KK** (4 hrs, RM26).

Background

History
Sarawak earned its place in the archaeological textbooks when a 37,000-year-old human skull belonging to a boy of about 15 was unearthed in the Niah Caves in 1958 (see page 354), predating the earliest relics found on the Malay Peninsula by about 30,000 years. The caves were continuously inhabited for tens of thousands of years and many shards of palaeolithic and neolithic pottery, tools and jewellery as well as carved burial boats have been excavated at the site. There are also prehistoric cave paintings. In the first

millennium AD, the Niah Caves were home to a prosperous community, which traded birds' nests, hornbill ivory, bezoar stones, rhinoceros horns and other jungle produce with Chinese traders in exchange for porcelain and beads.

Some of Sarawak's tribes may be descended from these cave people, although others, notably the Iban shifting cultivators, migrated from Kalimantan's Kapuas River valley from the 16th to 19th centuries. Malay Orang Laut, sea people, migrated to Sarawak's coasts and made a living from fishing, trading and piracy. At the height of Sumatra's Srivijayan Empire in the 11th and 12th centuries, many Sumatran Malays migrated to north Borneo. Chinese traders were active along the Sarawak coast from as early as the seventh century: Chinese coins and Han pottery have been discovered at the mouth of the Sarawak River.

From the 14th century right up to the 20th century, Sarawak's history was inextricably intertwined with that of the neighbouring Sultanate of Brunei, which, until the arrival of the White Rajahs of Sarawak, held sway over the coastal areas of north Borneo. For a more detailed account of how Sarawak's White Rajahs came to whittle away the sultan's territory and expand into the vacuum of his receding empire, see Robert Payne's *The White Rajahs of Sarawak*.

Enter James Brooke

As the Sultanate of Brunei began to decline around the beginning of the 18th century, the Malays of coastal Sarawak attempted to break free from their tributary overlord. They claimed an independent ancestry from Brunei and exercised firm control over the Dayak tribes inland and upriver. But in the early 19th century Brunei started to reassert its power over them, dispatching Pangiran Mahkota from the Brunei court in 1827 to govern Sarawak and supervise the mining of high-grade antimony ore, exported to Singapore to be used in medicine and as an alloy. The name 'Sarawak' is from the Malay word *serawak (antimony)*.

Mahkota founded Kuching, but relations with the local Malays became strained and Mahkota's problems were compounded by the marauding Ibans of the Saribas and Skrang rivers who raided coastal communities. In 1836 the local Malay chiefs, led by Datu Patinggi Ali, rebelled against Governor Mahkota, prompting the Sultan of Brunei to send his uncle, Rajah Muda Hashim to suppress the uprising. But Hashim failed to quell the disturbances and the situation deteriorated when the rebels approached the Sultan of Sambas, now in northwest Kalimantan, for help from the Dutch. Then, in 1839, James Brooke sailed up the Sarawak River to Kuching.

Hashim was desperate to regain control and Brooke, in the knowledge that the British would support any action that countered the threat of Dutch influence, struck a deal with him. He pressed Hashim to grant him the governorship of Sarawak in exchange for suppressing the rebellion, which he duly did. In 1842 Brooke became Rajah of Sarawak. Pangiran Mahkota – the now disenfranchised former governor of Sarawak – formed an alliance with an Iban pirate chief on the Skrang River, while another Brunei prince, Pangiran Usop, joined Illanun pirates. Malaysian historian J Kathirithamby-Wells wrote: "... piracy and politics became irrevocably linked and Brooke's battle against his political opponents became advertised as a morally justified war against the pirate communities of the coast."

The suppression of piracy in the 19th century became a full-time job for the Sarawak and Brunei rulers, although the court of Brunei was well known to have derived a large chunk of its income from piracy. Rajah James Brooke believed that as long as pirates were free to pillage the coast, commerce wouldn't grow and his kingdom would never develop; ridding Sarawak's estuaries of pirates – both Iban (Sea Dayaks) and Illanun – became an act of political survival. In *The White Rajahs of Sarawak*, Robert Payne wrote:

"Nearly every day people came to Kuching with tales about the pirates: how they had landed in a small creek, made their way to a village, looted everything in sight, murdered everyone they could lay their hands on, and then vanished as swiftly as they came. The Sultan of Brunei was begging for help against them."

Anti-piracy missions afforded James Brooke an excuse to extend his kingdom, as he worked his way up the coasts, 'pacifying' the Sea Dayak pirates. Brooke declared war on them and with the help of Royal Naval Captain Henry Keppel (of latter-day Singapore's Keppel Shipyard fame), he led a number of punitive raids against the Iban Sea Dayaks in 1833, 1834 and 1849. "The assaults", wrote DJM Tate in *Rajah Brooke's Borneo*, "largely achieved their purpose and were applauded in the Straits, but the appalling loss of life incurred upset many drawing room humanitarians in Britain." There were an estimated 25,000 pirates living along the North Borneo coast when Brooke became Rajah. He led many expeditions against them, culminating in his notorious battle against the Saribas pirate fleet in 1849.

In that incident, Brooke ambushed and killed hundreds of Saribas Dayaks at Batang Maru. The barbarity of the ambush (which was reported in the *Illustrated London News*) outraged public opinion in Britain and in Singapore; a commission in Singapore acquitted Brooke, but badly damaged his prestige. In the British parliament, he was cast as a 'mad despot' who had to be prevented from committing further massacres. But the action led the Sultan of Brunei to grant him the Saribas and Skrang districts (now Sarawak's Second Division) in 1853, marking the beginning of the Brooke dynasty's relentless expansionist drive. Eight years later, James Brooke persuaded the sultan to give him what became Sarawak's Third Division, after he drove out the Illanun pirates who disrupted the sago trade from Mukah and Oya, around Bintulu.

In 1857, James Brooke ran into more trouble. Chinese Hakka goldminers, who had been in Bau (further up the Sarawak River) longer than he had been in Kuching, had grown resentful of his attempts to stamp out the opium trade and their secret societies. They attacked Kuching, set the Malay kampongs ablaze and killed several European officials; Brooke escaped by swimming across the river from his astana. His nephew, Charles, led a group of Skrang Dayaks in pursuit of the Hakka invaders, who fled across the border into Dutch Borneo; about 1000 were killed by the Ibans on the way; 2500 survived. Robert Payne writes: "The fighting lasted for more than a month. From time to time Dayaks would return with strings of heads, which they cleaned and smoked over slow fires, especially happy when they could do this in full view of the Chinese in the bazaars who sometimes recognized people they had known." Payne says Brooke was plagued by guilt over how he handled the Chinese rebellion, for so many deaths could not easily be explained away. Neither James nor Charles ever fully trusted the Chinese again, although the Teochew, Cantonese and Hokkien merchants in Kuching never caused them any trouble.

The second generation: Rajah Charles Brooke

Charles Johnson (who changed his name to Brooke after his elder brother, Brooke Johnson, had been disinherited by James for insubordination) became the second Rajah of Sarawak in 1863. He ruled for nearly 50 years. Charles did not have James Brooke's forceful personality, and was much more reclusive – probably as a result of working in remote jungle outposts for 10 years in government service. Robert Payne noted that "in James Brooke there was something of the knight errant at the mercy of his dream. Charles was the pure professional, a stern soldier who thought dreaming was the occupation of fools. There was no nonsense about him." Despite this he engendered great loyalty in his administrators, who worked hard for little reward.

Charles maintained his uncle's consultative system of government and formed a Council Negeri, or national council, of his top government officials, Malay leaders and tribal headmen, which met every few years to hammer out policy changes. His frugal financial management meant that by 1877 Sarawak was no longer in debt and the economy gradually expanded. But it was not wealthy, and had few natural resources; its soils proved unsuitable for agriculture. In the 1880s, Charles's faith in the Chinese community was sufficiently restored to allow Chinese immigration, and the government subsidized the new settlers. By using 'friendly' downriver Dayak groups to subdue belligerent tribes upriver, Charles managed to pacify the interior by 1880.

When Charles took over from his ailing uncle in 1863 he proved to be even more of an expansionist. In 1868 he tried to take control of the Baram River valley, but London did not approve secession of the territory until 1882, when it became the Fourth Division. In 1884, Charles acquired the Trusan Valley from the Sultan of Brunei, and in 1890, he annexed Limbang ending a six-year rebellion by local chiefs against the sultan. The two territories were united to form the Fifth Division, after which Sarawak completely surrounded Brunei. In 1905, the British North Borneo Chartered Company gave up the Lawas Valley to Sarawak too. "By 1890," writes Robert Payne, "Charles was ruling over a country as large as England and Scotland with the help of about 20 European officers." When the First World War broke out in 1914, Charles was in England and he ruled Sarawak from Cirencester.

The third generation: Charles Vyner Brooke

In 1916, at the age of 86, Charles handed power to his eldest son, Charles Vyner Brooke, and he died the following year. Vyner was 42 when he became Rajah and had already served his father's government for nearly 20 years. "Vyner was a man of peace, who took no delight in bloodshed and ruled with humanity and compassion," wrote Robert Payne. He was a delegator by nature, and under him the old paternalistic style of government gave way to a more professional bureaucracy. On the centenary of the Brooke administration in September 1941, Vyner promulgated a written constitution, and renounced his autocratic powers in favour of working in cooperation with a Supreme Council. This was opposed by his nephew and heir, Anthony Brooke, who saw it as a move to undermine his succession. To protest against this, and his uncle's decision to appoint a mentally deranged Muslim Englishman as his Chief Secretary, Anthony left for Singapore. The Rajah dismissed him from the service in September 1941. Three months later the Japanese Imperial Army invaded; Vyner Brooke was in Australia at the time, and his younger brother, Bertram, was ill in London.

Japanese troops took Kuching on Christmas Day 1941 having captured the Miri oilfield a few days earlier. European administrators were interned and many later died. A Kuching-born Chinese, Albert Kwok, led an armed resistance against the Japanese in neighbouring British North Borneo (Sabah) – see page 485 – but in Sarawak, there was no organized guerrilla movement. Iban tribespeople instilled fear into the occupying forces, however, by roaming the jungle taking Japanese heads, which were proudly added to much older longhouse head galleries. Despite the Brooke regime's century-long effort to stamp out headhunting, the practice was encouraged by Tom Harrisson (see box, page 383) who parachuted into the Kelabit Highlands towards the end of the Second World War and put together an irregular army of upriver tribesmen to fight the Japanese. He offered them 'ten-bob-a-nob' for Japanese heads. Australian forces liberated Kuching on 11 September 1945 and Sarawak was placed under Australian military administration for seven months.

After the war, the Colonial Office in London decided the time had come to bring Sarawak into the modern era, replacing the anachronistic White Rajahs, introducing an

Tom Harrisson: life in the fast lane

Reputed to be one of the most important figures in the development of archaeology in Southeast Asia, Tom Harrisson, the charismatic 'egomaniac', put Borneo and Sarawak on the map.

Tom Harrisson loved Sarawak and, it would seem, Sarawak loved him. He first visited Sarawak in 1932 as part of a Royal Geographical Expedition sent, along with around 150 kg of Cadbury's chocolate, to collect flora and fauna from one of the world's great natural treasure stores. Instead Harrisson found himself entranced by the territory's human populations and so the love affair began.

By all accounts, Harrisson was a difficult fellow – the sort that imperial Britain produced in very large numbers indeed. He was a womaniser with a particular penchant for other people's spouses, he could be horribly abusive to his fellow workers and he apparently revelled in putting down uppity academics. But he was also instrumental in putting Sarawak, and Borneo on the map and in raising awareness of the ways in which economic and social change was impacting on Sarawak's tribal peoples.

Before taking up the curatorship of the Sarawak Museum in 1947 Harrisson also distinguished himself as a war hero, parachuting into the jungle and organizing around 1000 headhunters to terrorize the Japanese. All in all, Tom Harrisson led life in the fast lane.

Those wanting to read a good biography of Harrisson should get hold of *The Most Offending Soul Alive* by Judith M Heimann, Honolulu, Hawaii University Press, 1998.

education system and building a rudimentary infrastructure. The Brookes had become an embarrassment to the British government as they continued to squabble among themselves. Anthony Brooke desperately wanted to claim what he felt was his, while the Colonial Office wanted Sarawak to become a crown colony or revert to Malay rule. No one was sure whether Sarawak wanted the Brookes back or not.

The end of empire

In February 1946 the ageing Vyner shocked his brother Bertram and his nephew Anthony, the Rajah Muda (or heir apparent), by issuing a proclamation urging the people of Sarawak to accept the King of England as their ruler. In doing so he effectively handed the country over to Britain. Vyner thought the continued existence of Sarawak as the private domain of the Brooke family an anachronism; but Anthony thought it a betrayal. The British government sent a commission to Sarawak to ascertain what the people wanted. In May 1946, the Council Negeri agreed – by a 19-16 majority – to transfer power to Britain, provoking protests and demonstrations and resulting in the assassination of the British governor by a Malay in Sibu in 1949. He and three other anti-cessionists were sentenced to death. Two years later, Anthony Brooke, who remained deeply resentful about the demise of the Brooke Dynasty, abandoned his claim and urged his supporters to end their campaign.

As a British colony, Sarawak's economy expanded and oil and timber production increased, which funded the much-needed expansion of education and health services. As with British North Borneo (Sabah), Britain was keen to give Sarawak political independence and, following Malaysian independence in 1957, saw the best means to this end as being through the proposal of Malaysian Prime Minister Tunku Abdul Rahman. The prime minister suggested the formation of a federation to include Singapore, Sarawak, Sabah and

Brunei as well as the Peninsula. In the end, Brunei opted out, Singapore left after two years, but Sarawak and Sabah joined the federation, having accepted the recommendations of the British government. Indonesia's President Sukarno denounced the move, claiming it was all part of a neo-colonialist conspiracy. He declared a policy of confrontation – **Konfrontasi**. A United Nations commission which was sent to ensure that the people of Sabah and Sarawak wanted to be part of Malaysia reported that Indonesia's objections were unfounded.

Communists had been active in Sarawak since the 1930s. The Konfrontasi afforded the Sarawak Communist Organization (SCO) Jakarta's support against the Malaysian government. The SCO joined forces with the North Kalimantan Communist Party (NKCP) and were trained and equipped by Indonesia's President Sukarno. But following Jakarta's brutal suppression of the Indonesian Communists, the Partai Komunis Indonesia (PKI), in the wake of the attempted coup in 1965, Sarawak's Communists fled back across the Indonesian border, along with their Kalimantan comrades. There they continued to wage guerrilla war against the Malaysian government throughout the 1970s. The Sarawak state government offered amnesties to guerrillas wanting to come out of hiding. In 1973 the NKCP leader surrendered along with 482 other guerrillas. A handful remained in the jungle, most of them in the hills around Kuching. The last surrendered in 1990.

Politics and modern Sarawak

In 1957 Kuala Lumpur was keen to have Sarawak and Sabah in the Federation of Malaysia and offered the two states a degree of autonomy, allowing their local governments control over state finances, agriculture and forestry. Sarawak's racial mix was reflected in its chaotic state politics. The Ibans dominated the Sarawak National Party (SNAP), which provided the first chief minister, Datuk Stephen Kalong Ningkan. He raised a storm over Kuala Lumpur's introduction of Bahasa Malaysia in schools and complained bitterly about the federal government's policy of filling the Sarawakian civil service with Malays from the Peninsula. An 'us' and 'them' mentality developed: in Sarawak, the Malay word *semenanjung* (Peninsula) was used to label the newcomers. To many, *semenanjung* was Malaysia, Sarawak was Sarawak.

In 1966 the federal government ousted the SNAP, and a new Muslim-dominated government led by the Sarawak Alliance took over in Kuching. But there was still strong political opposition to federal encroachment. Throughout the 1970s, as in Sabah, Sarawak's strongly Muslim government drew the state closer and closer to the Peninsula: it supported *Rukunegara* – the policy of Islamization – and promoted the use of Bahasa Malaysia. Muslims make up less than one-third of the population of Sarawak. The Malays, Melanaus and Chinese communities grew rich from the timber industry; the Ibans and the Orang Ulu (the upriver tribespeople) saw little in the way of development. They did not reap the benefits of the expansion of education and social services, they were unable to get public sector jobs and, to make matters worse, logging firms were encroaching on their native lands and threatening their traditional lifestyles.

It has only been in more recent years that the tribespeoples' political voice has been heard at all. In 1983, Iban members of SNAP – which was a part of former Prime Minister Dr Mahathir Mohamad's ruling Barisan Nasional (National Front) coalition – split to form the Party Bansa Dayak Sarawak (PBDS), which, although it initially remained in the coalition, became more outspoken on native affairs. At about the same time, international outrage was sparked over the exploitation of Sarawak's tribespeople by politicians and businessmen involved in the logging industry. The plight of the Penan hunter-gatherers came to world attention due to their blockades of logging roads and the resulting publicity highlighted the rampant corruption and greed that characterized modern Sarawak's political economy.

The National Front remain firmly in control in Sarawak. But unlike neighbouring Sabah, Sarawak's politicians are not dominated by the centre. The chief minister of Sarawak is Abduly Taib Mahmud, a Melanau, and his Parti Pesaka Bumiputra Bersatu is a member of the UMNO-dominated (United Malays National Organisation) National Front. But in Sarawak itself UMNO wields little power.

The ruling National Front easily won the 1999 election in Sarawak, successfully playing on voters' local concerns and grievances. The problem for the opposition is that local people think it is the state legislature that can help, not the federal parliament in KL, which seems distant and ineffective. So UMNO does not have a presence and it is the Parti Pesaka Bumiputra Bersatu which represents Sarawak in the National Front.

The challenge of getting the voters out in the most remote areas of the country was clearly shown in Long Lidom. There it cost the government RM65,000 to provide a helicopter to poll just seven Punan Busang in a longhouse on the Upper Kajang, close to the border with Indonesia. Datuk Omar of the Election Commission said that mounting the general election in Sarawak, with its 28 parliamentary seats, was a "logistical nightmare". Along with a small air force of helicopters, the Commission used 1032 long boats, 15 speed boats and 3054 land cruisers. The Commission's workforce numbered a cool 13,788 workers in a state with a population of just two million.

The 2006 state elections in Sarawak was won convincingly by the Barisan Nasional, winning 62 out of the 71 contested seats.

Today there are many in Sarawak as well as in Sabah who wish their governments had opted out of the Federation, as did Brunei. Sarawak is of great economic importance to Malaysia, thanks to its oil, gas and timber. The state now accounts for more than one-third of Malaysia's petroleum production (worth more than US$800 million per year) and more than half of its natural gas. As with neighbouring Sabah however, 95% of Sarawak's oil and gas revenues go directly into federal coffers.

Culture

People

About a third of the population is made up of Iban tribespeople who live in longhouses on the lower reaches of the rivers. Chinese immigrants, whose forebears arrived during the 19th century, make up another third. A fifth of the population is Malay; most are native Sarawakians, but some came from the Peninsula after the state joined the Malaysian Federation in 1963. The rest of Sarawak's inhabitants are indigenous tribal groups, of which the main ones are the Melanau, the Bidayuh and upriver Orang Ulu such as the Kenyah, Kayan and Kelabits; the Penan are among Southeast Asia's few remaining hunter-gatherers. The population of the state is almost 2.2 million. The people of the interior are classified as Proto-Malays and Deutero-Malays and are divided into at least 12 distinct tribal groups including Iban, Murut (see page 491), Melanau, Bidayuh, Kenyah, Kayan, Kelabit and Penan.

Bidayuh In the 19th century, Sarawak's European community called the Bidayuh Land Dayaks, mainly to distinguish them from the Iban Sea Dayak pirates. The Bidayuh make up 8.4% of the population and are concentrated to the west of the Kuching area, towards the Kalimantan border. There are also related groups living in west Kalimantan. They were virtually saved from extinction by the White Rajahs, because the Bidayuh were quiet, mild-mannered people, they

The Iban in Borneo

The Iban are an outgoing people and usually extend a warm welcome to visitors. Iban women are skilled weavers; even today a girl is not considered eligible until she has proven her skills at the loom by weaving a ceremonial textile, the *pua kumbu* (see page 394). The Ibans love to party and, during the harvest festival in June, visitors are welcome to drink copious amounts of *tuak* (rice wine) and dance through the night.

Probably because they were shifting cultivators, the Iban remained in closely bonded family groups and were a classless society. Historian Mary Turnbull said: "they retained their pioneer social organization of nuclear family groups living together in long-houses and did not evolve more sophisticated political institutions. Long-settled families acquired prestige, but the Ibans did not merge into tribes and had neither chiefs, rakyat class, nor slaves".

The Iban have a very easygoing attitude to love and sex, which is best explained in Redmond O'Hanlon's book *Into the Heart of Borneo*. Free love is the general rule among Iban communities that have not become evangelical Christians although, once married, the Iban divorce rate is low and they are monogamous.

were at the mercy of the Iban headhunters and the Brunei Malays who taxed and enslaved them. The Brookes afforded them protection from both groups.

Most live in modern longhouses and are dry rice farmers. Their traditional long-houses are exactly like Iban ones, but without the tanju veranda. The Bidayuh tribe comprises five sub-groups: the Jagoi, Biatah, Bukar-Sadong, Selakau and Lara, all of whom live in far west Sarawak. They are the state's best traditional plumbers and are known for their ingenious gravity-fed bamboo water systems. They are bamboo specialists, making it into everything from cooking pots to finely carved musical instruments. Among other tribal groups, the Bidayuh are renowned for their rice wine and sugarcane toddy. Henry Keppel, who with Rajah James Brooke fought the Bidayuh's dreaded enemies, the Sea Dayaks, described an evening spent with the Land Dayaks thus: "They ate and drank, and asked for everything, but stole nothing."

Chinese Hakka goldminers had already settled at Bau, upriver from Kuching, long before James Brooke arrived in 1839. Cantonese, Teochew and Hokkien merchants also set up in Kuching, but the Brookes did not warm to the Chinese community, believing the traders would exploit the Dayak communities if they were allowed to venture upriver. In the 1880s, however, Rajah Charles Brooke allowed the immigration of large numbers of Chinese – mainly Foochow – who settled in coastal towns like Sibu. Many became farmers and ran rubber smallholdings. The Sarawak government subsidized the immigrants for the first year. During the Brooke era, the only government-funded schools were for Malays and few tribal people ever received a formal education. The Chinese, however, set up and funded their own private schools and many attended Christian missionary schools, leading to the formation of a relatively prosperous, educated elite. Today the Chinese comprise nearly a third of the state's population and are almost as numerous as the Iban; they are the middlemen, traders, shopkeepers, timber towkays (magnates) and express boat owners.

Iban Sarawak's best-known erstwhile headhunters make up nearly a third of the state's population and while some have moved to coastal towns for work, many remain in their

Skulls in the longhouse

Although headhunting has been largely stamped out in Borneo, there is still the odd reported case once every few years. But until the early 20th century, headhunting was commonplace among many Dayak tribes and the Iban were the most fearsome of all.

Following a headhunting trip, the freshly taken heads were skinned, placed in rattan nets and smoked over a fire, or sometimes boiled. The skulls were then hung from the rafters of the longhouse and they possessed the most powerful form of magic.

The skulls were considered trophies of manhood (they increased a young bachelor's eligibility) and symbols of bravery. They also testified to the unity of a longhouse. The longhouse had to hold festivals – or *gawai* – to appease the spirits of the skulls. Once placated, the heads were believed to bring great blessing – they could ward off evil spirits, save villages from epidemics, produce rain and increase the yield of rice harvests. Heads that were insulted or ignored were

capable of wreaking havoc in the form of bad dreams, plagues, floods and fires. To keep the spirits of the skulls happy, they would be offered food and cigarettes and made to feel welcome in their new home. As the magical powers of a skull faded with time, fresh heads were always in demand. Tribes without heads were seen as spiritually weak.

Today, young Dayak men no longer have to take heads to gain respect. They are, however, expected to go on long journeys (the equivalent of the Australian aborigines' Walkabout), or *bejalai* in Iban. The one unspoken rule is that they should come back with plenty of good stories, and, these days, as most *bejalai* expeditions translate into stints at timber camps or on oil rigs, they are expected to come home bearing video recorders, TVs and motorbikes.

Many Dayak tribes continue to celebrate their headhunting ceremonies. In Kalimantan, for example, the Adat Ngayau ceremony uses coconut shells, wrapped in leaves, as substitutes for freshly cut heads.

traditional longhouses. But with Iban men now earning good money in the timber and oil industries, it is increasingly common to see longhouses bristling with TV aerials, equipped with fridges and flush toilets and Land Cruisers in the car park. Even modern longhouses retain the traditional features of gallery, veranda and doors. ▸▸ *See also box opposite.*

The Iban are shifting cultivators who originated in the Kapuas River basin of west Kalimantan and migrated into Sarawak's Second Division in the early 16th century, settling along the Batang Lupar, Skrang and Saribas rivers. By the 1800s, they had begun to spill into the Rejang River valley. It was this growing pressure on land as more migrants settled in the river valleys that led to fighting and headhunting (see box above).

The Iban joined local Malay chiefs and turned to piracy, which is how Europeans first came into contact with them. They were dubbed Sea Dayaks as a result, which is really a misnomer as they are an inland people. The name stuck, however, and in the eyes of Westerners, it distinguished them from Land Dayaks, who were Bidayuh people from the Sarawak River area (see page 385). While Rajah James Brooke only won the Iban's loyalty after he had crushed them in battle (see page 381), he had great admiration for them and they bore no bitterness. He described them as "good-looking a set of men, or devils ... Their wiry and supple limbs might have been compared to the troops of wild horses that followed Mazeppa in his perilous flight."

The Kelabit in Borneo

The Kelabit, who live in the highlands at the headwaters of the Baram River, are closely related to the Murut (see page 491) and the Lun Dayeh and Lun Bawang of interior Kalimantan.

They are skilled hill-rice farmers. The hill climate also allows vegetable cultivation.

Kelabit parties are also famed as boisterous occasions, and large quantities of *borak* (rice beer) are consumed, despite the fact that the majority of Kelabit has converted to Christianity. They are also regarded as among the most hospitable people in Borneo.

Kelabit Tom Harrisson parachuted into Kelabit territory with the Allied Special Forces towards the end of the Second World War. The Kelabit Highlands around Bario were chosen because they were so remote. Of all the tribes in Sarawak, the Kelabit have the sturdiest, strongest builds, which is usually ascribed to the cool and invigorating mountain climate. Their fragrant Bario rice is prized throughout Sarawak. ▶▶ See also box above.

Kenyah and Kayan These probably originally migrated into Sarawak from the Apo Kayan district in East Kalimantan. Kenyah and Kayan raids on downriver people were greatly feared, but their power was broken by Charles Brooke, just before he became the second White Rajah, in 1863. The Kayan had retreated upstream above the Pelagus Rapids on the Rejang River (see page 340), to an area they considered out of reach of their Iban enemies. In 1862 they killed two government officers at Kanowit and went on a killing spree. Charles Brooke led 15,000 Iban past the Pelagus Rapids, beyond Belaga and attacked the Kayan in their heartland. Many hundreds were killed. In November 1924, Rajah Vyner Brooke presided over a peace-making ceremony between the Orang Ulu and the Iban in Kapit (there is a photograph of the ceremony on display in the Kapit Museum). ▶▶ See also box opposite.

The Kenyah and Kayan in Sarawak live in pleasant upriver valleys and are settled rice farmers. Subgroups include the Kejaman, Skapan, Berawan and Sebop.

Malay About half of Sarawak's 300,000-strong Malay community lives around the state capital; most of the other half lives in the Limbang Division, near Brunei. The Malays traditionally live near the coast, although today there are small communities far upriver. There are some old wooden Malay houses with carved façades in the kampongs along the banks of the Sarawak River in Kuching. In all Malay communities, the mosque is the centre of the village, but while their faith is important to them, the strictures of Islam are generally less rigorously enforced in Sarawak than on the Peninsula. During the days of the White Rajahs, the Malays were recruited into government service, as they were on the Malay Peninsula. They were renowned as good administrators and the men were mostly literate in Jawi script. Over the years there has been much intermarriage between the Malay and Melanau communities. Traditionally, the Malays were fishermen and farmers.

Melanau The Melanau are a relaxed and humorous people. Rajah James Brooke, like generations of men before and after him, thought the Melanau girls particularly pretty. He said that they had "agreeable countenances, with the dark, rolling, open eye of the Italians, and nearly as fair as most of that race". The Melanau live along the coast between the Baram and Rejang rivers; originally they lived in magnificent communal houses built high off the ground, like the one that has been reconstructed at the Sarawak Cultural Village in

The Kenyah and Kayan in Borneo

These two closely related groups now live mainly in Sarawak and Kalimantan. They were the traditional rivals of the Iban and were notorious for their warlike ways. Historian Robert Payne, in his history *The White Rajahs of Sarawak*, described the Kayan of the upper Rejang as "a treacherous tribe, [who] like nothing better than putting out the eyes and cutting the throats of prisoners, or burning them alive".

They are very different from other tribal groups, have a completely different language (which has ancient Malayo-Polynesian roots) and are class conscious, with a well-defined social hierarchy. Traditionally their society was composed of aristocrats, nobles, commoners and slaves (who were snatched during raids on other tribes). One of the few things they have in common with other Dayak groups is the fact that they live in longhouses, although even these are of a different design, and are much more carefully constructed, in ironwood. Many have now been converted to Christianity (most are Protestant).

In contrast to their belligerent history, the Kenyahs and Kayans are much more introverted than the Ibans; they are slow and deliberate in their ways and are very artistic and musical. They are also renowned for their parties; visitors recovering from drinking *borak* rice beer have their faces covered in soot before being thrown in the river. This is to test the strength of the newly forged friendship with visitors, who are ill-advised to lose their sense of humour on such occasions.

Their artwork is made from wood, antlers, metal and beads. They use a lot of wooden statues and masks to scare evil spirits at the entrances to their homes.

Kuching, but these have long since disappeared. The houses were designed to afford protection from incessant pirate raids (see page 380), for the Melanau were easy pickings, being coastal people. Their stilt-houses were often up to 12 m off the ground. Today most Melanau live in Malay-style pile-houses facing the river. Hedda Morrison, in her classic 1957 book *Sarawak*, wrote: "As a result of living along the rivers in swamp country, the Melanaus are an exceptionally amphibious people. The children learn to swim almost before they can walk. Nearly all progress is by canoe, sometimes even to visit the house next door."

The traditional Melanau fishing boat is called a *barong*. Melanau fishermen employed a unique fishing technique. They would anchor palm leaves at sea as they discovered that shoals of fish would seek refuge under them. After rowing out to the leaves, one fisherman would dive off his *barong* and chase the fish into the nets which his colleague hung over the side. The Melanaus were also noted for their production of sago, which they ate instead of rice. At Kuching's Cultural Village there is a demonstration of traditional sago production, showing how the starch-bearing pith is removed, mashed, dried and ground into flour. Most Melanau are now Muslim and have assimilated with the Malays through intermarriage. Originally, however, they were animists (animist Melanau are called Likaus) and were particularly famed for their elaborately carved 'sickness images', which represented the form of spirits which caused specific illnesses (see page 393).

Orang Ulu The jungle, or upriver, people comprise a range of different small tribal groups. Orang Ulu longhouses are usually made of *belian* (ironwood) and are built to last. They are well-known swordsmiths, forging lethal parangs from any piece of scrap metal they find. They are also very artistic people – skilled carvers and painters and famed for their

Tribal tattoos

Tattooing is practised by many indigenous groups in Borneo, but the most intricate designs are those of the upriver Orang Ulu tribes.

Designs vary from group to group and for different parts of the body. Circular designs are mostly used for the shoulder, chest or wrists, while stylized dragon-dogs (*aso*), scorpions and dragons are used on the thigh and, for the Iban, on the throat.

Tattoos can mean different things; for the man it is a symbol of bravery and for women, a good tattoo is a beauty feature. More elaborate designs often denote high social status in Orang Ulu communities –

the Kayan, for example, reserved the *aso* design for the upper classes and slaves were barred from tattooing. In these Orang Ulu groups, the women have the most impressive tattoos; the headman's daughter has her hands, arms and legs completely covered in a finely patterned tattoo.

Designs are first carved on a block of wood, which is then smeared with ink. The design is printed on the body and then punctured into the skin with needles dipped in ink, usually made from a mixture of sugar, water and soot. Rice is smeared over the inflamed area to prevent infection, but it usually swells up for some time.

beadwork – taking great care decorating even simple household utensils. Most Orang Ulu are decorated with traditional tattoos (see box above).

Penan Perhaps Southeast Asia's only remaining true hunter-gatherers live mainly in the upper Rejang area and Limbang. They are nomads and are related, linguistically at least, to the Punan, former nomadic forest dwellers who are now settled in longhouses along the upper Rejang. The Malaysian government has long wanted the Penan to settle too, but has had limited success in attracting them to expensive new longhouses. Groups of Penan hunter-gatherers still wander hunt wild pigs, birds and monkeys and search for sago palms to make their staple food, sago flour. The Penan are considered to be the jungle experts by all the other inland tribes. As they live in the shade of the forest, their skin is relatively fair. They have a great affection for the coolness of the forest and until the 1960s were rarely seen by the outside world. For them sunlight is extremely unpleasant. They are broad and more stocky than other river people and are extremely shy, having had little contact with the outside world. Most trade is conducted with remote Kayan, Kenyah and Kelabit longhouse communities on the edge of the forest.
▸ *See also box, page 317.*

In the eyes of the West, the Penan have emerged as the 'noble savages' of the late 20th century for their spirited defence of their lands against encroachment by logging companies. This spirited defence continues today. But it is not just recently that they have been cheated: they have long been the victims of other upriver tribes. A Penan, bringing baskets full of rotan to a Kenyah or Kayan longhouse to sell, may end up exchanging his produce for one bullet or shotgun cartridge. In his way of thinking, a bullet will kill one wild boar which will last his family 10 days. In turn, the buyer knows he can sell the same rotan downstream for RM50-100. Penan still use the blowpipe for small game, but shotguns for wild pig. If they buy the shotgun cartridges for themselves, they have to exchange empties first. Some of the Penan's shotguns date back to the Second World War, when the British supplied them to upriver tribespeople to fight the Japanese. During the Brooke era, a large annual market would be held which both Chinese traders and

The palang

One of the more exotic features of upriver sexuality is the *palang* (penis pin), which is the versatile jungle version of the French tickler.

Traditionally, women suffer heavy weights being attached to their ear lobes to enhance their sex appeal. In turn, men are expected to enhance their physical attributes and entertain their womenfolk by drilling a hole in their organs, into which they insert a range of items, aimed at heightening their partner's pleasure.

Tom Harrisson, a former curator of the Sarawak Museum, was intrigued by the *palang*; some suspect his authority on the subject stemmed from first-hand experience. He wrote: "When the device is put into use, the owner adds whatever he prefers to elaborate and accentuate its intention. A lively range of objects can so be employed – from pigs' bristles and bamboo shavings to pieces of metal, seeds, beads and broken glass. The effect, of course, is to enlarge the diameter of the male organ inside the female."

It is said that many Dayak men, even today, have the tattoo man drill a hole in them. As the practice is now centuries old, one can only assume that its continued popularity proves it is worth the agony.

Orang Ulu (including Penan) used to attend; the district officer would have to act as judge to ensure the Penan did not get cheated.

Those wishing to learn more about the Penan should refer to Denis Lau's *The Vanishing Nomads of Borneo* (Interstate Publishing, 1987). Lau has lived among the Penan and has photographed them for many years; his photographs appear in *Malaysia – Heart of Southeast Asia* (Archipelago Press, 1991).

Dance

Dayak tribes are renowned for their singing and dancing, most famously for the hornbill dance. In her book *Sarawak*, Hedda Morrison wrote: "The Kayans are probably the originators of the stylized war dance now common among the Ibans but the girls are also extremely talented and graceful dancers. One of their most delightful dances is the hornbill dance, when they tie hornbill feathers to the ends of their fingers which accentuate their slow and graceful movements. For party purposes everyone in the longhouse joins in and parades up and down the communal room led by one or two musicians and a group of girls who sing." On these occasions, drink flows freely. With the Ibans, it is *tuak* (rice wine), with the Kayan and Kenyah it is *borak*, a bitter rice beer. After being entertained by dancers, a visitor must drink a large glassful, before bursting into song and doing a dance routine themselves. The best guideline for visitors on how to handle such occasions is provided by Redmond O'Hanlon in his book *Into the Heart of Borneo*. The general rule of thumb is to be prepared to make an absolute fool of yourself. This will immediately endear you to your hosts.

The following are the most common dances in Sarawak. **Kanjet Ngeleput** (Orang Ulu) dance is performed in full warrior regalia, traditionally celebrating the return of a hunter or headhunters. **Mengarang Menyak** (Melanau) dance depicts the processing of sago from the cutting of the tree to the production of the sago pearls or pellets. **Ngajat Bebunuh** (Iban) war dance is performed in full battledress, armed with sword and shield. **Ngajat Induk** (Iban) is performed as a welcome dance for those visiting longhouses. Ngajat Lesong (Iban) dance of the *lesong* or mortar is performed during gawai. **Tarian Kris**

(Malay) dance is of the *kris*, the Malay dagger, which symbolizes power, courage and strength. **Tarian Rajang Beuh** (Bidayuh) dance is performed after the harvesting season as entertainment for guests to the longhouse. **Tarian Saga Lupa** (Orang Ulu) is performed by women to welcome guests to the longhouse, accompanied by the *sape* (see Music below). **Ule Nugan** (Orang Ulu) dance is to the sound of the *kerebo bulo*, or bamboo slates. The music is designed to inspire the spirit of the paddy seeds to flourish. The male dancers hold a dibbling stick used in the planting of hill rice.

Music
Gongs range from the single large gong, the *tawak*, to the *engkerumong*, a set of small gongs, arranged on a horizontal rack, with five players. An *engkerumong* ensemble usually involves five to seven drums, which include two suspended gongs (*tawak* and *bendai*) and five hour-glass drums (*ketebong*). They are used to celebrate victory in battle or to welcome home a successful headhunting expedition. Sarawak's Bidayuh also make a bamboo gong called a *pirunchong*. The *jatang uton* is a wooden xylophone which can be rolled up like a rope ladder; the keys are struck with hardwood sticks.

The Bidayuh, Sarawak's bamboo specialists, make two main stringed instruments: a three-stringed cylindrical bamboo harp called a *tinton* and the *rabup*, a rotan-stringed fiddle with a bamboo cup. The Orang Ulu (Kenyah and Kayan tribes) play a four-stringed guitar called a *sape*, which is also common on the Kalimantan side of the border. It is the most common and popular lute-type instrument, whose body, neck and board are cut from one piece of softwood. It is used in Orang Ulu dances and by witch doctors. It is usually played by two musicians, one keeping the rhythm, the other the melody. Traditional *sapes* had rotan strings; today they use wire guitar strings and electric pick-ups. Another stringed instrument, more usually found in Kalimantan, or deep in Sarawak's interior, is the *satang*, a bamboo tube with strings around the outside, cut from the bamboo and tightened with pegs.

One of the best-known instruments is the *engkerurai* (or *keluri*), the bagpipes of Borneo, which is usually linked with the Kenyah and Kayan, but is also found in Sabah (where it is called a *sompoton*). It is a hand-held organ in which four bamboo panpipes of different lengths are fixed to a gourd, which acts as the wind chamber. Simple *engkerurai* can only play one chord; more sophisticated ones allow the player to use two pipes for the melody, while the others provide a harmonic drone. The Bidayuh are specialists in bamboo instruments and make flutes of various sizes; big thick ones are called *branchi*, long ones with five holes are *kroto* and small ones are called *nchiyo*.

Arts and crafts
Bamboo carving The Bidayuh (Land Dayaks) are best known for their bamboo carving. The bamboo is usually carved in shallow relief and then stained with dye, which leaves a pattern in the areas which have been scraped out. The Bidayuh carve utilitarian objects as well as ceremonial shields, musical instruments and spirit images used to guard the longhouse. The Cultural Village (Kampong Budaya) in Kuching is one of the best places to see demonstrations of Bidayuh carving.

Basketry A wide variety of household items are woven from rotan, bamboo, bemban reed as well as nipah and pandanus palms. Malaysia supplies 30% of the world's demand for *manau rotan* (rattan). Basketry is practised by nearly all the ethnic groups in Sarawak and they are among the most popular handicrafts in Sarawak. A variety of baskets are made for harvesting, storing and winnowing paddy as well as for collecting and storing other items. The Penan are reputed to produce the finest rattan sleeping mats – closely plaited and pliable – as well as the *ajat* and *ambong* baskets (all-purpose jungle rucksacks, also produced by the Kayan and Kenyah). Many of the native patterns used in basketry are derived from Chinese patterns and take the form of geometrical shapes and stylized birds. The Bidayuh also make baskets from either rotan or sago bark strips. The most common Bidayuh basket is the *tambok*, which is simply patterned and has bands of colour; it also has thin wooden supports on each side.

Beadwork Among many Kenyah, Kayan, Bidayuh, and Kelabit groups, beads have long been symbols of status and wealth; necklaces, skullcaps and girdles are handed down from generation to generation. Smaller glass or plastic beads, usually imported from Europe, are used to decorate baby carriers, baskets, headbands, jackets, hats, sheaths for knives, tobacco boxes and handbags. Beaded baby carriers are mainly used by the Kelabit, Kenyah and Kayan and often have shells and animals' teeth attached, which make a rattling sound to frighten away evil spirits. Rounded patterns require more skill than geometric ones; the quality of the pattern is used to reflect the status of the owner. Only upper classes are permitted to have beadwork depicting 'high-class' motifs such as human faces or figures. Early beads were made from clay, metal, glass, bone or shell (the earliest found in Niah Caves). Later on, many of the beads that found their way upriver were from Venice, Greece, India and China – even Roman and Alexandrian beads have made their way into Borneo's jungle. Orang Ulu traded them for jungle produce. Tribes attach different values to particular types of beads.

Blowpipes These are made by several Orang Ulu tribes in Sarawak and are usually carved from hardwood – normally *belian* (ironwood). The first step is to make a rough cylinder about 10 cm wide and 2.5 m long. This is tied to a platform, from which a hole is bored through the rod. The bore is skilfully chiselled by an iron rod with a pointed end. The rod is then sanded down to about 5 cm in diameter. Traditionally, the sanding was done using the rough underside of macaranga leaves. The darts are made from the nibong and wild sago palms and the poison itself is the sap of the upas (Ipoh) tree (*Antiaris toxicari*) into which the point is dipped.

Hats The Melanau people living around Bintulu make a big colourful conical hat from nipah leaves called a *terindak*. Orang Ulu hats are wide-brimmed and are often decorated with beadwork or cloth appliqué. Kelabit and Lun Bawan women wear skullcaps made entirely of beads, which are heavy and extremely valuable.

Pottery Malaysia's most distinctive ceramic designs are found in Sarawak where Iban potters reproduce shapes and patterns of Chinese porcelain which was originally brought to Borneo by traders centuries ago (see page 311). Copies of these old Chinese jars are mostly used for brewing *tuak* (rice wine).

Sickness images The coastal Melanau, who have now converted to Islam but used to be animists, have a tradition of carving sickness images (*blum*), usually from sago or other softwoods. The image is believed to take the form of the evil spirit causing a specific illness. They are carved in different forms according to the ailment. The Melanau developed elaborate healing ceremonies; if someone was struck down by a serious illness, the spirit medium would perform the berayun ceremony, using the *blum* to extract the illness from the victim's body. Usually, the image is in a half-seated position, with the hands crossed over the part of the body which is affected. During the ceremony, the medium tries to draw the spirit from the sick person into the image, after which it is set adrift on a river in a tiny purpose-made boat or hidden in the jungle. These images are roughly carved and can, from time to time, be found in antique shops.

Textiles The weaving of cotton *pua kumbu*, literally 'blanket' or 'cover', is one of the oldest Iban traditions. Iban legend recounts that 24 generations ago the God of War, Singalang Burong, taught his son how to weave the most precious of all *pua*, the *lebor api*. Dyed deep red, this cloth was traditionally used to wrap heads taken in battle.

The weaving of *pua kumbu* is done by the women and is a vital skill for a would-be bride to acquire. There are two main methods employed in making and decorating *pua kumbu*: the more common is the ikat tie-dyeing technique, known as *ngebat* by the Iban. The other method is the *pileh*, or floating weft. The Iban use a warp-beam loom which is tied to two posts, to which the threads are attached. There is a breast-beam at the weaving end, secured by a back strap to the weaver. A pedal, beneath the threads, lowers and raises the alternate threads which are separated by rods. The woven material is tightly packed by a beater. The material is tie-dyed in the warp.

Because the *pua kumbu* is made by the warp-tie-dyeing method, the number of colours is limited. The most common are a rich browny-brick-red colour and black, as well as the undyed white sections; blues and greens are used in more modern materials. Traditionally, *pua kumbu* were hung in longhouses during ceremonies and were used to cover images during rituals. Designs and patterns are representations of deities which figure in Iban myths and are believed to protect individuals from harm; they are passed down from generation to generation. Such designs, with deep spiritual significance, can only be woven by wives and daughters of chiefs. Other designs and patterns are representations of birds and animals, including hornbills, crocodiles, monitor lizards and shrimps, which are either associated with worship or are sources of food. Symbolic representations of trees, plants and fruits are also included. A typical example is the zigzag pattern which represents the act of crossing a river – the zigzag course is explained by the canoe's attempts to avoid strong currents. Many of the symbolic representations are highly stylized and can be difficult to pick out.

Malay women in Sarawak are traditionally renowned for their *kain songket*, sarongs woven with silver and gold thread.

Woodcarvings Many tribal groups are skilled carvers, producing everything from huge burial poles (like the Kejaman pole outside the Sarawak Museum in Kuching) to small statues and masks. Kenyah's traditional masks, used during festivals, are elaborately carved and often have large protruding eyes. Eyes are always emphasized, as they frighten the enemy. Other typical items include spoons, stools, doors, walking sticks, *sapes* (guitars), shields, tattoo plaques and the hilts of *parang ilang* (ceremonial knives). The most popular Iban motif is the hornbill, which holds an honoured place in Iban folklore (see page 537), as the messenger for the sacred Brahminy kite, the ancestor of the Iban. Another famous carving is the sacred measuring stick, the *tuntun peti*, used to trap deer; it is carved to represent a forest spirit. The Kayan and Kenyah's most common motif is the *aso*, a dragon-like dog with a long snout. The Kenyah and Kayan carve huge burial structures (*salong*), as well as small ear pendants made of hornbill ivory. The elaborately carved masks used for their harvest ceremony are unique.

Contents

398 Kota Kinabalu
398 Ins and outs
401 Background
401 Sights
404 Around Kota Kinabalu
407 Listings

418 Off the coast and south of Kota Kinabalu
418 Tunku Abdul Rahman National Park
419 Pulau Tiga National Park
420 Pulau Labuan
423 South of Kota Kinabalu
427 Listings

435 North of Kota Kinabalu
435 Kota Belud
436 Kudat
437 Mantanani Island
438 Listings

439 Gunung Kinabalu National Park
447 Listings

450 East coast
450 Sandakan
454 Turtle Islands National Park
457 Sepilok Orang-Utan Sanctuary and Rehabilitation Centre
458 Gomantong Caves
459 Sungai Kinabatangan
460 Lahad Datu and around
461 Danum Valley Conservation Area
463 Semporna
464 Sipadan Island Marine Reserve
466 Tawau
467 Maliau Basin Conservation Area
470 Listings

483 Background
483 History
486 Modern Sabah
488 Culture

Sabah

Footprint features

396 Don't miss ...
402 Mat Selleh: fort builder and folk hero
424 Rafflesia: the world's largest flower
432 Sabah's markets and trade fairs
436 Tamus (markets) in Kota Belud District
454 Agnes Keith's house
456 The tough life of a turtle
462 The Sumatran rhinoceros
463 The gentler beast of Borneo
468 It's a bear's life
485 The Borneo Death March
489 The Kadazan in Borneo
490 The Murut in Borneo
491 Tapai: Sabah's rice wine

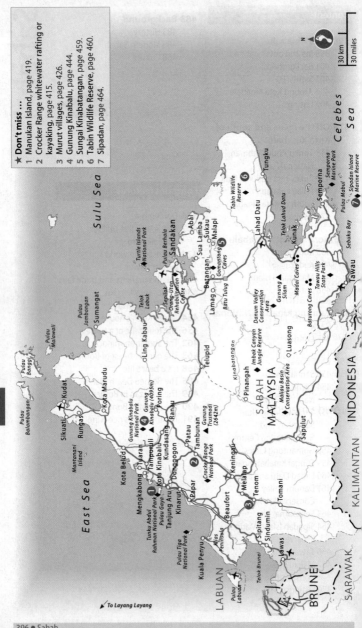

★ **Don't miss ...**
1 Manukan Island, page 419.
2 Crocker Range whitewater rafting or kayaking, page 415.
3 Murut villages, page 426.
4 Gunung Kinabalu, page 444.
5 Sungai Kinabatangan, page 459.
6 Tabin Wildlife Reserve, page 460.
7 Sipadan, page 464.

Celebes Sea

Sulu Sea

East Sea

Tungku

Tabin Wildlife Reserve

Semporna
Semporna Marine Park
Sipadan Island Marine Reserve
Pulau Mabul

Sebuku Bay

Tawau

Lahad Datu

Telok Lahad Datu
Kunak

Gunung Silam
Madai Caves
Tawau Hills State Park
Baturong Caves

Turtle Islands National Park

Pulau Berhala
Sandakan
Sepilok
Orang-Utan Rehabilitation Centre
Sukau
Malapi
Abai
Sua Lamba
Batangan
Gomantong Caves

Danum Valley Conservation Area

Luasong

Imbok Canyon Jungle Reserve
Pinangah

SABAH
MALAYSIA

Meliau Basin Conservation Area

Sapulut

Telok Labuk

Lamag
Batu Tulug

Kinabatangan

Telupid

Ling Kabau

Gunung Kinabalu (4095m)
Gunung Kinabalu National Park
Poring
Kundasang
Ranau

Gunung Trusmadi (2642m)

Tambunan

Patau

Keningau

Melalap
Tenom

Tomani

Crocker Range National Park

Papar
Kinarut
Donggogon

Tanjung Aru
Kota Kinabalu
Tamparuli
Tuaran
Mengkabong

Tunku Abdul Rahman National Park
Pulau Gaya
Pulau Tiga National Park

Kuala Penyu

LABUAN
Pulau Labuan

To Layang Layang

Kota Belud

Kota Marudu

Sikuati
Kudat
Rungus

Pulau Banggi
Pulau Malawali
Pulau Jambongan
Sumangat

Mantanani Island

Pulau Balambangan

Klias Peninsula
Beaufort
Sipitang
Sindumin
Lawas

Telok Brunei

BRUNEI
SARAWAK
KALIMANTAN
INDONESIA

N

30 km
30 miles

Introduction

Sabah may not have the colourful history of neighbouring Sarawak, but there is still a great deal to entice the visitor. It is the second largest Malaysian state after Sarawak, covering 72,500 sq km, making it about the size of Ireland. Occupying the northeast corner of Borneo, it is shaped like a dog's head, the jaws reaching out in the Sulu and Celebes seas, and the back of the head facing onto the South China Sea.

The highlights of Sabah are natural and cultural, from caves, reefs, forests and mountains to tribal peoples. The Gunung Kinabulu National Park is named after Sabah's (and Malaysia's) highest peak and is one of the state's most visited destinations. Also popular is the Sepilok Orang-Utan Rehabilitation Sanctuary outside Sandakan. Marine sights include the Turtle Islands National Park and Sipadan Island, one of Asia's finest dive sites.

While Sabah's indigenous tribes were not cherished as they were in Sarawak by the White Rajahs, areas around towns such as Kudat, Tenom, Keningau and Kota Belud still provide memorable insights into the peoples of the region.

Kota Kinabalu

→ *Colour map 4, A3. Population: 354,000.*

KK is most people's introduction to Sabah for the simple reason that it is the only town with extensive air links to other parts of the country as well as a handful of regional destinations. KK is a modern state capital with little that can be dated back more than 50 years. Highlights include the State Museum and the town's markets. Out of town, within a day's excursion, are beaches such as Tanjung Aru and those near Tuaran, as well as a number of Kadazan and Bajau districts, with their distinctive markets. While it is necessary to go further afield to get a real view of tribal life, this is better than nothing.

The city is strung out along the coast, with jungle-clad hills as a backdrop. Two-thirds of the town is built on land reclaimed from the shallow Gaya Bay and at spring tides it is possible to walk across to Gaya Island. Jalan Pantai, or Beach Road, is now in the centre of town. Successive land reclamation projects have meant that many of the original stilt villages, such as Kampong Ayer, have been cut off from the sea and some now stand in stinking, stagnant lagoons. The government is cleaning up and quickly reclaiming these areas and the inhabitants of the water villages are being rehoused. ›› *For listings, see pages 407-417.*

Ins and outs

Getting there

KK's **airport** ① *T088-238555*, the second busiest in Malaysia, is 6 km south of town. For buses into town, there is a bus stop five minutes' walk from the airport (RM1.50 to the city centre). Taxis from the airport cost RM20 to the city centre; buy coupons in advance from the booths outside the arrivals hall. ›› *See also Transport, page 416.*

Getting around

City buses and minibuses provide a service around town and to nearby destinations. Red taxis are unmetered, dark blue taxis metered. There are plenty of car hire firms.

Best time to visit

Sabah's equatorial climate means that temperatures rarely exceed 32°C or fall below 21°C, making it fairly pleasant all year. However, October to March is the rainy season, which spoils plans for the beach and makes climbing Mount Kinabalu or trekking in Sabah's national parks an unpleasant and slippery experience. For spotting turtles on the east coast islands, your best chance is between May and September. **Sabah Fest**, a big carnival of dancing, music and cow races, takes place in May, when the Kadazun/ Dusun celebrate their harvest festival. ›› *See also Festivals and events, page 31.*

Tourist information

Sabah Tourism Board ① *51 Jln Gaya, T088-212121, www.sabahtourism.com, Mon-Fri 0800-1700, Sat-Sun 0900-1600*, is a great first point for help when arriving in KK. It is well stocked with leaflets and information and has courteous and helpful staff. **Tourism Malaysia**① *ground floor, Uni Asia Building, 1 Jln Sagunting, T088-211732, mtpbki@tourism. gov.my*, is not as useful for Sabah, but still does its best. A great tourist website for Sabah is www.sabahtravelguide.com.

Tours that are widely available include: Kota Belud *tamu* (Sunday market), Gunung Kinabalu Park (including Poring Hot Springs), Sandakan's Sepilok Orang-Utan

Rehabilitation Centre, train trips to Tenom through the Padas Gorge and tours of the islands in the Tunku Abdul Rahman National Park. Several companies specialize in scuba diving tours. ▶ *See also Tour operators, page 414.*

Parks offices All accommodation and trekking at **Mount Kinabalu** and **Poring Hot Springs** is organized through **Sutera Sanctuary Lodges** ① *ground floor, Wisma Sabah, KK, T088-243629, www.suterasanctuarylodges.com, Mon-Fri 0900-1830, Sat 0900-1630, Sun 0900-1500.*

For **Danum Valley** and **Maliau Basin**, contact **Borneo Nature Tours** (connected to the Sabah Foundation, see below) ① *Block D, Lot 10, ground floor, Sadong Jaya Complex, T088-267637, www.borneonaturetours.com,* which deal with the majority of tourism-related activity in Danum Valley and Maliau Basin and are perhaps the easiest first point of contact. You can also contact **Sabah Parks** ① *Lot 3, Block K, Sinsuran Complex, T088-211881, www.sabahparks.org.my.* The official body that regulates the parks is the **Sabah Foundation (Yayasan Sabah Group)** ① *12th floor, Menara Tun Mustapha, KK, T088-326300, www.borneoforest heritage.org.my;* see Likas Bay, page 403, for details.

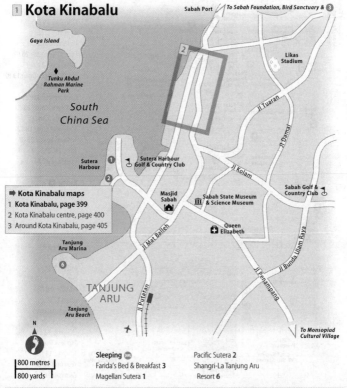

① Kota Kinabalu

Sleeping 😴
Farida's Bed & Breakfast **3**
Magellan Sutera **1**
Pacific Sutera **2**
Shangri-La Tanjung Aru
Resort **6**

➡ Kota Kinabalu maps
1 Kota Kinabalu, page 399
2 Kota Kinabalu centre, page 400
3 Around Kota Kinabalu, page 405

To 17 24, Inanam, Likas Bay & One Borneo Hypermall

➡ Kota Kinabalu maps
1 Kota Kinabalu, page 399
2 Kota Kinabalu centre, page 400
3 Around Kota Kinabalu, page 405

100 metres
100 yards

To Labuan & Tunku Abdul Rahman National Park

South China Sea

To Labuan

To Islands of Tunku Abdul Rahman National Park

British Consul

Jln Balai Polis

Jln Bukit Bendera

Nasalis Larvatus Tours & Riverbug Tours

Tourism Malaysia

Sabah Tourism Board

Gaya Centre

Wisma Sabah

Jln Pantai

Australia Pl

Jln Limabelas

Borneo Books

Jln Haji Saman

Lorong Bakau

Kinabalu Emporium

Jln Datuk Salleh Sulong

Milimewah Supermarket

Jln Gaya

Sunday

Atkinson's Clock Tower

Signal Hill (Bukit Bendera)

Segama Shopping & Complex

Jln Tujuhbelas

Central Market

Penampang, Tanjung Aru City Buses

City Hall

Taxis (Long Distance)

Padang

Jln Lapanbelas

State Library

Long-distance Bus Station

Minibuses

Filipino Market

Jln Sembilanbelas

City Park

Jln Tun Razak

Jln Merdeka

Jln Tun Fuad Stephens

Sinsuran Complex

Kampong Ayer

Jln Padang

Jln Tunku Abdul Rahman

Bandaran Berjaya Complex

Immigration

Taxis

Waterfront Esplanade

Jln Tun Chong Thian Vun

Night Market

Sedco Square

Jln Sapuloh

Warisan Square

Jln Duapuloh

Centrepoint Mall

Jln Tugu

Api-Api Centre

Kompleks Asia City

To 2

Plaza Wawasan

KK Region Bus Station

Sacred Heart Cathedral

To Airport & Sutera Harbour

To Masjid Sabah

Kompleks Karamunsing

Sleeping
Akinabalu 1 C2
Berjaya Palace 2 E2
Borneo Backpackers 25 B2
Borneo Gaya Lodge 8 B2
Borneo Xplorer
  Backpackers 15 C2
Capital 3 B1
Century 4 D2
City Inn 5 B1
Courtyard 17 A2
High Street Inn 7 B1
Hyatt Regency 9 B1
Jesselton 10 B2
Kinabalu Daya 11 B1
King Park 19 D2
KK 6 B1
Le Meridien 20 D1
Lucy's Homestay 26 B2
Mandarin 12 C2
North Borneo Cabin 13 B2
Promenade 14 E1
Rainforest Lodge 21 C1
Red Palm Hostel 23 C2
Shangri-La 16 D2
Summer Lodge 18 C2
Trekkers Lodge 28 B1
Tune 24 A2
Wah May 22 B1

Eating
Aesha Corner 3 D1
Aussie Bar &
  Barbecue 1 D1
Four Seasons 4 E2
La Manila Café 5 D1
Merdeka 6 B1
Nan Xing 7 B1
Nishiki 2 B2
Peppermint 10 B2
Port View 8 D1
Riza 11 D2
Sri Sempelang 9 D1
Tambayan At
  Kaining 12 E1
Tap Nok Thai 13 E1
Toscanis 14 D1
Yee Fung 15 C2
Zaminah 16 E1

Background

Kota Kinabalu started life as a trading post, established in 1881 by the **British North Borneo Chartered Company** under the directorship of William C Cowie (see page 451); not on the mainland, but on Gaya Island, opposite the present town, where a Filipino shanty town is today. On 9 July 1897 rebel leader Mat Salleh (see page 402), who engaged in a series of hit-and-run raids against the British North Borneo Chartered Company's administration, landed on Pulau Gaya. His men looted and sacked the settlement and Gaya township was abandoned.

Two years later the Europeans established another township but this time located on the mainland, opposite Pulau Gaya, adjacent to a Bajau stilt village. The kampong was called 'Api Api' ('Fire! Fire!') because it had been repeatedly torched by pirates over the years. After the Gaya experience, it was an inauspicious name. The Chartered Company rechristened it Jesselton, after Sir Charles Jessel, one of the company directors. However, for years, only the Europeans called it Jesselton; locals preferred the old name, and even today Sabahans sometimes refer to their state capital as Api.

Jesselton owed its raison d'être to a plan that backfired. William C Cowie, a former gun-runner for the Sultan of Sulu, became managing director of the Chartered Company in 1894. He wanted to build a trans-Borneo railway and the narrow strip of land just north of Tanjung Aru and opposite Pulau Gaya, with its sheltered anchorage, was chosen as a terminus.

Photographs in the Sabah State Museum chart the town's development from 1899, when work on the North Borneo Railway terminus began in earnest. By 1905, Jesselton was linked to Beaufort by a 92-km narrow gauge track. By 1911 it had a population of 2686, half of whom were Chinese and the remainder Kadazans and Dusuns; there were 33 European residents. Jesselton was of little importance in comparison to Sandakan, the capital of north Borneo.

When the Japanese Imperial Army invaded Borneo in 1942, Jesselton's harbour gave the town strategic significance and it was consequently completely flattened by the Allies during the Second World War. Jesselton followed Kudat and Sandakan as the administrative centre of north Borneo at the end of the Second World War, and the city was rebuilt from scratch. In September 1967 Jesselton was renamed Kota Kinabalu after the mountain; its name is usually shortened to KK.

Sights

Only three buildings remain of the old town: the old **General Post Office** on Jalan Gaya, **Atkinson's Clocktower** (built in 1905 and named after Jesselton's first district officer) and the old red-roofed **Lands and Surveys building**. The renovated post office now houses the **Sabah Tourism Board**.

Masjid Sabah and Sabah State Museum

ⓘ *To get to Masjid Sabah and the Sabah State Museum complex there are minibuses that stop near Wisma Kewangan on the Kota Kinabalu to Tanjung Aru road, and near Queen Elizabeth Hospital on the Kota Kinabalu to Penampang road.*

The golden dome of **Masjid Sabah** ⓘ *Jln Tunku Abdul Rahman*, is visible from most areas, although it is actually about 3 km out of town. Regular minibuses connect it with the town centre. Completed in 1975, it is the second biggest mosque in Malaysia and, like the Federal Mosque in Kuala Lumpur, a fine example of contemporary Islamic architecture. It can accommodate 5000 worshippers.

Mat Salleh: fort builder and folk hero

Mat Salleh was a Bajau, and son of a Sulu chief, born in the court of the Sultan of Sulu. He was the only native leader to stand up against the increasingly autocratic whims of the North Borneo government as it sequestrated land traditionally belonging to tribal chiefs. Under the British North Borneo Chartered Company and the subsequent colonial administration, generations of schoolchildren were taught that Mat Salleh was a rabble-rouser and troublemaker. Now Sabahans regard him as a nationalist hero.

In the *British North Borneo Herald* of 16 February 1899, it was reported that when he spoke, flames leapt from his mouth; lightning flashed with each stroke of his *parang* (cutlass) and when he scattered rice, the grains became wasps. He was said to have been endowed with 'special knowledge' by the spirits of his ancestors and was also reported to have been able to throw a buffalo by its horns.

In 1897 Mat Salleh raided and set fire to the first British settlement on Pulau Gaya (off modern day Kota Kinabalu). For this, and other acts of sabotage, he was declared an outlaw by the governor. A price tag of 700 Straits dollars was put on his head and an administrative officer, Raffles Flint, was assigned the unenviable task of tracking him down. Flint failed to catch him and Mat Salleh gained a reputation as a military genius.

Finally, the managing director of the Chartered Company, Scottish adventurer and former gunrunner, William C Cowie, struck a deal with Mat Salleh and promised that his people would be allowed to settle peacefully in Tambunan, which at that time was not under Chartered Company control.

Half the North Borneo administration resigned as they considered Cowie's concessions outrageous. With it looking increasingly unlikely that the terms of his agreement with Cowie would be respected, Mat Salleh retreated to Tambunan where he started building his fort; he had already gained a fearsome reputation for these stockades. West coast resident G Hewett described it as "the most extraordinary place and without [our] guns it would have been absolutely impregnable". Rifle fire could not penetrate it and Hewett blasted 200 shells into the fort with no noticeable effect. The stone walls were 2.5 m thick and were surrounded by three bamboo fences, the ground in front of which was studded with row upon row of sharpened bamboo spikes. Hewett's party retreated, having suffered four dead and nine wounded.

Mat Salleh had built similar forts all over Sabah and the hearts of the protectorate's administrators must have sunk when they heard he was building one at Tambunan. A government expedition arrived in the Tambunan Valley on the last day of 1899. There was intensive fighting throughout January, with the government taking village after village, until at last the North Borneo Constabulary came within 50 m of Mat Salleh's fort. Its water supply had been cut off and the fort had been shelled incessantly for 10 days. Mat Salleh was trapped. On 31 January 1900 he was killed by a stray bullet which hit him in the left temple.

Perched on a small hill overlooking the mosque is the relatively new purpose-built **Sabah State Museum** (and State Archives) ① *Jln Mat Salleh/Bukit Istana Lama (Old Palace Hill), www.mzm.sabah.gov.my, daily 0900-1700, RM15, also guided tours*, which is designed like a Rungus longhouse. It is divided into ethnography, natural history, ceramics, history and archaeology. The ethnographic section includes an excellent display on the uses of bamboo. There is also tribal brassware, silverware, musical instruments, basketry and pottery, as well as a collection of costumes and artefacts from Sabah tribes such as the Kadazan/Dusun, Bajau, Murut and Rungus.

One of the most interesting items in this collection is a *sininggazanak*, a sort of totem pole. If a Kadazan man died without an heir, it was the custom to erect a *sininggazanak* – a wooden statue supposedly resembling the deceased – on his land. There is also a collection of human skulls (*bangkaran*), which before the tribe's wholesale conversion to Christianity, would have been suspended from the rafters of Kadazan longhouses. Every five years a *magang* feast was held to appease the spirits of the skulls.

The museum's archaeological section contains a magnificently carved coffin found in a limestone cave in the Madai area. Upstairs, the natural history section provides a good introduction to Sabah's flora and fauna. Next door is a collection of jars, called *pusaka*, which are tribal heirlooms. They were originally exchanged by the Chinese for jungle produce, such as beeswax, camphor and birds' nests.

Next door to the State Museum is the **Science Museum**, containing an exhibition on Shell's offshore activities. The **Art Gallery and Multivision Theatre**, within the same complex, is also worth a browse. The art gallery is small and mainly exhibits works by local artists; among the more interesting items on display are those of Suzie Mojikol, a Kadazan artist, Bakri Dani, who adapts Bajau designs, and Philip Biji, who specializes in burning Murut designs onto chunks of wood with a soldering iron. The ethnobotanical gardens are on the hillside below the museum. There is a cafeteria in the main building.

Sabah has a large Christian population and the **Sacred Heart Cathedral** has a striking pyramidal roof that is clearly visible from the Sabah State Museum complex.

Viewpoints

Further into town nearer the coast are a series of water villages, including **Kampong Ayer**, although it has shrunk dramatically in recent years. **Signal Hill** (Bukit Bendera), just southeast of the central area, gives a panoramic view of the town and islands. In the past, the hill was used as a vantage point for signalling to ships approaching the harbour.

Likas Bay

There is an even better view of the coastline from the top of the **Sabah Foundation (Yayasan Sabah) Complex** ① *4 km northeast of town, overlooking Likas Bay*. This surreal glass sculpture houses the chief minister's office. The Sabah Foundation was set up in 1966 to help improve Sabahans' quality of life. The foundation has a 972,800 ha timber concession, which it claims to manage on a sustainable-yield basis (achievement of a high-level annual output without impairing the long-term productivity of the land). More than two-thirds of this concession has already been logged. Profits from the timber go towards loans and scholarships for Sabahan students, funding the construction of hospitals and schools and supplying milk, textbooks and uniforms to school children. The Foundation also operates a 24-hour flying ambulance service to remote parts of the interior. In recent years the Foundation has begun to invest more directly in conservation, seeing potential financial returns from ecotourism and rainforest-derived medicines amongst others. The major pristine areas that haven't been logged within the concession are Danum Valley, the Maliau Basin Conservation area and the Imbak Canyon.

Between the Yayasan Sabah and the city centre is one of Borneo's largest squatter communities, visibly demonstrating that not all share equally in the timber boom.

Over in Likas Bay is **Kota Kinabalu City Bird Sanctuary** ⓘ *Tue-Sun 0800-1800, RM10, children RM5*, a 24 ha spread of mangrove forest with a 1.5 km boardwalk that snakes inside. Possible sightings include egrets, kingfishers, green pigeons, purple herons, plover and redshanks. A pair of binoculars is recommended.

Markets

Gaya street market ⓘ *Sun 0600-1300*, sells a vast range of goods from jungle produce and handicrafts to pots and pans. The market almost opposite the main minibus station on Jalan Tun Fuad Stephens is known as the **Filipino market** (Pasar Kraftangan) as most of the stalls are run by Filipino immigrants. Filipino and local handicrafts are sold in the hundreds of cramped stalls along winding alleyways that are strung with low-slung curtains of shells, baskets and bags. The Filipino market is a good place to buy cultured pearls (RM5 each) and has everything from fake gems to camagong-wood salad bowls, fibre shirts and traditional Indonesian medicines. Further into town, on the waterfront, is the **central market** selling mainly fish, fruit and vegetables. The daily fishing catch is unloaded on the wharf near the market. There is a lively **evening market** selling cheap T-shirts and jewellery in front of the City Park.

Tanjung Aru Beach

This is the best beach near KK, after those in Tunku Abdul Rahman National Park, and is close to **Shangri-La Tanjung Aru Resort**, 5 km south of KK (see page 410). It is particularly popular at weekends and there is a good open-air food court that looks onto the beach. To get there take the Tanjung Aru (beach) bus from the station in front of City Hall.

Around Kota Kinabalu → *For listings, see pages 407-417.*

Penampang

The old town of Donggongon, 13 km southeast of KK, was demolished in the early 1980s and the new township built in 1982. The population is mainly Kadazan or Sino-Kadazan and about 90% Christian. The oldest church in Sabah, **St Michael's** Roman Catholic church, is on a steep hill on the far side of the new town. Turn left just before the bridge – and after the turn-off to the new town – through the kampong and turn left again after the school. It's a 20-minute walk. A granite building with a red roof, it was originally built in 1897 but is not dramatic to look at and has been renovated over the years. Services are in Kadazan but are fascinating, and visitors are warmly welcomed; hymns are sung in Kadazan and Malay. The social focus of the week is the Sunday **market**. To get to Penampang, take a green and white **Union Transport** bus from just in front of City Hall.

There are many **megaliths** in the Penampang area that are thought to be associated with property claims, particularly when a landowner died without a direct heir. Some solitary stones standing in the middle of paddy fields are more than 2 m tall. The age of the megaliths has not been determined. Wooden figures called *siningazanak* can also be seen in rice fields (see page 403). **Yun Chuan**, Penampang New Town (also known as Donggongon Township), specializes in Kadazan dishes such as *hinava* (raw fish), the Kadazan equivalent of sushi. *Tapai* chicken is also recommended.

Monsopiad Cultural Village

ⓘ *www.monsopiad.com, daily 0900-1700, cultural shows at 1100, 1400 and 1600, RM65.*
This is in Kampong Monsopiad – named after a fearsome Kadazan warrior-cum-

headhunter, Siou do Mohoing, the so-called Hercules of Sabah – just outside Penampang. There are 42 fragile human skulls, some of which are said to be 300 years old and possess spiritual powers. They are laced together with leaves of the hisad palm, representing the victims' hair. For those who have already visited longhouses in Sarawak, this collection of skulls, in the rafters of an ordinary little kampong house overlooking the village and the Penampang River, is a bit of an anticlimax. But Dousia Moujing and his son Wennedy are very hospitable and know much about local history and culture. They preside over their ancestor's dreaded sword (although Wennedy reckons it's not the original, even though there are strands of human hair hanging off it). A three-day, three-night feast is held in May, in the run-up to the harvest festival. Visitors should remove footwear and not touch the skulls or disturb the rituals or ceremonies in progress. A reconstruction of the original Monsopiad main house gives an insight into the life and times of the warrior and his

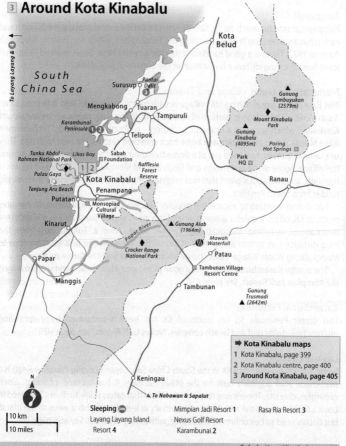

3 Around Kota Kinabalu

Kota Kinabalu maps
1 Kota Kinabalu, page 399
2 Kota Kinabalu centre, page 400
3 Around Kota Kinabalu, page 405

Sleeping
Layang Layang Island Resort 4
Mimpian Jadi Resort 1
Nexus Golf Resort Karambunai 2
Rasa Ria Resort 3

descendants. There is a good restaurant serving traditional dishes; the *kadazandusun hinara* is recommended. It consists of fresh sliced raw fish marinated in lime juice, mixed with chilli, garlic and shallots.

For more information, contact **Borneo Legends and Myths** ⓘ *5 km Ramaya-Putaton Rd, Penampang, T088-761336, www.monosopiad.com,* who manage the village. The house is hard to find; from the new town take the main road east past the Shell station and turn right at sign to Jabatan Air; past St Aloysus Church, the house is on the left about 1.5 km from the turn-off. Minibuses run from Donggongon Township, 10 km south of KK, to Kampong Monsopiad. Take a bus to Donggongon Town and then change to a bus for Monsopiad Cultural Village. A taxi from KK costs RM40. For RM80 you can catch a shuttle bus from the Sutera Magellan and back and get entrance to the village. Buses leave for the village from Sutera Magellan on Monday, Wednesday, Friday and Sunday at 0930 and 1400, and on Tuesday, Thursday and Saturday at 0900 and 1400.

Tamparuli
This popular stop for tour buses is 32 km north of KK at the junction of the roads north and east. It has a suspension bridge straddling the Tuaran River, which was built by the British Army in 1922. There is a good handicraft shopping centre here. Buses marked Tamparuli leave from the long-distance bus station at the bottom of Signal Hill.

Mengkabong Water Village and Tuaran
This Bajau (sea gypsy) fishing stilt village is within easy reach of KK and is likened to an Asian Venice. The village is particularly photogenic in the early morning, before Mount Kinabalu – which serves as a dramatic backdrop – is obscured by cloud. The fishermen leave Mengkabong at high tide and arrive back with their catch at the next high tide. They use sampan canoes, hollowed out of a single tree trunk, which are crafted in huts around the village. Some of the waterways and fields around Mengkabong are choked by water hyacinth, an ornamental plant that was originally introduced by Chinese farmers as pig fodder from South America.

For visitors wanting to escape the popular beaches close to KK, **Tuaran**, 45 minutes north of KK, offers a quieter alternative and is a good access point for several different destinations including Mengkabong. To get there, take a Tuaran bus from the long-distance bus station at the foot of Signal Hill, then change to a local minibus to Mengkabong Water Village. Taxis charge about RM45, or you can take a tour.

The nearby **Karambunai Beach** has a good picnic area, clean beach and sea. Close by is the **Mimpian Jadi Resort**, see page 410.

Karambunai Peninsula
This scenic Peninsula 30 km north of KK has been transformed by a sprawling multimillion-dollar golf and beach complex, **Nexus Golf Resort**, see page 409.

Layang Layang
Some 300 km northwest of KK in the South China Sea, Layang Layang (Swallow Reef) is a man-made atoll originally built for the Malaysian navy. It has become a famous, albeit expensive, dive site. There is one resort on the island that caters solely to divers. You need to book a flight through the resort; there are usually at least four flights a week to the island, but details need to be confirmed in advance, with plenty of notice. See also page 36.

For Sleeping and Eating price codes and other relevant information, see Essentials pages 25-30.

● **Sleeping**

Kota Kinabulu *p398, maps p399, p400 and p405*
Well-heeled tourists will seek the more refined out-of-town resorts; but in KK itself, mid-range hotels have improved immeasurably in recent years. The increased number of budget airlines flying into KK has prompted the opening of a number of budget guesthouses, and those on a fairly modest budget are well catered for in KK.

AL Hyatt Regency, Jln Datuk Salleh Sulong, T088-221234, www.kinabalu.regency. hyatt.com. With a/c, 288 rooms and 3 restaurants. Three's also a pool and kids' pool. It's in a central location. Rooms vary in standard. There's live entertainment (**Shenanigan's Fun Pub**) and Club Olympus, a popular spa and massage centre with views over the bay from the treadmills. Tours and treks organized. Good value.

AL Le Meridien, Jln Tun Fuad Stephens, Sinsuran, T088-322222, www.lemeridien.com/ kota kinabalu. Popular hotel with the well-heeled with 306 smart, modern rooms, some with superb views over the bay. There's a pool, gym and excellent restaurant and club. For the best prices, book online well in advance.

AL Promenade, 4 Lorong Api-Api 3, Api-Api Centre, T088-265555, www.promenade.com.my. 4-star hotel along the seafront, popular with domestic business travellers. Sea view rooms are only a fraction more expensive than the city view rooms and worth every ringgit for the sunset. There are 4 dining outlets, a large pool and gym. Wi-Fi available in room for a steep RM30 per 24 hrs.

AL Sutera Harbour Resort,1 Sutera Harbour Blvd, T088-318888, www.suteraharbour.com. South of the city centre, this resort was created from reclaimed land covering 156 ha that was previously the South China Sea. The **Harbour** is

2 hotels (1000 rooms in total): the **Magellan Sutera**, and the **Pacific Sutera**. The **Magellan Sutera** is the more relaxed, with many sports activities, including 27 holes of golf and a spa. The **Pacific Sutera** is more a business hotel, with superb conference facilities.

A Berjaya Palace, 1 Jln Tangki, Karamunsing, T088-211911, www.berjayaresorts.com.my. This distinctive, castellated hotel stands on a hill south of KK. 160 rooms, pool, sauna and gym, conference rooms. The proprietor James Sheng has a small resort with chalets on Pulau Gaya, at Maluham Bay, east of Police Bay, enquire at hotel.

A Capital, 23 Jln Haji Saman, T088-231999, capitalh@streamyx.com. 102 a/c rooms that are looking a little dated, TV, coffee shop, central position. Overpriced, given the competition in town.

A Jesselton, 69 Jln Gaya, T088-223333, www.jesseltonhotel.com. The first to open in KK, this classic hotel dates from 1954. With just 32 rooms, it was upgraded in the mid-1990s and is now considered KK's premier boutique-style hotel. It's an old establishment, with everything from a shiny red London cab to shoe shining at your service. There's an Italian restaurant on the ground floor and all rooms have Wi-Fi.

A Shangri-La, 75 Bandaran Berjaya, T088-212800, kkshang@po.jaring.my. Not part of the international **Shangri-La** group, and popular with business visitors. The rooms are a/c and comfortable but vastly overpriced.

A-B Courtyard, Unit G–800, One Borneo Hypermall, Jln Sulaiman, T088-528228, www.courtyardhotel1borneo.com. Super-slick rooms with gargantuan LCD TV, the same model of bed that was used by athletes in the Sydney Olympics and free access to their Elusion lounge. Wi-Fi in bar and lobby. The room rates are excellent value, but the compulsory breakfast at RM50 a room hikes prices up unnecessarily.

B Century, Jln Masjid Lama, T088-242222, www.firstcenturyhotel.com. Chinese hotel at the edge of town, backing on to a hill with a lobby area overlooking a verdant patch of greenery. Rooms are functional, clean and have TV and Wi-Fi. Fair value for this price range.

B Kinabalu Daya, 9 Jln Pantai, T088-240000, www.bestwestern.com. Owned by the Best Western chain, the 68 rooms are comfortable and modern with cable TV and a/c. Rooms on the top floor have good views over the city. Hunter's Bar downstairs is a popular watering hole with live music at weekends. Breakfast and daily paper included.

B King Park, Jln Masjid Lama, T088-270500, www.kingparkhotel.com.my. Newish place in a bright yellow tower block overlooking town. Rooms are a bit on the small side, but are clean, modern and elegant. Good value.

B Mandarin, 138 Jln Gaya, T088-225222, F225481. Functional place with gleaming marble floors, clean rooms with TV (local channels only), minifridge and attached bathroom with hot water. The de luxe and super-de luxe rooms are particularly spacious. The 6th-floor rooms have good views over town. Fair value.

B-C Wah May, 36 Jln Haji Saman, T088-266118, wahmayhtl.com.my. Modern, typical Chinese hotel with 24 functional and clean rooms with a/c, cable TV, Wi-Fi, minifridge and attached bathroom with hot water. Tight security with CCTV in operation.

B-D Rainforest Lodge, 48 Jln Pantai, T088-258228, www.rainforestlodgekk.com. Excellent new addition to the lodgings scene. Smart en suite rooms have spacious balconies overlooking the town and eatery below, cable TV, a/c and Wi-Fi. The comfortable a/c dorm room is fair value at RM30. Breakfast is included. Good promotional rates. Recommended.

C City Inn, 41 Jln Pantai, T088-218933, F218937. A/c, bathroom and TV. Good value, often full.

C High Street Inn, 38 Jln Pantai, T088-218111, F219111. Rooms with a/c, TV and hot water are soulless but functional and comfortable. Very typical of hotels in this price range.

C Red Palm Hostel, Jln Gaya, T088-211130, www.redpalmkk.com. With rooms built around a friendly common area, this new place is a cosy spot to relax. Rooms have a/c and Wi-Fi with shared bathroom facilities. TV and free internet available in the lounge. They can help with tours around the region.

C Tune, Unit G 803, One Borneo Hypermall, Jln Sulaiman, T03-7962 5888, www.tune hotels.com. New place at One Borneo 7 km from the city and run using the same model – book early, pay less – as budget airlines. This chain is the latest venture of Air Asia supreme Tony Fernandez. Rooms are comfortable and have attached bath but are plastered with advertisements. Pay extra for TV, a/c and Wi-Fi.

C-D North Borneo Cabin, 1st and 2nd floor, 74 Jln Gaya, T088-272800, F272900, www.northborneocabin.com. A collection of spacious, spartan rooms and dorms (RM23) with shared bathroom, free breakfast and Wi-Fi access. Friendly staff.

C-D Summer Lodge, 2nd/3rd and 4th floor, Lot 120 Gaya St, T088-244499, www.summer lodge.com.my. Spacious and popular hotel in the centre near a few good eating and drinking options. Rooms are simple, cleanish and have high ceilings and a/c. There's a rooftop garden for the smokers on the 4th floor and plenty of bathrooms scattered about the place, although more expensive rooms are en suite. There are often DVDs playing in the reception, and Beach St market kicks off in a colourful style on weekends. The friendly staff offer a range of tours and the reception is home to a few bounding kittens – strays adopted by the guesthouse – which further add to the cheery mood. Dorms (RM25) and Wi-Fi available.

C-E Akinabalu, Lot 133, Jln Gaya, T088-272188, www.akinabaluyh.com. Popular backpacker haunt with massive communal space and free internet access. Rooms are a bit gloomy, with windows onto a corridor only. Good spot to meet other travellers.

C-E Borneo Gaya Lodge, 78 Jln Gaya, T088-242477, www.borneogayalodge.com. Another new offering, this quiet and relaxed hotel has a selection of clean and comfortable a/c rooms and an a/c dorm. Rooms have TV with cable, Wi-Fi and breakfast is included. Many rooms are windowless. Tour information available.

C-E Borneo Xplorer Backpackers,
1st floor, 106 Jln Gaya, T088-538780,
www.xplobackpackers.com. Run by a couple
of friendly local guys, this guesthouse is
spread over 2 wings. Rooms in the newer
wing are the best bet, recently renovated and
with a common balcony. Dorms are not too
squashed and some sleep 4. Free breakfast
and Wi-Fi access. Guests get a 10% discount
at nearby **Gaya Reflexology**, see page 414.
C-E Farida's Bed & Breakfast, 413 Jln Saga,
Mile 4.5 Jln Tuaran, Likas, T088-428733,
www.homeaway.com.my/farida.htm. Friendly,
whitewashed lodge with 12 rooms, from
dorms to doubles with attached bathroom.
Internet, kitchen, laundry and free breakfast.
It's a 10-min drive north of KK in Inananam
and handy for early morning bus departures
to Sandakan and Tawau. They may be able to
offer free pickup; phone in advance, or take a
Likas bus from Plaza Wawasan and get off
before the mosque. It's a 5-min walk from there.
Run by tour company **Home Away from Home**.
C-E Trekkers Lodge, 30 Jln Haji Saman, T088-
252263, www.trekkerslodge.com. Very busy
place, so book ahead by several days to get a/c
or fan double room. En suite rooms (**B**) are not
good value. Well set up for travellers, with
helpful staff, sitting-out area, library, tour
information (good deals with **Borneo Divers**).
Due to its popularity, however, it feels cramped
and can get a bit grubby, particularly the dorms.
D Borneo Backpackers, 24 Lorong Dewan,
at the foot of Signal Hill on the corner with
the roundabout, T088-234009, www.borneo
backpackers.com. In a renovated 1950s
printing works. 50 beds, internet, laundry,
lounge, roof garden, and tourist information.
The ground floor houses a post-war era
coffee shop stacked with wartime photos
and antique-style furniture. A variety of
rooms, plus dorms with fan (RM20 per
person) or a/c (RM25 per person).
D KK, 46 Jln Pantai, 1st floor, T088-248587.
Just 2 floors down from **Beach Lodge**,
this place has cheap doubles with shared
bathroom, but is not geared towards
travellers. No travel information or communal

lounge, simply a cheap, basic place to stay if
all the other guesthouses are full.
D-E Lucy's Homestay (Backpacker Lodge),
Australia Pl, 25 Lorong Dewan (by the Atkinson
Clock Tower), T088-261495, www.welcome.to/
backpackerkk. Owned by the genial Lucy,
who gets rave reviews from her guests,
this sociable spot is one of the better budget
options in town, although when lots of
guests are staying, it can feel a bit cramped.
Accommodation is mainly in dorms, although
there are also 3 private rooms. Simple kitchen,
excellent library and small balcony. Due to its
popularity it's a good idea to book some days
in advance. Free breakfast with a large pot of
Marmite providing solace to the homesick.
Recommended.

Homestays
Homestays in Sabah are now organized
through **Nature Heritage Travel and Tours**,
ground floor, Wisma Sabah, T088-318747,
nhtt@nature-heritage.com.

Around Kota Kinabalu p404, map p405
L-A Nexus Golf Resort Karambunai,
Menggatal, Karambunai Peninsula, T088-
411222, www.nexusresort.com. Built on
13.5 sq km sprawling along the coast, with
490 ocean-view rooms and a full range of
facilities including 18-hole golf course,
3 pools and sports activities. Popular with
business guests and for conferences.
AL Layang Layang Island Resort, T088-
709121, www.layanglayang.com. Or book
through the reservation office in KL: Block A,
ground floor, A-0-3, Megan Av 11, 12 Jln Yap
Kwan Seng, 50450, KL, T03-2162 2877. This
3-star resort has 76 rather plain rooms and 10
suites, movie room, pool, restaurant and bar.
Apart from the resort the atoll is rather bleak
with only an airstrip. Most reservations are
included in an all-inclusive diving package.
In 2007 this was US$1260 for 6 days/5 nights
with 3 dives a day, plus a flight costing
US$256 per person. You have to enjoy your
diving to make the visit worthwhile, but the
underwater world is spectacular.

AL Rasa Ria Resort, overlooking Pantai Dalit Beach, near Tuaran (take a local bus to Tuaran), T088-792888, www.shangri-la.com. Top-class Shangri-La resort with 330 rooms, a free-form pool, water sports, an 18-hole golf course, a driving range, spacious gardens, conference facilities, horse riding, cultural events, several restaurants including an Italian and a seafood beachfront one and 30 ha of forest nature reserve with semi-tame orang-utans. There have been some complaints about the integrity of an orang-utan fostering programme run by the resort and the cleanliness of the surrounding beach away from the resort. Recommended.

A-B Mimpian Jadi Resort, No 1 Kuala Matinggi, Kampong Pulau, Simpangan, Karambunai Beach, T088-787799, F787775. Chalets, private beach, water sports, fishing, mini zoo, karaoke bar, horse riding, volleyball, children's playground, Malay/Chinese and Western food. To get there, take a bus to Menggatal, then a bus to Karambunai. **Surusup** is 10-15 mins beyond Tuaran. Ask at the store in Surusup for Haji Abdul Saman, who will take visitors by boat to the lesser-known Bajau fishing village, Kampong Penambawan, also likened to an Asian Venice, on the north bank of the river. Nearby there is a suspension bridge and rapids where it is possible to swim.

Tanjung Aru Beach *p404*
AL Shangri-La Tanjung Aru Resort, 20 Jln Aru, T088- 225800, www.shangri-la.com. With a/c, 500 rooms and a pool, this is one of the best hotels in Sabah, along with its sister hotel, the **Rasa Ria** at Tuaran. Tanjung Aru is a public beach 5 km from KK and frequented by kiteflyers, swimmers, joggers and lovers; the hotel is noticeably on the honeymoon circuit for Europeans. Recommended.

⊙ Eating

Kota Kinabalu *p398,*
maps p399, p400 and p405
The waterfront has a range of restaurants with outdoor seating facing the South China

Sea. Seafood is seasonally prone to toxic red tide. Locals will know when it's prevalent. Avoid all shellfish if there's any suspicion.

♔ Aussie Bar and Barbecue, Waterfront Esplanade, Jln Tun Fuad Stephens. Simple no-frills Australian bar-cum-steakhouse, with a bright green and yellow frontage. This is a good spot for carnivores on the hunt for steaks, but it also has fusion dishes and salads.

♔ Chinese Restaurant, Hyatt Hotel, Jln Datuk Salleh Sulong. Broad menu of good Chinese cuisine including Shanghainese, Sichuan and Cantonese, although its signature dish, the delicious Peking duck, hails from the north. Recommended.

♔ Four Seasons, Kompleks Asia City, Jln Tugu. Tucked away at the back of this shopping centre is this Cantonese place with excellent dim sum and steamboats. Good value.

♔ Gardenia Grill Room, Jesselton hotel, 69 Jln Gaya, T088-223333. Elegant dining.

♔ Little Italy, ground floor, **Hotel Capital**, 23 Jln Haji Saman, T088-232231. Open for lunch and dinner. Award-winning pizza and pasta place with Italian chef. Recommended.

♔ Nagisa, Hyatt Hotel, see page 407. Fancy Japanese place with tables facing the South China Sea. Open kitchen, sushi bar, teppanyaki counters and a private tatami room for the wealthy.

♔ Nishiki, Jln Gaya (opposite Wing On Life Building). Japanese. Friendly staff and good-sized portions.

♔ Port View, the Waterfront, T088-221753. Garish Chinese seafood palace with a gigantic bank of aquariums featuring the catch of the day including lobster, grouper, crab and more. The chilli crab is renowned. Very popular at weekends. Recommended.

♔ Seri Selera Kampung Air, Sedco Sq, Kampung Air, T088-210400. Open 1500-0200. Fun tourist-orientated place with 7 different seafood eateries, street stalls and nightly cultural shows.

♔ Sri Melaka, 9 Jln Laiman Diki, Kampong Ayer (Sedco Complex, near **Shiraz**). Popular with the fashionable KK set, serves great Malay and Nyonya food.

Tap Nok Thai, Unit 6, G/F Api Api Centre, T088-258328. Open 1130-1430 and 1800-2230. Authentic Thai restaurant with simple wooden decor and good soups, seafood and salads.

Toscanis, Lot 14, Waterfront Esplanade, Jln Tun Fuad Stephens. Small but popular Mediterranean eatery that draws locals and expats alike with Italian and Spanish seafood dishes, pasta, tapas and delicious desserts.

Aesha Corner, Anjung Perdana (the Waterfront). Cheap Malay canteen facing the sea.

Golf Field Seafood, 0858 Jln Ranca-Ranca. Better known by taxi drivers as **Ahban's Place**. Excellent marine cuisine. A local favourite. Recommended.

Korean, Jln Bandaran Berjaya, next to **Asia Hotel**. Large selection, barbecues a speciality.

La Manila Café, ground floor, Blk D, Warisan Sq, Jln Tun Fuad Stephens, T088- 488996. Open 1000-2200. Strange name for a restaurant specializing in Penang and Nyonya cuisine, but let the food do the talking. Well-priced dishes including Penang *char kway teow*, *asam laksa*, curry *mee* and Penang prawn *mee*.

Nan Xing, Jln Datuk Salleh Sulong, opposite the **Hyatt** and **Emporium**. Dim sum and Cantonese specialities.

Peppermint, Lot 25, G/F, Jln Pantai. A Vietnamese restaurant that is hugely popular lunchtime draw with local workers, arrive after 12 noon and you'll have to join the queue. Simple, short but effective menu of *pho* (noodle soup), beef stew, spicy chicken rice and spring rolls. Recommended.

Restoran Islam, Segama Complex, opposite Hyatt Hotel. Best in a string of coffee shops, all of which are good value for money and curries with a decidedly Indonesian flavour.

Riza, next to the **King Park Hotel** on Jln Masjid Lama. This large Malay canteen has big servings of tasty grub in a clean and friendly environment.

Shiraz, Lot 5, Block B, Sedco Sq, Kampong Ayer. Indian. Recommended.

Sri Sempelang, Sinsuran 2 (on the corner with Jln Pasar Baru). Great Malay canteen with enormous fruit juices and tables outside. Locals recommend it.

Tambayan At Kaining, G/F Api Api Centre, T016-818 5311. Outrageously authentic Filipino restaurant with lots of rattan furniture and leafy plants. Popular with overseas Filipinos, the menu includes *sinagang*, garlic rice, and *calderata*. Recommended.

Yee Fung, 127 Jln Gaya. Open 0630-1700. Local Chinese residents rave about this simple eatery, which gets packed out at lunch with hungry punters wanting their signature *yee fung laksa*, fragrant claypot chicken rice and, for those with a stomach for organs, the *ngau chap* should satisfy the craving. Recommended.

Zaminah, Api-Api Centre. Open 1000-2200. Fairly standard Malaysian Indian Muslim restaurant with the usual rotis and curries.

Foodstalls

There are stalls above the central market. **Sedco Square**, Kampong Ayer, is a large square filled with stalls, with a great atmosphere in the evenings, ubiquitous *ikan panggang* and satay. Night market on **Jln Tugu**, on the waterfront at the **Sinsuran Food Centre** and at **Merdeka Foodstall Centre**, Wisma Merdeka.

Tanjung Aru Beach *p404*

There are mainly seafood foodstalls in Tanjung Aru Beach – recommended for *ikan panggang* – and satay stalls. It's very busy at weekends, but on weekdays it is rather quiet, with only a few stalls to choose from.

Garden Terrace, Tanjung Aru Resort, T088-225800. Open 0600-2300. Asian and Western buffet (dim sum available) and à la carte, with tables facing pretty gardens.

Peppino, Tanjung Aru Resort, T088-225800. Tasty but expensive Italian, good Filipino cover band.

Seafood Market, Tanjung Aru Beach, T088-238313. Pick your own fresh seafood and get advice on how to have it cooked.

✿ Bars and clubs

Kota Kinabulu *p398,*
maps p399, p400 and p405
Bars
Many popular bars are along the **Waterfront
Esplanade**. Notable drinking venues along
this stretch include the **Cock and Bull**, an
English-style pub; **Shamrock's Irish Bar**, with
Kilkenny and Guiness; and **Aussie Bar and
Barbecue**. All are in a strip and make a
colourful short pub crawl. Bars and restaurants,
all with outdoor seating, are strung along
Beach St, a pedestrianized lane between
Jln Pantai and Jln Gaya.
BB Café, Beach St. Closes 2400. Live music,
Kenny G and cheap beer pulls in the punters.
Café Upperstar, Segama Complex (opposite
Hotel Hyatt). Sandwiches and fried food. Jugs
of Long Island iced tea for RM45.

Clubs
Bed, at the end of Waterfront Esplanade.
Popular late-night club with a big dance floor,
live music and lounge area. It gets a little wild
and is a great place to blow off some steam.
Shenanigan's at the Hyatt and **Rumba** at Le
Meridien are also good late-night venues.
    In Tanjung Aru is **Blue Note**, with chilled
grooves at the Tanjung Aru Resort, and
Tiffiny, opposite the Sacred Heart Church.
    Karaoke is very popular in KK; found in
Damai, Foh Sang and KK centre.

✿ Entertainment

Kota Kinabulu *p398,*
maps p399, p400 and p405
Cinemas
Cinema in Centrepoint Mall and at Golden
Screen Cinema and Mega Pavilion on Jln
Sepuluh. There's a large **Cineplex** at One
Borneo on Jln Sulaiman.

Cultural shows
Cultural Palace Theatre Restaurant, Jln
Tanjung Lipat, T088-251844. Dance shows by

Kadazan-Dusun, Bajau and Murut. Dinner and
show RM42 (from 1845, closed Mon). You'll
need a taxi to get there.
Kadazan-Dusun Cultural Centre (Hongkod
Koisaan), KDCA Bldg, Mile 4.5, Jln Penampang.
Restaurant open all year, but in late May,
during the harvest festival, the cultural
association comes into its own, with dances,
feasts and shows and lots of *tapai* (RM15).

✿ Festivals and events

Kota Kinabulu *p398,*
maps p399, p400 and p405
May Magavau (see page 34), a post-harvest
celebration, is carried out at Hongkod Koisaan
(cultural centre), Mile 4.5, Jln Penampang. To
get there, take a green and white bus from
the MPKK Building, next to the state library.

✿ Shopping

Kota Kinabulu *p398,*
maps p399, p400 and p405
Antiques
Good antiques shop at the bottom of the
Chun Eng Bldg on Jln Tun Razak, and a couple
on Jln Gaya. **Merdeka Complex** and **Wisma
Wawasan 2020** hold a number of antiques
shops. You need an export licence from Sabah
State Museum to export rare antiques.

Books
Borneo Books/ Borneo Books 2, Wisma
Merdeka ground and 2nd floor, T088-538077,
www.borneobooks.com. Eco-friendly books
on Borneo, plus a travellers' book exchange
and large collection of classic *National
Geographic* magazines, amongst others.
Times Books, Warisan Square. The best
selection of books in town, with fiction,
magazines, and a great choice of local
interest books.
Zenithway, 29 Jln Pantai. English books
and magazines, also Penguin books.

Clothes

Centrepoint Mall. Branded clothing.
House of Borneo Vou'tique, Lot 12A, 1st floor, Lorong Bernam 3, Taman Saon Kiong, Jln Kolam, T088-268398. For that ethnic, exotic and exclusive look for men and women; souvenirs, tablecloths, cushion covers, etc.

Electronic goods

VCDs, DVDs and stereo equipment are considered the cheapest in the country here. **Karamunsing Kompleks** and **Centrepoint** are the places to go.

Handicrafts

Mainly baskets, mats, tribal clothing, beadwork and pottery. **Api Tours**, Lot 49, Bandaran Berjaya, has a small selection of handicrafts. **Borneo Gifts**, ground floor, Wisma Sabah. **Borneo Handicraft**, 1st floor, Wisma Merdeka, local pottery and material made up into clothes. **Elegance Souvenir**, 1st floor, Wisma Merdeka, lots of beads of local interest (another branch on ground floor of Centrepoint). **Kampong Ayer Night Market**, mainly Filipino handicrafts. **Kraftangan Kompleks/Filipino Market**, Jln Tun Fuad Stephens (see page 404). **Malaysian Handicraft**, Cawangan Sabah, No 1, Lorong 14, Kg Sembulau, T088-234471, Mon-Sat 0815-1230, Fri 0815-1600. **Sabah Art and Handicraft Centre**, 1st floor, Block B, Segama Complex (opposite New Sabah Hotel). **Sabah Handicraft Centre**, Lot 49 Bandaran Berjaya (next to **Shangri-La**), good selection (also has branches at the museum and the airport). **The Crafts**, Lot AG10, ground floor, Wisma Merdeka, T088-252413. There is also a handicraft shop at the **airport**.

Jewellery

Most shops in Wisma Merdeka.

Shopping complexes

Kinabalu Emporium, Wisma Yakim, Jln Daruk Salleh Sulong. The main department store.
Likas Square, Likas. Pink monstrosity with 2 floors of shopping malls, foodstalls and restaurants. Cultural shows in central lobby.

One Borneo Hypermall, Jln Sulaiman (7 km outside the city, free shuttle buses from Warisan Square every hr), www.1borneo.net. The largest shopping mall in Borneo, this gargantuan mall has it all – designer boutiques, a handicraft centre, bowling lanes, hotels, a cineplex and some good eateries – making it ideal for people who want a day of hedonistic consumerism. East Malaysia's largest aquarium, **Aquatica KK** is currently being constructed here. Check www.aquaticakk.org for updates.
Segama, Jln Tun Fuad Stephens, and **Sinsuran**.
Warisan Square. New complex with eateries, boutiques and swimwear outlets.

Tanjung Aru Beach p404
Kaandaman Handicraft Centre, below Seafood Market Restaurant in Tanjung Aru Beach. **Tanjung Aru Resort**, a few handicraft shops in the arcade.

▲ Activities and tours

Kota Kinabalu p398,
maps p399, p400 and p405
The sports complex at Likas is open to the general public. It has volleyball, tennis, basketball, gym, badminton, squash, aerobics and a pool. To get there take a Likas-bound minibus from Plaza Wawasan. **Likas Square** (see above), the pink shopping complex north of Likas Sports Complex, has a recreation club with tennis, squash, jogging, golf, driving range, pool and children's playground.

Bowling

Centrepoint, Jln Lebuh Raya Pantai Baru and at **One Borneo**, Jln Sulaiman.

Diving

Do not believe dive shops if they tell you that you must book through their offices in KK – it's often cheaper to book through local offices in the area where you want to dive. One exception to this rule is Sipadan Island. Only limited numbers of divers are allowed to dive in the area per day due to conservation concerns. Diver limits only apply to Sipadan; Mabul and other islands have yet to impose restrictions. To obtain permits in advance, contact Sipadan tour operators, page 479.

Golf

Green fees are considerably higher over the weekend, up to double the weekday rate. Fees range from RM200 during the week at cheaper courses to RM450 or more over the weekend at flasher clubs. Prices drop considerably for night golf, which usually means a tee-off time after 1700. **Golf Booking Centre Malaysia**, nbtt@tm.net.my, provides escorted golf tours.

Sabah Golf and Country Club, Bukit Padang, T088-247533 www.sgccsabah.com. The oldest course in the state, this 18-hole championship course affords magnificent views of Mt Kinabalu.

Sutera Harbour Golf and Country Club, www.suteraharbour.com, on reclaimed land just to south of the city. A 27-hole layout with great views across to the islands of Tunku Abdul Rahman Park.

Sailing and water sports

Tanjung Aru Marina. Snorkelling RM35 per day, waterskiing RM250 per hr, fishing RM75 per day, sailing RM80 per hr, water scooter RM100 per hr.
Yacht club, Tanjung Aru, next to the hotel.

Spas

The big name hotels such as the **Hyatt** have their own spas.
Gaya Reflexology, 114 Jln Gaya. Offers good-value massage and other treatments, helpful to those who have stiff legs after a Kinabalu climb. A full body massage starts at RM60.

Tour operators

The Sabah Tourism Board has a full list of tour agents operating in the state, and also on its website, www.sabahtourism.com.
Api Tours Lorong Kacang, Jln Kolombong, Inanam, T088-424 156, www.apitours.com.

Wide variety of tours, treks in the Crocker Range, homestays and some more unusual ones such as overnight stays in longhouses. Recommended.
Borneo Divers, ground floor, Wisma Sabag, T088-222227, www.borneodivers.info. Operates exotic scuba-diving trips all over Borneo including Sipadan, accommodation on Mamutik Island (Tunku Abdul Rahman); they also have an office in Tawau, T089-761214. Dive trips are well organized but expensive, it's possible to bargain. **Trekker's Lodge** can sometimes help with good deals with this dive shop.
Borneo Eco Tours, Lot 1, Pusat Perindustrian, Kolombong Jaya, 88450, T088-438300, www.borneoecotours.com. Award-winning operator that specializes in environmentally aware tours. Their **Sukau Rainforest Lodge** (www.sukau.com) on the Kinabatangan River is highly recommended.
Borneo Nature Tours, Block D, Lot 10, ground floor, Sadong Jaya Complex, T088-267637, www.borneonaturetours.com. Official agent operating within the excellent Danum Valley Conservation Area (including Borneo Rainforest Lodge), see page 461, and the Maliau Basin, page 467.
Borneo Sea Adventures, 1st floor, 8a Karamunsing Warehouse, T088-230000, www.bornsea.com. Scuba-diving courses and diving and fishing trips around Sipadan (see page 464). They run **Mantanani Island Resort** on this island, see page 438.
Borneo Ultimate, ground floor, Wisma Sabah, www.borneoultimate.com.my. Adventure tours including whitewater rafting, mountain biking, jungle trekking, and sea kayaking.
Borneo Wildlife Adventures, Lot F, 1st floor, General Post Office building, T088-213668, www.borneo-wildlife.com. Specializing in nature tours, wildlife and cultural activities.
Diethelm Borneo Expeditions, Suite 303, 2nd floor, EON-CMG Life Building, 1 Jln Sagunting, T088-222271, dbex@tm.net.my.
Discovery Tours, ground floor, Wisma Sabah, Jln Haji Saman, T088-221244, www.infosabah.com.my/discovery/. Run by experienced tour

operator Albert Wong. Packages include trips to longhouses, whitewater rafting and wildlife trips. Recommended.

Down Below Marine and Adventures, KK Times Square, 3rd floor, Lot 12, Block B, T088-488997, www.divedownbelow.com. Run by a friendly British couple, this outfit has received plaudits from readers for their dive and snorkel trips out to Pulau Gaya (where they have a Five-Star PADI Dive Station), Pulau Tiga and the Usukan Bay Second World War wrecks. They can also arrange land tours to Kinabatangan and Gomantong. Recommended.

Exotic Borneo, Likas Post Office, Likas, T088-245920, www.exborneo.com. Runs well-run theme tours including culture, adventure and nature, at a price.

Intra Travel Service, Lot No A-1-7, Block A, 1st floor, Tanjung Aru Plaza, Jln Mat Salleh, T088-261558, www.intra-travel.com.my. Best place to book trips in the excellent Tabin Wildlife reserve, see page 460.

KK Tours & Travel, J-60-5, Signature Office, KK Times Square, Off Coastal Highway, T088-868818, www.kktours.com. Good operator with a wide range of tours, from golfing to island hopping around Pilau's Tiga and Mantanani and luxury helicopter rides in the mountains. Also have own tours and accommodation in the Klias Wetlands, see page 423.

Mountain Torq, Unit 3-49, 3rd floor, Asia City Complex, Jln Asia City, T088-268126, www.mountaintorq.com. Organizes Via Ferrata treks on the north face of Gunung Kinabalu.

Nasalis Larvatus Tours, contact General Manager Alexander Yee (friendly and genuinely interested in conservation), Lot 226, 2nd floor, Wisma Sabah, Jln Tun Abdul Razak, T088-230534, www.nasalislarvatus tours.com. For **Nature Lodge Kinabatangan**, www.naturelodgekinabatangan.com, excellent mid-range lodge about 1 hr upriver from Sukau. More luxurious accommodation is in the process of being built, recent upgrades include electric fences to keep out monkeys, new dining area and hot showers. Currently a fairly quiet part of the river with a wide range of activities including kayaking, nature walks including night-time trips and trips to a local oxbow lake, plus more typical river boat trips. At least 2-3 nights needed to get the most from the area. Great wildlife viewing, with elephants, orang-utans and many primates often spotted. Also plenty of crocodiles and many bird species.

Pan Borneo Tours & Travel, 1st floor, Lot 127, Wisma Sabah, T088-221221, www.panborneo.com. Sightseeing, diving and wildlife.

Riverbug/Traverse Tours, White Water Rafting Specialist, Lot 227-229, 2nd floor, Wisma Sabah, Jln Tun Fuad Stephen, T088-260501, www.traversetours.com. Well-organized 1-day rafting trips on the Padas (grade III-IV) river run from KK. Good guides, transport and safety equipment, plus a post-river barbecue (photos and 'in action' videos for extra fee). Good facilities including changing rooms and a dinner hut on the river. Not terrifying rapids for hardcore paddlers, but big waves, warm water and the spectacular scenery of the Crocker Range make this a fun day out for everyone. The smaller Kiulu River (grades II-III) is just as picturesque, but with smaller rapids and occasional slow moving sections interspersed with deep pools – a good river for learning basic kayaking skills or for racking up some of your first white water descents. They also run a probosis monkey wetland tour, climbing packages up Mount Trusmadi and trekking, biking and camping tours across Sabah.

Scuba Paradise, Lot G28, ground floor, Jln Tun Razak Wisma Sabah, T088-266695, www.scubaparadiseborneo.com.my. Reliable local dive operator offering both open water courses and fun dives around Tunku Abdul Rahman National Park, Mantanani Island and Sipadan/Mabul islands. Recommended for day dives in the TARP area and Mantanani.

Tanjung Aru Tours, The Marina, Tanjung Aru Resort, T088-214215, F240966. Fishing and island tours – particularly to Tunku Abdul Rahman National Park.

Whitewater rafting

Papar River (grades I and II), Kadamaian River (grades II and III), Padas River (grade IV). Usually requires a minimum of 3 people. Main operators include **Api Tours, Diethelm Borneo Expeditions, Traverse Tours/ Riverbug** and **Discovery Tours** (see above).

⊖ Transport

Kota Kinabulu *p398,*
maps p399, p400 and p405

Air

Air is the most widely used form of transportation between major towns in Sabah. MASwings connect KK with **Sandakan, Tawau** and **Lahad Datu** and it's cheap. Regular connections with **KL**. There are also connections from KK with **Bintulu, Johor Bahru, Kuching, Labuan, Miri** (and on to **Mulu National Park**) and **Sibu**. International connections are to **Singapore, Brunei, Hong Kong, Manila** (with Cebu Pacific), **Cebu, Seoul, Jakarta,** and various cities in China including **Shenzhen, Guangzhou** and **Kaohsiung (Taiwan)**. Singapore is now well connected to KK with budget airlines Tiger Airways, Air Asia and Jet Star Asia offering frequent connections. Air Asia plans to make KK its hub for China flights, with connections to **Guilin** and **Xiamen** expected by the time this guide is published.

Airline offices AirAsia, Jln Gaya, T088-438222. **Asiana**, Suite 7-7E, 7th floor, Menara MAA, 6 Lorong Api Api, T088-268677. **Cebu Pacific**, c/o Skyzone Tours, Suite G-02, Menara MAA, 6 Lorong Api Api, T088-448871. **Dragonair**, Lot G, G/F, Block C, Kompleks Kuwasa, T088-254733. **Korean Air**, Lot 2B, Airport, T088-251152. **Malaysia Airlines** (for MAS and MASwings), PO Box 10194, T088- 239111. **Royal Brunei**, Lot BG, 3B, G/F Kompleks Kuwasa, T088-242193. **Silk Air**, Tg Aru Plaza, 1st floor, Block B, Jln Mat Salleh, T088-265771.

Boat

Getting from Brunei overland takes 6 hrs including 2 ferries from Muara to Labuan and then on to Kota Kinabalu, or a 45-min flight.

There is a ferry service between KK and **Labuan** with departures at 0800 (daily), 1330 (Mon-Thu) and 1500 (Fri-Sun), the journey takes 3 hrs (RM31 one way). There are 6 daily ferries to **Serasa Muara (Brunei)** from the Labuan jetty between 0900 and 1630 (1 hr, RM30). For travellers heading through to Muara from KK, there is a package including both ferry tickets for RM53. This does not include the RM10 departure tax payable in Labuan. For travellers heading to Brunei, it's essential to catch the first departure of the day. From Muara's Serasa Ferry Terminal, minibuses run to Bandar Seri Begawan (45 mins, B$2).

Bus and minibus

There's no central bus station in KK. Buses further afield but still in the KK region leave from next to Plaza Wawasan. Destinations include **Sipitang, Beaufort** and **Lawas**.

Buses into the interior wait in the scruffy car park at the base of Signal Hill; destinations include **Tenom, Ranau, Kota Belud, Papan, Sipitang, Lawas, Tambunan** and **Keningan**.

City minibuses leave from the station on Jln Tun Razak, next to the City Park. Long-distance buses to **Sandakan, Semporna, Lahad Datau** and **Tawau** leave from the terminal in Inanam, 10 km from the centre. To get there, hop on local bus No 3, or take a taxi (RM15). Buses around the state are cheaper than minibuses but not as regular or efficient. The large buses go mainly to destinations in and around KK itself.

There are lots of bus companies and when you arrive at the bus station touts will try to get you to use their company. All the prices should be the same, and it's advisable to buy your ticket the day before. The time on the ticket is a rough guide only. Get there 10 mins before to guarantee your seat, but you may have to wait until the bus is full.

Buses to **Tenom** (0800, 1200, 1600, 3 hrs, RM17), **Keningau** (8 departures daily, 2½ hrs, RM13), **Beaufort** (more than 10 every day, 2 hrs RM10), **Tawau** (0730, 0745, 1400, 2000, 9 hrs, RM71.40), **Sandakan** (0730, 0800, 0930, 1130, 1200, 1400, 6 hrs, RM71.40), **Semporna** (0730, 0830, 0900, 2000, 9 hrs, RM75), **Lahud Datu** (0700, 0830, 0900, 2000, 8 hrs, RM52).

Daily buses leave at 0800 from the Wawasan Plaza Terminal for **Bandar Seri Begawan** (7 hrs, RM100) and **Miri** (10 hrs, RM90).

All minibuses have their destinations on the windscreen, most rides in town cost between RM1 and RM2 and they will leave when full. You can get off wherever you like.

Car
Not all roads in the interior of Sabah are paved and a 4WD vehicle is advisable for some journeys. Car hire is expensive (RM30-80 per hr) and rates often increase for use outside a 50-km radius of KK. All vehicles have to be returned to KK as there are no agency offices outside KK, although local car hire is usually available. Drivers must be between the ages of 22 and 60 and possess an international driving licence. ABAN-D Rent a Car, Lot 22, 1st floor, Taman Victory, Mile 4.5, Jln Penampang, T088-722300, F721959. Adaras Rent-a-Car, Lot G03, ground floor, Wisma Sabah, T088-2166671, F216010. Hertz, Level 1, Lot 39, Kota Kinabalu airport, T088-317740. Kinabalu Rent-a-Car, Lot 3.61, 3rd floor, Karamunsing Kompleks, T088-232602, www.kinabalurac.com/. Samzain Rent a Car, Lot 10, Tingkat 2 Putatan Point, Penampang, T088-765805.

Taxis
There are taxi stands outside most of the bigger hotels and outside the General Post Office, the Segama complex, the Sinsuran complex, next to the DPKK building, the Milemewah supermarket, the Capitol cinema and in front of the clocktower (for taxis to

Ranau, **Keningau** and **Kudat**). Approximate fares from town: RM15 to **Tanjung Aru Resort**, RM15 to **Sabah Foundation**, RM12 to the museum, RM15-20 to the airport. See also minibus, above.

Train
The station is 5 km out of town in Tanjung Aru. There is only 1 train line in Sabah, and rolling stock dates from the colonial era. At the time of writing no services were operating due to an upgrade. Services are expected to resume in late 2010.

❶ Directory

Kota Kinabalu p398, maps p399, p400 and p405

Banks There are money changers in main shopping complexes: HSBC, 56 Jln Gaya; Maybank, Jln Kemajuan/Jln Pantai; Sabah Bank, Wisma Tun Fuad Stephens, Jln Tuaran; Standard Chartered, 20 Jln Haji Saman. **Embassies and consulates** British Consul, Hong Kong Bank Building, 56 Jln Gaya; Indonesian Consulate, Lorong Kemajuan, Karimunsing, T088-218600, indocon@indocon.po.my; Japanese Consulate, Wisma Yakim, T088-428169. **Immigration** 4th floor, Government Building, Jln Haji Yaakub, visas can be renewed at this office, without having to leave the country. **Internet** Web access is easily available and cheap. Many of the more jazzy coffee shops (including Western chains like Starbucks) and many hotels and guesthouses offer free Wi-Fi for customers with their own laptops. Local internet cafés are often noisy and crammed with game-playing locals. Expect to pay RM3 per hr. **Post office** General Post Office, Jln Tun Razak, Segama Quarter (poste restante facilities). **Telephone** Telekom, Block C, Kompleks Kuwaus, Jln Tunku Abdul Rahma. International and local calls, fax service.

Off the coast and south of Kota Kinabalu

West of KK is the Tunku Abdul Rahman Park, a reef and coral marine park. Travelling south from KK, the route crosses the Crocker Range to Tambunan. Continuing south the road passes through the logging town of Keningau and on to Tenom, where the North Borneo railway used to run (which should be back in action late 2010), snaking down the Padas Gorge to Beaufort. The Padas River is the best place to go whitewater rafting in Sabah. Few towns are worth staying in for long on this route, but it is a scenic journey.

Pulau Tiga National Park is a forest reserve where the pied hornbill can be spotted and Pulau Labuan is a tax-free haven off the coast. >> *For listings, see pages 427-434.*

Tunku Abdul Rahman National Park → *For listings, see pages 427-434. Colour map 4, A3.*

The five islands in Gaya Bay, which make up Tunku Abdul Rahman Park (TAR), lie 3-8 km offshore. Coral reefs fringe all the islands in the park. The best reefs are between **Pulau Sapi** and **Pulau Gaya**, although there is also reasonable coral around **Manukan**, **Mamutik** and **Sulug**. Named after Malaysia's first prime minister, they became Sabah's first national park in 1923 and were gazetted in 1974 in an effort to protect their coral reefs and sandy beaches. Geologically, the islands are part of the Crocker Range formation, but as sea levels rose after the last ice age, they became isolated from the massif. The islands can be visited all year round.

Ins and outs

Getting there Boats for the park leave from Jesselton Point Ferry Terminal, 10 minutes' walk north of the town and cost RM23 return. There are frequent departures and the last boat back is at 1700. Ferries to Labuan leave from here too. There are also frequent boats from the Sutera Harbour Resort. >> *See also Transport, page 433.*

Tourist information **Park HQ** is on Pulau Manukan; there are ranger stations on Gaya, Sapi and Mamutik.

Flora and fauna

Some of the only undisturbed coastal dipterocarp forest left in Sabah is on Pulau Gaya. On the other islands most of the original vegetation has been destroyed and established secondary vegetation predominates, such as ferns, orchids, palms, casuarina, coconut trees and tropical fruit trees. Mangrove forests can be found at two locations on Pulau Gaya. Animal and birdlife includes long-tailed macaques, bearded pig and pangolin (on Pulau Gaya), white-bellied sea eagle, pied hornbill, green heron, sandpipers, flycatchers and sunbirds.

There is a magnificent range of marine life because of the variety of the reefs surrounding the islands. The coral reefs are teeming with exotica such as butterfly fish, Moorish idols, parrot fish, bat fish, razor fish, lion fish and stone fish, in stark contrast to the areas that have been depth-charged by Gaya's notorious dynamite fishermen.

The islands

By far the largest island, **Pulau Gaya** was the site of the first British North Borneo Chartered Company settlement in the area in 1881; the settlement lasted only 15 years before being destroyed in a pirate attack. There is still a large community on the island on the promontory facing KK, but today it is a shanty town, populated mainly by Filipino immigrants. On Pulau Gaya there are 20 km of marked trails including a plankwalk across a mangrove swamp and many beautiful little secluded bays. Police Bay is a popular, shaded beach. **Gayana Island EcoResort** is a big chalet development on the island with its own ferry from the KK jetty. **Pulau Sapi**, the most popular of the islands for weekenders, also has good beaches and trails. It is connected to Pulau Gaya at low tide by a sandbar. There are good day-use facilities but no accommodation except camping.

Pulau Mamutik, closer to the mainland, is the smallest island but has a well-preserved reef off the northeast tip. **Pulau Manukan** is the site of the Park HQ and most of the park accommodation. It has good snorkelling to the south and east and a particularly good beach on the east tip. It is probably the best of all the islands but is heavily frequented by day trippers and rubbish is sometimes a problem. There is accommodation here; book through **Sutera Sanctuary Lodges**, see page 399. Marine sports facilities stretch to the hire of mask, snorkel and fins (RM15, plus RM50 deposit for the day), and diving equipment. There's a swimming pool, water sports centre for sailing, banana boat and windsurfing. Glass-bottom boat trips are available. Fish feeding off the jetty attracts large shoals of fish, making it a good place for snorkelling. The best reefs are off **Pulau Sulug**, which is less developed as it is a bit further away. This small island has a sand spit, making it good for swimming. There are dive facilities and a restaurant. You can also camp here.

Pulau Tiga National Park → *For listings, see pages 427-434. Colour map 4, B2.*

This park is 48 km south of KK. Declared a forest reserve in 1933, the 15,864 ha park is made up of three islands: Pulau Tiga, Kalampunian Damit and Kalampunian Besar.

Ins and outs

Getting there and around Drive 140 km to Kuala Penyu at the tip of the Klias Peninsula (two hours, RM18), and then take a 30-minute boat ride (scheduled departures at 1000, 1030 and 1500 from Kuala Penyu – price usually included in resort packages – book in advance). Alternatively charter a speedboat from KK; contact **Sipadan Dive Centre** ⓘ *11th floor, Wisma Merdeka, Jln Tun Razak, KK, T088-240584, www.pulau-tiga.com*, who run the island's resort, to organize transport to the island. **Sabah Parks Office** can also help arrange the boat trip. Speedboats cost RM350 for 10 people, but it's possible to bargain down to RM250 for the boat if there are fewer people.

Tourist information The Park HQ, on the south side of Pulau Tiga, is mainly used as a botanical and marine research centre and tourism is not vigorously promoted; as a result there are no special facilities for tourists. The best time to visit is between February and April, when it is slightly drier and the seas are calmer.

National park

Pulau Tiga achieved notoriety as the location for the reality TV series *Survivor*, chosen for its unspoilt natural landscape. Pulau Tiga's three low hills were all formed by mud volcanoes. The last big eruption, in 1941, was heard 160 km away and covered the island in a layer of boiling mud. The bubbling mud pools that remain at three points across the island are a slightly bizarre but interesting bathing experience and something that distinguishes the island from others in the area. The dipterocarp forests on the islands are virtually untouched and they contain species not found on other west coast islands, such as a poisonous amphibious sea snake (*Laticauda colubrina*), also known as the banded sea krait, which comes ashore on Pulau Kalampunian Damit to lay its eggs. Rare birds such as the pied hornbill (*Anthracoceros convexus*) and the megapode (*Megapodus freycinet*) are found here, as well as flying foxes, monitor lizards, wild fruit trees and mangrove forest. A network of trails, marked at 50-m intervals, leads to various points of interest.

Underwater the island offers good diving at a diverse range of sites. There's excellent coral growth mid-channel and plenty of smaller marine life and fish making this a colourful spot. It's variable after storms and strong winds. The small offshore house reef is good, with lots of anemones, clown fish and the occasional turtle. As long as you're not expecting the vast underwater cliffs and crystal-clear conditions of the Sipadan area, Pulau Tiga has plenty to keep you entertained on the marine front.

Pulau Labuan → *For listings, see pages 427-434. Colour map 4, B2.*

Labuan is one of the historically stranger pieces of the Bornean jigsaw. Originally part of the Sultanate of Brunei, the 92-sq-km island, 8 km off the coast of Sabah, was ceded in 1846 to the British who were enticed to take it on by the discovery of rich coal deposits. It joined the Malaysian Federation in 1963, along with Sabah and Sarawak. In 1984 it was declared a tax-free haven – or an 'International offshore financial centre' – and hence this small tropical island with just 80,000-odd inhabitants has a plethora of name-plate banks and investment companies. For the casual visitor – rather than someone wanting to salt away

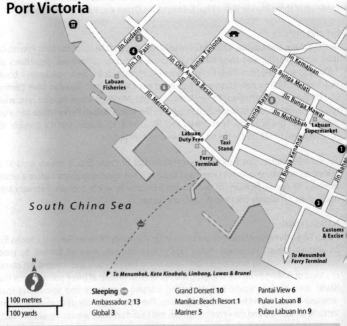

Port Victoria

South China Sea

► *To Menumbok, Kota Kinabalu, Limbang, Lawas & Brunei*

To Menumbok Ferry Terminal

Labuan Fisheries

Labuan Duty Free

Taxi Stand

Ferry Terminal

Labuan Supermarket

Customs & Excise

100 metres
100 yards

Sleeping
Ambassador 2 **13**
Global **3**

Grand Dorsett **10**
Manikar Beach Resort **1**
Mariner **5**

Pantai View **6**
Pulau Labuan **8**
Pulau Labuan Inn **9**

their million – it offers some attractions, but not many. There are good hotels, lots of duty-free shopping, a golf course, sport fishing and diving, plus a handful of historic and cultural sights.

Ins and outs

Getting there and around The airport is 5 km from town. There is a reasonable island bus network, a few car hire firms and a small number of taxis. ▸▸ *See also Transport, page 433.*

Tourist information **Tourist Information Office** ⓘ *Lot 4260, Jln Dewan/Jln Berjaya, T087-423445.* See also www.labuantourism.com.my.

Background

With a superb deep-water harbour, Labuan promised an excellent location from which the British could engage the pirates who were terrorizing the northwest Borneo coast. Labuan also had coal, which could be used to service steamships. Sarawak's Rajah James Brooke became the island's first governor in 1846 and two years later it was declared a free port. It also became a penal colony: long-sentence convicts from Hong Kong were put to work on the coal face and in the jungle, clearing roads. The island was little more than a malarial swamp and its inept colonial administration was perpetually plagued by fever and liver disorders. Its nine drunken civil servants provided a gold mine of eccentricity for novelists Joseph Conrad and Somerset Maugham. In *The Outstation*, Maugham describes the desperate attempt by Resident Mr Warburton to keep a grip on civilization in the wilds of

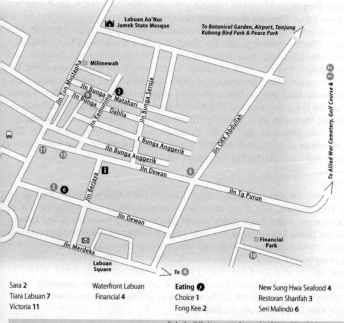

		Eating 🍴	
Sara **2**	Waterfront Labuan	Choice **1**	New Sung Hwa Seafood **4**
Tiara Labuan **7**	Financial **4**	Fong Kee **2**	Restoran Sharifah **3**
Victoria **11**			Seri Malindo **6**

Malaysia: "The only concession he made to the climate was to wear a white dinner jacket; but otherwise, in a boiled shirt and high collar, silk socks and patent leather shoes, he dressed as formally as though he was dining at his club in Pall Mall..."

By the 1880s ships were already bypassing the island and the tiny colony began to disintegrate. In 1881 William Hood Treacher moved the capital of the new territory of British North Borneo from Labuan to Kudat and eight years later the Chartered Company was asked to take over the administration of the island. In 1907 it became part of the Straits Settlements, along with Singapore, Malacca (Melaka) and Penang.

Modern Labuan

In 1946 Labuan became a part of British North Borneo and was later incorporated into Sabah as part of the Federation of Malaysia in 1963. Datuk Harris is thought to own half the island (including the **Hotel Labuan**). As chief minister, he offered the island as a gift to the federal government in 1984 in exchange for a government undertaking to bail out his industrial projects and build up the island's flagging economy. The election of a Christian government in Sabah in 1986, making it Malaysia's only non-Muslim-ruled state, proved an embarrassment to the then prime minister Doctor Mahathir Mohamad. Labuan has strategic importance as a federal territory, wedged between Sabah and Sarawak. It is used by garrisons of the Malaysian army, navy and air force.

In declaring Labuan a tax haven the Malaysian government set out its vision of Labuan becoming the Bermuda of the Asia-Pacific for the 21st century; 4065 offshore firms had set up on the island by the end of 2003, and in 2000, the **Labuan International Financial Exchange** (LFX), a wholly owned subsidiary of the Kuala Lumpur Stock Exchange, was established on the island. This, together with several five-star hotels, makes it seem that Labuan's days of being a sleepy rural backwater are over.

Included in the island's population of about 80,000 are 10,000 Filipino refugees, with about 21 different ethnic groups. The island is the centre of a booming 'barter' trade with the South Philippines; Labuan is home to a clutch of so-called string vest millionaires, who have grown rich on the trade. In Labuan, 'barter' is the name given to smuggling. The Filipino traders leaving the Philippines simply over-declare their exports (usually copra, hardwood, rotan and San Miguel beer) and under-declare the imports (Shogun jeeps, Japanese hi-fi and motorbikes), all ordered through duty-free Labuan. With such valuable cargoes, the traders are at the mercy of pirates in the South China Sea. To get round this, they arm themselves with M-16s, bazookas and shoulder-launched missiles. This ammunition is confiscated on their arrival in Labuan, stored in a marine police warehouse, and given back to them for the return trip.

Sights

Away from the busy barter jetty, Labuan Town, a name largely superseded by its name of **Port Victoria**, is a dozy, seedy and unremarkable Chinese-Malaysian mix of shophouses, coffee shops, sleazy karaoke bars and cheap booze shops. The **Labuan An'Nur Jamek State Mosque** is an impressive site, whilst the manicured **golf course** is popular with businessmen. Illegal cockfights are staged every Sunday afternoon. There is an old brick **chimney** at Tanjung Kubong, believed to have been built as a ventilation shaft for the short-lived coal mining industry established by the British in 1947 to provide fuel for their steamships on the Far Eastern trade route. Remnants of the industry, which had petered out by 1911, are to be found in a maze of **tunnels** in this area. Near Tanjung Kubong is a **Bird Park**.

On the west coast there are pleasant beaches, mostly lined with kampongs. There is a large **Japanese war memorial** on the east coast and a vast, well-tended, **Allied war cemetery** between the town and the airport with over 3000 graves, most of which are unknown soldiers. The **Peace Park** at Layang Layangan marks the Japanese surrender point on 9 September 1945, which brought the Second World War to an end in Borneo.

Boat trips can be made to the small islands around Labuan, although only by chartering a fishing vessel. The main islands are **Pulau Papan** (an uninspiring island between Labuan and the mainland), **Pulau Kuraman**, **Pulau Rusukan Kecil** (known locally as the floating lady) and **Pulau Rusukan Besar** (floating man). These last three have good beaches and coral reefs but none have any facilities.

Off the south coast of the island is the **Marine Park**; a great place to dive, especially as there are four shipwrecks scattered in these waters. The park has 20 dive sites. ▸ *See Activities and tours, page 432.*

South of Kota Kinabalu → *For listings, see pages 427-434.*

Papar → *Colour map 4, B3.*
Formerly a sleepy Kadazan village, 38 km south of KK, Papar is developing fast. In *bandar lama* (the old town) there are rows of quaint wooden shophouses, painted blue and set along spacious boulevards lined with palms. There is a large market in the centre. The Papar area is famous for its fruit and there is a good *tamu* every Sunday.

There is a scenic drive between Papar and KK, with paddy fields and jungle lining the roadside. Nearby, **Pantai Manis**, a 3-km stretch of golden sand with a deep lagoon good for swimming, can be reached easily from Papar. It is also possible to make boat trips up the Papar River, which offers gentle rapids for less energetic whitewater rafters. Rafting trips can be organized through tour agents in KK (see page 414).

The **Klias Wetlands** is a new destination promoted by **Sabah Tourism**, popular with visitors who do not have time to visit the east coast of Sabah. Boat trips operate through a mangrove swamp and the Klias River, with the chance to spot proboscis monkeys, long-tailed macaques, silver langur monkeys and an abundance of birdlife. The Klias Peninsula lies 120 km south of KK; trips down the Klias River depart from the Kota Klias jetty. Booking via a tour operator is recommended. Contact tour operators in KK such **Diethelm Borneo Expeditions** and **KK Tours & Travel**, see page 414 and page 415.

Tambunan → *Colour map 4, B3. Population: 28,000.*
The twisting mountain road that cuts across the **Crocker Range National Park** (see page 425) and over the Sinsuran Pass at 1649 m is very beautiful. There are dramatic views down over Kota Kinabalu and the islands beyond and glimpses of Mount Kinabalu to the northeast. The road itself, from KK to Tambunan, was the old bridleway that linked the west coast to the interior. Inland communities traded their tobacco, rattan and other jungle produce for salt and iron at the coastal markets. The road passes through Penampang. Scattered farming communities grow hill rice, pineapples, bananas, mushrooms and other vegetables that are sold at roadside stalls, where wild and cultivated orchids can also be found. After descending from the hills the road enters the sprawling flood plain of Tambunan – the Pegalam River runs through the plain – which, at the height of the paddy season, is a magnificent patchwork of greens.

The Tambunan area is largely Kadazan/Dusun, Sabah's largest ethnic group, and the whole area explodes into life each May during the harvest festival when copious

Rafflesia: the world's largest flower

The rafflesia (*Rafflesia arnoldi*), named after Stamford Raffles, the founder of modern Singapore, is the largest flower in the world. The Swedish naturalist Eric Mjoberg wrote in 1930 on seeing the flower: "The whole phenomenon seems so amazing, so unfamiliar, so fantastic, that we are tempted to explain: such flowers cannot be real!"

Stamford Raffles, who discovered the flower for Western science 100 years earlier during his first sojourn at Bengkulu

on the west coast of Sumatra, noted that it was "a full yard across, weighs 15 pounds, and contains in the nectary no less than eight pints [of nectar]...".

The problem is that the rafflesia does not flower for very long – only for a couple of weeks, usually between August and December. At other times of the year there is usually nothing to see. The plant is in fact parasitic, so appropriately its scent is more akin to rotting meat than any perfume. Its natural habitat is moist, shaded areas.

quantities of *lihing*, the famed local rice wine, are consumed and *Bobolians* (high priestesses) still conduct various rituals (see box, page 491). There is a *lihing* brewery inside the Tambunan Village Resort Centre. The Tambunan District covers an area of 134,540 ha. At 650 m to 900 m, it enjoys a spring-like climate during much of the year.

Tambunan (Valley of the Bamboo), so-called as there are at least 12 varieties of bamboo to be found here, also lays claim to the Kitingan family. Joseph was Sabah's first Christian chief minister until he was deposed in March 1994. His brother, Jeffrey, was formerly head of the Sabah Foundation. He entered politics in 1994 on his release from detention on the Malaysian Peninsula. He had been charged under Malaysia's internal security act of being a secessionist conspirator.

A concrete structure at Tibabar, just outside Tambunan, situated amongst the rice fields and surrounded by peaceful kampong houses, commemorates the site of **Mat Salleh's fort** ⓘ *daily 0900-1700, free*, and the place of his death. Mat Salleh, now a nationalist folk hero, led a rebellion for six years against the **Chartered Company** administration until he was killed in 1900 (see box, page 402). The memorial has been set up by the Sabah State Museum and houses some exhibits including weapons, Salleh paraphernalia and a photo of the man himself.

The Rafflesia Information Centre ⓘ *daily 0800-1500, T087-774691*, is located at the roadside on the edge of a forest reserve that has been set aside to conserve this remarkable flower (see box above). The information centre has a comprehensive and attractive display on the rafflesia and its habitat and information on flowers in bloom. If trail maps are temporarily unavailable, ask the ranger to point out the sites where blooms can be seen on the large relief model of the forest reserve at the back of the information centre. The blooming period of the flower is very short so, to avoid disappointment, it's worth phoning the centre first. Ranger guides are available at the centre and cost RM100 for a group of six or less.

Ahir Terjan Sensuron is a waterfall 4 km from the Rafflesia Information Centre on the Tambunan–KK road (heading towards KK). From the road, it is a 45-minute walk to the waterfall. Every Thursday morning a large market is held here, selling tobacco, local musical instruments, clothing, strange edible jungle ferns and yeast used to make fermented rice wine. There are also bundles of a fragrant herb known as *tuhau*, a member of the ginger family that is made into a spicy condiment or sambal redolent of the jungle. A smaller market is held on Sunday in Kampong Toboh, north of Tambunan.

Crocker Range National Park ① *no visitors' facilities have yet been developed*, incorporates 139,919 ha of hill and montane forest, which includes many species endemic to Borneo. It is the largest single totally protected area in Sabah. Private development is taking place along the narrow strips of land each side of the KK – Tambunan road, which were unfortunately overlooked when the park was gazetted. To get there, see Transport, page 433 (as for Tambunan).

The **Mawah Waterfall** is reached by following the road north towards Ranau to Kampong Patau, where a sign beside the school on the left indicates a gravel road leading almost to the waterfall (Mawah Airterjun). It is 15 minutes down the road by car and between five and 10 minutes' walk along the trail.

Gunung Trusmadi, 2642 m, 70 km southeast of Kota Kinabalu, is the second highest mountain in Malaysia, but very few people climb it: the route is difficult and facilities, compared with Gunung Kinabalu, are few. There are two main routes to the top: the north route, which takes four days to the summit (and three days down) and the south route, which is harder but shorter; two days to the summit. Trusmadi is famous for its huge, and very rare, pitcher plant *Nepethes trusmadiensis*, found only on one spot on the summit ridge. It is also known for its fantastic view north, towards Gunung Kinabalu, which rises above the Tambunan Valley. There is a wide variety of vegetation on the mountain as it rises from dipterocarp primary jungle through oak montane forest with mossy forest near the summit and heath-like vegetation on top. An expedition to Trusmadi requires careful planning and should not be undertaken casually. A more detailed account of the two routes is in *Mountains of Malaysia – A Practical Guide and Manual*, by John Briggs.

Keningau → *Colour map 4, B3.*

The Japanese built fortifications around their base in Keningau during the Second World War. It is now rather a depressing, shabby lumber town, smothered in smoke from the sawmills. The timber business in this area turned Keningau into a boom town in the 1980s and the population virtually doubled within a decade. The felling continues, but there is not much primary forest left these days. There are huge logging camps all around the town and the hills to the west. Logging roads lead into these hills off the Keningau–Tenom road, which are accessible by 4WD vehicles. It is just possible to drive across them to Papar, which is a magnificent route. If you do attempt the drive, steer well clear of log-laden trucks on their way down the mountain. There is an interesting weekly *tamu* held here on Sunday mornings, principally noted for its Kadazan handicrafts.

Sapulut is deep in Murut country and is accessible from Keningau by a rough road via Kampong Nabawan (4WD required). At Sapulut, follow the river of the same name east through Bigor and Kampong Labang to Kampong Batu Punggul at the confluence of Sungai Palangan, a 2½-hour journey. **Batu Punggul** is a limestone outcrop protruding 200 m above the surrounding forest, about 30 minutes' walk from the kampong; it can be climbed without any equipment, but with care. It is quite a dangerous climb, but there are plenty of handholds and the view of the surrounding forest from the top is spectacular. Both the forest and the caves in and around Batu Punggul are worth exploring. Nearby is the less impressive limestone outcrop, **Batu Tinahas**, with huge caves and many unexplored passages. It is thought to have at least three levels of caves and tunnels. Some tour operators in KK offer trips here.

There is a short stretch of road leading from Sapulut to Agis, just a four-hour boat ride from the Kalimantan border. There is even an immigration checkpoint at Pegalungan, which is a settlement en route. (**Note** It's not possible to cross into Indonesia from here.)

There are many rivers and longhouses worth exploring here. One particular longhouse is **Kampong Selungai**, only 30 minutes from Pegalungan. Here it is possible to see traditional boatbuilders at work, as well as weaving, mat making and beadwork. Given the luxury of time, it is a fascinating area where traditional lifestyles have not changed much. It is possible to charter a minibus along the Nabawan road to Sapulut, where you can hire boats upriver. At Sapulut, ask for Lantir (the headman, or *kepala*). He will arrange the trip upriver, which could take up to two days, with accommodation in Murut longhouses, through the gloriously named **Sapulut Adventurism Tourism Travel Company**, which he runs. As in neighbouring Sarawak, these long upriver trips can be prohibitively expensive unless you are in a decent-sized group.

Tenom → Colour map 4, B3.
Situated at the end of the North Borneo Railway, southwest of Keningau on the banks of the Sungei Lapas, Tenom is a hilly inland town, with a population of about 46,000, predominantly Chinese. Although it was the centre of an administrative district under the Chartered Company from the turn of the century, known as Fort Birch, most of the modern town was built during the Japanese occupation in the Second World War. It is in the heart of Murut country, but don't expect to see longhouses and Murut in traditional costume; many Murut have moved into individual houses, except in the remoter parts of the interior and their modernized bamboo homes are often well equipped.

The surrounding area is very fertile and the main crops are soya beans, maize and a variety of vegetables. Cocoa is also widely grown. The cocoa trees are often obscured under shade trees called *pokok belindujan*, with bright pink flowers. The durians from Tenom (and Beaufort) are thought to be the best in Sabah. *Tamu* (market) is on Sunday.

There are many **Murut villages** surrounding Tenom, all with their own churches. In some villages there is also an oversized mosque or *surau*. The **Murut Cultural Centre** ① *T088-734506*, is 10 km out of town. Run by the Sabah Museum, it displays the material culture of the Murut people including basketry, cloth and the famous Murut trampolines of *lansaran*. The *Pesta Kalimaran* is held for two days each year at the centre at the start of April and showcases the culture of the Murut through music, dance and art. It's very touristy but well worth a visit. The best longhouses are along the Padas River towards Sarawak at Kampong Marais and Kampong Kalibatang where blowpipes are still made. At **Kemabong**, 25 km south of Tenom, the Murut, who are keen dancers, have a *lansaran* dancing trampoline; a wooden platform sprung with bamboo which can support 10 Murut doing a jig.

Sabah Agricultural Park ① *T088-258529, www.sabah.net.my/agripark, 15 km northeast of Tenom, Tue-Sun 0900-1630, RM25, children RM10*, is a research initiative developed by the Sabah State Government. This is also the site of Tenom's **orchid farm**, which has been developed into an agro-tourism park. One of the more celebrated aspects of the park is the Bee Centre, highlighted in a Sir David Attenborough BBC documentary. Almost half of the world's bee species can be seen here.

Beaufort → Colour map 4, B3.
This small, sleepy, unexciting town is named after British Governor P Beaufort of the North Borneo Company, who was a lawyer and was appointed to the post despite having no experience of the East or of administration. He was savaged by Sabahan historian KG Tregonning as "the most impotent governor North Borneo ever acquired and who, in the manner of nonentities, had a town named after him." Beaufort is a quaint town, with

riverside houses built on stilts to escape the constant flooding of the Padas River. The *tamu* (market) is on Saturday.

Sipitang → *Colour map 4, B2.*

Located on the coast, Sipitang is a sleepy town with little to offer the traveller apart from a supermarket and a few hotels (see page 430). Sipitang is south of Beaufort and the closest town in Sabah to the Sarawak border. It is possible to take minibuses from Beaufort to Sipitang and on to Sindumin, where you can connect with buses bound for Lawas in Sarawak by walking across the border to Merapok. There is an immigration checkpoint here and month-long permits are given for visitors to Sarawak.

● Off the coast and south of Kota Kinabalu listings

For Sleeping and Eating price codes and other relevant information, see Essentials pages 25-30.

● Sleeping

Tunku Abdul Rahman National Park *p418*

There are significant discounts Mon-Fri.
AL Chalets, Pulau Manukan, contact **Sutera Sanctuary Lodges**, ground floor, Wisma Sabah, T088-243629, www.suterasanctuary lodges.com, for bookings on Manukan. Delightful wooden chalets, some 2 storey, with cable TV and jungle-themed bathrooms. There's a pool, restaurant, tennis and squash courts, football field, 1500-m jogging track and dive centre. Slightly overpriced.
A Gayana Island EcoResort, Lot 16, ground floor, Wisma Sabah, Jln Tun Razak, Pulau Gaya, T088-245158, www.gayana-ecoresort. com. Set on the east coast of the island, 44 a/c chalets, good service but slightly run down, restaurant serving Asian and Western dishes, private beach, reef rehabilitation research centre with some interactive programmes available for interested visitors. Activities include diving, snorkelling, fishing windsurfing, jungle trekking and yachting. Dank smelling mangroves and some reports of dirty water around the resort from the nearby shanty town.

Camping

It's possible to camp on any island. Obtain permission from the **Sabah Parks Office** in KK,

Lot 3, Block K, Sinsuran Complex, T088-211881, www.sabahparks.org.my. The island gets packed with tourists during the day, but if you camp you can enjoy a near-deserted island after 1700 when the rabble departs. Beware of leaving your clothing unattended at the edge of the forest, as monkeys have been known to run off with it!

Pulau Tiga National Park *p419*
AL-A Pulau Tiga Resort, T088-240584, www.pulau-tiga.com. Owned by **Sipadan Dive Centre** and with standard chalets, a/c superior rooms with comfortable kingsize beds and drink-making facilities. Budget triples in a longhouse. All rooms have sea views. The resort also organizes water sports, treks and trips to nearby islands. There is a Survivor package where visitors take part in numerous gruelling activities including challenges and building a shelter. Games room, **Survivor Bar** and restaurant. Many packages include meals, making it good value, especially for those staying in the cheaper rooms.

There is also a **hostel** that can hold up to 32 people. Book in advance through the Sabah Parks Office in KK, see above; there is also an attached canteen. It is possible to camp.

Pulau Labuan *p 420, map p420*
Hotels in Labuan are generally poor value compared to towns in Sabah and Sarawak. Prices at more expensive places drop during the week. There is little for budget travellers.

AL Grand Dorsett, 462 Jln Merdeka, T087-422000, www.dorsetthotels.com/labuan. This is Labuan's most upmarket offering, with a huge sparkling lobby, pool, fitness centre and an array of food and beverage outlets including **Victoria's Brasserie** with superb seafood and daily themed buffet dinners. The **Fun Pub** has live music and nightly drinks specials. Rooms are opulent and some have excellent views over the port. Wi-Fi access throughout. Staff are professional and offer top service with a smile. Recommended.

A Manikar Beach Resort, Jln Batu Manikar, T087-418700, manikar@tm.net.my. On the northwest tip of Labuan, 20 mins from town centre by free shuttle. A stylish resort built with polished wood (the owner is a timber tycoon), set in 15 ha of gardens dotted with tall palms which reach down to the beach. The 250 rooms, all sea facing with generous balconies, are very spacious, tastefully furnished, with a/c, minibar, TV, in-house video. Large pool at sea level with swim-up bar, separate children's pool, fitness centre, tennis, playroom, business centre, duty-free shop. The beach is regularly cleaned and sprayed so sandflies are not a problem, but the sea is not recommended for swimming due to jellyfish. Restaurant with excellent food and good value theme buffet nights.

A Tiara Labuan, Jln Tanjung Batu, T087-414300, F410195. On the west coast next to the golf course, 5-min taxi ride from town centre. Beautiful hotel and serviced apartments surrounding a large lotus pond and deep blue pool complete with jacuzzi. Built onto Adnan Kashoggi's old mansion, it has an Italian feel with terracotta tiles, putty pink stone, a glorious gilt fountain and long shady arcades. The original mansion now has the reception, restaurant (food mediocre) and acres of opulent lounge including an Arab section with low sofas, hubbly bubbly pipes and a marble fountain. All 25 rooms, and also the 48 serviced apartments (1 or 2 bedroom) have a/c, TV, minibar, electric hob, sink and a living room. Tanjung Batu beach across the road is rather muddy, but good for walks

when the tide is out. **Labuan Beach Restaurant** is here too. Holidaymakers, especially families, opt for the larger hotels as the **Tiara** has no organized activities or kiddy pool, but this is partly what makes it a haven of tranquillity. Recommended.

A Waterfront Labuan Financial, 1 Jln Wawasan, T087-418111, F413468. Overlooking the yacht marina (and also an industrial seascape), this place has a marina-look combined with the atmosphere of being on a luxury cruise. Over 200 rooms, all with a/c, minibar, TV and opulent fittings. The main restaurant, the **Clipper**, serves Western and local food. There is also a bar, the **Anchorage**, with live entertainment nearly every evening. Pool, tennis and health centre. The hotel manages the 50-berth marina with internationally rated facilities. The harbourmaster also organizes yacht charters and luxury cruises. Recommended.

B Ambassador 2, Lot 2 Jln Bunga Kesuma, T087-411711, F411337. Chinese-run hotel with a range of clean rooms, unfortunately reeking of cigarettes. The small single rooms are tiny and an extra RM10 will get a much more spacious 'superior' room. All rooms with TV and a/c and attached bath

B Global, U0017, Jln OKK Awang Besar (near market), T087-425201, www.skynary.com/globalhotel. Smallish rooms with cable TV, tatty carpet and attached hot-water bathroom. Many rooms are windowless. The staff are friendly enough, but this place is overpriced.

B Mariner, Jln Tg Purun (on crossroads opposite police HQ), T087-418822, mhlabuan@streamyx.net. Spic and span place with 60 clean a/c rooms with attached bathroom and TV with in-house movies. Staff are on the ball here. Fair value.

B Pantai View, Lot U0068, Jln OKK Awang Besar, T087-411339, hpv2009@hotmail.com. Recently renovated, this place is one of the better hotels in town with simple clean rooms, friendly staff and spacious rooms with Wi-Fi, cable TV, marble floor and attached hot-water bathroom. There are a couple of good Indian restaurants downstairs for late-night snacks. Free tea, coffee and mineral water. Recommended.

B Pulau Labuan, 27-28 Jln Muhibbah, T087-416288, F416255. Fair value hotel with limited character but clean a/c rooms with TV and attached bathroom. A coffee shop downstairs serves Western food and cold beer.

B Pulau Labuan Inn, Lot 8, Jln Bunga Dahlia, T087-416833, F441750. Downmarket sister of the **Pulau Labuan**, spotlessly clean but small a/c rooms.

B Sara, Jln Dewan, T087-417811, saratel@tm.net.my. Smart hotel popular with families and business folk without the seedy undertones of many other city hotels. Rooms have cable TV and attached bathroom and there is Wi-Fi on the 1st floor and lobby. Excellent Malay eatery (**Seri Malindo**).

B Victoria, U0360 Jln Tun Mustapha, T087-412411, F412550. The oldest hotel in town with an archaic lift with a concertina door. The carpets in the rooms are tatty and stained and the furniture is ancient. However, prices here are lower than most other places in town and rooms have TV, a/c and attached bathroom with lukewarm water. Seedy massage parlour leads off the lobby.

Homestays

The local government offers a variety of homestay packages with local families in traditional Malay kampongs, a great way to see the island and learn about Malay life. On offer is a stay at the water village opposite Port Victoria, a night at Sungai Labu village on the coast 12 km from the town and a 2-night stay at Bukit Kuda. Various activities are offered from joining a *gotong royong* (communal clean-up), cooking lessons, fishing trips and Kedayan cultural performances. Prices start at RM65 a night including all meals. Highly recommended. Contact **Labuan Tourism Action Council**, Labuan Sea Port Complex, T087-422622, www.labuantourism.com.my.

Papar *p423*

A Beringgis Beach Resort, Km 26, Jln Papar, Kampong Beringgis, Kinarut, T088-752333,

www.beringgis.com. Sprawling resort on the beach with spotless, stylish a/c rooms with TV, minibar and hot-water bathroom. There is a pool, restaurant, lots of Asian games such as *carom* and *congkak* and Wi-Fi access in the lobby. Very family-friendly place.

A Langkah Syabas Beach Resort, Jln Papar Baru, Kinarut, T088-752000, www.langkah syabas.com.my. 21 km south of KK. 18 chalets of varying size with spacious verandas set around the pool. A/c, fans, TV, tennis and riding centre close by, attractive tropical garden. 100 m to the beach.

B-D Seaside Travellers Inn, Km 20 Papar-KK Highway, Kinarut, T088-750555, www.infosabah.com.my/seaside. Fairly unexciting place with a/c rooms and a dorm set in a pleasant location off the beach. Tennis court, pool. Horse riding and tours can be organized.

C Mai Aman Country Rest House, Km 35, off Old Papar Rd, Kinarut, T088-914486, maiamanresort@hotmail.com. 6-room country resthouse and 12-room bush hostel. Fishing onsite in spacious grounds with an orchard and a nightclub with karaoke for those in a masochistic frame of mind.

Tambunan *p423*

The area is renowned for its rice wine (*lihing*); see it being brewed at the TVRC factory.

B-C Borneo Heritage Village Resort (also known as **TVRC**, or Tambunan Village Resort Centre), signposted off main road before town, on both sides of the Pegalam River, T088-774076, F774205. Chalets and a 'longhouse' dorm made of split bamboo. Restaurant, motel and entertainment centre (with karaoke and slot machines), hall and sports field. There are also a couple of retreat centres located about 10 mins' walk away.

C-E Gunung Emas Highlands Resort, Km 52 (about 7 km from the **Rafflesia Centre**), T013- 868 9830. Dorms, basic tree houses, a fresh climate and good views. Mini zoo and restaurant serving local food. To get there take the Rabunan or the Keningau minibus and then bus from Tambunan.

Keningau *p425*

A-L Juta, T087-337888, www.sabah.com.my/juta. The swankiest pad in town. Marble-lobbied business tower, de luxe rooms have minibar and circular beds. Attractive wooden theme. Bar with live crooners, café and restaurant. Business centre with internet access

A Perkasa, Jln Kampong Keningau, T088- 331045, www.perkasahotel.com.my. Business hotel with comfortable a/c rooms on the edge of town. There's a Chinese restaurant, coffee house and health centre.

B-C Hillview Garden Resort, 1 Jln Menawo, T087-333678, hillview@alfons.com. New place with 25 rooms. Good option.

C Kristal, Pegalan Shopping Complex, T087- 338888, F330562. Reasonable but a bit characterless. A relatively cheap option in a town lacking decent budget places.

Tenom *p426*

Orchid and Sri Jaya are both within walking distance of the bus stop.

B Perkasa, top of the hill above town, T087-735811, www.perkasahotel.com.my. A large, modern business hotel with superb views over Tenom and countryside. Rooms are spacious and attractively furnished, with TV, a/c and en suite bathroom. As guests are few and far between, the restaurant, **Tenom Perkasa**, has a limited but well-priced range of Chinese and Western dishes. Staff are friendly and helpful in arranging sightseeing. Excellent value. Recommended.

C Orchid, Block K, Jln Tun Mustapha, T087-737600, exceIng@tm.net.my. Small but friendly with clean, well-maintained rooms.

C-D Rumah Rehat Lagud Sebren (Agricultural Research Station Resthouse), agripark@sabah.net.my. Located in the heart of the agricultural park. Dorms and camping (RM10 per person). Dorms are packed during the school holidays, so book in advance.

C-D Sri Perdana, Lot 71, Jln Tun Mustapha, T087-734001. Cheap, standard rooms. Fair value.

D Sri Jaya, PO Box 47, T087-735007. The cheapest option in town, with 12 a/c rooms, shared bathroom, basic but clean.

Beaufort *p426*

A poor selection of hotels, all roughly the same and slightly overpriced. Rooms have a/c and bathrooms.

C Beaufort, Lot 19-20, Lochung Park, T087-211911, F212590. Central, a/c, 25 rooms.

C Mandarin Inn, Lot 38, Jln Beaufort Jaya, T087-212800. A/c rooms. It garners better reviews than the **Beaufort**.

Sipitang *p427*

A-B SFI Motel, SFI Housing Complex, 10 Jln Jeti, T087-802097. Clean place with a selection of a/c rooms with attached hot-water bathroom.

B-C Asanol, T087-821506. Good-value rooms with bathrooms.

B-C Shangsan, T088-821800. Comfortable rooms with a/c and TV. There is the ubiquitous coffee shop in the same street.

● Eating

Tunku Abdul Rahman National Park *p418*

Excellent restaurant on Pulau Manukan. Pulau Mamutik and Pulau Sapi each have a small shop selling limited and expensive food and drink and Sapi has some hawker-style food. For Pulau Sulug, Sapi and Mamutik take all the water you need – there is no drinkable water supply here – shower and toilet water is only provided if there has been sufficient rain.

Pulau Labuan *p420, map p420*

Several basic Chinese places to be found along Jln Merdeka and Jln OKK Awang Besar.
❤❤ Clipper, Waterfront Labuan Financial hotel. 24-hr upmarket coffee shop with local and Western cuisine. Recommended.
❤❤ Fisherman's Wharf, next to the Sara hotel on Jln Dewan Pusat Bandar. Open for lunch and dinner. This a/c place offers great

Cantonese-style seafood dishes and steamboats. Recommended.

Fong Kee, Lot 5 and 6, Jln Kemuning. While this place certainly won't win any awards for cleanliness, it's buzzing at lunchtimes as punters get stuck into generous plates of chicken rice, steaming bowls of delicious prawn mee and a daily dim sum selection.

Labuan Beach, Jln Tanjung Batu, T087-415611. International and local cuisine, breezy location on seashore, food not special but ambience makes up for it, as does well chilled draft Carlsberg. Recommended.

Pulau Labuan, Lot 27-28, Jln Muhibbah. Smart a/c interior with chandeliers. Fish sold by weight; good tiger prawns. Recommended.

Victoria's Brasserie, Grand Dorsett. Changing daily theme buffet selection that includes Penang street food, barbecue nights and, perhaps in celebration of the town's colonial past, English night. The steamboat buffet is the one to look out for though, with fresh seafood in chicken or *tom yam* broth. Recommended.

Choice, Jln Bahasa. Great selection of north and south Indian dishes from dosai to naan, and biryani to tender tandoori. The fish biryani is particularly good. Recommended.

New Sung Hwa Seafood, Jln Ujong Pasir, PCK Building. Amongst the best-value seafood restaurants in Malaysia, chilli prawns, superb grilled stingray steak, no menu. Recommended.

Restoran Sharifah, Jln Merdeka. Just opposite the ferry terminal, this busy place has a good choice of Malay and Indian Muslim dishes. The *roti prata* here fly out the kitchen at an alarming rate.

Seri Malindo, next to Sara hotel. Spotless a/c restaurant offering good *nasi campur*.

Foodstalls

Above wet market and at other end of town, along the beach next to the **Island Club**. Stalls on Jln Muhibbah opposite the end of Jln Bahasa, west of the cinema, and a few hawker stalls behind **Hotel Pulau Labuan**.

Papar *p423*

There are several run-of-the-mill coffee shops and restaurants in the old town.

Seri Takis, New Town (below the lodging house). Padang food.

Sugar Buns Bakery, Old Town. Sweet bread and thick coffee.

Keningau *p425*

Seri Wah Coffee Shop, on the corner of the central square and near some foodstalls.

Tenom *p426*

Curry Emas. Specializes in monitor lizard claypot curries, dog meat and wild cat.

Jolly, near the station. Serves Western food (including lamb chops), karaoke.

Restoran Chi Hin. Chinese coffee shop.

Sabah, Jln Datuk Yaseen. Muslim Indian food, clean and friendly.

Sapong, Perkasa hotel. Local and Western.

Y&L (Young & Lovely) Food & Entertainment, Jln Sapong (2 km out of town). Noisy, but easily the best restaurant in Tenom. Mainly Chinese food: freshwater fish (steamed *sun hok*, also known as *ikan hantu*) and venison; washed down with the local version of *air limau* (or *kitchai*) which comes with dried plums. Giant TV screen. Recommended.

Yong Lee. Coffee shop serving cheap Chinese fare in town centre.

Beaufort *p426*

Beaufort Bakery, behind Beaufort hotel, 'freshness with every bite'.

Ching Chin Restaurant. Chinese coffee shop in town centre.

Jin Jin Restaurant, behind Beaufort hotel. Chinese, popular with locals.

O Shopping

Pulau Labuan *p420, map p420*
Duty free

If you plan to take duty-free goods into Sabah or Sarawak, you have to stay on Labuan for a

Sabah's markets and trade fairs

In Sabah, an open trade fair is called a *tamu*. Locals gather to buy and sell jungle produce, handicrafts and traditional wares. *Tamu* comes from the Malay word *tetamu*, to meet, and the biggest and most famous is held at Kota Belud, north of Kota Kinabalu in Bajau country.

Tamus were fostered by the pre-war **British North Borneo Chartered Company**, when district officers would encourage villagers from miles around to trade among themselves. It was also a convenient opportunity for officials to meet with village headmen. They used

to be strictly Kadazan affairs, but today *tamus* are multicultural events. Sometimes public auctions of water buffalo and cattle are held. Some of the biggest *tamus* around the state are:
Monday: Tandek
Tuesday: Kiulu, Topokan
Wednesday: Tampuruli
Thursday: Keningau, Tambunan, Sipitang, Telipok, Simpangan
Friday: Sinsuran, Weston
Saturday: Penampang, Beaufort, Sindumin, Matunggong, Kinarut
Sunday: Tambunan, Tenom, Kota Belud, Papar, Gaya Street (KK)

minimum of 72 hrs. Labuan Duty Free, Bangunan Terminal, Jln Merdeka, T087-411573. Opened in Oct 1990, 142 years after Rajah James Brooke first declared Labuan a free port. The island's original duty-free concession did not include alcohol or cigarettes, but the new shop was given special dispensation to sell them. 2 months later the government extended the privilege to all shops on the island, which explains the absurd existence of a duty-free shop on a duty-free island. The shop claims to be the cheapest duty free in the world; however, you will find competitively priced shops in town too. **Monegain**, for example, can undercut most other outlets on the island due to the volume of merchandise it turns over: worth more than RM1 million a month. The shop owes its success to Filipino 'barter traders' who place bulk purchase orders for electronic goods or cigarettes. These are smuggled back to Zamboanga and Jolo and find their way onto Manila's streets within a week. Brunei's alcohol-free citizens also keep the shop in business; they brought liquor worth nearly RM2 million from Labuan into Brunei within the first 3 months of trading.

Handicrafts
Behind Jln Merdeka and before the fish market, there is a congregation of tin-roofed shacks housing a Filipino handicrafts and textile market and an interesting wet market.

Supermarkets
Financial Park, Jln Merdeka. Shopping complex with Milimewah supermarket. **Labuan Supermarket**, Jln Bunga Kenanga, centre of town. **Milimewah**, Lot 22-27, Lazenda Commercial Centre, Phase II, Jln Tun Mustapha, department store with supermarket on ground floor. **Thye Ann Supermarket**, central position below Sri Mutiara.

Tambunan *p423*
Handicrafts
There is a *tamu* (market) on Thu. The **Handicraft Centre**, just before the Shell petrol station, sells traditional local weaving and basketry.

▲ Activities and tours

Pulau Labuan *p420, map p420*
Diving
There are at least 10 popular dive sites around the TAR islands, with reef depths from

3-21 m, providing a variety of experiences. It's possible to dive all year with an average visibility of about 12 m. The water is cooler Nov-Feb, when visibility is not as good. For extensive information on the various coral/fish/dive sites, contact **Borneo Divers**. Borneo Divers, 1 Jln Wawasan, Waterfront Labuan Financial hotel, T087-415867, www.borneodivers.info. Specializes in 2-day packages diving on shipwrecks off Labuan for certified scuba divers. There are 4 wrecks in total and each wreck costs about RM100.

Fishing
Fishing with a hook and line is permitted but the use of spearguns and nets is not. Permits are not necessary.

Golf
Kelab Golf, Jln Tanjung Batu, T087-421810. Magnificent 9-hole golf course. You may be asked for proof of handicap or a membership card from your own club. Also tennis and a pool.

Horse riding
Labuan Horse Riding Centre, T087-466828. For a different way to go sightseeing. It offers beach and paddock rides plus lessons.

Snorkelling
Snorkel, mask and fins can be rented from boatmen at the KK jetty (although snorkelling equipment is for hire on Sapi and Manukan).

Sipitang *p427*
Tour operators
Sipitang Tours & Services, Lot 5, Tingkat 1, Kedai SEDCO, T013-869 1570.

⊖ Transport

Tunku Abdul Rahman National Park *p418*
Boat
All boats leave from the main jetty 10 mins' walk north of town.

There are regular speedboats to **KK** and **Menumbok** (used by those who want to take their car onto Labuan, 1 hr's drive from KK) and several daily boat connections with **Lawas** and **Limbang** (**Sarawak**) and **Sipitang**. There's also a regular ferry service with **Kota Kinabalu** and with **Muara** in **Brunei**.

Small boats carry 6 people and will leave for any of the islands (RM15 per person fixed price) when full, but everyone needs to agree a destination and a return time. It will cost an extra RM50 if you want to return the next day. There's a regular service for **Gayana** between 0800 and 2300, roughly every 2 hrs (RM23 return), 38 km. For 2 island hops it costs RM33 and for 3 hops, RM43. It's possible to charter a boat for tours, from RM350 for a 3-island tour or RM600 for a 5-island tour, for 12 passengers. It's possible to negotiate trips with local fishermen. Boats also leave from **Tanjung Aru Beach Hotel**. There is a RM3 park fee payable for entry to the park.

Pulau Labuan *p420, map p420*
Air
The airport is 5 km from town. There are regular flights to **KK** and **KL** (MAS and AirAsia) and to **Miri** with MASwings.

Airline offices AirAsia, c/o HMD Tours & Travel, T087-416117. MAS, airport, T087-412263.

Boat
From Bangunan Terminal Feri Penumpang next to the duty-free shop on Jln Merdeka. All times are subject to change, tickets are sold at arrival points at the ferry terminal, but can be bought in town at **Duta Muhibbah Agency**, T087-413827. 2 connections a day with **Menumbok** (RM10, the nearest mainland point) by speedboat (30 mins) or car ferry. It's a 2-hr bus ride from here to **KK**. Currently there are 2 boats a day to **Kota Kinabalu** (2½ hrs, RM31, 0830-1500). There are 2 daily boats to **Limbang** at 1230 and 1400 (1½ hrs, RM20) and one to **Lawas** (both Sarawak), at 1230 (1½ hrs, RM20).

To Brunei On weekends and public holidays in Brunei the ferries are packed and it's a scramble to get a ticket. You can reserve tickets to Brunei at the ticket office at the ferry terminal. 6 boats leave Labuan for Brunei (**Serasa Muara**) daily, 0830-1630, (1½ hrs, RM35).

Bus
Local buses around the island leave from Jln Bunga Raya.

Car
Adaras Rent-a-Car, T087-421590. Travel Rent-a-Car, T087-423600.

Taxi
Old Singapore NTUC cabs are not abundant, but are easy enough to get at the airport and around hotels. It is impossible to get a taxi after 1900 but minibuses abound.

Papar p423
Minibus
These leaves from the Bandar Lama area. There are regular connections with **KK**, 1 hr and **Beaufort**, 1 hr.

Tambunan p423
Minibus
Buses marked Tambunan go from the long-distance bus station at the bottom of Signal Hill in **KK** (1½ hrs).

Taxi
To **KK** for RM120.

Keningau p425
Minibus
These leave from the centre, by the market. Regular buses to **KK** and **Tenom**.

Taxi
KK costs around RM200

Tenom p426
Minibus
Minibuses leave from centre of town on Jln Padas. Regular connections with **Keningau** (45 mins) and **KK** (3 hrs).

Taxi
To **KK** costs around RM220 or shared taxis are available for a fraction of the price; they leave from the main street (Jln Padas).

Beaufort p426
Minibus
Minibuses leave from centre of town. Regular connections with **KK** (2 hrs, RM10).

Sipitang p427
There is a line of minibuses and taxis along the waterfront. The jetty for ferries to **Labuan** (daily departures) is a 10-min walk from the centre.

ⓞ Directory

Pulau Labuan p420, map p420
Banks HSBC, Jln Merdeka; Standard Chartered, Jln Tanjung Kubang (next to Victoria Hotel); Syarikat K Abdul Kader, money changer. **Post office** General Post Office Jln Merdeka.

Beaufort p426
Banks HSBC and Standard Chartered in centre of town. **Post office** General Post Office & Telekom, next to Hong Kong Bank.

North of Kota Kinabalu

From KK, the route heads north to the sleepy Bajau town of Kota Belud which wakes up on Sunday for its colourful tamu (market). Near the northernmost tip of the state is Kudat, the former state capital. The region north of KK is more interesting, with Gunung Kinabalu always in sight. From Kota Belud, the mountain looks completely different. It is possible to see its tail, sweeping away to the east, and its western flanks, which rise out of the rolling coastal lowlands. ▶▶ *For listings, see pages 438-439.*

Kota Belud → *For listings, see pages 438-439. Colour map 4, A3.*

This busy little town is in a beautiful location, nestling in the foothills of Mount Kinabalu on the banks of the Tempasuk River, but is of little interest except for its market. It is the heart of Bajau country, the so-called 'cowboys of the East', which is also lacking in sights.

The first Bajau to migrate to Sabah were pushed into the interior, around Kota Belud. They were originally a seafaring people but then settled as farmers in this area. The famed Bajau horsemen wear jewelled costumes, carry spears and ride bareback on ceremonial occasions. The ceremonial headdresses worn by the horsemen, called *dastars*, are woven on backstrap looms by the womenfolk of Kota Belud. Each piece takes four to six weeks to complete. Traditionally, the points of the headdress were stiffened using wax; these days, strips of cardboard are inserted into the points.

Sabah's largest **market** (*tamu*) is held every Sunday in Kota Belud behind the mosque, starting at 0600. A mix of people – Bajau, Kadazan/Dusun, Rungus, Chinese, Indian and Malay – come to sell their goods and it is a social occasion as much as a market. Aside from the wide variety of food and fresh produce on sale, there is a weekly water buffalo auction at the entrance. Visitors are strongly recommended to get there early, but don't expect to find souvenirs at these markets. However, the *tamu besar* (big market) held in November has cultural performances and handicrafts on sale.

This is an account of the market by a civil servant, posted to the KB district office in 1915: "The *tamu* itself is a babel and buzz of excitement; in little groups the natives sit and spread their wares out on the ground before them; bananas, langsats, pines and bread-fruit; and, in season, that much beloved but foul-smelling fruit, the durian. Mats and straw-hats and ropes; fowls, goats and buffaloes; pepper, gambia sirih and vegetables; rice (*padi*), sweet potatoes and *ubi kayu*; *dastars* and handkerchiefs, silver and brassware. In little booths, made of wood, with open sides and floors of split bamboos and roofs of *atap* (sago palm-leaf) squat the Chinese traders along one side of the *tamu*. For cash or barter they will sell; and many a wrangle, haggle and bargain is driven and fought before the goods change hands, or money parted with."

Tempasuk River has a wide variety of migrating birds and is a proposed conservation area. More than 127 species of bird have been recorded along this area of the coastal plain and over 500,000 birds flock here every year, many migrating from northern latitudes in winter. These include 300,000 swallows, 50,000 yellow longtails and 5000 water birds. The best period for birdwatching is October to March. Between Kota Belud and the sea are mangrove swamps with colonies of proboscis monkeys. You can hire small fishing boats in town to go down the Tempasuk River (RM20 per hour).

Tamus (markets) in Kota Belud District

Monday and Saturday: Kota Belud. Market time is 0600-1200. All *tamus* provide many places to eat.

Tuesday: Pandasan (along the Kota Belud to Kudat road).

Wednesday: Keelawat (along the Kota Belud to KK road).

Thursday: Pekan Nabalu (along the Kota Belud to Ranau road).

Friday: Taginambur (along the Kota Belud to Ranau road, 16 km from Kota Belud).

Kudat → *For listings, see pages 438-439. Colour map 4, A4.*

Kudat town, surrounded by coconut groves, is right on the northern tip of Sabah, 160 km from KK. The local people here are the Rungus, members of the Kadazan tribe. Gentle, warm and friendly, Rungus have clung to their traditions more than other Sabahan tribes and some still live in longhouses, although many are now building their own houses. Rungus longhouses are built in a distinctive style with outward-leaning walls; the Sabah State Museum incorporates many of the design features of a Rungus longhouse. The Rungus used to wear coils of copper and brass round their arms and legs and today the older generation still dress in black. They are renowned for their fine beadwork and weaving. A handful of Rungus longhouses are dotted around the Peninsula, away from Kudat town.

The East India Company first realized the potential of the Kudat Peninsula and set up a trading station on Balambanganan Island, to the north of Kudat. The settlement was finally abandoned after countless pirate raids. Kudat became the first administrative capital of Sabah in 1881, when it was founded by a Briton, AH Everett. William Hood Fletcher, the protectorate's first governor, first tried to administer the territory from Labuan, which proved impossible, so he moved to the newly founded town of Kudat which was nothing more than a handful of *atap* houses built out into the sea on stilts. It was a promising location, however, situated on an inlet of Marudu Bay, and it had a good harbour. Kudat's glory years were shortlived; it was displaced as the capital of North Borneo by Sandakan in 1883.

Today it is a busy town dominated by Chinese and Filipino traders (legal and illegal) on the coast and prostitutes trading downtown. Kudat was one of the main centres of Chinese and European migration in the late 19th century. Most of the Chinese who came to Kudat were Christian Hakka vegetable farmers: 96 of them arrived in April 1883 and they were followed by others, given free passages by the Chartered Company. More Europeans, especially the British, began to arrive on Kudat's shores with the discovery of oil in 1880. Frequent pirate attacks and an inadequate supply of drinking water forced the British to move their main administrative offices to Sandakan in 1883.

Sights

Kudat is dotted with family farms cultivating coconut trees, maize and groundnuts and keeping bees. Being by the sea, seafood is also a staple element in the diet and fisheries an important industry. Kudat is inhabited by many other ethnic groups: Bonggi, Bajau, Bugis, Kadazandusun, Obian, Orang Sungai and Suluk. The market is on Mondays.

There are some beautiful unspoilt white sand beaches north of town; the best known is **Bak-Bak**, 11 km north of Kudat. This beach, however, can get crowded at weekends and there are plans to transform it into a resort. It is signposted off the Kota Belud – Kudat road. You can take a minibus, but they are irregular; the best option is a taxi, but this is expensive.

Sikuati, 23 km west of Kudat on the northwest side of the Kudat Peninsula, has a good beach. Every Sunday, at 0800, the Rungus come to the market in this village. Local handicrafts are sold. You can get there by minibus.

Between Kota Belud and Kudat there is a marsh and coastal area with an abundance of birds. Costumed Bajau horsemen can sometimes be seen here.

The **Longhouse Experience** is possibly the most memorable thing to do in Kudat. A stay at a longhouse enables visitors to observe, enjoy and take part in the Rungus' unique lifestyle. There are two Baranggaxo longhouses with 10 units. Nearby are the village's only modern amenities, toilets and showers. During the day, the longhouse corridor is busy with Rungus womenfolk at work stringing elaborate beadworks and weaving baskets and their traditional cloth. Visitors can experience and participate in these activities. Longhouse meals are homegrown; fish and seafood come from nearby fishing villages, drinks are young coconuts and local rice wine. Evening festivities consist of the playing of gongs with dancers dressed in traditional Rungus costume. Tour companies organize trips. See box, page 334, for advice on visiting longhouses; for more details, contact **Sabah Tourism**, T088-212121, www.sabahtourism.com.

Matunggong is a less touristy area found on the road south of Kudat best known for its longhouses, though they are rather dilapidated now.

At **Kampong Gombizau**, visitors get to see bee keeping and the harvesting of beeswax, honey and royal jelly, while at **Kampong Sumangkap**, an enterprising little village, you can learn about traditional gong- and handicraft-making.

Mantanani Island → *For listings, see pages 438-439. Colour map 4, A3.*

One hour by speedboat from Kota Belud off Sabah's northwestern coast is Pulau Mantanani. The island and its surrounding islets offer a more rugged, unrestrained vibe than the sanitized upmarket resorts around Sabah's coastline. **Mantanani Island Resort** is run by **Borneo Sea**, a family business, offering a good chance to relax and get away from it all – just don't expect the island to be manicured exclusively for all your needs. While admiring another magnificent sunset, don't be surprised if all of a sudden a mother dairy cow and her calf wander up – just another resident of an island that boasts a couple of local fishing communities in addition to a diverse range of wildlife.

Mantanani also offers some more specific attractions. Surrounding waters can't be always be described as crystal clear, but they're renowned in the scuba community for their muck diving opportunities, nude branches and diverse underwater life, plus several interesting wrecks. Until recently, the waters were well known for the charming presence of Nick, a local and distinctive dugong (*Dugong dugon*) or sea cow with a small, unique indent or 'nick' – hence the name – in his tail. However, as of 2007 Nick and his friends seem to have migrated north to the southern Philippines.

Mantanani's remaining highlight has everything to do with location. Get yourself out of bed just before sunrise on a clear day and you'll be treated with a breathtakingly vast silhouette of Mount Kinabalu rising more than 4 km into the morning sky, framed in golden light as the sun rises behind it. Whilst daylight has already reached most of Sabah, a huge triangular shadow, tens of kilometres across, holds Mantanani and the nearby coast in darkness for a just a few minutes longer – a truly spectacular way to begin your day on the island. On the not uncommon overcast days, dark storm clouds laced with lightning around the mountains summit can also be quite beautiful.

For Sleeping and Eating price codes and other relevant information, see Essentials pages 25-30.

Sleeping

Kota Belud *p435*

B-C Impian Siu Motel, Kg Sempirai, Jln Kuala Abai, T088-976617. Just 10 rooms in this reasonable place.

B-C Kota Belud Travellers Lodge, Lot 6, Plaza Kong Guan, T088-977228. Simple place with a variety of clean rooms.

Homestays

There's no limit to your length of stay. Live with and be treated as part of the family, getting invited to celebrations such as weddings. Activities include buffalo riding, jungle trekking, river swimming, cultural dancing, visits to local *tamus*, padi planting. Contact **Nature Heritage Travel and Tours**, ground floor, Wisma Sabah, KK, T088-318747, nhtt@nature-heritage.com, or **Taginambur Homestay**, T088-976595, taginambur@gmail.com. Very affordable for young travellers and an excellent way to learn the language and gain an in-depth knowledge of the culture.

Kudat *p436*

The **Sunrise** and **Oriental** hotels are within walking distance of the bus stop.
A Kudat Golf & Marina Resort, off Jln Urus Setia, T088-611211, www.kudatgolf marinaresort.com. A spanking-new orange monster next to a marina. Main attraction is the 18-hole championship golf course.
C Greenland, Lot 9/10, Block E, Sedco Shophouse (new town), T088-613211, F611854. A/c, standard rooms, shared bath.
C Kinabalu, Kudat Old Town, Jln Melor, T088-613888, F615388. A/c, clean, average value.
D Southern, Kudat Old Town, T088-613133. 10 rooms, but quite cheap and reasonable value compared with others in this category.

Mantanani Island *p437*

Book through **KK Tours & Travel**, page 415, or directly through **Borneo Sea Adventures**, page 414.

KK-based dive operation **Scuba Paradise**, see page 415, also runs day trips diving (RM560 per person) and snorkelling (RM380 per person) around Mantanani.
L-AL Mantanani Resort, book at Borneo Sea Adventures, www.bornsea.com/mantanani. A bit rough round the edges, but the hexagonal en suite chalets are surprisingly elegant inside, and the home cooking is fresh and supplied in vast quantities. Prices are per person and usually sold in packages inclusive of food and activities: kayaking, snorkelling, up to 3 boat dives and unlimited shore dives per day. Good value if you use the island's facilities. Published rates are RM1900 (US$550) for a 3-day/2-night package (including transport to and from KK). Discounts for non-divers and children sharing with adults. Drinks and equipment hire are extra.

Eating

Kota Belud *p435*

There are several Indian coffee shops around the main square.
† **Bismillah Restoran**, 35 Jln Keruak (main square). Excellent *roti telur*.
† **Indonesia Restoran**, next to the car park behind the **Kota Belud Hotel**.

Festivals and events

Kota Belud *p435*

Nov The annual *Tamu Besar* includes a parade and equestrian games by the Bajau horsemen, a very colourful event. Contact Sabah Tourism for some more information.

O Shopping

Kota Belud p435
Daily market in main square, fish market south of the square. Large *tamu* every Sun and an annual *tamu besar* with a wide variety of local handicrafts.

⊖ Transport

Kota Belud p435
Minibus
From main square. Regular connections with **KK**, **Kudat** and Ranau. It takes 90 mins for **KK** to **Kudat** and Kota Belud could be a stop along the way, as connections are easy.

Kudat p436
Minibus
Minibuses leave from Jln Lo Thien Hock. Regular connections with **KK**, 4 hrs.

⊙ Directory

Kota Belud p435
Banks Bank Pertanian, Jln Kudat; Public Bank Berhad, Jln Kota Kinabalu; Sabah Finance, Jln Ranau.

Kudat p436
Banks Standard Chartered Bank, Jln Lo Thien Hock.

Gunung Kinabalu National Park

→ *Colour map 4, A3.*

Gunung Kinabalu is the pride of Sabah, the focal point of the national park and probably the most magnificent sight in Borneo. In recognition of this, the park was declared a World Heritage Site by UNESCO in 2000 – a first for Malaysia. Although Gunung Kinabalu has foothills, its dramatic rockfaces, with cloud swirling around them, loom starkly out of the jungle. The view from the top is unsurpassed and on a clear day you can see the shadow of the mountain in the South China Sea, over 50 km away – Mantanani Island, page 437, is a great spot to see the mountain and its shadow from a different perspective. Even if you're not planning on climbing Gunung Kinabalu itself, it's well worth spending a few days exploring the park, one of the most biodiverse areas in Borneo.
▶▶ *For listings, see pages 447-449.*

Best time to visit
The average rainfall is 400 cm a year, with an average temperature of 20°C at Park HQ but at Panar Laban it can drop below freezing at night. With the wind chill factor on the summit, it feels very cold. The best time to climb Gunung Kinabalu is in the dry season between March and April when views are clearest. The worst time has traditionally been November to December during the monsoon, although wet or dry periods can occur at any time of the year. Avoid weekends, school and public holidays if possible.

The park is occasionally closed to climbers. Contact the **Sutera Sanctuary Lodges**, see below, to check the mountain is open for climbing when you visit.

Note The climb has become extremely popular in the last few years and it is worth booking a slot as early as possible.

Permits, entrance fees and accommodation
It costs RM100 per person (RM40 per child) to climb Gunung Kinabalu; a RM15 entry fee must be paid on arrival by all park visitors and compulsory insurance costs RM7. The park

is run by **Sutera Sanctuary Lodges** ⓘ *ground floor of Wisma Sabah, Kota Kinabalu, T088-243629, www.suterasanctuarylodges,com, Mon-Fri 0900-1830, Sat 0900-1630, Sun 0900-1500*. All accommodation in the park must be booked in advance through its office.
▸▸ *See also Sleeping, page 447.*

Equipment

A thick jacket is recommended, but at the very least you should have a light waterproof or windcheater to beat the wind chill on the summit. You can hire jackets from Laban Rata but you need to book ahead as there are limited numbers. Carry a dry sweater and socks in your backpack and change just before you get to the peak – if it's raining the damp chill is worse than the actual cold. There are small shops at Park HQ and Laban Rata that sell gloves, hats, raincoats, torches and food for the climb (but it's cheaper if you stock up in KK). It is also best to bring a sweater or thick shirts; the shops in Wisma Merdeka sell cheap woollies. Walking boots are recommended, but not essential; many people climb the mountain in trainers. Stock up on food, chocolate and drinking water in KK the day before. Essential items include a torch, toilet paper, water bottle, plasters, headache pills and suntan lotion. A hat is good for guarding against the sun and the cold. Lockers are available, RM1 per item, at the Park HQ reception office. Sleeping bags are provided free of charge in the **Laban Rata Resthouse**; essential for a good night's sleep. The resthouse also has hot-water showers, but soap and towels are not provided. Some of the rooms are well heated, cheaper ones leave you to freeze.

Guides

Hiring a guide is compulsory: RM70 for the round trip (one to three people), RM80 for the Mesilau trail. Porters are available for between RM40 and RM62 (for 10 kg carried). Guides and porters should be reserved at least a day in advance at the Park HQ or at **Sutera Sanctuary Lodges**. On the morning of your climb, go to the HQ and a guide will be assigned to you. While a tour will cost around RM750 each (often excluding the RM100 climbing permit fee), a group of you can hire a taxi, book dorm accommodation and share a guide for the climb for slightly less per person than a tour, including all the fees. If you are doing it by yourselves it is best to get to the park a day in advance, and stay at Park HQ to get up early for the first part of the climb to Laban Rata. Alternatively, you can get up at 0600 in KK and try and arrive at the Park HQ before 0900 to be sure of finding a guide.

If you are desperate to go, short of time and have been informed that there is no accommodation available on the mountain in the next few days (as can happen during busy periods such as school holidays), it might still be worth turning up in person to enquire, but be aware that some hardy enthusiasts have spent nights sleeping on cold floors waiting for a spot. A shuttle bus to the park leaves from the Sutera Harbour in KK at 0715, and will drop you outside Park HQ around 0930; arrive no later if you are hoping to climb the mountain that day. You may still be able to pick up a guide if you are there before 1000, although you will be unlikely to find anyone else to share with; the climb should begin around 1100, allowing enough time to reach Laban Rata. Reports suggest that beds/mattresses up the mountain can sometimes be found if someone turns up in person. This method should be an absolute last resort, and it is by no means guaranteed to work. If things don't work out, accommodation will probably be available at Park HQ, or there are a number of good places within 2 km of the park.

Park HQ

These located a short walk from the main Ranau–KK road, and all the accommodation and restaurants are within 15 minutes' walk from the main compound. There is a shop next to the Park HQ that has good books on the mountain and its flora and fauna. Slide and film shows are held in the mini-theatre in the administration building at 1400 during the week

Gunung Kinabalu Trail

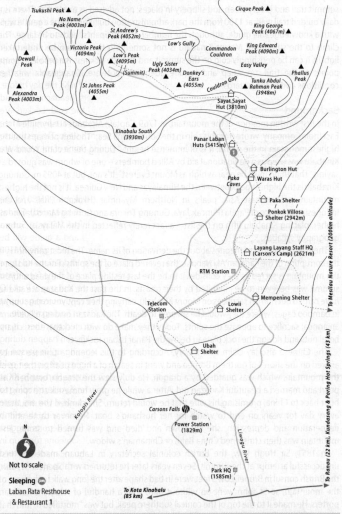

Tsukushi Peak ▲

No Name
Peak (4003m) ▲

Cirque Peak ▲

St Andrew's
Peak (4052m) ▲

King George
Peak (4067m) ▲

Victoria Peak
(4094m) ▲

Low's Gully

Commandon
Couldron

King Edward
Peak (4090m) ▲

Dewall
Peak ▲

Low's Peak
(4095m)
(Summit) ▲

Ugly Sister
Peak (4034m) ▲

Donkey's
Ears
(4055m) ▲

Easy Valley

Phallus
Peak ▲

St Johns Peak
(4055m) ▲

Couldron Gap

Tunku Abdul
Rahman Peak
(3948m) ▲

Alexandra
Peak (4003m) ▲

Sayat Sayat
Hut (3810m)

Kinabalu South
(3930m) ▲

Panar Laban
Huts (3415m)

Burlington Hut
Waras Hut

Paka
Caves

Paka Shelter

Ponkok Villosa
Shelter (2942m)

Layang Layang Staff HQ
(Carson's Camp) (2621m)

RTM Station

► To Mesilau Nature Resort (2000m altitude)

Mempening Shelter

Telecom
Station

Lowii
Shelter

Ubah
Shelter

Kolopis River

Carsons Falls

Power Station
(1829m)

Liwogu River

► To Ranau (22 km), Kundasang & Poring Hot Springs (43 km)

N

Not to scale

Park HQ
(1585m)

To Kota Kinabalu
(85 km)

Sleeping
Laban Rata Resthouse
& Restaurant **1**

and at 1930 on weekends and public holidays (RM2), while naturalists give escorted trail walks every morning at 1100 (RM3). The museum displays information on local flora and fauna, beetles and foot-long stick insects.

Treks

A small colour pamphlet, *Mount Kinabalu/A Guide to the Summit Trail*, published by Sabah Parks, are a good guide to the wildlife and the trail itself. Most treks are well used and are easy walks, but the **Liwagu Trail** is a good three- to four-hour trek up to where it joins the summit trail and is very steep and slippery in places; not advised as a solo trip. There is a daily guided trail walk at 1100 from the park administration building. This is a gentle walk with a knowledgeable guide, although the number of participants tends to be large. The climb to the summit of Mount Kinabalu is not something that should be undertaken lightly. It can be perishingly cold on the summit and altitude sickness is a problem. Some points of the trail are steep and require adequate footware. Changeable weather conditions add to the hazards.

Background

In the first written mention of the mountain, in 1769, Captain Alexander Dalrymple of the East India Company, wrote from his ship in the South China Sea: "Though perhaps not the highest mountain in the world, it is of immense height." During the Second World War Kinabalu was used as a navigational aid by Allied bombers – one of whom was quoted as saying "That thing must be near as high as Mount Everest". It's not, but at 4095 m, Gunung Kinabalu is the highest peak between the Himalayas and New Guinea. It is not the highest mountain in Southeast Asia: peaks in Northern Myanmar (Hkakabo Razi) and the Indonesian province of Papua (Puncak Jaya, Gunung Trikora and Gunung Mandala) are all higher, placing Kinabalu fifth on the list – a fact rarely reflected in the Malaysian school geography syllabus.

There are a number of theories about the derivation of its name. The most convincing is the corruption of the Kadazan Aki Nabulu, 'the revered place of the spirits'. For the Kadazan, the mountain is sacred as they consider it to be the last resting place of the dead and the summit was believed to be inhabited by their ghosts. In the past the Kadazan are said to have carried out human sacrifices on Mount Kinabalu, carrying their captives to the summit in bamboo cages, where they would be speared to death. The Kadazan guides still perform an annual sacrifice to appease the spirits. Today they make do with chickens, eggs, cigars, betel nuts and rice on the rock plateau below the Panar Laban rockface.

The Chinese also lay claim to a theory. According to this legend, a Chinese prince arrived on the shores of northern Borneo and went in search of a huge pearl on the top of the mountain, which was guarded by a dragon. He duly slew the dragon, grabbed the pearl and married a beautiful Kadazan girl. After a while he grew homesick and took the boat back to China, promising his wife that he would return. She climbed the mountain every day for years on end to watch for her husband's boat. He never came and in desperation and depression, she lay down and died and was turned to stone. The mountain was then christened China Balu, or Chinaman's widow.

In 1851, Sir Hugh Low, the British colonial secretary in Labuan, made the first unsuccessful attempt at the summit. Seven years later he returned with Spencer St John, the British consul in Brunei. Low's feet were in bad shape after the long walk to the base of the mountain, so St John went on without him, with a handful of reluctant Kadazan porters. He made it to the top of the conical southern peak, but was "mortified to find that the most westerly [peak] and another to the east appeared higher than where I sat." He retreated and returned three months later with Low, but again failed to reach the summit, now called Low's Peak (standing at 4095 m above sea level). It remained unconquered for another 30 years. The first to reach the summit was John Whitehead, a zoologist, in 1888. Whitehead spent several months on the mountain collecting birds and mammals and many of the more spectacular species bear either Low's or Whitehead's name. More scientists followed and then a trickle of tourists, but it was not until 1964, when Kinabalu Park (encompassing 75,000 ha) was gazetted, that the 8.5-km trail to the summit was opened. Today the mountain attracts 200,000 visitors a year. Although the majority are day visitors who do not climb the peak, the number of climbers is steadily increasing, with at least 30,000 making the attempt each year.

In plan, the top of the mountain is U-shaped, with bare rock plateaux. Several peaks stand proud of these plateaux, around the edge of the U; the space between the western and eastern arms is the spectacular gully known as Low's Gully. No one has ever scaled its precipitous walls, nor has anyone climbed the Northern Ridge (an extension of the eastern arm) from the back of the mountain. From Low's Peak, the eastern peaks, just 1.5 km away, look within easy reach. As John Briggs points out in his book *Mountains of Malaysia*, "It seems so close, yet it is one of the most difficult places to get to in the whole of Borneo".

Flora and fauna

The range of climatic zones on the mountain has led to the incredible diversity of plant and animal life. Kinabalu Park is the meeting point of plants from Asia and Australasia. There are thought to be more than 1200 species of orchid alone and this does not include the innumerable mosses, ferns and fungi. These flowering plants of Kinabalu are said to represent more than half the families of flowering plants in the world. Within the space of 3 km, the vegetation changes from lowland tropical rainforest to alpine meadow and cloud forest. The jungle reaches up to 1300 m; above that, to a height of 1800 m, is the lower montane zone, dominated by 60 species of oak and chestnut; above 2000 m is the upper montane zone with true cloud forest, orchids, rhododendrons and pitcher plants. Above 2600 m, growing among the crags and crevices of the summit rock plateau are gnarled tea trees (*Leptospermums*) and stunted rhododendrons. Above 3300 m, the soil disappears, leaving only club mosses, sedges and Low's buttercups (*Ranunculus lowii*), which are alpine meadow flowers.

Among the most unusual of Kinabalu's flora is the world's largest flower, the rust-coloured rafflesia (see box, page 424). It can usually only be found in the section of the park closest to Poring Hot Springs. Rafflesia are hard to find as they only flower for a couple of weeks between August and December.

Kinabalu is also famous for the carnivorous pitcher plants, which grow to varying sizes on the mountain. A detailed guide to the pitcher plants of Kinabalu can be bought in the shop at Park HQ. Nine different species have been recorded on Kinabalu. The largest is the giant Rajah Brooke's pitcher plant; Spencer St John claimed to have found one of these containing a drowned rat floating in four litres of water. Insects are attracted by the scent and, when they settle on the lip of the plant, they cannot maintain a foothold on the waxy, ribbed surface. At the base of the pitcher is an enzymic fluid which digests the 'catch'.

Rhododendrons line the trail throughout the mossy forest (there are 29 species in the park), especially above the Paka Cave area. One of the most beautiful is the copper-leafed rhododendron, with orange flowers and leaves with coppery scales underneath. There are an estimated 1000 species of orchid in the park, along with 621 species of fern and 52 palm species.

It is difficult to see wildlife on the climb to the summit as the trail is well used, although tree shrews and squirrels are common on the lower trails. There are, however, more than 100 species of mammal living in the park. The Kinabalu summit rats, which are always on cue to welcome climbers to Low's Peak at dawn, and nocturnal ferret badgers are the only true montane mammals in Sabah. As the trees thin with altitude, it is often possible to see tree shrews and squirrels, of which there are more than 28 species in the park. Large mammals, such as flying lemurs, red-leaf monkeys, wild pigs, orang-utan and deer, are lowland forest dwellers. Nocturnal species include the slow loris (*Nycticebus coucang*) and the mischievous-looking bug-eyed tarsier (*Tarsius bancanus*). If heading to Kinabalu specifically to spot wildlife, then the longer, less visited Mesilau Trail is almost certainly a more productive option.

More than half of Borneo's 518 species of bird have also been recorded in Kinabalu Park, but the variety of species decreases with height. Two of the species living above 2500 m are endemic to the mountain: the Kinabalu friendly warbler and the Kinabalu mountain blackbird.

More than 61 species of frog and toad and 100 species of reptile live here. Perhaps the most interesting frog in residence is the horned frog, which can be impossible to spot thanks to its mastery of camouflage. The giant toad is common at lower altitudes; it's covered with warts, which are poisonous glands. When disturbed, these squirt a stinking, toxic liquid. Other frogs found in the park include the big-headed leaf-litter frog, whose head is bigger than the rest of its body, and the green stream shrub frog, who has a magnificent metallic green body, but is deadly if swallowed by any predator.

The famous flying tree snake has been seen in the park. It spreads its skin flaps, which act as a parachute when the snake leaps blindly from one tree to another.

There are nearly 30 species of fish in the park's rivers, including the unusual Borneo sucker fish (*Gastomyzon borneensis*), which attaches itself to rocks in fast- flowing streams. One Sabah Parks publication likens them to 'underwater cows', grazing on algae as they move slowly over the rocks.

Walkers and climbers are more likely to come across the park's abundant insect life than anything else. Examples include pill millipedes, rhinoceros beetles, the emerald green and turquoise jewel beetles, stick insects, 'flying peapods', cicadas, and a vast array of moths (including the giant atlas moth) and butterflies (including the magnificent emerald green and black Rajah Brooke's birdwing).

Gunung Kinabalu

The climb to the summit and back should take two days; four to six hours from Park HQ at 1585 m to the **Laban Rata Resthouse** (3550 m) on the first day. It is three hours to the summit for dawn on the second day, returning to the Park HQ at around 1200 hours on the second day.

Note There is a slightly tougher walk starting from Mesilau which takes two to three hours longer to get to Laban Rata, but which has far less tourists; the guide fee is slightly higher on this route at RM84 per person and porter fees to Laban Rata from Mesilau are RM88 per person.

Asia's first **Via Ferrata** (iron road) ① *www.mountaintorq.com,* opened in 2007 and is also the world's highest. It is still relatively quiet with three possible routes taking between two to five hours to complete. The trail uses fixed rungs, rails, cables and stemples wrapped around the north face of the mountain. This slightly hair-raising adventure provides an experience akin to mountain climbing and a chance to see parts of the mountain usually never experienced by most visitors. The trail starts at Panar Laban Rock Face (3300 m) and reaches its highest point at 3800 m.

Gurkha soldiers and others have made it to the summit and back in well under three hours. For the really keen, or foolhardy, depending on your perspective, there is also the annual Kinabalu Climbathon (www.climbathon.sabahtourism.com) held in early October. Having said that the climb to the top requires no special skills, the death of a British teenage girl on the mountain in 2001 highlights the hazards of climbing an unfamiliar mountain where changes in the weather can be sudden and dramatic. Keep to the trails and keep your group together.

A minibus for 12 people can take groups from headquarters to the power station at 1829 m where the trail starts (RM5 per person). It is a 25-minute walk from the power station to the first shelter. The trail splits in two soon afterwards, the left goes to the radio station and the helipad and the right towards the summit. The next stop is **Layang Layang staff headquarters** (with drinking water, cooking facilities and accommodation), also known as **Carson's Camp** (2621 m). There is one more shelter, **Ponbok Villosa** at 2942 m, about 45 minutes from Carson's Camp, before the stop at the path to **Paka Caves**, which is really just an overhanging rock by a stream. Paka is a 10-minute detour to the left, where Low and St John made their camps.

From the cave/fifth shelter the vegetation thins out and it is a steep climb to **Panar Laban huts** – which includes the well-equipped **Laban Rata Resthouse** – affording magnificent views at sunset and in the early morning. The name Panar Laban is derived from Kadazan words meaning Place of Sacrifice: early explorers had to make a sacrifice here to appease the spirits and this ritual is still performed by the Kadazan once a year. **Sayat Sayat** (3810 m) hut – named after the ubiquitous shrubby tea tree – is an hour further on, above the Panar Laban rockface. Most climbers reach Panar Laban (or the other huts) in the early afternoon in order to rest up for a 0300 start the next morning to reach the summit by sunrise. This second part of the trail – 3 km long – is more demanding technically, but the trail is well laid out with regular resting points every 500 m. Ladders, handrails and ropes are provided for the steeper parts (essential in the wet, as the granite slabs can be very slippery). The final 1 km has no hand rails or ropes but is less steep. The first two hours after dawn are the most likely to be cloud free. For enthusiasts interested in alternative routes to the summit, John Briggs's *Mountains of Malaysia* provides a detailed guide to the climb.

Mountain Garden
ⓘ *Tours leave at 0900, 1200, 1500; the garden is closed at other times, RM5.*
Situated behind the park administration building, this landscaped garden has species from the mid-levels of the mountain, which have been planted in natural surroundings.

Mesilau Nature Resort
This rainforest resort nestles at the foot of Mount Kinabalu at 2000 m. The main attractions are the cool climate and the superb views up the mountain and across the plains toward Ranau and the sea. It is possible to scale the peaks of the mountain using the resort as a base, providing an alternative route to Low's Peak. Taking this new trail, one would join the main trail at Layang Layang. Alternatively, there are a number of walks to be made around the reserve in this secluded location.

Poring → *Colour map 2, A1.*

ⓘ *T088-878801, if you've already paid the entrance fee to the national park, keep your ticket for entrance to the hot springs; if staying at Poring there is no charge and the baths can be used all night; permits are not necessary.*

Poring lies 43 km from Gunung Kinabalu Park HQ and is part of the national park. The **hot sulphur baths** ⓘ *RM15 per hr; sulphur bath and jacuzzi, RM20 per hr*, were installed during the Japanese occupation of the Second World War for the jungle-weary Japanese troops. There are individual concrete pools that can fit two people, with taps for hot- and cold-spring mineral water; once in your bath you are in complete privacy. However, many visitors now complain that the water is no longer hot, more like lukewarm. The springs are on the other side of the Mamut River from the entrance, over a suspension bridge. They are a fantastic antidote to tiredness after a tough climb up Gunung Kinabalu. There is also a cold-water rock pool. The pools are in a beautiful garden setting of hibiscus and other tropical flowers, trees and thousands of butterflies. There are some quite luxurious private cabin baths available and also large baths which hold up to eight people. The de luxe cabins have lounge areas and jacuzzis. The Kadazans named the area Poring after the towering bamboos of that name nearby.

The **jungle canopy walk** ⓘ *daily 0900-1600, RM5, camera RM5, video RM30, guides available*, at Poring is a rope walkway 35 m above the ground, which provides a monkey's-eye view of the jungle; springy but quite safe. The entrance is five minutes' walk from the hot springs and the canopy walkway is 15 minutes' walk from the entrance. The canopy walkway at Danum Valley is far more exciting. If the weather is clear at Ranau, it is generally safe to assume that the canopy walk will also be clear.

Kipungit Falls are only about 10 minutes' walk from Poring and swimming is possible here. Follow the trail further up the hill and after 15 minutes you come to bat caves; a large overhanging boulder provides shelter and a home for the bats.

The **Langanan Waterfall** trail takes 90 minutes one way, is uphill, but worth it. There is another hard, 90-minute trail to **Bat Cave** (inhabited by what seems to be a truly stupendous number of bats) and a waterfall. The **Butterfly Farm** ⓘ *daily 0900-1600, RM4*, was established close to the springs by a Japanese-backed firm in 1992 and is very educational in the descriptions of butterflies and other insects.

There is also an information centre, a rafflesia centre, orchid centre, aviary and tropical garden at Poring. It is better not to visit the hot springs at the weekend or on public holidays if you want to relax in a peaceful atmosphere. Minibuses to the springs leave Park HQ at 0900, 1300, 1600; alternatively, flag down a bus/minibus to Ranau on the main road a two-minute walk from HQ and take a taxi from there to Poring.

Ranau and Kundasang → *Colour map 2, A1.*

The Ranau plateau, surrounding the Kinabalu massif, is one of the richest farming areas in Sabah and much of the forest not in the park has now been devastated by market gardeners. Even within the national park's boundaries, on the lower slopes of Mount Kinabalu itself, shifting cultivators have clear-felled tracts of jungle and planted their patches. More than 1000 ha are now planted out with spinach, cabbage, cauliflower, asparagus, broccoli and tomatoes, supplying much of Borneo.

Kundasang and Ranau are unremarkable towns a few kilometres apart; the latter is bigger. The **war memorial**, behind Kundasang, which unfortunately looks like Colditz, is in memory of those who died in the death march in the Second World War (see box, page 485). The walled gardens represent the national gardens of Borneo, Australia and the UK.

Mentapok and Monkobo are southwest of Ranau. Both are rarely climbed. Mentapok, 1581 m, can be reached in 1½ days from Kampong Mireru, a village at the base of the mountain. A logging track provides easy access halfway up the south side of the mountain. Monkobo is most easily climbed from the northwest, a logging track from Telupid goes up to 900 m and from here it is a two-hour trek to the top. It is advisable to take guides, organized from Ranau or one of the nearby villages.

Some 17 km on the road to Sandakan is the **Sabah Tea Garden** ① *Km 17, Ranau–Sandakan Rd, Kampung Nalapak, T088-440882, www.sabahtea.net,* the only organic tea farm in Borneo and offering a range of activities other than just sitting back with a cuppa and admiring the views. They offer a variety of packages including a rainforest adventure, where tourists sleep in a bamboo forest and swim in the Sapayon River before learning some survival cooking techniques. More genteel activities include tea tree planting and a factory visit. There is also some good accommodation available here.

⊚ Gunung Kinabalu National Park listings

For Sleeping and Eating price codes and other relevant information, see Essentials pages 25-30.

⊜ Sleeping

Gunung Kinabalu Park *p439, map p441*
Management of the park is privatized. It is managed by **Sutera Sanctuary Lodges**, all accommodation in the park must be booked in advance through its office: ground floor, Wisma Sabah, KK, T088-243629, www.sutera sanctuarylodges.com, Mon-Fri 0900-1830, Sat 0900-1630, Sun 0900-1500. Prices have shot up dramatically recently, putting what was quite reasonably priced accommodation out of the reach of many visitors.

Park HQ *p441*
Each cabin has a fireplace, kitchen, shower, gas cooker, fridge, and cooking and eating utensils. Electricity, water and firewood are provided free of charge. The rates quoted below are reduced on weekdays. The most expensive option at the Park HQ is the **Rajah Lodge**, sleeping 6 people, RM8000 for the whole lodge with all meals and a personal butler; very comfortable. **Kinabalu Lodge**, 6 people, RM3500 per night, all meals, cable TV, also very comfortable. The **Summit Lodge**, 4 people, RM2275 per night, and the **Garden Lodge**, 4 people, RM2275 per night, are both very comfortable and meals are included; also

cable TV; nice and toasty inside. **Nepenthes Lodge**, 4 people, RM760 per night. **Peak Lodge**, 4 people, RM660 per night. **Ligawu Suite**, 2 people, RM490 per night, cable TV, breakfast and hot showers. **Hill Lodge**, 2 people, RM390 per night. **Rock Twin Share**, 2 people, RM350 per night, has a shared bathroom and common area with fireplace. **Grace Hostel**, unheated dorms with shared bathroom for RM120 per bed, includes breakfast. The **Rock Hostel** offers much of the same for the same price.

The following are close to Park HQ.
A Haleluyah Retreat Centre, Jln Linouh, Km 61, Tuaran-Ranau Highway, T088-423993, kandiu@tm.net.my. This Christian centre is open to all, located at 1500 m close to the foot of Mount Kinabalu. It makes a good stop-off point before climbing the mountain. Set amidst natural jungle and approximately 15 mins' walk from the Park HQ, it is isolated but safe, clean, friendly and with a relaxing atmosphere. Cooking and washing facilities, camping area, multi-purpose hall and meeting rooms make it a suitable venue for seminars, meetings, youth camps or family holidays. Reasonably priced food in the canteen, dorm beds also available.
A-C Sonny's Cottage, T088-750555. 6 rooms with spectacular views.
A-D D'Villa Lodge (Rina Ria Lodge), Batu 36, Jln Tinompok, Ranau, T088-889282,

www.dvillalodge.com. About 1 km from the Kinabalu National Park, rooms have attached kitchen and basic bathroom, armchairs and beautiful views. There's also a shop. Prices increase at weekends. Dorms also available (RM30). Breakfast included.

B Kinabalu Rose Cabin, Km18, Ranau-Kinasaraban Rd, Kundasang, T088-889233, www.kinabalurosecabin.8m.com. A/c, restaurant, 2 km from the park, towards golf course (30% discount to golfers); range of rooms, suites all with mountain views, attached bathroom with hot water and TV. There's also a restaurant and internet access.

C Mountain View Motel, 5 km east of Kinabalu National Park on the Ranau-Tamparuli Highway, T088-875389, bbmt kinabalu@hotmail.com. Breakfast included, hot water, restaurant, laundry facilitites, local tours, climbing gear available for hire. The corrugated iron roof can be loud when it rains.

E Mountain Resthouse and Restaurant, T088-771109. Located just outside the park, this has small 4-person dorms that are cheaper, newer, cleaner and warmer than the park dorms. Spectacular views. Arguably preferable to the park accommodation.

Gunung Kinabalu *p444*

Laban Rata Resthouse, Panar Laban. 54 rooms (space is often made for extra people by laying out matresses on the restaurant floor), a good-quality though pricey canteen (but sometimes rather limited food – it all has to be walked up the mountain) and hot-water showers, plus electricity and heated rooms; bedding provided. Most expensive rooms are the heated de luxe Buttercup rooms at RM765 per night, beds in the heated dorms go for a pricey RM395 per bed. Rates include all meals and a packed lunch.

Mesilau Nature Resort *p445*

L-A Mesilau Nature Resort, managed by Sutera Sanctuary Lodges, T088-871733, www.suterasanctuarylodges.com. A range of tasteful wooden chalets that blend neatly into their surroundings, housing up to 4

people (RM2275 per unit) with all meals, personal butler, cable TV, heater and hot-water bathroom. More budget accommodation provided in dorms in the hostel (RM120 per bed). Laundry, gift shop and regular educational talks. The nature reserve is situated close to the **Mount Kinabalu Golf Club**, a few mins' drive away.

Poring *p446*

Booking recommended. Camping RM6. The following are all **E: Serindit Hostel**, dorms with space for 20 people, RM120 per person; **Serindit twin share**, 2 people, RM350 per chalet, shared bathroom; **Jungle Lodge**, 2 people, huge rooms, jungle shower, living room with cable TV, RM420 per unit; **River Lodge**, 4 people, RM740 per unit, comfortable, **Palm Villa** RM3500, 6 people, personal butler. All meals.

Ranau and Kundasang *p446*

L-A Zen Garden Resorts, Km 2, Jln Mohimboyan Kibas, T088-889242, www.zengarden resort.com/index.cfm. 3/4-room lodges with equipped kitchen, living room with TV and bedroom. Also, rooms with TV and some with fridge for considerably less. Very pleasant environment with some wonderful views of the mountains. The biggest resort in the area.

AL-A Mount Kinabalu Heritage Resort and Spa, visible on the hill above Kundasang (a further 1 km down the road from Kinabalu Pine), T088-889511, www.perkasahotel. com.my. Recently revamped with some lovely but pricey accommodation available in stilted chalets with excellent views. Other rooms in the main block are less impressive. Very professional spa centre on the 6th floor offering rejeuvnating therapies to tired walkers.

B Kinabalu Pine Resort, Kampong Kundasang, T088-889388, www.kinabalupine resort.com. A/c rooms with TV constructed from selangan batu hardwood and with great mountain views in this attractive but isolated area, 6 km from the national park. Good value.

B-D Sabah Tea House, KM 17 Ranau–Sandakan Rd, Kampung Nalapak, T088-

889330, www.sabahtea.com. Good selection of accommodation including clean chalets, funky Rungus longhouse with shared bathroom and a campsite with space for 100.

⦿ Eating

Gunung Kinabalu Park *p439, map p441*
The best places to stay are at Park HQ but the restaurants are rather spread out, requiring a walk between buffet and bed.

🍴 **Liwagu**. Open 1100-2130. Beer, chips, curries and other international treats.
🍴 **Balsam Cafeteria**. Open 0630-2130. The cheaper option for filling Malay staples. Breakfast is included in the price of all accommodation.

There are cooking facilities at the hostels plus good quality meals are provided for guests at Rajah Lodge, Summit Lodge, Garden Lodge and Kinabalu Lodge.

Mesilau Nature Resort *p445*
🍴 **Renanthera Terrace**. Open 0700-2200. Provides the 3 main meals.
🍴 **Renanthera Café**. Open 0700-2200. Has a stunning veranda offering great views of the mountain.

Poring *p446*
🍴 **Rainforest**. Open 0700-2200. Comfortable place to kick back and get stuck into Malay, Chinese and international fare.
🍴 **Restaurant**. Quite good Chinese and Malay food at the springs and stalls outside the park.

Ranau and Kundasang *p446*
There are several restaurants along the roads serving simple food in Kundasang. Open 0600-2100.
🍴 **Tinompok**, at the Mount Kinabalu Heritage Resort and Spa, Kundasang. Local and Western dishes, good service, excellent food.
🍴 **Five Star Seafood**, Ranau. Chinese, opposite the market.
🍴 **Sin Mui Mui**, top side of the square near the market. Closed Fri afternoons.

⦿ Shopping

Ranau and Kundasang *p446*
Cheap sweaters and waterproofs for the climb from **Kedai Kien Hin**, Ranau. A *tamu* (market) is held near Ranau on the 1st of each month and every Sat. Kundasang *tamu* is held on the 20th of every month and also every Fri.

▲ Activities and tours

Ranau and Kundasang *p446*
Kundasang Golf Course, 3 km behind Kundasang. Club hire from the **Perkasa Hotel**, Kundasang. The **Mount Kinabalu Heritage Resort and Spa** offers golfing packages which include golf fees, accommodation, breakfast and lunch, and transfer from hotel to course.

⊖ Transport

Gunung Kinabalu Park *p439, map p441*
Bus
All buses heading to **Sandakan** and **Ranau** will drop you off at the turn-off to the park.

Minibus
Regular connections from **KK** to **Ranau**, ask to be dropped at the park, 2 hrs. Return minibus (roughly every hour) must be waved down from the main road.

Taxi
RM160 negotiable, taxi from outside the Padang Merdeka in **KK**.

Poring *p446*
Minibuses can be shared from **Ranau** for RM5. Buses running between **KK** and **Sandakan** stop in town on Jln Kibarambang. Taxis are also available.

Ranau and Kundasang *p446*
Minibuses leave from the market place. Regular connections to **Park HQ**, **KK** and **Sandakan** (4 hrs).

East coast

From Ranau it is possible to reach Sandakan by road. Several key sights are within reach of Sandakan: the Turtle Islands National Park, 40 km north in the Sulu Sea; Sepilok Orang-Utan Rehabilitation Centre; and the Kinabatangan Basin, to the southeast. From Sandakan, the route continues south to the wilds of Lahad Datu and Danum Valley and on to Semporna, the jumping off point for Pulau Sipadan, an island that has achieved legendary status among snorkellers and scuba divers. Tawau Hills State Park has some unusual natural features that draw visitors at weekends.
▶▶ *For listings, see pages 470-482.*

Sandakan → *For listings, see pages 470-482. Colour map 4, B5.*

Sandakan is at the neck of a bay on the northeast coast of Sabah and looks out to the Sulu Sea. It is a postwar town, much of it rebuilt on reclaimed land, and is Malaysia's biggest fishing port; it even exports some of its catch to Singapore. Sandakan is often dubbed 'mini Hong Kong' because of its Cantonese influence; its occupants are well-heeled and the town sustains many prosperous businesses, despite being rather scruffy as a whole. It is now also home to a large Filipino community, mostly traders from Mindanao and the Sulu Islands. Manila still officially claims Sabah in its entirety – Sandakan is only 28 km from Philippines' territorial waters. Large numbers of illegal Indonesian workers have made Sandakan their home in recent years, further adding to the town's cosmopolitan atmosphere.

New developments are slowly encircling the generally charmless heart of the town, with bright, cheery blocks on the outskirts and the new Sandakan Harbour Square on the waterfront with a few fancy shops, a gleaming new hotel and smart promenade pointing the way to a more attractive future for the city.

Ins and outs

Getting there The airport is 10 km north of town. There are daily connections with KL, KK and several lesser destinations in Sabah. Minibuses travel from the airport to the station at the southern end of Jalan Pelabuhan. From the long-distance bus terminal 5 km to the west of town, there are connections with KK, Tawau, Ranau, Lahad Datu, Semporna and several other destinations. Boats from Zamboanga in the Philippines call into Sandakan twice a week.**▶▶** *See also Transport, page 480.*

Getting around Sandakan is not a large town and it is easy enough to explore the central area on foot, although it does stretch some way along the coast. Minibuses provide links with out-of-town places of interest.

Tourist information The privately run **Tourist Information Centre** ① *next to the municipal council building opposite Lebuh Empat, T089-229751, Mon-Fri 0800-1600*, should be the first port of call for any visitor to Sandakan. Despite limited resources, Elvina Ong is an absolute goldmine of information about Sandakan and its environs. She is extremely well organized and can help tourists arrange tours. It was opened by the owner of the **Sepilok Jungle Resort**, but it provides impartial advice.

Background

The Sandakan area was an important source of beeswax for the Sulu traders and came under the sway of the Sultans of Sulu. William Clarke Cowie, a Scotsman with a carefully waxed handlebar moustache who ran guns for the Sultan of Sulu across the Spanish blockade of Sulu (later becoming the managing director of the North Borneo Chartered Company), first set up camp in Sandakan Bay in the early 1870s. He called his camp, which was on Pulau Timbang, 'Sandakan', the Sulu name for the area for 200 years, but it became known as Kampong German as there were several German traders living there and early gunrunners tended to be German. The power of the Sulu sultanate was already waning when Cowie set up. In its early trading days, Europeans, Africans, Arabs, Chinese, Indians, Javanese, Dusun and Japanese all lived here. It was an important gateway to the interior and used to be a trading centre for forest produce like rhinoceros horn, beeswax and hornbill ivory, along with marine products like pearls and sea cucumbers (*tripang*, valued for their medicinal properties). In 1812, English visitor John Hunt estimated that the Sandakan/Kinabatangan area produced an astonishing 37,000 kg of wild beeswax and 23,000 kg of birds' nests each year.

The modern town of Sandakan was founded by an Englishman, William Pryer, in 1879. Baron von Overbeck, the Austrian consul from Hong Kong who founded the Chartered Company with businessman Alfred Dent, had signed a leasing agreement for the territory with the Sultan of Brunei, only to discover that large tracts on the east side of modern day Sabah actually belonged to the Sultan of Sulu. Overbeck sailed to Sulu in January 1878 and on obtaining the cession rights from the Sultan, dropped William Pryer off at Kampong German to make the British presence felt. Pryer's wife Ada later described the scene: "He had with him a West Indian black named Anderson, a half-caste Hindoo named Abdul, a couple of China boys. For food they had a barrel of flour and 17 fowls and the artillery was half a dozen sinder rifles." Pryer set about organizing the three existing villages in the area, cultivating friendly relations with the local tribespeople and fending off pirates. He raised the Union Jack on 11 February 1878.

Cowie tried to do a deal with the Sultan of Sulu to wrest control of Sandakan back from Pryer, but Dent and Overbeck finally bought him off. A few months later Cowie's Kampong German burned to the ground, so Pryer went in search of a new site, which he found at Buli Sim Sim. He called his new settlement Elopura, meaning 'beautiful city', but the name did not catch on. By the mid-1880s it was renamed Sandakan and, in 1884, became the capital of North Borneo when the title was transferred from Kudat. In 1891 the town had 20 Chinese-run brothels and 71 Japanese prostitutes; according to the 1891 census there were three men for every one woman. The town quickly established itself as the source of birds' nests harvested from the caves at Gomantong and shipped directly to Hong Kong, as they are today.

Timber was first exported from this area in 1885 and was used to construct Beijing's Temple of Heaven. Sandakan was, until the 1980s, the main east-coast port for timber and it became a wealthy town. In its heyday, the town is said to have boasted one of the greatest concentrations of millionaires in the world. The timber- boom days are over: the primary jungle has gone, and so has the big money. In the mid-1990s the state government adopted a strict policy restricting the export of raw, unprocessed timber. The hinterland is now dominated by vast plantations of cocoa and oil palm.

Following the Japanese invasion in 1942, Sandakan was devastated by Allied bombing. In 1946 North Borneo became a British colony and the new colonial government moved the capital to Jesselton (later to become Kota Kinabalu).

Sights

Sandakan is strung out along the coast but in the centre of town is the riotous **daily fish market**, which is the biggest and best in Sabah. The best time to visit is at 0600 when the boats unload their catch. The **Central Market** along the waterfront, near the local bus station, sells fruit, vegetables, sarongs, seashells, spices and sticky rice cakes.

The **Australian war memorial** ⓘ *take Labuk bus service Nos 8, 12 and 14 and stop at the Esso petrol station*, near the government building at Mile Seven on Labuk Rd, between Sandakan and Sepilok, stands on the site of a Japanese prison camp and commemorates Allied soldiers who lost their lives during the Japanese occupation. Each year on ANZAC day (24 April) crowds of former servicemen and their families come to the memorial park to commemorate the lives of those that died In the bloody conflict in Sabah. The Japanese invaded North Borneo in 1942 and many Japanese also died in the area. In 1989 a new **Japanese war memorial** ⓘ *walk 20 mins up Red Hill (Bukit Berenda)*, was built in the Japanese cemetery, financed by the families of the deceased soldiers.

St Michael's Anglican church is one of the very few stone churches in Sabah and is an attractive building, designed by a New Zealander in 1893. Most of Sandakan's stone churches were levelled in the war and, indeed, St Michael's is one of the few colonial-era buildings still standing. It is just off Jalan Singapura, on the hill at the south end of town. In

Sandakan

To Goddess of Mercy Temple

To Trig Hill & Ⓢ

✠ St Michael's

Sam Sing
Kung Temple

To Tanah Merah Town, Pertubuhan Ugama Buddhist
& Ⓢ ⑪ ① ③ ⑦

Three Saints Temple

Jln Utara

Jln Tokong

BUKIT
ELTON

Jln Singapura

Padang

Jln Leila

Night

Tun Razak
Park

Community
Centre

Minibuses

Lebuh Tiga   (3rd Av)

Jln Dua   (2nd Av)

Jln Europa

Minibuses

Centre
Point
Plaza

Local Bus
Station

Fisherr

N

100 metres

100 yards

Sleeping
City View **1**
Hsiang Garden **5**
London **3**
Mayfair **4**

Nak **2**
Sabah **8**
Sanbay **11**
Sandakan **6**
Sandakan Backpackers **7**

Sunset Harbour Botik
Hostel **9**
Swiss Inn **10**
Winho Lodge **12**

1988 a big **mosque** was built for the burgeoning Muslim population at the mouth of Sandakan Bay. The main Filipino settlements are in this area of town. The mosque is outside Sandakan, on Jalan Buli Sim Sim where the town began in 1879, just after the jetty for Turtle Islands National Park, and is an imposing landmark. There is also a large water village here.

There are a couple of other notable Chinese temples in Sandakan. The oldest one, the **Goddess of Mercy Temple** is just off Jalan Singapura, on the hillside. Originally built in the early 1880s, it has been expanded over the years. Nearby is **Sam Sing Kung Temple**, which becomes a particular focus of devotion during exam periods since one of its deities is reputed to assist those attempting examinations. The **Three Saints Temple**, further down the hill at the end of the padang, was completed in 1887. The three saints are Kwan Woon Cheung, a Kwan clan ancestor, the goddess Tien Hou (or Tin Hau, worshipped by seafarers) and the Min Cheong Emperor.

Sabah's only **Crocodile Farm** ⓘ *daily 0800-1730, RM5, children RM2, weekday crocodile shows at 1145 and 1600 and snake and crocodile shows at 1145, 1400 and 1600 at weekends, feeding times are throughout the day*, is a commercial licensed enterprise, set up in 1982 when the government made the estuarine crocodile a protected species. The original stock was drawn from a population of wild crocodiles found in the Kinabatangan River.

Visitors can see around 2000 crocs at all stages of maturity waiting in concrete pools for the day when their skins are turned into bags and wallets and their meat is sold to local butchers. There are numerous other animals to see here at their mini zoo including snakes, civets and sun bears. The farm, at Mile 8, Labuk Road, has about 200 residents. To get there take the Labuk Road bus.

The **Forest Headquarters** (Ibu Pejabat Jabatan Perhutanan) ⓘ *Mile 6 Labuk Rd, T089-660811*, next to the Sandakan Golf Course, contain an exhibition centre and a well-laid out and interesting mini-museum showing past and present forestry practice.

The **Sandakan Heritage Trail** is a loop which supposedly takes in the historical gems of this scruffy town including a good lookout point; the walk should take a leisurely 90 minutes. The tourist office has trail maps. It starts off at the town mosque and nips up the 'stairs with 100 steps', a nice shady climb with good views from the top where young local couples gather to whisper sweet nothings to each other and smoke clandestine cigarettes. It's rather dark here at night, so lone travellers are advised to climb in the day. A couple of tourists were mugged here in 2004.

To Airport, Australian & Japanese War Memorials, Crocodile Farm, Labuk Road, Sepilok & Forest HQ

Agnes Keith House 1

Town Mosque

100 steps

Sandakan Heritage Museum

Jln Empat

Lebuh Empat

Wisma Sandakan

Wisma Khoo Siak Chiew

To Long Distance Bus Station, Jln Buli Sim Sim, mosque & Turtle Islands Jetty

Lebuh Tiga

Jln Empat (4th St)

Jln Lima (5th St)

Jln Tiga (3rd St)

Air Asia

Jln Dua

Central Market

Fish Market

Jln Pryer

Sandakan Harbour Square

To Markets

Wharf

To Turtle Islands

Eating 🍴
English Tea House 1
King Cheong 4
New Seoul Garden 7
Ocean King Seafood 3

Santai 2

Agnes Keith's house

American authoress Agnes Keith lived with her English husband in Sandakan from 1934 to 1952. He was the conservator of forests in North Borneo and she wrote three books about her time in the colony.

The Land Below the Wind tells stories of dinner parties and tiffins in pre-war days. *Three Came Home* is about her three years in a Japanese internment camp during the war on Pulau Berhala, off Sandakan, and in Kuching, and was made into a film. *White Man Returns* tells the story of their time in British North Borneo. The Keiths' rambling wooden house on the hill above the town was destroyed during the war, but was rebuilt by the government to exactly the same design when Harry Keith returned to his job when the war ended.

From here the trail passes through **Agnes Keith's house** ① *daily 0900-1700, RM15 discounts for children*, see box above, the restored British colonial government quarters built on the site of her home. Inside the grounds, there's an **English Tea House** serving scones and pastries on manicured lawns. From here, the trail takes in the Goddess of Mercy Temple, St Michael's Anglican Church and ends up at the **Sandakan Heritage Museum** ① *next to the tourist office, daily 0900-1700, free*, a rather slipshod affair with some early photos of the town and an unexplained mannequin dressed in a kilt. There is, however, a good wall photo of Sandakan razed to the ground taken in 1945.

Tanah Merah

Pertubuhan Ugama Buddhist (Puu Jih Shih Buddhist temple) overlooks Tanah Merah town. The US$2 million temple was completed in 1987 and stands at the top of the hill, accessible by a twisting road that hairpins its way up the hillside. The temple is very gaudy, contains three large Buddha images and is nothing special, although the 34 teakwood supporting pillars, made in Macau, are quite a feature. There is a good view of Sandakan from the top, with Tanah Merah and the log ponds directly below, in Sandakan Bay. The names of local donors are inscribed on the walls of the walkway.

Pulau Lankayan

This dive resort is on a near uninhabited island, 90 minutes by boat from Sandakan in the Sulu Sea. **Lankayan Island Dive Resort**, see page 470, offers more than 40 dive sites including a couple of wrecks. Sightings of whale sharks are common from April to May.

Pulau Berhala

① *To get to the beach charter a boat from the fish market.*

Famed for its 200-m rust-coloured sandstone cliffs on the south end, with a beach at the foot, this island is within easy reach by boat, but there isn't a great deal to do here. There are plans to develop the island for tourism in the near future. The island was used as a leper colony before the Second World War and as a prisoner of war camp by the Japanese. Agnes Keith was interned here during the war, see box above.

Turtle Islands National Park → *For listings, see pages 470-482. Colour map 4, A5.*

Located 40 km north of Sandakan, Turtle Islands are at the south entrance to Labuk Bay. The park is separated from the Philippine island of Bakkungan Kecil by a narrow stretch of water. These eight tiny islands in the Sulu Sea are among the most important turtle-breeding spots in Southeast Asia. The turtle sanctuary is made up of three tiny islands (**Pulau Selingan**, **Pulau Bakkungan Kecil** and **Pulau Gulisan**) and also encompasses the surrounding coral reefs and sea, covering 1700 ha. On Pulau Bakkungan Kecil there is a small mud volcano.

Ins and outs

Best time to visit The driest months and the calmest seas are between March and July. The egg laying season is July to October. Seas are rough October to February.

Tourist information The number of visitors is restricted to 50 per night in an effort to protect the female turtles, that are easily alarmed by noise and light when laying. Visitors are asked not to build campfires, shine bright torches or make noise at night on the beach. The turtles should be watched from a distance to avoid upsetting the nesting process. The park is managed by **Sabah Parks** ① *Sabah Parks Office Room 906, 9th floor, Wisma Khoo, Lebuh Tiga, T089-273453, entrance fee RM10, plus a camera fee of RM10 (no flash photography permitted)*. All accommodation must be booked through **Crystal Quest** (see page 479). This is booked up weeks, sometimes months, in advance.

Sandakan Bay

The islands

The islands are famous for their green turtles (*Chelonia mydas*), which make up 80% of the turtles in the park, and hawksbill turtles (*Eretmochelys imbricata*), known locally as *sisik*. There were four reported landings of Olive Ridley turtle (*Lepidochelys Olivacea*) between 1996 and 1988, but none since. Most green turtles lay their eggs on Pulau Selingan. The green turtles copulate 50-200 m off Pulau Selingan and can be seen during the day, their heads popping up like submarine periscopes. Hawksbills prefer to nest on Pulau Gulisan.

Both species come ashore, year-round, to lay their eggs, although the peak season is between July and October. Even during the off-season between four and 10 turtles come up the beach each night to lay their eggs. Pulau Bakkungan Kecil and Pulau Gulisan can only be visited during the day but visitors can stay overnight on Pulau Selingan to watch the green turtles.

Only the females come ashore; the male waits in the sea nearby for his mate. The females cautiously crawl up to nest after 2000 or with the high tide. The nesting site is above the high-tide mark and is cleared by the female's front and hind flippers to

The tough life of a turtle

Historically, green and hawksbill turtles have been hunted for their meat, shells and their edible eggs (a Chinese delicacy). They were a favourite food of British and Spanish mariners for centuries. Japanese soldiers slaughtered thousands of turtles for food during the Second World War. Dynamite fishermen are also thought to have killed off many turtles in Indonesian, Malaysian and Philippines waters in recent years.

Malaysia, Hong Kong, Japan and the Philippines, where green turtle meat and eggs are in demand, are all signatories of the Convention in International Trade in Endangered Species (CITES) and trading in sea turtles has been banned under the Convention since 1981.

In his book *Forest Life and Adventures in the Malay Archipelago*, the Swedish adventurer and wildlife enthusiast Eric Mjoberg documents turtle egghunting and shell collecting in Borneo in the 1920s. He tells of how the Bajau would lie in wait for hawksbills, grab them and put them on the fire so their horny shields could be removed.

"The poor beasts are put straight on the fire so that their shield may be more readily removed, and suffer the tortures of the damned. They are then allowed to go alive, or perhaps half-dead into the sea, only to come back again after a few years and undergo the same cruel process."

The Bajau, he says, used an "ingenious contrivance" to hunt their prey. They would press pieces of common glass against their eyes "in a watertight fashion" and would lie face-down on a piece of floating wood, dipping their faces into the water, watching for hawksbills feeding on seaweed. They would then dive in, armed with a small harpoon, and catch them, knocking them out with a blow to the head.

make a 'body pit', just under a metre deep. She then digs an egg chamber with her powerful rear flippers after which she proceeds to lay her eggs. The clutch size can be anything between 40 and 200; batches of 50-80 are most common.

When all the eggs have been laid, she covers them with sand and laboriously fills the body pit to conceal the site of the nest, after which the exhausted turtle struggles back to the sea, leaving her Range Rover-like tracks in the sand. The egg-laying process can take about an hour or two to complete. Some say the temperature of the sand affects the sex of the young: if it is warm the batch will be mostly female and if cold, mostly male. After laying her eggs, a tag reading "If found, return to Turtle Island Park, Sabah, East Malaysia" is attached to each turtle by the rangers, who are stationed on each island. Over 27,000 have been tagged since 1970; the measurements of each turtle are recorded and the clutches of eggs removed and transplanted to the hatchery where they are protected from natural predators, like monitor lizards, birds and snakes.

The golf ball-sized eggs are placed by hand into 80 cm-deep pits, covered in sand and surrounded by wire. They take up to 60 days to hatch. The hatchlings mostly emerge at night when the temperature is cooler, breaking their shells with their one sharp tooth. There are hatcheries on all three islands and nearly every night a batch is released into the sea. Millions of hatchlings have been released since 1977. They are released at different points on the island to protect them from predators: they are a favoured snack for white-bellied gulls and sadly only about 1% survive to become teenage turtles.

Sepilok Orang-Utan Sanctuary and Rehabilitation Centre
→ *For listings, see pages 470-482. Colour map 4, B5.*

Sepilok, a reserve of 43 sq km of lowland primary rainforest and mangrove, was set up in 1964 to protect the orang-utan (*Pongo pygmaeus*) from extinction. It is the first and largest of only four orang-utan sanctuaries in the world and now has 40,000 visitors a year. Logging has seriously threatened Sabah's population of wild orang-utan, as has their capture for zoos and as pets. The orang-utan (see page 534) lives on the islands of Borneo and Sumatra and there are estimated to be as few as 10,000 still in the wild. In Sabah there are populations of orang-utan in the Kinabatangan basin region (see page 459), Danum Valley Conservation Area and a few other isolated tracts of jungle.

Ins and outs
Getting there There are several buses a day from Sandakan.

Park information Sepilok Orang-Utan Sanctuary ① *T089-5311180, soutan@po.jaring.my, Sat-Thu 0900-1230 and 1400-1600, Fri 0900-1100 and 1400-1600, RM30 (children RM5), camera RM10.* It is worth getting to the park early. The **Information Centre** ① *video viewing times at 0830, 1100, 1200, 1410 and 1530,* next to the Park HQ, runs a nature education exhibition with replicas of jungle mammals and videos. If you want to do the walks, arrive at the centre in the morning so you can get a permit. The pass is valid all day so you can see both feeds if you arrive early. Feeding times: Platform A, 1000 and 1500. For more details contact the coordinator, Sepilok Orang-Utan Rehabilitation Centre, Sabah Wildlife Department, T089-531180, F531189. **Note** The morning feed is packed with tour groups; the afternoon feed is generally quieter.

The sanctuary
Sepilok is an old forest reserve that was gazetted as a forestry experimentation centre as long ago as 1931, and by 1957 logging had been phased out. Orphaned or captured orang-utans that have become too dependent on humans through captivity are rehabilitated and protected under the Fauna Conservation Ordinance and eventually returned to their natural home. Many, for example, may have been captured by the oil-palm planters because they eat the young oil palm trees. Initially, the animals at the centre and in the surrounding area are fed every day but, as they acclimatize, they are sent further and further away or are re-released into the Tabin Wildlife Reserve near Lahad Datu. In 1996, researchers placed microchip collars on the orang-utans enabling them to be tracked over a distance of up to 150 km so that a better understanding of their migratory habits and other behaviour could be acquired.

After an initial period of quarantine at Sepilok, newly arrived orang-utans are moved to Platform A and taught survival skills by rangers. At the age of seven they are moved deeper into the forest to Platform B, about 30 minutes' walk from Platform A and not open to the public. At Platform B, they are encouraged to forage for themselves. Other animals brought here include Malay sun bears, wild cats and baby elephants.

Sepilok also has a rare Sumatran rhinoceros (*Didermoceros sumatrensis*), the Asian two-horned rhinoceros, see box page 462. This enclosure is sometimes closed to the public.

The **Mangrove Forest Trail** takes two to three hours one way and passes transitional forest, some pristine lowland rainforest, a boardwalk into a mangrove forest, water holes and a wildlife track. The visitors' reception centre provides other information.

Rainforest Discovery Centre

① *Jln Sepilok, T089-533780, www.forest.sabah.gov.my/rdc, daily 0800-1700, RM10, children RM5. A free booklet is available; for more details contact the Forest Research Centre, PO Box 14-07, T089-531522.*

This centre located within the Kabili-Sepilok Forest Reserve is 2 km from the Orang-utan Rehabilitation Centre and provides detailed displays about the vegetation in the area. It is run by the **Forest Research Centre**, also found on this road. Emphasis is on participation, with questionnaires, games and so on; it offers a wide range of information about all aspects of tropical rainforests and the need for conservation. It is situated in the Forest Research Centre's arboretum and there is an 800-m rainforest walk around the lake. There also a 150-m canopy walkway offering the opportunity to walk over the forest canopy and spot wildlife. Keep your eyes peeled for hornbills, kingfishers and the Bornean bristlehead.

Gomantong Caves → For listings, see pages 470-482.

The Gomantong Caves are 32 km south of Sandakan Bay, between the road to Sukau and the Kinabatangan River, or 110 km overland on the Sandakan–Sukau road. The name Gomantong means 'tie it up tightly' in the local language and the caves are the largest system in Sabah. They are located in the 3924 ha Gomantong Forest Reserve.

Ins and outs

At the Park HQ there is an information centre, a small cafeteria where drinks and simple dishes are sold and a pit latrine. Good walking shoes are essential, as is a torch. If you're squeamish about cockroaches give this cave a miss. If you arrive independently then one of the nest workers, a person from the information centre or a ranger will show you around. The bats can be seen exiting from the caves between 1800 and 1830; to request to see this it is necessary to ask at the **Gomantong Wildlife Department** ① *T011-817529*, at the information centre.

The caves and reserve

① *Daily 0800-1600, RM30.*

There are sometimes orang-utan, mouse deer, wild boar and wild buffalo in the reserve, which was logged in the 1950s. There are several cave chambers. The main limestone cave is Simud Hitam (Black Cave). This cave, with its ceiling soaring up to 90 m overhead, is just a five-minute walk from the registration centre and picnic area. The smaller and more complex Simud Putih (White Cave) is above. It is quite dangerous climbing up as there is no ladder to reach the caves and the rocks are slippery. Between 200,000 and 300,000 bats of two different species are thought to live in the caves; at sunset they swarm out to feed. Sixty-four species of bat have been recorded in Sabah; most in these caves are fruit- and wrinkled-lipped bats whose guano is a breeding ground for cockroaches. The squirming larvae make the floor of the cave seethe. The guano can cause an itchy skin irritation. The bats are preyed upon by birds like the bat hawk, peregrine falcon and buffy fish owl.

There are also an estimated one million swiftlets that swarm into the cave to roost at sunset, the birds of bird's nest soup fame (see box, page 355). The swiftlets of Gomantong have been a focus of commercial enterprise for 400 or 500 years. However, it was not until 1870 that harvesting birds' nests became a serious industry here. The caves are divided into five pitches and each is allocated to a team of 10-15 people. Harvesting periods last 10 days and there are two each year (February-April and July-September). Collecting nests from hundreds of feet above the ground is a dangerous business and deaths are not uncommon. Before each harvesting period a chicken or goat is sacrificed to the cave spirit; it is thought that deaths are not caused by human error, but by an angry spirit. Birdlife around the caves is rich, with crested serpent eagles, kingfishers, Asian fairy bluebirds and leafbirds often sighted. Large groups of richly coloured butterflies are also often seen drinking from pools along the track leading from the forest into the caves.

Sungai Kinabatangan → For listings, see pages 470-482.

At 560 km, this river is Sabah's longest. Much of the lower basin is gazetted under the Kinabatangan Wildlife Sanctuary and meanders through a flood plain, creating numerous oxbow lakes and an ideal environment for some of Borneo's best wildlife.

Ins and outs

Visitors who prefer an in-depth look at the area's wildlife can stay overnight at Sukau, two hours by road from Sandakan, where accommodation is provided by local tour operators. They take visitors by boat in the late afternoon through freshwater swamp forest to see proboscis monkeys and other wildlife. There are also walks through the jungle. Those who wish to visit for a day can charter a cab from Sandakan for around RM300.

Kinabatangan Riverine Forest area

One of the principal reasons why the Kinabatangan has remained relatively unscathed by Sabah's rapacious logging is because much of the land is permanently waterlogged and the forest contains only a small number of commercially valuable trees. Just some of the animals include: tree snake, crocodile, civet cat, otter, monitor lizard, long-tailed and pig-tailed macaque, silver-, red- and grey-leaf monkey and proboscis monkey. It is the most accessible area in Sabah to see proboscis monkeys, which are best viewed from a boat in the late afternoon, when they converge on treetops by the river banks to settle for the night. Sumatran rhinoceros have also been spotted (see box, page 462) and herds of wild elephant often pass through the park. The birdlife is particularly good and includes oriental darter, egret, storm's stork, osprey, coucal owl, frogmouth, bulbul, spiderhunter, oriole, flowerpecker and several species of hornbill. The night trip is well worth doing as you can get close to the sleeping birds and they look very colouful.

Because of the diversity of its wildlife, the Kinabatangan Riverine Forest area is becoming a wildlife reserve; however, there's some debate as to whether enough land is being set aside for the protection of the region's fauna. In addition, there has been little disturbance from human settlements: the Kinabatangan basin has always been sparsely inhabited because of flooding and the threat posed by pirates. The inhabitants of the Kinabatangan region are mostly Orang Sungai or people of mixed ancestry including Tambanua, Idahan, Dusun, Suluk, Bugis, Brunei and Chinese. A good destination for a jungle river safari is not on the Kinabatangan itself, but on the narrow, winding Sungai Menanggol tributary, about 6 km from Sukau. The Kinabatangan estuary, largely mangrove, is also rich in wildlife and is a haven for migratory birds. Boats can be chartered from Sandakan to Abai (at the river mouth).

Batu Tulug, also known as Batu Putih (white stone), on the Kinabatangan River 100 km upstream from Sukau, is a cave containing wooden coffins dating back several hundred years. Some of the better examples have been removed to the Sabah State Museum in KK. The caves are about 1 km north of the Kinabatangan Bridge, on the east side of the Sandakan–Lahad Datu road.

Lahad Datu is Malaysia's 'wild East' at its wildest and its recent history testifies to its reputation as the capital of cowboy country. The population is an intriguing mixture of Filipinos, Sulu islanders, Kalimantan migrants, Orang Bugis, Timorese and a few Malays. Most came to work on the palm oil plantations. Nowadays there are so many migrants few can find employment in this grubby and uninteresting town. There are reckoned to be more illegal Filipino immigrants in Lahad Datu than the whole population put together. Piracy in the Sulu Sea and the offshore islands in Kennedy Bay is rife; local fishermen live in terror. In October 2003, a band of Abu Sayyaf rebels kidnapped six Filipino and Indonesian workers from **Borneo Paradise Resort** near Kunak. Eight months later, four hostages were freed. It is thought a Malaysian businessman paid a ransom.

During the Second World War, the Japanese made Lahad Datu their naval headquarters for east Borneo. After the war, the timber companies moved in and the **British Kennedy Bay Timber Company** built Lahad Datu's first plywood mill in the early 1950s. Oil palm plantations grew up in the hinterland after the timber boom finished in the 1970s. As for the town, what it lacks in aesthetic appeal is made up for by its colourful recent history.

Kampong Panji is a water village with a small market at the end of Jalan Teratai, where many of the poorer immigrant families live.

The only good beaches are on the road to Tungku; Pantai Perkapi and Pantai Tungku. They can be reached by minibus from Lahad Datu or by boat from the old wharf. It is possible to get to the nearby islands from the old wharf behind the Mido Hotel, but because of lawlessness in the area, particularly at sea, a trip is not advisable. In April 2000, the Philippines-based radical Islamic group Abu Sayyaf kidnapped 21 people from Sipadan (see page 464).

Madai Caves are about 2 km off the Tawau–Lahad Datu road, near Kunak. The caves are an important archaeological site; there is evidence they were inhabited over 15,500 years ago. Birds' nests are harvested from the caves three times a year by local Idahan people whose lean-to kampong goes right up to the cave mouth. Your own transport is required for this trip as it's not catered for by tour operators.

Another 15 km west of Madai is **Baturong**, another limestone massif and cave system in the middle of what was originally Tingkayu Lake. The route is not obvious so it is advisable to take a local guide. Stone tools, wooden coffins and rock paintings have been found there. Evidence of humans dating from 16,000 years ago, after the lake drained away, can be found at the huge rock overhang (take a torch; it is possible to camp here). To get to Baturong, take a minibus from Lahad Datu.

At **Gunung Silam**, 8 km from Lahad Datu on the Tawau road, a track leads up the mountain to a Telekom station at 620 m and from there, a jungle trail to the summit. There are good views over the bay, when it isn't misty, and out to the islands beyond. It is advisable to take a guide. You can stay at **Silam Lodge** (see page 473).

Tabin Wildlife Reserve → *Colour map 4, B6.*

① *Book at Lot 11-1, Blk A, Damai Point, Jln Damai, KK, T088-267266, www.tabinwildlife.com.my.*
Gazetted in 1984 as a protected forest area, Tabin is one of Sabah's largest and most important wildlife reserves and, according to the WWF, one of the last refuges of the critically endangered Sumatran rhino; see box, page 462. Since the opening of **Tabin Jungle Resort** in 2002, around 50 km or one hour's drive from Lahad Datu, it's also one one of the easiest and most comfortable to visit. In addition, it's in one of the most

exciting settings, close to a large mud-volcano – favoured as a mineral lick by mammals. The reserve offers a wide variety of trails and various wildlife habitats. There are several huge bubbling mud volcanoes an easy trek from the resort.

Since the reserve consists of large areas of previously logged and now recovering forest and also due to its considerable size, covering 120,500 ha, it's particularly good for observing Bornean mammals. Pygmy elephants (see box, page 463), wild pigs, civets and macaques are often seen on evening safaris close to palm oil plantations; otters make their homes in the river below the jungle resort; and by staking out the mud volcano for a night even a close encounter is possible with a sun bear; see box, page 468. There are occasional sightings of the Sumatran Rhinoceros as Tabin is one of their last natural breeding spots. It is estimated that only 300 of these animals are left in the wild.

There are various packages available to visit the reserve, including day trips that start at RM285 per person (minimum two people) and include transfers from Lahad Datu.

Danum Valley Conservation Area → *For listings, see pages 470-482. Colour map 4, B5.*

Danum Valley's 438 sq km of virgin jungle is the largest expanse of undisturbed lowland dipterocarp forest in Sabah. Segama River runs through the area and past the field centre. Danum River is a tributary of the Segama joining it 9 km downstream of the field centre. Gunung Danum (1093 m) is the highest peak, 13 km southwest of the field centre. Within the area is a tightly controlled Yayasan Sabah timber concession.

Ins and outs

The field centre, 65 km west of Lahad Datu and 40 km from the nearest habitation, was set up by the Sabah Foundation (Yayasan) in 1985 for forest research, nature education and recreation; the centre is only open to visiting scientists and researchers. If you are a biologist or an educator you may be able to get permission to visit the centre; contact the **Sabah Foundation** ① *Likas Bay, T088-326327, www.ysnet.org.my*, for permission. Guides charge RM5 per hour. Tourists are allowed to visit only through the **Borneo Rainforest Lodge**, see Sleeping and Transport, pages 470 and 480 respectively.

The valley

This area has never been inhabited, although there is evidence of a burial site that is thought to have been for the Dusun people who lived here about 300 years ago. There is also growing evidence of prehistoric cave dwellers in the Segama River area. Not far downstream from the field centre, in a riverside cave, two wooden coffins have been found, together with a copper bracelet and a *tapai* jar, all of uncertain date. There is evidence of some settlement during the Japanese occupation; townspeople came upstream to escape from the Japanese troops. The area was first recommended as a national park by the WWF's Malaysia Expedition in 1975 and designated a conservation area in 1981. The field centre was officially opened in 1986.

The main aims of this large area are to research the impact of logging on flora and fauna and to try and improve forest management, to understand processes that maintain tropical rainforest and to provide wildlife management and training opportunities for Sabahans. Many are collaborative projects between Malaysian and foreign scientists.

The Sumatran rhinoceros

Although not as rare as its Javan brother, the Sumatran, or Asian two-horned rhinoceros (*Didermoceros sumatrensis*) is severely endangered. The species has suffered from the destruction of its natural habitat and the price placed on its head by the value that the Chinese attach to its grated horn as a cure-all. Should the Sumatran rhino disappear so, too, it is thought, will a number of plants whose seeds will only germinate after passing through the animal's intestines.

It was once widespread through mainland and island Southeast Asia but there are now only around 300 in the wild, mostly in the most remote forests of Sumatra but with small populations in Borneo (including Sepilok Orang-Utan Sanctuary, page 457, and Tabin Wildlife Reserve, page 460), Peninsular Malaysia and Vietnam. It is now a protected species. Only on Sumatra does it seem to have a chance of surviving.

The situation has become so serious that naturalists established a captive breeding programme as a precaution against extinction in the wild. Unfortunately this has been spectacularly unsuccessful. Around a third of animals have died during capture or shortly thereafter and, according to naturalists Tony and Jane Whitten, the only recorded birth in captivity was in Calcutta in 1872.

In a startlingly similar Darwinesque manner to Borneo's bears and elephants, these rhinos have evolved dwarf characteristics, a feature that has helped them to survive in dense undergrowth. The Sumatran rhino is the smallest of all the family, only growing to 600-900 kg. It is a shy, retiring creature, inhabiting thick forest. Tracks have been discovered as high as 3300 m in Mount Leuser National Park, Sumatra. It lacks the armoured skin of other species and has a soft, hairy hide. It also has an acute sense of smell and hearing, but poor eyesight.

Until recently the rhino's destiny continued looking bleak, but there has been recent evidence in Sabah that rhinos are breeding and in early 2007 some of the first wild footage of a Sumatran rhino was captured in Sabah with a WWF camera trap, giving hope that the rhino might be on the rebound from extinction.

However, much more help is still needed if that dream is going to become reality. Find out more at www.panda.org, www.sosrhino.com or www.tabinwildlife.com.my. Programmes are run by various organizations for fit and enthusiastic volunteers to make a contribution and **Intra Travel Service** runs tours out of their beautifully designed Tabin Jungle Resort, page 473, in Tabin Wildlife Reserve.

Flora and fauna

Due to its size and remoteness, Danum Valley is home to some of Sabah's rarest animals and plants. The dipterocarp forest is some of the oldest, tallest and most diverse in the world, with 200 species of tree per hectare; there are over 300 labelled trees. The conservation area is teeming with wildlife: Sumatran rhinoceros have been recorded, as have elephant, clouded leopards, orang-utans, proboscis monkeys, crimson langur, pig-tailed macaques, sambar deer, bearded pigs, Western tarsier, sun bears (see page 468) and 275 species of bird including hornbills, rufous picolet, flowerpeckers and kingfishers. A species of monkey, which looks like an albino version of the red-leaf monkey, was first seen on the road to Danum in 1988 and appears to be unique to this area. There are guided nature walks on an extensive trail system. Features include a

The gentler beast of Borneo

It was dung that eventually solved the mystery surrounding Borneo's rare elephants. For a long time scientists couldn't decide whether the animals were native to the island or introduced by human settlers. One argument suggested that the British East India Company gave the beasts as gifts to the Sultan of Sulu in the 17th century.

Using evidence gleaned from DNA analysis of the mucus which sticks to elephant droppings, scientists from Columbia University in the US discovered the pachyderm is indeed indigenous. From genetic data they concluded the Borneo variety is a distinct sub-species of Asian elephant, having been isolated from its cousins 300,000 years ago. In recognition of its new status, the animal was rechristened the Borneo pygmy elephant in 2003.

The animals are smaller than the Asian elephant, with larger ears, longer tails and straighter tusks. They are also said to be gentler in temper. Scientists believe elephants trooped across swampy land joining Borneo with Sumatra when sea levels were lower during the ice ages.

Conservation groups estimate there are only around 2000 of the endangered elephants left, which are threatened by ivory poachers and loss of habitat.

canopy walkway, a heart-stoppingly springy platform 107 m long and 27 m above the ground, ancient Dusun burial site, waterfalls and a self-guided trail.

Semporna → For listings, see pages 470-482. Colour map 4, B6.

Semporna is a small fishing Bajau town at the end of the Peninsula and is the main departure point for Sipadan Island. It has a lively and very photogenic market, spilling out onto piers over the water, and is known for its seafood. There are scores of small fishing boats, many with outriggers and square sails. There is a regatta of these traditional boats every March. The town is built on an old coral reef, said to be 35,000 years old, which was exposed by the uplift of the seabed. Many illegal Filipino immigrants pass through Semporna as it is only two hours from the nearest Philippine island, which gives the place quite a different feel from that of other Malaysian towns. The town is grubby and charmless with street corners populated by gangs of lingering youths. However, it's a friendly enough place with some good seafood on offer.

The islands off Semporna stand along the edge of the continental shelf, which drops away to a depth of 200 m to the south and east of Pulau Ligitan, the outermost island in the group. Darvel Bay and the adjacent waters are dotted with small, mainly volcanic, islands, which are all part of the 9300-ha **Semporna Marine Park**. The bigger ones are Pulau Mabul, Pulau Kapalai, Pulau Si Amil, Pulau Danawan and Pulau Sipadan. The attractive hilly island that can be seen on the horizon is affectionately termed the island of the sleeping beauty. With a little imagination, the island has the profile of a rather busty lady lying down. The reefs surrounding these islands have around 70 genera of coral, placing them, in terms of their diversity, on a par with Australia's Great Barrier Reef. More than 200 species of fish have also been recorded in these waters.

Locals live in traditional boats called *lipa-lipa* or in pilehouses at the water's edge and survive by fishing. In the shallow channels off Semporna there are three fishing villages built on stilts: Kampong Potok Satu, Kampong Potok Dua and Kampong Larus. There are many more islands than are marked on the map; most are hilly, uninhabited and have beautiful white sandy beaches.

Reefs in Semporna Marine Park include Sibuan Ulaiga, Tetugan, Mantabuan Bodgaya, Sibuan, Maigu, Selakan, Sebangkat and Bohey Dulang. The latter is a volcanic island with a Japanese-run pearl culture station. Visitors can only visit if there is a boat from the pearl culture station going out. The **Kaya Pearl Company** leases part of the lagoon and Japanese pearl oysters are artificially implanted with a core material to induce pearl growth. The oysters are attached to rafts moored in the lagoon. The pearls are harvested and exported direct to Japan. Some islands, like Sibuan, Sebangkat, Maigu and Selakan, can be reached by local fishing boats from the main jetty by the market.

Sipadan Island Marine Reserve → *For listings, see pages 470-482. Colour map 4, C6.*

The venerable French marine biologist Jacques Cousteau 'discovered' Sipadan in 1989 and, after spending three months diving around the island from his research vessel, *Calypso* said: "I have seen other places like Sipadan 45 years ago, but now no more. Now we have found an untouched piece of art." Since then Sipadan has become a sub-aqua shangri-la for serious divers. It is regularly voted one of the top dive destinations in the world by leading scuba magazines. The reef is without parallel in Malaysia. But Sipadan Island is not just for scuba divers: it is a magnificent, tiny tropical island with pristine beaches and crystal-clear water and its coral can be enjoyed by even the most amateur of snorkellers.

Ins and outs

The island's tourist facilities are run by a handful of tour companies, who control everything (see Activities and tours, page 414). In 2004, after much legal wrangling, the tour operators agreed to close all resort facilities on the island to protect the environment; although dive boats can still take visitors around the island, numbers are limited to 120 tourist permits per day. Park permits cost RM40 per day to visit Sipidan. Tourists can still stay on Mabul, Kapalai and Mataking, and these islands are likely to be developed further.

Best time to visit The best diving season is from mid-February to mid-December when visibility is greater (20-60 m); most of the dives involve drift diving; the night diving is said to be absolutely spectacular.

Note Due to the issuing of a limited number of permits per day, visitors are advised to book a trip at least two to three weeks in advance. Those showing up without a booking are unlikely to find a slot.

Background

While Sipadan may win lots of points from dive enthusiasts, it has also been in the news for less savoury reasons. In April 2000 Abu Sayyaf, a separatist group in the Philippines, kidnapped 21 people including 10 foreign tourists from the island. Abu Sayyaf, linked to Osama bin Laden's al-Qaeda, spirited the hostages to the Philippine island of Jolo. Here they remained under guard and threat of execution while the armed forces of the Philippines tried, sometimes incompetently, to rescue them. The hostages were freed in dribs and drabs with the final batch being released in September 2000, but it wasn't the sort of publicity that Sipadan was looking for. There is a heavy Malaysian navy presence on the island and around Semporna.

The island is disputed by the Indonesian and Malaysian governments. Indonesia has asked Malaysia to stop developing marine tourism facilities on Sipadan. Malaysia's claim to the island rests on historical documents signed by the British and Dutch colonial administrations. Periodically the two sides get around the negotiating table, but neither is prepared to make a big issue of Sipadan. Occasionally guests on the island see Indonesian or Malaysian warships just offshore. A third party also contests ownership of Sipadan: a Malaysian who claims his grandfather, Abdul Hamid Haji, was given the island by the Sultan of Sulu. He has the customary rights to collect turtles eggs on the island, although the Malaysian government disputes this.

Pulau Sipadan

Pulau Sipadan is the only oceanic island in Malaysia; it is not attached to the continental shelf and stands on a limestone and coral stalk, rising 600 m from the bed of the Celebes Sea. The limestone pinnacle mushrooms out near the surface, but a few metres offshore drops off in a sheer underwater cliff to the seabed. The reef comes right into the island's small pier, allowing snorkellers to swim along the edge of the coral cliff, while remaining close to the coral-sand beach. The edge is much further out around the rest of the island. The tiny island has a cool, forested interior and it is common to see flying foxes and monitor lizards. It is also a stopover point for migratory birds, and was originally declared a bird sanctuary in 1933. It has been a marine reserve since 1981 and a large wildlife department and anti-poaching group is now permanently stationed on the island. In addition, the island is a breeding ground for the green turtle; August and September are the main egg laying months. With the exception of the beach close to the jetty, beaches now also have restricted access in order to protect turtle nesting sites.

Sipadan is known for its underwater overhangs and caverns, funnels and ledges, all of which are covered in coral. A cavern, known as the Turtle Cave, is located on the drop-off in front of the island's accommodation area. The cave originally acquired its fame due to turtles being encountered deep within the cave's depths – some of these turtles had become disorientated and died in the caves and, with the deaths of a few panicked divers, venturing far into the caverns is now reserved for experienced divers only. The island's geography and location focus nutrient-rich upwellings towards the island, and in areas such as the South and Barracuda Points, large pelagic (open sea) species such as grey reef sharks and sometimes even hammerheads are spotted.

Mabul Island

Located between Semporna and Sipadan, this island of 21 ha is considerably larger than Sipadan and is partly home to Bajau fishermen who live in traditional palm-thatched houses. In contrast to Sipadan's untouched forest, the island is predominantly planted with coconut trees. Diving has been the most recent discovery; an Australian diver claims it is "one of the richest single destinations for exotic small marine life anywhere in the world". It has already become known as the world's best muck diving, so called because of the silt-filled waters and poor visibility (usually around 12 m, which is quite reasonable compared with many other places in the area). The island is surrounded by gentle sloping reefs with depths from 3-35 m and a wall housing numerous species of hard corals. Since the closure of Sipadan's luxury resorts, several companies have moved their accommodation to Mabul, only 20 minutes away by fast boat. Places to stay at affordable backpacker budget places are available with island homestays or Semporna tour operators; see page 479. Depending on your bargaining skills, RM100 should get you a return boat trip to the island. Bajau culture remains fairly traditional on the island and while visitors will be stared at, especially women in Western dress, people are friendly, albeit in an intense manner.

Mataking and Kapalai

Mataking has only been open as a dive resort for a few years, but with the closure of Sipadan its popularity is almost guaranteed to rocket. There are about 30 good dive sites around the island including various reefs (plenty of good shallow ones making it an ideal spot for beginner divers), a sea fan garden, a 100-m crevice called Alice Channel that runs to Pulau Sipadan and Sweet Lips rock, a good night-diving spot. Accommodation is at the upmarket **Mataking Island Reef Dive Resort**, see page 475.

Kapalai is a sandbar, heavily eroded and set on top of Ligitan Reefs between Sipadan and Mabul. Semporna tour operators take people diving in Sipadan and in the shallow waters around Kapalai. **Bohedulang** is a volcanic, mountainous island east of Semporna, reminiscent of many Thai islands in the Andaman Sea. You pass its thickly forested slopes if heading for dive sites or resorts at Mataking, Bohayan or Mantabuan. The area is exceptionally beautiful above and below the waves.

Tawau → *For listings, see pages 470-482. Colour map 4, C5.*

Tawau is a timber port in Sabah's southeastern corner. It is a busy commercial centre and the main entry point of Indonesian workers into Sabah. A great contrast to the newly built hotel and business area, the waterfront has plenty of colourful markets and foodstalls and some picturesque views across the bay, including to Kalimantan.

The town was developed in the early 19th century by the British who planted hemp. The British also developed the logging industry in Sabah using elephants from Burma. The **Bombay Burma Timber Company** became the **North Borneo Timber Company** in 1950, a joint British and Sabah government venture.

In the last few years Tawau has began to develop rapidly as a regional hub of transport and commerce. Tawau centre has been cleaned up and has a few decent hotels and restaurants. The town has wide, clean streets and an air of prosperity not seen in many other Sabahan towns. Many travellers heading for Semporna now fly directly to Tawau, with its daily air connections to KL. With a couple of days' notice you can obtain a 60-day Indonesian visa and cross into eastern Kalimantan. As with many sections of Indonesian Borneo, transport is poor and very few westerners make this journey; of those that do, a large proportion head for pre-booked and exclusive diving operations off the coast. Although mud logging tracks exist on the Indonesian side of Sebuku Bay, most people usually find boat transport to the Indonesian towns of Nunukan and Tarakan further south much more comfortable and efficient.

With the development of a new road cutting across the south of Sabah towards KK nearing completion (passing just to the south of Maliau Basin), Tawau is set to receive more foreign visitors.

Tawau is surrounded by plantations and smallholdings of rubber, copra, cocoa and palm oil. The local soils are volcanic and very fertile and palm oil has recently taken over from cocoa as the predominant crop. Malaysian cocoa prices dropped when its quality proved to be 20% poorer than cocoa produced in Nigeria and the Ivory Coast and this, coupled with disease outbreaks in the crop, caused many of the cocoa growers to emigrate to the Ivory Coast. KL is now an established research centre for palm oil where there are studies on using palm oil as a fuel.

Now that the Sandakan area has been almost completely logged, Tawau has taken over as the main logging centre on the east coast. The forest is disappearing fast but there are some reforestation programmes. At **Kalabakan**, west of Tawau, there is a well-established, large-scale reforestation project with experiments on fast-growing trees such as *Albizzia falcataria*, said to grow 30 m in five years. There are now large plantation areas. The tree is processed into, among other things, paper for making money.

Tawau Hills State Park

ⓘ *Contact Ranger Office, Tawau Hills Park, T089-810676, F011-884917, RM2.*

This park, 24 km northwest of Tawau, protects Tawau's water catchment area. The Tawau River flows through the middle of the 27,972 ha park and forms a natural deep-water pool, at Table Waterfall, which is good for swimming. There is a trail from there to hot springs and another to the top of Bombalai Hill, an extinct volcano. Most of the forest in the park below 500 m has been logged; only the forest on the central hills and ridges is untouched. The park is popular with locals at weekends. Camping is possible but bring your own equipment. Access to the park is via a maze of rough roads through the **Borneo Abaca Limited** agricultural estates. It is advisable to hire a taxi.

Maliau Basin Conservation Area → *For listings, see pages 470-482. Colour map 4, B3.*

ⓘ *Conservation and Environmental Management Division, Yayasan Sabah Group, PO Box 11622, T088-326300, www.borneoforestheritage.org.my. Obtain permission in advance. Entry permits (RM50) are sold at the Shell Maliau Basin Reception and Information Building.*

In the rugged forest-clad hills in Sabah's heart lies an area known as Sabah's Lost World. Covering an area of 390 km², the Maliau Basin is one of the state's last areas of primary rainforest largely unaffected by agriculture or large-scale logging. It has remained undisturbed partly due to the difficulty of access and the geography of the basin. From the air, it looks like a vast meteor crater, measuring up to 25 km in diameter and surrounded by steep cliffs up to 1700 m in height on all but the southern and southeastern sides. Scientists believe that the crater was made through sedimentary forces over 15 million years ago, combined with major geological shifts, creating more than 30 spectacular waterfalls in the valley. The conservation area covers 588 sq km.

Granted government protection in the late 1990s and subject to growing scientific interest, Maliau is finally opening its doors to the public with its state-of-the-art visitors' centre completed in 2007. A major logging road cutting across the south of Sabah, from Tawau to Keningau and the west coast, is close to completion as a major paved highway. This will improve access to the zone, but will also increase threats to wildlife.

Flora and fauna

Maliau Basin is an area of incredible biodiversity featuring areas of lowland rainforest, heath forests and oak conifer, with cloud forests on the higher elevations. With over 1800 species of plant being recorded here, including 80 species of orchid, it is also only one of two sites in Sabah to have the rare rafflesia.

For wildlife watchers the park contains the full range of Bornean mammals, with animals such as the sun bear (see box, page 468), clouded leopard, Bornean gibbon, proboscis monkey and orang-utan being recorded in the park. These and other wildlife like the rare banteng (Asian wild cattle), elephant and pangolin are sometimes spotted on night safaris. However, it's unlikely you'll ever be lucky enough to spot the rarest resident,

It's a bear's life

The least studied and understood of all the bears, the sun or honey bear has differing names in the scientific community. The largest potentially carnivorous mammal in Borneo, sun bears are nevertheless the smallest of the world's eight bear species. A male sun bear weighs up to 65 kg, the female up to 50 kg, and bears are covered in short black fur, except for a yellow chest patch, unique to each bear in shape. It roams the dense forests of Southeast Asia, from Assam in India to Southern China and the lush islands of Sumatra and Borneo.

Using outsized claws tailored for an arboreal lifestyle, sun bears are excellent climbers, sometimes reaching up to 50 m in the forest canopy in search of food as diverse as palm hearts, termites, birds, small mammals, eggs and wild honey, which they love, lapping it up with long tongues. Bears often use their long claws like safety hooks to sleep high in the branches. Rare to see on the forest floor, sun bears are quite aggressive if cornered or startled, and with poor eyesight, they have been known to charge. If you're lucky enough to find a bear in the forest, it would be advisable to back away quietly while facing the bear, keeping as calm as possible. Remember, this is the bear's territory, not yours.

Massive forest destruction in Southern Asia means that the habitat of sun bears is under threat. Bears are widely hunted for their body parts, for use in traditional medicines; claws, gall bladders and other bones are found in markets throughout China and Southeast Asia.

Bears also face competition from other predators – pythons and crocodiles in Borneo sometimes hunt bears and in mainland Asia they share a shrinking habitat with tigers and leopards, plus Asian black bears and sloth bears in Eastern India.

To protect bears, follow these rules:
→ Never buy bear products in markets. In many countries (including Malaysia) this is illegal. If you see these products, report them to the local authorities.
→ Support projects to protect the rainforest and its habitat. WWF's Heart of Borneo programme aims to protect and conserve national parks and Borneo's most valuable forest areas. See www.panda.org for more information.
→ Support environmentally sustainable ecotourism projects by visiting and perhaps volunteering to protect or replant forest areas.
→ Encourage local people to become involved in ecotourism or forest-friendly industries. Hiring local and especially indigenous guides such as those from Kelabit, Penan and Iban tribal groups helps both the people and the forest.
→ If you have to buy wooden products, choose sustainably produced forest products such as those certified by the FSC (Forest Stewardship Council).
→ The US-based Rainforest Action Network, www.ran.org, is another good source of information.

the secretive Sumatran rhino, which is on the verge of extinction (see box, page 462). There are also nearly 300 species of birds. After the rains this area becomes packed with leeches, so specialized leech socks are worth considering.

Trekking

A network of trails linking a series of comfortable but basic scientific camps provides some of the best, and toughest, trekking in Northern Borneo. The treks pass numerous spectacular waterfalls, including the famous multi-tiered Maliau Falls and Takob Akob Falls, over 38 m high. If you're lucky with the weather you should get some panoramic views of the conservation area from the ridge tops.

It's a long drive back to Tawau or Semporna; however, the roads are improving all the time. Make sure you budget for trekking costs, including the entry fee, food of RM80 per day (if you arrange it through the park), accommodation and guide fees. Porters are also available. Each trip has to be individually organized to match trekkers' needs.

To make the most of the conservation area's facilities, a trek of a minimum five days and four nights is recommended (see the sample itinerary below). For truly serious trekkers and those with lots of time (and money) it may be possible to arrange a two-week expedition to Strike Ridge Camp in the north of the basin. As well as trek-based activities there's also a canopy walkway at Belian Camp and an observation platform, 30m high up a huge primary forest tree close to Camel Trophy Camp. This is a suggested basic five-day itinerary, covering 30 km:

Day 1: Many visitors arrive at Agathis Camp after driving from the well-organized (and interestingly Shell-sponsored) reception and information centre, which sells entry permits. Keep your eyes open for wildlife along the road and get some rest for a tough trek the next day.

Day 2: There's a tough climb uphill for a few hours through magnificent primary forest to the ridge top bordering Maliau's southern edge. Gibbons are often heard calling in forest here, a beautiful, emotional sound that encapsulates the spirit of the jungle. The 7-km-long trail leads to the basic Camel Trophy Camp. Behind is the 33-m-high observation tower in an Agathis tree. Additional trails lead to the spectacular Takob Akob Falls, two hours' walk away, and the nearer Giluk Falls. Don't underestimate the hikes after the initial six hours. This is a wildlife-rich area worthy of time and exploration. **Note** Watch out for poisonous red centipedes.

Day 3: A big day. You hike over highlands, mist-clad montane forest and stunted heathlands. These areas are crammed with orchids and pitcher plants, a botanist's dream. A five-hour walk takes you to Lobah Camp. From here, you can get to Maliau Falls, another few hours' return hike to the spectacular multi-level cascade.

Day 4: Take a break to enjoy the forest and the falls. A couple of hours' walk to Ginseng Camp.

Day 5: Another six- to eight-hour hike brings you back to your starting point, Agathis Camp, a good spot for a night hike or a drive to spot some wildlife. Civets, pangolins, small cats and deer are often spotted. You can even get a certificate to state that you've completed the circuit.

For Sleeping and Eating price codes and other relevant information, see Essentials pages 25-30.

◉ Sleeping

Sandakan *p450, map p452*

AL-B Swiss Inn, Sandakan Harbour Square, T089-240888, www.swissgarden.com. New hotel on the waterfront. Rooms are elegant, bright and modern with large flatscreen TV, Wi-Fi access and minibar. The more expensive ones have expansive sea views. Good café and bar downstairs. Decent promotion rates available. Recommended.

A Sabah, Km 1, Jln Utara, T089-213299, www.sabahhotel.com.my. Surrounded by forest, and with some tremendous views over the treetops, this smart 4-star hotel has modern, comfortable rooms with a/c, cable TV and marble bathrooms. Facilities include gym, pool, tennis court, spa and its own nature trail.

A Sanbay, Mile 1.25, Jln Leila, T089-275000, www.sanbay.com.my. 3-star hotel with bright and spacious en suite rooms with piped music and cable TV.

A Sandakan, 4th Av, T089-221122, www.hotelsandakan.com.my. Despite the old-fashioned carpets and heavy decor, rooms here are comfortable and good value. De luxe rooms are spacious and have views over the rooftops of Sandakan and down to the Sulu Sea. Good Cantonese restaurant and bar. This hotel is efficiently run and has some excellent promotional rates. Recommended.

B Hsiang Garden, Km 1, T089-273122, F273127. A/c, restaurant, good bar.

B-C City View, Lot 1, Block 23, 3rd Av, T089-271122, www.citystar.com.my. Hotel with functional, comfortable rooms with a/c, cable TV, Wi-Fi and attached bathroom in the heart of town. Popular restaurant downstairs. Fair value, given the cost of backpacker accommodation in town. Recommended.

B-D Nak, Jln Pelabuhan Lama, T089-272988, www.nakhotel.com. Recently upgraded hotel with tasteful Chinese decor and spacious

rooms with slightly old, but clean bathrooms. Rooms have cable TV and Wi-Fi. Stylish rooftop café with excellent views. A/c dorm.

C London, Lot D1, Block 10, Jln Empat, T089-216372, www.hlondon.com.my. Excellent mid-range place offering a/c spotless, light rooms with cable TV with HBO movies, Wi-Fi and attached bathroom. There's a pleasant rooftop garden. Newly refurbished in classical style. Recommended.

C-D Mayfair, 24 Jln Pryer, T089-219855. Rooms with a/c, shower and TV. Owner has a vast collection of DVDs free to watch. As there's little to do in Sandakan after 2100, this hotel offers some welcome entertainment. Arranges transport to the airport and Sepilok for reasonable prices. The decor isn't great but it has a friendly atmosphere and a central location.

C-D Sandakan Backpackers, Lot 108, Sandakan Harbour Square, T089-221104, www.sandakanbackpackers.com. Miles ahead of the pack in this price range, this hostel has spacious bright rooms with Wi-Fi access and a/c, friendly common area with a pool table and rooftop garden. Can arrange tours to local attractions. Highly recommended.

C-D Winho Lodge, Lot 8, Jln Dua, T089-212310, www.winholodge.com. Large, old-school hostel with functional rooms, free Wi-Fi and internet access and 4-bed a/c dorms. Lacking in charm but reasonable value.

C-E Sunset Harbour Botik Hostel, Lot 125 Harbour Square, T089-229875, www.sunsethostels.com.Clean and friendly Malay-run place with a range of a/c rooms and a 10-bed dorm. There's also a kitchen. Internet access available. Fair value.

Pulau Lankayan *p454*

AL Lankayan Island Dive Resort, run by Pulau Sipadan Resort & Tours, 1st floor, Bandar Sabindo, Tawau, T089-765200, www.lankayan-island.com. The resort offers quiet chalets with electricity and attached bathroom by the beach and more than 40 dive sites including a couple of wrecks. Sightings of whale sharks are said to be common here Apr-May. There is an open-air café for meals and a TV room where dive fanatics gather to watch footage of the day's diving trip.

Turtle Islands National Park *p454*
The number of visitors to the islands is restricted, even in peak season. 3 chalets (one with 2 doubles, 2 with 6 doubles) on Pulau Selingan (RM260-370 per person, minimum 2 people). Book well in advance through **Crystal Quest**, page 479. Tour agencies can also organize trips to the island.

Sepilok Orang-Utan Sanctuary and Rehabilitation Centre *p457*
A-D Sepilok Jungle Resort (and Wildlife Lodge), Km 22 Labuk Rd, Sepilok Orang-Utan Sanctuary, 100 m behind the government resthouse, T089-533031, www.sepilokjungle resort.com. This resort is the realization of a dream for John and Judy Lim, who have gradually purchased all the land on the edge of the forest and landscaped the area surrounding 3 man-made lakes. They've planted many flowering and fruiting trees, attracting butterflies and birds. The resort offers dorms with shared hot-water bathrooms; double rooms with fan, a/c and hot-water bathrooms; comfortable a/c double and family rooms; and more luxurious rooms, with cable TV, a/c, large balcony and tasteful tropical flourishes, surrounded by forest. Pleasant restaurant and in a great setting. This place is clean and comfortable. Boats for fishing available. Campsite (see below). The resort also has a large pool, gym and jacuzzi (RM5 a day). The owners are actively involved in Sandakan tourism and opened the tourist information office in town. Recommended.
The same team have opened **Bilit Adventure Lodge**, offering mid-range rooms along the Kinabatangan River. Rooms, with either a/c or fan, are usually offered in combination with tour packages.
B-D Sepilok B&B, Jln Arboreum, off Jln Sepilok, Mile 14, PO Box 155, T089-534050,

www.sepilokbednbreakfast.com.
Comfortable and bright rooms with polished wooden floors and a variety of rooms from a dorm to a de luxe room with TV and private balcony. All have attached bathroom with hot water. Wi-Fi, free breakfast and campsite under construction at the time of writing. Around 1 km from the sanctuary. Fair value.
B-D Sepilok Resthouse, Mile 14 Labuk Rd, T089-534900. Octagonal wooden house next to the orang-utan sanctuary. Government owned and now privately run. Big rooms, with bathtub and balcony. It's mostly occupied by long-term residents (young foreigners volunteering at the sanctuary), so it can be a bit noisy.
C Sepilok Country Restouse, 22KM, Labuk Rd, Jln Sepilok, T089-535784, www.sepilok countryresthouse.com. It's a fair old trek to the sanctuary from here and the place is a little sterile, but if things are full elsewhere this place offers clean rooms, café, a communal area with pool table and a 22 ft-deep fish pond.
C Uncle Tan Bed and Breakfast, Jln Sepilok, Lot 1, Mile 14, T089-531639, www.uncletan.com. Recently moved from Sandakan, this bed and breakfast has dorm-only accommodation and the price includes 3 meals a day. Double rooms should be ready by the time you read this. The staff here have a wealth of knowledge and can help organize trips to their famed Wildlife Camp in Kinabatangan. Recommended.
C-D Sepilok Forest Edge Resort, Jln Rambutan off Jln Sepilok, Mile 14, T089-533245, www.sepilokforestedge.com. A 10-min walk from the bus stop on Jln Sepilok. Chalets here are new, with attached bathroom and fan. There's also a dorm and a jacuzzi (RM6). Good communal area and jungle trail. They also have their own small farm, and a large pond. One of the owners, Robert Chong, is a birdwatching guide and can arrange tailored trips for birders.

Camping
E There's a campsite at **Sepilok Jungle Resort**, but you must bring your own gear.

Sungai Kinabatangan p459

Most companies running tours to the Kinabatangan put their guests up in Sukau or in camps along the river. See also **Sepilok Jungle Resort** above.

A Sukau Rainforest Lodge, Borneo Eco-Tours, 2nd floor, Lorong Bernam, Taman Soon Kiong, KK, T088-234009, www.sukau.com. Award-winning operator with a large selection of packages. This resort is accessible by boat from Sukau, and is run with eco-friendly ideals. There's accommodation for 40 in traditional Malaysian-style chalets on stilts. All 20 rooms with solar-powered fans, twin beds, mosquito netting, and attached tiled bathroom with hot water. Excellent restaurant and two boardwalks, including the 1500ft Hornbill boardwalk. Pleasant garden and sundeck overlooking the rainforest, and gift shop. Internet and satellite phone available. Friendly, efficient service. A shining example of ecotourism at its best. It must be good – past visitors include the Prince of Denmark and S Club 7! Shoe-string package available for budget travellers – contact Borneo Ecotours for more information. Highly recommended.

B Bilit Rainforest Lodge, contact **Tropical Gateway Tours**, 117 Ground Floor, Sandakan Harbour, T089-202311, www.tropicalg.com. New operation offering excellent value accommodation in spacious wooden a/c chalets with attached bathroom and hot water. They also run the more basic **Bilit Safari Camp (D)**, an option for budget travellers with dorms and highly competitive rates.

B Nature Lodge Kinabatangan, usually booked via **Nasalis Larvatus Tours**, Lot 226, 2nd floor, Wisma Sabah, Jln Tun Adbul Razak, KK, T088-863 6263, www.naturelodge kinabatangan.com/index.php. Excellent wildlife viewing lodge on a quiet section of the river about 1 hr by boat from Sukau. Accommodation is in simple Orang Sungei huts with electricity. The posher Agamind chalets have attached bathrooms with hot water. Good night walks and knowledgeable

and professional guides. Variety of packages offered, including transfers from Sandakan and entrance to the Sepilok Orang-utan Sanctuary.

C Proboscis Lodge, run by Sipadan Dive Centre, 10th floor, Wisma Merdeka, KK, T088-240584, www.proboscislodge.com. A more upmarket Kinabatangan experience, near Sukau, not in the heart of the jungle like the jungle camps. Chalets with hot-water showers, a/c and 24-hr electricity. Lovely large airy main building for meals and socializing and sun deck for observing riverine happenings. Visitors are limited to a maximum of 47 at a time, so it never feels too hectic. Various packages available.

D Uncle Tan Wildlife Adventures, Jln Sepilok, Lot 1, Mile 14, T089-531639, www.uncletan.com. A long-established budget option for exploring the lower Kinabatangan Valley. The camp recently relocated to its present site on the Lokam river, upriver from their previous camp. Accommodation is in simple huts with no doors or window and lino flooring. Guests are provided a clean sheet, a thin mattress and a mosquito net and all rooms are shared. There is a bathouse with water pumped from the river for bathing and visitors are reminded not to leap in the river as several large crocodiles have been lingering. All meals are provided and vegetarians catered for. This is a great way to get back to nature. A 3-day, 2-night package including van transport to the river from the B&B on Jln Sepilok, several river cruises including an amazing night cruise, jungle treks and all meals (simple but hearty) costs RM380 (extra nights for RM80 each). Prepare to get very muddy; wellies are available. Bring raincoat and torch. The camp is very remote and in the middle of the jungle. It is run by enthusiastic young locals who speak pretty good English, love to mix with guests and, while not expert naturalists, are knowledgeable about the wildlife. Some have been working here for years. The camp was started by Uncle Tan, who began taking tourists out to the jungle in 1988. A colourful character, he fought stridently for conservation issues in the region.

He died in 2002 and the running of the resort has been taken over by his brother, based in Singapore. This place is deservedly popular, so book ahead. It's common to see proboscis monkeys and wild orang-utan sightings are not rare. Perhaps your best chance of seeing Sabah's wildlife. Recommended.

Lahad Datu and around p460

Lahad Datu is not a popular tourist spot and accommodation is poor and expensive. Avoid **Perdana** and **Venus** hotels on Jln Seroja.
A Tabin Jungle Resort, Tabin Wildlife Reserve, book at Lot 11-1, Blk A, Damai Point, Jln Damai, KK, T088-267266, www.tabinwildlife.com.my. Great for serious wildlife enthusiasts or anyone on a romantic weekend or escaping to nature for a few days. Beautifully designed wooden cabins with balconies overlooking the Lipad river in Tabin Wildlife Reserve. All cabins with ceiling fan and hot showers. Variety of packages available. Recommended.
B Silam Lodge, Gunung Silam, T088-243245, F254227. Owned by **Borneo Rainforest Lodge** and mostly used by people in transit to the Danum Valley. Minibuses from Lahad Datu.
B-C Jagokota, Jln Kampong Panji, T089-882000, F881526. A well-furnished place.
C Permaisaba, Block 1, Lot 3, 1/4 Jln Tengah Nipah, T089-883800, F883681. Five mins' drive from the airport and town. Seafood restaurant, Malaysian and Indian food, conference hall, free transfers to/from the airport and town. Large rooms with attached bathroom and hot water, information on the Danum Valley, characterless but convenient.

Danum Valley Conservation Area p461

AL Borneo Rainforest Lodge, c/o Borneo Nature Tours, Block 3, ground floor, Fajar Centre, Lahad Datu, T089-880207, F885051. KK office: Block D, Lot 10, 3rd floor, Sadong Jaya Complex, T088-243245, www.borneorainforestlodge.com. One of the finest tourism developments in Sabah. 18 bungalows in a magnificent setting beside the river, built on stilts from *belian* (ironwood) and based on traditional Kadazan design with connecting wooden walkways. 28 rooms with private bathroom and balcony overlooking the Danum River, good restaurant, jacuzzi (solar-heated water). Designed by naturalists, the centre aims to combine a wildlife experience in a remote primary rainforest with comfort and privacy and provide high-quality natural history information. There is a conference hall, excellent guides; visits to a centre for forest management, a library of resource books, after-dinner slide shows and a gift shop. Rafting is available and night drives can be organized. Mountain bikes, fishing rods and river tubes can be hired. Electricity is available all day. Expensive but well worth it. Price includes meals and guided jungle trips. If you get permission to stay at the centre, the **Sabah Foundation** has dorms for RM45 per night, or RM80 for a single room.

Semporna p463

AL-B Seafest, Jln Kastam, T089-782333, www.seafesthotel.com. A high-rise building on the waterfront, somewhat out of character with the rest of the town but a lack of business has forced them into offering very good walk-in promotional rates. Rooms are comfortable but characterless. There's a restaurant and a new pool. Wi-Fi is available up to the 6th storey. Front-facing rooms have great views of the bay.
A-B Sipadan Inn, Block D, Lot No19-24, seafront, T089-782766, www.sipidan-inn.com. Newish place near the main jetty, popular with people on dive courses. It has huge well-furnished de luxe rooms with massive TV, attached bathroom and lounge area. The smaller a/c standards are a bit of a squeeze, but comfortable and clean. Wi-Fi.
B-C City Inn, Lot 2, Block K, Bangunan, Hing Loong, close to the Dyana Express bus office, T089-784733, www.cityinn-semporna.com. This well-run place has spotless, slightly old rooms with TV, attached bathroom and a/c in the busy commercial heart of the town – it's a

good 5-min walk to the jetty, but handy for the bus station. Wi-Fi and internet access in the lobby. Recommended.

B-D Borneo Global Backpackers, Bangunan Seafest, Jln Causeway, T089-785088, www.bgbackpackers.com. New place right on the waterfront with large a/c dorms with attached bathroom and spacious family rooms. Rooms at the front have excellent views over the bay. Very clean and well managed. Arranges trips to Sipidan and Mabul.

B-D Dragon Inn, Jln (next to the jetty), T089-781088, F781099, www.dragoninnfloating com.my. All rooms are built in wooden longhouses over the sea. Unfortunately much of the sea here is filled with the detritus of urban coastal life, which detracts from the charm. Some very large, well-furnished doubles and smaller twins with a/c, TV and attached bathroom. Cavernous dorms are excellent value with over 20 beds that are often empty. Great experience to have a shower and see the green ocean through the wooden slatted floor. Recommended.

C Lee's Resthouse and Café, Pekau Baru, T/F089-784491. Clean guesthouse with pokey rooms with a/c, TV and attached bathroom. Some rooms are windowless. Slighty overpriced, but staff are very friendly and there is a superb restaurant next door.

C-D Damai Traveller's Lodge, TL 89, 3rd floor, town centre, T089-782011, F781525. Particularly unexciting place in the town centre. Rooms have a/c, attached bathroom and TV but many are windowless. Can arrange tours and trips to islands. Some rooms have sea views. Average value.

C-E Scuba Junkie Backpacker, PO Box 458, Block B Lot 36, seafront, T089-785372, www.scuba-junkie.com. Opposite Scuba Junkie's dive shop and with a bar/restaurant attached. Good location with a variety of rooms from dorms to en suites. Excellent value with breakfast and internet included and discounts for SJ's divers and snorkellers. Some private rooms are a little cave-like with no windows and not always perfectly clean. Book ahead as this place is often rammed.

Mabul Island *p465*

With the closure of all Sipidan resorts Mabul Island is a convenient place to stay. There are several resorts here, plus some cheaper options. Food is often included in the price.

L Mabul Water Bungalows, book via Explore Asia Tours, Lot A-1-G, Block A, Signature Office, KK Times Square, off Coastal Highway, T088-486389, www.mabul waterbungalows.com. A pricey and luxurious resort built on stilts above the Mabul reef. Dive packages and facilities including nitrox and cave diving are available. A good choice for people who want all their home comforts, with cable TV, minibar, a/c and business centre with internet access.

L Sipadan Mabul Resort, at the southern tip of the island overlooking Sipidan and a pleasant beach, the same company, contact address, website and phone number as Mabul Water Bungalows above. 25 newly refurbished beach chalets with a/c, hot-water showers, balcony, pool and jacuzzi, restaurant serving Chinese and Western buffet food, all-inclusive price, PADI diving courses, snorkelling, windsurfing, deep-sea fishing, volleyball, diving boats.

L Sipadan Water Village, reservations: PO Box 62156, T089-751777, www.sipadan-village.com.my. Stunning resort constructed on several wharves in Bajau, water village-style on ironwood stilts over the water. 45 chalets with private balconies, hot-water showers, restaurant serving good range of cuisine, well-organized dive shop and centre, deep-sea fishing tours. Relaxing, tranquil place, with no TV or unnecessary noise. 3 daily boat dives are usually included in packages and there's quite a bit of marine life on the house reef directly below the resort. Reserve in advance for Sipidan Island dives/licenses.

A Borneo Divers Mabul Resort, Head Office, 9th floor, Menara Jubili, 53 Jln Gaya, Kota Kinabalu, T088-222226, www.borneo divers.info. Small office just outside the entrance to Dragon Inn next to Uncle Chang's. One of the few mid-range places on the island, prices include food. Pool. Not particularly stylish, but decent value facing the beach and the **Seaventures** platform. All diving facilities.

A Seaventures Dive Resort, run by Sea Ventures Dives, 4th floor 422-423, Wisma Sabah, Kota Kinabalu, T088-261669, www.seaventuresdive.com. Just offshore is the strange site of a refurbished oil rig. A true diver's spot, it offers boat dives to Sipadan and other nearby islands and is locally famous for its excellent muck diving directly beneath the platform. Good value and an exciting location for divers who enjoy macrolife and underwater photography.

C per person. **The Longhouse** book through Scuba Junkie, Semporna, see page 480, price includes food if diving with **Scuba Junkie**. Very basic but superb value. Interesting location in Bajau village house. 6 new rooms constructed and a bar on the way. RM40 each way for transfer to the island if you're not diving.

C per person. **Uncle Chang's**, book through Uncle Chang's dive shop, see page 480. Another good backpacker option, located in the Bajau village on the far side of Mabul island. Rates include food and Uncle Chang has all the diving kit, plus years of experience above and below the waves in the region. He is currently trying to open a place on Maita island. Recommended.

Mataking and Kapalai *p466*

L Mataking Island Reef Dive Resort, book through Jln Bunga, Tawau, T089-770022, or ground floor, Wisma Sabah, KK, T088-318022, www.mataking.com. It also has a counter in Semporna at the jetty on Jln Kastam. The resort has 3 speedboats daily from Semporna jetty and the journey takes 45 mins. The resort has a/c chalets and de luxe rooms, some with sea view and balcony. Facilities at the resort include a *jammu* (native medicinal) spa, satellite TV, internet, bar and restaurant. In 2006 the resort sank an old cargo boat and renamed it the Mataking 1, with the hopes that this will encourage a new reef to grow.

The wreck is home to Malaysia's only underwater post office – now that's a postbox with a difference!

AL Sipadan-Kapalai Dive Resort, run by Pulau Sipadan Resort & Tours, 1st floor, Bandar Sabindo, Tawau, T089-765200, www.sipadan-kapalai.com. This resort straddles Kapalai's sandback on stilts. The resort, modelled as a water village, has 40 twin-sharing wooden chalets, with attached bathrooms, balconies and amazing sea views all round, linked by a network of wooden platforms. Dive centre, internet access.

Tawau *p466*

Rock-bottom places in Tawau are grim and visitors are advised to spend a few more ringgit to get somewhere safe and clean. There aren't any guesthouses to speak of, but a number of good value mid-range places aimed at local business travellers. Hotels are concentrated around the intersection of Jln Bunga and Jln Haji Karim.

A Belmont Marco Polo, Jln Abaca/Jln Clinic, T089-777988, F763739. Smart upmarket hotel primarily aimed at business travellers, but offering great walk-in promotional rates. Rooms are clean and feature cable TV, Wi-Fi access, and rather stiff, formal furnishings. Bathrooms have bathtubs. There's also a health centre, café and good Chinese restaurant.

A-B De Choice, Jln Masjid, T089-776655. Sterile business hotel with a selection of spacious clean rooms all with a/c, Wi-Fi access and attached bathroom. Fair value.

A-B Heritage, Jln Bunga, Fajar Complex, T089-766222, www.heritagehotel.com.my. Well-managed hotel with stylish, modern rooms. All rooms have sofas and complimentary daily newspapers. More expensive rooms have bathtubs, free Wi-Fi access and jacuzzi. Recommended.

B King Park, 30 Jln Haji Karim, T089-766699, kingpark@streamyx.com. Good mid-range option with 150 clean rooms in a mint green tower block overlooking the city. Rooms at the front have views of the sea in the distance. All

rooms have cable TV, a/c, attached bathroom and Wi-Fi access. Good promotional rates.
B MB, Jln Masjid, T089-701333, www.mavblossomhotel.com. New hotel with spotless, modern rooms. Limited in character but with all the facilities needed for a comfortable stay. Good promotional rates. Recommended.

B-C Monaco, 214 Jln Haji Karim (on the corner of Jln Bunga), T089-769912, F769922. The best value lodgings in town with carpeted a/c rooms (some windowless) with Wi-Fi access, cable TV and attached bathroom. Staff are friendly and rooms on the corner have good views over the rooftops to the hills surrounding Tawau. Recommended. This hotel is run by the same groups that runs the **Monaco Dynasty Hotel (B-C)** and **Istana Monaco Hotel (B-C)**, opposite on Jln Bunga. All 3 hotels have similar facilities, but the **Istana** has the newest rooms. Rooms at the **Dynasty** are looking a little tatty and are mostly windowless.

C First, 208 Jln Bunga, T089-778989, F761296. Popular with domestic travellers, this place is looking a little rough round the edges but has clean rooms with a/c and attached bathroom. There are better value options along the street.

C Grace, 4263 Jln Chester, T089-751555. Handy for the port for boats to Indonesia and in the bustling centre, this place has passable a/c rooms with TV and attached bathroom.

Maliau Basin *p467*

E per person. **Maliau Basin camps**. Basic dorms, beds must be booked in advance due to limited availability. Camps have 20-40 beds, apart from Camel Trophy Camp with only 8 places available.

● Eating

Sandakan *p450, map p452*
Sandakan is justifiably renowned for its inexpensive and delicious seafood; try the semi-outdoor restaurants situated at the top of Trig (Trigonometry) Hill.

♈ **English Tea House & Restaurant**, Agnes Keith House, T089-222544, www.englishtea house.org. Step back in time at this wonderful place with shady outdoor garden seating overlooking the bay, an immaculate croquet lawn and jugs of Pimms. An afternoon here could easily be mistaken for a freakishly hot day in Devon circa 1930. Scones, clotted cream and pots of tea are proffered alongside excellent fusion cuisine that makes this one of Malaysia's most charming eateries. Highly recommended.
♈ **New Seoul Garden**, Hsiang Garden Estate, Mile 1.5, Leila Rd. Korean food.
♈ **Ocean King Seafood**, Mile 2.5, Jln Batu Sapi, T089-618111. Great seafood place built on stilts over the water. Big, over-the-top statues of lobster and marine life Disney-up the place. But unbeatable for a relaxing sunset meal, great views.
♈ **Palm Garden**, Hotel Sandakan. Open for lunch and dinner. Well known for its steamboats and dim sum buffets, this place is a good spot to sample Sandakan's Cantonese cuisine. There's an international buffet every Friday in the **Palm Café** downstairs.
♈ **Pesah Putih Baru**, on the coast, nearly at the end of Sandakan Bay, about 5 km from the port. Great views of Sandakan and good food. Recommended.
♈ **Trig Hill Ming**, Sabah Hotel, Km 1, Jln Utara, T089-213299. Cantonese and Sichuan cuisine, renowned for dim sum (breakfast).
♉ **Balin Rooftop Garden**, Nak Hotel, Jln Pelabuhan Lama. Open 1630-2400. Lovely rooftop garden serving simple Western fare and cold beers, making this an ideal spot for a sundowner. Recommended.
♉ **Fairwood**, Jln Dua. A cheap, a/c fast-food place with all the local favourites, situated in the centre of town.
♉ **Fat Cat**, 206 Wisma Sandakan, 18 Jln Haji Saman. Several branches around town, breakfasts recommended.
♉ **Hawaii**, City View Hotel, Lot 1, Block 23, 3rd Av. Pseudo Western and local food, busy at 1200 as workers come for the cheap set lunch.
♉ **Kedai Makanan King Cheong**, Jln Dua. Open for breakfast and lunch. The quality

of this great place is testified to by the lunchtime crowds that ram in daily. Trolleys of dim sum weave between tables of punters getting stuck into simple Cantonese fare and some interesting oddities: Marmite fans will want try the *nasi ayam marmite*.

Restoran Hikmah, Jln Batu Empat, Mile 4. Reputed to be the best spot in town for Malay food, with good seafood dishes and some *asam pedas*.

Santai, Waterfront, Sandakan Harbour Sq. Cheap seafood dishes, including superb noodles and fried rice, this popular spot is right on the waterfront offering a relaxing view of the fishing boats on the horizon. Busy in the evenings. Recommended.

ZL Vegetarian Restaurant, Lot 6, Block 1, Bandar Pasar Raya, Batu Empat. Great value selection of Chinese vegetarian dishes on the edge of town.

Foodstalls

Next to minibus station, just before the community centre on the road to Ramai Ramai, also at summit of Trig Hill.

Sepilok Orang-Utan Sanctuary and Rehabilitation Centre *p457*

By far the best place to eat is the veranda restaurant at the **Sepilok Jungle Resort**, which serves international and Malaysian food. The food is OK but the setting is lovely.

Lahad Datu and around *p460*

Melawar, 2nd floor, Block 47, off Jln Teratai (around the corner from the **Mido Hotel**). Seafood restaurant, popular with locals.

Ping Foong, 1.5 km out of Lahad Datu, on Sandakan Rd. Open-air seafood restaurant, highly recommended by locals.

Ali, opposite **Hotel New Sabah**. Indian, good roti.

Evergreen Snack Bar and Pub, on 2nd floor, Jln Teratai, opposite Hap Seng Building. A/c, excellent fish and chips and best known for its tuna steaks. Recommended.

Golden Key, on stilts over the sea opposite the end of Jln Teratai. Just a tumbledown

wooden coffee shop, but well known for its seafood.

Good View, just over 500 m out of town on Tengku Rd. Recommended by locals.

Seng Kee, Block 39, opposite **Mido Hotel** and next to **Standard Chartered Bank**. Cheap and good.

Foodstalls

Pasar Malam, behind **Mido Hotel** on Jln Kastam Lama. Spicy barbecued fish (*ikan panggang*) and skewered chicken wings recommended.

The new market has foodstalls upstairs with attractive views out to sea.

Semporna *p463*

This grubby little town is no diner's fantasy, but there is some good seafood on offer and plenty of little eateries offering Malay curries. Don't leave it too late for dinner in the evening as Semporna goes to bed early.

Pearl City Restaurant, attached to **Dragon Inn**. Chinese-style seafood in a wooden restaurant over the sea. Verify prices before ordering. Great setting. Recommended.

Seafest, next to the **Seafest Inn**. Mainly Malay food with some excellent fish dishes. Good standard for very reasonable prices.

Anjung Paghalian, next to police station near bridge to jetty. Simple outdoor place with good, cheap seafood and giant iced avocado juices. Recommended.

Lee's Café, next to **Lee's Hotel**. This place is the best eatery in town with excellent Chinese dishes at very good prices. The prawns here are plump, the beer cold and the staff friendly. Simple Western breakfasts are available from 0700 onwards. Recommended.

Mabul Café (a few shops down from Scuba Junkie). Mainly a Chinese restaurant but with plenty of pseudo-Western dishes such as king prawn wrapped in a kraft cheddar slice, steaks, fries and all the usual suspects. The Asian dishes are the better choice here. Plenty of beer available.

Sinar Harapan, next to Mabul Café. Simple Malay place with curries, noodles and *tom* *yam*. Friendly spot to neck a plate of *pisang goreng* on a listless tropical afternoon.

Tawau *p466*
Foodstalls along the seafront.
† CJs Bistro, Jln Bunga (next to Heritage Hotel). Good pizza, coffee, naughty desserts and Western dishes in a convivial, clean restaurant with Wi-Fi access. Recommended.
† Kam Ling Seafood, Sabindo Square. Delicious fresh seafood including crab and huge prawns. The fresh lime juice here is excellent. Very popular.
† Kublai Khan, Marco Polo Hotel, Jln Clinic. Open for lunch and dinner. Large, traditionally furnished Chinese eating hall specialising in Cantonese food, with a good value weekly steamboat buffet (Sat, 1900). There is also the **Venice Coffee House** here serving a range of fair international cusine and huge weekend brunches.
† May Garden, 1 km outside town on road to Semporna. Outside seating.
† Asnur, 325B, Block 41, Fajar Complex. Thai and Malay, large choice.
† Dragon Court, 1st floor, Lot 15, Block 37 Jln Haji Karim. Chinese, popular with locals, lots of seafood.
† Olive, 1878 Jln Haji Karim. Open 1100-1430 and 1800-2230. Cheap eatery serving glasses of red wine, cold beer and a menu of pizza, tapas and pasta dishes. Don't expect the real deal with these prices, but not a bad spot nevertheless.
† Yasmin, Jln Chester. Excellent selection of *nasi campur* dishes served with an interesting cinnamon-infused chicken soup.
† Yassin Curry House, Sabindo Square (near the minibus terminal). Biryani, tandoori chicken, kebabs and outrageously sweet lassis, 10 mins' walk from the town centre. There is a/c seating.
† Yun Lo, Jln Abaca (below the Hotel Loong). Good Malay and Chinese. A popular spot with locals, good atmosphere. Recommended.

☺ Entertainment

Sandakan *p450, map p452*
There is a karaoke parlour on just about every street. **Tiffany Discotheatre and Karaoke**, Block C, 7-10, Jln Leila, Bandar Ramai-Ramai.

Tawau *p466*
Cinema, Jln Stephen Tan, next to central market. There are karaoke bars on every street corner. Several hotels have nightclubs and bars.

O Shopping

Sandakan *p450, map p452*
Almost everything in Sandakan is imported. There are some inexpensive batik shops and some good tailors. **Centre Point**, near the bus station, is even more down at heel than Wisma Sandakan. **Handicrafts Sabakraf**, opposite Hotel Sandakan, has basketry, pearls and souvenirs. **Wisma Sandakan**, next to the town mosque, has 3 floors of dimly lit shopping.

Lahad Datu and around *p460*
The central market is on Jln Bungaraya and there is a spice market off Jln Teratai where Indonesian smugglers tout Gudang Garam cigarettes and itinerant dentists and *bumohs* (witch doctors) draw large crowds.

Semporna *p463*
Cultured pearls are sold by traders in town. Filipino handicrafts.

Tawau *p466*
General and fish market at the west end of Jln Dunlop, near the customs wharf.

▲ Activities and tours

Sandakan *p450, map p452*
Bowling
Champion Bowl, Jln Leila, Bandar Ramai Ramai. Jln Leila is the main road that heads

out of Sandakan, **Champion Bowl** is just out of town at Mile 1¼, T089-211396.

Golf
Sandakan Golf Club, Jln Kolam, Bukit Padang, T088-247533, 10 km out of town. Open to non-members.

Social clubs
Sepilok Recreation Club, Bandar Ramai Ramai. Snooker, sauna, darts and karaoke.

Tour operators
Many tour operators have their offices in Wisma Khoo Siak Chiew.
Borneo Ecotours, c/o Hotel Hsiang Garden, PO Box 82, Jln Leila, T089-220210, F213614.
Capac Travel Service, ground floor, Rural District Building, Jln Tiga, T089-217288. Ticketing, tour and hotel services.
Crystal Quest, Sabah Park Jetty, Jln Buli Sim Sim, T089-212711, cquest@tm.net.my or cq1996@streamyx.net. The only company running accommodation on Pulau Selingan, Turtle Islands National Park.
SI Tours, 1st floor, Wisma Khoo Siak Chiew, T089-213501, www.sitours.com.my. Well-established company running tours to Gomantong Caves, Kinabatangan and Turtle Islands National Park. Recommended.
Tropical G, 117, Block 12, Sandakan Harbour Square, T089-202333, www.tropicalg.com. Offers Sabah-wide packages including trips to Kinabatangan, Gomontong caves and Selingan turtle islands, Danum Valley and Maliau Basin.
Wildlife Expeditions, Room 903, 9th floor, Wisma Khoo Siak Chiew, Lebuh Tiga, Jln Buli Sim-Sim, T089-219616, F214570 (in **Sabah Hotel**). The most expensive, but the most efficient, with the best facilities and guides.

Turtle Islands National Park p454
The average cost of a 1-night tour including accommodation and boat transfer is RM350 or more. An expedition to the islands needs to be well planned; the vagaries, such as bad weather, which can prevent you from leaving

the islands as planned, can mess up itineraries. Most visitors book trips well in advance.

Gomantong Caves p458
It is easiest to visit the caves on a tour, see Sandakan above. They are accessible by an old logging road, which can be reached by bus from the main Sandakan-Sukau Rd. The timing of the bus is inconvenient for those wishing to visit the caves. Alternatively take a taxi (around RM150 from Sandakan). It is a good idea to visit the caves on the way to Sukau, where you can stay overnight.

Sungai Kinabatangan p459
Tour operators will transport guests to the lodge or camp as part of the package, some offer tours of Gomantong and/or Sepilok en route. **Uncle Tan's** picks up from its base in Sepilok. Others have transport from Sandakan, Tawau, Danum Valley and Semporna. Book trips at tour operators in Sandakan, see above, or KK, page 414.

Lahad Datu and around p460
Tour operators
Borneo Nature Tours, Block 3, Fajar Centre, T089-880207, F885051.

Semporna p463
Tour operators
Today Travel Services, No 90, Lot 2, Tingkat Bawah, T089-781112. Sells **AirAsia** and MAS flights to KK and KL from Tawau, the nearest airport.

Sipadan Island Marine Reserve p464
Tour operators
Most dive centres here offer PADI courses. Each operator arranges permits, rents out equipment (RM50-75 per day) and provides all food and accommodation. Pre-arranged packages operated by the companies sometimes include air transfer to and from Kota Kinabalu. Walk-in rates are cheaper. Book trips to Sipidan well in advance as only 120 permits are issued daily.

Borneo Divers, Rooms 401-412, 4th floor, Wisma Sabah, KK, T088-222226, www.borneodivers.info. A major Sipadan player; it organizes trips from KK to Sipadan with accommodation on Mabul. However, some complain it has gone downhill. 3-day package with 10 dives and stay on Mabul around RM1200.

Pulau Sipadan Resort, 484, Block P, Bandar Sabindo, Tawau, T089-765200, www.sipadan-resort.com. Organizes dive tours, food and lodging and diving instruction, snorkelling equipment is also available, maximum of 30 divers at any one time. It also runs accommodation on Pulau Kapalai.

Scuba Junkie, Blk B, Lot 36, Semporna seafront, T089-785372, www.scuba-junkie.com. Well-run outfit that offers a variety of courses and trips to Mataking, Sipidan, Kapalai and Mabul. Accommodation on Mabul available. 2-dive trip to Sipidan (RM330), snorkelling to outer islands and night dives arranged.

Sipadan Dive Centre, A1103, 11th floor, Wisma Merdeka, Jln Tun Razak, KK, T088-240584, www.sipidandivers.com. Packages (all-in) approximately US$740 (5 days/4 nights). Recommended.

Uncle Chang's, entrance to **Dragon Inn**, Semporna, T089-781002. Uncle Chang, entrepreneur extraordinaire, offers the budget traveller everything. He can get discount bus tickets, offers shuttle service to the airport, gets discounts for the **Dragon Inn**, has an efficient laundry service and runs some great dive trips out to Sipadan including courses. 3 boat dives including all equipment hire and lunch for RM360 Snorkelling day trips to Sipdian (RM225) and Mabul (RM115), plus night diving at Mabul (RM115). Excellent value accommodation on Mabul. Recommended.

Tawau p466
Diving
Borneo Divers, 46, 1st floor, Jln Dunlop, T089-762259, F761691.
Pulau Sipadan Resort & Tours, 1st floor, Bandar Sabindo, Tawau, T089-765200, F763563.

Reef Dive Resort and Tours, Jln Bunga, T089-770022, www.mataking.com. Arranges packages to the upmarket **Reef Dive Resort** on Mataking.

Golf
9-hole golf course, modest green fees, even cheaper during the week.

Tour operators
GSU, T089-772531. This is the booking agent for Kalimantan.

⊖ Transport

Sandakan p450, map p452
Air
The airport is 10 km north of the town centre (RM20 by taxi into town). Early morning flights from **KK** to Sandakan allow breathtaking close-up views of Mt Kinabalu as the sun rises. **AirAsia** and **MAS** have daily connections with **KL** and KK. **MASwings** flies daily to **Tawau** and KK.

Airline offices MAS, ground floor, Sabah Bldg, Jln Pelabuhan, T089-273966; AirAsia, Jln Dua.

Boat
The MV Kristle Jane 3 sails to **Zamboanga** in the southern **Philippines**. The journey takes 12-16 hrs and leaves at 1700 every Tue and Fri from Sandakan (RM280 for a suite). Contact **Aleson Shipping Lines** (T089-212063 or T089-224009) for ticketing.

Bus and minibus
Local minibuses from the bus stop between the Esso and Shell stations on Jln Pryer.

Sandakan's a/c long-distance buses leave from the bus station at Mile 2.5. Some buses and all minibuses don't leave until they are full, so be prepared for a long wait. Regular connections with most towns in Sabah including **Kota Kinabalu**, (6 hrs, RM42), **Ranau**, (4 hrs, RM27), **Lahad Datu** (3-4 hrs, RM20). Buses start at 0715, and then several departures until 1100. After this you will have to take a Tawau bus, get off at Simpang Assam and take a minibus into Lahad Datu (RM1). **Tawau** (6 hrs, RM40), buses from 0630, every 30 mins until 1100. 1 bus at 1400. **Semporna** (6 hrs, RM40), departs 0800.

Turtle Islands National Park p454

Tour operators have their own boats and the fee is included with the package price, so times will vary.

Sepilok Orang-Utan Sanctuary and Rehabilitation Centre p457
Bus

There are 5 daily public buses from **Sandakan**, from the central minibus terminal in front of Nak Hotel from 0900-1400 (40 mins RM4). Ask for the Sepilok Batu 14 line. From the airport, the most convenient way to reach Sepilok is by taxi. Sepilok is 1.9 km from the main road. A taxi should cost around RM35 into Sandakan. You can charter a car for RM40 into Sandakan from **Sepilok Jungle Resort**. There are 6 buses to Sandakan from 0700-1600 (40 mins RM4).

Lahad Datu and around p460
Air

Connections with **KK**.

Airline offices MAS, ground floor, Mido Hotel, Jln Main, T089-881707.

Boat

Fishing boats take paying passengers from the old wharf (end of Jln Kastam Lama) to **Tawau** and **Semporna**, although time-wise (and, more to the point, safety-wise) it makes much more sense to go by road or air.

Minibus

Minibuses and what are locally known as wagons (7-seater, 4WD Mitsubishis) leave from the bus station on Jln Bunga Raya (behind Bangunan Hap Seng at the mosque end of Jln Teratai) and from opposite the Shell station. Regular connections with **Tawau** (2½ hrs), **Semporna**, **Sandakan** and **Madai**.

Danum Valley Conservation Area p461

From Lahad Datu, turn left along the logging road at Km 15 on the Lahad Datu – Tawau road to Taliwas and then left again to field centre, 85 km west of Lahad Datu. **Borneo Rainforest Lodge** is 97 km (not an easy trip) from **Lahad Datu**; it provides a transfer service (2 hrs); phone the lodge for details.

Semporna p463
Bus and minibus

Minibus station in front of USNO HQ. Regular connections with **Tawau** (1½ hrs, RM13) and **Lahad Datu**. Most departures are in the morning. Minibus to **Tawau airport**. 1 daily bus to Sandakan (6 hrs, RM40). 2 daily buses to **KK** (0730, 1930, 11 hrs, RM75). The mid-morning AirAsia flight from Tawau is a better option. Prices start at RM70.

Mataking and Kapalai p466
Air and boat

Flight to **Tawau**, minibus, taxi or resort van to Semporna (1½ hrs), from where speed boats depart for the islands (30-60 mins). Boats to the islands are taken either with dive companies or as a transfer to a resort. Lots of boats leave daily but generally only in the morning at around 0730, for day trips (RM100).

Tawau p466
Air

The airport is 2 km from town centre. Regular connections with MAS and Air Asia to **KK** and **KL** and MASwings to **Sandakan**.

Flights to **Tarakan** and elsewhere in Indonesia have been suspended. Those travelling to **Kalimantan** will have to take a boat to Nunukan.

Airline offices AirAsia office at the airport and on Jln Bunga opposite the Heritage Hotel. MAS, Lot 1A, Wisma SASCO, Fajar Complex, T089-765533.

Boat

Packed boats leave Tawau's customs wharf (behind Pasar Ikan) twice daily at 1100 and 1600 for **Pulau Nunukan Timur, Kalimantan**

(1 hr, RM75). More convenient is the boat to **Indonesia**'s **Tarakan** (daily at 1130 except Sun, 4 hrs RM140). There is limited transport available from Nunukan, and travellers will need to travel to Tarakan for more transport options (there are 2 daily **Kal Star** flights from Nunukan to Tarakan at 1330 and 1400, Rp250,000). Nunukan is connected to **Pare Pare**, **Pantoloan**, by PELNI ferry. Tarakan is connected to **Balikpapan** and **Surabaya** by air and with **Toli Toli Surabaya**, and **Jakarta** with PELNI ferry. All visitors need to get a visa before arriving in Indonesia. Tickets available from offices near the Pasar Ikan (fish market). Agents include **Saumdera Indah**, T089-753320.

Note PELNI ferries in Indonesia generally call in every 2 weeks. Travellers wishing to catch a ferry should time their arrival in Nunukan or Tarakan to meet the ferry. Schedules are available at www.pelni.co.id.

Bus

Station on Jln Wing Lock (west end of town). Minibus station on Jln Dunlop (centre of town). Direct service from Tawau to **Kota Kinabalu** leaving at 2000 to arrive 0500 in KK (RM75). It's a better option to take the mid-morning flight to KK on AirAsia, from RM70. Minibuses to **Semporna** leave when full from the Sabindo Complex (1½ hrs, RM13).

It's possible to drive from **Sapulut** (south of **Keningau**) across the interior to Tawau on logging roads (4WD vehicle is required).

Maliau Basin *p467*

There isn't much public transport to Maliau; however, due to road improvements this may change in the near future. If you don't have your own transport you can arrange to hire a 4WD and driver through the Maliau Basin Conservation Area organization, see page 467. Vehicles can carry up 5 people and their gear. The return 4-5 hr trip to the Basin from either Tawau or Keningau (on the west coast) will cost RM600-700 per vehicle.

Directory

Sandakan *p450, map p452*
Banks Most are situated on Lebuh Tiga and Jln Pelabuhan. HSBC, Lebuh Tiga/Jln Pelabuhan; Standard Chartered, Jln Pelabuhan. **Immigration** Federal Bldg, Jln Leila. **Internet** Sandakan Cybercafé, 2nd floor, Wisma Sandakan; also in Centre Point mall. **Parks Office** Sabah Parks Office, Room 906, 9th floor, Wisma Khoo, Lebuh Tiga, T089-273453. Bookings for Turtle Islands National Park. **Post office** General Post Office, Jln Leila, to the west of town; parcel post off Lebuh Tiga.
Telephone Telecom Office, 6th floor, Wisma Khoo Siak Chiew, Jln Buli Sim-Sim.

Lahad Datu and around *p460*
Banks Standard Chartered, in front of Mido Hotel. **Post office** Post office, Jln Kenanga, next to the Lacin cinema.

Semporna *p463*
Bank Maybank (near the mosque). The queues for the ATM here are horrendous on a daily basis. Visitors are recommended to bring enough cash with them or face a long wait to get on the machine.
Internet Cyber Planet (opposite Damai), 1st floor, 0800-2200, RM3 per hr; Zanna Computer, next to Maybank, 1st floor; @DCCN opposite bus station, RM2 per hr (often closed). **Post office** General Post Office next to minibus station.

Tawau *p466*
Banks Bumiputra, Jln Nusantor, on seafront; HSBC, 210 Jln Utara, opposite the padang; Standard Chartered, 518 Jln Habib Husein (behind HSBC); exchange kiosk at wharf. **Embassies and consulates** Indonesian Consulate, Jln Sinn On. Open from 0900. Taxi RM8 from the city centre, 60-day visa available here. **Immigration** Office on Jln Stephen. **Post office** Post Office off Jln Nusantor, behind the fish market.

Background

The name Sabah is probably from the Arabic *Zir-e Bad* (the land below the wind). This is appropriate, as the state lies just south of the typhoon belt. Officially, the territory has only been called Sabah since 1963, when it joined the Malay federation, but the name appears to have been in use long before that. When Baron Gustav Von Overbeck was awarded the cession rights to North Borneo by the Sultan of Brunei in 1877, one of the titles conferred on him was Maharajah of Sabah. In the *Handbook of British North Borneo*, published in 1890, it says: "In Darvel Bay there are the remnants of a tribe which seems to have been much more plentiful in bygone days – the Sabahans". From the founding of the Chartered Company until 1963, Sabah was British North Borneo.

Sabah has a population of just over 2.5 million plus a good number of illegal immigrants on top of that. Sabah's inhabitants can be divided into four main groups: the Kadazan Dusun, the Bajau, the Chinese and the Murut, as well as a small Malay population. These groups are subdivided into several different tribes (see page 488).

History

Prehistoric stone tools have been found in eastern Sabah, suggesting that people were living in limestone caves in the Madai area 17,000-20,000 years ago. The caves were periodically settled from then on; pottery dating from the late neolithic period has been found, and by the early years of the first millennium AD, Madai's inhabitants were making iron spears and decorated pottery. The Madai and Baturong caves were lived in continuously until about the 16th century and several carved stone coffins and burial jars have been discovered in the jungle caves, one of which is exhibited in the Sabah State Museum. The caves were also known for their birds' nests; Chinese traders were buying the nests from Borneo as far back as AD 700. In addition, they exported camphor wood, pepper and other forest products to Imperial China.

There are very few archaeological records indicating Sabah's early history, although there is documentary evidence of links between a long-lost kingdom, based in the area of the Kinabatangan River, and the Sultanate of Brunei, whose suzerainty was once most of North Borneo. By the early 18th century, Brunei's power had begun to wane in the face of European expansionism. To counter the economic decline, it is thought the sultan increased taxation, which led to civil unrest. In 1704 the Sultan of Brunei had to ask the Sultan of Sulu's help in putting down a rebellion in Sabah and, in return, the Sultan of Sulu received most of what is now Sabah.

The would-be White Rajahs of Sabah

It was not until 1846 that the British entered into a treaty with the Sultan of Brunei and took possession of the island of Labuan, in part to counter the growing influence of the Rajah of Sarawak, James Brooke. The British were also wary of the Americans; the US Navy signed a trade treaty with the Sultan of Brunei in 1845 and in 1860 Claude Lee Moses was appointed American consul-general in Brunei Town. However, he was only interested in making a personal fortune and quickly persuaded the sultan to cede him land in Sabah. He sold these rights to two Hong Kong-based American businessmen who formed the American Trading Company of Borneo. They styled themselves as rajahs and set up a base at Kimanis, just south of Papar. It was a disaster. One of them died of malaria, the Chinese labourers they imported from Hong Kong began to starve and the settlement was abandoned in 1866.

The idea of a trading colony on the North Borneo coast interested the Austrian consul in Hong Kong, Baron Gustav von Overbeck, who, in turn, sold the concept to Alfred Dent, a wealthy English businessman also based in Hong Kong. With Dent's money, Overbeck bought the Americans' cession from the Sultan of Brunei and extended the territory to cover most of modern-day Sabah. The deal was clinched on 29 December 1877, and Overbeck agreed to pay the sultan 15,000 Straits dollars a year. A few days later Overbeck discovered that the entire area had already been ceded to the Sultan of Sulu 173 years earlier, so he immediately sailed to Sulu and offered the sultan an annual payment of 5000 Straits dollars for the territory. On his return, he dropped three Englishmen off along the coast to set up trading posts; one of them was William Pryer, who founded Sandakan (see page 451). Three years later, Queen Victoria granted Dent a royal charter and, to the chagrin of the Dutch, the Spanish and the Americans, the British North Borneo Company was formed. London insisted that it was to be a British-only enterprise however, and Overbeck was forced to sell out. The first managing director of the company was the Scottish adventurer and former gunrunner William C Cowie. He was in charge of the day-to-day operations of the territory, while the British government supplied a governor.

The new chartered company, with its headquarters in the City of London, was given sovereignty over Sabah and a free hand to develop it. The British administrators soon began to collect taxes from local people and quickly clashed with members of the Brunei nobility. John Whitehead, a British administrator, wrote: "I must say, it seemed rather hard on these people that they should be allowed to surrender up their goods and chattels to swell even indirectly the revenue of the company". The administration levied poll tax, boat tax, land tax, fishing tax, rice tax, *tapai* (rice wine) tax and a 10% tax on proceeds from the sale of birds' nests. Resentment against these taxes sparked the six-year Mat Salleh rebellion (see box, page 402) and the Rundum Rebellion, which peaked in 1915, during which hundreds of Muruts were killed by the British.

Relations were not helped by colonial attitudes towards the local Malays and tribal people. One particularly arrogant district officer, Charles Bruce, wrote: "The mind of the average native is equivalent to that of a child of four. So long as one remembers that the native is essentially a child and treats him accordingly he is really tractable." Most recruits to the chartered company administration were fresh-faced graduates from British universities, mainly Oxford and Cambridge. For much of the time there were only 40-50 officials running the country. Besides the government officials, there were planters and businessmen: tobacco, rubber and timber became the most important exports. There were also Anglican and Roman Catholic missionaries. British North Borneo was never much of a money-spinner – the economy suffered whenever commodity prices slumped – but it mostly managed to pay for itself until the Second World War.

The Japanese interregnum

Sabah became part of Dai Nippon, or Greater Japan, on New Year's Day 1942, when the Japanese took Labuan. On the mainland, the Japanese Imperial Army and Kempetai (military police) were faced with the might of the North Borneo Armed Constabulary, about 650 men. Jesselton (Kota Kinabalu) was occupied on 9 January and Sandakan 10 days later. All Europeans were interned and when Singapore fell in 1942, 2740 prisoners of war were moved to Sandakan, most of whom were Australian, where they were forced to build an airstrip. On its completion, the POWs were ordered to march to Ranau, 240 km

The Borneo Death March

The four years of Japanese occupation ended when the Australian ninth division liberated British North Borneo. Sandakan was chosen by the Japanese as a regional centre for holding Allied prisoners. In 1942 the Japanese shipped 2750 prisoners of war (2000 of whom were Australian and 750 British) to Sandakan from Changi Prison, Singapore. A further 800 British and 500 Australian POWs arrived in 1944. They were ordered to build an airfield (on the site of the present airport) and were forced to work from dawn to dusk.

Many died, but in September 1944 2400 POWs were force- marched to Ranau, a 240-km trek through the jungle which only six Australians survived. This 'Death March', although not widely reported in Second World War literature, claimed more Australian lives than any other single event during the war in Asia, including the building of the notorious Burma-Siam railway.

For more information on the march, including details of sensitive tours and walks take a look at www.sandakan-deathmarch.com.

through the jungle. This became known as the Borneo Death March and only six men survived (see box above).

The Japanese were hated in Sabah and the Chinese mounted a resistance movement which was led by the Kuching-born Albert Kwok Hing Nam. He also recruited Bajaus and Sulus to join his guerrilla force which launched the Double Tenth Rebellion (the attacks took place on 10 October 1943). The guerrillas took Tuaran, Jesselton and Kota Belud, killing many Japanese and sending others fleeing into the jungle. But the following day the Japanese bombed the towns and troops quickly retook them and captured the rebels. A mass execution followed in which 175 rebels were decapitated. On 10 June 1945 Australian forces landed at Labuan, under the command of American General MacArthur. Allied planes bombed the main towns and virtually obliterated Jesselton and Sandakan. Sabah was liberated on 9 September and thousands of the remaining 21,000 Japanese troops were killed in retaliation, many by Muruts.

A British military administration governed Sabah in the aftermath of the war and the cash-strapped chartered company sold the territory to the British crown for £1.4 million in 1946. The new crown colony was modelled on the chartered company's administration and rebuilt the main towns and war-shattered infrastructure. In May 1961, following Malaysian independence, Prime Minister Tunku Abdul Rahman proposed the formation of a federation incorporating Malaya (ie Peninsular Malaysia), Singapore, Brunei, Sabah and Sarawak. Later that same year, Tun Fuad Stephens, a timber magnate and newspaper publisher formed Sabah's first-ever political party, the United National Kadazan Organization (UNKO). Two other parties were founded soon afterwards: the Sabah Chinese Association and the United Sabah National Organization (USNO). The British were keen to leave the colony and the Sabahan parties debated the pros and cons of joining the proposed federation. Elections were held in late 1962 in which a UNKO-USNO alliance (the Sabah Alliance) swept to power and the following August Sabah became an independent country ... for 16 days. Like Singapore and Sarawak, Sabah opted to join the federation to the indignation of the Philippines and Indonesia who both had claims on the territory. Jakarta's objections resulted in the Konfrontasi, an undeclared war with Malaysia (see page 384) that was not settled until 1966.

Politics

Sabah's political scene has always been lively and never more so than in 1994 when the then Malaysian prime minister, Doctor Mahathir Mohamad, pulled off what commentators described as a democratic coup d'état. With great political dexterity, he out-manoeuvered his rebellious rivals and managed to dislodge the opposition state government, despite the fact that it had just won a state election.

Following Sabah's first state election in 1967, the Sabah Alliance ruled until 1975 when the newly formed multi-racial party, Berjaya, swept the polls. Berjaya had been set up with the financial backing of the United Malays National Organization (UMNO), the mainstay of the ruling Barisan Nasional (National Front) coalition on the Peninsula. Over the following decade that corrupt administration crumbled and in 1985 the opposition Sabah United Party (PBS), led by the Christian Kadazan Datuk Joseph Pairin Kitingan, won a landslide victory and became the only state government in Malaysia that did not belong to the UMNO-led coalition. It became an obvious embarrassment to then Prime Minister Doctor Mahathir Mohamad to have a rebel Christian state in his predominantly Muslim federation. Nonetheless, the PBS eventually joined Barisan Nasional, believing its partnership in the coalition would help iron things out. It did not.

When the PBS came to power, the federal government and Sabahan opposition parties openly courted Filipino and Indonesian immigrants in the state, almost all of whom are Muslim, and secured identity cards for many of them, enabling them to vote. Doctor Mahathir has made no secret of his preference for a Muslim government in Sabah. Nothing, however, was able to dislodge the PBS, which was resoundingly returned to power in 1990. The federal government had long been suspicious of Sabahan politicians, particularly following the PBS's defection from Doctor Mahathir's coalition in the run-up to the 1990 general election, a move which bolstered the opposition alliance. Doctor Mahathir described this as "a stab in the back", and referred to Sabah as "a thorn in the flesh of the Malaysian federation". But in the event, the prime minister won the national election convincingly without PBS help, prompting fears of political retaliation. Those fears proved justified in the wake of the election.

Sabah paid heavily for its 'disloyalty'; prominent Sabahans were arrested as secessionist conspirators under Malaysia's Internal Security Act, which provides for indefinite detention without trial. Among them was Jeffrey Kitingan, brother of the chief minister and head of the Yayasan Sabah, or Sabah Foundation (see page 403). At the same time, Joseph Pairin Kitingan was charged with corruption. The feeling in Sabah was that the men were bearing the brunt of Doctor Mahathir's personal political vendetta.

As the political feud worsened, the federal government added to the fray by failing to promote Sabah to foreign investors. As investment money dried up, so did federal development funds; big road and housing projects were left unfinished for years. Many in Sabah felt their state was being short-changed by the federal government. The political instability had a detrimental effect on the state economy and the business community felt that continued feuding would be economic lunacy. Politicians in the Christian-led PBS, however, continued to claim that Sabah wasn't getting its fair share of Malaysia's economic boom. They said that the agreement which enshrined a measure of autonomy for Sabah when it joined the Malaysian federation had been eroded.

The main bone of contention was the state's oil revenues, worth around US$852 million a year, of which 95% disappeared into federal coffers. There were many other causes of dissatisfaction, too, and as the list of grievances grew longer, the state government exploited them to the full. By 1994, anti-federal feelings were running high. The PBS continued to promote the idea of 'Sabah for Sabahans', a defiant slogan in a country where the federal government was working to centralize power. Because Doctor Mahathir likes to be in control, the idea of granting greater autonomy to a distant, opposition-held state was not on his agenda. A showdown was inevitable.

It began in January 1994. As Datuk Pairin's corruption trial drew to a close, he dissolved the state assembly, paving the way for fresh elections. He did this to cover the eventuality of his being disqualified from office through a 'guilty' verdict: he wanted to have his own team in place to take over from him. He was convicted of corruption but the fine imposed on him was just under the disqualifying threshold and, to the prime minister's fury, he led the PBS into the election. Doctor Mahathir put his newly appointed deputy, Anwar Ibrahim, in charge of the National Front alliance campaign.

Datuk Pairin won the election, but by a much narrower margin than before. He alleged vote buying and ballot rigging. He accused Doctor Mahathir's allies of whipping up the issue of religion. He spoke of financial inducements being offered to Sabah's Muslim voters, some of whom are Malay, but most of whom are Bajau tribespeople and Filipino immigrants. His swearing-in ceremony was delayed for 36 hours; the governor said he was sick; Datuk Parin said his political enemies were trying to woo defectors from the ranks of the PBS to overturn his small majority. He was proved right.

Three weeks later, he was forced to resign; his fractious party had virtually collapsed in disarray and a stream of defections robbed him of his majority. Datuk Parin's protestations that his assemblymen had been bribed to switch sides were ignored. The local leader of Doctor Mahathir's ruling party, Tan Sri Sakaran Dandai, was swiftly sworn in as the new chief minister.

In the 1995 general election the PBS did remarkably well, holding onto eight seats and defeating a number of Front candidates who had defected from the PBS the previous year. Sabah was one area, along with the east coast state of Kelantan, which resisted the Mahathir/BN electoral steamroller.

The March 1999 state elections pitted UMNO against Pairin's PBS. Again the issues were local autonomy, vote rigging, the role of national politics and political parties in state elections, and money. A new element was the role that Anwar Ibrahim's trial might play in the campaign but otherwise it was old wine in old bottles.

The outcome was a convincing win for Mahathir and the ruling National Front who gathered 31 of the 48 state assembly seats – three more than the prime minister forecast. Mahathir once again used the lure of development funds from KL to convince local Sabahans where their best interests might lie. "We are not being unfair" Mahathir said. "We are more than fair, but we cannot be generous to the opposition. We can be generous to a National Front government in Sabah. That I can promise."

But, worryingly for the National Front, the opposition Parti Bersatu Sabah (PBS) still managed to garner the great bulk of the Kadazan vote and in so doing won 17 seats. As in Sarawak, the election, in the end, was more about local politics than about the economic crisis and the Anwar trial.

However, in the 2004 state and federal elections, the PBS rejoined the National Front and, faced only with the disunity of opposition parties, the BN-PBS coalition won resounding victories in both polls. A legitimate alternative to KL's ruling steamroller has all but died. The BN gave itself half the seats, one third to non-Malays, and distributed the rest between Chinese representatives. The message is that Sabahans accept dominance by the Malay minority from KL in return for money and development. The Sabah state elections were held simultaneously with the federal elections in 2008. and were again won comfortably by the BN-PBS coalition with only one of the 60 contested seats going to another party, the Democratic Action Party.

Culture

People

According to Malaysia's 2000 Population and Housing Census (next one due 2010), the main ethnic group in Sabah is Kadazan Dusun (18.4%), followed by Bajau (17.3%) and Chinese (13.2%). The Kadazan mostly live on the west coast, the Murut inhabit the southern interior and the Bajau are mainly settled around Gunung Kinabalu. There are more than 30 tribes, more than 50 different languages and about 100 dialects. Sabah also has a large Chinese population and many illegal Filipino immigrants.

Bajau The Bajau, the famous cowboys of the Wild East, came from the south Philippines during the 18th and 19th centuries and settled in the coastal area around Kota Belud, Papar and Kudat, where they made a handsome living from piracy. The Bajau who came to Sabah joined forces with the notorious Illanun and Balinini pirates. They are natural seafarers and were dubbed sea gypsies; today, they form the second largest indigenous group in Sabah and are divided into subgroups, notably the Binadan, Suluk and Obian. They call themselves 'Samah'; it was the Brunei Malays who first called them Bajau. They are strict Muslims and the famous Sabahan folk hero, Mat Salleh, who led a rebellion in the 1890s against British Chartered Company rule, was a Bajau (see box, page 402). Despite their seafaring credentials, they are also renowned horsemen and (very occasionally) still put in an appearance at Kota Belud's *tamu* (see page 435). Bajau women are known for their brightly coloured basketry – *tudong saji*. The Bajau build their *atap* houses on stilts over the water and these are interconnected by a network of narrow wooden planks. The price of a Bajau bride was traditionally assessed in stilts, shaped from the trunks of bakau mangrove trees. A father erected one under his house on the day a daughter was born and replaced it whenever it wore out. The longer the daughter remained at home, the more stilts he got through and the more water buffalo he demanded from a prospective husband.

Chinese The Chinese accounted for nearly a third of Sabah's population in 1960; today they make up just over a tenth. Unlike Sarawak, however, where the Chinese were a well-established community in the early 1800s, Sabah's Chinese came as a result of the British North Borneo Chartered Company's immigration policy, designed to ease a labour shortage. About 70% of Sabah's Chinese are Christian Hakka, who first began arriving at the end of the 19th century, under the supervision of the company. They were given free passage from China and most settled in the Jesselton and Kudat areas; today most Hakka are farmers. There are also large Teochew and Hokkien communities in Tawau, Kota Kinabalu and Labuan while Sandakan is mainly Cantonese, originating from Hong Kong.

Filipinos Immigration from the Philippines started in the 1950s and refugees began flooding into Sabah when the separatist war erupted in Mindanao in the 1970s. Today there are believed to be upwards of 700,000 illegal Filipino immigrants in Sabah (although their migration has been undocumented for so long that no one is certain) and the state government fears they could soon outnumber locals. There are many in Kota Kinabalu, the

The Kadazan in Borneo

Formerly known as Dusuns (peasants or orchard people), a name given to them by outsiders and picked up by the British, the Kadazan live in Sabah and East Kalimantan.

The Kadazans traditionally traded their agricultural produce at large markets, held at meeting points, called *tamus* (see box, page 432).

They used to be animists and were said to live in great fear of evil spirits; most of their ceremonies were rituals aimed at driving out these spirits. The job of communicating with the spirits of the dead, the *tombiivo*, was done by priestesses, called *bobohizan*. They are the only ones who can speak the ancient Kadazan language, using a completely different vocabulary from modern Kadazan. Most converted to Christianity, mainly Roman Catholicism, during the 1930s, although there are also some Muslim Kadazan.

The big cultural event in the Kadazan year is the harvest festival that takes place in May. The ceremony, known as the Magavau ritual, is officiated by a high priestess. These elderly women, who wear black costumes and colourful headgear with feathers and beads, are now rarely seen. The ceremony ends with offerings to the *Bambaazon* (rice spirit). After the ceremonies Catholic, Muslim and animist Kadazan all come together to play traditional sports such as wrestling and buffalo racing. This is about the only occasion when visitors are likely to see Kadazan in their traditional costumes. Belts of silver coins (*himpogot*) and brass rings are worn round the waist; a colourful sash is also worn. Men dress in a black, long-sleeved jacket over black trousers; they also wear a *siga*, colourful woven headgear. These costumes have become more decorative in recent years, with colourful embroidery.

state capital, and a large community – mainly women and children – in Labuan, but the bulk of the Filipino population is in Semporna, Lahad Datu, Tawau and Kunak (on the east coast) where they already outnumber locals by a majority of three to one. One Sabah government minister, referring to the long-running territorial dispute between Malaysia and the Philippines, was quoted as saying "We do not require a strong military presence at the border any more: the aliens have already landed".

Although the federal government has talked of its intention to deport illegal aliens, it is mindful of the political reality: the majority of the Filipinos are Muslim, and making them legal Malaysian citizens could ruin Sabah's predominantly Christian, Kadazan-led state government. The Filipino community is also a thorn in Sabah's flesh because of the crime wave associated with their arrival: the Sabah police claim 65% of crime is committed by Filipinos. The police do not ask questions when dealing with Filipino criminal suspects; about 40 to 50 are shot every year. Another local politician was quoted as saying: "The immigrants take away our jobs, cause political instability and pose a health hazard because of the appalling conditions in which some of them live".

There are six different Filipino groups in Sabah: the Visayas and Ilocano are Christian as are the Ilongo (Ilo Ilo), from Zamboanga. The Suluks are Muslim; they come from south Mindanao and have the advantage of speaking a dialect of Bahasa Malaysia. Many Filipinos were born in Sabah and all second-generation immigrants are fluent in Bahasa. Migration first accelerated in the 1950s during the logging boom and continued when the oil palm plantation economy took off. Many migrants have settled along the

The Murit in Borneo

The Murut live in the southwest of Sabah, in the Trusan Valley, North Sarawak and in Northeast Kalimantan. Some of those in more remote jungle areas retain their traditional longhouse way of life, but many Murut have opted for detached kampong-style houses.

Murut means hill people and is not the term used by the people themselves. They refer to themselves by individual tribal names.

The Nabai, Bokan and Timogun Murut live in the lowlands and are wet-rice farmers, while the Peluan, Bokan and Tagul Murut live in the hills and are mainly shifting cultivators. They are thought to be related to Sarawak's Kelabit and Kalimantan's Lun Dayeh people, although some of the tribes in the south Philippines have similar characteristics. The Murut staples are rice and tapioca; they are known for their weaving and basketry and have a penchant for drinking *tapai* (rice wine; see box, page 491). They are also enthusiastic dancers and devised the *lansaran*, a sprung dance floor like a trampoline. The Murut are a mixture of animists, Christians and Muslims and were the last tribe in Sabah to give up headhunting, a practice stopped by the British North Borneo Chartered Company.

roadsides on the way to the Danum Valley; it is easy to claim land since all they have to do is simply clear a plot and plant a few fruit trees.

Kadazan The Kadazan are the largest ethnic group in Sabah and are a peaceful agrarian people with a strong cultural identity. Until Sabah joined the Malaysian Federation in 1963, they were known as Dusuns. It became, in effect, a residual category including all those people who were not Muslim or Chinese. Kadazan identity is therefore not particularly straightforward. In Malaysia's 2000 census, they were called Kadazan Dusun. The 1991 census, however, lists both Kadazan (110,866) and Dusun (229,194). The 1970 census listed all as Kadazan, while the 1960 census listed all as Dusun. In 1995 the Malaysian government agreed to add the common language of these people to the national repertoire to be taught in schools. This they named Kadazandusun. The others are Malay, Chinese, Tamil and Iban.

Most Kadazans call themselves after their tribal names. They can be divided into several tribes including the Lotud of Tuaran, the Rungus of the Kudat and Bengkoka Peninsulas, the Tempasuk, the Tambanuo, the Kimarangan and the Sanayo. Minokok and Tengara Kadazans live in the upper Kinabatangan River basin, while those living near other big rivers are just known as Orang Sungai (river people).

The majority of Kadazans used to live in longhouses; these are virtually all gone now. The greatest chance of coming across a longhouse in Sabah is in the Rungus area of the Kudat Peninsula; even there, former longhouse residents are moving into detached, kampong-style houses while one or two stay for the use of tourists.

All the Kadazan groups used to have similar customs and modes of dress (see below). Up to the Second World War, many Kadazan men wore the *chawat* loin cloth. The Kadazans used to hunt with blowpipes and in the 19th century were still headhunting. Today, however, they are known for their gentleness and honesty; their produce can often be seen sitting unattended at roadside stalls and passing motorists are expected to pay what they think fair. The Kadazan are farmers, and the main rice producers of Sabah.

➤➤ *See also box, page 489.*

Tapai: Sabah's rice wine

Tapai, the fiery Sabahan rice wine, is much loved by the Kadazan and the Murut people of Borneo. It was even more popular before the two tribal groups converted to Christianity in the 1930s. Writer Hedda Morrison noted in 1957 that "The squalor and wretchedness arising from [their] continual drunkenness made the Murut a particularly useful object of missionary endeavour."

In the Sabah State Museum there is a recipe for *tapai*, which reads: "Boil 12 lbs of the best glutinous rice until well done. In a wide-mouthed jar, lay the rice in layers of no more than two fingers deep, and between layers, place about 20½-oz yeast cakes. Add two cups of water, tinctured with the juice of six beetroots. Cover jar with muslin and leave to ferment. Each day, uncover it and remove dew which forms on the muslin. On the fifth day, stir the mixture vigorously and

leave for four weeks. Store for one year, after which it shall be full of virtue and potence and smooth upon the palate."

Oscar Cook, a former district officer in the North Borneo civil service, noted in his 1923 book *Borneo: the Stealer of Hearts*: "As an alternative occupation to headhunting, the Murut possess a fondness for getting drunk, indulged in on every possible occasion…Births, marriages, deaths, sowing, harvesting and any occasion that comes to mind is made the excuse for a debauch. It is customary for Murut to show respect to the white man by producing their very best *tapai*, and pitting the oldest and ugliest women of the village against him in a drinking competition." Cook admits that all this proved too much for him and when he was transferred to Keningau, he had to employ an 'official drinker'. "The applicants to the post were many," he noted.

For the May harvest festival, villages send the finalists of local beauty contests to the grand final of the Unduk Ngadau harvest festival queen competition in Penampang, near Kota Kinabalu. It is the Kadazans who dominate the Pasti Bersatu Sabah (PBS), the critical piece in Sabah's political jigsaw.

Murut The Murut live around Tenom and Pensiangan in the lowland and hilly parts of the interior. They were the last tribe in Sabah to give up headhunting, a practice stopped by the British North Borneo Chartered Company. ▶ *See also box opposite.*

Arts and crafts

Compared with neighbouring Sarawak and Kalimantan, Sabah's handicraft industry is rather impoverished. Sabah's tribal groups were less protected from Western influences than Sarawak's and traditional skills quickly began to die out as the state modernized and the economy grew. In Kota Kinabalu today, the markets are full of Filipino handicrafts and shell products; local arts and crafts are largely confined to basketry, mats, hats, beadwork, musical instruments and pottery.

The elongated Kadazan backpack baskets found around Mount Kinabalu National Park are called *wakids* and are made from bamboo, rattan and bark. Woven food covers, or *tudong saji*, are often mistaken for hats, and are made by the Bajau of Kota Belud. Hats, made from nipah palm or rattan, and whose shape varies markedly from place to place, are decorated with traditional motifs. One of the most common motifs is the *nantuapan* (meeting), which represents four people all drinking out of the same *tapai* (rice wine) jar. The Rungus people from the Kudat Peninsula also make linago basketware from a strong wild grass; it is tightly woven and not decorated. At *tamus*, Sabah's big open-air markets (see box on page 432), there are usually some handicrafts for sale. The Kota Belud *tamu* is the best place to find the Bajau horseman's embroidered turban, the *destar*. Traditionally, the Rungus people, who live on the Kudat Peninsula, were renowned as fine weavers and detailed patterns were woven into their ceremonial skirts (*tinugupan*). These patterns all had different names but, like the ingredients of the traditional dyes, many have now been forgotten.

Contents

494 History
494 Precolonial Malaysia
494 The colonials arrive
494 British Malaya emerges
497 Japanese occupation
498 The British return
500 The rise of Communism
501 The road to Merdeka
502 Racial politics in the 1960s

503 Modern Malaysia
503 Politics

506 Economy

509 Culture
509 People
514 Art and architecture
515 Language and literature
517 Drama, dance and music
520 Crafts

522 Religion
522 Islam

529 Land and environment
529 Geography
530 Climate
531 Flora and fauna

541 Books

Footprint features

495 Putting Malaya on the map
498 The kris: martial and
    mystic masterpiece
518 Making a wayang kulit puppet
523 The practice of Islam:
    living by the Prophet
524 What's in a word?
526 In Siddhartha's footsteps:
    a short history of Buddhism
528 Malay magic and the spirits
    behind the prophet

Background

History

Precolonial Malaya

With the arrival of successive waves of Malay immigrants about five millennia ago, the earliest settlers – the Orang Asli aboriginals (see page 513) – moved into the interior. The Malays established agricultural settlements on the coastal lowlands and in riverine areas and from very early on were in contact with foreign traders, thanks to the Peninsula's strategic location on the sea route between India and China. Although the original tribal inhabitants of Malaya were displaced inland, they were not entirely isolated from the coastal peoples. Trade relations in which 'upriver' tribal groups exchanged forest products for commodities like salt and metal implements with 'downstream' Malays, were widespread. Malay culture on the Peninsula reflected these contacts, embracing Indian cultural traditions, Hinduism among them. In the late 14th century, the centre of power shifted from Sumatra's Srivijayan Empire across the Strait to Melaka. In 1430, the third ruler of Melaka embraced Islam and became the first sultan; the city quickly grew into a flourishing trading port. By the early 1500s it was the most important entrepôt in the region and its fame brought it to the attention of the Portuguese who, in 1511, ushered in the colonial epoch. They sacked the town and sent the sultan fleeing to Johor, where a new sultanate was established. But because of internal rivalries and continued conflict with the powerful trading sultanate of Aceh in north Sumatra as well as the Portuguese, Johor never gained the prominence of Melaka, and was forced to alternate its capital between Johor and the Riau archipelago.

The colonials arrive

The Portuguese were the first of three European colonial powers to arrive on the Malay Peninsula. They were followed by the Dutch, who took Melaka in 1641 (see page 194 for a history of Melaka). When Holland was occupied by Napoleon's troops at the end of the 18th century, Britain filled the vacuum and the British colonial era began.

During the 17th century, the Dutch came into frequent conflict with the Bugis, the fearsome master-seafarers who the Dutch had displaced from their original homeland in South Sulawesi. In 1784, in league with the Minangkabau of West Sumatra, the Bugis nearly succeeded in storming Melaka and were only stymied by the arrival of Dutch warships. The Bugis eventually established the Sultanate of Selangor on the west coast of the Peninsula and, in the south, exerted increasing influence on the Johor-Riau sultans until they had reduced them to puppet-rulers. By then however, offshoots of the Johor royal family had established the sultanates of Pahang and Perak. The Minangkabau-dominated states between Melaka and Selangor formed a confederacy of nine states, or Negeri Sembilan. To the northeast, the states of Kelantan and Terengganu came under the Siamese sphere of influence.

British Malaya emerges

The British occupied Dutch colonies during the Napoleonic Wars, including the Dutch East Indies (now Indonesia), following France's invasion of the Netherlands in 1794. Dutch King William of Orange, who fled to London, instructed Dutch governors overseas to end their rivalry with the British and to permit the entry of British troops to their colonies in a bid to keep the French out. Historian William R Roff writes: "From being an

Putting Malaya on the map

The names of most of Malaysia's states are older than the name Malaya; until the 1870s the scattered coastal sultanates were independent of each other. Many of the Malay areas were colonized by Sumatrans long ago and it is possible that the word 'Melayu' – or 'Malay' – derives from the Sungai Melayu (Melayu River) in Sumatra. The name in turn is derived from the Dravidian (Tamil) word *malai*, or 'hill'. As the Malays are coastal people, the paradox is explained by their pre-Islamic religion, which is thought to have been based on a cult in which a sacred mountain took pride of place.

The Graeco-Roman geographer Ptolemy called the Malay Peninsula Aurea Chersonesus, or the 'The Golden Chersonese': it was the fabled land of gold. By the early 1500s, European maps were already marking Melaka and Pulau Tioman, which were well known to Chinese mariners. During the Portuguese and Dutch colonial periods, the whole Peninsula was simply labelled 'Malacca', and the town was the only significant European outpost until the British took possession of Penang in 1786. There was very little mapping of the Peninsula until the early 19th century, and the names of states only gradually appeared on maps over the course of the 17th and 18th centuries.

According to cartographic historian RT Fell, the first maps of the interior of the Peninsula, beyond the bounds of the British Straits Settlements, did not appear until the late 19th century. In 1885 the Survey Department was founded and charged with mapping the interior – one of the tasks William Cameron was undertaking when he stumbled across the highland plateau named after him that same year. But right into the 20th century, large tracts of mountainous jungle were still unexplored.

Indian power interested primarily ... in the free passage of trade through the Malacca Straits and beyond to China, the East India Company suddenly found itself possessor not merely of a proposed naval station on Penang island but of numerous other territorial dominions and responsibilities."

The British had their own colonial designs, having already established a foothold on Penang where Captain Francis Light had set up a trading post in 1786 (see page 143). The Anglo-Dutch Treaty of London signed in 1824 effectively divided maritime Southeast Asia into British and Dutch spheres of influence. Britain retained Penang, Melaka (which it swapped for the Sumatran port of Bengkulu) and Singapore – which had been founded by Stamford Raffles in 1819 – and these formed the Straits Settlements. The Dutch regained control of their colonial territories in the Indonesian archipelago. Britain promised to stay out of Sumatra and the Dutch promised not to meddle in the affairs of the Peninsula, thus separating two parts of the Malay world whose histories had been intertwined for centuries.

The British did very little to interfere with the Malay sultanates and chiefdoms on the Peninsula, but the Straits Settlements grew in importance – particularly Singapore, which soon superceded Penang, which in turn had eclipsed Melaka. Chinese immigrants arrived in all three ports and from there expanded into tin mining, which rapidly emerged as the main source of wealth on the Peninsula. The extent of the tin rush in the mid-19th century is exemplified in the town of Larut in northwestern Perak. Around 25,000 Chinese speculators arrived in Larut between 1848 and 1872. The Chinese fought over the rights to mine the most lucrative deposits and organized into secret societies and kongsis, which by the 1860s were engaged in open warfare. At the same time, the Malay rulers in the states on the

Peninsula were busily taxing the tin traders while in the Straits Settlements, British investors in the mining industry put increasing pressure on the Colonial Office to intervene in order to stabilize the situation. In late 1873 Britain decided it could not rule the increasingly lawless and anarchic states by remote control any longer and the western-central states were declared a British protectorate. In his account of British intervention, William R Roff quotes a Malay proverb: 'Once the needle is in, the thread is sure to follow'.

In 1874, the Treaty of Pangkor established the residential system whereby British officers were posted to key districts; it became their job to determine all administrative and policy matters other than those governing Islam and Malay custom. This immediately provoked resentment and sparked uprisings in Perak, Selangor and Negeri Sembilan, as well as a Malay revolt in 1875. The revolts were put down and the system was institutionalized: in 1876 these three states plus Pahang became the Federated Malay States. By 1909 the north states of Kedah, Perlis, Kelantan and Terengganu – which previously came under Siamese suzerainty – finally agreed to accept British advisers and became known as the Unfederated Malay States. Johor remained independent until 1914. The British system of government relied on the political power of the sultans and the Malay aristocracy: residents conferred with the rulers of each state and employed the aristocrats as civil servants. Local headmen (known as penghulu) were used as administrators in rural areas.

Meanwhile, the British continued to encourage the immigration of Chinese, who formed a majority of the population in Perak and Selangor by the early 1920s. Apart from the wealthy traders based in the Straits Settlements, the Chinese immigrants were organized (and exploited) by their secret societies, which provided welfare services, organized work gangs and ran local government. In 1889 the societies were officially banned and while this broke their hold on political power, they simply re-emerged as a criminal underworld. In the Federated Malay States, there was an eight-fold population increase to 1.7 million between 1891 and 1931. Even by 1891 the proportion of Malays had declined to a fraction over a third of the population, with the Chinese making up 41.5% and Indians – imported as indentured labourers by the British (see page 512) – comprising 22%. To the south, Johor, which in the late 1800s was not even a member of the federation, had a similar ethnic balance.

For the most part, the Malay population remained in the countryside and were only gradually drawn into the modern economy. But by the 1920s Malay nationalism was on the rise, partly prompted by the Islamic reform movement and partly by intellectuals in secular circles who looked to the creation of a Greater Malaysia (or Greater Indonesia), under the influence of left-wing Indonesian nationalists. These Malay nationalists were as critical of the Malay élite as they were of the British colonialists. The élite itself was becoming increasingly outspoken for different reasons – it felt threatened by the growing demands of Straits-born Chinese and second-generation Indians for equal rights.

The first semi-political nationalist movement was the Kesatuan Melayu Singapura (Singapore Malay Union), formed in 1926. The Union found early support in the Straits Settlements where Malays were outnumbered and there was no sultan. They gradually spread across the Peninsula and held a pan-Malayan conference in 1939. These associations were the forerunners of the post-war Malay nationalist movement. In the run-up to the Second World War the left wing split off to form the Kesatuan Melayu Muda – the Union of Young Malays, which was strongly anti-British and whose leaders were arrested by the colonial authorities in 1940. The Chinese were more interested in business than politics and any political interests were focused on China. The middle class supported the Chinese nationalist Kuomintang (KMT), although it was eventually banned by the British, as it was becoming an obvious focus of anti-colonial sentiment. The KMT allowed Communists to join the movement until 1927, but in 1930 they split off to form the Malayan Communist Party (MCP) which drew its support from the working class.

Japanese occupation

Under cover of darkness on the night of 8 December 1941, the Japanese army invaded Malaya, landing in South Thailand and pushing into Kedah, and at Kota Bharu in Kelantan. The invasion, which took place an hour before the attack on Pearl Harbor, took the Allies in Malaya and 'Fortress' Singapore completely by surprise. The Japanese forces had air, land and sea superiority and quickly overwhelmed the Commonwealth troops on the Peninsula. Militarily, it was a brilliant campaign, made speedier by the fact that the Japanese troops stole bicycles in every town they took, thus making it possible for them to outpace all Allied estimates of their likely rate of advance.

By 28 December they had taken Ipoh and all of northern Malaya. Kuantan fell on 31 December, the Japanese having sunk the British warships *Prince of Wales* and *Repulse* and Kuala Lumpur on 11 January 1942. They advanced down the east coast, centre and west coast simultaneously and by the end of the month had taken Johor Bahru and were massed across the strait from Singapore. By 15 February they had forced the capitulation of the Allies in Singapore. This was a crushing blow, and, according to Malaysian historian Zainal Abidin bin Abudul Wahid, "the speed with which the Japanese managed to achieve victory, however temporary that might have been, shattered the image of the British, and generally the 'whiteman', as a superior people". Right up until the beginning of the Second World War, the British had managed to placate the aristocratic leaders of the Malay community and the wealthy Chinese merchants and there was little real threat to the status quo. The Japanese defeat of the British changed all that by altering the balance between conservatism and change. Because Britain had failed so miserably to defend Malaya, its credentials as a protector were irrevocably tarnished.

For administrative purposes, the Japanese linked the Peninsula with Sumatra as part of the Greater East Asia Co-Prosperity Sphere. All British officials were interned and the legislative and municipal councils swept aside. But because the Japanese had lost their command of the seas by the end of 1942, nothing could be imported and there was a shortage of food supplies. The 'banana' currency introduced by the Japanese became worthless as inflation soared. Japan merely regarded Malaya as a source of raw materials, yet the rubber and tin industries stagnated and nothing was done to develop the economy.

After initially severing sultans' pensions and reducing their powers, the Japanese realized that their co-operation was necessary if the Malay bureaucracy was to be put to work for the occupation government. The Indians were treated well since they were seen as a key to fighting the British colonial regime in India, but Malaya's Chinese were not trusted. The Japanese, however, came to recognize the importance of the Chinese community in oiling the wheels of the economy. The Chinese Dalforce militia (set up by the Allies as the Japanese advanced southwards) joined the Communists and other minor underground dissident groups in forming the Malayan People's Anti-Japanese Army. British army officers and arms were parachuted into the jungle to support the guerrillas. It was during this period that the Malayan Communist Party (MCP) broadened its membership and appeal, under the guise of a nationwide anti-Japanese alliance.

The brutality of the Japanese regime eased with time; as the war began to go against them, they increasingly courted the different communities, giving them more say in the run of things in an effort to undermine any return to colonial rule. But the Japanese's

The kris: martial and mystic masterpiece

The kris occupies an important place in Malay warfare, art and philosophy. It is a short sword – the Malay word *keris* means dagger – and the blade may be either straight or sinuous (there are over 100 blade shapes), sharpened on both edges. Such was the high reputation of these weapons that they were exported as far afield as India.

Krisses are often attributed with peculiar powers: one was reputed to have rattled violently before a family feud. Another, kept at the museum in Taiping, has a particularly bloodthirsty reputation. It would sneak away after dark, kill someone, and then wipe itself clean before miraculously returning to its display cabinet. As each kris has a power and spirit of its own, they must be compatible with their owners. Nor should they be purchased; a kris should be given or inherited.

The fact that so few kris blades have been unearthed has led some people to assume that the various Malay kingdoms were peaceful and adverse to war. The more likely explanation is that pre-Muslim Malays attributed such magical power to sword blades that they were only very rarely buried. The art historian Jan Fontein writes that "the process of forging the sword from clumps of iron ore and meteorite into a sharp blade of patterned steel is often seen as a parallel to the process of purification to which the soul is subjected after death by the gods".

The earliest confirmed date for a kris is the 14th century; they are depicted in the reliefs of Candi Panataran and possibly also at Candi Sukuh, both on Java. However, in all likelihood they were introduced considerably earlier, possibly during the 10th century.

Krisses are forged by beating nickel or nickeliferous meteoritic material into iron in a complex series of laminations (iron

favourable treatment of Malays and their general mistrust of the Chinese did not foster good race relations between the two. A Malay paramilitary police force was put to work to root out Chinese who were anti-Japanese, which exacerbated inter-communal hostility. The Japanese never offered Malaya independence but allowed Malay nationalist sentiments to develop in an effort to deflect attention from the fact they had ceded the North Malay states of Kedah, Perlis, Kelantan and Terengganu to Thailand.

The British return

During the war the British drew up secret plans for a revised administrative structure in Malaya. The plan was to create a Malayan Union by combining the federated and unfederated states as well as Melaka and Penang, leaving Singapore as a crown colony. Plans were also drawn up to buy North Borneo from the Chartered Company and to replace the anachronous White Rajahs of Sarawak with a view to eventually grouping all the territories together as a federation. As soon as the Japanese surrendered in September 1945, the plan was put into action. Historian Mary Turnbull noted that "Malaya was unique [among Western colonies] because the returning British were initially welcomed with enthusiasm and were themselves unwilling to put the clock back. But they were soon overwhelmed by the reaction against their schemes for streamlining the administration and assimilating the different immigrant communities."

from meteors is particularly prized because of its celestial origin). After forging, ceremonies are performed and offerings made before the blade is tempered. The *empu* (swordsmith) was a respected member of society, who was felt to be imbued with mystical powers. After forging the blade it is then patinated using a mixture of lime juice and arsenicum. Each part of the sword, even each curve of the blade, has a name and the best krisses are elaborately decorated. Inlaid with gold, the cross-pieces carved into floral patterns and animal motifs, grips made of ivory and studded with jewels, krisses are works of art.

But they were also tools of combat. In the Malay world, a central element of any battle was the amok. Taken from the Malay verb mengamok, the amok was a furious charge by men armed with krisses, designed to spread confusion within the enemy ranks. Amok warriors would be

committed to dying in the charge and often dressed in white to indicate self-sacrifice. They were often drugged with opium or cannabis. It was also an honourable way for a man to commit suicide.

Alfred Russel Wallace in *Malay Archipelago* (1869) writes: "He grasps his kris-handle, and the next moment draws out the weapon and stabs a man to the heart. He runs on, with the bloody kris in his hand, stabbing at everyone he meets. 'Amok! Amok!' then resounds through the streets. Spears, krisses, knives and guns are brought out against him. He rushes madly forward, kills all he can – men, women and children – and dies overwhelmed by numbers...". The English expression 'to run amok' is taken from this Malay word.

Recommended reading: Frey, Edward (1986) *The Kris: Mystic Weapon of the Malay World*, OUP: Singapore.

A unitary state was formed on the Peninsula and everyone regardless of race or origin who called Malaya 'home' was accorded equal status. But the resentment caused by British high-handedness was the catalyst which triggered the foundation of the United Malays National Organization (UMNO) which provided a focus for opposition to the colonial regime and, following independence, formed the ruling party. Opposition to UMNO, led by the Malay ruling class, forced the British to withdraw the Union proposal. The sultans refused to attend the installation of the governor and the Malays boycotted advisory councils. Mary Turnbull noted that the Malayan Union scheme was "conceived as a civil servant's dream but was born to be a politician's nightmare". Vehement Malay opposition prompted negotiations with Malay leaders which hammered out the basis of a Federation of Malaya which was established in February 1948. It was essentially the same as the Union in structure, except that it recognized the sovereignty of the sultans in the 11 states and the so-called 'special position' of the Malays as the indigenous people of Malaya. The federation had a strong central government (headed by a High Commissioner) and a federal executive council.

In this federal system, introduced in 1948, non-Malays could only become Malaysian citizens if they had been resident in Malaya for a minimum of 15 out of the previous 25 years, were prepared to sign a declaration of permanent settlement and were able to speak either Malay or English. This meant only three million of Malaya's five million population qualified as citizens, of whom 78% were Malay, 12% Chinese and 7% Indian. Historian Mary Turnbull said that while the British believed they had achieved their objective of common citizenship (even on more restricted terms), they had, in reality "accepted UMNO's concept of a Malay nation into which immigrant groups would have to be integrated, and many difficulties were to develop from this premise".

The rise of Communism

The Chinese and Indian communities were not consulted in these Anglo-Malay negotiations and ethnic and religious tensions between the three main communities were running high, unleashing the forces of racialism that had been lying dormant for years. Because their part in the political process had been ignored, many more Chinese began to identify with the Malaysian Communist Party (MCP), which was still legal. It was not until the Communist victory in China in 1949 that the Chinese began to think of Malaya as home. During the war the MCP had gained legitimacy and prestige as a patriotic resistance movement. The MCP's de facto military wing, the MPAJA, had left arms dumps in the jungle, but the Communist leadership was split as to whether negotiation or confrontation was the way forward. Then in 1947 the MCP suffered what many considered to be a disastrous blow: its Vietnamese-born secretary-general, Lai Teck, absconded with all the party's funds having worked as a double agent for both the Japanese and the British. He was suspected of having betrayed the entire MCP central committee to the Japanese in 1942. The new 26-year-old MCP leader, former schoolmaster Chin Peng, immediately abandoned Lai's soft approach.

In June 1948 he opted for armed rebellion and the **Malayan Communist Emergency** commenced with the murder of three European planters. According to John Gullick, the historian and former member of the Malayan civil service, it was called an 'Emergency' because the Malayan economy was covered by the London insurance market for everything other than war. Premiums covered loss of stock, property and equipment through riot and civil commotion, but not through civil war, so the misnomer continued throughout the 12 year insurrection. Others say it got its name from the Emergency Regulations that were passed in June 1948 which were designed to deny food supplies and weapons to the Communists.

The Emergency was characterized by indiscriminate armed Communist raids on economic targets – often rubber estates and tin mines – and violent ambushes which were aimed at loosening and undermining central government control. Chinese 'squatters' in areas fringing the jungle (many of whom had fled from the cities during the Japanese occupation) provided an information and supply network for the Communists. In 1950 the British administration moved these people into 500 'New Villages', where they could be controlled and protected. This policy, known as 'The Briggs Plan' after the Director of Operations, Lieutenant-General Sir Harold Briggs, was later adopted (rather less successfully) by the Americans in South Vietnam.

In much the same way as they had been caught unprepared by the Japanese invasion in 1941, the British were taken by surprise and in the first few years the MCP (whose guerrillas were labelled 'CTs' – or Communist Terrorists) gained the upper hand. In 1951 British morale all but crumbled when the High Commissioner, Sir Henry Gurney, was ambushed and assassinated on the road to Fraser's Hill (see page 109). His successor, General Sir Gerald Templer, took the initiative, however, with his campaign to 'win the hearts and minds of the people'. Templer's biographer, John Cloake, gave him Japanese General Tomoyuki Yamashita's old sobriquet 'Tiger of Malaya', and there is little doubt that his tough policies won the war. In his book *Emergency Years*, former mine-manager Leonard Rayner says the chain-smoking Templer "exuded nervous energy like an overcharged human battery". Within two years the Communists were on the retreat. They had also begun to lose popular support due to the climate of fear they introduced, although the Emergency did not officially end until 1960.

Historians believe the Communist rebellion failed because it was too slow to take advantage of the economic hardships in the immediate aftermath of the Second World War and because it was almost exclusively Chinese. It also only really appealed to the Chinese working class and alienated and shunned the Chinese merchant community and Straits-born Chinese.

The road to Merdeka

The British had countered the MCP's claim to be a multi-racial nationalist movement by accelerating moves towards Malayan independence, which Britain promised, once the Emergency was over. The only nationalist party with any political credibility was UMNO. Its founder, Dato' Onn bin Jaafar wanted to allow non-Malays to become members, and when his proposal was rejected he resigned to form the Independence of Malaya Party. The brother of the Sultan of Kedah, Tunku Abdul Rahman, took over as head of UMNO and to counter Onn's new party he made an electoral pact with the Malayan Chinese Association (MCA) and the Malayan Indian Congress (MIC). With the MCP out of the picture the Chinese community hesitantly grouped itself around the MCA. The Alliance (which trounced Onn's party in the election) is still in place today, in the form of the ruling Barisan Nasional (National Front). After sweeping the polls in 1955, the Alliance called immediately for *merdeka*, or independence, which the British guaranteed within two years.

With independence promised by non-violent means, Tunku Abdul Rahman offered an amnesty to the Communists. Together with Singapore's Chief Minister, David Marshall and Straits-Chinese leader Tan Cheng Lock (see page 194), he met Chin Peng in 1956. But they failed to reach agreement and the MCP fled through the jungle into the mountains in southern Thailand around Betong. While the Emergency was declared 'over' in 1960, the MCP only finally agreed to lay down its arms in 1989, in a peace agreement brokered by Thailand. The party had been riven by factionalism and its membership had dwindled to under 1000. In 1991, the legendary Chin Peng struck a deal with the Malaysian government allowing the former guerrillas to return home. Historian Mary Turnbull wrote: "When Malaya attained independence in 1957 it was a prosperous country with stable political institutions, a sound administrative system and a good infrastructure of education and communications – a country with excellent resources and a thriving economy based on export agriculture and mining". Under the new constitution, a king was to be chosen from one of the nine sultans, and the monarchy was to be rotated every five years. A two-tier parliament was set up, with a Dewan Rakyat (People's House) of elected representatives and a Dewan Negara (Senate) to represent the state assemblies. Each of the 11 states had its own elected government and a sultan or governor.

Politicians in Singapore made it clear that they also wanted to be part of an independent Malaya, but in Kuala Lumpur, UMNO leaders were opposed to a merger because the island had a Chinese majority (a straight merger would have resulted in a small Chinese majority in Malaya.) Increasing nationalist militancy in Singapore was of particular concern to UMNO and the radical wing of the People's Action Party, which was swept to power with Lee Kuan Yew at its head in 1959, was dominated by Communists. Fearing the emergence of 'a second Cuba' on Malaysia's doorstep, Tunku Abdul Rahman proposed that Singapore join a greater Malaysian Federation, in which a racial balance would be maintained by the inclusion of Sarawak, Brunei and British North Borneo (Sabah). Britain supported the move, as did all the states involved. Kuala Lumpur was particularly keen on Brunei joining the Federation on two scores: it had Malays and oil. But at the eleventh hour, Brunei's Sultan Omar backed out, mistrustful of Kuala Lumpur's designs on his sultanate's oil revenues and unhappy at the prospect of becoming another sultan in Malaya's collection of nine monarchs.

Prime Minister Tunku Abdul Rahman was disheartened, but the Malaysia Agreement was signed in July 1963 with Singapore, Sarawak and Sabah. Without Brunei, there was a small Chinese majority in the new Malaysia. The Tunku did not have time to dwell on racial arithmetic, however, because almost immediately the new federation was plunged into an undeclared war with Indonesia – which became known as Konfrontasi, or Confrontation (see page 384) – due to President Sukarno's objection to the participation of Sabah and Sarawak. Indonesian saboteurs were landed on the Peninsula and in Singapore and there were Indonesian military incursions along the borders of Sabah and Sarawak with Kalimantan. Konfrontasi was finally ended in 1966 after Sukarno fell from power. But relations with Singapore – which had been granted a greater measure of autonomy than other states – were far from smooth. Communal riots in Singapore in 1964 and Lee Kuan Yew's efforts to forge a nation-wide opposition alliance which called for 'a democratic Malaysian Malaysia' further opened the rift with Kuala Lumpur. Feeling unnerved by calls for racial equality while the Malays did not form a majority of the population, Tunku Abdul Rahman expelled Singapore from the federation in August 1965 against Lee Kuan Yew's wishes.

Racial politics in the 1960s

The expulsion of Singapore did not solve the racial problem on the Peninsula, however. As the Malay and Chinese communities felt threatened by each other – one wielded political power, the other economic power – racial tensions built up. Resentment focused on the enforcement of Malay as the medium of instruction in all schools and as the national language and on the privileged educational and employment opportunities afforded to Malays. The tensions finally exploded on 13 May 1969, in the wake of the general election.

The UMNO-led Alliance faced opposition from the Democratic Action Party (DAP), which was built from the ashes of Lee Kuan Yew's People's Action Party. The DAP was a radical Chinese-dominated party and called for racial equality. Also in opposition was Gerakan (the People's Movement), supported by Chinese and Indians, and the Pan-Malayan Islamic Party, which was exclusively Malay and very conservative. In the election, the opposition parties – which were not in alliance – deprived the Alliance of the two-thirds parliamentary majority required to amend the constitution unimpeded. Gerakan and DAP celebrations provoked counter-demonstrations from Malays and in the ensuing mayhem hundreds were killed in Kuala Lumpur.

The government suspended the constitution for over a year and declared a **State of Emergency**. A new national ideology was drawn up – the controversial New Economic Policy, which was an ambitious experiment in social and economic engineering aimed at ironing out discrepancies between ethnic communities. The Rukunegara, a written national ideology aimed at fostering nation-building, was introduced in August 1970. It demanded loyalty to the king and the constitution, respect for Islam and observance of the law and morally acceptable behaviour. All discussion of the Malays' 'special position' was banned as was discussion about the national language and the sovereignty of the sultans. In the words of historian John Gullick, "Tunku Abdul Rahman, whose anguish at the disaster had impeded his ability to deal with it effectively," resigned the following month and handed over to Tun Abdul Razak. Tun Razak was an able administrator, but lacked the dynamism of his predecessor. He did, however, unify UMNO and patched up the old Alliance, breathing new life into the coalition by incorporating every political party except the DAP and one or two other small parties into the newly named Barisan Nasional (BN), or National Front. In 1974 the Barisan won a landslide majority.

Tun Razak shifted Malaysia's foreign policy from a pro-Western stance to non-alignment and established diplomatic relations with both Moscow and Beijing. Yet within Malaysia Communist paranoia was rife: as Indochina fell to Communists in the mid-1970s, many Malaysians became increasingly convinced that Malaysia was just another 'domino' waiting to topple. There were even several arrests of prominent Malays (including two newspaper editors and five top UMNO politicians). But when Chin Peng's revolutionaries joined forces with secessionist Muslims in South Thailand, the Thai and Malaysian governments launched a joint clean-out operation in the jungle along the frontier. By the late 1970s the North Kalimantan Communist Party had been beaten into virtual submission too. In 1976 Tun Razak died and was succeeded by his brother-in-law, Dato' Hussein Onn (the son of Umno's founding father). He inherited an economy that was in good shape, thanks to strong commodity prices, and in the general election of 1978 the BN won another comfortable parliamentary majority. Three years later he handed over to Dr Mahathir Mohamad.

Modern Malaysia

Politics

On the face of it, Malaysia's political landscape is remarkably unchanging. In 2009 Najib Tun Razak succeeded Abdullah Ahmad Badawi, who had succeeded Dr Mahathir Mohamad in October 2003, Tun Razak heads the Barisan Nasional (BN), or National Front coalition (the party that Mahathir ruled for 22 years as Asia's longest-serving elected leader). Since the first general election was held back in 1959, the largest number of parliamentary seats won by an opposition party has been 31 – by the PKR in 2008. After a landslide victory in 2004, the BN won the most recent general election in 2008 by a slim margin, allowing Badawi to stay in power and hand over the reins to Najib Tun Razak in 2009.

With the rapid expansion of Malaysia's economy – and notwithstanding the recession associated with the Asian economic crisis of 1997-99, a global slump in 2001-2002 and the current global economic crisis – there has emerged a substantial nouveau riche middle class. There has, in turn, been the expectation in some quarters that a more open political system might evolve as prosperous, and increasingly well educated, people demand more of a political say. But the government does not readily tolerate dissent and during the premiership of Dr Mahathir power had, in fact, become increasingly concentrated in the hands of the government. Many Malaysians hoped that Badawi, who was seen as the 'nice guy' in Malaysian politics, would open up the arena. Opinions are divided as to whether or not this was actually the case. One sign of Badawi's potential was the release of Anwar Ibrahim (see below) who had been jailed on corruption and sodomy charges six years previously. However, given that Ibrahim faces another highly controversial jail term, it seems that Badawi might have thought he had made a mistake.

Anwar Ibrahim: Malaysia's trial of the century

It may have become commonplace in Malaysia for opposition politicians, free-thinking jurists, environmentalists and other assorted annoyances to be hounded, arrested, tried and jailed, but not mainstream Malay politicians. It is this that rocked Malaysia's political establishment when Anwar Ibrahim, former deputy prime minister and Mahathir's successor in waiting, was arrested in late 1998. Anwar was sacked by Mahathir on 2 September 1998. This was preceded by a series of murky allegations impugning Anwar's morals. In particular, there were whispers that he was bisexual. Not only is this beyond the pale in a largely Muslim country like Malaysia, but homosexuality remains a crime. Anwar's supporters saw this whispering campaign as politically motivated and the result of a widening gulf between Mahathir and his deputy over how to manage the economy.

A few days after he was sacked, Anwar was arrested and charged with five counts of sodomy and five charges of abuse of power. But before his second appearance in court Anwar appeared with bruised arms and a black eye, and accused the police of beating him. Mahathir seemed to imply that the injuries were self-inflicted. Anwar's treatment at the hands of the police as well as the crude and one-sided coverage in the government-controlled press angered many Malaysians. They did not believe the charges, and as the trial continued they became less and less credible. Nonetheless, on 14 April 1999, Anwar was convicted of corruption with a jail sentence for six years and convicted of sodomy and sentenced to nine years in jail. Anwar appealed against both convictions. In 2002, he lost his final appeal against the corruption charges in the federal court. In September 2004, a federal court of three judges overturned the sodomy conviction at 2 to 1 because of inconsistencies in the prosection's evidence. As Anwar had already served the six years for corruption, he was freed. Shortly after he was freed Anwar tried to have the corruption conviction lifted, but he failed in his appeal. The court found Anwar fairly convicted on those charges. Because his conviction was not lifted, Anwar could not return to politics until April 2008. Directly after Anwar was freed he flew to Germany for back treatment. He alleged the injuries came from abuse during his arrest and jail time. The then prime minister Badawi cautioned overseas leaders not to visit Anwar.

The immediate aftermath of the Anwar affair brought demonstrators onto the streets of Kuala Lumpur, created demands for *reformasi* and led to the creation of a new opposition party, the Justice Party (Keadilan), led by Anwar's wife Wan Azizah.

Whether the court had exerted its independence or the order for his release came from above, Anwar's freedom would have been unthinkable under Mahathir.

Anwar stormed back into politics in August 2008 with a crushing victory in the Permatang by-election, cementing his position in Malaysian political life, However, this victory was tinged with a bitter edge: in July 2008 Anwar was again arrested having been accused by one of his aides of sodomy, a crime punishable with a jail sentence of 20 years and a punishment sure to end any effective opposition Anwar could offer to the BN. The doctor who examined the alleged victim claimed in August 2008 that there was no physical evidence to support the accuser's claims. After Anwar was released on bail, the case was transferred to the High Court with global notables including Al Gore and Condoleeza Rice expressing their alarm at the accusations and proceedings. Gore claimed that Anwar was the victim of a political character assassination. In June 2009 Anwar accused the public prosecutor of conspiring with the government against him. While the noose tightened around Anwar's political neck, he claimed to have enough BN dissenters to topple the ruling party and wished to push through a vote of no confidence against the government, However, any supporters in the ruling camp he might have had wished to remain silent. On 17 June 2009, an affidavit was filed at the KL High Court to throw out the case against Anwar with the evidence of two doctors to support Anwar's innocence.

In February 2010, the case went to trial at the Malaysian High Court, with Ibrahim claiming the judge was biased against him as he claimed to be the victim of a conspiracy. The judge refused to vacate his position at the trial and postponed proceedings until March 2010. As the trial went to court, Anwar again saw huge support from the international community with 50 Australian lawmakers protesting the trial with warnings that the affair would only damage Malaysia's international standing, backed up by calls from former US presidential candidate John Kerry calling for a fair trial.

As the trial looks to stretch long into 2010, it seems that Anwar's return to political life is sure to be a rough and painful ride.

General elections

The 2004 general election was the first one since 1981 not contested by Mahathir, who had tearfully resigned and handed over to his deputy Abdullah Ahmad Badawi in October 2003. The sacking and imprisonment on allegedly trumped up charges of Anwar Ibrahim was not an issue. The public had forgotten him despite efforts by the opposition to revive his case. Also Badawi's face was on the election posters, and it was Mahathir who was associated with Anwar's treatment.

Most observers agree that BN's landslide victory came because it played the Islamic fundamentalism card. Many of Malaysia's Muslims follow a more moderate form of the religion and do not support the idea of an Islamic state. The Islamist PAS wanted to ban rock concerts, make dress even more conservative and separate sexes on beaches and even supermarkets. Moreover, the country's media is under government control.

The 2008 general elections started off controversially with the election committee announcing on 14 February that nominations for candidates would be announced on 24 February and the election proper held on 8 March, allowing only 13 days for campaigning. Anwar Ibrahim claimed this was 'a dirty trick', and that it was also too early for Ibrahim to legally return to politics and stand as a candidate. Again, using the Islamic card, the BN unsuccessfully tried to wrest Kelantan away from the PAS with promises of extensive mosque building and development projects. With claims of fraud ringing through the media and international organization Human Rights Watch claiming the process was 'grossly unfair', the BN claimed victory once more, although the opposition's gain of 36.9% of the seats was the first time since 1969 that the BN did not gain a two-thirds majority.

On 3 April 2009, Badawi handed over control of the country to the new prime minister and leader of UMNO Najib Tun Razak, son of former Malaysian prime minister Tun Abdul Razak, and immediately attracted the wrath of Matahir Mohamed for the inclusion of several 'unsavoury characters' in his 28-strong cabinet. Najib quickly unveiled his 1Malaysia scheme, an attempt to bridge many of the gaps between the ethnic groups of Malaysia. In July 2009 Najib Tun Razak outlined a plan to reduce the grip on economic power held by the Malays, who have long been given a favoured status as *bumiputeras* (sons of the soil). The new policy outlined by Razak changes the requirement that 30% of the shares of companies need to be held be ethnic Malays, allowing for a freer and fairer market. Many believe this change has been brought about by the resurgence in popularity of Anwar Ibrahim, who promises to undo Malaysia's system of racial preferences once and for all, allowing Chinese and Indians equal benefits and access to higher education as the Malays. The continuing policy of racial preferencing was seen as a key reason why the opposition parties gained a much larger numer of seats in the 2008 general election.

Money, politics and corruption

The entrenched position of UMNO and the BN has, in the eyes of the government's critics, allowed money politics and political patronage to flourish. It is argued that the use of political power to dispense favours and make money has become endemic, so much so that it is accepted as just another part of the political landscape.

Badawi made stamping out corruption one of his main policies. He strengthened a number of anti-corruption agencies and arrested some Mahathir-era cronies. However, critics comment that the pace of change is too slow.

Many suggested that Mahathir worsened the corruption problem. They blamed his style and his emphasis on wealth creation. Chandra Muzaffar, a political scientist at the Science University of Malaysia in Penang, for example, argued that "He's created a culture that places undue emphasis on wealth accumulation for its own sake. The new heroes are all corporate barons".

Racial relations in the New Malaysia

Since the race riots of 1969, relations between Malaysia's Malay and Chinese populations have dominated political affairs. Now that Malaysia is fast attaining economic maturity, a debate is beginning to emerge about whether it is time to consign racial politics, and racial quotas, to the dust heap. Former Prime Minister Mahathir's Vision 2020 (see page 508), which sets out a path to developed country status by 2020, significantly talks of a 'Malaysian race working in full and equal partnership'. There is no mention here of 'bumiputras' and 'Chinese Malaysians', but of a single Malaysian identity which transcends race, further outlined in Najib Tun Razak's 1Malaysia policy.

In late 2007 Malaysia saw its biggest street demonstrations in years, when the ethnic Indian community gathered in protest about the affirmative-action policy favouring ethnic Malays. They argued that the Malay-dominated ruling coalition government discriminated against minority groups, denying them basic opportunities in education and business.

Foreign relations

In foreign affairs Malaysia follows a non-aligned stance and is fiercely anti-Communist. This, however, has not stopped its enthusiastic investment in Indochina and Myanmar. Malaysia is a leading light in the Association of Southeast Asian Nations (ASEAN).

Malaysia's most delicate relations are with neighbouring Singapore, a country with which it is connected by history and also by water pipelines and a causeway. Until it was ejected in 1965, Singapore was part of the Malaysian Federation and Singapore's status as a largely Chinese city state makes for an uneasy relationship with Malay-dominated Malaysia. In 1997 mutual sensitivities were made all too clear in a spat which threatened to escalate into a major diplomatic conflict. The cause? A dispute over whether Johor Bahru was a safe place or not.

Economy

Malaysia has an abundance of natural resources. Today, rubber, palm oil and timber are valuable exports, and it is also a major producer of electronic equipment. At the same time, the service sector is booming, and tourism is a large foreign exchange earner. Over recent years, Malaysia has been one of the fastest-growing economies in the world. The World Bank defines Malaysia as an upper-middle-income country. There is a Malay saying which goes: *ada gula, ada semut* (where there's sugar, there are ants) and from the late

1980s foreign investors swarmed to Malaysia, thanks to its sugar-coated investment incentives as well as its cheap land and labour, good infrastructure and political stability. Until 1997, the country's economy grew extraordinarily rapidly. But the Asian economic crisis, which began in Thailand in mid-1997 and then spread to Malaysia and other Asian countries, temporarily put a halt to this.

Malaysia once again has a strong economy, although growth has not returned to the (unsustainable) levels of the 1990s.

The evolution of the Malaysian economy

In the late 1800s, as the British colonial government developed the infrastructure of the Federated Malay States, they built a network of roads, railways, telephones and telegraphs, which served as the backbone of the export economy. In the 50 years following 1880, export earnings rose 30-fold. Most of the tin mines and plantations were in the hands of British-owned companies and remained foreign-owned until the Malaysian government restructured foreign equity holdings in the 1970s.

On independence in 1957, resource-rich Malaysia's future looked bright and foreign investment was encouraged, the capitalist system maintained and there was no threat to nationalize industry. The first national development plan aimed to expand the agricultural sector and begin to reduce dependence on rubber which, even then, was beginning to encounter competition from synthetic alternatives. But rubber and tin remained the main economic props. In 1963, when the Federation of Malaysia was formed, only 6% of the workforce was employed in industry and 80% of exports were contributed by tin, rubber, palm oil, timber, oil and gas.

The structure of Malaysia's economy has been radically altered since independence, and particularly since the 1980s. Commodity exports, which were the mainstay of the post-colonial economy, have declined in significance and within a few decades this sector is unlikely to contribute more than a few percent of Malaysia's export earnings. Manufacturing output has rapidly increased and the value of manufactured exports is growing even faster; today they are approaching three-quarters of Malaysia's export earnings. The country that used to be the world's biggest producer of rubber and tin is now the world's leading producer of semiconductors and air-conditioning units. In May 1993, another landmark was created in Malaysia's economic history: the Malaysia Mining Corporation, one of the country's biggest remaining tin producers, pulled out of tin mining.

The type of products Malaysia manufactures is also undergoing rapid change. One of the main reasons for this is Malaysia's labour squeeze. The main industrial boom zones (the Klang Valley around Kuala Lumpur, Johor and Penang) are already suffering shortages, and while infrastructural developments have just about kept pace with the flood of foreign manufacturing investment, the labour pool is drying up. There has been a continual flow of both legal and illegal migrant labour, although crackdowns on the latter has led to hundreds of thousands of illegal workers leaving the country.

Transforming the economy

A key element in Malaysia's development strategy is how to manage the transition from a production centre where comparative advantage is based on labour cost to an economy where high levels of education and skills provide the industrial impetus. Malaysia invariably looks to Singapore as both a role model in this regard and as a competitor.

One of former Prime Minister Mahathir's favoured programmes is the so-called MSC or 'Multimedia Super Corridor' – an attempt to build an Oriental Silicon Valley on a 15 km-by-

50 km stretch of land south of KL. This is linked to the new administrative capital of Putrajaya and the associated international airport at Sepang. When you add to these developments the technological centre of Cyberjaya the bill comes to a breathtaking US$20 billion. As Daniel Ng of Sun Microsystems was quoted as saying when the plans for Cyberjaya were in their infancy: "It's as if someone said, 'What would be the perfect Silicon Valley?' and then built it".

There are critics and sceptics aplenty. In particular there are those who say Malaysia lacks the human resources to justify such grandiose plans. Part of the problem is perceived to be the culture of education in the country. Malaysian students are not expected to challenge or contradict their teachers, but to conform. This is perceived to be unhealthy if Malaysia is to become a thinking economy where people are creative and innovative. More practically, Malaysian graduates are often not sufficiently fluent in English to take full advantage of the IT revolution. This dates back to the 1970s when the government switched from English to Bahasa Malaysia as the medium of instruction in secondary schools. Further, the tertiary level enrolment rate in Malaysia is low: just 7.2% of the relevant age group are in higher education. But these sort of criticisms have also be levelled at neighbouring Singapore, and that can hardly be counted an economic failure.

Tourism

Tourism has grown to assume a critical role in Malaysia's economy in the past few years. In 1990, Malaysia launched itself into big league tourism with a bang, joining the swelling ranks of Southeast Asian countries to host 'tourism years'. Visit Malaysia Year (VMY) was a big success: 7.4 million tourists arrived – half as many again as in 1989 and receipts rose 61% to US$1.5 billion. This made tourism Malaysia's third biggest earner after manufacturing and oil – up from sixth position the previous year. The latest catchy slogan is the banal 'Malaysia: truly Asia'. Now, it seems, one marketing campaign follows on seamlessly from the last.

While the vast majority of tourists still come from neighbouring Singapore and Thailand, the government is targeting the big spenders – the 'high-yield markets' like the Japanese, who spend 70% more than the average tourist. Smart new hotel and resort complexes have been built and scores of golf courses are being carved out of the jungle. Until fairly recently, the government paid scant regard to the lower-middle end of the tourism market, favouring sparkling new five-star complexes to (in their view) grotty little low-return guesthouses. Among European countries the most enthusiastic visitors to Malaysia are the British (equalled by the Australians).

Mapping out the future: Vision 2020

Mahathir's long-term economic blueprint, continued by Badawi, appropriately labelled 'Wawasan 2020' or 'Vision 2020' aims to quadruple per-capita income, double the size of the economy and make Malaysia a fully developed industrialized country by the end of the second decade of this century. Vision 2020 is full of lofty ambitions, grand goals and fuzzy rhetoric and it reads more like a corporate mission statement than a well-defined policy. Yet while it was undeniably ambitious, few people questioned whether Malaysia could not achieve the annual average economic growth rate of 7% necessary to meet the plan's targets. That, though, was before the economic crisis in the late 1990s.

However 2000 saw a bounce-back and consumer confidence recovered with a surge in demand for luxury items. Because all this was linked to Prime Minister Mahathir's decision to go against the IMF (and most economists') recommendations, he personally gained considerable prestige from the economy's robust recovery.

Falling tigers

Malaysia's economic crisis came quick on the heels of Thailand's fall from economic grace in July 1997, which led to the devaluation of the baht and a US$15 billion IMF rescue package. Though Thailand's problems were uniquely serious there were enough commonalities to cause concern in KL's financial district: a high current account deficit; a currency linked to the US dollar; a booming property sector; and a lack of transparency in some aspects of financial management. It was these similarities with Thailand – and perhaps also a sense that the economies of ASEAN, having boomed together would also fall together – which led currency speculators to attack the ringgit.

Unlike the other countries of the region, Mahathir did not stick with the IMF's medicine. Instead he imposed tight currency controls in September 1998. While his actions were widely condemned in the international press, the recovery of the Malaysian economy by mid-1999, in Mahathir's eyes at least, vindicated his actions. Of course, opponents of the controls maintained that the country's economic recovery had little to do with the controls per se. Indeed, they say that of all the countries of the region Malaysia was best placed to deal with the crisis and that the currency controls were an irrelevance in the broader economic context. The danger, these critics of Malaysian economic policies maintain, is that because the country was affected least by the crisis it also did the least to confront the structural problems that created the conditions for the crisis in the first place. In other words they wonder if it could all happen again.

Malaysia is ranked as a newly developed economy with a 2008 per capita GDP of US$8141, almost twice that of Thailand and four times larger than Indonesia.

Culture

People

Visitors sometimes get confused over the different races that make up Malaysia's population. All citizens of Malaysia are 'Malaysians'; they are comprised of Malays, Chinese and Indians as well as other 'tribal' groups, most of whom live in the East Malaysian states of Sabah and Sarawak.

Malaysia had a total population in 2009 of 28.2 million, of whom more than 8% live on the Peninsula, 8% in Sabah and 9% in Sarawak. Statistics on the ethnic breakdown of Malaysia's multi-racial population tend to differ and because politics is divided along racial lines, they are sensitive figures. For Malaysia as a whole, Malays and other indigenous groups make up roughly 62% of the population, Chinese 24% and Indians 8%. The Malays and indigenous groups are usually lumped together under the umbrella term *bumiputra* – or 'sons of the soil'. This includes both Malays and tribal groups such as the assorted Dayaks of East Malaysia. On the Peninsula the Chinese make up a rather large share of the population, amounting to some 31%, while *bumis* comprise 58% and Indians 9%.

In theory, being a *bumi* bestows certain advantages. The New Economic Policy (NEP) introduced after the race riots in 1969, discriminates in favour of the indigenous population – mostly the Malays, but also the non-Malay tribal peoples of East Malaysia and the Orang Asli of the Peninsula. They receive preferential treatment when it comes to university places, *bumi* entrepreneurs have an inside track securing government contracts, and they also benefit from discounts on houses. However there have been stories of non-Malay *bumiputras* not being accorded the affirmative action rights of Malay *bumis*. In 1997, for example, it was revealed that an Iban ('tribal' Dayak from East Malaysia) man was refused the 5-7% discount that *bumis* are entitled to when he tried to buy a house in Melaka. The federal government was appalled, but many commentators were not altogether surprised. What it means to qualify as a *bumi* has never been adequately defined. It appears that for some people being a *bumi* not only means being indigenous, it also means being Muslim, and many of the non-Malay *bumis* are Christian.

Malaysia's population is growing by just over 2% per annum and the total fertility rate – the number of children born to each woman – stands at 3.24. This fertility rate, however, is not equally distributed between the ethnic groups. Since 1970, the *bumiputra* population has grown fastest, and, on the Peninsula, their proportion of the total population has increased from 53%. In the same period, the proportion of the Chinese population has declined from 36% while the proportion of Indians has remained roughly the same. The higher average fertility rate of the Malay compared with the Chinese population means that the delicate racial balance that was such a potential source of instability at independence is becoming less of a worry. It has been estimated that by 2020 the *bumiputra* population will comprise 70% of the total population of the country. The fear that the Chinese might represent a political threat to Malay domination is receding as each year passes.

Malays

The Malay people probably first migrated to the Peninsula from Sumatra. Anthropologists speculate that the race originally evolved from the blending of a Mongoloid people from Central Asia with an island race living between the Indian and Pacific oceans. They are lowland people and originally settled around the coasts. These 'Coastal Malays' are also known as 'Deutero-Malays'. They are ethnically similar to the Malays of Indonesia and are the result of intermarriage with many other racial groups, including Indians, Chinese, Arabs and Thais. They are a very relaxed, warm-hearted people who had the good fortune to settle in a land where growing food was easy. For centuries they have been renowned for their hospitality and generosity as well as their well-honed sense of humour. When Malays converted to Islam in the early 15th century, the language was written in Sanskrit script which evolved into the Arabic-looking Jawi.

Because Malays were traditionally farmers and were tied to rural kampongs, they remained insulated from the expansion of colonial Malaya's export economy. Few of them worked as wage labourers and only the aristocracy, which had been educated in English, were intimately involved in the British system of government, as administrators. "… In return for the right to develop a modern extractive economy within the negeri [states] by means of alien immigrant labor," writes historian William R Roff, "the British undertook to maintain intact the position and prestige of the ruling class and to refrain from catapulting the Malay people into the modern world". Rural Malays only began to enter the cash economy when they started to take up rubber cultivation on their smallholdings – but this was not until after 1910. In 1921, less than 5% of Malays lived in towns.

On attaining independence in 1957, the new constitution allowed Malays to be given special rights for 10 years, enabling them to become as prosperous as the Chinese 'immigrants'. To this end, they were afforded extra help in education and in securing jobs. The first economic development plan focused on the rural economy, with the aim of improving the lot of the rural Malays. It was the Malay community's sense of its own weakness in comparison with the commercial might of the Chinese that led to ethnic tensions erupting onto the streets in May 1969. Following the race riots, the Malays were extended special privileges in an effort to increase their participation in the modern economy. Along with indigenous groups, they were classed as bumiputras, usually shortened to 'bumis' – a label many were able to use as a passport to a better life.

Chinese

The Chinese community account for about a quarter of Malaysia's population. In 1794, just eight years after he had founded Georgetown in Penang, Sir Francis Light wrote: "The Chinese constitute the most valuable part of our inhabitants: ... they possess the different trades of carpenters, masons, smiths, traders, shopkeepers and planters; they employ small vessels. They are the only people from whom a revenue may be raised without expense and extraordinary effort by the government. They are a valuable acquisition ...". Chinese immigrants went on to become invaluable members of the British Straits Settlements – from the early 1820s they began to flood into Singapore from China's southern provinces. At the same time they arrived in droves on the Malay Peninsula, most of them working as tin prospectors, shopkeepers and small traders.

Although the great bulk of Chinese in Malaysia arrived during the massive immigration between the late 19th and early 20th centuries, there has been a settled community of Chinese in Melaka since the 15th century. Many arrived as members of the retinue of the Chinese princess Li Poh who married Melaka's Sultan Mansur Shah in 1460 (see page 204). Over the centuries their descendants evolved into a wealthy and influential community with its own unique, sophisticated culture (see page 194). These **Straits Chinese** became known as **Peranakans** (which means 'born here', although it's not known when this term originated); men were called **Babas** and women, **Nyonyas**. Baba came into common usage during the 19th century and it is thought that Peranakan was already a well-established label at that time. 'Baba' does not seem to be of Chinese origin but is probably derived from Arabic, or perhaps Turkish, roots. To begin with Baba was used to refer to all local-born foreigners in Malaya, whether they were ethnic Chinese, Indians or Europeans. However, before long it became solely associated with the Straits Chinese.

The centres of Peranakan Chinese culture were the Straits Settlements of Melaka, Penang and Singapore. There were, however, significant differences between the communities in the three settlements. For example, Nyonya food in Penang shows culinary influences from Thailand, while food in Melaka and Singapore does not.

The Peranakans of Malaysia and Singapore saw their futures being intimately associated with the British. They learnt English, established close links with the colonial administration system and colonial businesses, and even their newspapers were written in English rather than Chinese. With the massive infusion of new Chinese blood from the mainland beginning at the end of the 19th century there emerged a two-tier Chinese community. The Peranakans were concentrated in the commercial and professional sectors, and the 'pure' Chinese in the manual sectors. But as the 20th century progressed so the influence of the Peranakans declined. Competition from non-Baba Chinese became stronger as their businesses expanded and as sheer weight of numbers began to tell. The Straits Chinese British Association (SCBA) was eclipsed by the Malaysian Chinese Association (MCA) as a political force and the Peranakans found themselves marginalized. As this occurred, so the Babas found themselves the object, increasingly, of derision by non-Baba Chinese. They were regarded as having 'sold out' their Chinese roots and become ridiculous in the process. Today the Straits Chinese, in terms of political and economic power, have become – to a large extent – an irrelevance.

Today Peranakan culture is disappearing. Few Baba Chinese identify themselves as Baba; they have become Chinese Malaysians. Only in Melaka (and to some extent in Singapore) does the Baba cultural tradition remain strong. In Penang the numbers of people who see their Baba roots as anything but historical are dwindling. But although Peranakan culture is gradually disappearing, it has left an imprint on mainstream Malaysian culture. For example the custom among Peranakan women of wearing the sarong and kebaya has become subsumed within Malay tradition and has, in the process, become inter-ethnic. Baba cuisine has also been incorporated within Malay/Chinese cuisine.

The Peranakans may be the most colourful piece in Malaysia's Chinese mosaic, but the vast majority of modern Malaysia's prosperous Chinese population arrived from China rather later, as penniless immigrants. They left China because of poverty, over-population and religious persecution – and were attracted by the lure of gold. In the mid-19th century, these newly arrived immigrants came under the jurisdiction of secret societies and kongsis (clan associations). Some of the most striking examples of the latter are in Penang (see, for example, the Khoo Kongsi, page 148). The secret societies sometimes engaged in open warfare with each other as rival groups fought over rights to tin mining areas.

The overseas Chinese have been described as possessing these common traits: the ability to smell profits and make quick business decisions; a penchant for good food (they prefer to sit at round tables to facilitate quicker exchange of information); and a general avoidance of politics in favour of money-making pursuits. Like many stereotypes, these characteristics break down when put to the detailed test but at a certain level of generalization, hold true. It is also true to say – broadly speaking – that the Chinese population felt little loyalty to their host society. At least, that is, until the 1949 Communist take-over in China, which effectively barred their return. Despite the community's political and economic gripes and traumas in the intervening years, Chinese culture has survived and the community enjoys religious freedom; Chinese cuisine is enthusiastically devoured by all races and the mahjong tiles are still clacking in upstairs rooms. Today about 80% of Chinese schoolchildren attend private Chinese primary schools – although all secondary and tertiary education is in Malay.

Indians

Indian traders first arrived on the shores of the Malay Peninsula more than 2000 years ago in search of Suvarnadvipa, the fabled Land of Gold. There was a well-established community of Indian traders in Melaka when the first sultanate grew up in the 1400s – there was even Tamil blood in the royal lineage. But most of the 1½ million Indians in modern Malaysia – who make up nearly 8% of the population – are descendants of indentured Tamil labourers shipped to Malaya from South India by the British in the 19th century. They were nicknamed 'Klings' – a name which today has a deeply derogatory connotation. Most were put to work as coolies on the roads and railways or as rubber tappers.

About 100 years on, four out of five Indians are still manual labourers on plantations or in the cities. This has long been explained as a colonial legacy, but as modern Malaysia has grown more prosperous, the Tamils have remained at the bottom of the heap. Other Indian groups – the Keralans (Malayalis), Gujeratis, Bengalis, Sikhs and other North Indians, who came to colonial Malaya under their own volition, are now well represented in the professional classes. The South Indian Chettiar money-lending caste, which was once far more numerous than it is today, left the country in droves in the 1930s. Their confidence in British colonial rule was shaken by events in Burma, where anti-Indian riots prompted tens of thousands of Chettiars to return to India. While most of Malaysia's Indian community are Hindus, there are also Indian Muslims, Christians and Sikhs. In Melaka there is a small group of Indians with Portuguese names – known as Chitties.

Today the chanted names of the Hindu pantheon echo around the cool interior of the Sri Mariamman Temple in the heart of the capital Kuala Lumpur as they have since its construction in 1873. But large numbers of Tamils still live in the countryside, where they still make up more than half the plantation workforce. Because the estates are on private land, they fall outside the ambit of national development policies and Malaysia's economic boom has passed them by. The controversial New Economic Policy gave the Malays a helping hand, and although it was aimed at eradicating poverty generally, it did not help the Indians much – who often, and justifiably, feel that they are the group who have missed out most. They lack the economic clout of the Chinese, and the political might of the Malays, and can, it seems, conveniently be forgotten.

The new policy document which replaced the NEP in 1991 officially recognizes that Indians have lagged behind in the development stakes. Education is seen as the key to broadening the entrepreneurial horizons of Tamils, getting them off the plantations, out of the urban squatter settlements and into decent jobs. But in the privately run Tamil shanty schools on the estates, the drop-out rate is double the national average. Critics accuse the Malaysian Indian Congress (MIC), which is part of the ruling coalition, of perpetuating this system in an effort to garner support. Because Indians are spread throughout the country and do not form the majority in any constituency, tplantations have been the MIC's traditional support base. It is not in the MIC's interests to see them move off the estates.

But things are beginning to change on the plantations: an unprecedented national strike in 1990 guaranteed plantation workers a minimum wage for the first time. Workers are becoming more assertive and aware of their individual and political rights. A new party, the Indian Progressive Front, has drawn its support from working class Indians. It seems that these stirrings of new assertiveness represent rising aspirations on the estates, which will have to continue to rise if the Tamils are ever going to escape from their plantation poverty trap. In 1970 ethnic Indians controlled about 1.1% of the country's wealth. By 1992, at the end of the 20-year NEP, this figure had declined to 1%. It has been estimated that two-thirds of Indians still live in poverty and for the Indians the NEP has been largely irrelevant. While Malays have enjoyed cumulative gains from the NEP and the Chinese have seen their slice of the cake grow in size if not in proportion, the Indian community have been left trailing and marginalized – a classic 'excluded' community.

Orang Asli (aboriginals)

While the Malay population originally settled on the coasts of the Peninsula, the mountainous, jungled interior was the domain of the oldest indigenous groups – the aboriginals. They are probably of Melanesian origin, possibly related to Australian aborigines. During the Pleistocene ice age, when a land-bridge linked the Philippines to Borneo and mainland Southeast Asia, these people spread throughout the continent. Today they are confined to the mountains of the Malay Peninsula, Northeast India, North Sumatra, the Andaman Islands and the Philippines. The **Negrito** aboriginals – who in Malay are known as Orang Asli (Indigenous People) – were mainly hunter-gatherers. As the Malays spread inland, the Orang Asli were pushed further and further into the mountainous interior. Traditionally, the Negritos did not build permanent houses – preferring makeshift shelters – and depend on the jungle and the rivers for their food.

A second group of Orang Asli, the **Senoi** – who are also known as the **Sakai** – arrived later than the Negritos. They practised shifting cultivation to supplement their hunting and gathering and built sturdier houses. The third aboriginal group to come to the Peninsula were the **Jakuns** – or **proto-Malays** – who were mainly of Mongoloid stock.

They were comprised of several subgroups, the main ones being the Mantera and Biduanda of Negeri Sembilan and Melaka and the Orang Ulu, Orang Kanak and Orang Laut (Sea People) of Johor. Their culture and language became closely linked to that of the coastal Malays, and over the centuries many of them assimilated into Malay society. Most practised shifting cultivation; the Orang Laut were fishermen.

Malaysia's aborigines have increasingly been drawn into the modern economy. Along with the Malays, they are classified as bumiputras and as such became eligible, as with other tribal groups in East Malaysia, for the privileges extended to all bumiputras following the introduction of the New Economic Policy (NEP) in 1970. In reality, however the NEP offered few tangible benefits to the Orang Asli, and while the government has sought to integrate them – there is a Department of Aboriginal Affairs in Kuala Lumpur – there is no separate mechanism to encourage entrepreneurism among the group.

Art and architecture

Unlike the countries of mainland Southeast Asia and its neighbour Indonesia, Malaysia is not known for its art and architecture. Arriving at Kuala Lumpur's Sabang International Airport and driving into town, there is apparently scarcely anything worth an aesthetic second glance. Many of Malaysia's artistic treasures have either been torn down to make way for modern buildings with scarcely a concrete ounce of artistic merit, or have simply rotted away through sheer neglect. However, the country is far from being the artistic desert that a cursory glance might suppose. The sadness, though, is that much of what is deemed to be 'worth seeing' (ie a 'sight') is not Malaysian per se, but colonial. The most attractive towns – particularly Georgetown (Penang) and Melaka – are notable mainly for their Chinese shophouses, and Dutch, Portuguese and English colonial buildings. Vernacular Malay houses must be sought out more carefully; few are preserved, and most are being demolished to make way for structures perceived to be more fitting of a thrusting young country on the verge of developed nation status.

In his book *The Malay House*, architect Lim Jee Yuan wrote that traditional houses, which are built without architects, "reflect good housing solutions, as manifested by the display of a good fit to the culture, lifestyle and socio-economic needs of the users; the honest and efficient use of materials; and appropriate climatic design". Classic Malay houses are built of timber and raised on stilts with wooden or bamboo walls and an *atap* roof – made from the leaves of the nipah palm. It should have plenty of windows and good ventilation – the interior is usually airy and bright. It is also built on a prefabricated system and can be expanded to fit the needs of a growing family. Malay houses are usually simple, functional and unostentatious, and even those embellished by woodcarvings blend into their environment. Lim Jee Yuan said "the Malay house cannot be fully appreciated without its setting – the house compound and the kampong". Kampong folk, he says, prefer "community intimacy over personal privacy" which means villages are closely knit communities.

Most Malays on the Peninsula traditionally lived in pile houses built on stilts along the rivers. The basic design is called the *bumbung panjangi* (long roof), although there are many variations and hybrids; these are influenced both by the Minangkabau house-forms (of West Sumatra) and by Thai-Khmer designs. The differences in house-styles between regions is mainly in the shape of the roof. The bumbung panjang is the oldest, commonest, simplest and most graceful, with a long gable roof, thatched with *atap*. There are ventilation grills at either end, allowing a throughflow of air. From the high apex, the eaves slope down steeply, then, towards the bottom, the angle lessens, extending out over the walls. Bumbung panjang are most commonly found in Melaka, but the design is used widely throughout the Peninsula.

These days it is more usual to find the *atap* replaced with corrugated zinc roofs that require less maintenance and are a measure of status in the community. But zinc turns houses into ovens during the day, makes them cold at night and makes a deafening noise in rainstorms. On the east coast of the Peninsula, the use of tiled roofs is more common. Towards the north, Thai and Khmer influences are more pronounced in roof style. As in Thai houses, walls are panelled; there are also fewer windows and elaborate carving is more common. Because Islam proscribes the use of the human figure in art, ornamental woodcarvings depict floral and geometric designs as well as Koranic calligraphy. Most are relief-carvings on wood panels or grilles. In Melaka, colourful ceramic tiles are also commonly used as exterior decoration.

The oldest surviving Malay houses date from only the 19th century. The traditional design is the *rumah berpanggung*, which is built high off the ground on stilts with an A-shaped roof. The basic features include: *Anjung*: covered porch at the top of entranceway stairs where formal visitors are entertained; *Serambi gantung*: veranda, where most guests are entertained; *Rumah ibu* ('the domain of the mother of the house'): private central core of the house, with raised floor level, where the family talks, sleeps, prays, studies and eats (particularly during festivals); *Dapur*: kitchen, always at the back, and below the level of the rest of the house; most meals are taken here. The *dapur* is connected to the *rumah ibu* by the *selang*, a closed walkway. Near the *dapur*, there is usually a *pelantar*, with a washing area for clothes, a mandi and a toilet.

The best places to see traditional Malay houses are Melaka and Negeri Sembilan, on the west coast, and Terengganu and Kelantan states to the northeast. Minangkabau influence is most pronounced in Negeri Sembilan state, between Kuala Lumpur and Melaka. There, houses have a distinctive elegant curved roofline, where the gable sweeps up into 'wings' at each end – the so-called Minangkabau 'buffalo horns'.

Today the traditional Malay house has lost its status in the kampong – now everyone wants to build in concrete and brick. Many planned modern kampongs have been built throughout Malaysia, with little regard for traditional building materials or for the traditional houseforms. Many like-minded architects despair of the 'vulgarization' of the Malay houseform, which has been used as an inspiration for many modern buildings (notably in Kuala Lumpur, see page 62). The curved Minangkabau roof, for example, which has been borrowed for everything from modern bank buildings to toll-booths, has merely become a cultural symbol, and has been deprived of its deeper significance.

Peranakan

The Straits Chinese (Peranakan) communities of Melaka, Penang and Singapore developed their own architectural style to match their unique cultural traditions (see page 194). The finest Peranakan houses can be seen along Jalan Tun Tan Cheng Lock in Melaka (see page 203), notably the Baba-Nyonya Heritage Museum. Typical Peranakan houses were long and narrow, and built around a central courtyard. Their interiors are characterized by dark, heavy wood and marble-topped furniture, often highly decorated, and made by Chinese craftsmen who were brought over from China.

Language and literature

Bahasa Melayu (Malay Language) – or to give the language its official title, Bahasa Kebangsaan (National Language) – is an Austronesian language that has been the language of trade and commerce throughout the archipelago for centuries. It is the parent language of, and is closely related to, modern Indonesian. In 1972, Indonesia and Malaysia came to an agreement to standardize spelling, although many differences still remain.

Modern Malay has been affected by a succession of external influences – Sanskrit from the seventh century, Arabic from the 14th and English from the 19th century. These influences are reflected in a number of words, most of them of a religious or technical nature. All scientific terminology is directly borrowed from the English or Latin. However, there are many common everyday words borrowed from Arabic or English: *pasar*, for example, comes from the Arabic *bazaar* (market) and there are countless examples of English words used in Malay – particularly when it comes to modern modes of transport – *teksi*, *bas* and *tren*. Where a Malay term has been devised for a 20th-century phenomenon, it is usually a fairly straightforward description. An alternative word for train, for example is *keretapi* (literally, fire car) and the word for aeroplane is *kapalterbang* (flying ship).

From the seventh century, the Indian Pallava script was in restricted use, although few examples survive. The Jawi script, adapted from Arabic, was adopted in the 14th century, with the arrival of Muslim traders and Sufi missionaries in Melaka. To account for sounds in the Malay language which have no equivalent in Arabic, five additional letters had to be invented, giving 33 letters in all. Jawi script was used for almost all Malay writings until the 19th century, and romanized script only began to supplant Jawi after the Second World War. Many older Malays still read and write the script and it is not uncommon to see it along the streets. Some Chinese-owned banks, for example, have transliterated their names into Jawi script so as to make Malays feel a little more at home in them.

Malay literature is thought to date from the 14th century – although surviving manuscripts written in Jawi only date from the beginning of the 15th century. The first printed books in Malay were produced by European missionaries in the 17th century. The best known of Malay literary works are the 16th-century Sejara Melayu or Malay Annals; others include the romantic Hikayat Hang Tuah and the 19th century Tuhfat al-Nafis.

The first of Malaysia's 'modern' authors was the 19th century writer Munshi Abdullah – who has lent his name to a few streets around the country. Although he kept to many of the classical strictures, Abdullah articulated a personal view and challenged many of the traditional assumptions underlying Malay society. His best known work was his autobiography, Hikayat Abdullah. However, it was not until the 1920s that Malayan authors began to write modern novels and short stories. Among the best known writers are Ahmad bin Mohd. Rashid Talu, Ishak Hj. Muhammad and Harun Aminurrashid. Their work laid the foundations for an expansion of Malaysian literature from the 1950s and today there is a prodigious Malay-language publishing industry.

Since independence, the government has promoted Bahasa Melayu at the expense of Chinese dialects and English. However in 1994 then Prime Minister Mahathir signalled a switch in strategy when he declared that university courses in the sciences and technology would be taught in English rather than Bahasa. The emphasis on Bahasa is regarded to some extent as yesterday's battle – the battle to build a national, Malaysian identity. Today's battle is to produce an educated workforce conversant and at home in the world of international business – in other words, people who can use English. When comparisons are made between Malaysian and other overseas students, Malaysian students come out poorly. This is one reason why so many wealthy Malays and Chinese send their children to private English language schools. Now the government appears to have realized the necessity for state schools and universities to reintroduce English. In mid-1997 the government ruled that Islamic civilization would become a mandatory course for all university students – they would need to take and pass it in order to graduate. Needless to say, non-Muslim Malaysians, and some Muslim Malaysians, thought this a step backwards and going against the trend towards a modern, outward-looking, and inclusive Malaysia. Later it was announced that the course would also include study of other Asian civilizations. In 2009 the government controversially reversed the policy of English-language maths and science lessons back to Bahasa Malaysia much to the distress of critics who lamented Malaysia's ever-changing and experimental education policies were leaving the country far behind its neighbour Singapore, which is regarded as having one of the best education systems in the world.

Drama, dance and music

Drama

Wayang Kulit Wayang means 'shadow', and the art form is best translated as 'shadow theatre' or 'shadow play'. Shadow plays were the traditional form of entertainment in Malay kampongs. Although film and television have replaced the wayang in many people's lives – especially the young – they are still performed in some rural parts of the Peninsula's east coast and are regular fixtures at cultural events. Some people believe that the wayang is Indian in origin, pointing to the fact that most of the characters are from Indian epic tales such as the *Ramayana* and *Mahabharata*.

By the 11th century wayang was well established in Java. A court poet of the Javanese King Airlangga (1020-1049), referred to it in *The Meditation of King Ardjuna*: "There are people who weep, are sad and aroused watching the puppets, though they know they are merely carved pieces of leather manipulated and made to speak. These people are like men, thirsting for sensual pleasures, who live in a world of illusion; they do not realize the magic hallucinations they see are not real."

It seems that by the 14th century the art form had made the crossing from the Javanese Majapahit Empire to the courts of the Malay Peninsula and from there spread to kampongs across the country.

There are many forms of wayang – and not all of them are, strictly speaking, shadow plays – but the commonest and oldest form is the wayang kulit. Kulits are finely carved and painted leather, two-dimensional puppets jointed at the elbows and shoulders and manipulated using horn rods (see box above). In order to enact the entire repertoire of 179 plays, 200 puppets are needed. A single performance can last as long as nine hours. The plays have various origins. Some are animistic, others are adapted from the epic poems. The latter are known as 'trunk' tales or pondok and include the *Ramayana*. Others have been developed over the years by influential puppet masters. They feature heroic deeds, romantic encounters, court intrigues, bloody battles and mystical observations, and are known as *carangan* or 'branch' tales.

The *gunungan* (tree of life) is an important element of wayang theatre. It represents all aspects of life and is always the same in design: shaped like a stupa, the tree has painted red flames on one side and a complex design on the other (this is the side which faces the audience). At the base of the tree are a pair of closed doors, flanked by two fierce demons or *yaksas*. Above the demons are two garudas and within the branches of the tree there are monkeys, snakes and two animals – usually an ox and a tiger. The *gunungan* is placed in the middle of the screen at the beginning and end of the performance – and sometimes between major scene changes. During the performance it stands at one side, and flutters across the screen to indicate minor scene changes.

Making a wayang kulit puppet

Wayang kulit puppets are made of buffalo hide, preferably taken from a female animal of about four years of age. The skin is dried and scraped, and then left to mature for as long as 10 years to achieve the stiffness required for carving. After carving, the puppet is painted in traditional pigments.

In carving the puppet, the artist is constrained by convention. The excellence of the puppet is judged according to the fineness of the chisel-work and the subtlety of painting. If the puppet is well made it may have *guna* – a magical quality which is supposed to make the audience suspend its disbelief during the performance.

Puppets accumulate *guna* with age; this is why old puppets are preferred to new ones.

Each major character has a particular iconography, and even the angle of the head and the slant of the eyes and mouth determine the character. Some puppets may perform a number of minor parts, but in the main a knowledgeable wayang-goer will be able to recognize each character immediately.

The cempurit or rods used to manipulate the puppet are made of buffalo horn, while the studs used to attach the limbs are made of metal, bone or bamboo. Court puppets might even be made of gold, studded with precious stones.

Traditionally, performances were requested to celebrate particular occasions – for example the seventh month of pregnancy (*tingkep*) – or to accompany village festivities. Admission was free as the individual commissioning the performance would meet the costs. Of course, this has changed now and tourists invariably have to pay an entrance charge.

In the past, the shadows of the puppets were reflected onto a white cotton cloth stretched across a wooden frame using the light from a bronze coconut oil lamp. Today, electric light is more common – a change which, in many people's minds, has meant the unfortunate substitution of the flickering, mysterious shadows of the oil lamp, with the constant harsh light of the electric bulb. There are both day and night wayang performances. The latter, for obvious reasons, are the more dramatic, although the former are regarded as artistically superior.

The audience sits on both sides of the screen. Those sitting with the puppet master see a puppet play; those on the far side, out of view of the puppet master and the accompanying gamelan orchestra, see a shadow play. It is possible that in the past, the audience was segregated according to sex: men on the *to' dalang*'s side of the screen, women on the shadow side.

The puppet-master is known as the *to' dalang*; he narrates each story in lyrical classical Malay and is accompanied by a traditional gamelan orchestra of gongs, drums, *rebab* (violins) and woodwind instruments. He slips in and out of different characters, using many different voices throughout the performances, which lasts as long as three to four hours. The words *to' dalang* are said to be derived from *galang*, meaning bright or clear, the implication being that the *to' dalang* makes the sacred texts understandable. He sits on a plinth, an arm's length away from the cloth screen. From this position he manipulates the puppets, while also narrating the story. Although any male can become a *to' dalang*, it is usual for sons to follow their fathers into the profession. The *to' dalang* is the key to a successful performance: he must be multi-skilled, have strength and stamina, be able to manipulate numerous puppets simultaneously, narrate the story, and give the lead to the accompanying gamelan orchestra. No wonder that an adept *to' dalang* is a man with considerable status.

Dance

Silat (or, more properly, *bersilat*) is a traditional Malay martial art, but is so highly stylized that it has become a dance form and is often performed with the backing of a percussion orchestra. *Pencak silat* is the more formal martial art of self-defence; *seni silat* is the graceful aesthetic equivalent. A variety of the latter is commonly performed at ceremonial occasions – such as Malay weddings – it is called *silat pulut*. *Silat* comprises a fluid combination of movements and is designed to be as much a comprehensive and disciplined form of physical exercise as it is a martial art. It promotes good blood circulation and deep-breathing, which are considered essential for strength and stamina. The fluidity of the body movements require great suppleness, flexibility and poise.

The **Mak Yong** was traditionally a Kelantanese court dance-drama, performed only in the presence of the sultan and territorial chiefs. Performed mainly by women (the *mak yong* being the 'queen' and lead dancer), it is accompanied by an orchestra of gongs, drums and the *rebab* (violin). There are only ever two or three male dancers who provide the comic interludes. The dance is traditionally performed during the Sultan of Kelantan's birthday celebrations. Unlike the wayang kulit shadow puppet theatre (see page 517), the stories are not connected to the Hindu epics; they are thought to be of Malay origin. Other Kelantanese court dances include: the *garong*, a lively up-tempo dance by five pairs of men and women, in a round (a *garong* is a bamboo cow bell). The *payang*, a folk dance, is named after the distinctive east coast fishing boats; traditionally it was danced on the beach while waiting for the kampong fishing fleet to return.

The **joget** dance is another Malay art form which is the result of foreign cultural influence – in this case, Portuguese. It has gone by a variety of other names, notably the *ronggeng* and the *branyo*. It is traditionally accompanied by the gamelan orchestra. Arab traders were responsible for importing the **zapin** dance and Indonesians introduced the *inang*. Immigrants from Banjarmasin (South Kalimantan), who arrived in Johor in the early 1900s, brought with them the so-called Hobbyhorse Dance – the **Kuda Kepang** – which is performed at weddings and on ceremonial occasions in Johor. The hobbyhorses are made of goat or buffalo skin, stretched over a rotan frame. There are countless other local folk dances around Malaysia, usually associated with festivals – such as the **Wau Bulan** Kite Dance in Kelantan.

The **Lion Dance** is performed in Chinese communities, particularly around Chinese New Year, and is accompanied by loud drums and cymbals – hard to miss. The lion dance originated in India, where tamed lions were led around public fairs and festivals as entertainment, but because lions were in short supply, dancers with lion masks took their place. The dance was introduced to China during the Tang Dynasty. The lion changed its image from that of a clown to a symbol of the Buddha and is now regarded as 'the protector of Buddhism'. The lion dance developed into a ceremony in which demons and evil spirits are expelled (hence the deafening cymbals and drums).

Bharata Natyam (Indian classical dance) is performed by Malaysia's Indian community and is accompanied by Indian instruments such as the *tambura* (which has four strings), the *talam* (cymbals), *mridanga* (double-headed drum), *vina* (single stringed instrument) and flute. In Malaysia, the Temple of Fine Arts in Kuala Lumpur is an Indian cultural organization which promotes Indian dance forms. The Temple organizes an annual Festival of Arts (see page 96).

Music

Traditional Malay music, which accompanies the various traditional dances, offers a taste of all the Peninsula's different cultural influences. The most prominent of these were

Indian, Arab, Portuguese, Chinese, Siamese and Javanese – and finally, Western musical influence which gave birth to the all-pervasive genre 'Pop Melayu' – typically melancholic heavy rock. Traditional musical instruments reflect similar cultural influences, notably the *gambus* or lute (which has Middle Eastern origins and is used to accompany the zapin dance), the Indian harmonium, the Chinese *serunai* (clarinet) and gongs, the *rebana* drums, also of Middle Eastern origin, and the Javanese gamelan orchestra. Because Malays have traditionally been so willing to absorb new cultural elements, traditional art forms have been in danger of extinction. Most traditional Malay instruments are percussion instruments; there are very few stringed or wind instruments. There are six main Malay drums, the most common of which is the cylindrical, double-headed *gendang*, which is used to accompany wayang kulit performances and silat. Other drums include the *geduk* and the *gedombak*; all three are played in orchestras.

Rebana, another traditional Malay drum, is used on ceremonial occasions as well as being a musical instrument. Traditionally, drumming competitions would be held following the rice-harvesting season (in May) and judges award points for timing, tone and rhythm. The best place to see the *rebana* in action is during Kelantan's giant drum festivals at the end of June. The drums are made from metre-long hollowed-out logs and are brightly painted. In competitions, drummers from different kampongs compete against each other in teams of up to 12 men. Traditionally the *rebana* was used as a means of communication between villages, and different rhythms were devised as a sort of morse code to invite distant kampongs to weddings or as warnings of war. *Kertok* are drums made from coconuts whose tops are sliced off and replaced with a block of nibong wood (from the sago palm) as a sounding board; these are then struck with padded drumsticks.

There are three main gongs; the biggest and most common, the *tawak* or *tetawak* is used to accompany wayang kulit shadow puppet theatre and Mak Yong dance dramas. The other smaller gongs are called *canang* and also accompany wayang kulit performances. The only Malay stringed instrument is the *rebab*, a violin-type instrument found throughout the region. The main wind instrument is the *serunai*, or oboe, which is of Persian origin and traditionally accompanies wayang kulit and dance performances. Its reed is cut from a palm leaf.

The **Nobat** is the ancient royal orchestra which traditionally plays at the installation of sultans in Kedah, Perak, Selangor, Terangganu and Brunei. It is thought to have been introduced at the royal court of Melaka in the 15th century. The instruments include two types of drums (*negara* and *gendang*), a trumpet (*nafiri*), a flute (*serunai*) and a gong. The Nobat also plays at the coronation of each new king, every five years.

Crafts

The Malay heartland, on the east coast of Peninsular Malaysia, is the centre of the handicraft industry – particularly Kelantan. An extensive variety of traditional handicrafts, as well as batiks, are widely available in this area, although they are also sold throughout the country, notably in Kuala Lumpur and other main towns (see individual town entries). In East Malaysia, Sarawak has an especially active handicraft industry (see page 392).

Kites Kite-making and kite-flying (*main wau*) are traditional pursuits in the northern Malaysian states of Perlis, Kedah, Kelantan and Terengganu. (Most kite-flying competitions take place after the rice harvest in May, when kampongs compete against each other.) Malaysia's most famous kite is the crescent-shaped Kelantanese *wau bulan* (moon kite) which has a wingspan of up to 3 m and a length of more than 3 m; they can reach altitudes of nearly 500 m. Bow-shaped pieces of bamboo are often secured underneath, which make a melodious humming noise (*dengung*) in the wind. *Wau* come in all shapes and sizes however, and scaled-down versions of *wau bulan* and other kites can be bought. It is even possible to find batik-covered *wau cantik* or *wau sobek*, which are popular wallhangings but make for awkward hand luggage. There are often kite-flying competitions on the east coast, where competitors gain points for height and manoeuvering skills. Kites are also judged for their physical attributes, their ability to stay in the air and their sound. On the east coast, all kites are known as *wau*, a word which, it is said, is derived from the arabic letter of the same sound, which is shaped like a kite. Perhaps the most recognizable one is Terengganu's *wau kucing* (cat kite), which Malaysia Airlines adopted as its logo. There are also *wau daun* (leaf kites) and *wau jala budi* (which literally means 'the net of good deeds kite'). Elsewhere in Malaysia, kites are known as *layang- layang* (floating objects).

Tops Top-spinning (*main gasing*) is another traditional form of entertainment, still popular in rural Malay kampongs – particularly on the east coast of the Peninsula. There are two basic forms of tops. The heart-shaped *gasing jantung* and the flattened top, *gasing uri*. The biggest tops have diameters as big as frisbees and can weigh more than 5 kg; the skill required in launching a top is considerable. Top-making is a precision craft, and each one can take up to three days to make; they are carved from the upper roots and stem-bases of merbau and afzelia trees.

Woodcarving Originally craftsmen were commissioned by sultans and the Malay nobility to decorate the interiors, railings, doorways, shutters and stilts of palaces and public buildings. In Malay woodcarving, only floral and animal motifs are used as Islam prohibits depiction of the human form. But most widely acclaimed are the carved statues of malevolent spirits of the Mah Meris, an Orang Asli tribe.

Batik (Batek) The word batik may be derived from the Malay word *tik* (to drip). It is believed that batik replaced tatooing as a mark of status in the Malay archipelago. (In eastern Indonesia the common word for batik and tattoo are the same.) Although batik technology was actually imported from Indonesia several centuries ago, this coloured and patterned cloth is now a mainstay of Malaysian cultural identity. Traditionally, the wax was painted onto the woven cloth using a *canting* (pronounced 'janting'), a small copper cup with a spout, mounted on a bamboo handle. The cup is filled with melted wax, which flows from the spout like ink from a fountain pen – although the canting never touches the surface of the cloth. Batik artists have a number of canting with various widths of spout, some even with several spouts, to give varied thicknesses of line and differences of effect.

In the mid-19th century the 'modern' batik industry was born with the invention (in Java, but quickly adopted in Malaysia) of the *cap* (pronounced 'jap'). This is a copper, or sometimes a wooden, stamp which looks something like a domestic iron, except that it has an artistically patterned bottom, usually made from twisted copper and strips of soldered tin. Dripping with molten wax, the *Jap* stamps the same pattern across the length and breadth of the cloth, which is then put into a vat of dye. The waxed areas resist the dye and after drying, the process is repeated several times for the different colours. The cracking effect is produced by crumpling the waxed material, which allows the dye to penetrate the cracks. The cloth is traditionally printed in 12 m lengths.

Recent years have seen a revival of hand-painted batiks (*batik tulis*), particularly on silk. Price depends on the type of material, design, number of colours used and method employed: factory-printed materials are cheaper than those made by hand. Batik is sold by the sarung-length or made up into shirts – and other items of clothing.

Kain songket is Malaysia's 'cloth of gold', although it is also woven in other parts of the region, particularly coastal southern Sumatra. Originally cloth made from a mix of cotton and silk was inter-woven with supplementary gold or silver thread. Today, imitation thread is generally used although the metallic thread from old pieces is also removed to provide yarn for new lengths.

The *songket* evolved when the Malay sultanates first began trading with China (where the silk came from) and India (where the gold and silver thread derived). Designs are reproduced from Islamic motifs and Arabic calligraphy. It was once exclusive to royalty, but is used today during formal occasions and ceremonies (such as weddings). In Kelantan, Terengganu and Pahang the cloth can be purchased directly from workshops. Prices increase with the intricacy of the design and the number of threads used. Each piece is woven by hand and different weavers specialize in particular patterns – one length of cloth may be the work of several weavers.

Pewterware Pewter-making was introduced from China in the mid-19th century; it was the perfect alloy for Malaysia, which until recently, was the world's largest tin-producer: pewter is 95% tin. Straits tin is alloyed with antimony and copper. The high proportion of tin lends to the fineness of the surface. It is made mainly into vases, tankards, water jugs, trays and dressing-table ornaments. The dimpling effect is made by tapping the surface with a small hammer. Selangor Pewter is the world's biggest and best pewter manufacturer, there are factories in KL and Singapore.

Wayang kulit (shadow puppets; see box, page 518) are crafted from buffalo hide and represent figures from the Indian epic tales. They are popular handicrafts as they are light and portable.

Silverware Silverwork is a traditional craft and is now a thriving cottage industry in Kelantan. It is crafted into brooches, pendants, belts, bowls and rings. Design patterns incorporate traditional motifs such as wayang kulit (see above) and hibiscus flowers (the national flower). The Iban of Sarawak also use silver for ceremonial headdresses and girdles, and some Iban silvercraft can be found for sale on the Peninsula.

Religion

Islam

Malays are invariably Muslims and there is also a small population of Indian Muslims in Malaysia. The earliest recorded evidence of Islam on the Malay Peninsula is an inscription in Terengganu dating from 1303, which prescribed penalties for those who did not observe the moral codes of the faith. Islam did not really gain a foothold on the Peninsula, however, until Sri Maharaja of Melaka – the third ruler – converted in 1430 and changed his name to Mohamed Shah (see page 197). He retained many of the ingrained Hindu traditions of the royal court and did not attempt to enforce Islam as the state religion. The Arab merchant ships that made regular calls at Melaka probably brought Muslim missionaries to the city. Many of these were Sufis – belonging to a mystical order of Islam that was tolerant of local customs and readily synthesized with existing animist and Hindu beliefs. The adoption of this form of Islam is one reason why animism and the Muslim faith still go hand in hand in Malaysia (see below). Mohamad Shah's son, Rajah Kasim, was the first ruler to adopt the title 'Sultan', and he became Sultan Muzaffar; all subsequent rulers have continued to preserve and uphold the Islamic faith. The Portuguese and Dutch colonialists, while making a few local converts to Christianity, were more interested in trade than proselytizing.

The practice of Islam: living by the Prophet

Islam is an Arabic word meaning 'submission to God'. It is not just a religion but a total way of life. The main Islamic scripture is the Koran or Quran, the name being taken from the Arabic *al-qur'an* or 'the recitation'. The Koran is divided into 114 *sura*, or 'units'. In addition to the Koran there are the hadiths, from the Arabic word *hadith* meaning 'story', which tell of the Prophet's life and works. These represent the second most important body of scriptures.

The practice of Islam is based upon five central tenets, known as the Pillars of Islam: Shahada (profession of faith), Salat (worship), Zakat (charity), saum (fasting) and Haj (pilgrimage). The mosque is the centre of religious activity. The two most important mosque officials are the *imam* (leader) and the *khatib* (preacher) who delivers the Friday sermon.

The **Shahada** is the confession, and lies at the core of any Muslim's faith. It involves reciting, sincerely, two statements: 'There is no god, but God', and 'Mohammad is the Messenger [Prophet] of God'. A Muslim will do this at every **Salat**. This is the daily prayer ritual which is performed five times a day, at sunrise, midday, mid-afternoon, sunset and at night. There is also the important Friday noon worship. The Salat is performed by a Muslim bowing and then prostrating himself in the direction of Mecca (in Malaysian *kiblat*, in Arabic *qibla*). In hotel rooms throughout Malaysia there is nearly always a little arrow, painted on the ceiling – or sometimes inside a wardrobe – indicating the direction of Mecca and labelled *kiblat*. The faithful are called to worship by a mosque official. Beforehand, a worshipper must wash to ensure ritual purity. The Friday midday service is performed in the mosque and includes a sermon given by the *khatib*.

A third essential element of Islam is **Zakat** – charity or alms-giving. A Muslim is supposed to give up his 'surplus'; through time this took on the form of a tax levied according to the wealth of the family. In Malaysia there is no official Zakat as there is in Saudi Arabia, but good Muslims are expected to contribute a tithe to the Muslim community.

The fourth pillar of Islam is **saum** or fasting. The daytime month-long fast of Ramadan is a time of contemplation, worship and piety – the Islamic equivalent of Lent. Muslims are expected to read one-thirtieth of the Koran each night. Muslims who are ill or on a journey have dispensation from fasting, but otherwise they are only permitted to eat during the night until "so much of the dawn appears that a white thread can be distinguished from a black one".

The **Haj** (Pilgrimage to the holy city of Mecca in Saudi Arabia) is required of all Muslims once in their lifetime if they can afford to make the journey and are physically able to. It is restricted to a certain time of the year, beginning on the eighth day of the Muslim month of *Dhu-l-Hijja*. Men who have been on the Haj are given the title *Haji*, and women *Hajjah*.

The Koran also advises on a number of other practices, in particular the prohibitions on usury, the eating of pork, the taking of alcohol, and gambling.

There is quite a powerful Islamic revival and the use of the veil is becoming de rigeur. The Koran says nothing about the need for women to veil, it only stresses the necessity of women dressing modestly.

The British colonial system of government was more 'progressive' than most colonial regimes in that it barred the British residents from interfering in 'Malay religion and custom'. So-called Councils of Muslim Religion and Malay Custom were set up in each

What's in a word?

In 2007, the government of Malaysia created a storm by outlawing the use of the word *Allah* in any context other than anything Islamic. However, with a large Christian minority that had been using the word *Allah* for the past 400 years since the Bible translations of Frances Xavier, it was clear that this law wouldn't be passed without a struggle. *Allah* arrived in the Bible as a translation from the Hebrew *Elohim*, meaning 'God'. It's widely used amongst indigenous (but considered politically *bumiputeras*, sons of the soil) groups in Sabah and Sarawak, throughout the Indonesian archipelago and Middle Eastern countries such as Egypt and Syria that have large Christian communities.

The Malaysian Catholic newspaper *The Herald* was told to cease printing the Malay version of its paper and decided to challenge the government's ruling in the High Court as being unconstitutional. Shortly after this, 15,000 Malay bibles imported from Indonesia were confiscated by the government. The government contested that one of the reasons for the ban on the use of the word out of context was that its use in a non-Islamic context would confuse believers, in a country where it is illegal for Christians to proselytize Muslims. *The Herald* won a major legal victory in February 2009 when it was given the right to print the word in its masthead, as long as it was stated that the magazine was 'for Christians only'. However, two days after being given this permission, the Home Ministry rescinded the right.

In December 2009, the Kuala Lumpur High Court ruled that despite Islam being the federal religion of the nation, the government does not have the right to stop others using it, stating that their ban on the word was illegal and unconstitutional, and that the word was not for the exclusive use of Muslims.

January 2010 saw tensions running high in the streets with Muslims calling for Christians to respect the name of Allah with Muslim students claiming exclusive use of the word for their religion. Ten churches were attacked throughout the country, including well-publicized arson attacks on churches in KL. No one was hurt in the attacks, but they prompted united responses of condemnation from all the major political parties, with Anwar Ibrahim publishing a scathing criticism of the government's policy in the *Wall Street Journal* entitled 'Muslims have no Monopoly over 'Allah''.

state answerable to the sultans. These emerged as bastions of Malay conservatism and served to make Islam the rallying point of nascent nationalism. The Islamic reform movement was imported from the Middle East at the turn of the 19th century and Malays determined that the unity afforded by Islam transcended any colonial authority and the economic dominance of immigrant groups. The ideas spread as increasing numbers of Malays made the Haj to Mecca, made possible by the advent of regular steamer services. But gradually the sultans and the Malay aristocracy – who had done well out of British rule – began to see the Islamic renaissance as a threat.

On Fridays, the Muslim day of prayer, Malaysian Muslims congregate at mosques in their 'Friday best'. The 'lunch hour' starts at 1130 and runs through to about 1430 to allow Muslims to attend the mosque; in big towns and cities, Friday lunchtimes are marked by traffic jams. In the fervently Islamic east coast states, Friday is the start of the weekend. Men traditionally wear *songkoks* (black velvet hats) to the mosque and often wear their best *sarung* (sometimes *songket*) over their trousers. Those who have performed the Haj pilgrimage to Mecca wear a white skullcap. However, at least until recently (see below), Malaysia's Islam has been moderate by Middle Eastern standards. Traditionally, for example, women were not required to wear the head scarf (*tudung*).

But Malaysia has emerged as an outspoken defender of Muslims and Islamic values around the world. On occasions, former prime minister Mahathir made outspoken attacks on Western attitudes towards Islam, in which, he says, Muslims are cast as pariahs and bogeymen. Partly this can be viewed as part of his efforts to polish his own Islamic credentials. At home, the BN feels threatened by the rise of fundamentalist sentiments – particularly in the northeastern state of Kelantan, where the Islamic government has approved a bill calling for the introduction of a strict Islamic penal code (see page 292). Hardline Islam is perceived as a threat to secular society in Malaysia. The former deputy Prime Minister, Anwar Ibrahim – once a young Islamic firebrand himself – became during his time in office an eloquent proponent of Islamic moderation. He appealed in articles submitted to international newspapers for less rhetoric in the name of political expediency from Muslim leaders around the world and for greater understanding of Islam in the West.

All of this, of course, has taken on even greater significance in the light of the events of 11 September. But it is worth remembering that the debate over the role and place of Islam in modern Malaysia dates back before the attacks in New York and Washington.

In 1994, then prime minister Mahathir was forced to clamp down on a fundamentalist Islamic sect known as **Al Arqam** with 10,000 followers, an estimated 200,000 sympathizers, and assets of RM15 million in businesses ranging from property firms to textile factories. Ashaari Muhammed, the leader of the sect, was arrested after being deported from Thailand and then held in detention under the Internal Security Act. Unlikely liberals leapt to defend Mr Ashaari who taught that women should be kept in their place, and operated his sect almost like a secret society. Why there was an order for Mr Ashaari's arrest was a point of dispute. The prime minister's office maintained that the sect's teachings were 'deviationist' 's support. The arrest was not, in their view, anything to do with religion, but a great deal to do with politics. Nonetheless the government were able to get Ashaari Muhammed to renounce his teachings on television, thereby preventing him becoming a martyr.

Mahathir was concerned that radical Islam might destabilize Malaysia's delicate racial and religious cocktail. Sects like Al Arqam, and the spread of Shia theology, are closely watched by a government that wishes to maintain its secular credentials and to control what has been termed 'creeping Islamization'. In mid-1997, Mahathir showed his displeasure at the enforcement of a fatwa in the state of Selangor banning all beauty contests. In June, three Malay contestants were arrested and handcuffed on stage after they had competed in the Miss Malaysia Petite contest. The prime minister rebuked the religious officials who had exceeded their 'little powers'. Earlier he had set in motion a wide-ranging review of Islamic jurisprudence (*fiqh*). In confronting the clerics and their supporters Mahathir took on a powerful conservative group closely allied with the opposition PAS and, until 11 September, there were those who wondered whether the *ulamas* (Muslim theologians) might successfully challenge the prime minister for the hearts and minds of ordinary Malaysians. But events since then have played into Mahathir's hands.

In Siddhartha's footsteps: a short history of Buddhism

Buddhism was founded by Siddhartha Gautama, a prince of the Sakya tribe of Nepal, who probably lived between 563 and 483 BC. He achieved enlightenment and the word buddha means 'fully enlightened one', or 'one who has woken up'. Siddhartha Gautama is known by a number of titles. In the West, he is usually referred to as The Buddha, ie the historic Buddha (but not just Buddha); more common in Southeast Asia is the title Sakyamuni, or Sage of the Sakyas (referring to his tribal origins).

Over the centuries, the life of the Buddha has become part legend, and the Jataka tales which recount his various lives are colourful and convoluted. But, central to any Buddhist's belief is that he was born under a sal tree (Shorea robusta), that he achieved enlightenment under a bodhi tree (Ficus religiosa) in the Bodh Gaya Gardens, that he preached the First Sermon at Sarnath, and that he died at Kusinagara (all in India or Nepal).

The Buddha was born at Lumbini (in present-day Nepal), as Queen Maya was on her way to her parents' home. She had had a very auspicious dream before the child's birth of being impregnated by an elephant, whereupon a sage prophesied that Siddhartha would become either a great king or a great spiritual leader. His father, being keen that the first option of the prophecy be fulfilled, brought him up in all the princely skills (at which Siddhartha excelled) and ensured that he only saw beautiful things, not the harsher elements of life.

Despite his father's efforts, Siddhartha saw four things while travelling between palaces – a helpless old man, a very sick man, a corpse being carried by lamenting relatives, and an ascetic, calm and serene man as he begged for food. These episodes made an enormous impact on the young prince, and he renounced his princely origins and left home to study under a series of spiritual teachers. He finally discovered the path to enlightenment at the Bodh Gaya Gardens in India. He then proclaimed his thoughts to a small group of disciples at Sarnath, near Benares, and continued to preach and attract followers until he died at the age of 81 at Kusinagara.

Buddhism

While Buddhism is the formal religion of most of Malaysia's Chinese population, many are Taoists, who follow the teachings of the three sages – Confucius, Mencius and Lao Tse. Taoism is characterized by ancestor worship and many deities. As with Islam, this has been mixed with animist beliefs and spirit worship forms a central part of the faith. See also box above.

Hinduism

Hindu (and Buddhist) religions were established on the Malay Peninsula long before the religion of Islam arrived. Remains of ancient Hindu-Buddhist temples dating from the kingdom of Langkasuka in the early years of the first millennium have been found in the Bujang Valley, at the foot of Gunung Jerai (Kedah Peak) in Kedah. The majority of Malaysia's Indian population is Hindu, although there are also many Indian Muslims.

Religion in Borneo

In Sabah and Sarawak, apart from the Malays, Bajaus, Illanuns and Suluks, who accepted Islam, all the inland tribes were originally animists. The religion of all the Dayak tribes in

In the First Sermon at the deer park in Sarnath, the Buddha preached the Four Noble Truths, which are still considered the root of Buddhist belief and practical experience. These are the 'Noble Truth' that suffering exists, the 'Noble Truth' that there is a cause of suffering, the 'Noble Truth' that suffering can be ended, and the 'Noble Truth' that to end suffering it is necessary to follow the 'Noble Eightfold Path' – namely, right speech, livelihood, action, effort, mindfulness, concentration, opinion and intention.

Soon after the Buddha began preaching, a monastic order – the Sangha – was established. As the monkhood evolved in India, it also began to fragment as different sects developed different interpretations of the life of the Buddha. An important change was the belief that the Buddha was transcendent: he had never been born, nor had he died; he had always existed and his life on earth had been mere illusion. The emergence of these new concepts helped to turn what up until then was an ethical code of conduct, into a religion. It eventually led to the appearance of a new Buddhist movement, Mahayana Buddhism, which split from the more traditional Theravada 'sect'.

Despite the division of Buddhism into two sects, the central tenets of the religion are common to both. Specifically, the principles pertaining to the Four Noble Truths, the Noble Eightfold Path, the Dependent Origination, the Law of Karma and nirvana. In addition, the principles of non-violence and tolerance are also embraced by both sects. In essence, the differences between the two are of emphasis and interpretation. Theravada Buddhism is strictly based on the original Pali Canon, while the Mahayana tradition stems from later Sanskrit texts. Mahayana Buddhism also allows a broader and more varied interpretation of the doctrine. Other important differences are that while the Thervada tradition is more 'intellectual' and self-obsessed, with an emphasis upon the attaining of wisdom and insight for oneself, Mahayana Buddhism stresses devotion and compassion towards others.

Borneo boiled down to placating spirits, and the purpose of tribal totems, images, icons and statues was to chase bad spirits away and attract good ones, which were believed to be capable of bringing fortune and prosperity. Headhunting (see page 387) was central to this belief, and most Dayak tribes practised it, in the belief that freshly severed heads would bring blessings to their longhouses. Virtually everything had a spirit, and complex rituals and ceremonies were devised to keep them happy. Motifs associated with the spirit world – such as the hornbill bird – dominate the artwork and textiles and many of the woodcarvings for sale in art and antique shops in the country had religious significance. Islam began to spread to the tribes of the interior from the late 15th century, but mostly it was confined to coastal districts or those areas close to rivers like the Kapuas and Barito where Malays penetrated into the interior to trade. Christian missionaries arrived with the Europeans but did not proselytize seriously until the mid-19th century. The Dutch, particularly, saw missionaries fulfilling an administrative function, drawing the tribal peoples close to the Dutch and, by implication, away from the Muslim Malays of the coast: it was a policy of divide and rule by religious means. Both Christianity and Islam had enormous influence on the animist tribes, and many converted en masse to one or the other. Despite this, many of the old superstitions and ceremonial traditions, which are

Malay magic and the spirits behind the prophet

Despite the fact that most Malays are Muslims, some traditional, pre-Islamic beliefs are still practised by Malays – particularly in the northeast of the Peninsula, the conservative Islamic heartland.

The *bomoh* – witch doctor and magic-man – is alive and well in modern Malaysia. The use of *ilmu* (the malay name for magic), which is akin to voodoo, is still widely practised and *bomohs* are highly respected and important members of kampong communities. They are often called in to perform their ancient rituals – to bring rain, to determine the site of a new house, to make fields or (married couples) fertile or to heal sickness. The healing ceremony is called the main *puteri*: there are certain illnesses which are believed to be caused by spirits – or *hantu* – who have been offended and must be placated.

The *bomoh's* job is to get the protective, friendly spirits on his side, in the belief that they can influence the evil ones. He knows many different spirits by name; some are the spirits of nature, others are spirits of ancestors. Many *bomohs* are specialists in particular fields. Some, known as *pewangs*, traditionally concentrated on performing spells to ensure fruitful harvests or safe fishing expeditions. *Bomohs* are still consulted and contracted to formulate herbal remedies, charms, love potions and perform traditional massage (*urut*). The *belian* – or shaman – specializes in more extreme forms of magic, conducting exorcisms and spirit-raising seances, or *berhantu*. In Kelantan, a *bomoh* who acts as a spirit medium is known as a *Tok Peteri* and once a spirit has entered him, during a seance, his assistant, called the *Tok Mindok*, is required to question the spirit, present offerings and address the spirit in a secret language of magic formulae. Seances are always held in front of the whole village after evening prayers.

Manipulation of the weather is one area where the magic is still widely used. In 1991 actors from Kuala Lumpur's Instant Café Theatre Company called on a *bomoh* to ensure their open-air production of *A Midsummer Night's Dream* was not washed out. The only occasion on which rain interrupted the play was during an extra performance, not covered in the *bomoh's* contract.

All natural and inanimate objects are also capable of having spirits and Malays often refer to them using the respectful title *Datuk*. Other spirits, like the *pontianak* (the vampire ghost of a woman who dies in childbirth) are greatly feared. Any suspicion of the presence of a *pontianak* calls for the immediate intervention of a *belian*, who is believed to inherit his powers from a *hantu raya* – great spirit – which attaches itself to a bloodline and is subsequently passed from generation to generation.

deeply ingrained, remain a part of Dayak culture today. (The traditional beliefs of Kalimantan's Dayaks is formalized in the Kaharingan faith, which, despite the in-roads made by Christianity and Islam, is still practised by some Mahakam and Barito river groups. The Indonesian government recognizes it as an official religion.)

Land and environment

Geography

Malaysia covers a total land area of 329,054 sq km and includes Peninsular Malaysia (131,587 sq km) and the Borneo states of Sarawak (124,967 sq km) and Sabah (72,500 sq km). Geologically, both the Peninsula and Borneo are part of the Sunda shelf, although the mountains of the Peninsula were formed longer ago than those in Borneo. This 'shelf', which during the Pleistocene ice age was exposed forming a land bridge between the two halves of the country, was inundated as the glaciers of the north retreated and sea levels rose.

The **Malay Peninsula** is about 800 km north-south, has a long narrow neck, a tapered tail and a bulging, mountainous, middle. The neck is called the Kra Isthmus, which links the Peninsula to the Southeast Asian mainland. The isthmus itself is in southern Thailand – Peninsular Malaysia comprises only the lower portion of the Peninsula and covers an area larger than England and a little smaller than Florida. Nestled into the southernmost end of the Peninsula is the island of **Singapore**, separated from the Peninsula by the narrow Strait of Johor. The thin western coastal plain drains into the Strait of Melaka, which separates the Peninsula from Sumatra (Indonesia), and is one of the oldest shipping lanes in the world. The eastern coastal lowlands drain into the South China Sea.

The **Barisan Titiwangsa (Main Range)** comprises the curved jungle-clad spine of Peninsular Malaysia. It is the most prominent of several roughly parallel ranges running down the Peninsula. These subsidiary ranges include the Kedah-Singgora Range in the northwest, the Bintang Range (stretching northeast from Taiping) and the Tahan Range (which includes the Peninsula's highest mountain, Gunung Tahan, 2187m). In the northern half of the Peninsula, the mountainous belt is very wide, leaving only a narrow coastal strip on either side.

The Main Range – or Barisan Titiwangsa – runs south from the Thai border for nearly 500 km, gradually receding as it approaches the coastal plain, near Melaka. The average elevation is about 1000 m and there are several peaks of more than 2000 m. The southern end of the range is much narrower and the mountains lower; the most prominent southern 'outlier' is Gunung Ledang (Mount Ophir) in Johor. Until just over a century ago, when William Cameron first ventured into the mountains of the Main Range, this was uncharted territory – British colonial Malaya was, in fact, little more than the west coastal strip. Not only was the west coast adjacent to the important trade routes (and therefore had most of the big towns), its alluvial deposits were also rich in tin. Because roads and railways were built along this western side of the Peninsula during the colonial period, it also became the heart of the plantation economy.

In addition to the mountain ranges, the Malay Peninsula also has many spectacular limestone outcrops. These distinctive outcrops are mainly in the Kuala Lumpur area, such as Batu Caves and those in and around Templer Park, and in the Kampar Valley near Ipoh, to the north. The erosion of the limestone has produced intricate solution-cave systems, some with dramatic formations. The vegetation on these hills is completely different to the surrounding lowland rainforest.

Malaysia's year-round rainfall has resulted in a dense network of rivers. The Peninsula's longest river is the Sungai Pahang, which runs for just over 400 km. Most rivers flood regularly, particularly during the northeast monsoon season, and during the heavy rain the volume of water can more than double in the space of a few hours. It is thought that the flooding of Malaysian rivers has become more pronounced due to logging and mining. Waterfalls are very common features in Peninsular Malaysia; these occur where rivers, with their headwaters in the hills, encounter resistant (usually igneous) rocks as they cut their valleys.

Three countries have territory on **Borneo**, but only one of them – the once all-powerful and now tiny but oil-rich sultanate of Brunei – is an independent sovereign state in itself. It is flanked to the west by the Malaysian state of Sarawak and to the east by Sabah. Sarawak severs and completely surrounds Brunei. Sabah, formerly British North Borneo, and now a Malaysian state, occupies the northeast portion of Borneo. The huge area to the south is Kalimantan, Indonesian Borneo, which occupies about three-quarters of the island.

Borneo is the third largest island in the world after Greenland and New Guinea and covers almost 750,000 sq km. During the Pleistocene period, Borneo was joined to mainland Southeast Asia, forming a continent which geologists know as Sundaland. The land bridge to mainland Asia meant that many species, both flora and fauna, arrived in what is now Borneo before it was cut off by rising sea levels. Borneo is part of the Sunda shelf. Its interior is rugged and mountainous and is dissected by many large rivers, navigable deep into the interior. The two biggest rivers, the Kapuas and Mahakam, are both in Kalimantan, but there are also extensive river systems in the East Malaysian states of Sabah and Sarawak. About half of Borneo's land area is under 150 m, particularly the swampy south coastal region.

Borneo's highest mountain, Gunung Kinabalu in Sabah (4101 m) is often declared the highest mountain in Southeast Asia. Despite this claim being repeated so many times that it has taken on the status of a truth, it isn't: there are higher peaks in Indonesia's province of Irian Jaya and in Myanmar (Burma). Kinabalu is a granite mound called a pluton, which was forced up through the sandstone strata during the Pliocene period about 15 million years ago. The mountain ranges in the west and centre of the island run east-to-west and curve around to the northeast. Borneo's coal, oil and gas-bearing strata are Tertiary deposits which are heavily folded; most of the oil and gas is found off the northwest and east coasts. The island is much more geologically stable than neighbouring Sulawesi or Java – islands in the so-called 'ring of fire'. Borneo only experiences about four mild earthquakes a year compared with 40-50 on other nearby islands. Although, as there are no active volcanoes, Borneo's soils are not particularly rich.

Climate

The Malay Peninsula has an equatorial monsoon climate. Temperatures are uniformly high throughout the year, as is humidity, and rainfall is abundant and well distributed, although it peaks during the northeast monsoon period from November to February.

Mean annual temperature on the coastal lowlands is around 26°C. The mean daily minima in the lowlands is between 21.7°C and 24.4°C; the mean daily maxima is between 29.4°C and 32.8°C. The maxima are higher and the minima, lower, towards the interior. In the Cameron Highlands, the mean annual temperature is 18°C. Temperatures dip slightly during the northeast monsoon period. The highest recorded temperature, 39.4°C, was taken on Pulau Langkawi in March 1931. The lowest absolute minimum temperature ever recorded on the Peninsula was in the Cameron Highlands in January 1937 when the temperature fell to 2.2°C. The Cameron Highlands also claims the most extreme range in temperature – the absolute maximum recorded there is 26.7°C.

The developed west coast of the Peninsula is sheltered from the northeast monsoon that strikes the east coast with full force between November and February. The east coast's climatic vagaries have reinforced its remoteness: it is particularly wet and the area north of Kuantan receives between 3300 mm and 4300 mm a year. About half of this falls in the northeast monsoon period. The northwest coast of the Peninsula is also wet and parts receive more than 3000 mm of rain a year. Bukit Larut (Maxwell Hill), next to Taiping, has an annual rainfall of more than 5000 mm. The west coast receives its heaviest rainfall in March and April. October and April are the transitional months between the southwest and northeast monsoons.

In the more heavily populated coastal districts of the Peninsula, the temperature is ameliorated by sea breezes that set in about 1000 and gather force until early afternoon. In the evenings, a land breeze picks up. These winds are only felt for distances up to 15 km inland. Another typical weather feature on the Malay Peninsula is the squall, which is a sudden, violent storm characterized by sharp gusts of wind. These can be very localized in their effect, highly unpredictable and, from time to time, extremely hazardous to light fishing vessels. Squalls are caused by cool air either from sea breezes in the late morning or land breezes in the evening undercutting warmer air; squall lines are marked by stacks of cumulo-nimbus clouds. Most squalls occur between May and August; the ones that develop along the west coast between Port Klang and Singapore during this period are called 'Sumatras' and produce particularly violent cloudbursts. Most Sumatras occur at night or in the early morning, while squalls between November and February usually occur in the afternoon.

Borneo

Borneo has a typical equatorial monsoon climate: the weather usually follows predictable patterns, although in recent years it has been less predictable, a phenomenon some environmentalists attribute to deforestation and others to periodic changes to the El Niño Southern Oscillation. Temperatures are fairly uniform, averaging 23-33°C during the day and rarely dropping below 20°C at night, except in the mountains, where they can drop to below 10°C. Most rainfall occurs between November and January during the northeast monsoon; this causes rivers to burst their banks, and there are many short, sharp cloudbursts. The dry season runs from May to September. It is characterized by dry south-easterly winds and is the best time to visit. Rainfall generally increases towards the interior; most of Borneo receives about 2000-3000 mm a year, although some upland areas get more than 4000 mm.

Flora and fauna

Originally 97% of Malaysia's land area was covered in closed-canopy forest. According to the government, about 56% of Malaysia is still forested – although it is difficult to ascertain exactly how much of this is primary rainforest. Only 5% of the remaining jungle is under conservation restrictions. The Malaysian jungle, which, at about 130 million years old, is believed to be among the oldest forests in the world, supports more than 145,000 species of flowering plant (well over 1000 of which are already known to have pharmaceutical value), 200 mammal species, 600 bird species and countless thousands of insect species. The rainforest is modified by underlying rock type (impervious rocks and soils result in swamp forest) and by altitude (lowland rainforest gives way to thinner montane forest on higher slopes). All the main forest types are represented on the Peninsula, including mangrove swamp forest, peat swamp forest, heath forest, lowland and hill mixed Dipterocarp forest and montane forest. Where primary forest has been logged, burned or cleared by shifting cultivators or miners, secondary forest grows up quickly. The fields cultivated by shifting cultivators are known as swiddens – a word which is derived from an old English term meaning 'burnt field'. In Malaysia, the secondary regrowth is known as *belukar*. It can take up to 250 years before climax rainforest is re-established. The pioneer plant species colonizing abandoned *ladang* (sites cleared by shifting cultivators) is called *lalang* (elephant grass).

Borneo's ancient rainforests are rich in flora and fauna, including more than 9000-15,000 species of seed plants (of which almost half may be endemic), 200 species of mammals, 570 species of birds, 100 species of snake, 250 species of freshwater fish and 1000 species of butterfly. The theory of natural selection enunciated by Victorian naturalist Alfred Russel Wallace – while that other great Victorian scientist Charles Darwin was coming to similar conclusions several thousand miles away – was influenced by Wallace's observations in Borneo. He travelled widely in Sarawak between 1854 and 1862.

Flora

As late as the middle of the 19th century, the great bulk – perhaps as much as 95% – of the land area of Borneo was forested. Alfred Russel Wallace, like other Western travellers, was enchanted by the island's natural wealth and diversity: "ranges of hill and valley everywhere", he wrote, "everywhere covered with interminable forest". But Borneo's jungle is disappearing fast and since the mid-1980s there has been a mounting international environmental campaign against deforestation. The campaign has been particularly vocal in Sarawak but other parts of the island are also suffering rapid deforestation, notably Sabah and also Indonesia's province of East Kalimantan. Harold Brookfield, Lesley Potter and Byron state in their hard-headed book *In place of the forest* (1995): "Concerning those large areas of forest that have been totally cleared and converted to other uses or that lie waste [in Borneo] a great resource has been squandered, and the major part of the habitat of a great range of plant and animal species has been destroyed. Moreover, this has been done with far less than adequate economic return to the two nations [Malaysia and Indonesia] concerned."

How extensive has been the loss of species as a result of the logging of Borneo's forests is a topic of heated debate. Brookfield et al in the volume noted above suggest that there "is very little basis in firm research for the spectacular figures of species loss rates that appear not infrequently in sections of the conservationist literature and that readily attract media attention". But they do admit that the flora and fauna of Borneo is especially diverse with a high degree of endemism and that there has been a significant loss of biodiversity as a result of extensive logging. It has been estimated that 32% of terrestrial mammals, 70% of leaf beetles, and 50% of flowering plants are endemic to Borneo; in other words, they are found nowhere else.

The best-known timber trees fall into three categories, all of them hardwoods. Heavy hardwoods include selangan batu and resak; medium hardwoods include kapur, keruing and keruntum; light hardwoods include madang tabak, ramin and meranti. There are both peat-swamp and hill varieties of meranti, which is one of the most valuable export logs. Belian, or Bornean iron wood (Eusideroxylon zwageri) is one of the hardest and densest timbers in the world. It is thought that the largest belian may be 1000 years or more old. They are so tough that when they die they continue to stand for centuries before the wood rots to the extent that the trunk falls. On average, there are about 25 commercial tree species per ha, but because they are hard to extract, 'selective logging' invariably results in the destruction of many unselected trees.

Lowland rainforest (mixed dipterocarp) predominates up to 600 m. Dipterocarp forest is stratified into three main layers, the top one rising to heights of 45 m. In the top layer, trees' crowns interlock to form a closed canopy of foliage. The word 'dipterocarp' comes from the Greek and means 'two-winged fruit' or 'two [di]-winged [ptero] seed [carp]'. The leaf-like appendages of the mature dipterocarp fruits have 'wings' which makes them spin as they fall to the ground, like giant sycamore seeds. Some species have more than two wings but are all members of the dipterocarp family. It is the lowland rainforest which comes closest to the Western ideal of a tropical 'jungle'. It is also probably the most species rich forest in Borneo. A recent study of a dipterocarp forest in Malaysia found that an area of just 50 ha supported no less than 835 species of tree. In Europe or North America a similar area of forest would support less than 100 tree species. The red resin produced by many species of dipterocarp, and which can often be seen staining the trunk, is known as damar and was traditionally used as a lamp 'oil'. Another characteristic feature of the trees found in lowland dipterocarp rainforest is buttressing, the flanges of wood that protrude from the base of the trunk. For some time the purpose of these massive buttresses perplexed botanists who arrived at a whole range of ingenious explanations. Now they are thought, sensibly, to provide structural support. Two final characteristics of this type of forest are that it is very dark on the forest floor (explaining why trees take so long to grow) and that it is not the impenetrable jungle of Tarzan fantasy. The first characteristic explains the second. Only when a gap appears in the forest canopy, after a tree falls, do light-loving pioneer plants get the chance to grow. When the gap in the canopy is filled by another tree, these grasses, shrubs and smaller trees die back once more.

Many of the rainforest trees are an important resource for Dayak communities. The jelutong tree, for example, is tapped like a rubber tree for its sap ('jungle chewing gum') which is used to make tar for waterproof sealants – used in boat-building. It also hardens into a tough, but brittle, black plastic-like substance used for *parang* (machete) handles.

Montane forest occurs at altitudes above 600 m, although in some areas it does not replace lowland rainforest until considerably higher than this. Above 1200 m mossy forest predominates. Montane forest is denser than lowland forest with smaller trees of narrower girth. Moreover, dipterocarps are generally not found while flowering shrubs like magnolias and rhododendrons appear. In place of dipterocarps, tropical latitude oaks as well as other trees that are more characteristic of temperate areas, like myrtle and laurel, make an appearance. Other familiar flora of lowland forest, like lianas, also disappear while the distinctive pitcher plant (Nepenthes) become common.

The low-lying river valleys are characterized by **peat swamp forest**, where the peat is up to 9 m thick, which makes wet-rice agriculture impossible. **Heath forest** or *kerangas* – the Iban word meaning 'land on which rice cannot grow' – is found on poor, sandy soils. Although it mostly occurs near the coast, it is also sometimes found in mountain ranges, but almost always on level ground. Here, trees are stunted and only the hardiest of plants can survive. Some trees have struck up symbiotic relationships with animals – like ants – so as to secure essential nutrients. Pitcher plants (Nepenthes) have also successfully colonized heath forest. The absence of bird calls and other animal noises make heath forest rather eerie, and it also indicates their general biological poverty.

Along beaches there are often stretches of **casuarina forest**; the casuarina grows up to 27 m, and looks like a conifer, with needle-shaped leaves. **Mangrove** occupies tidal mud flats around sheltered bays and estuaries. The most common mangrove tree is the bakau (Rhizophora) which grows to heights of about 9 m and has stilt roots to trap sediment. Bakau wood is used for pile-house stilts and for charcoal. Further upstream, but still associated with mangrove, is the nipah palm (Nipa fruticans), whose light-green leaves come from a squat stalk; it was traditionally of great importance as it provided roofing and wickerwork materials.

Fauna

Mammals The continual development of forested areas has destroyed many habitats in recent years. The biggest mammal in Malaysia and Asia is the Asiatic **elephant**. Adult elephants weigh up to three to four tonnes; they are rarely seen, although the carnage caused by a passing herd can sometimes be seen in Taman Negara National Park. Borneo's wild elephants until recently posed a zoological mystery. They occur only at the far northeast tip of the island, at the furthest possible point from their Sumatran and mainland Southeast Asian relatives. No elephant remains have been found in Sabah, Sarawak or Kalimantan. It is known that some animals were introduced into Sabah – then British North Borneo – by early colonial logging concerns and certainly that there were already populations established in the area. Another theory has it that one of the sultans of Sulu released a small number of animals several centuries ago. The difficulty with this explanation is that experts find it difficult to believe that just a handful of elephants could have grown to the 2000 or so that existed by the end of the last century. Some zoologists speculate that they were originally introduced at the time of the Javan Majapahit Empire, in the 13th and 14th centuries. Antonio Pigafetta, an Italian historian who visited the Sultanate of Brunei as part of Portuguese explorer Ferdinand Magellan's expedition in July 1521, tells of being taken to visit the sultan on two domesticated elephants, which may have been gifts from another ruler.

Borneo's male elephants are up to 2.6 m tall; females are usually less than 2.2 m. Males' tusks can grow up to 1.7 m in length and weigh up to 15 kg each. Mature males are solitary creatures, only joining herds to mate. The most likely places to see elephants in the wild are the Danum Valley Conservation Area and the lower Kinabatangan basin, both in Sabah. See also box, page 463.

Walt Disney's film of Rudyard Kipling's Jungle Book made the orang-utan a big-screen celebrity, dubbing him "the king of the swingers" and "the jungle VIP". Borneo's **Orang-Utan** (*Pongo pygmaeus*) is also known as 'man of the jungle', after the translation from the Malay: orang (man), utan (jungle). The orang-utan is endemic to the tropical forests of Sumatra and Borneo although at the beginning of the historic period it was distributed from tropical China to Java. The Sumatran animals tend to keep the reddish tinge to their fur, while the Bornean ones go darker as they mature. It is Asia's only great ape; it has four hands, rather than feet, bow-legs and has no tail. The orang-utan moves slowly and deliberately, sometimes swinging under branches, although it seldom travels far by arm-swinging. Males of over 15 years old stand up to 1.6 m tall and their arms span 2.4 m. Adult males (who make loud roars) weigh 50-100 kg – about twice that of adult females (whose call sounds like a long belch). Orang-utans are said to have the strength of seven men but they are not aggressive. They are peaceful, gentle animals, particularly with each other. Orang-utans have bluey-grey skin and their eyes are close together, giving them an almost human look. Males develop cheek pouches when they reach maturity, which they fill with several litres of air; this is exhaled noisily when they demarcate territory.

Orang-utans mainly inhabit riverine swamp forests or lowland dipterocarp forests. Their presence is easily detected by their nests of bent and broken twigs woven in much the same fashion as a sun bear's, in the fork of a tree. They are solitary animals and always sleep alone. Orang-utans have a largely vegetarian diet consisting of fruit and young leaves, supplemented by termites, bark and birds' eggs. They are usually solitary but the young remain with their mothers until they are five or six years old. Two adults will occupy an area of about 2 sq km and are territorial, protecting their territory against intruders. They can live up to 30 years and a female will have an average of three to four young during her lifetime. Females reach sexual maturity between seven and nine years, and the gestation period is nine months. Female orang-utans usually have only one young at a time although twins and even triplets have been recorded. After giving birth, they do not mate for around another seven years.

Estimates of the numbers of orang-utan vary. One puts the figure at 14,000 animals; another at up to 25,000 in the wild in Borneo and Sumatra. Part of the difficulty is that many are thought to live in inaccessible and little researched areas of peat swamp. But this is just a very rough estimate, based on one ape for each 1.5 sq km of forest. No one, so far, has attempted an accurate census. What is certain is that the forest is disappearing fast, and with it the orang-utan's natural habitat. Orang-utans' favoured habitat is lowland rainforest and this is particularly under threat from logging. The black market in young apes in countries like Taiwan means that they fetch relatively high returns to local hunters. At the village level an orang-utan might command US$100; in local markets, around US$350; and at their international destination, along with all the necessary forged export permits, travel costs and so on, from US$5000 to as much as US$60,000.

The five species of **monkeys** found in Malaysia are the long-tailed macaque, pig-tailed macaque, and three species of leaf monkey (langur) – the banded, dusky and silvered varieties. Malaysia's cutest animal is the little slow loris, with its huge sad eyes and lethargic manner; among the most exotic is the flying lemur, whose legs and tail are joined together by a skin membrane. It parachutes and glides from tree to tree, climbing each one to find a new launch-pad.

The **proboscis monkey** (*Nasalis larvatus*) is an extraordinary-looking animal, endemic to Borneo, which lives in lowland forests and mangrove swamps all around the island. Little research has been done on proboscis monkeys; they are notoriously difficult to study as they are so shy. Their fur is reddish-brown and they have white legs, arms, tail and a ruff on the neck, which gives the appearance of a pyjama-suit. Their facial skin is red and the males have grotesquely enlarged, droopy noses; females' noses are shorter and upturned. The male's nose is the subject of some debate among zoologists: what ever else it does, it apparently increases their sex-appeal. To ward off intruders, the nose is straightened out, "like a party whoopee whistle", according to one description. Recently a theory has been advanced that the nose acts as a thermostat, helping to regulate body temperature. But it also tends to get in the way: old males often have to resort to holding their noses up with one hand while stuffing leaves into their mouths with the other.

Proboscis' penises are almost as obvious as their noses – the proboscis male glories in a permanent erection, which is probably why they are rarely displayed in zoos. The other way the males attract females is by violently shaking branches and making spectacular – and sometimes near-suicidal – leaps into the water, in which they attempt to hit as many dead branches as they can on the way down, so as to make the loudest noise possible. The monkeys organize themselves into harems, with one male and several females and young – there are sometimes up to 20 in a group. Young males leave the harem they are born into when the adult male becomes aggressive towards them and they rove around in bachelor groups until they are in a position to form their own harem.

Proboscis monkeys belong to the leaf monkey family, and have large, pouched stomachs to help digest bulky food – they feed almost entirely on the leaves of one tree –

the Sonneratia. The proboscis is a diurnal animal, but keeps to the shade during the heat of the day. The best time to see them is very early in the morning or around dusk. They can normally be heard before they are seen: they make loud honks, rather like geese; they also groan, squeal and roar. Proboscis monkeys are good swimmers; they even swim underwater for up to 20 m – thanks to their partially webbed feet. Males are about twice the size and weight of females. They are known fairly ubiquitously (in both Malaysian and Indonesian Borneo) as 'Orang Belanda', or Dutchmen – which is not entirely complimentary. In Kalimantan they also have other local names including Bekantan, Bekara, Kahau, Rasong, Pika and Batangan.

Other monkeys found in Borneo include various species of leaf monkey – including the **grey leaf monkey, the white-fronted leaf monkey**, and the **red leaf monkey**. One of the non-timber forest products formerly much prized was bezoar stone which was a valued cure-all. Bezoars are green coloured 'stones' which form in the stomachs of some herbivores, and in particular in the stomachs of leaf monkeys. Fortunately for the leaf monkeys of Southeast Asia though, these stones – unlike rhino horn – are no longer prized for their medicinal properties. One of the most attractive members of the primate family found in Borneo is the tubby slow loris or kongkang. And perhaps the most difficult to pronounce – at least in Dusun – is the tarsier which is locally known as the *tindukutrukut*.

The ape family includes the **white-handed gibbon** (known locally as *wak-wak*), the **dark-handed gibbon** (which is rarer) and **siamang**, which are found in more mountainous areas.

The two-horned Sumatran **rhinoceros**, also known as the hairy rhinoceros, is the smallest of all rhinos and was once widespread throughout Sumatra and Borneo. The population has been greatly reduced by excessive hunting. The horn is worth more than its weight in gold in Chinese apothecaries, and that of the Sumatran rhino is reputedly the most prized of all. But the ravages of over-hunting have been exacerbated by the destruction of the rhino's habitat. Indeed, until quite recently it was thought to be extinct on Borneo. Most of Borneo's remaining wild population is in Sabah, and the Malaysian government is attempting to capture some of the thinly dispersed animals to breed them in captivity, for they remain in serious danger of extinction (see page 462).

One of the strangest Malayan mammals is the **tapir**, with its curled snout – or trunk – and white bottom. The starkly contrasting black and white is good camouflage in the jungle, where it is effectively concealed by light and shade. Young tapirs are dark brown with light brown spots, simulating the effect of sun-dappled leaf-litter.

Other large mammals include the **common wild pig** and the **bearded pig**, and the **seladang** (or gaur) wild cattle; the latter live in herds in deep jungle. There are two species of deer on the Malay Peninsula: the **sambar** (or rusa) and the **kijang** (barking deer); the latter gets its English name from its dog-like call. The **mouse deer** (kanchil and napoh) are not really deer; they are hoofed animals, standing just 20 cm high. The mouse deer has legendary status in Malay lore – for example, the Malay Annals tell of Prince Parameswara's decision to found Melaka on the spot where he saw a mouse deer beat off one of his hunting dogs (see page 195). Despite their reputation for cunning, they are also a favoured source of protein.

Malaysia's most famous carnivore is the **tiger** – *harimau* in Malay. Tigers still roam the jungle in the centre of the Peninsula, and on several occasions have made appearances in the Cameron Highlands, particularly during the dry season, when they move into the mountains to find food. Other members of the cat family are the clouded leopard and four species of wild cat: the leopard cat, the golden cat, the flat-headed cat and the marbled cat. Other jungle animals include the **Malayan sun bear** (which have a penchant for honey), the **serigala** (wild dog), **civet cats** (of which there are many different varieties), mongooses, weasels and otters.

Malaysia has several species of fruit bats and insect-eating bats, but the best-known insect-eater is the **pangolin** (scaly anteater), the animal world's answer to the armoured car. Its scales are formed of matted hair (like rhinoceros horn) and it has a long thin tongue which it flicks into termite nests. More common jungle mammals include rodents, among which are five varieties of **giant flying squirrels**. Like the **flying lemur**, these glide spectacularly from tree to tree and can cover up to about 500 m in one 'flight'.

Birds In ornithological circles, Malaysia is famed for its varied birdlife. The country is visited by many migratory water birds, and there are several wetland areas where the Malayan Nature Society has set up birdwatching hides; the most accessible to Kuala Lumpur is the Kuala Selangor Nature Park (see page 77). Migratory birds winter on Selangor's mangrove-fringed mudflats from September to May. There are also spectacular birds of prey, the most common of which are the **hawk eagles** and **brahminy kites**. Among the most fascinating and beautiful jungle species are the **crested firebacks**, a kind of pheasant; the **kingfisher** family, with their brilliantly coloured plumage; the **hornbills** (see below); **greater racquet-tailed drongos** – dark blue with long, sweeping tails; and **black-naped orioles**, saffron-coloured lowland residents. There are also **wagtails, mynas, sunbirds, hummingbirds (flower-peckers), bulbuls, barbets, woodpeckers** and **weaver-birds**.

There are nine types of **hornbill** on Borneo, the most striking and biggest of which is the rhinoceros hornbill (*Buceros rhinoceros*) – or kenyalang. They can grow up to 1.5 m long and are mainly black with a white belly. The long tail feathers are white too, crossed with a thick black bar near the end. They make a remarkable, resonant "GERONK" call in flight, which can be heard over long distances; they honk when resting. Hornbills are usually seen in pairs and are believed to be monogamous. After mating, the female imprisons herself in a hole in a tree, building a sturdy wall with her own droppings. The male bird fortifies the wall from the outside, using a mulch of mud, grass, sticks and saliva, leaving only a vertical slit for her beak. She remains incarcerated in her cell for about three months, during which the male supplies her and the nestlings with food – mainly fruit, lizards, snakes and mice. Usually, only one bird is hatched and reared in the hole and when it is old enough to fly, the female breaks out of the nest hole. Both emerge looking fat and dirty.

The 'bill' itself has no known function, but the males have been seen duelling in mid-air during the courting season. They fly straight at each other and collide head-on. The double-storeyed yellow bill has a projection, called a casque, on top, which has a bright red tip. In some species the bill develops wrinkles as the bird matures: one wrinkle for each year of its life. For this reason they are known in Dutch, and in some eastern Indonesian languages as 'year birds'. The hornbill is the official state emblem of Sarawak.

Most Dayak groups consider the hornbill to have magical powers and the feathers are worn as symbols of heroism. In tribal mythology the bird is associated with the creation of mankind, and is a symbol of the upper world. The best place to see hornbills is near wild fig trees – they love the fruit and play an important role in seed dispersal. The helmeted hornbill's bill is heavy and solid and can be carved, like ivory. These bills were highly valued by the Dayaks, and have been traded for centuries. The third largest hornbill is the wreathed hornbill which makes a yelping call and a loud – almost mechanical – noise when it beats its wings. Others species on Borneo include the wrinkled, black, bushy-crested, white-crowned and pied hornbills.

Reptiles

The kings of Malaysia's reptile population are the giant **leatherback turtles** (see page 268), **hawksbill** and **green turtles**; there are several other species of turtle and three species of land tortoise. The most notorious reptile is the **estuarine crocodile** (*Crocodilus porosus*) – which can grow up to 8 m long. The largest population of estuarine crocodiles are found in the lower reaches of Borneo's rivers. However, they have been so extensively hunted that they are rarely a threat, although people do very occasionally still get taken. The **Malayan gharial** (*Tomistoma schlegeli*) is a fish-eating, freshwater crocodile which grows to just under 3 m.

Lizards include common house geckos (*Hemidactylus frenatus* – or *cikcak* in Malay), green-crested lizards (*Calotes cristatellus*), which change colour like chameleons, and flying lizards (*Draco*), which have an extendable undercarriage allowing the lizard to glide from tree to tree. Monitors are the largest of Malaysian lizards, the most widespread of which is the common water monitor (*Varanus salvator*), which can grow to about 2.5 m.

The Malaysian jungles also have 140 species of frogs and toads, which are more often heard than seen. Some are dramatically coloured, such as the appropriately named **green-backed frog** (*Rana erythraea*) and others have particular skills, such as **Wallace's flying frog** (*Rana migropalmatus*) which parachutes around on its webbed feet.

Of Malaysia's 100-odd land snakes, only 16 are poisonous; all 20 species of sea snake are poisonous. There are two species of python, the **reticulated python** (*Python reticulatus*) – which can grow to nearly 10 m in length and has iridescent black and yellow scales – and the **short python** (*Python curtus*), which rarely grows more than 2.5 m and has a very thick, rusty-brown body. Most feared are the venomous snakes, but the constrictors can also pose a threat to humans.

Among the most common non-poisonous snakes is the dark brown **house snake** (*Lycodon aulicus*) which likes to eat geckos, and the common **Malayan racer** (*Elaphe flavolineata*), which grows to about 2 m and is black with a pale underbelly. The most beautiful non-poisonous snakes are the **paradise tree snake** (*Chrysopelea paradisi*), which is black with an iridescent green spot on every scale and the **mangrove snake** (Boiga dendrophilia) which grows to about 2 m long and is black with yellow stripes. The former is famed for its gliding skills: it can leap from tree-to-tree in a controlled glide by hollowing its underbelly, trapping a cushion of air below it. In the jungle it is quite common to see the dull brown **river snake** which goes by the unfortunate name of the dog-faced water snake (*Cerberus rhynchops*); it has an appetite for fish and frogs.

The most feared venomous snake is the **king cobra** (*Naja hannah*), which grows to well over 4 m long and is olive-green with an orange throat-patch. They are often confused with non-poisonous rat snakes and racers. The king cobra eats snakes and lizards – including monitor lizards. Its reputation as an aggressive snake is unfounded, but its venom is deadly. Both the king cobra and the common cobra (*Naja naja*) are hooded; the hood is formed by loose skin around the neck and is pushed outwards on elongated ribs when the snake rears to its strike posture.

Other poisonous snakes are the **banded krait** (*Bungarus fasciatus*) with its distinctive black and yellow stripes and the **Malayan krait** (*Bungarus candidus*) with black and white stripes. Kraits are not fast movers and are said to bite only under extreme provocation. **Coral snakes** (of the genus *Maticora*) have extremely poisonous venom, but because the snake virtually has to chew its victim before the venom can enter the bite (its poison glands are located at the very back of its mouth), there have been no recorded fatalities. **Pit vipers** have a thermo-sensitive groove between the eye and the nostril which can detect warm-blooded prey even in complete darkness. The bite of the common, bright green **Wagler's pit viper** (*Trimeresurus wagleri*) is said to be extremely painful, but is never fatal. They have broad, flattened heads; adults have yellow bars and a bright red tip to the tail.

Insects

Malaysia has a literally countless population of insect species; new ones are constantly being discovered and named. There are 120 species of **butterfly** in Malaysia. The king of them is the male **Rajah Brooke's birdwing** (*Troides brookiana*) – the national butterfly – with its iridescent, emerald zig-zag markings on jet-black velvety wings. It was named by Victorian naturalist Alfred Russel Wallace after his friend James Brooke, the first White Rajah of Sarawak. The males can be found along rivers while the much rarer females (which are less spectacularly coloured), remain out of sight among the treetops.

There are more than 100 other magnificently coloured butterflies, including the **black and yellow common birdwing**, the **swallowtails and swordtails**, the **leaf butterflies** (which are camouflaged as leaves when their wings are folded) such as the blue and brown saturn and the rust, white and brown tawny rajah. Among the most beautiful of all is the delicately patterned **Malayan lacewing** (*Cethosia hypsea*) with its jagged markings of red, orange, brown and white. There are several butterfly farms around the country, including in Kuala Lumpur (see page 69), Penang (see page 151) and the butterfly capital of Malaysia, the Cameron Highlands (see page 116).

The most spectacular moths are the huge **atlas moth** (*Attacus atlas*) and the **swallow-tailed moth** (*Nyctalemon patroclus*); these can be found on exterior walls illuminated by strip-lights late at night, particularly in remoter parts of the country.

The Malaysian beetle population is among the most varied in the world. The best known is the **rhinoceros beetle** (*Oryctes rhinoceros*), which can grow to nearly 6 cm in length and is characterized by its dramatic horns. The empress cicada (*Pomponia imperatoria*) is the biggest species in Malaysia and can have a wingspan of more than 20 cm. The male cicada is the noisiest jungle resident. The incredible droning and whining noises are created by the vibration of membranes in the body, the sound of which is amplified in the body cavity.

One of the most famous insects is the **praying mantis**. In *Malayan Animal Life*, MWF Tweedie wrote: "They owe their name to the deceptively devotional appearance of their characteristic pose, with the fore legs held up as if in prayer. In reality the mantis is, of course, waiting for some unwary insect to stray within reach; if it does, the deadly spined fore limbs will strike and grasp and the mantis will eat its victim alive, daintily, as a lady eats a sandwich." There are several other species of mantis, and the most intriguing is the flower mantis (Hymenopus coronatus) which is bright pink and can twist and extend itself to resemble a four-petalled flower, a camouflage which protects it from predators, while attracting meals such as bees.

Of the less attractive insect life, it is advisable to be wary of certain species of wasps and hornets. The most dangerous is the **slender banded hornet** (*Polistes sagittarius*) which is big (3 cm long) and has a black and orange striped abdomen. Its nests are paper-like, and hang from trees and the eaves of houses by a short stalk. They are extremely aggressive and do not need to be provoked before they attack. The **golden wasp** (*Vespa auraria*) is found in montane jungle – notably the Cameron Highlands – and, like the hornet above, will attack anything coming near its nest. The wasp is a honey-gold colour, it nests in trees and shrubs and its sting is vicious. There are several other wasp species which attack ferociously, and stings can be extremely painful. One of the worst is the **night wasp** (*Provespa anomala*), which is an orangy-brick colour and commonly flies into houses at night, attracted by lights. Bee stings can also be very serious, and none more so than that of the **giant honey bee**, which builds pendulous combs on overhanging eaves and trees. It is black with a yellow mark at the front end of the abdomen; multiple stings can be fatal.

Another insect species to be particularly wary of is the **fire ant** (*Tetraponera rufonigra*). It has a red body and a big black head; it will enthusiastically sting anything it comes into contact with, and the pain is acute. **Weaver ants** (*Oecophylla smaragdina*) are common but do not sting. Instead, their powerful jaws can be used as jungle sutures to stitch up open wounds. The bites alone are very painful, and the ant (which is also known as the kerengga) adds insult to injury by spitting an acidic fluid on the bite. It is difficult to extract the pincers from the skin, and once attached, the ant will not let go. The biggest of all ants, the **giant ant** (*Camponotus gigas*), can be nearly 3 cm in length; (it is also variously known as the elephant ant and the 'big-bum ant'). They are largely nocturnal, however, so tend to cause less trouble in the jungle.

Other jungle residents worth avoiding are the huge, black, hairy **Mygalomorph spiders**, whose bodies can be about 5 cm long. Their painful bites cause localized swelling. **Scorpions** are dangerous but not fatal. The biggest scorpion, the wood scorpion (*Hormurus australasiae*) can grow to about 16 cm long. It is black, lives under old logs and is mainly nocturnal. In rural areas, the particularly paranoid might shake their shoes for the spotted house-scorpion (*Isometrus maculatus*), which is quite common. **Centipedes** (*Chilopoda*) have a poisonous bite and can grow up to about 25 cm in length.

The environmental costs of growth

As Malaysia has become more wealthy, and the middle class has burgeoned, so environmental concerns have gained greater prominence. In 1993 the Department of the Environment released figures revealing that of Peninsular Malaysia's 116 major rivers, 85 were either 'biologically dead' or 'dying'. Air quality is also a source of concern, especially in the Klang Valley, an agglomeration of industrial activity around Kuala Lumpur. Environmental Impact Assessments (EIAs) are now, in theory, compulsory for every development project, but most companies undertake to do them only grudgingly, if at all. The claim that, as a developing country, Malaysia can ill-afford the 'luxury' of such things is wearing very thin as wealth spreads with each year of 8% growth. The government recognizes that the environment is fast becoming a political issue, and like any good political party is trying to climb aboard the bandwagon.

Most accounts of Malaysia's environmental problems – some would characterize it as a 'crisis' – concentrate on the East Malaysian states of Sarawak and Sabah. In a sense the Peninsula is a lost cause: deforestation has been so extensive that the only large areas remaining are already gazetted as national parks. In East Malaysia, though, there is a sense that if only logging could be better controlled then the natural wealth of Malaysian Borneo could be preserved.

The haze

For years now, Malaysia (and Singapore) has had to deal with what is locally called 'the haze': a choking fog that reduces visibility to no more than a few metres and causes severe health problems.

In 2010 haze is still an issue, with the hottest months of June and October. People in Singapore, KL and Penang regularly suffer the smell of acrid burning in the air, breathing difficulties and sore throats with a kind of fatalistic acceptance. It is thought that the worst years are those when the fires burning in Kalimantan and Sumatra combine with the drying effects of El Nino. The year 2006 saw another particularly bad year when Malaysia was again severely affected with places in Negeri Sembilan recording Air Pollution Index (API) numbers of over 190. Sarawak was also badly affected with authorites threatening to close schools. Rain in mid-October brought API numbers down and doused many of the slow-burning fires. Singapore saw its API briefly rising to an unhealthy 150 in early October, the highest level since 1997.

The Indonesian government was accused of doing little to ease the fires, and although had sent fire dousing planes to control burning on state-controlled land, it conceded that it could do little about fires on private land. A Malaysian news agency, BERNAMA, quoted one Indonesian villager as being unconcerned about living in perpetual smog: "If we do not burn the forest, where are we going to get our food from?"

If you are concerned about haze affecting your trip or suffer from asthma, you can check daily haze readings for the region and find out more at www.weather.gov.sg/wip/web/ASMC/Haze_Information.

Books

Fiction

Burgess, Anthony Burgess lived in Malaysia between 1954 and 1957, learnt Malay, and mixed with the locals to a far greater extent than Maugham or Conrad, and this is reflected in a much more nuanced understanding of the Malay character. After leaving Malaya in 1957, he taught in Brunei until 1960. Among his books are *Time for a Tiger* (1956), *The Enemy in the Blanket* (1958) and *Beds in the East* (1959) which were later published together by Penguin as *Malayan Trilogy*.

Conrad, Joseph Perhaps the finest novelist of the Malay archipelago. Books include *Lord Jim*, the tale of Jim, who abandons his ship and seeks refuge from his guilt in Malaya, earning in the process the sobriquet Lord, and *Victory*, arguably Conrad's finest novel, based in the Malay Archipelago. Both are widely available in paperback editions from most bookshops. Also worth reading is *The Rescue*, Penguin: London. Set in the Malay Archipelago in the 1860s; the hero, Captain Lingard, is forced to choose between his Southeast Asian friend and his countrymen.

Godshalk, CC *Kalimantaan* (1998) Little Brown). A fictional account of an ambitious Englishman's quest to build his own kingdom on the north Borneo coast in the mid-19th

century. It's a superb book, detailing the violence, duplicity, waves of pitiless disease and dark colonial attitudes that epitomized the lives of the first white settlers in Borneo.

Keith, Agnes *Land below the Wind* (1969) Ulverscroft: Leicester. Perhaps the best-known English-language book on Sabah.

Maniam, KS *The Return* (1983) Skoob Books: London. The novel, by an Indian Malaysian, is about the difficulties a Hindu has in finding a home in Malaysia, especially since the Indian in question is educated at a British colonial school.

Maugham, William *Somerset Maugham's Malaysian Stories* (1969) Heinemann: London and Singapore. Another English novelist who wrote extensively on Malaysia. These stories are best for the insight they provide into colonial life, not Malay life.

Theroux, Paul *The Consul's File* (1979) Penguin. A selection of short stories based on Malaysia.

Travel

Bird, Isabella *The Golden Chersonese* (1883 and reprinted 1983) Murray: London, reprinted by Century paperback. The account of a late 19th-century female visitor to the region who shows her gumption facing everything from natives to crocs.

Bock, Carl *The Headhunters of Borneo* (1985, first published 1881) OUP: Singapore. Bock was a Norwegian naturalist and explorer and was commissioned by the Dutch to make a scientific survey of southeastern Borneo. His account, though, makes much of the dangers and adventures that he faced, and some of his 'scientific' observations are, in retrospect, clearly highly faulty. Nonetheless, this is an entertaining account.

Hose, Charles *The Field Book of a Jungle Wallah* (1985, first published 1929) OUP: Singapore. Hose was an official in Sarawak and became an acknowledged expert on the material and non-material culture of the tribes of Sarawak. He was one of that band of highly informed, perceptive and generally benevolent colonial administrators.

King, Victor T (edit) *The Best of Borneo Travel* (1992) OUP: Oxford. A compilation of travel accounts from the early 19th century through to the late 20th. An excellent companion to take while exploring the island. Published in portable paperback.

Mjoberg, Eric *Forest Life and Adventures in the Malay Archipelago*, OUP: Singapore.

O'Hanlon, Redmond *Into the Heart of Borneo* (1984) Salamander Press: Edinburgh. This highly amusing and perceptive romp through Borneo in the company of poet and foreign correspondent James Fenton, includes an ascent of the Rejang River and does much to counter the more romanticized images of Bornean life.

History

Barber, Noel *The War of the Running Dogs: Malaya 1948-1960* (1971) Arrow Books. This is one of numerous accounts of the Malayan Emergency and the successful British efforts to defeat the Communist Party of Malaya.

Barley, Nigel *White Rajah* (2003) Abacus. Extemely readable account of the life and extraordinary achievements of James Brooke, filled with ingenuity and dark, bloody violence.

Chapman, F Spencer *The Jungle is Neutral.* An account of a British guerrilla force fighting the Japanese in Borneo – not as enthralling as Tom Harrisson's book, but still worth reading.

Harrisson, Tom *World Within* (1959) Hutchinson: London. During the Second World War, explorer, naturalist and ethnologist Tom Harrisson was parachuted into Borneo to help organize Dayak resistance against the occupying Japanese forces. This is his extraordinary account.

Payne, Robert *The White Rajahs of Sarawak.* Readable account of the extraordinary history of this East Malaysian state.

Turnbull, Mary C *A History of Malaysia, Singapore and Brunei* (1989) Allen and Unwin. A very orthodox history of Malaysia, Singapore and Brunei, clearly written for a largely academic/student audience.

Natural history

Briggs, John *Mountains of Malaysia: a Practical Guide and Manual* (1988) Longman: London. Briggs has also written Parks of Malaysia, useful for anyone intending to especially visit the country's protected areas (Longman: Kuala Lumpur).

Cranbrook *Earl of Riches of the Wild: Land Mammals of South-East Asia* (1987) Oxford University Press.

Cubitt, Gerald and Junaidi, Payne *Wild Malaysia* (1990) London: New Holland. Large-format, coffee-table book, lots of wonderful colour photos, reasonable text, short background piece on each national park.

Hanbury-Tenison, Robin *Mulu, the Rain Forest* (1980) Arrow/Weidenfeld. This is the product of a Royal Geographical Society trip to Mulu in the late 1970s; semi-scholarly and useful.

Payne, Junaidi et al *A Field Guide to the Mammals of Borneo*, World Wildlife Fund/Sabah Society. Good illustrations, reasonable text, but very dry.

Payne, Junaidi et al *Pocket Guide to Birds of Borneo*, World Wildlife Fund/Sabah Society.

Tweedie, MWF and Harrison, JL
Malayan Animal Life (1954 with new editions) Longman.

Wallace, Alfred Russel *The Malay Archipelago* (1869). A classic of Victorian travel writing by one of the finest naturalists of the period. Wallace travelled through all of island Southeast Asia over a period of some years. The original is now reprinted.

Other books

Craig, Jo Ann *Culture Shock Malaysia.* One in a series of Culture Shock books, this examines and assesses the do's and don'ts of Malaysian and Singapore society. Useful for those going to live or spend an extended period in the region.

Lat Lat is Malaysia's foremost cartoonist. His images of the effects of social and economic change on a simple kampong boy are amusing and highly perceptive. His cartoons are compiled in numerous books including *Kampong boy* and *Town boy*, published by Straits Times Publishing.

Leee, Kit *Adoi* (1989) Times Books: Singapore. An amusing book of Malaysian attitudes to most things.

Southeast Asian region

Buruma, Ian *God's Dust* (1989) Jonathan Cape: London. Enjoyable journey through Burma, Thailand, Malaysia and Singapore along with the Philippines, Taiwan, South Korea and Japan; journalist Buruma questions how far culture in this region has survived the intrusion of the West.

Caufield, C *In the Rainforest* (1985) Heinemann: London. This readable and well-researched analysis of rainforest ecology and the pressures on tropical forests is part-based in the region.

Dingwall, Alastair *Traveller's Literary Companion to South-east Asia* (1994)

In Print: Brighton. Experts on Southeast Asian language and literature select extracts from novels and other books by Western and regional writers. The extracts are brief, but it gives a good overview of what is available.

Fraser-Lu, Sylvia *Handwoven Textiles of South-East Asia* (1988) OUP: Singapore. Well-illustrated, large-format book with informative text.

King, Ben F and Dickinson, EC *A Field Guide to the Birds of South-East Asia* (1975) Collins: London. Best regional guide to the birdlife of the region.

Osborne, Milton *Southeast Asia: an Introductory History* (1979) Allen & Unwin: Sydney. Good introductory history, clearly written, published in a portable paperback edition and recently revised and reprinted.

Pentes, Tina and Truelove, Adrienne *Travelling with Children to Indonesia and South-East Asia* (1984) Hale & Iremonger: Sydney.

Reid, Anthony *Southeast Asia in the Age of Commerce 1450-1680* (1988 and 1993) Yale University Press: New Haven. Perhaps the best history of everyday life in Southeast Asia, looking at such themes as physical well-being, material culture and social organization; meticulously researched.

Sesser, Stan *The Lands of Charm and Cruelty: Travels in Southeast Asia* (1993) Picador: Basingstoke. A series of collected narratives first published in the New Yorker including essays on Singapore, Laos, Cambodia, Burma and Borneo. Finely observed and thoughtful, the book is an excellent travel companion.

Young, Gavin *In Search of Conrad* (1991) Hutchinson: London. This well-known travel writer retraces the steps of Conrad; part travel-book, part fantasy, it is worth reading but is not up to the standard of his other books.

Contents

552 Planning your trip
  552 Where to go
  553 When to go

553 Getting there
  553 Air
  555 Rail
  555 Road
  557 Sea and river

558 Getting around
  558 Rail
  558 Road
  560 Sea
  560 Maps and guides

561 Sleeping

562 Eating

565 Festivals and events

567 Shopping

570 Essentials A-Z

576 Sights
  576 Colonial Core
  585 Singapore River
      and the City
  589 Chinatown
  595 Orchard Road and
      Botanic Gardens
  598 Little India
  601 Arab Street
  603 HarbourFront and Sentosa
  607 Singapore West
  610 East Coast
  612 North of the island

616 Listings
  616 Sleeping
  622 Eating
  631 Bars and clubs
  634 Entertainment
  636 Shopping
  639 Activities and tours
  640 Directory

641 History

647 Modern Singapore

Singapore

Footprint features

548 Don't miss...
561 Sleeping price codes
563 Eating price codes
581 24 hours in Singapore
651 Capital punishment

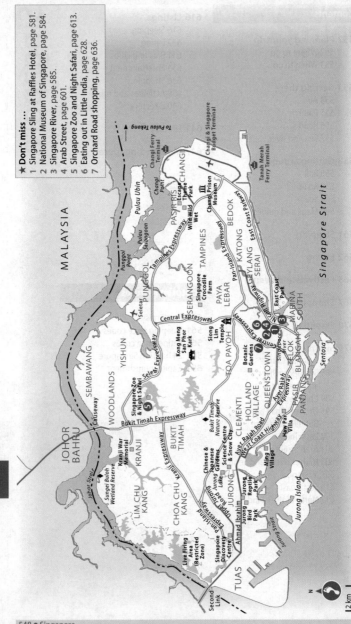

★ Don't miss ...
1 Singapore Sling at Raffles Hotel, page 581.
2 National Museum of Singapore, page 584.
3 Singapore River, page 585.
4 Arab Street, page 601.
5 Singapore Zoo and Night Safari, page 613.
6 Eating out in Little India, page 628.
7 Orchard Road shopping, page 636.

MALAYSIA

JOHOR BAHRU

Causeway

Second Link

Johor Strait

Sungei Buloh Wetland Reserve

TUAS

Live Firing Area (Restricted Zone)

Singapore Discovery Centre

Ahmad Ibrahim

LIM CHU KANG

CHOA CHU KANG

Jurong Bird Park

Jurong Reptile Park

Upper Jurong Road

Jurong Island

Jurong Strait

Ming Village

West Coast Highway

Haw Par Villa

Ayer Rajah Expressway

PASIR PANJANG

KRANJI

Kranji War Memorial

Kranji Expressway

BUKIT TIMAH

Chinese & Japanese Gardens

Jurong Lake

Science Centre & Snow City

JURONG

CLEMENTI

West Coast Highway

WOODLANDS

SEMBAWANG

YISHUN

Seletar Expressway

Bukit Timah Expressway

Singapore Zoo & Night Safari

Bukit Timah Nature Reserve

Botanic Gardens

HOLLAND VILLAGE

QUEENSTOWN

Ayer Rajah Expressway

Pulau Ubin

Pulau Seragoon

PUNGGOL

Punggol Point

Seletar

Central Expressway

Kong Meng San Phor Kark

Siong Lim Temple

TOA PAYOH

PAYA LEBAR

SERANGOON

Singapore Crocodile Farm

Central Expressway

Singapore River

TELOK BLANGAH

Sentosa

Singapore Strait

PASIR RIS

Changi Point

CHANGI

Wild Wild Wet

Escape Theme Park

Changi Prison Museum

To Pulau Tekong

Changi Ferry Terminal

Changi & Singapore Budget Terminal

Tanah Merah Ferry Terminal

BEDOK

TAMPINES

Tampines Expressway

Pan-Island Expressway

KATONG

GEYLANG

SERAI

MARINA SOUTH

East Coast Parkway

East Coast Park

Nicoll Highway

Singapore Strait

N

2 km
2 miles

Introduction

To some, it has all the ambience of a supermarket checkout lane. It has been described as a Californian resort town run by Mormons and even more famously as Disneyland with the death penalty. It has frequently been dubbed sterile and dull and for those who fail to venture beyond the plazas that line Orchard Road, or spend their 3½ days on coach trips to the ersatz cultural extravaganzas, this is not surprising. But there is a cultural and architectural heritage in Singapore beyond the one that the government tries so hard to manufacture. Despite its brash consumerism and toy-town mentality, Singapore is certainly not without its charm.

Singapore is difficult to fathom, especially from afar. Beneath its slick veneer of westernized modernity, many argue that its heart and soul are undoubtedly Asian. Behind the computers, hi-tech industries, marble, steel and smoked-glass tower blocks, highways and shopping centres is a society ingrained with conservative Confucian values.

For those stopping over in Singapore for just a few days – en route, as most of the island's tourists are, to somewhere else – there are several key sights that should not be missed. Many who visit, however, consider that it is far more important to enjoy the food. The island has an unparalleled variety of restaurants to suit every palate and wallet and offers possibly the greatest variety and quality in Asia. Hawker centres in particular are a highly recommended part of the Singapore epicurean experience – they are inexpensive, and many are open into the early hours.

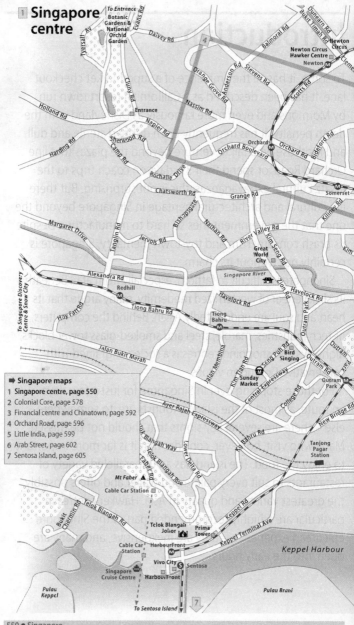

To Entrance
Botanic
Gardens &
National
Orchid
Garden

Evans Rd

Dunearn Rd

Bukit Timah Rd

Newton
Circus

Tyersall Av

Daivey Rd

Balmoral Rd

Newton Circus
Hawker Centre

Newton

Clemen

Cluny Rd

Orange Grove Rd

Anderson Rd

Stevens Rd

Scotts Rd

Holland Rd

Nassim Rd

Napier Rd

Entrance

Sherwood Rd

Camp Rd

Harding Rd

Orchard Boulevard

Orchard

Orchard Rd

Bideford Rd

Rochalie Drive

Chatsworth Rd

Grange Rd

Somerset

Margaret Drive

Tanglin Rd

Jervois Rd

Bishopsgate

Nathan Rd

Grange Rd

River Valley Rd

Kim Seng Rd

Kim

Killiney

Kim

Alexandra Rd

Great
World
City

Singapore River

Zion Rd

Havelock Rd

To Singapore Discovery
Centre & Snow City

Redhill

Havelock Rd

Outram Park

Hoy Fatt Rd

Tiong Bahru Rd

Tiong
Bahru

Outram Rd

Outram

Jalan Bukit Merah

Jalan Membina

Kim Tian Rd

Seng Poh Rd

Bird
Singing

Outram
Park

Sunday
Market

Kim Seng Rd

Central Expressway

College Rd

Ayer Rajah Expressway

New Bridge Rd

➡ **Singapore maps**

1 Singapore centre, page 550
2 Colonial Core, page 578
3 Financial centre and Chinatown, page 592
4 Orchard Road, page 596
5 Little India, page 599
6 Arab Street, page 602
7 Sentosa Island, page 605

Kg Bahru Rd

Tanjong
Pagar
Station

Mt Faber

Cable Car Station

Telok Blangah Way

Telok Blangah Rise

Lower Delta Rd

Bukit Chermin Rd

Telok Blangah Rd

Telok Blangah
Johor

Prima
Tower

Keppel Rd

Keppel Terminal Ave

Cable Car
Station

HarbourFront

Keppel Harbour

Singapore
Cruise Centre

Vivo City

HarbourFront

Sentosa

Pulau
Keppel

Pulau Brani

To Sentosa Island

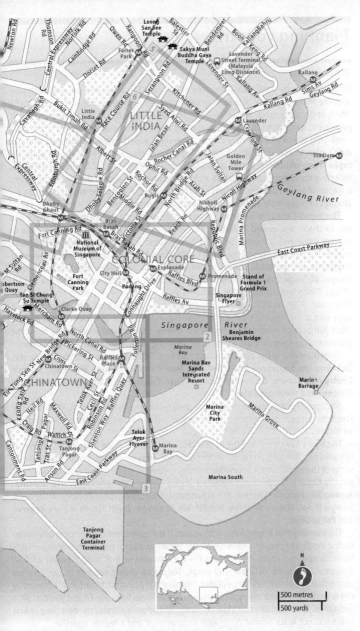

Planning your trip

Where to go

Singapore is a city state with a land area of just over 710 sq km and growing each year with the implementation of land reclamation projects. Moreover, public transport in the city is impeccably quick and efficient, so nowhere is exactly off the beaten track. It is possible to get a good feel for the place and to enjoy many of Singapore's sights on a week-long stay; if you stop over for just a weekend, expect to leave wondering why you didn't plan to remain a little longer. Singapore is also a nifty jumping-off point for exploring neighbouring Malaysia and Indonesia. Indeed, parts of Peninsular Malaysia, including the historic city of Melaka and the Indonesian islands of the Riau archipelago, are accessible on a day trip. Below is a slightly contrived – and by no means exhaustive – attempt to pigeonhole and categorize Singapore's attractions.

The popular image of Singapore as a city state is that it is so well managed that it has lost its charm and erased its history. This is not true, and there is a great deal here to interest those with a historic bent. The best historic sights in the central colonial core include the two branches of the **Asian Civilisations Museum**, the **National Museum of Singapore**, and the **Battle Box** in Fort Canning Park. Slightly further afield are **Fort Siloso**, **Images of Singapore** and **Surrender Chambers**, all of which are on **Sentosa Island**. Changi Prison and the Kranji War Memorial and Cemetery are also worth visiting. In the 1960s and 1970s, as its leaders tried to create a new, modern post-colonial Singapore, a large slice of the republic's colonial heritage was bulldozed for apartment blocks and the other symbols of modernity. Singapore's diverse architectural styles range from the grandeur of the **colonial core** to skyscrapers towering over the shophouses of **Chinatown**.

Singapore is a great place to bring children. There are plenty of things to see, including the **Singapore Flyer**, **Sentosa**, **Haw Par Villa**, **Jurong Bird Park**, **Science Centre**, **Singapore Discovery Centre**, **East Coast Park**, **Singapore Zoological Gardens** and the **Night Safari**.

Singaporeans have taken shopping to their hearts and to new heights. While the city is not the bargain-basement place it once was, it is still a great place to browse and buy with care.

The tigers have gone and the largest creature left alive, aside from Homo sapiens, is the wild pig, hanging on by its trotters on some outlying islands. But there are parks, some of the world's most accessible primary rainforest, gardens and a great zoo; check out the **Botanic Gardens** and **National Orchid Garden**, **Underwater World**, **Sentosa**, **Jurong Bird Park**, the **Chinese and Japanese Gardens**, **Singapore Zoological Gardens**, **Sungei Buloh Nature Reserve**, **MacRitchie Reservoir**, **Bukit Timah Nature Reserve** and **Pulau Ubin**.

The memory that lingers most with visitors is the gastronomic delights on offer. With such a medley of people – Chinese, Malay, Indian and large populations of expatriates from Europe and other Asian nations – considerable victual buying power and an unappeasable desire to snack and binge, Singapore must have one of the greatest concentrations of eateries on the planet. Cleanliness is a byword (foodstalls are graded by the government health ministry according to cleanliness from A to D) and you can get a great meal for a few dollars (or a few hundred). Singapore is possibly the best place in Asia to learn about Asian cuisine; come with an open mind and a healthy appetite.

When to go

There is no best season to visit Singapore and it is hot throughout the year. It gets even stickier before the monsoon breaks in November, while the hottest months are July and August. The wettest months are November, December and January, during the period of the north-east monsoon, when it is also coolest – but even 'cool' days are hot by most temperate people's standards. As one would expect, the hottest time of day is early afternoon when the average temperature is around 30°C, but even during the coolest time of the day, just before dawn, the temperature is still nearly 24°C.

Getting there

Air

Airport information

Almost all visitors arrive at Singapore's **Changi Airport** ⓘ *www.changiairport.com*, which is regularly voted the world's leading or favourite airport. It is the region's busiest and best connected airport and most major airlines fly here. Located at the extreme eastern tip of the island, it's about 20 km from town. There are three terminals and a budget terminal for low-cost carriers (imaginatively named The Budget Terminal), divided between airlines (all clearly indicated). The new S$1.5 billion third terminal opened in January 2008 with typical Singaporean efficiency. The airport's stress-free terminals belie its status as one of the world's most hectic transit hubs. The new terminal increased the number of annual arrivals by 22 million, bringing the total number of passenger arrivals processed up to 70 million passengers per year – around 16 times the population of Singapore. It takes only 20 minutes from touchdown to baggage claim, called 'accelerated passenger through-flow'.

Changi's facilities are excellent and include banks, desks for hotel reservations and the Singapore Tourist Board, a medical centre, business centre, children's discovery corner, free internet centre, day rooms, restaurants, left-luggage facilities, mail and telecommunications desks, shopping arcades, supermarkets, sports facilities (health centre and pool), hairdresser, nature trails in seven different themed gardens, a movie theatre, full service hotel and transit hotels in every terminal. Everything is clearly signposted in English and the three terminals are connected by skytrains (0500-0230, one to three minutes between terminals). There is an excellent canteen/food centre in Terminal 2, reached via the multi-deck car park. A tourist information pack is available just after Immigration, near the Customs Hall.

Over 80 airlines service Singapore, connecting the city state with 116 cities in 59 countries. As well as major long-haul airlines including **British Airways**, **Cathay Pacific**, **Singapore Airlines**, **Qantas** and **American Airlines**, Changi is a hub for cheap budget Asian airlines including **AirAsia**, **Tiger Airways**, **Jet Star Asia** and **Firefly**, which connect Singapore with destinations as far away as India, China and Australia. If you want to work out connections with specific cities, the Changi website has a useful flight-planning facility. Under Flight Information click on Passenger Flight Planner, then type in your city of origin and it will show the flights, airlines and routes.

The **Budget Terminal** ⓘ *www.btsingapore.com*, lacks the debonair ambience of Changi, but has all the mod cons such as free internet, money exchange and dining options. At the time of research only **Tiger Airways**, **Firefly** and **Cebu Pacific** were using this terminal.

Seletar Airport is a military airport, but is also used for connections with Pulau Tioman and Pulau Redang off Malaysia's east coast and for some charter flights. Although the authorities do not allow photos on the tarmac, checking in is very informal, in contrast to Changi's brusque efficiency. There are no public buses here so most people take taxis and, as at Changi, there is a S$3 surcharge (S$5 Friday-Sunday 1700-2400). When a scheduled flight arrives from Tioman the airline usually calls so that the required number of taxis are waiting.

Airport tax
This is payable on departure and is S$21 for all flights to all countries (but most airlines incorporate this into the ticket prices). Transit passengers staying less than 24 hours do not have to pay. The 7% **Goods and Sales tax** (GST) is refundable at the airport for goods bought (over US$100) with appropriate receipts.

From Southeast Asia
As an international crossroads, Singapore is within easy reach of all the region's key points and there are flights to Changi Airport from destinations throughout Southeast Asia. It is possible to get special deals to selected destinations from discount travel agents and Singapore's *Yellow Pages*, but tickets bought in Bangkok and Penang are generally cheaper. The most competitive deals are with the budget airlines AirAsia, Tiger Airways and Jet Star. The monopoly held by Singapore Airlines and Malaysian Airlines on the busy Singapore–KL route has thankfully been broken, and all the budget carriers fly there, with fares often working out cheaper than a bus ticket. For the best value, book budget tickets online.

AirAsia flies between Singapore and Penang, Langkawi, KL, Kuching and Kota Kinabalu, as well as destinations in Indonesia and Thailand. AirAsia also has cheap deals between Johor Bahru, just across the causeway from Singapore, with most major cities in Malaysia. Tickets can be bought online, via AirAsia's call centre, from their office or from one of 20 post offices (surcharge; see www.singpost.com.sg). They now have a booking office in Peninsula Plaza (nearest MRT: City Hall); tickets bought here have a S$10 surcharge.

Firefly flies to some smaller cities in Malaysia such as Alor Star, Ipoh, Kuantan and Kuala Terengganu. Other budget airlines flying here include Tiger Airways with flights from Kuching, Kota Kinabalu, KL, Penang and Langkawi in Malaysia and cities in Australia, India, Indonesia, China and Vietnam. Jet Star Asia flies from Kuching, Kota Kinabalu, KL, Hong Kong and cities in Australia, Thailand, Myanmar, Cambodia, Malaysia, Vietnam and Indonesia. Cebu Pacific flies from Manila, Cebu and has seasonal flights from Davao in the Philippines.

Transport to town
See also www.changiairport.com, under Airport Guide, for more information. Hotels will only meet guests with a previous arrangement; some charge, but others offer the service free. The car pick-up area is outside the arrivals halls of the terminals. **Buses** run between the airport and nearby bus interchanges. Bus No 36 loops along Orchard Road passing many hotels including the YMCA (0600-2400, S$2). Another option is the **airport shuttle** ⓘ *every 15 mins 0600-2400, every 30 mins 2400-0600, S$9, children S$6, booking counters in arrivals halls*. These minibuses will drop off at various destinations, including hotels, within the central business district; make sure your hotel is covered by the door-to-door service. If you are in a group of three or four, it is probably cheaper to take a taxi (see below).

The airport is connected to the **MRT underground line**. Trains to the centre of Singapore take approximately 27 minutes. The fare is S$2.70 inclusive of a refundable S$1 deposit for a single-trip ticket. Trains runs every 12 minutes between 0530 and 2318.

Taxis queue up outside the arrival halls. As a general rule taxi drivers in Singapore are straightforward and honest folk, and unless you're on an incredibly tight budget they offer the most painless and hassle-free method to find a bed for the night. They are metered but there is an airport surcharge of S$3, which increases to S$5 on Friday, Saturday and Sunday between 1700 and 2400. A trip to the centre of town should cost from S$18 to S$28 – the only exception being a further 50% fee for late arrivals between 2400 and 0600. Most taxi companies operate a **limousine service** (London cab or Mercedes) with a fee of S$16 plus the metered fare. To book limousine service from your hotel, call **Comfort City Cab** ① T6552 1111, or **Comfort Premier Cab** ① T6552 2828.

For **car hire**, **Avis** ① T6545 0800, and **Hertz** ① T6542 5300, desks open 0700 to 2300, are in the arrivals hall in all three main terminals.

Budget Terminal Other than taxi, the best way to get here is to jump on the free shuttle bus service linking it with Terminal 2, where there are comprehensive transport options. The service runs every 10 minutes 0500-0200, and 0200-0500 every 30 minutes.

Rail

The **Tanjong Pagar Railway Station** ① Keppel Rd, T6221 3390, is to the south of the city centre. Singapore is the last port of call for the Malaysian railway system, **Keretapi Tanah Melayu (KTM)** ① www.ktmb.com.my. Visitors have to clear Singaporean immigration at the Woodlands and then continue for another 30 minutes, before clearing Malaysian immigration and customs at Tanjong Pagar; see page 595.

There are two main lines connecting Singapore and Malaysia: one up the west coast to KL and another line that goes through the centre of Peninsular Malaysia and on to Kota Bharu on the northeast coast. Three fully air-conditioned express trains make the trip daily between Singapore and Kuala Lumpur, taking 6½ hours (S$34-68, and S$19 for third class seat) and departing at 0740, 1400 and 2200. The overnight sleeper arrives in Kuala Lumpur at 0623. The 0740 train continues through to Butterworth (for Penang and connections to Thailand). It is possible to take a train (for S$2.90) to Johor Bahru – just across the border in Malaysia – and then catch a (much cheaper) connection further north, which requires a wait, but is significantly healthier on the wallet. Trains are clean and efficient and overnight trains have cabins in first class, sleeping berths in second class, and restaurants. The service to Kota Bharu takes 12 hours (S$41-51 and S$33 for a third-class seat). It leaves daily at 1800.

Transport to town

From the station, bus 10 travels up Robinson Road, past Collyer Quay to Empress Place and the Nicoll Highway; bus 100 goes up Robinson, Fullerton and Beach roads; bus 30 travels west; bus 84 goes to HarbourFront; and buses 97 and 131 travel through the centre of town and then up Serangoon Road and through Little India.

Road

Bus

From Malaysia There are services to Singapore from a number of towns in Malaysia. These include: Kuala Lumpur (S$33), Melaka (S$17), Butterworth (S$45), Mersing (S$30), Ipoh (S$38), Penang (S$55) and Genting (S$40). (The fares quoted here are from Singapore; tickets bought in Larkin Terminal in Johor Bahru in Malaysia are around half the price.) Malaysian long-distance buses arrive at the Lavender Street Terminal at the junction of Lavender Street and Kallang Bahru, while tour group buses (including those from Thailand) arrive outside the Golden Mile Tower on Beach Road Junction. From Singapore it is cheaper to buy a ticket from the Malaysian buses on Lavender Road (for KL, Mersing, and Melaka). **Golden Mile** buses are more expensive as they are organized by tour agencies. **707** ① *T6292 3633*, for KL, Melaka, Penang, Cameron Highlands and Ipoh, has a booking office at Lavender Street and the Golden Mile Complex. **Transnasional** ① *T6294 7034*, run comfortable coaches to Mersing, Kota Bahru and Kuala Terengganu from Lavender Street.

There are three bus companies leaving at least every 10 minutes between **Johor Bahru**'s Larkin Bus Terminal and Singapore. Boarding in JB is only permitted at Larkin and at immigration. The service passes through the new and efficient Sultan Islakandar border crossing in JB and pauses at the Woodlands immigration point for Singaporean border and customs checks and on to Singapore's Ban San Terminal at the northern end of Queen Street (at the junction with Arab Street; see map, page 602) or Kranji MRT station. The journey from JB takes about an hour, including customs and immigration formalities at the border. **SBS** No 170 runs every 15 minutes from Singapore's Ban San Terminal, between Queen Street and Rochor Canal Road. Tickets are all priced around RM1.70 from JB, or S$1.70 (twice as much) from Singapore. The **Johor Singapore Express** is air conditioned, faster and more frequent and also leaves from Ban San S$2.40. There are two **Causeway Link** services. The yellow CW1 bus with a smiley face runs between Kranji MRT station in Singapore and the Larkin terminal. It only takes 20 minutes from the border to the MRT station. The CW2 is an express service that runs from Ban San Street Terminal through to Larkin, S$3.40. All three bus companies require you to get off twice: for the Malaysian border point and its Singaporean counterpart. You have to take all your luggage with you since the bus does not wait for you. You wait for the next bus to come along; each bus has its own stop after exiting immigration. Keep your ticket or you will have to buy a new one. Also have a pen handy to fill in immigration forms as they are not provided.

If leaving Singapore for destinations in Malaysia, note that buses to more distant destinations such as Butterworth, Terengganu and Ipoh tend to leave in the late afternoon. It is best to book tickets a few days ahead of departure, especially if intending to travel over a holiday period. Many bus companies use the Second Link at Tuas when travelling north into Malaysia. This saves considerable time. It is worth asking the company if they travel via Tuas or JB. If they travel via JB, you can be assured of a stop in Larkin to pick up more passengers.

Note Crossing into Singapore from JB on a Sunday evening can be nightmarish with huge queues and traffic jams.

From Thailand As well as **buses** from destinations in Malaysia, there are also long-distance services from Bangkok and Hat Yai in Thailand. These obviously route their journeys through Malaysia. Services from Thailand arrive outside the Golden Mile Tower on Beach Road and fares from Singapore are S$49 to Hat Yai and S$80 to Bangkok. There are scores of agents selling tickets close to the station. Note that if you are leaving Singapore for Thailand, it is cheaper to book a ticket to Hat Yai and then pay for the rest of the journey in Thai baht; or even cheaper still to catch a bus to JB, one from JB to Hat Yai and then a third from Hat Yai to Bangkok.

Taxis

Rather than taking a bus, it is possible to take a long-distance taxi from Malaysia to Singapore. However, this usually requires a change of vehicle in Johor Bahru. (In other words, it is necessary to take a taxi from, say, Melaka, Kuantan, KL or Butterworth to JB, and then another taxi on to Singapore.) From JB there are scores of taxis to the Rochor Road terminus (S\$8 per person, but if you need a full cab, S\$32).

Sea and river

A small fraction of Singapore's visitors arrive by ship into the world's busiest port. Passenger liners serve Singapore from Australia, Europe, USA, India and Hong Kong. Ships either dock at the Singapore Cruise Centre at HarbourFront or anchor in the main harbour with a launch service to shore. Entry requirements are the same as those described on page 575. **Star Cruises** ① *T6223 0002, www.starcruises.com*, is one of the biggest companies operating in the region. **Orient Lines** ① *P&O Travel Singapore, T6317 2800, www.orientlines.com*, and **Silversea Cruises** ① *T6276 3556, www.silversea.com*, also dock at Singapore.

From Indonesia and Malaysia

There are regular high-speed ferry connections between Singapore and Indonesia's Riau islands of Batam (Sekupang and Batam Centre) Tanjung Balai (Karimun) and Bintan (Tanjung Pinang). A one-way fare to Batam costs around S\$30 and the journey takes 45 minutes. Ferries leave from the **Singapore Cruise Centre** ① *T6513 2200, www.singapore cruise.com*, at HarbourFront, south of town, just a short walk from the HarbourFront MRT. Tickets can be booked online at www.penguin.com.sg. Ferries to the resorts on the north shore of Bintan leave from Tanah Merah ferry terminal (East Coast), and cost S\$64 for a peak return (1½ hours). It's a little cheaper during the week. Tickets can be booked online at www.brf.com.sg. From the Riau islands it is possible to travel by boat to Sumatra or by air to many other destinations in Indonesia including Kalimantan.

Ferry operators have their offices in the Singapore Cruise Centre, on the second level of the HarbourFront Tower, and include **Penguin Ferries** ① *T6271 4866*, and **WaveMaster** ① *T6546 8830*. Penguin and **Bintan Resort Ferries** ① *T6542 4369*, are two of the companies that operate ferries to Bintan. Intending passengers should arrive at the terminal one hour before departure if they do not already have a booked ticket. **Indo Falcon** ① *T6270 6778, www.indofalcon.com*, offer cheap package tours to Batam.

If travelling from Tanjung Belungkur, fares are much cheaper (payable in ringgit). **Note** Most EU citizens and citizens of Australia, Canada, USA and New Zealand need a visa to enter Indonesia. You can get a visa on arrival at Batam and Bintan's resort immigration point. There are no visa processing points on Karimun. Check the latest situation before travel.

There is also a ferry from Changi Ferry Terminal to Tanjung Belungkor, east of Johor Bahru in Malaysia. Most people use this service to get to the beach resort of Desaru. Passengers S\$22; journey time 30 minutes. There are daily departures from Changi at 1000, 1700 and 2000, and from Tanjung Belungkur to Changi at 0815, 1530 and 1845. Contact **Cruise Ferries** ① *T6546 8518*, for reservations. To get to the terminal, take bus No 2 to Changi Village and then a taxi.

It is possible to enter Singapore from Malaysia by bumboat from Johor Bahru (S\$5), Tanjung Pengileh or Tanjung Surat (S\$9) in southern Johor to Changi Point, on the northeast tip of Singapore, which is a good way of beating the bottleneck at the causeway. The first boat is at 0700 and the last at 1900. Bicycles can be brought aboard for S\$2. Boats depart as soon as they have 12 passengers.

Getting around

In an attempt to discourage Singaporeans from clogging the roads with private cars, the island's public transport system was designed to be cheap and painless. **Buses** go almost everywhere, and the **Mass Rapid Transit** (**MRT**) underground railway provides an extremely efficient subterranean back-up.

Contact **TransitLink** ① *T1800-2255 663, daily 0800-1800* or check *www.transitlink. com.sg*, for bus, MRT and LRT information. A useful guide to Singapore's transport system is the *TransitLink Guide* (S$2), listing all bus and MRT routes and stops, available at news outlets, bookshops, MRT stations and many hotels.

An **Ez-link card** ① *www.ezlink.com.sg*, costs S$15 (S$10 stored value and S$5 non-refundable card deposit) from MRT stations and TransitLink ticket offices (see www.transitlink.com.sg for locations). It can be used on buses, the MRT and LRT, some taxis, 7-Eleven stores and McDonald's; it's worth buying if you plan to use public transport extensively.

Rail

Singapore's **Mass Rapid Transit (MRT)** is one of the most technologically advanced, user-friendly light railway systems in the world and about a third of the system is underground. The designer stations of marble, glass and chrome are cool, spotless and suicide-free, thanks to the sealed-in, air-conditioned platforms. Nine of the underground stations serve as self-sufficient, blast-proof emergency bunkers for Singaporeans, should they ever need them. Smoking is strictly banned on all public transport – transgression is punishable by a large fine. Eating or drinking inside stations is also strictly forbidden.

There are four MRT lines: the North-East line runs from HarbourFront through Chinatown and Little India to Punggol in the northeast. The North-South line runs from Jurong East (for the Singapore Science Centre) in a loop north passing Kranji (for buses to Johor Bahru in Malaysia) and down to Marina Bay passing through Orchard Road, City Hall and Raffles Place. The East-West line runs from Joo Koon in the west through City Hall, Bugis and onto Changi Airport. The Circle line was only partially open at the time of writing, from Marymount to Dhoby Ghaut via Bras Basah. When this line is completed it will run through central and southern Singapore from HarbourFront to Dhoby Ghaut. The main interchanges are at Outram Park, Raffles Place, Dhoby Ghaut and City Hall.

The MRT's 106 fully automated trains operate every 2½ to eight minutes, depending on the time of day, between 0600 and 2400. Fare stages are posted in station concourses, and tickets dispensed, with change, from the vending machines. Fares range from 90¢ to S$2.10. ▶▶ *See also Singapore MRT and LRT colour map in the centre of the book.*

Road

Bus

For anyone visiting Singapore for more than a couple of days, the bus is a great way to get to the spots not yet covered by the MRT. **SBS (Singapore Bus Service)** ① *T1800-287 2727, www.sbstransit.com.sg*, is efficient, convenient and cheap. Fares range from 80¢ (non air conditioned) to S$1.80 (cheaper with an Ez-link card). Buses run daily with a Nite Owl service operating after 2400. Nite Owl buses charge a flat rate of S$3. **SMRT**

ⓘ www.smrtbuses.com.sg, fares range from 80¢ to S$1.80. It runs a NightRider service, S$3 flat rate. Routes for all buses are listed (with a special section on buses to tourist spots) in the aforementioned *Transit Link Guide*. Tourists can get the useful **Singapore Tourist Pass** ⓘ T6223 2282, www.thesingaporetouristpass.com, giving unlimited travel on Singapore buses and MRT lines. The passes are valid for up to five days and can be topped up at a Transit Link Office. The pass costs S$8 per day, excluding a one-off refundable S$10 card rental fee.

Note For new arrivals in Singapore, make sure you have the correct change in coins for buses. Bus drivers don't give you change from notes.

Car hire

This is one of the most expensive ways to get around. It is not worth it unless you are travelling to Malaysia since parking is expensive in Singapore (parking coupons can be bought in shops and daily licence booths). If travelling to Malaysia, it is cheaper, in any case, to hire a car in Johor Bahru, Malaysia. Rental agencies require a licence, passport and for drivers to be over 20. Car rental cost is anything from S$90 to S$350 per day, depending on size and comfort, plus mileage. Vans and pickups are much cheaper as they are classified as commercial vehicles and are taxed at a lower rate. Driving is on the left, the speed limit is 50 km per hour (80 km per hour on expressways) and wearing a seat belt is compulsory. Avoid bus lanes (indicated by an unbroken yellow line) during rush hour. Driving into the city centre and core business district, drivers will pass under ERP gantries, a government-managed toll-collection system. Cars and taxis are fitted with a stored value card from which the toll fee is deducted. There are over 80 gantries in Singapore, making driving through the city an expensive proposition. In addition to car-hire counters at the airport and booking offices in top hotels, the *Yellow Pages* lists local firms under 'Motorcar Renting and Leasing'.

Cycling

This is not a bicycle-friendly city. Bicycles are available for hire at a number of public parks and other quieter spots on the island, including East Coast Parkway, Sentosa, Pasar Ris, Bishan and Pulau Ubin. Expect to pay S$5 per hour or S$20 per day; some ask for a deposit.

East Coast Bicycle Centre ⓘ *East Coast Parkway, open 0800-1830*, has bikes for rent including tandems (S$3 per hour). **Sentosa Island Bicycle Station** ⓘ *near Ferry Terminal, Mon-Fri 0900-1800, Sat-Sun 0900-1900*, charges S$3 per hour. Pulau Ubin off Singapore's northeast coast offers some good cycling along tranquil jungle roads. Bikes can be rented for around S$5 a day here. To get to Pulau Ubin, take a bumboat from Changi Village (S$2).

Hitchhiking

The idea is alien to most Singaporeans and those trying are unlikely to be successful.

Taxis

Taxis are the fastest and easiest way to get around the island in comfort. However, with the continued erection of ERP gantries they are losing their competitive edge. Nevertheless, compared with the UK they are excellent value. There are more than 24,000 taxis, all of them metered and air conditioned, which ply the island's roads completing almost 600,000 road trips daily. Taxis can only be hailed at specified points; it's best to go to a taxi stand or about 50 m from traffic lights. The taxis' bells are an alarm warning cabbies they've exceeded the 80 km per hour expressway speed limit, but drivers rarely pay attention to this.

Fares start at S$2.80 for the first kilometre and rise 20¢ for every subsequent 385 m up to 10 km, after which they rise by 20¢ every 330 m. 20¢ is also added for every 30 seconds waiting time. There is a peak period surcharge of 35% added to the metered fare for trips commencing between 0700 and 0930 Monday-Friday and between 1700 and 2000 Monday-Saturday. These surcharges do not apply on public holidays. A surcharge of S$3 is levied on all trips beginning from the Central Business District (CBD) between 1700 and 2400 on Monday-Saturday. If there are more than four passengers there is a S$2 surcharge; luggage costs S$1 extra and there's a 50% 'midnight charge' from 2400 to 0600. There is also a S$3 (S$5 at peak times) surcharge for journeys starting from (but not going to) Changi Airport or Seletar Airport. Trips paid for with credit cards incur a 10% surcharge on top of the fare and taxis hired between 1800 on the evening before a public holiday and 2400 on the day of the public holiday also get hit with a S$1 surcharge. Passengers also need to reimburse the taxi driver for charges incurred by passing through ERP gantries around the city centre. Charges for these vary depending on location and time of day.

Even with this veritable extravaganza of surcharges, Singapore's taxis are fairly good value for money and are definitely the best way to get around. They provide a view of Singapore that is absent from the MRT (at least in the city centre) and are a great source of information. Drivers are usually polite and will even round down fares to the nearest dollar. Unlike most of the rest of Asia, language is not a barrier to communication.

For taxi services ring: **Comfort and City Cab** ① T6552 1111; **Premier Cab** ① T6363 6888; **Smart** ① T6485 7777; **SMRT** ① T6555 8888. Charges for advance telephone booking apply.

Trishaws

Descendants of the rickshaw, trishaws have all but left the Singapore street scene. The biggest population of trishaws is around the Bugis area and lingering outside the Raffles Hotel; they cater for tourists only these days and charge accordingly, making trishaws the most expensive form of public transport. Agree a price before climbing in and expect to pay about S$30 for a 45-minute ride. Top hotels offer top-dollar trishaw tours. **Trishaw Tours** ① T6339 6833, also offers trishaw tours starting from Chinatown.

Sea

Ferries to the southern islands, such as Sentosa, Kusu and St John's, leave from Marina South Pier. Boats for the northern islands go from Changi Point or Punggol Point.

Maps and guides

A plethora of city maps are available free from Singapore Tourism Board (STB) offices and many hotels. The best street map to Singapore is the Periplus Map, available at bookshops. Another useful map is the Singapore Street Directory, www.streetdirectory.com.sg.

The STB produces the general official guide, which is updated each month. It is worth making a visit to one of the STB offices or pick up brochures and maps on arrival at Changi Airport. Other free maps can be picked up from hotels and tourist offices.

Invaluable for making the most of Singapore's public transport is the *TransitLink Guide*, S$2, listing all bus and MRT routes and stops.

Sleeping price codes

L	Over US$200	AL	US$91-200
A	US$41-90	B	US$21-40
C	US$12-20	D	US$7-11

Price codes refer to the cost of two people sharing a double room in the high season.

Top-end hotels (L-AL)
Singapore has some of the very best hotels in the world. These offer unrivalled personal service, sumptuous extras, luxury rooms and just about every amenity that you can think of. Most of the top hotels provide Wi-Fi, 24-hour business facilities, several pools, jacuzzis, health spas, tennis courts, numerous restaurants serving incredible cuisine, and much else besides.

Most of the middle to upper range hotels in the **AL** category will provide a business centre (although it is worth checking whether these operate 24 hours). There will be an executive floor or two, with a lounge for private breakfast and evening cocktails or for entertaining clients. They will also have a fitness centre and pool and may have several restaurants.

Mid-range hotels (A-B)
In Singapore, the better guesthouses and budget hotels are priced at the top of this bracket. Places in the **A** category will range from very comfortable to functional. Rooms in the top end of this bracket will have most extras, such as a minibar, cable TV, Wi-Fi and tea- and coffee-making facilities. They may also have a pool, but it's likely to be small, and a coffee shop and perhaps a restaurant.

There are not many hotels in the **B** category, but it's possible to get a smallish air-conditioned room with a shared bathroom in a guesthouse. You can get a bed in a decent dorm in this bracket at one of the better guesthouses in Little India, with Wi-Fi and good showers. Rooms in the **B** category should still be clean, comfortable and serviceable.

Budget hotels (C-D)
This is strictly dorm-only accommodation. There are a few bargains out there in these price codes so it's worth hunting around.

Sleeping → *See also box above and listings, page 616.*

Many of the excellent international-class hotels are concentrated in the main shopping and business areas, including Orchard and Scotts roads, and near Raffles City and the Marina complexes. They are all run to a very high standard and room rates range between S$200 and S$650, although discounts are almost always on offer and few people pay the full rate. Enquire at the airport hotel desk on arrival whether there are any special offers. Singapore is currently experiencing a lull in tourism arrivals, due to the general poor state of the global economy. As a result, mid-range and more expensive hotels have not been filling their rooms and prices have been slashed. However, during holiday periods and major events such as the Grand Prix race, occupancy is very high and those without a reservation face a long and tiring hunt. As a general rule, it is always better to book accommodation in advance. Taxes of 10% (government) plus 5% (goods) plus 1% (services) are added to bills in all but the cheapest of hotels.

Singapore offers an excellent choice of hotels in our upper categories, from luxury to tourist class. Though rooms may be more expensive than equivalent classes of hotels elsewhere in the region, they try to make up for this in terms of service. It is rare to stay in a hotel that does not offer attentive and professional care. Budget hotels have improved immeasurably in Singapore over the last decade, from the bed bug-riddled pits of the start of the century to an excellent selection of comfortable, bright and clean guesthouses and hostels, often staffed by cheery and enthusiastic folk. The majority of budget guesthouses are located around Little India, Arab Street and Bugis Junction. Compared to other places in Southeast Asia, Singapore's budget guesthouses and hostels aren't budget at all. Private rooms usually start at S$55 and a dorm bed can be had for S$15 and upwards. It is imperative to book ahead as the better places fill up fast and walking under the blazing midday sun with a backpack is no fun at all.

Eating → See also box, opposite, and listings, page 622.

Eating is the national pastime in Singapore and has acquired the status of a refined art. The island is a tropical paradise for epicureans of every persuasion and budget. While every country in the region boasts national dishes, none offers such a delectably wide variety as Singapore. Fish-head curry must surely qualify as the national dish although others will adamantly tell you it should be black pepper crab or Hainan chicken rice. You can sample countless Chinese cuisines, North and South Indian, Malay and Nonya (Straits Chinese) food, plus Indonesian, Vietnamese, Thai, Japanese, Korean, French, Italian (and other European), Russian, Mexican, and even find a good old British roast dinner at several places on a Sunday. There's a very respectable selection of Western food at the top end of the market, a few good places in the middle bracket and swelling ranks of cheaper fast food restaurants. For young and hip Singaporeans, coffee culture has replaced food court fare and the favoured spots are places like The Coffee Bean, Spinelli's and Starbucks, which are giving a buzz to thousands. For a full list of eateries, see page 622.

Don't be put off by characterless, brightly lit restaurants in Singapore; the food can be superb. Eating spots range from high-rise revolving restaurants to neon-lit pavement seafood extravaganzas. A delicious dinner can cost as little as S$3 or more than S$100 and the two may be just yards away from each other. For example, it is possible to have a small beer in one of the bars of the Raffles Hotel for S$12, or more, and then nip 20 m across the road and indulge in a huge plate of curry and rice for S$3.

For a listing of Singapore's more pricey restaurants, www.bestsingaporerestaurants.com is worth checking out; it gives a description of the food and restaurant ambience, but frustratingly little information is given about prices. Wine and Dine's *Singapore's Top Restaurants* is a handy guide to the city's most exclusive eateries and is available at most good bookshops for S$10. One of the most interesting guides available for food lovers is *Our Makan Places*, a light-hearted romp through the heartlands (Singapore's residential neighbourhoods) in search of the country's best hawker stalls; essential reading for those in search of authentic Singaporean food and ambience. It's available at MPH Bookstores for S$5. For details of Singapore's varied cuisines, see page 660.

Eating price codes

♦♦♦ Over US$12   **♦♦** US$4-12   **♦** Under US$4

Prices refer to the average cost of a two-course meal for one person, not including drinks or service charge.

Chinese meals are eaten with chopsticks and Malays and Indians traditionally eat with their right hands. It is just as acceptable, however, to eat with spoons and forks. In Malay and Indian company, do not use your left hand for eating.

Coffee shops

Mainly family concerns, traditional Singaporean coffee shops or *kopi tiam* are in the older part of the city, usually in old Chinese shophouses. They serve breakfast, lunch and dinner, as well as beer, at only slightly higher prices than hawker centres.

Fast-food cafés

Despite Singapore's gourmet delights, fast-food outlets do a roaring trade in Singapore. As well as the standard names in fast-food fare, there are now chains of more sophisticated 'cafés', selling a wider range of European food. In particular, there is **The Coffee Bean and Tea Leaf**, who provide a good selection of fresh coffees (ground or beans). Modern takes on the Singapore *kopitiam* include **Toast Box** and **Killiney Kopitiam**, both serving coffee, tea and traditional Singaporean snacks such as laksa and toast with half-boiled eggs in air-conditioned comfort.

Hawker centres and food courts

The government might have cleared hawkers off the streets, but there are plenty of hawker centres in modern Singapore. Food courts are the modern, air-conditioned, sanitized version of hawker centres. They provide the local equivalent of café culture and the human equivalent of grazing. Large numbers of stalls are packed together under one roof. Hawker centres are found beneath HDB blocks and in allocated areas in the city while food courts are usually found in shopping malls. The seats and tableware may be basic, but the food is always fresh and diners are spoilt for choice. Customers claim a table, then graze their way down the rows of Chinese, Malay and Indian stalls. It is not necessary to eat from the stall you are sitting next to. Most are self service but vendors will deliver to your table when the food is ready; payment is on receipt. The food is cheap and prices are non-negotiable. Note that napkins are not provided, but easily available from the drinks stall. Two of the best are the **Lau Pa Sat Festival Market** ① *www.laupasat.biz*, and the **Maxwell Food Centre**.

Note Chope (v): To *chope* a table. Food courts and hawker centres are invariably busy places and often get packed at lunch and dinner. To reserve a table, a Singaporean will *chope* it. They will leave a possession such as an umbrella, or bag on the seat or table and from that point on, the table is considered reserved whilst the diner heads off to choose his meal. In more recent times, people have been using tiny items such as tissue packets to *chope* tables, causing a bit of a fuss in the media. Invariably foreigners find the system a bit rude, and rarely *chope* tables themselves. Also, Singaporeans will often hover around a table waiting for the diners to slurp their dinner down and make way. Don't feel pressurized by this behaviour, it's just the way things are done in the hectic city state.

While Singapore is well known for its three main populations of Indians, Chinese and Malays, there are significant communities of other Asian nationalities that have their own hang-out areas. If you want some good authentic Asian cuisine head to the Golden Mile Complex on Beach Rd for Thai food, City Plaza near Paya Lebar MRT for Indonesian, Tanjong Pagar Rd for hearty Korean fare, Lucky Plaza on Orchard Rd for Filipino, Peninsula Plaza near City Hall MRT for authentic Burmese and for Middle Eastern flavours, head to Arab Street, which has a smattering of Arabic eateries. The Japanese form one of the largest communities of foreigners in Singapore and their food can be found all over the city.

Drink

Every hawker centre has at least a couple of stalls selling fresh fruit juice, a more wholesome alternative to the ubiquitous bottles of fizzy drink. A big green apple, pear or papaya juice costs S$3. You can choose any combination of fruits to go in your fruit punch. Freshly squeezed fruit juices are widely available at stalls and in restaurants. Fresh lime juice is served in most restaurants, and is a perfect complement to the banana-leaf curry, tandoori and dosai. Carbonated soft drinks, cartons of fruit juice and air-flown fresh milk can be found in supermarkets. For local flavour, the Malay favourite is *rose bandung* (a sickly sweet, bright pink concoction of rose essence and condensed milk), found in most hawker centres, as well as the Chinese thirst quenchers, soya bean milk or chrysanthemum tea. Red Bull (Krating Daeng) is also widely available and is the toast of Singapore's army of Thai building site labourers.

Tiger and Anchor beers are the local brews and Tsingtao, the Chinese nectar, is also available. Tiger Beer was first brewed at the Malayan Breweries with imported Dutch hops and yeast on Alexandra Road in 1932, and was the product of a joint venture between Singapore's Fraser & Neave and Heineken. Anchor was the result of German brewers Beck's setting up the rival Archipelago Brewery. Because of its German roots, Archipelago was bought out by Malayan Breweries in 1941. Nowadays Tiger and Anchor are produced by Asia Pacific Breweries, whereas Archipelago produces a range of hand-crafted beers with a heavy Southeast Asian influence. Archipelago beers can be found at select restaurants around town as well as at their shop in Circular Road. Brewerkz on Clarke Quay has its own microbrewery and produces some delicious beers. It also has one of the best happy hours in the city. Some bars specialize in imported beers, but even local beer is expensive (around S$8 a bottle in hawker centres and S$10 a glass in bars and pubs). There is an international selection of drinks at top bars, but they're often pricey. Coffee houses, hawker centres and small bars or coffee shops around Serangoon Road, Jalan Besar and Chinatown have the cheapest beer. Expect to pay around S$12 for half a pint of beer in most smart bars. However, most bars and restaurants do have a happy hour (or hours) when punters can get two for the price of one.

There is no shortage of wine available in Singapore, but it is extraordinarily expensive; Australian and Chilean wines are generally a better deal than imported European ones. Supermarkets all have good wines and spirits sections.

The Singapore Sling is the island's best known cocktail. It was invented in the Raffles Hotel in 1915 and contains a blend of gin, cherry brandy, sugar, lemon juice and angostura bitters. For an authentic experience, head to the long bar at Raffles Hotel, drink and throw monkey nut shells over the floor with wild abandon, but be prepared to dig deep into your wallet.

Festivals and events

Singapore's cultural diversity gives Singaporeans the excuse to celebrate plenty of festivals, most of which visitors can attend. The Singapore Tourist Board produces a brochure every year on festivals, with their precise dates, or check the STB's website, www.visitsingapore.com.

Jan

New Year's Day (**1 Jan**). Public holiday.
Chingay Parade (**late Jan**). Held from City Hall to Raffles Ave, the Singaporean version of Notting Hill Carnival, with floats, acrobats and live music. Tickets cost S$30-50.

Feb

Chinese New Year (movable). Public holiday. This 5-day lunar festival is celebrated in **Jan** or **Feb**. Each new year is given the name of an animal in a 12-year rotation and each has a special significance. The seasonal Mandarin catch-phrase is *Gong Xi Fa Chai* (Happy New Year).
Thaipusam (movable – in the Hindu month of Thai, usually **Feb**). In honour of the Hindu deity Lord Subramaniam, or Murgham, the son of Lord Siva. Held during the full moon in the month of Thai, it is a festival of penance and thanksgiving celebrated with a procession between Chettiar Temple on Tank Rd and Vinayagar Temple on Keong Saik Rd. The highlight of Thaipusam is the second day, when devotees assemble in their thousands at the Sri Perumal Temple on Serangoon Rd. Devotees pay homage to Lord Subramaniam by piercing their bodies, cheeks and tongues with sharp skewers (*vel*) and hooks, weighted with oranges and carrying steel structures bearing the image of Lord Subramaniam.
Hari Raya Haji (movable public holiday, falls on the 10th day of Zulhiah, the 12th month of the Muslim calendar). This festival honours Muslims who have made the pilgrimage to Mecca. The feast day is marked by prayers at mosques and the sacrificial slaughter of goats and buffalo for distribution to the poor as a sign of gratitude to Allah.
Jade Emperor's Birthday (movable). Crowds converge on the Giok Hong Tian Temple on Havelock Rd to celebrate the Jade Emperor's birthday. A Chinese opera is performed in the courtyard of the temple and lanterns are lit in the doorways of houses.
T'se Tien Tai Seng's (the Monkey God's) Birthday (movable – but celebrated twice a year, in **Feb** and **Oct**). Participants go into a trance and pierce their cheeks and tongues with skewers before handing out paper charms. Celebrated at the Monkey God Temple, Eng Hoon St, near Seng Poh market, Tiong Bahru Rd, South Chinatown.

Mar-Apr

Mosaic Music Festival (**mid-Mar**). An annual event since 2005, this 10-day festival (www.mosaicmusicfestival.com) brings together an eclectic mixture of artists from around the world playing a number of stages in and around the Esplanade. Artists in 2009 included the Indigo Girls, Brian McKnight, Electro Green and George Duke.
Kwan Yin's Birthday (movable). Chinese visit temples dedicated to the goddess of Mercy (like the one on Waterloo Rd). Childless couples come to pray for fertility.
Qing Ming (movable, **early Apr**). A Chinese ancestor-worship extravaganza in which family graves are spruced up and offerings of food and wine placed on tombs to appease their forebears' spirits.
Tamil New Year (movable, **Apr/May**). Begins at the start of the Hindu month of Chithirai. Pujas are held at main temples to honour Surya, the sun god. An almanac containing the Hindu horoscope is published at this time.
Easter (movable, Good Friday is a public holiday). Services are held in the island's churches. There is a candlelit procession in the grounds of St Joseph's Catholic Church, Victoria St.

May-Jun

Labour Day (1 May). Public holiday.

Great Singapore Sale (May-Jul). A nationwide event, with massive sales, super discounts on everything from jewellery to spa treatments as the city goes into consumerist summer overload. See www.greatsingaporesale.com.

Singapore Arts Festival (1 month **May-Jun**) Art, dance, theatre, live music and more from Asia and beyond. Held at various locations around the city (www.singaporeartsfest.com).

Vesak Day (movable – public holiday, usually in **May**, on the full moon of the 5th lunar month). Commemorates the Buddha's birth, death and enlightenment and is celebrated in Buddhist temples everywhere. Kong Meng San Phor Kark. See Temple in Bright Hill Drive and the Temple of a Thousand Lights in Race Course Rd are particularly lively. In Singapore celebrations begin before dawn, monks chant *sutras* (prayers) and lanterns and candles are lit to symbolize the Buddha's enlightenment.

Jul

Singapore Food Festival A month-long series of events encouraging visitors to eat even more. See www.singapore foodfestival.com.

Aug-Sep

Hari Raya Puasa or Aidil Fitri (movable – public holiday). Marks the end of Ramadan, the month of fasting for Muslims and is a day of celebration. Once the Muftis have confirmed the new moon of Syawal, the 10th Islamic month, Muslims don traditional clothing and spend the day praying in the mosques and visiting friends and family. During Ramadan, Muslims eat at stalls after dark; Geyland Serai and Bussorah St (near Arab St) are favourite *makan* stops, see page 603.

National Day (9 Aug, public holiday). To celebrate the Republic's independence in 1965. There's a military parade, air force fly-past and carnival procession around the Matrina Bay and Esplanade. If you want to get into the patriotic nature of things, wear red and white.

Festival of the Hungry Ghosts, Yu Lan Jie (movable, runs for 30 days after the last day

of the 6th moon). Banquets are given by stallholders, lavish feasts are laid out on the streets and there are roving bands of Chinese street opera singers, puppet shows and lotteries. Then there is the ritual burning of huge incense sticks and paper 'hell money' to appease the spirits, who are believed to wander around on earth for a month after the annual opening of the gates of hell.

Mooncake or Lantern Festival (movable – midway through the Chinese 8th moon). This Chinese festival commemorates the overthrow of the Mongul Dynasty in China. Children parade with elaborate candlelit lanterns and eat mooncakes filled with lotus seed paste. According to Chinese legend, secret messages of revolt were carried inside these cakes and led to the uprising that caused the overthrow of their oppressors. A gentler interpretation is that the round cakes represent the full moon, the end of the farming year and an abundant harvest, a bucolic symbolism that must be lost on most city-born Singaporeans.

Navarathri Festival (movable). 9 days of prayer (*navarathiri* means 9 lights), temple music and classical dance honour the consorts of Siva, Vishnu and Brahma (the Hindu trinity of Gods). Music and dance performances can be viewed at all Hindu temples from around 1930-2200 each night of the festival. The festival is celebrated notably at the Chettiar Temple on Tank Rd, ending with a procession on the 10th day along River Valley Rd, Killiney Rd, Orchard Rd, Clemenceau Av and returning to the temple.

Singapore Formula 1 Grand Prix (late Sep). The world's first ever Grand Prix night race is quite a spectacle with some dangerous-looking bends, a beautiful backdrop and deafening motor hum. The race takes place around Marina Bay and the Colonial Core. Hotels in this area are booked well in advance. Tickets from S$128 to S$1488, available online (www.singaporegp.sg).

Oct-Nov

Deepavali (movable – public holiday, usually in **Oct** or **Nov** in the Hindu month of Aipasi). The Hindu festival of lights commemorates the victory of Lord Krishna over the demon king Narakasura, symbolizing the victory of light over darkness and good over evil. Every Hindu home is brightly lit and decorated for the occasion. Shrines are swamped with offerings and altars piled high with flowers. Rows of little earthen oil lamps are lit to guide the souls of departed relatives in their journey back to the next world, after their brief annual visit to earth during Deepavali.

Thimithi Festival (movable, in the Hindu month of Aipasi). This Hindu festival, in honour of the goddess Draupadi, often draws a big crowd to watch devotees fulfil their vows by walking over a 3 m-long pit of burning coals in the courtyard of the Sri Mariamman Temple on South Bridge Rd. Fire walking starts at 1600.

Dec

Zouk Out (**Dec**, movable). All-night raving on the beach in Sentosa attracting over 20,000 usually restrained party beasts. See www.zoukout.com. Good selection of international DJs and the largest dance festival in Southeast Asia. Be warned that getting a taxi home from this event can take up to 2 hrs of queuing.

Christmas Day (**25 Dec**, public holiday). Christmas here is a spectacle of dazzling lights, the best along Orchard Rd, where trees are bejewelled with fairy lights. Shopping centres and hotels compete to have the year's most extravagant or creative display. These seasonal exhibitions are often conveniently designed to last through to Chinese New Year. It would not be untypical, for example, to find Santa riding on a man-eater in the year of the tiger. In shopping arcades, sweating tropical Santa Clauses dash through the fake snow. Choirs from Singapore's many churches line the sidewalks and Singaporeans go shopping.

Shopping → *See also listings, page 636.*

Singapore is a shopper's paradise. There is an endless variety of consumer goods and gimmicks. The choice seems almost unlimited, but don't be deluded that there are bargains galore with rock-bottom prices to match the variety. With the global economy in tatters, local shoppers seem to be spending their disposable income in other ways (or themselves go shopping abroad) and tourists no longer come with empty suitcases to stuff them full of goodies. Even the people who used to come here from places like Manila, Bangkok and Jakarta can buy just about everything at home and often cheaper. That said, there are some good buys, and sales can throw up the odd bargain.

Probably the best area for window shopping is around Scotts and Orchard roads (see page 636), where many of the big complexes and department stores are located. This area comes alive after dark and most shops stay open late. The towering Raffles City Complex, Bugis Junction, Suntec City, Marina Square and Vivo City are the other main shopping centres. Serangoon Road (or Little India), Arab Street and Chinatown offer a more exotic shopping experience with a range of 'ethnic' merchandise.

Singapore has all the latest electronic gadgetry and probably as wide a choice as you will find anywhere. It also has a big selection of antiques (although they tend to be overpriced), arts and crafts, jewellery, silks and batiks. For branded goods, Singapore is still marginally cheaper than most other places, but for Asian-produced products it is no longer the cheapest place in the region. Head to Sim Lim Square between Little India and Bugis, or the Funan Digitalife Mall at City Hall for the best selection of goods. Be prepared to bargain furiously at Sim Lim Square – the salesmen there are masters of the art.

Singapore Service Star has been set up by the Singapore Tourism Board, as a mark of quality assurance; shops who are members of the scheme display a sticker of a pink lotus.

Feel you've been unfairly ripped off? Then contact the **Small Claims Tribunal** ① *No 1 Havelock Sq, 1st level Subordinate Courts, Havelock Rd, T1800-736 2000*. There's a fast-track claims mechanism where visitors, after paying a S$10 fee, can have their cases against errant retailers heard, often within 24 hours.

Tips on buying

It doesn't take long to get the feel of where you can bargain and where you cannot. Department stores are fixed price, but most smaller outfits – even those in smart shopping complexes – can sometimes be talked into discounts. As ever, it is best not to buy at the first shop; compare prices and get an idea of what you should be paying from big department stores – **Tang's Department Store** on Orchard Road is a good measuring rod – that you can nearly always undercut. In ordinary shops, 20-30% can be knocked off the asking price, sometimes more. Keep smiling, joking and teasing when bargaining and never believe a shopkeeper who tells you they are giving you something at cost or is not making a profit. The golden rule is to keep a sense of humour. Bargaining occurs especially in Chinatown and you're in a strong negotiating position if you're the first customer of the day. The Chinese believe it is inauspicious for the first customer to leave their shop without buying something!

For big purchases, ask for an international guarantee (they're often extra), although sometimes you'll have to do with Singapore-only guarantees. Generally once goods are sold they are not returnable, unless faulty; make sure you keep your receipt. Deposits, not usually more than 50% of the value of the goods, are generally required when orders are placed for custom-made goods. Make sure electrical goods are compatible with the voltage back home.

Complaints about retailers (who sometimes exhibit aggressive tendencies when selling merchandise to tourists) can be registered at the **Consumers' Association of Singapore** ① *T6222 4165*. Or contact the **Retail Information Centre** ① *Block 528, Ang Mo Kio Ave 10, #02-2387, T6450 2114*.

Antiques Singapore's antique shops stock everything from opium beds, planters' chairs, gramophones, brass fans, porcelain, jade, Peranakan marble-top tables and 17th-century maps, to smuggled Burmese Buddhas, Sulawesian spirit statues and Dayak masks. There are few restrictions on bringing antiques into Singapore or exporting them. Many top antique shops are in Tanglin Shopping Centre, Orchard Road. The *Guide to Buying Antiques, Arts and Crafts in Singapore* by Anne Jones is recommended, available in most bookshops.

Art galleries With the arrival of both Christie's and Sotheby's and the increased interest in home decorating, art has taken on a new meaning for Singaporeans. For information on contemporary art shows, contact the **Art Galleries Association** ① *T6235 4113, www.agas.org.sg*, which represents the interests of 20 commercial galleries.

Batik and silk Malaysian and Indonesian batiks are sold by the metre or in sarong lengths. Arab Street and Serangoon Road are the best areas for batik and silk lengths; big department stores usually have batik ready-mades. Ready-made Chinese silk garments can be found all over Singapore in Chinese emporia. If you want silk without the hassle, at reasonable prices, big department stores (such as **Tang's** on Orchard Road) have good selections. **China Silk House** designers come up with new collections every month.

If you're travelling widely in Southeast Asia, Bangkok remains an excellent location for clothing bargains, with tailored silk garments available at a fraction of Singapore prices.

Cameras There are several places dedicated to electronics and they usually house camera shops. **Cathay Photo**, **Marina Square** and **Max Photo** on the third floor of Centrepoint (Orchard Road) or **Peninsula Plaza** (colonial core) provide a good range and advice.

Children Singapore is a great place to shop for children, from cheap knick-knacks in the markets of Little India or Chinatown, to the chi chi boutiques in the shopping malls. The best choice of children's clothes is to be found at **The Forum**, corner of Cuscaden and Orchard roads, where there are at least 20 shops selling children's clothes. Ngee Ann City, Marina Square and Suntec City also offer lots of choice.

Clothes Singapore boasts all the international designer labels as well as standard international high street chains. Many of the shops are strung out along Orchard Road, with the Paragon Shopping Centre having the largest selection of designer stores. There are now also quite a few shops in Vivo City, Raffles City, Marina Square and Suntec City. Designer fashion comes a bit cheaper in Singapore than other Southeast Asian capitals as no duty is levied. Locally designed clothes keep up with the catwalk and are reasonably priced. For exceptional value, slightly damaged clothes and factory seconds can be purchased from **Fashion Export**, which has branches in Tanglin Mall and in Holland Village, and **FOS**, which has branches in Holland Village, Millenia Walk and Specialist Shopping Centre.

Electronic goods Singapore has all the latest electronic equipment, hot from Japan at duty-free prices. Prices are still cheaper than in Europe, but can vary enormously. Check that items come with an international guarantee. The centres for electronic goods are Sim Lim Tower (corner of Jalan Besar, Little India) and Sim Lim Square (corner of Rochor Canal Road, south of Little India). The Japanese **Best Denki** stores are in most shopping centres or Singapore's **Harvey Norman** stores also offer a wide variety of electronic goods in a more conventional manner at competitive prices. The weekend newspapers often feature huge adverts detailing the weekend's big bargains.

Furniture Singapore now has a good range of old (or distressed) and new furniture. Antique furniture in varying states of decay can be found at Upper Paya Lebar Road, just north of Macpherson Road; **Chin Yi Antique House**, **Mansion Antique House** and **Tech Huat Antique House** can all be found here. **Just Anthony** is also on this road, south of Upper Serangoon Road; it sells antique and reproduction furniture. River Valley Road, just up from Tank Road, has several antique and second-hand furniture dealers. Reproduction antique furniture can also be found on Kelantan Lane.

Interior decorating There is now fantastic choice for kitting out your home, from small to large pieces, most of it imported from around the region (or further afield). Park Mall on Penang Road (parallel to Orchard Road) offers an eclectic mix of Asian-inspired furniture and lighting. Also **The John Erdos Gallery**, Kim Yam Road, at the corner of Moh'd Sultan Road, and **The Shophouse** in Gillman Village are popular choices for expats furnishing their homes.

Jewellery Gold (mostly Asian; 18, 22 or 24 carat), precious stones and pearls (freshwater and cultured) are all easily found in Singapore and good value. Styles and designs are quite different from the West. Gold is a good buy, but it too looks different. The Singapore Assay Office uses a merlion head as a hallmark. Most of the jewellery shops are in South Bridge Road, Chinatown and Little India. All the major shopping malls have jewellery shops.

Sports goods There are plenty of branded goods and one of the most popular choices is the **Royal Sporting House** in many of the malls. The Queensway shopping centre on Alexandra Road has a great selection of branded sports footwear at competitive prices.

Tailoring Quick, efficient and usually high-quality tailoring can be found in most shopping centres. The tailors in the main tourist shopping belt along Orchard and Scotts roads, notably **Far East Plaza** and **Lucky Plaza**, are as good a bet as any. You can design virtually what you want for yourself, but it is worth shopping around for the best deal. For more upmarket tailoring, hotel tailors are recommended.

Watches A huge range of watches are available at duty-free prices in most shopping centres. Copy watches do not officially exist in Singapore, where most people prefer the real thing. The government frequently takes steps to eliminate the trade in copies now often taking a hard line against the purchaser as well as the trader.

Wet markets The most accessible market of interest is the Zhujiao Market, also known as Tekka Market, on the corner of Bukit Timah and Serangoon roads, at the southern end of Little India. It is a hive of activity and sells everything from flowers to fish and meat to spices, and every conceivable vegetable and fruit. There's also a good hawker centre here. An excellent Sunday market is on Seng Poh Road, Tiong Bahru, between Tiong Bahru and Outram Park MRT stations, which is worth taking in if you go to see the singing birds. A good place to buy orchids is the small Holland Village wet market; it is much cheaper than the more touristy flower shops downtown and will pack them for shipment.

Esssentials A-Z

Accidents and emergencies
Police T999.
Ambulance/Fire T995.
Contact the relevant emergency service and your embassy (see page 640). Make sure that you obtain police/medical reports required for insurance claims.

Children
Singapore is one of the most child-friendly cities in Asia. It is clean and safe, there are good hospitals, you can drink the water, drivers take notice of pedestrian crossings, there's a very efficient transport system and lots of a/c refuges to cool off. Just bear in mind that if children are not used to the tropical heat it can be exhausting, so don't expect them to keep going for a full day, and make sure they are regularly topped up with fluids and coated in sun protection.

Singapore also has a number of swimming complexes, great for cooling off after a day in the heat. See also page 552 and www.travelforkids.com.

Customs and duty free
Singapore is a duty-free port. The duty-free allowance is 1 litre of liquor, 1 litre of wine and 1 litre of beer or stout provided you are not arriving from Malaysia, from where there is no duty-free allowance. Note that due to the government's strict anti-smoking policy, there is no duty-free allowance for tobacco.

There is no limit to the amount of Singapore and foreign currency or TCs you can bring in or take out.

There is no export duty, but export permits are required for arms, ammunition, explosives, animals, gold, platinum, precious stones and jewellery, poisons and drugs. No permit is needed for the export of antiques.

Visitors can claim back their 7% Goods and Services Tax (GST) from shops displaying the 'Tax Free for Tourists' sign when they spend S$100 or more. Ask for a Global Refund Cheque when you pay and this is then presented at customs on leaving the country, when visitors are reimbursed minus a handling fee. It is also possible to claim by post; the refund is paid either by bank cheque or to a credit card account. The Singapore Tourism Board publishes a brochure, *Tax refund for Visitors to Singapore*.

Narcotics are strictly forbidden in Singapore and, as in neighbouring Malaysia, trafficking is a capital offence which is rigorously enforced. Dawn hangings at Changi prison are regularly reported and Singapore has one of the highest execution rate per head of population in the world. Trafficking in more than 30 g of morphine or cocaine, 15 g of heroin, 500 g of cannabis or 200 g of cannabis resin, 250 g of ice (methamphetamine hydrochloride) and 1.2 kg of opium is punishable by death. Those convicted of lesser drug-related offences face 20-30 years in Changi prison and 15 strokes of the rotan, a punishment devised by the British colonial administration. Passengers arriving from Malaysia by rail may have to march, single-file, past sniffer dogs.

The Singapore government has banned the importation and sale of chewing gum, after the MRT Corporation claimed the substance threatened the efficient running of its underground trains. Chewing tobacco, toy currency, pornographic material and seditious literature are also prohibited items.

Disabled travellers

Singapore is the most wheelchair-friendly city in Southeast Asia. Singapore Medicine produces a brochure especially for physically impaired visitors. An online PDF version is at www1.singaporemedicine.com under 'Resources'. The guide lists taxi and van services designed for wheelchair use (public transport is not wheelchair friendly) and lists hotels with facilities for the disabled.

Electricity

220-240 volts, 50 cycle AC; most hotels can supply adapters.

Gay and lesbian travellers

Singapore is a pretty straight place. There are 2 clauses in Singapore's penal code that deal with homosexual sex, namely: Section 377: 'Whosoever voluntarily has carnal intercourse against the order of nature with any man, woman or animal, shall be punished with imprisonment for life, or with imprisonment for a term which may extend to 10 years, and shall also be liable to a fine'; and Section 377(a): 'Any male person who, in public or private, commits or abets the commission of or procures the commission by any male person of, any act of gross indecency with another male person, shall be punished with imprisonment for a term which may extend to 2 years'.

However, it is not illegal to be gay. The law only criminalizes the homosexual act.

And, despite the law and the city's surface conservatism, the government appears to be actively courting the pink dollar. This is based on the theory that encouraging a more cultured and creative environment that is tolerant of homosexuality will improve a city's economy. Ironically, one of the most closed states in Asia has the most vibrant gay scenes. There are plenty of openly gay and lesbian bars and clubs around town, a bloom of gay saunas, gay and lesbian film festivals and lots of gay-themed theatre. Look out for the rainbow flag which is often, but not always, hung outside a gay establishment. The best website for events and contacts is the Singapore-based www.fridae.com. Also check out www.plu.sg, set up by People Like Us (PLU), a lesbian and gay advocacy group, which has lots of background information on homosexuality in Singapore.

The hugely popular LGBT Nation parties that ran from 2001 to 2004 were cancelled by the Public Entertainment Licensing Unit, after police reportedly received complaints about same sex couples kissing and hugging. The nation party was moved to

Thailand in 2005, but only received about a tenth of the number of partygoers of the nation parties in Singapore.

Health

The water in Singapore, most of which is pumped across the causeway from Johor, Malaysia, and treated in Singapore, is clean and safe to drink straight from the tap.

Singapore's medical facilities are among the best in the world. See page 640 for a listing of medical facilities or see the *Yellow Pages* for all public and private hospitals.

Most big hotels have their own doctor on 24-hr call. Other doctors are listed under 'Medical Practitioners' in the *Yellow Pages*. Pharmaceuticals are readily available over the counter and registered pharmacists work 0900-1800.

Vaccinations Certificates of vaccination against cholera and yellow fever are necessary for those coming from endemic areas within the previous 6 days. Otherwise, no certificates are required for Singapore. There is no longer any malarial risk on the island, although sometimes there are outbreaks of dengue fever. Vaccination services are available at the Tan Tock Seng Hospital, see page 640.

Internet

Singapore is very well wired and there are loads of internet cafés; see page 640 . Most cafés and hotels routinely offer free Wi-Fi. It's often worth the price of a coffee.

Language

Malay is the national language of Singapore although the government recognizes 4 official languages: English, Mandarin,Tamil and Malay. Many of the Chinese community, particularly the older generation, speak their dialect group as their mother tongue. The most commonly spoken Chinese dialects in Singapore are Hokkien, Teochew, Hakka and Cantonese. Mandarin is becoming increasingly heard as the government pushes it at schools and Singapore continues to

accept waves of migrants from China. English – or rather Singlish – is spoken by almost everybody. Singlish is a love-it-or-loathe-it musical variant of English, which despite sharing 98% of its vocabulary with the Queen's tongue sounds remarkably different; sentences often end in 'lah' or 'leh' or 'meh'. Malay, Tamil and Hindi are also widely spoken by members of their respective ethnic groups. For an entertaining look at Singlish and its vocabulary see the following website: www.talkingcock.com and follow the links to the Coxford Singlish Dictionary.

For a list of Malay words and phrases, see page 654.

Media

The 2 main media organizations, Singapore Press Holdings and Mediacorp, merged their mass-market TV and free newspaper operations in late 2004, somewhat narrowing the choice for readers and viewers.

The press is privately owned and legally free, but is carefully monitored and strictly controlled. It runs on Confucianist principles – respect for one's elders – which translates as unwavering support of the government. In the past, papers that were judged to have overstepped their mark, such as the former *Singapore Herald*, were shut down. The *Straits Times* has been likened to Beijing's *People's Daily* for the degree to which it is a mouthpiece of the government.

The English-language daily **newspapers** are the *Straits Times* (www.straitstimes.com); the *Sunday Times*, which runs better foreign news pages than any other regional newspaper; the *Business Times* (www.businesstimes.com.sg); and the *New Paper* (www.newpaper.asia1.com.sg), Singapore's very own tabloid. The *Today* (www.today online.com) is a freebie, available Mon-Sat.

English-language **radio** stations are easy listening *Gold* (90.5FM), *Class* (95FM) for yuppies, *Perfect Ten* (98.7FM) for teens, *NewsRadio* (93.8FM), and *Symphony* (92.4FM) with classical offerings. *Radio Singapore*

International (6080KHZ shortwave) has English news broadcasts. *Lush* (99.5FM) has 24-hr chillout music including New Age and chilled beats. The *International Channel* (96.3FM) caters to French, German, Japanese and Korean expats. The *BBC World Service* broadcasts 24 hrs a day on 88.9FM. There are also local Chinese, Indian and Malay language stations. For an overview of radio stations, see www.mediacorpradio.sg.

English-language **TV** channels are *Channel 5*, which shows imported shows from the US, movies and homegrown light entertainment. Okto has a range of English-language TV shows, mostly imported from America. Okto Day caters mainly for kids, and Okto Nite has programmes with a more mature theme. *Channel News Asia* is a 24-hr news channel on the CNN model. Many hotels receive STARHUB cable TV which shows *HBO*, *StarTV*, *MTV*, *Discovery*, *CNN*, *BBC World* and *ESPN* among others. Programmes are listed in the daily newspapers.

Money
Currency
Local currency is dollars and cents. Bank notes are available in denominations of S$2, 5, 10, 20, 50, 100, 500, 1000 and 10,000. Coins are in 5, 10, 20 and 50 cent and 1 dollar denominations. In March 2010, the Singapore dollar was valued at S$1.40 to US$1, S$2.10 to £1 and S$0.42 to RM1. Brunei currency is interchangeable with Singapore currency.

Exchange
It is possible to change money at banks, licensed money changers and hotels, although a service charge may be added. Licensed money changers often give better rates than banks. Singapore is one of the most plastic-friendly countries in the region and there are ATMs (cash point machines), seemingly, on every street corner. Cash can be withdrawn using a credit or debit card. Singapore is a major regional banking centre, so it's relatively easy to get money wired from home. There is no black market.

Bank opening hours are Mon-Fri 0930-1500, Sat 0930-1130. Some banks do not offer foreign exchange dealings on Sat, although money changers operate throughout the week and for longer hours.

Most of Singapore's hotels, shops, restaurants and banks (and even some taxis) accept the major international **credit cards**, and many cash machines allow you to draw cash on Visa or MasterCard. Many banks charge set fees for withdrawing cash with cards so check before leaving home. However, you can often minimize these charges by taking more cash out per transaction and thus reducing the overall number of times you visit the cashpoint. Notification of credit card loss: American Express, T1800-732 2244; MasterCard, T800-110 0113; Visa, T800-110 0344.

Cost of living
Singapore is a thoroughly first world city. It is an expensive place to live, particularly when compared to its neighbours in Southeast Asia, but with wages more or less in line with costs, most Singaporeans enjoy a fairly high standard of living. The average monthly salary for a doctor is around S$8000, while a receptionist – one of the lowest paid jobs – earns around S$1500. While poverty still exists, it is hard to find as the government has systematically cleared slums and built housing estates offering low cost public flats.

Cost of travelling
Singapore is comparatively more expensive place than its neighbours in Southeast Asia. While accommodation and hotel rooms are pricey, and fine dining, cigarettes and alcohol will burn a hole in your pocket, no-frills food (which is still great) and transport are relatively cheap. You can feast at a hawker stall for around S$5 (although this is still twice the price of an equivalent slap-up meal in Malaysia). Transport is a bargain and there are plenty of attractions that can be enjoyed cheaply or for free.

Opening hours
Most shops in the tourist area open around 1030 and close at 2100. Sun is a normal working day around Orchard and Scotts rds.

Post
The main post office is the Singapore Post Centre at No 8, 10 Eunos Rd (take Paya Lebar MRT), Mon-Fri 0900-2100, Sat 0900-1800, and Sun 0900-1600. There are 1300 postal outlets. Post Office opening hours are Mon-Fri 0900-1700, Sat 0900-1400. A few open later. The Killiney Rd branch (just off Orchard Rd near Somerset MRT) opens Mon-Sat 0900-2100, Sun 0900-1700. The Changi Airport branch (departure hall, terminal 2), opens daily 0800-2100.

Local postal charges start at 26¢ (20 g). International postal charges are 50¢ (postcard), 50¢ (aerogramme), S$1.10 (letter, 20 g). For the latest charges see www.singpost.com.sg. The Singapore Post Office provides 5 sizes of sturdy carton, called Postpacs, for sending parcels abroad. **Note** AirAsia and Jetstar Asia flights can be booked and paid for at 20 post offices. There is a S$5 handling fee.

Safety
Singapore is probably the safest big city in Southeast Asia. Women travelling alone need have few worries. It is wise, however, to take the normal precautions and not wander in lonely places after dark.

Smoking
Smoking is discouraged and prohibited by law in many public places, such as buses, taxis, lifts, government offices, cinemas, theatres, libraries, department stores, shopping centres and all a/c restaurants. First offenders can be fined up to S$1000 for lighting up in prohibited places. Many hotels provide non-smoking floors.

Student travellers
Student travellers will find Singapore a generally expensive place, with no great savings on entrance fees or public transport.

Telephone
In public payphones the minimum charge is 10¢ for 3 mins. Card phones are quite widespread; cards can be bought in post offices, supermarkets and newsagents, and come in units of S$5, S$10, S$20 and S$50.

Singapore has 3 mobile phone networks (GSM and UMTS), and 3 mobile phone providers (SingTel, M1 and Starhub). Access codes are: SingTel, 001; for M1, 002; and Starhub, 008. Pre-paid SIM cards can be bought from money changers, 7-Elevens, and many other stores, starting at S$15.

International calls can be made from most public phones; phones take 50¢ and S$1 coins or phonecards. International Phone Home Cards are available at all post offices and come in units of S$10 and S$20. The most widely available card is Singtel's Worldcard, but there are many other brands which often have cheaper IDD rates. Credit card phones are also available. IDD calls made from hotels are free of any surcharge.

Singapore's IDD code is 65. For details on country codes, dial 162. Directory enquiries is T103.

Time
8 hrs ahead of GMT.

Tipping
Tipping is virtually non-existent and any attempt will be met with a bewildered stare. Most hotels and restaurants add 10% service charge and 5% government tax to bills. In general, only tip for special personal services.

Tourist information
The Singapore Tourism Board operates a Touristline number, T1800-736 2000 (24-hr toll-free information number with automated information in English, Mandarin, Japanese and German); T+65-67362000 if calling from overseas, or see www.visitsingapore.com.

It produces a good free official guide called the *Visitor's Guide to Singapore*. The main office is at Tourism Court, 1 Orchard Spring Lane (well signposted at the junction of Orchard and Cairnhill rds, MRT Orchard), open daily 0930-2230. It's crammed with useful city maps and brochures and the excellent staff are happy to help new arrivals book hotels, arrange itineraries and provide advice ranging from special events to newly opened bars and clubs. Recommended.

Other offices at: Liang Court Shopping Centre, 177 River Valley Road, Level 1, T6336 2888, daily 1000-2200, MRT Clarke Quay; Changi Airport, arrivals halls 1, 2 and 3, daily 0600-0200; The Galleria at Suntec City Mall, T6333825, daily 1000-1800, MRT City Hall and The InnCrowd Backpacker's Hostel, 73 Dunlop St, Little India, T6296 4280, daily 1000-2200, MRT Little India. All are good sources of brochures and maps. Complaints can also be registered at these offices.

The Indonesian Tourist Board can be contacted on T6737 7422. The Malaysian Tourist Board is at Ocean Building, 11 Collyer Quay, T6532 6351.

Below is a selection of websites. Note that websites in Asia are multiplying like rabbits and this makes searching a sometimes frustrating business.
www.asiatravel.com/singapore.html This is useful for hotel reservations, weather reports, the latest travel information and exchange rates, and has a map detailing sights.
www.singaporeexpats.com A portal geared at expats. Property for rent, entertainment listings, jobs and more.
www.singstat.gov.sg For the truly pedantic: a site devoted to statistics regarding Singapore.
www.straitstimes.com The website of Singapore's strait-laced English daily. To make the most of the site you must register; S$15 for a month. For more English-language newspaper websites, see page 572. The forums here are filled with surprisingly racist rants and offer a glimpse into the frustrations of life in modern multicultural Singapore.
www.streetdirectory.com Website featuring Singapore maps. Excellent navigation tool.
www.visitorsguide.com.sg Published by the city state's *Yellow Pages*,

www.yellowpages.com.sg, this website has tourist information and business contacts.

Visas and immigration
Visitors must possess a passport valid for at least 6 months, a confirmed onward/return ticket, sufficient funds to support themselves in Singapore and, where applicable, a visa. For all of the latest visa information, you should check www.ica.gov.sg.

No visa is required for citizens of the Commonwealth, USA or Western Europe. On arrival in Singapore by air, citizens of these countries are granted a 1 to 3 month visitor's permit. Tourists entering Singapore via the causeway from Johor Bahru in Malaysia or by sea are allowed to stay for 14 days. Nationals of most other countries (except India, China and the Commonwealth of Independent States) with confirmed onward reservations may stop over in Singapore for up to 14 days without a visa. It is necessary to keep the stub of your immigration card until you leave.

Visas can be extended for up to 3 months either online (if you meet certain conditions, such as this being your first extension) at the website above. Or visit the Visitor Services Centre, 4th floor, ICA building 10 Kallang Rd, next to Lavender MRT, T63916100, Mon-Fri 0800-1700, Sat 0800-1300. Application takes around a day and costs S$40. It can be just as easy to nip across the causeway to Johor Bahru (in Malaysia) and then re-enter Singapore on a 2-week permit.

Weights and measures
The metric system is used.

Women travellers
Singapore is safe and it's rare for women to be harassed. Unlike some neighbouring countries, it's not seen as strange for young women to travel alone. Apart from entering temples, there's no conservative dress code. It's not unusual to see local women wear fairly revealing clothes (for Asia). See also Safety, page 574.

Sights

The city's main attraction, particularly for Asian tourists, is its shopping. For air-conditioned malls head to Orchard Road, while the more aromatic market bargaining experience can be found at stalls in Little India, Chinatown and Arab Street. The city state's colonial core stretches from the world-famous Raffles Hotel to stately government and court buildings near the river. The river itself is lined with restaurants, bars and leafy walkways. For fun day trips, head west of the city for Jurong Bird Park and Japanese gardens and north to the zoo and the night safari. South of the centre, Sentosa Island is linked to the mainland by a cable car and offers beaches, an oceanarium, a fun park, musical fountain and Southeast Asia's first luge ride. ▶▶ *For listings, see pages 616-640.*

Colonial core

Situated to the north of the Singapore River, the colonial core is bordered to the northeast by Rochor Road and Rochor Canal Road, to the northwest by Selegie Road and Canning Hill, and to the southeast by the sea. The area is small enough to walk around – just. To walk from the Singapore Art Museum in the far northwest corner of this area to the mouth of the Singapore River shouldn't take more than 30 minutes. You may want to take a cab to get over to Fort Canning Park if it is a particularly hot and humid day.

The Padang

The Padang (playing field in Malay), the site of most big sporting and other events in Singapore – including the National Day parades – is at the centre of the colonial area. Many of the great events in Singapore's short history have been played out within sight or sound of the Padang. It was close to here that Stamford Raffles first set foot on the island on the morning of 28 January 1819, where the Japanese surrendered to Lord Louis Mountbatten on 12 September 1945, and where Lee Kuan Yew, the first prime minister of the city state, declared the country independent in 1959.

The Padang originally fronted on to the sea, but due to land reclamation now stands 1 km inland. After the founding of Singapore in 1819, English and Indian troops were quartered here and the area was known as The Plain. The name was only later changed to Padang. In 1942, when Singapore fell to the invading Japanese, all the European population of the colony were massed on the Padang before the troops were marched away to prisoner-of-war camps, some to camps in Malaya and Siam (where they helped to build the infamous Bridge over the River Kwai), others to Changi (see page 611). The **Cricket Club**, at the end of the Padang, was the focus of British activity. A sports pavilion was first constructed in 1850 and a larger Victorian clubhouse was built in 1884 with two levels, the upper level being the ladies' viewing gallery. The **Singapore Recreation Club** (the SRC) building, at the northern end of the Padang, has been built on the site of a former club built in 1883 by the Eurasian community, who were excluded from the Cricket Club. The building is a modern, green-glass affair with polished brown columns: a nouveau antidote to the venerable Cricket Club at the other end of the Padang. In 1963 the club lifted its membership restrictions and fewer than a fifth are now Eurasian.

Flanking the Padang are the houses of justice and government: the domed **Supreme Court** (formerly the Hotel de l'Europe) and the City Hall. The neo-classical **City Hall** ① *enter via the lower entrance at the front, hearings usually start at 1000 and the public are* *allowed to sit at the back and hear cases in session*, was built with Indian convict labour for a trifling S$2m and was finished in 1929. The Japanese surrendered here to Lord Louis Mountbatten and on the same spot, Lee Kuan Yew declared Singapore's independence. Today it contains law courts – the overflow from the Supreme Court next door.

On the seaward side of the Padang from the City Hall is **Tan Kim Seng's Fountain**. Along the base the following words are inscribed: "This fountain is erected by the municipal commissioners in commemoration of Mr Tan Kim Seng's donation towards the cost of the Singapore Water Works". This tells only part of the story for the fountain is a remnant of pristine Singapore's filthy past. Mr Tan, a prosperous Straits Chinese, made a gift of S$13,000 in 1857 to finance the island's first municipal water works on the condition that the water be available to all, free of charge. At the time it was just beginning to be recognized that Singapore's appallingly high mortality rate – which was higher than the island's birth rate (only immigration kept the population growing) – was linked to dirty water. Unfortunately, the terms of Mr Tan's gift were not adhered to; indeed, some people suggest that money was, so to speak, siphoned off for some other nefarious purpose. Certainly, it was not for another 60 years that mortality rates declined significantly, especially among Singapore's Chinese, Indian and Malay communities. Perhaps the city fathers erected this fountain when their guilt got the better of them.

Esplanade and the river

Stretching right along the seafront, looking like a pair of giant metal durians, is **Esplanade – Theatres on the Bay** ① *T6828 8377, ticket sales T6348 5555, www.esplanade.com; walk along the underground shopping centre of CityLink Mall (from City Hall MRT)*, the centre of Singapore's performing arts scene, completed in 2002. Within the durians there's a 1800-seater concert hall, a 2000-seat theatre, and various outdoor performing spaces and, of course, a shopping plaza. After a shaky start the theatres are increasingly attracting world-class performances, with luminaries such Ian McKellen as King Lear for the RSC in 2007, plus epic musicals and resurgent, newly hip local theatre adding to the diverse line-up. The annual Mosaic Music Festival is held here.

Located a 20-minute walk from the Esplanade along Raffles Avenue is one of Singapore's newer attractions, the **Singapore Flyer** ① *30 Raffles Ave, T6738 3338, www.singaporeflyer.com.sg, S$29.50, children S$20.65, daily 0800-2200, shuttle bus every 30 mins from City Hall MRT*. This rotating wheel, similiar to the London Eye, stands at 165 m above sea level and is currently the largest Ferris wheel on Earth. The ride offers outstanding views over the city, the busy shipping lanes and the islands of Indonesia's Riau province beyond. Rides last 30 minutes and the capsules are filled with mellow beats. The Flyer has had many problems since opening with financial troubles (locals claim it is too expensive) and five breakdowns including the dramatic incident in 2008 when a short circuit caused the wheel to stop, trapping 173 passengers for six hours.

Between High Street and Singapore River there are a number of architectural legacies of the colonial period: Old Parliament House, the Victoria Theatre, and Empress Place. It was in this area that the Temenggongs, the former Malay rulers of Singapore, built their kampong; the royal family was later persuaded to move out to Telok Blangah. The **Victoria Theatre** was originally built as the Town Hall in 1856, but was later adapted by Swan and Maclaren to celebrate Queen Victoria's jubilee, integrating a new hall (the Memorial Hall) and linking the two with a central clocktower. During the Japanese Occupation the clock, like those in other occupied countries, was set to Tokyo time. The buildings are still venues for Singapore's multi-cultural dance, drama and musical

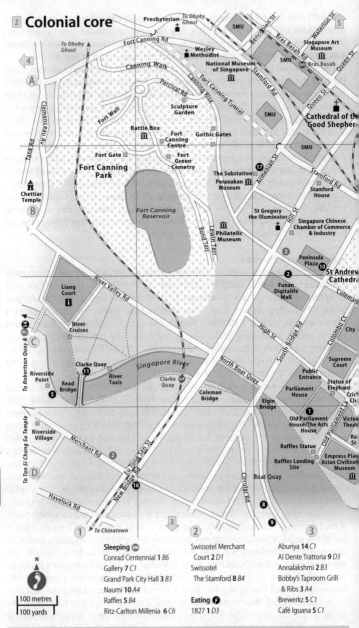

Colonial core

To Dhoby Ghaut

Presbyterian

Fort Canning Rd

SMU

Bras Basah St

Waterloo St

SMU

Singapore Art Museum

Wesley Methodist

National Museum of Singapore

Stamford Rd

SMU

Queen St

Canning Walk

Bras Basah

Queen St

Percival Rd

Canning Rise

Fort Canning Tunnel

SMU

Cathedral of the Good Shepher

Sculpture Garden

Fort Wall

Battle Box

Fort Canning Centre

Gothic Gates

The Substation

Armenian St

Stamford Rd

Fort Gate

Fort Green Cemetery

Peranakan Museum

Stamford House

Fort Canning Park

St Gregory the Illuminator

Hill St

Singapore Chinese Chamber of Commerce & Industry

Chettiar Temple

Philatelic Museum

Lewin Terr

Band Terr

Peninsula Plaza

St Andre Cathedr

Fort Canning Reservoir

Clemenceau Av

Tank Rd

River Valley Rd

Funan Digitalife Mall

Coleman

Liang Court

High St

South Bridge Rd

Colombo Ct

City

River Cruises

Supreme Court

To Robertson Quay &

Clarke Quay

River Taxis

Singapore River

North Boat Quay

Public Entrance

Statue of Elephant

Cric Clu

Read Bridge

Clarke Quay

Coleman Bridge

Parliament House

Riverside Point

Elgin Bridge

Old Parliament House/The Arts House

Victo Thea

Riverside Village

Merchant Rd

Eu Tong Sen St

Raffles Statue

Ra St

To Tan Si Chong Su Temple

Raffles Landing Site

Empress Plac Asian Civiliza Museum

New Bridge Rd

Havelock Rd

Circular Rd

Boat Quay

To Chinatown

Boat Quay

Sleeping

Conrad Centennial **1** *B6*
Gallery **7** *C1*
Grand Park City Hall **3** *B3*
Naumi **10** *A4*
Raffles **5** *B4*
Ritz-Carlton Millenia **6** *C6*

Swissotel Merchant Court **2** *D1*
Swissotel The Stamford **8** *B4*

Eating

1827 **1** *D3*

Aburiya **14** *C1*
Al Dente Trattoria **9** *D3*
Annalakshmi **2** *B3*
Bobby's Taproom Grill & Ribs **3** *A4*
Brewerkz **5** *C1*
Café Iguana **5** *C1*

100 metres
100 yards

N

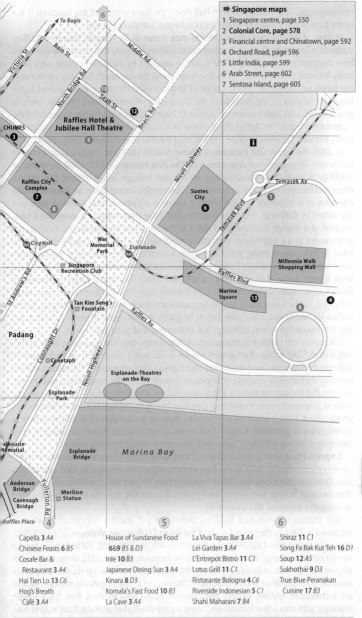

➡ **Singapore maps**

1 Singapore centre, page 550
2 **Colonial Core, page 578**
3 Financial centre and Chinatown, page 592
4 Orchard Road, page 596
5 Little India, page 599
6 Arab Street, page 602
7 Sentosa Island, page 605

To Bugis

Victoria St

Bain St

Middle Rd

North Bridge Rd

Seah St

CHIJMES

Raffles Hotel & Jubilee Hall Theatre

Beach Rd

Nicoll Highway

Temasek Av

Raffles City Complex

Suntec City

City Hall

War Memorial Park

Esplanade

Singapore Recreation Club

Millennia Walk Shopping Mall

Raffles Blvd

St Andrew's Rd

Tan Kim Seng's Fountain

Raffles Av

Temasek Blvd

Padang

Connaught Dr

Cenotaph

Nicoll Highway

Marina Square

Esplanade Park

Esplanade-Theatres on the Bay

Dalhousie Memorial

Esplanade Bridge

Marina Bay

Anderson Bridge

Cavenagh Bridge

Fullerton Rd

Merlion Statue

Raffles Place

④

Capella 3 *A4*
Chinese Feasts 6 *B5*
Cosafe Bar &
  Restaurant 3 *A4*
Hai Tien Lo 13 *C6*
Hog's Breath
  Café 3 *A4*

⑤

House of Sundanese Food
  6&9 *B5 & D3*
Inle 10 *B3*
Japanese Dining Sun 3 *A4*
Kinara 8 *D3*
Komala's Fast Food 10 *B3*
La Cave 3 *A4*

La Viva Tapas Bar 3 *A4*
Lei Garden 3 *A4*
L'Entrepot Bistro 11 *C1*
Lotus Grill 11 *C1*
Ristorante Bologna 4 *C6*
Riverside Indonesian 5 *C1*
Shahi Maharani 7 *B4*

⑥

Shiraz 11 *C1*
Song Fa Bak Kut Teh 16 *D1*
Soup 12 *A5*
Sukhothai 9 *D3*
True Blue Peranakan
  Cuisine 17 *B3*

extravaganzas. The Victoria Concert Hall (the right-hand section of the building) is the home base of the Singapore Symphony Orchestra. See also page 635.

In front of the theatre is the original **bronze statue of Sir Thomas Stamford Raffles**, sculpted in bronze by Thomas Woolner in 1887. There is a story that the statue was saved from destruction at the hands of the invading Japanese by a cunning curator, who hid it away. It seems, however, that the truth is more banal: the colonnade formerly surrounding the statue was destroyed during the fall of Singapore and the statue was removed to the National Museum for the duration of the Occupation. When Lee Kuan Yew first came to power in 1965, his Dutch economic adviser Dr Albert Winsemius told him to get rid of the Communists but to "let Raffles stand where he is today. Say publicly that you accept the heavy ties with the West because you will need them in your economic programme".

In 2003 the former **Old Parliament House**, built in 1827 and the oldest government building in Singapore, was converted into **The Arts House** ⓘ *T6332 6900, ticket hotline T6332 6919, www.theartshouse.com.sg*, an arts and heritage venue hosting film, drama, music and literary events and art exhibitions. Designed by George Coleman, it was originally intended as a residence for the wealthy Javanese merchant John Maxwell, who was appointed by Raffles as one of Singapore's first three magistrates. He never lived here, because of a dispute over the legal rights to the land, and he later leased it out to the government as a Court House. With the construction of a Supreme Court in St Andrews Road in 1939, the building stood empty for a decade, before becoming the Assembly Rooms in the 1950s and later Parliament House. Just to the north of Parliament House is a small bronze statue of an **elephant** – a gift from Siam's (Thailand's) King Chulalongkorn, Rama V, who visited Singapore in 1871. (At the time, King Chulalongkorn was itching to get to Europe, but he had to make do with Singapore and one or two other colonial possessions in Asia. He had to wait a few years before he got to the real centre of *siwilai* – civilization.) The Arts House has a shop, café and Thai, Vietnamese and pizza restaurants.

Old Parliament House became too small to accommodate the expanding body of MPs and a new S$80 million **Parliament House** ⓘ *the public entrance is on Parliament Pl, opposite the Supreme Court, www.parliament.gov.sg*, was opened in 1999 next to the old building. Parliamentary debate in Singapore is modelled on the Westminster system and, as in the Old Parliament, there is a Strangers' Gallery where the public – and visitors – can witness Singapore's version of democracy in action. In an attempt to educate Singapore's youth about their parliamentary system, there is a soundproofed gallery where a commentary is provided, a Moot Parliament where schoolchildren can sharpen their debating skills and a History Corner with interactive computer programmes.

Empress Place, on the river and near to the Old Parliament, was one of Singapore's first conservation projects. Built as the East India Company courthouse in 1865 and named after Queen Victoria, Empress of the Empire, it later housed the legislative assembly and then became, in turn, part of the immigration department, the offices of other assorted government agencies, and a museum.

This thoroughly confused building underwent yet another reincarnation when it reopened in 2003 as the second wing of the **Asian Civilisations Museum** ⓘ *T6332 2982, www.acm.org.sg, Mon 1300-1900, Tue-Sun 0900-1900, Fri 0900-2100, S$8 (admission fees for various exhibitions vary), joint ticket for ACM and Pernakan Museum S$12, under 6s free, over 60s free entry on Mon, reduced entry fee Fri 1900-2100*. As its name suggests, the focus of the museum is Asian culture and civilization – 5000 years of it. The 11 galleries explore religion, art, architecture, textiles, writing and ceramics from China to West Asia. It's a superb museum, with interactive features and some superb displays of artefacts from around Asia.

24 hours in Singapore

After a dawn stroll along the beach at the East Coast Park head to Still Road for a breakfast of half boiled eggs and toast washed down with sweet tea at a *kopitiam*. Take some time to wander around Katong and enjoy the beautiful architecture of the shophouses. Shoppers will want to head smartly over to Orchard Road and pick from a selection of Singapore's finest malls including Ion, Ngee Ann City and Wisma Atria, great for window shopping, people-watching and credit-card crunching.

End your shopping spree with a gentle walk around the **Botanic Gardens**. Hop across the river to **Chinatown** for a tour of Singapore's backbone Chinese community, with its traditional medicine shops, funeral stores, antique shops and shuttered traders' homes, now beautifully restored. On nearby Neil Road, enjoy a delicate Chinese brew at the **Tea Chapter**.

It's a few stops on the MRT line to **Little India**, whose muddle of streets are packed with astrologers, tailors, spice sellers, gaudy jewellers, stalls of sequinned fabrics, thumping Bollywood DVD stores and vendors of Hindu paraphernalia.

As dusk falls head to the **Singapore Flyer** for superlative sunset views over the city before moving on to the **Singapore River**, to enjoy a cocktail followed by dinner at one of the waterside restaurants.

Dinner does not spell the end of the night, however. Take a taxi to Singapore's **Night Safari** for a tour of the zoo in the dark – complete with roaring lions and flapping bats.

The city has tried hard to pump life into its party scene, to some success. If you feel like dancing and you have the cash, head to **Zouk**, **New Asia Bar** or **The Butter Factory** – all very cool spots that attract the glam set.

On your way home, chat to your taxi driver, who, in perfect Singlish, will no doubt extol the virtues of his clean, ordered city.

This is a good place to get an overall view of Singapore and its history within the regional framework. Guided tours are available in many languages; tours in English depart on Monday at 1400, Tuesday-Friday 1100 and 1400 and Saturday and Sunday at 1330. Check the website for tours in other languages and details of special guided tours.

In front of Empress Place stands the **Dalhousie Memorial**, an obelisk erected in honour of Lord James Dalhousie, governor-general of India, who visited Singapore for three days in 1850. He is credited on the plaque as having emphatically recognized the wisdom of liberating commerce from all restraints.

Raffles Hotel

ⓘ *1 Beach Rd, City Hall MRT, www.singapore.raffles.com, museum daily 1000-1800, free.*
The iconic Raffles Hotel – with its 875 designer-uniformed staff (a ratio of two staff to every guest) and 104 suites (each fitted with Persian carpets), eight restaurants (and a Culinary Academy), five bars, playhouse and custom-built, leather-upholstered cabs – is the jewel in the crown of Singapore's tourist industry. Founded by four Armenian brothers, the Sarkies, the hotel has seen it all, barely surviving the Great Depression of the 1930s, and was the venue for a mass suicide of over 300 Japanese soldiers at the end of the Second World War. It was used as a transit camp for prisoners of war, and has played host to notables such as Queen Elizabeth II, Charlie Chaplin, Elizabeth Taylor, Michael Jackson and Noel Coward. The hotel was fully renovated in the late 80s and is now a fixture on the tourist trail, with visitors

indulging in Singapore Slings in the Long Bar. In true Singapore style, it has a 5000 sq m shopping arcade and there's even a museum of Rafflesian memorabilia on the third floor. The museum has a beautiful collection of early guidebooks, tickets, party photos, evening gowns and signed pictures of notable guests. A visit is highly recommended. Next to the museum is the **Jubilee Hall Theatre**, named after the old Jubilee Theatre that was demolished to make way for the Raffles extension (see below).

Raffles Hotel's original (but restored) billiard table today stands in the Billiard Room. It is claimed that the last tiger ever shot in Singapore met its end under the billiard table here in 1902, having escaped from a show. Palm Court is also still there and as is the Tiffin Room, which unsurprisingly serves tiffin (a snack or lunch). Teams of restoration consultants undertook painstaking research into the original colours of paint, ornate plasterwork and fittings. A replica of the cast-iron portico, known as cad's alley, was built to the original 19th-century specifications of a Glasgow foundry.

There has been a vigorous debate over whether or not in the process of its lavish restoration Raffles has lost some of its atmosphere and appeal. There is no doubt that it has been done well; architecturally it can hardly be faulted and the lawns and courtyards are lush with foliage. It's also clearly an immensely comfortable and well-run hotel, but critics say they've tried a little too hard.

Cathedrals and churches

South of Raffles lies **St Andrew's Cathedral** ① *T6337 6104, several daily services in different languages (see the noticeboard in the northwest corner of the plot for times),* designed by Colonel Ronald MacPherson and built in the 1850s by Indian (Tamil) convict labourers in early neo-gothic style. Its interior walls are coated with a plaster called Madras chunam, a decorative innovation devised by the Indian labourers to conceal the deficiencies of the building materials. The recipe for Madras chunam was egg white, egg shell, lime and a coarse sugar (called jaggery), mixed with coconut husks and water into a paste. Once the paste had hardened, it was polished and then moulded to give many buildings their ornate façades. Note the window commemorating Raffles as the founder of modern Singapore. The cathedral is often packed; 7% of Singapore's population over 15 are Christian. There's a visitor centre with pictures and artefacts and there are daily guided tours.

Built in 1835 (the spire was added in 1850), the **Armenian Church of St Gregory the Illuminator** (the first monk of the Armenian church), on Hill Street, is the island's oldest church and was designed by Irish architect George Coleman. This diminutive church seats 50 people at a squeeze. The construction of the church was largely funded by Singapore's small Armenian community, although a number of non-Christian Asians also contributed. Agnes Joaquim is buried here – she discovered what is now the national flower of Singapore, the Vanda Miss Joaquim orchid. On the other side of the road from the church is a strange pagoda-roofed block – the **Singapore Chinese Chamber of Commerce & Industry** building. This rather unhappy edifice was erected in 1964. Two stone lions imported from mainland China guard the entrance and the murals on either side of the gate are copies of similar murals in Beijing.

One of George Coleman's pupils, Denis McSwiney, designed the **Roman Catholic Cathedral of the Good Shepherd**, on the junction of Queen Street and Bras Basah Road. It was used as an emergency hospital during the Second World War. The building has been gazetted as a national monument.

CHIJMES or the **Convent of Holy Infant Jesus**, opposite the Cathedral on Victoria Street, is a complex consisting of the convent, chapel and **Caldwell House** (designed by

George Coleman). It has been redeveloped by a French architect into a sophisticated courtyard of handicraft shops, as well as bars and restaurants. Originally, the convent was run by four French Catholic nuns, opening its doors to 14 fee-paying pupils, nine boarders and 16 orphans in 1854. As well as being an orphanage and school for older girls, the convent became a home for abandoned babies, who were often left at the gates of the convent at the point of death. The gothic-style church, designed by French Jesuit priest Father Beurel, was added at the turn of the 20th century. The church is now used for concerts and wedding ceremonies (and photo opportunities). Even the stained glass was painstakingly dismantled and renovated to a high standard.

Armenian Street to Coleman Street

On Armenian Street, close to Stamford Road, is a restored school. Tao Nan School was built in 1910 and became one of the first Chinese schools in Singapore. It has been taken over by the Singapore Museums Department and in 1997 opened as the first branch of the Asian Civilisations Museum. The **Peranakan Museum** ① *39 Armenian St, T6332 7591, www.peranakanmuseum.sg, Mon 1300-1900, Tue-Sun 0900-1900, Fri 0900-2100, S$6, joint ticket Perenakan Museum and ACM $12, free entry Fri 0900-2100*, has exhibits describing Peranakan life in the Straits Chinese-dominated cities of Singapore, Melaka and Penang. The Perenakans or Straits Chinese have been one of the region's most important cultures, coming about through centuries of intermarriage between Malays and Chinese. The clothes, food and arts are a wonderful fusion of colours and tastes with gorgeous ceramics, tasty fusion-style cooking and bright fashion.

Almost next door to the museum is **The Substation** ① *45 Armenian St, T6337 7535, www.substation.org*, an offbeat cinema that also mounts small art exhibitions.

Nearby, the **Singapore Philatelic Museum** ① *23B Coleman St, T6337 3888, www.spm.org.sg, Mon 1300-1900, Tue-Sun 0900-1900, S$5, 3-12 year-olds S$4, 10-min walk from City Hall MRT station*, is a small but extremely well-run museum and is not just of interest to philatophiles. It shows the history of Singapore's – and, more widely, the world's – postal system. Children (or adults for that matter) can design their own stamps and print them out, use touch-screen computers to test their knowledge of philately, tackle puzzles or just admire the collection of stamps and envelopes. There is a good 'Room of Rarities' gallery, which uses stamps to recount aspects of Singapore's history.

Singapore Art Museum

① *71 Bras Basah Rd, T6332 3222, www.nhb.gov.sg/SAM, Sat-Thu 1000-1900, Fri 1000-2100, S$8, students (with card) and senior citizens S$4, free for under 6s, free Fri 1800-2100, 10-min walk from Dhoby Ghaut or City Hall MRT stations.*

Built in 1867, the former Catholic boys' school, St Joseph's Institution, opposite the RC Cathedral, is a good example of colonial religious architecture and is now home to the Singapore Art Museum. There are travelling exhibitions every month or so, both modern and classical. The Singapore Art Museum's own collection is modest and, understandably, predominantly features Singaporean and Malaysian artists' work. There are always pieces from the collection on show providing an interesting insight into how Singaporean and Malaysian artists have selectively absorbed Western and Eastern influences.

While St Joseph's was being renovated, a feature wall was discovered behind a row of built-in cupboards. Two supporting columns bear an entablature emblazoned with the words *Santa Joseph Ora Pro Nobis* (Saint Joseph Pray For Us) and it is presumed that the school chapel was located here.

Bras Basah Road was so-called because wet rice – *bras basah* in Malay – was dried here on the banks of the Sungai Bras Basah (now Stamford Canal).

National Museum of Singapore

ⓘ *93 Stamford Rd, T6332 3659, www.nationalmuseum.sg, daily 1000-2000 (History Gallery), 1000-2000 (Living Galleries), S$10, children S$5, free admission 1800-2000 (Living Galleries only), Dhoby Ghaut MRT.*

A beautiful colonial structure originally built in 1887, the museum sits handsomely at the meeting point of Orchard Road, Bencoolen Street and Fort Canning Park and makes for a fascinating visit. One of Asia's finest museums, this shouldn't be missed. It provides an insight into a city that is a fusion of a fascinating, surprisingly brutal history and state-of-the-art technology and both of these aspects are beautifully encapsulated in this hi-tech renovation. At the Stamford Road entrance beneath the elegant glass dome, visitors are given an audiovisual guide. In the History Gallery, Singapore's past is covered from its 14th-century beginnings through the colonial years, the Second World War, to Independence and life as commercial superpower. What makes this so effective is its seamless multimedia execution, combining dramatic recreations of events, historical footage, memoirs and interviews with well-presented artefacts. Allow three to four hours to do the museum justice. Upstairs in the Living Galleries are displays of Singapore's 'living' culture, exploring Singapore through its food, photography and fashion. Singaporean and world cinema screenings are also held (some on the lawn outside). Downstairs – and it wouldn't be Singapore without it – are an array of shops and mouthwatering, if pricey, eateries.

Fort Canning Park

Behind the National Museum of Singapore is Fort Canning Park. The British called it Singapore Hill, but its history stretches back centuries earlier. It is known as Bukit Larangan, or Forbidden Hill, by the Malays, as this was the site of the ancient fortress of the Malay kings and reputedly contains the tomb of the last Malay ruler of the kingdom of Singapura, Sultan Iskandar Shah. Archaeological excavations in the area have uncovered remains from the days of the Majapahit Empire. It is thought that the palace was built in the early 14th century and then abandoned in 1396 in the wake of Siamese (Thai) and Majapahit (Javanese) attacks. Furthermore, when Raffles and his companions landed in 1819, it is said that Malay oral history still recalled the former 14th-century palace and its sultans and would not accompany the British up the hill for fear of the spirits. In a letter written to Sir William Marsden at the time of his first landing on Singapore, Raffles mentions the ruins of the Malay fortress. The name Canning Hill was given to this slight geological protuberance in the 1860s in honour of the first Viceroy of India, Viscount George Canning.

Over the last few years Canning Hill has evolved into something a little more ambitious than just a park. The **Battle Box** ⓘ *T6333 0510, www.legendsfortcanning.com, daily 1000-1800, last admission 1700, S$8, under 12s S$5, Dhoby Ghaut MRT,* opened in 1997, is a museum contained within the bunker where General Percival directed the unsuccessful campaign against the invading Japanese in 1942. Visitors are first shown a 15-minute video recounting the events that led up to the capture of Singapore. They are then led into the Malaya Command headquarters – the Battle Box – where the events of the final historic day, 15 February 1942, are re-enacted. Visitors are given earphones and are then taken from the radio room, to the cipher rooms and on to the command room, before arriving at the bunker where Percival gathered his senior commanders for their final, fateful, meeting. It is very well done with a good commentary, figures and film. The bunker is also air conditioned, a big plus after the hot walk up. During the Second World War, though, it was stiflingly hot – air was inefficiently re-circulated in case of gas attack. There is also a small traditional museum and a souvenir shop.

Above the Battle Box are the **ruins of Fort Canning**; the Gothic gateway, derelict guardhouse and earthworks are all that remain of a fort which once covered 3 ha. There are now some 40 modern sculptures here. Below the sculpture garden to the south is the renovated **Fort Canning Centre** (built 1926), home venue of Theatre Works and the Singapore Dance Theatre. In front of Fort Canning Centre is an old Christian cemetery, **Fort Green**, where the first settlers, including the architect George Coleman, are buried.

The graves of these early settlers have been exhumed. Along with George Coleman, there was a Russian and, unusually, a Chinese – for this was a Christian burial ground – and it may indicate an early convert to Christianity. While Sir Stamford Raffles may have lived here, he did not die here. He fell out with the East India Company, and died of a presumed brain tumour the day before his 45th birthday. His funeral in North London went unnoticed by London society and it was only later that he was reburied in Westminster Abbey.

Chettiar Temple

ⓘ *T6737 9393, www.sttemple.com, many Hindu temples close in the heat of the day, so are best seen before 1100 and after 1500, 5 mins' walk from Dhoby Ghaut MRT.*

Below Canning Hill, on Clemenceau Avenue, is the Hindu **Chettiar Temple**, also known as the **Sri Thendayuthapani Temple**. The original temple on this site was built in the 19th century by wealthy Chettiar Indians (money lending caste). It has been superseded by a modern version, finished in 1984, and is dedicated to Lord Subramaniam (also known as Lord Muruga). The ceiling has 48 painted glass panels, angled to reflect sunset and sunrise. Its gopuram, the five-tiered entrance, aisles, columns and hall all sport rich sculptures depicting Hindu deities, carved by sculptors trained in Madras. This Hindu temple is the richest in Singapore – some argue, in all of Southeast Asia. Thousands flock here to witness the spectacular Kavadi procession of the Thaipusam festival (see page 31).

Singapore River and the City

The mouth of the river is marked by the bizarre symbol of Singapore: the grotesque Merlion statue, a lion's head on a fish's body. The financial heart of the city is just south of here; tall towers cast shadows on streets which on weekdays are a frenzy of suited traders, bankers and office workers. The most pleasant area is along the river, which offers peaceful walks along its banks. The riverside is dotted with restaurants and bars making it a lively place at night.

Merlion

Standing guard at the mouth of the **Singapore River** – though rather dwarfed now by the Esplanade bridge – is the mythical Merlion, half-lion, half-fish, the grotesque saturnine symbol of Singapore. The statue was sculpted by local artist Lim Nang Seng in 1972 and stands in the miniscule **Merlion Park**, an unaccountably popular stop for tour groups, where there is a souvenir shop which is sometimes rather ambitiously billed a museum. It is inspired by the two ancient (Sanskrit) names for the island: Singa Pura (lion city) and Temasek (sea-town). The confused creature is emblazoned on many a trinket and T-shirt. In a bizarre move, the 8.6-m symbol was shifted 120 m in 2002 to a finger of reclaimed land, still in the park, in front the Fullerton Hotel. The relocation was the combined effort of a barge, two 500-tonne lifting capacity cranes and 20 engineers.

Directly behind the Merlion stands the imposing **Fullerton Hotel** (see page 616), in prime position, overlooking the mouth of the river, formerly the General Post Office. Until 1873 this site was occupied by Fullerton Fort, built to defend the Singapore River from seaborne attack. Fullerton Building was erected in 1925-1928 by a firm of Shanghai-based architects. The heavy, almost Scottish, design seems a little out of place in tropical Singapore and, perhaps appropriately, the firm left the colony in the early 1930s after they had been struck off the architect's register for professional misconduct.

Cavenagh Bridge, erected in 1869 by convict labourers (the last big project undertaken by convicts here), was originally called Edinburgh Bridge to commemorate the visit of the Duke of Edinburgh. It was later renamed Cavenagh in honour of Governor WO Cavenagh, the last India-appointed governor of Singapore. The bridge was constructed from steel shipped out from Glasgow (supplied by the same company that furnished the Telok Ayer Market) and was built to provide a link between the government offices on the north side of the river and Commercial Square to the south. However, it was apparently built without a great deal of thought to the tides: *tongkangs*, the lighters that transferred cargo from ships to the godowns (warehouses) at Boat Quay, and vice versa, could not pass under the bridge at high tide and would have to wait for the water level to drop. It became a footbridge in 1909 when the Anderson Bridge superseded it, but it still bears its old sign that forbids bullock carts, horses and heavy vehicles from crossing.

One of the more striking buildings on the river, for its sheer size, is the headquarters of the **United Overseas Bank** (UOB) backing onto Chulia Street, which towers to the maximum permissible height of 280 m (to avoid collision with low-flying aircraft). The octagonal tower is said to represent a pile of coins, although this seems simply too crass to believe. Below, in the open under-court area, is a large bronze statue by **Salvador Dalí** entitled Homage to Newton, cast in 1985. A bronze statue of a squat bird, by **Fernando Botero**, sits on the waterfront, while behind the UOB, on Chulia Street and next to the OCBC Centre, is a giant reclining figure by Henry Moore.

Boat Quay

Along the south bank of the river, facing Empress Place, is Boat Quay – commercially speaking, one of the most successful restoration projects of the Urban Redevelopment Authority (URA). In the early 19th century this part of the river was swamp and the original roomah (*rumah* means house) rakits were rickety, stilted affairs, built over the mud. However, by the mid-1850s Boat Quay had emerged as the centre of Singapore River's commercial life, with three-quarters of the colony's trade being transferred through the godowns here. The opening of the Suez Canal in 1869 increased trade still further, but the development of the steamship around the same time threatened the commercial vitality of the area: vessels became too large to dock here. Merchants, worried that shipping companies would move their business to the new port of Tanjong Pagar which opened in 1852, began to use lighters, or *tongkangs*, to load and unload ships moored outside the river. *Tongkangs*, barges and sampans once littered the river, but they were cleared out to Marina Bay, or destroyed and scuttled, as part of the government's river-cleaning programme over a period of 10 years during the 1990s. Singapore River is now said to be pollution-free (although it only takes a quick glance to see that this is blatantly untrue), but what it gained in cleanliness it has lost – some would argue – in aesthetics.

With technological advances threatening to undermine Boat Quay's vitality, it is perplexing that the area's merchants didn't sell up and move on. One popular explanation is that the curve of the river made it look like the belly of a carp – a sure indicator of commercial success according to Chinese folk wisdom. The wealthier the merchant the higher their godowns were constructed, giving the frontage an attractively uneven appearance. By the time the URA announced its conservation plans in 1986, Boat Quay had fallen on hard times. The original inhabitants were encouraged to leave, the shophouses and godowns were restored and renovated, and a new set of owners moved in. The strip now provides a great choice of drinking holes and restaurants for Singapore's upwardly mobile young, expats and tourists alike, although the area's hipness has faded in recent years and is predominantly patronised by tourists only.

Elgin Bridge marks the upriver end of Boat Quay. The bridge was built in 1929 to link the community of Chinese merchants settled on the south side of the river with the Indian traders of the High Street on the north side, and was named after Lord Elgin, governor-general of India. It is, in fact, the fifth bridge to be built on this site. The first was constructed in 1819 and was the only bridge across the river at that time. Note the roundels depicting the Singapore lion, which are under a palm tree on the bases of each cast iron lamp at either end of the bridge. They were designed by Cavalieri Rodolofo Nolli.

Clarke Quay

Further upriver, the newly hip Clarke Quay has also been renovated at great expense and is lined with colourful shops, bars and restaurants that are particularly popular with the large expat crowd and Singapore's young and trendy elite. At night Clarke Quay is lit up like a perpetual Christmas tree shaded by giant rainproof mushrooms – it's worth checking out just for the spectacle. A further stop up the river takes you to the forest of plush hotels around Robertson Quay – trendy, but somehow quieter, more relaxed and in tune with the wine bar and bistro lovers. This was once godown country – in colonial days, the streets around the warehouses would have been bustling with coolies. It is now a pleasant pedestrian area, with 150-odd shops, restaurants and bars. Clarke Quay has a slightly different feel to Boat Quay; while the latter consists of individual enterprises, the former is controlled by a single company that keeps close tabs on which shops and food outlets open. The atmosphere is more contrived, more managed and controlled. In the pedestrian lanes, overpriced hawker stalls and touristy knick-knack carts set up from lunchtime onwards, selling all manner of goods that people could do without. Despite this, it is still a lot of fun, especially at night, and unlike Boat Quay it is possible to snack from stalls while wandering the alleys of the area.

It is also the site of Singapore's first bungee jump, the **G-Max** ① *T6338 1146, www.gmax.com.sg, open 1300-0100, S$45 per ride*. Daredevils are strapped into a chair to be launched 60 m in the air at 200 km per hour. The screams can be heard from across the river. Next to the G-Max is the **GX-5** ① *S$40 per ride*, offering punters the chance to fly across the Singapore River at over 100 km per hour.

A good way of seeing the sights along Singapore River is on a **Riverboat Cruise** ① *www.rivercruise.com.sg, bumboats operate 0900-2300, S$13, children $8, 30 min, a river taxi operates from here, S$1 (morning) and S$3 (afternoon)*, which can be taken from Clarke Quay or Boat Quay. A rather banal recorded commentary points out the godowns, shophouses, government buildings and skyscrapers lining the riverbank.

Riverside Point

Spanning the river at Clarke Quay is a pedestrian bridge, **Read Bridge**, erected in the 1880s and named after a famous businessman of the day. The antique lamps have been added to a structure which, when it was built, looked more modern than it does now. Read Bridge leads to **Riverside Point**, an arcade of upmarket shops and restaurants.

Across Merchant Road via an aerial walkway is yet another shopping centre-cum-restaurant complex – **Riverside Village** – with its component parts, **Merchant Square** and **Central Mall**. This was reputedly once a centre of prostitution and racketeering, which is hard to believe now that fornication and fraud have given way to fusion cuisine and fashion. At the northwest corner of the complex is the attractive **Tan Si Chong Su Temple**, which has successfully resisted attempts at modernization. The temple was built in 1876 as an ancestral temple and assembly hall of the Hokkien Tan clan. The money was donated by Tan Kim Cheng (1829-1892) and Tan Beng Swee (1828-1884), sons of the wealthy philanthropist Tan Tock Seng. The temple faces the Singapore River – as feng shui (geomancy) dictates – and it is particularly rich in carvings and other decoration. The series of two courtyards and two altar halls symbolizes li, the admired characteristic of humbling oneself in deference to others. The dragon-entwined columns, round windows and granite panels are comparatively unusual. Above the main altar table are four Chinese characters that translate as 'Help the world and the people'.

Financial centre

ⓘ *Raffles Place MRT station is in the heart of the financial district, just south of the Singapore River. Bus Nos 124 and 174 run direct from Orchard Rd. Tanjong Pagar is the nearest MRT stop to the Tanjong Pagar container terminal. It is best to explore this from Cavenagh Bridge, near the mouth of the Singapore River, to Clarke Quay; this takes about 20 mins.*

Shenton Way (Singapore's equivalent of Wall Street), **Raffles Place**, **Robinson Road** and **Cecil Street**, all packed tight with skyscrapers, form the financial heart of modern Singapore. These streets contain most of the buildings that give the city its distinctive skyline and it is best seen from the **Benjamin Sheares Bridge** or from the boat coming back from Batam Island. The first foreign institutions to arrive on the island still occupy the prime sites: the Hong Kong and Shanghai Banking Corporation and Standard Chartered Bank. A short walk away down Philip Street is the small **Wak Hai Cheng Bio Temple**, built in 1826, looking particularly diminutive against the buildings around it. The name means 'Guangdong Province Calm Sea Temple' and the purpose is pretty clear: to ensure that Chinese immigrants making the voyage through the dangerous South China Seas arrived safely. The two key gods depicted here are Xuan Tien Shang Di (the Heavenly Father) in the right-hand hall and Tien Hou (the Heavenly Mother) in the left. Tien Hou (Tin Hau) is a particular favourite of sailors. The figures on the roof are extremely vivid and so is some of the carving inside.

Another piece of old Singapore amidst the new is the **Lau Pa Sat Festival Market**, once known as Telok Ayer, between Robinson Road and Raffles Quay. This was the first municipal market in Singapore. The first market here was commissioned by Stamford Raffles in 1822, but the present structure was designed by James MacRitchie and built in cast-iron shipped out from a foundry in Glasgow in 1894. (The same foundry cast the iron for Cavenagh Bridge.) It is said to be the last remaining Victorian cast-iron structure in Southeast Asia and was declared a national monument in 1973, but was dismantled in 1985 to make way for the MRT, before being rebuilt. It is now a thriving food centre.

Marina Bay and the Integrated Resorts

At the time of research the Singapore skyline was changing dramatically as the three Integrated Resorts were being constructed, due for completion in 2010. The resorts will house Singapore's first ever casinos, the world's largest aquarium and thousands of hotel rooms and shopping opportunities. Despite the creation of an estimated 35,000 jobs for

Singaporeans, there are grave concerns by activist groups about how the casinos will affect Singaporean society as a whole, with fears of an upsurge of gambling-related crime. See page 607 for Resort World Sentosa.

The Marina Barrage

Completed in 2008, this is an impressive 350 m-long dam built across the Marina Channel between Marina South and Marina East. This award-winning project created Singapore's 15th reservoir, forming the new downtown Marina Reservoir out of the Kallang Basin. The dam is made up of nine gates to block the tide. Each 30m-long gate has a pump capable of pumping out the equivalent volume of water per minute as an Olympic swimming pool. There is an **information centre** ⓘ *daily 1000-1800*, tours can be arranged. Kids – and adults who feel like cooling off – will love the water play area with its fountains and paddling pools. To get there, hop on an MRT to Marina Bay where there are free shutte buses going to the barrage.

Cementing Singapore's reputation as the 'Garden City', **Gardens By The Bay** ⓘ *www.gardensbythebay.org.sg*, is a national parks project that will house three distinctive gardens at Marina South. The first phase is due to open in 2011 and should be quite spectacular.

Chinatown

The area known as Kreta Ayer encompasses Smith, Temple, Pagoda, Trengganu and Sago streets. This was the area that Raffles marked out for the Chinese kampong and it became the hub of the Chinese community, deriving its name from the ox-drawn carts that carried water to the area. Renovation by the URA has meant that these streets still retain their characteristic baroque-style shophouses, with weathered shutters and ornamentation.

Background

After Raffles' initial foray to Singapore in 1819, he left the fledgling colony in the hands of Major Farquhar with instructions on how it should be developed. When Raffles returned from Bengkulu in October 1822, he was horrified to find his instructions being ignored and the city expanding in an alarmingly haphazard fashion with the settlement gaining a reputation for crime and thuggery. He countermanded Farquhar's plans and orders and established a committee with even more explicit instructions. The committee allocated an area to each ethnic group and the Chinese were awarded this slice of land, southwest of the river.

Immigrants from China settled in Singapore in the latter half of the 19th century and recreated much of what they had left behind. Clan groups began migrating from the southern provinces of China to the Nang Yang or 'Southern Seas' in successive waves from the 17th century. By 1849 the Chinese population had reached 28,000, but the area they inhabited was largely confined to a settlement between Telok Ayer and Amoy streets. The greatest numbers migrated in the 40 years after 1870, mostly coming from the southeastern coastal provinces, with the Hokkiens forming the majority. Each dialect group established their own temple. The Hokkiens founded **Thian Hock Keng** in 1821, the Cantonese established **Fu Tak Chi** on Telok Ayer Street around the same time, as did the Teochews who built **Wak Hai Cheng Bio** on Philip Street. Streets, too, were occupied by different Chinese groups, with clubs and clan houses (*kongsi*) aiding family or regional ties. The *kongsi* were often affiliated with secret societies (*tongs*), which controlled the gambling and prostitution industries and the drug trade.

Expansion of the financial district meant that Chinatown was being demolished so rapidly that by the time the authorities realized that tourists actually wanted to see its crumbling buildings, many of the streets had already been destroyed. In any case, Chinatown had become a slum, with overcrowding and poor sanitation being very real problems. A clean-up campaign was undertaken; its markets were cleared out, shops and stalls relocated, shophouses refurbished and the smells and noises of Chinatown banished to a world that only a few confused grandparents care to remember. Many residents have moved out to new, modern flats in HDB (Housing Development Board) estates scattered around the island. To preserve what was left of the city's architectural history, the Urban Redevelopment Authority (URA) was established in the 1970s to list old buildings and provide a framework for restoration and conservation.

Chinatown architecture

The typical Straits Chinese house accommodated the family business on the ground floor, leaving the second and third floors as family living quarters – sometimes accommodating two families (and in later years, as Chinatown became desperately overcrowded, up to five families). A few wealthy Chinese merchants (*towkays*) built their houses according to traditional Chinese architectural conventions, but almost all of these have long since been demolished. One which has survived is **Tan Yeok Nee's mansion** on Tank Road, at the eastern end of Orchard Road. Another is the **Thong Chai Medical Institute** on Eu Tong Sen Street, at the corner of Merchant Road. It was built in southern Chinese palace style with three halls, two inner courts and ornamental gables, and was completed in 1892. By the late-19th century it had become a centre for traditional medicine, offering its services free to the poor; *thong chai* means 'benefit to all'. In 1911, during a malaria outbreak, it distributed free quinine. The building also became a focal point for the Chinese community, being the headquarters for the Chinese guilds. The Chinese Chamber of Commerce began life here (its headquarters are now on Hill Street, see page 582). The building was made a national monument in 1973 and has been expertly renovated.

Chinatown streets

In **Sago Street** (or 'death house alley' as it was known in Cantonese, after its hospices for the dying), **Temple Street** and **Smith Street**, there are shops making paper houses and cars, designed to improve the quality of the after-life for dead relatives (by burning the models after the funeral, it is believed that one's worldly wealth hurries after you into the next world). Also on these streets, shops sell all the accoutrements needed for a visit to a Chinese temple. At Number 36 Smith Street there is a three-storey building that was originally home to a famous Cantonese opera theatre – Lai Chun Yen – and formerly Smith Street was also known as 'Hei Yuen Kai', or Theatre Street. The English probably gave Sago Street its name in the early 19th century, as Singapore became a centre of high-quality sago (a multi-purpose palm yielding starch) production for export to India and Europe. By 1849, there were 15 Chinese and two European sago factories here.

Perhaps because death and health go hand-in-hand, there are also a number of **Chinese medicine shops** in this area – for example, Kwang Onn Herbal at 14 Trengganu Street and others on Sago Street. Chinese traditional medicine halls still do a roaring trade, despite the advantages of Medisave schemes and 21st-century pharmaceuticals. On show are antlers and horns, dried frogs and flying lizards, trays of mushrooms and fungi, baskets of dried seahorses and octopus, sharks' fins and ginseng. Presumably more rare, and because they are illegal, body parts such as tiger penis and ground rhino horn are kept out of sight. Looking at this cornucopia of the dried and the pickled, it is easy to wonder how the Chinese ever discovered that flying lizard seeped in tea is good for athlete's foot. The **Hong Lim Complex** on **Upper Cross Street** has several more such medicine halls. There are also a few skilled Chinese calligraphers still working from shops around Upper Cross Street. **Note** Due to habitat loss and demand for shark-fin products, many species of these magnificent predators are now severely endangered. Please do not encourage the continuation of this business by purchasing shark-based products in any form. Hunting has reduced Javan rhinos to around 50 and Sumatran rhinos now number a few hundred. Please report any incidents of illegal wildlife trade to the Singapore authorities.

For anyone looking for a full range of Chinese products, one of the best bets is to visit the **Yue Hwa Chinese Emporium** on the corner of Eu Tong Sen and Upper Cross streets. Yue Hwa is an Aladdin's Cave of Chinese goodies, from silk camisoles, to herbal medicines, to beaded bags and Chinese tea. Just north of here, between Upper Pickering Street and North Canal Road, is a small area of green called **Hong Lim Park**.

Sri Mariamman Temple
As if to illustrate Singapore's reputation as a racial and religious melting-pot, the Hindu Sri Mariamman Temple is situated nearby at 244 South Bridge Road. There was a temple on this site as early as 1827, making it Singapore's oldest Hindu place of worship. Stamford Raffles is said to have granted the land to Narian Pillai, a Tamil who accompanied Raffles to Singapore during his second visit on board the *Indiana*, and set up Singapore's first brickworks. The basic layout of the present, gaudy Dravidian (South Indian) structure dates from 1843, although it has been much renovated and extended over the years. The temple shop is piled high with books on Hindu philosophy and cosmology and, unsurprisingly, is run by a Chinese family. The building is dedicated to Sri Mariamman, a manifestation of Siva's wife Parvati. (She is believed to be particularly good at curing epidemics and other major health scares, which at that time in Singapore were the norm rather than the exception.) The gopuram, or tower, here is particularly exuberant and the sacred cows seated along the top of the boundary wall add a rather pleasing bucolic touch to the affair. The temple is the site of the annual Thimithi festival, which takes place at the end of October or the beginning of November. Devotees cleanse their spirits by fasting beforehand and then show their purity of heart by walking over hot coals (see page 567). To the north of the temple, also on South Bridge Road, is the **Jamae Mosque**, built in 1826 by the Chulias from southern India. It harnesses an eclectic mix of Anglo-Indian, Chinese and Malay architecture.

Chinese temple-carvers still live on **Club Street**, which also has a number of *kongsi* along it. Many buildings along **Mosque Street** were originally stables. It was also home to Hakkas, who traded in second-hand paper and scrap metal – today it is better known for its Chinese restaurants. Number 37 Pagoda Street was one of the many coolie quarters in the area – home to Chinese immigrants, who lived in cramped conditions, sleeping in bunk spaces.

Also on Pagoda Street (No 48) is the **Chinatown Heritage Centre** ① *T6325 2878, www.chinatownheritagecentre.sg, daily 0900- 2000, last admission 1900, S$10, children S$6*, which is well worth a visit. The centre evocatively captures the lives of early Chinese settlers with mock-ups of boats, coffee houses, opium dens and squalid housing through the ages including kitchens, bedrooms, and even a prostitute's boudoir. Everything is captured down to the finest detail, including fake cockroaches in the kitchens and soiled toilets. Electronic sensors that switch on swinging lamps and start taps make the experience a little creepy.

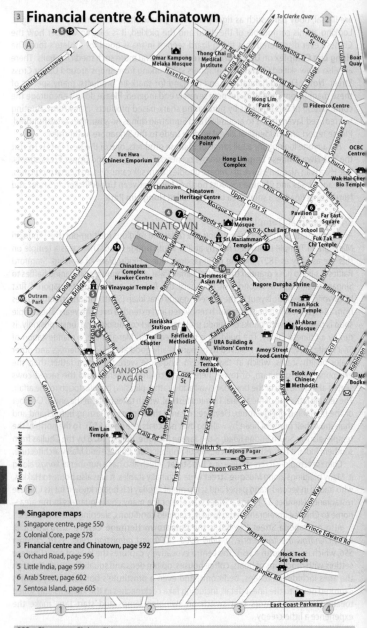

To 8 15

To 2

A

Central Expressway

Omar Kampong
Melaka Mosque

Thong Chai
Medical
Institute

Merchant Rd

Hongkong St

Carpenter St

Boat Quay

Havelock Rd

Eu Tong Sen St

New Bridge Rd

North Canal Rd

South Bridge Rd

Circular Rd

B

Yue Hwa
Chinese Emporium

Chinatown
Point

Hong Lim
Complex

Hong Lim
Park

Upper Pickering St

Hokkien St

Pidemco Centre

Synagogue St

Church St

OCBC
Centre

Wak Hai Cher
Bio Temple

C

M Chinatown

Chinatown
Heritage Centre

CHINATOWN

Mosque St

Pagoda St

Smith St

Trengganu St

Temple St

Sago St

Banda St

Upper Cross St

Jamae
Mosque

Sri Mariamman
Temple

South Bridge Rd

Chin Chew St

Club St

Chui Eng Free School

Mohd Ali Ln

Chin Chew St

China St

Pekin St

Pavilion

6

Far East
Square

Fuk Tak
Chi Temple

Gemmill Ln

Amoy St

Telok Ayer St

Boon Tat St

14

Chinatown
Complex
Hawker Centre

Sri Vinayagar Temple

Kreta Ayer Rd

Lajeunesse
Asian Art

Ang Siang Hl

Erskine Rd

Nagore Durgha Shrine

12

Thian Hock
Keng Temple

D

Outram
Park M

5

New Bridge Rd

Keong Saik Rd

Teck Lim Rd

Kadayanallur St

URA Building &
Visitors' Centre

Al-Abrar
Mosque

Amoy Street
Food Centre

McCallum St

Cecil St

Robinson Rd

Mf
Books

Jinriksha
Station

Tea
Chapter

Fairfield
Methodist

Murray
Terrace
Food Alley

Duxton Rd

Kak St

Chuan Rd

Neil Rd

TANJONG
PAGAR

4

Cook St

Maxwell Rd

Telok Ayer
Chinese
Methodist

Telok Ayer St

E

Cantonment Rd

10

17

Duxton Rd

Tanjong Pagar Rd

Tras St

Peck Seah St

Craig Rd

Kim Lan
Temple

Wallich St

Tanjong Pagar

Shenton Way

Parsi Rd

Prince Edward Rd

To Tiong Bahru Market

F

1

Choon Guan St

Anson Rd

Hock Teck
See Temple

Palmer Rd

East Coast Parkway

➡ Singapore maps

1 Singapore centre, page 550
2 Colonial Core, page 578
3 Financial centre and Chinatown, page 592
4 Orchard Road, page 596
5 Little India, page 599
6 Arab Street, page 602
7 Sentosa Island, page 605

Sleeping
1929 6 D1
Amara 1 F2
Fullerton 7 B6
Grand Copthorne
  Waterfront 8 A1
Inn at Temple St 4 C2
Keong Saik 5 D1
Scarlet 2 D3

Eating
Bamboo Court 6 C4
Blue Ginger 2 E2
Da Paolo's 4 C3, E2
Indochine 8 C3

Kintamani at Furama
  Riverfront Hotel 15 A1
Pasta Brava 10 E2
Pierside 5 B6
Senso 11 C3
Swee Kee Fishhead
  Noodle House 12 D4
Tiong Shiang 14 C2
Wan Tang Eating
  House 7 C2

Bars & clubs
Beaujolais
  Winebar 16 D3
The Butter Factory 13 B6

Telok Ayer Street

This street is full of shophouses and fascinating temples of different religions and was once one of the most important in Singapore. The city's oldest Chinese temple, the Taoist **Thian Hock Keng Temple** ① T6423 4616, or Temple of Heavenly Happiness, is a gem (notwithstanding the naff fibreglass wishing well in one corner). The temple is also very popular; the coaches lined up outside give the game away – but don't let this put you off. Telok Ayer Street was the perfect place for merchants and traders to establish themselves, as it was right on the seafront. (It also became notorious for its slave trade in the 1850s.) The temple was funded by a wealthy merchant of the same name and building commenced in 1839. Skilled craftsmen and materials were all imported from China, the cast-iron railings came from Glasgow and the decorative tiles from Holland. The building was modelled on 19th-century southern Chinese architectural traditions, with a grouping of pavilions around open courtyards, designed to comply with the dictates of geomancy (feng shui).

The main deity of the temple is Tien Hou (Tin Hau), the Goddess of Seafarers, and she is worshipped in the central hall. The image here was imported from China in the 1840s and the temple soon became a focal point for newly arrived Hokkien immigrants who would gather to thank Tien Hou for granting them a safe journey. In the left-hand hall there is an image of the Lord of Laws (Fa Zhu Gong) and in the right is the Prince of Prominence, Zai Si Xian He. The ubiquitous Kuan Yin, the Goddess of Mercy, is also here. The temple's position on the waterfront quickly came to an end, in the 1880s, when one of Singapore's first land reclamation projects moved the shore several blocks east. It's well worth a visit.

A little way north of Thian Hock Keng is another much smaller Chinese temple, the Fuk Tak Chi temple. This is situated in an area that has been gentrified and is now known as **Far East Square**. Within the square is a jumble of renovated shophouses, with bars and bistros and a handful of shops. The two buildings of interest here are the **Chui Eng Free School** ① *131 Amoy St*, one of the first free schools in Singapore – although sadly only the façade remains – and the **Fuk Tak Chi Temple** ① *76 Telok Ayer St, daily 1000-2200, free*, (now a museum) one of the oldest of Singapore's temples, restored in 1998. Coolies arriving in Singapore made this their first stop, giving thanks for safe arrival. This modest but elegantly proportioned temple, with just one court and shrine room, was built in 1824 by the Hakkas and Cantonese. Telok Ayer means water bay in Malay; before land reclamation, this temple stood on the waterfront and was constantly under attack from processes of coastal erosion. It's a little oasis of calm amidst the frenetic life of the city and holds a limited display of exhibits, including some Peranakan jewellery, Chinese stone inscriptions, a pair of porcelain pillows, a model of a Chinese junk and an excellent 'diorama' of Telok Ayer Street, as it must have been in the mid-1850s. **The Pavilion**, also within the square, is on the site where Chinese opera was once performed and is now used as a centre for the performing arts.

The **Al-Abrar Mosque**, also on Telok Ayer Street, was built between 1850 and 1855 by Indian Muslims, who were also responsible for the fancy turrets of the **Nagore Durgha Shrine** – a little further up the street – which was built in 1829. Designated a national monument, the shrine is a blend of architectural styles – Palladian doors and Doric columns combined with more traditional Indian-Islamic touches like the perforated roof grilles ... and then there are the fairy lights. An intriguing architectural sight is the **Telok Ayer Chinese Methodist Church** ① *235 Telok Ayer St*. The church was built in 1924 and combines a mixture of Eastern and Western influences. There is a flat roof with a Chinese pavilion and a colonnaded ground floor. It is all rather odd. During the Second World War it was used as a refugee camp.

Tea Chapter
① *9A/11 Neil Rd, T6226 3026, www.tea-chapter.com.sg, daily 1100-2300*.
One of Chinatown's more interesting places to visit is the Tea Chapter where visitors are introduced to the intricacies of tea tasting in elegant surroundings. You are invited to remove your shoes (sometimes an aromatic experience in itself) and can choose either to sit in one of their special rooms or upstairs on the floor. Relaxing Chinese plink-plink music, muffled feet, a tiny cup of delicious Supreme Grade Dragon Well, Scarlet Robe, Dong Ding Oolong or Green Iron Goddess of Mercy at your lips and the cool atmosphere (it's air conditioned upstairs) all add towards a soothing experience. As the brochure rather extravagantly puts it: "It is a mythical dream come true for those seeking solace from a harsh and unfeeling existence". This is a popular place for young Singaporeans to visit on a Sunday afternoon. There is a range of teas available to buy in the shop. For those interested in learning more about Chinese tea culture, there are workshops held. Check the website for more details.

Jinriksha Station
The white building on the corner of Tanjong Pagar and Neil Road was the Jinriksha Station, built in 1903, and now the **Dragontown Seafood Restaurant**. It served as the administration centre for the *jinriksha* pullers. *Jinrickshas* (rickshaws) arrived from Japan via Shanghai in the 1880s and soon became the most popular way to travel. By 1888 there were 1800 in use, pulled by immigrants who lived in Sago and Banda streets. By the 1900s, the fare for a 30-minute trip would have been 3 cents.

West and south of Chinatown

① *MRT to Tiong Bahru or Outram Park, or the bus stops right opposite this spot – bus Nos 16 (stop outside YMCA) and 33 (stop outside CJIMES).*

On Sunday mornings, bird lovers gather at the corner of Tiong Bahru and Seng Poh roads for **traditional bird singing competitions**, where row upon row of thrushes, merboks and sharmas sing their hearts out, in antique bamboo cages with ivory and porcelain fittings, hung from lines. The birds are fed on a carefully controlled diet to ensure the quality of their song. Owners place their younger birds next to more experienced songsters, to try to improve their voices and pick up new tunes. Birds start twittering at 0730 and are spent by 1000. On the opposite side of the road, there's a shop selling everything you need for your pet bird – including porcelain cage accoutrements. Come here early and combine a visit to hear the birds with breakfast in one of the traditional coffee shops nearby: fresh baked roti washed down with sweet black or milky coffee. If you walk on down Seng Poh Road you will come to a fabulous **wet market**; every conceivable vegetable, fruit, fish, meat, beancurd you could ever want to purchase is available here.

The domed **Railway Station** – apparently inspired by Helsinki's – opened in 1932 and was renovated in 1990, though you wouldn't know it. The design, with its rubber-covered walls and their images of rubber tappers, tin miners and other Malay scenes, was heralded when it opened. Also notable are the four fine art deco images on the front of the station depicting commerce, agriculture, industry and shipping – suitably industrious for the new, as well as the old, Singapore. The station is notable in another respect too: the building and the land are Malaysian, not Singaporean. This was contrived as part of the deal when Singapore left the Malaysian Federation in 1965 and Malaysia ended up controlling the KTM. The two countries have been wondering how to handle this oddity of history ever since. In August 1998, Singapore moved its immigration officials from the Tanjong Pagar station to new purpose-built facilities at Woodlands, near the causeway on the Straits of Johor. But Malaysia refused to do the same. They are still trying to sort out their differences.

Orchard Road and Botanic Gardens

Orchard Road is a long curl of air-conditioned malls, the spine of modern-day Singapore and home to its national pastime: shopping. This glass-fronted materialism is nicely juxtaposed at its western edge with the Botanic Gardens, an elegant park planted with rubber trees and hundreds of orchids and popular with joggers and stretching tai chi practitioners.

Ins and outs

There are 3 **MRT** stations on, or close to, Orchard Road. Dhoby Ghaut MRT station lies at the eastern end of the road, close to the northwest corner of the colonial core. The Somerset MRT stop is on Somerset Road, which runs parallel to Orchard Road. The Orchard MRT station is at the intersection of Orchard Road and Scotts Road, towards the western end of the strip and close to the main concentration of hotels. A profusion of **bus** services run eastwards along Orchard Road – at last count, 20 in all. For routes west, walk 1 block south of Orchard Road. To walk Orchard Road from end to end is quite a slog – from Dhoby Ghaut to the northwestern end of Orchard Road past Scotts Road is around 2.5 km. This is fine if you're taking it slowly, stopping off for brief respites in one of the many air-conditioned shopping arcades. Otherwise, consider hopping on a bus or taking the MRT.

Botanic Gardens and National Orchid Garden

ⓘ *T6471 7361, www.sbg.org.sg, gardens daily 0500-2400, free. Download a map from the website or ask at the ranger's office, 5 mins' walk into the garden. Many buses run past including No 7, 75, 77, 105, 106, 123 and 174, alighting at the junction of Cluny and Napier rds, next to Gleneagles Hospital. Suitable for wheelchairs, telephone for further information.*

At the western end of Orchard Road, on Cluny Road, not far from Tanglin, are the Botanic Gardens. The gardens contain almost 500,000 species of plants and trees from around the world in its 47 ha of landscaped parkland, primary jungle, lawns and lakes. In 1963 former Prime Minister Lee Kuan Yew launched the successful Garden City campaign and most of the trees lining Singapore's highways were supplied by the Botanic Gardens. The gardens now cater for the recreational needs of modern Singapore. Every morning and evening, the park fills with joggers and tai chi fanatics. During the day, wedding parties pose for pictures among the foliage. The bandstand in the centre of the gardens is used for live music performances at the weekends.

The Botanic Gardens were founded by an agri-horticultural society in 1859. In the early years they played an important role in fostering agricultural development in Singapore

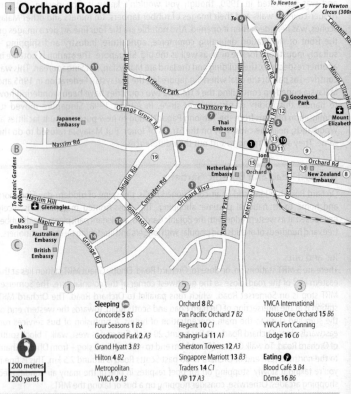

④ Orchard Road

Sleeping
Concorde **5** *B5*
Four Seasons **1** *B2*
Goodwood Park **2** *A3*
Grand Hyatt **3** *B3*
Hilton **4** *B2*
Metropolitan
YMCA **9** *A3*

Orchard **8** *B2*
Pan Pacific Orchard **7** *B2*
Regent **10** *C1*
Shangri-La **11** *A1*
Sheraton Towers **12** *A3*
Singapore Marriott **13** *B3*
Traders **14** *C1*
VIP **17** *A3*

YMCA International
House One Orchard **15** *B6*
YWCA Fort Canning
Lodge **16** *C6*

Eating
Blood Café **3** *B4*
Dôme **16** *B6*

and Malaya, as successive directors collected, propagated and distributed plants with economic potential, the most famous of which was rubber. Henry Ridley, director of the gardens from 1888 to 1912, pioneered the planting of the Brazilian para rubber tree (*Hevea brasiliensis*). In 1877, 11 seedlings brought from Kew Gardens in London were planted in the Singapore gardens. An immediate descendant of one of the 11 originals is still alive in the Botanic Gardens today, near the main entrance. By the lake at the junction of Tyersall and Cluny roads, there is a memorial to Ridley on the site where the original trees were planted. Ridley was known as 'Mad Ridley' because of the proselytizing zeal with which he lobbied Malaya's former coffee planters to take up rubber instead, often slipping rubber tree seeds into planters' pockets at dinner parties.

The Botanic Gardens also house the **National Orchid Garden** ① *daily 0830-1900, S$5, students and senior citizens S$1, under 12s free, the closest entrance to the Botanic Gardens for the Orchid Garden is on Tyersall Av*, where 700 species and 2100 hybrids of Singapore's favourite flower are lovingly cultivated. It is billed as the 'Largest Orchid Showcase in the World'. The gardens began to breed orchids back in 1928 and those on show include Singapore's national flower, Miss Vanda Joaquim orchid, discovered in the late-19th

➡ **Singapore maps**
1 Singapore centre, page 550
2 Colonial Core, page 578
3 Financial centre and Chinatown, page 592
4 **Orchard Road, page 596**
5 Little India, page 599
6 Arab Street, page 602
7 Sentosa Island, page 605

Esmirada's **2** *B5*
Lei Garden **13** *B4*
Les Amis **1** *B3*
Nanbantei **10** *B3*
Orchard Maharajah **6** *B5*
Sakura **10** *B3*
Sushi Tei **3** *B4*

Bars & clubs 🍸
Hard Rock Café **4** *B2*
Ice Cold **8** *B4*
Number 5 **9** *B4*
Que Pasa **11** *B4*

Shopping 🛍
Park Mall **1** *C6*

Plaza Singapura **2** *B6*
Centrepoint **4** *B5*
Heeren **6** *B4*
Paragon **7** *B4*
Ngee Ann City **8** *B3*
Lucky Plaza **9** *B3*
Wisma Atria **10** *B3*
Tang's **11** *B3*

Scotts **12** *B3*
Far East Plaza **13** *B3*
Wheelock Place **15** *B3*
Tanglin **19** *B2*

century by the eponymous Miss Joaquim in her garden. The Mist House contains a collection of rare orchids, whilst the Yuen-Peng McNeice Bromeliad Collection houses 300 species and 500 hybrids from Central and South America.

Goodwood Park Hotel, Emerald Hill and Dhoby Ghaut

Situated on Scotts Road off the western end of Orchard Road is Goodwood Park, which – apart from Raffles – is the only other colonial hotel in Singapore. It has had a chequered history, beginning life in 1856 as the German Recreation Club, the *Teutonia*. During the First World War it was declared enemy property and was seized by the government. In 1929 it was converted into a hotel, but then during the Second World War it was occupied by the Japanese. After the war it became a War Crimes Trial Court and did not resume functioning as a hotel until 1947.

Further east, Emerald Hill was laid out by 30 different owners between 1901 and 1925; conforming to the established theme was considered good manners, which has resulted in a charming street of Peranakan (Straits Chinese) shophouses. These have been carefully restored to their original condition and combine European and Chinese architectural elements.

At the end of Orchard Road is Dhoby Ghaut, which got its name from the Bengali and Madrasi *dhobis* who used to wash the clothes of local residents in the stream that ran down the side of Orchard Road and dry them on the land now occupied by the YMCA. *Ghaut* is a Hindi word meaning 'landing place' or 'path down to a river', while *dhoby* is from the Sanskrit word *dhona*, meaning 'to wash'. The *dhobis* would walk from house to house collecting their clients' washing, noting each piece down in a little book using a series of marks (they were illiterate). Dhoby Ghaut MRT is now an interchange linking the northeast with City Hall.

Little India

The city's South Asian community has its roots in the grid of streets branching off Serangoon Road. Tourist-spruced handicraft shops are packed into the Little India Arcade opposite the more gritty wet market of the Tekka Centre. The best Indian restaurants lie shoulder to shoulder along Race Course Road, while a bit of exploring will unearth theatres, a Bengali temple and a hand-operated spice mill. Dunlop Street connects the main arteries of Serangoon Road and Jalan Besar – it deserves a mention as the heart of backpacker land, with plenty of cheap bars and guesthouses and hostels melding with the Indian bustle.

Ins and outs

Little India **MRT** station on the Northeast line has an exit that opens onto the Tekka Centre market. Numerous buses run up Jalan Besar (parallel to Serangoon Road), including Nos 64 and 65 from Orchard Road; No 139 runs along Serangoon Road from Orchard Road.

Serangoon Road

Serangoon Road was named after the Rongong stork that used to inhabit swampland in the area. By 1828, Serangoon Road was established as 'the road leading across the island', but the surrounding area remained swampland until the 1920s when its brick kilns and lime pits attracted Indian (mainly Tamil) labourers to the area. In 1840 the racecourse was completed, which drew Europeans to settle here. (The road names Cuff, Dickson and Clive would have been private lanes to the European residences.)

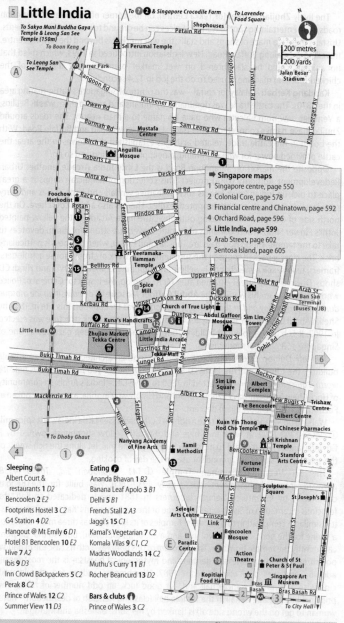

5 Little India

To ❼ ❷ & Singapore Crocodile Farm
To Lavender Food Square

Pétain Rd — Shophouses

To Sakya Muni Buddha Gaya Temple & Leong San See Temple (150m)

To Boon Keng

To Leong San See Temple

A

Sri Perumal Temple

Farrer Park

Rangoon Rd

Owen Rd

Kitchener Rd

Burmah Rd

Birch Rd

Mustafa Centre

Sam Leong Rd

Maude Rd

Roberts La

Anguillia Mosque

Kinta Rd

Desker Rd

B

Foochow Methodist

Rowell Rd

Rotan La

Race Course La

Hindoo Rd

Norris Rd

Sri Veeramaka-liamman Temple

Veerasamy Rd

Belilios Rd

Cuff Rd

Kerbau Rd

Spice Mill

Upper Dickson Rd

Upper Weld Rd

Weld Rd

C

Dickson Rd

Church of True Light

Kuna's Handicrafts

Dunlop St

Abdul Gaffoor Mosque

Mayo St

Sim Lim Tower

Little India

Zhujiao Market/ Tekka Centre

Buffalo Rd

Campbell La

Little India Arcade

Bukit Timah Rd

Hastings Rd

Tekka Mall

Sungei Rd

Rochor Canal

Bukit Timah Rd

Rochor Canal Rd

Sim Lim Square

Albert Complex

Mackenzie Rd

Albert St

Rochor Rd

D

Short St

Selegie Rd

Niven Rd

The Bencoolen

New Bugis St

Albert Centre

Trishaw Centre

To Dhoby Ghaut

Nanyang Academy of Fine Arts

Prinsep St

Kuan Yin Thong Hod Cho Temple

Chinese Pharmacies

Tamil Methodist

Bencoolen Link

Sri Krishnan Temple

Stamford Arts Centre

Fortune Centre

Bencoolen St

E

Selegie Arts Centre

Selegie Link

Middle Rd

Waterloo St

Sculpture Square

St Joseph's

Bencoolen Mosque

Action Theatre

Church of St Peter & St Paul

Queen St

Paradiz Centre

Kopitiam Food Hall

Bras Basah

Singapore Art Museum

Bras Basah Rd

To City Hall

Arab St — Ban San Terminal (Buses to JB)

Ophir Rd

Rochor Rd

6

To Bugis

➡ **Singapore maps**

1 Singapore centre, page 550
2 Colonial Core, page 578
3 Financial centre and Chinatown, page 592
4 Orchard Road, page 596
5 Little India, page 599
6 Arab Street, page 602
7 Sentosa Island, page 605

200 metres
200 yards

Jalan Besar Stadium

N

Sleeping 🛌
Albert Court & restaurants **1** D2
Bencoolen **2** E2
Footprints Hostel **3** C2
G4 Station **4** D2
Hangout @ Mt Emily **6** D1
Hive **7** A2
Hotel 81 Bencoolen **10** E2
Ibis **9** D3
Inn Crowd Backpackers **5** C2
Perak **8** C2
Prince of Wales **12** C2
Summer View **11** D3

Eating 🍴
Ananda Bhavan **1** B2
Banana Leaf Apolo **3** B1
Delhi **5** B1
French Stall **2** A3
Jaggi's **15** C1
Kamal's Vegetarian **7** C2
Komala Vilas **9** C1, C2
Madras Woodlands **14** C2
Muthu's Curry **11** B1
Rocher Beancurd **13** D2

Bars & clubs 🍸
Prince of Wales **3** C2

The lively **Zhujiao Market** (or Tekka Centre), on the corner of Buffalo and Serangoon roads, is an entertaining spot to wander. Spices can be ground to your own requirements. Upstairs there is a maze of shops and stalls; the **wet market** is beyond the hawker centre, travelling west along Buffalo Road. New legislation introduced in 1993, which ruled that no animals could be slaughtered on wet market premises, saw the end of the chicken-plucking machine. It used to do the job in 12.4 seconds.

Kandang Kerbau – Malay for corral – was the centre of Singapore's cattle-rearing area in the 1870s. The cattle trade was dominated by Indians and among them was IR Belilios, a Venetian Jew from Calcutta who gave his name to a road nearby. The roads around Zhujiao have names connected to the trade: Lembu (cow) Road and Buffalo Road. With the boom in the cattle trade, related activities established themselves in the area; the cattle provided power for wheat grinding, pineapple preserving and so on.

Opposite the market on Serangoon Road is the **Little India Arcade**, another Urban Redevelopment Authority (URA) project. This collection of handicraft shops is a great place to pick up Indian knick-knacks such as leather sandals and bags, spices and curry powders, incense, saris and other printed textiles. There is also a food court here. On the north side of Campbell Road, facing onto the Little India Arcade, is the yellow-painted Jothi's Flower Shop, where garlands of jasmine flowers are strung for Hindu devotees to take to the temple. Hindu holy days are Tuesday and Friday, when business is particularly brisk. The closely packed shops in the surrounding network of streets house astrologers, framers, tailors, spice merchants, jewellers and pumping Bollywood DVD and Hindi CD shops. Down Dunlop Street – named after Mr AE Dunlop, the Inspector General of Police whose private road this was – is the **Abdul Gaffoor Mosque** ⓘ *avoid visiting the mosque during Fri prayer day and in the evenings*. A mosque was first built on this site in 1859 by Sheikh Abdul Gaffoor bin Shaikh Hyder, although the current brick structure was erected in 1907. It is hardly a splendid building, but nonetheless has been gazetted as one of Singapore's 58 national monuments.

Just off Dunlop Street, on Perak Road, is another architecturally unremarkable building, the **Church of True Light** ⓘ *Sat-Sun 0900-1300; if you pass by at this time it's worth a quick look*, which was erected in 1850 to serve Little India's Anglican community of Hock Chew (modern-day Fuzhou, Fujian) and Hinghwa (Xinghua, a language spoken in Fuzhou and Quanzhou, Fujian) descent.

Walking up Serangoon Road, take a right at Cuff Road to see Little India's last **spice mill** ⓘ *closed 1300-1400*, at work in a blue and mustard yellow shophouse, owned by P Govindasamai Pillai. It's hard to miss the chugging of the mill, let alone the rich smells of the spices. Here spices are ground for use on the day of cooking.

The **Sri Veeramakaliamman Temple** ⓘ *141 Serangoon Rd, T6295 4538, www.sriveeramakaliamman.com, closed daily 1230-1600*, was built for the Bengali community by indentured Bengali labourers in 1881 and is dedicated to Kali, the ferocious incarnation of Siva's wife. The name of the temple means 'Kali the courageous'. It is similar in composition to most other temples of its kind and has three main elements: a shrine for the gods, a hall for worship and a *goporum* (or tower), built so that pilgrims can identify the temple from afar. The *goporum* of this temple – with its cascade of gaudy, polychromed gods, goddesses, demons and mythological beasts – is the most recent addition and was only completed in 1987. Worshippers and visitors should walk clockwise around the temple hall and, for good luck, an odd number of times. The principal black image of Kali in the temple hall (clasping her club of destruction – not a woman to get on the wrong side of) is flanked by her sons, Ganesha and Murugan.

Further up Serangoon Road is another Indian temple, **Sri Perumal** ① *daily 0630-1200, 1800-2100*, with its high *goporum* sculptured with five manifestations of Vishnu. The temple was founded in 1855, but much of the decoration is more recent. This carving was finished in 1979 and was paid for by local philanthropist P Govindasamy Pillai, better known as PGP, who made his fortune selling saris. Like other Hindu temples, the greatest activity is on the holy days of Tuesdays and Fridays. For the best experience of all, come here and to the Sri Veeramakaliamman and Hindu Chettiar (see above and page 585) temples during the two-day festival of **Thaipusam** – generally held in February (see page 31) – which celebrates the birthday of Murugan, one of Kali's sons.

Sakya Muni Buddha Gaya Temple

① *366 Race Course Rd (parallel to Serangoon Rd), T6294 0714, daily 0800-1645; dress conservatively and remove shoes before entering. Take a taxi from Dhoby Ghaut MRT or bus No 64, 65, 106 or 111 from Orchard Rd.*

Further north is the Buddhist Sakya Muni Buddha Gaya Temple – or Temple of One Thousand Lights – dominated by a 15 m-high, 300 tonne, rather crude, statue of the Buddha surrounded by 987 lights (the lights are turned on if you make a donation). The image is represented in the attitude of subduing Mara – the right hand touches the ground, calling the Earth Goddess to witness the historic Buddha's resistance of the attempts by Mara to tempt him with his naked dancing daughters. At the back of the principal image is a smaller reclining Buddha. Devotees come here to worship the branch of the sacred Bodhi tree – under which the Buddha gained enlightenment – and a replica mother-of-pearl footprint of the Buddha showing the 108 auspicious signs of the Enlightened One.

Across the road is the Chinese Mahayana Buddhist **Leong San See Temple** – or Dragon Mountain Temple – with its carved entrance (where you don't have to remove your shoes). It is dedicated to Kuan Yin (the goddess of mercy) who had 18 hands, which are said to symbolize her boundless mercy and compassion. The principal image on the altar shows her modelled, as usual, in white, surrounded by a mixed bag of Chinese Mahayana folk gods and Theravada images of the Buddha.

Arab Street

The smallest of Singapore's ethnic quarters, Arab Street is a pedestrianized tourist market strip with shops hawking all manner of Middle Eastern and Islamic goods – prayer rugs, Egyptian perfume bottles, baskets, rattan, silk, velvets and jewellery, as well as textiles from Indian and Indonesia. There are a couple of great Middle Eastern eateries and the imposing golden-domed Sultan Mosque. Remember to dress modestly.

Background

Originally this area was a thriving Arab village known as Kampong Glam (Glam Village). There is some disagreement over the origins of this name. Some commentators have attributed it to the Gelam tribe of sea gypsies who once lived in the area. More likely, it refers to the glam tree from which Bugis seafarers extracted resin to caulk their ships.

Singapore's Arabs were among the area's earliest settlers, the first being a wealthy merchant called Syed Mohammad bin Harum Al-Junied who arrived in 1819, a couple of months after Stamford Raffles. The Alkaffs were another important local Arab family, who built their ostentatious mansion on Mount Faber. Arab merchants began settling in the area around Arab Street in the mid-19th century.

Mosques

① 0900-1300, 1400-1600. Visitors will not be permitted to enter if dressed in shorts, short skirts or sleeveless T-shirts , but suitable clothing is provided on the door.

The **Sultan Mosque**, with its golden domes, on North Bridge Road, attracts thousands of the faithful every Friday. Completed in 1928 and designed by colonial architect Denis Santry of Swan & Maclaren, it is an eclectic mixture of classical, Moorish and Persian. The original building, constructed in the 1820s, was part of a deal between the Temenggong of Johor and the East India Company, in which the company donated S$3000 towards its construction and the Temenggong leased the land to the trustees of the mosque. Next door is the old **Kampong Glam Istana**, built in the early 1840s as the Temenggong Ali Iskander Shah's palace.

Stalls and shops

In the maze of side streets around the Sultan Mosque, there is a colourful jumble of Malay, Indonesian and Middle Eastern merchandise. Excellent selections of batik (which is sold in sarong lengths of just over 2 m) jostle for space with silk and Indian textiles (especially

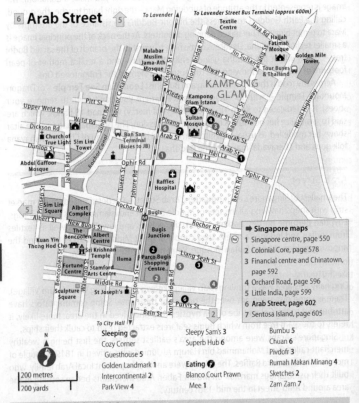

6 Arab Street

To Lavender
To Lavender Street Bus Terminal (approx 600m)

➡ **Singapore maps**

1 Singapore centre, page 550
2 Colonial Core, page 578
3 Financial centre and Chinatown, page 592
4 Orchard Road, page 596
5 Little India, page 599
6 Arab Street, page 602
7 Sentosa Island, page 605

200 metres
200 yards

Sleeping 🛏
Cozy Corner
Guesthouse 5
Golden Landmark 1
Intercontinental 2
Park View 4

Sleepy Sam's 3
Superb Hub 6

Eating 🍴
Blanco Court Prawn
Mee 1

Bumbu 5
Chuan 6
Pivdofr 3
Rumah Makan Minang 4
Sketches 2
Zam Zam 7

along Arab Street), wickerwork, jewellery, perfumes and religious paraphernalia. In the weeks before Hari Raya Puasa, which marks the end of the fasting month of Ramadan (see page 566), Bussorah Street is lined with stalls selling all kinds of traditional Muslim and Malay foods; after dark it is a favourite haunt of famished Muslims. Bussorah Street is a pedestrianized, tree-lined street of elegant shophouses.

Bugis Street

Bugis Street is southwest of Arab Street, right across the road from the Bugis Street MRT station. It is packed with stalls selling cheap T-shirts, copy watches and handicrafts – like a street market you might see in Thailand or Malaysia, but something that seems rather out of place in modern-day Singapore. For those who like to see Singapore not just as a giant shopping plaza but also as a real life experiment in ersatz existence, then Bugis Street offers more than keyrings and Oriental flim-flam. The whole street has been recreated from a road that was demolished for the MRT in the 1980s. Some people maintain that the reason it was demolished, and then brought back from the dead, sums up Singapore's approach to life.

On the opposite side of Victoria Street is the **Parco Bugis Junction**, a shopping plaza (in reconstructed air-conditioned shophouses) bustling with life, and containing restaurants, shops, a cinema and one of Singapore's fabulous fountains.

Temples

Waterloo Street, much of which has been pedestrianized, cuts across New Bugis Street and is also worth a modest detour. The **Sri Krishnan Temple** at 152 Waterloo Street dates back to the 1870s, when a simple *atap* hut protected two Hindu images (Krishna didn't arrive until the 1880s). Over the years it has been expanded and refined as the Hindu population of the surrounding area has prospered. Almost next door is a large, modern Mahayana pagoda, dedicated to **Kuan Yin** – the **Kuan Yin Thong Hod Cho Temple**. This temple is especially popular; try visiting at lunchtime (1200-1300) when scores of worshippers come here to pray for good fortune. The central image is of multi-limbed Kuan Yin, while on either side are Ta Ma Tan Shith and Hua Tua. The latter was an important Han Dynasty figure (third century BC) who is now the patron saint of Chinese medics.

Perhaps not coincidentally, on the other side of the street in Cheng Yan Court is a collection of **traditional Chinese pharmacies**, selling the usual range of dried fungi, bones, herbs, roots like ginseng, desiccated sea horses and other unidentified body parts.

HarbourFront and Sentosa

To the west of Tanjong Pagar port (see page 586), on Keppel Road, is HarbourFront (formerly the World Trade Centre). Most people visit the centre either to get to Sentosa, to take the boat to Batam and Bintan islands in Indonesia's Riau Archipelago (see page 557), or to use the cable car that connects Sentosa with Mount Faber.

Opposite HarbourFront's exhibition halls lies the **Telok Blangah Johor State Mosque**, dating from the 1840s. It was the focal point of the pre-Raffles Malay royalty in Singapore. Nearby is the tomb of the Temenggong Abdul Rahman (the Tanah Kubor Rajah or Tanah Kubor Temenggong), who was partly responsible for negotiating Singapore's status as a trading post with Stamford Raffles. The Johor royal family lived at Telok Blangah until 1855, when the town of Iskandar Putri was founded on the other side of the straits; it was renamed Johor Bahru in 1866.

Sentosa Island

ⓘ T1800-736 8672, www.sentosa.com.sg, daily 0900-2100, many attractions close before 2100, at 1800 or 1900. S$3, plus a charge for each attraction. There are combination tickets available; some of which also tie you in to a tour. Apart from battling with the hordes of people, another downside to Sentosa is that a day here tends to be an expensive, as well as an entertaining, experience. A family of 4 can easily get through S$200.

Sentosa is a tourist resort island with three beaches stretching along its southern coast and various activities including a man-made volcano, a 4D theatre, a luge ride, a laser-lit merlion statue, an oceanarium, a butterfly park and a Second World War museum. There are also five-star resorts and a couple of golf courses.

Getting there and around The orange **Sentosa bus** operates from the HarbourFront Bus Terminal to Sentosa Sunday-Thursday 0700-2400, Friday-Saturday 0700-2430. Ticket costs S$3 (includes Sentosa entrance fee). You can also take the **SIA Hop-on shuttle** from five stops; see siahopon.asiaone.com.sg for route and timetable information. The **Sentosa Express monorail** ⓘ daily 0800-2200, S$3 including admission to Sentosa, links Sentosa Station in VivoCity with the Imbiah and Beach stations on Sentosa. HarbourFront has its own MRT station, from where you can take the Sentosa bus or Sentosa Express. The **cable car** ⓘ daily 0830-2100, return S$11.90, children S$6.50 (normal cabin), S$18, children S$11 (glass-bottomed cabin), admission to Sentosa is not included in these fares, has three stops: Mount Faber (the highest point in Singapore, with scenic views and seafood restaurants – worthwhile), the Cable Car Tower adjacent to the HarbourFront and the Cable Car Plaza on Sentosa. **Taxis** are charged a toll of S$3 and can only drop off/pick up at the hotels on Sentosa.

Once on Sentosa, there are three free **bus** lines, and two free tram lines. The blue line (Sunday-Thursday 0700-2300, until 2430 Friday-Saturday) does a loop from the Visitor Arrival Centre past the Merlion to Underwater World and Siloso Beach. The green line (daily 0900-2100) runs between the Ferry Terminal, the cable car and Underwater World. The yellow line (Sunday-Thursday 0700-2300, until 2430 Friday-Saturday) links the Visitor Arrival Centre with Dolphin Lagoon. The red line (daily 0900-2200) links Underwater World with Dolphin Lagoon. The Siloso Beach Tramline (daily 0900-2300) runs between Siloso Beach and the Beach Station, while the Palawan-Tanjong Beach Line (daily 0900-2300) shuttles between the Beach Station and Tanjong beach. **Tandems** and **trishaws** are for hire from the ferry terminal and near Palawan Beach, open 1000-1800. There is also a 6-km **cycle track** around the island.

Sights Travelling anti-clockwise around the island, the first attraction of interest is the **Underwater World** ⓘ www.underwaterworld.com.sg, 0900-2100, S$22.90, children S$14.60, which includes entry to Dolphin Lagoon. It's highly recommended and is the highlight of any visit to Sentosa. A 100-m tunnel, with a moving conveyor, allows a glimpse of some of its 350 underwater species and 5000 specimens. Giant rays glide overhead, while thick-lipped garoupa and spooky moray eels hide in caves and crevices. The 'creatures of the deep' tank, with giant octopus and spider crabs, is impressive. Smaller tanks house turtles, reef fish, corals, sea urchins and others. There is also a touch pool where the curious can have a close encounter with starfish and baby sharks. It is possible to dive with sharks and dugongs here. Prices start at S$120 per dive. Book in advance.

Fort Siloso ⓘ 1000-1800, S$8, children S$5, free guided tours Sat, Sun 1100 and 1600, on the westernmost point, is Singapore's only preserved coastal fort, built in the 1880s to guard the narrow western entrance to Keppel Harbour. It provides an informative visit, especially if you're interested in the fall of Singapore. It is possible to explore the underground tunnels, artillery nests and bunkers, experience a mock firing of a seven-inch gun, run riot over the assault course and play various interactive computer games with a martial tinge. The fort was built to guard against a seaward attack, but, as every amateur student of Singapore's wartime history knows, the Japanese assault was from the north. The guns of Fort Siloso were turned landwards, but could do little to thwart the Japanese advance. When news of the surrender came through, the soldiers of the Royal Artillery (many from the Indian subcontinent) sabotaged the guns to prevent them falling into enemy hands.

MegaZip Adventure Park ① *T6884 5602, www.megazip.com.sg, daily 1400-1700, S$10-S$60, take blue line bus to Imbiah Lookout from where it's a 3-min walk*, is a new park much loved by thrill seekers and corporations on team-building days. Of the four rides, the most fun is the 450 m-long Megazip flying fox, the steepest in Asia, which goes up to 50 kph. There are three wires, so you can race your pals over the jungle canopy. Other rides include the ClimbMax, climbing obstacles 40 m up with superb views over the shipping lanes (for those without vertigo); North Face, a 16 m-high climbing wall; and Parajump, a freefall simulator involving a complex arrangement of wires and a 15-m drop.

7 Sentosa Island

➡ **Singapore maps**
1 Singapore centre, page 550
2 Colonial Core, page 578
3 Financial centre and Chinatown, page 592
4 Orchard Road, page 596
5 Little India, page 599
6 Arab Street, page 602
7 Sentosa Island, page 605

200 metres
200 yards

Sleeping 🛏
Amara Sanctuary **4**
Sentosa Resort & Spa **2**
Shangri-La Rasa Sentosa **1**
Treasure Resort **3**

Eating 🍴
Prima Tower Revolving
Restaurant **3**

━━━Ⓢ Sentosa Express
- - - - Cable car
++++++ Beach tram

Float through the air with the greatest of ease on **Sentosa's Flying Trapeze** ① *Tue-Fri 1600-1800, Sat, Sun and public holidays 1600-1900, S$10 per swing, S$20 for 3 swings, under 4s and pregnant women are not allowed to take part*. Daredevils wear safety harnesses to enjoy heart-stopping swings.

Sentosa Luge and Skyride ① *daily 1000-2130, S$11, Skyride only S$7, family packages available*, is Southeast Asia's first luge, a bizarre mix of sledging and go-karting that kids will love. To get to the Luge, take the scenic chairlift – the Skyride – up the hill.

The **Butterfly Park and Insect Kingdom Museum** ① *daily 0900-1830, S$16, children S$10*, is a 1-ha park containing 1500 butterflies from 50 species at all stages in their life cycle. Also here is a rather antiseptic museum of dead butterflies and insects.

Poking up like a giant needle, the **Tiger Sky Tower** ① *daily 0900-2100, last entry 2045, S$12, children S$8*, next to the cable-car station, has a small glass-sided cabin which rotates at 131 m above sea level giving good views of the island.

Songs of the Sea ① *daily 1940 and 2040, S$10, likely to sell out at weekends and public holidays*, is an award-winning night spectacular featuring pyrotechnics, lasers and 40 m-high water jets. Shows last 25 minutes.

The 37 m, 12 storey-tall **Merlion** ① *climb: 1000-2000, last admission 1930, S$8, children S$5*, is a stupendous symbol of Singapore. The Merlion can be climbed either up to its mouth or its crown for views over Sentosa, the city and port. There is a shop here – since nothing can be built on Sentosa without some merchandising outlet – themed as a Bugis shipwreck. The Bugis were the feared Malay seafarers who sailed from southern Sulawesi and controlled the seas of the Malay archipelago long before the Europeans arrived. They have often been likened to the Vikings and, like the Vikings, they were famed for their fearlessness and for their seafaring skills and for the terror they instilled in the hearts of coastal communities.

Images of Singapore, **Pioneers of Singapore** and the **Surrender Chambers** ① *daily 0900-1900, last admission 1830, S$10, children S$7*, offer a well-displayed history of Singapore, focusing on key figures from the origins of the city state as an entrepôt, through to the modern period and also telling the traumatic Second World War story. The wax models are not up to Madame Tussaud's standard, but the history is well told.

The southwest 'coast' of the island has been redeveloped, with tens of thousands of cubic metres of golden sand shipped in from Indonesia, along with 300 mature coconut palms and over 100 ornamental shrubs and flowering trees. Three **beaches** have been created: Palawan, Siloso and Tanjong. The beach trams run between them.

The **Dolphin Lagoon** ① *daily 1030-1800, S$22.90, children S$14.60, price includes entry into Underwater World*, near Tanjong Beach, provides 'Meet the Dolphin' sessions at 1100, 1300, 1530 and 1730. So-called pink (although they are more white in colour) Indo-Pacific humpback dolphins have been trained to do rather banal and demeaning tricks.

The **Sentosa Orchid Gardens** ① *free*, very close to the ferry terminal, have 10,000 plants and over 200 species of orchid. Within the gardens is a restaurant, a fish pond with koi carp, a Japanese tea room and various other gazebos, boulders and associated paraphernalia, and – yes, you've guessed it – a souvenir shop.

Cineblast ① *www.cineblast.com.sg, show every 30 mins, 1000-1900, last show starts 2045, S$16, children S$9.50*, a high-tech movie extravaganza. Combining high-definition film with state-of-the-art sound and seats, raised on hydraulic jacks, it creates what is rather ambitiously called 'hyper reality'.

Golf ① *T6275 0022, www.sentosagolf.com, 0700-1900*, is available on one of two 18-hole courses – Serapong or Tanjong.

Resort World Sentosa, an integrated resort costing Genting International almost US$5 billion, is made up of six hotels, a casino, the world's largest oceanarium (not open at the time of going to press) and Southeast Asia's first Universal Studios. The beginning of 2010 saw the opening of the Michael Graves-designed Hotel Michael, with abundant light wood touches, mosaic showers and arty furniture and the Hard Rock Hotel, with the usual bright and garish faux rock-and-roll theme and gorgeous pool surrounded by white sand imported from Australia. Other hotels recently opened here include Crockford's Tower, Spa Villas, Equarius Hotel and the family-oriented Festive Hotel. Reservations can be made through the Resort World site, www.rwsentosa.com.

Southeast Asia's first **Universal Studios theme park** ① *11 Sentosa East Mall, T6577 8888, www.rwsentosa.com, Mon-Fri 0900-1800, Sat-Sun 0900-2100, week day/weekend S$66/S$72, children S$48/S$52, take the RWS8 from outside VivoCity and before Seah Im Road, S$2.00*, is carved up into different themed zones. This sweaty day out is guaranteed to have you gulping down ice cream as you wander through a disturbingly tropical New York Street, a Hollywood and a sci-fi city based on the TV show *BattleStar Galactica* that no sci-fi fan can afford to miss. One of the park's star attractions is the world's tallest Duelling roller coaster at over 43 m. Other attractions in the park include the highly popular indoor Revenge of the Mummy roller coaster, the Jurassic Park River Adventure, and those in the mood to experience a tsunami can check out Waterworld.

If you fancy a flutter, visit the controversial **casino** at the resort. It's open 24/7, has a smart dress code and is expected to contribute S$2.7 billion to the country's GDP by 2015. The casino met with opposition from social workers and Christian groups who had serious concerns over the effect of a casino on the Singaporean population and on a possible increase in organized crime. Within a week of opening, over 100 Singaporeans had voluntarily banned themselves from entry. Singaporeans and Singapore Permananet Residents are charged a S$100 entry fee in order to discourage low income locals frittering their hard-earned dollars away.

The other integrated resort is at Marina Bay and can clearly be seen from the bridges near Clarke Quay. This resort, the Marina Bay Sands Resort (www.marinabaysands.com), features three 55-storey hotel towers topped with a 1-ha sky garden on the roof with what promise to be spectacular city views. The resort opened in mid-2010.

Singapore West

Haw Par Villa

① *262 Pasir Panjang Rd, T872 2694, daily 0900-1900, free (outside), S$1 for entrance to Ten Courts of Hell. Don't even think about visiting Haw Par Villa over Chinese New Year, when about 12,000 people visit in 4 days. MRT westbound to Buona Vista, then bus No 200.*

The gloriously tacky Haw Par Villa (formerly **Tiger Balm Gardens**) is on the way out to Jurong. Built by Aw Boon Haw and Aw Boon Par, brothers of Tiger Balm fame, it was their family home until they opened it to the public. The delightful estate was finally sequestrated by the Singapore government in 1985 and turned into a theme park. Boon Haw originally designed the gardens for his family's enjoyment. But his gory sculptures have instilled a sense of traditional morality in generations of Singaporeans. Sequences depict wrongdoers being punished in creative ways, most notably in the Ten Courts of Hell: one is having his tongue cut out, another is galled by a spear, others are variously impaled on spikes, gnawed by dogs, boiled in oil, bitten by snakes, sliced in two, drowned in the Filthy Blood Pond or ground into paste by enormous millstones. Some of the allegories and stories are obscure to say the least. Though doubtless highly significant to the cognoscenti of Chinese mythology, many of the stories will be lost on the uninitiated.

Its 9-ha site is five times the size of the original villa and its grounds. There is a large section on ancient China, with pagoda-roofed buildings, craft shops and restaurants serving authentic cuisine, as well as traditional theatre in which lion dances and wayangs are performed. The 'Creation of the World Theatre' tells classic tales from the Qin Dynasty; in the 'Legends and Heroes Theatre', a lifelike robot is programmed to relate stories; and a video in the 'Spirit of the Orient Theatre' explains Chinese folklore, customs, traditions and festivals. There is also a museum on the arrival of Chinese immigrants to Singapore.

Holland Village
ⓘ *Take the MRT to Buona Vista and then walk up Commonwealth Av to Holland Av (about 15 mins) or take bus No106 from Orchard Rd (stop outside YMCA).*

This is really a residential area – and was once the home to the British forces barracked in Singapore – but it also developed into one of the trendier parts of suburban Singapore and is a pleasant area to explore. It is very popular with expats, especially at weekends. There are restaurants and bars, small craft and antique shops, and a good wet market called Pasar Holland. The Holland Village Shopping Centre, on the first floor of Holland Avenue, is a good stop for Asian arts and crafts and there are ample places to eat (see page 630).

Jurong Bird Park
ⓘ *Jln Ahmad Ibrahim, T6265 0022, www.birdpark.com.sg, daily 0830-1800, last admission 1730. S$18, children aged 3-12 S$9, 3-in1 tickets to the bird park, zoo and night safari S$45, children S$22.50 (tickets valid for 1 month). There are several bird shows every hour. MRT westbound to Boon Lay then SBS bus No 194 or 251 from Boon Lay Bus Interchange. There is a monorail service round the park for those who find the heat too much, S$4, children S$2.*

Jurong Bird Park is a beautifully kept 20-ha haven for more than 8000 birds of 600 species from all over the world, including a large collection of Southeast Asian birds. As it is now difficult to see most of these birds in the wild in Southeast Asia, a trip here is well worthwhile. Highlights include the world's largest collection of Southeast Asian hornbills and South American toucans, a new African wetlands section and an entertaining air-conditioned penguin corner, complete with snow. Another main attraction is one of the largest walk-in aviaries in the world, with a 30-m-high man-made waterfall and 1500 birds, many of which will happily come and perch on guests and eat papaya chunks from their hands. Kids will enjoy the Birds and Buddies show at 1100 and 1500. There is also an interesting nocturnal house, with owls, herons, frogmouths and kiwis and bird shows throughout the day (the birds of prey show – at 1000 and 1600 – is particularly good).

Chinese and Japanese Gardens
ⓘ *T6261 3632, daily 0600-2300. Free, including the Bonsai Garden (daily 0900-1800), but there is a charge to enter the Garden of Abundance (S$2) and the Tortoise Museum (S$5). MRT to Chinese Gardens (W10) and then walk 200 m across the open-grassed area to the east gate.*

On Yuan Ching Road are these gardens, which extend over 13 ha on two islands in Jurong Lake. The Chinese garden (Yu-Hwa Yuan) is said to be modelled on an imperial Sung Dynasty garden and specifically on the classical style of Beijing's Summer Palace. There are artfully scattered boulders, Chinese pavilions and a brace-and-a-half of pagodas to give it that Oriental flavour, but it is hard to believe that the Sung emperors would have been happy with this. Rather more refined is the Penjing Garden (Yun Xiu Yuan – or Garden of

Beauty), a walled bonsai garden, which reputedly cost S$6 million to develop. The garden contains 3000 miniature potted *penjing* (bonsai) trees, sourced from all over Asia. The two outside the entrance are said to come from Sichuan and to be around 300 years old. They symbolize male and female lions guarding the entrance, but just in case these arboreal defenders should fail, there is also a pair of stone lions to act as back-up. Close to the main entrance is a large statue of the sage Confucious (551-479 BC), looking suitably studious and wise, and a stone boat craftily concealing a food outlet. On a small rise in the middle of the Chinese garden is the main pagoda, which towers up through six levels. It is possible to sweat your way to the top for a great view of HDB blocks.

Science Centre

ⓘ *15 Science Centre Rd, T6425 2500, www.science.edu.sg, Tue-Sun 1000-1800, S$6, children aged 3-16 S$3; Science Centre and 40-min IMAX film at the Omni Theatre (Tue-Sun 1000-2000) S$12.80, children aged 3-12 S$6.40; Science Centre and Snow City, S$16, children aged 3-16 S$14. Jurong East MRT and then bus No 335 or it's an 8-min walk.*

This centre might be aimed more at children than adults – it is usually packed with schoolchildren enjoying a few hours away from cramming – but there is plenty of fun for grown-ups too. The central hub of the museum has a figure of Einstein talking in a rather forced German accent, hatching chicks and various other exhibits, including a computer screen where it is possible to conduct plastic surgery on your face. From this hub radiates the Hall of Life Sciences, a Virtual Science Centre, the Aviation Centre, a children's Discovery Centre and a Physical Science Hall. In the Aviation Centre, where Changi Airport makes a predictably significant appearance, visitors are guided around the wonders of flight by Archie the Archaeopteryx – a sort of avine dinosauric maître d'. For an extra charge it is possible to fly a simulator. The Hall of Life Science's theme is humanity's impact on the earth and here there are some live animals along with a few talking dummies, including a dinosaur (spouting surprisingly unscientific rubbish) and Charles Darwin (far too thin) talking with an American-accented gorilla. Disney's *Jungle Book* has a lot to answer for. Overall, the centre succeeds in its mission to make science come alive, with plenty of gadgets and hands-on exhibits. It makes most sense to come here with children who will be able to spend several hours having fun and maybe even learn something.

Next door, in the **Omni-theatre** ⓘ *Tue-Sun 1000-2000, S$10, children aged 3-12 S$5,* the marvels of science, technology and the universe can be viewed in a 284-seat amphitheatre with a huge IMAX screen. Films have a scientific, geographical or natural history flavour – usually space exploration, an underwater journey or a flying adventure over some geological marvel. Excellent films and very popular.

Singapore Discovery Centre

ⓘ *510 Upper Jurong Rd, T6792 6188, www.sdc.com.sg, Tue-Sun 0900-1800, S$10, children aged 3-12 S$6, family (2 adults and 2 children) S$28 (includes on iWERKS movie screening); iWERKS S$8, children S$5. Westbound MRT to Joo Koon and then a 10-min walk, or MRT to Boon Lay (W12) and then connecting bus No 182 or 193.*

Located at the western end of the island, the Singapore Discovery Centre provides a hands-on insight into the past, present and possible future of the city state. Lots of high-tech interactive machines and play things make the centre popular with kids, such as a paintball set-up, which is great fun and plenty of exercise, plus a theatre and **iWERKS** ⓘ *T6792 6188, www.sdc.com.sg/iwerks,* a 3D cinema screening a wide variety of shows, from wildlife documentaries to Hollywood blockbusters.

Snow City

ⓘ *21 Jurong Town Hall Rd, T6560 2306, www.snowcity.com.sg, Tue-Sun 0945-1715, 1 hr S$16 (2 hrs S$27), children S$14 (2 hrs S$22), family (2 adults and 2 children) S$49. All prices include rental of jacket and boots and entry to the Science Centre. Jurong East MRT then bus No 335, 66 or a 10-min walk.*

Sun-bound Singapore now has its own indoor snow centre at Snow City, next to the Singapore Science Centre. Visitors can snowboard, snow-tube or ski up and down slopes covering 1200 sq m with walls rather kitschly painted with alpine snow scenes. There is an airlock at 10°C to get you acclimatized to the -5°C environment of the snow slopes. There's also a giant (so-called life-size – how do they know?) model of the Yeti, slides for children and permission to have snowball fights. Snow is made with an aptly named snow gun where water is shot out and cooled with liquid nitrogen. Around 15 tons of the white stuff are made every week to keep the slopes topped up with around 40-cm depth of crunchy snow. Guests are required to wear long trousers (pants) or will be forced to rent them. In an attempt to attract a more mature clientele, there is the **Ice Bar** ⓘ *Tue-Sun from 1900-2400*, with vodka in ice glasses and cheap beer promos. Also, occasional blizzard parties with house music, -5°C temperatures and falling snow.

East Coast

Katong and Geylang Serai

ⓘ *MRT to Eunos and then bus No 15 or a taxi, or take bus No 33 from Orchard Rd.*

Katong is an enclave of Peranakan architecture and there are still streets of well- preserved shophouses and terraced houses in their original condition. Restaurants in Katong serve some of the best Peranakan food in Singapore, including delicious pastries and sweets. **Joo Chiat Road**, which runs south down to the sea, is interesting for its unchanged early 20th-century shophouse fronts and famed for its girlie bars. The extravagant façades, found both here and on Koon Seng Road, are an excellent example of the Singapore Eclectic Style which evolved in the 1920s and 1930s. This whole area was originally a coconut plantation owned by a family of Arab descent – the Alsagoffs. A portion was purchased by a wealthy Chinese, Chew Joo Chiat, after whom a number of the roads are named (not just Joo Chiat Road; also Joo Chiat Lane, Joo Chiat Terrace and Joo Chiat Place). While most of the traditional businesses here have closed down or moved out, there are still some candlemakers struggling to make a living and a few other craftspeople.

Peter Wee's Katong Antique House ⓘ *268 East Coast Rd*, is well worth a visit if you are in the area, with its unsurpassed collection of Peranakan antiques and an owner who is probably the most knowledgeable person in Singapore on the Peranakan culture.

East Coast Park

ⓘ *Open 24 hrs, the park is lit from 1900-0700, free; bus No 16 from Orchard Rd and get off at Marine Terrace and walk under the underpass.*

This popular recreation area has beaches and gardens, as well as a tennis centre, a driving range, a sailing centre and a food centre. The sand along these beaches was imported from nearby Indonesian islands. The **East Coast Recreation Centre**, in the park, has the usual array of crazy golf, foodstalls, cycling, canoes and fun rides. A good half-day excursion, especially if you are with children, is to hire bicycles and ride along the track that winds its way up the East Coast. There are no hills and lots of food and drink stops. It's more fun than battling with the crowds and cars and is also relatively quiet Monday to Friday.

Ski 360° ⓘ *1206A East Coast Parkway, T6442 7318, www.ski360degree.com, daily 1000-2200, S$32 per hr Mon-Fri, S$42 per hr Sat-Sun*, is Singapore's first cable ski park, with participants tied to a cable and pulled around a lake at up to 58 kph on skis or a wakeboard. It's brilliant fun and much cheaper than hiring a boat and skis or board. Visit on a weekday morning when you're likely to have the park to yourself; weekends can be hellish.

The **Singapore Crocodile Farm** ⓘ *790 Upper Serangoon Rd, T6288 9385, www.singaporecrocfarm.com, daily 0900-1800, free; Kovan or Serangoon MRT or bus No 80, 81, 82, 107, 136 or 153*, is a commercial set-up. Here, visitors can learn about skinning techniques and various other methods of transforming scary reptiles into quiescent handbags and shoes. This farm, with its population of about 800 crocodiles, has been on the same site since 1945, importing crocodiles from rivers in Sarawak.

Changi Museum
ⓘ *1000 Upper Changi Rd, T6214 2451 www.changimuseum.com, daily 0930-1700, free, guided tours and audio tours S$8, children S$4. MRT to Tanah Merah and then bus No 2 or Tampines MRT then bus No 29.*

Changi prison, as featured on the 'Go to Jail' square in the Singapore version of Monopoly, is where Singapore's hangman dispenses with drug traffickers at dawn on Fridays with gruesome regularity. It was originally built to house 600 prisoners, but during the war more than 3500 civilians were incarcerated here. This museum tells the story of the prison and is mostly visited by Second World War veterans. In 1944, POWs were moved into the prison, and 12,000 American, Australian and British servicemen were interned in and around it. There are reproductions of WRM Haxworth's paintings and the then 17-year-old trooper George

East Coast

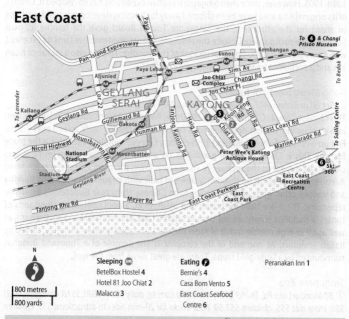

To ④ & Changi Prison Museum

Sleeping 🛏
BetelBox Hostel 4
Hotel 81 Joo Chiat 2
Malacca 3

Eating 🍴
Bernie's 4
Casa Bom Vento 5
East Coast Seafood Centre 6

Peranakan Inn 1

800 metres
800 yards

Aspinall's photographs, which record the misery of internment. A replica of the atap-roofed Changi Prison chapel stands in the prison yard. The memorial chapel's original altar cross, whose base was made from a Howitzer shell casing, was returned to the chapel in 1992.

Escape Theme Park
ⓘ *1 Pasir Ris Close, T6581 9112, www.escapethemepark.com.sg, Sat, Sun and public holidays only 1000-2000. S$16.50, children $8.30. MRT to Pasir Ris and then a 10-min walk.*
This park features 14 rides that vary from the mellow to the gut-wrenching, with a few classics such as the Pirate Ship and Asia's highest water flume. The Inverter flips passengers over in 360 degree circles – not good after a solid Indian pure-veg lunch.

Next door is **Wild Wild Wet** ⓘ *T6581 9112, www.wildwildwet.com, Mon and Wed-Fri 1300-1900, Sat-Sun 1000-1900, S$15.50, children S$10.50*, a water theme park with a selection of rides including the Ular-lah flume, the Waterworks and rides for toddlers.

North of the island

Siong Lim Temple
ⓘ *184 Jln Toa Payoh. Take the MRT to Toa Payoh, then bus No 8 or 26, getting off at HDB block 195, 1 stop past the Toa Payoh stadium.*
This temple lies due north of the city, within the modern suburb of Toa Payoh. This Fujian temple's full name is Lian Shan, Shuang Lin (meaning Lotus Hill, Twin Groves) referring to the sal grove in Kunisnara, near Patna, where the Buddha attained enlightenment. It is the largest Buddhist temple in Singapore, originally built 1898-1905. However, since then Singapore's urban expansion has enveloped it. Chunks of its original 4 ha area have been chipped away for housing development and, perhaps to atone for the effrontery, the Singapore Tourist Board gave the temple its own Suzhou-style rock garden. Despite the redevelopments, the temple retains its excellent wood carvings and some fine Thai images of the Buddha. There is also a statue of Kuan Yin and a corpulent image of the Maitreya Buddha.

Kong Meng San Phor Kark
ⓘ *Get off at Bishan MRT station and take bus No 410.*
This Chinese Temple Complex (Bright Hill Drive) has, since its construction in 1989, grown into a sprawling, million-dollar religious centre whose golden roofs spread over 7.5 ha. Fed up with tastefully mouldering 19th-century Chinese temples? Then this is the place for you. This is Chinese temple garishness on a truly gargantuan scale; restraint was clearly not a word in the architect's vocabulary. From the main entrance on Sin Ming Avenue, pilgrims climb up through a series of halls with images of the historic Buddha and various other gods and goddesses from Chinese Mahayana Buddhism's extensive repertoire. There are halls for prayer and meditation, a pool containing thousands of turtles, a Buddhist library, an old-people's home (and, appropriately, a crematorium), as well as a 9 m-high marble statue of Kuan Yin, the 15-headed goddess of mercy, carved by Italian sculptors. At one end of the complex is The Temple of a Thousand Buddhas surmounted by a large gold stupa. There are great views from the roof.

Singapore Zoo
ⓘ *80 Mandai Lake Rd, T6269 3411, www.zoo.com.sg, daily 0830-1800, S$18, children (3-12) S$9; tram ride S$5, children S$2.50. Boat docks for 20-min rides to attractions, S$5, children*

S$2.50. For a 3-in-1 ticket for the zoo, night safari and Jurong Bird Park, see the bird park on page 608; combined Zoo and Night Safari, S$32, children S$16. Take the MRT to Ang Mo Kio and then bus No 138 from the station. A taxi from the city costs S$20 and takes 30 mins.

These zoological gardens have one of the world's few open zoos – with moats replacing bars – making it also one of the most attractive zoos, with animals in environments vaguely reminiscent of their habitats. Only the polar bears and the tigers seem unhappy in their surroundings. It contains over 332 species of animals (about 3000 actual animals), some of them rare – like the dinosauric Komodo dragons and the golden lion tamarin – as well as many endangered species from Asia, such as the Sumatran tiger and the clouded leopard. The pygmy hippos are relatively recent newcomers; they live in glass-fronted enclosures (as do the polar bears), so visitors can watch their underwater exploits. Animals are sponsored by companies; Tiger Beer, for example, sponsors the tigers and Qantas the kangaroos.

There are animal shows throughout the day carrying a strong ecological message: elephants (at 1130 and 1530) and penguins, sea lions and manatees at the newly revamped Splash Ampitheatres (at 1100, 1430 and 1700). Animal feeding times are provided upon arrival. There is a Treetops Trail, where visitors can view primates, crocodiles, squirrels and pheasants from a 6 m-high boardwalk. There is a children's area too, with farm animals, a miniature train and play equipment. There are tram tours for those too weary to walk (S$5 and S$2.50), with recorded commentaries, and several restaurants. Elephant, camel and pony rides are on offer at various times each afternoon. A shop sells environmentally sound T-shirts and cuddly toy animals. Overall, it is a well-managed and informative zoo; it's well worth the trip out here.

Night Safari

ⓘ www.nightsafari.com.sg, daily 1900-2400, S$22, children S$11; with tram ride S$32, children S$16. The last tram leaves at 2315. No flash cameras permitted. 3-in-1 park combination tickets for Night Safari, Zoo and Jurong Bird Park, see the bird park on page 608, 2-in-1 combination ticket S$32, children S$16. To get there, see Singapore Zoo, above.

The unique Night Safari is situated adjacent to the zoo, covering 40 ha of secondary growth tropical forest. The area has been cunningly converted into a series of habitats, populated with wildlife from the Indo-Malayan, Indian, Himalayan and African zoogeographical regions. The park supports 1200 animals belonging to 110 species, including the tiger, Indian lion, great Indian rhinoceros, fishing cat, Malayan tapir, Asian elephant, bongo, striped hyena, Cape buffalo and giraffe. Visitors can either hop on a tram to be taken on a 40-minute guided safari through the jungle, lit by moonglow lighting and informed by a rather earnest commentary, or they can walk along three short trails at their own pace. It's extremely well conceived and managed, with 'tribal' performances, opportunities to meet and sometimes touch animals such as pythons, and also a 'creatures of the night show', which on busy nights may become overbooked, so arrive early. The experience is rewardingly authentic – possibly because the night-time ambience hides the seams that are usually so evident in orthodox zoos. Children love the safari experience, believing that they truly are chancing upon animals in the jungle. At the entrance 'lodge' there is a good noodle bar. There is also another small café at the East Lodge. Bear in mind that the combined zoo and night safari tickets, although offering good value, don't include the additional tram ride, which most consider a highlight.

The Kranji War Memorial and Cemetery

ⓘ *Woodlands Rd, bus 170 goes direct from Rochor Rd; alight opposite the entrance to the cemetery. On weekends, bus No 181 also stops here.*

The Kranji War Memorial and Cemetery, on a gentle hillside overlooking the Straits of Johor, is where Allied soldiers killed in Singapore in the Second World War are buried. In the heart of the cemetery is the war memorial, bearing the names of 24,346 Allied servicemen who died in the Asia-Pacific region during the war. The design of the memorial is symbolic, representing the three arms of the services – the army, navy and air force. The upright section represents a conning tower, the lateral elements are wings, and the walls symbolize army lines. Flowers are not allowed to be placed on graves, in case tiger mosquitoes breed in the jars.

Nature reserves

For Singapore's green areas, see www.wildsingapore.com or www.ulusingapore.com.

The 87-ha **Sungei Buloh Wetland Reserve** ⓘ *Neo Tiew Cres, T6794 1401, www.sbwr.org.sg, Mon-Fri 0730-1900, Sat-Sun and public holidays, 0700-1900, S$1, children S$0.50. Take MRT to Kranji and then bus No 925, on Sat and Sun bus No 925 runs to the park entrance, but Mon-Fri it's a further 20-min walk,* is Singapore's first designated wetland nature reserve. It is an important stopover point for birds migrating along the East Asian Flyway. Carefully constructed hides give excellent observation points to view birds such as sea eagles, kites and blue herons. There are four walks, from 500 m to 7 km, including a boardwalk through a mangrove swamp. There are guided tours that need pre-booking or free tours on Saturday at 0930 and 1530.

Bukit Timah Nature Reserve ⓘ *Hindhede Drive off Upper Bukit Timah Rd, T6468 5736, www.nparks.gov.sg, open 0630-1900, though the visitors' centre isn't open until 0830, it is possible to enter the reserve earlier, free; from Newton MRT station take bus Nos 67, 170 or 171,* nestles in the centre of the island and has a resident population of wild monkeys, pythons and scorpions. It was one of the first forest reserves, established in 1883 for the purposes of protecting the native flora and fauna. The naturalist Alfred Russel Wallace collected beetles at Bukit Timah in 1854. Jungle trails go through the forested terrain (130-million-year-old tropical rainforest) that once covered the whole island. The artificial lakes supply the city with much of its water. Clearly marked paths (one of them metalled) in the 81-ha reserve lead to Singapore's highest point (164 m) for scenic views. A visitor centre includes an exhibition on natural history. The nature reserve is at its quietest and coolest in the early mornings. It's possible to hike through to the MacRitchie Reservoir from here, but check with park rangers on the state of the trail first. It's a wonderful walk and well worth a day to do.

Bukit Batok Nature Park ⓘ *0700-1900, the park is a 5-min walk from Bukit Gombak MRT Station,* is a very beautiful secondary forest with trails leading up the main hill. It was developed around an abandoned quarry – the quarry has been filled in to create a small lake. There is a durian orchard (which is pungent during durian season) and picnic areas. At the top of Batok hill are the remains of two Japanese war memorials.

Pulau Ubin

ⓘ *T6542 4108, www.nparks.gov.sg; from Changi Point it costs S$2 to go to Pulau Ubin; bumboats go when they're full – very frequently at the weekends – and operate between 0600 and 2300. It is possible to charter the whole vessel if you want to be alone, or are bored waiting for the boat to fill up. For transport to and from Changi Village, see page 611.*

The source of granite for the causeway and Singapore's earlier buildings and skyscrapers, the name Pulau Ubin derives from the Javanese word for 'squared stone'. Ubin village affords a taste of Singapore in bygone days, with dilapidated wooden shophouses, coffee shops and community spirit. The island, with its beaten-up cars and old taxis, quarry pits, jungle tracks, hills, beaches and challenging trails, is a mountain-biker's paradise and has become a popular destination for that reason, as the trails are quite challenging; it is possible to hire bicycles in the village. There is also an **outward bound centre** ① *T6546 1197*, on the island. Wildlife on the island includes the red jungle-fowl (from which domesticated chickens are descended), straw-headed bulbul, Brahminy kites, white-bellied fish eagles, mangrove pitta, flying fox bats, fruit bats and tomb bats, the Oriental whip snake (an unmissable bright yellow colour), long-tailed macaques, house musang, civet and wild pigs. The hill in the centre of the island provides great views over to Singapore. There are some sandy beaches on the north shore, though they can be dirty at low tide.

The Urban Redevelopment Authority (URA) has also published plans to reclaim an additional 2694 ha on Pulau Ubin and Pulau Tekong (the majority on Tekong, which houses a military training camp and is not open to the public).

Canoes, kayaks and mountain bikes are all available for hire on the island. Mountain bikes can also be hired from Changi Village – S\$20 per day (S\$10 returnable deposit).

Outer islands

The little-visited southern islands of St Johns, Kusu, Sister Islands and Pulau Hantu (Ghost Island) are great getaways from the hustle and bustle of the city. There are scheduled ferry services to Kusu and St Johns from Marina South Pier with **Singapore Island Cruises** ① *T6534 9339, www.islandcruise.com.sg, S\$15, check website for scheduled departures*. This company also charter boats to Sister Islands and Pulau Hantu from West Coast Pier.

Kusu Island is also known as Tortoise Island after a legend that describes how a turtle turned itself into an island to save two shipwrecked mariners. Da bo Gong, a Chinese temple on the island, was built in 1923 and dedicated to Kuan Yin and Dab o Gong. Ethnic Chinese flock to the island around the ninth lunar month to pray for good health. It is not permitted to stay overnight. St Johns, formerly known by its Malay name of Pulau Sekijang Bendara, is a mellow 39-ha island 6.5 km from Singapore and used by Singaporeans for a little relaxation. There are some excellent **holiday bungalows** ① *T1800-736 8672, S\$107 weekend, half price weekdays, bring your own food*, on the island that can be rented cheaply for the weekend.

A Malay myth tells of the formation of **Sister Islands**. Two sisters who were very close couldn't bear to be separated. One was kidnapped by a lovestruck Orang Laut chief. As she was being forced into the boat, the sky turned black and a storm broke. The other sister weeping on the jetty was engulfed by a huge wave. On seeing this, the kidnapped sister wrestled free from her sea gyspy captor and leapt into the waves. Neither sister was ever seen again, and these mysterious islets rose from the depths of their final resting place.

Pulau Hantu was thought to be formed from the bodies of two fighting warriors sucked into the sea by a whirlpool. It is possible to camp on both these islands, and those with the right equipment could enjoy a beautifully tranquil stay. Campers must first register with the Southern Islands Management at administrator@sentose.com.sg.

Singapore listings

Hotel and guesthouse prices
L Over US$200 AL US$91-200 A US$41-90
B US$21-40 C US$12-20 D US$7-11

Restaurant prices
††† over US$12 †† US$4-12 † under US$4
See pages 561-563 for further information.

Sleeping

Most budget accommodation is in the Little India and Arab Street areas to the north of town. See also Sleeping, page 561.

Colonial core p576, map p578

L **Conrad Centennial**, 2 Temasek Blvd, T6334 8888, www.conradhotels.com. Close to Suntec City and good for the business traveller. A total of 509 beautifully designed contemporary rooms, with lots of space, big windows and a large desk. Superb service, excellent meeting rooms and an impressive mezzanine level for functions. There is a fabulous collection of around 3000 expensive artworks throughout the hotel. Decent-sized pool for lengths and adequate fitness centre. Recommended.

L **Raffles**, 1 Beach Rd, T6337 1886, www.singapore-raffles.raffles.com. Singapore's most famous hotel and, despite criticisms, it is still a great place to stay – if you can afford it. There are 8 restaurants and a Culinary Academy, 5 bars (see entries under Eating, page 622) and it's surrounded by 70 shops. The 104 suites have been immaculately refurbished, with wooden floors, high ceilings, stylish colonial furniture and plenty of space. Bathrooms are the ultimate in luxury and the facilities are excellent, including a peaceful rooftop pool with jacuzzis and a (rather small) gym, both 24 hr. Very exclusive and highly recommended. See also page 581.

L **Ritz-Carlton Millenia**, 7 Raffles Av, Marina Bay, T6337 8888, www.ritzcarlton.com/hotels/singapore. Both this hotel and the **Conrad Centennial** were designed by US Hirsch Bedner. There are ultra-modern furnishings, major investment in artworks (notably the

Frank Stella and the Dele Chihuly glass balls below the lobby area) and attractive rooms with wooden floors and big bathrooms that provide stunning views of the harbour and river. Large pool area with jacuzzi in well-landscaped grounds and a huge fitness centre. Good business facilities. Recommended.

L **Swissotel The Stamford**, 2 Stamford Rd, T6338 8585, www.singapore-stamford.swissotel.com. Designed by Chinese architect IM Pei, who also designed the futuristic Bank of China building in Hong Kong, this hotel stands tall over with city with the **New Asia Bar** on the top floor providing stunning views over 3 countries: Singapore, Malaysia and Indonesia. There are 13 restaurants, an attractive triple circular pool (great for children) and a high-tech fitness centre. But with over 1200 rooms and a vast echoing lobby, it's all a little over-whelming and too large for a personal touch. It has a good reputation in the business world.

L-AL **Grand Park City Hall**, 10 Coleman St, T6336 3456, www.parkhotel group.com. This marble-cladded monster has a huge echoing lobby and dreamy spa. Despite its size (327 rooms), it feels quite intimate. There are 2 restaurants, a bar, an attractive but smallish pool and jacuzzi, gym and spa. It also has a business centre. Recommended.

AL **Naumi**, 41 Seah St, T6403 6000, www.naumihotel.com. Gorgeous, intimate boutique hotel with ultra-modern decor, well set up for business travellers. The executive patio suites are huge and have an outdoor terrace, perfect for an evening drink. There is a contemporary fitness centre, rooftop infinity pool with delightful views over the city and bar and restaurant. Recommended.

Singapore River and the City p585, maps p578 and p592

L-AL **Fullerton Hotel**, 1 Fullerton Square, T6733 8388, www.fullertonhotel.com. Great position at the head of the Singapore River, this 5-star hotel has 400 rooms in Philippe Starck style, very functional and well equipped, but slightly on the small side compared (say) with the **Ritz Carlton**. There are excellent restaurants and a stunning infinity pool with views over Singapore River, the CBD and Boat Quay.

L-AL Grand Copthorne Waterfront, 392 Havelock Rd, T6733 0880, www.grand copthorne.com.sg. This rather overblown monster has a rambling lobby, a good gym, 2 tennis courts and a small but attractive pool. There are also extensive business services, a sushi bar and a fusion restaurant. With 574 rooms, there's no sense of intimacy here, but it does a roaring trade, so they must have got something right.

L-AL The Scarlet Hotel, 33 Erskine Rd, T6511 3333, www.thescarlethotel.com. Super-swish award-winning boutique hotel of dark red fabrics and jet black marble, this hotel resembles a luxury cross between *Pirates of the Caribbean* and *Dracula*. Helpful staff and a lovely colonial building make for a pricey but memorable base camp in Singapore. Good for a romantic weekend.

AL Gallery, 1 Nanson Rd, Robertson Quay, T6849 8686, www.galleryhotel.com.sg. This Philippe Starck-styled hotel with 223 minimalist rooms. Brightly coloured cushions provide light relief from the austerity in the standard rooms, with showers only. Free internet access in all rooms and 'smart wired rooms' have sensor- controlled lighting and a/c. The pool is original, with glass on all sides. Superb Japanese and French eateries. Chill-out lounges and bars including the popular **EM Studio** club and **EM by the River** bar. A thoroughly funky choice.

AL Swissotel Merchant Court, 20 Merchant Rd, T6337 9993, www.swissotel.com. This 500-room hotel has an attractive freeform pool in a rooftop garden setting with slides and a separate jacuzzi overlooking the river. Excellent fitness centre. Great location.

Chinatown p589, map p592
Chinatown accommodation has more individuality, but rooms can be small.

AL Amara, 165 Tanjong Pagar Rd, T6879 2555, www.amarahotels.com.

Well maintained, with 380 average-sized rooms and good extras such as self-service launderette. Several restaurants (with one of the best Thais in town, **Thanying**, see page 626), an excellent Vietnamese restaurant called **Hue**, and a coffee shop serving a good buffet (mid-range), decent-sized pool with a café area for steamboat and barbecues. There are also 4 tennis courts, a jogging track and a gym. Business centre. Good location to explore Chinatown or for business visitors.

AL Hotel 1929, 50 Keong Saik Rd, T6347 1929, www.hotel1929.com. Tasteful, slick boutique hotel with well-furnished rooms. The owners have used their own collection of retro and designer furniture for this quirkily restored shophouse. The 32 rooms are small, but so chic that size does not matter. There's a small rooftop jacuzzi, and excellent restaurant, **Ember**. Highly recommended.

AL The Inn at Temple Street, 36 Temple St, T6221 5333, www.theinn.com.sg. Billing itself as a boutique hotel, the 42 rooms do have a certain charm, each well appointed with safe, cable TV, Wi-Fi and Peranakan-style furniture and attached shower (in standard rooms) or bath (in de luxe rooms). On the downside, rooms are very small; not even de luxe rooms have space for a desk (except in the few single rooms), which will deter business travellers.

AL-A Keong Saik, 69 Keong Saik Rd, T6223 0660, www.keongsaikhotel.com.sg. An intimate little 'business' hotel in a sensitively restored shophouse. 25 a/c immaculately presented rooms with attractive wooden furniture. It is let down by small room size, with little space for anything other than the bed. Standard rooms have no windows, or skylights in the attic rooms. Wi-Fi in lobby only (chargeable).

Orchard Road and Botanic Gardens
p595, map p596
There is little to differentiate the numerous 4- and 5-star hotels strung out along the road, concentrated towards the western end.

L Concorde, 100 Orchard Rd, T6733 8855, www.concordehotel.com.sg. Open-plan lobby filled with a bewildering array of furniture, with 4 terraces of rooms and garlands of orchids. Good-sized rooms with queen-sized beds and attractive decor; ask for a room overlooking the pool, as these have a balcony. Pool and gym.

L Four Seasons, 190 Orchard Blvd, T6734 1110, www.fourseasons.com/singapore. Hard to beat, this intimate hotel of 254 rooms and more than 300 staff, provides exceptional personal service. Rooms are elegantly decorated in traditional European style, with feather pillows, writing desk, and spacious bathrooms. The hotel has a unique Asian art collection, with 1500 pieces, including artwork in all the rooms. There are 2 pools (one is for lengths), the only a/c tennis courts in Singapore, a golf simulator and a well-equipped fitness centre. Full spa service with Thai masseuses. Restaurants include Cantonese and international cuisine. The weekend brunch at Jiang-Nan Chun is a real treat with over 100 dishes to choose from. Although mainly a business hotel, children are well catered for. Recommended.

L Goodwood Park, 22 Scotts Rd, T6737 7411, www.goodwoodparkhotel.com. Apart from Raffles Hotel, this is the only other colonial hotel in Singapore. The exterior is rakish rather than modern and the lobby isn't very encouraging, but the 233 rooms are exceptional. Colonial-style rooms have ceiling fans, windows that can be opened, stylish minimalist decor and lots of space. The modern ones are slightly smaller, but overlook a pool. Some ground-level rooms lead straight out to the poolside. All are fitted with the latest electronic equipment. There is a lovely pool area, set in a garden with pagodas, and another larger pool for lengths. It has several restaurants (see page 627). Recommended.

L Grand Hyatt, 10 Scotts Rd, T6738 1234, www.singapore.grand.hyatt.com. Owned by the Sultan of Brunei, this hotel has larger than average rooms – all with an alcove sitting area (some with poolside view) – and separate showers. Its selling points are its garden and fitness facilities. There is a spectacular large 5th-floor garden, with a roaring waterfall and lovely pool area, poolside bar and restaurant.

The executive-class rooms have their own private Balinese garden (good for families), while those on the 5th floor open out onto a large terrace area. There are also squash courts, 2 tennis courts, huge fitness centre with aerobics classes, fabulous jacuzzi and sauna. There is a popular nightclub, **Brix**, a good restaurant, **Mezza9**, and the glassy **Mezza9** martini bar. It's mainly for business clients, but good discounts are available. Recommended.

L Hilton, 581 Orchard Rd, T6737 2233, www.hilton.com. The first international hotel in Singapore. It has 434 average-sized rooms and despite its age it has a good reputation. It's especially popular with business people and Japanese tour groups. The **Kaspia Bar** has live jazz. Small, dated rooftop pool and good gym.

L Orchard, 442 Orchard Rd, T6734 7766, www.orchardhotel.com.sg. Rooms are decent sized and the bathrooms have separate showers; a luxury in Singapore. Large pool but no shade, excellent fitness centre and sauna. Its main highlight is its magnificent ballroom.

L Pan Pacific Orchard, 10 Claymore Rd, T6737 0811, www.panpacific.com. This 206-room hotel, quieter and away from the crowds, prides itself on an intimate atmosphere. It pampers business visitors with a personalized service (no reception counters here) and a very high standard throughout. There are no 'club' floors; but rooms are unusual and larger than average. Bathrooms are spacious and there are separate showers. There is a large mineral water swimming pool (but rather exposed sitting area), a very sophisticated fitness centre and a jacuzzi. Recommended.

L Regent, 1 Cuscaden Rd, T6733 8888, www.regenthotels.com. Huge ostentatious lobby with bubble lifts and sterile atmosphere, reminiscent of tenement blocks. In a quiet location at western end of Orchard Rd, this hotel is notable for its excellent service and attention to detail. There are gloomy corridors, 439 large but quite plain rooms, an excellent fitness centre and a circular pool with a barren sunbathing area.

L Shangri-La, 22 Orange Grove Rd, T6737 3644, www.shangri-la.com. One of Singapore's finest hotels, set in 15 acres of beautifully maintained and spacious landscaped gardens. There are 750 stylish rooms; the ones in the refined and relaxed Valley Wing are superior and the service is exceptional. Superb facilities include a spacious pool area surrounded by greenery and waterfalls, jacuzzi, indoor pool, good fitness centre, squash and tennis courts, and 3-hole pitch-and-putt golf. There are 4 good restaurants: **Shang Palace** for dim sum, the Japanese **Nadamon**, **The Line**, serving excellent international fare, and the outstanding **Blu**, a Californian-French eatery. Recommended. **L Sheraton Towers**, 39 Scotts Rd, T6737 6888, www.sheratonsingapore.com. Quietly sophisticated lobby, with waterfalls and beautiful flowers everywhere, 412 rooms with bare corridors but good rooms. The more expensive rooms provide an exceptional service, with lots of extras thrown in. The Cabana rooms on the rooftop overlook the pool. Attractive pool area with bar. Italian restaurant and exclusive Cantonese restaurant. **AL Singapore Marriott**, 320 Orchard Rd, T6735 5800, www.marriott.com/sindt. Another vast hotel towering over Orchard Rd with its iconic green pagoda roof. This place has 393 rooms with LCD TV and broadband internet access. Good fitness centre, large pool with separate whirlpool. Extensive business services, efficient but unwelcoming. Central. **AL Traders**, 1A Cuscaden Rd, T6738 2222, www.shangri-la.com. Lavish pots of orchids at the entrance makes it feel special, but there isn't much to mark this hotel apart from the competition. It has 546 rooms and about three-quarters of its guests are business people. Rooms are average, but there is an attractive large freeform pool. Fitness centre, business centre and 4 bars and restaurants. Nothing special and a bit stuck out on its own near the western section of Orchard Rd. **A VIP**, 5 Balmoral Crescent, T6235 4277, www.viphotel.com.sg. Set in a quiet area close to the **Garden Hotel** and west of the Newton MRT station, about 2.5km from Orchard road, this place has added new rooms lately and

now has 57 with a/c, rather floral chairs and colour TV. There's also a restaurant and pool with jacuzzi, spa, café, internet facilities. Wi-Fi is available in rooms at S$3 per day. **A-B Metropolitan YMCA**, 60 Stevens Rd, T6839 8333, www.mymca.org.sg. All rooms are a/c. A no-frills place, providing efficient service and clean serviceable private rooms and single-sex dorms. The added bonus is a large pool. Excellent value. Massive discounts for online bookings. Recommended. **A-B YMCA International House One Orchard**, 1 Orchard Rd, T6336 6000, www.ymca.org.sg. Facilities are well above the usual YMCA standards, with a/c, restaurant, rooftop pool, squash courts, badminton, billiards and fitness centre. Very clean, efficient and in an unbeatable position at the head of Orchard Rd next to the National Museum. Rooms are minimalist but clean, spacious and light. Good coffee shop, but the constant religious soundtrack can be a bit much. Not cheap, but good value for the location. Recommended. **A-B YWCA Fort Canning Lodge**, 6 Fort Canning Rd, T6338 4222, www.nof.ywca.org.sg. Large modern building with 175 plus rooms, pool, tennis courts, ballroom, exhibition hall and Wi-Fi in the lobby and café. It's not your average youth hostel. Dorms available.

Little India *p598, map p599*

This area offers the best selection of budget digs in town. With some excellent new hostels opening in recent years, this vibrant area is a great place to base yourself and has excellent facilities for those travelling on a shoestring, or anyone seeking a bit of local style away from the glassy towerblocks. **AL Perak**, 12 Perak Rd, T6299 7733, www.peraklodge.net. One of Singapore's better mid-range options, this early 19th-century building has an archipelago flavour, wooden overtones and comfortable rooms with cable TV, minifridge and Wi-Fi. Some of the rooms are a little dim, so ask to see a selection. Friendly atmosphere, excellent buffet breakfast with daily newspapers and good location down a side street in the heart of Little

India. There's a pleasant reception area and 2 family suites/ apartments make the most of the attic space. Highly recommended.

AL-A Albert Court, 180 Albert St, T6339 3939, www.albertcourt.com.sg. Hotel filled with fusion accents, a mix of Western and Peranakan styles and motifs lying behind a courtyard of renovated shophouses. This is an intimate place built to high specifications, with attractive extras. Ask for a room with big windows. Right next to a good range of restaurants in Albert Court. Recommended.

AL-A Bencoolen, 47 Bencoolen St, T6336 0822, www.hotelbencoolen.com. Popular mid-range choice with good bathrooms and breakfast included. Rooms here are inoffensively bland, but perfectly comfortable. There's a small rooftop pool and chill-out area on the 1st floor.

AL-A Ibis, 170 Bencoolen St, T6593 2888, www.ibishotel.com. Over 530 rooms in an excellent location between Bugis and Little India. This functional hotel isn't wildly exciting, but rooms have all the mod cons for a comfortable stay. Bar and restaurant on the ground floor. Good promotional rates often available; check the website.

AL-A Summer View, 173 Bencoolen St, T6338 1122, www.summerviewhotel.com.sg. Decent mid-range hotel offering with comfortable rooms with bathtub and Wi-Fi access. Good Thai restaurant.

AL-B Hangout @ Mt Emily, 10A Upper Wilkie Rd, T6438 5588, www.hangouthotels.com. Accessed by a steep set of steps and resting on top of a hill, this is prime flashpacker accommodation with comfy, bright modern rooms and dorms with free Wi-Fi access; a patio area with games and a chill-out lounge with TV, newspapers and magazines to browse. Excellent range of facilities. Significant discounts available for online reservations. Highly recommended.

A Hotel 81 Bencoolen, 41 Bencoolen St, T6336 8181, www.hotel81.com.sg. Singaporean version of a love hotel, with lots of intriguing noises late at night and queues of lovers waiting in the lobby at weekends for a short-time room, this place manages to keep its head above sleaze, with professional staff, spotless rooms with cable TV, and attached bathroom. Wi-fi is available for an extra daily charge, This hotel is a good value option if the guesthouses are full. There are branches all over the island including on Rochor Rd and Dickson Rd in Little India. Most rooms are windowless. Fair value.

A-B G4 Station, 11 Mackenzie Rd, T6334 5644, www.g4station.com. Sparkling new hostel that has taken the Singapore backpacker scene by storm with its spotless dorms and double rooms, friendly staff and superb location on the edge of Little India. Free Wi-Fi, and a handy coin-operated laundry. Recommended.

A-C Footprints Hostel, 25A Perak Rd, T6295 5134, www.footprintshostel.com.sg. Friendly hostel with a range of 6-12 bed dorms and a couple of private doubles. The communal toilets are kept clean and there are enough of them to ensure no leg crossing in the morning. Free Wi-Fi access, breakfast. Friendly staff and communal TV area. Recommended.

B-C The Hive, 624 Serangoon Rd, T6341 5041, www.thehivebackpackers.com. Good value lodgings near Boon Keng MRT. Rooms here vary a lot from airy and bright to dark and sad, so check a selection. The de luxe rooms, at S$5 more than the standards, are worth the money in terms of extra space and natural light. Beds can be a bit creaky. Free Wi-Fi and internet access, breakfast, loads of travel information and friendly staff.

B-C (dorms **D** pp) **Inn Crowd Backpackers Hotel**, 73 Dunlop St, T6296 9169, www.the-inncrowd.com. State-of-the-art backpackers' hostel. Colourful and welcoming with all the facilities you need: internet, kitchen, communal lounge with TV and plenty of DVDs, breakfast included and a bar next door. Dorms are basic but clean and there are good showers. The only slight problem is its own success, with rooms often booked weeks in advance.

B-C Prince Of Wales,101 Dunlop St, T6229 0130, www.pow.com.sg. Prime backpacker lodgings with a mixture of clean dorms and a few newly renovated doubles in the depths of Little India. Modelled on an Australian pub/inn, the **POW** has live music downstairs most nights (fairly noisy). Convivial vibes and friendly staff. Recommended.

Arab Street p601, map p602

In Arab Street, budget accommodation in Rochor Rd and North Bridge Rd (on the corner of Liang Seah St) is nicely juxtaposed with the bustling upmarket Parco Bugis shopping complex and the glitzy **Intercontinental**.

L Intercontinental, 80 Middle Rd, Bugis Junction, T6338 7600, www.singapore.inter continental.com. This beautifully designed hotel is one of Singapore's best. It is situated at the edge of the colonial core in the Arab St area, in an attractively renovated and extended block of art deco shophouses, with a high-rise block behind. It has over 400 good-sized rooms with spacious bathrooms and every luxury provided, attractive rooftop pool with jacuzzi and well-equipped fitness centre. There's a business centre with small meeting room. The Shophouse Rooms are the hotel's showpiece with original Peranakan and colonial furniture and parquet floors.

AL Golden Landmark, 390 Victoria St, T6297 2828, www.goldenlandmark.com.sg. This 400-room tower block (with Arabic overtones) has a façade more retro than its 1980s birthdate would indicate. It has an Indonesian restaurant, a big pool and a business centre. It caters mainly for tours and corporate clients.

A Park View, 81 Beach Rd, T6338 8558, www.parkview.com.sg. Medium-sized hotel without pool or gym, but with well-appointed rooms. The de luxe rooms are a good size and better value than the cramped standard (no windows) and superior rooms.

A-C Sleepy Sam's, 55 Bussorah St, T9277 4988, www.sleepysams.com. Quiet and charming location away from the crowds, these lodgings provide clean private rooms and dorms (including a women-only dorm), internet access and helpful staff.

B Superb Hub, 144 Arab St, T9669 9990, www.superbhub.co.cc. Whilst rooms here are good value and spotlessly clean, they are small and many are windowless. The place needs an injection of charm, but if it's quiet, simple, safe and clean lodgings you're after, this place is more than adequate. Free Wi-Fi.

B-D Cozy Corner Guesthouse, 490 North Bridge Rd, 2nd floor, T6224 6859, www.cozycornerguest.com. This is serious backpacker territory with some of the cheapest rooms in town. Don't expect anything other than a room to crash in and cleanish shared toilets. Dorms available, and free internet access. The location is good, above Muslim and Indian restaurants on North Bridge Rd, just south of Liang Seah St. Free breakfast.

HarbourFront and Sentosa p603, map p605

Staying in these hotels, as Stan Sesser put it in his *New Yorker* piece on Singapore, is rather like being a prisoner in a theme park.

L Amara Sanctuary, 1 Larkhill Rd, T6825 3888, www.amarahotels.com. Award-winning hotel set in lush tropical greenery on a hillside overlooking Pahlawan beach. The 121 rooms and villas are extraordinarily well furnished, some with private garden and plunge pool. Of the 3 pools, the rooftop infinity pool has gorgeous views over the busy shipping lanes to the Riau Islands. Gym, spa and a handful of top-draw Asian and Western dining options.

L Sentosa Resort and Spa, 2 Bukit Manis Rd, T6275 0331, www.thesentosa.com. A/c, restaurants, large (33 m) pool, gym, tennis courts, archery, volley ball court, squash courts, access to the 18-hole Tanjong golf course, luxurious spa and 27 acres of grounds. The most refined of the hotels on Sentosa; smaller, quieter and more elegant than the Rasa Sentosa, with excellent service.

L Siloso Beach Resort, 51 Imbiah Walk, T6722 3333, www.silosobeachresort.com. With promises of eco-friendly principles, including a heat absorbing garden and pool filled with water from an underground reservoir, this sleek hotel is good for those seeking a bit of romance, a stone's throw from hip Siloso beach. Rooms are modern and functional and most have sea views and branded Posturepedic mattresses. Those with a bit of cash to splash can check out the rooftop suites with their gardens featuring fabulous views, bathtub, sun loungers and jacuzzi.

AL Shangri-La Rasa Sentosa, 101 Silosa Rd, T6275 0900, www.shangri-la.com. At the western tip of the island, facing the beach, a/c, restaurant, freeform pool, sports facilities, crèche, clean beach (sterilized sand imported from Indonesia) with water OK for swimming. Built in a curve, behind Fort Siloso, this hotel has first-class facilities and an unsurpassed view of the oil refinery just across the water, competitive weekend package deals available – though it can get very busy then.

AL Treasure Resort, 23 Beach View, T6271 2002, www.treasure-resort.com. Situated close to the action by the 37-m-high Merlion, this hotel has charming colonial architecture, a decent beer garden and bistro and comfy, modern rooms with huge TVs and Wi-Fi. Good package deals available online.

East Coast p610, map p611

If booking a **Hotel 81** or **Fragrance Hotel** in this area, particularly in Geylang, bear in mind that the area is one of Singapore's 3 designated red-light areas and has streets full of prostitutes after dark. The hotels have hourly rates and are used by the prostitutes and clients.

A Hotel 81 Joo Chiat, 305 Joo Chiat Rd, T6348 8181, www.hotel81.com.sg. Good-value place to stay. See **Hotel 81 Bencoolen**, page 620, for more on this chain.

A Malacca, 97 Still Rd, T6345 7411, www.malacca.com.sg. Another good-value business hotel in this area of town, 20 mins' walk from nearest MRT station (Eunos). Rooms are very well appointed at the price, with a/c, TV, and attached bathrooms. Great place to stay for those interested in the Peranakan cultural and dining delights of Katong.

B-C BetelBox Hostel, 200 Joo Chiat Rd, T6247 7340, www.betelbox.com. Bus No 24 from terminal 2 at the airport, get off at Joo Chiat complex, then it's a 7-min walk. Closest MRT is Payar Lebar, a 15-min walk away. A joint venture by a Singaporean and a Dutch former backpacker based in a converted shophouse.

Asian-style furnishings, with a massive, well-equipped lounge and kitchen area, breakfast included with deep bowls full of tropical fruits. Dorms and 1 double, with shared hot-water showers. Free internet (30 mins daily per guest) and lots of free tours. Recommended.

Airport p553

AL Changi Village, 1 Netheravon Rd, T6379 7111, www.changivillage.com.sg. Very well run, award-winning, first-class hotel, situated on Changi Beach, just north of the airport. Recommended for efficiency.

AL Crowne Plaza Airport Hotel, Changi Airport, 75 Airport Blvd 01-01, T6823 5300, www.ichotelsgroup.com. Changi airport's first full-service hotel, it's easily accessed from all 3 terminals. Rooms are uber-stylish and, when booked well in advance, superb value for those overnighting in Singapore. Pool, gym and expensive internet access.

A Ambassador Transit Hotel Terminal 1, in transit malls of each of Changi's 3 terminals, T6542 5538, www.airport-hotel.com.sg. Short-term rate quoted (6 hrs). A good place to take a break if you're stuck at Changi for a while and don't need to clear immigration. It also provides a 'freshen-up' service including showers, sauna and gym. Excellent budget room rates available (shared bathroom and showers). Booking is recommended.

⊘ Eating

Colonial core p576, map p578

Ⅷ **1827**, the Arts House, Old Parliament House, 1 Parliament Lane, T6337 1871, www.theartshouse.com.sg. Elegant Thai restaurant on the ground floor of the beautifully renovated Parliament House, also a well-regarded arts venue. Great ambience.

Ⅷ **Annalakshmi**, 133 New Bridge Rd, Chinatown Point, B1-02, T6339 9993. Open for lunch and dinner until 2130. North and South Indian vegetarian cuisine. Staffed by women volunteers, with profits going to the Kalamandhir Indian cultural group. The health drinks are excellent, especially *mango tharang* (mango juice, honey and ginger) and Annalakshmi special (fruit juice, yoghurt, honey and ginger). There's another branch at 104 Amoy St.

ŤŤŤ Bobby's Taproom Grill and Ribs, Fountain Court, CHIJMES, 30 Victoria St, T6337 5477. Inspired by a Halrme jazz club, this is a great place to satisfy blood lust with juicy steaks and ribs. There's also German and Irish beer and some naughty desserts. Some alfresco seating available. Booking recommended.

ŤŤŤ Capella, CHIJMES, 01-29, 30 Victoria St, T6334 9927. Large Italian restaurant with earthy copper overtones and sleek modern furnishings. Some excellent pasta and risottos to choose from and fair set lunches. Prices are intimidating. Popular at weekends.

ŤŤŤ Chinese Feasts, Suntec City Mall, 3 Temasek Blvd, T6337 6921. Traditional Sichuan fare served in grand surroundings next to Suntec's fountain. Those needing a little spicy warmth will relish the Chongqing hotpot, a chilli and Sichuan peppercorn-infused broth with meat, tofu and vegetables.

ŤŤŤ Cosafe Bar and Restaurant, 01-11 CHIJMES, 30 Victoria St, T6339 2276. Owned by a Singaporean teen with an obsession with Japanese *cosplay* (costume play), this restaurant is staffed by young women in maid uniforms with impeccable service, and is notable in that it is one of the only *cosplay* cafés outside Japan to have survived more than a couple of years. The food is a strange mixture of Asian and Western, and the novelty factor high. It's a friendly, quirky spot for a light meal or drink.

ŤŤŤ Hai Tien Lo, Pan Pacific Hotel, 37th floor, Marina Sq, T6826 8338. Cantonese restaurant in elegant surroundings, with stunning views of the city. Steamed lobster and Kobe beef are specialities. Dim sum lunches on Sun.

ŤŤŤ Hog's Breath Café, 01-27 CHIJMES, 30 Victoria St, T6338 1387. Daily 1130-2400. Fun Aussie-themed steakhouse with large portions of ribs, thick steaks and excellent burgers.

ŤŤŤ Jaan, Swissotel The Stamford, 2 Stamford Rd, T6837 3322. Great venue for a romantic

dinner or business lunch atop Singapore's tallest hotel building. Features visiting international chefs with 'an altitude'. Adjoining **New Asia Bar** is an atmospheric place for a drink with some of Singapore's best views.

ŤŤŤ Japanese Dining Sun, 02-01 CHIJMES, 30 Victoria St, T6336 3166. Lunch and dinner. Good bet for high-quality Japanese food with a menu changing with the seasons of Japan. Busy at weekends.

ŤŤŤ Lei Garden, 01-24, CHIJMES, 30 Victoria St, T6339 3822. A menu claiming to comprise 2000 dishes. Outstanding Cantonese food: silver codfish, emperor's chicken and regulars like dim sum and Peking duck. Dignitaries, royalty and film stars dine here. Tasteful decor and a 2-tier aquarium displaying the day's offerings. Despite seating for 250, you need to book in advance. Worth every cent. Recommended.

ŤŤŤ Raffles Grill, Raffles Hotel, 1 Beach Rd (main building, lobby), T6412 1185. Superb French cuisine in elegant colonial surroundings, with silver plate settings, chandeliers and reproduction Chippendale furniture.

ŤŤŤ Ristorante Bologna, Marina Mandarin Hotel, 6 Raffles Blvd, Marina Square, T6845 1127. Award-winning Italian restaurant, house specialities include *spaghetti alla marinara* and baked pigeon. Diners lounge amidst sophisticated decor while wandering minstrels strum.

ŤŤŤ Shahi Maharani, 03-21B, Raffles City, 252 North Bridge Rd, T6235 8840. North Indian tandoori, especially good seafood dishes. Live performances during dinner; a cosy place.

ŤŤŤ Tiffin Room, Raffles Hotel, 1 Beach Rd (main building, ground floor). North Indian curry buffet (plus à la carte menu) in pristine white, overlit, ersatz Victorian grandeur. The food is good, but at S$56 for the buffet, you're paying a lot more for the surroundings than for the curry. Reservation recommended. No sleeveless T-shirts or shorts.

ŤŤŤ True Blue Peranakan Cuisine, 47/49 Armenian St, T6440 0449. In a beautifully restored shophouse near the Peranakan Museum, this restaurant offers sensual, colourful Peranakan style in abundance, award-winning chefs and the city's most authentic Nyonya dining. Highly recommended.

House of Sundanese Food, several outlets spread around town, such as Suntec City Boat Quay. Typical Sundanese dishes from West Java, with a real home-cooked taste including spicy salad, charcoal-grilled seafood (*ikan sunda* and *ikan mas*) and curries. Simply decorated non-a/c restaurant.

La Cave, B1-10 Fountain Court, CHIJMES, 30 Victoria St, T6337 9717. Fusion cuisine with generous servings and a lovely ambience. Good value and excellent service. A bar, open 1700-2300, serves food from 1900.

La Viva Tapas Bar, 01-12, CHIJMES, 30 Victoria St, T6339 4290. Funky little tapas bar with regional Spanish dishes. The gazpacho here is excellent, and weekends see jugs of sangria being gulped liberally. Friendly service. Recommended.

Seah Street Deli, ground floor, Raffles Hotel, 1 Beach Rd. T6412 1816. New York-style deli counter with plenty of Americana, gleaming white tiles and some of Singapore's juiciest burgers with a range of fillings. Also sandwiches and salads. Recommended.

Soup, 39 Seah St. A chain of popular Cantonese restaurants serving herbal soups and Guangdong favourites.The steamed chicken is excellent.

Inle, Peninsula Plaza, Basement, Coleman St. One of Singapore's rare Burmese restaurants. Simple canteen style, with Burmese coffee and Shan noodles. There are a couple of other Burmese cheapies down here worth a try; sample the sour, spicy curries.

Komala's Fast Food, Peninsula Plaza, Basement, Coleman St. One of Komala's fast-food outlets, serving good South Indian delicacies including thalis, masala dosas and *idlis*, served at competitive prices; a/c. Next door is the more upmarket **Ganges**, which lays on a superb eat-as-much-as-you-can Indian vegetarian buffet at lunchtime.

Cafés and bakeries
Ah Teng's Bakery, Raffles Arcade. Pricey, but it has all the goodies you dream about at the end of a long trip away from home.

Hawker centres and food courts
There's a good outdoor food court where Bain and Victoria streets merge, next to the **Allson Hotel**. There are mostly Chinese stalls, but also one serving fabulous fresh juices served by the slightly cranky old couple furthest from the road.

Fountain Terrace, Suntec City, Marina Square. Trendy food court situated under the enormous fountain.

Funan Digitalife Mall, South Bridge Rd. This big shopping plaza contains one of the better food courts in Singapore in its basement, with a huge range of foods to choose from; in particular, an excellent Indian stall.

Water Court, basement of Raffles City. Sophisticated food court, mostly frequented by business people with a penchant for extravagant sandwiches, crêpes and patisseries. There is a superb selection of stalls and restaurants to suit all budgets including **Din Tai Fung**, Taiwanese cusine; **Chippy British Takeaway**, with semi-authentic fish and chips and deep-fried Mars Bars; and an excellent Japanese dining complex, **Kuriya**.

Singapore River and the City *p585, maps p578 and p592.*
Restaurants overlooking the river at Boat Quay (bargains sometimes available), Clarke Quay and Robertson Quay are hugely popular, as much for the river breeze and views as anything else – a casual stroll along the riverbank is as good method as any to find your perfect spot. Boat Quay can get a bit rowdy on weekend evenings.

Al Dente Trattoria , 71 Boat Quay, T6536 5336. Good pizza and lobster pasta. Also has a Holland Village branch and a branch at the Esplanade offering superb views at night,.

Brewerkz, Riverside Point, opposite Clarke Quay, T6438 2311. This very popular American-style restaurant and bar provides most of its seating under awnings by the riverfront. Great place for lunch, with a menu of satay, buffalo wings, nachos, burgers, steaks and pizza. Also has a children's menu. However, it is the beer from their mirco-brewery that is the best offering here.

Indochine Waterfront Restaurant, 1 Empress Place (next to Asian Civilisations Museum), T6339 1720, www.indochine.com.sg. Delightful decor and Indochinese food; plenty of fish on the menu here, from squid to mussels to tiger prawns. It's filled with the sumptuous hues of the Mekong, Shan antiques and Czech chandeliers. Superb river views at night further enhance the romantic ambience. The restaurant has sister establishments at Wisma Atria on Orchard Rd, Club St and on Clarke Quay.

Kinara, 57 Boat Quay, T6533 0412. North Indian frontier cuisine, good choice of tandoori-baked meat or vegetarian options. There's a couple of good south Indian dishes too, including the rich Keralan fish curry. Equally atmospheric **Fez** bar upstairs, often quiet and with a big screen showing football matches.

L'Entrepot Bistro, Clarke Quay, Block E, Unit 01-02, T6337 5585. French-style bistro with a decent wine cellar, hearty fare and dainty wooden tables. It's all a little contrived, but makes for a fun escape from the tropics.

Pierside, One Fullerton, T6438 0400. Mainly seafood and some fusion dishes. The main attraction here is the alfresco dining with views of Marina Bay. Try the spiced crab cakes.

Shiraz, 1-6 Clarke Quay, Block 3A River Valley Rd, T6334 2282. Excellent Iranian cuisine with strong flavours, large portions and plenty of meaty traditional dishes. Some very sweet desserts on offer. A refreshingly different dining experience.

Sukhothai, 47 Boat Quay, T6538 2422. Extensive Thai menu, but the food can be a little hit and miss; booking recommended.

Aburiya, 60 Robertson Quay, T6735 4862. Japanese barbecued meat. Quiet location just in front of the **Gallery Hotel**.

Café Iguana, Riverside Point, opposite Clarke Quay, T6236 1275. A funky bar and restaurant with a classic choice of Mexican dishes and a good choice of margaritas; try the horny toad. They also serve the delicious beers from Brewerkz here.

Lotus Grill, 3 Clarke Quay, T6338 0902. A slickly organized restaurant serving a mix of Asian food, with an emphasis on grilled Indonesian-style seafood. Good satay.

Riverside Indonesian, Riverside Point, opposite Clarke Quay. Bright functional interior, with some alfresco dining overlooking the river, serving Indonesian food: baked pomfret, chilli crabs, grilled chicken. An attractive location.

Song Fa Bak Kut Teh, 111 New Bridge Rd, T6533 6128. Small and busy eatery with traditional Chinese decor, alfresco seating and bowls of delicious *bak kut teh* (a Hokkien pork rib herbal soup) and range of Chinese teas. Highly recommended.

House of Sundanese Food, 55 Boat Quay. See page 624.

Cafés and bakeries
The Book Café, 20 Martin Rd. Just behind the Gallery Hotel. Light meals, sandwiches, soups and rich desserts in a relaxing lounge setting with books and magazines to browse.

Hawker centres and food courts
Food Court, basement of Liang Court, next door to Clarke Quay. Good choice of Asian stalls and a play area for children.

Lau Pa Sat Festival Market (formerly the Telok Ayer Food Centre), at the Raffles Quay end of Shenton Way in the old Victorian market (see page 588). Good range of food on offer including: Chinese, Indian, Nonya, Korean, Penang, ice creams and fruit drinks. It's best in the evening when Boon Tat St is closed off and satay stalls serve up cheap, tasty sticks of chicken, beef, mutton or prawns washed down with jugs of Tiger beer.

Chinatown *p589, map p592*
The last couple of years has seen a burgeoning of restaurants along Club St. All are top-end eateries, catering for city business

people, and all seem to be vying to create the most ostentatious menu (foie gras, venison and seafood are standard fare). Having said this, the standard of cuisine is extremely high.

Blue Ginger, 97 Tanjong Pagar Rd, T6222 3925. In a restored shophouse; good home-cooked Nonya (Peranakan) food and relaxed atmosphere.

Da Paolo's, 80 Club St. There are 5 Da Paolo's in Singapore; 2 are in Chinatown, in restored shophouses decorated in contemporary fashion. Popular with expats. Italian home-made pasta, but overpriced.

Indochine, 49B Club St, T6323 0503. Sister to the Indochine at Empress Place. The Sa Vanh Bar (1700-0300) is ethnically decorated with a laid-back feel. Running water adds to the serene atmosphere, which is somewhat undermined by arranging the tables too close together for comfort.

Senso, 21 Club St, T6224 3534. An all-Italian experience, with 'neo-classical Italian cooking'. Superb cuisine, great atmosphere, sophisticated London-style joint.

Thanying, Amara hotel, T6227 7856. A hallmark of Singaporean fine dining, Thanying provides the best Thai food in town, with an extensive menu (the 15 female chefs are all said to have trained in the royal household in Bangkok). Specialities include deep-fried garoupa, *yam som-o* (spicy pomelo salad), *khao niaw durian* (durian served on a bed of sticky rice – available from May-Aug), as well as such classics as *tom yam kung* (spicy prawn soup with lemongrass). Booking necessary.

Bamboo Court, 130 Amoy St, Far East Square. A Thai-Chinese eatery set in former temple grounds. There's an a/c section or tables in the garden around a fountain.

Pasta Brava, 11 Craig Rd, Tanjong Pagar, T6227 7550. Tastiest Italian in town in an equally tasty shophouse conversion; fairly expensive, but good choice of genuine Italian fare. Recommended.

Sanur, 3rd floor, 133 New Bridge Rd. Malay/Indonesian restaurant, one of a chain. Specialities include fish-head curry and spicy grilled chicken.

Swee Kee Fishhead Noodle House, 96 Amoy St, T6224 9920. This Chinese restaurant has acquired some degree of local renown due to the owner Tang Kwong Swee – known to his friends as 'Fish-head' – having run the same place for 60 years (although the location has changed). Recommended are the deep-fried chicken, Hainanese style, fish-head noodle soup and prawns in magi sauce; very popular.

Tiong Shiang, corner of Keong Saik and New Bridge roads. Popular Hainanese corner café, with tables spilling out onto the street.

Wan Tang Eating House, 2 Trengganu St. A rowdy Cantonese restaurant serving seafood and cheap Tiger beer with tables on the street at the corner of Trengganu and Pagoda streets. Popular.

Cafés and bakeries

Tea Chapter, 9A-11A Neil Rd, T6226 1175. An excellent little place on 3 floors with a choice of seating (on the floor or at tables). Peaceful atmosphere, plenty of choice of teas as well as sweet and savoury snacks, games for those who want to tarry, and the director, Lee Peng Shu, and his wife enthusiastically talk you through the tea-tasting ceremony (if you wish). Recommended. See also page 594.

Hawker centres and food courts

Amoy Street Food Centre, just south of Al-Abrar Mosque at southern end of Amoy St. Excellent little centre, worth a graze.

Chinatown Complex Hawker Centre, Block 335, 1st floor, Smith St. Recommended stall: Ming Shan (No 179), for its *kambing* (mutton) soup; famed for decades, though this is a pretty scruffy food centre. A pleasant place to snack at night is along Trengganu St where hawkers set up stalls.

Tanjong Pagar Plaza Food Centre, Tanjong Pagar Rd, southern end.

Orchard Road and Botanic Gardens

p595, map p596

Au Jardin, EJH Corner House, Singapore Botanic Gardens Visitors' Centre, 1 Cluny Rd,

T6466 8812. Situated in the former garden director's black and white bungalow, with only 12 tables, this French restaurant is elegant and sophisticated, with a menu which is changed weekly. Booking essential.

ŦŦŦ Blu, Shangri-La, 22 Orange Grove Rd, T62134598. Situated on the 24th floor, **Blu** provides stunning views, great service and excellent Californian food. Recommended.

ŦŦŦ Esmirada's, corner of Peranakan Pl and Orchard Rd, T6735 3476. Mediterranean food in Spanish-style taverna, good salads, paella, Moroccan couscous. Always packed, reservations recommended. There is a Greek plate-smashing ceremony on busy nights.

ŦŦŦ Gordon Grill, Lobby, Goodwood Park, 22 Scotts Rd, T6730 1744. One of the best grills in town known for its meat trolley. Plenty of choice cuts of meat to choose from. Superb desserts. Those in the know head here to enjoy well-prepared steaks. Recommended.

ŦŦŦ Harbour Grill and Oyster Bar, Hilton, 581 Orchard Rd, T6730 3393. Contemporary surroundings with nautical theme, serving international food. Delicacies include foie gras, Hokkaido scallops and roasted prime rib; monthly guest chef. Impeccable service. Highly recommended.

ŦŦŦ Kintamani, Furama Riverfront hotel, 405 Havelock Rd, T6333 8898. Award-winning restaurant with Balinese-style interior, extensive Indonesian lunch and dinner buffet.

ŦŦŦ Les Amis, Shaw Centre, 1 Scotts Rd, T6733 2225. Closes at 2200. Great French food, excellent service and extensive wine list.

ŦŦŦ Mezza9, Grand Hyatt, 10-12 Scotts Rd, T6416 7189. Incorporates Western Grill, Japanese food, Chinese, a salad bar and a patisserie. À la carte during the week and a set-price buffet brunch on Sun, 1100-1500.

ŦŦŦ Min Jiang, Goodwood Park, 22 Scotts Rd, T6730 1704. Large, noisy room, expansive Szechuan menu, with an excellent reputation. Delicious hot and sour soup, and good choice of seafood and 7 private rooms. Booking recommended.

ŦŦŦ Nanbantei, 5/F Far East Plaza, 12 Scotts Rd, T6733 5666. Japanese eatery, famous for

its *yakitori*. Tables divided by *shoji* screens. A little overpriced, but delicious nonetheless.

ŦŦŦ One Ninety, Four Seasons, 190 Orchard Blvd, T6734 1110. Sophisticated surroundings and unusual international food combinations make this a relaxed and pleasurable gastronomic experience.

ŦŦŦ Pete's Place, Grand Hyatt, Scott's Rd, basement, T6732 1234. One of the oldest Italian restaurants in Singapore, huge helpings of home-made pasta, popular Sun brunch.

ŦŦŦ Singapore Polo Club, 80 Mt Pleasant Rd (just off Thomson Rd). If you're not put off by the polo set or visiting sultans, this is a great place to dine (or drink Pimms) on the veranda, especially on match days (for upcoming matches, see www.singapore poloclub.or). There is a snack menu (steak sandwich, fish and chips, etc) for the veranda and a smarter restaurant inside.

ŦŦ Blood Café, 290 Orchard Rd, Paragon, T6735 6765. Funky café with style and fashion magazines to browse behind the Project ShockBloodBrothers clothes shop on the 2nd floor. Relaxing place, with an inventive menu featuring couscous, roasted vegetables and chunky sandwiches. Very hip and healthy. Good veggie choices. Recommended.

ŦŦ Lei Garden, Orchard Shopping Centre, 321 Orchard Rd, T6734 3988. Another branch of this famous Cantonese restaurant. Book in advance. Recommended.

ŦŦ Orchard Maharajah, 27 Cuppage Terrace, T6732 6331. Excellent North Indian food – tandoori and Kashmiri – and 7 different types of bread to choose from. This family-run place is conveniently located in a converted shophouse close to some good bars.

ŦŦ Sakura, 5/F Far East Plaza. Packed restaurant with no pretensions serving halal Thai-Chinese fare. Extraordinarily popular.

ŦŦ Sushi Tei, Paragon, 290 Orchard Rd. Japanese; great conveyor-belt sushi.

Cafés

Checkers Deli, Hilton Hotel, Orchard Rd, for a fabulous selection of cheesecakes, cakes and pastries. Dôme, Lane Crawford House,

Orchard Rd, and The Promenade on Orchard Rd. Delicious focaccia sandwiches, patisseries and some of the best coffee in town, good café atmosphere and a pleasant stop for a mid-morning break. **Goodwood Park Hotel**, Scotts Rd. Sophisticated buffet tea, served on the lawn by the pool. **Rose Veranda**, Shangri-La Hotel, 22 Orange Grove Rd, said to offer the best tea in town. **Spinelli Coffee**, The Heeren, Orchard Rd. Relaxing coffee shop with outdoor seating and friendly staff.

Hawker centres and food courts

Newton Circus, Scotts Rd, north of Orchard Rd. Despite threats of closure by the government, this huge food centre of over 100 stalls is still surviving and dishing up some of the best food of its kind. Open later than others so very popular with tourists. Chinese actress (and now Singapore citizen) Gong Li is known to frequent here. Many of the plazas along Orchard Rd provide food courts in their basements. Convenient and cheap.

Little India p598, map p599

Restaurants here range from sophisticated a/c places to the simplest of banana plate eateries. For North Indian cuisine, the best option is to trot down to the southern end of Race Course Rd, where there are several good restaurants in a row, all competing for business, including the most famous of all, **Muthu's**. Some of the best vegetarian restaurants – South Indian particularly – are found on the other side of Serangoon Rd, along Upper Dickson Rd.

Ⓣ The French Stall, 544 Serangoon Rd, T6299 3544. Closed Mon. Charming place owned by a former 5-star hotel French chef who cooks up 'no-frills French cuisine' in a rather Gallic *kopitiam*. The set menu is excellent value and the chocolate mousse rich, heavy and sinful. Recommended.

Ⓣ Ananda Bhavan, 95 Syed Alwi Rd, T6297 9522. Pure veg Indian dishes served in spotless environs with walls covered with info on the benefits of vegetarianism. The food is excellent with a range of filling thalis, dosai and a selection of *chaat*. Open 24 hrs.

Ⓣ Banana Leaf Apollo, 56-58 Race Course Rd. North Indian food, another popular fish-head curry spot, a/c and more sophisticated than the name might imply, although the food is still served on banana leaves to justify the name. Recommended.

Ⓣ Delhi, Race Course Rd. North Indian food including chicken tikka, various tandooris, as well as creamy Kashmiri concoctions. Popular and award-winning restaurant.

Ⓣ Jaggi's, 34 Race Course Rd. North Indian cuisine, immaculately clean and very popular.

Ⓣ Komala Vilas, 76-78 Serangoon Rd, T6293 6980, and 12 Buffalo Rd. South Indian thalis and masala dosas, bustling café, with a little more room upstairs. Recommended.

Ⓣ Muthu's Curry, 138 Race Course Rd, T6392 1722. North Indian food, one of the finest authentic Indian restaurants in town, not catering for bloated expats in search of standard London curries, but Indians on the look out for contemporary flavours, good presentation and lively ambience. Muthu's fish heads are famous. Highly recommended. Another branch in Suntec City.

Ⓣ Kamal's Vegetarian, Cuff Rd. Vegetarian restaurant; excellent paper and masala dosas.

Ⓣ Madras Woodlands, 22 Belilios Lane. Good vegetarian Indian food, very clean, the staff can be a little abrupt. Great value buffet lunch.

Ⓣ Rochor Beancurd, corner of Middle Rd and Short St. Popular noodle joint.

Hawker centres and food courts

Albert Centre, between Waterloo and Queen streets. There's a huge area of hawker stalls.

Kopitiam Food Hall, corner of Bras Basah Rd and Bencoolen St. Bang in the centre and popular with locals and travellers, this place offers everything from pig's organ soup to fresh juices and vegetarian curry. A bit lacking in character, but a/c and good for a breather.

Lavender Food Square, Lavender Rd, north of Little India. One of the best hawker centres in town. Recommended.

Tekka Food Court, Selegie Rd. Excellent selection of dishes from Indian to Thai. Not the cleanest of spots, but the food is great.

Zhujiao Food Centre, on the corner of Buffalo and Serangoon roads. Wide range of dishes, and the best place for Indian Muslim food: curries, rotis, dosai and *murtabak* are hard to beat (beer can be bought from the Chinese stalls on the other side).

Arab Street *p601, map p602*

Arab St is the best area for Muslim food of all descriptions – Malay, Indonesian, Indian or Arabic. There are some good restaurants around the Sultan Mosque and many more on noisy North Bridge Rd. Try the Parco Bugis Shopping Centre for non-Muslim restaurants including good Italian ones, and New Bugis St for simple open-air fare and jugs of cold beer.

The basement of **Parco Bugis Junction** has a good selection of stalls and restaurants, the stalls are in the style of a Chinese eating street where you can snack away on numerous dishes from cheese-covered chips to Hangzhou dumplings and Cantonese sausages. There's a clean foodcourt on the 3rd floor of the mall.

††† Bumbu, 44 Kandahar St, T6392 8628. Beautifully decorated with Peranakan antiques and screens. Fare is a Thai and Indonesian mix, famous for its deep-fried fish and *tahu telor*.

††† Olive Tree Restaurant and Café, Intercontinental Hotel, 80 Middle Rd, T6431 1061. The café is situated in the Parco Bugis shopping mall, whilst the restaurant is cosier and separate from all those frantic shoppers. Both serve the same good Mediterranean food – there's a good buffet.

††† Pasta Fresca da Salvatore, Shaw Centre. Open 24 hrs. Fresh Italian food: tasty pizzas and a good range of pasta dishes.

††† Pimai Thai, Intercontinental Hotel, 80 Middle Rd, T6431 1064. Excellent Thai menu with unusually extensive dessert buffet.

†† Chuan, 9 Purvis St, T6338 4755. Sichuan hotpot that promises to set your mouth on fire.

†† Pivdofr, 1 Liang Seah St, T6336 2995. A shophouse café serving classic international fare such as pizza, macaroni cheese or pork chops. Good service.

††† Sketches, Parco Bugis Shopping Centre, 80 Middle Rd, T6339 8386. A novel approach to ordering Italian, with boxes to tick for 9 types of pasta, 8 sauces and some garnishes. Quick and fairly basic food.

† Blanco Court Prawn Mee, 243 Beach Rd. Simple tiled eatery serving excellent steaming bowls of prawn noodles. Very popular with locals. Highly recommended.

† Rumah Makan Minang, Kandahar St (facing onto the Istana Kampong Glam). Small restaurant serving cheap Padang (West Sumatran) dishes, including beef *rendang* (dry beef curry), spicy grilled fish and *kangkung*.

† Zam Zam, junction of Arab St and North Bridge Rd. Muslim Malay-Indian dishes served in busy and chaotic coffee shop. Very popular and recommended for a taste of the other Singapore – spicy meats, chargrilled seafood and creamy curries.

HarbourFront and Sentosa *p603, map p605*

††† The Cliff at the Sentosa Resort & Spa, T6275 0331. Good sea views from dining perches. It's worth splashing out on the buffet at the adjoining terrace.

††† Long Beach Seafood, 31 Marina Park, Marina South, T6323 2222. One of the island's most famous seafood restaurants, specializing in pepper and chilli-crabs, drunken prawns and baby squid cooked in honey.

††† Prima Tower Revolving Restaurant, 201 Keppel Rd, T6272 8822. Revolving restaurant atop a huge silo that looks out over the harbour and city. Established over 30 years ago with the same chef still working here. Beijing cuisine, particularly good Peking duck, book in advance.

†† Imperial Herbal, Vivo City, 03-08 Lobby G (HarbourFront MRT), T6337 0491. Unusual, delicately flavoured Chinese food. A resident in-house herbalist takes your pulse (for a fee) and recommends a meal with the appropriate rejuvenating ingredients to balance your yin and yang. Booking recommended for dinner.

† Han's, 8 branches around the city including HarbourFront. This chain is Singapore's answer to the greasy spoon, single-dish Chinese meals, simple (largely fried) breakfasts, some European food including such things as steaks, burgers and fries, all served in large helpings at very competitive prices.

Hawker centres and food courts

Food Republic, level 3, VivoCity, T6276 0521, close to the HarbourFront MRT station. Food court very popular with locals, cheap, but very busy at lunchtimes. Recommended.

Singapore West *p607*

♥♥♥ **Au Petit Salut**, 40C Harding Rd, T6475 1976. French patisserie-style restaurant. Some main course dishes, but come here for the pastries and cakes.

♥♥♥ **Brazil Churrascaria**, 16 Sixth Av (off Bukit Timah Rd), T6463 1923. If meat's your thing, come to this Brazilian restaurant, with its huge skewers of barbecued (*churrascaria* is Portuguese for barbecue) meat and as much as you can eat.

♥♥♥ **Cha Cha Cha**, 35 Lorong Mambong, Holland Village, T6462 1650. Small and informal Mexican restaurant, with some outdoor seating and an extensive menu. Always bustling with locals. Food is reputedly more authentic than the adjoining Mexican place which sports poncho tablecloths.

♥♥♥ **Lucerne**, 224 Pasir Panjang Rd, Pasir Panjang Village, T6776 1221. Sophisticated Swiss restaurant.

♥♥♥ **Michelangelo's**, Jln Merah Saga, Holland Village, T6475 9069. Under the same management as **Zambuca Italian Restaurant** and **Original Sin**, Italian, with a range of pasta dishes and other specialities. Pleasant surroundings (both indoor or terrace seating), but fairly average food for the price. Booking recommended, especially at the weekend.

♥♥♥ **Original Sin**, Jln Merah Saga, Holland Village, T6475 5605. Mediterranean vegetarian restaurant, with some really intriguing dishes. Try the lentil tower, packed with lentils, aubergine, roasted peppers and haloumi cheese. Indoor or terrace dining. Booking recommended, especially at the weekend.

♥♥♥ **Shayray Punjab**, Lorong Mambong, Holland Village. Rich North Indian Punjabi cuisine, including excellent tandoori chicken. Friendly service. Recommended.

♥♥♥ **Wala-Wala**, 31 Lorong Mambong, Holland Village, T6462 4288. Buzzy atmosphere and pretty tiles on the tables in this Mexican restaurant; good, honest, unpretentious.

♥♥ **Westlake Eating House**, Empress Drive, off Farrer Rd, 1st floor of an HDB block, T6474 7283. Big indoor and outdoor restaurant serving Singapore-Chinese food. Extensive menu, including delicious black-peppered prawns and baby *kailan*. Great value for money.

♥♥ **Samy's Curry**, Civil Service Club, Dempsey Rd, T6472 2080. A wonderful Indian establishment where food is served at your table on a banana leaf – you pay for what you take – great value and very atmospheric. Highly recommended, especially by Indians.

East Coast *p610, map p611*

The east coast is a particularly good place to experience seafood in one of the large, casual-style restaurants, where customers pick their own fish from tanks and then choose how they'd like it cooked.

♥♥♥ **Al Forno East Coast**, 400 East Coast Rd, T6348 8781. Authentic Italian cuisine with fine but pricey Italian wine to match.

♥♥♥ **Casa Bom Vento**, 467 Joo Chiat Rd, T6348 7786. Eurasian and Peranakan cuisine. Famous for its Katong jelly drink – unique to this restaurant. Presentation of dishes here is somewhat off, but the flavours make up for this. An interesting and informal option.

♥♥♥ **East Coast Seafood Centre**, East Coast Park Service Rd, T6345 1211. There are 10 outlets here and they're all good. Trolleys are provided to choose your fish. Not for the squeamish. There are drunken prawns, chilli and pepper crab and bamboo clams. One of the most celebrated eateries here is **Jumbo Seafood**, a veritable Singaporean institution. Highly recommended.

♥♥ **Bernie's**, 961A Upper Changi Rd, T6542 2232. American fare in a laid-back setting, with friendly staff and big American-style helpings.

Kim's Seafood, 37 Joo Chiat Place. T6742 1119. Mon-Fri until 0130, Sat until 0230. Claypot pepper crabs are the speciality in Mr Tan's cheap and informal restaurant. Cheese crabs make for an interesting alternative.

Peranakan Inn, 210 East Coast Rd, T6440 6195. Service is prompt in this popular restaurant, selling classic Peranakan food such as galangal, *ayam buah keluak*, *chap chye* and *itek tim*.

Charlie's Corner, Block 2, 01-08, Changi Village, T6542 0867. Bus to Changi Point from Tampines MRT. Closed Sat-Sun. Charlie's folks, who were first-generation immigrants from China, set up the Changi Milk Bar in the 1940s, then Charlie's Corner became the favoured watering hole and *makan* stop for sailors and riggers for decades. His mum still fries the chips that gave them the reputation as the best chippies east of London's Isle of Dogs. Excellent chilli-dogs, spicy chicken wings and other international food, as well as 70 beers to choose from. Recommended.

◑ Bars and clubs

The bar and club scene changes fast in Singapore so check local papers, *TimeOut Singapore*, www.timeoutsingapore.com/sg/en, or just ask around for the latest tips on the local gigs and DJs. The Singapore Tourism Board also provides a free 'Where to Eat and Party' guide or see www.visitsingapore.com.

Most big hotels have discos; the cover charge is usually S$25-30.

Colonial core *p576, map p578*

Bar and Billiard Room, Raffles Hotel, Beach Rd, T6337 1886. Relocated from its original position, the bar is lavishly furnished with teak tables, oriental carpets and 2 original billiard tables.

Insomnia, CHIJMES, 30 Victoria St. Popular late-night drinking den with live music, top-40 hits and a fairly wild crowd. Gets rammed at weekends.

Le Baroque, B1-07 CHIJMES, 30 Victoria St . Blend of upmarket eatery-cum-club with decent menu, theme nights and good live music. Wed is Guy and Girls night with free-flow drinks from 2100-2330.

The Long Bar, Raffles Hotel, 1-3 Beach Rd. The home of the Singapore Sling, originally concocted by bartender Ngiam Tong Boon in 1915 (see page 564), now on 2 levels and very popular with tourists and locals, gratuitous, tiny, dancing, mechanical *punkah-wallahs* sway out of sync to the cover band.

Loof, Odeon Towers Rooftop, 331 North Bridge Rd, 03-07. Individualistic lounge bar with unique seating plan, gorgeous rooftop garden with superb city views and chilled beats soundtrack. This place is popular with the well-heeled arty set and is a good spot to meet some of Singapore's less conventional types. Range of promotions include 1 for 1 when it rains and free flow of satay on Mon.

New Asia Bar, atop Swissotel Stamford. Suave drinking locale with a good happy hour and ice-cold cans of Caffreys. As the bar is on the 71st floor, the real reason to come here is for the views over the city, which are simply stunning. You can come here during the day for a coffee and to snap some pics, but don't expect to be let in wearing flip flops. S$25 admission on Fri and Sat after 2100, including a drink.

Paulaner Brauhaus, Time-Square@Millenia Walk, 9 Raffles Blvd. Microbrewery serving a massive range of freshly brewed German beers to expat Germans and merry boozers from around the planet. German sausage and other Teutonic delicacies such as fatty pork knuckle. The weekly Sun brunch here is excellent value and great fun.

Writers' Bar, Raffles Hotel, 1 Beach Rd (just off the main lobby). In honour of the likes of Somerset Maugham, Rudyard Kipling, Joseph Conrad, Noel Coward and Herman Hesse, who were said either to have wined, dined or stayed at the hotel. Bar research indicates that other literary luminaries from James A Michener to Noel Barber and the great Arthur Hailey are said to have sipped Tigers at the bar, as the bookcases and mementoes attest.

Singapore River and the City *p585, maps p578 and p592*

There are lots of bars on Boat and Clarke quays; those at the former are wilder and less packaged, although the last few years has seen a slight deterioration in quality as locals have moved on and tourists have become the dominant clientele. One of the more dramatic changes over the past few years is the development along the riverfront westwards. Both Robertson's Walk and The Quayside are gradually filling up with shops and restaurants, and the nearby Mohammed Sultan Rd is a popular watering hole; the street is lined with bars and clubs. The west side is a row of restored shophouses, whilst the east is a modern high-rise block.

Archipelago Craft Beer Hub, 79 Circular Rd. Singapore's first commercial brewery now offers a range of freshly brewed beers influenced by the smells and tastes of Southeast Asia. The Java Ale is spot on. Excellent happy hour promotions.

Attica, 01-03 3A River Valley Rd, Clarke Quay. A Singapore institution, this frequently packed bar attracts a mixed crowd of party animals looking for love. **Attica Too**, upstairs, has a laser show and dance music.

Bar Cocoon, 01-02, 3 River Valley Rd, Clarke Quay. Owned by the IndoChine group, this opulent bar has plenty of tasteful oriental flourishes, an extensive list of cocktails and well-heeled expats with cash to splash. There's also a good bar here, for those in need of a shot of vodka in a freezing room.

Brewerkz, Riverside Point. Microbrewery with good beer, including a delicious IPA. The happy hour here is one of Singapore's best.

The Butter Factory, 02-02 One Fullerton, T6333 8243. Large bar/club with an urban decor of skyscrapers and tower blocks, 2 rooms playing hip hop and electro and a massive smokers' room. The main downside is that the toilets are located outside the club.

The Clinic, 3C River Valley Rd, Clarke Quay. Somewhat faddish place with a trendy crowd lounging on white furniture and drinking cocktails from hospital drinks and syringes.

Crazy Elephant, 3E River Valley Rd, Clarke Quay. Live music, graffiti-scrawled walls and a popular place for a drink following a meal.

Dbl O (pronounced 'Double O'), Robertson Walk, 11 Unity St. Open 2000 to 0300. Not too far removed from a Newcastle meat market, this place has plenty of young 'uns in micro minis, cheap cheap booze and bops to a raucous dance soundtrack.

eM Studio, 1 Nanson Rd at the **Gallery Hotel**. Wed-Sat. Awfully hip bar popular with models and the glam crew, this place has a superb music policy and a huge range of spirits to choose from. **eM By the River** is a chilled bar downstairs.

Harry's at Far East Square, 01-01 Pekin St, Far East Square. Decent food, range of beers and popular with an after-work expat crowd.

Harry's Bar, 28 Boat Quay. Large bar with seating outside overlooking the river, popular with City boys, pricey food, jazz band.

Molly Malone's, 42 Circular Rd (behind Boat Quay). Irish pub, complete with stout and Irish folk music (also serves food).

Nihonshu, 33 Mohamed Sultan Rd. Japanese bar with over 100 different types of sake to choose from. Worth a visit for something a little different.

Penny Black, 26 Boat Quay. A stylized English Victorian London pub, with some classic English food. This is the place to go to watch Premiership matches at weekends.

Siam Supperclub, UE Square, 207 River Valley Rd. A tastefully decorated place (a reputed 56 Buddha images are on display), with spirit mixes such as 'Buddha jumps over the wall'.

Tivoli Beer Bar, Robertson Walk, 11 Unity St, 01-23. Friendly Danish-themed bar with plenty of big TVs for football fans and alfresco seating. Be warned: Liverpool games take priority.

Velvet Underground, 17 Jiak Kim St (off Kim Seng Rd), next door to **Zouk** and under the same management. Tue-Sat 2100-0300. Small nightclub, cover S$25-30, playing contemporary dance music. If you're in the mood for some Summer of Love vibes, drop in on Thu for the Balearic night. Recommended. Often has gay or lesbian parties.

Yard, 294 River Valley Rd. The Singaporean version of a London pub, complete with darts, dominos, fish 'n' chips and Newcastle Brown Ale.

Zouk, 17 Jiak Kim St, opposite the **Concorde Hotel**. Huge quirky club, with a fun design. The place for hard clubbing. Attracts big name international DJs. Hosts one of Singapore's most popular nights on Wed, called Mambo Jambo. Women free on Wed.

Chinatown p589, map p592

There are several quiet bars on Duxton Hill, Chinatown, in a pleasant area of restored shophouses – a retreat from the hustle and bustle of Boat Quay or the city. Duxton Rd and Tanjong Pagar Rd also provide a dozen or so bars in restored shophouses.

Beaujolais Winebar, 1 Ann Siang Hill, T6224 2227. Very pleasant, atmospheric wine bar in restored shophouse, with reasonably priced wine, candles in wine bottles on the windowsills, good cheese and charcuterie platters. Recommended.

Tantric Bar, 78 Neil Rd. Double shots for the price of singles, lethal Long Island Ice Teas and comfy day beds make this is good spot to get thoroughly wasted.

Orchard Road and Botanic Gardens p595, map p596

Peranakan Place just off Hollywood Rd is home to a string of funky New York-style bars carved out of restored shophouses. At S$15 a pint, these places aren't cheap, but they are very stylish and good for posing.

Acid Bar, 180 Orchard Rd, Peranakan Pl, T6738 8828. Tastefully decorated in Peranakan style, these flourishes can be difficult to spot as this place gets absolutely rammed at weekends. Great drinks promotions and live music from 2200.

Alley Bar, 1 Emerald St, T6738 8818. Faux alleyway with clever lighting, hip music, and L-shaped bar. Mellow beats and a terrace to escape the crowds.

Balcony Bar, The Heeren, 260 Orchard Rd. Uber-trendy hangout in the centre of town

with good food, extensive drink selection, daybeds and a jacuzzi.

Dubliner, Winsland Conservation House, 165 Penang Rd, T6735 2220. Irish pub set in a beautifully restored colonial house. It's very friendly, serving good hearty Irish food and the compulsory pints of Guinness and Kilkenny. Recommended.

Hard Rock Café, HPL House, 50 Cuscaden Rd, west end of Orchard Rd. Complete with limo in suspended animation and queues to enter.

Ice Cold, 9 Emerald Hill. If you like a slightly anarchic feel to your bars, with loud music and darts, then this is a good place. Occupying a refurbished shophouse built in 1910 at the top of the pedestrianized section of Emerald Hill, a good place for a drink away from Orchard Rd, popular with locals, 35 beers to choose from.

Kaspia Bar, Hilton Hotel, Orchard Rd. For the widest selection of vodkas in Singapore and live jazz.

Martini Bar@Mezza9, Grand Hyatt Hotel, Orchard Rd. A selection of 30 Martinis.

Muddy Murphy's, Orchard Hotel Shopping Arcade. Rowdy Irish pub full of tourists and expats.

Number 5, 5 Emerald Hill. Happy hours Mon-Sat 1200-2100, Sun 1700-2100. At the top of the pedestrianized part of Emerald Hill, retro-chic restored shophouse bar and restaurant, popular with young expats. Regular drink promotions and busy pool table upstairs.

Que Pasa, 7 Emerald Hill. A wine bar in a converted shophouse, with a small snack menu of tapas, oysters and olives and good wine list.

Top Ten Club, Orchard Towers, 400 Orchard Rd. Huge converted cinema, often has live black-American or Filipino disco bands. Part of the Orchard Towers complex, known locally as '4 floors of whores' – one of Singapore's most notorious pick-up areas.

Woodstock, Rooftop, Far East Plaza, 14 Scotts Rd. Open until 0200. Take the bullet lift up the outside of the building. Expect to hear hard rock.

Little India p598, map p599

Prince of Wales, 101 Dunlop St. Cheap and cheerful no-frills boozer. Popular with backpackers. Live music and Aussie beers. Great spot to meet other travellers.

HarbourFront and Sentosa *p603, map p605*

Also worth checking out at Sentosa are **KM8** on Tanjong Beach and **Club Islander** on Palawan Beach.

Café Del Mar, Siloso Beach. Located on the beach, this cousin of Ibiza's renowned chillout bar also plays mellow beats in a stylish setting with dipping pool.

St James Power Station, HarbourFront. Located in Singapore's first coal-fired power station, the coal has now been replaced by this mega complex of bars and sophisticated clubs. Places worth a look include Cuban-inspired **Movida**, **Dragonfly** for Mandarin pop music, commercial dance at mega club **Powerhouse** and live music in the **Boiler Room**.

Singapore West *p607*

There are pubs and bars in a row of restored shophouses in Pasir Panjang Village, along what is known as the Pub Row. Singapore's newest posh nightlife hub can be found at Dempsey Hill, the quiet and green site of the former British army barracks, but now the place to be seen. Try **Red Dot Brewhouse**, 0101 Dempsey Rd, an excellent microbrewery; **Camp**, 8D Dempsey Rd renowned for its cocktails – check out the Tiffin Punch; and **Oosh**, 22 Dempsey Rd, with water features, waiter call buttons and a stern dress code.

East Coast *p610, map p611*

Changi Sailing Club, Changi Village. Pleasant and, surprisingly, one of the cheapest places for a quiet beer, overlooking the Strait of Johor. **Charlie's Corner**, Block 2, 01-08, Changi Village. Closed weekends. Charlie Han describes his bar as 'the pulse of the point', tucked away behind the local hawker centre, he is a teetotaller but serves 70 brands of beer from all over the world, which you can sip as you watch the red-eyes touchdown on runway 1; Charlie's Corner is best known for its fish and chips; see page 631. Recommended.

Gay and lesbian venues

Regular parties for gay and lesbians are held throughout the month, usually at **Zouk**. Check www.fridae.com for an update or ask at one of the establishments listed below. **Backstage**, 13A Trengganu St, T6227 1712. A funky chill-out bar for men, very boutique-like with drapes and candlesticks. **Cow & Coolies**, 30 Mosque St, T6221 1239. A scruffy karaoke pub for lesbians. **Why Not**, 56-58 Tras St, Tanjong Pagar. A disco karaoke bar with a small stage. Mainly gay male crowd.

⊙ Entertainment

Singapore *maps p550, 578, 592, 596, 599, 602, 605, 611*

Cinema

Singaporeans are cinema mad. There is a profusion of cinemas for such a small place, and ticket prices are very reasonable. For the latest schedules see www.sg.movies.yahoo.com or the *Straits Times Life* section, which publishes listings daily.

With more than 50 cinemas, Singapore gets most blockbusters soon after their US release. Tickets cost about S$10 and shows run throughout the day, with late-night viewing at weekends. Censors have relaxed in recent years; there's an RA category for those over 21 years old, which means a little more sex and violence hits the screens. When the **Cathay**, at the southeastern end of Orchard Rd, opened in 1939 and became the first a/c public building in Singapore, local celebs turned up in fur coats. It stopped screening films for many years, but after 6 years of redevelopment, opened its doors in 2006 incorporating many of the cinema's original design features.

GV Grand, top floor of Great World City, Zion Rd, T6735 8484, booking recommended. Good for a real cinema experience. You can relax in an easy chair and dine at the same time.

There are several other multiplex cinemas, including: **Parco Bugis Junction** on Victoria

St, opposite Bugis MRT; the **Lido Cineplex** at the Shaw Centre; **Orchard Rd** and **Suntec City**, Marina Sq; the **Screening Room**, 12 Ann Siang Rd, T6221 1694, www.thescreening room.com.sg, offers quality food, 12 screens including 1 on the roof, a lounge bar and a selection of art-house and classic films.

Classical, opera and other music

Chinese classical and folk music are organized by the **Nanyang Academy of Fine Arts** (NAFA), T6337 6636 for performance details.

Classical music performances are held at the Esplanade (www.esplanade.com), **Singapore Cultural Theatre** and the **Victoria Theatre** (see page 577). The Singapore Symphony Orchestra gives regular performances and there are often visiting orchestras, quartets and choirs. The Singapore Symphony Orchestra also performs in many free open-air shows in the Botanic Gardens. The National Theatre Trust promotes cultural dance performances and local theatre as well as inviting international dance and theatre groups to Singapore. **Chinese Street Opera (Wayang)** Traditional Chinese street operas mostly take place during the 7th lunar month, following the Festival of the Hungry Ghosts (see page 33). They are regularly staged on makeshift wooden platforms that are erected in vacant lots all over the city. To the sound of clashing cymbals and drums, wayang actors, adorned in ornate costumes and with faces painted, act out roles of gods and goddesses, heroes and heroines, and more, from Chinese folklore.

Kala Mandhir, Temple of Fine Arts, 1st floor, **Excelsior Hotel** shopping centre, T6339 0492. Classes available in dance, instrumental music, percussion and singing. Fabulous array of Indian instruments.

Live music

Brix Hyatt Regency Hotel, 10/12 Scotts Rd. Open until 0300, Fri-Sat 0400. Popular American-style, touristy bar with loud live music and good wine and whisky selections.

Fabrice's World Music Bar, Basement, Marriott Hotel, 320 Orchard Rd. One of Singapore's most celebrated live music venues with an eclectic selection of world music acts.
Hard Rock Café, HPL House, 50 Cuscaden Rd. AOR covers (Boston, Chicago and the like); forget conversation. Queues to get in.
Harry's Quayside, 28 Boat Quay. Jazz Wed-Sat, blues on Sun. Also on Orchard Rd (covers, classic rock), the Esplanade and Changi Airport.
Kaspia Bar, Hilton Hotel, Orchard Rd. Jazz.
Molly Malone's, 42 Circular Rd, behind Boat Quay. Irish folk Tue-Fri.
St James Power Station, 3 Sentosa Gateway, HarbourFront, T6270 7676, www.stjames powerstation.com. 9 different boozy venues, with lots of live music to choose from, including hip hop and hard rock all under one roof.

Theatre, dance and comedy

Most theatrical and dance performances are held at the Esplanade or Victoria Theatre (see page 577). Tickets for many performances can be bought from SISTIC, T6348 5555, www.sistic.com.sg, as well as from the box offices themselves.

There are often open-air performances at Fort Canning Park, which is a magical venue. Check local media for lisitings. A full listing of venues can be found at www.nac.gov.sg.
Action Theatre, 42 Waterloo St, next to the Synagogue, T6837 0842, www.action.org.sg. Provides small-scale productions on an outdoor stage or in a small auditorium.
The Arts House, Old Parliament House, see page 580. Arts venue staging contemporary theatre productions.
Esplanade – Theatres on the Bay, see page 577. The majority of performances will be held in the theatres apparently enclosed in a pair of giant durians.
Raffles Jubilee Hall, 328 North Bridge Rd, T6331 1732. Occasional theatrical performances.
Sculpture Square, 155 Middle Rd, www.sculpturesq.com.sg. Mon-Fri 1100-1800 and Sat-Sun 1200-1800. Housed in Middle Rd church, which has been converted into an exhibition space.

Stamford Arts Centre, 155 Waterloo St. A centre for the performing arts, with Chinese opera, Nrityalaya performances, and traditional Indian dance and drama. **The Substation**, 45 Armenian St, set up in a former power station, T6337 7800, www.substation.org. Intimate small theatre staging plays and showing avant garde films.

O Shopping

The colonial core *p576, map p578*

Art galleries

Many contemporary galleries have opened up and some can be found in the Tanglin shopping centre.

Gajah Gallery, MICA Building, 140 Hill St, T6737 4202, www.gajahgallery.com. Contemporary Southeast Asian art. There are a few others in the same building.

Books

National Museum Shop, 53 Armenian St. Source of Asian art books and postcards.

Electronic goods

Funan Digitalife Mall, North Bridge Rd, and Peninsula Plaza, next to Grand Plaza Hotel, Coleman St. Both have dozens of shops dedicated to cameras, phones, MP3s, video cameras and computers.

Furniture

Pacific Link Shopping Centre, Marina Square. Shops here sell a range of contemporary furniture and furnishings. **Pennsylvania House**, Stamford House, Stamford Rd. New England furniture and smaller items, with a contemporary section.

Handicrafts

Natraj's Arts & Crafts, 03-202 Marina Square Shopping Centre, in a row of Far Eastern handicraft shops. By far the best shop for Indian exotica, Natraj's specialities are papier mâché Bharata Natayam dancing girl dolls, which wobble and shake just like the real thing.

Chinatown *p589, map p592*

Handicrafts

Shops on Smith and Sago streets sell assorted Chinese knick-knacks, including kites, lanterns, silk dressing gowns, opera masks, incense sticks, candle holders, lucky money and all the paraphernalia required for visiting a Chinese temple and attending a funeral. It is cheap and prices are not negotiable.

People's Park Complex, Eu Tong Sen St. One of the biggest Chinese emporia.

Orchard Road *p595, map p596*

Antiques

Many of the top antique shops are to be found on levels 2 and 3 of the **Tanglin Shopping Centre**. They include the old map shop, **Antiques of the Orient**, level 2, T6734 9351. This is probably the best place to buy antique maps and prints in Southeast Asia and is a wonderful place to browse. It also has a library. **Apsara**, for lacquerware chests. **Tiepolo**, T6732 7924, was established over 20 years ago and David Mun has a fabulous range of Chinese and Indonesian porcelain, wooden pieces and bronze. This is well worth a visit and Mr Mun is a mine of information and fascinating to talk with. **Kensoon**, has exclusive Asiatic pieces. **Tatiana**, on the floor above, is a long-established treasure trove of mostly 'primitive' art. A considerable proportion is from Indonesia: antiques, great wooden sculptures and textiles, baskets, Vietnamese drums and jewellery. **Spiritual Antique Land**, for quality Tibetan and Chinese furniture and accessories with the main shop on the 1st floor. **Lopburi**, on the ground floor of Tanglin Place, Orchard Rd, sells a good range of Thai art and antiquities.

For general antiques, there are shops dotted around Cuppage Terrace behind **Centrepoint** (upstairs, above Saxophone, there are several good shops, selling antique Melaka furniture, porcelain, and Peranakan pieces). There are also some good shops (selling antiques and restored/imitation items) at Binjai Park, off Bukit Timah Rd, which is rather off the beaten track to the north of Orchard Rd.

Art galleries

Gauguin Gallery, Orchard Hotel Shopping Arcade, 442 Orchard Rd, T6-733 4268. Mounts changing exhibitions of international artists.
Tzen Gallery, Tanglin Shopping Centre, 19 Tanglin Rd, T6734 4339. Shows mainland Chinese watercolours and pen and ink drawings, and has a wide selection of scrolls, reasonable prices. Also check out the **Yang Gallery** and **Ha Karen ART gallery**.

Books

Singapore has some excellent bookshops with a selection of titles as good as can be found in the UK.
Borders Books & Music, ground floor of Wheelock Place, Orchard Rd. The best place to browse, with 140,000 titles, books that are not sealed in polythene, a café and seating.
Select Books, Tanglin Shopping Centre, Orchard Rd. Sells a good range of coffee-table glossies of the region.
Tango Mango, 3rd floor, Tanglin Mall. Sells a selection of local-interest books. There is also **Kinokuniya** in Ngee Ann City.

Children

The Forum, corner of Orchard Rd and Cuscaden Rd. An entire shopping plaza for children, with Toys 'R' Us on the top floor and lots of other individual shops on the other 3 floors. The best choice of children's clothes is to be found here; there are over 20 shops selling children's clothes.
Magic Wand, Orchard Point, Orchard Rd. A treasure trove of goodies.
Tanglin Mall, at the western end of Orchard Rd. Also has several excellent little shops for children; eg a great beanie baby and wooden toy shop on the ground floor.

Electronic goods

Lucky Plaza, Orchard Rd, and **Far East Plaza**, Scotts Rd. Both have many electronics shops.

Furniture

Barang Barang, Plaza Singapura. A wide range of contemporary furnishings, from bedding to kitchenware to items for sitting rooms or the garden. Branches all over town.
Planters House, 2nd Floor, Tanglin Shopping Centre, 19 Tanglin Rd (western end of Orchard Rd), T6734 8938. Excellent choice of furniture, very stylish with olde worlde accents. Also try **Antquaro** on the 2nd floor.

Handicrafts

Boon's Pottery, level 1, Tanglin Mall, Orchard Rd. An outlet for 50 or so local artists. Some are pretty ghastly, but there's something here to suit most tastes. There is a larger storage area in Tanglin Place, almost next door, on the lower ground level.
Ju-I Antiques and **Moon Gate**, both at Tanglin Shopping Centre (Orchard Rd) are good shops for porcelain.
Singapore Handicrafts, in the somewhat pricey but slightly tacky mock Tudor Court, at the far western end of Orchard Rd.

Jade

Kwok Gallery, Far East Shopping Centre, Orchard Rd.

Music

The Heeren, on the corner of Cairnhill Rd and Orchard Rd. 4 floors of HMV; another branch in the CityLink Mall.

Persian rugs

Salam Carpets, 2nd floor, The Tanglin Mall; **Mohammed Akhtar**, Tanglin Shopping Centre, Orchard Rd; **Hassan's Carpets**, Tanglin Shopping Centre, Orchard Rd, also has an extensive range.

Shopping centres

Centrepoint, 176 Orchard Rd, dominated by Robinsons department store, **Marks & Spencer**, **Gap**, **Esprit**, and food and beverage stalls on the 5th floor.
Far East Plaza, Scotts Road. One of the older plazas with a maze of small boutiques, plenty of shops selling electronic goods, cameras and watches. Money changers, tailors and a small food court. Popular with a young crowd.

Iluma Mall, Bugis MRT. A brand new mall with incredible exterior lighting that has to be seen to be believed. Mainly boutiques, but 60% of the space is entertainment venues including eateries, a cinema and clubs.

Ion Orchard, Orchard MRT. A new mall with insanely modern architecture that you'll either love or hate. Walls are covered with the Media Façade, allowing films and trippy lights to further intensify the shopping experience. Head up to the IonSKY observation deck on the 56th floor for wonderful views over the city. There's an art gallery on the 4th floor, and high-end designer goods, high-street fashion, a Hong Kong supermarket and food court.

Marina Square, 6 Raffles Blvd. Tiny boutiques, cinema, 10-pin bowling and food outlets.

Ngee Ann City, Orchard Rd. This massive complex houses the Takashimaya department store and over 100 speciality shops, mainly boutiques. The **Kinokuniya** bookshop here is excellent. Expensive food court in the basement.

The Paragon, Bras Basah Rd. Includes **Marks & Spencer**, **Miss Sixty**, **Armani**, **Diesel** and a few good eateries including **Lawry's Prime Rib** and **Thai Express**.

Park Mall, Penang Rd. Interior design items such as furniture and textiles. Food in basement.

Plaza Singapura, next door to Dhoby Ghaut MRT. **Carrefour** hypermarket, **John Little** department store, **Times Bookstore**, **Spotlight**, **Best Denki** lingerie shops, and numerous eateries together with a multi-screen cinema complex.

Raffles City, City Hall MRT. Huge mall featuring mid- to high-end boutiques and a few interesting anomalies. Tenants include **Robinson's**, **Marks & Spencer**, a bookshop, a food court and lots of stalls selling interesting bits and pieces. The biggest spa in Asia, the **Raffles Amrita Spa**, is on the 6th floor of the hotel complex next door. **Jason's supermarket** in the basement has the best collection of imported foodstuffs in Singapore; it's not cheap but is good to fulfil any food cravings.

Scotts, 6 Scotts Rd. Department store, **Picnic** food court in basement, smart, female

boutiques with contemporary designers. Good electronics shops.

Suntec City, City Hall MRT. Packed at weekends, this maze-like mall has a massive **Carrefour**, countless eateries, a feng shui musical fountain, excellent book and music shops and more. To get there, walk through the subterranean CityLink mall from City Hall MRT.

Tanglin Shopping Centre, top end of Orchard Rd. A treasure trove of Asian antiques and curios and Persian rugs. There are also high-end eateries, jewellers and tailors.

Tang's, next to Marriott Hotel. A very smart department store, the Harrods of Singapore.

Vivo City, near HarbourFront MRT station. Huge award-winning mall covering over 24 ha and featuring outdoor dining along the waterfront, Singapore's largest cinema complex, an excellent book shop (**Page One**) boutiques and shops galore, 2 huge food courts and the Sentosa Express terminal on Level 3. Absolutely rammed at weekends.

Wheelock Place, 501 Orchard Rd. **Borders** bookshop dominates the ground level, but it also houses **Marks & Spencer**, **Sakae Sushi** and **NYDC**.

Wisma Atria, Orchard Rd. One of the best places for boutique browsers, though not necessarily top brands. Tenants include **Top Shop**, **Isetan** and **Food Republic**.

Silk

If you want silk without the hassle, at good prices, big department stores (such as **Tang's** on Orchard Rd) have good selections. The best known of the silk boutiques, with fine silks at high prices, is **China Silk House**, which has shops in Tanglin, Scotts and Centrepoint shopping centres on Orchard Rd.

Tailoring

Far East Plaza and **Lucky Plaza**, along Orchard and Scotts roads.

Textiles

Spotlight. The large Australian-owned shop is on the 5th Floor of Plaza Singapura (see above).

Little India *p598, map p599*
Electronic goods
Sim Lim Tower (upper floors) and the nearby Albert Complex, both just off Bukit Timah on Rochor Canal Rd. Good for computers.

Handicrafts
Kuna's, Buffalo Rd. Sells Indian handicrafts. There are other shops around here where Indian knick-knacks can be found.

Shopping centres
Mustafa Centre, corner of Serangoon Rd and Styed Alwi Rd. Open 24 hrs. This department store is popular for cheap electronics, clothes, textiles, gold and household goods. Insanely busy on Sun.

Textiles
Serangoon Rd is one of the best areas for reasonably priced batik and silk lengths, but you should bargain.

Arab Street *p601, map p602*
Textiles
Along with Serangoon Rd (see above), Arab Street is one of the best areas for reasonably priced batik and silk lengths. But, again, you should bargain.

Singapore West *p607*
Antiques
Dempsey Rd, off Holland Rd, is a great place to browse amongst the furniture warehouses in some of the old army barracks there (though it's a bit of a tourist trail these days). Furniture from Indonesia, plantation chairs, opium couches, Burmese Buddhas and so on are all available. Warehouse shops include: **Asian Passion**, Block 13, T6473 1339, good for tables and cabinets; **Woody Antique House**, Block 7, 01-01 Dempsey Rd; **Eastern Discoveries**, Block 26, T6475 1814, for wooden sculptures among other things; **Journey East**, Block 13, T6473 1693, for chests, planters chairs – old and new; **Pasardina**, Block 13, T6472 0228, good range of new and old cabinets, planters chairs, beds

and small-scale Indonesian pieces (spice boxes and baskets); **Renaissance**, Block 15, T6474 0338, has restored Chinese furniture.

Handicrafts
Holland Village Shopping Centre, Holland Av. An excellent place for Asian arts and crafts, Vietnamese lacquerware, Balinese goods, etc. **Lim's**, is also here, see below.

Linen
Lim's, 1st floor, Holland Village Shopping Centre, Holland Av.

East Coast *p610, map p611*
Antiques
Geylang has a number of good antique junk shops where occasional treasures can be found. Peter Wee's **Katong Antique House** (aka Katong Antiques House, at 268 East Coast Rd, T6435 8544 (half museum, half shop), has one of the best selections of Peranakan antiques. The shop has been established for 20 years and has become a focal point for Peranakan culture. He has established a Peranakan Association and publishes a newsletter. Groups from the National Museum visit him. He has a considerable collection of beaded shoes and holds classes on how to make them every Wed.

▲ Activities and tours

Singapore *maps p550, 578, 592, 596, 599, 602, 605, 611*
There are some excellent tours on offer in Singapore, opening a window to the city's fascinating history and culture, and even pubs and hawker centres. Three of the more notable companies are listed below.
Duck Tours, Suntec City Gate 5, T6338 6111 www.ducktours.com.sg. Using an American amphibious military vehicle that saw action in Vietnam, these popular tours dip in and out of the water around the Colonial Core, Marina Bay and the Merlion Park. Departures hourly, S$33, children S$17.

The Original Singapore Walks, 170 Tyrwhitt Rd, T6325 1631, www.singaporewalks.com. Award-winning company with humorous and knowledgeable guides and interesting tours including Changi Museum War Trails, spicy Little India Walk, Colonial District Walk, a wander around the old red-light districts of Chinatown and the Boat Quay Historical Pub Walk. Prices vary according to the tour, from S$25, children S$15. Highly recommended.
Tour East Singapore, T6738 2622. Tours of 3½ hrs to the Singapore heartlands and around the Peranakan areas in the East Coast area. It's a great way to find some of the city's best hawker centres and local culinary delights. Tours cost S$40, children S$20, minimum 2 adults.

ⓓ Directory

See also Essentials A-Z, page 570.

Singapore maps p550, 578, 592, 596, 599, 602, 605, 611

Embassies and consulates
Australia (High Commission), 25 Napier Rd, T6836 4100, www.australia.org.sg. **Austria**, 600 North Bridge Rd, T6396 6350. **Belgium**, 8 Shenton Way, 1401 Temasek Tower, T6220 7677 www.diplomatie.be/Singapore. **Canada** (High Commission), 1 George St, 1101, T6854 5900. **Denmark**, 1301 United Square, 101 Thomson Rd, T6355 5010. **France**, 101-103 Cluny Park Rd, T6880 7800, www.ambafrance-sg.org. **Germany**, 1200 Singapore Land Tower, 50 Raffles Pl, T6533 6002, www.sing.diplo.de. **Indonesia**, 7 Chatsworth Rd, T6737 7422, www.kbri singapura.com. **Israel**, 24 Stevens Cl, T6834 9200. **Italy**, 101 Thomson Rd, No 27-02 United Square, T6250 6022. **Japan**, 16 Nassim Rd, T6235 8855. **Malaysia** (High Commission), 301 Jervois Rd, T6235 0111. **Netherlands**, 1301 Liat Towers, 541 Orchard Rd, T67371155.

New Zealand (High Commission), 391A Orchard Rd, T6235 9966. **Norway**, 1401 Hong Leong Building, 16 Raffles Quay, T6220 7122. **South Africa** (High Commission), 15th floor, Odeon Towers, 331 North Bridge Rd, T6339 3319. **Spain**, 3800 Suntec Tower One, 7 Temasek Blvd, T6725 9220. **Sweden**, 05-01 Singapore Power Building, 111 Somerset Rd, T6415 9720. **Thailand**, 370 Orchard Rd, T6737 2644. **UK** (High Commission), 100 Tanglin Rd, T6424 4270, www.ukinsingapore.fco.gov.uk. **USA**, 27 Napier Rd, T6476 9100.

Internet
There are internet cafés everywhere. In Little India, try **AJs Internet**, with several branches charging S$2 per hr. Those with Wi-Fi should be able to log in at most cafés and hotels.

Medical facilities
Alexandra, 378 Alexandra Rd, T6472 2000, www.alexhosp.com.sg. **East Shore**, 321 Joo Chiat Pl, T6735 5000. **Gleneagles**, 6A Napier Rd (at the end of Orchard Rd), T6470 5700, the best place to go in an emergency. Large A&E, 24-hr medical clinic for longer care. **Mount Alvernia**, 820 Thomson Rd, T02-534818. **Mount Elizabeth**, 3 Mount Elizabeth, T6731 2218. Has a good reputation. **National University**, 5 Lower Kent Ridge Rd, T6772 5000. **Raffles Hospital**, 585 North Bridge Rd, T6311 1555, www.raffleshospital.com. Pricey but professional private facility including specialist emergency, heart, cancer, dental and eye centres. High standard accommodation for long-term patients. **Singapore General**, Outram Rd, T6321 4311. **Traveller's Health and Vaccination Clinic**, Tan Tock Seng Hospital Medical Centre, Level 1, 11 Jln Tan Tock Seng, T6357 8766, www.ttsh.com.sg. Mon-Fri 0800-1700, Sat 0800-1200. Specialist advice and treatment for travel-related illnesses and a walk-in vaccination service. Phone ahead to arrange consultation.

History

What is perhaps unusual is the ease with which Singaporeans have come to terms with their history. The psychology of decolonization, so evident elsewhere, seems not to have afflicted the average Singaporean. Perhaps this is because all the population are the sons and daughters of relatively recent immigrants; perhaps because of the self-evident social and economic achievements of the country; or perhaps it is because there is general acceptance that the colonial experience was beneficial. It is reflected in such things as place names. After independence, there was no rush to rename streets after resistance fighters and nationalist figures from history. Empress Place, Connaught Drive, Alexander Road, Clive Street and Dalhousie Pier remain with the names that the British gave them.

Early records

Although Singapore has probably been inhabited for the past two millennia, there are few early records. In the third century, Chinese sailors mention *Pu-luo-chung*, 'the island at the end of the Peninsula', and historians speculate that this may have been Singapore. Even its name, *Singapura*, from the Sanskrit for 'Lion City', is unexplained – other than by the legendary account in the *Sejara Melayu*. It was originally called Temasek – or 'Sea Town' – and may have been a small seaport in the days of the Sumatran Srivijayan Empire. Following Srivijaya's decline in the late 13th century, however, Singapore emerged from the shadows to become, for a short while, a locally important trading centre in its own right.

Marco Polo, the Venetian adventurer, visited Sumatra in the late 1200s and referred to *Chiamassie*, which he says was a 'very large and noble city'. Historians believe this was probably Temasek. According to the 16th-century *Sejara Melayu*, Temasek was a thriving entrepôt by the 14th century, when it changed its name to Singapura. Whatever prosperity it may have had did not last. In the late 1300s it was destroyed by invading Siamese and Javanese, for Singapura fell in the middle ground between the expanding Ayutthaya (Siamese) and Majapahit (Javanese) empires. The ruler – called Parameswara, who was said to be a fugitive prince from Palembang in Sumatra – fled to Melaka, where he founded the powerful Malay sultanate in the 1390s. Following Parameswara's hasty departure, Singapura was abandoned except for a few *Orang Laut* ('Sea People'), who made a living from fishing and piracy. While trade flourished elsewhere in the region, the port, which today is the busiest in the world, was a jungled backwater, and it remained that way for four centuries.

Raffles steps ashore

In the early 1800s, the British East India Company occupied Dutch colonies in the east, to prevent them falling into French hands: Napoleon had occupied Holland and the Dutch East India Company had gone bankrupt. In January 1819, Sir Thomas Stamford Raffles arrived in Singapore with the hope that he could set up a trading post at the mouth of the Singapore River. He was relieved to hear that the Dutch had never been there and promptly struck a deal with the resident *temenggong* (Malay chief) of the Riau-Johor Empire. To seal this agreement, he had to obtain official approval from the Sultan of Riau-Johor.

Due to a succession squabble following the previous sultan's death in 1812, there were two claimants, one on Pulau Lingga (far to the south), who was recognized by the Dutch, and one on Pulau Bintan. Realizing that the Dutch would bar the Lingga sultan from sanctioning his settlement on Singapore, Raffles approached the other one, flattering him, offering him money and pronouncing him Sultan of Johor. He agreed to pay Sultan Hussein Mohammad Shah 5000 Spanish dollars a year in rent and a further 3000 Spanish dollars to the *temenggong*. The Union Jack was officially raised over Singapore on 6 February 1819, and Raffles set sail again the next day – having been there less than a week – leaving in charge the former Resident of Melaka, Colonel William Farquhar. It was this act of Raffles' that led to him being accorded the title 'Founder of Singapore'. Yet some historians would give the title to another great, although lesser known, British colonialist, Sir John Crawfurd. Ernest Chew, Professor of History at the National University of Singapore, argues that all Raffles secured in his negotiations was permission to establish a trading post. It was not until Crawfurd became the second Resident of Singapore in 1824 that Britain acquired the island by treaty.

The Treaty of London

The Dutch were enraged by Raffles' bold initiative and the British government was embarrassed. But after a protracted diplomatic frisson, the Treaty of London was finally signed in 1824 and the Dutch withdrew their objection to the British presence on Singapore in exchange for the British withdrawal from Bencoolen (Benkulu) in Sumatra, where Raffles had served as governor. Seven years later, the trading post was tied with Penang (which had been in British hands since 1786) and Melaka (which the Dutch had swapped with Bencoolen). They became known as the Straits Settlements and attracted traders and settlers from all over Southeast Asia, and the world.

Raffles' vision

Although Sir Thomas Stamford Raffles spent little time in Singapore, his vision for the city can still be seen today: "Our object is not territory but trade; a great commercial emporium and a fulcrum whence we may extend our influence politically as circumstances may hereafter require." Each time Raffles departed, he left strict instructions on the layout of the growing city; stipulating, for example, that the streets should be arranged on a grid structure wherever possible. Houses were to have a uniform front and "a veranda open at all times as a continued and covered passage on each side of the street" (the so-called 'five-foot ways') – stipulations which resulted in the unique character of Singapore. During his second visit in 1819, he divided the town into distinct districts, or kampongs. Raffles firmly believed that the different ethnic groups should be segregated. The Europeans were to live in the Beach Road area between Stamford canal and Arab Street, the Chinese were to live south of the river (in fact, Chinatown was divided into three separate areas for the different dialect groups), and the *temenggong* and the 600-odd Malays were to live along the upper reaches of the river. To the northeast of the European enclave, Kampong Glam housed Sultan Hussein and his Arab followers. The land on the north side of the river was set aside for government buildings. A mere six months after Raffles had landed, more than 5000 people had settled around the mouth of the river. Much of the area to the south was mangrove swamps, but that was reclaimed and settled too.

European merchants soon realized that the beach was inappropriate as a landing area because of the swell. In agreement with Farquhar, they started to unload from the north bank of the river. When Raffles returned for his third and final visit in October 1822, he was horrified by the chaos of the town. He fell out with Farquhar and had him replaced by John Crawfurd.

From fishing village to international port

Within four years of its founding, Singapore had overshadowed Penang in importance and had grown from a fishing village to an international trading port. Thanks to its strategic location, it expanded quickly as an entrepôt, assuming the role Melaka had held in earlier centuries. But by 1833 the East India Company had lost its China trade monopoly, and consequently its interest in Singapore and the other Straits Settlements declined. Whilst Penang and Melaka declined, however, Singapore boomed. When the Dutch lifted trade restrictions in the 1840s, this boosted Singapore's economy again. New trade channels opened up with the Brooke government in Sarawak and with Thailand. The volume of trade increased fourfold between 1824 and 1868. However, due to the lack of restrictions and regulation, Singapore descended into a state of commercial anarchy, and in 1857 the merchants, who were dissatisfied with the administration, petitioned for Singapore to come under direct British rule.

Ten years later, the Colonial Office in London reluctantly made Singapore a crown colony. Then, in 1869, the Suez Canal opened, which meant that the Strait of Melaka was an even more obvious route for east-west shipping traffic than the Sunda Strait, which was controlled by the Dutch. Five years after that, Britain signed the first of its protection treaties with the Malay sultans on the Peninsula. The governor of Singapore immediately became the most senior authority for the Straits Settlements Colony, the Federated Malay States and the British protectorates of Sarawak, Brunei and North Borneo. In one stroke, Singapore had become the political capital of a small empire within an empire. As Malaysia's plantation economy grew (with the introduction of rubber in the late 19th century) and as its tin-mining industry expanded rapidly, Singapore emerged as the expanding territory's financing and administrative centre and export outlet. By then Singapore had become the uncontested commercial and transport centre of Southeast Asia. Between 1873 and 1913 there was an eightfold increase in Singapore's trade. Joseph Conrad dubbed it "the thoroughfare to the East".

The Japanese invasion

The First World War gave Singapore a measure of strategic significance and by 1938 the colony was bristling with guns; it became known as Fortress Singapore. Unfortunately, the impregnable Fortress Singapore had anticipated that any attack would be from the sea and all its big guns were facing seawards. The Japanese entered through the back door. Japan attacked Malaya in December 1941 and, having landed on the northeast coast, they took the entire Peninsula in a lightning campaign, arriving in Johor Bahru at the end of January 1942.

The Japanese invasion of Singapore was planned by General Tomoyuki Yamashita and was co-ordinated from the Sultan Ibrahim tower in Johor Bahru, which afforded a commanding view over the strait and north Singapore. Yamashita became known as the 'Tiger of Malaya' for the speed with which the Japanese Army overran the Peninsula. The northeast coast of Singapore was heavily protected, but the northwest was vulnerable and this is where the Japanese found their opening. On 13 February 1942, the Japanese captured Kent Ridge and Alexandra Barracks on Alexandra Road. They entered the hospital, where they bayoneted the wounded and executed doctors, surgeons and nurses. The Allies and the local people were left in little doubt as to what was in store.

With their water supplies from the Peninsula cut off by the Japanese, and facing an epidemic because of thousands of rotting corpses, British Lieutenant-General Arthur Percival was forced to surrender in the Ford Motor Company boardroom on Bukit Timah Road, at 1950 on 15 February 1942. The fall of Singapore, which was a crushing humiliation for the British, left 140,000 Australian, British and Indian troops killed, wounded or captured. Japan had taken the island in one week.

Following the defeat, there were accusations that Sir Winston Churchill had 'abandoned' Singapore and let it fall to the Japanese when reinforcements were diverted elsewhere. The motivation for this, it has been suggested, was to get America to join the war. It is significant that Churchill never pressed for an inquiry into the fall of Singapore – the historian Peter Elphick suggests that Churchill was worried that he would emerge as the prime factor behind the capitulation. Apart from Churchill's supposed involvement in the surrender, there were other manifold reasons why Singapore fell. There is little doubt that the defence of Singapore itself, and Malaya more widely, was poorly handled. There was a widespread lack of appreciation of the martial skills of the Japanese. The forces defending Singapore lacked sufficient air cover and were poorly equipped, and training and morale were poor. The massive surrender certainly stands in stark contrast to Churchill's orders issued to General Wavell on 10 February: "There must at this stage be no thought of saving the troops or sparing the population. The honour of the British Empire and of the British Army is at stake."

The occupation

The Japanese ran a brutal regime and their occupation was characterized by terror, starvation and misery. They renamed Singapore *Syonan* – meaning 'light of the south'. The intention was to retain Syonan as a permanent colony, and turn it into a military base and centre in its 'Greater East Asia Co-Prosperity Sphere'. During the war, Singapore became the base of the collaborationist Indian National Army and the Indian Independence League.

In the fortnight that followed the surrender, the Japanese required all Chinese males aged 18-50 to register. 'Undesirables' were herded into trucks and taken for interrogation and torture by the Kempetai military police to the old YMCA building on Stamford Road, or were summarily bayoneted and shot. The purge was known as *sook ching* – or 'the purification campaign'. Thousands were killed (Singapore says 50,000, Japan says 6000), and most of the executions took place on Changi Beach and Sentosa. The sand on Changi Beach is said to have turned red from the blood.

Allied prisoners-of-war were herded into prison camps, the conditions of which are vividly described in James Clavell's book *King Rat*; the author was himself a Changi POW. Many of the Allied troops who were not dispatched to work on the Burma railway or sent to Sandakan in North Borneo, where 2400 died, were imprisoned in Selarang Barracks on the northeast side of the island.

After Hiroshima and Nagasaki

Following the dropping of atomic bombs on Hiroshima and Nagasaki, the Japanese surrendered on 12 September 1945. The Japanese 5th and 18th Divisions, which had spearheaded the invasion of Singapore and had carried out civilian massacres, were from the towns of Hiroshima and Nagasaki respectively. Lord Louis Mountbatten, who took the surrender, described it as the greatest day of his life.

In the wake of the war, the Japanese partially atoned for their 'blood debt' by extending 'gifts' and 'special loans' to Singapore, totalling some US$50 million. But Japanese war crimes were neither forgiven nor forgotten. Older Singaporeans noted with dismay and concern how Japan had rewritten its historical textbooks to gloss over its wartime atrocities, and many Singaporeans harbour a deep-seated mistrust of the Japanese. Among the most outspoken of them is former Prime Minister Lee Kuan Yew.

This mistrust remains, despite former Japanese Prime Minister Toshiki Kaifu's public apology in 1991 for what his countrymen had done 50 years before.

After the war

Following a few months under a British military administration, Singapore became a crown colony and was separated from the other Straits Settlements of Penang, Melaka and Labuan. The Malay sultanates on the Peninsula were brought into the Malayan Union. The British decision to keep Singapore separate from the Malayan Union sparked protests on the island and resulted in the founding of its first political party, the Malayan Democratic Union (MDU), which wanted Singapore to be integrated into a socialist union. The Malayan Union was very unpopular on the mainland too and the British replaced it with the Federation of Malaya in 1948. Singapore was excluded again because Malaya's emergent Malay leaders did not want to upset the Peninsula's already delicate ethnic balance by incorporating predominantly Chinese Singapore.

In the same year, elections were held for Singapore's legislative council. The MDU, which had been heavily infiltrated by Communists, boycotted the election, allowing the Singapore Progressive Party (SPP) – dominated by an English-educated élite – to win a majority. The council was irrelevant to the majority of the population, however, and did nothing to combat poverty and unemployment and little to promote social services. When the Communist Emergency broke out on the Peninsula later the same year, the Malayan Communist Party of Malaya (CPM) was banned in Singapore and the MDU disbanded.

Lee Kuan Yew ('Harry Lee' to the British and Americans) returned from study in England in 1950. In 1954, as his political aspirations hardened, he let it be known that he wished to be called Lee Kuan Yew. Ten years later, the British foreign secretary George Brown is still alleged to have remarked to him: "Harry, you're the best bloody Englishman east of Suez".

Political awakening

In 1955 a new constitution was introduced, which aimed to jolt the island's apathetic electorate into political life. Two new parties were formed to contest the election – the Labour Front under lawyer David Marshall (descended from an Iraqi Jewish family) and the People's Action Party (PAP), headed by Lee Kuan Yew. These two parties routed the conservative SPP and Marshall formed a minority government. His tenure as Chief Minister was marked by violence and by tempestuous exchanges in the Legislative Assembly with Lee. Marshall resigned in 1956, after failing to negotiate self-government for Singapore by his self-imposed deadline. His deputy, Lim Yew Hock (who later became a Muslim), took over as Chief Minister and more Communist-instigated violence followed.

The rise of the PAP

The influence of the PAP grew rapidly, in league with the communists and radical union leaders, and through the Chinese-language schools and trade unions. For the anti-communist Lee, it was a machiavellian alliance of convenience. He mouthed various anti-colonial slogans, but the British, at least, seemed to realize he was playing a long, and cunning, game. The communists came to dominate the PAP central committee and managed to sideline Lee before their leaders were arrested by Marshall's government. At the same time, Singapore's administration was rapidly localized: the four main languages (Malay, Chinese, Tamil and English) were given parity within the education system and locals took over the civil service. In 1957, as Malaya secured independence from the British, Singapore negotiated terms for full self-government. In 1959 the PAP swept the polls, winning a clear majority, and Lee became prime minister, a post he was to hold for more than three decades.

The PAP government began a programme of rapid industrialization and social reform. Singapore also moved closer to Malaysia, which Lee considered a vital move in order to guarantee free access to the Malaysian market and provide military security in the run-up to its own independence. But the PAP leaders were split over the wisdom of this move, and the extreme left wing, which had come to the forefront again, was becoming more vociferous in its opposition. Malaysia, for its part, felt threatened by Singapore's large Chinese population and by its increasingly Communist-orientated government. Tunku Abdul Rahman, independent Malaysia's first Prime Minister, voiced concerns that an independent Singapore could be 'a second Cuba', a Communist state on Malaysia's doorstep. Instead of letting the situation deteriorate, however, Tunku Abdul Rahman cleverly proposed Singapore's inclusion in the Federation of Malaysia.

The Federation of Malaysia and independence

Rahman hoped the racial equilibrium of the Federation would be balanced by the inclusion of Sarawak, Brunei and North Borneo. Lee liked the idea, but the radical left wing of the PAP were vehemently opposed to it, having no desire to see Singapore absorbed by a Malay- dominated, anti-Communist regime, and in 1961 they tried to topple Lee's government. Their bid narrowly failed and resulted in the left-wing dissenters breaking away to form the Barisan Sosialis (BS), or Socialist Front. Despite opposition to the merger, a referendum showed that a majority of Singapore's population supported it. In February 1963, in *Operation Coldstore*, more than 100 Communist and pro-Communist politicians, trades unionists and student leaders were arrested, including half the BS Central Executive Committee.

On 31 August 1963, Singapore joined the Federation of Malaysia. The following month, Singapore declared unilateral independence from Britain. The PAP also won another victory in an election and secured a comfortable majority. Almost immediately, however, the new Federation ran into trouble due to Indonesian objections, and Jakarta launched its Konfrontasi – or Confrontation. Indonesian saboteurs infiltrated Singapore and began a bombing spree which severely damaged Singapore's trade. In mid-1964, Singapore was wracked by communal riots which caused great concern in Kuala Lumpur, and Lee and Tunku Abdul Rahman clashed over what they considered undue interference in each others' internal affairs. Tensions rose still further when the PAP contested Malaysia's general election in 1964, and Lee attempted to unite all Malaysian opposition parties under the PAP banner. While the PAP won only one of the 10 seats, it petrified many Malay politicians on the mainland. Finally, on 9 August 1965, Kuala Lumpur forced Singapore to agree to pull out of the Federation, and it became an independent state against the wishes of the government. At a press conference announcing Singapore's expulsion from the Federation, Lee Kuan Yew wept.

As a footnote to Singapore's expulsion from the Federation, in June 1996 Lee Kuan Yew suggested that the island republic might rejoin the Federation should certain conditions be met – like no racial favouritism. Few other politicans, either in Singapore or Malaysia, took the proposal seriously.

Modern Singapore

Singapore still believes in extended families, filial piety, discipline and respect, but above all, it believes in the Asian work ethic. The man who has instilled and preserved these values is former Prime Minister and now Minister Mentor (or MM for short) Lee Kuan Yew. But to some – and it should be added that most of these are non-Singaporeans – his far-sighted vision has transformed this clockwork island into a regimented city state. In this view of things, modern, automated Singapore has spawned a generation of angst-ridden, over-programmed people, who have given their country the reputation of being the most crushingly dull in Asia.

But now, all has changed. The architect of modern Singapore has allowed a new generation of Singaporeans to step up to the drawing board. That Lee Kuan Yew's own son, Lee Hsien Loong, took office in 2004, as part of a handover of power without elections, may give the impression that what goes round, comes round, the first Singaporean dynasty is in the making.

Politics

In 1965, the newly independent Republic of Singapore committed itself to non-Communist, multi-racial, democratic socialist government, and secured Malaysian co-operation in trade and defence. The new government faced what most observers considered impossible: forging a viable economy in a densely populated micro-state with no natural resources. At first, Singapore hoped for re-admission to the Malaysian Federation, but as Lee surprised everyone by presiding over one of the fastest-growing economies in the world, the republic soon realized that striking out alone was the best approach. Within a few years, independent Singapore was being hailed as an 'economic miracle'. Nonetheless, the government had to work hard to forge a sense of nationhood. As most Singaporeans were still more interested in wealth creation than in politics, the government became increasingly paternalistic, declaring that it knew what was best for the people, and because most people agreed, few raised any objections.

Singapore's foreign policy has been built around regional co-operation. It was a founder member in 1967 of the Association of Southeast Asian Nations (ASEAN) and has also been a leading light in the wider Asia-Pacific Economic Cooperation (APEC) grouping. Friendly international relations are considered of paramount importance for a state that relies so heavily on foreign trade and which, in terms of size and population, is a minnow among giants. Although Singapore continued to trade with the former Communist states of Eastern Europe and the Soviet Union throughout the period of the Cold War, Lee had a great fear and loathing of Communism. At home, 'Communists' became bogeymen; 'hard-core' subversives were imprisoned without trial, under emergency legislation enshrined in the Internal Security Act, a legacy of the British colonial administration.

Singapore's political stability since independence, which has helped attract foreign investors to the island, has been tempered by the government's tendency to stifle criticism. The media are state-owned and are so pro-government that they have become rigidly self-censoring. Foreign publications are summarily banned or their circulation restricted if they are deemed to be meddling in (ie critical of) Singapore's internal affairs. Probably because the People's Action Party (PAP) have been so successful at bringing about economic success, no major political opposition has emerged. Politicians who have stood out against PAP's autocratic style of government have been effectively silenced as the government sets about undermining their credibility in the eyes of the electorate. For 13 years, between 1968 and 1981, PAP held every single seat in parliament. In 2001 the general election saw less than a third of the constituency seats contested, making losing an impossibility for PAP. (This in a country where, if you're eligible to vote, voting is compulsory.) The 2006 elections saw more than half of the constituency seats contested (a first); PAP won 82 out of 84, taking 60% of the popular vote. Opposition won an impressive 30% of the vote and a high proportion of votes cast – 8% – were declared void.

Lee's succession

As Lee Kuan Yew came to be regarded as one of the region's 'elder statesmen', questions were raised over his succession. The PAP's old guard gradually made way for young blood, but Lee clung on until November 1990. Three months after Singapore's extravagant 25th anniversary, he finally handed over to his first deputy prime minister Goh Chok Tong. Lee, though, remained PAP's chairman. Subsequently a new post was created especially for him; Lee is now the 'Minister Mentor'.

When Lee senior stepped down in late 1990, a new era began. Goh promised to usher in a more open, 'people-oriented', consensus-style of government. Among his first acts was the creation of a new Ministry for the Arts, and to underscore his faith in Singapore's maturity, he permitted the showing of porn films, which proved very popular. He also began encouraging a more free press (particularly with regard to foreign publications), as well as releasing long-term political prisoners and allowing ageing exiles to return home. But relaxation in government attitudes should not be regarded as a shift to Western-style liberalism. Indeed, analysts perceived a slight hardening of attitude as Goh's premiership wore on.

The PAP – losing its way or regaining the initiative?

Perhaps a sign that the PAP was in danger of losing its way came with the country's first presidential election of August 1993, which was billed as a PAP stitch-up. Virtually all observers predicted that the result would be a foregone conclusion. In the event, the favoured candidate, former deputy prime minister Ong Teng Cheong (Lee Kuan Yew, despite much speculation, decided not to stand) did win, but he managed to attract less than 60% of the vote, against more than 40% won by his virtually unknown challenger, a former government accountant, Chua Kim Yeoh. As he did not actively campaign, analysts attributed his sudden popularity not to genuine support but to a protest against the PAP, which had barred two opposition candidates from standing.

Singapore's most recent general election was held in 2006 and some commentators were predicting a further erosion of PAP support, as the republic's increasingly sophisticated electorate bristled at the restrictions placed upon them. Despite increased votes cast for opposition, however, PAP has obviously retained its appeal for the majority of voters, see above. The next election is due in 2012.

Lee Hsien Loong

Although Singapore has been run as a meritocracy since independence, Goh was widely assumed to be a seat-warmer for Lee Kuan Yew's eldest son, Brigadier-General Lee Hsien Loong. Lee Hsien, like his father, got a first at Cambridge, returned to Singapore, joined the army as a platoon commander and within eight years was a Brigadier-General in charge of the Joint Operations Planning Directorate. During that period he obtained a Master's degree at Harvard and then in 1984, at the age of 32, was elected to parliament.

The following year he became a cabinet minister and head of the Ministry of Trade and Industry. At 38, he became deputy prime minister and then head of the critical Monetary Authority of Singapore. He celebrated his 54th birthday in 2006.

But Lee Hsien's life has not been one of an inexorable rise to the top. In 1982 his first wife died (he has since remarried). And in 1992 it was revealed that Lee had been diagnosed with lymphoma (in 1997 he was given a clean bill of health).

Since coming to power Lee Hsien has introduced a number of policies, some more popular than others. In 2005 he introduced the five-day week, abolishing the half working day on Saturday, and in 2006 PAP distributed a S$2.6 billion budget surplus termed the 'Progress Package'. This was given as cash to a huge number of eligible people and led to Lee Hsien being accused by critics and opposition of vote buying, as a general election was just around the corner.

Birth incentives have also been increased. Due to the historically low birth rate (1.26 children per mother, compared with 5.8 in the 60s), Singapore now finds itself incentivising families that have more than two children; an ironic position when you consider that just a few decades ago the governement was strongly encouraging sterilisation after the second child. The low birth rate has also led to a softening of immigration policies. Singapore has thrown its gates open to workers, particularly from India and China, as well as less skilled workers from all around Asia. Media reports state claims from Singaporean bosses who claim that the new migrants make better workers than Singaporeans, who are more likely to grumble at low wages and long hours than the recent arrivals from China. Diplomatic relations with China have improved with the Singapore-China Free Trade Agreement signed in 2008.

Singapore and its neighbours

Singapore is a member of the 10-member Association of Southeast Asian Nations (ASEAN) and enjoys generally good relations with its neighbours. However, there have been times of friction, particularly during the mid-1960s when Singapore left the Malaysian Federation and had a diplomatic spat with President Sukarno of Indonesia. As a minute city state with a population less that 2% of Indonesia's, Singapore's leaders have always been acutely aware of the need to build and maintain good relations with its regional neighbours.

Even so, Singapore has not always managed to avoid offending its larger neighbours. This particularly applies to Malaysia, a country with which it shares a common colonial history, but from which it is divided in so many other ways. Malaysia's majority are Malay and Muslim; Singapore's are Chinese. Malaysia has a national policy of positive discrimination in favour of ethnic Malays; Singapore is a meritocracy. Malaysia is still a developing country; Singapore's standard of living is among the highest in the world. This makes for a fierce competitiveness between the two countries, which disguises a lingering bitterness that some commentators trace back to Singapore's ejection from the Malaysian Federation in the mid-1960s. Malaysia is quick to take offence at anything that smacks of Singaporean superiority.

Between 1996 and 1998, relations between Malaysia and Singapore sunk to their lowest level for some years. In June 1996, Lee Kuan Yew offered the thought that Singapore could, conceivably, merge once more with Malaysia. Two months later, Goh Chok Tong seemed to use this as a threat when he warned that if Singapore slipped up, "we will have no option but to ask Malaysia to take us back". The Malaysian government took this as a slight. In their view, the prime minister was threatening the electorate with the possibility that they might be absorbed into Malaysia. In March 1997, Senior Minister

Lee Kuan Yew suggested that the Malaysian state of Johor Bahru was "notorious for shootings, muggings and car-jackings" (this was in relation to opposition politician Tang Liang Hong's decision to flee there from Singapore). The Malaysian press and some sections of the government reacted with outrage. Singapore's *Straits Times* then compounded Lee's insensitivity by publishing an article listing recent crimes in Johor – which Malaysians saw as a crass attempt to justify his comments. Just as this spat had run its course, the Asian crisis created further tensions. Malaysia felt Singapore was not doing enough to help the poor economy of its neighbour across the Strait of Johor.

Today, relations are stable, several outstanding disputes notwithstanding. Singapore and Malaysia are members of the Five Power Defence Arrangements, and undertake military exercises together in order to strengthen the ties between their armed forces. Both countries export to each other, with Malaysia supplying much of Singapore's drinking water (another source of tension, as Malaysia is signatory to a historical treaty guaranteeing Singapore's right to buy water from them at what is now below the market rate). Many Malaysians also work in Singapore.

There are lots of jokes about Singapore, many dreamt up by Singaporeans themselves. One concerns what it is like being a miniscule place with a massive collective ego, where boosterism has become a defining feature. It is said that Lee Kuan Yew was given, on a trip to India, a bolt of the finest silk cloth. When he got home he took it to his tailor, where he was measured up and told that there was sufficient material for a single suit. Not sure what to do, he took the cloth with him on an official trip to Hong Kong and asked Tung Chee Hwa whether his tailor could make up the cloth. Tung's tailor let Lee know that yes, he would be delighted to make up the cloth, and that he could make a suit and an extra pair of trousers. Mightily impressed with the tailor's skill, he nonetheless decided to take the cloth with him on a trip to Japan. Here the prime minister's tailor said he could make a suit, two pairs of trousers, and a fancy waistcoat. Even more impressed with the Japanese tailor's skills, he decided to take the bolt of cloth with him to the US where he was due to meet President George W Bush. Bush's tailor quickly let Lee know that he could make up two suits, two pairs of trousers, a fancy waistcoat and a cummerbund. Perplexed, Lee asked President Bush how on earth his tailor could make so much more from the bolt of cloth than his own tailor. Bush answered: "Well, you see Harry, it just goes to show that the further you are from Singapore the smaller you become."

Singapore in the 21st century

Singapore's political system fits no neat category. It is both democratic and authoritarian; although it is tempting to characterize Singapore as a totalitarian state, it is not. Whether the People's Action Party will be able to continue to dominate Singapore's political landscape, as it has done throughout the period since independence, is a key question. There are certainly challenges that the PAP will have to confront. To begin with, social differentiation is making it harder for the PAP to please almost all the people almost all of the time. People's interests are diverging as Singapore's affluence grows. Second, there is the question of whether the PAP, in creating a 'thinking society' necessary for economic success, is not also creating a society that will be more politically creative and combative. Third, and related, there is the question of whether the population will continue to accept such a low level of public debate and the continued ban on public street demonstrations.

Singapore ministers are the highest paid in the world, further adding to the impression that this city state is run as a company with its minsters as executives. In 2007 ministers received a 60% pay rise, bringing Lee Hsien Loong's paypacket to a staggering S$3.1

Capital punishment

With its reputation as being a 'fine city' splashed over T-shirts in Little India and Chinatown, Singapore has long been proud of its security and moral cleanliness when compared with its more edgy Southeast Asian neighbours. Those flying into the city state get their first taste of Singapore's stance on crime when filling in the landing card, emblazoned with 'Warning: death for drug traffickers under Singapore law'.

Between 1994 and 1999, Singapore had the dubious distinction of having the world's highest execution rate per capita, at 13.54 per one million of the population. Executions in Singapore are by hanging, taking place at Changi Prison at dawn on a Friday, a method much influenced by the British systems in use in the 1950s, in the pre-independence era, with the executioner still referring to the long drop table developed in the UK by William Marwood.

Capital cases are tried at court by a single judge with no jury. Those found guilty are allowed one appeal in the Court of Appeal. If this fails, the last chance lies with clemency being granted by the president, an extremely rare action last thought to have occurred in 1998. Prisoners and their families are notified of the upcoming execution four days before and from this point the condemned is allowed extra privileges such as watching TV, listening to the radio and having special meals (within the prison budget).

State Executioner Darshan Singh has held the post since 1959. It is alleged that he has tried to resign on numerous occasions but no suitable replacement can be found. Having hanged over 850 people in his career, he is known by the last words that he says to every condemned prisoner "I am going to send you to a better place than this. God bless you". In 2005, controversy surrounded Singh when his identity was revealed by an Australian newspaper prior to the execution of Australian Van Tuong Nguyen. Having been identified and quoted by an Australian newspaper, Darshan was not asked to perform the execution, many believing the job was given to a Malaysian executioner. Singh's response was "with me [prisoners] ... don't struggle. If [the executioner] ... is a raw guy they will struggle like chickens, like fish out of water", much to the anger of Australian Foreign Minister Alistair Downing.

There is virtually no public debate in Singapore about the death penalty, with the former opposition leader, the late Joshua Jayaretnam, being given mere minutes to express any counterviews before being rebuffed by the Minister of State for Law and Home Affairs. A survey carried out by the *Straits Times* in 2007 showed that 95% of Singaporeans support the death penalty. Singaporean leaders' defence is that it's their international right to punish criminals using capital punishment, and the Prime Minister Lee Hsien Loong states that the penalty protects citizens from the "evil inflicted on thousands of people which drug trafficking demands". With such little debate and scant public awareness, it seems as though the Friday hangings will remain a fixture on the island for some time to come.

million, five times the salary of the US president. The government claimed that such salaries prevent corruption, and the meek local population were unable to do anything other than complain in coffee shops to their friends.

In 2005, Reporters Without Borders ranked Singapore 140th out of 167 nations in their press freedom index. *The Economist* considers Singapore to be a hybrid nation, containing elements of democracy and authoritarianism. Those who have fought hard battles against the government on issues of democracy and freedom have often suffered greatly as a result. Believing the courts to be in the pockets of the PAP, political activists such as the late JB Jeyaratnam campaigned for separation of power between the courts and the ruling party, but found himself sued to bankruptcy and officially disqualified from opposing the government politically. In his final few years he could often be seen standing outside Raffles City selling his anti-government, pro-freedom books. In 2005 filmmaker Martyn Lee created a documentary about the leader of the opposition Singapore Democratic Party, Chee Soon Juan, the 'Singapore Rebel', but as the PAP got wind of this Lee found himself threatened with a lawsuit for making a partisan film, illegal in Singapore. In 2008, Chee found himself sued to oblivion, bankrupted, prohibited from leaving the country and sentenced to serve jail time.

Contents

654 Malaysian words
and phrases

657 Glossary

660 Malaysian and
Singaporean food glossary

663 Index

672 Credits

Malaysian words and phrases

Basic phrases
Yes/No ia/tidak
Thank you Terimah kasih
You're welcome Sama-sama
Good morning/Good afternoon (early) Selamat pagi/Selamat tengahari
Good afternoon (late)/Good evening/night Selamatpetang/Selam at malam
Welcome Selamat datang
Goodbye (said by the person leaving/said by the person staying) Selamat tinggal/
    Selamat jalan
Excuse me/sorry Ma'af saya
Where's the...? Dimana...?
How much is this...? Ini berapa?
I [don't] understand Saya [tidak] mengerti
I want.../I don't want Saya mahu/Saya tak mahu
My name is... Nama saya...
What is your name? Apa nama anda?
Bon Appetit! Selamat makan!

Sleeping
How much is a room? Bilik berapa?
Does the room have air-conditioning? Ada bilik yang ada air-con-kah?
I want to see the room first please Saya mahu lihat bilik dulu
Does the room have hot water? Ada bilik yang ada air panas?
Does the room have a bathroom? Ada bilik yang ada mandi-kah?

Travel
Where is the railway station? Stesen keretapi dimana?
Where is the bus station? Stesen bas dimana?
How much to go to...? Berapa harga ke...?
I want to buy a ticket to... Saya mahu beli tiket ke...
How do I get there? Bagfaimanakah saya?
Is it far? Ada jauh?
Turn left / turn right Belok kiri /belok kanan
Go straight on! Turus turus!

Time and days
Monday Hari Isnin (Hari Satu)
Tuesday Hari Selasa (Hari Dua)
Wednesday Hari Rabu (Hari Tiga)
Thursday Hari Khamis (Hari Empat)

Friday Hari Jumaat (Hari Lima)
Saturday Hari Sabtu (Hari Enam)
Sunday Hari Minggu (Hari Ahad)

Today Hari ini
Tomorrow Esok
Week Minggu

Month Bulan
Year Tahun

Numbers

1	satu	9	sembilan
2	dua	10	sepuluh
3	tiga	11	se-belas
4	empat	12	dua-belas...etc
5	lima	20	dua puluh
6	enam	21	dua puluh satu...etc
7	tujuh	30	tiga puluh
8	lapan	100	se-ratus

101	se-ratus satu
150	se-ratus limah puluh
200	dua ratus...etc
1,000	se-ribu
2,000	dua ribu...
100,000	se-ratus ribu
1,000,000	se-juta

Basic vocabulary

a little sedikit
a lot banyak
all right/good baik
and dan
bank bank
bathroom bilek mandi
beach pantai
beautiful cantik
bed sheet cadar
big besar
boat perahu
broken tak makan/rosak
bus bas
bus station setsen bas
buy beli
can boleh
cannot tak boleh
cheap murah
chemist rumah ubat
cigarette rokok
clean bersih
closed tutup
cold sejuk
crazy gila
day hari
delicious sedap
dentist doktor gigi

dirty kotor
doctor doktor
eat makan
excellent bagus
expensive mahal
food makan
he/she dia
hospital rumah sakit
hot (temperature) panas
hot (chilli) pedas
I/me saya
ice air batuais
island pulau
male lelaki
man laki
market pasar
medicine ubat ubatan
more lagi/lebeh
open masuk
please sila
police polis
police station pejabat polis
post office pejabat pos
railway station
  stesen keretapi/tren
restaurant
  restoran/kedai makanan

room bilik
sea laut
ship kapal
shop kedai
sick sakit
small kecil
stand berdiri
stop berhenti
taxi teksi
they mereka
that itu
ticket tiket
toilet (female)
  tandas perempuan
toilet (male) tandas lelaki
town bandar
trishaw beca
very sangat
wait tunggu
water air
we kami
what apa
when bila
woman perempuan
you awak/anda

A practical alternative

Malaysian English, which has been dubbed 'Manglish', as opposed to Singaporean English ('Singlish'), has evolved its own usages, abbreviations and expressions. Its very distinctive pronunciation can be almost unintelligible to visitors when they first arrive. The first thing many visitors notice is the use of the suffix *lah* which is attached to just about anything and means absolutely nothing. English has been spoken in the Malay world since the late 18th century, but over time, it has been mixed with local terms. The converse has also happened: English has corrupted Malay to such a degree that it is now quite common to hear the likes of 'you pergi-mana?' for 'where are you going?' In abbreviated Malaysian- Chinese English, can is a key word. 'Can-ah?' (inflection) means 'may I?'; can-lah means yes; cannot means no way; also can means 'yes, but I'd prefer you not to' and how can? is an expression of disbelief.

The man who first applied the term Manglish to mangled Malaysian English was Chinese-Malaysian satirist Kit Leee, in his book *Adoi* (which means ouch). It gives an uncannily accurate and very humorous pseudo-anthropological rundown on Malaysia's inhabitants. His section on Manglish, which should be pronounced exactly as it is written, is introduced: Aitelyu-ah, nemmain wat debladigarmen say, mose Malaysians tok Manglish... Donkair you Malay or Chinese or Indian or everyting miksup... we Malaysians orways tok like dis wan-kain oni. Below are extracts from his glossary of common Manglish words and phrases (which will help decipher the above).

atoyu (wat) gentle expression of triumph: 'What did I tell you?'

baiwanfriwan ploy used mainly by shop assistants to promote sales: 'If you buy one you'll get one free'.

betayudon mild warning, as in 'You'd better not do that'.

debladigarmen contraction of 'the bloody government'; widely used scapegoat; for all of life's disappointments, delays, denials, and prohibitions.

hauken another flexible expression applicable in almost any situation, eg 'That's not right!', 'Impossible!' or 'Don't tell me!'.

izzenit from 'isn't it?' but applied very loosely at the end of any particular statement to elicit an immediate response, eg Yused you will spen me a beer, izzenit?

kennonot request or enquiry, contraction of 'can or not': 'May I?' or 'Will you?' or 'Is it possible?'

nola a dilute negative, used as a device to interrupt, deny or cancel someone else's statement.

oridi contraction of already.

sohau polite interrogative, usually used as a greeting, as in 'Well, how are things with you?'

tingwat highly adaptable expression stemming from 'What do you think?'

wan-kain adjective denoting uniqueness; contraction of 'one of a kind'. Sometimes rendered as wan-kain oni ('only').

watudu rhetorical question: 'But what can we do?'

yala non-committal agreement, liberally used when confronted with a bore.

yusobadwan expression of mild reproach: 'That's not very nice!'

With thanks to Kit Leee and his co-etymologists: Rafique Rashid, Julian Mokhtar and Jeanne MC Donven. Leee, Kit (1989) *Adoi*, Times Books International: Singapore)

Glossary

A

Adat   custom or tradition

Amitabha   the Buddha of the Past (see Avalokitsvara)

Atap   thatch

Avalokitsvara   also known as Amitabha and Lokeshvara, the name literally means 'World Lord'; he is the compassionate male Bodhisattva, the saviour of Mahayana Buddhism and represents the central force of creation in the universe; usually portrayed with a lotus and water flask

B

Bahasa   language, as in Bahasa Malaysia

Barisan Nasional   National Front, Malaysia's ruling coalition comprising UMNO, MCA and MIC along with seven other parties

Batik   a form of resist dyeing common in Malay areas

Becak   three-wheeled bicycle rickshaw

Bodhi   the tree under which the Buddha achieved enlightenment (Ficus religiosa)

Bodhisattva   a future Buddha. In Mahayana Buddhism, someone who has attained enlightenment, but who postpones nirvana in order to help others reach the same state

Brahma   the Creator, one of the gods of the Hindu trinity, usually represented with four faces, and often mounted on a hamsa

Brahmin   a Hindu priest

Budaya   cultural (as in Muzium Budaya)

Bumboat   small wooden lighters, now used for ferrying tourists in Singapore

Bumiputra   literally, 'sons of the soil'; Malays as opposed to other races in Malaysia

C

Cap   batik stamp

Chedi   from the Sanskrit cetiya (Pali, caitya) meaning memorial. Usually a religious monument (often bell-shaped) containing relics of the Buddha or other holy remains. Used interchangeably with stupa

Cutch   see Gambier

D

Dalang   wayang puppet master

DAP   Democratic Action Party, Malaysia's predominantly Chinese opposition party

Dayak/Dyak   collective term for the tribal peoples of Borneo

Dharma   the Buddhist law

Dipterocarp   family of trees (Dipterocarpaceae) characteristic of Southeast Asia's forests

Durga   the female goddess who slays the demon Mahisa, from an Indian epic story

E

Epiphyte   plant which grows on another plant (but usually not parasitic)

F

Feng shui   the Chinese art of geomancy

G

Gambier   also known as cutch, a dye derived from the bark of the bakau mangrove and used in leather tanning

Gamelan   Malay orchestra of percussion instruments

Ganesh   elephant-headed son of Siva

Garuda   mythical divine bird, with predatory beak and claws, and human body; the king of birds, enemy of naga and mount of Vishnu

Gautama   the historic Buddha

Geomancy   or feng shui, the Chinese art and science of proper placement

Godown   Asian warehouse

Goporum tower in a Hindu temple

Gunung mountain

H

Hamsa sacred goose, Brahma's mount; in Buddhism it represents the flight of the doctrine

Hinayana 'Lesser Vehicle', major Buddhist sect in Southeast Asia, usually termed Theravada Buddhism

I

Ikat tie-dyeing method of patterning cloth

Indra the Vedic god of the heavens, weather and war; usually mounted on a three headed elephant

J

Jataka(s) birth stories of the Buddha, of which there are 547; the last 10 are the most important

K

Kajang thatch

Kala (makara) literally, 'death' or 'black'; a demon ordered to consume itself; often sculpted over entranceways to act as a door guardian, also known as kirtamukha

Kampung or kampong, village

Kerangas from an Iban word meaning 'land on which rice will not grow'

Keraton see kraton

Kinaree half-human, half-bird, usually depicted as a heavenly musician

Kongsi Chinese clan house

Kris traditional Malay sword

Krishna an incarnation of Vishnu

Kuti living quarters of Buddhist monks

L

Laterite bright red tropical soil/stone sometimes used as a building material

Linga phallic symbol and one of the forms of Siva. Embedded in a pedestal shaped to allow drainage of lustral water poured over it, the linga typically has a succession of cross sections: from square at the base through octagonal to round. These symbolize, in order, the trinity of Brahma, Vishnu and Siva

Lintel a load-bearing stone spanning a doorway; often heavily carved

Lokeshvara see Avalokitsvara

Lunggyi Indian sarong

M

Mahabharata a Hindu epic text written about 2,000 years ago

Mahayana 'Greater Vehicle', major Buddhist sect

Mandi Malay bathroom with water tub and dipper

Maitreya the future Buddha

Makara a mythological aquatic reptile, somewhat like a crocodile and sometimes with an elephant's trunk; often found, along with the kala, framing doorways

Mandala a focus for meditation; a representation of the cosmos

MCA Malaysian Chinese Association

Meru the mountain residence of the gods; the centre of the universe, the cosmic mountain

MIC Malaysian Indian Congress

Mudra symbolic gesture of the hands of the Buddha

N

Naga benevolent mythical water serpent, enemy of Garuda

Naga makara fusion of naga and makara

Nalagiri the elephant let loose to attack the Buddha, who calmed him

Nandi/Nandin bull, mount of Siva

NDP New Development Policy

Negara kingdom and capital, from the Sanskrit

Negeri also negri, state

NEP New Economic Policy

Nirvana 'enlightenment', the Buddhist ideal

O

Orang Asli indigenous people of Malaysia

P

Paddy/padi unhulled rice

Pantai beach

Pasar market, from the Arabic 'bazaar'

Pasar malam night market

Perahu/prau boat

Peranakan 'half caste', usually applied to part Chinese and part Malay people

Pradaksina pilgrims' clockwise circumambulation of a holy structure

Prang form of stupa built in the Khmer style, shaped rather like a corncob

Prasat residence of a king or of the gods (sanctuary tower), from the Indian prasada

Pribumi indigenous (as opposed to Chinese) businessmen

Pulau island

Pusaka heirloom

R

Raja/rajah ruler

Raksasa temple guardian statues

Ramayana the Indian epic tale

Ruai common gallery of an Iban longhouse, Sarawak

Rumah adat customary or traditional house

S

Sago multi-purpose palm

Sal the Indian sal tree (Shorea robusta), under which the historic Buddha was born

Sakyamuni the historic Buddha

Silat or bersilat, traditional Malay martial art

Singha mythical guardian lion

Siva one of the Hindu triumvirate, the god of destruction and rebirth

Songket Malay textile interwoven with supplementary gold and silver yarn

Sravasti the miracle at Sravasti when the Buddha subdues the heretics in front of a mango tree

Sri Laksmi the goddess of good fortune and Vishnu's wife

Stele inscribed stone panel or slab

Stucco plaster, often heavily moulded

Stupa see chedi

Sungai river

T

Tamu weekly open-air market

Tanju open gallery of an Iban longhouse, Sarawak

Tara also known as Cunda; the four-armed consort of the Bodhisattva Avalokitsvara

Tavatimsa heaven of the 33 gods at the summit of Mount Meru

Theravada 'Way of the Elders'; major Buddhism sect also known as Hinayana Buddhism ('Lesser Vehicle')

Tiffin afternoon meal – a word that was absorbed from the British Raj

Timang Iban sacred chants, Sarawak

Tong or towkay, a Chinese merchant

Totok 'full blooded'; usually applied to Chinese of pure blood

Towkay Chinese merchant

Triads Chinese mafia associations

Tunku also tuanku and tengku, prince

U

Ulama Muslim priest

Ulu jungle

UMNO United Malays National Organization

Urna the dot or curl on the Buddha's forehead, one of the distinctive physical marks of the Enlightened One

Usnisa the Buddha's top knot or 'wisdom bump', one of the physical marks of the Enlightened One

V

Vishnu the Protector, one of the gods of the Hindu trinity, generally with four arms holding the disc, the conch shell, the ball and the club

W

Waringin banyan tree

Warung a foodstall – a simple place to eat on the street – the alernative Malay name is Kedai Makan. The word originally comes from Indonesia.

Wayang traditional Malay shadow plays

Malaysian and Singaporean food glossary

Malay

assam sour
ayam chicken
babi pork
belacan hot fermented prawn paste
buah fruit
daging meat
Es avocado chilled avocado shake
Es delima dessert of water chestnut in sago and coconut milk
Gado-gado cold dish of bean sprouts, potatoes, long beans, tempeh, bean curd, rice cakes and prawn crackers, topped with a spicy peanut sauce
garam salt
gula sugar
Ice kachang similar to *chendol* (see Chinese food) but with evaporated milk instead of coconut milk
ikan fish
ikan bilis anchovies
ikan panggang spicy barbecued fish
kambing mutton
Kepala ikan fish head, usually in curry or grilled
kerupak prawn crackers
ketupat cold, compressed rice
kopi coffee
kueh cakes
lemang glutinous rice in bamboo
limau lime
manis sweet
mee noodles
minum drink
roti canai pancakes with lentils and curry
roti john baguette filled with sardine/eggmixture
roti kosong plain pancake
sambal spicy paste of pounded chillis, onion and tamarind
sayur manis sweet vegetables
sayur masak lemak deep-fried marinated prawns
sejuk crab
soto ayam spicy chicken soup

sotong squid
susu milk
tahu beancurd
telur egg
udang prawn

Rice dishes
nasi campur Malay curry buffet of rice served with meat, fish, vegetables and fruit.
nasi goreng rice, meat and vegetables fried with garlic, onions and *sambal*.
nasi lemak a breakfast dish of rice cooked in coconut milk and served with prawn *sambal*, *ikan bilis*, a hard-boiled egg, peanuts and cucumber.
nasi padang plain rice served with a selection of dishes.
nasi puteh plain boiled rice.
nasi dagang popular on the east coast for breakfast; glutinous rice cooked in coconut milk and served with fish curry, cucumber pickle and *sambal*.

Soup
soto ayam popular for breakfast in Johor and Sarawak, a spicy chicken soup served with rice cubes, chicken and vegetables.
lontong popular in the south, particularly for breakfast. Cubed compressed rice served with mixed vegetables in coconut milk. *Sambal* is the accompaniment.

Meat
satay chicken, beef or mutton marinated and skewered on a bamboo, barbecued over a brazier. Usually served with *ketupat*.

Noodles
kway teow flat noodles fried with seafood, egg, soy sauce, beansprouts and chives.
laksa johor noodles in fish curry sauce and raw vegetables.
mee goreng fried noodles.
mee jawa noodles in gravy, served with prawn fritters, potatoes, tofu and beancurd.

mee rebus noodles with beef, chicken or prawn with soybean in spicy sauce.

Curries
rendang dry beef curry (a Sumatran dish).
longong vegetable curry made from rice cakes cooked in coconut, beans, cabbage and bamboo shoots.

Salad
rojak Malaysia's answer to Indonesia's gado gado – mixed vegetable salad served in peanut sauce with *ketupat*.

Vegetables
kang-kong belacan water spinach fried in chilli shrimp paste
sayur manis sweet vegetables; vegetables fried with chilli, *belacan* and mushrooms.

Sweets (kueh)
apam steamed rice cakes.
pulut inti glutinous rice served with sweetened grated coconut.
nyonya kueh Chinese *kueh*, among the most popular is *yow cha koei* – deep-fried kneaded flour.

For more information on cuisine, see Eating, page 27.

Chinese and local food

Bak chang local rice dumpling filled with savoury or sweet meat and wrapped in leaves
Bak choy Chinese cabbage
Bak kut the local pork rib soup, with garlic and Chinese five spice
Belachan fermented prawn paste
Bird's nest edible nest of the swiftlet, made from glutinous secretions of their salivary glands
Char kway teow broad rice noodles fried with sweet sauce and additions of cockels, Chinese sausage, bean sprouts or fish cake
Char siew Sweet barbecued pork slices
Chendol a dessert: a cone of ice shavings topped with coloured syrups, brown syrup,

coconut milk, red beans, attap seeds and jelly
Cheng ting a Chinese dessert of a bowl of syrup with herbal jelly, barley and dates
Chicken rice rice in chicken stock and ginger, served with steamed chicken slices
Chilli padi an extremely hot variety of chilli
Choi sum Chinese vegetable served steamed with oyster sauce
Claypot rice rice cooked in a clay casserole with pieces of chicken, Chinese mushroom, Chinese sausage and soy sauce
Congee Chinese porridge
Dian sin/dim sum Chinese sweet and savoury dumplings served at breakfast and lunch.
Dow see Chinese fermented salted black beans
Fish sauce known as *nampla* in Thai, a brown sauce made from salted dried fish, used as a salt seasoning
Garoupa white fish popular in Asia
Gula malacca coarse palm sugar sold in lumps, from the sap of the Palmyra palm
Hainanese chicken rice chicken served with spring onions, ginger dressing, soup and rice boiled in chicken stock or coconut milk
Hoisin sauce Chinese thick seasoning with a sweet-spicy flavour
Hokkien mee yellow noodles fried with sliced meat, squid, prawns and garnished with strips of fried egg
Kang kong a Chinese vegetable
Kway teow broad rice noodles
Laksa spicy coconut soup of thin white noodles garnished with bean sprouts, quail's eggs, prawns, shredded chicken and dried bean curd
Lor mee a dish of noodles served with slices of meat, eggs and a dash of vinegar in a dark brown sauce
Rojak salad of cucumber, pineapple, turnip, fried beancurd tossed in a prawn paste with peanuts, tamarind and a sugary sauce
Sio bee a pork filling in a paper-thin wrapping
Tau hui a dessert made from a byproduct of soya bean, served with syrup
Teh tarek tea made with evaporated milk
Yu char kway deep-fried Chinese breadsticks

Indian

Aloo gobi potato and cauliflower dish
Bhindi okra or lady's fingers
Biryani North Indian dish of basmati rice and meat, seafood and vegetables
Brinjal aubergine or eggplant
Daun pisang a Malay/South Indian thali – curry and rice, with poppadoms and chutneys all served on a banana leaf
Dhal pureed lentils
Dhosas large crispy pancakes served with potatoes, onions and spices
Gulab jumun fried milk balls in syrup
Idli steamed rice cake
Keema spicy minced meat
Kofta minced meat or vegetable ball
Lassi yoghurt-based drink
Murgh chicken
Murtabak roti (bread) which has been filled with pieces of mutton, chicken or vegetables
Nasi biriyani rice cooked in ghee, spices and vegetable, served with beef or chicken
Nasi kandar Mamak's version of *nasi campur*
Pakora vegetable fritter
Pilau rice fried in ghee mixed with nuts
Pudina mint sauce
Raita side dish of cucumber, yoghurt, mint
Rogan josh spicy lamb curry with yoghurt
Roti prata flat round pancake-like bread
Saag spinach
Sambar fiery mixture of vegetables, lentils and split peas
Tandoori style of cooking: meat is marinated in spicy yoghurt and then baked in a clay oven
Tikka small pieces of meat or fish served off the bone, marinated in yoghurt and baked

Nyonya

kapitan chicken cooked in coconut milk
otak otak minced fish, coconut milk and spices, steamed in a banana leaf
laksa rice noodles in spicy coconut milk and prawn-flavoured gravy blended with spices and served with shellfish, chicken, beancurd and *belacan*

assam laksa the specialized Penang version – rice noodles served in fish gravy with shredded cucumber, pineapple, raw onions and mint

Sabahan

hinava marinated raw fish
sup manuk on hiing chicken soup with rice wine
tapai chicken cooked in rice wine
pakis ferns, which are fried with mushrooms and *belacan*. Sometimes ferns are eaten raw, with a squeeze of lime (*sayur pakis limau*)
sup terjun jumping soup – salted fish, mango and ginger
hinompula a dessert made from tapioca, sugar, coconut and the juice from screwpine leaves

Sarawakian

Ternbok fish, either grilled or steamed
pan suh manok chicken cooked in bamboo cup, served with *bario* (Kelabit mountain rice)
Lontong rice cakes in a spicy coconut-milk topped with grated coconut and sometimes bean curd and egg
Manis sweet
Mee rebus yellow noodles served in a thick sweet sauce made from sweet potatoes. Garnished with sliced hard-boiled eggs and green chillies
Mee siam white thin noodles in a sweet and sour gravy made with tamarind
Nasi biryani saffron rice flavoured with spices and garnished with cashew nuts, almonds and raisins
Rijsttafel Indonesian meal consisting of a selection of rice dishes, to which are added small pieces of meat, fish, fruit and pickles
Sambal spicy paste of pounded chillis, onion and tamarind
Sayur masak lemak deep-fried marinated prawns
Tempeh preserved deep-fried soya bean

Index → *Entries in bold refer to maps*

A

accommodation
  Malaysia 25
  Singapore 561
Ahir Terjan Sensuron 424
air travel
  discount flight agents 18
  domestic 20
  international 17
Al Arqam 525
Alor Star 167, **169**
Anwar Ibrahim 504
Api, Gunung 373
architecture 514
art 514
Ashaari Muhammed 525
Asian Art Museum, KL 75
Astana 310
atlas moth 539
ATMs
  Malaysia 48
Aur
  Pulau 228
Australian war memorial 452
Ayer Batang 224, **231**
Ayer Itam Dam 152
Ayer Keroh 206

B

Babas 194, 511
Babi Besar, Pulau 228
Bahasa Melayu 47, 515
Bajau
  Sabah 488
Bako National Park 318, **319**
  beaches 320
  flora and fauna 319
  listings 323
  treks 320
Bakun Dam 343
Balik Pulau 154
bamboo carving
  Sarawak 392
Bandar Sri Aman 331
  Fort Alice 331
  ins and outs 331
  listings 335
  sights 331
Bank Negara Money Museum 63
banks
  Malaysia 48

Baram River 356
Bario 375
  background 375
  listings 377
  treks 376
basketry
  Sarawak 392
Bat Temple 152
Batang Ai National Park 332
  listings 335
Batang Ai River 332
batik 521
bats 353
Batu Bungan 371
Batu Buruk 275
Batu Caves 74
Batu Ferringhi 150
Batu Mandi 352
Batu Maung 153
Batu Tulug 459
Baturong 460
Bau 314
beadwork
  Sarawak 393
Beaufort 426
  listings 430
Belaga 341
  listings 346
Beremban, Gunung 112
Berhala, Pulau 454
Besar, Pulau 207
Beserah 251
Bharata Natyam
  dance 519
Bidayuh, Sarawak 385
Bintulu 351, **351**
  listings 360
  longhouses 352
birds 537
birds' nests 355
birdwatching 36
blowpipes
  Sarawak 393
Blue Valley Tea Estate 116
boat travel
  international 20
  within Malaysia 24
books 541
border crossings
  Brunei 20
  Kalimantan 20

  Sabah-Sarawak 427
  Thailand 19
Borneo pygmy elephant 463
Brickfields
  Kuala Lumpur 68
Brinchang 115
Brinchang, Gunung 112
British Malaya 494
Brooke, Charles 381
Brooke, Charles Vyner 382
Brooke, James 307, 380, 483
Buddhism 526
Bujang Valley 169
Bukit Anak Takun 74
Bukit Batu Lawi 375
Bukit Larut 130
Bukit Singapore
  Bukit Timah Nature
    Reserve 614
Bukit Takun 74
bumiputra 509
Buntal 315
Burau Bay 177
bus travel
  Malaysia 19, 22
  Singapore 555, 558
Butterfly Park 69
Butterworth 154

C

Cameron Highlands 110, **111**
Cape Rachado 80
car hire
  Malaysia 22
  Singapore 559
Casino de Genting 109
Cendering 274
ceramics 311
Chan See Shu Yuen Temple 66
Changi Airport 553
Charah Caves 250
Cherating 265
children, travelling with
  Malaysia 43
  Singapore 570
Chinese
  culture 511
  Sabah 488
  Sarawak 386
Chinese New Year
  Singapore 565

Chow Kit 66
Clan Piers 148
Clearwater Cave 374
climate
    Borneo 531
    Malaysia 17, 530
    Singapore 553
climbing 41
clothing 41
cobra 538
Colonial Malaya 494
Commonwealth War
    Cemetery 130
Communism 500
Communist Emergency 500
consulates
    Malaysia 44
    Singapore 640
cookery courses 36
corruption 506
crafts 520
    Sabah 491
    Sarawak 392
credit cards
    Malaysia 48
    Singapore 573
Crocker Range National Park 425
crocodile farm 453
cuisine
    see food
currency
    Malaysia 48
    Singapore 573
customs
    Malaysia 44
    Singapore 570
cycling
    Malaysia 22, 23
    Singapore 559

D

Damai Peninsula 315
    listings 322
dance 519
    Sarawak 391
Danum Valley Conservation
    Area 461
    flora and fauna 462
    listings 473
Datai Bay 178
Dayabumi Complex 65
Dayang, Pulau 179
Death March 485
Deepavali, Singapore 566

Deer Cave 374
dengue fever 46
disabled travellers
    Malaysia 44
    Singapore 571
diving 36
    Pulau Tioman 227
drama 517, 635
drink
    Malaysia 29
    Singapore 564
drugs
    Singapore 571
Dusun 490
duty free
    Malaysia 44
    Singapore 570
Duyung Besar, Pulau 275

E

electricity
    Malaysia 44
    Singapore 571
elephant 534
    Borneo Pygmy 463
embassies
    Malaysia 44
    Singapore 640
emergency numbers 43
Endau Rompin National Park 240

F

festivals
    Malaysia 31
    Malaysia, when to go 17
    Singapore 565
Filipinos
    Sabah 488
flight agents 18
Flor de la Mar 196
flora
    Borneo 532
    Malaysia 531
Foo Lin Kong Temple 132
food 29
    Malaysia 27
    Singapore 562
    glossary 660
Fort Alice 331
Fort Altingberg 77
Fort Margherita 311
Fraser's Hill 109

G

gay travel
    Malaysia 45
    Singapore 571
Gaya, Pulau 418
Gedung Rajah Abdullah 76
Genting Highlands 108
Georgetown 144, 146
glossary 657
Golden Triangle 72
Gomantong Caves 458
gongs 520
Grik 296
Gua Musang 295
Gua Tambun 127
guano 353
Gunung Gagau
    Taman Negara National
    Park 261
Gunung Api 373
Gunung Gading National Park 314
    listings 322
Gunung Jerai 170
Gunung Kinabalu National
    Park 439, 441
    flora and fauna 443
    listings 447
    Mount Kinabalu 444
    practicalities 439
    treks 442
Gunung Ledang 207
Gunung Mulu National
    Park 369, 370
    background 371
    flora and fauna 371
    listings 377
Gunung Penrissen 313
    listings 322
Gunung Santubong 317
Gunung Silam 460
Gunung Tahan
    Taman Negara National
    Park 259
Gunung Tahan trek
    Taman Negara National
    Park 259
Gunung Tapis Park 251
Gunung Trusmadi 425

H

handicrafts
    Malaysia 35
Harrisson, Tom 383, 391
Harvest Festival 489

Hawaii Beach 359
hawker centres 29
haze, the 305, 540
headhunting 387
health
    Malaysia 45
    Singapore 572
Hibiscus and Reptile Garden 153
Hinduism
    religion 526
history
    Malaysia 494
    Sabah 483
    Sarawak 379
    Singapore 641
hitchhiking
    Malaysia 24
    Singapore 559
holidays
    Malaysia 31
    Singapore 565
homestays
    Kuala Lumpur 81
hornbill 537
hotels
    see accommodation

I
Iban, Sarawak 386
Ibrahim, Anwar 504
immigration
    Malaysia 51
    Singapore 575
internet
    Malaysia 47
    Singapore 572
Ipoh 124, 125, 133
ISIC 49
Islam
    religion 522
Istana Alam Shah 76

J
Jade Museum 73
Jakuns 513
Jalan Ampang 69, 71
Jalan Tun Tan Cheng Lock 203
Japanese interregnum 484
Japanese occupation 497
Japanese war memorial 452
Jasar, Gunung 112
Jerai, Gunung 170
Jerak Warisan Heritage Trail 192
Jeram Pasu 295

Jerantut 262
Johor Bahru 216, 216
Jonker Street 202

K
Kadazan, Sabah 490
Kain songket 521
Kampong Ayer 403
Kampong Ayer Batang 224
Kampong Cherating 265, 266
Kampong Genting 225
Kampong Gombizau 437
Kampong Juara 226, 233
Kampong Kraftangan 293
Kampong Kuala Tahan 259
Kampong Lalang 224
Kampong Morten 204
Kampong Mukut 226
Kampong Nipah 226
Kampong Panuba 224
Kampong Paya 224
Kampong Pulau Rusa 275
Kampong Salang 224, 232
Kampong Sumangkap 437
Kampong Sungai Ular 251
Kampong Tekek 224, 230
Kampung Cherating 265
Kampung Panji 460
Kampung Paya 233, 236
Kampung Selungai 426
Kanching Falls 74
Kapalai 466
    diving 37
    listings 475
Kapas, Pulau 275
Kapit 338, 339
    Fort Sylvia 339
    listings 345
    longhouses 340
Karambunai Beach 406
Karambunai Peninsula 406
Karyaneka Handicraft Centre 73
Kayan, Sarawak 388
Keith, Agnes 454
Kek Lok Si Temple 152
Kelabit Highlands 375
Kelabit, Sarawak 388
Kelantan 292
Kellie's Castle 126
Kemabong 426
Kemasik 267
Keningau 425
    listings 430
Kenong Rimba National Park 262

Kenyah, Sarawak 388
Ketam, Pulau 76
Khoo Kongsi 148
Kinabalu, Mount 444
Kinabatangan River 459
Kipungit Falls 446
KL Tower 71
Klang 76
Klias Wetlands 423
Konfrontasi 384, 485
Kong Mek 294
kongsis 512
Kota Belanda 132
Kota Belud 435
    listings 438
Kota Bharu 290, 291
Kota Kinabalu 398, 399, 400, 405
    history 401
    ins and outs 398
    listings 407
    Masjid Sabah 401
    Sabah Foundation 403
    Sabah State Museum 401
    sights 401
    viewpoints 403
Kota Tampan 296
krait 538
kris 498
Kuah 175
Kuala Abang 267
Kuala Besut 285
Kuala Dungun 267
Kuala Kangsar 127
Kuala Kedah 171
Kuala Likau 352
Kuala Lipis 262
Kuala Lumpur 53-104, 58, 64, 67, 70, 72
    bars 94
    Central Market 65
    Chinatown 66
    eating 88
    excursions 73
    history 61
    Jalan Ampang 69
    KLCC 69
    Kuala Lumpur Textile Museum 63
    Lake Gardens 68
    Little India 68
    Masjid Jamek 68
    Masjid Negara 65
    Museum of National History 65
    Muzium Negara 68
    sights 63

sleeping 81
Sultan Abdul Samad
    Building 63
The Colonial core 63
tourist information 60
tours 100
Kuala Perlis 171
Kuala Selangor 76
Kuala Selangor Nature Park 77
Kuala Sepetang 129
Kuala Terengganu 273, **273**
Kuala Woh 113
Kuantan 247, **248**
Kubah National Park 314
    listings 322
Kuching 304, **308**, **313**
    Astana 310
    Chinatown 309
    Chinese History Museum 310
    Civic Centre and
        Planetarium 310
    Fort Margherita 311
    history 305
    ins and outs 304
    kampongs 312
    listings 320
    national parks information 305
    Petra Jaya 312
    Sarawak Islamic Museum 306
    Sarawak Museum 306
    sights 306
    Timber Museum 312
    tourist information 304
    transport 329
    waterfront 306
Kuching Wetlands National
    Park 318
Kudat 436
    listings 438
Kukup 218
Kundasang 446
    listings 448

L
Labuan, Pulau 420
Lahad Datu 460
    listings 473
Lake Gardens 68
Lake Tasek Bera 250
Lambir Hills National Park 359
Lang Tengah, Pulau
    diving 38
Lang's Cave 375
Langanan Waterfall 446

Langkasuka 170
Langkawi 174
    diving 39
language 654
    Malaysia 47, 515
    Singapore 572
Lankayan, Pulau 454
    diving 37
Lata Iskandar Waterfall 114
Lawas 376
    listings 378
Layang Layang 406
    diving 36
leatherback turtle 268
Ledang, Gunung 207
leptospirosis 46
Likas Bay 403
Limbang 376
    listings 377
    sights 376
Ling Nam Temple 129
Lion Dance 519
literature
    Malaysia 515
Little India
    Kuala Lumpur 68
    Singapore 598
Loagan Bunut National Park 359
    longhouse tours 340
Lumut 130
Lundu 314
    listings 322

M
Mabul Island 465
    diving 37
    listings 474
Madai Caves 460
Mak Yong dance 519
Malay language 47
Malays
    culture 510
    Sarawak 388
Malaysian Armed Forces
    Museum 75
Malaysian Communist Party
    (MCP) 500
Malaysian dollar 48
Malaysian Indian Congress
    (MIC) 513
Maliau Basin Conservation
    Area 467
Mamutik, Pulau 419
Mantanani Island 437

Manukan, Pulau 419
maps
    Malaysia 25
    Singapore 560
Marang 275
martial art 498
Marudi 360
    listings 363
    longhouses 360
Marudi-Kampong Teraja log
    walk 360
Masjid Jamek, Kuala Lumpur 68
Masjid Kampung Laut 295
Masjid Negara, Kuala Lumpur 65
Masjid Sultan Salahuddin Abdul
    Aziz Shah 76
Mat Salleh 402
Mat Salleh's fort 424
Mataking 466
    listings 475
Matang Wildlife Centre 315
Matunggong 437
Mawah Waterfall 425
media
    Malaysia 47
Melaka 192, **193**, **201**
Melanaus, Sarawak 388
Melinau Gorge 373
Menara KL 313
Mengkabong Water Village 406
Merang 281
Merdeka Square 63
Merlion 585
Mersing 221, 222, **222**
Mesilau Nature Resort 445
    listings 448
Minangkabau 80
Mines Wonderland 77
Miri 356, **358**
    diving 37
    history 357
    listings 360
    sights 357
money
    Malaysia 48
    Singapore 573
monkeys 535
monsoons, Malaysia 530
Monsopiad Cultural Village 404
Mount Kinabalu 444
Mountain Garden 445
MRT, Singapore 558
Muka Head 151
Mulu, Gunung 372

Murut
  Sabah 491
  Murut villages 426
Museum of Islamic Arts
  Malaysia 65
music 519, 635
  Sarawak 392
Muzium Negara, KL 68

N

National Art Gallery, KL 73
national parks
  Endau Rompin 240
  Taman Negara 257
National Planetarium, KL 69
National Zoo and Aquarium, KL 75
newspapers
  Malaysia 47
  Singapore 572
Niah Caves 356
Niah National Park 353
Nobat 520
Nyonyas 194, 511

O

Ophir, Mount 207
Orang Asli (Aboriginals)
  culture 513
Orang Asli Museum, KL 74
Orang Ulu
  Sabah 390
  Sarawak 389
orang utan 534

P

palang 391
Pangkor Laut 132
Pantai Air Papan 222
Pantai Cahaya Bulan 294
Pantai Cenang 176, **177**
Pantai Dalam Rhu 295
Pantai Kok 177
Pantai Kundor 206
Pantai Rhu 178
Pantai Tengah 176
Papar 423
  listings 429
Parliament House, KL 69
Pasang Rapids 344
Pasir Mas 352
Payar, Pulau 179
Pekan 249
Peladang Setiu Agro Resort 277

Pelagus Rapids 340
  listings 345
Pemanggil, Pulau 228
Penampang 404
Penan 317
Penan, Sarawak 390
Penang 141, **142**, **151**
  listings 154
Penang Bridge 149
Penang Hill 152
Penang National Park 154
penis pin 391
Perak Museum 129
Perak Tong 127
Peranakans 511
  art and architecture 515
Perhentian Islands 284
  diving 38
Petaling Jaya 75
Petra Jaya 312
Petronas Towers, KL 70
pewterware 522
  craft 522
Pinnacles 373
politics 647
  Malaysia 503
  Sabah 486
  Sarawak 384
  Singapore 647
Poring 446
  listings 448
Port Dickson 79
Port Klang 76
Port Victoria 422, **420**
post
  Malaysia 49
  Singapore 574
pottery 311
  Sarawak 393
prohibitions 49
public holidays
  Malaysia 31
  Singapore 565
Pulau Aur 228
Pulau Babi Besar 228
Pulau Berhala 454
Pulau Besar 207
Pulau Dayang Bunting 179
Pulau Duyung Besar 275
Pulau Gaya 418
Pulau Kapas 275
Pulau Ketam 76
Pulau Labuan 420
  diving 38

listings 427
  sights 422
Pulau Lang Tengah 282
Pulau Langkawi 174, **175**
Pulau Lankayan 454
  listings 470
Pulau Mamutik 419
Pulau Manukan 419
Pulau Pangkor 130, **131**
Pulau Payar 179
  diving 39
Pulau Pemanggil 228
Pulau Perhentian Besar 284
Pulau Perhentian Kecil 284
Pulau Raja 275
Pulau Rawa 228
Pulau Redang 281
Pulau Sapi 419
Pulau Satang Besar 315
Pulau Sembilan 132
Pulau Sibu 228
Pulau Sibuh Tengah 228
Pulau Sipadan 465
Pulau Sulug 419
Pulau Tenggol 267
Pulau Tiga National Park 419
  listings 427
Pulau Tinggi 228
Pulau Tioman 222, **225**
  diving 227
Putra World Trade Centre 66

R

rabies 46
radio
  Malaysia 48
  Singapore 572
Raffles, Sir Thomas Stamford 580
rafflesia 314, 424
  Rafflesia Information
    Centre 424
rafting 41
Rainforest Interpretation
  Centre 458
Rainforest Music Festival 316
Raja, Pulau 275
Rajah Brooke's birdwing 539
Ramadan, Malaysia 33
Ranau 446
  listings 448
Rantau Abang 267
Rawa, Pulau 228
Rebana 520
  music 520

Redang archipelago 281
    diving 38
Rejang River 336
restaurants
    Malaysia 29
    Singapore 562
rhinoceros 536
    Sumatran 462
rhinoceros beetle 539
ringgit 48
Ringlet 114
road travel
    Malaysia 19, 22
    Singapore 555, 558
Royal Selangor Complex 75
Rumah Belor 342
Rumah Penghulu Abu Seman 72
Rumah Tuan Lepong Balleh 341

S
Sabah 395–492
    crafts 491
    culture 488
    history 483
    politics 486
Sabah Agricultural Park 426
Sabah State Museum 401
safety
    Malaysia 49
    Singapore 574
    Southern Thailand 290
Salleh, Mat 402
Salleh's fort 424
Sam Poh Buddhist Temple 115
Sam Poh Tong 127
Sandakan 450, 452, 455
    crocodile farm 453
    history 451
    listings 470
    sights 452
Santubong 315
Santubong, Gunung 317
Sapi, Pulau 419
Sapulut 425
Sarawak 301–394
    ceramics 311
    crafts 392
    culture 385
    dance 391
    history 379
    music 392
    national parks information 305
    people 385
    politics 384

Sarawak Chamber 375
Sarawak Cultural Village 316
scuba diving 36
Selangor Club 63
Seletar airport 554
Sematan 314
    listings 322
Semonggoh Orang-Utan
    Sanctuary 312
Semporna 463
    listings 473
Senoi 513
Sentosa Island 604
Sepilok Orang-Utan Sanctuary 457
Seremban 78, 78
Seribuat Archipelago 222
Shah Alam 76
Shenton Way 588
shopping
    Malaysia 35
    Singapore 567
Sibu 337, 336
    listings 344
Sibu, Pulau 228
Sikuati 437
Silverware 522
Similajau National Park 352
    flora and fauna 353
    listings 361
    treks 353
Singapore 547–652, 550, 578,
592, 596, 599, 602, 605, 611
    accommodation 561
    air travel 553
    airport tax 554
    Arab Street 601
    Arts House 580
    Asian Civilizations Museum 580
    bars and clubs 631
    Battle Box 584
    bird singing 595
    Boat Quay 586
    Botanic Gardens 595, 596
    Bugis Street 603
    Bukit Batok Nature Park 614
    bus travel, getting there 555
    car hire 559
    cathedrals 582
    Cavenagh Bridge 586
    Changi Airport 553
    Changi Museum 611
    Chettiar Temple 585
    children, travelling with 570
    Chinatown 589

Chinese and Japanese
    Gardens 608
    churches 582
    City Hall 576
    City, The 585
    Clarke Quay 587
    climate 553
    Colonial core 576
    credit cards 573
    Cricket Club 576
    currency 573
    customs 570
    cycling 559
    Dhoby Ghat 598
    disabled travellers 571
    drink 562, 564
    drugs 571
    duty-free 570
    East Coast 610
    East Coast Park 610
    eating 622
    electricity 571
    embassies and consulates 640
    Emerald Hill 598
    Empress Palace 580
    Esplanade 577
    ferries 560
    festivals 565
    Financial centre 588
    food 562
    Fort Canning Park 584
    gay travel 571
    guides 560
    HarbourFront 603
    Haw Par Villa 607
    health 572
    hitchhiking 559
    Holland Village 608
    hotels 561
    internet 572
    Jinriksha station 594
    Joo Chiat Road 610
    Jurong Bird Park 608
    Katong 610
    Kong Meng San Phor Kark 612
    Kranji War Memorial 614
    language 572
    Lau Pa Sat Festival Market 588
    Little India 598
    maps 560
    media 572
    medical facilities 640
    Merlion 585
    money 573

mosques 602
MRT 558
National Museum of Singapore 584
National Orchid Garden 597
North of the island 612
Orchard Road 595
Padang, The 576
Parliament House 580
post 574
public holidays 565
Pulau Ubin 614
Raffles Hotel 581
rail travel, international 555
Railway Station 595
Riverside Point 587
safety 574
Sakya Muni Buddha Gaya Temple 601
Science Centre 609
sea, getting there 557
Seletar Airport 554
Sentosa 603
Serangoon Road 598
shopping 567
sights 576
Singapore Art Museum 583
Singapore River 585
Singapore sling 564
Siong Lim Temple 612
sleeping 616
Snow City 610
Sri Mariamman Temple 591
student travellers 574
Sungai Buloh Wetland Reserve 614
Supreme Court 576
Tan Kim Seng's Fountain 577
tax 571
taxi 557, 559
Tea Chapter 594
telephone 574
Telok Ayer Street 593
Telok Blangah Johor State Mosque 603
temples 603
tipping 574
tourist board 574
transport 558
trishaw 560
vaccinations 572
visa 575
wet markets 600
women travellers 575

Zhujiao 600
Zoo 612
Singapore Sling 564
Sipadan Island Marine Reserve 464
  background 464
  diving 37
  listings 474
Sipitang 427
  listings 430
Skrang longhouses 332
Skrang River 332
smoking
  Singapore 574
Snake Temple, 153
Sri Mahamariamman Temple, KL 66
Sri Menanti 79
Sri Pantai 222
Sri Pathirakaliaman 132
Stadthuys 200
Straits Chinese 511
student travellers
  Malaysia 49
  Singapore 574
Sultan Abu Bakar Museum 249
Sultan Iskandar Planetarium 310
Sulug, Pulau 419
Sumatran rhinoceros 462
sun bear 468
Sungai Karang 251
Sungai Lembing 251
Sungai Likau 352
Sungai Palas 116
Sungai Petani 169
Sze Ya Temple 66

T
Tabin Wildlife Reserve 460
Taiping 128, **129**
Talang Talang 314
Taman Burung 69
Taman Burung (Bird Park), KL 69
Taman Negara National Park 257, **258**
Tambunan 423
  listings 429
Tampuruli 406
Tamu Muhibba 357
tamus 432
Tanah Merah 454
Tanah Rata 114, **114**
Tanjong Sapi 320
Tanjung Aru 404
  listings 409

Tanjung Datu National Park 315
Tanjung Jara 270
Tanjung Kling 206
Tapah 113
tapai 491
tapir 536
Tasek Cini 250
tattoos 390
Tawau 466
  listings 475
Tawau Hills State Park 467
tax
  Malaysia 49
  Singapore 571
taxis
  Malaysia 24
  Singapore 559
telephone
  Malaysia 49
  Singapore 574
Telok Assam 320
Telok Paku 320
Telok Pandan Kecil 320
Teluk Bahang 150
Teluk Bahang Recreation Forest 151
Teluk Batik 130
Teluk Cempedak 249
Teluk Rubiah 130
Temerloh 250
Tempasuk River 435
Temple of the Goddess of Heaven 73
Templer Park 74
Tengah, Pulau 228
Tenggol, Pulau 267
  diving 39
Tenom 426
  listings 430
textiles, Sarawak 394
Thaipusam
  Malaysia 31
  Singapore 565
Thaipusam festival 74
tiger 536
time
  Malaysia 50
  Singapore 574
Tinggi, Pulau 228
Tioman, Pulau 222
  diving 39
tipping
  Malaysia 50
  Singapore 574

Titi Kerawang 154
tourist information
    Malaysia 50
    Singapore 574
train travel
    domestic 21
    to Malaysia 19
transport
    air, Malaysia 17, 20
    air, Singapore 553
    rail, Malaysia 19, 20
    rail, Singapore 555, 558
    road, Malaysia 19, 22
    road, Singapore 555, 558
    sea, Malaysia 20, 24
    sea, Singapore 557, 560
trekking 41
Trusmadi, Gunung 425
Tuaran 406

Tumpat 295
Tun Razak Memorial 69
Tunku Abdul Rahman National
    Park 418
    listings 427
Turtle Islands National Park 454
    listings 471
turtles 267, 455
    giant leatherback 268

V

vaccinations
    Malaysia 45
    Singapore 572
visas
    Malaysia 51
    Singapore 575
Vision 2020 508

W

Wah Aik Shoemaker Shop 203
Wat Chayamangkalaram 150
Wat Phothivian 295
Wayang kulit 518, 522
    craft 522
    drama 517
whitewater rafting 41
women travellers
    Malaysia 52
    Singapore 575
working
    in Malaysia 52

Notes

Credits

Footprint credits
Project Editor: Jo Williams
Layout and production: Emma Bryers
Maps: Kevin Feeney
Colour section: Robert Lunn, Kevin Feeney
Series design: Mytton Williams
Proofreader: Jen Haddington
Cover design: Robert Lunn

Managing Director: Andy Riddle
Commercial Director: Patrick Dawson
Publisher: Alan Murphy
Publishing managers: Felicity Laughton, Jo Williams
Digital Editor: Alice Jell
Marketing: Liz Harper, Hannah Bonnell
Sales: Jeremy Parr
Advertising: Renu Sibal
Finance and administration:
Elizabeth Taylor

Photography credits
Front cover: age fotostock/Superstock
Back cover: Ahmed Faizal Yahya/Alamy
Page 1: Jim Zuckerman/Alamy; page 2:
Art Directors & Trip/Alamy; page 6: Robert
Harding PL/Superstock, oversnap/iStock,
faberfoto/Shutterstock, Jeffrey Ong Guo Xiong/
Shutterstock; page 7: Hemis.fr/Superstock,
Robert Harding PL/Superstock, Photononstop/
Superstock, Westend61/Superstock; page 8:
Khoroshunova Olga/Shutterstock

Manufactured in India by Nutech
Pulp from sustainable forests

Footprint feedback
We try as hard as we can to make each
Footprint guide as up to date as possible
but, of course, things always change. If you
want to let us know about your experiences –
good, bad or ugly – then don't delay, go to
footprinttravelguides.com and send in
your comments.

Publishing information
Footprint Malaysia & Singapore
7th edition
© Footprint Handbooks Ltd
June 2010

ISBN: 978 1 906098 9 95
CIP DATA: A catalogue record for this book
is available from the British Library

® Footprint Handbooks and the Footprint
mark are a registered trademark of Footprint
Handbooks Ltd

Published by Footprint
6 Riverside Court
Lower Bristol Road
Bath BA2 3DZ, UK
T +44 (0)1225 469141
F +44 (0)1225 469461
footprinttravelguides.com

Distributed in the USA by Globe Pequot Press,
Guilford, Connecticut